Words Made fr

You can see what words with **ly, ness, er, est, less, like, ing,** and **ed** added to them mean by these:

ly:

bad badly. John acted badly.
beautiful beautifully. The rose bloomed beautifully.
soft softly. The cat purred softly.

ness:

fresh freshness. The freshness of fish makes it taste better.
big bigness. The bigness of a desk makes it hard to carry.
red redness. The redness of an apple makes it pretty.

er and **est:**

long longer longest. A month is longer than a week. A year is the longest of all.
rich richer richest. He became rich and richer until he was the richest man in the world.

er meaning a person or thing that does:

A fighter fights. A leader leads. A painter paints.

less:

hairless means having no hair, or without any hair.
motherless means having no mother, or without any mother.
treeless means having no trees, or without any trees.

like:

doglike means like a dog or like a dog's. A wolf is a doglike animal. Tom followed his big brother with doglike devotion.
fairylike means like a fairy or like a fairy's. Lily was a fairylike girl. She danced with fairylike steps.

ing and **ed:**

He is laughing now. He laughed at the joke.
Laughing is better than crying.
I am buttering my bread. His has been buttered.
The buttering of a hundred sandwiches kept Mother busy.
Buttered toast is good.
Do you like hunting? The hunted fox ran into his hole.
A forested hill is a hill with a forest on it.
Painting is fun if you can do it well.
A painted face is a face that has paint on it or a face that has been painted.
A curtained window is one that has curtains.
A frosted window is one that has frost or has been frosted.

THORNDIKE CENTURY
BEGINNING DICTIONARY

by

E. L. Thorndike

Scott, Foresman and Company

Chicago Atlanta Dallas New York

Printed in the United States of America

Contents

Editorial Advisory Committee

Sir William Craigie, Professor Emeritus, University of Chicago, Coeditor of the Oxford English Dictionary, Chairman
Professor Albert C. Baugh, University of Pennsylvania
Professor Leonard Bloomfield, Yale University
Dean Francis M. Crowley, Fordham University
Professor Charles C. Fries, University of Michigan
Professor Archibald A. Hill, University of Virginia
Professor Arthur G. Kennedy, Stanford University
Professor George S. Lane, University of North Carolina
Professor Kemp Malone, Johns Hopkins University
Professor George H. McKnight, Ohio State University
Professor Charles S. Pendleton, George Peabody College for Teachers
Professor Robert C. Pooley, University of Wisconsin
Professor Robert L. Ramsay, University of Missouri
Professor William A. Read, Louisiana State University
The late Professor Edward Sapir, Yale University
Professor George Watson, University of Chicago
Professor George K. Zipf, Harvard University

Advisory Committee on Pronunciation

Professor Miles L. Hanley, University of Wisconsin, Chairman
Professor Leonard Bloomfield, Yale University
Professor Charles C. Fries, University of Michigan
Professor W. Cabell Greet, Barnard College, Columbia University
Professor R-M. S. Heffner, University of Wisconsin
Professor Archibald A. Hill, University of Virginia
Professor Lee S. Hultzén, University of Missouri
Professor Hans Kurath, Brown University
Professor William F. Luebke, University of Denver
Professor Kemp Malone, Johns Hopkins University
Professor C. E. Parmenter, University of Chicago
Professor Robert C. Pooley, University of Wisconsin
Professor Louise Pound, University of Nebraska
Professor William A. Read, Louisiana State University
The late Professor Edward Sapir, Yale University
Professor C. K. Thomas, Cornell University
Professor Claude M. Wise, Louisiana State University
Mrs. Jane Dorsey Zimmerman, Teachers College, Columbia University

Introduction

Realizing the immense resources of the dictionary for self-help in language, classroom teachers have for generations sought ways of training the child to make better use of the dictionary. In the elementary grades this challenging problem has two phases. First is the matter of content, of putting into the child's hands a dictionary designed for his own use. Second is the matter of method, of how best to teach the child the skills necessary to effective use of the dictionary.

Until recent years the only children's dictionaries available were merely "cut-down" editions of complicated lexicons—written for adults in the language of adults. In fact, the *Thorndike-Century Junior Dictionary*, published in 1935, was the first dictionary designed especially for children and written in language they could understand. It set new standards in the selection of entry words, in the simplification of definitions, in the use of illustrative sentences and pictures, in the recording of pronunciation by means of easily understood symbols, and in typography.

The *Thorndike-Century Beginning Dictionary*, designed for use in the fourth and fifth grades, represents a still further simplification. Definitions are easier to understand. More illustrative sentences are included. Careful selection of entry words insures their usefulness to young learners. An improved format increases legibility.

But simplification of dictionary content is only one phase of the problem. The other phase—how best to teach the skills necessary to effective use of the dictionary—has heretofore received only scant attention from the makers of dictionaries. The all-important contribution of the *Thorndike-Century Beginning Dictionary* is the inclusion of seventy lessons for the child on "How to Use Your Dictionary." These lessons provide for adequate step-by-step instruction in all the necessary dictionary skills. No lesson introduces more than one new dictionary skill; and each skill is developed through simple explanations, examples, illustrations, and practice involving actual, individual use of the dictionary.

Most noteworthy, perhaps, is the flexibility that results from presenting the lessons in two levels of difficulty. The major dictionary skills—locating entry words, comprehending word meanings, and deriving pronunciations—are covered at each level. Level One (pages 15–59) may be used in the fourth grade, and Level Two (pages 60–85) in the fifth. Or Level One may be used for slow groups, and both levels for fast groups. In either case the lessons have been so organized that children who complete the first level are able to make intelligent, though somewhat limited, use of the dictionary.

Thus the *Thorndike-Century Beginning Dictionary* is truly a dictionary for the beginner. Designed especially to meet his needs, it contains a carefully selected list of the words he is most likely to need in his reading, speaking, and writing; clear explanations of meanings that he can understand; a simple pronunciation system that he can use. Given a dictionary with these features, the young learner can, by means of the carefully planned lessons and exercises, soon acquire the special skills needed to make effective, individual use of the dictionary in solving his language problems.

Notes to the Teacher

Level One (Pages 15-59)

These pages provide for the development at simple levels of the major dictionary skills—locating entry words, comprehending word meanings, and deriving pronunciations. Level One may be used throughout the fourth grade or it may be used in the first half of the year and Level Two in the second half.

Pages 15–20 . . . *introduce the dictionary to the child as a book in which he will find the meanings of words. These first six pages acquaint the pupil with the general format of the dictionary, and with four methods of explaining word meanings: namely, definitions, pictures, illustrative sentences, and illustrative phrases.*

Page 15 involves learning the meaning of a word by reading one simple definition.

In discussing the picture, call attention to the signs and pronounce the word *aviary*, but do not explain its meaning.

After pupils have read the page, ask them to answer the two questions at the bottom of the page.

Suggest that many other interesting words are explained in the dictionary. After the pupils have looked through the dictionary, ask them to turn to pages 150–151. Call attention to the pictures and encourage pupils to read what the dictionary says about any words that interest them.

Page 16 presents a picture and a definition as aids to deriving meaning for a word.

Guide the study of the first half of the page and discuss the picture of a weasel and the information given about the size of the animal. Make sure children understand the abbreviation *in.* Ask a pupil to read aloud the definition and discuss what it tells about a weasel.

When children have located the word *dromedary* on page 230, discuss the picture and definition given.

Be sure that pupils understand the directions given for the exercise at the bottom of page 16 before they begin to work independently. When they have written their responses to the five questions, take time to talk over their answers. Encourage discussion of new things learned about the six animals.

Page 17 presents an illustrative sentence, a picture, and a definition for a word.

Direct group study and discussion of the first half of the page. Pupils may then complete the page independently, or they may work it out in a group situation. Lead children to compare their definitions and sentences with those given in the dictionary. They should notice that the dictionary gives a very brief explanation of the meaning of a word. Then discuss how the pictures and illustrative sentences help clarify word meanings.

Page 18 presents words with more than one definition, and introduces the illustrative phrase.

Guide the study and discussion of the entries for *canary* and *cherry*. Then have pupils read the directions for the exercise at the bottom of the page. After they have located *football* in the dictionary and read the two definitions, ask several children to give oral sentences using *football* with these two meanings. Have them complete the exercise independently.

Page 19 is designed to promote skill in determining approximate size from dictionary pictures.

Guide the study of the first half of the page, and then have pupils complete the page independently.

Discuss responses to the questions, and encourage children to tell *how* the size of each object is shown in the picture.

Page 20 involves the comprehension of one or more definitions to derive a general meaning for a word.

After pupils have completed the first half of the page, let them discuss their responses and tell what each word means.

Continue in the same way with the second exercise on the page.

PAGES 21–31 . . . *are designed to develop skill in locating entry words through the use of alphabetical order and guide words.*

Page 21 presents the term "entry word" and develops the meaning of "alphabetical order."

After the exercise has been completed, lead pupils to compare their lists of words.

Make sure at this point that all pupils know the letters of the alphabet in order.

Page 22 gives practice in using alphabetical sequence. In working out the code messages, the child must repeatedly think "What letter comes before __ in the alphabet?"

Introduce the page by asking children if they have ever used secret codes. Clarify the meaning of "code" and make sure that all children understand the directions for figuring out the message. Check to see if all pupils write the correct words for the first sentence; then let them continue independently. The two messages are:

"We will go to Mystery Cave by ourselves next Saturday. Do not tell anybody. Fred."

"We know your code. Have a good time at Mystery Cave."

Page 23 explains and gives practice in alphabetizing by second and third letters.

Guide the study and discussion of the first two paragraphs and of the model given at the right of the page.

Check pupils' responses to the exercise on alphabetizing by second letters before proceeding to the study of alphabetizing by third letters.

If some pupils have difficulty with these exercises, provide more practice before introducing page 24. These pupils may be asked to alphabetize the following lists of words:

1. go, kill, you, am, do, cat, two, now, his, use, for, red, we, sit, look, put, me.
2. ball, cellar, clean, box, brown, came, berry, city, cut, but, big, crumb, blow, cog.
3. faint, fade, fault, fall, fan, face, fate, far.

Pages 24 and 25 give practice in alphabetizing by first, second, and third letters.

In discussing the list of twenty-four words on page 24, attention may be called to words 9–12 which show alphabetizing by fourth and fifth letters.

Page 26 explains and gives practice in alphabetizing by fourth letters.

Direct attention to words 13 and 14 which show alphabetizing by fifth letter.

Page 27 involves comprehending definitions and pictures and gives practice in locating words on given pages of the dictionary.

The following are shown in the picture: cask, cascade, casement, castle, casque, javelin, jig, jerkin.

Page 28 gives practice in using alphabetical sequence. In working out the code message, children must repeatedly think "What letter comes after __ in the alphabet?"

Suggest that pupils write the alphabet before they start to figure out the message.

The message is:

"Can you meet me at Mystery Cave after school about half past four? I think it would be fun to explore the cave. Do not let your sister Jean get hold of this message. She might figure out our new code. Joe."

Pages 29 and 30 introduce guide words and give practice in using them.

On page 30 attention is directed to the index on the inside back cover of this book. Ask children to turn to this index, and discuss how they may use it in finding entry words.

Page 31 involves comprehension of the general meanings of words and gives practice in using guide words and alphabetical order to locate entry words.

If desired, the last part of this page may be discussed before the "Voice? Eyes? Feet?" exercise is introduced. Ask children to find the first and last "*l* word" in the dictionary—note that they are near the middle of the book. Continue with the *c* and *r* words.

PAGES 32–39 . . . *provide a step-by-step developmental program in comprehending defined meanings and adapting these meanings to fit given contexts.*

Page 32 is designed to promote skill in (1) the interpretation of part-whole diagrams and (2) the comprehension of definitions that involve part-whole relationships.

Guide the study of the diagram and the discussion of the four questions given under it. Encourage pupils to look up *aileron, fuselage, propeller,* and *rudder.* Discuss with the group what the dictionary tells about each.

When pupils have read the directions for the last part of the page and looked up the word *bowsprit,* ask some child to tell what a bowsprit is a part of. Children may then continue independently.

Page 33 gives practice in substituting a defined meaning for a word in context. This exercise involves only the substitution of a synonym for a word.

Before pupils start independent work, be sure they know what is meant by "italics."

Page 34 presents the problem of changing the order of words to fit a defined meaning into a given context.

Guide the study of the first half of the page. After children have rewritten the five sentences, have several pupils read aloud their versions of the first sentence. If any pupils have written "You can mend the toy with that sticks tape," lead them to compare this with the meaningful sentence "You can mend the toy with tape that sticks." Discuss the other sentences.

Pages 35 and 36 develop the ability to select the definition that fits a given context. On these pages only noun meanings are used.

Page 37 is designed to promote the ability to select the defined meaning that fits a given context. This page involves discrimination between noun and verb meanings.

Page 38 introduces the problem of adapting the definition of a verb to fit into a context that uses an inflected form of the verb.

In discussing the sentences pupils write, commend especially those children who have written smooth, readable sentences.

Page 39 gives further practice in selecting the appropriate meaning to fit a given context.

After the correct definitions have been read aloud, see if pupils can restate each sentence without using the word printed in italics.

PAGES 40–54 . . . *develop basic concepts and skills needed for the interpretation of dictionary pronunciations. These pages introduce the following aspects of phonetic spelling: omission of silent letters, single consonant sounds and their symbols, eleven vowel sounds and their symbols, syllabication, and accent.*

At Level One only eleven vowel symbols are introduced, but these eleven are so useful that they will enable the pupils to derive the pronunciation of a large proportion of the words given in this dictionary.

Page 40 develops the idea that there are no silent letters in pronunciations.

After the children have read the page independently, discuss with them the spellings and the pronunciations shown. Call attention to silent letters which appear in the spellings but not in the pronunciations.

Have the children write the exercise at the bottom of the page. Then in a group situation check their spellings and pronunciations.

The correct pronunciations are: 1. (bel), 2. (pin), 3. (glas), 4. (eg), 5. (shel).

Page 41 aids the child in making the generalization that in pronunciations a consonant letter stands for its most common sound.

After pupils have read the first part of the page, have them pronounce the words listed under the letter *g*. Then ask them to give other words that begin with this sound of *g*. Develop the idea that this is the most common sound of the letter *g*. Continue in the same way with the other letters.

In discussing the pronunciations (jam), (jump), and (jem), make sure that children understand why *j* is used in the pronunciation of *gem*.

Continue in the same way with the words *sat, sit,* and *his*. Ask the children to suggest other words in which they hear the *s* sound as in *sat* and the *z* sound as in *his*.

Page 42 strengthens understanding of differences between spellings and pronunciations.

When pupils have completed the study of the page, discuss their responses to the nine questions. Then ask children to tell some of the differences between regular spellings and pronunciations.

Page 43 introduces the concept of diacritical marks and promotes association of sounds with the symbols i, ī, a, ā.

Direct the study of the entire page in a group situation. Make sure children understand that with vowels, as with consonants, the letter itself stands for its most common sound and that marks are added above the vowel letters to indicate other sounds.

Give pupils time to study the fifteen pronunciations at the bottom of the page. Encourage them to ask for help on any pronunciation they are not sure of. Then have individual children pronounce the words.

Page 44 further strengthens the understanding of diacritical marks and promotes the association of correct sounds with the symbols a, ā, e, ē, i, ī, o, ō, u, ū.

In a group situation discuss with the children the way their dictionary shows the six vowel sounds of e, ē, o, ō, u, and ū.

Give the pupils time to study silently the pronunciations of the nine words before they say them aloud.

The picture key illustrates: cat, cage, bell, tree, pig, pie, top, goat, duck, mule.

If additional practice is needed, write the following pronunciations on the blackboard one at a time and ask pupils to say each.

(lāk)	(hed)	(pik)	(hōld)
(fan)	(bēt)	(snō)	(krum)
(hā)	(pīp)	(kot)	(fūm)

Page 45 involves the use of a key for ten vowel sounds—a, ā, e, ē, i, ī, o, ō, u, ū.

Show the children how to use the vowel key in working out the pronunciation of *dredge.* After the other pictures and pronunciations have been studied independently, ask individual children to pronounce each word. If desired, pupils may be asked to tell what some of the words mean. If any child has difficulty in formulating definitions, encourage him to find and read those given in the dictionary.

Page 46 is designed to strengthen association of the proper sound with each of the ten vowel symbols previously introduced.

The teacher should pronounce each word clearly so that the pupils are given the correct auditory stimulus as they look at the pronunciation. Then individual children, or the class as a group, may pronounce the words.

The pronunciations called for at the bottom of the page are:

1. (mēt)	5. (not)	9. (kup)
2. (met)	6. (nōt)	10. (kūt)
3. (stik)	7. (ran)	11. (ōld)
4. (fīv)	8. (rān)	12. (fēt)

Page 47 gives the teacher an opportunity to check children's ability to derive pronunciation and meaning of words looked up in the dictionary.

Discuss the directions with the children, using the first two lines of the poem as an example. Have the pupils work out the rest of the poem and then read it aloud.

The correct pronunciations are: *quay* (kē), *clique* (klēk), *deign* (dān), *mien* (mēn), *mauve* (mōv).

Page 48 develops understanding of what a syllable is and how a syllable is shown in the dictionary.

Guide the study of the first half of the page. Then have the children pronounce each word in the left-hand column and tell how many vowel sounds they heard in each. Continue in the same way with the column at the right. Have pupils answer the questions.

Ask the pupils to pronounce the words at the bottom of the page and to tell how many vowel sounds and how many syllables are in each word.

Page 49 introduces the concept of accent and develops understanding of the function of the accent mark.

Give several pupils an opportunity to pronounce the words *awake, locate, dollar,* and *darkness.* Then ask the class to tell which syllable was emphasized in each word. Guide the study of the accent mark.

After the exercise at the bottom of the page has been completed, check the responses by having the children pronounce the words aloud and tell where they put the accent marks.

Page 50 gives practice in interpreting pronunciations. It involves the use of accent, syllabication, the ten known vowel symbols, and single consonant symbols.

Use the procedure suggested for page 45 for the pictured words.

Page 51 introduces the soft unstressed vowel sound represented by the symbol ə.

Direct the study of the entire page. Make sure that children understand that the symbol ə is not a letter, but a special sign that represents the soft unaccented vowel sound. Avoid calling this symbol the "upside-down e." It may be called "unaccented vowel sign" or "schwa."

Continue with group discussion of the rest of the page.

Page 52 gives practice in recognition of the unstressed vowel sound represented by the symbol ə.

In pronouncing the twelve words at the top of the page, say them as in conversation, avoiding undue emphasis of any sound.

After children have studied the directions for the exercise at the bottom of the page, ask them to pronounce the words under the first picture and choose the correct one. They may then complete the exercise independently.

Page 53 gives practice in identifying an accented syllable.

When pupils have completed the exercise at the bottom of the page, they may check their own work by looking up these words in the dictionary.

Page 54 gives the teacher an opportunity to check each child's ability to use the pronunciation skills developed at Level One.

These pronunciations may be written on the blackboard for additional practice:

(med′ō)	(par′ət)	(tōn)
(mel′ən)	(pet′əl)	(fū′əl)
(mū′zik)	(rē′əl)	(fun′əl)
(pad′əl)	(rī′fəl)	(pə rād′)

Page 55 presents the problem of homographs as entry words and gives additional practice in selecting meaning to fit context.

Guide the study of the first half of the page and then suggest that children look through their dictionaries for other entry words that have small numbers after them.

Children should understand that when they find an entry word with a small number after it, they should look for other words that are spelled in the same way.

Page 56 presents words that have identical spellings but different pronunciations. Pupils are asked to select both meaning and pronunciation to fit context.

PAGES 57–59 . . . *develop skill in using the dictionary to find spellings of words.*

Page 57 involves locating the spelling of a word from its sound. Initiate informal discussion about the use of the dictionary for meanings and pronunciations. Explain that the dictionary can also be used to find spellings of words. Ask pupils to pronounce the words given under the pictures, and then let each child write the spellings.

Page 58 gives practice in choosing one of two homonyms to fit a given context.

Page 59 develops ability to find spellings of words that begin with silent letters or with sounds for which there are common variant spellings.

Guide the study of the first two exercises on this page. Supplement the discussion of the *ca* and *ka* words with such questions as, "If you wanted to find the spelling of the word *calico,* would you turn first to the entry words that begin with the letters *ca* or to those that begin with *ka?* Why?"

LEVEL TWO (Pages 60-85)

Level Two is designed to develop each of the dictionary skills at an advanced level. These pages may be used in the last half of the fourth grade with average or superior pupils. With slow learning groups use of the lessons in Level Two may be postponed until the fifth grade.

PAGES 60–68 . . . *complete the introduction of all symbols used in pronunciations and give practice in their use. Pages 65 and 66 combine locating, pronunciation, and meaning skills.*

Pages 60 and 61 present eight vowel sounds and the pronunciation symbols that represent them: ã, ä, ėr, ô, oi, ou, ů, ü.

Both pages should be developed in a group-teaching situation.

On page 60, after the teacher has pronounced the twelve words given, she may ask first individual children and then the class as a group to pronounce each word.

The pronunciations on page 61 represent:
1. few, 2. pull, 3. doubt, 4. pool, 5. full, 6. fool, 7. toil, 8. tomb, 9. row, 10. noon, 11. took, 12. noise, 13. bushel, 14. however, 15. crowd, 16. whoever.

Pages 62 and 63 present a summary of the vowel sounds, first in sentences and then in a short key.

After these pages have been read and discussed by the group, give children practice in using the short key. Write on the blackboard such words as *balm, churl, buoy, barque, dirge.* Have children look up the words, pronounce them, and tell what key word shows the vowel sound in each.

Page 64 gives the teacher an opportunity to check each child's ability to interpret pronunciations. Check each child's work carefully and give more practice to those pupils who need it.

Children are required to derive the pronunciations of the following words:

2. plume, plum	10. mare, mar
3. restraint, restaurant	11. stark, stork
4. hockey, hookey	12. certain, curtain
5. hut, hoot	13. careful, curfew
6. geography, geology	14. carve, curve
7. Pacific, pacify	15. horse, harsh
8. allegiance, alliance	16. absurd, absorb
9. turn, torn	17. ruler, roller

Page 65 presents the problem of one word with two pronunciations and gives practice in selecting both meaning and pronunciation to fit context.

Page 66 provides additional practice in selecting meaning to fit a given context.

In a group situation discuss pupils' answers to the seven questions.

Page 67 promotes recognition of the consonant symbols ch, ng, sh, th, ᴛʜ, and zh.

Give children time to study the pronunciations given at the bottom of the page before asking them to pronounce the words.

Page 68 explains the function of the full pronunciation key and calls attention again to the short key.

The key words called for in the exercise on this page are: 1. age, 2. far, 3. hat, 4. care, 5. be, 6. let, 7. term, 8. it, 9. ice, 10. hot, 11. open, 12. order, 13. oil, 14. out, 15. cup, 16. use, 17. put, 18. rule.

PAGES 69–72 . . . *are designed to promote ability in locating and using special meanings of words and phrases given in the dictionary, and to give practice in adapting definitions to context.*

Page 69 introduces special meanings of words that are listed as definitions of entry words, and gives practice in adapting defined meanings to context.

Page 70 introduces special meanings of phrases that are given as definitions under entry words, and gives practice in adapting defined meanings to context.

Discuss the definition of the phrase "hedge in." Then have children read the directions for the exercise at the bottom of the page, and find the definition given for "in search of." Ask two or three pupils to give orally their version of sentence 1. If desired, the entire group of eleven sentences may be worked out orally in a group situation. Note individual pupil's ability to restate ideas in meaningful sentences.

Page 71 introduces special meanings of words and phrases that are listed as entries under the main entry word.

Page 72 involves paraphrasing to adapt defined meanings to context.

Pages 73 and 74 introduce the secondary accent, and promote the ability to interpret primary and secondary accent marks.

PAGES 75–78 . . . *present the problem of determining the root word in order to find the meaning of variant forms and derivatives. These pages give practice in finding the right entry word and in adapting its definition to a context that uses a variant form or derivative of the entry word.*

Page 75 introduces the concept of root word.

The page "Words Made from Other Words" should be read and discussed by the group. Ask children to give other sentences using each of the forms listed.

Page 76 involves deriving the meaning of variant forms from definitions of the root word.

Pages 77 and 78 are designed to develop skill in determining the spelling and in finding the correct root word as an entry word in the dictionary. Page 78 also involves adapting defined meanings to context.

PAGES 79–85 . . . *give practice in using the dictionary for meaning, pronunciation, and spelling of words.*

Pages 79 and 80 present the problem of learning the meaning of an unknown word that may be encountered in a definition.

Page 81 involves a detailed study of two entries and the use of both common and special meanings in context.

Pages 82 and 83 are designed to develop ability to solve spelling problems individually through use of the dictionary.

In discussing this page, point out to children that they may need to look in more than one place in the dictionary to find the spelling of a word.

Page 84 involves a detailed study of the meanings of three words that are spelled *light.*

Page 85 gives practice in deriving pronunciation and word meaning through the use of the dictionary.

The first paragraph of the story should be worked out in a group-teaching situation. Ask several pupils to read aloud the first paragraph and then to explain in their own words what it tells about Paddy. Children may then continue independently. When they have completed their study, ask them to read the story aloud. Then ask several children to tell it in their own words.

How to Use Your Dictionary

Illustrators

William Mark Young and *Gregory Orloff*

At the Zoo

Bob and his father were spending the day at the zoo. They had been watching the bears for a long time.

"Let's look at something else now," Father said at last. "What would you like to see next? Here are some signs that show us where to go."

Bob looked at the three signs. "I've seen elephants and lions," he said, "but I've never seen an aviary. Let's see what kind of animal that is."

Bob's father laughed.

Do you know why he laughed? You can find out by reading what your dictionary says about an aviary. On page 116 of this book you will find:

aviary (ā′vi ãr′i), place where many birds are kept.

The first thing after *aviary* is (ā′vi ãr′i). This shows how the word *aviary* is pronounced. Then the dictionary explains the meaning of the word.

Now do you know why Bob's father laughed? What do you think he told Bob about an aviary?

Do You Know?

At the zoo Bob saw some animals that he had never seen before. One of them was a weasel. Do you know what a weasel looks like? Do you know what it eats and how big it is? Your dictionary tells you. On page 627 you will find:

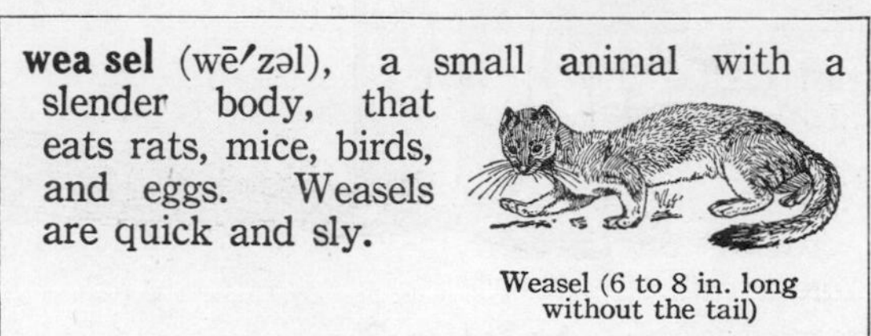

wea sel (wē′zəl), a small animal with a slender body, that eats rats, mice, birds, and eggs. Weasels are quick and sly.

Weasel (6 to 8 in. long without the tail)

Bob also saw a dromedary at the zoo. Do you know what a dromedary looks like? You can find out if you turn to page 230. There you will see *drizzle* and *droll* and many other words in large type. Find the word *dromedary* in large type. Read what your dictionary says about this animal and look at the picture.

The names of four other animals are printed below. There is a number after each name. This number shows you on what page in the dictionary you can learn about the animal.

copperhead (187)	heron (303)
eel (235)	opossum (409)

Read what the dictionary says about each animal and look at the picture of it. Then write the answers to these questions:

1. Which animal is dangerous?
2. About how long is a copperhead?
3. Why do we say "as slippery as an eel"?
4. Which animal lives in trees?
5. Which animal is a bird?

Can You Do It?

Have you ever tried to tell or show someone what a word means? If you have, you know that it is hard to do. Do you think you could make someone else understand what a raft is? How would you do it?

Let's see how your dictionary does it.

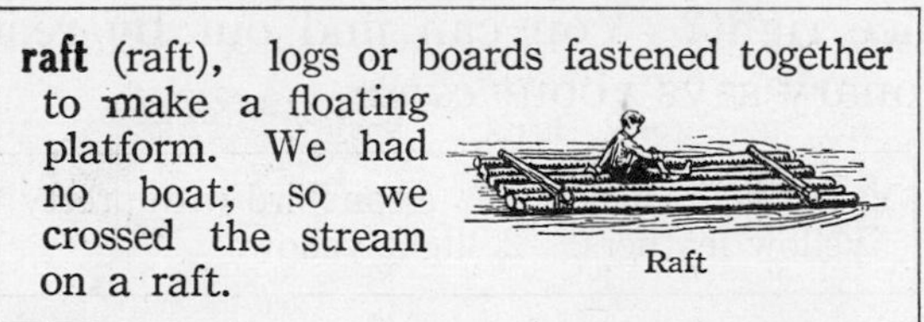
raft (raft), logs or boards fastened together to make a floating platform. We had no boat; so we crossed the stream on a raft.

Raft

Your dictionary does three things to show the meaning of the word *raft*.

It gives a picture of a raft.
It gives a definition that explains what a raft is.
It uses the word *raft* in a sentence.

The sentence is "We had no boat; so we crossed the stream on a raft." What does this tell you about a raft?

Do you think you could tell or show someone what a ladder is? Try to do these three things:

1. Draw a picture of a ladder.
2. Write a definition that explains what a ladder is.
3. Use the word *ladder* in a sentence.

Now read what your dictionary tells you about the word *ladder* on page 343.

Suppose someone asked you to explain the meaning of *afraid*. Could you draw a picture of *afraid?* Write a definition and sentence of your own for *afraid* or copy those given in your dictionary on page 97.

Read the definition of *affable* on page 96 and write a sentence using the word.

Who Was Right?

"My mother is going to buy me a new dress," said Alice. "I think I'll get a canary one."

"You can't buy a canary dress," laughed Susan. "A canary is a bird!"

"It's a color, too," Alice replied.

Was Alice right? You can find out by reading what your dictionary says about *canary*.

ca nar y (kə nãr′i), 1. a songbird with pretty yellow feathers. 2. light yellow.

Alice knew that the word *canary* has two meanings. They are numbered 1 and 2 in your dictionary.

Now read what your dictionary tells you about the word *cherry*.

cher ry (cher′i), 1. a small, round fruit with a hard seed in the middle. Cherries are good to eat. 2. the tree it grows on. 3. bright red; as, cherry ribbons.

Look at the third definition again. How do the words "as, cherry ribbons" help you understand that the word *cherry* may mean a color?

Copy the six words and page numbers that are printed below. In your dictionary you will find two definitions for each of these words. Read both definitions for the word *football*. Then write a sentence using this word with its first meaning. Next write a sentence using the word with its second meaning.

Continue in the same way with the other words.

1. football (269)
2. erect (243)
3. jacket (333)
4. handy (296)
5. kerchief (339)
6. kite (341)

How Big?

These four pictures are from your dictionary. Notice how your dictionary tells or shows you the size of the thing in each picture.

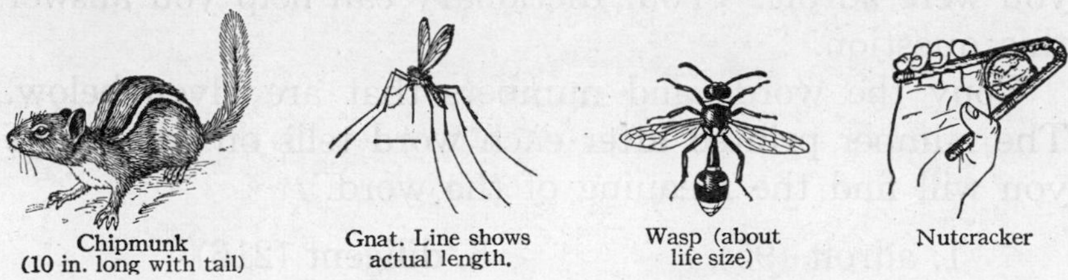

Chipmunk (10 in. long with tail) — Gnat. Line shows actual length. — Wasp (about life size) — Nutcracker

Now write the answers to these questions:

1. How does your dictionary tell the size of a chipmunk?
2. How does your dictionary show you about how long a real gnat is?
3. How does your dictionary tell you how big a wasp is?
4. What is there in the picture that shows you about how big a nutcracker is?

Copy the six questions and page numbers given below. Read the first question and find the picture of *bamboo* on page 119. Study the picture. Then write "Yes" or "No" after the question.

Now continue in the same way with each of the other questions.

1. Does bamboo grow over six feet tall? (119)
2. Is a badger smaller than a chipmunk? (118)
3. Is the picture of a caterpillar about the size of a real caterpillar? (156)
4. Is the picture of a crayfish smaller than a crayfish really is? (193)
5. Is a harp a large instrument? (297)
6. Is a marten larger than a mouse? (369)

Yes or No?

If a friend told you that you were kind, you would be pleased. But if he said that you were lazy, you would not be pleased. Would you like to have a friend say that you were adroit? Your dictionary can help you answer this question.

Copy the words and numbers that are given below. The number printed after each word tells on what page you will find the meaning of the word.

1. adroit (95)
2. deceitful (204)
3. frivolous (275)
4. dauntless (203)
5. diligent (216)
6. impertinent (317)
7. generous (281)
8. surly (566)

Find in your dictionary each of the words you have copied and read all the definitions given. If you would like to have your friends use the word to describe you, write "Yes" after it. If you would not like to have them use the word to describe you, write "No" after it.

Copy the seven questions and numbers printed at the bottom of this page. Read the first question and find the meaning of *foxglove* on page 273 of your dictionary. Then write "Yes" or "No" after the question. Go on to the other questions. Use your dictionary to help you give the right answers.

1. Do foxes have foxgloves? (273)
2. Could you climb a hillock? (304)
3. Is brocade a cheap cloth? (142)
4. Does meditation mean "quiet thought"? (373)
5. Is an edifice a small truck? (234)
6. Is bullion valuable? (145)
7. Would you find rabbits in a warren? (624)

The words explained in the dictionary are called entry words. These words are printed in large type.

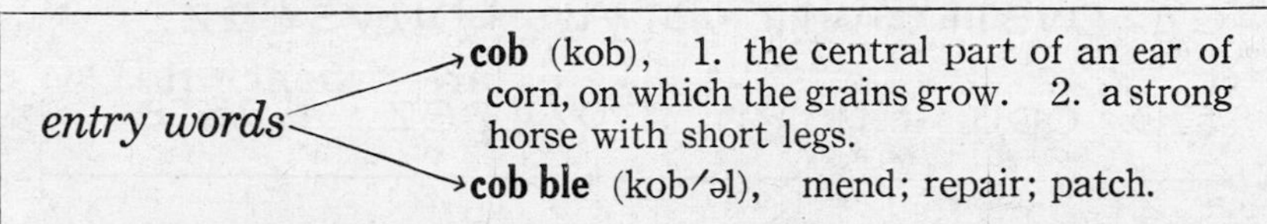
entry words

cob (kob), 1. the central part of an ear of corn, on which the grains grow. 2. a strong horse with short legs.

cob ble (kob′əl), mend; repair; patch.

In your dictionary the entry words are arranged in a certain order. The words beginning with *a* come on pages 89 to 117. The words that begin with *b* are on pages 117 to 148, and the words that begin with *c* are on pages 149 to 201.

You can find an entry word in the dictionary if you know the order of the letters in the alphabet. At the top of this page the letters are shown in alphabetical order.

Write the letters *a* through *z* in a column like this:

a
b
c

After each letter write a word which begins with that letter. For example, after the letter *a*, write *apple;* and after the letter *b*, write *ball*.

If you can't think of a word that begins with a certain letter, use your dictionary to help you. When you have finished, you will have a list in which the words are arranged in alphabetical order by their first letters.

Secret Messages

Fred and Joe often wrote secret messages to each other. When they wrote, they used the order of letters in the alphabet to make a code.

One day Mary and Jean found a secret note that Fred had written to Joe. It looked like this:

Xf xjmm hp up Nztufsz Dbwf
cz pvstfmwft ofyu Tbuvsebz.
Ep opu ufmm bozcpez. Gsfe

"Look at this!" cried Mary. "It's nonsense!"

But Jean said, "I think the boys have a code. Let's try to figure it out. First we need to see the alphabet."

a b c d e f g h i j k l m n o p q r s t u v w x y z

Jean studied the alphabet and Fred's note carefully. At last she said, "I think I know their code. I'm going to try putting *a* for *b*, *b* for *c*, *c* for *d*, *d* for *e*, and so on. Then maybe I can read the note."

For *Xf*, Jean wrote *We.* For *xjmm*, she wrote *will.* For *hp*, she wrote *go.*

Write *We will go.* Then see if you can write the real words for the rest of the message.

A few days later Jean and Mary wrote a note to Fred, using the boys' secret code. The note is shown below. Write what the girls told the boys in their message.

Xf lopx zpvs dpef. Ibwf b
hppe ujnf bu Nztufsz Dbwf.

Second and Third Letters

You can arrange the words *ago*, *doll*, *been*, and *fat* in alphabetical order by their first letters. Can you put the words *act*, *able*, *age*, and *add* in alphabetical order?

These four words are in alphabetical order in the box at the right. Since they all begin with the same letter, they are arranged in alphabetical order by their second letters. *Able* comes before *act* because *b* is before *c* in the alphabet. *Act* comes before *add* because *c* comes before *d* in the alphabet. Why does *add* come before *age?*

able
act
add
age

See how quickly you can write in alphabetical order the words that are printed below.

cat	crate	coat
cheese	clock	center
city	cut	cyclone

All the words in the box at the right begin with the same two letters. These four words are arranged in alphabetical order by their third letters. Look at the third letter in each word. *Drain* comes before *dream* because *a* is before *e* in the alphabet. *Dream* comes before *drill* because *e* is before *i* in the alphabet. Why does *drill* come before *drop?*

drain
dream
drill
drop

See how quickly you can write in alphabetical order the words that are printed below.

four	date	hall
dance	egg	feet
fever	fence	double

Where Does It Go?

Look at the twenty-four numbers that are printed below. Most of the numbers have words after them, and the words are arranged in alphabetical order. But the list is not complete. These words were left out of it:

yam	yonder	yes	yawl
yoke	yucca	yell	yap

Can you put these words into the list in alphabetical order? Try it. Copy the number 2, which is the first number without any word printed after it. Then find the word above that comes between *yacht* and *Yankee* in an alphabetical list. Write this word after the number 2.

Do it this way: 2. yam

Continue in the same way with the rest of the list.

1. yacht	9. year	17. yield
2. . . .	10. yearly	18. . . .
3. Yankee	11. yearn	19. yolk
4. . . .	12. yeast	20. . . .
5. yard	13. . . .	21. you
6. . . .	14. yeoman	22. young
7. ye	15. . . .	23. . . .
8. yea	16. yet	24. Yule

The words *violate*, *vibrate*, *vim*, and *vie* were left out of the list of words printed below. Copy the numbers 2, 4, 7, and 9. After the number 2, write the word that comes in an alphabetical list between *viand* and *vicar*.

Continue in the same way with the rest of the list.

1. viand	4. . . .	7. . . .
2. . . .	5. vigil	8. vintage
3. vicar	6. villain	9. . . .

Ted was having a birthday party. "Now we will play a new game," he said. "It's a treasure hunt. Here are directions that tell where to find the treasure." Each sheet of paper Ted handed out had these words on it:

gate basket from treasure a
bush east directly feet holds
garden real beside secret eight

"What funny directions!" Ted's friends cried. "These words don't tell us where to hunt."

"Oh, yes, they do," laughed Ted. "I'll tell you a secret about them. You have to put them in alphabetical order to find out what they say. The one who puts the words in alphabetical order first will find the treasure first."

The boys got busy. In a few minutes Tom jumped up and shouted, "I know where it is!" Quick as a flash he came back, proudly carrying a box of candy.

Where had Tom found the treasure? Find out by writing the words of the directions in alphabetical order.

Fourth Letters

The words *card*, *car*, *care*, and *carbon* all begin with the letters *c a r*. Since the first three letters are the same, the words must be arranged in alphabetical order by their fourth letters. But *car* doesn't have four letters. Do you know which of these words would come first in an alphabetical list?

car
carbon
card
care

In the box at the right the four words are in alphabetical order. The one with only three letters is first. The other words are arranged in order by their fourth letters.

Most of the twenty-four numbers given at the bottom of this page have words after them. These words are in alphabetical order. But the list is not complete. The following words were left out of it:

pathway	panda	pang	pause
panama	patch	paw	path

Can you put these words into the list in alphabetical order? Copy the number 2, which is the first number without any word after it. Then find the word above that comes between *pan* and *pancake* in an alphabetical list. Write this word after the number 2.

Continue in the same way with the rest of the list.

1. pan	9. pat	17. pattern
2. . . .	10. . . .	18. pauper
3. pancake	11. pate	19. . . .
4. . . .	12. . . .	20. pave
5. pane	13. pathetic	21. pavement
6. . . .	14. pathos	22. paving
7. panic	15. . . .	23. . . .
8. pantry	16. patient	24. pawn

You are familiar with many of the things shown in this picture of England long ago. But there are other things pictured that you may never have seen before.

Some of the nine words printed below are names of objects in the picture, and some are not. Copy these words on a sheet of paper. Then use pages 154 and 155 of your dictionary to find out what the words mean.

Is there a cask shown in the picture? When you have decided, write "Yes" or "No" after the word *cask*.

Continue in the same way with the other words.

1. cask	4. cashew	7. catapult
2. cartoon	5. cart	8. castle
3. cascade	6. casement	9. casque

Copy the words given below. Use pages 334 and 335 of your dictionary to find out what the words mean.

Is there a javelin shown in the picture? When you have decided, write "Yes" or "No" after the word *javelin*.

Continue in the same way with the other words.

1. javelin	3. jig	5. jaguar
2. jib	4. jetty	6. jerkin

You have read about Fred and Joe and the messages they wrote to each other. You will remember that Jean learned how to read their secret messages.

When the boys discovered that Jean and Mary knew their code, they made up a new one. A message in the new code is shown below. The picture helps you know what Joe said to Fred in this secret note.

You can figure out the message by writing *b* for *a*, *c* for *b*, *d* for *c*, and so on. You must write *a* for *z*. The first two words in the note are *Can you*. Write *Can you*. Then write the real words for the rest of the message.

Bzm xnt ldds ld zs Lxrsdqx
Bzud zesdq rbgnnk zants gzke
ozrs entq? H sghmj hs vntkc
ad etm sn dwoknqd sgd bzud.
Cn mns kds xntq rhrsdq Idzm
fds gnkc ne sghr ldrrzfd. Rgd
lhfgs ehftqd nts ntq mdv bncd.
Ind

Guide Words

At the top of each page in the dictionary are two words that are called guide words. The one at the left is the same as the first entry word on the page. The one at the right is the same as the last entry word on the page. All the entry words that come between the guide words in an alphabetical list can be found on that page.

Here are the guide words that are on pages 225, 227, and 229 of your dictionary.

domain	225	**dose**

downward	227	**drank**

dresser	229	**driver**

Use these guide words in deciding on what page you would find each entry word printed below. Copy each entry word and, after it, put the correct page number.

1. done	**4. drift**	**7. dowry**
2. dragon	**5. drink**	**8. door**
3. domino	**6. doze**	**9. dressing**

Write the answers to these questions:

1. Would you find the entry word *dove* on page 226 or on page 228?
2. On what page would you find the word *doubt?*
3. On what page would you find the word *dream?*
4. Would you find the word *drawl* on page 226 or on page 228?
5. Would *dream* come before *drawl* or after it?

Finding Entry Words

export	250	**extinction**
headdress	300	**heartless**
legitimate	350	**let**
nought	400	**numeral**

These guide words and page numbers are taken from the tops of pages in your dictionary. They will help you find the entry words that are printed below. The index on the inside of the back cover of your dictionary will also help you find pages that you need.

1. dart	**6. ladybug**	**11. furtive**
2. iris	**7. lemon**	**12. export**
3. orifice	**8. palace**	**13. hearty**
4. hyena	**9. jockey**	**14. nestle**
5. gallop	**10. marine**	**15. knight**

Copy these numbers and entry words in one column on a sheet of paper.

Would you look before or after page 250 for the word *dart?* Open your dictionary near where you think *dart* will be. Look at the guide words, and then turn ahead or back until you find the page that *dart* is on. You can tell by the guide words when you have found the right page. Copy these guide words after the word *dart.*

Do it this way: 1. dart (darling — dazzle)

Continue in the same way with the other words.

Voice? Eyes? Feet?

Each of the words below tells about something that is done with the voice or with the eyes or with the feet.

1. caper
2. berate
3. chant
4. plod
5. saunter
6. leer
7. lope
8. retort
9. amble
10. coo
11. espy
12. scrutinize

Do you caper with your voice, your eyes, or your feet? One of the meanings of the word is "to leap or skip in a playful way." You use your feet; so in the chart shown below, *caper* is written in the column under *Feet.*

Voice	Eyes	Feet
		caper

Make a chart like this one. Then look up the other words that are printed in the list at the top of the page. Find out what each word means and write the word in the correct column on your chart.

Your dictionary ends on page 645. Words beginning with the letter *l* are near the middle of the book on pages 343 to 362.

Words beginning with *c* are on pages 149 to 201.

Words beginning with *r* are on pages 464 to 497.

Would you look before or after page 149 to find the word *berate?*

Would you look before or after page 201 to find the word *espy?*

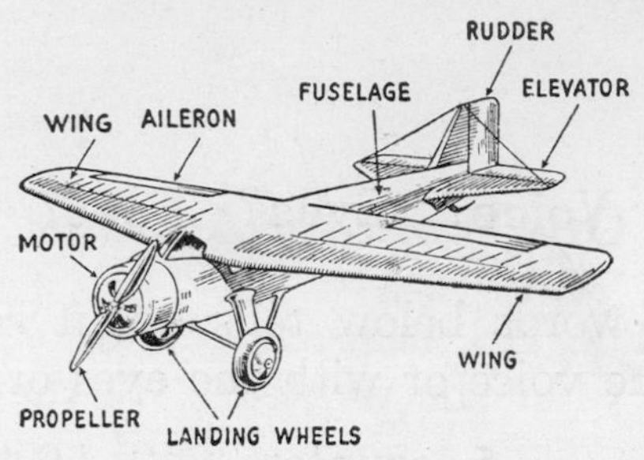

This picture of an airplane is in your dictionary on page 98. It tells you the names of several parts of an airplane. Use the picture to help you answer these four questions:

1. Is an aileron a part of the fuselage or a part of a wing of an airplane?
2. Is the propeller larger or smaller than the fuselage?
3. Where is the rudder located?
4. How many ailerons are shown on this airplane?

If you would like to know more about any of these parts of an airplane, look up the name of that part in your dictionary.

The word *fuselage* is the name of a part of an airplane. Each word in the list below is the name of one part of something else.

1. bowsprit	5. pistil
2. stamen	6. steeple
3. shin	7. twig
4. gunwale	8. gable

The first word in the list is *bowsprit.* Do you know what a bowsprit is? Do you know what it is a part of? Your dictionary will tell you.

When you have found the word *bowsprit,* read the definition and study the picture. Then write a sentence telling what a bowsprit is a part of.

Continue in the same way with each of the other words in the list.

One Word for Another

Jim read "The girl begged for succor," but he was not at all sure what she wanted. He thought maybe it was sugar, or perhaps a piece of hard candy. But when he looked up *succor*, he found:

suc cor (suk′ər), help; aid.

Then he knew that the sentence meant "The girl begged for help."

Do you know the meaning of the first sentence printed at the bottom of this page? Use the guide words to help you find the word *avaricious* in your dictionary. Read the definition carefully. Then write the first sentence, but instead of *avaricious*, write another word that has the same meaning.

Write each of the other sentences, using another word in place of the word that is printed in italics.

1. He was a very *avaricious* man.
2. It was a *murky* night.
3. If there is *aught* you need, tell me now.
4. Mr. Kay was known for his *benevolent* deeds.
5. The *firmament* was clear and blue.
6. "Ask the *proprietor*," said the clerk.
7. The *morose* boy refused to talk.
8. The man had a strange *malady*.
9. Her *vivacious* chatter amused the group.
10. "I won't *chastise* you," he promised.
11. We stared at the huge *portal*.
12. He liked to *rove* through the country.
13. Lucy's face looked *pallid* in the dim light.
14. The soldier fought with great *valor*.

"Look at this, Mother!" cried Ann as she pointed to an announcement in the newspaper.

"The Garden Club," Mrs. Wilson read slowly, "will give a prize for the best floral arrangement made by a boy or girl under twelve years of age."

"Yes," nodded Ann, "and I'm going to win that prize!"

Do you know what the Garden Club meant by "floral arrangement"? In your dictionary the meaning of the word *floral* is "of flowers." How would you use this definition to explain the meaning of the announcement? Would you say "the best of flowers arrangement"? Or would you change the order of the words in the sentence and say "The Garden Club will give a prize for the best arrangement of flowers"?

Read the first sentence printed at the bottom of this page, and find the definition of *sticky* that is given in your dictionary. Then write a sentence that means the same thing as the first sentence below, but use other words instead of the word *sticky*.

Continue in the same way with the other sentences.

1. You can mend the toy with *sticky* tape.
2. Fires often *imperil* many people.
3. We must *saturate* the lawn with water.
4. *Coöperative* people are needed for this job.
5. On the bank there were many *mossy* stones.

Many Meanings

Read the definitions that your dictionary gives for the word *cutter:*

> **cut ter** (kut′ər), 1. person who cuts; as, a garment cutter, a woodcutter. 2. machine made to cut; as, a meat cutter, a bread cutter. 3. small sleigh. 4. small sailboat with one mast. 5. boat belonging to a warship, used for carrying supplies and passengers to and from shore. 6. a small, armed ship used by the coast guard.
>
> Cutter (def. 3)

How many definitions are given for the word *cutter?* How many pictures are there? What does "(def. 3)" under the picture mean?

Pictures of other kinds of cutters are given below. Look at the pictures and then see if you can find the definition that describes each one.

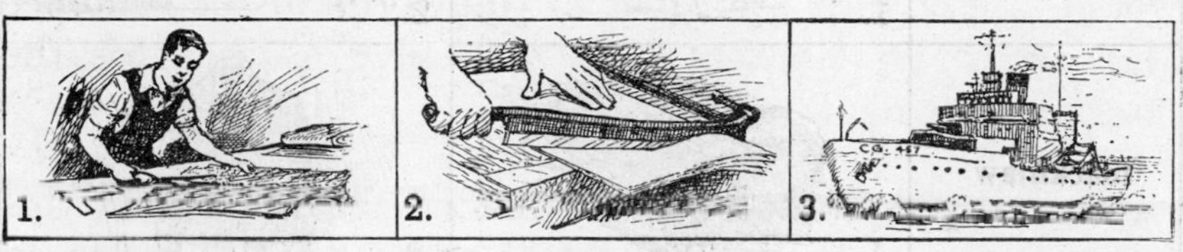

Find the entry word *coach* in your dictionary and read all the definitions given for the word. Which definition explains the meaning shown in picture 1 below? Which gives the meaning shown in picture 2? In picture 3?

Two meanings of the word *gem* are pictured above. Find the entry word *gem* in your dictionary and read the five definitions that are given. Which definition describes picture 1 above? Which describes picture 2? When you have decided, write the word *gem*. Then tell which definition describes each picture.

Do it this way:

gem	picture 1 (def. 1)
	picture 2 (def. 5)

Continue in the same way with the words and pictures given below.

crane	 1.	 2.
mackinaw	 1.	 2.
nut	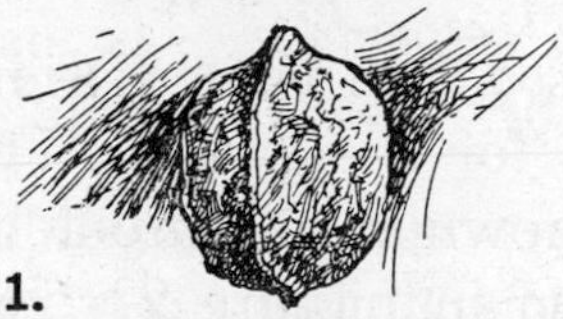 1.	 2.
gondola	 1.	 2.

1. The nurse put the baby in the *cradle.*
2. The boys watched the little girl *cradle* the tired puppy in her arms.

The two sentences in the box use different meanings of the word *cradle.* Find the entry word *cradle* in your dictionary and read all the definitions given. Which definition explains the meaning of *cradle* in sentence 1? In sentence 2? When you have decided, write the word *cradle.* Then tell which definition explains the word in each sentence.

Do it this way:

cradle	sentence 1 (def. 1)
	sentence 2 (def. 5)

Continue in the same way with the pairs of sentences given below.

1. The nurse started to *bandage* Jim's hand.
2. Jack put a clean *bandage* on his finger.

1. Let us *sojourn* here for a while.
2. Our *sojourn* was very pleasant.

1. The boy had to *cart* away the leaves.
2. One wheel of the farmer's heavy *cart* was broken.

1. You must *peel* the banana before you can eat it.
2. The orange *peel* was hard to get off.

1. The thief decided to *reform.*
2. Miss Scott noticed the *reform* in John's behavior.

1. They *gossip* about everyone they know.
2. The *gossip* spread through the town like wildfire.

1. This is a good *pasture* for the cows.
2. The farmer turned the cows out to *pasture.*

1. He put the *chisel* on the shelf.
2. The workman started to *chisel* the piece of stone.

In Other Words

Your dictionary gives two definitions for the word *avert.* After each definition, there is a sentence which uses that particular meaning of the word *avert.* Read each definition and sentence carefully.

> **a vert** (ə vėrt′), 1. turn away; turn aside. She averted her eyes from the wreck. 2. prevent. The driver averted an accident by a quick turn of his car.

Can you use the first definition of *avert* to explain the meaning of *averted* in the sentence "She averted her eyes from the wreck"? Would you say "She turn away her eyes from the wreck"? Or would you say "She turned her eyes away from the wreck"?

Now read the second definition and sentence again. If you wanted to use another word instead of *averted* in this second sentence, what would you say? Would you say "The driver prevent an accident by a quick turn of his car"? Or would you say "The driver prevented an accident by a quick turn of his car"?

Read the first sentence printed below and look up the word *restrain* in your dictionary. Write a sentence that means the same thing as "John has difficulty in restraining his temper," but use another word instead of the word *restraining.*

Continue with the other sentences.

1. John has difficulty in *restraining* his temper.
2. We *anticipated* a cold winter.
3. Four hours *elapsed* before they heard the news.
4. Sunshine helps in *purifying* the air.
5. Betty *altered* her plans.
6. The boys were *discussing* their problems.

One of the meanings of *galley* is pictured above. Read all the definitions of *galley* and tell which one goes with this picture.

gal ley (gal′i), 1. long, narrow ship of former times having oars and sails. Galleys were often rowed by slaves or prisoners. 2. a large rowboat. 3. the kitchen of a ship.

Galley (def. 1)

Read the first sentence given below and look up the word *smoke* in your dictionary. How many definitions are given for the word? Which definition explains the meaning of *smoke* in the first sentence below?

Look up the word printed in italics in each of the other sentences. Be ready to read aloud the definition that explains its meaning in the sentence on this page.

1. Before the man could get the honey, he had to *smoke* the bees out of the hollow tree.
2. I'd like to *reflect* on your question before I answer it.
3. The tall, *spare* soldier ate very little.
4. If the wind changes, we must *trim* the sails.
5. "*Shadow* that man," the officer ordered.
6. The *magazine* of the fort was filled with ammunition.
7. They stored the grain in the *crib*.
8. It is not polite to *elbow* your way through the crowd.

Here is a picture of something. Your dictionary tells you three things about its name:

how to spell it
how to pronounce it
what it means

Of course you know how to spell the word *hat*, how to pronounce it, and what it means. When we write *hat*, we write a letter for each sound that we make when we say the word. The letter *h* stands for the first sound, *a* for the second one, and *t* for the third.

Some words have silent letters in them. We spell the word *till* with four letters, but when we say this word, we say only three sounds. The last *l* in *till* is a silent letter. The word is pronounced *til*.

Look at the spellings and pronunciations printed below.

led (led)	**add** (ad)	**fill** (fil)
gnat (nat)	**knit** (nit)	**nod** (nod)

Now look at the five pictures below. Think of the name of each and then write the name twice. First, show how to spell it and, next, show how to pronounce it.

Do it this way: 1. bell (bel)

Do you remember your old A B C books? In the one above you see a fan after the letter F. Maybe your book had a picture of a fox or a fairy. But the letter F stood for the first sound in the name of the picture.

Say to yourself the three words in the first list below and think of the first sound in each word. The letter *g* usually has this sound. See if you can think of other words that begin with this sound of *g*.

Continue in the same way with the other lists of words.

g	j	k	s
got	jam	kid	sat
get	jump	keep	sit
goat	just	kind	see

You know the sound of the letter *g* in the words *got* and *get*. Do you know what letter usually stands for the first sound we say in the word *gem?* You can find out by studying the words and pronunciations below.

jam (jam) **jump** (jump) **gem** (jem)

In the words *sat* and *sit* the letter *s* has one sound, but in the word *his* it has a different sound. Of course you know what sound to say for the letter *s* in each of these words. But could you show someone what sound to say? Your dictionary does it this way:

sat (sat) **sit** (sit) **his** (hiz)

Think of the sound of the letter *z* in the words *buzz* and *zero*. Now do you see why your dictionary uses the letter *z* to show the last sound in *his?*

See and Say

It would be very easy to pronounce words if a letter always stood for just one sound. But, as you know, in some words we see one letter, and we say the sound of another. And in many words we see letters that we do not say at all.

Your dictionary prints the spelling and pronunciation of each entry word. Look carefully at the spelling and pronunciation of each word below. In the spelling you may see letters that you do not say when you pronounce the word. But in the pronunciation you will see only letters that stand for the sounds you say.

puff (puf)	**kick** (kik)	**sack** (sak)
knock (nok)	**kiss** (kis)	**lass** (las)
lamb (lam)	**cap** (kap)	**cent** (sent)

Now write the answers to these questions:

1. How many letters do you see in the spelling of *puff?* How many sounds do you say in the word?
2. How many letters do you see in the spelling of *knock?* How many sounds do you say in the word?
3. What letter is silent in *lamb?*
4. How many sounds do you say in the word *kick?* How many letters do you see in its pronunciation?
5. In the pronunciation of *cap* what letter is used to show the first sound?
6. What letter would you use to show the first sound in the word *can?*
7. How many sounds do you say in *lass?*
8. In the pronunciation of *cent* what letter is used to show the first sound?
9. What letter would you use to show the first sound you say in *city?*

Which Sound Is It?

Think of the first sound you say in the four words that are printed below.

it (it) **is** (iz) **in** (in) **if** (if)

The letter *i* has this sound more often than it has any other. So in the pronunciations in your dictionary the letter *i* stands for this sound.

Now think of the last sound you say in the four words that are printed below.

pie (pī) **tie** (tī) **lie** (lī) **my** (mī)

The letter *i* with a line above it stands for the last sound you say in *pie, tie, lie,* and *my.*

Can you say the pronunciations that are printed below? A line above the letter *i* tells you to say the last sound you say in *pie.*

1. (dim)	3. (bīt)	5. (lik)	7. (hīd)
2. (dīm)	4. (bit)	6. (līk)	8. (hid)

Look at the words and pronunciations below. Think of the first sound you say in each word.

am (am) **ant** (ant) **ate** (āt) **age** (āj)

The letter *a* without any line above it stands for the first sound you say in *am* and *ant.* The letter *a* with a line above it stands for the first sound you say in *ate* and *age.*

Now pronounce each of these words:

1. **played** (plād)	6. **build** (bild)	11. **sigh** (sī)
2. **plaid** (plad)	7. **clay** (klā)	12. **gay** (gā)
3. **hymn** (him)	8. **pack** (pak)	13. **scan** (skan)
4. **gate** (gāt)	9. **skein** (skān)	14. **ridge** (rij)
5. **guide** (gīd)	10. **fight** (fīt)	15. **gauge** (gāj)

Vowel Sounds

Notice the first sound you say in each of these words:

end eat on over up use

You say a different sound at the beginning of each of these six words. Each of the sounds is a vowel sound. This is the way your dictionary shows these six vowel sounds in pronunciations:

e stands for the sound of *e* in *end* and *let*
ē stands for the sound of *e* in *be* and *equal*

o stands for the sound of *o* in *on* and *hot*
ō stands for the sound of *o* in *open* and *go*
u stands for the sound of *u* in *up* and *cup*
ū stands for the sound of *u* in *use* and *music*

Pronounce each of these words:

1. **said** (sed)	4. **loaf** (lōf)	7. **few** (fū)
2. **deed** (dēd)	5. **lock** (lok)	8. **view** (vū)
3. **team** (tēm)	6. **moat** (mōt)	9. **love** (luv)

Now you know the signs your dictionary uses for ten vowel sounds. They are: a, ā; e, ē; i, ī; o, ō; u, ū.

The picture key below may help you remember the signs for these common vowel sounds.

What Is It?

Do you know the name of each thing that is pictured on this page?

The picture tells you what the word means.
The letters in large type tell you how to spell it.
The pronunciation tells you how to say it.

Say the name that is printed under each picture. Here is a pronunciation key to help you with the vowel sounds:

hat, āge; let, bē; it, īce; hot, ōpen; cup, ūse

dredge (drej) | **brig** (brig) | **clog** (klog)

vise (vīs) | **cube** (kūb) | **jack** (jak)

skis (skēz) | **ruff** (ruf) | **cleat** (klēt)

troll (trōl) | **sleigh** (slā) | **lyre** (līr)

Can You Say It?

The pronunciations of twelve words are printed below. Your teacher will say "One" and pronounce the first word. Then she will say "Two" and pronounce the second word. Look carefully at the pronunciation of each of the twelve words as she says it.

1. (bid)	5. (gras)	9. (hut)
2. (bīd)	6. (grāz)	10. (hū)
3. (bed)	7. (boks)	11. (ūz)
4. (bēd)	8. (pōk)	12. (hej)

Now your teacher will say each number, and you are to say the pronunciation that is given after the number.

Look at each of these pronunciations and listen as your teacher says it.

1. (jib)	5. (kot)	9. (sēz)
2. (juj)	6. (hōp)	10. (glōb)
3. (pek)	7. (trā)	11. (luk)
4. (klas)	8. (mū)	12. (rāj)

Now your teacher will say each number, and you are to say the pronunciation that is given after the number.

There is only one vowel sound in each word printed below. Pronounce each word to yourself and think of the vowel sound. Then write each word twice. First, show how to spell it and, next, show how to pronounce it.

Do it this way: 1. meat (mēt)

1. meat	5. knot	9. cup
2. met	6. note	10. cute
3. stick	7. ran	11. old
4. five	8. rain	12. feet

The tall old ship that's by the quay
Was once the queen of all the (sea, bay).

What is a *quay?* How do you say this word? Find *quay* in your dictionary and learn its pronunciation and meaning. Does *sea* or *bay* rhyme with *quay?* Now read the two lines given above, but at the end of the second line, say only the word that rhymes with *quay*.

If you can make each pair of lines below rhyme, you will have a poem about the picture.

The men who sailed her formed a clique
Of sailors, bronzed and trim and (quick, sleek).

Her famous crew would never deign
To halt for wind or sleet or (rain, brine).

A stately ship with gallant mien,
Her hulk stands now stripped bare and (plain, clean).

Against a sky of blue and mauve
She's now at rest in this small (cove, grave).

Parts of Words

Some of the entry words in your dictionary are divided into parts, and some are not. Do you know why? Look at the entry words given below.

stream (strēm)
please (plēz)
brain (brān)

un tie (un tī′)
fin ish (fin′ish)
dis may (dis mā′)

You will see and say at least one vowel in every word in our language. In each of the three entry words given at the left above, you say only one vowel sound. These words are not divided into parts.

You say two vowel sounds in each of the three entry words printed at the right above. These entry words are divided into two parts. Study the pronunciations of the words at the right and answer these questions:

How many vowel sounds do you say in the first part of *untie?* How many do you say in the second part?
Do you say a vowel sound in each part of *finish?*
How many vowel sounds do you say in *dismay?*

A part of a word in which you say a vowel sound is called a syllable. Each word in the first list above has only one syllable. Each word in the second list has two syllables. You can pronounce one syllable without the rest of the word. Say the first syllable in *untie* and in *finish.* Say the last syllable in *dismay.*

Look at the entry words and pronunciations printed below. Notice that each word has the same number of vowel sounds as it has syllables.

rab bit (rab′it)
mer it (mer′it)
bas ket (bas′kit)

rest less (rest′lis)
las so (las′ō)
in di cate (in′di kāt)

Accent

When you pronounce a word that has two or more syllables, you usually accent one of the syllables. That is, you say it with more force or emphasis than you do the other syllables in the word.

The accented syllable is underlined in each of the four words printed below. Say each word to yourself just as you would say it if you were talking. See if you say the accented syllable with more force than you say the unaccented one.

a wake — dol lar

lo cate — dark ness

Look at the entry words and pronunciations that are printed below.

lo cate (lō′kāt) — **in vade** (in vād′)

rob in (rob′in) — **be hold** (bi hōld′)

You know the meaning of every sign that is used in these pronunciations except this one: (′). This mark is called an accent mark. Your dictionary uses it to show which syllable is accented. In the pronunciations this mark is placed after each accented syllable.

Each of the twelve words printed below is divided into syllables. Say each word to yourself just as you would say it if you were talking. Can you tell which syllable you accent as you say the word?

Copy each word in syllables, writing an accent mark just after the accented syllable.

1. sand wich
2. un til
3. es cape
4. cap tain
5. no tice
6. ba by
7. be came
8. mag ic
9. cab in
10. mis take
11. na vy
12. sick ness

Name It

Look at the pronunciation and listen carefully as your teacher says each word. Notice the syllable she accents.

1. **ber ry** (ber′i)
2. **be lieve** (bi lēv′)
3. **re late** (ri lāt′)
4. **vague ly** (vāg′li)
5. **re veal** (ri vēl′)
6. **read i ly** (red′i li)
7. **be lat ed** (bi lāt′id)
8. **de cay** (di kā′)
9. **de light** (di līt′)
10. **sen si tive** (sen′si tiv)
11. **ray on** (rā′on)
12. **plas tic** (plas′tik)

Now your teacher will say each number, and you are to pronounce the word that is given after the number.

The meaning, spelling, and pronunciation of nine words are shown below. Pronounce the name of each picture.

wren (ren) — **volcano** (vol kā′nō) — **butte** (būt)

tepee (tē′pē) — **giraffe** (ji raf′) — **kayak** (kī′ak)

doublet (dub′lit) — **frigate** (frig′it) — **dory** (dō′ri)

Say to yourself the name of each picture. There are two vowels in each word. Each of these three words has a different vowel sound in the first syllable. But all three words have the same vowel sound in the last syllable.

Say the words *sofa*, *kitten*, and *cannon* just as you say them when you talk. The first syllable in each word is accented. The last syllable is unaccented. We say a very soft vowel sound in the last syllable of these words. Can you hear it?

Your dictionary does not use a letter of the alphabet to show this sound. It uses a special sign to show the soft unaccented vowel sound. The sign is ə. It stands for the sound of *a* in *sofa*, *e* in *kitten*, *i* in *pencil*, *o* in *cannon*, and *u* in *minus*.

You will see the ə sign in each of the pronunciations shown below. Pronounce each word and listen for the unaccented vowel sound.

(sō′fə) (kit′ən) (pen′səl) (kan′ən) (mī′nəs)

In each of the three words at the left below you will see the syllable *on*. Look at the pronunciations and say each word. Listen carefully to the three different pronunciations of the syllable *on*.

Pronounce each word that is printed at the right below. Notice the two pronunciations of the syllable *con*.

lem on (lem′ən)	**con ceal** (kən sēl′)
on ly (ōn′li)	**con stant** (kon′stənt)
on ward (on′wərd)	**ba con** (bā′kən)

Which Pronunciation?

Look at each pronunciation and listen carefully as your teacher says it. Notice the syllable she accents.

1. (ə flōt′)	5. (jen′ təl)	9. (rē′ zən ə bəl)
2. (fit′ ər)	6. (rē′ zən)	10. (av′ ər ij)
3. (ə gen′)	7. (ə tōn′)	11. (on′ ər ə bəl)
4. (on′ ər)	8. (jen′ ər əs)	12. (kən tān′)

Now your teacher will say each number, and you are to say the pronunciation that is printed after the number.

Underneath the picture in each box below you will see the pronunciations of three words. One of these words is the name of the thing that is pictured. Which of the three pronunciations shown in the first box is the name of the picture? Write the number 1 and, after it, copy the pronunciation of the correct word.

Do it this way: 1. kan′ dəl

Where Does the Accent Go?

Words sound very strange when we place the accent on the wrong syllable. Say the words that are printed below just as you would say them if you were talking. Notice which syllable you accent.

over	under	mountain	accident
below	began	wagon	surprise

Which did you say?

o′ver or o ver′	moun′tain or moun tain′
be′low or be low′	wag′on or wag on′
un′der or un der′	ac′ci dent or ac ci dent′
be′gan or be gan′	sur′prise or sur prise′

Say to yourself "beautiful picture of a river valley." Did you say "beau ti′ful pic ture′ of a riv er′ val ley′," or did you say "beau′ti ful pic′ture of a riv′er val′ley"?

Below are twenty words divided into syllables. Say the first word to yourself and notice which syllable you accent. Then copy this word in syllables and put an accent mark after the accented syllable.

Continue in this way with the other words.

1. po ta to
2. mu si cal
3. el e phant
4. ad ven ture
5. hap pi ness
6. pro tec tion
7. a rith me tic
8. cal en dar
9. syl la ble
10. re mem ber
11. lis ten
12. neigh bor hood
13. fur ni ture
14. A mer i can
15. No vem ber
16. un grate ful
17. per mis sion
18. sat is fy
19. mag nif i cent
20. prop er ty

Say the Word

Look at the picture, the word, and the pronunciation in each box. Pronounce the word that is printed under the picture. Be sure to accent the right syllable.

The pronunciation key given below will help you with the vowel sounds in the twelve words.

hat, āge; let, bē; it, īce; hot, ōpen; cup, ūse;
ə represents *a* in about, *e* in taken, *i* in pencil, *o* in lemon, *u* in circus.

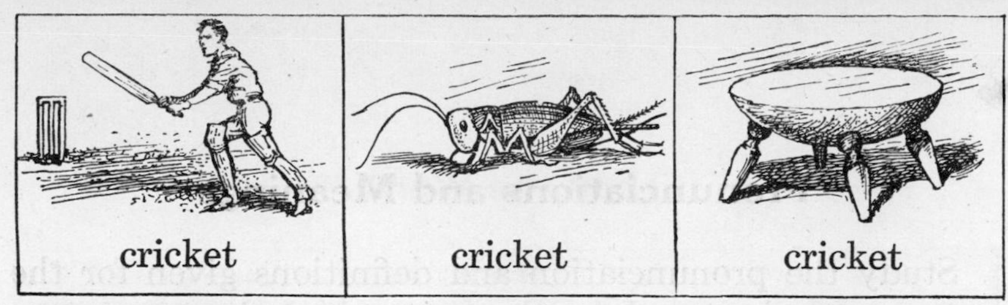

The pictures show that *cricket* may be the name of a game, an insect, or a small stool. Read the definitions under the entry words *cricket*^{1}, *cricket*^{2}, and *cricket*^{3}.

Which definition describes the first picture? Which describes the second picture? The third picture?

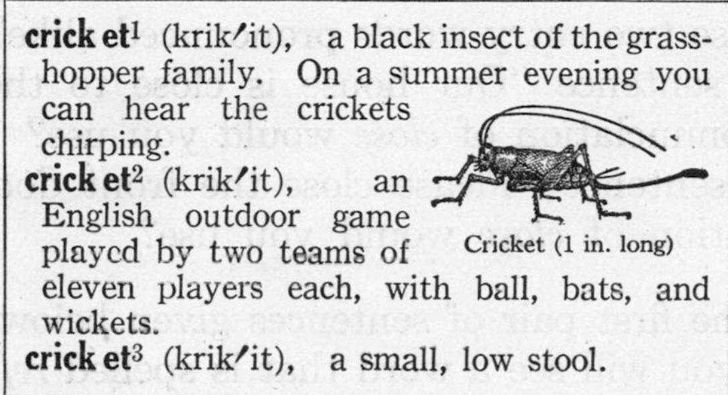
crick et^1 (krik′it), a black insect of the grass-hopper family. On a summer evening you can hear the crickets chirping.
crick et^2 (krik′it), an English outdoor game played by two teams of eleven players each, with ball, bats, and wickets.
crick et^3 (krik′it), a small, low stool.

Cricket (1 in. long)

Read the definitions given in your dictionary under the entry words *box*^{1}, *box*^{2}, and *box*^{3}. How many meanings of *box* are given under *box*^{1}? How many are given under *box*^{2}? Under *box*^{3}?

You will see *box* in each sentence below. Read the first sentence and find the meaning of *box* that fits the sentence. Is this meaning given under the entry word *box*^{1}, the entry word *box*^{2}, or the entry word *box*^{3}? Copy the sentence and, after it, write the correct entry word.

Do it this way: | 1. The boys liked to box. box^2 |

Continue in the same way with the other sentences.

1. The boys liked to box.
2. I put the things into a box.
3. A row of box grew along the walk.
4. Help me box these oranges.

Pronunciations and Meanings

Study the pronunciation and definitions given for the entry word *close*[1] and for the entry word *close*[2].

> **close**[1] (klōz), 1. shut. 2. bring together. 3. come together. 4. bring to an end. 5. an end.
> **close**[2] (klōs), 1. with little space. 2. with little fresh air. 3. near. 4. nearly equal. 5. stingy.

Are these two entry words pronounced alike?

In the sentence "Our house is close to the school," which pronunciation of *close* would you use?

In the sentence "Please close the front door," which pronunciation of *close* would you use?

Copy the first pair of sentences given below. In each sentence you will see a word that is spelled *refuse*. Find the entry words *refuse*[1] and *refuse*[2] in your dictionary. Study the pronunciations and definitions given.

How would you pronounce *refuse* in the first sentence you have copied? In the second sentence? After each sentence copy the correct pronunciation. Be sure to put the accent mark in the right place.

Continue in the same way with each of the other pairs of sentences.

1. People should not dump *refuse* in the park.
2. Please don't *refuse* to go.

3. Fish breathe through *gills.*
4. Two *gills* of water will almost fill a cup.

5. This book will *entrance* you.
6. They looked for the *entrance.*

7. Patty tried to *console* her friend.
8. The organist seated himself at the *console.*

Can You Spell It?

Your dictionary tells you how words are pronounced and what they mean. It also shows you how to spell words. Pronounce the name of the first picture below. Do you know how to spell this word? If not, find it in your dictionary and see how it is spelled. Then write the number 1 and, after it, write the correct spelling of the name of the picture.

Do it this way: 1. bonnet

Continue in this way with the other pictures.

Jack is carrying the hose.
Bill is carrying the hoes.

Which boy in the picture is Jack? Which is Bill? You can tell if you know the meanings of the words *hoes* and *hose.* These words sound alike, but they are different in spelling and in meaning. You may need to use your dictionary to learn which boy is Jack and which is Bill.

Write each sentence that is printed below, but write the correct spellings instead of the pronunciations that are printed in each. Use your dictionary to help you.

one won	Jack (wun) a prize (wun) day.
scene seen	The (sēn) was the loveliest I had ever (sēn).
peace piece	I'll have no (pēs) until I give him a (pēs) of pie.
seam seem	She didn't (sēm) to be able to sew a (sēm).
strait straight	The boat sailed (strāt) through the (strāt).
whole hole	There wasn't a (hōl) in the (hōl) piece.

Finding Spellings

All the entry words on page 93 in your dictionary begin with the letters *ac*. The letter *c* is the second letter in each spelling, but *k* is the second sign in each pronunciation. Turn to page 93 and look at each entry word and its pronunciation.

Now turn to page 99 and find all the entry words that begin with the letters *ak*. How many are there?

Suppose you wanted to find the spelling of the word that is pronounced (ak′ū rit). Would you turn first to the entry words that begin with the letters *ac*, or would you turn to those that begin with *ak?* Why?

Look at the pronunciations printed below and think of the sounds in each word.

(ak′sent) (ak′shən) (āk) (ak sept′)

Write the spelling of each word, and then look up the word in your dictionary to see if you spelled it right. Correct any errors in your spellings.

Find the entry words that begin with the letters *ca*, and notice the first sign in the pronunciations. Now look at the entry words that begin with the letters *ka*.

Write the spellings of the words that are pronounced (kā′bəl), (kāj), (kam′ər ə), and (kan′vəs). Use your dictionary to help you find and correct any errors in your spellings.

Find the entry words that begin with the letters *kn*. What is the first sound in all these words?

Each pronunciation given below begins with the sound of *n*. Use your dictionary to help you write the correct spelling for each word. If you do not find the spelling under the *n* words, look under the *kn* words.

1. (nik′əl)
2. (nīf)
3. (nar′ō)
4. (nēl)
5. (noz′əl)
6. (nuk′əl)

bear (bãr) **barn** (bärn) **fern** (fėrn) **horn** (hôrn)

You can pronounce the word printed under each of the four pictures above. Look at the pronunciations and notice the sign that your dictionary uses for the vowel sound in each word.

ã stands for the sound of *a* in *care*, *dare*, and *fare*

ä stands for the sound of *a* in *far* and *father*

ėr stands for the sound of *er* in *term*, *ir* in *bird*, *or* in *worm*, and *ur* in *turn*

ô stands for the sound of *o* in *order* and *a* in *all*

Look at each pronunciation given below and listen carefully as your teacher says the word.

1. **work** (wėrk)
2. **law** (lô)
3. **fair** (fãr)
4. **calm** (käm)
5. **ear nest** (ėr′nist)
6. **tar get** (tär′git)
7. **talk er** (tôk′ər)
8. **gui tar** (gi tär′)
9. **nurse** (nėrs)
10. **par ty** (pär′ti)
11. **pause** (pôz)
12. **whirl** (hwėrl)

Say the names of the animals that are pictured below.

llama (lä′mə) **falcon** (fô′kən) **burro** (bėr′ō)

fawn (fôn) **hare** (hãr) **sturgeon** (stėr′jən)

Four More Vowel Sounds

The picture key below shows the signs your dictionary uses for four more vowel sounds.

boy (boi)	**house** (hous)	**bush** (bu̇sh)	**stool** (stül)

This picture key and the key printed below will help you with the vowel signs oi, ou, u̇, and ü.

oil	out	pu̇t	rüle

Look at each pronunciation and listen carefully as your teacher says the word.

1. (fū)	5. (fu̇l)	9. (rou)	13. (bu̇sh′əl)
2. (pu̇l)	6. (fül)	10. (nün)	14. (hou ev′ər)
3. (dout)	7. (toil)	11. (tu̇k)	15. (kroud)
4. (pül)	8. (tüm)	12. (noiz)	16. (hü ev′ər)

Now your teacher will say each number, and you are to say the pronunciation that is printed after the number.

Think of the pronunciations of the words given below. Then when your teacher says "One," pronounce the first word in the list. When she says "Two," pronounce the second word.

Continue in this way with the other words in the list.

1. voice (vois)	**5. bough** (bou)	**9. an y how** (en′i hou)
2. shoot (shüt)	**6. ex cuse** (eks kūz′)	**10. bar be cue** (bär′bə kū)
3. would (wu̇d)	**7. cru el** (krü′əl)	**11. boil er** (boil′ər)
4. bull (bu̇l)	**8. un ru ly** (un rü′li)	**12. bul let** (bu̇l′it)

Vowel Letters and Vowel Sounds

In the three numbered sentences given on this page and in the four on the next page, you will see only five different vowel letters. If you read these sentences aloud, you will say nineteen different vowel sounds. Your dictionary uses a different sign to show each of these nineteen sounds.

Four of the words in sentence 1 contain the letter *a*. In each word the letter *a* has a different sound. In the pronunciations under the sentence, four different signs are used to show the four sounds.

1. Bill *stared at* the *face* in the *car* window.
   (stãrd) (at) (fās) (kär)

   In *stared* you say *a* as in *care*.
   In *at* you say *a* as in *hat*.
   In *face* you say *a* as in *age*.
   In *car* you say *a* as in *far*.

2. Susan has on *her green dress* and hat.
   (hėr) (grēn) (dres)

   In *her* you say *er* as in *term*.
   In *green* you say *e* as in *be*.
   In *dress* you say *e* as in *let*.

3. John could not *find his* new roller skates.
   (fīnd) (hiz)

   In *find* you say *i* as in *ice*.
   In *his* you say *i* as in *it*.

4. The *cold north* wind was *not* pleasant.

(kōld) (nôrth) (not)

In *cold* you say *o* as in *open*.
In *north* you say *o* as in *order*.
In *not* you say *o* as in *hot*.

5. *Ruth cut* a *huge* rose from the *bush*.

(Rüth) (kut) (hūj) (bu̇sh)

In *Ruth* you say *u* as in *rule*.
In *cut* you say *u* as in *cup*.
In *huge* you say *u* as in *use*.
In *bush* you say *u* as in *put*.

6. A sudden *loud noise* frightened me.

(loud) (noiz)

In *loud* you say *ou* as in *out*.
In *noise* you say *oi* as in *oil*.

7. A *medal* was *given* to a *pupil* who sang *tenor* in the school *chorus*.

(med′əl) (giv′ən) (pū′pəl) (ten′ər) (kō′rəs)

In the last syllable of *medal*, *given*, *pupil*, *tenor*, and *chorus*, you say a soft unaccented vowel sound. Your dictionary uses the sign ə to show this sound. This sign is used only in unaccented syllables.

The key below shows all the nineteen signs that your dictionary uses for vowel sounds in pronunciations. This key is printed at the bottom of every right-hand page in your dictionary.

hat, āge, cãre, fär; let, bē, tėrm; it, īce; hot, ōpen, ôrder; oil, out; cup, pu̇t, rüle, ūse; takən

Which Is It?

In sentence 1 the word *warm* is printed in italics. After the sentence you will see the pronunciations of two different words. They look something alike, but one is the pronunciation of *warm*, and the other is the pronunciation of *worm*. Use the key given at the bottom of this page to help you find out which is which. Then write the word *warm* and copy its pronunciation.

Do it this way: | 1. warm (wôrm) |

Continue in the same way with the other sentences.

1. It was a *warm* day. (wôrm) (wėrm)
2. Bob liked *plum* jam. (plüm) (plum)
3. I ate in a *restaurant.* (ri strānt′) (res′tə rənt)
4. We won the *hockey* game. (hok′i) (hu̇k′i)
5. An owl began to *hoot.* (hut) (hüt)
6. Here is my *geography* book. (ji og′rə fi) (ji ol′ə ji)
7. They saw the *Pacific* Ocean. (pə sif′ik) (pas′i fī)
8. Say the Pledge of *Allegiance.* (ə lē′jəns) (ə lī′əns)
9. His coat was *torn.* (tėrn) (tōrn)
10. My heavy shoes may *mar* the floor. (mãr) (mär)
11. That is *stark* foolishness. (stärk) (stôrk)
12. The *curtain* fell. (sėr′tən) (kėr′tən)
13. The *curfew* rings at nine o'clock. (kãr′fəl) (kėr′fū)
14. The car went around a *curve.* (kärv) (kėrv)
15. He put the harness on the *horse.* (hôrs) (härsh)
16. A sponge will *absorb* water. (ab sėrd′) (ab sôrb′)
17. The *ruler* was twelve inches long. (rül′ər) (rōl′ər)

hat, āge, cãre, fär; let, bē, tėrm; it, īce; hot, ōpen, ôrder; oil, out; cup, pu̇t, rüle, ūse; takən

One Word—Two Pronunciations

Your dictionary gives two pronunciations and four definitions for the word *rebel.*

> **reb el** (reb′əl for 1 and 2, ri bel′ for 3 and 4), 1. person who resists or fights against authority instead of obeying. The rebels armed themselves against the government. 2. defying law or authority; as, the rebel army. 3. resist or fight against law or authority. 4. feel a great dislike or opposition. We rebelled at having to stay in on so fine a day.

The phrase (reb′əl for 1 and 2) tells you that the word *rebel* is pronounced (reb′əl) if it has meaning 1 or 2. The 3 and 4 after the second pronunciation tell you that the word is pronounced (ri bel′) if it has meaning 3 or 4.

In the sentence "The rebel finally escaped," which pronunciation of *rebel* would you use?

In the sentence "I rebel against cruelty to animals," which pronunciation of *rebel* would you use?

Copy the first pair of sentences given below. Then look up the word *annex* in your dictionary. How would you pronounce *annex* in sentence 1? In sentence 2? Copy the right pronunciation after each sentence.

Continue in this way with the other sentences.

1. The *annex* had fewer rooms than the main building.
2. Bob wanted to *annex* my stamp collection to his own.

3. Mosquitoes *frequent* swamps.
4. Fogs are *frequent* along the seacoast.

5. His actions were an *insult* to the hostess.
6. We should never *insult* anyone.

7. I cannot *permit* you to go.
8. You must have a *permit* to enter the army camp.

One day when Tom and Ed were lost in the woods they met a girl who knew the country well.

"Hello, there," said Tom. "We want to get back to Camp Forest."

"All right," replied the girl. "There's Ghost Rivulet. Follow it through the scrub till you come to a shelf of granite. Then turn left and go through the alders till you see a path. When you come to the path, turn right and follow it for about ten rods till it crosses a gully. Go down the gully till you come to a blazed trail. Take that trail up the hill, and there you are! Got it?"

"Got it!" thought Tom. "Write it out and give us a dictionary, and maybe we'd get it!" But all he said was, "Thank you. Won't you go with us as far as the trail?"

If the girl had written the directions and given the boys a dictionary, what words do you think they would have looked up? Write the answers to these questions.

1. What is a rivulet?
2. Which *scrub* did the girl mean, *scrub*¹ or *scrub*²?
3. What is granite? What color is it usually?
4. What are alders?
5. Which definition of *rod* would have helped the boys?
6. What is a gully?
7. Which *blaze* did the girl use, *blaze*¹, *blaze*², or *blaze*³?

Consonant Signs and Sounds

Your dictionary uses forty-three signs to show sounds in pronunciations. Nineteen of these are vowel signs that you already know. The other twenty-four are signs for consonant sounds. You know the sounds for eighteen of these signs. You know what sound to say for:

b d f g h j k l m n p r s t v w y z

Your dictionary also uses six two-letter signs to show consonant sounds. The key printed below shows the sounds for the six two-letter signs.

ch stands for *ch* as in *child* and *much*

ng stands for *ng* as in *long* and *bring*

sh stands for *sh* as in *she* and *rush*

th stands for *th* as in *thin* and *both*

TH stands for *th* as in *then* and *smooth*

zh stands for *s* as in *measure* and *leisure*

Twelve words and their pronunciations are printed below. Look carefully at the pronunciation of each word as your teacher says it.

1. **choose** (chüz)
2. **quench** (kwench)
3. **young** (yung)
4. **bron co** (brong′kō)
5. **na tion** (nā′shən)
6. **sug ar** (shu̇g′ər)
7. **worth** (wėrth)
8. **e ther** (ē′thər)
9. **both er** (boTH′ər)
10. **wheth er** (hweTH′ər)
11. **pleas ure** (plezh′ər)
12. **ex po sure** (eks pō′zhər)

Now your teacher will say each number, and you are to say the word that is given after the number.

Pronounce each of these words:

1. **vi sion** (vizh′ən)
2. **lank** (langk)
3. **un cle** (ung′kəl)
4. **choir** (kwīr)
5. **wretch** (rech)
6. **teth er** (teTH′ər)
7. **ma chine** (mə shēn′)
8. **treas ure** (trezh′ər)
9. **tho rax** (thō′raks)

Long and Short Keys

There is a long pronunciation key on the inside front cover of this book. This long key will help you with any pronunciation, for it gives all the signs that your dictionary uses in pronunciations. Turn to the inside front cover and study the long key.

A short pronunciation key is printed at the bottom of every right-hand page in your dictionary. Turn to a right-hand page and study the short key. Then write the answers to these questions:

1. Which key would you use for vowel sounds?
2. In which key is the sound of zh shown? Turn to this pronunciation key and copy the key words for the zh sound.
3. Do you say the ng sound in the word *ink?* In *thing?*
4. Where would you look to find key words for the sign ᴛʜ? Write the key words for this sign.
5. Do you say the ch sound in *chart?* In *chamois?*

Copy the words that are printed below. Then find the pronunciation of *vein* in your dictionary. Study the short key at the bottom of the right-hand page, and copy the key word that helps you know what vowel sound to say in *vein*.

Do it this way: | 1. vein – age |

Continue in the same way with the other words.

1. vein	7. pearl	13. troy
2. alms	8. sieve	14. fowl
3. adz	9. aisle	15. flood
4. prayer	10. wan	16. queue
5. thief	11. beau	17. soot
6. says	12. fraught	18. snood

Special Meanings

Many, many years ago people knew about the useful material that we call *glass*. For a long time *glass* had only one meaning. But slowly the word came to have other meanings, too. Today, *glass* may mean a looking glass, a drinking glass, and so on.

At one time the word *glasses* meant just "more than one glass." Later it came to have a special meaning of its own. Find the word *glasses* in heavy type in the entry below and learn its special meaning.

> **glass** (glas), 1. a hard substance that breaks easily and can usually be seen through. Windows are made of glass. 2. thing or things made of glass. This shop sells china and glass. 3. something to drink from made of glass. 4. the amount a glass can hold. Drink a glass of water. 5. mirror. Look at yourself in the glass. 6. **Glasses** often means eyeglasses. 7. made of glass; as, a glass dish. 8. cover or protect with glass.

Which definition explains the meaning of *glasses* in the sentence "She filled the glasses with lemonade"?

Which definition explains the meaning of *glasses* in the sentence "He can't see without his glasses"?

Read the first sentence that is given at the bottom of this page and look up the word *trunk* in your dictionary. Then write a sentence that means the same thing as "Basketball players wear trunks," but use other words instead of the word *trunks*.

Continue in this way with the other sentences.

1. Basketball players wear *trunks*.
2. What were the *gains* from the sale?
3. Please give me my *instructions*.
4. *Flannels* are very comfortable to wear.

More Special Meanings

You know what *in* means in sentence 1 below, and you know what *hedge* means in sentence 2. But do you know what *hedge in* means in sentence 3?

1. The present was *in* the box.
2. There was a beautiful *hedge* around the yard.
3. The army attempted to *hedge in* the enemy.

When the two words *hedge* and *in* are used together, they sometimes have a special meaning. Look up the entry word *hedge* and find the definition of the phrase *hedge in*. How would you use this definition to explain the meaning of the sentence "The army attempted to hedge in the enemy"?

The words *in search of* are printed in italics in the first sentence below. Look in your dictionary under the entry word *search* to find the meaning of this phrase. Then write a sentence that means the same as "He went in search of food," but use other words instead of *in search of*.

Continue in the same way with the other sentences.

1. He went *in search of* food.
2. My old blue dress is *out of date* now.
3. Helen couldn't *figure out* the problem.
4. Suddenly the pilot ordered us to *bail out*.
5. Don't *harp on* the subject.
6. The driver's *presence of mind* prevented a wreck.
7. Mr. Miller bought his house *for a song*.
8. I go to the movies *off and on*.
9. The people were *at the mercy of* the cruel king.
10. The signal came for us to *sign off*.
11. The athlete *prides himself on* his strength.

Finding Special Meanings

In your dictionary, words with special meanings are sometimes listed separately as entry words. Look up the words *shorts*, *spectacle*, and *spectacles*. Then tell what these two sentences mean:

The pigs ate the shorts in a very short time.

The first time I wore spectacles, I thought I was a spectacle.

Sometimes groups of words with special meanings are printed as entry phrases below the definitions of the entry word. Under *high* you will find several of these.

high (hī), 1. up above the ground; as, a high jump. 2. up above others. A general has high rank. Washington was a man of high character. 3. great; greater or stronger than others; as, a high price, a high wind. 4. chief; main; as, the high altar. 5. at or to a high point, place, rank, amount, degree, price, etc. The eagle flies high. Strawberries come high in winter. Gamblers play high. 6. shrill; sharp. 7. Some special meanings are:
high and dry, 1. up out of water. 2. alone; without help.
high seas, the open ocean.
high spirits, cheerfulness; gaiety.
high tide, the time when the ocean comes up highest on the shore.
high time, the time just before it is too late.
high words, angry words.

Write a sentence that means the same as sentence 1 below, but use other words instead of *high seas*.

Continue in this way with the other sentences.

1. The old sailor longed to sail the *high seas* again.
2. They left me *high and dry* with all this work.
3. The fishing was good at *high tide*.
4. He showed his *high spirits* by whistling.

Problems and Answers

Study the following "problems and answers" so that you can solve other problems of the same kind.

PROBLEM: Write a sentence that means "The prince had many obedient servants." Do not use the word *obedient*.

WHAT TO DO: Read the definition of *obedient* and think of the meaning of the sentence.

> **o be di ent** (ō bē′di ənt), doing what one is told; willing to obey.

ANSWER: The prince had many servants who did what he told them to do.

PROBLEM: Write a sentence that means "All the employees of Mr. Jones came to the picnic." Do not use the word *employees*.

WHAT TO DO: Read the definition of *employee* and think of the meaning of the sentence.

> **em ploy ee** (em ploi′ē), person who works for some person or firm for pay.

ANSWER: All the people who work for Mr. Jones came to the picnic.

Write a sentence that means the same as the first sentence below, but do not use the word *birthplace*.

Continue in the same way with the other sentences.

1. Mr. Green visited his *birthplace*.
2. Do not light matches near *inflammable* things.
3. He *emigrated* to China when he was a young man.
4. The wrist watch had a *flexible* gold band.
5. He would not tell us his *destination*.

Two Accents

lad der (lad′ər)	**step lad der** (step′lad′ər)

When we say the word *ladder*, we accent only the first syllable, *lad*. So in the pronunciation an accent mark is placed after *lad*.

The word *stepladder* is made up of the two words *step* and *ladder*. When we say this word, we accent the first syllable, *step*, more strongly than we do the syllable *lad*. In the pronunciation of *stepladder*, there is a regular accent mark after the syllable *step* and a lighter accent mark after the syllable *lad*.

A word like *stepladder* which is made by putting two words together is called a compound word. Three other compound words and their pronunciations are printed below. Pronounce each word and listen for the heavy and the light accent.

air ship (ãr′ship′) **mo tor boat** (mō′tər bōt′) **hill side** (hil′sīd′)

There is a compound word in each of the sentences printed below. Each of these compound words has only two syllables. One of the syllables has a heavy accent, and one has a light accent. Find the compound word in each sentence. Then write the word, putting in accent marks to show the heavy and the light accent. Use your dictionary to help you.

Do it this way: | 1. rain′coat′ |

1. John wore his new raincoat to school.
2. The streetcar jumped the track.
3. Frank knew the lifeguard.
4. Jack threw a snowball at the tree.
5. The sailboat looked like a huge white bird.

Heavy and Light Accents

Can you say the names of the three animals shown in the pictures? Notice the heavy and the light accent mark in the pronunciation of *dromedary*, of *alligator*, and of *kangaroo*.

In each of the sentences printed below you will see a long word. Some of these words have one accent, and some of them have two accents.

Find the long words in the sentences and copy them in a column on a sheet of paper. Look up each word in your dictionary and copy it in syllables. Then show how the word is accented by putting a heavy or a light accent mark after each accented syllable.

Do it this way: | 1. elevator — el′e va′tor |

1. We rode up and down on the elevator.
2. No heat came from the radiator.
3. The sympathetic woman helped the lost child.
4. The noise of the cataract grew louder and louder.
5. St. Louis is a busy metropolis.
6. The little girl wore a pinafore.
7. I read a good story about a buccaneer.
8. The catastrophe will never be forgotten.
9. Jack thanked his friends for their hospitality.
10. Snakes hold a fascination for some people.
11. A strong palisade was built around the fort.

Root Words

The word *root* has many meanings. One meaning is "a part from which other things grow and develop." We call *smooth* a root word because other words have grown and developed from it. The words *smoother*, *smoothest*, *smoothed*, *smoothes*, and *smoothing* are all formed from the root word *smooth*.

Write a sentence that means the same thing as the first sentence below, but use one of the words formed from *smooth* instead of the words *made flat*.

Continue in this way with the other sentences.

1. Helen *made* her napkin *flat* before she folded it.
2. Mary was *making* the tablecloth *flat*.
3. Jack *makes* his hair *flat* with a brush.
4. Father *made* the way *easy* for Joe to get a job.

In the very front of this book you will find a page that is called "Words Made from Other Words." Turn to this page and study the sentences given there.

Write sentences that mean the same as those given below, but use one word instead of the words that are printed in italics in each sentence.

1. The *person who read* had a good voice.
2. The poor old man was *without a home*.
3. Her walk was *like that of a fairy*.
4. He talked *in a quiet way*.
5. An author is a *person who writes*.

Finding Meanings

In your dictionary four definitions are given for the word *cup*. These definitions can help you figure out the meanings of words that are formed from *cup*.

> **cup** (kup), 1. dish to drink from. Most cups have handles. 2. as much as a cup holds. She drank a cup of milk. 3. something shaped like a cup; as, the cup of a flower. 4. shape like a cup. He cupped his hands to catch the ball.

In sentence 1 below, for example, the word *cups* is used. The meaning of *cup* in this sentence is given in definition 1. The *s* on the word shows that more than one cup was on the table. Read the other sentences and study the definition that gives the meaning of *cup* in each. Notice how these definitions help you know what *cups*, *cupped*, or *cupping* means in each sentence.

1. There were two *cups* on the table. (def. 1)
2. He drank two *cups* of water. (def. 2)
3. The tulip *cups* nodded in the breeze. (def. 3)
4. The bird nestled in my *cupped* hands. (def. 4)
5. He was *cupping* his hands to catch the water. (def. 4)

Copy the five sentences below, underlining the words that are printed in italics. Look up the root word from which *latches* is formed. Which definition gives the meaning of the word *latch* in sentence 1? Write "def." and the number of this definition after the sentence.

Continue in the same way with the other sentences.

1. Jim *latches* the gate every night.
2. An elephant was *clumping* along through the jungle.
3. Four *letters* in the word were printed in large type.
4. George *mapped* out his entire vacation.
5. "He *quoted* my favorite poem," she whispered.

What Is the Root Word?

We make many words just by adding endings to root words, but we change the spelling of some root words before we add endings to them. Look at the groups of words below and answer the questions that are printed under them.

hope	hop	hurry	dry
hopes	hops	hurries	dries
hoped	hopped	hurried	drier
hoping	hopping	hurrying	driest

What letter is dropped from *hope* before *ing* is added?
What letter is added to *hop* before *ing* or *ed* is added?
What letter is changed in *hurry* before *es* or *ed* is added?
What letter is changed in *dry* before *er* or *est* is added?

Words ending in *ied*, *ies*, *ier*, and *iest* often come from root words that end in *y*.

Read each sentence below and notice the word that is printed in italics. Copy this word and, after it, write the root word from which it is formed. If you are not sure of the spelling of the root word, find it in your dictionary. Read the definitions given to be sure that you have the right word.

1. The word *parried* means "turned aside."
2. The word *hustling* means "hurrying."
3. The word *canopies* means "coverings or shelters."
4. The word *leased* means "rented."
5. The word *tinier* means "smaller."
6. The word *tidied* means "put in order."
7. The word *occurred* means "happened."
8. The word *puniest* means "weakest."
9. The word *musing* means "thinking in a dreamy way."

Finding the Root Word

Many words that end in *s*, *ed*, *ing*, etc., are not given as entry words in your dictionary. You may need to look up the root word in order to find the meanings of words that are formed from it. For example:

You will not find *lecturing* as an entry word, but you will find *lecture*.

You will not find *lopping* as an entry word, but you will find *lop*.

You will not find *coaxes*, but you will find *coax*.

You will not find *braved*, but you will find *brave*.

You will not find *abilities*, but you will find *ability*.

Read the first sentence printed at the bottom of this page, and learn the meaning of *tarnishes* by reading the definition of *tarnish* that is in your dictionary. Then write a sentence that means the same thing as sentence 1 below, but use other words instead of the word *tarnishes*.

Continue in the same way with the other sentences.

1. Silver *tarnishes* very easily.
2. Martha got her hair *bobbed*.
3. We expect snow *flurries* during the night.
4. The sweet old lady *doted on* the baby.
5. Since her illness Jean has not *craved* food.
6. A cat *relaxes* its muscles by stretching.
7. The story about the pioneers *enchanted* us.
8. "Why are you *denouncing* the book?" he asked.
9. *Hurdling* the fence was no trick for Bob.
10. I *jotted* down the address of my friend.
11. When they saw the storm, they *furled* the sails.
12. Bill would not listen to his sister's *entreaties*.

Dictionary Detective

Sometimes when you look up the meaning of a word, you find in the definition a word that you do not know.

Read the definition of *stadium* that is given below.

> **sta di um** (stā′di əm), place for athletic games, consisting of tiers of seats around an open field.

Do you know what "tiers of seats" are? This is what your dictionary says about the word *tier*.

> **tier** (tēr), one of a series of rows arranged one above another; as, tiers of seats at a baseball game.

Can you tell in your own words what *stadium* means? You might say, "A stadium is an open field with rows of seats built around it. Games are played in a stadium."

Look at the first word given below. Do you know what it means? Find the word *mesa* in your dictionary and read its definition. If there is a word in the definition that you do not know, look it up and learn its meaning. Then write the meaning of *mesa* in your own words.

Continue in this way with each of the other words.

1. mesa
2. prediction
3. bracken
4. translucent
5. treacle
6. mullet

What Does the Definition Mean?

Read the definitions that your dictionary gives for the word *exaggeration.*

> **ex ag ger a tion** (eg zaj′ər ā′shən), 1. an exaggerating. 2. a being exaggerated. 3. an exaggerated statement. It is an exaggeration to say that you would rather die than touch a snake.

Each of these three definitions uses some form of the root word *exaggerate.* Read what your dictionary says about *exaggerate* and notice how the meaning of this word helps you understand the definitions given under *exaggeration.*

> **ex ag ger ate** (eg zaj′ər āt), make too large; say or think something is greater than it is; go beyond the truth. The little boy exaggerated when he said there were a million cats in the back yard.

Now read the definitions that your dictionary gives for the word *exclusion.* What word will you need to look up to understand the definitions? Find this root word, write its spelling, and copy its definitions.

> **ex clu sion** (eks klü′zhən), 1. an excluding. 2. a being excluded. Amy's exclusion from the club hurt her feelings.

Suppose you read "The cruel king smote the old man," and you wanted to learn the meaning of *smote.* This is what your dictionary says about *smote.*

> **smote** (smōt). See **smite.** God smote the wicked city with fire from heaven.

Find the word *smite* and read the definition. Then tell what "The cruel king smote the old man" means.

Eyes and Ears

You know what *eye* means when it means a part of the body. Can you think of other meanings of this word? Use what your dictionary says under *eye* to help you tell what words go in the blanks in these sentences.

The eye of a needle is a ______.
The eye of a potato is a ______.
The eye of a hook and eye is a ______.

Read the special meanings given for *eye*. Then write a sentence that means the same as the first sentence below, but use other words instead of "keep an eye on." Continue in the same way with the other sentences.

1. Mother asked me to *keep an eye on* the baby.
2. The two boys *saw eye to eye.*
3. The yellow sweater *caught* Nell's *eye.*
4. Sally had never *set eyes on* it before.
5. "*Have an eye to* your manners," said Grandmother.

Now read what your dictionary says about *eyebrow, eyeglass, eyelash, eyelet, eyelid, eyepiece,* and *eyesight.* To understand these definitions, you must know several meanings of the word *eye.*

Which meaning of the word *eye* helps you understand the meaning of *eyelet?*

Which two meanings of *eye* help you understand the meaning of the word *eyeglass?*

Find the entry words *ear*[1] and *ear*[2] in your dictionary and read the definitions. Then tell what each of these sentences means.

1. Give ear to my story.
2. Tom says that he has no ear for music.
3. "The corn will ear soon," said the farmer.
4. Joe ate four ears of corn for dinner last night.

Aunt Lucy sent Mary a gift for her birthday. Mary wanted to write a note thanking her for the gift. But Mary was not a good speller. As soon as she started to write, she began to ask her mother how to spell first one word and then another.

"How do you spell *Aunt?*"

"A-u-n-t, dear," replied her mother.

"How do you spell *Lucy?*"

"L-u-c-y."

"How do you spell. . . ?"

"Please, Mary, don't bother me now," said Mother. "You just go ahead and write your letter on scratch paper. If you don't know how to spell a word, leave a blank. Then after I finish what I'm doing, I'll help you spell all the words you don't know."

When Mary had finished, her letter looked funny. It was full of blanks! Mary's note is printed on the next page, and each blank in it is numbered. Under the note are three spellings for the word Mary wanted to put in each blank. One of the three spellings is correct. The other two are wrong.

If you use your dictionary to help you, you can write Mary's letter and spell every word correctly. Try it.

Dear Aunt Lucy,

I was so happy when I ___(1)___ the lovely ___(2)___ you ___(3)___ me. It just matches my new ___(4)___. Mother says she is going to get me a new ___(5)___ this fall. I hope it will be the same ___(6)___ as my pretty ___(7)___.

Bill is a first ___(8)___ now. He is hoping to come home on ___(9)___ before long. All of us are ___(10)___ to see him. I can hardly ___(11)___.

Thank you for the ___(12)___. I will carry it when you come to see us next ___(13)___.

Your loving ___(14)___,

Mary

1. received, reseived, recieved
2. perse, pearse, purse
3. cent, sent, scent
4. swetter, sweter, sweater
5. soot, suit, siut
6. kuller, color, coulor
7. pocutbuk, poketbook, pocketbook
8. lootenant, lutcnant, lieutenant
9. lieve, leave, leav
10. ankshus, angkious, anxious
11. wait, wate, waight
12. present, preasant, pressent
13. munth, month, mounth
14. niece, neece, neice

How Much Do You Know?

Do you know all the meanings of the word *light?* Read the definitions that your dictionary gives under *light*^{1}, and write the numbers of the meanings that are new to you. Do the same with *light*^{2} and *light*^{3}.

Copy the four sentences that are printed below.

1. It was so light that I could see to read.
2. The moon gives light at night.
3. A glass door helped light the room.
4. A newspaper will light from a match.

Which sentence fits definition 1 under *light*^{1}? After this sentence, write "def. 1."

Which fits definition 3 of *light*^{1}? Mark it "def. 3."

Which fits definition 13 of *light*^{1}? Mark it "def. 13."

Which fits definition 15 of *light*^{1}? Mark it "def. 15."

Now copy the phrases that are printed below.

5. light infantry
6. a light heart
7. light on her feet

Which phrase fits definition 6 under *light*^{2}? After this phrase, write "def. 6."

Which fits definition 7 of *light*^{2}? Mark it "def. 7."

Which fits definition 10 of *light*^{2}? Mark it "def. 10."

Copy these sentences.

8. His searching glance lighted on a broken twig.
9. The balloon lighted on its side in a cornfield.
10. The aviator and his parachute lighted in a tree.

Which sentence fits definition 1 under *light*^{3}? After this sentence, write "def. 1."

Which fits definition 2 of *light*^{3}? Mark it "def. 2."

Which fits definition 3 of *light*^{3}? Mark it "def. 3."

A Story Puzzle

This story may seem like a puzzle to you because it has so many big words in it. Read the story, looking up the meanings and pronunciations of words you do not know. Then write or tell the story in your own words.

Paddy was an amiable canine, but he was filled with an insatiable curiosity about everything he encountered. His innocent appearance was misleading, for back of his placid demeanor there was an indomitable spirit of mischief.

Paddy looked even more complacent than usual as he started on his habitual afternoon stroll up the avenue. Little did he know that he was about to meet a most formidable adversary.

Rascal, the tigerlike pussy of the neighborhood, was sleeping quietly as Paddy trotted by. Now on one point Rascal was positively violent. He was a four-footed lunatic when his siesta was interrupted.

The sight of Rascal dozing peacefully roused all the latent mischief in Paddy. Cautiously he approached the bundle of contentment. A malicious gleam lighted his eyes as he deliberately nipped Rascal's ear.

The bundle of contentment was instantly transformed into a terrifying hump of wrath. One look at the blazing green eyes and the bristling back and Paddy knew that he had made an error. Emitting a startled yelp, he raced across the front yard, a flying brown streak against the green grass.

Stretching himself in haughty majesty, Rascal cast an annihilating look of scorn in the general direction of the interloper's flight. Paddy, from a safe distance, ventured one backward glance and then, with complete composure, resumed his stroll.

Your Dictionary

Contents of Your Dictionary

In this dictionary, entry words that begin with the letter *a* start on page 89, words that begin with *b* start on page 117, words that begin with *c* start on page 149, and so on.

ILLUSTRATORS

Martha Colley, Nellie Starkson, Raymond E. Craig, Warner Sallman, and George White, general artists; R. J. Rice and Leon Pray, special artists for animals; Helen Snyder, special artist for plants.

THORNDIKE CENTURY

BEGINNING DICTIONARY

a (ə or ā), 1. You write with a pen or a pencil. 2. Christmas comes once a year.

a back (ə bak′), 1. backward. 2. **Taken aback** means suddenly surprised.

a ban don (ə ban′dən), 1. give up entirely. 2. desert, forsake, or leave (any place, person, or thing) without intending to return. He abandoned his farm and went to sea. A good mother will not abandon her baby.

a ban doned (ə ban′dənd), deserted; forsaken.

a base (ə bās′), bring down; make lower; make humble. A man who betrays a friend abases himself.

a bashed (ə basht′), disturbed by shyness and somewhat ashamed. The boy was abashed when he saw the room filled with strangers.

a bate (ə bāt′), 1. become less. The storm has abated. 2. make less. The medicine abated his pain. 3. do away with. We can abate the smoke nuisance by burning oil.

ab bess (ab′is), woman who is the head of an abbey of nuns.

ab bey (ab′i), 1. the building or buildings where monks or nuns live a religious life. 2. a church that was once an abbey or a part of it.

ab bot (ab′ət), man who is the head of an abbey of monks.

ab bre vi ate (ə brē′vi āt), make shorter. We can abbreviate *hour* to *hr.*

ab bre vi a tion (ə brē′vi ā′shən), 1. a shortened form, such as *hrs.* and *hr.* for *hours,* or *ft.* for *foot* or *feet.* 2. making shorter.

ab do men (ab′də men), 1. lower part of the human body, which contains the stomach and the intestines; belly. 2. last of the three parts of an insect's body.

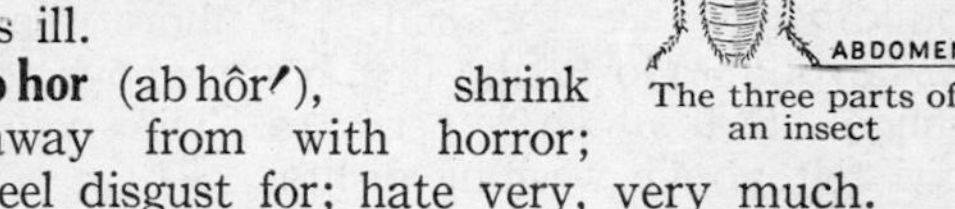

The three parts of an insect

a bed (ə bed′), in bed. Mary lies abed because she is ill.

ab hor (ab hôr′), shrink away from with horror; feel disgust for; hate very, very much.

a bide (ə bīd′), 1. stay. 2. **Abide by** means remain faithful to. He will abide by his promise. 3. dwell; continue to live (in a place). The fairy abode in a bird's nest. 4. wait for. He will abide my coming. 5. endure. A good housekeeper can't abide dirt. **abode** is formed from **abide.**

a bid ing (ə bīd′ing), permanent; lasting.

a bil i ty (ə bil′i ti), 1. power. A horse has ability to work. 2. skill. Washington had great ability as a general.

ab ject (ab′jekt), 1. wretched; miserable; degraded; very discouraged. 2. deserving contempt. Shame on you for your abject fear!

a blaze (ə blāz′), 1. on fire. 2. blazing. The room was ablaze with lights.

a ble (ā′bəl), 1. having power. Little children are able to walk, but they are not able to earn a living. 2. having the power or skill that is needed. She is an able teacher.

a bly (ā′bli), in an able manner; with skill; well.

ab nor mal (ab nôr′məl), not as it should be; very different from the ordinary conditions; unusual. It is abnormal for a man to have six fingers on each hand, or to walk in his sleep.

a board (ə bōrd′), on board; on a ship, train, airplane, etc.

a bode (ə bōd′), 1. place to live in; dwelling; house. 2. See **abide.** He abode there one year.

a bol ish (ə bol′ish), do away with; put an end to. Many people wish that nations would abolish war.

ab o li tion (ab′ə lish′ən), putting an end to; abolishing. The abolition of slavery in the United States occurred in 1865.

a bom i na ble (ə bom′i nə bəl), disgusting; hateful.

a bound (ə bound′), be plentiful. Fish abound in the ocean.

a bout (ə bout′), 1. This story is about horses. 2. He has about finished his work. 3. A collar goes about the neck. Look about and tell me what you see. 4. He is about to go. 5. Turn about is fair play.

a bove (ə buv′), 1. in a higher place. 2. higher than; over. Look above the tall building to see the sun. 3. more than. 4. beyond. Go to the first house above the school. 5. too high; superior to. The spoiled girl felt above washing dishes.

a breast (ə brest′), side by side. The soldiers marched four abreast.

a bridge (ə brij′), make shorter; make less. This long story must be abridged.

a broad (ə brôd′), 1. outside one's country. He is going abroad this summer to travel in England. 2. widely. The news of his coming spread abroad. 3. outside the house. He walks abroad only at night.

a brupt (ə brupt′), 1. sudden. He made an abrupt turn to avoid another car. 2. short and blunt. He was very gruff and had an abrupt way of speaking. 3. changing one's thoughts suddenly. 4. very steep. The road made an abrupt rise up the hill.

ab sence (ab′səns), being away. His absence from school was caused by illness.

ab sent (ab′sənt for 1 and 3, ab sent′ for 2), 1. away; not present. Three members of the class were absent. 2. keep (oneself) away. Do not absent yourself from school without reason. 3. lacking. Snow is absent in some countries.

ab so lute (ab′sə lüt), 1. complete; perfect. Try to tell the absolute truth. 2. not limited in any way. A long time ago some rulers had absolute power.

ab so lute ly (ab′sə lüt li), 1. completely. His frozen hand was absolutely useless. 2. certainly. David spoke only when it was absolutely necessary.

ab solve (ab solv′), 1. declare free from sin or blame. 2. set free from a promise or duty.

ab sorb (ab sôrb′), 1. take in or suck up (liquids). A sponge absorbs water. A blotter absorbs ink. 2. take in and hold. Anything black absorbs light that falls on it. 3. take up all the attention of; interest very much. The boy was absorbed in building a dam in the brook.

ab sorb ing (ab sôr′bing), extremely interesting; as, an absorbing story.

ab sorp tion (ab sôrp′shən), 1. act or process of absorbing; as, the absorption of ink by a blotter. 2. condition of being absorbed; great interest. Everybody noticed the absorption of the children in their game.

ab stain (ab stān′), do without something; hold yourself back; refrain. If you abstain from eating candy and rich foods, you will not be so fat.

ab sti nence (ab′sti nəns), partly or entirely giving up certain pleasures, food, drink, etc.

ab stract (ab strakt′ for 1, ab′strakt for 2, 3, and 4), 1. take away. Can you abstract the watch from my pocket without my knowing it? 2. thought of apart from any real thing. The idea of perfection is an abstract idea. 3. hard to understand; difficult. 4. a brief statement of the main ideas in an article, book, etc.

ab surd (ab sėrd′), plainly not sensible or true; foolish; ridiculous.

ab surd i ty (ab sėr′di ti), 1. foolishness; lack of sense. You can see the absurdity of wearing shoes on your head and hats on your feet. 2. something absurd. To say that every father has a daughter is an absurdity.

ab surd ly (ab sėrd′li), foolishly; against reason; to an absurd degree.

a bun dance (ə bun′dəns), great plenty; a quantity that is more than enough. There was such an abundance of apples that year that many were fed to the pigs.

a bun dant (ə bun′dənt), more than enough; very plentiful.

a bun dant ly (ə bun′dənt li), in large quantities; with more than enough. He supplied them abundantly, and nobody went hungry.

a buse (ə būz′ for 1, 3, and 6, ə būs′ for 2, 4, 5, and 7), 1. make bad use of. 2. bad or wrong use. 3. treat badly. 4. bad treatment. 5. a bad practice or custom. 6. scold very severely. 7. a severe scolding; harsh language.

a byss (ə bis′), a very deep crack in the earth; a bottomless hole.

a cad e my (ə kad′ə mi), 1. a place for instruction. 2. a private high school. 3. school where some special subject can be studied.

ac cel er a tor (ak sel′ər ā′tər), thing or person that increases the speed of anything.

ac cent (ak′sent), 1. the greater force or stronger tone of voice given to certain syllables or words. 2. a mark (′). 3. pronounce or write with an accent. 4. a peculiar manner of pronouncing heard in different parts of the same country, or in the speech of a person speaking a language not his own. Hans is German and speaks English with a German accent. 5. tone. She speaks to him in tender accents.

ac cept (ak sept′), 1. take what is offered or given to one. 2. consent to; say yes to. 3. take as satisfactory. We accepted her excuse.

ac cept a ble (ak sep′tə bəl), worth accepting; satisfactory; agreeable. Flowers are an acceptable gift to a sick person.

ac cept ance (ak sep′təns), 1. taking what is offered or given to one. Her acceptance of the flowers they brought delighted the children. 2. approval; taking as right, true, and sufficient; as, the acceptance of a plan or a new idea.

ac cess (ak′ses), approach to places, things, or persons. Access to mountain towns is often difficult because of bad roads. Has he access to men who could help him get work?

ac ces si ble (ak ses′i bəl), easy to get at; easy to reach. A public library makes good books accessible. A telephone is put where it will be accessible.

ac ces so ry (ak ses′ə ri), 1. something added; a finishing touch. All the accessories to her costume—gloves, stockings, handkerchiefs, and purse—were perfectly matched. 2. added; helping the general effect. His tie supplied an accessory bit of color which was very pleasing. 3. person who has helped in a crime.

ac ci dent (ak′si dənt), 1. an event not wanted, intended, or planned to happen, such as dropping a dish, a shipwreck, or the killing of a dog by an automobile. 2. chance. I cut my foot by accident. We found that the front door had been left open by accident and a thief had got in.

ac ci den tal (ak′si den′təl), happening by chance. Breaking May's doll was accidental; John did not mean to do it.

ac ci den tal ly (ak′si den′təl i), by chance; without being planned; not on purpose.

ac claim (ə klām′), 1. applaud; shout welcome; show approval of. The crowd acclaimed the fireman for rescuing two babies from the burning house. 2. applause; welcome.

ac com mo date (ə kom′ə dāt), 1. hold; have room for; lodge. This big bedroom will accommodate six beds. Can you accommodate a party of five for two weeks? 2. oblige; help out. He wanted some change, but I could not accommodate him.

ac com mo dat ing (ə kom′ə dāt′ing), obliging. The man was accommodating enough to lend me a quarter.

ac com mo da tion (ə kom′ə dā′shən), 1. room; lodging for a time. This hotel has accommodations for one hundred people. 2. a help; a convenience. It will be an accommodation to me if you will meet me tomorrow instead of today.

ac com pa ni ment (ə kum′pə ni mənt), anything that goes along with something else. The rain was an unpleasant accompaniment to our ride. She sang to a piano and violin accompaniment.

ac com pa ny (ə kum′pə ni), 1. go along with. He will accompany you on your walk. The rain was accompanied by a high wind. 2. make music along with other music.

ac com pa ny ing (ə kum′pə ni ing), going with. The soldiers and the accompanying band made a fine show.

ac com plice (ə kom′plis), person who shares in a crime.

ac com plish (ə kom′plish), do; carry out. Did you accomplish your purpose? He can accomplish more in a day than any other boy in his class.

ac com plished (ə kom′plisht), 1. done; carried out; completed. 2. expert; skilled; as, an accomplished dancer.

ac com plish ment (ə kom′plish mənt), 1. accomplishing; doing. The accomplishment of his purpose took two days. 2. a completed act or undertaking. 3. something that has been done with knowledge, skill, and ability. It was a real accomplishment to finish housecleaning in two days. 4. special skill. She was a girl of many accomplishments. She could play, sing well, and also sew and cook.

ac cord (ə kôrd′), 1. agree. His account of the day accords with yours. 2. agreement. Their opinion of war was in accord with his. 3. **Of one's own accord** means without being asked or without suggestion from anyone else. A boy who washes his hands of his own accord is indeed unusual.

ac cord ance (ə kôr′dəns), agreement; harmony. What he did was in accordance with what he said.

ac cord ing ly (ə kôr′ding li), 1. in agreement with something that has been stated. These are the rules. You can act accordingly or leave the club. 2. therefore. He was too sick to stay. Accordingly, we sent him home.

according to, 1. in agreement with. He came according to his promise. You will be ranked according to the work you do. 2. on the authority of. According to this book a tiger is really a big cat.

ac cost (ə kôst′), step up to and speak to. A stranger accosted him, asking him the way to church.

ac count (ə kount′), 1. statement of money received and spent; record of business. Jack keeps a written account of the way he spends his money. All stores, banks, and factories keep accounts. 2. statement; explanation; story. The boy gave his father an account of the ball game. 3. reason. The game was put off on account of rain. George was brought up not to lie on any account. 4. sake. Don't wait on my account. 5. consider. Solomon was accounted wise. 6. Some special meanings are:

account for, 1. tell what has been done with; answer for. The treasurer of a club has to account for the money paid to him. 2. explain. Late frosts accounted for the poor fruit crop.

of no account, of no use or importance.

on account of, because of.

on no account, under no conditions; certainly not.

turn to account, make useful or helpful.

ac cou ter (ə kü′tər), equip; array.

ac cu mu late (ə kū′mū lāt), heap up; collect. He accumulated a fortune by hard work. Dust had accumulated during the weeks she was gone.

ac cu mu la tion (ə kū′mū lā′shən), 1. collection. The accumulation of useful knowledge is one result of reading. 2. material collected; mass. His accumulation of old papers filled two closets.

ac cu ra cy (ak′ū rə si), exactness; correctness; being without errors or mistakes.

ac cu rate (ak′ū rit), exactly right. You must be accurate in arithmetic.

ac curs ed (ə kėr′sid or ə kėrst′), 1. cursed. 2. detestable; hateful.

ac cu sa tion (ak′ū zā′shən), a charge of being or doing something bad. The accusation against him was that he had stolen ten dollars from the store.

ac cuse (ə kūz′), 1. charge with being or doing something bad. The children accused Fred of being a tattletale. The man was accused of speeding. 2. find fault with; blame.

ac cus tom (ə kus′təm), make familiar by use or habit; get used. You can accustom yourself to almost any kind of food.

ac cus tomed (ə kus′təmd), 1. usual. By Monday he was back in his accustomed place. 2. **Accustomed to** means used to; in the habit of. He was accustomed to hard work.

ace (ās), 1. a playing card having one spot. The ace is the highest card. 2. a first-class aviator.

ache (āk), 1. continuous pain, such as a stomach ache, headache, or toothache. 2. suffer continuous pain; be in pain. My back aches.

a chieve (ə chēv′), 1. do; carry out. Did you achieve all that you expected to today? 2. reach (a certain end) by one's own efforts. George achieved fame as a swimmer.

a chieve ment (ə chēv′mənt), 1. achieving. 2. some plan or action carried out with courage or with unusual ability. Flying across the Atlantic for the first time was a great achievement.

ac id (as′id), 1. sour; sharp or biting to the

taste. Lemons are an acid fruit. Rhubarb has an acid taste. 2. sour substance.

ac knowl edge (ak nol′ij), 1. admit to be true. He acknowledges his faults. 2. recognize the authority or claims of. We acknowledged him to be the best player on the baseball team. 3. make known that one has received (a favor, gift, message, etc.). Mary acknowledged the gift with a pleasant letter.

ac knowl edg ment (ak nol′ij mənt), 1. an acknowledging. 2. something given or done for a service, favor, message, etc. A receipt is the acknowledgment that a bill has been paid.

ac me (ak′mi), highest point. A baseball player usually reaches the acme of his skill before he is thirty.

a corn (ā′kôrn), the nut of an oak tree. See the picture.

Acorns

ac quaint (ə kwānt′), 1. make familiar. "Let me acquaint you with the facts," means "Let me make the facts known to you." 2. **Be acquainted with** means have personal knowledge of (persons or things). I have heard about your friend, but I am not acquainted with him.

ac quaint ance (ə kwān′təns), 1. knowledge of persons or things gained from experience with them. I have some acquaintance with French, but I do not know it well. 2. person known to you, but not a close friend.

ac qui esce (ak′wi es′), accept without making objections; agree or submit quietly. John's parents acquiesced in the principal's decision that John should not be promoted.

ac quire (ə kwīr′), gain or get as one's own; get. By the time James was thirty he had acquired a store of his own.

ac qui si tion (ak′wi zish′ən), 1. acquiring. He spent hundreds of hours in the acquisition of skill with a rifle. 2. something acquired or gained. Mary's new acquisitions were two dresses, a hat, and a pair of shoes.

ac quit (ə kwit′), 1. declare not guilty. The man was acquitted of the crime. 2. **Acquit oneself** means do one's part; behave. The soldiers acquitted themselves bravely in battle.

a cre (ā′kər), 160 square rods or 43,560 square feet.

a cre age (ā′kər ij), the number of acres. The acreage of this park is over 800.

ac rid (ak′rid), 1. sharp, bitter, or stinging. Smoke feels acrid in your mouth and nose. 2. sharp in manner or temper.

ac ro bat (ak′rə bat), person who can dance on a rope or wire, swing on trapezes, turn handsprings, or do other such feats of bodily skill and strength.

a cross (ə krôs′). The man sawed the plank across. The cat walked across the street. The woods are across the river.

act (akt), 1. thing done; deed. Feeding the hungry is a kind act. 2. doing. The farmer caught the boys in the act of stealing his apples. 3. do something. The firemen acted promptly and saved the burning house. 4. have effect. Yeast acts on dough and makes it rise. 5. behave. The boy acted badly in school. 6. behave like. Most people act the fool now and then. 7. perform in a theater; play a part. The actor acts the part of the hero. He acts very well. 8. a main division in a play or opera. Most modern plays have three acts. 9. one of several performances on a program; as, the trained dog's act. 10. law; decree. 11. **Act as** or **act for** means do the work of; take the place of.

ac tion (ak′shən), 1. doing something; acting. The quick action of the firemen saved the building from fire. 2. thing done; act. Giving the dog food was a kind action. 3. way of working. This motor has a very easy action.

ac tive (ak′tiv), 1. acting; working; as, an active volcano, an active force. 2. showing much action; lively; moving rather quickly much of the time. Children are more active than grown people.

ac tiv i ty (ak tiv′i ti), 1. being active; movement; use of power; as, mental activity, physical activity, activity in club work. 2. action. 3. thing to do; as, outdoor activities, classroom activities.

ac tor (ak′tər), 1. person who acts on the stage or in moving pictures. 2. person who does something.

ac tress (ak′tris), woman actor.

ac tu al (ak′chü əl), real; existing as a fact. What he told us was not a dream but an actual happening.

ac tu al ly (ak′chü əl i), really; in fact.

a cute (ə kūt′), 1. sharp-pointed. 2. sharp and severe. A toothache can cause acute pain. 3. keen. Dogs have an acute sense of smell. An acute thinker is clever and shrewd. 4. less than a right angle.

ACUTE ANGLE RIGHT ANGLE

A.D., in the year of our Lord; since Christ was born. From 200 B.C. to 500 A.D. is seven hundred years.

Ad am (ad′əm), in the Bible, the first man.

ad a mant (ad′ə mant), 1. substance too hard to be cut or broken. 2. firm; unyielding.

a dapt (ə dapt′), make fit or suitable. The boys adapted the old barn for use by the club.

a dapt a ble (ə dap′tə bəl), 1. easily changed to fit different conditions. 2. changing easily to fit different conditions.

ad ap ta tion (ad′ap tā′shən), 1. an adapting or fitting. 2. a being adapted or made to fit. 3. something made by adapting. That book is an adaptation of old myths.

add (ad), 1. put together. When you add 4 and 2 and 3, you have 9. 2. **Add to** means put with. She added sugar to her tea. 3. **Add to** sometimes means make greater. The fine day added to our pleasure. 4. go on to say; say further.

ad der (ad′ər), 1. a poisonous snake of Europe. 2. a small, harmless snake of North America.

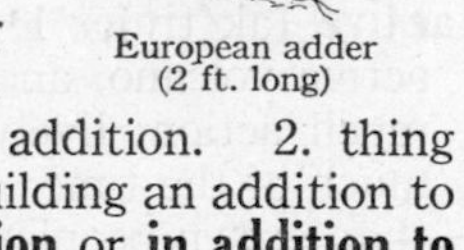
European adder (2 ft. long)

ad di tion (ə dish′ən), 1. adding one number or quantity to another. 2+2=4 is a simple addition. 2. thing added. Workmen are building an addition to this house. 3. **In addition** or **in addition to** means besides. In addition to the money for their work the girls received free lunches.

ad di tion al (ə dish′ən əl), added; extra; more. Mother will need additional help to do the work while there is so much company.

ad dress (ə dres′), 1. a speech, either spoken or written. The President gave an address to the nation over the radio. 2. speak to or write to. He will address you on the subject of war and peace. The king was addressed as "Your Majesty." 3. the place to which mail is directed. Write the name and address on the letter. 4. write on (an envelope or package) where it is to be sent. Please address this letter for me. 5. apply (oneself). He addressed himself to the task of cutting down the tree.

a dept (ə dept′), very skillful; expert. She is adept in music.

ad e quate (ad′i kwit), sufficient; enough; as much as is needed. His wages are adequate to support three people.

ad here (ad hēr′), stick fast (to a substance, a party, a person, or an opinion). Soft snow adheres to the branches. Most people adhere to the church of their parents.

a dieu (ə dū′ or ə dü′), good-by.

a dieux (ə dūz′ or ə düz′), good-bys.

ad ja cent (ə jā′sənt), near; adjoining. The house adjacent to ours has just been sold.

ad jec tive (aj′ik tiv), the name of a quality added to the name of a person, animal, or thing to describe it more fully. *Green, old, short, sweet,* and *sour* are adjectives.

ad join (ə join′), be next to; be close to; be side by side. His yard adjoins ours. New Jersey adjoins New York. We have adjoining desks.

ad journ (ə jérn′), 1. stop business for a time. The court adjourned from Friday until Monday. 2. put off until a later time. The president adjourned the meeting until all the members of the club could be present.

ad just (ə just′), arrange; set just right; change to make fit. These desks and seats can be adjusted to the height of ány child.

ad just ment (ə just′mənt), settlement; changing to make fit; setting right to fit some standard or purpose. The adjustment of seats to the right height for children is necessary for their comfort. Try to make some adjustment of your differences so that you can work together without quarrels.

ad min is ter (ad min′is tər), 1. manage. The Secretary of War administers a department of the government. A housekeeper administers a household. 2. give as medicine or treatment; apply; give (to). The nurse administers castor oil. Judges administer justice and punishment.

ad min is tra tion (ad min′is trā′shən), 1. management. 2. management of public affairs; government.

ad mi ra ble (ad′mi rə bəl), 1. worth admiring. 2. excellent; very good.

ad mi ral (ad′mi rəl), 1. officer in command of a fleet of ships. 2. officer of the highest rank in the navy.

ad mi ra tion (ad′mi rā′shən), 1. the feeling we have when we admire; delight or satisfaction at something fine or beautiful or well done. 2. person or thing that is admired. Helen's beautiful dress was the admiration of all her friends.

ad mire (ad mīr′), regard with wonder, pleasure, and satisfaction. We admire a brave boy, a beautiful picture, or a fine piece of work.

ad mir er (ad mīr′ər), person who admires.

ad mis sion (ad mish′ən), 1. an admitting or being admitted. We paid a dollar for admission to the concert. 2. the price of being admitted. 3. acknowledging. Tom's admission that he was to blame kept the other boys from being punished.

ad mit (ad mit′), 1. allow to enter. This ticket will admit you to the circus. He was admitted to school this year. 2. acknowledge. Tom admits now that he was wrong.

ad mon ish (ad mon′ish), warn or advise (a person) about his faults in order that he may be guided to improve.

ad mo ni tion (ad′mə nish′ən), admonishing; warning; advice concerning the faults a person has shown or may show.

a do (ə dü′), action; stir; fuss; trouble. There was much ado about the party by all the family. Alice made a great ado because her dress did not fit.

a do be (ə dō′bi), 1. sun-dried brick. 2. made of sun-dried brick. Many people in southwestern United States and in Mexico live in adobe houses.

Adobe house

a dopt (ə dopt′), take for your own or as your own choice. People adopt children into their families. I liked your idea and adopted it.

a dop tion (ə dop′shən), 1. adopting. Our club voted for the adoption of some new rules. 2. being adopted. John's adoption by his aunt changed his whole life.

a dor a ble (ə dōr′ə bəl), worthy of being adored.

ad o ra tion (ad′ə rā′shən), 1. worship. 2. the highest respect and love.

a dore (ə dōr′), respect and love very, very greatly; worship.

a dorn (ə dôrn′), add beauty to; decorate.

a dorn ment (ə dôrn′mənt), 1. act of adorning. Mary was busy with the adornment of the church. 2. thing that adds beauty; ornament.

a drift (ə drift′), drifting; floating without being guided.

a droit (ə droit′), skillful. Monkeys are adroit climbers. A good teacher is adroit in asking questions.

a dult (ə dult′ or ad′ult), 1. full-grown; grown-up; mature; having full size and strength. 2. a grown-up person.

ad vance (ad vans′), 1. move forward. The angry crowd advanced toward the building. 2. put forward. The plan he advanced was not good. 3. forward movement; progress. The army's advance was very slow. 4. go up. Sugar had advanced two cents a pound. 5. put up. The grocer advanced his prices on food when he had to pay more in the market. 6. rise in price or value. 7. personal approach; approach made to gain something. Frank made the first advances toward making up his quarrel with Jack. 8. **In advance** means in front, or ahead of time.

ad vanced (ad vanst′), 1. in advance. 2. ahead of most others. 3. far along in life; very old. His grandfather lived to the advanced age of ninety years.

ad vance ment (ad vans′mənt), advance; improvement; promotion.

ad van tage (ad van′tij), 1. anything that is desirable, or is a benefit. 2. help.

ad van ta geous (ad′vən tā′jəs), helpful; profitable; favorable. This advantageous position commands three roads.

ad vent (ad′vent), coming; arrival.

ad ven ture (ad ven′chər), 1. a bold and difficult undertaking, usually exciting and somewhat dangerous. A hunter of tigers has many adventures. 2. an unusual experience. The trip to Florida was an adventure for Mother. 3. dare to do; risk. 4. venture; dare.

ad ven tur er (ad ven′chər ər), person who has or seeks adventures.

ad ven tur ous (ad ven′chər əs), 1. fond of adventures; ready to take risks. Captain John Smith was a bold, adventurous explorer. 2. full of danger. The discovery of the North Pole was an adventurous undertaking.

ad verb (ad′vėrb), word that expresses time, place, manner, degree, or circumstances. *Soon, never, here, very,* and *gladly* are adverbs.

ad ver sar y (ad′vər sãr′i), enemy; person opposing another.

ad verse (ad vėrs′), 1. contrary; opposed. Adverse winds hinder ships. 2. unfavorable; harmful. Dirt and disease are adverse to the best growth of children.

ad ver si ty (ad vėr′si ti), distress; misfortune; hardship.

ad ver tise (ad′vər tīz), 1. give public notice of; announce. People advertise things that they wish to sell in newspapers, in magazines, over the radio, and in many other ways. 2. **Advertise for** means ask for by a public notice.

ad ver tise ment (ad′vər tīz′mənt), public announcement; printed notice. The store has an advertisement in the newspaper of a special sale.

ad vice (ad vīs′), 1. opinion about what should be done. To keep well, follow the doctor's advice. 2. news; information. Advices from China show that there will be war.

ad vis a ble (ad vīz′ə bəl), wise; sensible; suitable. It is not advisable for him to go while he is still sick. A hot-air furnace is not advisable for a large building.

ad vise (ad vīz′), 1. give advice to. He advised me to keep my money in the bank. 2. talk over plans; consult. 3. inform. We were advised of the dangers before we began our trip.

ad vis er or **ad vi sor** (ad vīz′ər), person who gives advice.

ad vo cate (ad′və kāt), 1. speak in favor of; recommend publicly. He advocates building more good roads. 2. person who speaks in favor; supporter. Mr. Smith is an advocate of better school buildings. 3. lawyer.

adz or **adze** (adz), tool somewhat like an ax. The blade is set across the end of the handle and curves inward.

Adz used by coopers

aer i al (ãr′i əl), 1. of the air; in the air. 2. like air. 3. a device with a radio set to receive the electric waves. 4. the wire or wires used in sending by radio.

aer o plane (ãr′ə plān), airplane.

a far (ə fär′), far; far away; far off; from a distance.

a feard (ə fērd′), afraid.

af fa ble (af′ə bəl), easy to talk to; courteous and pleasant.

af fair (ə fãr′), 1. thing to do; job; business. The President has many affairs to look after. 2. any thing or happening. The party Saturday was a jolly affair.

af fect[1] (ə fekt′), 1. produce a result or effect on; influence. The amount of rain affects the growth of crops. The disease affected his mind so that he could not remember what he had done. 2. touch the heart of. The stories of starving children so affected him that he sent all his spare money for relief.

af fect[2] (ə fekt′), pretend to have or feel. He affected ignorance of the fight, but we knew that he had seen it all.

af fect ed[1] (ə fek′tid), acted upon; influenced.

af fect ed[2] (ə fek′tid), artificial; pretended.

af fec tion (ə fek′shən), 1. friendly feeling; love. 2. disease. He is suffering from an affection of the ear.

af fec tion ate (ə fek′shən it), loving; fond; showing affection.

af firm (ə fėrm′), say firmly; declare to be true; assert. The Bible affirms that God is love.

af firm a tive (ə fėr′mə tiv), 1. saying yes; affirming. His answer was affirmative. 2. the side that says yes or affirms in an argument.

af flict (ə flikt′), cause pain to; trouble very much; distress greatly.

af flic tion (ə flik′shən), 1. pain; trouble; distress. 2. misfortune.

af flu ent (af′lü ənt), abundant; rich.

af ford (ə fōrd′), 1. have the means; have the money, time, or strength. Can we afford to buy a new car? He cannot afford to waste so much time. 2. yield; give. His own garden affords fresh vegetables for the family. Reading this story will afford real pleasure.

af fright (ə frīt′), frighten; excite with sudden fear.

af front (ə frunt′), 1. insult openly and purposely. The boy affronted the teacher by making a face at her. 2. offend the modesty or self-respect of. 3. an open insult. To be called a coward is an affront.

a field (ə fēld′), 1. in or on the field; to the field. 2. away; away from home. He wandered far afield in foreign lands.

a fire (ə fīr′), on fire.

a float (ə flōt′), 1. floating. John had ten

balloons afloat at one time. 2. on shipboard. On our trip around the world, we were afloat 60 days and ashore 30 days. 3. going around. Rumors of a revolt were afloat.

a foot (ə fu̇t′), 1. on foot; walking. Did you come all the way afoot? 2. going on; in progress. Great preparations for the dinner were afoot in the kitchen.

a fore (ə fōr′), before.

a fore said (ə fōr′sed′), said before; spoken before.

a fraid (ə frād′), frightened; feeling fear. She is afraid of snakes.

a fresh (ə fresh′), again. The child began to cry afresh when he saw his mother.

Af ri ca (af′ri kə), the continent south of Europe. Egypt is in Africa.

Af ri can (af′ri kən), 1. of Africa; having to do with Africa; from Africa. 2. a native of Africa. 3. Negro.

aft (aft), at the stern; toward the stern.

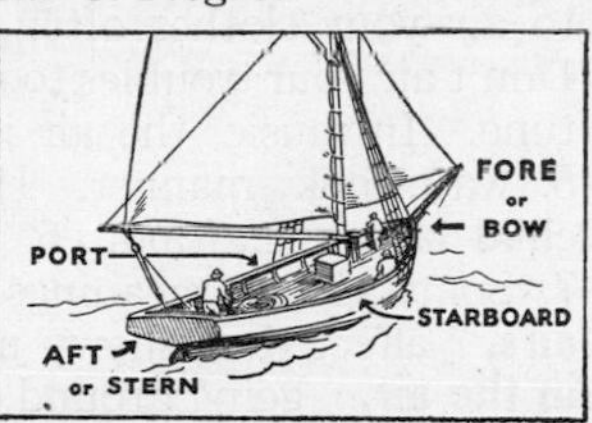

af ter (af′tər), 1. Jill came running after. You come after me in the line. 2. After dinner we can go. 3. After the way she has acted, how can you like her? 4. later; following. The after results of the storm were terrible. 5. in search of; in pursuit of. The dog ran after the rabbit.

af ter noon (af′tər nün′), the time from noon to evening.

af ter ward (af′tər wərd), afterwards; later.

af ter wards (af′tər wərdz), later. The bud was small at first, but afterwards it became a large flower.

a gain (ə gen′), another time; once more. Say that again. Come again to play.

a gainst (ə genst′). The dogs fought against the lion. Rain beats against the window. **Against** sometimes means in preparation for. Squirrels store up nuts against the winter.

ag ate (ag′it), 1. a stone with colored stripes or cloudy colors; a kind of quartz. 2. a marble used in games that looks like agate.

Agate, polished, showing stripes.

age (āj), 1. time of life; as, the age of ten. 2. length of life. The great trees of California have the greatest age of any living thing. 3. a particular period of life; as, old age. **Of age** means 21 years old or over. 4. period in history; as, the age of machinery. 5. a long time. 6. grow old. He is aging fast. 7. make old.

a ged (ā′jid for 1, ājd for 2), 1. old; having lived a long time. The aged woman was wrinkled and bent. 2. of the age of. She was aged six when she first went to school.

a gen cy (ā′jən si), 1. the office or business of some person or company that acts for another. An agency rented my house for me. Employment agencies help workers to get jobs, and find workers for people who need them. 2. means; action. Through the agency of friends he was set free.

a gent (ā′jənt), 1. person or company that acts for another. I made my brother my agent while I was out of the city. 2. any power or cause that produces an effect. Heat and electricity are important agents in the life of today.

ag gra vate (ag′rə vāt), 1. make worse; make more severe. His bad temper was aggravated by his headache. 2. annoy; irritate; provoke.

ag gre gate (ag′ri gāt), 1. collect; unite. Granite is made of small particles aggregated together. 2. collection; mass of separate things joined together. 3. amount to. The money collected will aggregate $1000. 4. total. The aggregate of all the gifts was over a hundred dollars.

ag gres sion (ə gresh′ən), 1. an attack. 2. the first step in an attack or quarrel.

ag gres sive (ə gres′iv), 1. taking the first step in an attack or quarrel; attacking. 2. active; energetic. When people grow old, they become less aggressive.

ag gres sor (ə gres′ər), one that begins an attack or quarrel.

ag grieve (ə grēv′), injure unjustly; oppress; cause grief or trouble to. He was aggrieved at the insult from his friend.

a ghast (ə gast′), frightened; struck with surprise or horror.

ag ile (aj′il), moving quickly and easily. An acrobat has to be agile. You need an agile mind to solve puzzles.

a gil i ty (ə jil′i ti), ability to move quickly and easily.

ag i tate (aj′i tāt), 1. move or shake. The slightest wind will agitate the leaves of some trees. 2. disturb; excite. She was much agitated by the loss of her purse.

ag i ta tion (aj′i tā′shən), 1. a moving or shaking. 2. noisy confusion; disturbance of body or mind; excitement.

a go (ə gō′), 1. gone by; past. I met her two years ago. 2. in the past; as, long ago.

ag o nize (ag′ə nīz), 1. feel very great pain. 2. pain very much; torture. 3. struggle.

ag o ny (ag′ə ni), very great suffering of body or mind; as, the agony of a severe toothache.

a gree (ə grē′), 1. consent. They agreed to do the work at a low price. 2. have the same opinion. We all agree in liking the teacher. I agree with you that arithmetic is hard. 3. be in harmony.

a gree a ble (ə grē′ə bəl), pleasant; pleasing.

a gree ment (ə grē′mənt), 1. an agreeing; an understanding reached by two or more nations, persons, or groups of persons. Nations make treaties; certain persons make contracts. Both are agreements. 2. harmony.

ag ri cul tur al (ag′ri kul′chər əl), of agriculture; having something to do with farming.

ag ri cul ture (ag′ri kul′chər), farming; cultivating the soil to make crops grow.

a ground (ə ground′), on the ground; on the shore; on the bottom in shallow water. The ship ran aground and stuck in the sand.

a gue (ā′gū), 1. fever caused by malaria with fits of chills. 2. a fit of shivering; a chill.

ah (ä). You sometimes say "ah" suddenly when you express your feeling of sorrow, regret, surprise, admiration, dislike, or contempt.

a ha (ä hä′), exclamation of triumph, satisfaction, surprise, joy, etc.

a head (ə hed′), 1. straight in front of you. There is danger ahead on this road. 2. forward. Go ahead with this work for another week. 3. in advance. Jim was ahead of his class in reading.

a hoy (ə hoi′), a call used by sailors to attract attention. Sailors say, "Ship, ahoy!" when they call to a ship.

aid (ād), 1. help. The Red Cross gives aid to many people. Jane aided me in my spelling. 2. helper; assistant. Our teacher chooses two aids from the class.

aide (ād), army or navy officer who acts as an assistant to a superior officer.

ail (āl), 1. to trouble; be the matter with. What ails the child? 2. be ill; feel sick. She has been ailing for a week.

ai ler on (ā′lər on), the movable part of a wing of an airplane. It helps to keep the airplane balanced while flying.

ail ment (āl′mənt), illness; sickness.

aim (ām), 1. point or direct (a gun, a blow, etc.) in order to hit. He aimed at the lion but missed. 2. act of aiming. His aim was so poor that he missed the lion. 3. to direct acts or words so as to influence a certain person or action. His speech was aimed at the boys who had not played fair. 4. try; intend; direct one's efforts. Mary aimed to please her teachers. 5. purpose; intention. Ruth's aim was to do two years' work in one.

ain't (ānt), 1. am not; are not; is not. 2. have not; has not. Careful speakers do not use *ain't*.

air (ãr), 1. Birds fly in the air. 2. It is good to air your clothes often. 3. make known. Don't air your troubles too often. 4. melody; tune. In music, the air is the leading part. 5. way; look; manner. He had the air of a child who was afraid. 6. light wind; breeze. 7. Some special meanings are:

airs, affected or showy manners.

in the air, going around.

on the air, broadcasting.

air base, airport and headquarters for military airplanes.

air castle, daydream; something that is only imagined.

air craft (ãr′kraft′), 1. airplanes, airships, or balloons. 2. any airplane, airship, or balloon.

air drome (ãr′drōm′), airport.

air plane (ãr′plān′), a flying machine that has one or more planes or wings and is driven by a motor.

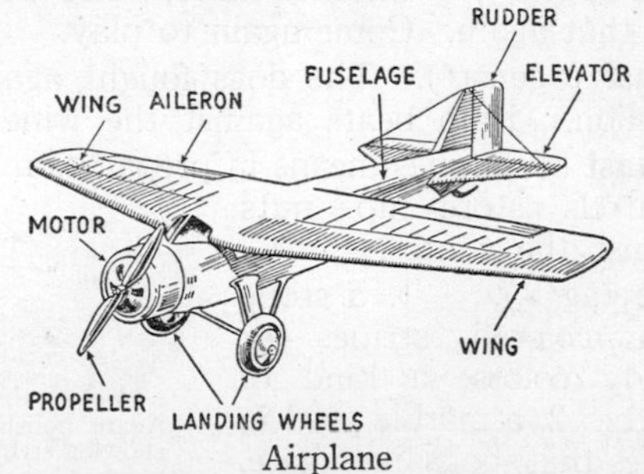

Airplane

air port (ãr′pōrt′), station with a field for airplanes to land at and start from, and buildings for keeping, inspecting, and repairing airplanes.

air ship (ãr′ship′), a dirigible, a balloon that can be steered.

air tight (ãr′tīt′), 1. so tight that no air can get in or out. 2. leaving no opening.

air way (ãr′wā′), route for airplanes.

air y (ãr′i), 1. of air; in the air. 2. breezy; with air moving through it; as, a large, airy room. 3. like air; not solid or substantial. 4. light as air; graceful; delicate. 5. gay; light-hearted; as, airy laughter.

aisle (īl), 1. a passage between rows of seats in a church, theater, etc. 2. long, narrow passage. A long space between trees in a forest is an aisle.

a jar[1] (ə jär′), slightly open.

a jar[2] (ə jär′), not in harmony.

a kim bo (ə kim′bō), with the hand on the hip and the elbow bent outward. See the picture.

Boy with arms akimbo

a kin (ə kin′), 1. belonging to the same family; related. They are akin to me; in fact, they are my cousins. 2. alike. Most boys are akin in their love of sports.

al a bas ter (al′ə bas′tər), 1. a white mineral somewhat like marble. 2. white and smooth like alabaster.

a lack (ə lak′), alas.

a larm (ə lärm′), 1. a call to arms or action. Paul Revere gave the alarm to the towns near Boston. 2. the warning sound or signal used to give an alarm. 3. the thing that makes the sound or signal; as, a fire alarm. 4. giving an alarm; as, an alarm clock. 5. make uneasy; frighten. The breaking of a branch under my foot alarmed the deer. 6. sudden fear; excitement caused by fear of danger. The deer darted off in alarm.

a las (ə las′), Oh dear!; an exclamation of sorrow, grief, regret, pity, or dread.

A las ka (ə las′kə), a territory in northwestern North America belonging to the United States.

al be it (ôl bē′it), although; even though. Albeit he has failed twice, he is not discouraged.

al bum (al′bəm), a book with blank pages for holding things like photographs, pictures, and stamps.

al co hol (al′kə hôl), 1. the colorless liquid in wine, beer, whiskey, gin, etc., which makes them intoxicating. Alcohol is used in medicines, as a fuel, and in manufacturing. Wood alcohol is a different substance. 2. any liquor containing alcohol.

al co hol ic (al′kə hôl′ik), 1. of alcohol. 2. containing alcohol.

Alcove

al cove (al′kōv), a small room opening into a larger room.

al der (ôl′dər), a tree or shrub somewhat like a birch. Alders usually grow in wet land.

al der man (ôl′dər mən), person who represents the people of a certain district on a council or board that governs a city, town, or borough. Our city has ten aldermen.

ale (āl), a strong, light-colored beer made from malt and hops.

a lert (ə lėrt′), 1. watchful; wide awake. The dog was alert. 2. lively; nimble. A sparrow is very alert in its movements. 3. **On the alert** means watchful; ready at any instant for what is coming.

a lert ness (ə lėrt′nis), 1. watchfulness. 2. liveliness; nimbleness.

al fal fa (al fal′fə), a plant with deep roots, leaves like clover, and bluish-purple flowers. It is used as a food for horses and cattle.

Alfalfa

al gae (al′jē), seaweeds and some fresh-water plants like them.

al ien (āl′yən), 1. foreigner. A person who is not a citizen of the country in which he lives is an alien. 2. of another country; foreign. 3. entirely different; strange. Unkindness was alien to his nature.

a light[1] (ə līt′), 1. get down; get off; as, to alight from a horse, to alight from a train. 2. come down from the air; come down from flight. The bird alighted on our window sill.

a light[2] (ə līt′), on fire; lighted up. Her face was alight with happiness.

a like (ə līk′), 1. similar; like one another. These twins are very much alike. 2. in the same way. Robert and his father walk alike.

a live (ə līv′), 1. living. Was the snake alive or dead? 2. active; lively; brisk. **Look alive!** means "Be active!" or "Hurry up!" 3. full of people or things in motion; swarming. The streets were alive with people.

all (ôl), 1. All dogs have heads. 2. The pin was all gold. 3. All is well. 4. They came after all. 5. **At all** means in any way or under any conditions.

al lay (ə lā′), make less; check; quiet; relieve. His fears were allayed by news that his family was safe. His fever was allayed by the medicine. Water allays thirst.

al lege (ə lej′), 1. assert; declare. This man alleges that his watch has been stolen. 2. assert without proof. The alleged theft really never happened.

al le giance (ə lē′ jəns), 1. the loyalty owed by a citizen to his government or by a subject to his ruler. 2. loyalty; faithfulness; devotion. Jack's allegiance to his brother lasted all his life.

al ley (al′i), 1. a narrow back street in a city or town. 2. a path in a park or garden, bordered by trees. 3. a long, narrow, enclosed place for bowling.

al li ance (ə lī′əns), 1. union formed by agreement; joining of interests. A joining of national interests by treaty is an alliance. A marriage may be a family alliance. 2. the nations, persons, etc., that belong to such a union.

al lied (ə līd′), 1. united by agreement; as, allied nations, allied armies. 2. connected. His business is allied with several banks.

al li ga tor (al′i gā′tər), a large crawling animal with a long body, four short legs, a thick skin, and a long tail. See the picture. Alligators live in rivers and marshes of warm parts of America.

Alligator (12 ft. long)

al lot (ə lot′), 1. divide and distribute in parts or shares. The profits from the candy sale have been allotted equally to the Boy Scouts and the Camp Fire Girls. 2. give to (a person) as his share; assign. The principal allotted each class a part in the Christmas program.

al low (ə lou′), 1. let; permit. Mrs. Smith allows her children to go swimming. Dogs are not allowed in this car. 2. give; let have. Grace is allowed 20 cents a day for lunch at school. 3. add or subtract to make up for something. The trip will cost you only $20; but you ought to allow $5 more for extra expenses. 4. **Allow for** sometimes means take into consideration. In making the dress large, she allowed for shrinking.

al low ance (ə lou′əns), 1. a limited share set apart; a definite portion or amount given out. Mary has an allowance of 25 cents a week. Our allowance of candy is two pieces after dinner. 2. amount added or subtracted to make up for something. 3. **Make allowance for** means take into consideration; allow for. You must make allowance for the wishes of others.

al loy (al′oi), 1. a mixture of two or more metals. Brass is an alloy of copper and zinc. 2. an inferior metal mixed with a more valuable one. This is not pure gold; there is some alloy in it.

al lude (ə lüd′), refer indirectly; mention slightly. Do not ask him about his failure; do not even allude to it.

al lure (ə lür′), 1. tempt by the offer of some pleasure or reward. The circus so allured Jim that he wished to join it. 2. fascinate; attract or charm.

al lu sion (ə lü′zhən), indirect reference; slight mention. John was hurt by any allusion to his lameness.

al ly (ə lī′ for 1, al′ī for 2), 1. combine or unite for some special purpose. One country will ally itself with another to protect its people or its interests. 2. a person or state united with another for some special purpose. England and France have been allies in some wars though they have fought against each other in others.

al ma nac (ôl′mə nak), a calendar of days, weeks, and months, often with information about the weather, the sun, moon, stars, tides, church days, and other facts.

al might y (ôl mīt′i), possessing all power. God is often called **the Almighty.**

al mond (ä′mənd), 1. the nut or seed of a fruit growing in warm regions. 2. the tree it grows on.

Almond with and without its shell

al most (ôl′mōst), nearly. Nine is almost ten.

alms (ämz), money or gifts to help the poor.

a loft (ə lôft′), 1. far above the earth; up in the air; high up. 2. above the deck of a ship; high up among the sails and masts.

a lone (ə lōn′), 1. apart from other persons or things. One tree stood alone on the hill. 2. without anyone else. One boy alone can do this work. 3. without anything more. Meat alone is not the best food for children. 4. **Let alone** means (1) not touch; not do; not pay attention to. (2) not to mention.

a long (ə lông′), 1. from one end of to the other. Trees are planted along the street. 2. further; onward. March along quickly. 3. **Along with** means in company with. 4. **All along** means all the time.

a long side (ə lông′sīd′), 1. at the side; close to the side; side by side. 2. by the side of; side by side with. The boat was alongside the wharf.

a loof (ə lüf′), away; apart. One boy stood aloof from the other boys. He kept aloof because he did not like them.

a loud (ə loud′), 1. loud enough to be heard; not in a whisper. He spoke aloud, although he was alone. She read the story aloud to the others. 2. loudly; in a loud voice.

al pha bet (al′fə bet), 1. a set of letters used in writing a language. 2. the letters of a language arranged in a certain order, not as they are in words. The English alphabet is a b c d e f g h i j k l m n o p q r s t u v w x y z.

al pha bet i cal (al′fə bet′i kəl), arranged by letters in the order of the alphabet.

al pha bet i cal ly (al′fə bet′i kəl i), according to the alphabet.

al read y (ôl red′i), before this time; by this time; even now. You are half an hour late already. The child has already broken his new toy.

al so (ôl′sō), too; in addition. That dress is pretty, and cheap also.

al tar (ôl′tər), 1. a stand or table in the most sacred part of a church. 2. a raised place built of earth or stone on which to make sacrifices or burn offerings to gods.

al ter (ôl′tər), change; make different; become different. If this coat is too large, a tailor can alter it to fit you.

al ter a tion (ôl′tər ā′shən), change. Mother made some alterations in her new dress.

al ter nate (ôl′tər nāt for 1 and 2, ôl′tər nit for 3 and 4), 1. arrange one after the other; be arranged by turns. Squares and circles alternate in this row:

□ ○ □ ○ □ ○ □ ○

2. take turns. Lucy and her sister will alternate in setting the table. 3. first one and then the other by turns. The row has alternate squares and circles. 4. every other. We buy ice on alternate days because we do not need it every day.

al ter nate ly (ôl′tər nit li), by turns.

al ter na tive (ôl tėr′nə tiv), 1. giving or requiring a choice between things. Father offered the alternative plans of having a picnic or taking a trip on a steamboat. 2. a choice between things. John's father gave him the alternative of staying in high school or going to work. 3. one of the things to be chosen. John chose the first alternative and stayed in school.

al though or **al tho** (ôl ᴛʜō′), though.

al ti tude (al′ti tūd or al′ti tüd), 1. height. What altitude did the airplane reach? 2. height above sea level. The altitude of Denver is 5300 feet. 3. a high place. In some altitudes the snow never melts.

al to (al′tō), part in music sung by the lowest female voice or the highest male voice.

al to geth er (ôl′tə geᴛʜ′ər), 1. completely; entirely. The house was altogether destroyed by fire. 2. on the whole. Altogether, he was well pleased.

a lu mi num (ə lü′mi nəm), a silver-white, very light metal that does not tarnish easily. Aluminum is much used for making kettles and pans.

al ways (ôl′wāz), at all times; all the time. Night always follows day.

am (am), John said, "I am 6 years old. I am going to school."

A.M. or **a.m.**, before noon; the time from midnight to noon.

a main (ə mān′), 1. with force or violence. 2. at full speed.

a mass (ə mas′), heap together; pile up; accumulate. The miser amassed a fortune.

am a teur (am′ə tūr), 1. person who does something for pleasure, not for money. 2. person who does something rather poorly. 3. of amateurs; by amateurs; as, an amateur play.

a maze (ə māz′), surprise greatly; strike with sudden wonder. The boy who had seemed so stupid amazed us all by his fine examination. She was so amazed by the surprise gift that she could not think of anything to say.

a maze ment (əmāz′mənt), great surprise; sudden wonder. The little girl was filled with amazement when she first saw the ocean.

am bas sa dor (am bas′ə dər), 1. a representative of highest rank sent by one government or ruler to another. An ambassador lives in a foreign country and speaks and acts in behalf of his ruler or his government. 2. official messenger with a special errand; messenger; agent.

am ber (am′bər), 1. a yellow or yellowish-brown gum, used for jewelry and in making stems of pipes. 2. made of amber; as, amber beads. 3. yellow or yellowish brown.

am bi tion (am bish′ən), 1. strong desire for fame or success; seeking after a high position or great power. 2. the thing for which one has a strong desire. Her ambition was to be a great actress.

am bi tious (am bish′əs), 1. having ambition. John is ambitious to get through high school in three years, so he works hard. 2. showing ambition. Mary had the ambitious plan of walking across the United States.

am ble (am′bəl), 1. the way a horse goes when it first lifts the two legs on one side and then lifts the two on the other side. 2. go in that manner. 3. an easy, gentle gait. 4. go with an easy, gentle gait.

am bu lance (am′bū ləns), wagon or automobile used to carry sick or wounded people.

am bus cade (am′bəs kād′), ambush.

am bush (am′bůsh), 1. soldiers hidden so that they can make a surprise attack on an approaching enemy. 2. place where the soldiers are hidden. 3. attack from an ambush. 4. act or condition of lying in wait. The Indians often trapped their enemies by ambush instead of meeting them in a regular battle.

a men (ā′men′ or ä′men′). Amen is a word said at the end of a prayer. Perhaps it means "May it become so" or "Be it so!"

a mend (ə mend′), 1. change for the better; correct. It is time you amended your ways. 2. change. Each time that they amended the law, they made it worse.

a mend ment (ə mend′mənt), 1. a change for the better; correction. 2. a change. There have been many amendments to the Constitution of the United States.

a mends (ə mendz′), payment for loss; satisfaction for an injury; compensation. If you carelessly took more than your share of the money, you should at once make amends by returning the extra amount.

A mer i ca (ə mer′i kə), 1. the United States. 2. North America. 3. North America and South America.

A mer i can (ə mer′i kən), 1. of the United States; belonging to the United States. 2. citizen of the United States. 3. of America; in America. 4. person born or living in America.

am e thyst (am′i thist), 1. a purple or violet quartz used for jewelry. 2. purple; violet.

a mi a ble (ā′mi ə bəl), friendly; agreeable. May is a sweet, gentle, amiable girl.

a mid (ə mid′), in the middle of; among. The little church stood unharmed amid the ruins of the bombed village.

a mid ships (ə mid′ships), in the middle of a ship.

a midst (ə midst′), amid.

a miss (ə mis′), wrong; wrongly; not the way it should be; out of order. Something is amiss when a boy will not eat for days. To do something amiss is to do it in the wrong way.

am mo ni a (ə mō′ni ə), 1. a colorless gas with a strong smell. 2. water with ammonia gas dissolved in it. Ammonia is very useful for cleaning and for many other purposes.

am mu ni tion (am′ū nish′ən), powder, shot, bullets, balls, bombs, and shells; military supplies.

a mong (ə mung′). His brothers were among the crowd. Divide the fruit among the boys. Was John among those present? The children quarreled among themselves.

a mongst (ə mungst′), among.

a mount (ə mount′), 1. reach; be equal. The loss from the flood amounts to ten million dollars. Keeping what belongs to another amounts to stealing. 2. sum; quantity. No amount of coaxing would make the dog leave his master. 3. total sum; full value.

PONTOON WHEELS

Amphibian airplane

am phib i an (am fib′i-ən), 1. an animal living both on land and in water. Frogs are amphibians. 2. an airplane so made that it can start from or alight on either land or water.

am phib i ous (am fib′i əs), able to live both on land and in water.

am ple (am′pəl), 1. large. 2. abundant; more than enough. Take an ample supply of food, for we shall be gone all day. 3. enough. The money her mother gave her was ample for fares and lunches.

am pli fi er (am′pli fī′ər), 1. one that amplifies. 2. vacuum tube in a radio set for strengthening the electrical impulses.

am ply (am′pli), abundantly.

a muse (ə mūz′), 1. entertain; turn to pleasant thoughts and feelings; cause to feel cheerful and happy. The sailor amused the little boy by telling him a story. 2. cause to laugh or smile.

a muse ment (ə mūz′mənt), 1. condition of being amused. The boy's amusement was so great that we all had to laugh with him. 2. anything that amuses; entertainment; sport. Most outdoor games are healthy amusements.

an (an), 1. Is there an apple for me? 2. James earns ten cents an hour.

an a con da (an′ə kon′də), a large snake that crushes its prey. See the picture.

a nal y ses (ə nal′i sēz), more than one analysis.

a nal y sis (ə nal′i sis), separation of anything into its parts or elements. You can make an analysis of a book, a person's character, a medicine, water, soil, etc.

Anaconda (25 ft. long)

an a lyze or **an a lyse** (an′ə līz), 1. separate into its parts. We can analyze water into two colorless gases. 2. examine the parts or elements of; find out the essential features of. Many men have tried to analyze the causes of success.

an ar chy (an′ər ki), 1. absence of a system of government and law. 2. disorder; confusion.

a nat o my (ə nat′ə mi), 1. structure of an animal or plant. The anatomy of an earthworm is much simpler than that of a man. 2. the science of the structure of animals or plants. Anatomy is a part of biology.

an ces tor (an′ses tər), person from whom you are directly descended. Your father, your mother, your grandfathers, your grandmothers, and so on back, are your ancestors.

an ces tral (an ses′trəl), 1. of ancestors. The ancestral home of the Pilgrims was England. 2. inherited from ancestors. Curly hair is an ancestral trait in that family.

an chor (ang′kər), 1. shaped piece of iron fastened to a ship by a long chain or rope and dropped to the bottom of the water. The anchor grips the earth or rocks and so keeps the ship from drifting. See the picture. 2. hold (a ship) fast by dropping an anchor to the bottom. 3. drop anchor. 4. fix firmly; as, to anchor a tent to the ground. 5. anything that makes you feel sure and safe. His mother's letters were an anchor to the boy at this time.

Anchor

an chor age (ang′kər ij), a place to anchor.

an cient (ān′shənt), belonging to times long past. **The ancients** means peoples who lived long ago.

and (and). You can come and go on the car. 4 and 2 make 6.

and i rons (and′ī′ərnz), pair of metal supports for wood in a fireplace. See the picture.

Andirons

an ec dote (an′ik dōt), a short account of some interesting incident or event. Many anecdotes are told about Abraham Lincoln.

a nem o ne (ə nem′ə ni), plant with slender stems and white flowers that blossoms early in the spring.

a new (ə nū′ or ə nü′), 1. again; once more. He made so many blots on his paper that he had to begin his long letter anew. 2. in a new way. The architect planned the building anew.

an gel (ān′jəl), 1. messenger from God. 2. person like an angel in goodness, innocence, loveliness, etc.

an gel ic (an jel′ik), 1. of angels; heavenly. 2. like an angel; pure; innocent; good and lovely.

an ger (ang′gər), 1. the feeling which you have when you are angry. 2. make angry. The boy's disobedience angered his father.

an gle[1] (ang′gəl), 1. the space between two lines or surfaces that meet. 2. the figure formed by two such lines or surfaces. 3. corner.

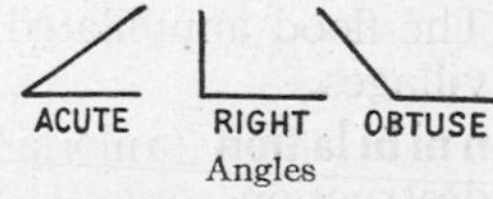

Angles

an gle[2] (ang′gəl), 1. fish with hook and line. 2. try to get something by using tricks or schemes. She angled for an invitation to his party by flattering him.

an gler (ang′glər), person who fishes with hook and line.

an gle worm (ang′gəl wėrm′), earthworm.

an gri ly (ang′gri li), in an angry manner.

an gry (ang′gri). You are angry when you slap, kick, or bite at people. You are angry when someone tries to keep you from doing something which you want to do, or from going where you want to go.

an guish (ang′gwish), very great pain or grief. Fred was in anguish until the doctor set his broken leg.

an gu lar (ang′gū lər), having angles; having sharp corners; jagged.

an i mal (an′i məl), 1. creature that can feel and move. A dog, a bird, a fish, a snake, a fly, and a worm are all animals. All living things are animals or plants. 2. If we call a person an animal, we usually mean that he is like a beast in the way he acts or thinks.

an i mate (an′i māt), 1. give life to. Don't you wish that we could animate our dolls? 2. make lively and gay. Jim's arrival served to animate the whole party. 3. be a motive or a reason for. Love for her mother animated Alice's work.

an i mat ed (an′i māt′id), 1. living; alive. 2. lively; gay; vigorous.

an i ma tion (an′i mā′shən), 1. life. 2. liveliness; spirit.

an i mos i ty (an′i mos′i ti), violent hatred; ill will.

an kle (ang′kəl), joint connecting the foot with the leg.

an klet (ang′klit), 1. band around the ankle. An anklet may be an ornament, a brace, or a fetter. 2. short sock.

an nex (ə neks′ for 1, an′eks for 2), 1. join or add (a small thing) to a larger thing. The United States annexed Texas in 1845. 2. something annexed; an added part; as, an annex to a building.

an ni hi late (ə nī′i lāt), destroy completely. The flood annihilated over thirty towns and villages.

an ni hi la tion (ə nī′i lā′shən), complete destruction.

an ni ver sa ry (an′i vėr′sə ri), 1. the yearly return of a date. Your birthday is one anniversary you like to have remembered. 2. a celebration of the yearly return of a date.

an nounce (ə nouns′), 1. make known formally. Please announce to the children that there will be no school this afternoon. 2. make known the presence or arrival of. The servant announced each guest in a loud voice.

an nounce ment (ə nouns′mənt), what is announced or made known by private or public notice. The announcement was published in the newspapers.

an noy (ə noi′), tease; vex; disturb; make angry. The baby annoys her sister by pulling her hair.

an noy ance (ə noi′əns), 1. act of annoying. 2. being annoyed; vexation; feeling of dislike or trouble. 3. thing that annoys.

an nu al (an′ū əl), 1. coming once a year. Your birthday is an annual event. 2. in a year; for a year. Mr. White's annual income is $2000. 3. living one year or season. Corn and beans are annual plants.

an nu al ly (an′ū əl i), yearly; each year; year by year.

a noint (ə noint′), 1. put oil on; rub. Anoint sunburned places with cold cream. 2. apply ointment or oil to (a person) as a part of a ceremony. The bishop anointed the new king.

a non (ə non′), 1. soon. 2. again; at another time. I won't say good-by; for I shall see you anon.

an oth er (ə nuᴛʜ′ər), 1. one more. Drink another glass of milk. 2. a different. Show me another kind of hat. 3. a different one; someone else.

an swer (an′sər), 1. Who can answer the question? The boy gave a quick answer. Answer the bell by going to the door. Any response by speaking, writing, or doing something is an answer. 2. be responsible. A father must answer for his child's acts. 3. serve. A piece of paper answered for a tablecloth. 4. correspond. This boy answers to your description.

Small red ant. Line shows actual length.

ant (ant), a small insect. See the picture. Ants live together in large groups or communities called colonies. Ants, bees, and wasps are alike in many ways.

an tag o nism (an tag′ə nizm), active opposition; conflict.

an tag o nist (an tag′ə nist), one who fights, struggles, or contends against another in a combat or contest of any kind; opponent; adversary; rival. The knight defeated each antagonist who came against him.

ant arc tic (ant ärk′tik), 1. at or near the South Pole; of the south polar region. There is an antarctic continent. 2. the south polar region.

Antelope (2½ ft. high at the shoulder)

an te lope (an′ti lōp), any one of certain animals somewhat like deer. See the picture just above.

an ten na (an ten′ə), 1. feeler on the head of an insect, spider, scorpion, lobster, etc. See the picture. 2. long wire or wires used in radio for sending out or receiving electric waves; aerial.

an ten nae (an ten′ē), more than one antenna.

Antennae of a beetle

an te room (an′ti rüm′), room leading to another room; a waiting room.

an them (an′thəm), 1. song of praise, devotion, or patriotism. "The Star-Spangled Banner" is the national anthem. 2. piece of sacred music usually with words from some passage in the Bible.

ant hill, heap of dirt piled up by ants around the entrance to their underground nest.

an thra cite (an′thrə sīt), hard coal; coal that burns with very little smoke and flame.

anti-, prefix meaning against or opposed to.

an tic i pate (an tis′i pāt), 1. expect; look forward to. He had anticipated a good vacation in the mountains; but when the time came, he was sick. 2. do before others do; be ahead of in doing. The Chinese anticipated some modern discoveries. 3. use, tell, realize, or consider in advance. When Mother has a headache, Mary anticipates all her wishes.

an tic i pa tion (an tis′i pā′shən), act of anticipating; looking forward to; expectation. He cut more wood than usual, in anticipation of a long winter.

an tics (an′tiks), funny gestures and actions; silly tricks; capers. The clown amused us by his antics.

an tip a thy (an tip′ə thi), strong dislike. He felt an antipathy to snakes.

an tique (an tēk′), 1. of times long ago; from times long ago. This antique chair was made in 1750. Mother made Mary an antique costume. 2. something made long ago. This carved chest is a real antique.

an tiq ui ty (an tik′wi ti), 1. oldness; great age. That vase is of such great antiquity that nobody knows how old it is. 2. times long ago, especially those before 476 A.D. Moses and Caesar were two great men of antiquity. 3. the people of ancient times; the customs, events, things, etc., from times long ago.

Antlers

ant ler (ant′lər), 1. horn of a deer. See the picture just above. 2. branch of a deer's horn.

an vil (an′vil), an iron block on which metals are hammered and shaped. See the picture.

anx i e ty (ang zī′ə ti), 1. uneasy thoughts or fears about what may happen; troubled, worried, or uneasy feeling. Mothers feel anxiety when their children are sick. 2. eager desire. Nell's anxiety to succeed led her to work hard.

Man using an anvil

anx ious (angk′shəs), 1. uneasy because of thoughts and fears about what may happen; troubled; worried. Mother felt anxious about the children who had been gone an hour too long. The week of the flood was an anxious time for all of us. 2. wishing very much; eager. Dick was anxious for a bicycle. Mary was anxious to please her mother.

anx ious ly (angk′shəs li), 1. uneasily. 2. eagerly.

an y (en′i), 1. one out of many. Choose any book you like. 2. some. Have you any fresh fruit? We haven't any. 3. at all. Did she cry any?

an y bod y (en′i bod′i), 1. any person; anyone. 2. important person.

an y how (en′i hou), 1. in any way whatever. It is wrong anyhow you look at it. 2. in any case; at any rate; anyway. I can see as well as you can, anyhow.

an y one or **any one** (en′i wun), anybody; any person. Anyone may come to the party.

an y thing (en′i thing), 1. any thing. 2. thing of any kind. 3. at all. Is your doll anything like mine?

an y way (en′i wā), 1. in any way whatever. 2. in any case. I am coming anyway, no matter what you say.

an y where (en′i hwãr), in any place.

a pace (ə pās′), swiftly; fast. The summer flew by, and school days were coming on apace.

a part (ə pärt′), 1. to pieces; in pieces; in separate parts. The boy took the watch apart to see how it runs. 2. to one side; aside; off or away from others. He sets some money apart for a vacation each year. All joking apart, do you mean that? 3. away from each other.

a part ment (ə pärt′mənt), 1. room or group of rooms to live in. 2. single room.

ap a thy (ap′ə thi), 1. lack of feeling; dullness of feeling; indifference. The stingy old miser heard the beggar's story with apathy. 2. lack of interest and activity; as, the apathy of a lazy, stupid boy.

ape (āp), 1. a tailless, long-armed animal somewhat like a monkey. Apes are able to stand almost erect and to walk on two feet. 2. one who imitates or mimics. 3. imitate; mimic. The girl aped the movie star.

ap er ture (ap′ər chər), opening; gap; hole. A window is an aperture for light and air.

a pex (ā′peks), the highest point; the tip.

a piece (ə pēs′), each; for each one. These apples are five cents apiece. The boys received a dollar apiece for the work.

a pol o get ic (ə pol′ə jet′ik), making an apology; expressing regret; acknowledging a fault; excusing failure.

a pol o get i cal ly (ə pol′ə jet′i kəl i), in an apologetic manner.

a pol o gize (ə pol′ə jīz), make an apology; offer an excuse. She apologized for hurting my feelings.

a pol o gy (ə pol′ə ji), 1. words of regret for an offense, fault, or accident; explanation; saying one is sorry; asking pardon. Make an apology to the lady for hitting her. We made our apologies for being late. 2. poor substitute. She thinks lamps are only an apology for sunlight.

a pos tle or **A pos tle** (ə pos′əl), 1. one of the twelve men chosen by Christ to go forth and preach the gospel to all the world. 2. Christian leader or missionary. 3. leader of any reform or belief.

a poth e car y (ə poth′i kãr′i), person who prepares and sells drugs and medicines; druggist.

ap pall or **ap pal** (ə pôl′), terrify; fill with horror; dismay. She was appalled when she saw the river had risen to the doorstep. We were appalled at the thought of another war.

ap pa ra tus (ap′ə rā′təs or ap′ə rat′əs), anything necessary to carry out a purpose. Tools, special instruments, and machines are apparatus. A chemical set is apparatus; so are a grocer's scales and the equipment in a gymnasium.

ap par el (ə par′əl), 1. clothing; dress. 2. clothe; dress up. The horseback riders, gaily appareled, formed part of the circus parade.

ap par ent (ə par′ənt), 1. plain to see; so plain that you cannot help seeing it; easily understood. It is apparent that day is the best time for outdoor work. 2. seeming; that appears to be. The apparent truth was really a lie.

ap par ent ly (ə par′ənt li), 1. seemingly; as far as one can judge by appearances. 2. clearly; plainly.

ap pa ri tion (ap′ə rish′ən), 1. ghost. The apparition, clothed in white, glided through the wall. 2. appearance of something strange or unexpected.

ap peal (ə pēl′), 1. an earnest request; a call to the feelings. She made one last appeal to her father to forgive her. 2. ask earnestly. The children appealed to their mother to know what they could do on a rainy day. 3. call on some person to decide some matter in your favor. When Mother said "No," Johnny would appeal to Father. 4. a call on some person to decide some matter in your favor. Sometimes Johnny's appeals were successful. 5. be interesting, attractive, or enjoyable. Blue and red appeal to me, but I don't like gray or yellow.

ap pear (ə pēr′), 1. be seen. One by one the stars appear. 2. seem; look. The apple appeared sound, but it was rotten. 3. be published. This poet's latest book appeared a year ago.

ap pear ance (ə pēr′əns), 1. act of coming

in sight. John's appearance in the doorway was welcomed with shouts. 2. coming before the public. She made her first appearance in a concert in Boston. 3. outward look (of a person, object, animal, country, city). The appearance of the old gray house made us think it was empty. 4. thing that appears in sight; object seen. 5. ghost.

ap pease (ə pēz′), make calm; satisfy; quiet. He tried to appease his father's anger by promising to obey. His hunger was appeased by a good dinner.

ap pend age (ə pen′dij), 1. thing attached; addition. 2. tail.

ap pe tite (ap′i tīt), 1. desire for food. Mary had no appetite; so they had to coax her to eat. 2. desire. The lively boys had a great appetite for excitement and amusement.

ap plaud (ə plôd′), 1. express approval by clapping hands, shouting, etc. The audience applauds anything that pleases it in a play or concert. 2. approve; praise. Frank's mother applauded his decision to remain in school.

ap plause (ə plôz′), 1. approval expressed by clapping hands, shouting, etc. 2. approval; praise.

ap ple (ap′əl), 1. a common fruit. See the picture. 2. the tree it grows on.

Apple

ap pli ance (ə plī′əns), thing like a tool, small machine, etc., used in doing something; device. A can opener is an appliance for opening tin cans.

ap pli cant (ap′li kənt), person who applies (for a job, money, position, help, etc.).

ap pli ca tion (ap′li kā′shən), 1. applying; putting on; as, the application of paint to a house, the application of salve to a sore. 2. act of using; use. The application of what you know will help you solve new problems. 3. the thing applied. This application is made of cold cream and ointment. 4. a request. I have put in my application to become a Boy Scout. 5. continued effort in work; close attention. By application to his work he got a better job.

ap ply (ə plī′), 1. put on. You can apply paint to a house, a remedy to a mosquito bite, and force to a pump. 2. use. Bill knows the rule but does not know how to apply it. Fred knows it and applies it. 3. be useful or suitable; fit. When does this rule apply? 4. ask. She applied for help. 5. set to work and stick to it. She applied herself to her music.

ap point (ə point′), 1. decide on; set (a time or a place to be somewhere or meet someone). He appointed the schoolhouse as the place for the meeting. We shall appoint 8 o'clock as the hour to begin. 2. choose. This man was appointed postmaster. 3. equip; furnish; as, a well-appointed guest room.

ap point ment (ə point′mənt), 1. an appointing or being appointed. The appointment of Anna as secretary pleased all her friends. 2. office or position. 3. engagement to be somewhere or to meet someone.

ap pre ci a ble (ə prē′shi ə bəl), that can be appreciated; enough to be felt or estimated. A slight hill makes an appreciable difference in the ease of walking.

ap pre ci ate (ə prē′shi āt), 1. value; enjoy; think highly of. Almost everybody appreciates good food. 2. be thankful for. We appreciate your kindness. 3. estimate; have an opinion of the value, worth, or quality of. A musician can appreciate small differences in sounds. 4. estimate correctly.

ap pre ci a tion (ə prē′shi ā′shən), 1. appreciating; valuing. 2. valuing highly; sympathetic understanding. She has an appreciation of art and music.

ap pre ci a tive (ə prē′shi ā′tiv), having appreciation; showing appreciation; recognizing the value.

ap pre hend (ap′ri hend′), 1. seize; arrest. The thief was apprehended and put into jail. 2. understand; grasp with the mind. I apprehended his meaning more from his gestures than from the queer sounds he made. 3. fear; dread. A guilty man apprehends danger in every sound.

ap pre hen sion (ap′ri hen′shən), 1. seizing or arrest; as, the apprehension of a thief. 2. understanding; grasp by the mind. Tom has a clear apprehension of arithmetic. 3. fear; dread; as, the guilty man's apprehension that he would be found out.

ap pren tice (ə pren′tis), 1. person who is learning a trade, profession, or art. The apprentice had to serve his master seven years to pay for his instruction. 2. bind as an apprentice. Franklin's father apprenticed him to a printer. 3. beginner; learner.

ap pren tice ship (ə pren′tis ship), 1. condition of being an apprentice. 2. time during which one is an apprentice.

ap proach (ə prōch′), 1. come near (in space or time). Walk softly as you approach the bed. Sunday is approaching. 2. come near to (in character, condition, or amount). The wind was approaching a gale. 3. act of coming near. 4. way by which a place or a person can be reached. The approach to the house was a narrow path. His best approach to the great man lay through a friend.

ap pro pri ate (ə prō′pri it for 1, ə prō′pri āt for 2 and 3), 1. suitable; proper. Plain, simple clothes are appropriate for school wear. 2. take for oneself. You should not appropriate other people's belongings without their permission. 3. set apart for some special use. The town appropriates money for the care of its roads.

ap pro pri a tion (ə prō′pri ā′shən), 1. act of appropriating. His appropriation of the money was not right. 2. the fact of being appropriated. The appropriation of the land made it possible to have a park. 3. thing or sum of money appropriated. The school received an appropriation of a thousand dollars for a new playground.

ap prov al (ə prüv′əl), 1. approving; praise; favorable opinion. We all like others to show approval of what we do. 2. consent. The principal gave his approval to the plans for a holiday.

ap prove (ə prüv′), 1. think well of; be pleased with. The teacher approved Helen's work. 2. consent to. Father approved our plans for the summer. 3. give approval.

ap prox i mate (ə prok′si mit for 1, ə prok′si māt for 2), 1. nearly correct. Forty is the approximate number of books needed in our class. 2. come near to; approach. This lumber approximates first-class, but it still has some defects. The crowd approximated a thousand people.

ap prox i mate ly (ə prok′si mit li), nearly; about.

a pri cot (ā′pri kot or ap′ri kot), 1. a pale orange-colored fruit, somewhat like a peach but smaller. 2. the tree it grows on. 3. pale orange-yellow.

A pril (ā′pril), the fourth month. It has 30 days.

a pron (ā′prən), garment worn over the front part of the body to cover or protect clothes; as, a kitchen apron, a carpenter's apron.

apt (apt), 1. fitted by nature; likely. A careless person is apt to make mistakes. 2. suitable; fitting. His apt reply to the question showed that he had understood it very well. 3. quick to learn. Some pupils are more apt than others.

a quar i um (ə kwãr′i əm), 1. a pond, tank, or glass bowl in which living fish, water animals, and water plants are kept. 2. a building used for showing collections of living fish, water animals, and water plants. The aquarium had many tanks with glass fronts.

a quat ic (ə kwat′ik), 1. growing or living in water. Water lilies are aquatic plants. 2. taking place in or on water. Swimming and sailing are aquatic sports.

aq ue duct (ak′wi dukt), 1. artificial channel or large pipe for bringing water from a distance. 2. structure that supports such a channel or pipe.

ar a ble (ar′ə bəl), fit for plowing. There is not much arable land on the side of a rocky mountain.

ar bi trar y (är′bi trãr′i), based on one's own wishes, notions, or will; not going by any rule or law. A good judge tries to be fair and does not make arbitrary decisions.

ar bi tra tion (är′bi trā′shən), settlement of a dispute by the decision of a judge, umpire, or committee.

ar bor (är′bər), 1. a naturally shaded place in the woods. 2. a shaded place formed by vines and plants growing on frames or supports.

arc (ärk), 1. part of a circle. 2. part of a curved line. 3. the stream of brilliant light or sparks formed as an electric current goes from one conductor to another.

Arcs of circles

arch[1] (ärch), 1. a curved structure that bears the weight of the material above it. Arches often form the tops of doors, windows, and gateways, or the foundations of a bridge. 2. a monument forming an arch or arches. 3. bend into an arch; curve. Doris arched the branch of apple blossoms over her head.

Bridge showing three arches

arch[2] (ärch), 1. chief. The arch rebel of all was Patrick Henry. 2. playfully mischievous. The little girl gave her mother an arch look and ran away.

arch bish op (ärch′bish′əp), chief bishop.

arched (ärcht), having arches; made with arches.

arch er (är′chər), person who shoots with bow and arrows.

arch er y (är′chər i), 1. shooting with bows and arrows. 2. archers. The archery advanced, shooting steadily.

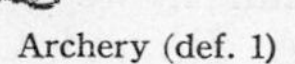

Archery (def. 1)

ar chi pel a go (är′ki pel′ə gō), 1. a sea having many islands in it. 2. a group of many islands.

ar chi tect (är′ki tekt), person who makes plans for buildings and sees that these plans are followed by the people who actually put up the buildings.

ar chi tec ture (är′ki tek′chər), 1. science and art of building. Architecture has to do with the planning of houses, churches, schools, and public and business buildings. 2. style or special manner of building. Greek architecture made much use of columns.

arch way (ärch′wā′), an entrance or passage with an arch above it; passage under an arched or curved roof.

Arch with three archways

arc tic (ärk′tik), 1. at or near the North Pole; of the north polar region; as, the arctic fox. 2. the north polar region.

ar dent (är′dənt), 1. eager; very enthusiastic. He became an ardent scout. 2. burning; fiery; hot.

ar dor (är′dər), warm feeling; eagerness; zeal; enthusiasm; as, the ardor of a saint, patriotic ardor.

ar du ous (är′jü əs), 1. hard to do; requiring much effort; as, an arduous lesson. 2. using up much energy; as, an arduous effort to learn the lesson.

are (är). You are next. We are ready. They are waiting. We say: I am, you are, thou art, he is, she is, it is, we are, you are, they are.

ar e a (ãr′i ə), 1. amount of surface; extent. The area of this floor is 600 square feet. 2. region. The Rocky Mountain area is the most mountainous in the United States.

a re na (ə rē′nə), 1. a space where contests or shows take place. Men fought with lions in the arena. 2. a place of conflict.

aren't (ärnt), are not.

ar gue (är′gū), 1. discuss with someone who disagrees; give reasons for or against something. 2. try to prove by reasoning. Columbus argued that the world was round.

ar gu ment (är′gū mənt), 1. arguing; discussion by persons who disagree. 2. reason or reasons offered for or against something.

ar id (ar′id), dry; as, arid soil, an arid, tiresome speech.

a right (ə rīt′), correctly; rightly.

a rise (ə rīz′), 1. rise up; get up. 2. move upward. Smoke arose from the chimney. 3. come into being; come about. Trouble had arisen over the ball game.

a ris en (ə riz′ən). See **arise.** John has not yet arisen from his bed.

ar is toc ra cy (ar′is tok′rə si), 1. the ruling body of nobles. 2. the upper class; any class that is superior because of birth, intelligence, culture, or wealth. 3. government in which an upper class rules. 4. nation having such a government.

a ris to crat (ə ris′tə krat), 1. person who belongs to the aristocracy; a noble. 2. person who has the tastes, opinions, manners, etc., of the upper class.

a ris to crat ic (ə ris′tə krat′ik), 1. belonging to the upper classes; superior in birth, intelligence, or wealth. 2. like an aristocrat in manners; proud. 3. having something to do with an aristocracy.

a rith me tic (ə rith′mə tik), the science and art of numbers.

ark (ärk), 1. the large boat in which Noah saved himself, his family, and a pair of each kind of animals from the Flood. 2. chest or box.

arm[1] (ärm), 1. the part of a person's body between the shoulder and the hand. 2. something that is shaped or used like a person's arm; as, the arm of a chair, an arm of the sea.

arm[2] (ärm), 1. a weapon of any kind. A gun, a sword, an ax, a stick—any of these might be arms for defense or attack. 2. provide with weapons; supply with any means of fighting. "Arm yourselves and be ready to fight," said our leader. 3. take up arms; prepare for war. The soldiers armed for battle.

ar ma da (är mä′də), 1. a fleet of warships. 2. a fleet of airplanes.

ar ma dil lo (är′mə dil′ō), a small burrowing animal that has a very hard shell. Some kinds can roll themselves up into a ball. Armadillos are found in South America and in some parts of southern North America.

Armadillo walking and also rolled up (2½ ft. long, with the tail).

ar ma ment (är′mə mənt), 1. war equipment and supplies. 2. a navy or army.

arm chair (ärm′chãr′), a chair with side-pieces to support a person's arms or elbows. See the picture.

Armchair

arm ful (ärm′fu̇l), as much as one arm can hold; as much as both arms can hold.

ar mi stice (är′mi stis), a stop in fighting; temporary peace; truce.

ar mor (är′mər), 1. covering worn to protect the body in fighting. See the picture just below. 2. any protective covering. The steel plates of a warship and the scales of a fish are armor.

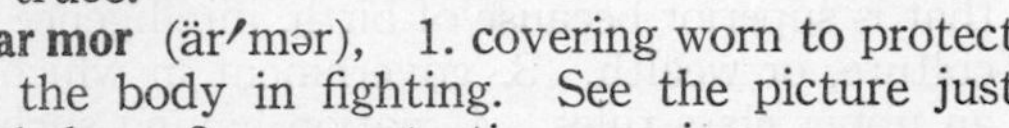

ar mored (är′mərd), covered or protected with armor.

ar mor er (är′mər ər), person who made or repaired armor.

ar mor y (är′mər i), 1. place where arms are kept. 2. place where arms are made. 3. a building with rooms for the militia to drill in.

Armor

arm pit (ärm′pit′), the hollow under the arm at the shoulder.

ar my (är′mi), 1. an organized group of soldiers trained and armed for war. American armies fought bravely in many lands. 2. any organized group of people. 3. multitude; very large number; as, an army of ants.

a ro ma (ə rō′mə), fragrance; spicy odor.

ar o mat ic (ar′ə mat′ik), fragrant; spicy. The cinnamon tree has an aromatic bark.

a rose (ə rōz′). See **arise.** She arose from her chair.

a round (ə round′), 1. The tree measures four feet around. He walked around the house. The sun shines all around us. 2. here and there; about. 3. somewhere about; near.

a rouse (ə rouz′), 1. awaken. 2. excite; stir to action.

ar range (ə rānj′), 1. put in proper order. The table is arranged for dinner. 2. settle. Mother arranged the dispute between Jim and Henry. 3. plan; form plans. Can you arrange to be at my house by six o'clock? 4. adapt; fit. This music for the violin is also arranged for the piano.

ar range ment (ə rānj′mənt), 1. arranging. The arrangement of all our baggage in one car took some time. 2. the way or order in which things or persons are put. You can make six arrangements of the letters A, B, and C. 3. plan; preparation. All arrangements have been made for our trip to Chicago. 4. something arranged in a particular way; as, a musical arrangement for the piano and violin.

ar ray (ə rā′), 1. order. Have your troops formed in battle array. 2. put in order. The general arrayed his troops for the battle. 3. display of persons or things. The array of good players on the other team made our side look weak. 4. clothes; dress; as, bridal array, gorgeous array. 5. to dress; dress in fine clothes; adorn. Elsie was arrayed like a queen.

ar rest (ə rest′), 1. stop; check. The driver could not arrest the horses' speed. 2. seize by legal authority; take to jail or to court. Policemen arrest thieves. 3. catch and hold. 4. stopping; seizing; arresting. We saw the arrest of a spy.

ar riv al (ə rīv′əl), 1. act of arriving; a coming. She is waiting for the arrival of the steamboat. 2. person or thing that arrives.

ar rive (ə rīv′), come; come to the end of a journey; come to a place.

ar ro gance (ar′ə gəns), too great pride; haughty behavior.

ar ro gant (ar′ə gənt), boastfully proud; too proud; boasting too much.

ar row (ar′ō), 1. a slender, pointed shaft or stick which is shot from a bow. 2. a sign (⟶) used to show direction or position in maps, on road signs, and in writing. 3. anything shaped like an arrow.

Arrow

ar se nal (är′si nəl), a building for storing or making weapons and ammunition for an army or navy; place for keeping guns powder, etc.

ar se nic (är′si nik), 1. a grayish-white chemical element. 2. a compound of arsenic that is a violent poison.

art[1] (ärt), 1. skill. 2. human skill. This well-kept garden owes more to art than to nature. The pupil tried to learn his master's art. 3. some kind of skill or practical application of skill. Cooking, sewing, and housekeeping are household arts. 4. a branch of learning that depends more on special practice than on general principles. Writing compositions is an art; grammar is a science. 5. The **fine arts** include painting, drawing, sculpture, architecture, literature, music, and dancing. 6. drawing, painting, or sculpture. Nell is studying art and music. 7. principles or methods; as, the art of making friends, the art of war. 8. skillful act; cunning; trick. The witch deceived the youth by her arts. **Black art** means evil magic.

art[2] (ärt), an old form meaning are. "Thou art" means "You are."

ar ter y (är′tər i), 1. any of the tubes that carry blood from the heart to all parts of the body. 2. a main road; important channel. Main Street and Broadway are the two arteries of traffic in our city.

art ful (ärt′fəl), 1. crafty; deceitful. That cheat uses artful tricks to get people's money away from them. 2. skillful; clever.

ar ti choke (är′ti chōk), a plant whose flowering head is cooked and eaten.

Artichoke

ar ti cle (är′ti kəl), 1. a literary composition that is part of a magazine, newspaper, or book. This newspaper has a good article on gardening. 2. a separate part of anything written; as, the third article of the Constitution. 3. a particular thing. Bread is an important article of food.

ar ti fice (är′ti fis), 1. skill; craft. 2. clever device; trick.

ar ti fi cial (är′ti fish′əl), not natural; made by the art of man; as, artificial flowers, artificial light, artificial ice, an artificial voice or manner.

ar til ler y (är til′ər i), 1. mounted guns; cannon. 2. the part of an army that uses and manages cannon.

ar ti san (är′ti zən), workman skilled in some industry or trade; craftsman. Carpenters, masons, plumbers, and electricians are artisans.

art ist (är′tist), 1. person who paints pictures. 2. person who is skilled in any of the fine arts, such as sculpture, music, or literature. 3. person who does work with skill and good taste.

ar tis tic (är tis′tik), 1. done with skill and good taste. 2. having good color and design. 3. having or showing appreciation of beauty. Tony is much more artistic than Jim. 4. of art or artists.

art less (ärt′lis), 1. natural; simple; without any trickery. Small children ask many artless questions, such as, "Mother, did you want this lady to come to see you?" 2. without art; unskilled; ignorant.

as (az), 1. Treat others as you wish them to treat you. 2. Mary will act as teacher today. 3. As they were walking, the rain began. 4. He was well paid, as he had done the work well. 5. Mary is as tall as Nell. 6. Our dog eats such food as we give him. 7. Some animals, as dogs and cats, eat meat.

as bes tos (as bes′təs), a substance which will not burn and which comes in fibers that can be made into a sort of cloth or felt. Asbestos is used for mats to put under hot dishes.

as cend (ə send′), go up; rise; climb. He watched the airplane ascend higher and higher. Few people ascend high mountains.

as cent (ə sent′), 1. a going up; upward movement; act of rising. 2. place that slopes up.

as cer tain (as′ər tān′), find out.

as cribe (əs krīb′), assign (to a cause or a source). **Ascribe to** means think of as caused by; think of as belonging to. The discovery of America is usually ascribed to Columbus. The police ascribed the automobile accident to fast driving.

ash[1] (ash), what remains of a thing after it has been thoroughly burned.

ash[2] (ash), a kind of shade tree that has a tough wood.

a shamed (ə shāmd′), 1. feeling shame; disturbed by a feeling of guilt or failure, or by being made fun of. Mary was ashamed of her dirty, ragged dress, but it was the only one she had. 2. unwilling because of shame. Tom was ashamed to tell his mother he had failed.

ash es (ash′iz), what remains of a thing after it has been burned. Ashes have to be removed from fireplaces and furnaces or there would be no space for a fire.

a shore (ə shōr′), on shore; to the shore.

A sia (ā′zhə), the largest continent. China and India are in Asia.

a side (ə sīd′), 1. on one side; to one side; away. Move the table aside. John spoke aside to Tom and nobody else heard what he said. 2. words spoken aside.

ask (ask), 1. Ask as many questions as you like. Ask him how old he is. 2. Ask for what you want. Ask Kate to sing. 3. Nell asked ten girls to her party. 4. She asked about our health, and asked after you, too.

a skance (ə skans′), 1. with suspicion or disapproval. The students looked askance at the suggestion of having classes on Saturday. 2. sideways; to one side.

a skew (ə skū′), to one side; out of the proper position; turned or twisted the wrong way. Her hat is on askew.

a sleep (ə slēp′), 1. sleeping. The cat is asleep. 2. into a condition of sleep. The tired boy fell asleep. 3. numb. My foot is asleep.

as par a gus (əs par′ə gəs), 1. a plant whose shoots are used for food. 2. the shoots.

Asparagus shoot

as pect (as′pekt), 1. look; appearance. The judge has a sober aspect. 2. one side or part or view (of a subject). We must consider this plan in its various aspects.

as phalt (as′fôlt), 1. dark-colored substance much like tar, that is found in various parts of the world. 2. a smooth hard mixture of this substance with crushed rock. Asphalt is used for pavements, roofs, etc.

as pir ant (əs pīr′ənt), person who aspires; person who seeks a position of honor.

as pi ra tion (as′pi rā′shən), longing; desire. She had aspirations to be an actress.

as pire (əs pīr′), have an ambition for something; desire earnestly; seek. Tom aspired to be captain of the team. Scholars aspire after knowledge.

ass (as), 1. donkey. 2. a fool; a stupid, silly, or stubborn person.

as sail (ə sāl′), attack.

as sail ant (ə sāl′ənt), person who attacks. The injured man did not know who his assailant was.

as sas sin (ə sas′in), murderer, especially one hired to murder.

as sas si nate (ə sas′i nāt), kill; murder.

as sas si na tion (ə sas′i nā′shən), murder.

as sault (ə sôlt′), 1. an attack; a sudden, vigorous attack. 2. to attack.

as say (ə sā′), 1. analyze (an ore, alloy, etc.) to find out the quantity of gold, silver, or other metal in it. 2. try; test.

as sem blage (ə sem′blij), assembly.

as sem ble (ə sem′bəl), 1. gather together; bring together; come together; meet. 2. put together; fit together.

as sem bly (ə sem′bli), 1. group of people gathered together for some purpose; meeting. A reception or a ball may be called an assembly. 2. a meeting of lawmakers. 3. putting together; fitting together. In Detroit we saw the assembly of the parts of an automobile to make an automobile.

as sent (ə sent′), 1. agree; express agreement. 2. agreement; acceptance of a proposal, statement, etc.

as sert (ə sėrt′), 1. declare; state positively. 2. defend or insist on (a right, a claim, etc.). 3. put (oneself) forward.

as ser tion (ə sėr′shən), 1. positive declaration; very strong statement. 2. an insisting on one's rights, a claim, etc.

as set (as′et), something that has value. Money, jewels, health, and strength are assets.

as sign (ə sīn′), 1. give as a share. The teacher assigned the next ten problems for today. 2. appoint. The captain assigned two soldiers to guard the gate. 3. name definitely; fix; set. The judge assigned a day for the trial.

as sign ment (ə sīn′mənt), 1. assigning; appointment; as, the assignment of a soldier to a place of danger. 2. something assigned. Today's assignment in arithmetic is ten examples.

as sim i late (ə sim′i lāt), absorb; digest. Alice does so much reading that she cannot assimilate it all. The human body will not assimilate sawdust.

as sist (ə sist′), help.

as sist ance (ə sis′təns), help; aid.

as sist ant (ə sis′tənt), 1. helper; aid. 2. helping; assisting.

as so ci ate (ə sō′shi āt for 1, 2, and 3, ə sō′shi it for 4 and 5), 1. join as a companion, partner, or friend; keep company. Never associate with bad companions. 2. connect in thought. We associate giving presents with Christmas. 3. join; combine; unite. 4. companion; partner; ally. 5. thing connected with another.

as so ci a tion (ə sō′si ā′shən), 1. act of associating. 2. fact or condition of being associated. 3. companionship. 4. connection; relation; combination; union. 5. group of people joined together for some common purpose; a society.

as sort ed (ə sôr′tid), 1. selected so as to be of different kinds. 2. arranged by kinds; classified. 3. matched; as, a well-assorted couple.

as sort ment (ə sôrt′mənt), 1. an assorting. 2. a collection of various sorts.

as suage (ə swāj′), make easier or milder; quiet; calm.

as sume (ə süm′), 1. take upon oneself; undertake. Next month we assume new duties. 2. take on; put on. 3. pretend; as, assumed ignorance. 4. take for granted; suppose. He assumed that the train would be on time.

as sump tion (ə sump′shən), 1. act of assuming. She bustled about with an assumption of authority. 2. thing assumed. John's assumption that he would win the prize proved incorrect.

as sur ance (ə shür′əns), 1. making sure or certain. 2. security; certainty; confidence. 3. confidence in one's own ability. 4. impudence; too great boldness. 5. insurance.

as sure (ə shür′), 1. make sure or certain. The leader assured himself that the bridge was safe before crossing it. 2. tell positively. The captain of the ship assured the passengers that there was no danger.

as sured (ə shürd′), 1. sure; certain. 2. confident; bold.

as sur ed ly (ə shür′id li), 1. surely; certainly. 2. confidently; boldly.

as ter (as′tər), a common flower with white, pink, or purple petals around a yellow center. Some asters are very small; others are large with many petals.

a stern (ə stėrn′), 1. at or toward the rear of a ship. 2. backward. 3. behind.

a stir (ə stėr′), in motion.

as ton ish (əs ton′ish), surprise greatly; amaze. The gift of ten dollars astonished me.

as ton ish ing (əs ton′ish ing), very surprising; amazing.

as ton ish ment (əs ton′ish mənt), great surprise; amazement; wonder.

as tound (əs tound′), surprise very greatly; amaze.

a stray (ə strā′), out of the right way; wandering. We are looking for the cows that went astray.

a stride (ə strīd′), with one leg on each side of. He sits astride his horse.

as tron o mer (əs tron′ə mər), person skilled in the science of the sun, moon, planets, stars, etc.

as tron o my (əs tron′ə mi), the science that deals with the sun, moon, planets, stars, and other heavenly bodies.

a sun der (ə sun′dər), 1. apart; separate. 2. in pieces; into separate parts. Lightning split the tree asunder.

a sy lum (ə sī′ləm), 1. institution for the support and care of the insane, the blind, orphans, or other classes of unfortunate persons. 2. refuge; shelter. In olden times a church might be an asylum for a debtor or a criminal, since no one was allowed to drag a person from the altar.

at (at), 1. At is used to show where. Mary is at home. The dog ran at the cat. 2. At is sometimes used to show when. Tom goes to bed at nine o'clock. 3. England and France were at war. We were sad at hearing such bad news.

ate (āt). See **eat.** John ate his dinner an hour ago.

a thirst (ə thėrst′), thirsty.

ath lete (ath′lēt), person trained in exercises of strength, speed, and skill. Ballplayers, runners, boxers, and swimmers are athletes.

ath let ic (ath let′ik), 1. active and strong. 2. of an athlete; like or suited to an athlete. 3. having something to do with active games and sports.

ath let ics (ath let′iks), exercises of strength, speed, and skill; active games and sports.

a thwart (ə thwôrt′), 1. across. 2. across the line or course of. The tug steamed athwart the steamer. 3. across from side to side.

At lan tic (at lan′tik), 1. the ocean east of North and South America. 2. of the Atlantic Ocean. 3. on or near the Atlantic Ocean.

at las (at′ləs), a book of maps. A big atlas has maps of every country.

at mos phere (at′məs fēr), 1. air. 2. the air that surrounds the earth. 3. mental and moral surroundings. Nuns live in a religious atmosphere.

at om (at′əm), 1. very small particle; tiny bit. 2. very small particle of a chemical element. Water is made of two atoms of hydrogen for every one atom of oxygen.

a tone (ə tōn′), make up; make amends. Tom atoned for his unkindness to Dick by taking Dick to the movies.

a tone ment (ə tōn′mənt), making up for something; amends; giving satisfaction for wrong, loss, or injury. The sufferings and death of Christ are called **the Atonement.**

a top (ə top′), 1. on the top; at the top. 2. on the top of.

a tro cious (ə trō′shəs), very wicked or cruel; very savage or brutal.

at tach (ə tach′), 1. fasten (to). The boy attached a rope to his sled. 2. join. 3. add. The signers attached their names to the Constitution. 4. bind by affection. May is much attached to her cousin. 5. stick; belong; fasten itself. The blame for this accident attaches to the man who destroyed the signal.

at tach ment (ə tach′mənt), 1. an attaching. 2. being attached. 3. thing attached. A sewing machine has various attachments, such as a hemmer and a darner. 4. means of attaching; fastening. 5. affection.

at tack (ə tak′), 1. set upon to hurt; go against as an enemy. The dog attacked the cat. 2. go at with vigor; as, to attack a hard lesson, to attack one's dinner. 3. attacking. The attack of the enemy took us by surprise. 4. make an attack; begin fighting.

at tain (ə tān′), 1. arrive at; reach. 2. gain; accomplish.

at tain ment (ə tān′mənt), 1. act of attaining. 2. something attained. 3. accomplishment; ability. Benjamin Franklin was a man of varied attainments; he was a writer, inventor, and statesman.

at tempt (ə tempt′), 1. try. 2. try to take or destroy. 3. a trying; an effort.

at tend (ə tend′), 1. be present at. Children must attend school. 2. give care and thought; apply oneself. Attend to your lessons. 3. wait on; go with. Noble ladies attend the queen. 4. go with as a result. Success often attends hard work.

at tend ance (ə ten′dəns), 1. attending. Our class has perfect attendance today. 2. company present. There was a large attendance of fairies at Queen Mab's party. 3. persons attending. The attendance at church was over two hundred.

at tend ant (ə ten′dənt), 1. waiting on another to help or serve; as, an attendant nurse. 2. person who waits on another, such as a servant or a follower. 3. accompanying; going with as a result; as, attendant circumstances, weakness attendant on illness. 4. present; as, attendant hearers. 5. person who is present.

at ten tion (ə ten′shən), 1. act of attending. The children gave attention to the teacher. 2. power of attending. James called my attention to the cat trying to catch the mouse. 3. care; consideration. The boy shows his mother much attention. 4. courtesy. The pretty girl received many attentions, such as invitations to parties, candy, and flowers. 5. military attitude of readiness. **Come to attention** and **stand at attention** mean stand straight and still.

at ten tive (ə ten′tiv), 1. giving attention; observant. 2. courteous; polite. Alice was attentive to her mother's guests.

at test (ə test′), testify; give proof of; certify. The child's good health attests his mother's care.

at tic (at′ik), space just below the roof in a house.

at tire (ə tīr′), dress; array. The queen wears rich attire. She is attired in purple.

at ti tude (at′i tūd or at′i tüd), 1. way of thinking, acting, or feeling. His attitude toward school changed from dislike to great enthusiasm. 2. position of the body. Standing, sitting, lying, and stooping are attitudes.

at tor ney (ə tėr′ni), 1. person who has power to act for another. 2. lawyer.

at tract (ə trakt′), 1. draw to oneself. A magnet attracts iron. 2. be pleasing to; win the attention and liking of. Bright colors attract children.

Magnet attracting nails

at trac tion (ə trak′shən), 1. act or power of drawing to oneself. 2. thing that attracts. The elephants were the chief attraction at the circus.

at trac tive (ə trak′tiv), 1. pleasing; winning attention and liking. 2. attracting.

at trib ute (at′ri būt for 1 and 2, ə trib′ūt for 3), 1. a quality considered as belonging to a person or thing; a characteristic.

Kindness is an attribute of a good teacher. 2. symbol. 3. assign. **Attribute to** means consider as belonging to or appropriate to; regard as an effect of; think of as caused by. We attribute Edison's success to intelligence and hard work.

at tune (ə tūn′ or ə tün′), tune; put in tune.

au burn (ô′bərn), reddish brown.

auc tion (ôk′shən), 1. public sale in which each thing is sold to the person who offers the most money for it. 2. sell at an auction.

au da cious (ô dā′shəs), 1. bold; daring. 2. too bold; impudent.

au dac i ty (ô das′i ti), 1. boldness. 2. rude boldness; impudence.

au di ble (ô′di bəl), that can be heard; loud enough to be heard.

au di ence (ô′di əns), 1. people gathered in a place or building to hear or see; as, the audiences at moving-picture shows, theaters, or speeches. 2. any persons within hearing. People who hear over the radio may be called an audience. 3. a chance to be heard; hearing. He should have an audience with the committee, for his plan is good. 4. an interview with a person of high rank. The king granted an audience to the famous general.

au di tor (ô′di tər), 1. hearer; listener. 2. person who examines and checks business accounts.

au ger (ô′gər), tool for boring holes. See the picture.

Auger

aught (ôt), anything. Has he done aught to help you?

aug ment (ôg ment′), increase. The heat usually augments during the forenoon. John bought some stamps to augment his collection.

Au gust[1] (ô′gəst), the eighth month of the year. It has 31 days.

au gust[2] (ô gust′), inspiring reverence and admiration; majestic; venerable.

aunt (ant). Your father's sister or your mother's sister or your uncle's wife is your aunt.

aus pic es (ôs′pis iz), 1. omens. 2. favoring influence. The school fair was held under the auspices of the Parents' Association.

aus pi cious (ôs pish′əs), with signs of success; favorable; fortunate.

aus tere (ôs tēr′), 1. harsh; stern. Frank's father was a silent, austere man, very strict with his children. 2. strict in morals. Some of the ideas of the Puritans seem to us too austere. 3. severely simple. The tall columns stood against the sky in austere beauty.

Aus tral ia (ôs trāl′yə), 1. a continent southeast of Asia. 2. the British dominion that includes this continent and Tasmania.

au then tic (ô then′tik), 1. reliable. We heard an authentic report of the wreck, given by one of the ship's officers. 2. genuine; real. We saw an authentic letter by George Washington.

au thor (ô′thər), 1. person who writes books, stories, or articles. 2. person who creates or begins anything.

au thor i ta tive (ô thor′i tā′tiv), 1. having authority; officially ordered. Authoritative orders came from the general. 2. commanding. In authoritative tones the policeman shouted, "Keep back!" 3. that ought to be believed or obeyed; having the authority of expert knowledge.

au thor i ty (ô thor′i ti), 1. power. A father has authority over his children. 2. right. A policeman has the authority to arrest fast drivers. 3. person who has power or right. Who are the proper authorities to give permits to hunt or fish? 4. source of correct information or wise advice. A good dictionary is an authority on the meanings of words.

au thor ize (ô′thər īz), 1. give power or right. The President authorized him to do this. 2. make legal. Congress authorized the spending of money for a new post-office building. 3. give authority for; justify. The dictionary authorizes the two spellings *traveler* and *traveller*.

au to (ô′tō), automobile.

au to crat (ô′tə krat), absolute ruler; ruler having entire power.

au to graph (ô′tə graf), 1. a person's name written by himself. 2. write one's name on or in. 3. something written in a person's own handwriting.

au to mat ic (ô′tə mat′ik), 1. moving or acting of itself; as, an automatic lock, an automatic pump. 2. done without thought or attention. Breathing and swallowing are usually automatic. 3. pistol that throws out the empty shell and reloads by itself when the trigger is pulled.

au to mat i cal ly (ô′tə mat′i kəl i), in an automatic manner. Electric refrigerators work automatically. The girl knitted automatically, chattering with her friend all the time.

au to mo bile (ô′tə mō bēl′), motorcar; car that carries its own engine.

au tumn (ô′təm), 1. the season of the year between summer and winter. 2. of autumn; coming in autumn; as, autumn flowers and fruits, autumn rains.

aux il ia ry (ôg zil′yə ri), 1. helping; assisting. 2. a helper; an aid.

a vail (ə vāl′), 1. help. Talk will not avail without work. 2. be of use or benefit to. Money will not avail you after you are dead. 3. help; use. Crying is of no avail now. 4. **Avail oneself of** means take advantage of; profit by; make use of.

a vail a ble (ə vāl′ə bəl), 1. that can be used. The saw is not available for the job; father is using it. 2. that can be had. All available tickets were sold.

av a lanche (av′ə lanch), a large mass of snow and ice, or of dirt and rocks, sliding or falling down the side of a mountain.

av a rice (av′ə ris), greed; greedy desire for money.

av a ri cious (av′ə rish′əs), greedy.

a venge (ə venj′), get revenge for. The Indian will avenge the murder of his brother by killing the murderer.

a veng er (ə ven′jər), one who avenges a wrong.

av e nue (av′i nū or av′i nü), 1. wide street. 2. road or walk bordered by trees. 3. way of approach. Hard work is a good avenue to success.

a ver (ə vėr′), state to be true; assert.

av er age (av′ər ij), 1. The average of several quantities is found by dividing the sum of the quantities by the number of quantities. The average of 3 and 10 and 5 is 6. 2. find the average of. 3. obtained by averaging. The average temperature for the week was 82. 4. have as an average; be on the average. The cost of our lunches at school averaged one dollar a week. 5. usual sort or amount. His mind is about like the average. 6. usual; ordinary.

a verse (ə vėrs′), opposed; unwilling. She was averse to fighting.

a ver sion (ə vėr′zhən), 1. dislike. 2. thing or person that is disliked.

a vert (ə vėrt′), 1. turn away; turn aside. She averted her eyes from the wreck. 2. prevent. The driver averted an accident by a quick turn of his car.

a vi ar y (ā′vi ãr′i), place where many birds are kept.

a vi a tion (ā′vi ā′shən), flying in airplanes.

a vi a tor (ā′vi ā′tər), person who flies an airplane.

a void (ə void′), keep away from; keep out of the way of. We avoided driving through large cities on our trip.

a void ance (ə void′əns), act of avoiding; keeping away from. Mary's avoidance of her old friends was noticeable.

a vow (ə vou′), declare frankly and openly. Tom avowed that he could not sing.

a wait (ə wāt′), 1. wait for; look forward to. He has awaited your coming for a week. 2. be ready for; be in store for. Many pleasures await you.

a wake (ə wāk′), 1. wake up; arouse. We awoke from a sound sleep. 2. not asleep.

a wak en (ə wāk′ən), awake; wake up; rouse from sleep; stir up.

a wak en ing (ə wāk′ən ing), a waking up; an arousing.

a ward (ə wôrd′), 1. give after careful consideration; assign. The sum of $5000 was awarded to the injured man. Gold stars were awarded to the children who did well. 2. something given after careful consideration; a prize. Frank's dog won the highest award. 3. a decision by a judge. We all thought the award was fair.

a ware (ə wãr′), knowing; realizing; conscious. I was too sleepy to be aware how cold it was. He is not aware of his danger.

a way (ə wā′), 1. not at; not near; at a distance. Go away! The sailor was far away from home. Mary stays away from the fire. My mother is away today. 2. without stopping. Fred worked away at his writing.

awe (ô), 1. great fear and wonder; fear and reverence. We feel awe when we stand near vast mountains, or when we think of God's power and glory. 2. cause to feel awe; fill with awe.

aw ful (ô′fəl), 1. dreadful; causing fear; as, an awful storm with thunder and lightning 2. impressive; deserving great respect; as, the awful power of God.

aw ful ly (ô′fəl i), terribly; dreadfully.

a while (ə hwīl′), for a short time. He stayed awhile.

awk ward (ôk′wərd), 1. clumsy; not graceful in movement or shape. Seals are very awkward on land, but are graceful in the water. 2. not well suited to use. The handle of this pitcher has an awkward shape. 3. not easily managed. This is an awkward corner to turn. He asked me an awkward question.

Awl

awk ward ly (ôk′wərd li), in a clumsy way.

awk ward ness (ôk′wərd nis), awkward behavior; awkward quality.

awl (ôl), a tool used for making small holes in leather or wood. See the picture just above.

awn ing (ôn′ing), piece of canvas spread over or before a door, window, porch, etc., for protection from the sun or rain.

Awnings

a woke (ə wōk′), waked up. Mary awoke us at seven. John has not yet awoke.

a wry (ə rī′), 1. with a twist or turn to one side. Her hat was blown awry by the wind. 2. wrong. Our plans have gone awry.

ax or **axe** (aks), tool for chopping wood. See the picture.

Ax

ax is (ak′sis), the straight line about which a thing turns. The axis of the earth is a line from the North Pole to the South Pole.

ax le (ak′səl), 1. bar on which or with which a wheel turns. 2. crossbar on the two ends of which wheels turn.

AXLE

ay[1] or **aye**[1] (ā), always; ever. A mother's love lasts forever and ay.

ay[2] or **aye**[2] (ī), yes. Aye, aye, sir. The ayes won when the vote was taken.

a zal ea (ə zāl′yə), any one of certain plants bearing many showy flowers.

az ure (azh′ər), blue; blue like the sky.

B

baa (bä), the sound a sheep makes; bleat.

bab ble (bab′əl), 1. make sounds like a baby. 2. talk that cannot be understood. 3. talk foolishly. 4. foolish talk. 5. talk too much; tell secrets. 6. murmur; as, the babble of the brook.

babe (bāb), baby.

ba boon (ba bün′), a kind of large, fierce monkey with a doglike face and a short tail. Baboons live in the rocky hills of Arabia and Africa.

Baboon (body 2 ft. high, 2 ft. long; tail 18 in.)

ba by (bā′bi), 1. a very young child. Some babies cry a good deal. 2. person who acts like a baby. 3. of or for a baby. 4. young; small; as, a baby lamb. 5. treat as a baby.

ba by hood (bā′bi hu̇d), condition or time of being a baby.

bach e lor (bach′ə lər), man who has not married.

back (bak), 1. the part of a person's body opposite to his face or the front part of his body. In animals, the upper part from the neck to the end of the backbone is the back. 2. the side of anything away from you. 3. support or help. Many of his friends backed his plan. 4. move away from the front. He backed his car slowly. He backed away from the gun. 5. behind in space or time. Please walk back three steps. They are often back in their work. Have you read the back numbers of this paper? Some years back this land was all in farms. 6. in return. You should pay back what you borrow.

back bone (bak′bōn′), 1. the main bone along the middle of the back in man, mammals, birds, reptiles, and fishes. The backbone consists of many separate bones called vertebrae. 2. the most important part. 3. strength of character.

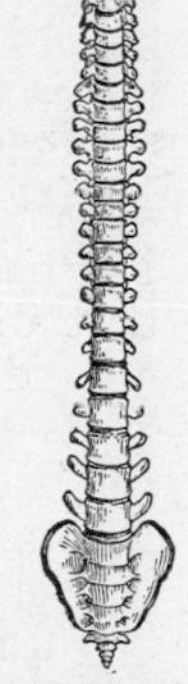
Human backbone

back ground (bak′ground′), 1. the part in the back. The cottage stands in the foreground with the mountains in the background. 2. part which shows off the chief thing or person. Her dress had pink flowers on a white background. 3. **In the background** sometimes means out of sight or not in clear view. The shy boy kept in the background. 4. past experience, knowledge, and training. Dan had the background of life on a farm.

back ward (bak′wərd), 1. away from one's front. 2. with the back first; as, to tumble over backward. 3. toward the back; as, to look backward, a backward motion. 4. toward the starting point. 5. from better to worse. 6. dull; slow in development. Backward children need a special kind of schooling. 7. late; behind time. This is a backward season; spring is two weeks late. 8. shy; bashful.

back ward ness (bak′wərd nis), 1. slowness. 2. lateness. 3. bashfulness; shyness.

back wards (bak′wərdz), backward (definitions 1, 2, 3, 4, and 5).

back woods (bak′wůdz′), uncleared forests or wild regions far away from towns.

back woods man (bak′wůdz′mən), man who lives in the backwoods.

ba con (bā′kən), salted and smoked meat from the back and sides of a hog.

bac te ri a (bak tēr′i ə), very, very tiny living plants, some of which cause disease. Other kinds of bacteria cause milk to sour or turn cider into vinegar.

SPHERE ROD SPIRAL
Bacteria

bad (bad), not good; not as it ought to be.

bad blood, unfriendly feeling; hate.

bade (bad), 1. commanded. 2. invited. 3. told. Helen bade us good-by.

badge (baj), 1. something worn to show that a person belongs to a certain school, class, club, society, occupation, etc. Policemen wear badges. The Red Cross badge is a red cross on a white background. 2. a symbol or sign. Chains are a badge of slavery.

Badge

badg er (baj′ər), 1. a hairy, gray animal that digs holes in the ground to live in. 2. its fur. 3. question persistently; keep on teasing or annoying. An agent has been badgering father for the last two weeks to buy a new car.

Badger (2 ft. long)

bad ly (bad′li), in a bad way.

bad-tem pered (bad′tem′pərd), having a bad temper or disposition.

baf fle (baf′əl), 1. be too hard for (a person) to understand or solve. This puzzle baffles me. 2. hinder.

bag (bag), 1. paper, cloth, or other material fastened together to hold something. 2. put in a bag. 3. swell; bulge. 4. game killed or caught by a hunter. 5. kill or catch in hunting. The hunter bagged many ducks.

bag gage (bag′ij), 1. the trunks, bags, suitcases, etc., that you take with you when you travel. 2. the equipment that an army takes with it, such as tents, blankets, dishes, etc.

bag pipe (bag′pīp′), musical instrument made of a tube, a bag for air, and pipes, now used chiefly in Scotland.

Scottish bagpipe

bail[1] (bāl), 1. set (a person) free from arrest by agreeing to pay a certain sum of money if he does not appear at his trial or whenever he is wanted. 2. the guarantee of money necessary to set a person free from arrest until he is to appear for trial. Mr. Jones gave bail for his son, who was accused of setting fire to a barn.

bail[2] (bāl), the handle of a kettle or pail. See the picture.

BAIL

bail[3] (bāl), throw (water) out of a boat with a bucket, pail, dipper, or any kind of container. **Bail out** sometimes means to drop from an airplane with a parachute.

bail iff (bāl′if), 1. assistant to a sheriff. 2. an officer of a court who has charge of prisoners when they are brought into court. 3. overseer or steward of an estate. The bailiff collects rents for the owner.

bairn (bãrn), child.

bait (bāt), 1. anything, especially food, used to attract fish or other animals so that they may be caught. 2. put bait on (a hook) or in (a trap). 3. thing used as a temptation or in order to get a person to begin something he would not wish to do. 4. torment.

bake (bāk), 1. cook (food) by dry heat without exposing it directly to the fire. We bake bread and cake in an oven. 2. harden by heat; as, to bake bricks or china. 3. become baked. These cakes will bake very quickly.

bak er (bāk′ər), person who makes and sells bread, pies, cakes, etc.

bak er y (bāk′ər i), baker's shop; place where bread, cake, etc., are made or sold.

bak ing (bāk′ing), 1. cooking in dry heat. 2. amount baked at one time; batch.

baking powder, mixture of various chemicals, used to cause biscuits, cakes, etc., to rise.

bal ance (bal′əns), 1. instrument for weighing. See the picture. 2. weigh two things against each other on scales, in your hands, or in your mind, to see which is heavier or more important. Let us balance the advantages and disadvantages before we decide. 3. a condition of not falling over in any direction; steadiness. It is hard to keep your balance when standing on a fence. 4. keep or put in a steady condition. 5. all-around development and steadiness of character. John's balance kept him from doing anything foolish or queer. 6. equality in weight, amount, etc. 7. **In the balance** sometimes means undecided.

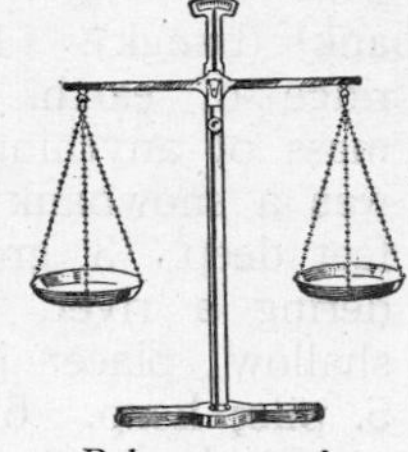
Balance or scale for weighing

bal co ny (bal′kə ni), 1. an outside projecting platform with an entrance from an upper floor of a building. 2. an upper floor in a theater or hall with seats for an audience.

Balcony

bald (bôld), 1. wholly or partly without hair on the head. 2. without its natural covering. The top of a mountain with no trees or grass on it is bald. 3. bare; plain. The bald truth is that he is a thief. 4. having white on the head; as, the bald eagle.

bale (bāl), 1. a large bundle of merchandise or material securely wrapped and tied for shipping or storage; as, a bale of cotton. 2. make into bales. We saw a big machine bale hay.

bale ful (bāl′fəl), evil; harmful. The wicked witch gave the children a baleful glance.

balk (bôk), 1. stop short and stubbornly refuse to go on. My horse balked at the bridge. 2. bring to a standstill; prevent from going on; hinder. The robber's plans were balked by the police. 3. hindrance.

balk y (bôk′i), stopping short and stubbornly refusing to go on. Mules are balky animals.

ball[1] (bôl), 1. anything round. 2. game in which some kind of ball is thrown, hit, or kicked. 3. a bullet for firearms; a round, solid object to be shot from a gun. 4. form into a ball.

ball[2] (bôl), large, formal party for dancing.

bal lad (bal′əd), 1. simple song. 2. poem that tells a story. Ballads are often sung.

bal last (bal′əst), 1. something heavy carried in a ship to steady it. 2. gravel or crushed rock used in making the bed for a railroad track. 3. something heavy carried in a balloon or dirigible to steady it. Our balloon used bags of sand for ballast. 4. furnish with ballast.

bal loon (bə lün′), 1. airtight bag filled with some gas that is lighter than air, so that it will rise and float in the air. 2. swell out like a balloon.

Child with a toy balloon

bal lot (bal′ət), 1. piece of paper or other object used in voting. 2. the whole number of votes cast. 3. to vote or decide by using ballots.

ball room (bôl′rüm′), a large room for dancing.

balm (bäm), 1. a fragrant, oily substance obtained from certain kinds of trees, used to heal or to relieve pain. 2. preparation for relieving pain or for healing. 3. anything that heals or soothes. My praise was balm to her wounded feelings.

balm y (bäm′i), 1. mild; soft; gentle; as, a balmy breeze. 2. fragrant.

bal sam (bôl′səm), 1. a kind of fir tree. Balsam firs are much used as Christmas trees. 2. balm.

bam boo (bam bü′), a treelike plant belonging to the grass family. It is very tall, and the stiff hollow stems, which have hard thick joints, are used for making canes, furniture, and even houses.

Bamboo growing

ban (ban), 1. prohibit; forbid. The police banned swimming in this lake. 2. the forbidding of an act or speech by authority of the law, the church, or public opinion. There is a ban on parking cars in this narrow street.

ba nan a (bə nan′ə), a slightly curved yellow or red fruit with firm, creamy flesh. Bananas are about five inches long and grow in large bunches. The plant is like a tree with great long leaves. It grows in warm countries.

Bunch of bananas growing on the plant

band (band), 1. thin, flat strip of material for binding, trimming, or some other purpose. The oak box was strengthened with bands of iron. 2. a stripe; as, a white cup with a gold band. 3. put a band on. 4. number of persons or animals joined together; as, a band of robbers, a band of wild dogs. 5. unite in a group. 6. a company of players upon musical instruments.

band age (ban′dij), 1. a strip of cloth or other material used in dressing and binding up a wound, injured leg or arm, etc. 2. to dress or tie up with a bandage.

Bandage on the leg

ban dan na or **ban dan a** (ban dan′ə), large, colored handkerchief.

ban dit (ban′dit), highwayman; robber.

ban dy (ban′di), throw back and forth; hit to and fro; give and take. Do not bandy words with a foolish person.

ban dy-leg ged (ban′di leg′id), having legs that curve outward.

bane (bān), cause of death, ruin, or harm. Wild animals were the bane of the mountain village.

bane ful (bān′fəl), deadly; harmful.

bang[1] (bang), 1. He gave the drum a bang. 2. The baby was banging on the dishpan with a tin cup. 3. Tom banged the door as he went through. 4. We heard the bang of a gun. 5. My trunk was banged in the accident. 6. Bang! went the gun.

bang[2] (bang), 1. cut squarely across. She wears her hair banged. 2. a fringe of banged hair.

Child wearing bangs

ban ish (ban′ish), 1. condemn to leave a country. The king banished some of his enemies. 2. force to go away; send away; drive away. The children banished Tim from their game because he always cried. Now let's banish all our cares and have a happy time.

ban ish ment (ban′ish mənt), 1. act of banishing. 2. state of being banished; exile. Banishment made him sick at heart.

ban jo (ban′jō), stringed musical instrument played with the fingers.

Man playing a banjo

bank[1] (bangk), 1. shelf or ridge of earth. 2. great mass of anything. There was a snowbank over ten feet deep. 3. ground bordering a river. 4. shoal; shallow place in water. 5. pile; heap. 6. slope. 7. make (an airplane) slope. 8. cover (a fire) with ashes so that it will burn slowly.

bank[2] (bangk), 1. place for keeping, lending, exchanging, and issuing money. A savings bank is a good place to put money. 2. keep money in a bank. 3. put (money) in a bank.

bank[3] (bangk), bench; row; tier. Some organs have two banks of keys.

bank er (bangk′ər), person or company that runs a bank.

ban ner (ban′ər), 1. flag. John carried our school banner in the parade. 2. piece of cloth with some design or words on it.

ban quet (bang′kwit), 1. feast. 2. formal dinner with speeches.

ban ter (ban′tər), 1. joking. 2. talk in a joking way. 3. make fun of.

bap tism (bap′tizm), dipping a person into water or sprinkling water on him, as a sign of the washing away of sin and of admission into the Christian church.

Bap tist (bap′tist), 1. member of a Christian church that believes in baptism by dipping the whole person under water. 2. of or having something to do with the Baptists.

bap tize (bap tīz′), 1. dip into water or sprinkle with water as a sign of the washing away of sin and of admission into the Christian church. 2. purify; cleanse. 3. give a first name to (a person) at baptism.

bar (bär), 1. an evenly shaped piece of some solid, longer than it is wide or thick; as, a bar of iron, a bar of soap, a bar of chocolate. 2. a pole or rod across a door, window, etc., or across any opening. Let down the pasture bars so the cows can come in. 3. put bars across; fasten or shut off. Bar the doors. 4. anything that blocks the way or prevents progress. A bar of sand kept boats out of the harbor. A bad temper is a bar to making friends. 5. band of color; stripe. 6. mark with stripes or bands of color; as, a chicken with barred feathers. 7. a unit of rhythm in music. 8. the dividing line between two bars on the musical staff. 9. the place where a prisoner stands in a law court. Brought before the bar of conscience, his action could not be defended. 10. the whole group of practicing lawyers. After passing his law examinations, he was admitted to the bar. 11. law court. 12. anything like a law court. The bar of public opinion condemns dishonest people. 13. a counter or place where drinks are served to customers. 14. except; not including. He is the worst boy in town, bar none. 15. exclude; forbid. Rough play is barred.

BAR BAR DOUBLE BAR

barb (bärb), a point sticking out and back from the main point. See the picture.

BARBS BARB

Barbs on fishhooks

bar bar i an (bär bãr′i ən), 1. person who is not civilized. 2. not civilized; cruel and coarse; almost savage.

bar bar ic (bär bar′ik), rough and rude; suited to a barbarous people.

bar ba rous (bär′bə rəs), 1. not civilized. 2. cruel. Teasing and bullying smaller children are barbarous customs.

bar be cue (bär′bə kū), 1. a feast at which animals are roasted whole. 2. an animal roasted whole. 3. roast (an animal) whole. 4. meat roasted before an open fire. 5. roast in this way.

barbed (bärbd), having a barb or barbs; as, a barbed fishhook. Barbed wire has sharp points every few inches.

bar ber (bär′bər), person whose business is cutting hair, shaving men, and trimming beards.

bard (bärd), 1. poet and singer of long ago. Bards sang their own poems to the music of their harps. 2. poet.

bare[1] (bãr), 1. not clothed; naked; uncovered. His bare hands were blue with the cold. The top of the hill was bare, although trees grew part way up the hill. 2. empty; not furnished. The room was bare of furniture. 3. plain; not adorned. He lived in a bare little house. 4. just enough and no more; mere. He earns a bare living by his work. 5. uncover; reveal; strip. He bared his sword.

bare[2] (bãr), bore. See **bear**[1].

bare back (bãr′bak′), without a saddle; on a horse's bare back.

bare foot (bãr′fu̇t′), without shoes and stockings.

bare head ed (bãr′hed′id), wearing nothing on the head.

bare ly (bãr′li), only just; scarcely. He has barely enough money to live on.

bare ness (bãr′nis), being bare; lack of covering; lack of furnishings and contents.

bar gain (bär′gin), 1. an agreement to trade or exchange. Will you take $5 for it? Then it's a bargain. 2. something offered for sale cheap or bought cheap. 3. make a bargain. 4. try to get good terms. She stood bargaining for ten minutes with the man for the vegetables. 5. **Bargain for** sometimes means expect or be prepared for. It is raining, and that is more than I bargained for. 6. **Into the bargain** means moreover. It is raining, into the bargain.

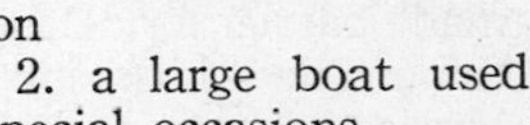
Barge used for freight

barge (bärj), 1. large, flat-bottomed boat for carrying freight on rivers and canals. 2. a large boat used for excursions and special occasions.

bark[1] (bärk), 1. the tough outside covering of the trunk, branches, and roots of trees. 2. strip the bark from (a tree). 3. scrape the skin from. I fell down the steps and barked my knees.

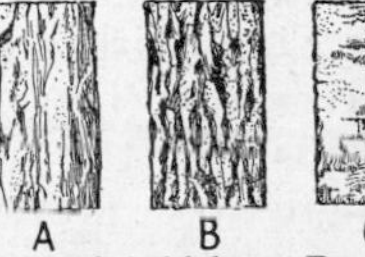

Bark of: A, hickory; B, white oak; C, white birch.

bark[2] (bärk), 1. the short, sharp sound a dog makes; a sound like this, such as the bark of a fox, a squirrel, a gun, or a cough. 2. make this sound or one like it. 3. shout sharply. Some officers bark out their orders.

bark[3] (bärk), barque.

bar ley (bär′li), a grasslike plant or its grain. Barley will grow in cool climates. It is used for food. See the picture.

Barley

barn (bärn), building for storing hay and grain and for sheltering cows and horses.

barn yard (bärn′yärd′), the yard around a barn.

bar on (bar′ən), a nobleman of the lowest rank.

bar on et (bar′ən it), a person below a baron in rank, but above a knight.

barque (bärk), 1. a kind of ship with three masts. 2. any boat or ship.

Barque

bar racks (bar′əks), 1. building or group of buildings for soldiers to live in. 2. large plain building in which many people live.

bar rel (bar′əl), 1. a container with round, flat top and bottom and slightly curved sides. It is usually made of boards held together by hoops. See the picture. 2. the amount that a barrel can hold. 3. put in barrels. We plan to barrel the cider next Wednesday. 4. the metal tube of a gun.

Barrel

bar ren (bar′ən), 1. not producing anything. A desert is barren. 2. a barren stretch of land. 3. not able to have children. 4. without interest; not attractive; dull.

bar ri cade (bar′i kād′), 1. a rough, hastily made barrier for defense. 2. barrier; obstruction. The soldiers cut trees down to make a barricade across the road. 3. block or obstruct with a barricade. We barricaded the door with a bureau.

bar ri er (bar′i ər), 1. something which stands in the way; something stopping progress or preventing approach. A dam is a barrier holding water back. Lack of water is a barrier to the settlement of a region. 2. something that separates or keeps apart. The Atlantic Ocean is a barrier between Europe and America.

bar row (bar′ō), 1. a frame with two short handles at each end, used for carrying a load. 2. wheelbarrow. 3. cart that a man pushes; handcart.

bar ter (bär′tər), 1. trade by exchanging goods for other goods without using money. The Indians bartered furs for beads and guns. 2. carry on trade by exchanging one kind of thing for other things.

base[1] (bās), 1. the part of a thing on which it rests; the bottom. The machine rests on a wide base of steel. 2. basis; foundation; groundwork. 3. a station or goal in certain games, such as baseball or hide-and-seek. 4. headquarters; starting place; place from which an army goes forth to fight and from which it is supplied. 5. establish; found. His large business was based on good service.

base[2] (bās), 1. low; mean; selfish; cowardly. To betray a friend is a base action. 2. inferior. Iron and lead are base metals; gold and silver are precious metals.

base ball (bās′bôl′), 1. a game played with bat and ball by two teams of nine players each, on a field with four bases. 2. the ball used in this game.

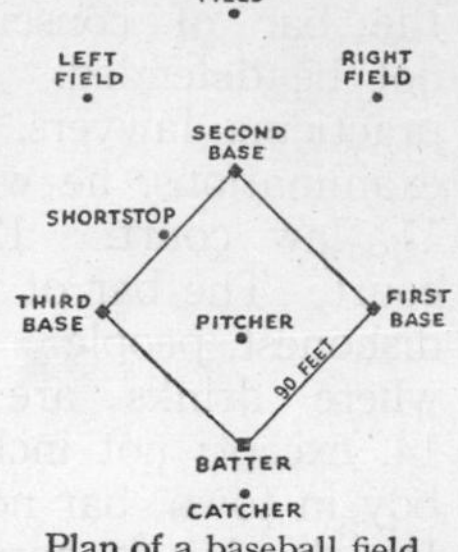

Plan of a baseball field

base ment (bās′mənt), the lowest story of a building, partly or wholly below ground.

bash ful (bash′fəl), uneasy and awkward in the company of strangers; shy.

ba sic (bā′sik), fundamental.

ba sin (bā′sən), 1. a wide, shallow bowl; bowl. 2. the amount that a basin can hold. He has eaten a basin of oatmeal already. 3. a hollow place containing water. 4. all the land drained by a river and the streams that flow into it.

ba sis (bā′sis), foundation; main part. The basis of this medicine is an oil. Knowledge of words and intelligence are the bases of ability in reading.

bask (bask), warm oneself pleasantly. The cat basks before the fire.

bas ket (bas′kit), 1. container made of twigs, grasses, fibers, strips of wood, etc., woven together. 2. amount that a basket holds. We ate a basket of peaches. 3. anything that looks or is shaped like a basket.

bas ket ball (bas′kit bôl′), 1. a game played with a large, round leather ball between two teams of five players each. The players try to toss the ball through a net shaped like a basket. 2. the ball used in this game.

bass[1] (bās), 1. having a deep, low sound; as, a bass voice. 2. the lowest part in music; the man's voice that sings the part; any singer or instrument that has a bass voice, part, or range.

bass[2] (bas), a fish used for food, living in fresh water or in the ocean.

bass vi ol (bās′ vī′əl), a big violin as tall as a man.

baste[1] (bāst), drip or pour melted fat or butter on (meat, etc.) while roasting. Meat is basted to keep it from drying out and to improve its flavor.

baste[2] (bāst), sew with long, loose stitches. These stitches are usually removed after the final sewing.

bat[1] (bat), 1. a stout wooden stick or club, used to hit the ball in baseball, cricket, etc. 2. hit with a bat; hit. I batted the balloon over to him with my hand. He bats well.

bat[2] (bat), a flying animal that looks somewhat like a mouse with skinlike wings. Bats fly at night and feed on insects and fruit.

Bat

batch (bach), 1. quantity of bread made at one baking. 2. quantity of anything made as one lot or set. Our second batch of candy was better than the first. 3. number of persons or things taken together.

bate (bāt), abate; lessen; hold back. The boys listened with bated breath to the sailor's story.

bath (bath), 1. a washing of the body. 2. water, towels, etc., for a bath. Your bath is ready. 3. a tub, a room, or other place for bathing. The house had no bath, so we had one built.

bathe (bāᴛʜ), 1. take a bath. 2. give a bath to. 3. go in swimming; go into a river, lake, or ocean for sport or to get cool. 4. pour over; cover. The valley was bathed in sunlight.

bath room (bath′rüm′), a room fitted up for taking baths.

ba ton (ba ton′), 1. a staff or stick used as a mark of office or authority. 2. the stick used by the leader for beating time to the music.

bat tal ion (bə tal′yən), any large part of an army organized to act together.

bat ter[1] (bat′ər), beat with repeated blows so as to bruise, break, or get out of shape; pound. The fireman battered down the door with a heavy ax.

bat ter[2] (bat′ər), a liquid mixture of flour, milk, eggs, etc., that thickens when cooked. Cakes, pancakes, muffins, etc., are made from batter.

bat ter[3] (bat′ər), person whose turn it is to bat in baseball, cricket, etc.

bat ter y (bat′ər i), 1. any set of similar or connected things. 2. a set of one or more electric cells which produce electric current. 3. a set of big guns for combined action in attack or defense. Four batteries began firing on the enemy.

bat tle (bat′əl), 1. a fight between two armies; a contest. 2. struggle; fight.

bat tle-ax or **bat tle-axe** (bat′əl aks′), an ax used as a weapon in battle. See the picture.

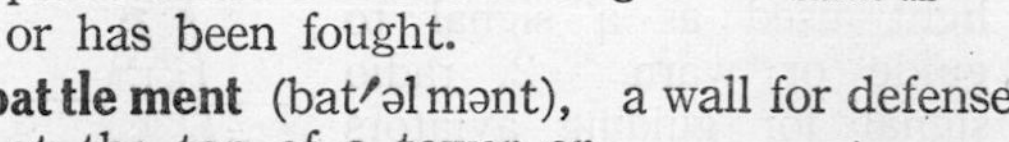
Head of a battle-ax

bat tle field (bat′əl fēld′), place where a battle is fought or has been fought.

bat tle ment (bat′əl mənt), a wall for defense at the top of a tower or wall, lower in some places so that men could shoot through them.

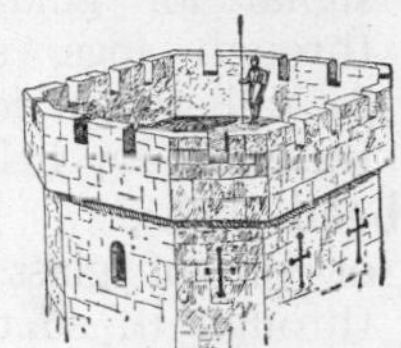
Battlement

bat tle ship (bat′əl ship′), very large warship having the heaviest armor and the most powerful guns.

bau ble (bô′bəl), showy trifle having no real value. Useless toys and trinkets are baubles.

bawl (bôl), 1. shout or cry out in a noisy way. The peddler bawled his wares in the street. 2. a loud shout or cry.

bay[1] (bā), part of a sea or lake extending into land. See the picture under **cove.**

bay[2] (bā), 1. long deep bark of a dog. The hunters heard the distant bay of the hounds. 2. bark; bark at. Dogs sometimes bay the moon. 3. a stand made by a hunted animal to face those hunting it. The stag stood at bay on the edge of the cliff. 4. position of pursuers or foe thus kept off. The stag held the hounds at bay.

bay[3] (bā), small evergreen tree with smooth, shiny leaves; laurel tree.

bay[4] (bā), 1. reddish-brown; as, a bay horse. 2. reddish-brown horse.

bay o net (bā′ə nit), 1. a blade for piercing or stabbing, attached to a gun. 2. pierce or stab with a bayonet.

Bayonet

bay ou (bī′ü), marshy inlet of a lake, river, or gulf in the southern United States.

ba zaar or **ba zar** (bəzär′), 1. street or streets full of shops in Oriental countries. 2. place for the sale of many kinds of goods. 3. sale of things given for some special purpose.

B.C., before Christ. B.C. is used for times before Christ. A.D. is used for times since Christ was born. From 20 B.C. to 50 A.D. is 70 years.

be (bē). He will be here all the year. She tries to be good. They will be punished.

beach (bēch), 1. an almost flat shore of sand or little stones over which the water washes when high. 2. run (a boat) ashore; draw up on the shore. We beached our boat and got out.

bea con (bē′kən), 1. fire or light used as a signal to guide or warn. 2. radio signal for guiding aviators through fogs, storms, etc. 3. tall tower for a signal; watchtower; lighthouse.

Beacon light over a rock at sea

bead (bēd), 1. small ball or bit of glass, metal, etc., with a hole through it, so that it can be strung on a thread with others like it. Beads are used for ornament or for counting prayers. 2. any small round body like a drop or bubble; as, beads of sweat. 3. a bit of metal at the front end of a gun to aim by. 4. ornament with beads.

bea gle (bē′gəl), a kind of a small hunting dog.

beak (bēk), 1. a bird's bill, especially one that is strong and hooked and useful in striking or tearing. Eagles, hawks, and parrots have beaks. 2. anything like a beak, such as the projecting prow of an ancient warship.

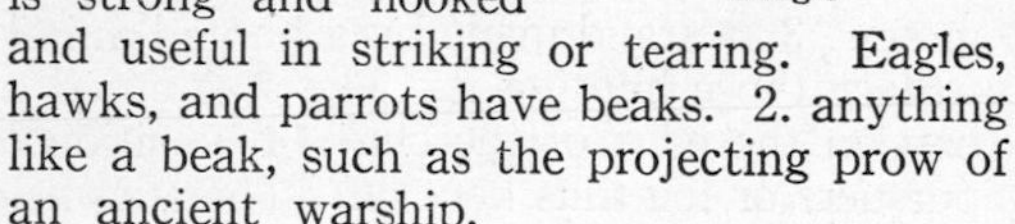

Beagle

beak er (bēk′ər), large cup or glass.

beam (bēm), 1. large, long piece of timber or metal, ready for use in building. 2. any long piece or bar; as, the beam of a plow, the beam of a balance. 3. the main horizontal support in a building or ship. 4. the widest part of a ship. 5. a ray of light. 6. send forth rays of light; shine. 7. a bright look; a smile. 8. to smile.

bean (bēn), 1. smooth, somewhat flat seed used as a vegetable. 2. long pod containing such seeds. The green or yellow pods are also used as a vegetable. 3. plant that beans grow on. 4. any seed shaped somewhat like a bean. Coffee beans are seeds of the coffee plant.

bean stalk (bēn′stôk′), the stem of a bean plant.

bear[1] (bãr), 1. carry. It takes two men to bear that stone. That board is too thin to bear your weight. 2. endure. He cannot bear any more pain. 3. have an effect on; have something to do with. This story does not bear on the question. 4. bring forth; produce. This tree is bearing fine apples. 5. press; thrust; drive. Don't bear down so hard. **bore** and **borne** are formed from **bear.**

bear[2] (bãr), 1. a large, clumsy animal with coarse hair and a very short tail. 2. gruff or surly person.

American black bear (4½ ft. long; 3 ft. tall)

beard (bērd), 1. hair growing on a man's face. 2. something resembling or suggesting this. The chin tuft of a goat is a beard; so are the stiff hairs around the beak of a bird. 3. hairs on the heads of plants like oats, barley, and wheat. 4. face boldly; defy.

bear ing (bãr′ing), 1. way of standing, sitting, walking, etc.; manner. 2. reference; relation. His foolish question has no bearing on the problem. 3. direction; position in relation to other things. "I have lost my bearings" means "I do not know in which direction to go." 4. part of a machine on which another part turns or slides.

beast (bēst), 1. any animal except man, especially a four-footed animal. 2. coarse, dirty, or brutal person.

beast ly (bēst′li), like a beast; brutal; vile.

beat (bēt), 1. strike; strike again and again. The cruel man beats his horse. He has beaten it many times. 2. a stroke or blow made again and again. We heard the beat of a drum. We saw the beat of waves on a beach. 3. defeat; get the better of. Jack's school beat Tom's at baseball. 4. make flat. 5. mix by stirring or striking with a fork, spoon, or other utensil; as, to beat eggs. 6. move up and down. The bird beat its wings. 7. make a sound by being struck. The drums beat loudly. 8. in music, the division of time or accent; as, three beats to a measure. A good dancer never misses a beat. 9. regular round or course made by a policeman or watchman. 10. go through in a hunt. They were beating the woods in search of the bear. 11. move against the wind by a zigzag course. The ship beat along the coast. 12. did beat; did strike; did defeat; etc. **Beat a retreat** means run away or ran away.

beat en (bēt′ən), 1. whipped; struck. The beaten dog crawled to his master's feet. 2. much walked on or traveled; as, a beaten path across the grass. 3. defeated; overcome; as, a beaten fighter. 4. shaped by blows of a hammer. This bowl is made of beaten silver. 5. See **beat.**

beau (bō), 1. lover; young man who is courting a young woman. 2. man who dresses with great care in the latest fashion.

beau te ous (bū′ti əs), beautiful.

beau ti ful (bū′ti fəl), very pleasing to see or hear; delighting the mind or senses; as, a beautiful picture, beautiful music.

beau ti fy (bū′ti fī), make beautiful; make more beautiful. Flowers beautify a garden.

beau ty (bū′ti), 1. good looks. 2. that which pleases in flowers, music, pictures, etc. 3. something beautiful; as, the beauties of nature.

bea ver[1] (bē′vər), 1. a soft-furred animal once common in North America. It has a broad, flat tail and feet adapted to swimming or walking. Beavers live both in water and on land and build dams across streams. 2. its soft brown fur; as, a coat trimmed with beaver. 3. man's high silk hat, formerly made of beaver fur. 4. a heavy woolen cloth.

Beaver (3½ ft. long, with the tail)

bea ver[2] (bē′vər), the movable lower part of a helmet, protecting the chin and lips.

B, beaver.

be came (bi kām′). See **become.** The seed became a plant.

be cause (bi kôz′). Boys play ball because it's fun. He cannot go to school because of sickness.

beck (bek), a motion of the head or hand meant as a call or command. An errand boy is at the beck and call of his boss.

beck on (bek′ən), signal (to a person) by a motion of the hand or head. He beckoned me to follow him.

be come (bi kum′), 1. come to be; grow to be. It is becoming colder. 2. **Become of** means happen to. What has become of the box of candy? 3. suit; look well on. A white dress becomes her. **became** is formed from **become.**

be com ing (bi kum′ing), fitting; suitable; looking well on the wearer. A becoming dress makes a girl look her best.

bed (bed), 1. anything to sleep or rest on. 2. any place where people or animals sleep or rest. 3. base on which anything rests. They set the pole on a bed of concrete. 4. layer. 5. the ground under a body of water; as, the bed of a stream. 6. space in a garden filled with plants. 7. provide with a bed; put to bed; put in a bed. The man bedded down his horse with straw. These plants should be bedded in rich soil.

bed cham ber (bed′chām′bər), bedroom.

bed clothes (bed′klōz′), sheets, blankets, quilts, etc.

bed ding (bed′ing), 1. bedclothes. 2. material for beds. Straw is used as bedding for cows and horses.

bed lam (bed′ləm), 1. uproar; confusion. 2. insane asylum; madhouse.

be drag gle (bi drag′əl), wet or soil (a garment) by dragging it or trailing it. The woman's long skirt was bedraggled from the wet streets.

bed room (bed′rüm′), a room to sleep in.

bed side (bed′sīd′), the side of a bed. The nurse sat by the sick woman's bedside.

bed spread (bed′spred′), cover that is spread over the blankets on a bed to make the bed look better.

bed stead (bed′sted), wooden or metal framework of a bed.

bed time (bed′tīm′), time to go to bed. His regular bedtime is nine o'clock.

bee (bē), 1. an insect that makes honey and wax. A bee has four wings and a sting, and usually lives with many other bees. 2. a gathering for work or amusement; as, a spelling bee, a husking bee.

Worker honeybee (about ½ life size)

beech (bēch), 1. a tree with smooth, gray bark and glossy leaves. It bears a sweet nut that is good to eat. 2. its wood.

beef (bēf), 1. meat from a steer, cow, or bull, used for food. 2. a steer, cow, or bull when full-grown and fattened for food.

beef steak (bēf′stāk′), slice of beef for broiling or frying.

beef y (bēf′i), fleshy; solid; heavy.

bee hive (bē′hīv′), 1. a hive or house for bees. 2. busy, swarming place.

Beehives

been (bin). He has been here for years. This boy has been present every day. The books have been read by every girl in the room. The two boys have been friends for many years.

beer (bēr), 1. an alcoholic drink made from malt, barley, and hops. 2. a drink made from roots or plants, such as root beer, ginger beer.

beet (bēt), a plant, grown for its thick, fleshy root; its root. Red beets are used as vegetables. Sugar is made from white beets.

Beet

bee tle (bē′təl), insect that has two hard, shiny cases to cover its wings when folded. See the picture just below.

beeves (bēvz), beef cattle. Beeves are shipped from the farm to the city.

be fall (bi fôl′), happen; happen to. Be careful that no harm befalls you. **befell** and **befallen** are formed from **befall.**

Beetle

be fall en (bi fôl′ən). See **befall.** An accident must have befallen them.

be fell (bi fel′), did befall. Evil befell the knight upon his lonely trip.

be fit (bi fit′), suit; be fit for; be proper for.

be fore (bi fōr′), 1. in front of. Before him sat a great crowd. 2. in front. He went before to see if the road was safe. 3. earlier than. Before the bell rings, you may play games. 4. earlier. Come at two o'clock, not before. 5. before now; in time past. You were never late before. 6. rather than; sooner than. I'd starve before I'd surrender.

be fore hand (bi fōr′hand′), ahead of time. I am going to get everything ready beforehand.

be friend (bi frend′), act as a friend to; help. The kind man befriended the lost boy.

beg (beg), 1. ask for (food, clothes, or money) as a charity. The old man said that he had no way to live but by begging. 2. ask earnestly or humbly. He begged his mother to forgive him.

be gan (bi gan′), did begin. Snow began to fall early in the evening. His mother began to worry when he did not come home.

be get (bi get′), 1. be the father of. 2. produce; cause to be. Hate begets hate and love begets love. **begot, begotten,** and **begetting** are formed from **beget.**

beg gar (beg′ər), 1. person who lives by begging. 2. a very poor person. 3. make a beggar of; make poor. Your reckless spending will beggar your father.

be gin (bi gin′). School begins at nine. We begin breakfast at seven. I am beginning to feel hungry. **began, begun,** and **beginning** are formed from **begin.**

be gin ner (bi gin′ər), person who is doing something for the first time; one who lacks skill and experience. You skate well for a beginner.

be gin ning (bi gin′ing), 1. time when anything begins. 2. first part. 3. first cause; source; origin. 4. See **begin.**

be gone (bi gôn′), go away. "Begone," said the prince.

be got (bi got′), 1. was the father of. 2. produced. See **beget.**

be got ten (bi got′ən), produced. See **beget.**

be guile (bi gīl′), 1. deceive; cheat. He beguiled me into thinking that he was my friend. 2. charm; amuse. The old sailor beguiled the boys with stories about his life at sea. 3. while away (time) pleasantly.

be gun (bi gun′), commenced. The work was begun Monday. It has begun to rain.

be half (bi haf′), side; interest; favor. **In behalf of** means for or in the interest of. I am speaking in behalf of my friend John.

be have (bi hāv′), 1. act. Don't behave like a fool. 2. act well; do what is right. "Behave, or I'll take you home," said Lulu's mother.

be hav ior (bi hāv′yər), way of acting; conduct; action; acts. His behavior showed that his feelings were hurt. The little boat's behavior was perfect on the trial trip.

be head (bi hed′), cut off the head of.

be held (bi held′), 1. saw. We beheld the approaching storm. 2. seen. You have all beheld beautiful sunsets.

be hest (bi hest′), command. The knight vowed to carry out every behest of his king.

be hind (bi hīnd′). Stand behind me. He is behind his usual time. The men are behind in their work.

be hold (bi hōld′), see; look; take notice. Behold! the king! **beheld** is formed from **behold.**

be hold er (bi hōl′dər), onlooker. The man's strength amazed all the beholders.

be ing (bē′ing). The dog is being fed. Being hungry, he eats much. Men, women, and children are human beings. This world came into being long ago.

be la bor (bi lā′bər), beat vigorously. The man belabored his poor donkey.

be lat ed (bi lāt′id), delayed; too late. Your belated letter arrived at last.

belch (belch), 1. throw out gas from the stomach through the mouth. 2. throw out with force. The volcano belched fire and smoke. 3. a belching.

bel fry (bel′fri), 1. tower for a bell or bells. 2. the space for the bell in a tower.

Belfry

be lie (bi lī′), 1. give a false idea of. His scowl belied his usual good nature. 2. fail to come up to; disappoint. Roy is stealing again, and so is belying our hopes.

be lief (bi lēf′), 1. what is held true; thing believed; as, Christian beliefs. 2. acceptance as true or real. 3. faith; trust. He expressed his belief in the boy's honesty.

be lieve (bi lēv′), 1. think (something) is true or real. We all believe that the earth is round. 2. have faith; trust. Believe in God. 3. think (somebody) tells the truth. His friends believe him.

be liev er (bi lēv′ər), person who believes.

be like (bi līk′), very likely; perhaps.

be lit tle (bi lit′əl), make little; make less important.

bell (bel), 1. a hollow metal cup that makes a musical sound when struck by a clapper or hammer. 2. the stroke or sound of a bell. On shipboard a bell indicates a half hour of time. 3. anything shaped like a bell. 4. put a bell on.

Hand bell

belle (bel), 1. a beautiful woman or girl. 2. the prettiest or most admired woman or girl.

bel lig er ent (bə lij′ər ənt), 1. at war; engaged in war. 2. a nation or person engaged in war. 3. warlike; willing to fight. Boys are more belligerent than girls.

bel low (bel′ō), 1. roar as a bull does. 2. shout angrily. 3. roar with pain. 4. a deep bellowing noise; a roar.

bel lows (bel′ōz), an instrument for producing a strong current of air, used for blowing fires or sounding an organ.

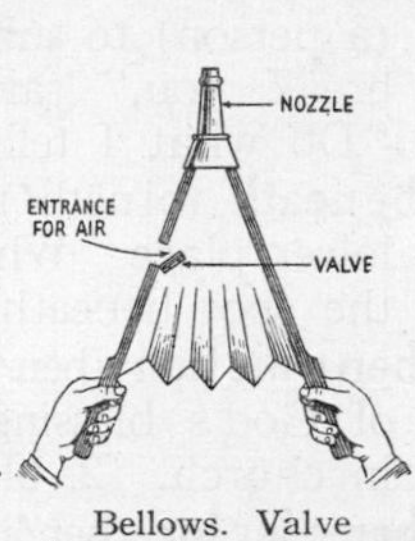

Bellows. Valve closes when sides are pushed together.

bel ly (bel′i), 1. the lower part of the human body, which contains the stomach and bowels. 2. the under part of an animal's body. 3. stomach. 4. the bulging part of anything, or the hollow in it. 5. swell out; bulge. The sails bellied in the wind.

be long (bi lông′), 1. **Belong to** means be the property of. Does this cap belong to you? 2. **Belong to** also means be a part of or be a member of. Mary belongs to the Girl Scouts. 3. have one's or its proper place. That book belongs on this shelf.

be long ings (bi lông′ingz), things that belong to a person; possessions.

be lov ed (bi luv′id or bi luvd′), 1. dearly loved; dear. 2. person who is loved; darling.

be low (bi lō′), 1. under; in a lower place than; not so high as. 2. beneath; lower down.

belt (belt), 1. a strip of leather, cloth, etc., worn around the body to hold in or support clothes or weapons. 2. any broad strip or band. The cotton belt is the region where cotton is grown. 3. an endless band that moves the wheels and pulleys it passes over. A belt moves the fan in our automobile. 4. put a belt around. 5. fasten on with a belt. 6. beat with a belt.

be moan (bi mōn′), moan about; bewail.

bench (bench), 1. long seat, usually of wood or stone. 2. worktable of a carpenter, or of any worker with tools and materials. Dick worked at his bench in the cellar. 3. judge or a group of judges sitting in a law court.

bend (bend), 1. a curve or turn; a part that is not straight. There is a sharp bend in the road here. 2. to curve; be crooked. The branch began to bend as I climbed along it. 3. make crooked; force out of a straight line. The strong man had bent the iron bars and escaped. 4. move or turn in a new direction. His steps were bent toward home now. 5. to bow; to stoop. She bent to the ground and picked up a stone. 6. submit. I bent to his will. 7. force (a person) to submit. "I will bend you or break you," said the cruel master. "Do what I tell you or you die tonight."

be neath (bi nēth′), below; under; in a lower place. What you drop will fall upon the spot beneath.

ben e dic tion (ben′i dik′shən), 1. the asking of God's blessing at the end of a service in church. 2. blessing.

ben e fac tor (ben′i fak′tər), person who has given money or kindly help.

be nef i cent (bi nef′i sənt), kind; doing good.

ben e fi cial (ben′i fish′əl), favorable; helpful; productive of good. Sunshine is beneficial to plants.

ben e fit (ben′i fit), 1. advantage; anything which is for the good of a person or thing. Good roads are of great benefit to travelers. 2. do good to. The sea air will benefit you. 3. receive good; profit. He benefited from the medicine. He will benefit from the new way of doing business. 4. act of kindness; favor. My new friend showered more benefits upon me than I could repay.

be nev o lence (bi nev′ə ləns), 1. good will; kindly feeling. 2. act of kindness; something good that is done.

be nev o lent (bi nev′ə lənt), charitable; kindly.

bent (bent), 1. See **bend.** He bent the wire. 2. determined. Tom is bent on being a sailor. 3. inclination; tendency. He has a decided bent for drawing.

be numb (bi num′), make numb.

be queath (bi kwēᴛʜ′), give when one dies. The father bequeathed his home to his son.

be rate (bi rāt′), scold sharply.

be reave (bi rēv′), deprive; leave desolate. People are bereaved by the death of relatives and friends.

be reft (bi reft′), deprived; bereaved; left desolate. Bereft of hope and friends, the old man led a wretched life.

ber ry (ber′i), 1. small, juicy fruit with many seeds. 2. gather berries. 3. a dry seed or kernel; as, coffee berries.

berth (bėrth), 1. a place to sleep on a ship, train, or airplane. See the picture. 2. a ship's place at a wharf. 3. a place for a ship to anchor conveniently or safely. 4. appointment; position; job.

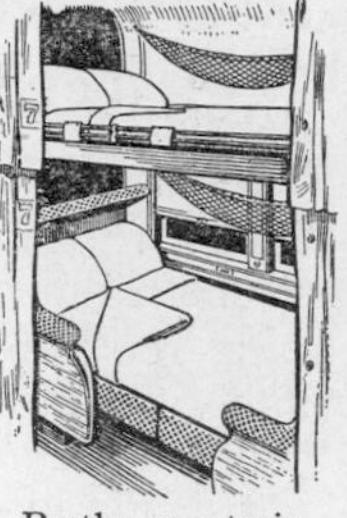
Berths on a train

be seech (bi sēch′), ask earnestly; beg. She besought the doctor to stop the pain. **besought** is formed from **beseech.**

be seem (bi sēm′), be proper for; suit; be fitting to. It does not beseem you to leave your friend without help.

be set (bi set′), 1. attack; attack on all sides; attacked. In the swamp we were beset by mosquitoes. 2. surround; hem in; surrounded. We may be beset by enemies or beset by fears.

be set ting (bi set′ing), habitually attacking. Laziness is his besetting sin.

be side (bi sīd′), 1. by the side of; near; close to. Grass grows beside the brook. 2. compared with. Nell seems dull beside her sister. 3. away from. That question was beside the mark and need not be answered. 4. **Beside oneself** means out of one's senses.

be sides (bi sīdz′), 1. also; more than that; moreover. 2. in addition to. Besides his gun, he took two pistols.

be siege (bi sēj′), 1. try for a long time to take (a place) by armed force; surround and try to capture. The Greeks besieged the city of Troy for ten years. The Indians besieged the blockhouse. 2. crowd around. Hundreds of admirers besieged the famous aviator. 3. overwhelm with requests, questions, etc. During the flood, the Red Cross was besieged with calls for help.

be sieg er (bi sēj′ər), person who besieges.

be smirch (bi smėrch′), make dirty; soil; sully.

be som (bē′zəm), 1. broom made of twigs. 2. a broom.

Besom

be sought (bi sôt′), asked earnestly; begged. I have besought her more than once not to work so hard.

be speak (bi spēk′), 1. engage in advance; order; reserve. We have bespoken two tickets for tomorrow. 2. show; indicate. The neat appearance of his room bespeaks care.

bespoke and **bespoken** are formed from **bespeak.**

best (best), 1. Mary's work is good; John's work is better; Helen's is the best. Who reads best? We want the best. 2. **Make the best of** means do as well as possible with. 3. defeat. 4. **Get the best of** means defeat.

bes tial (bes′tyəl), beastly; brutal.

be stow (bi stō′), 1. give. **Bestow on** means give to. 2. put safely; put; place. I bestowed my bundle under the hedge, and went to seek Robin.

be strew (bi strü′), 1. strew. The children bestrewed the path with flowers. 2. strew (things) around; scatter about. **bestrewn** is formed from **bestrew.**

be stride (bi strīd′), 1. get on or sit on (something) with one leg on each side. You can bestride a horse, a chair, or a fence. 2. stand over with one leg on each side. 3. stride across; step over. **bestrode, bestrid,** and **bestridden** are formed from **bestride.**

bet (bet), 1. say you will give (some money or a certain thing) to another if he is right and you are wrong. I bet you two cents I won't pass this test. 2. a promise to give some money or a certain thing to another if he is right and you are wrong. I made a bet that I shouldn't pass. 3. the money or thing promised. I did pass; so I lost my bet (lost my two cents). **betting** is formed from **bet.**

be take (bi tāk′). **Betake oneself** means (1) go. They betake themselves to the mountains every summer. (2) try doing; apply oneself. He betook himself to hard study.

be think (bi thingk′), think about; call to mind. **Bethink oneself** means think or remember. I bethought me that I must study.

be thought (bi thôt′). See **bethink.**

be tide (bi tīd′), happen to. Woe betide you if you hurt my dog!

be times (bi tīmz′), early. He rose betimes in the morning.

be to ken (bi tō′kən), be a sign of; show. His smile betokens his satisfaction.

be took (bi tük′). See **betake.**

be tray (bi trā′), 1. give away to the enemy. Some wicked soldiers betrayed their general. 2. be unfaithful to. She betrayed her promises. 3. show; reveal. Harry's wet shoes betrayed the fact that he had not worn his rubbers.

be troth (bi trōᴛʜ′), promise or engage to marry. Bess and Tom are betrothed. He betrothed his daughter to a rich man.

be troth al (bi trōᴛʜ′əl), engagement to be married.

bet ter (bet′ər), 1. We say good, better, best. Try to do better next time. 2. less sick. The sick child is better today. 3. improve. We can better that work by being more careful next time. 4. person or thing that is better. Which is the better of these two dresses? 5. Some special meanings are:
better off, in a better condition.
get the better of, defeat; be superior to.
had better, should; ought to. I had better go before it rains.

bet ter ment (bet′ər mənt), improvement.

be tween (bi twēn′). Between the two trees is a space of ten feet. The two boys shared the cake between them. There is no difference between the two dresses. We could not see the moon, for a cloud came in between. She earned between ten and twelve dollars.

be twixt (bi twikst′), between.

bev el (bev′əl), 1. a sloping edge. There is a bevel on the frame for a picture, on a piece of plate glass, etc. 2. cut a square edge to a sloping edge; make slope. Some mirrors have beveled edges. 3. an instrument or tool for measuring angles.

bev er age (bev′ər ij), drink. Milk, coffee, tea, wine, and beer are beverages.

bev y (bev′i), small group. He shot at a bevy of quail. She was talking to a bevy of girls.

be wail (bi wāl′), mourn for; weep for; complain of. The little girl was bewailing the loss of her doll.

be ware (bi wãr′), be careful; be on your guard against. Beware! danger is here. Beware the dog!

be wil der (bi wil′dər), confuse completely; puzzle; perplex. Grandma was bewildered by the crowds and noises. Some problems in arithmetic bewilder me.

be wil der ment (bi wil′dər mənt), bewildered condition; confusion; perplexity.

be witch (bi wich′), 1. put under a spell; use magic on. The wicked fairy bewitched the princess, and made her fall into a long sleep. 2. charm; delight very much. We were all bewitched by our pretty little cousin.

be yond (bi yond′). Your ball did not fall here; look beyond for it. The road is beyond that hill. It is an hour beyond the time you should stay. He was beyond the help of the doctor. The meaning of this story is beyond him. The price of the suit was beyond what he could pay. The day at the beach was beyond all we had hoped.

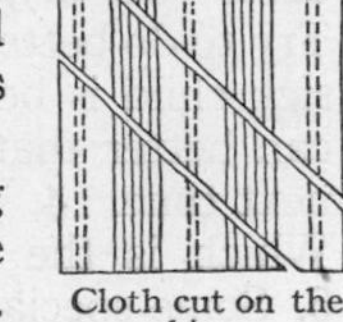
Cloth cut on the bias

bi as (bī′əs), 1. a slanting line. 2. slanting across the threads of cloth; diagonal. 3. opinion before there is reason for it; prejudice; a leaning of the mind.

bi ased (bī′əst), favoring one side too much; warped; prejudiced.

bib (bib), 1. a cloth worn under the chin by babies and small children to protect the clothing. 2. the part of an apron above the waist. See the picture.

Bib for a baby

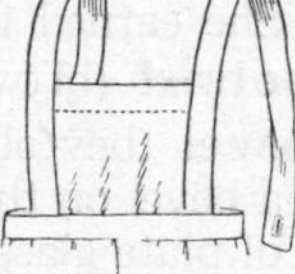
Bib of an apron

Bi ble (bī′bəl), 1. the book of sacred writings of the Christian religion; the Old Testament and the New Testament. 2. a book of the sacred writings of any religion.

bi cy cle (bī′si kəl), 1. See the picture. 2. ride a bicycle.

Boy riding a bicycle

bid (bid), 1. command. The captain bids his men go forward. Do as I bid you. 2. invite. Our friends gave us strawberries and bade us come again in apple time. 3. say; tell. His friends are bidding him good-by. 4. offer to pay (a certain price). First she bid $5 for the table. He then bid $6. 5. an offer; amount offered for a thing. My bid was $7. **bade, bidden,** and **bidding** are formed from **bid.**

bid den (bid′ən). See **bid.** Twelve guests were bidden to the feast.

bid ding (bid′ing), 1. command. 2. invitation. 3. offering of a price at an auction. Also see **bid.**

bide (bīd). **Bide one's time** means wait for a good chance.

bier (bēr), movable stand on which a coffin or dead body is placed.

big (big), 1. large. Dogs are bigger than mice. 2. grown up. 3. important.

bile (bīl), 1. a bitter, yellowish liquid secreted by the liver to aid digestion. 2. ill humor; anger.

bill[1] (bil), 1. account of money due for work done or things supplied. Pay your bills promptly. 2. send a bill to. 3. a piece of paper money; as, a dollar bill. 4. written or printed public notice; advertisement; poster. 5. announce by bills. 6. written or printed statement; list of items.

bill[2] (bil), 1. the mouth of a bird; beak. 2. anything shaped somewhat like a bird's bill; as, the bill of a turtle. 3. join beaks; touch bills. 4. show affection.

bil liards (bil′yərdz), a game played with balls on a special table. A long stick called a cue is used in hitting the balls.

bil lion (bil′yən), 1,000,000,000 in France and the United States; 1,000,000,000,000 in England.

bil low (bil′ō), 1. a big wave. 2. rise or roll in great waves.

bil low y (bil′ō i), rising in billows; surging.

bin (bin), a box or enclosed place for holding grain, coal, etc.

bind (bīnd), 1. tie together; hold together; fasten. 2. oblige; oblige by law. Parents are bound to send their children to school. 3. put a border or edge on to strengthen or ornament. Helen bound the sleeves of her dress with red ribbon. 4. bandage. Bind up their wounds. 5. fasten (sheets of paper) into a cover; put a cover on (a book). **bound** is formed from **bind.**

bi og ra phy (bī og′rə fi), the written story of a person's life.

bi ol o gy (bī ol′ə ji), the science of life or living things; study of plant and animal life.

birch (bėrch), 1. a slender tree with smooth bark and hard wood, used in making furniture. The Indians used birch bark to cover the framework of their canoes. 2. bundle of birch twigs or a birch stick used for whipping. 3. to whip with a birch.

White birch

bird (bėrd), an animal that has wings and feathers. A **bird of prey** eats flesh. Eagles, hawks, vultures, and owls are birds of prey.

birth (bėrth), 1. a coming into life; being born. 2. a beginning; as, the birth of a nation. 3. a bringing forth; as, the birth of a plan. 4. descent; family. He was a man of humble birth.

birth day (bėrth′dā′), 1. the day on which a person was born. 2. the day on which something began. July 4th, 1776, was the birthday of a nation. 3. the yearly return of the day on which a person was born, or on which something began. Tomorrow is my birthday; I shall be ten years old then.

birth place (bėrth′plās′), the place where a person was born.

birth right (bėrth′rīt′), rights belonging to a person because he is the oldest son, or because he was born in a certain country, or because of any other fact about his birth.

bis cuit (bis′kit), 1. soft bread dough baked in small shapes. 2. a thin, flat, dry bread or cake; a cracker.

bish op (bish′əp), a clergyman of high rank, at the head of a church district.

bi son (bī′sən), the American buffalo. See the picture.

American bison (about $5\frac{1}{2}$ ft. high at the shoulder)

bit (bit), 1. small piece; small amount. 2. somewhat; a little. 3. a short time. People often say, "Wait a bit." 4. $12\frac{1}{2}$ cents. Some people speak of 25 cents as two bits. 5. the part of a bridle that goes in the horse's mouth. 6. anything that curbs or restrains. 7. See **bite.** Tom bit off more than he could chew. The strong trap bit the leg of the fox. The tramp was bit by our dog. 8. tool for boring or drilling.

Bit

bite (bīt), 1. seize, cut into, or cut off with the teeth. 2. a cut or hold with the teeth; a nip. The dog gave a bite or two at the bone. 3. mouthful; the amount one bites off. 4. a wound made by biting or stinging. 5. cause a smarting, sharp pain to. His fingers are bitten by frost. 6. take a strong hold of. The jaws of a vise bite the wood they hold. **bit** and **bitten** are formed from **bite.**

bit ing (bīt′ing), 1. sharp; cutting. 2. sarcastic; sneering. Biting remarks hurt people's feelings.

bit ten (bit′ən). See **bite.** The dog has bitten Jack.

bit ter (bit′ər), 1. Grass and quinine taste bitter. 2. Failure is bitter. 3. A cold wind is sometimes called bitter. 4. A bitter cry shows that a person feels pain or grief.

bit ter ly (bit′ər li), in a very unpleasant way. Lulu spoke bitterly about Grace.

biv ou ac (biv′ü ak), camp outdoors without tents. **bivouacked** and **bivouacking** are formed from **bivouac.**

black (blak), 1. without any light. The room was black as night. 2. the opposite of white. This print is black. 3. make black. 4. black person; Negro. 5. very dark; as, black clouds. 6. unhappy; gloomy. 7. evil; as, black magic, a black look.

Blackberries

black ber ry (blak′ber′i), 1. small, black or dark-purple fruit of certain bushes and vines. See the picture. 2. thorny bush or vine that it grows on.

black bird (blak′bėrd′), any of several different kinds of birds. They are named blackbirds because the male birds are largely black.

Red-winged blackbird (9 in. long)

black board (blak′bōrd′), dark, smooth surface for writing or drawing on with chalk.

black en (blak′ən), 1. make black. 2. become black. 3. speak evil of. Don't blacken my family with false gossip.

black guard (blag′ärd), scoundrel.

black ness (blak′nis), being black; black color; darkness.

black smith (blak′smith′), man who works with iron. Blacksmiths can mend tools and shoe horses.

blad der (blad′ər), a soft, thin bag in which liquid collects in the body.

blade (blād), 1. the cutting part of anything like a knife or sword. 2. sword. 3. a leaf of grass. 4. the flat, wide part of a leaf. 5. the flat, wide part of anything; as, the blade of an oar or paddle. 6. a smart or dashing fellow.

blame (blām), 1. hold responsible. We blamed the fog for our accident. 2. responsibility. Lack of care deserves the blame for many mistakes. 3. find fault with. He will not blame us if we do our best. 4. finding fault. 5. **Be to blame** means deserve to be blamed. Each person said somebody else was to blame.

blame less (blām′lis), that cannot be blamed; free from fault; innocent. The saint led a blameless life.

blanch (blanch), 1. make white. 2. turn white; become pale. The boy blanched with fear when he saw the bear coming.

bland (bland), 1. smooth; mild; soft; gentle. Olive oil has a bland taste. Our minister has a bland manner. 2. agreeable; polite.

blank (blangk), 1. space left empty or to be filled in. Leave a blank after each word. 2. not written or printed on; as, blank paper. 3. a paper with spaces to be filled in. Fill out this application blank and return it at once. 4. with spaces left for filling in; as, a blank form for you to fill in. 5. empty. 6. without interest or meaning. There was a blank look on his face.

blan ket (blang′kit), 1. a soft, heavy covering woven from wool or cotton. Blankets are used to keep people or animals warm. 2. anything like a blanket. A blanket of snow covered the ground. 3. cover with a blanket. The snow blanketed the ground.

blare (blãr), 1. make a loud, harsh sound. The trumpets blared, announcing the king's arrival. 2. loud, harsh sound.

blast (blast), 1. strong sudden rush of wind or air; as, the icy blasts of winter. 2. the sound made by blowing a horn or trumpet. 3. blow up (rocks, earth, etc.) by dynamite, etc. The old building was blasted. 4. explosion. We heard the blast a mile away. 5. the amount of dynamite, etc., used. 6. wither; shrivel; destroy. A disease has blasted our grapes.

blaze[1] (blāz), 1. bright flame or fire. He could see the blaze of the campfire across the beach. 2. burn with a bright flame. A fire was blazing in the fireplace. 3. show bright colors or lights. On Christmas Eve the big house blazed with lights. 4. bright display. The tulips made a blaze of color in the garden. 5. burst out in anger or excitement. 6. violent outbreak.

blaze[2] (blāz), 1. a mark made on a tree by cutting off some of its bark. 2. to mark (a tree or a path) by chipping the bark of trees.

blaze[3] (blāz), make known; proclaim.

bleach (blēch), make white by leaving (it) out in the sun or by a chemical process. We bleach linen. Bleached bones lay on the hot sands of the desert.

bleak (blēk), 1. bare; swept by winds. The rocky peaks of high mountains are bleak. 2. chilly; cold. 3. dreary; dismal.

bleat (blēt), 1. cry made by a sheep, goat, or calf, or a sound like it. 2. make the cry of a sheep, goat, or calf, or a sound like it.

bled (bled). See **bleed.** The cut bled for ten minutes.

bleed (blēd), 1. lose blood. This cut is bleeding. 2. take blood from. Doctors used to bleed people when they were sick. 3. lose sap, juice, etc. 4. feel pity, sorrow, or grief. My heart has bled for the poor little orphan.

blem ish (blem′ish), 1. a stain; scar; injury; defect. **Without blemish** means perfect. 2. injure; mar. One bad deed can blemish a good reputation.

blend (blend), 1. mix together; become mixed; mix or become mixed so thoroughly that the things mixed cannot be distinguished or separated. 2. shade into each other. Yellow and orange blend into one another. 3. thorough mixture made by blending. The flavor of a soup is a blend.

bless (bles), 1. make holy. 2. ask God's favor for. 3. wish good to. 4. make happy or successful. 5. praise. **blest** is formed from **bless.**

bless ed (bles′id or blest), 1. holy; sacred. 2. happy; fortunate.

bless ed ness (bles′id nis), great happiness; bliss.

bless ing (bles′ing), 1. a prayer asking God to show His favor. The priest gave them his blessing. 2. a wish for happiness or success. 3. anything that makes people happy and contented. A good temper is a great blessing.

blest (blest), blessed.

blew (blü), did blow. All night long the wind blew.

blight (blīt), 1. any disease that causes plants to wither or decay. 2. anything that checks good fortune or withers hopes. 3. cause to wither or decay; ruin; destroy. Rain blighted our hopes for a picnic.

blind (blīnd), 1. not able to see. 2. take away one's sight; make blind. 3. hard to see; as, a blind track. A blind stitch is one that shows only on one side. 4. without judgment or good sense; as, a blind rage. 5. take away the power to understand or judge. His prejudices blinded him. 6. without an opening; as, a blind wall. 7. with only one opening; as, a blind alley. 8. something that keeps out light or hinders sight. A window shade or shutter is a blind.

blind fold (blīnd′fōld′), 1. cover the eyes of. 2. with the eyes covered.

blind ly (blīnd′li), in a blind way; as a blind person does; without vision.

blind ness (blīnd′nis), lack of sight; being unable to see.

blink (blingk), 1. look with the eyes opening and shutting. Mary blinked at the sudden light. 2. shut the eyes to. You cannot blink the fact that there is a war. 3. shine with an unsteady light. A lantern blinked through the darkness.

bliss (blis), very great happiness; perfect joy. What bliss it is to plunge into the cool waves on a hot day!

bliss ful (blis′fəl), very, very happy.

blis ter (blis′tər), 1. a little baglike place under the skin filled with watery matter. Blisters are often caused by burns or rubbing. My new shoes have made blisters on my heels. 2. a swelling on the surface of a plant, on metal, or on painted wood. 3. raise a blister on. The mustard plaster has blistered baby's chest. 4. become covered with blisters; have blisters.

blithe (blīᴛʜ), gay; happy; cheerful.

blithe some (blīᴛʜ′səm), joyous; gay; cheerful.

blitz krieg (blits′krēg′), warfare in which the attack is extremely rapid, violent, and hard to resist.

bliz zard (bliz′ərd), a violent, blinding snowstorm with a very strong wind and very great cold.

bloat (blōt), 1. swell; puff up. 2. preserve (herring) by salting and smoking.

block (blok), 1. a solid piece of wood or stone. 2. fill up so as to prevent passage. The country roads were blocked with snow. The city streets are blocked with traffic. 3. put things in the way of. Her sickness blocks my plans for the party. 4. anything or any group of persons that keeps something from being done. A block in traffic keeps cars from moving on. 5. number of buildings close together; a collection of buildings side by side bounded by four streets; as, one city block. 6. the length of one side of a city square. Walk one block east. 7. a pulley on a hook.

block ade (blok ād′), 1. control of who and what goes into or out of a place by the use of an army or navy. A blockade of all the harbors of the United States would require thousands of warships. 2. put under such control. 3. anything that blocks up or obstructs. 4. block up; obstruct. 5. **Run the blockade** means sneak into or out of a port that is being blockaded.

block head (blok′hed′), a stupid person; dunce; fool.

block house (blok′hous′), fort or building with loopholes to shoot from.

Blockhouse: A, loopholes for guns.

blond or **blonde** (blond), 1. light-colored; as, blond hair. 2. having yellow or light-brown hair, blue or gray eyes, and a fair skin. 3. person with such hair, eyes, and skin. Blonds are men or boys; blondes are women or girls.

blood (blud), 1. the red liquid in the veins and the arteries; the red liquid that flows from a cut. 2. temper; state of mind. **In cold blood** means cruelly or on purpose. 3. family; parentage; descent. Isaac is proud of his Jewish blood.

blood less (blud′lis), 1. without blood. 2. without spirit or feeling. 3. without bloodshed.

blood shed (blud′shed′), the shedding of blood; slaughter.

blood thirst y (blud′thėrs′ti), eager to shed blood; cruel; murderous. Wolves and tigers are bloodthirsty.

blood vessel, tube in the body through which the blood circulates. Arteries and veins are blood vessels.

blood y (blud′i), 1. bleeding; covered with blood. Jack came home with a bloody nose. 2. accompanied by much killing. It was a bloody battle.

bloom (blüm), 1. a flower; a blossom. 2. produce flowers; to blossom. Many plants bloom in the spring. 3. to flourish. 4. blooming or flourishing condition. She was in the bloom of youth. 5. the glow of health and vigor. 6. coating like fine powder on some fruits and leaves. There is a bloom on grapes, plums, and peaches.

blos som (blos′əm), 1. a flower, especially of a plant which produces fruit. 2. time of blooming; early stage of growth. 3. open into flower; have flowers. My pansies are blossoming. 4. open out; develop. Little Ruth blossomed into a beautiful girl.

blot (blot), 1. a spot of ink; a stain of any kind. 2. to spot with ink; to stain; make blots. Jack's pen slipped and blotted his paper in two places. 3. to dry ink with paper that will soak up the extra ink. 4. **Blot out** means (1) cover up entirely; hide. (2) wipe out; destroy.

blotch (bloch), a large, irregular blot.

blot ter (blot′ər), piece of blotting paper.

blouse (blous), 1. a loose upper garment worn by women and children as a part of their outer clothing. 2. a workman's loose upper garment for the protection of clothing during work.

Girl wearing a blouse

blow[1] (blō), 1. He struck the man a blow that sent him to the floor. 2. His mother's death was a great blow to him. 3. The army struck a swift blow at the enemy.

blow[2] (blō), 1. send forth a strong current of air. 2. move rapidly or with power. The wind blows. 3. be carried or moved by the wind. The curtains blew in the wind. 4. force a current of air into or through. 5. break open by an explosion. 6. sound. The whistle blows at noon. 7. pant; cause to pant. 8. puff; swell. 9. a blowing. **blew** and **blown** are formed from **blow**[2].

blow er (blō′ər), 1. one that blows; as, a glass blower. 2. machine for forcing air into a building, furnace, mine, etc.; fan.

blown (blōn), 1. out of breath; exhausted. 2. stale; tainted. 3. carried or driven by the wind. 4. swollen; puffed up; puffed out.

blow out (blō′out′), 1. a sudden or violent escape of air, steam, or the like. 2. the bursting of an automobile tire.

blub ber (blub′ər), 1. fat of whales and other sea animals. 2. weep noisily.

bludg eon (bluj′ən), 1. a short club with a heavy end. 2. strike with a heavy club.

blue (blü), 1. the color of the clear sky in daylight. 2. having this color. 3. sad; discouraged. I felt blue when I failed. 4. **The blue** means the sky or the sea.

blue bell (blü′bel′), a plant with blue flowers shaped like bells. The bluebell of Scotland and the wild hyacinth are two common bluebells.

blue ber ry (blü′ber′i), 1. small, blue berry that is good to eat. 2. shrub that it grows on.

blue bird (blü′bėrd′), a small songbird of the northern United States. The male is bright blue on the back and wings and has an orange breast.

blue grass (blü′gras′), grass with bluish-green stems.

blue jack et (blü′jak′it), a sailor in the navy.

blue jay (blü′jā′), a noisy, chattering bird with a blue back. See the picture.

Bluejay (11 in. long)

bluff[1] (bluf), 1. a high, steep bank or cliff. 2. rising with a straight, broad front. 3. abrupt, frank, and hearty in manner.

bluff[2] (bluf), 1. confidence of action or speech put on to deceive others. We say it is a bluff when a person lets others think he knows more than he really does, or has more money, or has better cards, etc., than he really has. 2. deceive by an air of confidence. 3. a threat that one knows he cannot carry out.

blu ish (blü′ish), somewhat blue.

blun der (blun′dər), 1. stupid mistake. 2. make a stupid mistake. 3. stumble; move as if blind. The injured boy blundered through the woods.

blun der buss (blun′dər bus), a short gun with a wide muzzle. It is no longer used. See the picture.

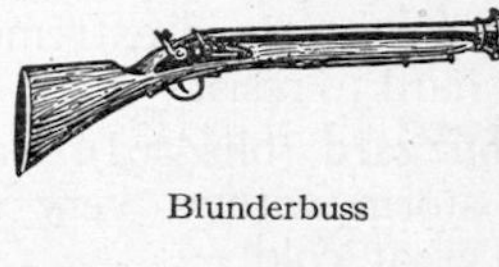
Blunderbuss

blunt (blunt), 1. without a sharp edge or point; dull. 2. make less sharp; make less keen. 3. saying what one thinks very frankly and without trying to be tactful.

blur (blėr), 1. make confused in form or outline. Mist blurred the hills. 2. dim. Tears blurred my sight. 3. blurred condition; dimness. 4. smear. He blurred the page with ink in two places. 5. a blot or stain.

blurt (blėrt), say suddenly or without thinking. In his anger he blurted out the secret.

blush (blush), 1. reddening of the skin caused by shame, confusion, or excitement. 2. become red from excitement, shame, or confusion. She was so shy that she blushed every time she was spoken to. 3. rosy color. The blush of dawn showed in the east. 4. become or be red or rosy.

blus ter (blus′tər), 1. storm noisily. The

wind blustered around the house. 2. boisterous blowing. 3. talk with noise and violence. Uncle John was very excited and angry, and blustered for a while. 4. noisy, boastful talk.

boar (bōr), 1. a male pig or hog. 2. a wild pig or hog. See the picture.

Wild boar (2½ ft. tall at the shoulder)

board (bōrd), 1. a broad, thin piece of wood. Boards are used much in building. 2. cover with boards. 3. flat piece of wood used for one special purpose; as, an ironing board. 4. table to serve food on. 5. food served on a table. 6. meals provided for pay. Mrs. Jones gives good board. 7. give food for pay. 8. get food for pay. 9. council; group of persons managing something; as, a board of health, a school board. 10. get on (a ship, train, etc.). 11. **On board** means on a ship or train.

board er (bōr′dər), person who pays for meals or for room and meals at another's house.

board ing (bōr′ding), 1. eating away from home. A person gets tired of boarding. 2. providing room and meals; as, a boarding house, a boarding school.

boarding school, a school with buildings where the pupils live, for pupils not ready to go to college.

boast (bōst), 1. speak too well of yourself. 2. a statement in praise of yourself that goes far beyond the truth. 3. something that you are proud of. "Let independence be our boast." 4. be proud of. 5. have (something) to be proud of. Our town boasts a new school building.

boast ful (bōst′fəl), 1. speaking too well about yourself. 2. fond of boasting.

boat (bōt), 1. a small, open vessel for water travel; as, a motorboat, a rowboat. 2. ship; as, a steamboat, a sailboat. 3. go in a boat. 4. put or carry in a boat.

boat house (bōt′hous′), house or shed for boats.

boat man (bōt′mən), 1. man who rows or sails boats for pay; man who rents boats. 2. man who works on boats; man who takes care of boats.

boat swain (bō′sən or bōt′swān′), an officer of a ship who has charge of the anchors, ropes, and rigging.

bob (bob), 1. move up and down, or to and fro, with short, quick motions. The bird bobbed its head up and down, and its tail bobbed, too. 2. a short, quick motion up and down, or to and fro. 3. cut hair short. 4. a short haircut. 5. a weight on the end of a line.

bob o link (bob′ə lingk), a common American songbird. See the picture.

Bobolink (7 in. long)

bob white (bob′hwīt′), the common American quail. The name bobwhite is given in imitation of the sound it makes.

bode (bōd), 1. be a sign of. The crow's cry bodes rain. 2. **Bodes well** means is a good sign; promises well.

bod i ly (bod′i li), 1. of the body; in the body; as, bodily pain. 2. in person. The man whom we thought dead walked bodily into the room. 3. as one group; entirely; as a whole. The audience rose bodily to cheer the hero.

bod y (bod′i), 1. the whole material part of a man or animal. This boy has a strong, healthy body. 2. the main part of anything. 3. group of persons or things. A large body of children sang at the church. 4. mass. A lake is a body of water. The moon, the sun, and the stars are heavenly bodies. 5. person. 6. substance.

bod y guard (bod′i gärd′), man or men who guard a person.

bog (bog), 1. piece of wet, soft, spongy ground; a marsh or swamp. 2. **Be bogged** or **get bogged** means sink in or get stuck so that one cannot get out without help.

bo gus (bō′gəs), counterfeit; sham.

boil[1] (boil), 1. bubble up and give off steam. Water boils when heated. Liquids boil when they bubble up and turn to steam or vapor through the action of heat. 2. bring anything to the heat at which it bubbles up. 3. cook by boiling. 4. be excited; be stirred up. He boiled with anger. 5. boiling condition.

boil[2] (boil), a red, painful swelling on the body, having a hard core with pus around it. Boils are caused by infection.

boil er (boil′ər), 1. container for heating liquids. 2. tank for making steam to heat buildings or drive engines. 3. tank for holding hot water.

bois ter ous (bois′tər əs), 1. violent; rough; as, a boisterous wind, a boisterous child. 2. noisily cheerful; as, a boisterous laugh.

bold (bōld), 1. without fear. The bold boy stood in front of his mother, ready to protect her from danger. 2. too free in manners. The bold little boy made faces at us as we passed. 3. vigorous; free; clear. The bold outline of the mountain appeared ahead of us. 4. steep; abrupt. Bold cliffs overlooked the sea.

bold ness (bōld′nis), 1. being bold. 2. being rude. 3. vigor; freedom; clearness.

bol ster (bōl′stər), 1. a long pillow for a bed. 2. cushion or pad. 3. To **bolster up** means to support; prop; keep from falling.

bolt (bōlt), 1. a strong pin of metal or wood with a head at one end and a place for a nut to be screwed on at the other. Bolts are used to fasten things together or to hold something in place. 2. a sliding fastening for a door; the sliding piece in a lock. 3. fasten with a bolt. 4. a short arrow with a thick head. Bolts were shot from crossbows. 5. discharge of lightning. It came like a bolt from the sky. 6. sudden start; running away. 7. dash off; run away. The horse bolted. 8. swallow without chewing. A dog bolts his food. 9. **Bolt upright** means stiff and straight.

BOLT NUT
Bolt with nut screwed on

Door bolt

bomb (bom), 1. a hollow iron ball filled with gunpowder or some other explosive. A bomb is exploded by a fuse or by the force with which it strikes. 2. hurl bombs at; drop bombs on.

bom bard (bom bärd′), 1. attack with heavy fire of shot and shell from big guns. 2. keep attacking vigorously. She bombarded me with many questions.

bom bard ment (bom bärd′mənt), an attack with heavy fire of shot and shell or with bombs.

bon bon (bon′bon′), piece of candy, usually soft and often having a fancy shape.

bond (bond), 1. anything that ties, binds, or unites; as, a bond of affection between sisters. 2. a written agreement by which a person says he will pay a certain sum of money if he does not perform certain duties properly. 3. a certificate issued by governments or private companies which promises to pay back with interest the money borrowed from the person who owns the certificate.

bond age (bon′dij), being held against your own wish under the control or influence of some person or thing.

bone (bōn), 1. the hard substance forming the framework of the body of a person or animal. 2. piece of this; as, the bones of the hand, a beef bone for soup. 3. something like a bone. Ivory is sometimes called bone. Dice and pieces of wood used to mark time are called bones. 4. take out the bones of; as, to bone fish.

bon fire (bon′fīr′), a fire built outdoors. The boys built a bonfire at the picnic.

bon net (bon′it), 1. a head covering with strings, worn by women and children. 2. a cap worn by men in Scotland.

bon ny or **bon nie** (bon′i), 1. healthy-looking; fair to see; rosy and pretty. What a bonny baby! 2. gay or cheerful; excellent.

bon y (bōn′i), 1. of bone. 2. like bone. 3. full of bones. 4. having big bones that stick out. 5. very thin.

boo by (bü′bi), 1. fool; dunce. 2. a kind of sea bird.

book (bu̇k), 1. sheets of paper bound together. Nell read the first ten pages in her book. You can keep your accounts in this book. 2. enter in a book or list so as to engage service or get tickets. He had booked a passage from New York to England. 3. part of a book; as, the books of the Bible.

book case (bu̇k′kās′), piece of furniture with shelves for holding books.

book let (bu̇k′lit), little book; thin book. Booklets often have paper covers.

boom[1] (büm), 1. a deep hollow sound like the roar of cannon or of big waves. 2. make a deep hollow sound like cannon or big waves. The big man's voice boomed out above the rest. 3. sudden activity and increase in business, prices, or values of property. Our town is having such a boom that it is likely to double its size in two years. 4. increase suddenly in activity; grow rapidly.

boom[2] (büm), a long pole or beam.

boon[1] (bün), 1. blessing. Those warm stockings were a boon to me in the cold weather. 2. something asked or granted as a favor.

boon[2] (bün), pleasant; jolly. Tom and Bill were boon companions.

boor (bür), rude person; person with bad manners.

boost (büst), 1. a push or shove that helps a person in rising or advancing. 2. to lift or push from below or behind.

boot (büt), 1. a leather or rubber covering for the foot and leg. 2. put boots on. The hunter was booted and spurred. 3. place for baggage in a coach.

booth (büth), 1. place where goods are sold or shown at a fair, market, etc. 2. small, closed place for a telephone, etc.

boot less (büt′lis), useless.

boo ty (bü′ti), 1. things taken from the enemy in war. 2. plunder. The pirates got much booty from the raided town. 3. any valuable thing or things obtained.

bor der (bôr′dər), 1. the side, edge, or boundary of anything, or the part near it. We pitched our tent on the border of the lake. 2. a strip on the edge of anything for strength or ornament. Her handkerchief has a blue border. 3. put a border on. 4. touch at the edge or boundary. Canada borders on the United States.

bore[1] (bōr), 1. make a hole in anything; hollow out evenly like a tube. 2. make a hole by pushing through or digging out. A mole has bored its way under my rose-bed. 3. a hole made by a revolving tool. 4. the hollow space inside a pipe, a tube, or a gun barrel. He cleaned the bore of his gun. 5. the distance across the inside of a hole or a tube. The bore of this pipe is 2 inches.

bore[2] (bōr), 1. weary by tiresome talk or by being dull. This book bores me, so I shall not finish it. 2. a tiresome or dull person or thing. It is a bore to have to wash dishes three times a day.

bore[3] (bōr). See **bear**[1]. She bore her loss bravely.

born (bôrn), 1. brought forth. A baby born on Sunday is supposed to be lucky. 2. by birth; by nature; as, born rich, a born poet.

borne (bōrn). See **bear**[1]. I have borne it as long as I can. I have borne the load for two miles. She has borne three children.

bor ough (bėr′ō), 1. a town that has certain privileges. 2. one of the five divisions of New York City.

bor row (bor′ō), 1. get (something) from another person with the understanding that it must be returned. If you lend your book to John, John has borrowed the book from you. 2. take; take and use as your own. The word *canoe* was borrowed from the Indians.

bos om (bu̇z′əm), 1. the upper front part of the human body; breast. 2. the part of a garment worn over the upper front of the body. She drew a handkerchief from her bosom. 3. the center or inmost part. He did not mention it even in the bosom of his family. 4. close; trusted. Very dear friends are bosom friends.

boss (bôs), 1. person who hires workers or watches over and directs them; foreman; manager. 2. person who controls a political organization. 3. be the boss of; direct; control. Who is bossing this job?

bo tan i cal (bə tan′i kəl), having to do with the study of plant life.

bot a ny (bot′ə ni), the science of plants; the study of plants and plant life.

both (bōth), 1. the two. Both boys may go. 2. alike; equally. John is both ready and willing to help.

both er (boTH′ər), 1. worry; fuss; trouble. 2. take trouble; concern oneself. Don't bother about my breakfast; I'll eat what is here. 3. person or thing that causes trouble or worry. A door that will not shut is a bother.

bot tle (bot′əl), 1. See the picture. We use bottles to hold milk, ink, etc. 2. He could drink a whole bottle of milk. 3. put into bottles; as, to bottle milk. **Bottle up** sometimes means hold in or control; as, to bottle up one's anger.

Bottle

bot tom (bot′əm), 1. the lowest part. These berries at the bottom of the basket are smaller. 2. part on which anything rests. The bottom of that cup is wet. 3. the ground under water; as, the bottom of the sea. 4. low land along a river. 5. seat. This chair needs a new bottom. 6. basis; foundation; origin. We'll get to the bottom of the mystery. 7. the part of a ship under water; ship. 8. lowest; last.

bot tom less (bot′əm lis), 1. without a bottom. 2. very, very deep; as, sunk in the bottomless depths of the sea, a bottomless lake in the mountains.

bough (bou), 1. one of the main branches on a tree. 2. branch cut from a tree. She held an apple bough in her hand.

bought (bôt). See **buy.** We bought apples from the farmer. I have bought two new pencils.

boul der (bōl′dər), large rock rounded or worn by the action of water and weather.

boul e vard (bu̇l′ə värd), broad street.

bounce (bouns), 1. bound like a ball. The baby likes to bounce up and down on the bed. 2. cause to bounce. 3. a bound; a spring.

bound[1] (bound), 1. put in covers; as, a bound book. 2. certain; sure. 3. See **bind.** The men bound their prisoners with ropes.

bound[2] (bound), 1. spring back. The ball bounded from the wall. I caught the ball on the first bound. 2. leap; spring lightly along; jump. Mountain goats can bound from rock to rock. With one bound the deer went into the woods.

bound[3] (bound), 1. boundary; limiting line; limit; as, the farthest bounds of the earth. Keep your hopes within bounds. 2. form the boundary of; limit. The country was bounded by the sea on two sides and by the mountains on the other two. 3. name the boundaries of.

bound[4] (bound), going; on the way. Where are you bound? I am bound for home.

bound a ry (boun′də ri), a limiting line; anything that limits. Lake Michigan forms part of the boundary between Canada and the United States.

bound en (boun′dən), required.

bound less (bound′lis), not limited; as, the boundless ocean.

boun te ous (boun′ti əs), 1. generous; giving freely. 2. plentiful.

boun ti ful (boun′ti fəl), 1. generous; giving freely. 2. plentiful; abundant; more than enough.

boun ty (boun′ti), 1. whatever is given freely. 2. generosity. 3. reward; premium. The State government gives a bounty of ten cents for each skunk killed.

bou quet (bü kā′), 1. bunch of flowers. 2. fragrance.

bout (bout), 1. trial of strength; contest. 2. length of time; spell. I have just had a long bout of illness.

bow[1] (bou), 1. bend the head or body in greeting, respect, submission, etc. 2. a bending of head or body in this way. 3. express by a bow. She bowed her thanks. 4. bend. The man was bowed with old age. 5. submit; yield. Dan bowed to his parents' wishes.

bow[2] (bō), 1. weapon for shooting arrows. A bow consists of a strip of elastic wood bent by a string. See the picture of a **bowman.** 2. slender rod with horsehairs stretched on it for playing the violin. 3. curve; as, the bow of one's lips. 4. loop or knot; as, a bow of ribbon.

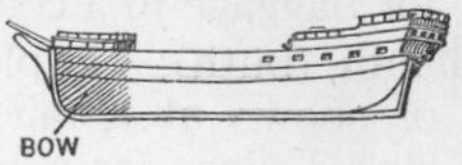

bow[3] (bou), the forward part of a ship, boat, or airplane.

BOW

bow els (bou′əlz), 1. the tube in the body into which food passes from the stomach; the intestines. 2. the inner part of anything. Miners dig for coal in the bowels of the earth.

bow er (bou′ər), 1. shelter of leafy branches. 2. arbor. 3. bedroom.

bowl[1] (bōl), 1. a hollow, rounded dish. 2. amount that a bowl can hold. 3. the hollow, rounded part of anything. The bowl of a pipe holds the tobacco.

bowl[2] (bōl), 1. a wooden ball used in games. 2. **Bowls** is a game played with wooden balls and wooden bottle-shaped pins on grass or in a special place indoors. 3. play bowls. 4. roll or move along rapidly and smoothly. Our car bowled merrily along on that good road.

Bowman

bowl der (bōl′dər), boulder.

bow man (bō′mən), archer; soldier armed with bow and arrows. See the picture just above.

bow sprit (bou′sprit), a pole or spar projecting forward from the bow of a ship. Ropes from it help to steady sails and masts.

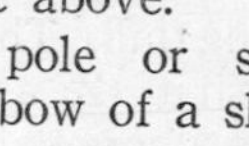

bow string (bō′string′), the string of a bow.

box[1] (boks), 1. container made of wood, metal, or paper to pack or put things in. 2. the amount that a box can hold. Strawberries cost 20 cents a box. 3. pack in a box; put into a box. 4. driver's seat on a coach. 5. a small boxlike space with chairs in a theater. 6. a small shelter; as, a box for a sentry.

box[2] (boks), 1. a blow with the open hand. A box on the ear hurts. 2. to fight with the fists.

box[3] (boks), an ornamental shrub or small tree which stays green all winter.

box er (bok′sər), man who fights with fists in padded gloves, according to special rules. Boxers fight for fun, for exercise, or to provide a show for others.

boy (boi), 1. male child from birth to about eighteen. 2. male servant.

boy hood (boi′hu̇d), 1. the time when one is a boy. 2. boys; as, the boyhood of the nation.

boy ish (boi′ish), 1. of a boy. 2. like a boy. 3. like a boy's. 4. fit for a boy.

Boy Scouts, organization for boys to develop manliness and usefulness to others.

brace (brās), 1. thing that holds parts together or in place. An iron rod or a timber used to strengthen a building, a tight bandage for the wrist, and an iron frame to hold the ankle straight are all braces. 2. give strength or firmness to; support. Jack braced the roof with four poles. 3. a pair; a couple; as, a brace of ducks. 4. a handle for a tool used in boring.

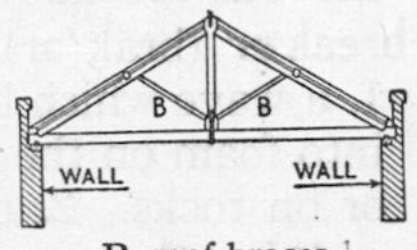

B, roof braces.

BRACE
BIT
Brace and bit

brace let (brās′lit), band or chain worn for ornament around the wrist or arm.

brack en (brak′ən), a large fern.

brack et (brak′it), 1. flat piece of stone, wood, or metal projecting from a wall as a support for a shelf, a statue, etc. 2. to support with a bracket. 3. a shelf supported by brackets. 4. either of these signs [ ], used to enclose words or figures. 5. enclose in brackets. 6. think of together; mention together; group.

Bracket for a shelf

brag (brag), 1. boast. 2. boasting talk.

braid (brād), 1. a band formed by weaving together three or more strands of hair, ribbon, straw, etc. 2. to weave or twine (three or more strands of hair, ribbon, straw, etc.) together. 3. a narrow band of fabric used to trim or bind clothing.

brain (brān), 1. the mass of cells enclosed in the skull. The brain is used in thinking. 2. dash the brains out of.

brake[1] (brāk), 1. anything used to check by pressing or scraping or by rubbing against. The brakes on a railroad train press against the wheels. 2. slow up or stop by using a brake.

brake[2] (brāk), thick growth of bushes.

brake[3] (brāk), any large fern.

bram ble (bram′bəl), a shrub with slender, drooping branches covered with little thorns that prick. Blackberry and raspberry plants are brambles.

bran (bran), the broken covering of grains like wheat and rye, which is separated from the finer part called flour.

branch (branch), 1. part of a tree that grows out from the trunk; any large, woody part of a tree above the ground except the trunk. A very small branch is called a twig. 2. a division; as, a branch of a river, a branch of a family, a branch of a library. Arithmetic is a branch of learning. 3. put out branches; spread in branches. 4. divide. The road branches at the bottom of the hill.

brand (brand), 1. piece of wood that is burning or partly burned. 2. a mark made on the skin by a hot stamp. Cattle and horses on big ranches are marked with brands to show who owns them. 3. an iron stamp for burning a mark. 4. to mark by burning with a hot iron. 5. a mark of disgrace. 6. set a mark of disgrace on. 7. a certain kind. Do you like this brand of coffee?

bran dish (bran′dish), shake or wave in a threatening manner. He brandished his sword and rushed at the enemy.

bran dy (bran′di), 1. a strong alcoholic liquor made from wine. 2. a similar alcoholic liquor made from fruit juice.

brass (bras), 1. a yellow metal made of two parts copper and one part zinc. 2. anything made of brass, such as brass instruments, ornaments, and dishes. Mary polished all the brasses.

brat (brat), 1. child. 2. unpleasant child.

brave (brāv), 1. without fear; having courage; showing courage. 2. brave person. 3. meet without fear. Soldiers brave much danger. 4. dare; defy. He braved the king's anger. 5. a North American Indian warrior. 6. making a fine appearance.

brav er y (brāv′ər i), 1. courage; being brave. 2. fine appearance; finery. Look at all the bravery in that display of dresses.

brawl (brôl), 1. noisy quarrel. 2. quarrel noisily.

brawn (brôn), 1. muscle; firm strong muscles. 2. muscular strength. Football requires brain as well as brawn.

brawn y (brôn′i), strong; muscular.

bray (brā), 1. the loud harsh cry or noise of a donkey. 2. a noise like it. 3. make a loud harsh cry or noise.

bra zen (brā′zən), 1. made of brass. 2. like brass in sound, color, or strength. 3. shameless; having no shame. The brazen girl told lie after lie. 4. **Brazen a thing out** means act as if one did not feel ashamed of it.

bra zier (brā′zhər), pan for holding burning charcoal. In some countries, braziers are used to heat rooms.

breach (brēch), 1. an opening made by breaking down something solid; gap. There is a breach in the hedge where I ran into it with my bicycle. 2. break through; make an opening in. The enemy's fierce attack finally breached our lines. 3. breaking or neglect. For me to go away today would be a breach of duty. 4. breaking of friendly relations; quarrel. There never was a breach between the two friends.

bread (bred). Bread is made of flour or meal. We eat bread and butter. Bread sometimes means food in general.

bread fruit (bred′früt′), a large, round fruit grown in the islands of the Pacific Ocean. When it is cooked, it tastes much like bread.

breadth (bredth), how broad a thing is; distance across; width.

break (brāk), 1. The plate broke into pieces when it fell on the floor. 2. May has broken her doll. 3. fail to keep; act against. He never breaks a promise. People who break the law are punished. 4. force a way. The man broke loose from prison. A thief broke into the house. 5. dig or plow (the ground). 6. stop; put an end to; as, to break one's fast, to break off relations with a friend. 7. lessen the force of. Someone must break the news of the boy's accident to his mother. The force of the wind is broken by the trees. 8. to tame; train to obey; as, to break a colt, to break a person's spirit. 9. come suddenly. War broke out. The storm broke within ten minutes. 10. fail; become weak; give way. The dog's heart broke when his master died. 11. go beyond. The speed of the new train has broken all records. 12. a breaking. 13. broken place. 14. interruption. 15. Some special meanings are:

break down, 1. have an accident; fail to work. 2. collapse; become weak; lose one's health. 3. begin to cry.

break in, 1. train; prepare for work or use. 2. enter by force. 3. interrupt.

break out, 1. start; begin. 2. have pimples, rashes, etc., on the skin.

break up, 1. scatter. 2. stop; put an end to.

break with, stop being friends with.

broke and **broken** are formed from **break.**

break down (brāk′doun′), 1. failure to work. There was a breakdown in the machinery. 2. collapse; weakness; loss of health; as, a nervous breakdown.

break er (brāk′ər), 1. a wave which breaks into foam on the beach or on rocks. 2. person or thing that breaks.

Breaker

break fast (brek′fəst), 1. the first meal of the day. 2. eat breakfast.

break neck (brāk′nek′), likely to cause a broken neck; very dangerous. The car traveled at breakneck speed.

break wa ter (brāk′wô′tər), wall or barrier to break the force of waves.

Breakwater

breast (brest), 1. the upper front part of the body between the neck and the waist; the chest. 2. the heart or feelings. Pity tore his breast. **Make a clean breast of** means confess all. 3. face or oppose; struggle with. He breasted the waves with powerful strokes. 4. a gland that gives milk.

breast plate (brest′plāt′), piece of armor for the breast.

breast work (brest′wėrk′), a low, hastily built wall for defense.

breath (breth), 1. air drawn into and forced out of the lungs. 2. ability to breathe easily. Running fast makes a person lose his breath. 3. slight movement in the air. Not a breath was stirring. 4. **Below** or **under one's breath** means in a whisper.

breathe (brēᴛʜ), 1. draw air into the lungs and force it out. 2. stop to take breath or rest after hard work or exercise. 3. whisper. Mother breathes words of love.

breath less (breth′lis), 1. out of breath. Running upstairs very fast makes you breathless. 2. unable to breathe because of fear, interest, or excitement. The beauty of the scenery left her breathless. 3. without breath; dead.

bred (bred). See **breed.** He bred cattle for market. Our parents have bred us to follow in their footsteps.

breech es (brich′iz), short trousers fastened below the knee.

breed (brēd), 1. produce young. Rabbits breed rapidly. 2. raise. This farmer is breeding cattle and hogs for market. 3. produce; be the cause of. Careless driving breeds accidents. 4. bring up; train. Dick was bred to be a soldier. Well bred means well brought up. 5. race; stock. Jerseys and Guernseys are breeds of cattle. **bred** is formed from **breed.**

breed ing (brēd′ing), 1. producing animals, especially to get improved kinds. 2. the result of training; behavior; manners. His good breeding showed in everything he did.

breeze (brēz), a stirring of air; light wind.

breez y (brēz′i), 1. having many breezes; with light winds blowing. 2. brisk; lively; jolly. We like his breezy, joking manner.

breth ren (breᴛʜ′rin), brothers; fellow members of a church or society.

brev i ty (brev′i ti), shortness.

brew (brü), 1. make (beer, ale, etc.) by soaking, boiling, and fermenting. 2. make by boiling, mixing, etc.; as, to brew tea. 3. bring about; plan; plot. Those boys are brewing some mischief. 4. be forming; gather. Dark clouds show that a storm is brewing. 5. the thing brewed.

bri ar (brī′ər), brier.

bribe (brīb), 1. anything given or offered to get someone to do something he thinks it is wrong to do. The thief offered the policeman a bribe to let him go. 2. reward for doing something that a person does not want to do. A child should not need a bribe to obey his parents. 3. offer a bribe to; give a bribe.

brib er y (brīb′ər i), 1. giving bribes. 2. taking bribes.

brick (brik), 1. block of clay baked by sun or fire. Bricks are used to build houses and pave streets. 2. bricks; material bricks are made of. 3. anything shaped like a brick. Ice cream is often sold in bricks. 4. cover or fill with bricks; build or pave with bricks. He bricked up the opening.

bride (brīd), woman just married or about to be married.

bride groom (brīd′grüm′), man just married or about to be married.

brides maid (brīdz′mād′), a young unmarried woman who attends the bride at a wedding.

bridge (brij), 1. something built that carries a road, railroad, or path across a river, road, or the like. 2. make (a way) over a river or anything that hinders; make or form a bridge over. A log bridged the brook. 3. the platform above the deck of a ship for the officer in command. 4. the upper bony part of the nose.

Bridge

bri dle (brī′dəl), 1. the head part of a horse's harness, used to hold back and control a horse. See the picture. 2. put a bridle on. 3. anything that holds back or controls. 4. hold back; check; bring under control. Bridle your temper. 5. hold the head up high with the chin drawn back.

Bridle

brief (brēf), 1. short. 2. short statement.

brief ly (brēf′li), 1. in few words. 2. for a short time.

bri er (brī′ər), a thorny or prickly plant or bush, especially the wild rose.

brig (brig), 1. ship with two masts and square sails. 2. prison on a warship.

Brig

bri gade (bri gād′), 1. part of an army, usually made up of two or more regiments. 2. any group of persons organized for some purpose; as, a fire brigade.

brig and (brig′ənd), robber; a robber who lives in the country, not in the city, and robs travelers especially.

bright (brīt), 1. Sunshine is bright. A new tin pan is bright. 2. The fire shines bright. 3. A bright girl learns quickly. 4. Everybody was bright and gay at the party. 5. Dandelions are bright yellow.

bright en (brīt′ən), 1. make bright or brighter. 2. grow bright or brighter. 3. make happy or cheerful.

bright ness (brīt′nis), being bright; shining quality; clearness; intelligence.

bril liance (bril′yəns), great brightness; glitter.

bril lian cy (bril′yən si), brilliance.

bril liant (bril′yənt), 1. sparkling; shining brightly; as, brilliant jewels, brilliant sunshine. 2. splendid; as, a brilliant party. 3. having great ability; as, a brilliant musician. 4. a diamond or other gem cut as shown in the picture.

Brilliant

brim (brim), 1. the edge of a cup or bowl; the edge of anything shaped like a cup or bowl. You have filled my glass to the brim. 2. fill to the brim; be full to the brim. 3. the projecting edge of a hat.

brim stone (brim′stōn′), sulphur.

brine (brīn), 1. very salty water. Some pickles are kept in brine. 2. the sea.

bring (bring), 1. come with (some thing or person) from another place. Bring me a clean plate and take the dirty one away. 2. cause to come. 3. influence; lead. He was brought to agree by our arguments. 4. Some special meanings are:

bring about, cause; cause to happen.

bring forth, 1. give birth to; bear. 2. reveal; show.

bring up, 1. care for in childhood. She brought up four children. 2. educate. He was well brought up. 3. stop suddenly.

brought is formed from **bring.**

brink (bringk), 1. the edge at the top of a steep place. 2. the edge. **On the brink of** means very near.

brin y (brīn′i), salty.

brisk (brisk), quick and active; lively. A brisk walk brings Jim home from school in ten minutes.

bris tle (bris′əl), 1. one of the short, stiff, coarse hairs of hogs. Bristles are used to make brushes. 2. any short, stiff hair of an animal or plant. 3. stand up straight like bristles. The dog's hair bristled. 4. be thickly set. Our path bristled with difficulties.

Brit ish (brit′ish), 1. of Great Britain, the British Empire, or its people. 2. people of Great Britain or the British Empire.

brit tle (brit′əl), very easily broken; breaking with a snap; apt to break. Thin glass and thin ice are brittle.

broach (brōch), 1. a tool to make and shape holes with. 2. open by making a hole. He broached a barrel of cider. 3. begin to talk about. Mary broached the subject of a picnic to her parents.

broad (brôd), 1. wide; large across. Many cars can go on that broad road. 2. large; not limited or narrow; of wide range. Our minister has broad views and does not insist that everyone believe just as he does. 3. main; general. Give the broad outlines of what the speaker had to say. 4. clear; full; as, broad daylight.

broad cast (brôd′kast′), 1. send out by radio. 2. speech, music, etc., sent out by radio. 3. radio program. 4. scatter widely. 5. scattering far and wide.

broad cloth (brôd′klôth′), 1. a cotton cloth with a smooth finish. 2. a fine woolen cloth with a smooth finish.

broad en (brôd′ən), 1. make broad or broader. 2. become broad or broader. The river broadens at its mouth.

broad side (brôd′sīd′), 1. all the side of a ship that shows above the water. 2. the discharge of all the guns on one side of a ship. 3. with the side turned. The ship drifted broadside to the wharf.

broad sword (brôd′sōrd′), sword with a broad, flat blade.

bro cade (brō kād′), expensive cloth woven with raised designs on it; as, silk brocade.

broc co li (brok′ə li), a variety of cauliflower with green stems and flower heads. See the picture.

Broccoli

broi der (broi′dər), embroider.

broil[1] (broil), 1. cook by direct heat, not in a pan or pot. We usually broil steaks and chops. 2. make very hot. 3. be very hot. We broiled in the hot sun.

broil[2] (broil), quarrel; fight; brawl.

broil er (broil′ər), 1. pan or rack for broiling. 2. young chicken for broiling.

broke (brōk). See **break.** She broke her doll.

bro ken (brō′kən), 1. in pieces; separated into parts by a break; as, a broken cup. 2. acted against; not kept; as, a broken promise. 3. not even; not regular. 4. imperfectly spoken. The French boy speaks broken English. 5. weakened in strength, spirit, etc.; tamed; crushed. His courage was broken by his failure. 6. See **break.** The window was broken by a ball. His sleep was broken by the noise of the party upstairs.

bron co or **bron cho** (brong′kō), a pony of the western United States. Broncos are often wild or half tamed.

bronze (bronz), 1. a brown alloy of copper with tin. 2. a similar alloy of copper with zinc or other metals. 3. a statue, medal, disk, etc., made of bronze. 4. made of bronze. 5. the color of bronze; yellowish brown; reddish brown. 6. make or become bronze in color. His skin is bronzed from the sun.

brooch (brōch or brüch), an ornamental pin fastened by a catch. Brooches are often made of gold, silver, or jewels.

Brooch

brood (brüd), 1. the young birds hatched at one time in the nest, or cared for together; as, a brood of chicks. 2. young who are cared for. 3. sit on. Hens and birds brood their eggs till the young hatch out. 4. think a long time about some one thing. The man had been brooding over his losses.

brook[1] (brůk), small stream.

brook[2] (brůk), put up with; endure; tolerate. We will not brook any more of your insults.

brook let (brůk′lit), little brook.

broom (brüm), 1. a brush with a long handle for sweeping floors. 2. a bush with slender branches, small leaves, and yellow flowers.

broom stick (brüm′stik′), the long handle of a broom.

broth (brôth), water in which meat has been boiled; soup made of this water.

broth er (bruᴛʜ′ər), 1. A boy is brother to the other children of his parents. 2. close friend. 3. Members of the same church or club are often called brothers.

broth er hood (bruᴛʜ′ər hůd), 1. the bond between brothers; the feeling of brother for brother. 2. persons joined as brothers; an association of men with some common aim or characteristic.

broth er-in-law (bruᴛʜ′ər in lô′), 1. the brother of one's husband or wife. 2. the husband of one's sister.

broth er ly (bruᴛʜ′ər li), 1. of a brother. 2. like a brother. 3. very friendly. He talked to me in a brotherly way.

brought (brôt). See **bring.** He brought his lunch yesterday. She was brought to school in a car.

brow (brou), 1. forehead. 2. arch of hair over the eye; eyebrow. 3. edge of a steep place; top of a slope. His house is on the brow of the hill.

brown (broun), 1. a dark color like that of toast, potato skins, or coffee. 2. having this color. Many Americans have brown hair. 3. make brown; become brown.

brown ie (broun′i), a good-natured, helpful elf or fairy.

Brownies

browse (brouz), 1. feed; graze. 2. read here and there in a book, library, etc.

bru in (brü′in), a bear.

bruise (brüz), 1. an injury to the body, caused by a fall or a blow which does not break the skin. The bruise on my arm turned black and blue. 2. an injury to the outside of a fruit, vegetable, plant, etc. 3. injure the outside of. 4. injure; hurt. His harsh words bruised her. 5. become bruised. Her flesh bruises easily. 6. pound; crush.

bru nette or **bru net** (brü net′), 1. dark-skinned, dark-haired, and dark-eyed. 2. person having a dark skin, dark-brown or black hair, and brown or black eyes.

brunt (brunt), 1. main force or violence. Company C bore the brunt of the attack. 2. hardest part.

brush[1] (brush), 1. A brush is made of bristles, hair, or wire, set in a stiff back or fastened to a handle. Brushes are used for scrubbing, cleaning, sweeping, and for putting on paint. 2. something like a brush; as, the brushes on an electric motor. 3. clean, rub, paint, etc., with a brush; use a brush on. 4. a brushing; a rub with a brush. 5. remove; wipe away. The child brushed the tears from his eyes. 6. touch lightly in passing. 7. light touch in passing. 8. short, brisk fight or quarrel. 9. move quickly.

Brushes: A, clothesbrush: B, paintbrush.

brush[2] (brush), 1. shrubs, bushes, and small trees growing in the woods. 2. branches broken or cut off.

brush wood (brush′wůd′), 1. small trees or bushes growing rather thickly together. 2. branches broken or cut off.

bru tal (brü′təl), cruel; like a brute.

bru tal i ty (brü tal′i ti), 1. savageness; brutal conduct. Some Indians carried on war with brutality. 2. a brutal act.

brute (brüt), 1. an animal without power to reason. 2. like an animal. 3. a stupid or cruel person. 4. without feeling; cruel; coarse.

bu., bushel; bushels.

bub ble (bub′əl), 1. A bubble is round and full of air or gas which is held in by the liquid around it. When water boils, it is full of bubbles which come to the top and break. 2. a round space filled with air. Sometimes there are bubbles in ice or in glass. 3. make sounds like water boiling; send up or rise in bubbles. Water bubbled up between the stones.

Bucking bronco

buc ca neer (buk′ə nēr′), pirate.

buck (buk), 1. male deer, goat, hare, or rabbit. 2. jump into the air with back curved and come down with the front legs stiff. His horse began to buck, but Tom managed to stay on. See the picture just above. 3. throw by bucking.

Bucket

buck et (buk′it), 1. pail made of wood or metal. Buckets are used for carrying water, milk, coal, etc. 2. the amount that a bucket can hold. Pour on about four buckets of water.

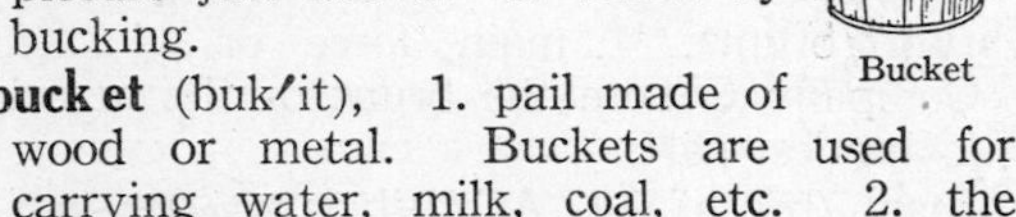

buck le (buk′əl), 1. a catch to hold together two loose ends of a belt, strap, or ribbon. 2. fasten together with a buckle. 3. bend; wrinkle. 4. **Buckle down to** means work hard at.

buck ler (buk′lər), small, round shield.

buck wheat (buk′hwēt′), 1. a plant with triangular seeds. The seeds of buckwheat are fed to horses and fowls; they also are ground into flour for pancakes. 2. the flour made from buckwheat.

BRANCH

SEED

Buckwheat

bud (bud), 1. the small beginning of a flower, leaf, or branch. 2. a flower partly opened. 3. put forth buds. The rosebush has budded. 4. begin to grow. 5. graft a branch from one tree into another.

budge (buj), move even a little. The stone was so heavy that the child could not budge it.

Budding or grafting

budg et (buj′it), 1. an estimate of the amount of money that can be spent, and the amounts to be spent for various purposes, in a given time. Governments, schools, companies, and persons often make budgets. 2. make a plan for spending. 3. a stock or collection; as, a budget of news.

buff (buf), 1. a strong, soft leather, dull-yellow in color, formerly made from buffalo skin. 2. made of buff. 3. dull yellow. 4. polish with a wheel covered with leather.

buf fa lo (buf′ə lō), 1. in America, the bison, a wild ox with a great, shaggy head and strong front legs. See the picture of **bison.** 2. any of several kinds of wild ox.

Buffalo of India (body 6 ft. long)

buf fet[1] (buf′it), 1. a blow of the hand. 2. to strike with the hand. 3. a knock, stroke, or hurt. 4. to knock about, strike, or hurt. The waves buffeted him. He buffeted his way through the waves.

buf fet[2] (bu̇ fā′), 1. piece of dining-room furniture with a flat top, for holding dishes, silver, and table linen. 2. counter where food and drinks are served.

bug (bug), 1. a crawling insect. 2. any insect.

Bug (def. 1)

bug a boo (bug′ə bü), an object of fright, usually imaginary. The foolish nurse frightened the child with tales of witches, ghosts, and other bugaboos.

bug bear (bug′bãr′), something feared without reason.

bug gy (bug′i), a light carriage with one seat. See the picture.

Buggy

bu gle (bū′gəl), a musical instrument like a small trumpet, made of brass or copper. Bugles are used in the army and navy for sounding calls and orders, and in band music.

bu gler (bū′glər), person who blows a bugle.

Soldier blowing a bugle

build (bild), 1. Men build houses and ships. Birds build nests. 2. An elephant has a heavy build. A giraffe has a slender build. **built** and **building** are formed from **build.**

build er (bil′dər), 1. person or animal that builds. 2. person whose business is building.

build ing (bil′ding), 1. See **build.** 2. thing built. Barns, houses, sheds, factories, and hotels are all buildings. 3. act of one that builds. 4. art of making houses, stores, bridges, ships, etc.

built (bilt). See **build.** The bird built a nest. It was built of twigs.

bulb (bulb), 1. the round, underground bud or stem from which certain plants grow. Onions, tulips, and lilies grow from bulbs. 2. rounded, swelling part; as, an electric light bulb, the bulb of a thermometer.

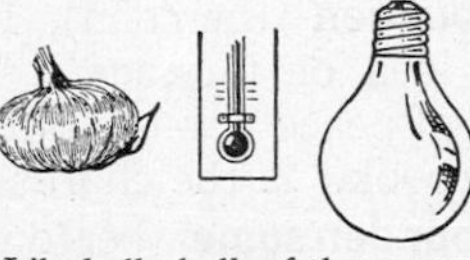
Lily bulb; bulb of thermometer; electric light bulb.

bulb ous (bul′bəs), 1. having bulbs; growing from bulbs. Daffodils are bulbous plants. 2. shaped like a bulb. The clown's mask had a big, red, bulbous nose.

bulge (bulj), 1. swell outward. His pockets bulged with apples and candy. 2. outward swelling. There is a bulge on the end of this tent.

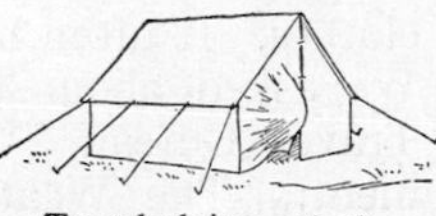
Tent bulging out at the end

bulk (bulk), 1. size; especially great size. 2. a large shape, person, or body. 3. The **bulk of** means the greater part of. The ocean forms the bulk of the earth's surface. 4. have size; be of importance. 5. mass; large mass.

bulk head (bulk′hed′), one of the upright partitions dividing a ship into compartments. Bulkheads are often made very tight.

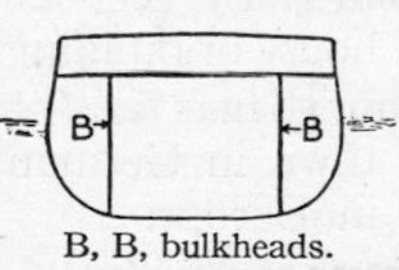

B, B, bulkheads.

bulk y (bul′ki), 1. large; taking up much space. 2. hard to handle.

bull (bůl), 1. the male of beef cattle. 2. the male of the whale, elephant, seal, and other large animals.

bull dog (bůl′dôg′), 1. heavily built dog with a large head and short hair. Bulldogs are not large, but they are very muscular and courageous. 2. like that of a bulldog; as, bulldog courage, a bulldog grip.

Bulldog (13 to 17 in. tall)

bul let (bůl′it), shaped piece of lead or steel to be shot from a gun.

bul le tin (bůl′ə tin), 1. a short statement of news. Newspapers print bulletins about a war, famine, the things the President does, and other events of public importance. Doctors issue bulletins on the progress of a sick person. 2. a small magazine or newspaper.

bull fight (bůl′fīt′), fight between men and a bull in an enclosed arena. It is a popular sport among Spanish people.

bull finch (bůl′finch′), a European songbird with handsome plumage and a short, stout bill.

bull frog (bůl′frog′), a large frog that makes a loud, croaking noise.

Bullfrog (7 in. long)

bul lion (bůl′yən), lumps or bars of gold or silver.

bull ock (bůl′ək), ox; steer.

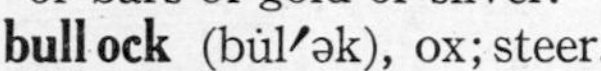

bul ly (bůl′i), 1. person who teases, frightens, or injures others who are not as strong as he is. 2. frighten into doing something by noisy talk or threats. Tim was bullied into giving away his candy.

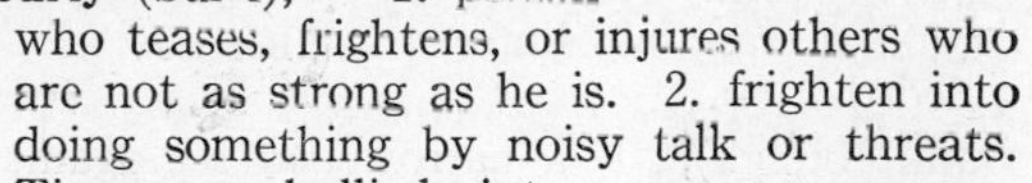
Bulwark for defense

bul rush (bůl′rush′), a tall, slender plant that grows in wet places.

bul wark (bůl′wərk), 1. person, thing, or idea that is a defense or a protection. 2. earthwork or other wall for defense against the enemy. 3. breakwater for protection against the force of the waves. 4. a ship's side above the deck.

Bulwark of a ship

bum ble bee (bum′bəl bē′), a kind of large bee.

Bumblebee (about life size)

bump (bump), 1. push, throw, or strike (against something fairly large or solid). The children all bumped against one another in their eagerness to be first. 2. move (along) with bumps. The cart bumped along the rough road. 3. hit or come against with heavy blows. The truck bumped the gray car. 4. a heavy blow or knock. The bump knocked the gray car across the road. 5. a swelling caused by a bump. 6. a swelling.

bump er (bump′ər), 1. a bar or rod that protects a car from bumps. 2. glass filled to the brim. 3. unusually large; as, a bumper crop of cotton.

bun (bun), bread or cake in small shapes. Buns are often slightly sweetened and contain spice, raisins, etc.

bunch (bunch), 1. group of things of the same kind growing or fastened together, placed together, or thought of together; as, a bunch of grapes, a bunch of thieves. 2. come together in one place. 3. bring together and make into a bunch.

bun dle (bun′dəl), 1. number of things tied together or wrapped together. 2. parcel; package. 3. tie together; make up into a bundle. 4. to wrap. 5. send or go in a hurry.

bun ga low (bung′gə lō), a one-story house.

Bungalow

bun gle (bung′gəl), do or make in a clumsy way. John tried to make a trap, but bungled the job.

bunk (bungk), 1. a narrow bed set against a wall like a shelf. 2. sleep in a bunk; occupy a bunk. 3. sleep in rough quarters. We bunked in an old barn.

bun ny (bun′i), pet name for a rabbit.

bunt (bunt), 1. strike with the head or horns, as a goat does. 2. a push; a shove.

bun ting[1] (bun′ting), 1. a thin cloth used for flags. 2. flags; long pieces of cloth in flag colors and designs, used to decorate buildings and streets on holidays.

bun ting[2] (bun′ting), a small kind of bird, somewhat like a sparrow.

buoy (boi), 1. something kept in a certain place on the water to show what is safe and what is dangerous. 2. A life buoy is something to keep a person from sinking. 3. **Buoy up** means hold up or keep from sinking.

Bell buoy

buoy an cy (boi′ən si), 1. power to float. Wood has more buoyancy than iron. 2. power to keep things afloat. Salt water has greater buoyancy than fresh. 3. tendency to rise. 4. tendency to be cheerful and hopeful.

buoy ant (boi′ənt), 1. able to rise to the top of the water and float easily. Cork is buoyant. 2. able to recover easily; light-hearted; cheerful and hopeful. Children are more buoyant than old people.

bur (bėr). See **burr.**

bur den[1] (bėr′dən), 1. what is carried; a load (of things, care, work, duty, or sorrow). 2. a load too heavy to carry easily. 3. to load; load too heavily; weigh down; oppress (said of things, care, work, duty, or sorrow). 4. the quantity of freight a ship can carry; the weight of a ship's cargo.

bur den[2] (bėr′dən), 1. the main idea or message. The value of peace was the burden of her book. 2. the chorus of a song.

Burdock

bur den some (bėr′dən səm), wearying; hard to bear; too heavy. The President's many duties are burdensome.

bur dock (bėr′dok′), a coarse weed with prickly heads or burrs and broad leaves. See the picture.

bu reau (būr′ō), 1. a chest of drawers for clothes. It often has a mirror. 2. an office. We asked about the railroad fares at the Travel Bureau. 3. a government department. The Weather Bureau makes daily reports on weather conditions.

burgh er (bėr′gər), citizen.

bur glar (bėr′glər), person who breaks into a house or building, usually to steal.

bur glar y (bėr′glər i), act of breaking into a house or building, usually to steal.

bur go mas ter (bėr′gō mas′tər), mayor of a town in Germany and some other countries in Europe.

bur i al (ber′i əl), 1. act of burying. 2. having to do with burial; as, a burial service.

bur ied (ber′id). See **bury.** The dog buried his bone. Many nuts were buried under the leaves.

bur lap (bėr′lap), coarse material used for bags, wrappings, and coverings.

bur ly (bėr′li), strong; sturdy; big.

burn[1] (bėrn), 1. be on fire; be very hot. 2. set on fire; cause to burn. 3. destroy by fire. Please burn those old papers. 4. injure by fire or heat. He burned his hand on the hot iron. 5. an injury caused by fire or heat. 6. make by fire or heat. He burned a hole in the wood. 7. feel hot; give a feeling of heat.

burn[2] (bėrn), Scotch word meaning brook.

burn er (bėr′nər), 1. man whose work is burning something. 2. thing or part that burns, or works by heat. Some stoves are oil burners; others are gas burners.

bur nish (bėr′nish), polish.

bur noose or **bur nous** (bėr nüs′), a cloak with a hood worn by Moors and Arabs. See the picture in the next column.

burnt (bėrnt), burned.

burr (bėr), 1. prickly, clinging seed case or flower of some plants. Burrs stick to anything they touch. 2. plant or weed that has burrs.

bur ro (bėr′ō), donkey. See the picture.

Burro (3 ft. high at the shoulder)

bur row (bėr′ō), 1. hole dug in the ground. Rabbits live in burrows. 2. dig a hole in the ground. The mole quickly burrowed out of sight. 3. dig. John used to burrow around in the ash heap. 4. search. John's father burrows in libraries.

burst (bėrst), 1. break open; break out suddenly; fly apart suddenly with force. The bomb will burst. The trees had burst into bloom. 2. go, come, do, etc., by force or suddenly. Don't burst into the room without knocking. 3. be full. The barns were bursting with grain. 4. a bursting; an outbreak; as, a burst of feeling.

bur then (bėr′ᴛʜən), burden.

bur y (ber′i), 1. put in the earth, in a tomb, or in the sea. A dead body is usually buried. 2. put away; cover up; forget. Many nuts were buried under the dead leaves.

bus (bus), a large vehicle with seats inside and sometimes also on the roof. Busses are used to carry passengers between fixed stations along a route.

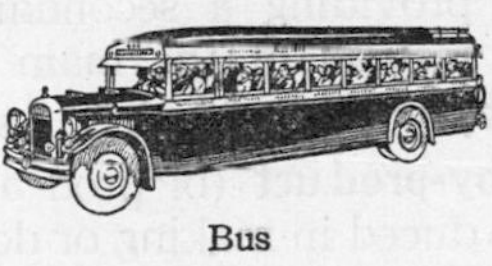
Bus

bush (bůsh), 1. a woody plant smaller than a tree, often with many separate stems starting near the ground. 2. open forest or wild land. **Beat about the bush** means avoid coming to the point of a matter.

bush el (bůsh′əl), a measure for grain, fruit, vegetables, and other dry things, containing 4 pecks or 32 quarts.

bush y (bůsh′i), 1. growing thickly. 2. overgrown with bushes.

bush y-tailed (bůsh′i tāld′), having a thick furry tail.

bus i ly (biz′i li), actively.

busi ness (biz′nis), 1. thing one is busy at; work; occupation. Business comes before pleasure. A carpenter's business is building. 2. matter; affair. Mind your own business. Taking chances is bad business. 3. trade; buying and selling. This store does a big business. 4. a commercial enterprise; industrial establishment. They sold their business for ten million dollars.

busi ness like (biz′nis līk′), having system and method; well-managed.

bust (bust), 1. statue of a person's head, shoulders, and chest. 2. the upper front part of the body, especially of a woman.

bus tle (bus′əl), 1. be noisily busy and in a hurry. 2. noisy or excited activity.

bus y (biz′i), 1. working; active; having plenty to do. 2. full of work or activity; as, a busy day, a busy street. 3. make busy; keep busy. The bees busied themselves at making honey. **busier** and **busiest** are formed from **busy.**

Man wearing a burnoose

bus y bod y (biz′i bod′i), meddler; person who interferes in the affairs of others.

but (but), 1. on the other hand. You may go, but you must come home at six o'clock. 2. except. Father works every day in the week but Sunday. 3. only. We can but try. Jack is but a small boy. 4. who not; which not. None come to his doors but are fed.

butch er (bůch′ər), 1. man whose work is killing animals for food. 2. man who sells meat. 3. kill (animals) for food. 4. kill (people, wild animals, or birds) wholesale, needlessly, or cruelly. 5. spoil. Don't butcher that song!

butch er y (bůch′ər i), 1. murder. 2. great slaughter.

but ler (but′lər), male servant in charge of pantry and table service in a household; head servant.

butt[1] (but), 1. thicker end of a tool or weapon. 2. end that is left; stub or stump. 3. object, aim, or target. That queer boy was the butt of many jokes.

butt² (but), 1. strike, push, or fight by pushing or knocking hard with the head. A goat butts. 2. a push or blow with the head.

butte (būt), a steep hill standing alone.

Butte

but ter (but′ər), 1. the yellowish fat obtained from cream by churning. 2. put butter on. 3. something like butter in looks or use. Do you like peanut butter?

but ter cup (but′ər kup′), a common plant with bright-yellow flowers shaped like cups.

but ter fly (but′ər flī′), an insect with a slender body and four large, usually bright-colored, wings. Many butterflies are very beautiful.

Butterfly (about ½ life size)

but ter milk (but′ər milk′), the sour liquid left after butter has been taken from milk or cream.

but ter nut (but′ər nut′), 1. oily kind of walnut that is good to eat. 2. tree that bears butternuts.

but ton (but′ən), 1. a knob, or a round flat piece of any material, fastened on clothing, shoes, and other things, to hold them closed or to decorate them. 2. a knob used as a handle or catch, either to take hold of, or push, or to turn so that it holds or closes something. 3. fasten the buttons of. Please button my dress for me.

but ton hole (but′ən hōl′), 1. the hole or slit through which a button is passed. 2. make buttonholes in. 3. detain in conversation, as if we held a man by the buttonhole of his coat and made him listen.

but tress (but′ris), 1. a support built against a wall or building to steady it; a support like this. See the picture. 2. to support and strengthen.

Buttresses: A, ordinary; B, flying.

bux om (buk′səm), plump and good to look at; healthy and cheerful.

buy (bī), get by paying a price. You can buy a pencil for five cents. I bought two.

buy er (bī′ər), person who buys.

buzz (buz), 1. the humming sound made by flies, mosquitoes, or bees. 2. the low confused sound of many people talking quietly. 3. make a steady humming sound; hum loudly. 4. to sound in a low confused way. 5. **Buzz about** means move about busily.

buz zard (buz′ərd), 1. a kind of heavy hawk. 2. a kind of vulture.

Buzzard (def. 1) (2½ ft. long)

buzz er (buz′ər), 1. thing that buzzes. 2. electrical device that makes a buzzing sound as a signal.

by¹ (bī), 1. near. Stand by me. He lives close by. 2. along; over; through. They went by the hill road. 3. through the means of. The sewing was done by machine. 4. past; as, days gone by. 5. aside; away. 6. during. 7. as soon as; not later than. 8. according to. Work by rule. 9. in relation to. She did well by her children. 10. **By and by** means after a while.

by-and-by (bī′ənd bī′), future.

bye or **by²** (bī), 1. **By the bye** means by the way. 2. aside; out of the main way. By in this meaning is usually a part of a compound word; as, by-path, by-product, byword.

by gone (bī′gôn′), 1. gone by; past; former. 2. something in the past. Let bygones be bygones.

by law (bī′lô′), secondary law or rule, not one of the main rules. Our club has a constitution and bylaws.

by-pass (bī′pas′), road, channel, pipe, etc., providing a secondary passage to be used instead of the main passage.

by-path (bī′path′), side path; byway.

by-prod uct (bī′prod′əkt), something produced in making or doing something else; not the main product.

by-road (bī′rōd′), side road.

by stand er (bī′stan′dər), person who stands near or looks on but does not take part.

by way (bī′wā′), side path; way that is little used.

by word (bī′wėrd′), 1. object of contempt; thing people scorn. His cowardice made him a byword to all who knew him. 2. common saying; proverb.

C

cab (kab), 1. automobile that can be hired; taxicab. 2. carriage that can be hired, pulled by one horse. 3. covered part of a locomotive where the engineer sits.

Cabbage

cab bage (kab′ij), a vegetable whose thick leaves are closely folded into a round head.

cab in (kab′in), 1. a small, roughly built house; hut. See the picture just below. 2. a room in a ship. The 500 passengers slept in 200 cabins. 3. place for passengers in an airplane or airship.

Log cabin

cab i net (kab′i nit), 1. piece of furniture with shelves or drawers, used to contain articles for display or use, such as jewels, dishes, letters. A kitchen cabinet is used to hold food supplies and dishes. 2. council of advisers, especially of advisers to lead the nation.

ca ble (kā′bəl), 1. a strong, thick rope, often made of wires twisted together. 2. a protected bundle of wires, used for sending telegraph messages under the ground or under the ocean. 3. message sent across the sea by cable. 4. send a message across the sea by cable.

ca boose (kə büs′), 1. small car on a freight train in which the trainmen can rest and sleep. 2. kitchen on the deck of a ship.

ca ca o (kə kä′ō), 1. a small tree from whose seeds cocoa and chocolate are made. 2. the seeds of the tree.

cache (kash), 1. hiding place for food or other things. 2. hidden store of food or supplies. 3. put in a cache; hide.

cack le (kak′əl), 1. the shrill, broken sound that a hen makes after laying an egg. 2. make this sound. 3. broken or harsh laughter. 4. laugh with broken or harsh sounds, like a hen cackling. 5. noisy chatter; silly talk.

cac tus (kak′təs), a plant with a fleshy stem, usually having spines but no leaves. Cactuses grow in dry, hot regions.

Common cactus

ca det (kə det′), 1. young man who is training to be an officer in the army or navy. 2. younger son or brother.

ca fé (ka fā′), restaurant; place to buy and eat a meal.

caf e te ri a (kaf′ə tēr′i ə), café or restaurant where people wait on themselves.

cage (kāj), 1. prison for animals or birds, made of wire, strong iron bars, or wood. 2. anything shaped or used like a cage; as, the cage or car of an elevator. 3. put or keep in a cage; as, a caged lion.

cai tiff (kā′tif), 1. a mean, bad person; coward. 2. vile; cowardly; mean.

cake (kāk), 1. a baked mixture of flour, sugar, eggs, and other things; as, a layer cake, a spice cake, a fruit cake. 2. a flat, thin mass of dough baked or fried. Joe ate ten pancakes. 3. a shaped, flat mass of food or other substance; as, a fish cake, a cake of soap, a cake of ice. 4. form into a compact mass. Mud cakes as it dries.

ca lam i ty (kə lam′i ti), a great misfortune such as a flood, a fire, the loss of one's sight or hearing, or of much money or property.

cal ci um (kal′si əm), a substance which is part of lime, chalk, milk, bone, and many other things. You need to have enough calcium in what you eat.

cal cu late (kal′kū lāt), 1. reckon; add, subtract, multiply, divide, etc., in order to find out something; as, to calculate the cost of furnishing a house. 2. find out beforehand by any process of reasoning. Can you calculate the day of the week on which Christmas will fall? 3. plan; intend. That remark was calculated to hurt someone's feelings.

cal cu la tion (kal′kū lā′shən), 1. adding, subtracting, multiplying, or dividing to find a result. 2. the result found by calculating. 3. careful thinking; deliberate planning. The general spent much time in calculation.

cal dron (kôl′drən), large kettle or boiler.

cal en dar (kal′ən dər), a table showing the months, weeks, and days of the year. A calendar shows the day of the week on which each day of the month falls.

DECEMBER						
S	M	T	W	T	F	S
..	..	..	..	..	..	1
2	3	4	5	6	7	8
9	10	11	12	13	14	15
16	17	18	19	20	21	22
23	24	25	26	27	28	29
30	31	..	..	..	..	..

Page of calendar

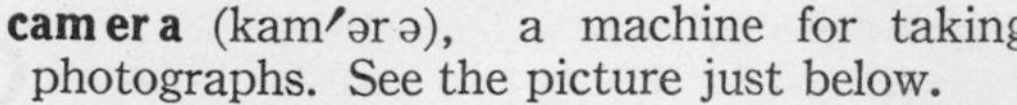

calf[1] (kaf), 1. a young cow or bull. 2. a young elephant, whale, deer, etc. 3. leather made of the skin of a calf.

calf[2] (kaf), the thick, fleshy part of the back of the leg below the knee.

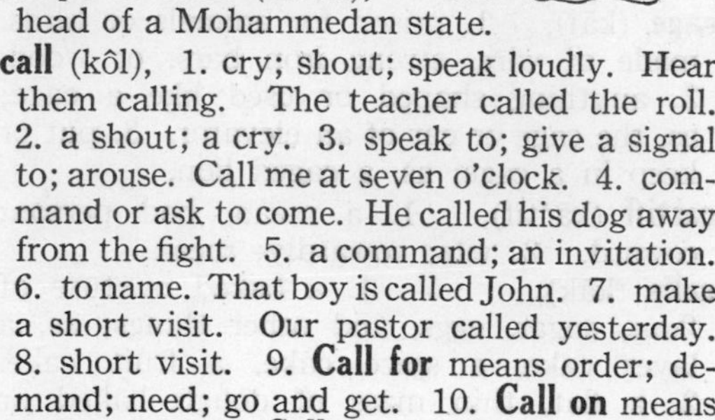

cal i co (kal′i kō), cotton cloth printed with colored patterns; plain white cotton cloth.

ca liph or **ca lif** (kā′lif), the head of a Mohammedan state.

call (kôl), 1. cry; shout; speak loudly. Hear them calling. The teacher called the roll. 2. a shout; a cry. 3. speak to; give a signal to; arouse. Call me at seven o'clock. 4. command or ask to come. He called his dog away from the fight. 5. a command; an invitation. 6. to name. That boy is called John. 7. make a short visit. Our pastor called yesterday. 8. short visit. 9. **Call for** means order; demand; need; go and get. 10. **Call on** means appeal to. 11. **Call up** means bring to mind or telephone to.

call er (kôl′ər), 1. person who makes a short visit. 2. person who calls out names, etc., in a loud voice.

call ing (kôl′ing), 1. profession, occupation, or trade. 2. summons; invitation.

cal lous (kal′əs), 1. hard; hardened. Going barefoot makes the bottoms of your feet callous. 2. unfeeling. Only a callous person can see people suffering without trying to help them.

calm (käm), 1. quiet; still; not stormy or windy; not stirred up; peaceful. 2. quietness; stillness; absence of wind or motion. 3. make calm; become calm. She soon calmed the baby. The baby calmed down.

calm ly (käm′li), in a calm way; without excitement.

calves (kavz), more than one calf.

ca lyx (kā′liks), a part of a flower. See the picture. The calyx is made of the sepals and is a sort of holder for the petals.

Calyx

cam bric (kām′brik), a fine, thin linen or cotton cloth.

came (kām). See **come.** He came to school late this morning.

cam el (kam′əl), a large, four-footed animal with one or two humps on its back. Camels are used in the deserts of Africa and Arabia because they can go a long time without drinking water.

cam er a (kam′ər ə), a machine for taking photographs. See the picture just below.

cam ou flage (kam′ə fläzh), 1. disguise; deception. The white fur of a polar bear is a natural camouflage, for it prevents its being easily seen against the snow. 2. in warfare, giving things a false appearance to deceive the enemy. 3. to disguise; give a false appearance to in order to conceal.

Camera

camp (kamp), 1. live away from home for a time in a tent or hut or outdoors. 2. a place where one lives in a tent or hut or outdoors. 3. persons living in a camp. 4. pitch tents and stay for a time. The Boy Scout troop camped at the foot of the mountain for two weeks. 5. the camping ground where an army is camping.

cam paign (kam pān′), 1. a number of related military operations. The summer campaign of our army resulted in opening a way into the enemy's country. 2. series of connected activities to do or get something. Our town had a campaign to raise money for our hospital. 3. take part or serve in a campaign.

cam phor (kam′fər), a white substance with a strong odor and a bitter taste.

can[1] (kan), 1. be able to. He can read rapidly. 2. may. You can go at 4 o'clock.

can[2] (kan), 1. a container of metal or glass in various forms; as, an oil can, a milk can, a can of fruit. 2. to preserve by putting up in airtight containers. Mother is canning fruit.

Milk can and ash can

Can a da (kan′ə də), the country north of the United States.

ca nal (kə nal′), waterway dug across land for ships or small boats to go through, or to carry water to places that need it.

ca nar y (kə nãr′i), 1. a songbird with pretty yellow feathers. 2. light yellow.

can cel (kan′səl), 1. cross out; mark so that it cannot be used again; as, a canceled stamp. 2. wipe out; do away with. He canceled his order for the books. This money will cancel your debt to me.

can cer (kan′sər), a very harmful growth in the body.

can did (kan′did), frank; sincere. Please be candid and tell me just what you think.

can di date (kan′di dāt), person who is proposed for some office or honor. There are three candidates for president of the club.

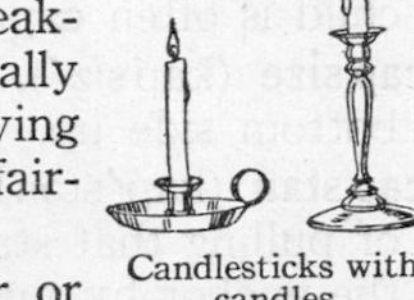
Birthday cake with candles

can dle (kan′dəl), a stick of tallow or wax with a wick in it, burned to give light. Long ago, before there was gas or electric light, people burned candles to see by.

can dle light (kan′dəl līt′), 1. light of a candle. 2. time when candles are lighted.

can dle stick (kan′dəl stik′), holder for a candle, to make it stand up straight.

can dor (kan′dər), 1. speaking openly what one really thinks; honesty in giving one's view or opinion. 2. fairness.

Candlesticks with candles

can dy (kan′di), 1. sugar or syrup boiled with water and flavoring, cooled, and made into pieces for eating. Most children eat all the candy they can get. 2. form into sugar. This honey has candied.

cane (kān), 1. a long, jointed stem. The stems of bamboo and sugar cane are canes. 2. a stick made from a cane stem; any slender stick used as an aid in walking. 3. beat with a cane.

ca nine (kā′nīn), 1. dog. 2. of a dog; like a dog. The four pointed teeth are called canine teeth.

can ker (kang′kər), 1. a sore in the mouth. 2. anything that causes rot or decay or destroys by a gradual eating away.

can na (kan′ə), a plant with large leaves and large, showy flowers.

canned (kand), preserved in airtight containers of glass, tin, etc.

can ner y (kan′ər i), factory where meat, fish, fruit, vegetables, etc., are canned.

can ni bal (kan′i bəl), 1. person who eats human flesh. 2. animal that eats others of its own kind.

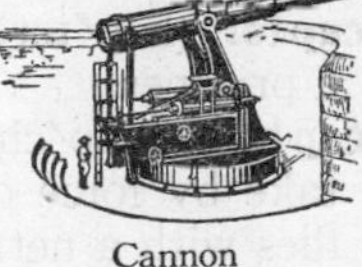
Cannon

can non (kan′ən), big mounted gun or guns.

can non ade (kan′ən ād′), 1. a continued firing of cannons. 2. attack with cannons.

can not (kan′not), can not.

can ny (kan′i), shrewd; cautious.

ca noe (kə nü′), a light boat moved with paddles. Lucky Sam owns two canoes. See the picture below.

Indian paddling a canoe

can on (kan′ən), 1. law of a church. 2. standard; rule by which a thing is judged. 3. list of saints. 4. member of a group of clergymen living according to a certain rule.

ca ñon (kan′yən), canyon.

can o py (kan′ə pi), 1. a covering fixed over a bed or a throne; a covering carried on poles over a person. 2. covering; shelter; shade. Trees formed a canopy over the old road.

Canopy over a bed

canst (kanst), an old form meaning **can.** "Thou canst" means "you can."

can't (kant), cannot.

can ta ta (kən tä′tə), music to be sung by a chorus, telling a story or drama.

can teen (kan tēn′), 1. small container to carry water or other drinks in. 2. place where food and drink are sold to soldiers and sailors.

can ter (kan′tər), 1. gallop gently. 2. an easy gallop.

can ton (kan′tən), a small part or division of a country. Switzerland is made up of 22 cantons.

can vas (kan′vəs), 1. strong cloth with a rather coarse, even weave. Canvas is used for sails and tents, and for painting on. 2. made of canvas. 3. anything made of canvas. 4. a picture painted on canvas. That little canvas cost $100.

can yon (kan′yən), narrow valley with high, steep sides, usually with a stream at the bottom.

cap (kap), 1. a soft, close-fitting covering for the head with little or no brim. Men and boys often wear caps instead of hats. 2. a special headdress showing rank, occupation, etc.; as, a nurse's cap, a student's cap and gown, a fool's cap. 3. anything like a cap. The top of a mushroom is called a cap. 4. highest part; top. 5. put a cap on; cover. 6. do or follow up with something as good or better. Each of the two clowns capped the last joke of the other. 7. small quantity of explosive in a wrapper of some kind.

ca pa bil i ty (kā′pə bil′i ti), ability; power; fitness; capacity.

ca pa ble (kā′pə bəl), able; having fitness or ability. Some airplanes are capable of going 300 miles an hour.

ca pa cious (kə pā′shəs), roomy; able to hold much.

ca pac i ty (kə pas′i ti), 1. the amount of room or space in a dish, a basket, a room, or a container of any kind. This can has a capacity of 4 quarts. This room has a seating capacity of 100 people. 2. ability to learn or do; power; fitness. 3. position or relation. He is here in the capacity of a teacher.

Caparison

ca par i son (kə par′i sən), 1. an ornamental covering for a horse. See the picture just above. 2. dress; equipment. 3. to dress richly.

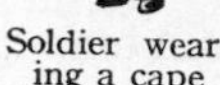

cape[1] (kāp), an outer garment, or a part of one, without sleeves, worn falling loosely from the shoulders.

cape[2] (kāp), a point of land extending into the water.

Soldier wearing a cape

ca per (kā′pər), 1. to leap or skip in a playful way. 2. a playful leap or skip.

cap i tal (kap′i təl), 1. the city where the government of a country or State is located. Washington is the capital of the United States. Each State of the United States has a capital. 2. A **capital** or **capital letter** is used to begin a sentence or the name of a person or place. 3. important; leading. 4. of the best kind; excellent. A maple tree gives capital shade. 5. **Make capital of** means use to one's own advantage. 6. involving death; punishable by death. Murder is a capital crime. 7. the top part of a column. See the picture just above. 8. money or property used in business, etc.

Capital

cap i tal ize (kap′i təl īz), write or print in capital letters.

Cap i tol (kap′i təl), 1. the building at Washington in which Congress meets. 2. the building in which a State legislature meets.

ca pit u late (kə pich′ů lāt), surrender on certain terms or conditions. The men in the fort capitulated, on the condition that they should be allowed to go away unharmed.

ca pon (kā′pən), rooster specially raised to be eaten.

ca price (kə prēs′), a sudden change of mind without reason; notion; fancy. If you decided that all your clothes must be blue, and would wear nothing else, that would be called a caprice.

Sailors turning a capstan

ca pri cious (kə prish′əs), guided by one's fancy; changeable. A spoiled child is often capricious.

cap size (kap sīz′), upset; overturn; turn bottom side up.

cap stan (kap′stən), a machine for lifting or pulling that stands upright. Sailors hoist the anchor by turning the capstan. See the picture just above.

cap sule (kap′səl), small case or covering. Medicine is often given in capsules made of gelatin. The seeds of some plants grow in capsules.

Capsule for medicine

cap tain (kap′tin), 1. leader; chief. 2. army officer in command of a company. 3. navy officer in command of a warship. 4. commander of a ship. 5. leader of a team in sports. 6. lead or command as captain. Tom will captain the team.

cap ti vate (kap′ti vāt), charm; fascinate. The beautiful music captivated him. The children were captivated by the animal story.

cap tive (kap′tiv), 1. prisoner. The army brought back a thousand captives. 2. held as prisoner; made a prisoner. The captive soldiers were shut up in a pen.

cap tiv i ty (kap tiv′i ti), 1. being in prison. 2. being held against one's will. Some animals cannot bear captivity, and die after a few weeks in a cage.

cap tor (kap′tər), man who takes or holds a prisoner.

cap ture (kap′chər), 1. make a prisoner of; take by force or trick. We capture butterflies with a net. 2. the thing or person captured. Captain Jones's first capture was an enemy ship. 3. act of capturing; fact of capturing or being captured. The capture of this ship took place on July 6.

car (kär), 1. vehicle moving on wheels. 2. automobile. 3. a railroad car, a streetcar, etc. 4. chariot. 5. part of a balloon, elevator, etc., for carrying passengers.

car a ba o (kä′rə bä′ō), water buffalo of the Philippine Islands.

car a mel (kar′ə məl or kär′məl), 1. burnt sugar used for coloring and flavoring. 2. a kind of candy.

car at (kar′ət), 1. one 24th part. Gold in watches is often 18 carats fine or pure and 6 parts alloy. 2. a unit of weight for precious stones equaling about 3 grains or $\frac{1}{150}$ ounce troy.

car a van (kar′ə van), 1. a group of merchants, pilgrims, tourists, etc., traveling together for safety through a desert or a dangerous country. 2. a large covered wagon for people or goods; a house on wheels; a van.

car a way (kar′ə wā), a plant whose seeds are used in cooking and medicine.

car bine (kär′bīn), short rifle or musket.

car bon (kär′bən), the substance that coal, charcoal, and graphite are made of. Carbon united with other substances is found in most animals and plants.

car cass (kär′kəs), dead body of an animal.

card (kärd), 1. flat piece of stiff paper or thin cardboard. Cards are used for various purposes. There are post cards, visiting cards, and cards of admission. 2. one of a pack of cards used in playing games.

card board (kärd′bōrd′), a stiff material made of paper and used for making cards, boxes, etc.

car di nal (kär′di nəl), 1. of first importance; chief; principal. The **cardinal points** of the compass are north, south, east, and west. 2. one of seventy high officials in the Roman Catholic Church, appointed by the Pope. 3. bright, rich red. 4. an American songbird whose feathers are red, black, and white.

care (kãr), 1. thought. A mother has care for her baby's health. 2. worry. I wish I could be free from care. 3. attention. A good cook does her work with care. 4. charge. Mary was left in her sister's care. 5. food, shelter, and protection. Your child will have the best of care. 6. something that requires care. 7. feel interest. He cares about music. 8. wish; like. A cat does not care to be washed. 9. **Care for** means (1) like. (2) take charge of. The nurse will care for him now.

ca reer (kə rēr′), 1. general course of action through life. It is interesting to read of the careers of great men and women. 2. occupation; profession. 3. rush along wildly. The runaway horse careered through the streets, banging the carriage behind him.

care free (kãr′frē′), without worry; happy; gay.

care ful (kãr′fəl), 1. full of care for something; taking pains; watchful; cautious. 2. done with care; showing care.

care ful ly (kãr′fəl i), in a careful manner; with care.

care less (kãr′lis), 1. not thinking or watching what you say or do. One careless step may cost a life. 2. not exact in doing work; not exactly done; as, a careless worker, careless work. 3. not caring or troubling.

care less ly (kãr′lis li), in a careless way.

Caribou (4 ft. high at the shoulder)

ca ress (kə res′), 1. a touch showing affection; tender embrace or kiss. 2. to touch or stroke tenderly; kiss.

car go (kär′gō), freight carried by a ship; load.

car i bou (kar′i bü), North American reindeer. See the picture just above.

car nage (kär′nij), the killing of a great number of people.

car na tion (kär nā′shən), 1. a garden flower with a spicy fragrance. 2. rosy pink.

Carnation

car ni val (kär′ni vəl), 1. place of amusement having merry-go-rounds, games, etc. 2. feasting and merrymaking; noisy and unrestrained revels. 3. time of feasting and merrymaking just before Lent.

car ol (kar′əl), 1. song of joy. 2. Christmas hymn. 3. sing; sing joyously; praise with carols. The birds carol in the early morning.

carp[1] (kärp), find fault.

carp[2] (kärp), a fresh-water fish that lives in ponds and slow streams.

car pen ter (kär′pən tər), worker who builds the wooden parts of houses, barns, ships, etc.

car pet (kär′pit), 1. heavy, woven fabric used for covering floors and stairs. 2. a smooth, soft, or bright stretch of grass, flowers, etc.; as, a carpet of leaves. 3. to cover with a carpet. In the spring, the ground was carpeted with violets.

car riage (kar′ij), 1. a vehicle having wheels. Carriages are usually drawn by horses and are used to carry people. 2. manner of holding the head and body; bearing. She has a queenly carriage. 3. the taking of persons or goods from one place to another. 4. the cost of taking anything from one place to another. 5. the support of a gun. See the picture just above. 6. a sliding part of machinery.

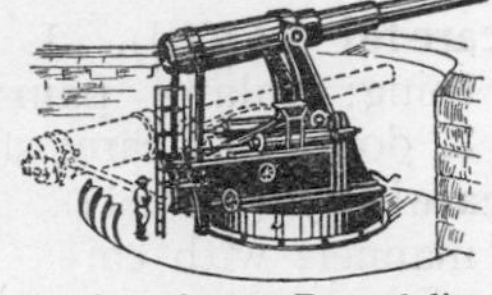

Gun carriage. Dotted lines show position of gun before it is raised for firing.

car ried (kar′id). See **carry.**

car ri er (kar′i ər), 1. person or thing that takes goods, packages, and messages from one place to another. The mail carriers deliver mail twice a day in our town. 2. anything that carries something. Water and milk are often carriers of disease germs.

car ri on (kar′i ən), dead and decaying flesh.

car rot (kar′ət), a vegetable which is the long, tapering, orange-colored root of a plant. Rabbits like to eat carrots.

Carrot

car ry (kar′i), 1. take (a thing or person) from one place to another. Railroads carry coal from the mines to your town. The man carried the child home. This story will carry your thoughts back to the first of the year. 2. cover the distance. His voice will carry to the back of the room. This gun will carry a mile. 3. win. Our side carried the election for club president. 4. hold or bear. This boy carries himself well. 5. **Carry away** means arouse strong feeling in; influence beyond reason. 6. **Carry on** means (1) do; manage; conduct. (2) go ahead with; go on with after being stopped. (3) keep going; not stop; continue. 7. **Carry out** means do; get done; complete.

cart (kärt), 1. strong vehicle with two wheels, used in farming and for carrying heavy loads. 2. light wagon used for delivering goods or for general business. 3. small vehicle on wheels, moved by hand. 4. carry in a cart. Cart away this rubbish.

Cart (def. 1)

cart er (kär′tər), man whose work is driving a cart.

car ti lage (kär′ti lij), a firm, elastic, flexible substance forming parts of a skeleton.

car ton (kär′tən), box made of pasteboard.

car toon (kär tün′), a sketch or drawing which interests or amuses us by showing public persons or events in an exaggerated way.

car tridge (kär′trij), a case made of metal or cardboard for holding gunpowder.

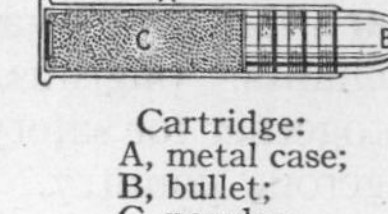

Cartridge: A, metal case; B, bullet; C, powder.

carve (kärv), 1. cut. To carve a statue is to cut it out of stone or wood, etc. A picture may be carved on the surface of wood or stone. 2. ornament with cut figures and designs; as, a carved box. 3. cut into slices or pieces. Father carves the meat at the table.

carv er (kär′vər), 1. person who carves. 2. knife for carving meat.

carv ing (kär′ving), 1. carved work; as, wood carving, stone carving, carvings in ivory. 2. See **carve.**

cas cade (kas kād′), small waterfall. See the picture.

Cascade

case[1] (kās), 1. A case of measles keeps a child away from school. The children agreed that every case of cheating should be punished. The man told of the sad case of starving children in India. Any special condition of a person or thing can be called a case. In case of fire walk quietly to the nearest door. 2. a matter for a law court to decide. 3. **In any case** means anyhow or no matter what happens.

case[2] (kās), 1. covering. Put the knife back in its case. 2. box. There is a big case full of books in the hall. 3. frame.

case ment (kās′mənt), a window opening on hinges like a door.

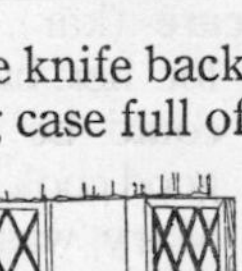

Casement

cash (kash), 1. ready money; coins and bills. 2. change into cash; give cash for. The bank will cash your five-dollar check. 3. get cash for. I cashed three checks for $10 each, and got $30.

cash ew (kash′ü), a tree that grows in tropical America. The cashew nut is soft and good to eat.

cash ier[1] (kash ēr′), person in charge of money in a bank, or in any business.

cash ier[2] (kash ēr′), dismiss from service; discharge in disgrace. A dishonest army or navy officer is deprived of his rank and cashiered.

cask (kask), 1. barrel. A cask may be large or small, and is usually made to hold liquids. 2. the amount a cask holds.

cas ket (kas′kit), 1. a small box, often fine and beautiful, used to hold jewels or letters. 2. coffin.

casque (kask), helmet.

cast (kast), 1. throw; throw off; let fall off. 2. threw; threw off. Yesterday that snake cast its skin. 3. thrown; thrown off. The thieves were cast into jail. 4. a throw; the distance a thing is thrown. 5. let harden in a mold. 6. thing that is molded. 7. select to take a part in a play. 8. the actors in a play. 9. form; appearance. 10. sort; kind. 11. hue; a slight amount of some color. 12. Some special meanings are:

cast a ballot, vote.

cast about, 1. search; look. 2. make plans.

cast down, 1. turn downward. 2. made sad or discouraged.

cast off, throw away; threw away; thrown away.

cast up, 1. turn upward. 2. add up.

cas tle (kas′əl), 1. a large building or group of buildings with thick walls, towers, and other defenses against attack. 2. a palace that once had defenses against attack. 3. large and stately residence.

Castle

cas u al (kazh′ü əl), **1.** happening by chance. A casual meeting at a party began our long friendship. 2. careless; not planned. I gave a casual glance in his direction. 3. irregular. A casual laborer is one who has no steady job.

cat (kat), 1. small animal often kept as a pet or for catching mice. Cats, lions, tigers, and leopards all belong to the same group of animals. 2. any animal belonging to this group. 3. a whip made of rope.

cat a logue or **cat a log** (kat′ə lôg), 1. a list. A library usually has a catalogue of its books. Some business companies print catalogues showing pictures and prices of what they have to sell. 2. make a list of; enter in the proper place in a list. Fred catalogued all the insects in his collection.

cat a pult (kat′ə pult), 1. ancient weapon for shooting stones, arrows, etc. 2. slingshot. 3. device for launching an airplane from the deck of a ship. 4. shoot from a catapult; throw; hurl. The jeep stopped so suddenly that Bill was catapulted out onto the road.

cat a ract (kat′ə rakt), 1. a large, steep waterfall. 2. a violent rush or downpour of water. 3. a disease of the eye that makes a person partly or entirely blind.

Cataract

ca tas tro phe (kə tas′trə fi), a sudden, widespread, or extraordinary disaster; great calamity or misfortune. A big earthquake or flood is a catastrophe; so is a big fire.

catch (kach), 1. take and hold (something moving); seize; capture. Catch the ball with both hands. The cat catches mice. The policeman caught the thief. The rat was caught in the trap. We were caught in the storm. Bright colors catch a baby's eye. 2. take; get. Paper catches fire easily. Put a warm coat on, or you will catch cold. He spoke so rapidly that I didn't catch the meaning of what he said. The soldiers suddenly caught sight of the enemy behind a wall. You have just five minutes to catch your train. 3. come upon suddenly; surprise. Mother caught me just as I was hiding her present. "Don't catch me up on every little mistake," said Dick to his big sister. 4. **Catch up with** means come up to while going the same way. Our dog ran as hard as he could to catch up with our car. 5. to act as catcher. John catches for our school team. 6. act of catching. Dick made a fine catch with one hand. 7. thing that catches. The catch on that door is broken. There is a catch to that question. 8. thing that is caught. A catch of fish is the amount caught. 9. a kind of song. "Three Blind Mice" is a catch.

caught is formed from **catch.**

catch er (kach′ər), 1. person or thing that catches. 2. baseball player who stands behind the batter.

cat e chism (kat′i kizm), 1. book of questions and answers about religion. 2. set of questions and answers about any subject. 3. set of questions.

ca ter (kā′tər), 1. provide food or supplies. He runs a restaurant and also caters for weddings and parties. 2. supply means of enjoyment. Some magazines cater to boys.

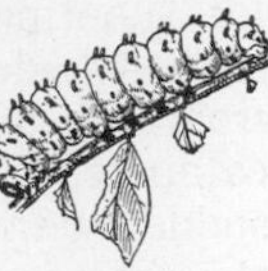

Caterpillar on a twig (about ½ life size)

cat er pil lar (kat′ər pil′ər), the larva or wormlike form in which insects such as the butterfly and the moth hatch from the egg.

cat fish (kat′fish′), any of several fishes without scales and with slender feelers about the mouth.

ca the dral (kə thē′drəl), 1. official church of a bishop. The bishop has a throne in the cathedral. 2. large or important church. See the picture.

Cathedral

Cath o lic (kath′ə lik), 1. of the Christian church governed by the Pope; Roman Catholic. 2. a member of this church.

cat kin (kat′kin), soft, downy, pointed cluster of flowers of the willow or birch. See the picture just below.

cat nip (kat′nip), a plant somewhat like mint. Cats like to eat catnip.

cat sup (kat′səp or kech′əp), a sauce to use with meat, fish, etc. Tomato catsup is made of tomatoes, onions, salt, sugar, and spices.

Catkin

cat tle (kat′əl), farm animals; livestock; oxen, bulls, cows, calves, etc.

caught (kôt). See **catch.** He caught the ball. The mouse was caught in a trap.

cau li flow er (kô′li flou′ər), a vegetable having a solid, white head with a few leaves around it.

Cauliflower

cause (kôz), 1. person or thing or event that makes something happen. One little mistake was the cause of all her trouble. 2. make happen; make do; bring about. A fever caused her death. A loud noise caused me to jump back. 3. reason or occasion for action. You have no cause to complain. 4. subject or movement in which many people take an interest. World peace is the cause she works for.

cause way (kôz′wā′), 1. a raised road or path. 2. a main road.

cau tion (kô′shən), 1. being very careful; taking care to be safe; never taking chances. Use caution in crossing streets. 2. a warning. A sign with "Danger!" on it is a caution. 3. warn. The policeman cautioned us against playing in that street.

cau tious (kô′shəs), careful.

cav al cade (kav′əl kād′), procession of persons riding on horses or drawn by horses.

cav a lier (kav′ə lēr′), 1. horseman; knight. 2. courteous gentleman. 3. a courteous escort for a lady. 4. haughty.

cav al ry (kav′əl ri), soldiers who fight on horseback.

cave (kāv), 1. hollow space underground. John found four caves on the side of Lime Hill. 2. **Cave in** means fall in.

cav ern (kav′ərn), large cave.

cav ern ous (kav′ər nəs), 1. like a cavern; large and hollow. 2. full of caverns.

cav i ty (kav′i ti), hole; hollow place. Most cavities in teeth are caused by decay.

ca vort (kə vôrt′), prance about. A horse cavorts when he feels excited.

caw (kô), 1. harsh cry made by a crow or raven. 2. make this cry.

cease (sēs), stop.

Cedar

cease less (sēs′lis), never stopping; going on all the time.

ce dar (sē′dər), an evergreen tree with hard, reddish, fragrant wood which is used for posts, clothes closets, cedar chests, pencils, and cigar boxes.

cede (sēd), give up; surrender; hand over to another. Spain ceded the Philippine Islands to the United States.

ceil ing (sēl′ing), 1. the inside top covering of a room. 2. greatest height to which an airplane or airship can go under certain conditions. 3. top limit. The ceiling price for the meat was 52 cents a pound.

cel e brate (sel′i brāt), observe (a special time or day) with activities of a proper kind. We celebrated Christmas with a tree and presents.

cel e brat ed (sel′i brāt′id), famous; well-known; much talked about.

cel e bra tion (sel′i brā′shən), 1. special services or activities in honor of a particular man, act, time, or day. A Fourth of July celebration often includes fireworks. 2. act of celebrating.

ce leb ri ty (si leb′ri ti), 1. famous person. 2. being talked about or praised; fame.

ce ler i ty (si ler′i ti), swiftness; speed.

cel er y (sel′ər i), vegetable whose long stalks are usually whitened by keeping the stalks covered while they grow. Celery is eaten raw or cooked.

ce les tial (si les′chəl), 1. of the sky; having something to do with the sky. The sun and moon are celestial bodies. 2. heavenly; very good or beautiful; as, celestial music.

cell (sel), 1. a small room in a prison, convent, or monastery. 2. any small, hollow space. Bees store honey in the cells of a honeycomb. 3. a container holding materials for producing electricity by chemical action. We bought four cells for our electric bells.

cel lar (sel′ər), underground room or rooms, usually under a building, used for storing fuel and food.

cel list or **'cel list** (chel′ist), person who plays the cello.

cel lo or **'cel lo** (chel′ō), violoncello, a musical instrument like a violin, but much larger; a bass violin. A cello is held between the knees while being played.

Man playing a cello

cel lo phane (sel′ə fān), transparent substance made from cellulose. It is used as a wrapping for food, candy, tobacco, and many other things.

cel lu lose (sel′ū lōs), the woody part of all plants and trees. Wood, cotton, hemp, and flax are made of cellulose.

ce ment (si ment′), 1. a substance made by burning clay and limestone. Cement is mixed with sand and water and used for holding stones and bricks together in the walls of buildings and for making hard walls, floors, and walks. Cement becomes hard like stone. 2. anything applied soft, which hardens to make things stick together. 3. fasten together with cement. A broken plate can be cemented. 4. spread cement over.

cem e ter y (sem′i ter′i), place for burying the dead; graveyard.

cen ser (sen′sər), container in which incense is burned.

cen sure (sen′shər), 1. expression of unfavorable opinion; blame. Censure is sometimes harder to bear than punishment. 2. to blame; find fault with. The man Fred worked for censured him for being late.

cen sus (sen′səs), an official count of the people of a country taken to find out the number of people, their ages, sex, what they do to make a living, and many other facts about them.

cent (sent), 1. a copper coin of the United States and Canada. 100 cents make one dollar. 2. a similar coin not made of copper.

cen taur (sen′tôr), a monster in Greek myths having the head, arms, and chest of a man, and the body and legs of a horse.

Centaur

cen ter (sen′tər), 1. a point within a circle or sphere equally distant from all points of the circumference or surface. 2. middle point; as, the center of a room. 3. person, thing, or group in a middle position. 4. principal point or place. New York City is a center of trade. 5. place in or at a center. 6. collect at a center.

cen ti me ter or **cen ti me tre** (sen′ti mē′tər), a measure of length equal to $\frac{1}{100}$ of a meter; .3937 inch.

cen tral (sen′trəl), 1. at the center; near the center. 2. equally distant from all points; easy to get to or from. 3. main; chief; principal. 4. telephone exchange.

cen tral ly (sen′trəl i), at the center; near the center.

cen tre (sen′tər), center.

cen tu ry (sen′chə ri), 1. each 100 years, counting from some special time like the birth of Christ. The first century is 1 to 100; the nineteenth century is 1801 to 1900; the twentieth century is 1901 to 2000. 2. a period of 100 years. From 1824 to 1924 is a century. From 1492 to 1892 is four centuries.

ce re al (sēr′i əl), 1. any grass producing grain which is used as a food. Wheat, rice, corn, oats, and barley are cereals. 2. grain. 3. food made from grain. Oatmeal, corn meal, and rice are cereals. 4. of grain; having something to do with grain or the grasses producing it.

cer e mo ni al (ser′i mō′ni əl), 1. formal. She received me in a ceremonial way. 2. of or having something to do with ceremony. The ceremonial costumes were beautiful. 3. the formal actions proper to an occasion. Bowing the head and kneeling are ceremonials of religion.

cer e mo ni ous (ser′i mō′ni əs), very formal; extremely polite.

cer e mo ny (ser′i mō′ni), 1. a special form or set of acts to be done on special occasions such as weddings, funerals, graduations, Christmas, or Easter. The marriage ceremony was performed in the church. Girls like ceremonies better than boys do. 2. very polite conduct; a way of conducting oneself that follows all the rules of polite social behavior. The old gentleman showed us to the door with a great deal of ceremony.

ce rise (sə rēz′), bright, pinkish red.

cer tain (sėr′tən), 1. sure. It is certain that 3 and 2 do not make 6. 2. some. Certain plants will not grow in this country. She uses a certain sort of perfume.

cer tain ly (sėr′tən li), surely; without doubt.

cer tain ty (sėr′tən ti), 1. a fact that you are sure of. "Death and taxes are certainties," said father. 2. freedom from doubt; being certain. The man's certainty was amusing, for we could all see that he was wrong.

cer tes (sėr′tēz), an old word meaning certainly.

cer tif i cate (sər tif′i kit), written or printed statement that may be used as proof of some fact. This certificate shows that John Williams has completed the schoolwork of the eighth grade.

cer ti fied (sėr′ti fīd). See **certify.**

cer ti fy (sėr′ti fī), 1. declare (something) true or correct by a spoken, written, or printed statement. 2. guarantee.

ces sa tion (se sā′shən), ceasing; pause; stop. During the summer there is a cessation of schoolwork.

chafe (chāf), 1. rub. The mother chafes her child's cold hands to warm them. 2. make sore or become sore by rubbing. This stiff collar chafes my neck. 3. make angry. His big brother's teasing chafed him. 4. get angry. He chafed under his brother's teasing.

chaff[1] (chaf), 1. stiff, strawlike bits around the grains of wheat, rye, or oats. Chaff is separated from the grain by threshing. 2. hay or straw cut fine for feeding cattle. 3. worthless stuff; rubbish.

chaff[2] (chaf), 1. make fun of in a good-natured way before one's face. The boys chaffed the French boy a good deal about his mistakes in speaking English. 2. good-natured joking about a person to his face. The French boy did not mind their chaff.

cha grin (shə grin′), a feeling of disappointment, failure, or humiliation. John felt chagrin because he did not get a prize.

chain (chān), 1. row of links joined together. The dog is fastened to a post by a chain. 2. series of things linked together; as, a chain of mountains, a chain of happenings. 3. fasten with a chain. 4. anything that binds or restrains. 5. bind; restrain. 6. keep in prison; make a slave of. 7. **Chains** sometimes means imprisonment or bondage.

Chain with eleven links

chair (chãr), 1. single seat with a back. 2. seat of position, dignity, or authority. 3. chairman.

chair man (chãr′mən), 1. person who is in charge of a meeting. 2. person at the head of a committee.

chair men (chãr′mən), more than one chairman.

chaise (shāz), a light carriage, usually with a folding top.

Chaise

chal ice (chal′is), cup.

chalk (chôk), 1. a soft, white or gray limestone, made up mostly of very small sea shells. Chalk is used for writing and for making lime. 2. material like chalk used to make white and colored crayons for writing or drawing on a blackboard. 3. to mark with chalk.

chalk y (chôk′i), 1. of chalk; containing chalk. 2. like chalk; white as chalk. The clown's face was chalky.

chal lenge (chal′inj), 1. a sudden questioning or calling to answer. "Who goes there?" is the challenge of a soldier on guard. 2. stop a person and question his right to do what he is doing or to be where he is. When I tried to enter the building, the guard at the door challenged me. 3. doubt; demand proof of before one will accept. The teacher challenged my statement that rice grows in Oregon. 4. a demand for proof of the truth of a statement; a doubting or questioning of the truth of a statement. 5. invitation to a game or contest of any kind. Giving a challenge often means that one undertakes to beat everybody else. 6. invite to a contest. The champion swimmer challenged anyone in the world to beat him.

chal leng er (chal′in jər), person who challenges.

cham ber (chām′bər), 1. a room, especially a bedroom. 2. any enclosed space in the body of animals or plants, or in some kinds of machinery. The heart has four chambers. 3. group of persons who make laws for a state or nation.

cham ber lain (chām′bər lin), person who manages the household of a king or of a great noble.

cha me le on (kə mē′li ən), 1. a lizard with the power of changing its color. 2. a changeable or fickle person.

Chameleon (6 in. long)

cham ois (sham′i), 1. a small, goatlike antelope, which lives in the high mountains of Europe and southwestern Asia. Six chamois were jumping from rock to rock. 2. a soft leather made from the skin of sheep, goats, deer, etc.

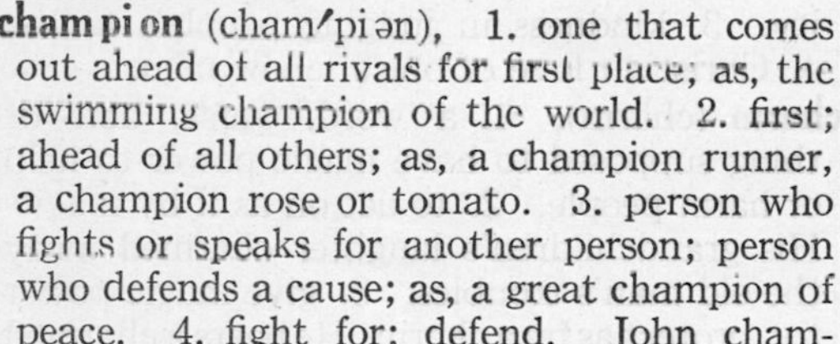

Chamois (2 ft. high at the shoulder)

champ (champ), 1. bite and chew noisily. 2. bite impatiently. The race horse champed at its bit.

cham pi on (cham′pi ən), 1. one that comes out ahead of all rivals for first place; as, the swimming champion of the world. 2. first; ahead of all others; as, a champion runner, a champion rose or tomato. 3. person who fights or speaks for another person; person who defends a cause; as, a great champion of peace. 4. fight for; defend. John championed his friend.

cham pi on ship (cham′pi ən ship′), the position of champion; first place. Our school won the championship in baseball.

chance (chans), 1. opportunity; as, a chance to make some money. 2. possibility; probability. There is a chance that the sick child will get well. The chances are against snow in May. 3. fate; luck. 4. a happening. Chance led to the finding of the diamond mine. 5. happen. 6. risk. 7. not expected; accidental; as, a chance visit.

chan cel lor (chan′sə lər), a very high official. Chancellor is the title used for the chief man in the government of some countries, for the chief judge in some courts, and for the president in some universities.

chan de lier (shan′də lēr′), fixture with branches for lights, usually hanging from the ceiling.

Chandelier

change (chānj), 1. put (something) in place of another; take in place of. You change your soiled clothes for clean ones. You can change a dollar bill for ten dimes. 2. make different; become different. She changed the room by painting the walls green. The wind changed from east to south. 3. passing from one form or place to a different one. The change from flower to fruit is interesting to watch. A change from the city to the country in the summer is good for children. 4. money returned to you when you have given a larger amount than the price of what you buy. If you buy an eight-cent loaf of bread and give the baker a dime, he will give you two cents in change. 5. small coins. Please give me change for this fifty-cent piece.

change a ble (chān′jə bəl), that can change; that does change; likely to change; variable; varying; fickle. April weather is changeable. Do not trust her love; she is changeable. Silk is called changeable when it looks different in different lights.

change less (chānj′lis), not changing.

chan nel (chan′əl), 1. the bed of a stream, river, etc. 2. body of water joining two larger bodies of water. The English Channel lies between two seas. 3. the deeper part of a waterway. There is shallow water on both sides of the channel in this river. 4. passage for liquids; a groove. 5. the means by which something is carried. The information came through secret channels. 6. form a channel in; cut out as one does a channel. The river had channeled its way through the rocks.

chant (chant), 1. song. 2. to sing. 3. a kind of tune used as part of a church service. 4. say a psalm or a prayer in a singing voice. 5. psalm, prayer, or other song for chanting.

chan ti cleer (chan′ti klēr), rooster.

cha os (kā′os), very great confusion; complete disorder. The whirlwind left chaos behind it.

chap[1] (chap), 1. crack open; become rough. The skin often chaps in cold weather. 2. make rough. Cold weather chapped his hands.

chap[2] (chap), fellow; man; boy. Hello, old chap!

chap el (chap′əl), 1. a building for Christian worship, not so large as a church. 2. a small place for worship in a larger building.

chap lain (chap′lin), clergyman on duty with a family, court, regiment, warship, etc.

chaps (chaps), strong leather trousers worn by cowboys.

chap ter (chap′tər), 1. a main division of a book, written about a particular part of the subject or story. 2. local division of an organization, which holds its own meetings.

char (chär), 1. burn to charcoal. 2. scorch; burn slightly. The fire was so hot that the meat got charred.

char ac ter (kar′ik tər), 1. nature. What is the character of the plan you suggest? The trees on those islands are of a peculiar character. 2. moral nature; moral strength or weakness. The special ways in which any person feels, thinks, and acts, considered as good or bad, make up his character. 3. a special thing or quality which makes one person, one animal or thing, or a group of any kind, different from others. The trunk is a character found only in elephants. 4. a letter, figure, or sign used in writing or printing. There are 52 characters in our alphabet, 26 small letters and 26 capitals. 5. a person in a play or book. 6. person who attracts attention because he is different or odd. The old captain was a character in the village.

char ac ter is tic (kar′ik tər is′tik), 1. marking off or distinguishing a certain person or thing from others; as, the characteristic smell of bananas. 2. special quality or feature. The characteristic I like best in him is his cheerfulness.

char ac ter ize (kar′ik tər īz), 1. describe the special qualities or features of (a person or thing). 2. distinguish; mark out. The camel is characterized by the humps on its back and an ability to go without water for days.

char coal (chär′kōl′), a black substance made by partly burning wood or bones in a place from which the air is shut out. Charcoal is used as fuel, in filters, and in drawing.

charge (chärj), 1. load; fill. He charged the gun with powder and shot. 2. a load. A gun is fired by exploding the charge of powder. 3. order; give a task or duty to. Mother charged Alice to take good care of the baby. 4. duty; responsibility. 5. care. Dr. Brown is in charge of the case. 6. an order; direction; as, the charge of a judge to a jury. 7. blame; accuse. The driver was charged with speeding. 8. an accusing. He admitted the charge and paid the fine. 9. ask as a price; put a price on. The grocer charged 40 cents a dozen for eggs. 10. price; expense. 11. put down as a debt. The store will charge things bought and send a bill at the end of the month. 12. rush at; attack. The soldiers charged the enemy. 13. an attack. The charge drove the enemy back.

charg er[1] (chär′jər), horse ridden in war.

charg er[2] (chär′jər), large, flat dish; platter.

char i ot (char′i ət), a two-wheeled car pulled by horses. The chariot was used in ancient times for fighting, for racing, and in processions.

Roman chariot

char i ta ble (char′i tə bəl), 1. generous in giving to the poor. 2. of charity; for charity. 3. kindly in judging people and their actions.

char i ty (char′i ti), 1. generous giving to the poor, or to institutions which look after the sick, the poor, and the helpless. 2. institution for helping the sick, the poor, and the helpless. A free hospital is a noble charity. 3. kindness in judging people's faults. 4. Christian love of one's fellow men.

charm (chärm), 1. a word, verse, act, or thing supposed to have magic power to help or harm people. 2. to act on as if by magic. His grandchildren's laughter charmed away the old man's troubles. 3. give magic power to; protect as by a charm. He bears a charmed life. 4. a quality or feature in persons, in books, or in conduct which delights or fascinates; the power of delighting. Our grandmother did not lose her charm for us as she grew old. 5. please greatly; delight. The boys were charmed by the sailor's tales of adventure.

charm ing (chär′ming), delightful; fascinating.

chart (chärt), 1. a sailor's map of the sea which shows the coasts, rocks, and shallow places. 2. map. 3. a sheet of information arranged in pictures, diagrams, etc. 4. make a map or chart of.

char ter (chär′tər), 1. an official written grant of certain rights. 2. give a charter to. 3. hire. He chartered a sailboat for a month.

chase (chās), 1. run after to catch or kill. 2. act of running after to catch or kill. We watched the chase. 3. act of hunting wild animals. 4. a hunted animal. The chase escaped the hunter. 5. drive; drive away. English sparrows chase other birds from their nests.

chasm (kazm), 1. a deep opening or crack in the earth. 2. wide difference of feeling or interests between two persons, two groups, or two parties.

Chasm

chaste (chāst), 1. pure. 2. pure in taste or style; simple; not ornamented.

chas ten (chās′ən), 1. punish to improve. God chastened Moses. 2. restrain from excess or crudeness.

chas tise (chas tīz′), punish; beat.

chat (chat), 1. easy, familiar talk. 2. to talk in an easy, familiar way.

châ teau (sha tō′), 1. castle. 2. country residence.

châ teaux (sha tōz′), more than one château.

chat ter (chat′ər), 1. talk constantly in a quick, foolish way. 2. quick, foolish talk. 3. make quick, indistinct sounds. The monkey chattered in anger. 4. quick, indistinct sounds. The chatter of sparrows annoyed her. 5. rattle together. Cold makes your teeth chatter.

chat ty (chat′i), fond of friendly, familiar talk.

chauf feur (shō′fər or shō fėr′), man who drives an automobile for a living.

cheap (chēp), 1. costing little. 2. costing less than it is worth. 3. easily obtained. 4. common; of low value. **Feel cheap** means feel inferior and ashamed.

cheap en (chēp′ən), make cheap; lower the value of.

cheap ly (chēp′li), at a low price; without spending much money or effort.

cheat (chēt), 1. deceive or trick; play or do business in a way that is not honest. 2. person who is not honest and does things to deceive and trick others. 3. fraud; trick.

check (chek), 1. stop suddenly. They checked their steps. 2. sudden stop. The message gave a check to our plans. 3. hold back; control; as, to check one's anger. 4. any person or thing that controls or holds back action; as, the check on a furnace. 5. proving or proof by comparing. My work will be a check on yours. 6. prove true or right by comparing. Check your answers with mine. 7. a mark showing that something has been examined or compared. 8. a written order directing a bank to pay money to the person named. 9. a ticket or metal piece given in return for baggage or a package, to show ownership or the right to claim again later. Show your trunk check when you want your trunk. 10. a pattern made of squares. Do you want a check or a stripe for your new dress? 11. a single one of these squares. The checks are small in this pattern.

check ers (chek′ərz), a game played by two people, each with 12 flat, round pieces of wood, ivory, etc., on a board marked off into 64 squares of two alternating colors.

cheek (chēk), 1. side of the face below either eye. 2. bold talk or action, especially from a child or an inferior; impudence.

cheep (chēp), 1. make a noise like a young bird; chirp; peep. 2. a young bird's cry.

cheer (chēr), 1. good spirits; hope; gladness. The warmth of the fire and a good meal brought cheer to our hearts again. 2. to comfort; make glad. It cheered the old woman to have us visit her. 3. **"Cheer up!"** means "Don't be sad; be glad!" 4. a shout of sympathy and support or praise. Give three cheers for the boys who won the game for us. 5. urge on by cheers or other means. 6. show praise and approval by cheers. 7. food.

cheer ful (chēr′fəl), 1. full of cheer; joyful; glad. 2. pleasant; bringing cheer. 3. willing; as, a cheerful helper.

cheer ful ness (chēr′fəl nis), 1. good spirits. 2. pleasantness. 3. willingness.

cheer i ly (chēr′i li), in a cheerful or cheery manner; in a way suggesting or bringing cheer. The children sang cheerily around the Christmas tree.

cheer less (chēr′lis), without comfort or happiness; gloomy; dreary.

cheer y (chēr′i), cheerful; pleasant; bright; gay. Sunshine and the singing of birds are cheery.

cheese (chēz), a solid food made from the thick part of milk.

chem i cal (kem′i kəl), 1. of chemistry. 2. made by chemistry; used in chemistry. 3. any substance that is used in chemistry. Oxygen, hydrogen, and calcium are chemicals.

chem ist (kem′ist), 1. person who makes chemistry his occupation or who knows a great deal about it. 2. in England, a druggist.

chem is try (kem′is tri), science that deals with the characteristics of simple substances, the changes that take place when they combine to form other substances, and the laws of their behavior.

cher ish (cher′ish), 1. hold dear; treat with tenderness; aid or protect. A mother cherishes her baby. 2. keep in mind; cling to. She cherished the hope of her son's return.

cher ry (cher′i), 1. a small, round fruit with a hard seed in the middle. Cherries are good to eat. 2. the tree it grows on. 3. bright red; as, cherry ribbons.

cher ub (cher′əb), 1. angel. 2. child with wings. 3. beautiful or innocent child.

Cherub

chess (ches), a game played by two persons, each with 16 pieces which can be moved in various ways on a board marked off into 64 squares.

chest (chest), 1. part of a person's or an animal's body enclosed by ribs. 2. large box with a lid, used for holding things; as, a linen chest, a medicine chest, a tool chest.

chest nut (ches′nut), 1. a nut that is good to eat. 2. the tree it grows on. 3. the wood of this tree. 4. deep, reddish brown.

chew (chü), 1. crush or grind with the teeth. 2. a bite.

chick (chik), 1. young chicken. 2. young bird. 3. child.

chick a dee (chik′ə dē), a small bird. See the picture.

Chickadee (5 in. long)

chick en (chik′in), 1. young hen or rooster. 2. any hen or rooster. 3. any young bird. 4. the flesh of a chicken.

chid (chid), chided.

chide (chīd), reproach; blame; scold. The nurse chided the princess for soiling her dress.

chief (chēf), 1. head of a tribe or group; leader; person in authority. 2. **In chief** means at the head or in the highest position. 3. highest in rank or authority; at the head; most important.

chief ly (chēf′li), 1. mainly; mostly. We visited Washington chiefly to see the Capitol. 2. first of all; above all.

chief tain (chēf′tən), 1. the chief of a tribe or clan. 2. leader.

child (chīld), 1. baby. 2. young boy or girl. 3. son or daughter. 4. **Child's play** sometimes means something very easy to do. **children** is formed from **child.**

child hood (chīld′hu̇d), 1. being a child. 2. time during which one is a child.

child ish (chīl′dish), 1. of a child. 2. like a child. 3. not proper for a grown person; silly; weak. Crying for things you can't have is childish.

chil dren (chil′drən), 1. young boys and girls. 2. sons and daughters.

chill (chil), 1. unpleasant coldness. Put some hot water in the milk to take the chill off. 2. unpleasantly cold. 3. make cold. 4. become cold; feel cold. 5. a sudden coldness of the body with shivering. I had a chill yesterday and still feel ill.

chill y (chil′i), 1. cold; unpleasantly cool. 2. not kind. Our club gives boasting a chilly reception.

chime (chīm), 1. a set of bells tuned to the musical scale and played usually by hammers or simple machinery. 2. the music made by a set of tuned bells. 3. ring out musically. 4. be in harmony or agreement. His ideas chimed in beautifully with mine.

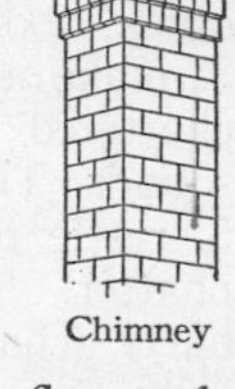
Chimney

chim ney (chim′ni), 1. an upright structure to make a draft and carry away smoke. Alice's house has two chimneys. 2. a glass tube placed around the flame of a lamp.

chim pan zee (chim pan′zi or chim′pan zē′), an African ape as big as a large dog. Chimpanzees are very intelligent.

Chimpanzee (4½ ft. tall when standing)

chin (chin), the front of the lower jaw below the mouth.

chi na (chī′nə), 1. a fine, white ware made of clay baked by a special process, first used in China. Colored designs can be baked into china. 2. dishes, vases, ornaments, etc., made of china.

Chi na (chī′nə), a large country in eastern Asia.

Chi nese (chī nēz′), 1. of China, its people,

or their language. 2. a member of the native race of China. 3. language of China.

chink[1] (chingk), 1. narrow opening; crack. The chinks in the cabin let in wind and snow. 2. fill up (narrow openings). The cracks in the log wall were chinked with mud.

chink[2] (chingk), 1. a sound like glasses or coins striking against one another. 2. make such a sound. I could hear the spoons chink in the glasses. 3. cause to make such a sound. He chinked the coins in his pocket.

chip (chip), 1. a small, thin piece cut from wood or broken from stone or china. 2. a place in china or stone from which a small piece has been broken. 3. cut or break (small pieces) from wood, stone, or dishes. Tom chipped off the old paint. 4. become chipped easily. These cups chip if they are not handled carefully. 5. shape by cutting at the surface or edge with an ax or chisel.

chip munk (chip′mungk), small, striped American squirrel.

Chipmunk (10 in. long with tail)

chirp (chėrp), 1. the short, sharp sound made by some small birds and insects. 2. make a chirp. Crickets chirp. Sparrows chirp.

chis el (chiz′əl), 1. a tool with a steel cutting edge at the end of a strong blade. Chisels are used for shaping wood, stone, or metal. 2. cut or shape with a chisel.

Chisels

chiv al rous (shiv′əl rəs), like an ideal knight; gallant, courteous, helpful, and honorable.

chiv al ry (shiv′əl ri), 1. the qualities of an ideal knight; skill in fighting with arms, bravery, honor, protection of the weak, devotion to women, and fairness to an enemy. 2. the rules, customs, and beliefs of knights.

chlo ro phyll or **chlo ro phyl** (klō′rə fil), the green coloring matter of plants.

choc o late (chôk′ə lit), 1. a substance that has a strong, rich flavor and much value as food. 2. a drink made from chocolate with sugar and hot water or milk. 3. candy made of chocolate. 4. dark brown.

choice (chois), 1. act of choosing. Use careful choice in buying dresses. 2. person or thing chosen. This is my choice. 3. power or chance to choose. Sam's father gave him his choice between a bicycle and a pony. 4. quantity and variety to choose from. You haven't much choice now. 5. excellent; of fine quality. The choicest fruit has the highest price.

choir (kwīr), 1. the group of singers used in a church service. 2. the part of the church set apart for the singers. 3. any group of singers.

choke (chōk), 1. stop the breath of (an animal or person) by squeezing the throat or by blocking it up. 2. be unable to breathe. 3. check or put out by cutting off air; smother; as, to choke a fire. 4. hold; control. He choked down his anger and choked back a sharp reply. 5. fill up or block. Sand is choking the river. 6. act or sound of choking. The man gave a few chokes and then got his breath.

chol er a (kol′ər ə), 1. a painful disease of the stomach and intestines that is not infectious. 2. a more dangerous disease that is infectious. Both kinds of cholera are marked by vomiting and cramps.

choose (chüz), 1. pick out; select from a number. Choose the cake you like best. He chose coconut. 2. prefer and decide; think fit. She did not choose to go with us. **chose** and **chosen** are formed from **choose.**

chop[1] (chop), 1. cut by blows. You chop wood with an ax. The boys chopped down five trees. 2. cut into small pieces; as, to chop up cabbage. 3. cutting blow. 4. slice of meat, especially of lamb, veal, or pork with a piece of rib. 5. move in small, jerky waves.

chop[2] (chop), jaw. The dog licked his chops.

chord[1] (kôrd), a combination of three or more notes of music sounded at the same time in harmony.

chord[2] (kôrd), 1. a structure in an animal body that looks like a string. 2. the string of a harp.

chore (chōr), odd job; small task. Feeding the chickens and milking cows are chores on the farm.

cho rus (kō′rəs), 1. group of singers who sing together, such as a choir. 2. music sung by many singers together. 3. a repeated part of a song coming after each stanza. 4. sing or speak all at the same time. The birds were chorusing around me. 5. a saying by many at the same time. My question was answered by a chorus of No!'s. 6. group of singers and dancers.

chose (chōz). See **choose.** Mary chose the pink dress.

cho sen (chō′zən). See **choose.** Have you chosen a book from the library? Six chosen scouts marched in front.

chow der (chou′dər), a thick soup or stew made of clams or fish with potatoes, onions, etc.

Christ (krīst), Jesus, the founder of the Christian religion.

chris ten (kris′ən), 1. baptize as a Christian. 2. give a first name to (a person) at baptism. The child was christened James. 3. give a name to.

Chris ten dom (kris′ən dəm), 1. Christian countries; Christian part of the world. 2. all Christians.

chris ten ing (kris′ən ing), baptism; act or ceremony of baptizing and naming.

Chris tian (kris′chən), 1. person who believes in Christ. 2. person whose life follows the teachings of Christ. 3. believing in or belonging to the religion of Christ; as, the Christian church, Christian countries. 4. showing a gentle, humble, helpful spirit; as, Christian kindness. 5. of Christ, His teachings, or His followers.

Chris ti an i ty (kris′chi an′i ti), 1. the religion taught by Christ and His followers. 2. Christian beliefs or faith; Christian spirit or character.

Christ mas (kris′məs), the yearly celebration of the birth of Christ on December 25. A **Christmas tree** is an evergreen tree hung with decorations.

chron ic (kron′ik), continuing a long time.

chron i cle (kron′i kəl), 1. history or story; an account of events in the order that they took place. 2. write or tell the story of.

chron i cler (kron′i klər), person who writes a chronicle; historian.

chrys a lis (kris′ə lis), 1. a stage in the life of an insect when it is in a case. It comes between the larva (caterpillar) and the winged adult stage (butterfly). 2. the case.

Chrysanthemum

chry san the mum (kri san′thi-məm), a round flower with many petals, which blossoms in the fall. The chrysanthemum plant was brought from Japan.

chub by (chub′i), round and plump; as, a chubby child.

chuck (chuk), 1. pat; tap; as, a chuck under the chin. 2. throw; toss.

chuck le (chuk′əl), 1. laugh to oneself. Father always chuckles when he sees a funny movie. 2. a soft laugh; quiet laughter.

chum (chum), 1. very close friend. 2. be on very friendly terms. 3. roommate.

chunk (chungk), a thick piece or lump; as, a chunk of wood, bread, etc.

church (chėrch), 1. a building for public Christian worship. 2. public worship of God in a church. 3. group of Christians with the same beliefs and under the same authority; as, the Methodist church, the Baptist church.

church man (chėrch′mən), 1. minister or priest. 2. member of a church.

church yard (chėrch′yärd′), the ground around a church. A churchyard is sometimes used for a burial ground.

churl (chėrl), 1. a rude, surly person. 2. peasant; person of low birth.

churn (chėrn), 1. container or machine in which butter is made from cream by beating and shaking. 2. beat and shake (cream, etc.) in a churn. 3. move as if beaten and shaken. The water churns in the rapids.

ci ca da (si kā′də), a large insect with transparent wings. The male makes a shrill sound in hot, dry weather.

Cicada (about ⅓ life size)

ci der (sī′dər), the juice of apples, used as a drink and in making vinegar.

ci gar (si gär′), tight roll of tobacco leaves for smoking.

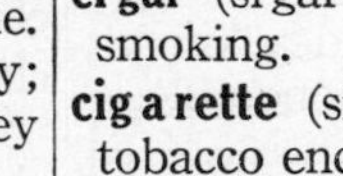

cig a rette (sig′ə ret′), small roll of finely cut tobacco enclosed in a thin sheet of paper for smoking.

cinch (sinch), 1. a strong girth for a saddle or pack. 2. put on with a cinch; bind firmly. 3. a firm hold or grip. 4. something sure and easy.

cin der (sin′dər), 1. wood or coal partly burned and no longer flaming. 2. burned-up wood or coal; ash. Cinders are made up of larger and coarser pieces than ashes are.

Cin der el la (sin′dər el′ə), the girl in the story who was forced to work very hard, but was rescued by her fairy godmother and married to a prince.

cin e ma (sin′i mə), moving picture.

cin na mon (sin′ə mən), 1. the inner bark of a tree, used as a spice and in medicine.

2. spice made from this bark. 3. the tree itself. 4. light, reddish brown; as, a cinnamon bear.

ci pher (sī′fər), 1. zero; 0. 2. person or thing of no importance. 3. do arithmetic. Mary can read, write, and cipher. 4. work by arithmetic. 5. secret writing. He sent me a telegram in cipher. 6. something in secret writing. 7. the key to a secret writing.

cir cle (sėr′kəl), 1. a line every point of which is equally distant from a point within called the center. 2. a plane figure bounded by such a line. 3. something flat and round or nearly so. 4. a ring. The girls danced in a circle. 5. move in a circle. An airplane circles before it lands. 6. enclose in a circle; surround. A ring of forts circled the city. 7. complete series; as, the circle of the months. 8. a group of people bound by the same interests; as, the family circle, a circle of friends.

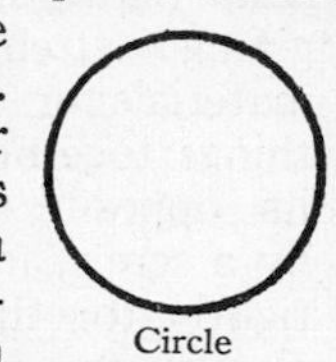

Circle

cir cuit (sėr′kit), 1. a going around; a moving around. 2. the distance around any space; the line enclosing an area. 3. a way over which a person or a group makes repeated journeys at certain times; the part of the country through which such journeys are made. 4. the complete path over which an electric current flows.

cir cu i tous (sər kū′i təs), roundabout.

cir cu lar (sėr′kū lər), 1. round like a circle. 2. moving in a circle; as, a circular trip. 3. a notice or advertisement sent around to a number of people.

cir cu late (sėr′kū lāt), 1. go around. A newspaper circulates among people who read it. Water circulates in the pipes of a building. Money circulates as it goes from person to person. 2. send around from person to person or place to place. The children circulated the news of the holiday. This book has been widely circulated among boys.

cir cu la tion (sėr′kū lā′shən), 1. a going round; circulating. Open windows increase the circulation of air in a room. 2. the movement of the blood from the heart through the body and back to the heart. 3. sending around books, papers, news, etc., from person to person or place to place.

cir cum fer ence (sər kum′fər əns), 1. boundary line of a circle or of certain other surfaces. Every point in the circumference of a circle is at the same distance from the center. 2. the distance around. The circumference of the circle shown here is a little over two inches. That of the circle in the other column is about $2\frac{1}{2}$ inches.

cir cum nav i gate (sėr′kəm-nav′i gāt), sail around. Magellan's ship circumnavigated the earth.

cir cum stance (sėr′kəm stans), 1. condition of an act or event. The place, the weather, and the other circumstances made the picnic a great success. 2. fact or event. It was a lucky circumstance that she found her money. **Circumstances** sometimes means condition or state of affairs. A rich man is in good circumstances; a poor man is in bad circumstances. 3. ceremony; display. The king was crowned with much circumstance.

cir cum vent (sėr′kəm vent′), get the better of.

cir cus (sėr′kəs), 1. a traveling show of acrobats, clowns, horses, riders, and wild animals. The performers who give the show and the show that they give are both called the circus. 2. a round or oval space with seats around it in rows, each row higher than the one in front of it.

cis tern (sis′tərn), tank or reservoir for storing water.

cit a del (sit′ə dəl), fortress, especially one in a city.

ci ta tion (sī tā′shən), 1. quotation. 2. honorable mention for bravery in war.

cite (sīt), 1. quote. He cited the Bible and Shakespeare to prove his statement. 2. refer to; mention; bring up as an example. Can you cite another case like this one?

cit i zen (sit′i zən), 1. person who by birth or by choice is a member of a state or nation which gives him certain rights and which claims his loyalty. Many foreigners have become citizens of the United States. 2. inhabitant of a city or town.

cit i zen ry (sit′i zən ri), citizens as a group.

cit i zen ship (sit′i zən ship′), the duties, rights, and privileges of a citizen.

cit ron (sit′rən), 1. a pale-yellow fruit somewhat like a lemon but larger, less acid, and with a thicker rind. 2. the shrub or small tree it grows on. 3. the rind of citron cooked in sugar and ready for use in fruit cake, plum pudding, etc.

cit y (sit′i), 1. a large, important town that manages its own affairs. New York, Chicago, London, and Paris are cities. 2. the people living in a city. The city was alarmed by the great fire. 3. of a city. 4. in a city.

civ ic (siv′ik), 1. of a city. 2. of citizenship. Every person has some civic duties, such as obeying the laws, voting, and paying taxes. 3. of citizens.

civ il (siv′il), 1. of a citizen or citizens; having something to do with citizens. Civil war is war between two groups of citizens in the same country. 2. not naval, military, or connected with the church. 3. polite; courteous. The boy pointed out our road in a civil way.

ci vil ian (si vil′yən), 1. person who is not a soldier or sailor. All men not in the army or navy are civilians. 2. of civilians; not military or naval.

ci vil i ty (si vil′i ti), politeness; courtesy.

civ i li za tion (siv′i li zā′shən), 1. civilized condition. 2. the ways of living of a race or nation. There are differences between Chinese civilization and our own.

civ i lize (siv′i līz), change from being savage and ignorant to having good laws and customs and knowledge of the arts and sciences. Schools will help to civilize the wild tribes of Africa.

clack (klak), 1. make a short, sharp sound. The old lady's needles clacked as she knitted. 2. short, sharp sound. We heard the clack of her heels on the sidewalk. 3. chatter.

clad (klad), clothed.

claim (klām), 1. demand as one's own or one's right. Does anyone claim this pencil? 2. such a demand. Mary makes a claim to the pencil. 3. a right or title to a thing; a right to demand something. She has a claim on us because she is my mother's cousin. 4. piece of land which someone claims; as, a miner's claim. 5. When things claim your attention, they deserve or require it. The care of the baby claims half my time. 6. **Claim to be** means maintain that one is. He claims to be the best player on the team.

clam (klam), 1. an animal somewhat like an oyster, with a soft body and hinged double shell, living in sand along the seashore, or in the edges of rivers, lakes, etc. Many kinds are good to eat. 2. go out after clams; dig for clams.

Shell of a clam

clam ber (klam′bər), climb, using both hands and feet; scramble. The boys clambered up the cliff.

clam my (klam′i), cold and damp. A frog is a clammy creature.

clam or (klam′ər), 1. loud noise, especially of voices; confused shouting. 2. make a loud noise. 3. noisy demand. 4. **Clamor for** means demand noisily. The children were clamoring for candy.

clam or ous (klam′ər əs), loud and noisy.

clamp (klamp), 1. an iron brace or band for giving strength to other materials or for holding two things together. 2. tool with its opposite sides connected by a screw, for holding things tightly together. 3. fasten together with a clamp; fix in a clamp; strengthen with clamps. A picture frame must be clamped together while the glue is drying.

Clamp (def. 2)

clan (klan), 1. group of related families that claim to be descended from a common ancestor. 2. group of people closely joined together by some common interest.

clang (klang), 1. a loud, harsh, ringing sound like metal being hit; as, the clang of the dinner gong. 2. make a loud, harsh, resounding sound. The fire bells clanged.

clank (klangk), 1. a sound like the rattle of a heavy chain. 2. make such a sound. The swords clashed and clanked as the men fought together.

clap (klap), 1. a sudden noise, such as a single burst of thunder, the sound of the hands struck together, or the sound of a loud slap. 2. make such a noise, especially with the hands. When the show was over, we all clapped. 3. strike with a quick blow. He clapped his friend on the back.

clap per (klap′ər), 1. person or thing that claps. 2. part that strikes a bell. 3. device for making noise.

clar i on (klar′i ən), 1. clear and shrill. 2. a trumpet with clear, shrill tones.

clar i ty (klar′i ti), clearness.

clash (klash), 1. a loud, harsh sound like that of two things running into each other, of striking metal, or of bells rung together but not in tune. 2. hit with a clash. In her haste, she clashed the saucepans against the stove. 3. a strong disagreement; a conflict. There are many clashes of opinion in that family, for no two of them think alike. 4. disagree strongly; conflict; go badly together.

clasp (klasp), 1. a thing for fastening that is somewhat like a buckle or a hook. 2. fasten together with a clasp. 3. hold closely with the hand or the arms. The mother clasped her baby to her breast. He clasped a knife in his hand. 4. a grasp of the hand. He gave my hand a warm clasp. 5. a close hold. I could not escape from the bear's clasp.

Clasp

class (klas), 1. group of persons or things of the same kind. 2. group of pupils taught together. 3. their time of meeting. 4. rank of society; as, upper class, middle class, working class. 5. put in a class.

clas sic (klas′ik), 1. an author or an artist of acknowledged excellence. 2. a fine book or painting produced by such a man. 3. of the first class; excellent. 4. simple and fine in form. 5. classical.

clas si cal (klas′i kəl), 1. first-class. She likes classical literature and music. 2. having to do with the culture of the ancient Greeks and Romans.

clas si fi ca tion (klas′i fi kā′shən), arrangement in classes or groups; grouping according to some system.

clas si fied (klas′i fīd). See **classify.**

clas si fy (klas′i fī), arrange in groups or classes. Children in school are classified into grades, according to how much they know. Mother classifies the clean clothes, and Mary puts them away. In the post office mail is classified according to the places where it is to go.

class mate (klas′māt′), member of the same class in school.

class room (klas′rüm′), room in which classes are held; schoolroom.

clat ter (klat′ər), 1. confused noise like many plates being struck together. The clatter in the big dining room was so great that we could hardly hear one another speak. 2. move or fall with confused noise; make a confused noise. The horses clattered over the stones. 3. noisy talk. 4. talk fast and noisily.

clause (klôz), 1. part of a sentence, with a subject and a verb. In "He came before we left," "He came" is a main clause, and "before we left" is a subordinate clause. 2. a single provision of a law, a treaty, or any other written agreement; short sentence. There is a clause in our contract that says we may not keep a dog in the building.

claw (klô), 1. a sharp, hooked nail on a bird's or animal's foot. 2. a foot provided with these sharp, hooked nails. 3. thing like a claw. The pincers of lobsters or crabs are claws. The part of a hammer used for pulling nails is the claw. 4. to scratch, tear, seize, or pull with claws or hands. The kitten was clawing the screen door.

Claws of a bird

clay (klā), a sticky kind of earth which hardens when it is baked. Bricks and dishes are made from various kinds of clay.

clean (klēn), 1. Soap and water make us clean. 2. The saint had a clean heart. 3. The cat is a clean animal. 4. Washing cleans clothes. Clean up the yard. Clean out your desk. 5. Anything well shaped and neat is called clean. 6. Anything well done may be called clean. 7. The new owner of the newspaper made a clean sweep by dismissing all the workers and hiring new ones. 8. The horse jumped clean over the brook. Boards of the bridge were cut clean through.

clean er (klēn′ər), 1. person whose work is keeping buildings, windows, or other objects clean. 2. anything that removes dirt, grease, or stains.

clean li ness (klen′li nis), cleanness; being always, or nearly always, clean. Cleanliness is good for health.

clean ly (klen′li), clean; habitually clean. A cat is a cleanly animal.

clean ness (klēn′nis), being clean. The cleanness of the rooms pleased the good housekeeper.

cleanse (klenz), make clean.

clear (klēr), 1. A clear sky is free from clouds. Healthy children have clear skins. There is a clear view of the sea from that hill. He told a clear story. 2. He will clear the land of trees. 3. It rained and then it cleared. **Clear up** sometimes means explain. 4. The bullet went clear through the door.

clear-cut (klēr′kut′), 1. having clear, sharp outlines. 2. clear; definite; distinct. Fred had clear-cut ideas about his work.

clear ing (klēr′ing), open space of cleared land in a forest.

clear ly (klēr′li). We could understand Mary because she spoke clearly. You cannot see clearly in a fog. Mud pies are clearly not fit to eat.

clear ness (klēr′nis), being clear. The clearness of the air made it possible to see the distant mountains. The clearness of the directions helped us to put the machine together easily.

cleat (klēt), 1. strip of wood or iron fastened across anything for support or for sure footing. Some shoes have cleats to keep people from slipping. 2. small, wedge-shaped block fastened to a spar, etc., as a support, check, etc. 3. piece of wood or iron used for securing ropes or lines.

Cleat securing a rope

cleav age (klēv′ij), 1. the way in which a thing tends to split. Slate shows a marked cleavage and can easily be separated into layers. 2. split; division.

cleave[1] (klēv), cut or split open. A blow of the whale's tail clove our boat in two. **cleaved, cleft, clove,** and **cloven** are formed from **cleave**[1].

cleave[2] (klēv), hold fast (to); cling; be faithful. He was so frightened that his tongue cleaved to the roof of his mouth.

cleft (kleft), 1. cut. His blow had cleft the bear's head in two. 2. split; divided. 3. space or opening made by splitting; crack.

clench (klench), 1. close tightly together; as, to clench one's teeth, to clench one's hand, a clenched fist. 2. grasp firmly. He clenched my arm. 3. tight grip. I felt the clench of his hand on my arm. 4. clinch.

cler gy (klėr′ji), persons ordained for religious work; ministers, pastors, and priests.

cler gy man (klėr′ji mən), minister; pastor; priest. We have clergymen to help us in religion just as we have doctors to help us in health or teachers to help us in education.

cler i cal (kler′i kəl), 1. of a clerk; of clerks; for clerks. A big bank employs many persons for clerical work. 2. of a clergyman or the clergy. A priest wears clerical robes in church.

clerk (klėrk), 1. man or woman employed to sell goods in a store or shop. 2. person employed in an office to file records, copy letters, keep accounts, etc. 3. public official in charge of files or records. 4. work as a clerk.

clev er (klev′ər), 1. intelligent. 2. skillful in doing some particular thing. Mr. Jones is a clever carpenter. 3. showing skill or intelligence; as, a clever trick, a clever answer.

clev er ness (klev′ər nis), being clever; quickness of mind; skill; ability.

clew (klü), 1. a guide to the solving of a mystery or problem. 2. a ball of thread or yarn. The old legend is that a clew was used as a guide out of a maze.

click (klik), 1. a short, sharp sound like that of a key turning in a lock. We heard the click as he cocked his pistol. 2. make such a sound. The soldier clicked his heels together and saluted.

cli ent (klī′ənt), 1. person for whom a lawyer acts. 2. customer.

cliff (klif), a high, steep rock.

cli mate (klī′mit), 1. the kind of weather a place has. Climate includes conditions of heat and cold, moisture and dryness, clearness and cloudiness, wind and calm. 2. a region with certain conditions of heat and cold, rainfall, wind, sunlight, etc. The doctor ordered him to go to a drier climate.

cli max (klī′maks), the highest point of interest; the most exciting part. We had had two punctures and a blowout, but the climax came when both front wheels fell off.

climb (klīm), 1. go up; as, to climb a hill, to climb a ladder. 2. grow up. A vine climbs by twining about a support of some kind. 3. the act of going up. Our climb took two hours. 4. go in any direction, especially with the help of the hands. He climbed down the rope.

clime (klīm), country; region; climate. Let us go to a sunny clime.

clinch (klinch), 1. fasten (a driven nail) by bending down the point. 2. fasten firmly; settle decisively. A deposit of five dollars clinched the bargain. 3. hold on tight in fighting or wrestling. 4. act of clinching.

cling (kling), stick or hold fast. A vine clings to its support. Wet clothes cling to the body. The child clung to his mother's skirt. We cling to the beliefs of our fathers. **clung** is formed from **cling.**

clink (klingk), 1. a light, sharp, ringing sound, like that of glasses hitting together. 2. make a sharp, ringing sound. The spoons and glasses clinked. 3. cause to clink. Baby likes to clink two spoons.

clink er (klingk′ər), large, rough cinder.

clip[1] (klip), 1. cut; cut short; trim with shears or scissors; as, to clip the hair, to clip the fleece of sheep. 2. cut a person's hair; cut the hair of a horse or dog; cut the fleece of a sheep. The dog has been clipped too short. 3. the amount of wool clipped from a sheep or flock of sheep. 4. a rapid motion.

clip[2] (klip), 1. hold or grip tightly; as, to clip papers together. 2. thing used for clipping. A clip for papers is often made of a piece of bent wire.

clip per (klip′ər), 1. an instrument for clipping; as, hair clippers, a nail clipper. 2. a fast sailing ship. American clippers used to sail all over the world.

Clippers for bushes

clip ping (klip′ing), piece cut out of a newspaper, magazine, etc.

clique (klēk), small, exclusive group of people.

cloak (klōk), 1. loose outer garment with or without sleeves. 2. to cover with a cloak. 3. anything that covers or hides. 4. hide. He cloaked his evil purpose under friendly words.

Man wearing a cloak

clock[1] (klok), instrument for measuring and showing time. A clock is not made to be carried about as a watch is.

clock[2] (klok), ornament on each side of a stocking, extending from the ankle up.

clock work (klok′wėrk′), machinery of a clock or like that of a clock. Toys that move are often run by clockwork.

clod (klod), 1. lump of earth. 2. stupid person.

clog (klog), 1. fill up; choke up. Grease clogged the drainpipe. 2. hinder. Heavy clothes clogged the swimmer. 3. any weight or other thing that hinders. 4. a shoe with a wooden sole.

clois ter (klois′tər), 1. a covered walk having one side walled and the other with windows or rows of pillars, built in a part of a church, college, or convent. 2. convent or monastery. 3. a quiet place shut away from the world. 4. shut away in a quiet place.

Cloister

close[1] (klōz), 1. shut. 2. bring together. 3. come together. 4. bring to an end. 5. an end.

close[2] (klōs), 1. with little space. 2. with little fresh air. 3. near. 4. nearly equal. 5. stingy.

close ly (klōs′li), 1. with little difference; almost the same. 2. snugly; tightly. Her coat fits closely.

close ness (klōs′nis), 1. narrowness. 2. lack of fresh air. 3. nearness. 4. stinginess.

clos et (kloz′it), 1. a small room used for storing clothes or household supplies, such as canned fruits, china, or linen. 2. a small, private room for prayer, study, or interviews with people. 3. shut up in a room for a secret talk. He was closeted with the lawyer for over an hour.

clot (klot), 1. half-solid mass; as, a clot of blood. 2. form into clots. Milk clots when it becomes sour. The cream had clotted, but we ate it all.

cloth (klôth), 1. Cloth is made in sheets or webs from wool, silk, linen, cotton, or other fiber. Cloth is used for clothing, curtains, bedding, and many other purposes. 2. piece of cloth used for a special purpose; as, a cloth for the table, a dishcloth, a washcloth.

clothe (klōᴛʜ), 1. put clothes on; cover with clothes; dress. 2. provide with clothes. 3. cover. The trees are clothed in green leaves. We clothe our thoughts in words. 4. provide; furnish; equip. A policeman is clothed with the authority of the government. **clothing** and **clad** are formed from **clothe.**

clothes (klōz or klōᴛʜz), coverings for the body. Lucy has pretty clothes.

cloth ing (klōᴛʜ′ing), clothes.

cloud (kloud), 1. a white or gray or almost black mass in the sky, made up of tiny drops of water. Sometimes when it rains, the sky is completely covered with dark clouds. 2. a mass of smoke or dust in the air. 3. cover with a cloud or clouds. 4. grow cloudy. The sky clouded over. 5. anything like a cloud; as, a cloud of arrows, a cloud of birds in flight. The dark veins in marble are sometimes called clouds. We may speak of a person as being under a cloud of disgrace or suspicion. 6. make dark; become gloomy. His face clouded with anger.

cloud less (kloud′lis), clear; bright; sunny; without a cloud.

cloud y (kloud′i), 1. covered with clouds; having clouds in it; as, a cloudy sky. 2. not clear; as, a cloudy liquid, cloudy ideas.

clout (klout), 1. cloth; rag. 2. the mark shot at in archery. 3. a shot that hits this. 4. a rap or knock. 5. hit.

clove (klōv), 1. strong, fragrant spice, made from the dried flower buds of a tree grown in the tropics. 2. the flavor of clove.

clo ven (klō′vən), split; divided into two parts. Cows have cloven hoofs.

clo ver (klō′vər), a plant with leaves of three small leaflets and sweet-smelling rounded heads of red or white flowers. Clover is grown as food for horses and cattle and to make the soil better.

Clover

clown (kloun), 1. man who makes a business of making people laugh by tricks and jokes. The clowns in the circus were very funny. 2. act like a clown; play tricks and jokes; act silly. 3. awkward person with bad manners. That clown does not know how to behave.

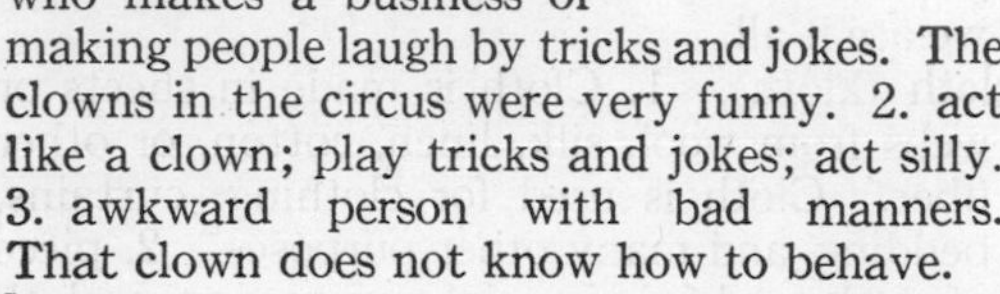

cloy (kloi), 1. weary by too much, too sweet, or too rich food. My appetite was cloyed by all the candy I had eaten. 2. weary by too much of anything pleasant.

club (klub), 1. a heavy stick of wood, thicker at one end, used as a weapon. 2. a stick or bat used in some games played with a ball; as, golf clubs. 3. beat with a club or something similar. 4. group of people joined together for some special purpose; as, a social club, tennis club, yacht club, scientific club. 5. the building or rooms used by a club. 6. combine for some purpose. The children clubbed together to buy their mother a plant for her birthday.

cluck (kluk), 1. the sound that a hen makes when calling to her chickens. 2. make such a sound.

clue (klü), a guide to the solving of a mystery or problem.

clump (klump), 1. a cluster; as, a clump of trees. 2. walk with a heavy, clumsy, noisy tread. The lame man clumps along.

clum sy (klum′zi), 1. awkward in moving. 2. not well-shaped or well-made. Jack's rowboat was a clumsy affair, for he had made it himself.

clung (klung), held fast. The child clung to her mother. The sticky mud had clung to my fingers.

clus ter (klus′tər), 1. a number of things of the same kind growing or grouped together; as, a cluster of grapes, a cluster of curls, a little cluster of houses. 2. be in a bunch; gather in a group. The girls clustered around their teacher.

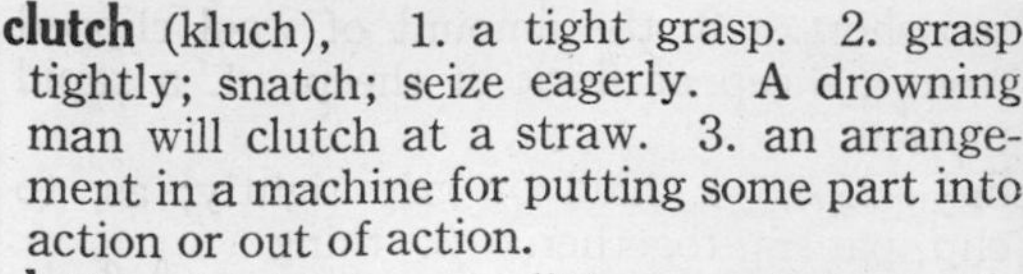

clutch (kluch), 1. a tight grasp. 2. grasp tightly; snatch; seize eagerly. A drowning man will clutch at a straw. 3. an arrangement in a machine for putting some part into action or out of action.

clut ter (klut′ər), 1. litter; confusion; disorder. 2. to litter with things. His desk was all cluttered with old papers, strings, and trash.

coach (kōch), 1. a large, old-fashioned, closed carriage with seats inside. Those which carried passengers along a regular run, with stops for meals and fresh horses, often had

Coach

seats on top too. 2. a passenger car of a railroad train. 3. a teacher. The football coach and the baseball coach are brothers. 4. train or teach.

coach man (kōch′mən), man who drives a coach or carriage for a living.

co ag u late (kō ag′ū lāt), change from a liquid to a thickened mass; thicken. Cooking coagulates the white of egg.

coal (kōl), 1. black mineral that burns and gives off heat. We use coal in our furnace. 2. a piece of glowing, partly burned, or burned material. The big log had burned down to a few red coals. 3. supply with coal. 4. take in a supply of coal. The ship stopped just long enough to coal.

coarse (kōrs), 1. not fine; made up of fairly large parts; as, coarse sand. 2. rough; as, coarse cloth. 3. common; poor; inferior; as, coarse food. 4. not delicate; crude; vulgar; as, coarse manners.

coarse ly (kōrs′li), in a coarse way.

coars en (kōr′sən), make coarse; become coarse.

coarse ness (kōrs′nis), coarse condition; vulgarity.

coast (kōst), 1. land along the sea; seashore. Many ships were wrecked on that rocky coast. 2. go along or near the shore of. We coasted South America on our trip last winter. 3. sail from harbor to harbor of a coast. 4. ride down a hill without using effort or power. 5. slide downhill on a sled.

coast al (kōs′təl), at the coast; along a coast; near a coast.

coat (kōt), 1. outer garment with sleeves. 2. any outer covering; as, a dog's coat, a coat of bark on a tree. 3. thin layer; as, a coat of paint. 4. cover or provide with a coat. 5. cover with a thin layer. The floor is coated with varnish. The pill is coated with sugar.

coat ing (kōt′ing), layer of any substance spread over a surface; as, a coating of paint.

coat of arms, a shield with pictures and designs on it. Each knight or lord had his own coat of arms.

coat of mail, garment made of metal rings or plates, worn as armor.

coax (kōks), persuade by soft words; influence by pleasant ways. She coaxed her father to let her go to the dance. I coaxed a smile from the baby. We coaxed the squirrel into his cage with peanuts.

cob (kob), 1. the central part of an ear of corn, on which the grains grow. 2. a strong horse with short legs.

cob ble (kob′əl), mend; repair; patch.

cob bler (kob′lər), 1. man whose work is mending shoes. 2. clumsy workman. 3. a fruit pie baked in a deep dish.

cob ble stone (kob′əl stōn′), a rounded stone that was formerly much used in paving.

co bra (kō′brə), a very poisonous snake, found most often in India.

cob web (kob′web′), 1. a spider's web, or the stuff it is made of. 2. anything thin and slight or entangling like a spider's web.

Cobweb

cock[1] (kok), 1. a male chicken; a rooster. 2. a male bird; as, a turkey cock. 3. a faucet used to turn the flow of a liquid or gas on or off. 4. the hammer of a gun. 5. the position the hammer is in when it is pulled back ready to fire. 6. pull back the hammer of (a gun), ready to fire.

cock[2] (kok), 1. turn or stick up, especially as if to defy. The little bird cocked his eye at me. 2. an upward turn or bend of the nose or eye. 3. the turn of the brim of a hat.

cock[3] (kok), 1. a small, round pile of hay that rises to a point at the top. 2. pile in cocks.

cock le (kok′əl), 1. a small shellfish that is good to eat. 2. its shell. 3. a small, light, shallow boat.

cock pit (kok′pit′), small, open place in an airplane, boat, etc., where the pilot or passengers sit.

Coco palm

co co or **co coa**[1] (kō′kō), a tall palm tree on which coconuts grow.

co coa[2] (kō′kō), 1. a powder made from the seeds of the cacao tree that tastes much like chocolate. 2. a drink made from this powder with sugar and milk or water.

co co nut or **co coa nut** (kō′kənut′), the large, round, brown, hard-shelled fruit of the coco palm. Coconuts have a white lining that is good to eat and a white liquid called coconut milk. The white lining is cut up into shreds and used for cakes, puddings, and pies.

Half of a coconut

co coon (kəkün′), silky case or shell made by worms and caterpillars to live in while they are turning into moths or butterflies.

Cocoons of: B, butterfly; S, silkworm.

cod (kod), an important food fish found in the cold parts of the northern Atlantic Ocean.

cod dle (kod′əl), 1. treat tenderly; pamper. Sick children are often coddled. 2. cook in hot water without boiling; as, a coddled egg.

code (kōd), 1. a collection of the laws of a country arranged in a clear way so that they can be understood and used. 2. any set of rules. 3. a system of military or naval signals. 4. an arrangement of words or figures to keep a message short or secret. 5. arrangement of long and short sounds used in telegraphing. 6. translate into a code.

co erce (kōėrs′), compel; force. Dick was coerced into learning to dance.

cof fee (kôf′i), 1. a common drink. 2. the seeds from which the drink is made. Coffee is roasted and ground. 3. the tree or shrub whose seeds are used to make coffee.

Coffee: A, branch; B, seed.

cof fer (kôf′ər), a box, chest, or trunk, especially one used to hold money or other valuable things.

cof fin (kôf′in), a box in which a dead person is put to be buried.

coil (koil), 1. wind round and round into a pile, a tube, or a curl. A snake can coil itself up or coil around a branch. A wire spring is evenly coiled. 2. anything that is coiled; as, a coil of rope. One wind or turn of a coil is a single coil. 3. a wire wound round and round into a spiral for carrying electric current.

Coil of pipe in a heater

coin (koin), 1. piece of metal stamped by the government for use as money. Pennies, nickels, dimes, and quarters are coins. 2. metal money. 3. make (money) by stamping metal. 4. make (metal) into money. 5. make up; invent; as, to coin a new word or phrase.

coin age (koin′ij), 1. the making of coins. 2. coins. 3. system of coins. 4. making or inventing. The coinage of new words in connection with radio has gone on very fast.

co in cide (kō′in sīd′), 1. occupy the same place in space. If these triangles △△ were placed one on top of the other, they would coincide. 2. occupy the same time. The working hours of Mr. Adams and Mr. Black coincide. 3. be just alike; correspond exactly. Her opinion coincides with mine.

co in ci dence (kō in′si dəns), 1. exact correspondence; agreement; especially, the chance occurrence of two things at such a time as to seem remarkable, fitting, etc. My cousin was born on the very same day that I was. Isn't that a coincidence? 2. a coinciding; occupying the same time or place.

coke (kōk), the black substance that is left after coal has been heated in an oven from which most of the air has been shut out.

cold (kōld), 1. much less warm than the body. Snow and ice are cold. 2. less warm than it usually is. This coffee is cold. 3. coldness; being cold. Warm clothes protect against the cold of winter. 4. a common sickness that causes a running at the nose and a sore throat. **Catch cold** means become sick with a cold. 5. not kind and cheerful.

cold-blood ed (kōld′blud′id), 1. having blood that is about as cold as the air or water around the animal. Turtles are cold-blooded; dogs are warm-blooded. 2. lacking in feeling; cruel.

cold cream, a simple, white oily preparation to put on the skin to make it feel better or be smoother or softer.

cole (kōl), a plant somewhat like cabbage.

col lapse (kə laps′), 1. fall in; shrink together suddenly. The little chair collapsed when my uncle sat down on it. 2. falling in. Six people were killed by the collapse of the building. 3. break down; fail suddenly. Both his health and his business collapsed within a year. 4. breakdown; failure.

Collar of a shirt

col lar (kol′ər), 1. the part of a coat, a dress, or a shirt that makes a band around the neck. See the picture. 2. a separate band of linen, lace, or other material worn around the neck. 3. a leather or metal band for a dog's neck. 4. a leather roll for a horse's neck to bear the weight of the loads he pulls. 5. any of the various kinds of rings, bands, or pipes in machinery. 6. put a collar on. 7. seize by the collar; capture.

Collar for machinery

col league (kol′ēg), associate; fellow worker.

col lect (kə lekt′), 1. bring together; come together. Do you collect stamps? Dust collects under beds. A crowd collects when there is an accident. 2. ask and receive pay for (debts, bills, dues, or taxes).

col lec tion (kə lek′shən), 1. bringing together; coming together. The collection of these stamps took ten years. 2. a group of things gathered from many places and belonging together. The library has a large collection of books. 3. money gathered from people; as, to take up a collection in church. 4. mass; heap.

col lec tor (kə lek′tər), person or thing that collects. Mr. Gray is a tax collector.

col lege (kol′ij), 1. a school that gives degrees. 2. school.

col lide (kə līd′), 1. rush against; hit or strike hard together. In running around the corner, John collided with another boy. 2. clash; conflict.

col lie (kol′i), an intelligent kind of dog used for tending sheep and as a pet.

col li sion (kə lizh′ən), 1. violent rushing against; hitting or striking hard together. Eight people were killed in the automobile collision. 2. clash; conflict.

Collie (about 2 ft. high at the shoulder)

co logne (kə lōn′), fragrant liquid, not so strong as perfume.

col o nel (kėr′nəl), officer who commands a regiment of soldiers.

co lo ni al (kə lō′ni əl), 1. of a colony; having something to do with colonies. 2. having something to do with the thirteen British colonies which became the United States of America. 3. person who lives in a colony.

col o nist (kol′ə nist), 1. person who helped to found a colony. 2. person who lives in a colony; settler. The first colonists in New England suffered from cold and hunger.

col o ni za tion (kol′ə ni zā′shən), the establishment of a colony or colonies. The English, French, and Spanish took part in the colonization of North America.

col o nize (kol′ə nīz), establish a colony in. The English colonized New England.

col o ny (kol′ə ni), 1. a group of people who leave their own country and go to settle in another land, but who still remain citizens of their own country. 2. the settlement made by such a group of people. 3. territory distant from the country that governs it. 4. group of people of one country or occupation living in their own part of a city. There is a Chinese colony in San Francisco. There is a colony of artists in Paris. 5. group of animals or plants of the same kind, living or growing together. We found two colonies of ants under the steps.

col or (kul′ər), 1. Red, yellow, blue, green, purple, etc., are colors. 2. give color to; put color on; change the color of. 3. paint; stain; dye. 4. outward appearance. His story has some color of truth. 5. change to give a wrong idea. The dishonest general colored his report of the battle. 6. **The colors** often means the flag.

col ored (kul′ərd), 1. having color. 2. belonging to some other race than the white. 3. of the Negro race. See also **color.**

col or ful (kul′ər fəl), picturesque; vivid.

col or ing (kul′ər ing), 1. way in which something is colored. 2. substance used to color. 3. false appearance. He lies with a coloring of truth.

col or less (kul′ər lis), 1. without color. 2. not vivid; not interesting; as, a colorless person.

co los sal (kə los′əl), huge; gigantic; vast.

colt (kōlt), young horse, donkey, etc.

Co lum bi a (kə lum′bi ə), 1. a river flowing between Washington and Oregon into the Pacific Ocean. 2. a name for the United States.

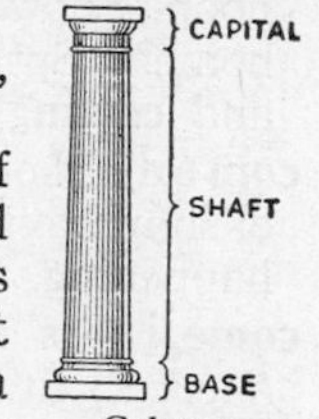

Column

col umn (kol′əm), 1. a slender, upright structure; a pillar. Columns are usually made of stone, wood, or metal, and used as supports or ornaments to a building. 2. anything that seems slender and upright like a column. A column of smoke rose from the fire. You add a column of figures. 3. soldiers or ships following one another in a single line. 4. slender part of a page reading from top to bottom, separated by lines or by blank spaces. This page has two columns. Some newspapers have eight columns to a page. 5. part of a newspaper used for a special subject or written by a special writer; as, the children's column.

Comb for hair

comb (kōm), 1. a narrow, short piece of metal, rubber, some plastic, etc., with teeth, used to arrange or clean the hair or to hold it in place. 2. anything shaped or used like a comb, especially an instrument for combing wool. 3. clean; take out tangles in; arrange with a comb. You comb your hair every morning. 4. search through. We had to comb the whole city before we found our lost dog. 5. the thick, red, fleshy piece on top of the head of chickens and some other fowls. 6. the arrangement of cells made by bees, in which they store honey.

Comb of rooster

Honeycomb

com bat (kom′bat), fight; struggle; battle.

com bat ant (kom′bə tənt), 1. a fighter. The two combatants let loose of one another to take breath. 2. fighting. A good football team has a combatant spirit.

com bi na tion (kom′bi nā′shən), 1. a combining or being combined; union. 2. one whole made by combining two or more different things. 3. a united set of things or persons. The farmers are forming a combination to market their goods at better prices.

com bine (kəm bīn′), join together.

com bus tion (kəm bus′chən), act or process of burning. We heat houses by the combustion of coal. The body does work by the slow combustion of food.

come (kum). Two boys have come; the others will come soon. The train comes at noon. Snow comes in winter. Are you coming home? Spring came late this year. **came** and **coming** are formed from **come.**

com e dy (kom′ə di), 1. a light, amusing play or show having a happy ending. 2. an amusing happening.

come li ness (kum′li nis), 1. pleasant appearance. 2. fitness; suitable behavior; propriety.

come ly (kum′li), pleasant to look at.

com er (kum′ər), one who comes. First comers will be served first.

com et (kom′it), a heavenly body with a shining point and often with a tail of light. Comets move around the sun like planets, but in a long oval course. We can see comets only when they come close to the earth.

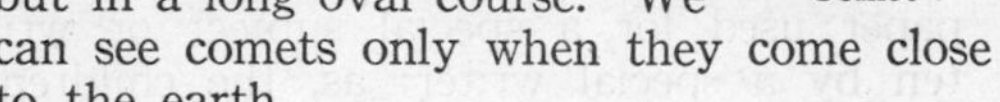

Comet

com fort (kum′fərt), 1. ease the grief or sorrow of. Her mother's words of love and help comforted the sobbing child. 2. anything that makes trouble or sorrow easier to bear; as, to bring comfort to a suffering family. 3. person or thing that makes life easier or takes away hardships. My sister is a great comfort to me. 4. ease; freedom from hardships; as, to live in comfort.

com fort a ble (kum′fər tə bəl), 1. giving comfort; as, a comfortable chair or room. 2. in comfort; at ease; free from pain or hardship. A warm fire makes you feel comfortable after a cold day outdoors. I feel comfortable about Mary now that she is with you.

com fort a bly (kum′fər tə bli), in a comfortable manner; easily.

com fort er (kum′fər tər), 1. person who makes pain and sorrow easier to bear; person who brings help and cheer in time of trouble. 2. a padded covering for a bed. 3. a long woolen scarf.

com ic (kom′ik), 1. amusing; funny. 2. funny story told by pictures. 3. any story told by pictures. 4. of comedy; in comedies.

com i cal (kom′i kəl), amusing; funny. A story or an action which makes you laugh is comical.

com ing (kum′ing), 1. approach; arrival. 2. approaching; next.

com ma (kom′ə), a mark (,) of punctuation.

com mand (kə mand′), 1. order; bid; direct. The captain commanded the men to fire. 2. an order; a bidding. "Halt!" was the sentry's command. 3. be in authority over; have power over; be master of. The captain commands his ship. The general commands the army. 4. possession of authority; power; control. The general is in command of the army. 5. body of troops or district under a commander. The captain knew every man in his command. 6. control by position; overlook. The fortress commanded the plain beneath. The house stood on a hill commanding the sea. 7. be able to have and use. He cannot command so large a sum of money. 8. ability to have and use. "She has an excellent command of English" means that she speaks it unusually well. 9. deserve and get. Such sufferings command our sympathy. Food commands a higher price when it is scarce.

com mand er (kə man′dər), 1. person who commands. Anyone who has people or supplies under his control is the commander of them. 2. officer in charge of an army or a part of an army. 3. in the navy, officer ranking next below a captain.

com mand ment (kə mand′mənt), a law; especially, one of the ten laws of Moses in the Old Testament. "Thou shalt not kill" is one of the Ten Commandments.

com mem o rate (kə mem′ə rāt), preserve the memory of. Christmas commemorates Christ's birth.

com mence (kə mens′), begin.

com mence ment (kə mens′mənt), 1. beginning; start. 2. the day or the ceremonies during which diplomas, certificates, etc., are given by colleges and schools to persons who have completed certain work.

com mend (kə mend′), 1. praise. 2. hand over for safe keeping. She commended the child to her aunt's care.

com men da tion (kom′ən dā′shən), praise.

com ment (kom′ent), 1. a note or remark that explains, praises, or finds fault with a book, a person, or a thing. 2. write notes or remarks that explain, praise, or find fault (with a book, a play, a concert, etc.). 3. make remarks (about persons or things). We all noticed the cut on Jack's face, but no one dared to comment on it.

com merce (kom′ərs), trade; buying and selling in large amounts between different places.

com mer cial (kə mėr′shəl), 1. having something to do with trade or business. 2. made to be sold.

com mis sion (kə mish′ən), 1. a written paper giving certain powers, privileges, and duties. My brother has just received his commission as lieutenant in the army. 2. give (a person) the right, the power, or the duty (of doing something). The club commissions one of its members to buy supplies. 3. the thing a person is trusted to do; errand. Mary gave me the commission of selecting a birthday present for her mother. 4. a group of persons appointed or elected with authority to do certain things. The President can appoint a commission to find out why food costs so much. 5. committing; as, the commission of a crime. 6. put into active service; make ready for use; as, to commission a warship. 7. **In commission** means in working order. I must get my broken bicycle in commission again. **Out of commission** means not in working order.

com mis sion er (kə mish′ən ər), 1. member of a commission. 2. person in charge of some public department; as, a police commissioner. Some counties have road commissioners.

com mit (kə mit′), 1. hand over for safe keeping. Commit yourself to the doctor's care; commit a poem to memory; commit a thought to writing; commit a thief to prison. 2. perform; do (something wrong); as, to commit a crime. 3. bind or involve (oneself); pledge. I have committed myself now and cannot draw back.

com mit tee (kə mit′i), group of persons appointed or elected to do some special thing. Our club has a committee on entertainments.

com mo di ous (kə mō′di əs), roomy.

com mod i ty (kə mod′i ti), anything that is bought and sold. Groceries are commodities.

com mon (kom′ən), 1. belonging equally to all. The house is the common property of the three brothers. 2. general; of all; from all; by all. By common consent of the class, Dick was chosen for president. 3. public; generally known. Throwing garbage into the street is a common nuisance. 4. often met with; usual. Snow is common in cold countries. 5. without rank. A common soldier is a private. 6. below ordinary; mean; low. 7. land owned or used by all the people of a village, etc. 8. **In common** means equally with another or others; owned, used, done, etc., by both or all.

com mon ly (kom′ən li), usually; generally. Arithmetic is commonly taught in schools.

com mon place (kom′ən plās′), 1. everyday thing. The commonplaces of our civilization, from watches to automobiles, are objects of wonder to savages. 2. ordinary remark. 3. ordinary; not new or interesting.

com mon wealth (kom′ən welth′), 1. the citizens of a state. 2. a state in which the people make the laws; a republic. The United States is a commonwealth. 3. one of the 48 States of the United States.

com mo tion (kə mō′shən), violent movement; confusion; tumult; noisy moving about; disturbance.

com mune (kə mūn′), talk in an intimate way.

com mu ni cate (kə mū′ni kāt), 1. pass or transfer. A stove communicates heat to a room. 2. give (information or news) by speaking or writing. I asked your sister to communicate my wishes to you. 3. be connected. The dining room communicates with the kitchen.

com mu ni ca tion (kə mū′ni kā′shən), 1. giving information or news by speaking or writing. Communication with people who are deaf is difficult. 2. the information or news given; letter, message, etc., which gives information or news. Your communication came in time to change all my plans. 3. passage; means of going from one to the other. There is no communication between these two rooms.

com mun ion (kə mūn′yən), 1. exchange of thoughts and feelings; fellowship. 2. quiet talk between persons who are dear to one another or are devoted to the same purpose; spiritual conversation. 3. **The Communion** is the celebration of the Lord's Supper.

com mu ni ty (kə mū′ni ti), 1. the people of any district or town. This lake provides water for six communities. 2. a group of people living together; as, a community of monks. 3. the public; as, the approval of the community. 4. ownership together; sharing together; as, community of food supplies, community of ideas.

com mute (kə mūt′), 1. exchange; substitute. 2. change (an obligation, penalty, etc.) for an easier one. The governor commuted the prisoner's sentence of death to one of life imprisonment.

com pact[1] (kəm pakt′), 1. closely and firmly packed together. The leaves of a cabbage are folded into a compact head. 2. using few words; brief.

com pact[2] (kom′pakt), agreement.

com pan ion (kəm pan′yən), 1. one who goes along with or accompanies another; one who shares in what another is doing. The twins were companions in work and play. 2. anything that matches or goes with another in kind, size, and color.

com pan ion a ble (kəm pan′yən ə bəl), fitted to be a companion; sociable; pleasant as a companion.

com pan ion ship (kəm pan′yən ship), being a companion; fellowship.

com pa ny (kum′pə ni), 1. group of people. A great company came to church. 2. group of people joined together for some purpose, such as carrying on a business or acting plays. 3. companions. You are known by the company that you keep. 4. companionship. 5. guest or guests; visitor or visitors. 6. the part of an army commanded by a captain. Major Reid led three companies against the enemy. 7. a ship's crew.

com pa ra ble (kom′pə rə bəl), 1. able to be compared. A fire is comparable with the sun; both give light and heat. 2. fit to be compared. A cave is not comparable to a house for comfort.

com par a tive (kəm par′ə tiv), 1. that compares. Fred made a comparative study of bees and wasps. 2. measured by comparison with something else. Screens give us comparative freedom from flies. 3. *Fairer*, *faster*, and *better* are the comparatives of *fair*, *fast*, and *good*.

com par a tive ly (kəm par′ə tiv li), by comparison; relatively; somewhat. Mountains are comparatively free from mosquitoes.

com pare (kəm pãr′), 1. find out or point out how persons or things are alike and how they are different. We compare one teacher with another. She compared several samples of silk for a dress. 2. liken; say (something) is like (something else). The fins of a fish may be compared to the legs of a dog. 3. **Cannot compare with** means cannot appear well when compared with. No artificial light can compare with daylight for general use.

com par i son (kəm par′i sən), 1. act of comparing; finding out the likenesses and the differences. The teacher's comparison of the heart to a pump helped the children to understand its action. 2. **In comparison with** means compared with. 3. **There is no comparison between them** means that one is plainly better than the other.

com part ment (kəm pärt′mənt), a separate division set off in any enclosed space. Your pencil box has several compartments for holding different things.

com pass (kum′pəs), 1. an instrument for showing directions, consisting of a needle that points to the magnetic north. 2. boundary; circumference. A prison is within the compass of its walls. 3. space within limits; area; extent; range. The old sailor had many adventures within the compass of his lifetime. 4. in music, the range of a voice or an instrument. 5. **Compasses** are an instrument for drawing circles and measuring distances. 6. go around; move around. 7. hem in; surround. 8. grasp with the mind.

Compass for showing directions

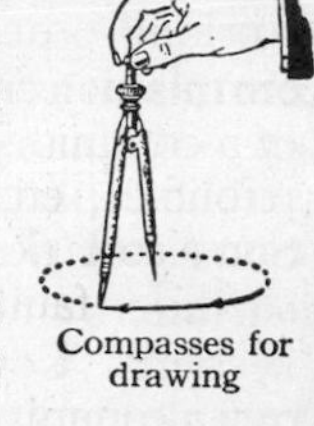
Compasses for drawing

com pas sion (kəm pash′ən), pity; feeling for another's sorrow or hardship that leads to help; sympathy.

com pas sion ate (kəm pash′ən it), pitying; wishing to help those that suffer.

com pel (kəm pel′), 1. force. The rain compelled us to stop our ball game. 2. bring about by force. A policeman can compel obedience.

com pen sate (kom′pən sāt), 1. make an equal return to; give an equivalent to. The hunters compensated the farmer for killing his cow by giving him a fine gun. 2. balance by equal weight or power; make up (for). Skill sometimes compensates for lack of strength. 3. pay. The company compensated Ruth for the extra work that she did.

com pen sa tion (kom′pən sā′shən), 1. something given to make up for something else; something which does make up for something else. Tom gave me a new knife as compensation for the one of mine he lost. 2. pay.

com pete (kəm pēt′), 1. try to win. John was competing against James for the prize in arithmetic. 2. take part (in a contest). Will you compete in the race?

com pe tent (kom′pi tənt), able; fitted. A competent cook gets high wages. A doctor should be competent to treat many diseases.

com pe ti tion (kom′pi tish′ən), rivalry; competing; trying to win or gain something for which others are trying at the same time. There is competition in many games.

com pet i tive (kəm pet′i tiv), 1. decided by

competition; using competition. A competitive examination for the job of postal clerk will be held January 10. 2. of competition; as, the competitive spirit.

com pet i tor (kəm pet′i tər), person who tries to win something for which others are trying at the same time; rival. There are many competitors for the United States golf championship.

com pile (kəm pīl′), 1. collect and bring together in one list or account. 2. make (a book, report, etc.) out of various materials.

com pla cen cy (kəm plā′sən si), 1. self-satisfaction. Grace solved the puzzle and smiled with complacency. 2. contentment.

com pla cent (kəm plā′sənt), pleased with oneself.

com plain (kəm plān′), 1. say something is wrong; find fault. 2. talk about one's pains, troubles, etc.

com plaint (kəm plānt′), 1. a complaining; finding fault. 2. accusation. 3. illness; disease. A cold is a very common complaint.

com ple ment (kom′pli mənt for 1 and 2, kom′pli ment for 3), 1. something that completes or makes perfect. 2. number required to fill. The ship now had its full complement of men, and no more could be taken on. 3. supply a lack of any kind; complete.

com plete (kəm plēt′), 1. with all the parts; whole; entire; as, a complete set of garden tools. 2. make whole or perfect; make up the full number or amount of. She completed her set of dishes by buying the cups and saucers. 3. perfect; thorough; as, a complete surprise. 4. finish. 5. finished.

com plete ly (kəm plēt′li), 1. entirely; wholly. 2. thoroughly; perfectly.

com ple tion (kəm plē′shən), 1. finishing; act of completing. After the completion of the job, the workman went home. 2. condition of being completed. The work is near completion.

com plex (kom′pleks), 1. made up of a number of parts. A complex sentence has one or more clauses besides the main clause. 2. complicated. The directions for reaching the house were so complex that we could not understand them. 3. strong prejudice. Mr. Pierce has a complex against foreigners.

com plex ion (kəm plek′shən), 1. the color, quality, and general appearance of the skin, particularly of the face. 2. general appearance; nature; character. The complexion of the war was changed by two great victories.

com plex i ty (kəm plek′si ti), a being complex. The complexity of the road map puzzled Tom.

com pli cate (kom′pli kāt), 1. mix up; make hard to understand or to settle. The fact that no two of us have the same hours free complicates the arrangement of a meeting of all five of us. 2. make worse or more mixed up. Her headaches were complicated by eye trouble.

com pli cat ed (kom′pli kāt′id), 1. mixed up; hard to understand; hard to settle. 2. made worse.

com pli ca tion (kom′pli kā′shən), 1. confused state of affairs hard to understand or settle. Such a complication of little rules and restrictions you never saw. 2. something that makes matters harder to untangle or settle.

com pli ment (kom′pli mənt for 1 and 3, kom′pli ment for 2), 1. something good said about you; something said in praise of your work. 2. pay a compliment to. He complimented my mother on the way she had trained her children. 3. **Compliments** sometimes means greetings.

com pli men ta ry (kom′pli men′tə ri), 1. expressing a compliment; praising. 2. given free. Father received two complimentary tickets to the circus.

com ply (kəm plī′), act in agreement with a request or a command. We should comply with the doctor's request. Father said, "Please turn down the radio," and we complied.

com pose (kəm pōz′), 1. make up. The ocean is composed of salt water. Our party was composed of three grown-ups and four children. 2. put together. To compose a story or poem is to construct it from words. To compose a piece of music is to invent the tune and write down the notes. To compose in a printing office is to set up type to form words and sentences. To compose a picture is to get an artistic arrangement of the things in it. 3. make calm. You look crazy; try to compose yourself.

com posed (kəm pōzd′), calm; quiet.

com pos er (kəm pōz′ər), 1. person who composes. 2. writer of music.

com pos ite (kəm poz′it), made up of various parts; compound.

com po si tion (kom′pə zish′ən), 1. the make-up of anything; what is in it. The composition of this candy includes sugar, chocolate, and milk. There is no meanness in his composition. 2. the putting together of a whole. Writing sentences, making pictures, and setting type in printing are all forms of composition. 3. thing composed, such as a piece of music, writing, etc.

com po sure (kəm pō′zhər), calmness; quiet; self-control.

com pound (kom′pound for 1, 2, and 3, kom pound′ for 4), 1. having more than one part. A palm leaf is a compound leaf. Steamship is a compound word. 2. a mixture. Many medicines are compounds. 3. a substance formed by chemical combination of two or more substances. Water is a compound of hydrogen and oxygen. 4. mix; combine. The man in the drug store compounds medicines and drinks.

com pre hend (kom′pri hend′), 1. understand. 2. include; contain.

com pre hen sion (kom′pri hen′shən), act or power of understanding. Philosophy is beyond the comprehension of most fourth-grade pupils.

com pre hen sive (kom′pri hen′siv), 1. including; including much. The term's work ended with a comprehensive review. 2. comprehending.

com press (kəm pres′ for 1, kom′pres for 2), 1. squeeze together; make smaller by pressure. Cotton is compressed into bales. 2. pad of wet cloth applied to the throat or other parts of the body in sickness; as, a cold compress, a hot compress.

com prise or **com prize** (kəm prīz′), consist of; include. The United States comprises 48 States.

com pro mise (kom′prə mīz), 1. settle (a quarrel or difference of opinion) by agreeing that each will give up part of what he demands. 2. settlement of a quarrel or a difference of opinion by a partial yielding on both sides. George and Tom both wanted the apple; their compromise was to share it. 3. put under suspicion. You will compromise your good name if you go around with thieves and liars.

com pul sion (kəm pul′shən), compelling; use of force. John can be made to take his medicine only by compulsion. A promise made under compulsion is not binding.

com pul so ry (kəm pul′sə ri), 1. compelled; required. Attendance at school is compulsory. 2. compelling; using force.

com pute (kəm pūt′), do by arithmetic; reckon; calculate. Mother computed the cost of our trip.

com rade (kom′rad or kom′rid), 1. companion and friend. 2. person who shares in what another is doing; partner; fellow worker. **Comrades at arms** means fellow soldiers.

con[1] (kon), 1. against. 2. a reason against. The pros and cons of a question are the arguments for and against it.

con[2] (kon), study; learn well enough to remember. The children were busy conning their lessons.

con ceal (kən sēl′), hide.

con ceal ment (kən sēl′mənt), 1. hiding. 2. means or place for hiding.

con cede (kən sēd′), 1. admit; admit as true. Everyone concedes that 2 and 2 make 4. 2. allow (a person) to have; grant. He conceded us the right to walk through his land.

con ceit (kən sēt′), too much pride in yourself or your ability to do things.

con ceit ed (kən sēt′id), having too high an opinion of oneself; vain.

con ceiv a ble (kən sēv′ə bəl), imaginable. We take every conceivable precaution against fire.

con ceive (kən sēv′), 1. form in the mind; think up; imagine. 2. have an idea or feeling; think.

con cen trate (kon′sən trāt), 1. bring together to one place. Our general concentrated his troops to attack the enemy's center. 2. make stronger. A concentrated solution of acid is one which has very much acid in it. 3. pay close attention. He concentrated upon the problem.

con cen tra tion (kon′sən trā′shən), 1. a concentrating. 2. close attention.

con cep tion (kən sep′shən), 1. conceiving; being conceived. 2. thought; notion; idea.

con cern (kən sėrn′), 1. have to do with; belong to. This letter concerns nobody but me. 2. Anything that touches or has to do with your work or your interests is your concern. 3. interest. We are all concerned about the school play. 4. troubled interest; anxiety. The mother's concern over her sick child kept her awake all night. 5. make anxious. 6. business company; firm. We wrote to two big concerns for their catalogues.

con cerned (kən sėrnd'), 1. interested. 2. troubled; anxious.

con cern ing (kən sėr'ning), about.

con cert (kon'sėrt), 1. musical entertainment. 2. agreement; harmony. 3. **In concert** sometimes means all together.

con ces sion (kən sesh'ən), 1. a conceding; a yielding. As a concession, mother let Nell stay up an hour longer. 2. anything conceded or yielded.

con cil i ate (kən sil'i āt), 1. win over; soothe. Mrs. Lee conciliated her cook with a present. 2. reconcile; bring into harmony.

con cise (kən sīs'), expressing much in few words; brief but full of meaning.

con clude (kən klüd'), 1. end. The book concluded happily. 2. reach (certain facts or opinions) by reasoning. We concluded that the animal must have been a deer. 3. settle; arrange. The two nations concluded a treaty of peace. 4. decide; resolve. I concluded not to go.

con clu sion (kən klü'zhən), 1. end; as, the conclusion of the story. A book or article often has a conclusion summing up all of the important points. 2. decision reached by reasoning. Jack came to the conclusion that he must work harder to succeed. 3. settlement; arrangement; as, the conclusion of a peace between two countries.

con clu sive (kən klü'siv), decisive; convincing; final.

con cord (kong'kôrd), agreement; peace; harmony.

con course (kong'kōrs), 1. running or coming together. The fort was built at the concourse of two rivers. 2. a crowd. 3. a place where crowds come.

con crete (kon'krēt or kon krēt'), 1. real; existing as an actual object. 2. a mixture of cement, sand or gravel, and water that hardens as it dries. Concrete is used for foundations, whole buildings, sidewalks, roads, dams, and bridges. 3. made of this mixture; as, a concrete sidewalk.

con cur (kən kėr'), 1. agree; be of the same opinion. The judges all concurred in giving John the prize. 2. work together. The events of the boy's life concurred to make him what he was. 3. come together.

con demn (kən dem'), 1. express strong disapproval of. We condemn cruelty and cruel people. 2. pronounce guilty of crime or wrong. The prisoner is sure to be condemned. 3. to doom; as, condemned to death. 4. declare not sound or suitable for use. This bridge has been condemned because it is no longer safe.

con dem na tion (kon'dem nā'shən), condemning; being condemned; as, the condemnation of a prisoner by a judge, the condemnation of an unsafe bridge.

con dense (kən dens'), 1. make denser; become more compact. 2. increase the strength of. Light is condensed by means of lenses. 3. change from a gas or a vapor to a liquid. If steam touches cold surfaces, it condenses into water. 4. put into fewer words. A long story can sometimes be condensed into a few sentences.

con dens er (kən den'sər), 1. person or thing that condenses something. 2. device for receiving and holding a charge of electricity.

con de scend (kon'di send'), come down willingly or graciously to the level of one's inferiors in rank. The king condescended to eat with the beggars.

con di tion (kən dish'ən), 1. state in which a person or thing is. The condition of John's health kept him from going to camp. 2. put in good condition. This man conditions dogs for dog shows. 3. rank in society. Lincoln's parents were people of humble condition. 4. thing on which something else depends; thing without which something else cannot be. Ability is one of the conditions of success. 5. to subject to a condition. The gift to the boy was conditioned on his good behavior. 6. **On condition that** means if.

con di tion al (kən dish'ən əl), depending on something else. "You may go if the sun shines" is a conditional promise.

con dor (kon'dər), large vulture with a bare neck and head.

Condor (4 ft. long; wingspread 9 ft.)

con duct (kon'dukt for 1, kən dukt' for 2, 3, 4, and 5), 1. action; way of acting or guiding oneself; behavior thought of as good or bad. 2. **Conduct oneself** means behave or act. 3. guide or lead. Conduct me to your teacher. 4. manage; direct. He conducts an orchestra of fifty instruments. Mr. Jones conducts a big business. 5. be a channel for. Metals conduct heat and electricity.

con duc tor (kən duk′tər), 1. guide or leader; one who is conducting. The conductor of an orchestra or chorus trains the performers to work together, selects the music to be used, and beats time for the orchestra. 2. person in charge of passengers on a train, a streetcar, or a bus. 3. thing that transmits heat, sound, or electricity. Copper wire is used as a conductor of electricity.

cone (kōn), 1. a solid object that has a flat, round base and narrows to a point at the top. 2. anything shaped like a cone; as, an ice-cream cone, the cone of a volcano. 3. part that bears the seeds on pine, cedar, fir, and other evergreen trees.

Cone

Cone of fir Cone of pine

con fed er a cy (kən fed′ər ə si), a union of countries or states; a group of people joined together for a special purpose.

con fed er ate (kən fed′ər it), 1. joined together for a special purpose. 2. person or state joined with another for a special purpose, usually a bad one. The thief and his confederates escaped to another city.

Con fed er ate (kən fed′ər it), a person who fought for the South in the Civil War.

con fed er a tion (kən fed′ər ā′shən), 1. confederacy. 2. league; alliance.

con fer (kən fėr′), 1. consult; talk the matter over; take counsel. The teacher conferred with the principal about Dick's promotion. 2. bestow. **Confer on** means give to. The school confers a medal on any student who is not absent a single day during the year.

con fer ence (kon′fər əns), a meeting of interested persons to discuss a particular subject. A conference was called to discuss the best way of getting a playground for the school.

con fess (kən fes′), 1. acknowledge; admit; own up. Ben confessed to eating all the cake. I confess you are right on one point. 2. admit one's guilt. 3. tell one's mistakes and sins, especially to a priest.

con fes sion (kən fesh′ən), 1. owning up; confessing; telling one's mistakes or sins. Confession is good for the soul. 2. thing confessed.

con fide (kən fīd′), 1. tell as a secret. 2. give to another to be kept safe. She confides her baby to the day nursery while she is at work. 3. put trust. Confide in God.

con fi dence (kon′fi dəns), 1. firm belief or trust. We have no confidence in a liar. 2. boldness. The little boy's confidence in the water startled his parents. 3. thing told as a secret. I listened to her confidences for half an hour.

con fi dent (kon′fi dənt), fully trusting; certain. I feel confident that our team will win.

con fi den tial (kon′fi den′shəl), 1. spoken or written as a secret matter. The detective made a confidential report. 2. trusted with secret matters. A confidential secretary should be discreet.

con fine (kən fīn′ for 1, kon′fīn for 2), 1. keep in; hold in. He was confined in prison for two years. A cold confined him to the house. 2. boundary; limit. These people have never been beyond the confines of their own valley.

con fine ment (kən fīn′mənt), 1. confining; being confined; as, confinement indoors on account of a cold. 2. imprisonment.

con firm (kən fėrm′), 1. make certain; make more certain by putting in writing, by consent, or by encouragement. The written order confirmed his telephone message. The treaty was confirmed by the senate. He was confirmed in his opinions by all his friends. 2. **Be confirmed** sometimes means be admitted to full membership in a church.

con fir ma tion (kon′fər mā′shən), 1. making sure by more evidence. 2. a religious ceremony of various Christian churches. A baby is baptized, and when he grows old enough to understand, his confirmation allows him to share in all the privileges of the church.

con firmed (kən fėrmd′), settled; firmly established; habitual; as, a confirmed invalid.

con fis cate (kon′fis kāt), 1. seize for the public treasury. The traitor's property was confiscated. 2. seize by authority; take and keep. The policeman confiscated the robber's pistol.

con fla gra tion (kon′flə grā′shən), a big fire, especially one which destroys buildings or forests.

con flict (kon′flikt for 1 and 2, kən flikt′ for 3), 1. a fight; a struggle. 2. active opposition of persons or ideas. A conflict of opinion arose over what food was best for our rabbit. 3. be opposed; clash; differ in thought and action.

con form (kən fôrm′), 1. act according to law or rule; be in agreement with generally accepted standards of business, law, conduct, or worship. 2. be like; make like. Her dress conformed to the pattern.

con form i ty (kən fôr′mi ti), 1. likeness. 2. action in agreement with generally accepted standards of business, law, conduct, or worship; fitting oneself and one's actions to the ideas of others.

con found (kon found′), confuse; perplex. To confound two things means not to be able to tell them apart.

con front (kən frunt′), 1. meet face to face; stand facing. 2. face boldly; oppose. 3. bring face to face; place before. We confronted the girl with the dish she had broken.

con fuse (kən fūz′), 1. mix up; throw into disorder. So many people talking to me at once confused me. 2. mistake (one thing for another). People often confuse Mary with her twin sister.

con fu sion (kən fū′zhən), 1. a mixed-up condition of things or of the mind. The confusion in the room showed that he had packed in a hurry. 2. mistaking one thing for another. Words like *believe* and *receive* sometimes cause confusion in spelling. 3. tumult; as, the confusion in a busy street.

con geal (kən gēl′), freeze; thicken as if frozen.

con gen ial (kən jēn′yəl), 1. having similar tastes and interests; getting on well together. Congenial companions made the trip pleasant. 2. agreeable; pleasing. He seeks more congenial work.

con gest ed (kən jes′tid), 1. crowded; filled too full. 2. too full of blood.

con grat u late (kən grach′u̇ lāt), express your pleasure at the happiness or good fortune of. I congratulated my friend on her birthday.

con grat u la tion (kən grach′u̇ lā′shən), congratulating; wishing a person joy; expression of pleasure at the happiness or good fortune of another.

con gre gate (kong′gri gāt), come together in a crowd or mass. Bits of steel congregate around the end of a magnet. Many children congregated around the Christmas tree.

con gre ga tion (kong′gri gā′shən), 1. a gathering of people. 2. a gathering of people for worship. 3. a coming together in a crowd or mass. There was a congregation of bees around the hive.

con gress (kong′gris), 1. coming together; meeting. 2. a meeting of representatives for the discussion of some subject. 3. **Congress,** the national lawmaking body of the United States, composed of the Senate and the House of Representatives, with members elected from every state.

con i cal (kon′i kəl), cone-shaped.

con jec ture (kən jek′chər), guess.

con junc tion (kən jungk′shən), 1. union; connection. A severe illness in conjunction with the hot weather has left the baby very weak. 2. a word that connects sentences, clauses, phrases, or words. *And, or, but, though,* and *if* are conjunctions.

con jure (kən jür′ for 1, kun′jər for 2 and 3), 1. make a solemn appeal to. By all that is holy, I conjure you not to betray your country. 2. compel to appear or disappear by a set form of words. Nowadays we do not try to conjure up spirits or devils. 3. perform tricks by very quick deceiving movements of the hands; juggle.

con nect (kə nekt′), 1. join one thing to another. 2. think of one thing with another. 3. join with others in some business or interest; have any kind of practical relation with. Mr. Davis is connected with several clubs.

con nec tion (kə nek′shən), 1. act of connecting. The connection of our telephone took two days. 2. being joined together or connected; union. 3. thing that connects; connecting part; bond; tie. 4. any kind of practical relation with another thing. I have no connection with my brother's firm. 5. meeting of trains, ships, etc., so that passengers can change from one to the other without delay. 6. related person; relative. She is a connection of ours by marriage.

con quer (kong′kər), overcome by force; get the better of; take in war. We can conquer an enemy, a bad habit, or a country.

con quer or (kong′kər ər), person who conquers.

con quest (kong′kwest), 1. conquering; as, the conquest of a country, the conquest of a bad habit. 2. thing conquered.

con science (kon′shəns), sense of right and wrong. Your conscience is the ideas and feelings within you which tell you what is wrong and keep you from doing it, and which tell you what is right and lead you to do it.

con sci en tious (kon′shi en′shəs), 1. careful to do what one knows is right; controlled by conscience. 2. done with care to make it right. Conscientious work is careful and exact.

con scious (kon′shəs), 1. knowing; having experience; aware. She was not conscious of his presence in the room. 2. able to feel. After an hour he became conscious again. 3. known to oneself. Talking is more often conscious than breathing is.

con scious ness (kon′shəs nis), 1. being conscious; awareness. The injured man did not regain consciousness for two hours. 2. all the thoughts and feelings of a person. Everything of which you are conscious makes up your consciousness.

con se crate (kon′si krāt), 1. set apart as sacred; make holy. A church is consecrated to worship. 2. devote to a purpose. A doctor's life is consecrated to keeping people well.

con sec u tive (kən sek′ū tiv), following one right after another. Monday, Tuesday, and Wednesday are consecutive days.

con sent (kən sent′), 1. agree. My father would not consent to my leaving school. 2. agreement; permission. We have mother's consent to go swimming.

con se quence (kon′si kwens), 1. result. The consequence of his fall was a broken leg. 2. importance. The loss of that old hat is a matter of no consequence.

con se quent (kon′si kwent), resulting; following as an effect. His long illness and consequent absence put him far behind in his work.

con se quent ly (kon′si kwent li), as a result; therefore.

con ser va tion (kon′sər vā′shən), preservation; avoidance of waste. The conservation of forests is very important.

con serv a tive (kən sėr′və tiv), 1. inclined to keep things as they are. A conservative person distrusts and opposes change and too many new ideas. 2. cautious. 3. person opposed to change.

con serve (kən sėrv′), 1. keep from harm or decay; keep from loss or from being used up; preserve. 2. fruit preserved in sugar; jam.

con sid er (kən sid′ər), 1. think about in order to decide. Take till tomorrow to consider this offer. 2. think to be; regard as. I consider him a very able man. 3. allow for; take into account. This watch runs very well, if you consider how old it is. 4. take thought for (the feelings of others).

con sid er a ble (kən sid′ər ə bəl), 1. worth thinking about; important. Ten dollars is a considerable sum of money. 2. not a little; much. A break in a pipe may cause considerable trouble.

con sid er a bly (kən sid′ər ə bli), much; a good deal. The boy was considerably older than he looked.

con sid er ate (kən sid′ər it), thoughtful of others and their feelings.

con sid er a tion (kən sid′ər ā′shən), 1. thinking about things in order to decide them. Please give careful consideration to this question. 2. something thought of as a reason. Price and quality are two considerations in buying anything. 3. **Take into consideration** means take into account; consider; make allowance for. 4. **In consideration of** means (1) in return for. (2) on account of. 5. money paid; any payment. Dishonest people will do anything for a consideration. 6. thoughtfulness for others and their feelings.

con sid er ing (kən sid′ər ing), taking into account; making allowance for. Considering his age, the little boy reads very well.

con sign (kən sīn′), 1. hand over; deliver. The man was consigned to prison. The father consigned the child to his sister's care. 2. transmit; send. We will consign the goods to Mr. Clark by express.

con sist (kən sist′), 1. be made up. A week consists of seven days. A chair consists of a seat with a back, supported by four legs. 2. **Consist in** means be contained in; be made up of.

con sist en cy (kən sis′tən si), 1. degree of firmness. Frosting for a cake must be of the right consistency to spread easily without dripping. 2. agreement. 3. keeping to the same principles, course, etc.

con sist ent (kən sis′tənt), 1. thinking or acting today in agreement with what you thought yesterday; keeping to the same principles and habits. 2. harmonious; agreeing. So much noise is not consistent with comfort.

con so la tion (kon′sə lā′shən), 1. comfort. 2. comforting person, thing, or event.

con sole[1] (kən sōl′), comfort.

con sole[2] (kon′sōl), 1. the keyboard, stops, and pedals of an organ. 2. radio cabinet made to stand on the floor. 3. bracket. 4. table made with brackets.

con so nant (kon′sə nənt), any letter of the alphabet that is not a vowel. B, c, d, and f are consonants.

con sort (kon′sôrt for 1 and 3, kən sôrt′ for 2), 1. a husband or wife. 2. associate. Do not consort with thieves. 3. a ship accompanying another.

con spic u ous (kən spik′ū əs), 1. easily seen. A traffic sign should be conspicuous. 2. remarkable; attracting notice. Lincoln is a conspicuous example of a poor boy who succeeded.

con spir a cy (kən spir′ə si), secret planning with others to do something wrong; plot. All those in the conspiracy were punished.

con spir a tor (kən spir′ə tər), person who conspires; one who joins in a plot. Conspirators planned to kill the king.

con spire (kən spīr′), 1. plan secretly with others to do something wrong; plot. Six wicked men conspired to kill the governor. 2. act together. All things conspired to make her birthday a happy one.

con sta ble (kon′stə bəl or kun′stə bəl), police officer.

con stan cy (kon′stən si), faithfulness; firmness in belief or feeling. We admire the constancy of Columbus in looking for a way around the earth.

con stant (kon′stənt), 1. always the same; not changing. 2. continually happening; as, the constant ticking of the clock. 3. faithful. A constant friend helps you when you need help.

con stant ly (kon′stənt li), 1. always; without change. 2. without stopping. 3. often; again and again.

con stel la tion (kon′stə lā′shən), a group of stars. The Big Dipper is the easiest constellation to locate.

con ster na tion (kon′stər nā′shən), dismay; paralyzing terror. To our consternation the train rushed on toward the burning bridge.

con stit u ent (kən stich′ü ənt), 1. forming a necessary part; making up. Flour, liquid, salt, and yeast are constituent parts of bread. 2. a part of a whole; a necessary part. Sugar is the main constituent of candy. 3. voter.

con sti tute (kon′sti tūt or kon′sti tüt), 1. make up; form. Seven days constitute a week. 2. appoint. We constituted him our captain. 3. set up; establish. Schools are constituted by law to teach boys and girls.

con sti tu tion (kon′sti tū′shən or kon′sti tü′shən), 1. the way in which anything is organized; nature; make-up. John has a very healthy constitution. 2. the fundamental principles according to which a country, a state, or a society is governed. Many clubs have written constitutions. The **Constitution** is the written constitution by which the United States is governed.

con sti tu tion al (kon′sti tū′shən əl or kon′sti tü′shən əl), 1. of or in a person's constitution or nature. A constitutional weakness makes George likely to have colds. 2. of the constitution. 3. walk taken for the health.

con strain (kən strān′), control by force; compel.

con straint (kən strānt′), 1. compelling; being compelled. 2. holding back of natural feelings.

con struct (kən strukt′), put together; fit together; build.

con struc tion (kən struk′shən), 1. act of constructing; building; putting together. The construction of the bridge took nearly a month. 2. way in which a thing is constructed. Cracks and leaks are signs of poor construction. 3. thing built or put together. The dolls' house was a construction of wood and cardboard. 4. arrangement of words in a sentence. 5. meaning; interpretation. She dislikes me and puts a bad construction upon everything I say or do.

con struc tive (kən struk′tiv), tending to construct; building up; helpful; as, a constructive suggestion.

con strue (kən strü′), show the meaning of; explain; interpret.

con sul (kon′səl), 1. an officer appointed by a government to live in some foreign city. A consul looks after the business interests of his own country and protects citizens of his country who are traveling or living there. 2. either of the two chief magistrates of the ancient Roman republic; a similar official.

con sult (kən sult′), 1. seek information or advice from. You can consult persons, books, or maps to find out what you wish to know. 2. take into consideration; have regard for. A good teacher consults the interests of her class.

con sume (kən süm′), 1. use up. Mary consumes much of her time in reading. 2. eat or drink up. Animals consume food. 3. destroy; burn up. A fire can consume a forest. 4. spend; waste (time, money, etc.).

con sum er (kən süm′ər), 1. person who uses food, clothing, or any article which a producer makes. A low price for wheat should reduce the price of flour to the consumer. 2. person or thing that uses up, makes away with, or destroys.

con sum mate (kon′sə māt for 1, kən sum′it for 2), 1. to complete; fulfill. John's happiness was consummated when his father let him drive the new car. 2. complete; perfect; in the highest degree. The expert pilot showed consummate skill.

con sum ma tion (kon′sə mā′shən), completion; fulfillment; perfection.

con sump tion (kən sump′shən), 1. using up; use. This food is for our consumption on the trip. 2. amount used up. The consumption of coal in that factory is five tons a day. 3. a disease that destroys parts of the lungs; tuberculosis.

con tact (kon′takt), 1. touch; a touching. To bring fire into contact with gasoline may cause an explosion. 2. place where things touch; connection.

con ta gion (kən tā′jən), 1. spreading disease by touching. 2. a disease spread in this way. 3. communication of any influence from one to another. A contagion of fear swept through the audience and caused a panic.

con ta gious (kən tā′jəs), 1. spreading by touch. Scarlet fever is contagious. 2. easily spreading from one to another. Yawning is often contagious.

con tain (kən tān′), 1. have within itself; hold as contents. My purse contains money. Books contain information. 2. be capable of holding. That pitcher will contain a quart of milk. 3. be equal to. A pound contains 16 ounces. 4. include. 5. control; hold back; restrain (one's feelings). He contained his anger. She could hardly contain herself when the boy kicked her dog.

con tain er (kən tān′ər), box, can, jar, etc., used to hold or contain something.

con tam i nate (kən tam′i nāt), defile; pollute; taint; corrupt. Flies contaminate food.

con tem plate (kon′təm plāt), 1. look at or think about for a long time. Fred contemplated the puzzle for ten minutes before he touched it. 2. have in mind; expect; intend. She is contemplating a change of work.

con tem pla tion (kon′təm plā′shən), looking at or thinking about something for a long time; deep thought.

con tem po rar y (kən tem′pə rãr′i), 1. belonging to the same period of time. 2. person who belongs to the same period of time. Lincoln and Lee were contemporaries.

con tempt (kən tempt′), 1. despising; scorn; feeling that a person or act is mean and low. We feel contempt for a sneak. 2. condition of being despised; disgrace. A cowardly traitor is held in contempt.

con tempt i ble (kən temp′ti bəl), mean; deserving contempt; that is scorned. A cowardly bully is contemptible.

con temp tu ous (kən temp′chü əs), showing contempt; scornful. The police dog gave the kitten a contemptuous look.

con tend (kən tend′), 1. fight; struggle. The first settlers in America had to contend with the Indians, sickness, and lack of food. Five runners were contending in the first race. 2. argue. Columbus contended that the earth was round.

con tent[1] (kon′tent), 1. what is contained in anything; as, the contents of the room, the contents of a container or holder of any kind. 2. what is written in a book; what is said in a speech. Did you agree with the content of the speech? 3. amount contained.

con tent[2] (kən tent′), 1. satisfy. Will it content you if I let you have the candy tomorrow? 2. satisfied; contented. Will you be content to wait till tomorrow? 3. contented state; satisfaction. Kitty lay stretched out beside the fire in sleepy content.

con tent ed (kən ten′tid), satisfied.

con ten tion (kən ten′shən), 1. quarreling; disputing. Contention has no place in the schoolroom. 2. a statement or point which one has argued for. Columbus's contention that the earth was round turned out to be correct.

con tent ment (kən tent′mənt), satisfaction; being pleased; happiness.

con test (kən test′ for 1, kon′test for 2), 1. dispute; struggle; fight. 2. a trial of skill. A game or race is a contest.

con test ant (kən tes′tənt), person who contests; person who takes part in a contest.

con ti nent (kon′ti nənt), 1. one of the six great masses of land on the earth. The continents are Europe, Asia, Africa, North America, South America, and Australia. 2. The mainland of Europe is often called **the Continent.**

con ti nen tal (kon′ti nen′təl), of a continent; like a continent.

con tin u al (kən tin′ū əl), 1. never stopping;

as, the continual flow of the river. 2. repeated many times; very frequent.

con tin u al ly (kən tin′ū əl i), 1. always; without stopping. 2. again and again; very frequently. Careless Jane is continually losing things.

con tin u ance (kən tin′ū əns), 1. going on; lasting; as, during the continuance of the war. 2. remaining; stay. His continuance in school depends on his health.

con tin u a tion (kən tin′ū ā′shən), 1. act of going on with a thing after stopping; a beginning again. Continuation of my work was hard after I had been ill for a month. 2. anything by which a thing is continued; added part. The continuation of the story will appear in next month's magazine.

con tin ue (kən tin′ū), 1. keep up; keep on; not stop; last; cause to last. The rain continued all day. 2. maintain; retain. Mr. Roosevelt was continued in office for four terms. 3. stay. The children must continue at school till July. Jack continues sullen. 4. take up; carry on. The story will be continued next month.

con tin u ous (kən tin′ū əs), connected; unbroken; without a stop; as, a continuous line, a continuous sound, continuous work, a continuous line of cars.

con tin u ous ly (kən tin′ū əs li), without stopping.

con tor tion (kən tôr′shən), 1. twisting. 2. twisted condition. The acrobat went through various contortions.

con tour (kon′tür), outline. The contour of the Atlantic coast of America is very irregular.

Contour of Lake Michigan

con tra band (kon′trə band), 1. against the law; prohibited. The sale of stolen goods is contraband in the United States. 2. trading contrary to law; smuggling. 3. smuggled goods.

con tract (kon′trakt for 1 and 2, kən trakt′ for 3, 4, 5, and 6), 1. an agreement. In a contract two or more people agree to do or not to do certain things. 2. a written agreement that can be enforced by law. 3. make a contract. A builder contracts to build a new house for a certain price. 4. form; start. Try not to contract bad habits. 5. draw together; make shorter; as, to

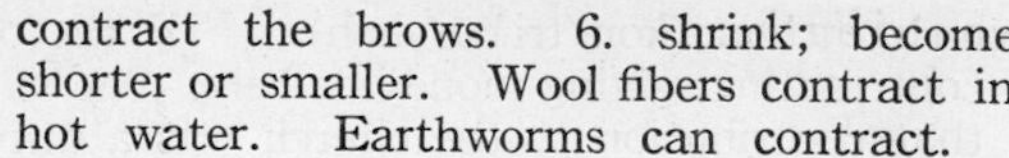

contract the brows. 6. shrink; become shorter or smaller. Wool fibers contract in hot water. Earthworms can contract.

con trac tion (kən trak′shən), 1. process of contracting. Cold causes the contraction of liquids, gases, metals, etc.; heat causes expansion. 2. state of being contracted. The contraction of mercury by cold makes it go down in thermometers. 3. something contracted; a shortened form. *Can't* is a contraction of *cannot.*

con trac tor (kon′trak tər or kən trak′tər), person who agrees to furnish materials or to do a piece of work for a certain price.

con tra dict (kon′trə dikt′), 1. deny; deny a statement. To contradict a statement is to say that it is not true. To contradict a person is to say the opposite of what he has said, or to say that his statement is not true. 2. be contrary to. Your story and your brother's story contradict each other.

con tra dic tion (kon′trə dik′shən), 1. denying what has been said. 2. a statement that contradicts. 3. disagreement.

con tra dic to ry (kon′trə dik′tə ri), contradicting; saying the opposite. Reports of the result of the battle were contradictory.

con tra ry (kon′trãr i), 1. opposed; opposite; completely different. My sister's taste in dresses is just contrary to my own. 2. the opposite. **On the contrary** sometimes means "No, the contrary is true." 3. opposing. A contrary boy often refuses to do what is suggested.

con trast (kon′trast for 1 and 2, kən trast′ for 3 and 4), 1. difference; a great difference. Anybody can see the contrast between black and white. There is a great contrast between life now and life a hundred years ago. 2. person, thing, event, etc., that shows differences when put side by side with another. Black hair is a sharp contrast to a light skin. 3. place (two things) side by side so as to show their differences. Contrast our climate with that of the tropics. 4. show differences when compared or put side by side. The black and the gold contrast well in that design.

con trib ute (kən trib′ūt), 1. give money or help. Will you contribute to the Red Cross? 2. write (articles, stories, etc.) for a newspaper or magazine. 3. **Contribute to** means help bring about. Poor food contributed to the child's illness.

con tri bu tion (kon′tri bū′shən), 1. act of contributing; giving money or help. She felt that contribution to the church was a duty and a pleasure. 2. money or help contributed; gift. Small contributions will be received with thanks. Her contribution to the picnic was a basket of apples. 3. something written for a newspaper or magazine.

con triv ance (kən trīv′əns), 1. thing invented; mechanical device. A can opener is a handy contrivance. 2. act or manner of contriving. By careful contrivance Fred made the old clock go. 3. plan; scheme.

con trive (kən trīv′), 1. invent; design. He contrived a new kind of engine. 2. plan; scheme; plot. 3. manage. I will contrive to be there by ten o'clock.

con trol (kən trōl′), 1. command; have in one's power. A captain controls his boat. Washington controlled the army. 2. power; authority. My oldest son is no longer under my control. 3. hold back. It is hard to control one's anger. 4. a holding back; a keeping down; restraint; check. He lost control of his temper. 5. device that controls a machine. The control of our furnace can be operated from the kitchen.

con tro ver sy (kon′trə vėr′si), a dispute; a long dispute; argument.

con vene (kən vēn′), 1. gather in one place; assemble. Congress convenes at least once a year. 2. call together.

con ven ience (kən vēn′yəns), 1. any thing or arrangement that is convenient. We find our folding table a great convenience. It will be a convenience if you can come to my house this time. 2. **At your convenience** means so as to be convenient for you. I will come any day at your convenience. 3. comfort; advantage. Many towns have camping places for the convenience of travelers by automobile.

con ven ient (kən vēn′yənt), 1. handy; suitable; saving trouble; well arranged; easy to reach or use. You can use a convenient tool, take a convenient bus, live in a convenient house, or meet at a convenient place. 2. easily done; done with advantage. Will it be convenient for you to bring your lunch to school?

con vent (kon′vent), 1. a group of women living together, who devote their lives to religion. 2. the building or buildings in which they live.

con ven tion (kən ven′shən), 1. a meeting arranged for some particular purpose. A political party holds a convention to choose candidates for public offices. 2. general consent; custom. Convention now permits short hair for women, but it used to be thought queer. 3. a custom or practice approved by convention. Using the right hand to shake hands is a convention. 4. an agreement.

con ven tion al (kən ven′shən əl), 1. depending on conventions; customary. "Good morning" is a conventional greeting. 2. formal; not natural; not original.

con ver sa tion (kon′vər sā′shən), talk.

con verse (kən vėrs′), talk.

con ver sion (kən vėr′zhən), 1. a change. Heat causes the conversion of water into steam. 2. a change from lack of belief to faith.

con vert (kən vėrt′ for 1 and 2, kon′vėrt for 3), 1. change; turn. These machines convert cotton into cloth. One last effort converted defeat into victory. 2. cause to change from lack of belief to faith. 3. person who has been converted.

con vey (kən vā′), 1. carry. A bus conveys passengers from the train to the boat. 2. communicate. Do my words convey any meaning to you? 3. give; make over; transfer. The old farmer conveyed his farm to his son.

con vey ance (kən vā′əns), 1. carrying; transmission; communication. Books are for the conveyance of ideas. 2. thing which conveys; vehicle; carriage. Railroad trains and busses are public conveyances. 3. transfer of property from one person to another.

con vict (kən vikt′ for 1 and 2, kon′vikt for 3), 1. prove guilty. 2. declare guilty. The prisoner was convicted of murder. 3. person serving a prison sentence for some crime.

con vic tion (kən vik′shən), 1. proving or declaring guilty. The trial resulted in the conviction of John Doe. 2. being proved or declared guilty. John Doe's conviction meant two years in prison for him. 3. firm belief. It was Lincoln's conviction that the Union must be preserved.

con vince (kən vins′), make (a person) feel sure; persuade firmly. The mistakes Nan made convinced me that she had not studied her lesson.

con voy (kon voi′ for 1, kon′voi for 2, 3, and 4), 1. go with and protect. Warships convoy merchant ships during time of war. 2. a convoying; protection. The gold was sent under convoy of troops. 3. thing that convoys. 4. thing that is convoyed.

con vulse (kən vuls′), 1. shake violently. 2. cause violent disturbance in. His face was convulsed with rage. 3. throw into convulsions. The sick child was convulsed before the doctor came. 4. throw into fits of laughter. The clown convulsed the audience with his funny acts.

con vul sion (kən vul′shən), 1. a violent contraction of the muscles; a fit. The sick child's convulsions frightened its mother. 2. a fit of laughter. 3. violent disturbance. An earthquake is a convulsion of the earth. A revolution is a convulsion in a nation.

con vul sive (kən vul′siv), 1. violently disturbing. 2. having convulsions. 3. producing convulsions.

coo (kü), 1. the soft, murmuring sound made by doves or pigeons. 2. make this sound. 3. murmur softly; speak in a soft, loving manner.

cook (kůk), 1. prepare (food) by using heat. We use coal, wood, gas, oil, and electricity for cooking. 2. undergo cooking; be cooked. Let the meat cook slowly. 3. person who cooks.

cook er y (kůk′ər i), cooking.

cook y or **cook ie** (kůk′i), a small, flat, sweet cake.

cool (kül), 1. somewhat cold; more cold than hot. 2. allowing or giving a cool feeling; as, a cool dress. 3. not excited; calm. 4. having little enthusiasm or interest; not cordial. I give beggars a cool reception. 5. something cool. 6. become cool. 7. make cool. 8. bold or impudent in a calm way.

coo lie or **coo ly** (kü′li), an unskilled laborer in China or India.

coon (kün), raccoon.

coop (küp), 1. a small cage or pen for chickens, rabbits, etc. 2. keep in a coop; confine. The children were cooped up indoors by the rain.

Chicken coop

coop er (küp′ər), man who makes or repairs barrels, tubs, casks, etc.

co öp er ate (kō op′ər āt), work together. The children coöperated with their teachers in keeping their rooms neat.

co öp er a tion (kō op′ər ā′shən), working together; united effort or labor. Coöperation can accomplish many things which no individual could do alone.

co öp er a tive (kō op′ər ā′tiv), wanting or willing to work together with others. John was the only child in the room who was not coöperative in keeping it neat.

cope (kōp), fight with some chance of success; struggle and not fail; get on successfully. Mother could not cope with all the housework and two sick children.

cop ied (kop′id). See **copy.**

co pi lot (kō pī′lət), pilot who works with another pilot.

co pi ous (kō′pi əs), plentiful; abundant.

cop per (kop′ər), 1. a reddish metal, easy to work with and hard to rust. Pennies were made of copper. 2. thing made of copper. 3. of copper; as, a copper kettle. 4. reddish brown.

cop per head (kop′ər hed′), a poisonous snake of the United States. It has a copper-colored head, and grows to be about three feet long.

Copperhead

copse (kops), a number of small trees or bushes growing together; a thicket or grove of small trees.

cop y (kop′i), 1. thing made to be just like another; thing made on the model of another. A written page, a picture, a dress, or a piece of furniture can be an exact copy of another. 2. make a copy of. Copy this page. She copied my hat. 3. be a copy of; be like; imitate. 4. something set or used as a pattern or model. 5. one of a number of books, of magazines, of pictures, etc., made at the same printing. Please get six copies of today's newspaper. 6. written material ready to be set in print in newspapers, magazines, or books.

cor al (kor′əl), 1. a hard red, pink, or white substance. Coral is made out of the skeletons of tiny sea animals. 2. the little sea animal which makes coral. It is mostly stomach and mouth. 3. deep pink or red.

cord (kôrd), 1. thick, well-made string; very thin rope. 2. fasten or tie up with a cord. 3. something resembling a cord. A pair of covered wires with fittings to connect an electric iron or lamp with a socket is a cord. 4. a measure of cut wood. A pile of wood 8 by 4 by 4 feet is a cord.

cor dial (kôr′jəl), sincere; hearty; warm; friendly.

cor dial i ty (kôr jal′i ti), cordial quality; cordial feeling; heartiness; warm friendliness. The cordiality of his welcome made Tom feel at home.

cor du roy (kôr′də roi), 1. thick cloth with close, raised ridges. 2. **Corduroys** is a name for corduroy trousers. 3. A **corduroy road** is one made of logs laid crosswise, often across low, wet land.

core (kōr), 1. the hard, central part containing the seeds of fruits like apples and pears. 2. the central or most important part. The core of the doctor's advice was that we should take care of our bodies. 3. take out the core of; as, to core apples.

cork (kôrk), 1. the light, thick, outer bark of a tree called the cork oak. Cork is used for bottle stoppers, floats for fishing lines, filling for some kinds of life preservers, and some floor coverings. 2. a shaped piece of cork; as, the cork of a bottle. 3. a stopper made of glass, rubber, etc. 4. stop up with a cork. Fill these bottles and cork them carefully.

cork screw (kôrk′skrü′), 1. tool used to pull corks out of bottles. 2. shaped like a corkscrew; spiral.

cor mo rant (kôr′mə rənt), a large, greedy sea bird with a long neck and a pouch under the beak for holding captured fish.

Cormorant (3 ft. long)

corn[1] (kôrn), 1. a grain or seed. 2. wheat, barley, rye, or oats. 3. a grain that grows on large ears; the plant it grows on. See the picture. Also called **maize** or **Indian corn.** 4. preserve (meat) with strong salt water or with dry salt. We boil corned beef and eat it with cabbage.

corn[2] (kôrn), a hardening of the skin with a tender sore spot. Shoes that do not fit properly often cause corns on the toes.

An ear of Indian corn

corn cob (kôrn′kob′), central, woody part of an ear of corn, on which the kernels grow.

corned (kôrnd), preserved with strong salt water or dry salt; as, corned beef.

cor ner (kôr′nər), 1. place where two lines or surfaces meet; as, the corner of a room. 2. place where two streets meet. 3. at a corner. 4. for a corner. 5. put in a corner; drive into a corner. 6. piece to protect a corner. The leather pocketbook has gold corners. 7. secret place; place away from crowds. The money was hidden in odd corners all over the house. 8. region; quarter; place that is far away; as, all the corners of the earth. 9. difficult place. His enemies had driven him into a corner. **Turn the corner** sometimes means pass the danger point. 10. force into a difficult position.

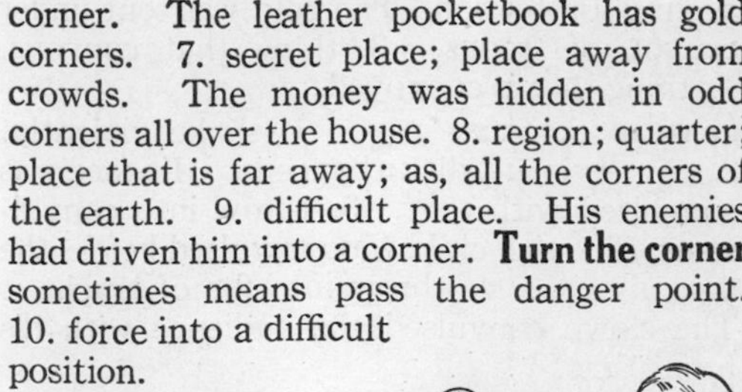

Boy playing a cornet

cor net (kôr net′), a musical wind instrument like a trumpet, usually made of brass.

cor nice (kôr′nis), molding along the top of a wall, pillar, or side of a building.

corn starch (kôrn′stärch′), a kind of flour made from corn, used to thicken puddings, custard, etc.

cor nu co pi a (kôr′nū kō′pi ə or kôr′nü kō′pi ə), 1. horn-shaped container or ornament. Cornucopias are hung on Christmas trees. 2. the horn of plenty, represented overflowing with fruits and flowers.

Cornucopia, or horn of plenty.

cor o na tion (kor′ə nā′shən), crowning (of a king or a queen).

cor o net (kor′ə net), 1. small crown worn as a mark of high rank. The king wears a crown; the prince, a coronet. 2. a circle of gold, jewels, or flowers worn around the head as an ornament.

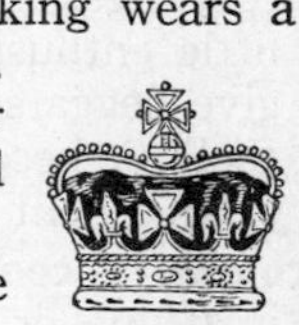

Coronet of the Prince of Wales

cor po ral[1] (kôr′pə rəl), of the body; as, corporal punishment.

cor po ral[2] (kôr′pə rəl), the lowest officer in the army. A corporal is higher than a private and lower than a sergeant. Most people do not think of corporals as officers.

cor po ra tion (kôr′pə rā′shən), a group of persons who obtain a charter giving them as a group certain rights and privileges. A corporation can buy, sell, etc., as if its members were a single person.

corps (kōr), 1. a division of an army; as, the Marine Corps, the Signal Corps. 2. group of people with special training, organized under a director. A large hospital has a corps of nurses. 3. (kōrz), more than one corps.

corpse (kôrps), a dead human body.

cor pu lent (kôr′pū lənt), fat.

cor pus cle (kôr′pus əl), 1. a very small particle. 2. any of the cells that form a large part of blood. Red corpuscles carry oxygen from the lungs to various parts of the body; some white corpuscles destroy disease germs.

Corral

cor ral (kə ral′), 1. pen for horses, cattle, etc. 2. drive into or keep in a corral. 3. hem in; surround; capture. We corralled the enemy's advance guard.

cor rect (kə rekt′), 1. true; right; as, the correct answer. 2. agreeing with a good standard of taste; proper; as, correct manners. 3. mark the mistakes in; change to what is right. Our teacher corrects our speech. 4. punish; set right by punishing; find fault with to improve.

cor rec tion (kə rek′shən), 1. a correcting; a setting right. The correction of all my mistakes took nearly an hour. 2. what is put in place of a mistake or an error. Write in your corrections neatly. 3. punishment. A prison is sometimes called a house of correction.

cor rect ly (kə rekt′li), in a correct manner; in the right way; without any errors.

cor re spond (kor′i spond′), 1. agree; be in harmony. Her white hat, shoes, and stockings correspond with her white dress. 2. agree in amount or position; be similar. Double doors usually correspond. 3. exchange letters; write letters to one another. Will you correspond with me while I am away?

cor re spond ence (kor′i spon′dəns), 1. agreement. Your account of the accident has little correspondence with the story John told. 2. exchange of letters; friendly letter writing. 3. letters. Bring me the correspondence concerning that order.

cor re spond ent (kor′i spon′dənt), 1. person who exchanges letters with another. Mabel and I have been regular correspondents for over two years; we write weekly. 2. person employed to send news from a distant place.

cor ri dor (kor′i dər), long hallway; passage in a large building into which rooms open; as, the corridor in a school.

cor rob o rate (kə rob′ə rāt), make more certain; confirm. Witnesses corroborated the policeman's statement.

cor ru gate (kor′ə gāt), wrinkle.

cor rupt (kə rupt′), 1. rotten. 2. start decay in. 3. wicked; as, a corrupt man, corrupt desires. 4. make evil. Bad company may corrupt a good boy. 5. influenced by bribes; dishonest; as, a corrupt judge. 6. to bribe.

cor rup tion (kə rup′shən), 1. decay. 2. evil conduct. 3. bribery; dishonesty.

corse let or **cors let** (kôrs′lit), armor for the body. See the picture.

C, corselet.

cor set (kôr′sit), a close-fitting undergarment worn about the waist and hips to support the body, or to shape it to the prevailing style.

cost (kôst), 1. price paid. The cost of this hat was $10. 2. loss; sacrifice. The poor fox escaped from the trap at the cost of a leg. 3. be obtained at the price of; require. This hat costs $10. The school play had cost much time and effort. Courtesy costs little and means much.

cost ly (kôst′li), 1. of great value. The queen had costly jewels. 2. costing much. The fool made costly mistakes.

cos tume (kos′tūm or kos′tüm for 1 and 2, kos tūm′ or kos tüm′ for 3), 1. dress; outer clothing; style of dress, including the way the hair is worn. In our play the characters wore Colonial costumes. 2. complete set of outer garments; as, a street costume, a hunting costume. 3. provide a costume for.

Cot

co sy (kō′zi), cozy.

cot[1] (kot), a small, light bed. See the picture just above.

cot[2] (kot), 1. cottage. 2. small building for shelter.

cote (kōt), a shelter for animals or birds.

cot tage (kot′ij), 1. small house. 2. house at a summer resort.

cot ton (kot′ən), 1. the cotton plant. See the picture. 2. the soft, white fibers surrounding the seed of the cotton plant. 3. thread of cloth made from these white fibers. 4. made of cotton. She bought two cotton dresses.

Cotton plant

cot ton wood (kot′ən wůd′), a kind of American poplar with tufts that look like cotton on the seeds.

cot y le don (kot′i lē′dən), the first leaf, or one of the first pair of leaves, growing from a seed.

couch (kouch), 1. a bed or sofa for sleep or rest. 2. any place for sleep or rest. The deer got up from its grassy couch. 3. put in a position ready to attack; as, to couch a spear. 4. lie hidden ready to attack. 5. put in words; express. His thoughts were couched in beautiful language.

C C

C, cotyledon.

cou gar (kü′gər), puma; mountain lion.

cough (kôf), 1. force air from the lungs with sudden effort and noise. 2. act of coughing. 3. diseased condition that causes coughing. She has a bad cough.

could (kůd), was able; was able to. He could eat.

could n't (kůd′ənt), could not.

couldst (kůdst), old form meaning **could.** "Thou couldst" means "you could."

cou lee (kü′li), 1. deep ravine or gulch. A coulee is usually dry in summer. 2. stream of lava.

coun cil (koun′səl), 1. a group of persons called together to give advice, and discuss or settle questions. 2. a small group of persons elected by the people to make laws for and manage a town or city.

coun ci lor or **coun cil lor** (koun′sə lər), member of a council.

coun sel (koun′səl), 1. act of exchanging ideas; act of talking things over. 2. advice. A wise person gives good counsel. 3. person or group that gives advice about the law; lawyer or group of lawyers. 4. give advice to; advise. 5. recommend. He counseled acting at once. 6. **Take counsel** means exchange ideas; talk things over; consult together.

coun se lor or **coun sel lor** (koun′sə lər), 1. person who advises. 2. lawyer.

count[1] (kount), 1. name numbers in order. The child can count up to ten. 2. add up; find the number of. He counted the books and found there were fifty. 3. adding up; finding out how many. The count showed that more than 5000 votes had been cast. 4. total number; amount. The exact count was 5170. 5. use in reckoning; take account of. Let's not count that game. 6. consider. He counts himself fortunate in having good health. 7. depend. We count on your help. 8. be counted; be included in reckoning or consideration. Your first trial is only for practice; it won't count. 9. have an influence; be of account or value. Everything we do counts.

count[2] (kount), nobleman; a title or rank. A French count was about equal to an English earl.

coun te nance (koun′ti nəns), 1. face. 2. expression of the face. His angry countenance showed how he felt. **Keep one's countenance** means be calm or keep from smiling or laughing. 3. approve or encourage (a person, an action, or a person in doing something). Mother countenanced the boys' friendship. 4. approval.

count er[1] (koun′tər), 1. small piece of metal, etc., usually round, used to keep count in games of cards, etc.; imitation coin. 2. long table in a store or bank on which money is counted out, and across which goods are given to customers. 3. person or thing that counts.

coun ter[2] (koun′tər), 1. contrary; opposed. He acted counter to his promise. 2. oppose. He countered my proposal with one of his own.

coun ter act (koun′tər akt′), act against; hinder. A hot bath and a hot drink will sometimes counteract a chill.

coun ter feit (koun′tər fit), 1. copy (money, pictures, handwriting, etc.) in order to deceive. He was sent to prison for counterfeiting five-dollar bills. 2. something copied and passed as genuine. 3. not genuine; as, a counterfeit stamp. 4. pretend. Ruth counterfeited interest and pleasure in order to be polite.

coun ter part (koun′tər pärt′), 1. a copy or duplicate. 2. person or thing closely resembling another. This twin is her sister's counterpart. 3. thing that complements another. Night is the counterpart of day.

count ess (koun′tis), 1. wife or widow of a count or an earl. 2. lady equal in rank to a count or earl in her own right.

coun ties (koun′tiz), more than one county. See **county.**

count less (kount′lis), too many to count; as, the countless sands of the seashore.

coun tries (kun′triz), more than one country.

coun try (kun′tri), 1. land; region. The country around the mining town was rough and mountainous. 2. all the land of a nation.

He came from France, a country across the sea. 3. A person's country is the land where he was born or where he is a citizen. 4. the people of a country. All the country hated the king. 5. land without many houses. Bob likes the country better than the city. 6. of the country; in the country. He likes country food and country air.

coun try man (kun′tri mən), 1. man of one's own country. We will protect our countrymen. 2. man who lives in the country.

coun try side (kun′tri sīd′), rural district.

coun try wom an (kun′tri wu̇m′ən), 1. woman of one's own country. 2. woman who lives in the country.

coun ty (koun′ti), a division for purposes of government next smaller than a country or State. The county officers conduct local business, collect taxes, hold court, keep roads in repair, and maintain county schools. County may mean the land, the people, or the officers of the county.

cou ple (kup′əl), 1. two things of the same kind that go together; a pair. 2. man and woman who are married, engaged, or partners in a dance. 3. partners in a dance. 4. join together; as, to couple two freight cars.

cou pling (kup′ling), 1. joining together. 2. device for joining together parts of machinery. 3. device used to join together two railroad cars.

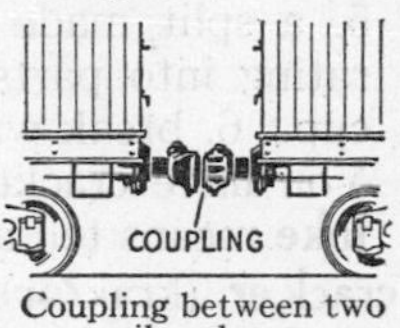

Coupling between two railroad cars

cou pon (kü′pon), part of a ticket, ration book, bond, etc., that gives the person who holds it certain rights.

cour age (kėr′ij), bravery; meeting danger without fear.

cou ra geous (kə rā′jəs), fearless; brave; full of courage.

cour i er (kėr′i ər or kür′i ər), 1. messenger sent in haste. 2. man hired by travelers to go with them and be in charge of the arrangements of the journey.

course (kōrs), 1. an onward movement. 2. direction taken. Our course was straight to the north. 3. line of action. The only sensible course was to go home. 4. track. 5. channel. 6. a number of like things arranged in some regular order. 7. regular order. Mother gets little rest in the course of her daily work. **Of course** means (1) surely; certainly. (2) naturally; as should be expected. 8. part of a meal served at one time. The first course was chicken soup. 9. row of bricks or stones in a wall. 10. hunt. 11. run.

cours er (kōr′sər), a swift horse.

court (kōrt), 1. space partly or wholly enclosed by walls or buildings. The apartment house is built around a court. 2. short street. 3. place marked off for a game; as, a tennis court, a handball court. 4. place where a king or other sovereign lives. 5. establishment and followers of a king, emperor, etc. The court of King Solomon was noted for its splendor. 6. a sovereign and his advisers as a ruling body or power. 7. assembly held by a sovereign. 8. place where justice is administered. The prisoner was brought to court for trial. 9. persons who administer justice; judge or judges. 10. assembly of such persons to administer justice. Several cases await trial at the next court. 11. **Pay court to** means try to please. 12. seek the favor of; try to please. 13. make love to; seek to marry; woo. 14. try to get; seek; as, to court applause. The brave soldier courted danger.

cour te ous (kėr′ti əs), polite. It is courteous to help an old lady.

cour te sy (kėr′ti si), 1. polite behavior; kind conduct. 2. a kindness; act of consideration; polite act. "Thanks for all your courtesies," said Aunt Bess. 3. curtsy.

court house (kōrt′hous′), 1. a building where judges do their work. 2. a building used for the government of a county.

cour ti er (kōr′ti ər), person often present at the court of a prince, king, emperor, etc.; court attendant.

court ly (kōrt′li), having manners fit for a king's court; polite; elegant.

court ship (kōrt′ship), making love; wooing.

court yard (kōrt′yärd′), space enclosed by walls, in or near a large building. In the courtyard stood two big trucks.

cous in (kuz′ən), the son or daughter of one's uncle or aunt. Your first cousins are other grandchildren of your grandparents. Your second cousins are the other great-grandchildren of your great-grandparents, and so for third cousins, fourth, etc.

cove (kōv), small bay; mouth of a creek; inlet on the shore.

cov e nant (kuv′ə nənt), 1. a solemn agreement between two or more persons or groups. 2. agree solemnly (to do certain things).

cov er (kuv′ər), 1. Cover this box with a wide board. Cover this sleeping child with your coat. Do not try to cover a mistake. 2. anything that protects or hides is a cover. Books have covers. Under cover of the dark night, the dog was stolen. 3. His clothes were covered with dirt. 4. The cars cover 200 miles a day. 5. This book covers all of the year's work in arithmetic.

cov er ing (kuv′ər ing), anything that covers.

cov er let (kuv′ər lit), an outer covering of a bed; bedspread.

cov ert (kuv′ərt), 1. secret; hidden; disguised. 2. a shelter; a hiding place; a thicket in which animals hide.

cov et (kuv′it), desire eagerly (something that belongs to another). The boys coveted John's new bat.

cov et ous (kuv′i təs), desiring things that belong to others.

cov ey (kuv′i), 1. small flock of partridges. 2. small flock; group.

cow[1] (kou), 1. common dairy animal that furnishes milk. 2. female of various other large animals; as, a buffalo cow, an elephant cow.

Cow (def. 1)

cow[2] (kou), make afraid; frighten.

cow ard (kou′ərd), person who lacks courage or is afraid; one who runs from danger.

cow ard ice (kou′ər dis), lack of courage; being easily made afraid.

cow ard ly (kou′ərd li), without courage; like a coward.

cow boy (kou′boi′), a man, usually on horseback, who looks after cattle on a ranch.

cow er (kou′ər), crouch in fear or shame. The whipped dog cowered under the table.

cow hide (kou′hīd′), 1. the hide of a cow. 2. leather made from it. 3. a strong, heavy whip made of rawhide or braided leather.

Cowl (def. 2)

cowl (koul), 1. monk's cloak with a hood. 2. the hood itself.

cow slip (kou′slip), a wild plant with yellow flowers.

cox swain (kok′sən or kok′swān), the man who steers a boat.

coy (koi), 1. shy; modest; bashful. 2. seeming more shy than one really is.

coy o te (kī ō′ti or kī′ōt), prairie wolf of western North America.

Coyote (4 ft. long, with tail)

co zi ly (kō′zi li), in a snug and comfortable manner.

co zy (kō′zi), warm and comfortable; snug.

crab (krab), water animal with eight legs, two claws, and a broad, flat, shell covering. See the picture. Many kinds of crabs are good to eat.

Crab

crab bed (krab′id), peevish; cross; surly.

crack (krak), 1. a sudden, sharp noise like that made by loud thunder, by a whip, or by something breaking. 2. make or cause to make a sudden, sharp noise; as, to crack a whip, the whip cracked. 3. break with a sharp noise. The tree cracked loudly and fell. We cracked the nuts. 4. a hard, sharp blow. 5. a split made by breaking without separating into parts. There is a crack in this cup. 6. break without separating into parts. You have cracked the window. 7. **Crack a joke** means tell a joke; say something funny.

crack er (krak′ər), 1. a thin, crisp biscuit. 2. firework that bursts with a sharp noise.

crack le (krak′əl), 1. make slight, sharp sounds. The papers crackled in the waste basket. A fire crackled on the hearth. 2. a slight, sharp sound, such as paper makes when crushed.

cra dle (krā′dəl), 1. a baby's little bed on rockers. 2. the place where anything begins its growth. 3. any kind of framework looking like or used as a cradle. The framework upon which a ship rests during building or repairs is a cradle. The rocking machine or trough in which gold-bearing earth is shaken in water is also a cradle. 4. a frame fastened to a scythe for laying grain evenly as it is cut. See the picture on the next page. 5. lay or rock as in a cradle. She cradled the child in her arms. 6. shelter or train in early youth.

Miner's cradle (def. 3)

craft (kraft), 1. skill. He shaped the bits of wood and fitted them together with loving craft. 2. a trade or art requiring skilled work; as, needlecraft. 3. members of a skilled trade. He belongs to the craft of masons. 4. skill in deceiving others; slyness; sly tricks. By craft he got all their money from them. 5. boat or boats; ship or ships. Craft of all kinds come into New York Harbor.

Man using a cradle (def. 4 of cradle)

crafts man (krafts′mən), skilled workman. Most makers of tools are craftsmen.

craft y (kraf′ti), skillful in deceiving others; as, the crafty fox.

crag (krag), a steep, rugged rock rising above others.

cram (kram), 1. force into; force down; stuff. He crammed all his clothes quickly into the bag. 2. fill too full. 3. eat too fast or too much.

cramp (kramp), 1. shut into a small space; limit. His work was cramped by the very short time he could spend on it. 2. sudden, painful contracting or pulling together of muscles from chill or strain. The swimmer was seized with cramps and had to be taken into the boat.

Crane for lifting

cran ber ry (kran′ber′i), a firm, sour, dark-red berry that grows on low shrubs in marshes. Cranberries are used in making sauce and jelly.

crane (krān), 1. machine with a long, swinging arm, for lifting and moving heavy weights. 2. a large wading bird with long legs, neck, and bill. 3. stretch (the neck) as a crane does, in order to see better.

crank (krangk), 1. part or handle of a machine connected at right angles to another part to set it in motion; as, the crank of an ice-cream freezer. 2. work or start by means of a crank; as, to crank an automobile. 3. odd person; person who has queer ideas.

White crane

cran ny (kran′i), crack; chink; crevice.

crape (krāp), a thin, light, crinkled cloth. Black crape is used for mourning.

crash (krash), 1. a sudden, loud noise like many dishes falling and breaking, or like sudden, loud band music. 2. make a crash. The dishes crashed to the floor. 3. the violent striking of one solid thing against another. 4. strike violently and shatter. The bullet crashed through the window. 5. sudden ruin; business failure. 6. fall to the earth in an airplane; make a very bad landing. 7. such a fall or landing.

crate (krāt), 1. a large frame, box, or basket made of wicker or of strips of wood, for shipping glass, china, fruit, household goods, or furniture. 2. pack in a crate for shipping.

Crate containing a bicycle

cra ter (krā′tər), 1. the opening of a volcano. 2. a big hole shaped like a bowl. The battlefield was full of craters made by exploding shells.

cra vat (krə vat′), 1. necktie. 2. scarf.

crave (krāv), 1. long for; desire very much. A thirsty man craves water. 2. ask earnestly for. He craved a favor of the king.

cra ven (krā′vən), 1. cowardly. 2. coward.

crav ing (krāv′ing), longing; yearning. A hungry man has a craving for food.

craw fish (krô′fish′), crayfish.

crawl (krôl), 1. move slowly, pulling the body along the ground. A worm or snake crawls. 2. move slowly on hands and knees. The boys crawled through a hole in the wall. 3. swarm with crawling things. The ground was crawling with ants. 4. feel creepy. My flesh crawled at the thought of the huge black snakes. 5. slow movement along the ground; any slow movement.

cray fish (krā′fish′), a fresh-water animal looking like a small lobster; a similar but larger salt-water shellfish.

Crayfish (3 to 6 in. long)

cray on (krā′ən), 1. a stick or pencil of chalk, charcoal, etc., for drawing or writing. 2. draw with crayons. 3. drawing made with crayons.

craze (krāz), 1. a short-lived, eager interest in doing some one thing. One year Sam had a craze for collecting beetles; the next year he had a craze for making models of ships. 2. make diseased or injured in mind; make crazy.

cra zy (krā′zi), 1. having a diseased or injured mind; insane. That crazy man thought he was George Washington. 2. not strong or sound; shaky. That crazy bridge ought to be repaired.

creak (krēk), 1. squeak loudly. Hinges creak when they need oiling. New shoes sometimes creak. 2. creaking noise.

cream (krēm), 1. the oily, yellowish part of milk which rises slowly to the top. Butter is made from cream. 2. form a thick layer like cream on the top; foam. 3. a fancy sweet dessert or candy; as, Spanish cream, chocolate creams. 4. make into a mixture like cream. The cook creamed butter and sugar together for a cake. 5. oily preparation put on the skin to make it smooth and soft. 6. yellowish white. 7. best part of anything.

cream er y (krēm′ər i), 1. place where butter and cheese are made. 2. place where cream, milk, and butter are bought and sold.

cream y (krēm′i), 1. like cream. 2. having much cream in it.

crease (krēs), 1. a line or mark produced by folding; fold; ridge; wrinkle. Men's pants are pressed with creases down the front. 2. make creases in; fall into creases.

cre ate (krē āt′), 1. make a thing which has not been made before; cause to be. She created this garden in the desert. 2. be the cause of. Do not create a disturbance.

cre a tion (krē ā′shən), 1. creating; the act of making a thing which has not been made before. 2. all things that have been created; the world; the universe. Let all creation praise the Lord. 3. a thing produced by intelligence or skill, usually an important or original one.

cre a tive (krē ā′tiv), having the power to create; inventive; productive.

cre a tor (krē ā′tər), person who creates.

crea ture (krē′chər), any living person or animal.

cred it (kred′it), 1. belief; trust. **Give credit to** a story means believe it. 2. believe in. I can credit all that you are telling me. 3. a trust in a person's ability and intention to pay. Buy **on credit** means buy without paying until later. 4. one's reputation in money matters. If you pay your bills, your credit will be good. 5. **Credit a person with** means think that he has. I credit him with some sense. 6. praise; honor. "It is to your credit" or "It does you credit" means that you may rightly be proud of it.

cred it a ble (kred′it ə bəl), bringing credit or honor. Alice's record of perfect attendance is very creditable to her.

cred i tor (kred′i tər), person to whom money or goods are due; one to whom a debt is owed.

cred u lous (krej′ů ləs), too ready to believe; easily deceived. Lola was so credulous that the other children could fool her easily.

creed (krēd), 1. a brief statement of Christian belief as approved by some church. 2. any statement of faith or belief. Part of John's creed was: "The U.S.A. is the best country in the world and Los Angeles is the best city in it."

creek (krēk), 1. small stream. 2. narrow bay running inland for some distance.

creep (krēp), 1. move slowly with the body lying close to the ground or floor; crawl. A baby learns to creep before it learns to walk. 2. move in a slow or sly way. When we were playing Indians, we crept silently through the bushes. 3. move timidly. 4. A plant that creeps is one that grows along the ground or over a wall by means of clinging stems. Ivy creeps. 5. feel as if things were creeping over the skin. It made my flesh creep to hear her moan. 6. creeping; slow movement. **crept** is formed from **creep.**

creep y (krēp′i), having or causing a creeping sensation of the skin. Ghost stories make some children creepy.

crepe or **crêpe** (krāp), 1. a thin cloth with a wavy surface. 2. tissue paper that looks like crepe.

crept (krept). See **creep.** The baby crept over to its mother. We had crept up on the enemy without their seeing us.

cres cent (kres′ənt), 1. shape of the moon when it is small and thin. 2. anything that curves in a similar way, such as a street or a row of houses. 3. shaped like the moon when it is small and thin; as, a crescent pin. 4. increasing.

Crescent moon

cress (kres), a plant whose leaves are used as a garnish or a salad.

crest (krest), 1. a tuft or mane on the head of an animal; a rooster's comb. 2. a decoration of plumes or feathers worn on a helmet. 3. decoration at the top of a coat of arms. 4. top of a hill or a wave.

crest ed (kres′tid), having a crest.

crest fall en (krest′fôl′ən), with bowed head; dejected; discouraged. Nell came home crestfallen because she had a poor report card.

cre vasse (krə vas′), 1. deep crack or crevice in the ice of a glacier. 2. a break in a dam or dike or levee.

crev ice (krev′is), a narrow split or crack. Tiny ferns grew in crevices in the stone wall.

Crevasse

crew[1] (krü), 1. the men needed to do the work on a ship, or to row a boat. 2. group of people working or acting together; as, a repairing crew on the railroad. 3. gang; mob. The boys on that street are a rough crew.

crew[2] (krü), crowed. The cock crew.

crib (krib), 1. small bed with high barred sides so that a baby cannot fall out. 2. barred manger for feeding animals. 3. a building or box for storing grain, salt, etc. 4. framework of logs or timbers used in building. 5. use somebody's words or ideas in an unfair way. Roy was marked zero because he cribbed.

Crib for a baby

crick et[1] (krik′it), a black insect of the grasshopper family. On a summer evening you can hear the crickets chirping.

Cricket (1 in. long)

crick et[2] (krik′it), an English outdoor game played by two teams of eleven players each, with ball, bats, and wickets.

crick et[3] (krik′it), a small, low stool.

cried (krīd). See **cry.** The baby cried for its mother. It has cried too much this week.

cries (krīz). See **cry.**

crime (krīm), 1. very wrong deed that is against the law. 2. evil act; sin. The preacher said that war was a crime against humanity. Slums are a crime against childhood.

crim i nal (krim′i nəl), 1. person who has committed a crime. 2. guilty of wrongdoing; that is a crime. Murder and stealing are criminal acts. 3. having something to do with crime; of crime.

crim son (krim′zən), 1. deep red. 2. turn deep red in color.

cringe (krinj), shrink; crouch in fear; bend down from lack of spirit. The dog cringed at the sight of the whip.

crin kle (kring′kəl), 1. wrinkle; ripple. Crepe paper is crinkled. 2. rustle. Paper crinkles when it is crushed.

crip ple (krip′əl), 1. lame person; person who cannot use his body properly because of injury or lack. 2. make a cripple of. 3. damage; weaken. The ship was crippled by the storm.

cri sis (krī′sis), 1. turning point in a disease, toward life or death. 2. deciding event in history. 3. time of danger or anxious waiting.

crisp (krisp), 1. hard and thin; breaking easily when bitten. Dry toast is crisp. Fresh celery is crisp. 2. make crisp; become crisp. 3. fresh; sharp and clear; bracing. The air was cool and crisp. 4. short and decided; as, a crisp manner. 5. curly and wiry; as, crisp hair.

crit ic (krit′ik), 1. person who makes a judgment, especially one concerning books, music, pictures, plays, acting, etc. 2. person who disapproves or finds fault. Dora was such a critic that the other girls did not like her.

crit i cal (krit′i kəl), 1. inclined to find fault or disapprove. Do not be so critical. 2. coming from one who is skilled as a critic. 3. of a crisis; being important at a time of danger and difficulty; as, the critical moment. His delay was critical.

crit i cism (krit′i sizm), 1. making judgments; approving or disapproving. 2. the work of a critic. 3. unfavorable remarks or judgments; finding fault.

crit i cize or **crit i cise** (krit′i sīz), 1. judge or speak as a critic. 2. blame; find fault with. Do not criticize him until you know all the circumstances.

croak (krōk), 1. the deep, hoarse sound made by a frog, a crow, or a raven. 2. make croaks. 3. be always prophesying evil. 4. be dissatisfied; grumble.

cro chet (krō shā′), make wool or cotton thread into sweaters, shawls, and other things in a way somewhat like knitting, but using only one needle, with a hooked end, called a crochet hook.

Crocheting

crock (krok), a pot or jar made of baked clay.

crock er y (krok′ər i), earthenware.

croc o dile (krok′ə dīl), a large animal with a long body, four short legs, a thick skin, and a long tail. See the picture. Crocodiles live in the rivers and marshes of the warm parts of Africa, Asia, Australia, and America.

Crocodile (14 ft. long)

cro cus (krō′kəs), 1. small plant that blooms very early in the spring and has white, yellow, or purple flowers. 2. the flower.

Crocuses

crone (krōn), old woman.

cro ny (krō′ni), very close friend; chum.

crook (krůk), 1. hook; bend; curve. There is a crook in the stream around the cliff. He crooked his arm. 2. the curved or bent part of anything. 3. a shepherd's hooked staff. 4. person who is not honest in his dealings.

crook ed (krůk′id), 1. not straight; bent; twisted. 2. not honest.

croon (krün), hum, sing, or murmur in a low tone. The mother was crooning to her baby.

crop (krop), 1. food plants grown or gathered by people for their use. 2. the whole amount (of wheat, corn, or the produce of any plant or tree) which is borne in one season. The potato crop was very small this year. 3. cut or bite off the top of. Sheep had cropped the grass very short. 4. clip or cut short (the tail, ear, hair, edge of book). 5. act or result of cropping; short hair. 6. a baglike swelling of a bird's food passage where food is prepared for digestion. 7. a short whip with a loop instead of a lash. 8. **Crop out** means appear or come to the surface. Ledges of white rock crop out on that hillside. 9. **Crop up** means appear or occur unexpectedly.

cro quet (krō kā′), an outdoor game played by knocking balls through arches with mallets. See the picture.

Girl playing croquet

cross (krôs), 1. a stick or post with another across it like a T or an X. Jesus died on the cross. 2. mark with a ×. 3. draw a line across. 4. move from one side to another; go across. 5. lying or going across; crossing. 6. make the sign of a cross. 7. mix breeds of (animals). 8. a mixing of breeds. 9. hinder; oppose. If you cross Percy he kicks and screams. 10. in a bad temper. 11. burden of duty or suffering.

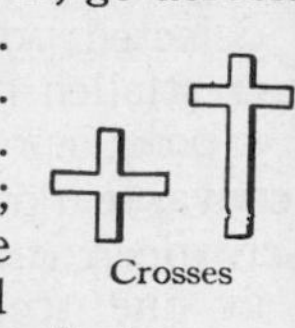
Crosses

cross bar (krôs′bär′), a bar, line, or stripe going crosswise.

cross bow (krôs′bō′), an old-time weapon for shooting arrows, stones, etc., consisting of a bow fixed across a wooden stock to direct the arrows.

Man using a crossbow

cross-eyed (krôs′īd′), having both eyes turned toward the nose.

cross ing (krôs′ing), 1. place where lines, tracks, etc., cross. "Railroad crossing! Stop! Look! Listen!" 2. place at which a street, river, etc., may be crossed. White lines mark the crossing.

cross piece (krôs′pēs′), piece of wood, metal, etc., that goes across.

cross road (krôs′rōd′), 1. road that crosses another. 2. road that connects main roads. 3. A **crossroads** is a place where roads cross. At the crossroads we stopped, and read the signboards.

cross wise (krôs′wīz′), 1. across. 2. in the form of a cross.

crotch (kroch), forked piece or part. The nest was in the crotch of a tree.

crouch (krouch), 1. stoop low with bent legs like an animal ready to spring, or like a person hiding. 2. shrink down in fear. 3. a crouching. 4. crouching position.

croup (krüp), a children's disease of the windpipe that causes a cough and difficult breathing.

crow[1] (krō), 1. the loud cry of a rooster. 2. make this cry. 3. happy sound made by a baby. 4. make this sound. 5. boast; show one's happiness and pride; as, to crow over one's victory, to crow over one's defeated enemy.

Crow (18 to 20 in. long)

crow[2] (krō), a kind of large black bird with a harsh cry. See the picture.

crow bar (krō′bär′), a bar of iron used to lift things or pry them apart.

crowd (kroud), 1. large number of people together. 2. people in general; the masses. 3. large number of things or animals together. 4. set; company. Tom and his crowd went to the dance. 5. collect in large numbers. 6. fill; fill too full. 7. push; shove; press; cram.

crown (kroun), 1. head covering for a king or queen. 2. royal power; supreme governing power in a monarchy. 3. of a crown; having to do with a crown; as, crown jewels. 4. wreath for the head. The winner of the race received a crown. 5. to honor; reward. His hard work was crowned with success. 6. head. 7. top part; as, the crown of a hat, the crown of a mountain. 8. top with a crown. A palace crowns the hill. 9. part of a tooth which appears beyond the gum, or an artificial substitute for it. 10. put a crown on. 11. a British coin worth 5 shillings, or about $1.24.

King wearing a crown

cru cial (krü′shəl), very important; critical; decisive. It is a crucial act for a nation to declare war.

cru ci ble (krü′si bəl), pot to melt metals in.

cru ci fix (krü′si fiks), cross with the figure of Christ crucified on it.

cru ci fix ion (krü′si fik′shən), 1. crucifying. 2. **The Crucifixion** means the putting to death of Christ on the cross.

cru ci fy (krü′si fī), 1. put to death by nailing the hands and feet to a cross. 2. torture.

crude (krüd), 1. in a natural or raw state. Oil, ore, sugar, etc., before being refined and prepared for use are crude. 2. rough; lacking finish, grace, taste, or refinement; as, a crude log cabin, a crude chair made out of a box, the crude manners of a boor.

cru el (krü′əl), 1. ready to give pain to others or to delight in their suffering; hardhearted; as, a cruel master. 2. showing a cruel nature; as, cruel acts. 3. causing pain or suffering; as, a cruel war, a cruel disease.

cru el ty (krü′əl ti), 1. readiness to give pain to others or to delight in their suffering; having a cruel nature. 2. cruel act or acts.

cruise (krüz), 1. sail about from place to place. Enemy ships cruised along the coast. 2. a voyage for pleasure with no special destination in view; a voyage in search of something whose position is not known exactly.

cruis er (krüz′ər), large warship of fair speed. An armored cruiser has less armor and greater speed than a battleship.

crumb (krum), 1. very small piece broken from a larger piece; as, a crumb of bread. 2. break into crumbs. 3. little bit; as, a crumb of comfort.

crum ble (krum′bəl), break into small pieces or crumbs; fall to bits. Do not crumble your bread on the table.

crum ple (krum′pəl), 1. crush together. He crumpled the letter into a ball. 2. wrinkle. "This is the cow with the crumpled horn."

crunch (krunch), 1. crush noisily with the teeth. Bill crunched the celery. 2. make such a sound. The hard snow crunched under our feet. 3. act or sound of crunching.

crup per (krup′ər), 1. a strap attached to the back of a harness and passing under a horse's tail. 2. the rump of a horse.

cru sade (krü sād′), 1. any one of the Christian military expeditions between the years 1096 and 1272 to recover the Holy Land from the Mohammedans. 2. vigorous movement against a public evil or in favor of some new idea. 3. take part in a crusade.

cru sad er (krü sād′ər), person who takes part in a crusade.

crush (krush), 1. squeeze together violently so as to break or bruise. 2. wrinkle or crease by wear or rough handling. 3. break into fine pieces by grinding, pounding, or pressing. 4. violent pressure like grinding or pounding. 5. mass of people crowded close together. There was a crush at the football game. 6. subdue; conquer.

crust (krust), 1. the hard surface of bread. 2. piece of the crust; any hard, dry piece of bread. 3. rich dough rolled out thin and baked for pies. 4. any hard outside covering; as, the crust of the earth. 5. cover with a crust; form into a crust; become covered with a crust. By the next day the snow had crusted over.

crutch (kruch), 1. a support to help a lame person walk. It is a stick with a padded piece at the top to fit under the arm, and often a place for the hand to hold lower down, so that a person can swing along on the crutches without having to touch the lame foot to the ground. 2. a support; prop; anything like a crutch in shape or use.

Two kinds of crutches

cry (krī), 1. call loudly. He cried, "Save me!" 2. make a noise from grief or pain, usually with tears. 3. shed tears. 4. yelp (said of hounds). 5. sell by calling on the streets, etc. The man is crying fish. 6. announce in public. 7. loud call. 8. noise of grief, pain, etc. 9. call for help; appeal; entreaty. 10. call that means things are for sale. 11. fit of weeping. 12. noise or call of an animal. 13. watchword.

crys tal (kris′təl), 1. a clear, transparent mineral that looks like ice. 2. piece of glass cut into form for use or ornament; as, crystals hung around the lights in a great hall. 3. very transparent glass. 4. the glass over the face of a watch. 5. made of crystal; as, crystal ornaments. 6. clear as crystal; as, crystal water. 7. one of the regularly shaped pieces with angles and flat surfaces into which many substances solidify. You have seen crystals of snow.

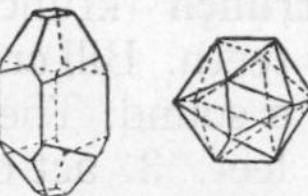
Crystal shapes

crys tal line (kris′təl in), 1. made of crystals. 2. as clear as crystal.

crys tal lize (kris′təl īz), 1. form into crystals. Honey crystallizes if kept too long. 2. form into definite shape. His vague ideas crystallized into a clear plan.

cub (kub), a young bear, fox, lion, etc.

cube (kūb), 1. a solid with six square faces or sides, all equal. 2. the product when a number is used three times as a factor. 125 is the cube of 5, for $5 \times 5 \times 5 = 125$. 3. make into a cube.

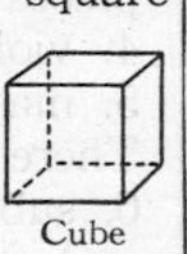
Cube

cu bic (kū′bik), 1. cube-shaped. 2. having length, breadth, and thickness. A cubic foot is the volume of a cube whose edges are each one foot long.

cu bit (kū′bit), an ancient measure of length, 18 to 22 inches. Once a cubit meant the length of the forearm, from the elbow down.

cuck oo (kuk′ü), 1. a bird which lays its eggs in the nests of other birds, one egg in each nest, instead of building a nest for itself. 2. the call of the cuckoo.

European cuckoo (about 14 in. long)

cu cum ber (kū′kum bər), 1. a long, fleshy, green vegetable eaten usually in thin slices as a salad, or used to make pickles. 2. the vine it grows on.

cud (kud), food brought back from the first stomach of cattle or similar animals for a slow second chewing in the mouth.

cud dle (kud′əl), 1. hold close and lovingly in one's arms or lap. Mary was cuddling the little kittens. 2. lie close and comfortably. Now cuddle down in bed and go to sleep.

cudg el (kuj′əl), 1. short, thick stick used as a weapon; a club. 2. beat with a cudgel. 3. **Cudgel your brains** means try very hard to think.

cue[1] (kū), 1. the last words of an actor's speech in a play which serve as the signal for another actor to come on the stage or to speak. 2. a signal like this to a singer or musician. 3. a hint as to what should be done.

cue[2] (kū), 1. braid of hair hanging down the back. 2. long stick used for striking the ball in the game of billiards.

cuff[1] (kuf), 1. a band of some material worn around the wrist. 2. the turned-up fold around the bottom of a sleeve or of a leg of a pair of trousers.

cuff[2] (kuf), hit with the hand; slap.

cui rass (kwi ras′), 1. piece of armor for the body made of a breastplate and a plate for the back fastened together. 2. Sometimes the breastplate alone is called a cuirass.

Cuirass (def. 1)

cull (kul), 1. pick out; select. 2. something inferior picked out. Poor fruit, stale vegetables, and animals not up to standard are called culls.

cul mi nate (kul′mi nāt), reach its highest point. The Christmas party at school culminated in the distribution of the presents.

cul pa ble (kul′pə bəl), deserving blame. The policeman was dismissed for culpable neglect of duty.

cul prit (kul′prit), 1. offender; person guilty of a fault or crime. Lulu was the culprit who had eaten all the candy. 2. prisoner in court accused of a crime.

cul ti vate (kul′ti vāt), 1. prepare and use (land) to raise crops by plowing it, planting seeds, and taking care of the growing plants. 2. help (plants) grow by labor and care. 3. loosen the ground around (growing plants) to kill weeds, etc. 4. improve; develop. It takes time, thought, and effort to cultivate your mind. 5. give time, thought, and effort to. She cultivated people who could help her.

cul ti va tion (kul′ti vā′shən), 1. preparing land and growing crops by plowing, planting, and necessary care. Better cultivation of soil will result in better crops. 2. giving time and thought to improving and developing (the body, mind, or manners). 3. culture; the result of improvement or growth through education and experience.

cul ti va tor (kul′ti vā′tər), 1. person or thing that cultivates. 2. a tool for loosening the ground and destroying weeds. A cultivator is pulled between rows of growing plants.

cul ture (kul′chər), 1. preparation of land and producing of crops. 2. proper care given to the production of bees, fish, silk, or germs. 3. training of the mind or of the body. 4. refinement of taste; the result of good education and surroundings.

cul tured (kul′chərd), cultivated; refined.

cul vert (kul′vərt), a drain crossing under a road or railroad.

Culvert

cum ber some (kum′bər səm), hard to manage; burdensome; troublesome. Ancient armor was cumbersome.

cum brous (kum′brəs), cumbersome.

cun ning (kun′ing), 1. skillful; clever in doing. With cunning hand he shaped the little pieces. 2. clever in deceit; sly; as, a cunning fox, a cunning thief. 3. skillful or sly ways of getting what one needs or wants, or of escaping one's enemies. Some animals have a great deal of cunning. 4. skill. We still say, "His hand has not lost its cunning." 5. pretty and dear; attractive. Kittens and babies are cunning.

cup (kup), 1. dish to drink from. Most cups have handles. 2. as much as a cup holds. She drank a cup of milk. 3. something shaped like a cup; as, the cup of a flower. 4. shape like a cup. He cupped his hands to catch the ball.

cup board (kub′ərd), closet or cabinet with shelves for dishes and food supplies.

Cu pid (kū′pid), 1. the Roman god of love, son of Venus. Cupid is usually represented as a winged boy with bow and arrows. 2. A **cupid** is a winged baby used as a symbol of love; as, cupids on a valentine.

cu po la (kū′pə lə), 1. a rounded dome on a roof. 2. a small dome or tower on a roof.

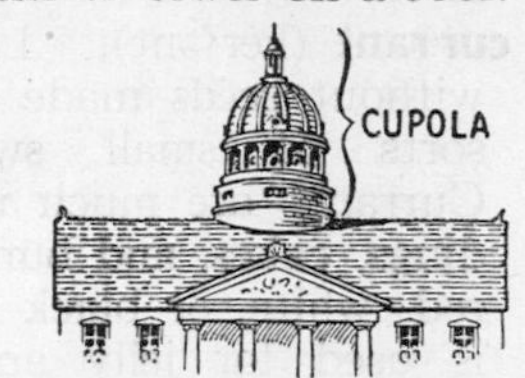

cur (kėr), worthless dog of mixed breed.

cu rate (kūr′it), an assistant clergyman; helper of a pastor, rector, or vicar.

cu ra tor (kū rā′tər), person in charge. The curator of an art museum knows much about pictures.

curb (kėrb), 1. a chain or a strap attached to a horse's bit and passing under the lower jaw, used as a check. 2. a check or restraint. 3. hold in check; restrain. You must curb your laughing when you are in church. 4. enclosing border of wood or stone along the edge of a pavement, or around the top of a well.

curd (kėrd), 1. the thick part of milk that separates from the watery part when the milk sours. Cheese is made from curds. 2. form into curds.

cur dle (kėr′dəl), form into curds. Milk curdles when kept too long.

cure (kūr), 1. bring back to health; make well; as, to cure a child of a cold. 2. get rid of; as, to cure a cold, to cure a bad habit. 3. remedy; something that removes or relieves disease or any bad condition; as, a cure for sore eyes, a cure for laziness. 4. preserve (bacon or other meat) by drying or salting. 5. religious oversight.

cur few (kėr′fū), 1. the ringing of a bell at a fixed time in the evening as a signal for children to leave the streets. 2. the time. 3. the bell. 4. law requiring children or others to be off the streets by a certain time.

cu ri os i ty (kūr′i os′i ti), 1. eager desire to know. Curiosity got the better of her, and she opened the forbidden door. 2. a strange, rare object. One of his curiosities was a cane made of the horn of a deer.

cu ri ous (kūr′i əs), 1. eager to know. Small children are very curious, and ask many questions. 2. strange; odd; unusual.

curl (kėrl), 1. twist into rings. Mother curls Mary's hair. Helen's hair curls naturally. 2. curve or twist out of shape. Paper curls up when it burns. You can curl up in a big chair. 3. rise in rings. Smoke curls slowly from the chimney. 4. a curled lock of hair. 5. anything curled or bent into a curve. A carpenter's shavings are curls.

curl y (kėr′li), 1. curling; as, curly hair. 2. having curls or curly hair; as, a curly head.

cur rant (kėr′ənt), 1. a small raisin without seeds made from certain sorts of small sweet grapes. Currants are much used in puddings, cakes, and buns. 2. a sour red, white, or black berry, which is used for jelly and preserves; the bush it grows on.

Currants (def. 2)

cur ren cy (kėr′ən si), 1. money in actual use in a country; as, paper currency, gold currency. 2. circulation; passing from person to person; as, the currency of a rumor. 3. general acceptance; prevalence.

cur rent (kėr′ənt), 1. flow of water, air, or any liquid; running stream; draft. 2. flow of electricity through a wire, etc. 3. the course or movement (of events or of opinions). Newspapers influence the current of thought. 4. of the present time. The current issue of a magazine is the latest one issued. 5. in general use; passing from person to person; as, current money, current jokes, current opinion.

cur ry[1] (kėr′i), 1. rub and clean (a horse) with a brush or scraper. 2. **Curry favor** means seek favor in ways that a self-respecting person would not use.

cur ry[2] (kėr′i), 1. a peppery sauce or powder. 2. food flavored with it.

curse (kėrs), 1. ask God to bring evil or harm on. He cursed his enemy solemnly. 2. the words that a person says when he asks God to curse someone or something. 3. bring evil or harm on; torment; as, cursed with blindness. He is cursed with a bad temper. 4. trouble; harm. My quick temper has been a curse to me all my life. 5. swear; say bad words. 6. words used in swearing.

curt (kėrt), short; short and rude; abrupt. Mr. Smith's curt way of speaking makes him seem rude.

cur tail (kėr tāl′), cut short; cut off part of. John's father curtailed his allowance.

cur tain (kėr′tən), 1. cloth hung at windows or in doors for protection or ornament. 2. a hanging screen which separates the stage of a theater from the part where the audience is. 3. provide with a curtain; hide by a curtain. We took off two sheets and curtained off a space in the corner.

curt sey (kėrt′si), curtsy.

curt sy (kėrt′si), 1. bow of respect or greeting made by bending the knees and lowering the body slightly. 2. make a curtsy. She curtsied low to the queen.

Lady curtsying

curve (kėrv), 1. line that has no straight part. 2. bend so as to form a line that has no straight part.

cush ion (ku̇sh′ən), 1. a soft pillow or pad for a couch, chair, etc. 2. anything that makes a soft place; as, a cushion of moss. 3. supply with a cushion.

cus tard (kus′tərd), a baked or boiled mixture of eggs, milk, and sugar. Custard is used as a dessert or as a food for sick persons.

cus to dy (kus′tə di), 1. keeping; care. Parents have the custody of their young children. 2. **In custody** often means in prison or in the care of the police.

cus tom (kus′təm), 1. any usual action. It was his custom to rise early. 2. a long-established habit having the force of law. The social customs of many countries differ from ours. 3. business support by being a customer. That store would like to have your custom. 4. for a special order. A custom tailor makes custom clothes.

cus tom ar y (kus′təm ãr′i), usual.

cus tom er (kus′təm ər), one who buys.

custom house, a government building, usually at a seaport, where customs are collected.

cut (kut), 1. a stroke or blow with a knife or any tool that has a sharp edge. 2. sharp stroke or blow. 3. opening made by a knife or sharp-edged tool. 4. make such an opening in; divide or wound with a sharp-edged tool. 5. strike sharply; hurt. 6. refuse to recognize socially. 7. an action or speech that hurts the feelings. 8. piece that has been cut off or cut out; as, a cut of meat. 9. place that has been made by cutting. The train went through a deep cut. 10. reduce. We cut expenses last month. 11. reduction. 12. A **short cut** is a quicker way. 13. go by a short cut; go. Let's cut through the woods and get ahead of them. 14. cross; divide by crossing. 15. an engraved block or plate used for printing; picture made from such a block. 16. the style or fashion of anything; as, the cut of a coat. 17. **Cut teeth** means have teeth grow through the gums.

cute (kūt), 1. pretty and dear. 2. clever; shrewd; cunning.

cu ti cle (kū′ti kəl), outer skin. The cuticle about the fingernails tends to become hard.

cut lass (kut′ləs), a short, heavy, slightly curved sword.

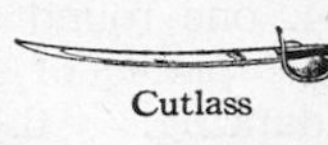
Cutlass

cut ter (kut′ər), 1. person who cuts; as, a garment cutter, a woodcutter. 2. machine made to cut; as, a meat cutter, a bread cutter. 3. small sleigh. 4. small sailboat with one mast. 5. boat belonging to a warship, used for carrying supplies and passengers to and from shore. 6. a small, armed ship used by the coast guard.

Cutter (def. 3)

cut ting (kut′ing), 1. a small shoot cut from a plant to grow a new plant. 2. a newspaper clipping. 3. an excavation through high ground. 4. that cuts. 5. hurting the feelings.

cy clone (sī′klōn), 1. very violent windstorm. 2. a storm moving around and toward a center of low pressure, which also moves.

cyl in der (sil′in dər), a hollow or solid body shaped like a roller.

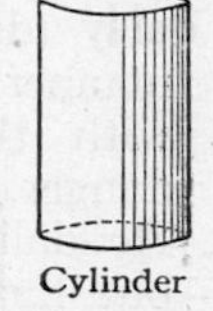
Cylinder

cy lin dri cal (si lin′dri kəl), shaped like a cylinder. Cans of fruit, candles, and water pipes are usually cylindrical.

cym bal (sim′bəl), one of a pair of brass plates which are struck together to make a ringing sound. See the picture.

Cymbals

cy press (sī′prəs), 1. an evergreen tree with hard wood and dark leaves. 2. the wood of this tree. Cypress is much used for boards and shingles.

czar (zär), emperor. When Russia had an emperor, his title was czar.

D

dab (dab), 1. tap; peck. The girl dabbed at her face with a powder puff. The cat made a dab at the butterfly. 2. a small soft or moist mass. The maid scraped the little dabs of butter from the plates.

dab ble (dab′əl), 1. wet by dabs; put in and out of water or mud; splash. We dabbled our bare feet in the pool. 2. play.

dachs hund (däks′hůnt′), a small hound with a long body and very short legs.

Daffodil (12 to 18 in. high)

dad (dad), father.

dad dy (dad′i), father.

daf fo dil (daf′ə dil), a yellow spring flower with long, slender leaves. It grows from a bulb. See the picture.

daft (daft), 1. silly. 2. crazy.

dag ger (dag′ər), a weapon for stabbing, with a short, pointed blade.

Dagger

dahl ia (dal′yə), a plant with showy flowers of many colors and varieties.

dai ly (dā′li), 1. done, happening, or appearing every day; as, a daily visit. 2. newspaper printed every day. The *Times* is a daily. 3. every day; day by day.

dain ti ly (dān′ti li), in a dainty way. Fairies eat daintily.

dain ty (dān′ti), 1. fresh, delicate, and pretty. A violet is daintier than a dandelion. 2. delicate in tastes and feeling. She is dainty about her eating. 3. good to eat. 4. choice bit of food; something very pleasing to eat. Candy and nuts are dainties.

dair y (dãr′i), 1. a room or building where milk and cream are kept and made into butter and cheese. 2. farm where milk and cream are produced and butter and cheese made. 3. store or company that sells milk, cream, butter, and cheese.

dair y maid (dãr′i mād′), girl or woman who works in a dairy.

dair y man (dãr′i mən), 1. owner or manager of a dairy. 2. man who works in a dairy.

Dais for a throne

da is (dā′is), raised platform at the end of a hall or large room, for a throne, seats of honor, a lecture desk, etc.

dai sy (dā′zi), a wild flower having a yellow center from which grow rays of white, pink, or yellow. We picked hundreds of daisies.

dal ly (dal′i), 1. act in a playful manner. The soft breeze dallies with the flowers. 2. flirt with danger, temptation, etc.; to trifle. He dallied with the offer for days but finally refused it. 3. be idle; loiter. Tom was late because he dallied along the way.

Daisy

dam[1] (dam), 1. wall built to hold back the water of a stream or any flowing water. 2. provide with a dam; hold back or block up with anything; as, to dam a stream.

dam[2] (dam), a mother animal in sheep, cattle, horses, and other four-footed animals.

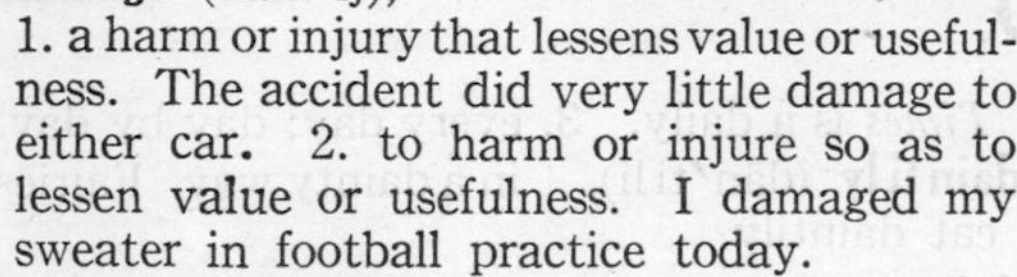
Dam

dam age (dam′ij), 1. a harm or injury that lessens value or usefulness. The accident did very little damage to either car. 2. to harm or injure so as to lessen value or usefulness. I damaged my sweater in football practice today.

dam ask (dam′əsk), 1. silk woven with an elaborate pattern; as, hangings of damask. 2. linen with woven designs. Spotless damask covered the table. 3. rose color; as, damask cheeks. 4. steel with a wavy pattern or markings.

dame (dām), 1. lady, especially in titles; as, Dame Fortune. 2. old woman.

damn (dam), 1. declare (something) to be bad; condemn. 2. doom to hell. 3. say "damn"; swear. 4. a curse.

damp (damp), 1. slightly wet; moist. 2. moisture. 3. make slightly wet. 4. to dull; check; put out. 5. a chill; a check. Mary's illness cast a damp over the party. 6. gas that gathers in mines. One kind of damp is likely to explode.

damp en (dam′pən), 1. make damp; become damp. We dampen clothes before we iron them. 2. depress; cast a chill over. The bad news dampened our spirits.

damp er (dam′pər), 1. person or thing that discourages or checks. 2. a movable plate to control the draft in a stove or furnace.

dam sel (dam′zəl), maiden.

dance (dans), 1. move in time with music. Helen can dance very well. 2. movement in time with music. 3. a party where people dance. 4. one round of dancing. 5. piece of music for dancing. 6. jump up and down; move in a lively way. See that boat dancing on the water.

Children dancing

danc er (dan′sər), 1. person who dances. 2. person who dances for pay.

dan de li on (dan′di lī′ən), a common weed with deeply notched leaves and bright-yellow flowers that bloom in the spring.

dan dle (dan′dəl), 1. move (a child) up and down on the knees or in the arms. 2. pet; pamper.

dan dy (dan′di), 1. man very careful of his dress and appearance. 2. excellent or first-rate thing; excellent; first-rate. Careful speakers do not use dandy with this second meaning.

dan ger (dān′jər), 1. chance of harm; nearness to harm; risk; peril. A soldier's life is full of danger. 2. thing that may cause harm. Hidden rocks are a danger to ships.

dan ger ous (dān′jər əs), likely to cause harm; not safe.

dan gle (dang′gəl), 1. hang loosely and sway. The curtain cord dangles. 2. hold or carry (a thing) so that it sways loosely. The nurse dangled the toys in front of the baby. 3. hang about; follow. Several dogs dangled near the butcher's truck.

dap ple (dap′əl), 1. spotted; as, a dapple horse. 2. mark or become marked with spots. Shadows of leaves dappled the path.

dare (dãr), 1. be bold; be bold enough. He does not dare to jump from that wall. 2. have courage to try; be bold enough for. The explorer dared the perils of the icy north. 3. challenge. I dare you to jump. 4. a challenge. 5. **I dare say** sometimes means probably or maybe.

dar ing (dãr′ing), 1. boldness; courage to take risks. 2. bold; fearless.

dark (därk). A night without a moon is dark. She has dark-brown eyes. Rain and clouds make a dark day. Do not be afraid of the dark. It was a dark secret. I am in the dark about his plan.

dark en (där′kən), make dark; become dark.

dark ness (därk′nis), lack of light.

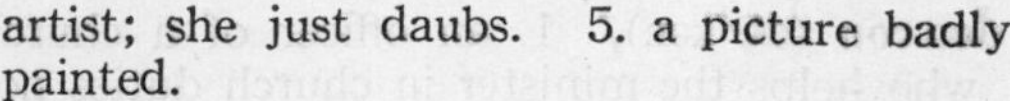

dar ling (där′ling), 1. person very dear to another; person much loved. 2. very dear; much loved.

darn (därn), 1. mend with rows of stitches back and forth. 2. place so mended.

dart (därt), 1. a slender, pointed weapon, thrown by the hand. 2. throw suddenly and rapidly. The savages darted spears at the lion. 3. a sudden, swift movement. 4. move swiftly. The deer saw us and darted away. 5. send suddenly. Ella darted an angry glance at her sister.

Dart

dash (dash), 1. throw. We dashed water over him. 2. splash. She dashed some paint on it. 3. rush. They dashed by in a hurry. 4. throw and break. He dashed the bowl to bits on a rock. 5. **Dash off** sometimes means do quickly. 6. ruin. Our hopes were dashed. 7. a short race; as, the 100-yard dash. 8. energy; spirit. 9. a mark like this (—) used in writing or printing. 10. small amount. Put in just a dash of pepper.

dash ing (dash′ing), 1. full of energy; lively. 2. showy. The band wore dashing uniforms.

da ta (dā′tə or dat′ə), facts; facts known or granted; information. Names, ages, and other data about the class are written in the teacher's book.

date[1] (dāt), 1. time; a statement of a time. 1492 is the date of the discovery of America by Columbus. 2. mark the time of; put a date on. Please date your letter. 3. find out the date of; give a date to. 4. be dated; have a date on it. 5. period of time. At that date there were no airplanes. **Out of date** means out of fashion. **Up to date** means in fashion or up to the present time. 6. belong to a certain period of time; have its origin. The oldest house in town dates from the 18th century.

date[2] (dāt), 1. the sweet fruit of a kind of palm tree. 2. the tree that bears it.

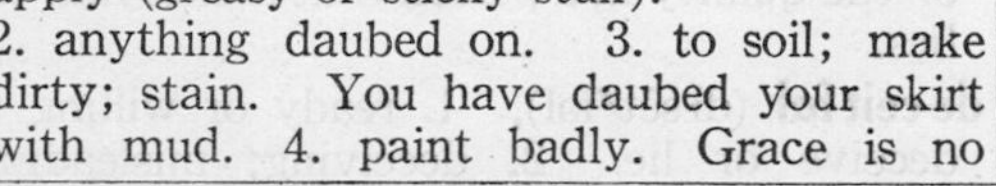

Date palm (40 to 80 ft. high)

daub (dôb), 1. coat or cover with plaster, clay, mud, or any soft material that will stick; apply (greasy or sticky stuff). 2. anything daubed on. 3. to soil; make dirty; stain. You have daubed your skirt with mud. 4. paint badly. Grace is no artist; she just daubs. 5. a picture badly painted.

daugh ter (dô′tər), 1. A girl is the daughter of her father and mother. 2. female child; as, daughters of Eve, a daughter of France.

daunt (dônt), frighten; discourage. Danger did not daunt the hero.

daunt less (dônt′lis), brave; not to be frightened or discouraged; as, a dauntless aviator.

daw dle (dô′dəl), waste time; be idle; loiter. Don't dawdle over your work.

dawn (dôn), 1. beginning of day; the first light in the east. 2. beginning; as, before the dawn of history. 3. grow bright or clear. Day dawns in the east. 4. grow clear to the eye or mind. The ocean dawned on our view. It dawned on me that Pearl was expecting to go with me. 5. begin; appear. A new era is dawning.

day (dā), 1. the time of light between sunrise and sunset. 2. Sometimes the 24 hours of day and night is called a day. 3. the hours given to work; the working day. An eight-hour day is common. 4. time; period; as, the present day. 5. **Win the day** means win the game, battle, or contest.

day break (dā′brāk′), dawn; the first light of day.

day dream (dā′drēm′), 1. dreamy thinking of pleasant things. 2. think of pleasant things in a dreamy way.

day light (dā′līt′), 1. the light of day. Lamplight is not so good for the eyes as daylight. 2. dawn; daybreak. He was up at daylight.

day time (dā′tīm′), the time when it is day and not night. Baby sleeps even in the daytime.

daze (dāz), 1. confuse; deaden in the mind; cause to feel stupid. A blow on the head dazed him so that he could not find his way home. The child was dazed by the sudden noise and bright lights. 2. dazed condition. He was in a daze and could not understand what was happening.

daz zle (daz′əl), 1. hurt (the eyes) with too bright light, or quick-moving lights. To look straight at the sun dazzles the eyes. 2. overcome the sight or the mind of with anything very bright. The poor little girl was dazzled by the richness of her new home. 3. a dazzling, bewildering brightness; as, the dazzle of powerful electric lights.

dea con (dē′kən), 1. an officer of a church who helps the minister in church duties not connected with preaching. 2. member of the clergy next below a priest in rank.

dead (ded), 1. with life gone from it. **The dead** means all who no longer have life. 2. without life. 3. dull; not active. 4. without force, power, spirit, feeling, activity, etc. This old battery is dead. 5. the time when there is the least life stirring; as, the dead of night. 6. sure; as, a dead shot, a dead certainty. 7. complete; as, a dead loss. 8. directly. Walk dead ahead two miles.

dead en (ded′ən), make weak. Some medicines are given to deaden pain. Thick walls deaden the noises from the street. The force of the blow was deadened by his heavy clothing.

dead ly (ded′li), 1. causing or likely to cause death; fatal; as, a deadly disease, deadly hatred, the deadly berries of a poisonous bush. 2. like that of death; as, deadly paleness, a deadly faintness. 3. extremely. "Washing dishes is deadly dull," said Lulu.

deaf (def), 1. not able to hear. 2. not able to hear well. 3. not willing to hear. A miser is deaf to all requests for money.

deaf en (def′ən), 1. make deaf. 2. stun with noise. The roar of the factory deafened us.

deaf ness (def′nis), being deaf.

deal (dēl), 1. have to do (with). Arithmetic deals with numbers. 2. act. Teachers should deal fairly with their pupils. 3. carry on business. This garage deals in gasoline, oil, tires, etc. 4. a bargain. 5. give. One fighter dealt the other a hard blow. 6. give out among several. Deal the cards. 7. a giving out; arrangement; plan; as, a new deal, a square deal. 8. part; portion; amount. A great deal of her money is spent for doctor's bills. **dealt** is formed from **deal.**

deal er (dēl′ər), 1. man who trades; any person engaged in buying and selling. 2. the person who distributes the cards to the players.

deal ing (dēl′ing), 1. way of doing business. 2. conduct toward others. Mr. Just is honored for his fair dealing.

dealt (delt). See **deal.** The knight dealt his enemy a blow. The cards are dealt.

dear (dēr), 1. His sister was very dear to him. "Come, my dear," said mother. 2. Fruit is still too dear to can. Tom's mistake cost him dear. 3. alas. Oh, dear! My head aches.

dear ly (dēr′li), 1. very much. Mother loves her baby dearly. 2. at a high price.

dearth (dėrth), scarceness; lack; too small a supply.

death (deth), 1. dying; the ending of life in people, animals, or plants. 2. any ending that is like dying. 3. being dead. 4. any condition like being dead.

death less (deth′lis), never dying; living forever; immortal; eternal.

death ly (deth′li), 1. like that of death. 2. causing death.

death's-head (deths′hed′), human skull.

de base (di bās′), make low or lower; lessen the value of. You can debase yourself or your character by evil actions.

de bate (di bāt′), 1. consider; discuss; talk about reasons for and against. I am debating buying a car. 2. discussion of reasons for and against. There has been much debate about which boy to choose for captain. 3. a public argument for and against a question in a meeting. We heard a debate over the radio. 4. hold a debate about.

de bris or **dé bris** (dā brē′), scattered fragments; ruins; rubbish. The street was covered with debris from the explosion.

debt (det), 1. something owed to another. 2. **In debt** means owing.

debt or (det′ər), person who owes something to another. If I borrow 10 cents from you, I am your debtor.

dec ade (dek′ād), ten years. Two decades ago means twenty years ago.

de cay (di kā′), 1. rot. Old fruits and vegetables decay. Your teeth decay if they are not cared for. The decay had not proceeded very far. 2. grow less in power, strength, wealth, or beauty. Many nations have grown great and then decayed. 3. growing less in power, strength, wealth, or beauty. The decay of her beauty was very gradual.

de cease (di sēs′), 1. death. 2. die.

de ceit (di sēt′), 1. deceiving; lying; making a person believe as true something that is false. 2. dishonest trick; a lie spoken or acted. 3. the quality in a person that makes him tell lies.

de ceit ful (di sēt′fəl), 1. ready or willing to deceive or lie. 2. deceiving; misleading. 3. meant to deceive.

de ceive (di sēv′), 1. make (a person) believe as true something that is false; mislead. The boy tried to deceive his mother, but she knew what he had done. 2. lie; use deceit.

De cem ber (di sem′bər), the 12th and last month of the year. December 25 is Christmas.

de cen cy (dē′sən si), 1. being decent; decent behavior. Common decency requires a healthy man to try to support his family. 2. something decent or proper. Washing your face, using good language, and going to church are some of the decencies of life.

de cent (dē′sənt), 1. respectable; modest; fit and proper. It is not decent to laugh at a funeral. 2. good enough; not wonderful and not very bad. I get decent marks at school. 3. not severe; rather kind. My boss was very decent about my being away when my mother was ill.

de cep tion (di sep′shən), 1. a deceiving. 2. trick; fraud; sham.

de cep tive (di sep′tiv), deceiving.

de cide (di sīd′), 1. settle. Let us decide it by tossing a penny. 2. give judgment. Mother decided in favor of the blue dress. 3. resolve; make up one's mind. John decided to be a sailor.

de cid ed (di sīd′id), 1. definite; unquestionable. 2. resolute; determined. 3. See also **decide.**

de cid ed ly (di sīd′id li), more than a little; distinctly; without question. John's work is decidedly better than Frank's. It was a decidedly warm morning.

dec i mal (des′i məl), 1. a fraction like $\frac{4}{100}$ or .04, .2 or $\frac{2}{10}$. 2. a number like 75.24, 3.062, .7, or .091. 3. of tens; proceeding by tens. United States money has a decimal system.

de ci pher (di sī′fər), 1. make out the meaning of (bad writing, an unknown language, or anything puzzling). 2. change (something in cipher) into ordinary writing; interpret by using a key.

de ci sion (di sizh′ən), 1. deciding; judgment; making up one's mind. The judge gives a decision in a lawsuit. 2. firmness; being decided. **With decision** means without any wavering or doubt; quickly and with force.

de ci sive (di sī′siv), 1. having a clear result; settling something beyond question; as, a decisive victory. 2. having or showing decision; as, a decisive answer.

deck (dek), 1. one of the floors or platforms extending from side to side and often from end to end of a ship. The upper, main, middle, and lower decks of a ship are somewhat like the stories of a house. Often the upper deck has no roof over it. 2. cover; dress; adorn. Grace was decked out in white linen. 3. a pack of playing cards.

dec la ra tion (dek′lə rā′shən), a statement; an open or public statement; a very strong statement.

de clare (di klãr′), say; make known; say openly or strongly. The boy declared that he would never go back to school again. Congress has the power to declare war. Travelers returning to the United States must declare the things which they bought abroad. Peace was declared at last. The boys declared themselves against cheating.

de cline (di klīn′), 1. refuse; turn away from doing. The man declined my offer. The boy declined to do what he was told. 2. bend or slope down. The high hill declines to a fertile valley. 3. grow less in strength and power; grow worse. A man's power declines as he grows old. Great nations have risen and declined. 4. falling to a lower level; losing strength; growing worse; as, the decline of a person's strength, the decline of the sun to the horizon, a decline in prices. 5. the last part of anything; as, the decline of the day, the decline of a person's life.

de cliv i ty (di kliv′i ti), a downward slope. A precipice is a very, very steep declivity.

de com pose (dē′kəm pōz′), 1. decay; rot. 2. separate (a substance) into what it is made of. A prism decomposes sunlight.

de com po si tion (dē′kom pə zish′ən), 1. act or process of decomposing. 2. decay.

dec o rate (dek′ə rāt), 1. make beautiful; trim; adorn. We decorated the Christmas tree with shining balls. 2. give a badge, ribbon, or medal to. The general decorated the soldier for his brave act.

dec o ra tion (dek′ə rā′shən), 1. decorating. 2. ornament. 3. a badge, ribbon, or medal given as an honor.

Decoration Day, Memorial Day. In most States it falls on May 30.

dec o ra tive (dek′ə rā′tiv), ornamental; helping to make beautiful.

de co rum (di kō′rəm), propriety of action, speech, dress, etc. You behave with decorum when you do what is fit and proper.

de coy (di koi′), 1. lead (wild birds, animals, etc.) into a trap or near the hunter. 2. a wooden bird used to entice birds into a trap or near the hunter. 3. a trained bird or other animal used for the same purpose. 4. entice; lead or tempt into danger. 5. any person or thing used to entice; a lure.

Wooden decoy for ducks

de crease (di krēs′ for 1 and 2, dē′krēs for 3 and 4), 1. grow or become less. Hunger decreases as one eats. 2. make less. Decrease the dose of medicine as you feel better. 3. growing less. Toward night there was a decrease of heat. 4. the amount by which a thing is made less. The decrease in heat was ten degrees.

de cree (di krē′), 1. something ordered or settled by authority; a decision; a law. By the king's decree all thieves were hanged. 2. order or settle by authority. The government decreed that Washington's birthday should be a holiday.

ded i cate (ded′i kāt), 1. set apart for a purpose. A minister or priest is dedicated to the service of God. The land on which the battle was fought was dedicated to the memory of the soldiers who had died there. 2. address (a book or other work) to a friend or patron.

de duct (di dukt′), take away; subtract.

de duc tion (di duk′shən), 1. act of taking away; subtraction. No deduction in pay is made for absence due to illness. 2. amount deducted.

deed (dēd), 1. something done; an act; an action. To feed the hungry is a good deed. Deeds, not words, are needed. 2. a written or printed agreement. The buyer of land receives a deed to the property from the former owner.

deem (dēm), think; believe; consider. The general deemed it wise to retreat.

deep (dēp). The ocean is deep here. The men dug a deep well to get pure water. The lot on which the house stands is 100 feet deep. She heard the low tones of the deep voice. A deep subject is one that is hard to understand. Deep feeling is hard to put into words. A deep sleep is one that is hard to be wakened from. The men dug deep before they found water. The color was a deep red. **The deep** sometimes means the sea.

deep en (dēp′ən), make deeper; become deeper.

deep ly (dēp′li), in a deep way; far down; in low tones; to a great extent; with much feeling.

deer (dēr), a graceful animal that chews the cud. The male deer has horns. See the picture. There are twenty tame deer in Lincoln Park.

Virginia deer (3½ ft. high at the shoulder)

def., definition.

de face (di fās′), spoil the looks of; mar. Thoughtless boys have defaced the desks by marking on them.

de feat (di fēt′), 1. overcome; gain the victory over; as, to defeat the enemy in battle, to defeat another school in basketball. 2. make useless; undo. Tom's effort to toughen himself by going without an overcoat defeated itself, for he caught a bad cold. 3. a defeating; as, Tom's defeat of Joe. 4. a being defeated; as, Joe's defeat by Tom.

de fect (di fekt′ or dē′fekt), 1. fault. A piece of cloth often shows defects in weaving. 2. the lack of something needed for completeness; falling short. A bad temper was the defect in Henry's kind and generous nature.

de fec tive (di fek′tiv), not complete; not perfect; faulty. This pump is defective and will not work.

de fence (di fens′), defense.

de fence less (di fens′lis), defenseless.

de fend (di fend′), 1. keep safe; protect. 2. act, speak, or write in favor of. The newspapers defended the governor's action.

de fend er (di fen′dər), person who defends; guardian.

de fense (di fens′), 1. any thing, act, or word that defends, guards, or protects. A wall around a city was a defense against enemies. A well-built house or a warm coat is a defense against cold weather. 2. defending. Thanks for your defense of Tim from that bully. 3. a being defended.

de fense less (di fens′lis), having no defense; helpless against attack. A baby is defenseless; he cannot prevent what is done to him.

A city without guns or water is defenseless against an army.

de fen sive (di fen′siv), 1. defending; ready to defend; intended to defend. France fought a defensive war. 2. defensive position or attitude. **On the defensive** means ready to defend but not to attack.

de fer[1] (di fėr′), put off; delay. Examinations were deferred because so many children were sick.

de fer[2] (di fėr′), yield in judgment or opinion. **Defer to** another person means put his opinion ahead of one's own; show respect to him. Children should defer to their parents' wishes.

def er ence (def′ər əns), 1. yielding to the judgment, opinion, wishes, etc., of another. 2. great respect. Boys and girls should show deference to persons who are much older and wiser. 3. **In deference to** means out of respect for the wishes or authority of.

de fi ance (di fī′əns), defying; standing up against authority and refusing to recognize or obey it; open resistance to power. He shouted defiance at the enemy. He goes without a hat all winter in defiance of the cold weather.

de fi ant (di fī′ənt), showing defiance; disobedient. The boy said, "I won't," in a defiant manner.

de fi cien cy (di fish′ən si), 1. a lack or absence of something needed. There is a deficiency of salt in this stew; put more in. 2. the amount by which a thing falls short or is too small. If a bill to be paid is $10 and you have only $6, the deficiency is $4.

de fi cient (di fish′ənt), lacking; incomplete; not enough. This milk is deficient in fat.

de file[1] (di fīl′), 1. make dirty, bad-smelling, or in any way disgusting. 2. destroy the pureness or cleanness of (anything sacred). The barbarians defiled the church by using it as a stable.

de file[2] (di fīl′), 1. to march in a line. 2. a narrow way through which troops can march only in narrow columns; a steep and narrow valley.

de fine (di fīn′), 1. explain the nature of; make clear the meaning of. A dictionary defines words. 2. settle the limits of. The powers of the courts are defined by law. The boundary between the United States and Canada is defined.

def i nite (def′i nit), clear; precise; not vague. Say "Yes" or "No", or give me some definite answer.

def i nite ly (def′i nit li), clearly; without doubt.

def i ni tion (def′i nish′ən), 1. explaining the nature of a thing; making clear the meaning of a word. 2. a statement in which the nature of a thing is explained or the meaning of a word is made clear.

de form i ty (di fôr′mi ti), 1. something in the shape of a body that is not as it should be, such as a hump on the back or a stump instead of a foot. 2. an ugliness of mind or body. 3. the state or fact of being deformed. Pearl said that she would prefer death to deformity.

de fraud (di frôd′), cheat; take away from by fraud.

deft (deft), skillful; nimble; clever. The fingers of a violinist must be deft.

de fy (di fī′), 1. challenge (a person) to do or prove something. We defy you to show that our game is not fair. 2. set oneself openly against (authority). As soon as the boy was earning his own living he defied his stepfather's strict rules. 3. withstand; resist. This strong fort defies capture.

de grade (di grād′), 1. reduce to a lower rank, often as a punishment; take away a position or an honor from. The captain was degraded for disobeying orders. 2. make worse; lower. You degrade yourself when you tell a lie.

de gree (di grē′), 1. a step in a scale; a stage in a process. By degrees the lake gets warm enough to swim in. 2. amount; extent. To what degree are you interested in reading? 3. rank. A princess is a lady of high degree. 4. a unit for measuring temperature. The freezing point of water is 32 degrees. 5. a unit for measuring the opening of an angle or an arc of a circle. A 90° angle is a right angle.

Degrees (def. 5)

deign (dān), condescend; think fit. So great a man would never deign to notice us.

de i ty (dē′i ti), 1. a god or goddess. Jove was a deity of the thunder. 2. **The Deity** means God.

de ject ed (di jek′tid), sad; discouraged.

de lay (di lā′), 1. put off till a later time. We will delay the party for a week. 2. putting off till a later time. The delay upset our plans. 3. make late; keep waiting; hinder the progress of. The accident delayed the train for two hours. 4. be late; go slowly; stop along the way. Do not delay on this errand. 5. a wait; making late; hindering; stopping along the way. We were so late that we could afford no further delay.

del e gate (del′i gāt), 1. person who acts for others; a representative. We sent two delegates to the meeting. 2. appoint or send (a person) as a representative. The children delegated Mary to buy the flowers. 3. give over (one's power or authority) to another so that he may act for one. The States delegated some of their rights to the nation.

del e ga tion (del′i gā′shən), 1. delegating; being delegated. 2. a group of delegates. Each club sent a delegation to the meeting.

de lib er ate (di lib′ər it for 1, 2, and 3, di lib′ər āt for 4 and 5), 1. intended; done on purpose; thought over beforehand. His excuse was a deliberate lie. 2. slow and careful in deciding what to do. Judges are more deliberate than sailors, as a rule. 3. slow; not hurried. The old man walked with deliberate steps. 4. think over; think over carefully. I was deliberating where to put up my new picture. 5. talk over reasons for and against; debate.

de lib er ate ly (di lib′ər it li), 1. on purpose. 2. slowly.

de lib er a tion (di lib′ər ā′shən), 1. careful thought. After long deliberation, he decided not to go. 2. talking about reasons for or against an action. 3. slowness. He aimed his gun with great deliberation.

del i ca cy (del′i kə si), 1. fineness of weave, quality, or make; slightness and grace; as, delicacy of silks or colors, the delicacy of a baby's skin. 2. fineness of feeling for small differences; as, delicacy of hearing or touch. 3. need of care, skill, or tact. A matter of great delicacy is one that requires careful handling. 4. thought for the feelings of others. 5. shrinking from what is offensive or not modest. 6. weakness; being easily hurt or made ill. The child's delicacy was a constant worry to his mother. 7. a dainty; a choice kind of food. Nuts and candy are delicacies.

del i cate (del′i kit), 1. pleasing to the taste; lightly flavored; mild; soft; as, delicate foods, delicate colors, delicate fragrance. 2. of fine weave, quality, or make; thin; easily torn. A spider's web is very delicate. 3. requiring careful handling; as, delicate flowers, a delicate situation, a delicate question. 4. finely sensitive; as, delicate instruments, a delicate sense of touch. 5. easily hurt or made ill; as, a delicate child.

de li cious (di lish′əs), very pleasing or satisfying; delightful, especially to taste or smell.

de light (di līt′), 1. great pleasure; joy. 2. something which gives great pleasure. Dancing is her delight. 3. please greatly. The circus delighted the children. 4. have great pleasure. Children delight in surprises.

de light ful (di līt′fəl), giving joy; very pleasing; as, a delightful ride, a delightful person.

de lir i ous (di lir′i əs), 1. out of one's senses; wandering in mind; raving. 2. wildly excited.

de liv er (di liv′ər), 1. carry and give out. The postman delivers letters. 2. give up; hand over. Dick delivered his mother's message to Mrs. Brown. 3. strike; throw. The fighter delivered a blow. 4. give forth in words. The traveler delivered a course of talks on his travels. The jury delivered its verdict. 5. set free; save from evil or trouble. "Deliver us from evil."

de liv er ance (di liv′ər əns), 1. release; freedom. The soldiers rejoiced in their deliverance from prison. 2. utterance; formal opinion or judgment.

de liv er er (di liv′ər ər), 1. rescuer; savior. 2. person who delivers.

de liv er y (di liv′ər i), 1. carrying and giving out letters, goods, etc.; as, parcel-post delivery. There are two deliveries of mail daily in our city. 2. giving over; handing over. The captive was released upon the delivery of his ransom. 3. manner of speaking. Our minister has an excellent delivery. 4. any act of delivering; as, the delivery of a hard blow.

Delta of the Mississippi River

dell (del), a small, sheltered glen or valley, usually with trees in it.

del ta (del′tə), the deposit of earth and sand that collects at the mouth of some rivers and is usually three-sided. See the picture above.

de lude (di lüd′), mislead; deceive.

del uge (del′ūj), 1. a great flood. 2. heavy fall of rain. 3. to flood; overflow. Water deluged our cellar when the big pipe broke.

de lu sion (di lü′zhən), a false belief or opinion. The crazy man had a delusion that he was President of the United States.

delve (delv), dig. That professor is always delving for knowledge in old books.

de mand (di mand′), 1. ask for as a right. The prisoner demanded a trial. 2. ask for with authority. The policeman demanded the boys' names. 3. call for; require; need. Training a puppy demands patience. 4. a claim. A mother has many demands upon her time. 5. a call; a request. Taxicabs are in great demand on rainy days. The supply of apples is greater than the demand this year.

de mean or (di mēn′ər), behavior; manner; the way one acts and looks. Amy has a quiet, modest demeanor.

dem i god (dem′i god′), a god; one who is partly divine and partly human.

de moc ra cy (di mok′rə si), 1. a government that is run by the people who live under it. 2. a country or town in which the government is a democracy. The United States is a democracy. 3. treating other people as one's equals. The old gentleman's democracy made him liked by all classes.

dem o crat (dem′ə krat), 1. person who believes that a government should be run by the people who live under it. 2. person who holds or acts on the belief that all people are his equals. 3. A **Democrat** is a member of the Democratic Party.

dem o crat ic (dem′ə krat′ik), 1. of a democracy; like a democracy. 2. treating all classes of people as one's equals. The queen's democratic ways made her dear to her people. 3. The **Democratic Party** is one of the two main political parties in the United States. 4. of the Democratic Party.

de mol ish (di mol′ish), pull or tear down; destroy.

de mon (dē′mən), 1. devil; evil spirit; fiend. 2. a very wicked or cruel person.

dem on strate (dem′ən strāt), 1. show clearly; prove. 2. teach by carrying out experiments, or by showing and explaining samples or specimens. 3. show, advertise, or make publicly known, by carrying out a process in public. He demonstrated his washing machine to us by washing some clothes with it. 4. show (feeling) openly. 5. show feeling by a parade, meeting, etc.

dem on stra tion (dem′ən strā′shən), 1. clear proof; as, a demonstration that the earth is round. 2. teaching by carrying out experiments, or by showing and explaining samples or specimens. 3. showing some new product or process in a public place; as, the demonstration of a washing machine. 4. open show or expression of feeling. He greeted them with every demonstration of joy. 5. a showing of feeling by a meeting, a procession, or the like.

de mure (di mūr′), 1. sober; serious; sedate. The modest maiden was demure. 2. falsely sedate or modest. A flirt may look demure.

den (den), 1. a wild animal's home. The bear's den was in a cave. 2. place where thieves have their headquarters. 3. a small, dirty room. 4. one's private room for reading and work, usually small and cozy.

de ni al (di nī′əl), 1. saying (a thing) is not so; as, a denial of the existence of fairies. 2. saying that one does not hold or accept a belief. When he was accused of heresy, he made a public denial. 3. refusing. His denial of our request seemed very rude.

de nied (di nīd′). See **deny.**

de nom i na tor (di nom′i nā′tər), the number below the line in a fraction, which states the size of the parts. In $\frac{3}{4}$, *4* is the denominator, and *3* is the numerator.

de note (di nōt′), indicate; be the sign of; mean. A fever usually denotes sickness. If I write "Excellent" on your paper, it denotes very good work.

de nounce (di nouns′), 1. speak against. The preacher denounced sin. 2. announce or report as something bad; give information against. He denounced his own brother as a thief.

dense (dens), 1. closely packed together; thick; as, a dense forest, a dense fog. 2. stupid.

den si ty (den′si ti), 1. closeness; compactness. The density of the woods prevented us from seeing more than a little way ahead. 2. the amount of matter to a unit of bulk. The density of lead is greater than the density of wood. 3. stupidity.

dent (dent), 1. a hollow made by a blow or pressure. The desk showed the dents of many years' use. 2. make a dent in. That table was dented in moving. 3. become dented. Soft wood dents easily.

den tal (den′təl), 1. of or for the teeth. 2. of or for a dentist's work.

den tist (den′tist), person who makes a business of filling, cleaning, and taking out teeth.

de ny (di nī′), 1. say (something) is not true. The prisoner denies the charges against him. They are denying the existence of disease in the town. 2. say that one does not hold or accept. 3. refuse. I could not deny her the favor. 4. disown; refuse to acknowledge. He denied his signature.

de part (di pärt′), 1. go away; leave. We arrived in the village in the morning, and departed that night. 2. turn away (from); change. He departed from his usual way of working. 3. die.

de part ment (di pärt′mənt), 1. a separate part of some whole; as, the fire department of a city government. 2. A **department store** sells many different kinds of things in separate departments under one management.

de par ture (di pär′chər), 1. act of going away. His departure was very sudden. 2. turning away; change; as, a departure from our old custom. 3. starting on a new course of action or thought. This dancing class will be a new departure for me, for I have never done anything like it.

de pend (di pend′), 1. rely; trust. You can depend on the timetable to tell you when trains leave. 2. **Depend on** means (1) be a result of. Health depends on good food, fresh air, and enough sleep. (2) have as a support; get help from. Children depend on their parents for food and clothing. 3. depend on something. Mary said, "That depends."

de pend ant (di pen′dənt), dependent.

de pend ence (di pen′dəns), 1. the fact or condition of being dependent; as, the dependence of crops on the weather. 2. trust. Do not put your dependence in him, for he may fail you. 3. living at the cost of another. The boy wished to go to work so that he could end his dependence on his uncle.

de pend ent (di pen′dənt), 1. trusting to or depending on another person or thing for support. A child is dependent on its parents. 2. a person who is supported by another. 3. depending; possible if something else takes place. Being promoted is dependent on doing good enough work in school. A farmer's success is dependent on having the right kind of weather for his crops.

de pict (di pikt′), represent by drawing, painting, or describing; portray. The artist and the author both tried to depict the splendor of the sunset.

de plore (di plōr′), be very sorry about; express great sorrow for. We deplore your misfortunes.

de port ment (di pōrt′mənt), behavior; conduct; way a person acts.

de pos it (di poz′it), 1. put down. He deposited his bundles on the table. 2. leave lying. The flood deposited a layer of mud in the streets. 3. a laying down of material by natural means; the material laid down. There is often a deposit of sand and mud at the mouth of a river. 4. put in a place to be kept safe. Deposit your money in the bank. 5. something put in a certain place to be kept safe. Money put in the bank is a deposit. 6. pay down as a pledge for carrying out a promise to do something or to pay more later. If you will deposit $5, we will hold the coat for you. 7. the money paid down as a pledge of this sort.

de pot (dē′pō), 1. railroad station. 2. storehouse. 3. place for storing military supplies.

de press (di pres′), 1. press down; lower. When you play the piano, you depress the keys. 2. make less active; weaken. Some medicines depress the action of the heart. 3. make sad. Rainy weather always depresses me. She was depressed by the death of her son.

de pres sion (di presh′ən), 1. a pressing down; a lowering or sinking. The heavy weight of snow caused a depression of the shed's roof. 2. a hollow. Water filled the depressions in the ground. 3. low spirits; sadness. In a fit of depression the sick man killed himself. 4. a lowering of activity. Many men lost their jobs during the business depression.

de prive (di prīv′). To deprive a person of a thing means (1) to take it away from him, or (2) to keep him from having it or doing it. The children were deprived of supper means that the children were not allowed to have their supper. His troubles deprived him of sleep means that his troubles kept him from sleeping.

depth (depth), 1. distance from the top to the bottom; as, the depth of a hole, the depth of a lake. 2. the deepest or most central part of anything; as, in the depths of the earth, in the depths of one's heart, in the depth of winter. 3. distance from front to back. The depth of our house lot is 125 feet. 4. deep quality; deepness.

dep u ty (dep′ū ti), person appointed to do the work or take the place of another. John was the teacher's deputy for half an hour.

der by (dėr′bi), a stiff hat with rounded crown and narrow brim.

Derby

de ride (di rīd′), make fun of; laugh at in scorn. The boys derided Percy because of his curls.

de ri sion (di rizh′ən), scornful laughter; ridicule. Children dread the derision of their playmates.

de rive (di rīv′), get; obtain. He derives much pleasure from his books. From the word *deep* you can derive *deeper*, *deeply*, and *deepen*.

der rick (der′ik), 1. a machine for lifting and moving heavy objects. A derrick has a long arm that swings at an angle from the base of an upright post or frame. 2. towerlike framework over an oil well, gas well, etc., that holds the drilling and hoisting machinery.

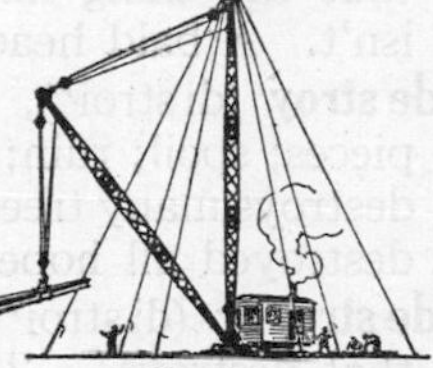

Derrick

de scend (di send′), 1. go or come down from a higher to a lower place. We descend the stairs, a mountain, a river. The river descends to the sea. 2. go from earlier to later time. 3. go from greater to less numbers; go from higher to lower on any scale. 4. make a sudden attack. The wolves descended on the sheep and killed them.

de scend ant (di sen′dənt), 1. person born of a certain family or group; as, a descendant of the Pilgrims. 2. offspring; child, grandchild, great-grandchild, etc. You are a direct descendant of your parents, grandparents, great-grandparents, etc.

de scent (di sent′), 1. coming or going down from a higher to a lower place. The descent of the balloon was more rapid than its rise had been. 2. downward slope. We climbed down a steep descent. 3. handing down from parent to child. We can trace the descent of this shape of lip through five generations. 4. family line; ancestors. 5. sudden attack.

de scribe (di skrīb′), 1. tell in words how a person looks, feels, or acts, or how a place, a thing, or an event looks; tell about in words. 2. trace or form; draw the outline of. The spinning top described a figure 8.

de scrip tion (di skrip′shən), 1. a telling in words how a person, place, thing, or event looks or behaves; a describing. 2. composition or account that describes or gives a picture in words. 3. kind; sort. I have seen no dog of any description today.

de scrip tive (di skrip′tiv), describing. Write a descriptive paragraph about a flower garden.

des ert[1] (dez′ərt), 1. a region without water and trees. There is a great desert in the northern part of Africa. 2. not inhabited or cultivated; barren and desolate. Robinson Crusoe was shipwrecked on a desert island.

de sert[2] (di zėrt′), forsake; go away and leave a person or a place, especially one which should not be left. The selfish man deserted his wife and children. A soldier who deserts is punished. The deserted house fell into ruins.

de sert[3] (di zėrt′), what one deserves; just reward or punishment. The thief was punished according to his deserts. The thief got his just deserts.

de sert er (di zėr′tər), 1. person who deserts. 2. a soldier or sailor who runs away from duty.

de serve (di zėrv′), have a right to; have a claim to; be worthy of. Good work deserves good pay. Bad acts deserve punishment.

de sign (di zīn′), 1. a drawing, plan, or sketch made to serve as a pattern from which to work. She is working now from my designs. 2. arrangement of details, form, and color in painting, weaving, building, etc.; as, a wallpaper design in tan and brown. 3. make a first sketch of; plan out; arrange form and color of. 4. a plan in mind to be carried out; a purpose. The thief was not able to carry out his designs because of the dog. 5. set apart; intend; plan. The nursery was designed for the baby's use. His parents designed him for the ministry.

Design for a calendar

des ig nate (dez′ig nāt), 1. mark out; point out; show. Will you designate the flowers you wish? 2. name. The ruler of a kingdom is designated a king.

de sir a bil i ty (di zīr′ə bil′i ti), desirable quality; condition to be wished for. Nobody doubts the desirability of good health.

de sir a ble (di zīr′ə bəl), 1. worth wishing for. 2. pleasant; satisfying; good.

de sire (di zīr′), 1. wish. 2. wish earnestly for. 3. ask for. 4. a long, earnest wish. 5. thing wished for.

de sir ous (di zīr′əs), desiring; wishing; eager. He was desirous of going to Europe then.

de sist (di zist′), stop; cease.

desk (desk), piece of furniture with a flat or sloping top on which to write or to rest books for reading.

des o late (des′ə lāt for 1 and 3, des′ə lit for 2 and 4), 1. make unfit to live in. 2. not lived in; as, a desolate house. 3. make unhappy. We are desolated to hear that you are going away. 4. unhappy; forlorn. The child looked desolate.

des o la tion (des′ə lā′shən), 1. making desolate. 2. a ruined, lonely, or deserted condition. 3. desolate place. 4. sadness; lonely sorrow.

de spair (di spãr′), 1. loss of hope; a being without hope; a dreadful feeling that nothing good can happen to you. Despair seized us as we felt the boat sinking under us. 2. lose hope; be without hope. The doctors despaired of saving the child's life. 3. something that causes loss of hope.

des patch (dis pach′), dispatch.

des per ate (des′pər it), 1. not caring what happens because hope is gone. 2. having little chance for hope or cure; very dangerous; as, a desperate illness. 3. ready to run any risk; as, a desperate robber.

des per a tion (des′pər ā′shən), 1. reckless feeling; readiness to try anything. In desperation he decided on a dash through the flames. 2. despair.

de spise (di spīz′), look down upon; scorn; think of as beneath your notice, or as too mean or low for you to do. Honest boys despise lies and liars.

de spite (di spīt′), 1. in spite of. The boys went for a walk despite the rain. 2. spite.

de spoil (di spoil′), rob; plunder.

des pot (des′pot), absolute ruler; tyrant; person who does just as he likes.

des sert (di zėrt′), a course of sweets or fruit at the end of a meal.

des ti na tion (des′ti nā′shən), the place to which a person or thing is going.

des tine (des′tin), 1. intend; reserve for a purpose or use. The prince was destined from his birth to be a king. 2. cause by fate. My letter was destined never to reach him. 3. **Destined for** means (1) intended to go to; bound for; as, ships destined for England. (2) intended for; as, destined for the ministry.

des ti ny (des′ti ni), 1. what becomes of a person or thing in the end. It was his destiny to die in battle. 2. fate; what is determined beforehand to happen. He struggled in vain against his destiny.

des ti tute (des′ti tūt or des′ti tüt), 1. needing necessary things such as food, clothing, and shelter. A destitute family needs help from charity. 2. **Destitute of** means having no; empty of. Destitute of usually implies that the thing might have been there but isn't. A bald head is destitute of hair.

de stroy (di stroi′), pull down; break to pieces; spoil; ruin; put an end to; kill. Fire destroys many trees every year. A heavy rain destroyed all hope of a picnic.

de stroy er (di stroi′ər), 1. person or thing that destroys. 2. small, fast warship with guns, torpedoes, and other weapons.

de struc tion (di struk′shən), 1. destroying. A crowd watched the destruction of the old building. 2. ruin. The storm left destruction behind it.

de struc tive (di struk′tiv), destroying; causing destruction. Fires and earthquakes are destructive. Destructive criticism shows things to be wrong, but does not show how to correct them.

de tach (di tach′), 1. unfasten; loosen and remove; separate. He detached his watch from the chain. A detached house is not joined to any other house. 2. in the army or navy, to send away on special duty. One squad of soldiers was detached to guard the road.

de tach ment (di tach′mənt), 1. separation. 2. lack of interest. 3. troops or ships sent away on special duty.

de tail (di tāl′ for 1, 2, 3, 4, and 5, or dē′tāl for 1, 2, and 4), 1. a small or unimportant part. All the details of her costume carried out the brown color scheme. 2. dealing with small things one by one. She does not enjoy the details of housekeeping. 3. tell fully; tell even the small and unimportant parts. The new boy detailed to us all the wonders he had seen in his travels. 4. in the army, a small group of men or officers sent on some special duty. The captain sent a detail of ten men to guard the bridge. 5. send on special duty. The captain detailed three soldiers to watch the road.

de tain (di tān′), keep back; delay; keep from going ahead; keep from going away. The police detained the suspected thief for further questioning.

de tect (di tekt′), find out; make out; discover; catch. Could you detect any odor in the room? Tom was detected stealing cookies in the pantry.

de tec tive (di tek′tiv), 1. a policeman or private person whose business is to get information secretly. 2. having something to do with detectives and their work.

de ter (di tėr′), discourage; keep back; hinder. The extreme heat deterred us from going downtown.

de ter mi na tion (di tėr′mi nā′shən), 1. deciding; settling beforehand. The determination of the list of things to prepare for that important trip took a long time. 2. finding out the exact amount or kind by weighing, measuring, calculating, etc. 3. fixed purpose; great firmness in carrying out a purpose. The boy's determination was not weakened by the difficulties he met.

de ter mine (di tėr′min), 1. make up one's mind very firmly. He determined to become the best Scout in his troop. 2. fix or settle beforehand. Can we now determine the date for our party? 3. be the deciding fact in reaching a certain result; settle. The number of examples you get right determines your mark on this test. Tomorrow's events will determine whether we are to go or stay.

de ter mined (di tėr′mind), 1. with one's mind firmly made up; resolved. The determined explorer kept on his way in spite of the storm. 2. firm; resolute. His determined look showed that he had made up his mind.

de test (di test′), dislike very much; hate.

de test a ble (di tes′tə bəl), deserving to be detested; hateful. Murder is a detestable crime.

de throne (di thrōn′), put off a throne; remove from ruling power.

de tour (dē′tür), 1. road that is used when the main or direct road cannot be traveled. 2. roundabout way. 3. use a detour.

dev as tate (dev′əs tāt), destroy; ravage; lay waste; make unfit to live in. A long war devastated Europe.

de vel op (di vel′əp), 1. grow; bring or come into being or activity. Plants develop from seeds. The seeds develop into plants. A boy may develop an interest in stamps. An interest in cooking developed in Mary when she was ten. 2. work out in greater and greater detail. Gradually we developed our plans for the Boys' Club. 3. treat (a photographic plate or film) with chemicals so that the picture shows.

de vel op ment (di vel′əp mənt), 1. developing; growth; bringing or coming to light. 2. outcome; result; news. A newspaper gives news about the latest developments. 3. working out in greater and greater detail.

de vice (di vīs′), 1. a mechanical invention used for a special purpose; machine; apparatus. A can opener is a device. So is an electric razor. 2. a plan; a scheme; sometimes, a trick. By some device or other the thief got the boy to let him into the house. 3. a drawing or figure used in a pattern or as an ornament. 4. **Left to one's own devices** means left to do as one thinks best.

dev il (dev′əl), 1. **The Devil** means the evil spirit, the enemy of goodness, or Satan. 2. any evil spirit. 3. person who is especially wicked, reckless, clever, active, etc. 4. person who has to work for others and stand their abuse. A printer's devil is the errand boy in a printing office. 5. bother; tease; torment.

dev il ish (dev′əl ish), 1. very evil; worthy of the devil; like a devil. 2. very; extremely; very great.

de vise (di vīz′), think out; plan; contrive; invent. The boys are trying to devise some scheme of earning money.

de void (di void′), empty. **Devoid of** means having no; without. A well devoid of water is useless.

de vote (di vōt′), give up (oneself, one's money, time, or efforts) to some person, purpose, or service. A mother devotes herself to her children. Mary devotes too much time to eating. He devoted his efforts to the improvement of the parks in his city.

de vot ed (di vōt′id), very loyal; as, a devoted friend.

de vo tion (di vō′shən), 1. deep, steady affection; as, the devotion of a mother to her child. 2. a giving up or being given up to some person, purpose, or service. Ruth's devotion to the Girl Scouts made her attend every meeting. 3. **Devotions** means worship, prayers, or praying.

de vour (di vour′), 1. eat (said of animals). The lion devoured the sheep. 2. eat like an animal; eat very hungrily. The hungry boy was devouring his dinner. 3. consume; destroy. The fire devoured the forest. 4. take in with eyes or ears in a hungry, greedy way; as, to devour a new book.

de vout (di vout′), 1. religious; active in worship and prayer. 2. earnest; sincere; hearty; as, devout thanks.

dew (dū or dü), 1. moisture condensed from the air. In the morning there are drops of dew on the grass and flowers. 2. something fresh or refreshing like dew; as, the dew of youth, the dew of sleep. 3. to wet with dew; moisten.

dew drop (dū′drop′ or dü′drop′), drop of dew.

dew y (dū′i or dü′i), 1. wet with dew. 2. looking as if wet with dew.

dex ter i ty (deks ter′i ti), skill in using the hands or mind. A good surgeon works with dexterity.

di a bol ic (dī′ə bol′ik), devilish; like the devil; very cruel or wicked.

di a dem (dī′ə dem), crown; band worn around the head by a king or queen.

Diadem

di ag o nal (dī ag′ə nəl), 1. a straight line that cuts across in a slanting direction, often from corner to corner. 2. taking the direction of a diagonal; slanting; as, a ship sailing on a diagonal course, a diagonal stripe in cloth.

Line AB is a diagonal.

di ag o nal ly (dī ag′ə nəl i), in a diagonal direction.

di a gram (dī′ə gram), 1. a drawing or sketch showing important parts of a thing. A diagram may be an outline, a plan, a drawing, a figure, a chart, or a combination of any of these, made to show clearly what a thing is or how it works. Tom drew a diagram to show us how to get to his house. A plan of a house or a steamship is a diagram. 2. put on paper in the form of a drawing or sketch; make a diagram of.

di al (dī′əl), 1. a marked surface on which a moving pointer shows how much there is of something. The face of a clock or of a compass is a dial. A dial may show the amount of water in a tank or the amount of steam pressure in a boiler. 2. plate, disk, etc., of a radio with numbers, letters, etc., on it for tuning in to a radio station. 3. the part of an automatic telephone used in making telephone calls. 4. call by means of a telephone dial. Martha dialed Main 2590 to call her father's office. 5. sundial.

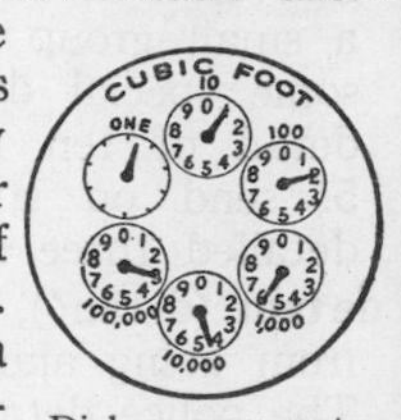

Dials on a gas meter

di a lect (dī′ə lekt), a form of speech peculiar to a district or class; as, the Scotch dialect or the Negro dialect.

di a logue or **di a log** (dī′ə lôg), 1. conversation. Two actors had a dialogue in the middle of the stage. 2. a conversation written out.

di am e ter (dī am′i tər), 1. a straight line passing through the center from one side of a circle, or other object, to the other side. 2. the length of such a line; measurement through the center. The diameter of the earth is about 8000 miles.

Line AB is a diameter.

di a mond (dī′ə mənd), 1. a colorless or tinted precious stone, formed of pure carbon in crystals. A diamond is the hardest substance known. 2. a figure shaped like this ◊. 3. the space inside the lines that connect the bases in baseball.

Diamond

di a ry (dī′ə ri), 1. an account, written down each day, of what has happened to one, or what one has done or thought, during that day. 2. a blank book with a space for each day in which to keep a daily record.

dice (dīs), 1. small cubes with a different number of spots (one to six) on each side. Dice are used in playing some games. 2. use dice in gambling. 3. cut into small cubes. Carrots are sometimes diced before being cooked.

Dice

dic tate (dik′tāt), 1. say or read aloud to another person or other persons who are to write what is said or read. The teacher dictated a spelling list. Mr. Jones dictates many letters to his secretary. 2. speak with authority; make others do what one says. Big nations sometimes dictate to little ones. No one shall dictate to me. 3. a direction or order that is to be carried out or obeyed; as, the dictates of a ruler or of the teacher.

dic ta tion (dik tā′shən), 1. dictating. The pupils wrote at the teacher's dictation. 2. words dictated. The girl took the dictation and wrote it out on the typewriter later. 3. giving orders; making rules. The boy was tired of his sister's constant dictation and refused to obey her.

dic ta tor (dik′tā tər), 1. person who dictates. 2. person exercising absolute authority. The dictator of a country has complete power over its people.

dic tion ar y (dik′shən ãr′i), a book that explains the words of a language, or some special kind of words. The children used their dictionaries often.

did (did). See **do**[1]. Did he go to school yesterday? Yes, he did.

did n't (did′ənt), did not.

didst (didst), an old form meaning **did.** "Thou didst" means "You did."

die[1] (dī), 1. stop living. 2. lose force or strength; come to an end. The music died away. 3. want very much. I am just dying to go with you.

die[2] (dī), 1. a carved metal block or plate. Different kinds of dies are used for coining money, for raising letters up from the surface of paper, and for giving a certain shape to articles made by forging and cutting. 2. a small cube used in games of chance. See **dice.**

Die for cutting threads of bolts

di et (dī′ət), 1. the usual food for a person or an animal. A rich diet is likely to make a person fat. The diet of the giraffe consists of young leaves and shoots. 2. any special selection of food eaten in sickness, or to make oneself fat, thin, etc. The doctor ordered a liquid diet for the sick child. 3. eat special food as a part of a doctor's treatment, or in order to gain or lose weight.

dif fer (dif′ər), 1. be unlike; be different. 2. hold or express a different opinion; disagree.

dif fer ence (dif′ər əns), 1. being different; as, the difference of night and day. 2. the amount or manner of being different. The difference between 6 and 15 is 9. 3. a dispute. The children had a difference over a name for the new puppy. 4. **Make a difference** means give or show different treatment, or be important.

dif fer ent (dif′ər ənt), 1. not alike; not like. People have different names. An automobile is different from a cart. 2. not the same; separate; distinct. We called three different times, but never found Alice at home.

dif fer ent ly (dif′ər ənt li), in a different way; in different ways.

dif fi cult (dif′i kult), 1. hard to do or understand. Arithmetic is difficult for some girls. 2. hard to manage; hard to please. Some movie stars are difficult.

dif fi cul ty (dif′i kul ti), 1. a thing that is hard to do or understand. 2. something which hinders. Our chief difficulties were lack of time and lack of money. 3. the degree to which a thing is difficult. The difficulty of the job was greater than we thought it would be. 4. hard work. Some children have a great deal of difficulty in learning how to spell. 5. trouble.

dig (dig), 1. use hands, spade, claws, or snout in making a hole or in turning over the ground. 2. make by digging. They dug a cellar. 3. make a way by digging; as, to dig through or under a mountain. 4. get by digging; as, to dig potatoes or clams. 5. thrust; poke. 6. work hard.

di gest (di jest′ for 1, 2, and 4, dī′jest for 3), 1. change (food) in the stomach and intestines, so that the body can use it. We digest our food; the food digests or is digested. 2. think over until you understand (it) clearly, or until (it) becomes a part of your own thought. 3. a brief statement of what is in a longer book or article. 4. make a brief statement of.

di ges tion (di jes′chən), 1. the digesting of food. 2. the power of digesting.

di ges tive (di jes′tiv), having something to do with digestion; as, digestive trouble, digestive tablets.

dig ger (dig′ər), 1. person or thing that digs. 2. the part of a machine that turns up the ground.

dig ni fied (dig′ni fīd), having dignity; noble; stately; of great worth.

dig ni fy (dig′ni fī), give dignity to; make noble, worth while, or worthy. The low farmhouse was dignified by the great elms around it.

dig ni ty (dig′ni ti), 1. quality of character or ability that wins the respect and high opinion of others; worth; being noble, worthy, or stately. A judge should maintain the dignity of his position. 2. high office, rank, or title; position of honor. He may attain the dignity of the presidency. 3. proud and self-respecting character or manner. 4. stately appearance; as, the dignity of a cathedral.

dike (dīk), 1. a bank of earth or a dam built as a defense against flooding by a river or the sea. 2. a ditch. 3. provide with dikes.

di lap i dat ed (di lap′i dāt′id), falling to pieces; partly ruined or decayed through neglect. The abandoned town was full of dilapidated houses.

di late (dī lāt′), 1. make or become larger or wider. The pupil of the eye dilates when the light gets dim. 2. speak or write at length. Mother was dilating on Johnnie's success.

dil i gence (dil′i jəns), working hard; being diligent; ability to work steadily.

dil i gent (dil′i jənt), hard-working; industrious; not lazy.

dill (dil), seed used in flavoring pickles.

di lute (di lüt′), 1. make weaker or thinner by adding water or some other liquid. 2. weakened or thinned by water or some other liquid.

dim (dim), 1. not bright; not clear; not distinct. 2. not clearly seen, heard, or understood. 3. not seeing, hearing, or understanding clearly. My eyesight is getting dimmer. 4. make or become dim. We dimmed our lights when we reached the city streets.

dime (dīm), silver coin of the United States and of Canada, worth 10 cents. Ten dimes make one dollar.

di men sion (di men′shən), 1. measurement of length, breadth, or thickness. If a room is 10 feet wide, 16 feet long, and 12 feet high, those are its dimensions. 2. **Dimensions** sometimes means size or extent.

di min ish (di min′ish), make or become smaller in size, amount, or importance. The heat diminished as the sun went down. Our diminishing supply of food had to be given out very carefully.

di min u tive (di min′ū tiv), 1. small; tiny. 2. a small person or thing. 3. a suffix expressing smallness, such as *-ling*, *-let*, or *-kin*.

dim ple (dim′pəl), 1. small hollow, usually in the cheek or chin. 2. form dimples. Alice dimples whenever she smiles. 3. make or show dimples in.

din (din), 1. a loud, confused noise that lasts. 2. make a din. 3. say (one thing) over and over. He was always dinning into our ears the importance of hard work.

dine (dīn), 1. eat dinner. 2. give dinner to; give a dinner for. The Chamber of Commerce dined the famous traveler.

din gy (din′ji), dirty-looking; lacking brightness or freshness. The old curtains were dingy.

din ner (din′ər), 1. the main meal of the day. In the city we have dinner at night, but in the country we have dinner at noon. 2. a formal meal in honor of some person or occasion.

di no saur (dī′nə sôr), one of a group of extinct reptiles. Some dinosaurs were bigger than elephants. Some were smaller than cats.

Dinosaur

dint (dint), 1. force. By dint of hard work the man became successful. 2. a dent. 3. make a dent in.

dip (dip), 1. put under water or any liquid and lift quickly out again. Mary dipped her head into the clear pool. 2. go under water and come quickly out again. 3. a dipping of any kind, especially, a plunge into and out of a tub of water, the sea, etc. 4. mixture in which to dip something. 5. make (a candle) by putting a wick into hot tallow or wax.

diph the ri a (dif thēr′i ə), a dangerous infectious disease of the throat. In former times many children died of diphtheria.

di plo ma (di plō′mə), a written or printed paper given by a school or college, which says that a person has completed a certain course of study, or has been graduated after a certain amount of work.

dip lo mat ic (dip′lə mat′ik), 1. having to do with the management of relations between nations. Ministers and consuls to foreign countries are in the diplomatic service. 2. skillful in dealing with people; tactful.

dip per (dip′ər), 1. person or thing that dips. 2. a long-handled cup or larger container for lifting water or liquids. 3. The **Big Dipper** and the **Little Dipper** are two groups of stars in the northern sky. See the picture just below.

Dipper for water

dire (dīr), dreadful; causing great fear or suffering.

di rect (di rekt′), 1. manage; control. The teacher directs the work of the pupils. 2. order; command. The captain directed his men to advance slowly. 3. tell or show the way. Can you direct me to the railroad station? Signposts direct travelers. 4. point (to); aim (at). We should direct our effort to a useful end. 5. address (a letter, package, etc.) to a person or place. 6. straight. Our house is in direct line with the school. A bee makes a direct flight home to the hive. 7. in an unbroken line. That man is a direct descendant of John Adams. 8. frank; truthful; plain. The boy gave direct answers. He made a direct denial of the charge of cheating. 9. directly.

Big Dipper and Little Dipper

di rec tion (di rek′shən), 1. guiding; managing; control. The school is under the direction of a good teacher. 2. order; command. 3. knowing or telling what to do, how to do, where to go, etc.; instruction. Can you give me directions how to reach the lake? 4. the address on a letter or package. 5. the course taken by a moving body, such as a ball or a bullet. 6. any way in which one may face or point. North, south, east, etc., are directions. Our school is in one direction and the post office is in another. 7. line of action; tendency, etc. The town shows improvement in many directions.

di rect ly (di rekt′li), 1. in a direct line or manner; straight. This road runs directly north. 2. exactly; absolutely; as, directly opposite. 3. immediately; at once. Come home directly.

di rec tor (di rek′tər), manager; person who directs.

di rec to ry (di rek′tə ri), a book of names and addresses. A telephone book is a directory.

dire ful (dīr′fəl), dire; terrible.

dirge (dėrj), funeral song or tune.

dir i gi ble (dir′i ji bəl), 1. a balloon that can be steered. See the picture. A dirigible is filled with a gas that is lighter than air. 2. capable of being directed.

Dirigible

dirk (dėrk), dagger.

dirt (dėrt), 1. mud, dust, earth, or anything like them which soils skin, clothing, houses, or furniture. 2. loose earth or soil. 3. an unclean thing, action, or speech.

dirt i ness (dėr′ti nis), dirty condition.

dirt y (dėr′ti), 1. not clean; soiled by mud, dust, earth, or anything like them. 2. not clean or pure in language or action; low; base. 3. not clear or pure in color; as, a dirty red. 4. stormy; rough. It was the dirtiest weather I ever saw. 5. make dirty; soil. **dirtier, dirtiest, dirtied,** and **dirtying** are formed from **dirty.**

dis a bil i ty (dis′ə bil′i ti), 1. something that disables. Deafness is a disability for a musician. 2. lack or weakness of some ability.

dis a ble (dis ā′bəl), deprive of ability or power; make useless; cripple.

dis ad van tage (dis′əd van′tij), 1. lack of advantage; unfavorable condition. Mary's shyness was a disadvantage in company. 2. loss; injury. Gossip to Mr. Brown's disadvantage was spread abroad by his enemies.

dis af fec tion (dis′ə fek′shən), disloyalty; discontent. Lack of food and supplies caused disaffection among the soldiers.

dis a gree (dis′ə grē′), 1. fail to agree; be different. Your story disagrees with his. 2. have unlike opinions; differ. Doctors sometimes disagree. 3. quarrel. 4. have a bad effect. Some foods disagree with him.

dis a gree a ble (dis′ə grē′ə bəl), 1. not to one's liking; not pleasant. A headache is disagreeable. 2. not friendly; unkind; cross. Mary is sometimes disagreeable until she has her breakfast.

dis a gree ment (dis′ə grē′mənt), 1. the state or fact of disagreeing; difference of opinion; dissent. 2. difference; unlikeness. 3. dissension; quarrel.

dis ap pear (dis′ə pēr′), pass from sight or from existence; be lost. The little dog disappeared down the road. When spring comes, the snow disappears.

dis ap pear ance (dis′ə pēr′əns), act of disappearing.

dis ap point (dis′ə point′), fail to satisfy one's desire, wish, or hope; leave (one) wanting something. The circus disappointed him, for there was no elephant. We were disappointed that our cousin could not come.

dis ap point ment (dis′ə point′mənt), 1. being disappointed; the feeling you have when you do not get what you expected or hoped for. When she did not find her mother, the disappointment seemed too great to bear. 2. person or thing that causes disappointment. Her lazy son was a disappointment to her. 3. act of disappointing. Ben's disappointment of our wishes was done on purpose.

dis ap prov al (dis′ə prüv′əl), having an opinion or feeling against; expressing an opinion against.

dis ap prove (dis′ə prüv′), consider not good or not suitable; express disapproval. Some girls disapprove of rough games.

dis arm (dis ärm′), 1. take weapons away from. The police captured the bandits and disarmed them. 2. stop having an army or navy; reduce the size of an army or navy. 3. remove anger, dislike, or suspicion. The little boy's smile could always disarm those who were about to scold or punish him. 4. make harmless.

dis as ter (di zas′tər), an event such as a flood, fire, shipwreck, earthquake, or great loss of money, which brings distress to many people; a great misfortune.

dis as trous (di zas′trəs), bringing disaster; causing danger, suffering, loss, pain, or sorrow to many people.

disc (disk), disk.

dis card (dis kärd′ for 1, dis′kärd for 2 and 3), 1. throw aside; give up as useless or worn out. You can discard clothes, ways of doing things, or beliefs. 2. act of throwing aside as useless. 3. thing or things thrown aside. That old book can go into the discard now; I don't want it.

dis cern (di zėrn′), perceive; distinguish; see clearly; recognize. I looked where he pointed, but could discern nothing. When there is so much gossip, it is hard to discern the truth.

dis charge (dis chärj′), 1. unload (a ship); unload (cargo) from a ship. 2. unloading. The discharge of this cargo will not take long. 3. fire off; as, to discharge a gun. 4. firing off a gun, a blast, etc. The discharge could be heard for three miles. 5. release; let go; dismiss; as, to discharge a patient from a hospital, to discharge a committee, to discharge a servant. 6. release; letting go; dismissing; as, the discharge of a prisoner from jail. 7. give off; let out. The wound discharges pus. 8. giving off; letting out. In a thunderstorm there is a discharge of electricity from the clouds. 9. thing given off or let out; as, the watery discharge from a sore. 10. pay (a debt). 11. payment of a debt. 12. perform (a duty). 13. the performing of a duty.

dis ci ple (di sī′pəl), 1. a believer in the thought and teaching of any leader; a follower. 2. in the New Testament, one of the followers of Jesus.

dis ci pline (dis′i plin), 1. training; especially, training of the mind or character. 2. a trained condition of order and obedience; order kept among school pupils, soldiers, or members of any group. When the fire broke out, the pupils showed good discipline. 3. train; bring to a condition of order and obedience; bring under control. 4. punishment. A little discipline would do him a world of good. 5. punish. You ought to discipline that rude boy for his bad behavior.

dis close (dis klōz′), 1. uncover. The lifting of the curtain disclosed a beautiful Christmas tree. 2. make known. This letter discloses a secret.

dis com fort (dis kum′fərt), 1. uneasiness; lack of comfort. 2. thing that causes discomfort.

dis con nect (dis′kə nekt′), separate; unfasten; undo or break the connection of. He disconnected the electric fan by pulling out the plug.

dis con tent (dis′kən tent′), 1. uneasy feeling; dissatisfaction; a dislike of what one has and a desire for something different. Discontent is the opposite of satisfaction. 2. displease.

dis con tent ed (dis′kən ten′tid), not contented; not satisfied; displeased and restless; disliking what one has and wanting something different.

dis con tin ue (dis′kən tin′ū), stop; give up. That train has been discontinued. After the patient got well, the doctor discontinued his visits.

dis cord (dis′kôrd), 1. harsh, clashing sounds. 2. in music, a lack of harmony in notes sounded at the same time. 3. difference of opinion; disputing. Angry discord spoiled the meeting.

dis cord ant (dis kôr′dənt), 1. harsh; clashing. Many automobile horns are discordant. 2. not in harmony; as, a discordant note in music. 3. not in agreement; not fitting together. Many discordant views were expressed.

dis cour age (dis kėr′ij), 1. take away the courage of; destroy the hopes of. Repeated failure discourages anyone. 2. try to prevent. All Nell's friends discouraged her from such a dangerous step. 3. frown on; make seem not worth while. The chill of coming winter soon discouraged our picnics.

dis cour age ment (dis kėr′ij mənt), 1. act of discouraging. 2. state of being or feeling discouraged. 3. something that discourages.

dis course (dis′kōrs for 1 and 2, dis kōrs′ for 3), 1. talk; conversation. 2. a long written or spoken discussion of some subject. Sermons and lectures are discourses. 3. to talk; converse.

dis cov er (dis kuv′ər), 1. find out; see or learn of for the first time. Columbus discovered America. No one has discovered a way to turn copper into gold. 2. make known; reveal. The knight would not discover his name to the prince.

dis cov er y (dis kuv′ər i), 1. finding out; seeing or learning of something for the first time. 2. the thing found out. One of Franklin's discoveries was that lightning was electricity.

dis cred it (dis kred′it), 1. cast doubt on; destroy belief in (a person, something thought to be true, a story told, or evidence offered). 2. doubt. Dick's story throws discredit on your account of the trip. 3. refuse to believe. We discredit Lulu because she has lied so often. 4. do harm to the reputation of; give a bad reputation to. Losing five battles discredited that general. 5. the loss of a good reputation.

dis creet (dis krēt′), prudent and careful in speech and action.

dis cre tion (dis kresh′ən), 1. freedom to judge or choose. It is within the principal's discretion to punish a pupil. 2. good judgment; care in speech and action; caution. My brother rushed in front of the car, but I showed more discretion.

dis crim i nate (dis krim′i nāt), 1. make or see a difference between; distinguish. Some boys cannot discriminate red from green easily. 2. make a distinction. Some unfair teachers discriminate against pupils whom they dislike.

dis cuss (dis kus′), talk over; consider from various points of view. The class discussed several problems. Bill's mother discussed his failure with his teacher.

dis cus sion (dis kush′ən), talk; talk about the reasons for and against; discussing things. His arrival caused much discussion in the village. After two hours' discussion, we seemed no nearer a decision.

dis dain (dis dān′), 1. to scorn; look down on; consider beneath one. He disdained our friendly offers. She disdains to speak to us. 2. scorn; looking down on a person or an act as beneath one. Dick treated his younger brothers and sisters with disdain.

dis dain ful (dis dān′fəl), proud and scornful.

dis ease (di zēz′), 1. sickness; illness. 2. any particular sickness, such as measles, scarlet fever, or whooping cough. A disease is killing all the chestnut trees.

dis eased (di zēzd′), having a disease.

dis fig ure (dis fig′yər), spoil the appearance of; hurt the beauty of. Huge advertising signs disfigure the countryside. A scar disfigured his face.

dis grace (dis grās′), 1. loss of favor; a lowering in position or esteem; loss of respect or honor. To be put in prison is usually a disgrace. 2. cause disgrace to; lower the worldly position of; bring shame upon. 3. anything that causes dishonor or shame.

dis grace ful (dis grās′fəl), shameful; causing dishonor or loss of respect; deserving disgrace.

dis guise (dis gīz′), 1. hide what one is by appearing as something else. In his Santa Claus costume my uncle was quite disguised. 2. the use of a changed or unusual dress and appearance in order not to be known. You will have to try disguise in order to succeed with that plan. 3. the clothes or actions used to hide or deceive. His disguise was perfect. 4. hide or cover up (purpose or thought) by seeming to have some other purpose or thought. For a time he disguised his hatred by a false show of friendly interest.

dis gust (dis gust′), 1. strong dislike; sickening dislike. We feel disgust for bad odors or tastes. 2. arouse disgust in. The smell of a pigpen disgusts many people.

dish (dish), 1. We eat from dishes. Cups, saucers, plates, bowls, and platters are dishes. 2. put (food) into a dish for serving at the table. You may dish the dinner now. 3. food served. Sliced peaches with cream is the dish I like best. 4. amount served in a dish. I ate two dishes of ice cream.

dis heart en (dis här′tən), discourage. Long illness is disheartening.

di shev eled (di shev′əld), hanging loosely or in disorder.

dis hon est (dis on′ist), 1. not fair play. Lying, cheating, and stealing are dishonest. 2. not honest; ready to cheat; not upright. A man who lies or steals is dishonest.

dis hon es ty (dis on′is ti), 1. lying, cheating, or stealing; disposition to lie, cheat, or steal. 2. dishonest act.

dis hon or (dis on′ər), 1. disgrace; shame; loss of reputation or standing in the world. 2. thing that causes dishonor. A lazy man is a dishonor to his family. 3. bring reproach or shame upon.

dis hon or a ble (dis on′ər ə bəl), without honor; disgraceful; shameful.

dis in ter est ed (dis in′tər es tid), free from selfish motives; as, disinterested kindness.

disk (disk), 1. a flat, thin, round plate shaped like a coin. 2. a round flat surface, or a surface that seems so.

Disk

dis like (dis līk′), 1. a feeling of not liking; a feeling against. I have a dislike of rain and fog. 2. not like; object to. Mice dislike cats.

dis lodge (dis loj′), drive or force out of a place, position, etc. The workman used a crowbar to dislodge a heavy stone from the wall. Violent attacks dislodged the enemy from the fort.

dis loy al (dis loi′əl), not loyal; faithless. A disloyal servant let robbers into the house.

dis loy al ty (dis loi′əl ti), unfaithfulness. The traitor was shot for disloyalty to his country.

dis mal (diz′məl), 1. dark; gloomy. A rainy day is dismal. 2. dreary; miserable. Sickness or bad luck often makes a person feel dismal.

dis man tle (dis man′təl), 1. strip of furniture, defenses, or equipment; as, to dismantle a house, a fort, or a ship. 2. pull down; take apart. We had to dismantle the bookcases in order to move them.

dis may (dis mā′), 1. a loss of courage because of dislike or fear of what is about to happen. 2. trouble greatly; make afraid. The thought that she might fail dismayed her.

dis miss (dis mis′), 1. send away; allow to go. At noon the teacher dismissed the class. 2. remove from office or service; not allow to keep a job. We dismissed the cook because her cooking was so poor. 3. put away; stop thinking about. Let us dismiss our troubles.

dis miss al (dis mis′əl), 1. act of dismissing. 2. state or fact of being dismissed. 3. written or spoken order dismissing someone.

dis mount (dis mount′), 1. get off a horse. The cavalry dismounted near the woods. 2. throw from one's horse. The first knight dismounted the second. 3. take (a thing) from its setting or support. The cannons were dismounted for shipping.

dis o be di ence (dis′ə bē′di əns), refusal to obey; failure to obey. Disobedience cannot be allowed in the army.

dis o be di ent (dis′ə bē′di ənt), failing to follow orders or rules; refusing or forgetting to obey.

dis o bey (dis′ə bā′), refuse to obey; fail to obey.

dis or der (dis ôr′dər), 1. lack of order; confusion. 2. disturb or confuse the regular order or working of. A series of accidents disordered the shop. 3. tumult; riot. 4. sickness; disease.

dis or der ly (dis ôr′dər li), 1. not orderly; untidy; confused. The troops fled in a disorderly rout. 2. causing disorder; making a disturbance; breaking rules; unruly.

dis or gan ize (dis ôr′gən īz), throw into confusion or disorder. Heavy snowstorms disorganized the train service.

dis own (dis ōn′), refuse to recognize as one's own; cast off. Mr. Jones disowned his wicked son.

dis patch (dis pach′), 1. send off to some place or for some purpose. He dispatched a messenger to tell the king what had happened. 2. sending off a letter, a messenger, etc. Hurry up the dispatch of this telegram. 3. a written message, such as special news or government business. This dispatch has been two days on the way. 4. get (something) done promptly. 5. prompt doing of anything. This boy works with neatness and dispatch. 6. kill. He dispatched the deer at his first shot. 7. finish off; eat up. The hungry boy quickly dispatched the meal.

dis pel (dis pel′), disperse; drive away and scatter. The captain's cheerful laugh dispelled our fears.

dis pense (dis pens′), 1. give out; distribute. The Red Cross dispensed food and clothing to the sufferers. 2. apply; carry out; cause to operate. Judges and law courts dispense justice. 3. prepare and give out. A druggist dispenses medicines for sick people. 4. **Dispense with** means (1) get rid of. (2) do without. I shall soon dispense with crutches.

dis perse (dis pėrs′), 1. scatter; send in different directions. 2. go in different directions. The crowd dispersed when the policeman came.

dis place (dis plās′), 1. take the place of; put something else in the place of. The automobile has practically displaced the horse and buggy. 2. remove from a position of authority. 3. put out of place; move from its usual place or position. Please do not displace any of my tools.

dis play (dis plā′), 1. show. He displayed his good nature by answering all our questions. The flag is displayed on the Fourth of July. He did not like the boy's display of bad temper. 2. show in a special way, so as to attract attention. The boys' suits were displayed in the big window of the store. 3. a planned showing of a thing, for some special purpose. Grade 5 had two displays of children's drawings.

dis please (dis plēz′), offend; annoy; not please. By failing to obey your mother you displeased her.

dis pleas ure (dis plezh′ər), annoyance; dislike; slight anger; dissatisfaction. We feel displeasure at something we dislike.

dis pos al (dis pōz′əl), 1. a placing in a certain order or position. 2. dealing with; settling. His disposal of the difficulty pleased everybody. 3. act of getting rid (of something); as, the disposal of garbage. 4. **At one's disposal** means ready for one's use or service at any time. I will put my room and my books at your disposal.

dis pose (dis pōz′), 1. put in a certain order or position. The ships were disposed in a straight line. 2. make ready or willing; influence. The good pay and short hours disposed him to take the new job. 3. **Be disposed** means be willing; be inclined. 4. **Dispose of** means (1) get rid of. Dispose of that rubbish. (2) give or sell. The agent disposed of all their property for $5000. (3) arrange; settle.

dis po si tion (dis′pə zish′ən), 1. natural way of acting toward others; as, a cheerful disposition, a selfish disposition, a changeable disposition. 2. a tending or natural bent; as, a disposition to argue. 3. a putting in order; arrangement. The disposition of the papers on my desk had been changed.

dis prove (dis prüv′), prove false. John disproved Tom's statement that he had less candy by weighing both boxes.

dis pute (dis pūt′), 1. argue; debate. 2. an argument; a debate. 3. quarrel because of a difference of opinion. 4. disagree with (a statement); say that (it) is false or doubtful. 5. fight against; oppose; resist. Our soldiers disputed every inch of ground when the enemy attacked. 6. try to win. Our team disputed the victory up to the last minute of play.

dis qui et (dis kwī′ət), 1. make uneasy; trouble; disturb; worry. Will's strange actions disquieted mother. 2. uneasy feelings; anxiety. Her disquiet made the rest of us uneasy, too.

dis re gard (dis′ri gärd′), 1. pay no attention to; take no notice of. Disregarding the child's screams, the doctor cleaned and bandaged the cut. 2. neglect; lack of attention. The boy's failure was due to continued disregard of his studies.

dis rep u ta ble (dis rep′ū tə bəl), 1. having a bad reputation; as, a disreputable dance hall. 2. not respectable; as, a disreputable old hat.

dis re spect (dis′ri spekt′), rudeness; lack of respect. I am sure he meant no disrespect by his remark.

dis sat is fac tion (dis′sat is fak′shən), the opposite of satisfaction; discontent; displeasure.

dis sat is fied (dis sat′is fīd), discontented, displeased. When we do not get what we want, we are dissatisfied.

dis sect (di sekt′), 1. cut up. 2. cut apart (an animal, plant, etc.) so as to examine. 3. examine part by part; analyze. One pupil dissected the other's composition.

dis sen sion (di sen′shən), disputing; quarreling; hard feeling caused by a difference in opinion. Differences in religion do not need to cause dissension between people.

dis sent (di sent′), 1. disagree; think differently; express a different opinion from others. Most of the class wanted to have a picnic, but three boys dissented. 2. disagreement; difference of opinion; expressing such a difference.

dis si pate (dis′i pāt), 1. scatter; spread in different directions. 2. disappear or cause to disappear; dispel. The sun dissipated the clouds. 3. spend foolishly; waste on things of little value. The extravagant son soon dissipated his father's fortune.

dis solve (di zolv′), 1. make liquid; become liquid, especially by putting or being put into a liquid. You can dissolve sugar in water. Sugar dissolves in water. 2. put an end to; as, to dissolve an agreement or a partnership. 3. fade away.

dis suade (di swād′), persuade not to do something. The father finally dissuaded his son from leaving school.

dis taff (dis′taf), 1. a split stick about a yard long that held the wool or flax for spinning into thread when this was done by hand. 2. the part of a spinning wheel that holds the wool or flax.

dis tance (dis′təns), 1. space in between. The distance from the farm to the town is five miles. 2. being far away. The farm is at a distance from any railroad. 3. a place far away. The sailors saw a light in the distance.

dis tant (dis′tənt), 1. far away in space. The moon is distant from the earth. 2. away. The town is three miles distant. 3. far apart in time, relationship, likeness, etc.; not close. A third cousin is a distant relative. 4. not friendly. She gave him only a distant nod.

dis taste (dis tāst′), dislike.

dis taste ful (dis tāst′fəl), unpleasant; displeasing; offensive; as, a distasteful medicine, a distasteful task.

dis tend (dis tend′), stretch out; expand; swell out. Blowing a horn distends your cheeks. The balloon was distended almost to the bursting point.

dis till or **dis til** (dis til′), 1. give off in drops. These flowers distill a sweet nectar. 2. make (a liquid) pure by turning it into a vapor by heat and then cooling it into liquid form again.

dis tinct (dis tingkt′), 1. separate; not the same. 2. different in quality or kind. Mice are distinct from rats. 3. clear; easily seen, heard, or understood. Your speech and writing should be distinct. 4. unmistakable; definite.

dis tinc tion (dis tingk′shən), 1. making a difference. He gave every servant ten dollars without distinction. 2. difference. What is the distinction between ducks and geese? 3. a mark or sign of honor. He won many distinctions for bravery. 4. excellence; superiority. A governor of any of our States should be a man of character and distinction.

dis tinc tive (dis tingk′tiv), distinguishing; characteristic. Boy Scouts wear a distinctive uniform.

dis tinct ly (dis tingkt′li), 1. so as to be easily seen, heard, or understood. Speak distinctly. 2. in a clear and definite way.

dis tin guish (dis ting′gwish), 1. see the differences in; tell apart. Can you distinguish cotton cloth from linen? 2. see or hear clearly; make out plainly. It is too dark for me to distinguish anything clearly. 3. make different; be a special quality or feature of. A trunk distinguishes the elephant. 4. make famous or well known. Tom distinguished himself by winning three prizes.

dis tin guished (dis ting′gwisht), great; well-known; as, a distinguished artist.

dis tort (dis tôrt′), 1. pull or twist out of shape; make crooked or ugly. Crying distorts the face. 2. change from the truth. The man distorted the facts of the accident to escape blame.

dis tract (dis trakt′), 1. draw away (the mind or attention). The talking of the other children distracts me from my studying. 2. confuse; disturb. Several people talking at once distract a listener. 3. **Distracted** sometimes means made almost insane.

dis tress (dis tres′), 1. great pain or sorrow; anxiety; trouble. 2. cause pain or sorrow to; make unhappy. 3. misfortune; dangerous condition; difficult situation. A sinking ship at sea is in distress.

dis trib ute (dis trib′ūt), 1. give some to each; deal out. I distributed the spelling papers for our teacher. 2. spread; scatter. Distribute your paint evenly over the wall. 3. divide into parts. 4. arrange; put each in its place. A mail clerk distributes mail when he puts each letter into the proper bag.

dis tri bu tion (dis′tri bū′shən), 1. act of distributing. After the contest the distribution of prizes to the winners took place. 2. way of being distributed. If some get more than others, there is an uneven distribution. 3. thing distributed.

dis trict (dis′trikt), 1. portion of a country; region. 2. portion of a country, a state, or a city, marked off for a special purpose, such as providing schools, electing certain government officers, or supporting a church.

dis trust (dis trust′), 1. have no trust in; not trust; not depend on; doubt. 2. lack of trust; lack of belief in the goodness of.

dis turb (dis tėrb′), 1. break in upon with noise or change. Do not disturb the baby; he is asleep. 2. put out of order. Someone has disturbed all my papers. 3. make uneasy; trouble. He was disturbed to hear of her illness.

dis turb ance (dis tėr′bəns), 1. a disturbing or being disturbed. 2. thing that disturbs. 3. confusion; disorder. 4. uneasiness; trouble; worry.

ditch (dich), 1. a long, narrow place dug in the earth. Ditches are usually to carry off water. 2. dig a ditch in. 3. run (into a ditch); throw into a ditch. The careless driver ditched his automobile.

di van (dī′van), long, low, soft couch or sofa.

dive (dīv), 1. plunge head first into water. 2. act of diving. 3. downward plunge of an airplane. 4. plunge (the body, the hand, or the mind) suddenly into anything. He dived into his pockets and fished out a dollar.

div er (dīv′ər), 1. one that dives. 2. person whose occupation is to work under water. 3. a diving bird.

A diver at work in a diving suit

di vers (dī′vərz), various; several different.

di verse (di vėrs′ or dī′vėrs), different.

di ver sion (di vėr′zhən), 1. a turning aside. A magician's talk creates a diversion of attention so that people do not see how he does his tricks. 2. relief from work, care, etc.; amusement; entertainment; pastime. Going to the movies is a popular diversion.

di ver si ty (di vėr′si ti), 1. being different; difference. Their diversity did not prevent them from being friends. 2. variety. The diversity of food on the table made it hard for him to choose.

di vert (di vėrt′), 1. turn aside. A ditch diverted water from the stream into the fields. He diverted trade to his own store when he could. The rattle diverted the baby's attention from the knife. 2. amuse; entertain. We were diverted by the clown's tricks.

di vide (di vīd′), 1. separate into parts. A brook divides the field. The river divides and forms two streams. 2. separate into equal parts. When you divide 8 by 2, you get 4. 3. to share. The children divided the candy. 4. to separate in feeling, opinion, etc. The school divided on the choice of a motto. 5. a ridge between the regions drained by two different river systems. The Rocky Mountains are called the Great Divide.

di vine (di vīn′), 1. of God or a god. 2. by or from God. 3. to or for God; sacred; holy. 4. like God or a god; heavenly. 5. very excellent; unusually good or great. 6. clergyman who knows much about theology; minister; priest. 7. find out or foretell by inspiration, by magic, or by guessing; predict.

di vin i ty (di vin′i ti), 1. divine being; a god. 2. divine nature or quality.

di vi sion (di vizh′ən), 1. dividing; being divided. 2. giving some to each; sharing; as, division of labor. 3. the process of dividing one number by another. $26 \div 2 = 13$ is a simple division. 4. dividing line; boundary. 5. one of the parts into which a thing is divided. Some divisions of the army fought in Africa. 6. a difference of opinion, thought, or feeling; disagreement.

di vorce (di vōrs′), 1. legal ending of a marriage. 2. end legally a marriage between. The judge divorced Mr. and Mrs. Jones. 3. get rid of by divorce. Mrs. Bush tried to divorce her husband. 4. separation. In this country there is a complete divorce of government and religion. 5. separate. In sports, exercise and play are not divorced.

di vulge (di vulj′), tell; reveal. The traitor divulged secret plans to the enemy.

Dix ie (dik′si), the Southern States of the United States.

diz zi ness (diz′i nis), dizzy condition.

diz zy (diz′i), 1. likely to fall, stagger, or spin around. When you spin round and round, and stop suddenly, you feel dizzy. 2. confused; not steady. 3. make dizzy. 4. likely to make dizzy; causing dizziness. The airplane climbed to a dizzy height.

do (dü), 1. When you carry through to an end any action or piece of work, you do it. Do your work well. 2. act; behave. He did very well today. 3. Do is used (1) to make what one says stronger. I do want to go. Do come, please. (2) to ask questions. Do you like milk? (3) to stand for another word. My dog goes where I do. Nell's sister walks just as Nell does. 4. **Do up** means wrap up. 5. be satisfactory. That knife will do. **does, did,** and **done** are formed from **do.**

doc ile (dos′il), 1. easily managed; obedient. 2. easily taught; willing to learn.

dock[1] (dok), 1. platform built on the shore or out from the shore; wharf; pier. 2. place where a ship may be repaired, often built watertight so that the water may be kept high or pumped out. 3. bring (a ship) to dock. The sailors docked the ship and began to unload it.

Ship loading at a dock

dock[2] (dok), 1. the solid, fleshy part of an animal's tail. 2. cut short; cut off the end of. 3. cut some off of. The company docked the men's wages if they came late to work.

dock[3] (dok), the place where an accused person stands in a law court to be tried.

dock[4] (dok), large weed with sour or bitter leaves.

doc tor (dok′tər), 1. person who knows how to treat diseases. When a man is very sick he sends for a doctor. 2. treat disease in. Mother doctors us for ordinary colds.

doc trine (dok′trin), 1. what is taught; teachings. 2. what is taught as the belief of a church, a nation, or a group of persons; a belief.

doc u ment (dok′ū mənt), something written or printed that gives information and can be used as evidence of some fact; any object used as evidence. Letters, maps, and pictures are documents.

dodge (doj), 1. move quickly to one side. 2. move quickly in order to get away from (a person, a blow, or something thrown). 3. a sudden movement to one side. 4. get away from by some trick. 5. a trick to cheat.

doe (dō), a female deer, rabbit, or hare.

does (duz). See **do.** He does all his work. Does she sing well?

does n't (duz′ənt), does not.

doff (dof), take off (hat, clothes, etc.). A man doffs his hat when he enters a house.

dog (dôg), 1. My dog guards the house. Tom's dog hunts rats. 2. something made to hold or grip like a dog's teeth. 3. hunt or follow like a dog. The police dogged the suspected thief.

Dog for gripping

dog ged (dôg′id), obstinate; persistent. Dick's dogged effort helped him to win the race.

dog wood (dôg′wůd′), a tree with large white or pinkish flowers in the spring and red berries in the fall.

do ings (dü′ingz), actions; conduct; proceedings.

dole (dōl), 1. a portion of money, food, etc., given in charity. 2. small portion. 3. give in small quantities. Mother doled out one piece of candy a day to each child.

dole ful (dōl′fəl), sad; dreary; dismal.

doll (dol). A doll looks like a baby, a child, or a grown person.

Doll wearing doll's clothes

dol lar (dol′ər), 1. the unit of United States money; one hundred cents. $1.00 means one dollar. 2. a silver coin or a paper note equal to 100 cents. 3. a large silver coin of Canada, Mexico, and some other countries.

doll y (dol′i), child's name for a doll. Baby loves her dollies.

dol or ous (dol′ər əs), 1. mournful; sorrowful. She uttered a little dolorous cry. 2. grievous; painful. The dolorous day was ending.

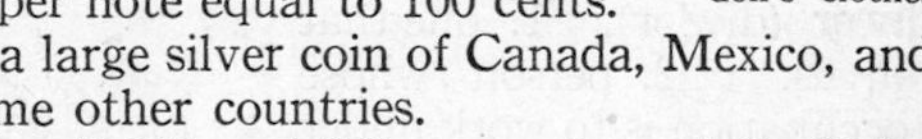
Dolphin (def. 1) (6 to 10 ft. long)

dol phin (dol′fin), 1. small whale that has a snout like a beak. See the picture above. 2. a large sea fish that changes color when it is taken out of the water.

dolt (dōlt), a dull, stupid person.

do main (dō mān′), 1. the lands belonging to a ruler, a nobleman, or a government, and under his or its rule. 2. a field of thought and action. Edison was a leader in the domain of invention.

dome (dōm), 1. a large, rounded roof on a circular or many-sided base. 2. thing shaped like a dome; as, the rounded dome of a hill.

Dome of a church

do mes tic (də mes′tik), 1. of the home, the household, or family affairs; as, domestic cares, a domestic scene. 2. fond of home. 3. household servant. 4. tame. Horses, dogs, cats, cows, and pigs are domestic animals. 5. of one's own country; not foreign.

do mes ti cate (də mes′ti kāt), to tame; make over (animals and plants) from a wild to a tame state.

dom i nant (dom′i nənt), 1. ruling; governing; controlling; most influential. The white race is dominant in the world today. 2. rising high above its surroundings; occupying a commanding position. A dominant cliff rose at the bend of the river.

dom i nate (dom′i nāt), 1. control or rule by strength or power; have or exercise control. The boy dominates his smaller friend. Dandelions will dominate over grass if they are not kept out. 2. hold a commanding position over. The town in the valley is dominated by a high mountain.

dom i na tion (dom′i nā′shən), control; rule; dominating.

do min ion (də min′yən), 1. rule; control. The English have dominion over a large part of the world. 2. lands under the control of one ruler or government.

dom i no (dom′i nō), 1. a loose cloak with a face mask worn as a disguise, especially at masquerade parties. 2. one of a set of small pieces of bone or wood marked with spots. **Dominoes** is the name of the game played with them.

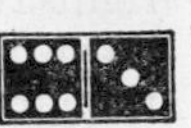
Dominoes

don[1] (don), 1. In Spain, Don is a title meaning Mr. or Sir. 2. In England, a don is the head of a college, or a tutor.

don[2] (don), put on (clothing, etc.). Sir Richard donned his armor.

do nate (dō′nāt), give; contribute.

do na tion (dō nā′shən), 1. act of giving. 2. gift; contribution. Every merchant was called upon to make donations to the Red Cross.

done (dun), 1. finished; completed. 2. worn out. 3. cooked. 4. See **do.**

don key (dong′ki), 1. a small animal somewhat like a horse but with longer ears, a shorter mane, and a tuft of hair at the end of its tail. 2. stubborn person; silly or stupid person. Don't act like donkeys.

Donkey (3 ft. high at the shoulder)

do nor (dō′nər), giver.

don't (dōnt), do not.

doom (düm), 1. fate. 2. terrible fate; ruin; death. The soldiers marched to their doom. 3. condemn to some fate. The prisoner was doomed to death. 4. judgment; sentence. The judge pronounced the guilty man's doom.

door (dōr), 1. A door closes the entrance of a house, a room, or a building. 2. doorway.

door step (dōr′step′), step leading from an outside door to the ground.

door way (dōr′wā′), an opening in the wall where a door is.

door yard (dōr′yärd′), yard about the door of a house; yard around a house.

dor mant (dôr′mənt), 1. sleeping. 2. quiet as if asleep. Bears are dormant during the winter. 3. inactive. Plant bulbs stay dormant during the cold of winter.

dor mi to ry (dôr′mi tō′ri), 1. a building containing a large number of sleeping rooms. 2. a sleeping room large enough for a number of beds. The lights in the dormitories are turned off at ten o'clock.

dor mouse (dôr′mous′), a small animal somewhat like a mouse and somewhat like a squirrel. It sleeps during cold weather.

do ry (dō′ri), a rowboat with a narrow, flat bottom and high sides, used for fishing, etc.

Dory

dose (dōs), 1. the amount of a medicine to be taken at one time. The usual dose of cod-liver oil is a spoonful. 2. give medicine to. The doctor dosed Maud with quinine.

dost (dust), an old form meaning **do.** "Thou dost" means "you do."

dot (dot), 1. small spot or point. There is a dot over each *i* in this line. 2. mark with a dot or dots. The bay was dotted with boats.

dote (dōt), 1. be weak-minded and childish because of old age. 2. **Dote on** means be foolishly fond of; be too fond of.

doth (duth), an old form meaning **does.**

dou ble (dub′əl), 1. twice as great, as large, as strong, etc. The man was given double pay for working overtime. 2. twice. 3. a number or amount twice as large. Four is the double of two. 4. make twice as much; make twice as many. Mr. Smith doubled his money in ten years by investing it wisely. 5. become twice as much. Money left in a savings bank will double in about twenty years. 6. made of two like parts; in a pair; as, double doors. 7. having two meanings, characters, etc. The word *fast* has a double meaning. 8. person or thing just like another. Here is the double of your lost glove. 9. fold over. Jack doubled his slice of bread to make a sandwich. The boy doubled his fists. 10. bend or turn sharply backward. The fox doubled on his track and escaped the dogs. 11. a sharp turn. 12. go around. The ship doubled Cape Horn. 13. having more than one set of petals. Some roses are double, others single.

dou blet (dub′lit), a man's close-fitting jacket. See the picture. Men wore doublet and hose in Europe from 1400 to 1600.

Doublet

dou bly (dub′li), in a double manner, amount, or degree. Doubly careful means twice as careful.

doubt (dout), 1. not believe; not be sure; feel uncertain. The captain doubted whether the sinking ship would reach land. 2. difficulty in believing; an uncertain state of mind. The men were in doubt as to the right road. **No doubt** sometimes means certainly.

doubt ful (dout′fəl), full of doubt; undecided; not certain. We are doubtful about the weather for tomorrow.

doubt less (dout′lis), without doubt; surely.

dough (dō), the mixture of flour, milk, fat, and other materials from which bread, biscuits, pie, etc., are made.

dough nut (dō′nut′), piece of sweetened dough cooked in deep fat. A doughnut is usually made in the shape of a ring.

douse (dous), 1. plunge into water. 2. throw water over.

dove[1] (duv), pigeon. Tame doves are often kept near a house. See the picture just below.

dove[2] (dōv), dived. He dove deep into the water.

Dove (about 1 ft. long)

dow dy (dou′di), 1. poorly dressed; shabby; not stylish. 2. a poorly dressed woman.

dow er (dou′ər), 1. the wife's share for life of her dead husband's property. 2. a gift of nature, such as ability, beauty, or any good or great quality. 3. provide with a dower.

down[1] (doun), 1. to a lower place; in a lower place. They ran down from the top of the hill. The stone step was worn down by many feet. 2. from an earlier time to a later time. The story has come down through many years. 3. down along. He went down the hill. 4. put down. Tom downed Percy and sat on top of him.

down[2] (doun), soft feathers; soft hair or fluff.

down[3] (doun), rolling, green land.

down cast (doun′kast′), 1. turned downward. She stood before us with downcast eyes. 2. dejected; sad; discouraged. He was downcast because of his failure.

down fall (doun′fôl′), 1. ruin; as, the downfall of an empire, the moral downfall of a person. 2. a heavy rain or snow.

down heart ed (doun′här′tid), discouraged; dejected; depressed.

down hill (doun′hil′), down the slope of a hill; downward.

down pour (doun′pōr′), heavy rain.

down right (doun′rīt′), 1. thorough; complete; as, a downright thief, a downright lie. 2. thoroughly; completely. He was downright rude to me. 3. plain; positive. His downright answer left no doubt as to what he thought.

down stairs (doun′stãrz′), 1. down the stairs. Bill slipped and fell downstairs. 2. on a lower floor. The downstairs rooms are dark. 3. lower floor or floors.

down stream (doun′strēm′), with the current of a stream; down a stream. It is easy to swim or row downstream.

down town (doun′toun′), 1. to or in the lower part of a town. 2. to or in the main part or business part of a town.

down ward (doun′wərd), 1. toward a lower place. 2. toward a later time.

down wards (doun′wərdz), downward.

down y (doun′i), 1. of soft feathers or fluff. 2. covered with down. 3. soft as down. A kitten's fur is downy.

dow ry (dou′ri), 1. the money or property that a woman brings to her husband when she marries him. 2. a gift of nature; a natural talent. Good health and intelligence are useful dowries.

doze (dōz), 1. sleep lightly; be half asleep. 2. light sleep; a nap.

doz en (duz′ən), 12; group of 12.

Dr. or **Dr,** Doctor; as, Dr. W. H. Smith.

drab (drab), 1. dull; not attractive; as, the drab houses of the smoky town. 2. dull, brownish gray.

draft (draft), 1. a current of air. 2. device for controlling a current of air. Opening the draft of a furnace makes the fire burn faster. 3. a plan; a sketch. 4. make a plan or sketch of. 5. rough copy. He made three different drafts of his speech before he had it in final form. 6. write out a rough copy of. 7. a selection of persons for some special purpose. In time of war men are often supplied to the army and navy by draft. 8. the persons chosen for special service. 9. select for some special purpose. The army drafted millions of young men. 10. act of pulling loads. 11. for pulling loads. A draft horse is used for pulling wagons and plows. 12. pulling of a net to catch fish. 13. all the fish caught in one drawing of a net. 14. the depth of water a ship requires to float it, or the depth it sinks into the water, especially when loaded. 15. amount drunk at a single drink. Also spelled **draught.**

drag (drag), 1. pull or move along heavily or slowly; pull or draw along the ground. A team of horses dragged the big log out of the forest. 2. go too slowly. A piece of music played too slowly drags. Time drags when you have nothing to do. 3. pull a net, hook, harrow, etc., over or along for some purpose. People drag a lake for fish or for a drowned person's body. 4. Anything that holds back or is pulled may be called a drag. Lazy, complaining boys are a drag on work or play.

drag gle (drag′əl), 1. make or become wet or dirty by dragging through mud, water, dust, etc. 2. follow slowly; lag behind; straggle.

drag net (drag′net′), a net pulled over the bottom of a river, pond, etc., or along the ground. Dragnets are used to catch fish and small birds.

Dragon with three heads

drag on (drag′ən), in old stories, a terrible creature like a huge winged snake with scales and claws, which often breathed fire.

drag on fly (drag′ən flī′), a large, harmless insect with a long, slender body and two pairs of gauzy wings.

Dragonfly (½ to 4 in. long)

dra goon (drə gün′), 1. soldier who fights on horseback. 2. compel by oppression or persecution. Some French were dragooned into working for the Germans.

drain (drān), 1. draw off (water or any liquid); draw liquid from; empty of liquid; as, to drain swamps, drain a cup. 2. dry by the flowing off of water. Set the dishes here to drain. 3. a channel or pipe for carrying off water or waste of any kind. 4. take away from slowly; use up little by little; deprive. War drains a country of its people and money. 5. a slow taking away; a using up little by little. Working or playing too hard is a drain on your strength.

drain age (drān′ij), 1. draining; drawing off water. The drainage of swamps improves a town. 2. a system of channels or pipes for carrying off water or waste of any kind. 3. what is drained off.

drake (drāk), male duck.

dra ma (drä′mə or dram′ə), 1. a play such as one sees in a theater; a story acted out by actors on the stage. 2. the art of writing and producing plays. 3. part of real life that seems to have been planned like a story. The history of America is a great and thrilling drama.

dra mat ic (drə mat′ik), 1. of drama; having to do with plays. 2. sudden; exciting; full of action or feeling.

dra mat i cal ly (drə mat′i kəl i), in a dramatic manner.

dram a tist (dram′ə tist), writer of plays.

drank (drangk). See **drink.** She drank her milk an hour ago.

drape (drāp), 1. cover or hang with cloth of any kind, especially as a decoration. The buildings were draped with red, white, and blue. 2. arrange to hang loosely in folds. Can you drape this skirt? 3. cloth hung in folds. Some curtains are drapes.

dra per y (drā′pər i), 1. cloths or fabrics, especially those used for hangings and garments. 2. clothing or hangings arranged in folds.

dras tic (dras′tik), acting with force or violence. The police took drastic measures to put a stop to the crime wave.

draught (draft), draft. See the meanings of **draft.**

draw (drô), 1. pull; drag; haul. The horses draw the wagon. 2. attract. Accidents in the streets always draw crowds. 3. pull out; pull up; cause to come out; take out; get. Draw a pail of water from this well. She drew ten dollars from the bank. Draw no conclusions now. 4. make a picture or likeness of anything with pen, pencil, or chalk. 5. tie. A game is a draw when neither side wins. 6. part of a drawbridge. Draw also has special meanings in special cases, as follows: 7. inhale; as, draw a breath. 8. make longer; stretch. The battle was long drawn out. 9. write. The lawyer drew up documents. 10. need for floating. The big ship draws 28 feet of water. 11. move. The car drew near. 12. make a draft of air to carry off smoke. The chimney does not draw well. 13. a kind of valley. **drew** and **drawn** are formed from **draw.**

draw back (drô′bak′), a disadvantage; anything which makes a situation or experience less complete or satisfying. Our trip was interesting, but the rainy weather was a drawback.

draw bridge (drô′brij′), bridge that can be entirely or partly lifted, lowered, or moved to one side.

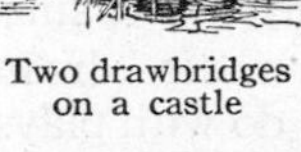
Two drawbridges on a castle

draw er (drô′ər for 1, drôr for 2 and 3), 1. person who draws. 2. a box with handles built to slide in and out of a table, desk, or bureau. 3. **Drawers** are a two-legged undergarment fastened about the waist.

draw ing (drô′ing), 1. a sketch, plan, or design done with pen, pencil, or crayon. 2. representing objects by lines.

drawing room, room for receiving or entertaining guests; parlor.

drawl (drôl), 1. talk in a slow, lazy way. 2. slow, lazy way of talking.

drawn (drôn). See **draw.** That old horse has drawn many loads.

dray (drā), a low, strong cart for carrying heavy loads.

dread (dred), 1. look forward to with fear; dislike to experience; fear greatly. Tom dreaded his visits to the dentist. Cats dread water. 2. fear, especially fear of something that will happen, or may happen. 3. dreaded; dreadful.

dread ful (dred′fəl), terrible; awful; fearful.

dread ful ly (dred′fəl i), in a dreadful manner; to a dreadful degree; terribly.

dream (drēm), 1. something thought, felt, or seen in sleep. 2. something as unreal as the fancies of sleep. The boy had dreams of being a hero. 3. think, feel, hear, or see in sleep. 4. form fancies; imagine. The girl dreamed of being in the movies. 5. suppose in a vague way. The day seemed so bright that we never dreamed there would be rain.

dream er (drēm′ər), 1. person who dreams. 2. person who does not fit his ideas to real conditions.

dreamt (dremt), dreamed.

dream y (drēm′i), 1. full of dreams; as, a dreamy sleep. 2. fond of daydreaming; fanciful; not practical; as, a dreamy person. 3. like a dream; vague; dim; as, a dreamy recollection.

drear (drēr), dreary.

drear y (drēr′i), dull; without cheer; gloomy. Which month do you think is the dreariest?

Dredge (def. 1)

dredge (drej), 1. machine for cleaning out or deepening a harbor or channel. 2. clean out or deepen with a dredge. 3. machine used for gathering oysters, etc., from the bottom of a river. 4. gather with a dredge.

dregs (dregz), 1. solid bits of matter that settle to the bottom of a liquid. After pouring the tea she rinsed the dregs out of the teapot. 2. most worthless part. Thieves and murderers are the dregs of humanity.

drench (drench), 1. wet thoroughly; soak. 2. a soaking.

dress (dres), 1. the usual outer garment

worn by women and girls. 2. clothing, especially outer clothing. Boys think less about dress than girls do. 3. put clothes on. 4. make ready to use; care for. The butcher will dress the chickens for you. To dress hair is to comb and brush and arrange it. To dress a cut or sore is to treat it with medicine and bandages. 5. form in a straight line. The captain ordered the soldiers to dress their ranks.

dress er[1] (dres′ər), 1. person who dresses (himself, another person, a shop window, or a wound). 2. tool or machine to prepare things for use.

dress er[2] (dres′ər), 1. piece of furniture with shelves for dishes. 2. a chest or set of drawers with a mirror, properly called a bureau.

dress ing (dres′ing), 1. medicine, bandage, etc., put on a wound or sore. 2. sauce for salads, fish, meat, etc. 3. a mixture of bread crumbs, seasoning, etc., used to stuff chickens, turkeys, etc.

dress mak er (dres′māk′ər), person, usually a woman, whose work is making women's or children's dresses.

drew (drü). See **draw.**

drib ble (drib′əl), 1. flow or let flow in drops or small amounts; trickle. That faucet dribbles. 2. drip from the mouth. The baby dribbles on his bib. 3. a dropping; a dripping. 4. very light rain. 5. move (a ball) along by bouncing it or giving it short kicks.

drib let (drib′lit), small amount.

dried (drīd). See **dry.** I dried my hands. This bread has been dried in the oven.

dri er (drī′ər), 1. thing or person that dries. 2. machine or person that removes water. 3. a substance mixed with paint or varnish to make it dry more quickly. 4. more dry.

drift (drift), 1. be carried along by currents of air or water. A raft drifts if it is not steered. 2. carry along. The current was drifting us along. 3. go along or live without a goal or without knowing where one will come out. Some people just drift through life. 4. being driven; the motion of being carried along by wind or water. 5. direction. The drift of this current is to the south. 6. meaning; direction of thought. I caught the drift of his words. 7. anything carried along by wind, water, or ice. 8. pile or be piled into heaps, like snow blown by the wind. 9. snow, sand, etc., heaped up by the wind.

drift wood (drift′wu̇d′), wood carried along by water; wood washed ashore from the water.

drill[1] (dril), 1. tool for boring holes; machine for using such a tool. 2. make (a hole) with a drill; use a drill. 3. teach by having the pupil do a thing over and over. 4. doing a thing over and over for practice. 5. group instruction and training in physical exercises or in marching, handling a gun, and other duties of soldiers. 6. do military or physical exercises. 7. cause to do such exercises. The sergeant drilled the new soldiers.

Drill

drill[2] (dril), machine for planting seeds in rows. It makes a small furrow, drops the seed, and then covers the furrow.

drink (dringk), 1. swallow anything liquid, such as water or milk. 2. anything liquid swallowed to make one less thirsty. 3. suck up; absorb. The soil drank water like a sponge. 4. take. Our ears had drunk in the music. 5. alcoholic liquor. 6. drink alcoholic liquor. **drank** and **drunk** are formed from **drink.**

drink er (dringk′ər), 1. person who drinks. 2. person who drinks alcoholic liquor often or too much.

drip (drip), 1. fall or let fall in drops. Rain drips from an umbrella. 2. falling in drops. 3. be wet enough to shed drops. His forehead was dripping.

drive (drīv), 1. make go. Drive the dog away. Drive the nail in. 2. make go where one wishes. Can you drive a car? 3. make go ahead; make succeed. He drove a good bargain at the store. 4. go in a car or carriage; carry in a car, etc. 5. a trip in a car or carriage. 6. road. He built a drive to his house. 7. go fast or violently. The ship drove on the rocks. 8. pressure; impelling force. Hunger is a drive to action. 9. special effort. Our church made a drive to get $10,000. **drove** and **driven** are formed from **drive.**

driv en (driv′ən). See **drive.** Mr. Jones has just driven past.

driv er (drīv′ər), 1. person who drives; especially, a driver of horses, of an automobile, or of an engine. 2. person who makes the people under him work very hard.

driz zle (driz′əl), 1. rain gently, in very small drops like mist. 2. very small drops of rain like mist.

droll (drōl), odd and amusing; quaint and laughable. We smiled at the monkey's droll tricks.

Dromedary (6 ft. high at the shoulder)

drom e dar y (drom′ədãr′i), a swift camel for riding, usually one that has only one hump.

drone (drōn), 1. male bee. Drones do no work. 2. person not willing to work; idler. 3. spend time idly; loaf. 4. make a deep, continuous, humming sound. Bees droned among the flowers. 5. such a sound. Soldiers listened for the drone of the airplane motors. 6. talk or say in a monotonous voice. The weary beggar droned a prayer.

Drone (about life size)

droop (drüp), 1. hang down; bend down. These flowers will soon droop if they are not put in water. Flags droop when there is no breeze. 2. hanging down; bending position. The droop of the branches brought them within our reach. 3. become weak; lose strength and energy. 4. become discouraged; be sad and gloomy.

drop (drop), 1. a small amount of liquid in a round shape; as, a drop of rain, a drop of blood. 2. fall in drops. 3. very small amount of liquid. Drink a drop of this. 4. sudden fall. 5. the distance down; a sudden fall in level; as, a drop of thirty feet. 6. take a sudden fall. The man dropped from the top of the building. The price of sugar will drop soon. 7. let fall. Drop that package. 8. cause to fall. 9. fall dead, wounded, or tired out. 10. cause to fall dead; kill. 11. go lower; sink. 12. make lower. Drop your voice. 13. let go; dismiss. The boss dropped six men Saturday. 14. leave out; omit. 15. stop; end; cease. We let the quarrel drop. 16. come. Drop in and see me some day. 17. go with the current or tide. The raft dropped down the river.

drought (drout), 1. long period of dry weather; lack of rain. 2. lack of water; dryness.

drouth (drouth), drought.

drove (drōv), 1. group of cattle, sheep, hogs, etc., moving or driven along together; herd; flock. We sent a drove of cattle to market. 2. many people moving along together; crowd. 3. See **drive.** We drove twenty miles yesterday.

dro ver (drō′vər), 1. man who drives cattle, sheep, etc., to market. 2. a dealer in cattle.

drown (droun), 1. die under water or other liquid because of lack of air to breathe. 2. kill by keeping under water. 3. be stronger than; keep from being heard. His loud voice drowned what the girl was trying to tell us.

drowse (drouz), be half asleep.

drow sy (drou′zi), 1. sleepy; half asleep. 2. making one sleepy. It was a warm, quiet, drowsy afternoon.

drudge (druj), 1. person who does hard, disagreeable work; a slave; an overworked servant. 2. do tiresome or disagreeable work.

drudg er y (druj′əri), work that is hard or without interest. Mary thinks that washing dishes every day is drudgery.

drug (drug), 1. a substance (other than food) that, when taken into the body, produces a change in it. If the change helps the body, the drug is a medicine; if the change harms the body, the drug is a poison. 2. give harmful drugs to, particularly drugs that cause sleep. The witch drugged the princess. 3. mix harmful drugs with (food or drink). She drugged her tea. 4. affect or overcome (the body or the senses) in a way not natural. The wine had drugged him.

drug gist (drug′ist), person who sells drugs, medicines, toilet articles, etc.

drum (drum), 1. a musical instrument that makes a sound when it is beaten. A drum is hollow with a cover stretched tight over the top. 2. the sound made by beating a drum; any noise like this. 3. play the drum; make a sound by beating a drum. 4. beat, tap, or strike again and again. He drummed on the table. 5. teach or drive into one's head by repeating over and over. Tom's lessons had to be drummed into him because he did not like school. 6. thing shaped like a drum.

drum mer (drum′ər), person who plays a drum.

drum stick (drum′stik′), 1. a stick for beating a drum. 2. the lower half of the leg of a cooked chicken, turkey, etc.

drunk (drungk), 1. overcome by alcoholic liquor. He was so drunk he could not stand up. 2. See **drink.**

drunk ard (drungk′ərd), person who is often drunk; person who drinks too much alcoholic liquor.

drunk en (drungk′ən), 1. drunk. 2. caused by being drunk; as, a drunken act, drunken words.

dry (drī), 1. not wet; not moist. Dust is dry. 2. make dry by wiping, draining, or heating. Helen was drying dishes. 3. not giving water or milk. The cow is dry. 4. make or become dry; stop giving water. 5. having little or no rain; as, a dry climate. 6. thirsty; wanting a drink. 7. solid; not liquid; as, on dry land. 8. not interesting; dull.

dry er (drī′ər), drier.

dry goods, cloth, ribbons, laces, and the like.

dub (dub), 1. make (a man) a knight by striking his shoulder lightly with a sword. 2. give a title to; name or call. The boys dubbed Tom "Fatty."

du bi ous (dū′bi əs or dü′bi əs), 1. doubtful; uncertain. Nell looked this way and that in a dubious manner. 2. of questionable character; probably bad; as, a dubious scheme for making money.

duch ess (duch′is), 1. the wife or widow of a duke. 2. a woman with a rank equal to a duke's.

duch y (duch′i), the territory ruled by a duke or a duchess.

duck[1] (duk), a wild or tame swimming bird with a flat bill and short neck and legs. See the picture. Ducks are very often kept to use as food and for their eggs.

Duck

duck[2] (duk), 1. plunge or dip the head or the whole body under water and come up quickly, as a duck does; put under water for a short time. 2. a quick plunge below the water. 3. lower the head or bend the body quickly to keep off a blow. Jane ducked to avoid a low branch. 4. a sudden lowering of the head or bending of the body.

duck[3] (duk), a strong cotton or linen fabric, lighter and finer in weave than canvas. Duck is used for small sails, and for outer clothing by sailors and by persons living in hot climates.

duck ling (duk′ling), young duck.

due (dū or dü), 1. owed as a debt; owing; to be paid. The money due him for his work was paid today. 2. a person's right; what is owed or due to a person. Courtesy is his due while he is your guest. 3. proper; rightful; fitting. He has his due reward for good work. 4. what a person owes. **Dues** sometimes means a fee or tax for some purpose; as, club dues. 5. **Due to** means caused by. The accident was due to Bill's careless use of the gun. 6. looked for; expected; set by agreement; promised to come or to do. The train is due at noon. He is due to speak twice tomorrow. 7. exactly; directly. The ship sailed due west.

du el (dū′əl or dü′əl), 1. a formal fight to settle a quarrel. Duels are fought with guns, swords, etc., between two persons in the presence of two others called seconds. 2. any contest between two. 3. fight a duel.

du et (dū et′ or dü et′), 1. piece of music for two voices or instruments. 2. two singers or players.

dug (dug). See **dig.** The dog dug a hole in the ground. The potatoes have all been dug. We dug them last week.

dug out (dug′out′), 1. rough shelter or dwelling formed by digging. 2. boat made by hollowing out a large log.

duke (dūk or dük), a nobleman of a very high rank.

duke dom (dūk′dəm or dük′dəm), the territory ruled by a duke.

dull (dul), 1. not sharp or pointed; as, a dull knife, a dull joke. 2. not bright or clear; as, dull eyes, a dull color, a dull day, a dull sound. 3. slow in understanding; stupid; as, a dull mind, a dull boy. 4. not interesting or pleasant; boring; as, a dull book. 5. not active. The coal business is dull in summer. 6. make dull. 7. grow dull.

dull ard (dul′ərd), dull, stupid person.

dul ly (dul′li), in a dull manner.

du ly (dū′li or dü′li), as due; according to what is due; rightly; suitably.

dumb (dum), 1. not able to speak. 2. silent; not speaking. 3. stupid; dull.

dump (dump), 1. empty out; throw down. The truck backed up to the curb and dumped the coal on the sidewalk. 2. place for throwing rubbish. 3. heap of rubbish.

dun[1] (dun), 1. demand payment of a debt from, again and again. 2. a demand for payment. 3. person who keeps demanding payment.

dun[2] (dun), dull, grayish brown.

dunce (duns), 1. child slow at learning his lessons in school. 2. stupid person.

dune (dūn or dün), a mound or ridge of loose sand heaped up by the wind.

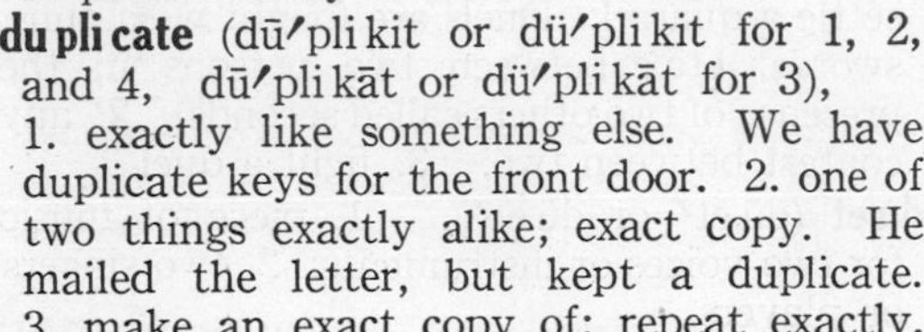
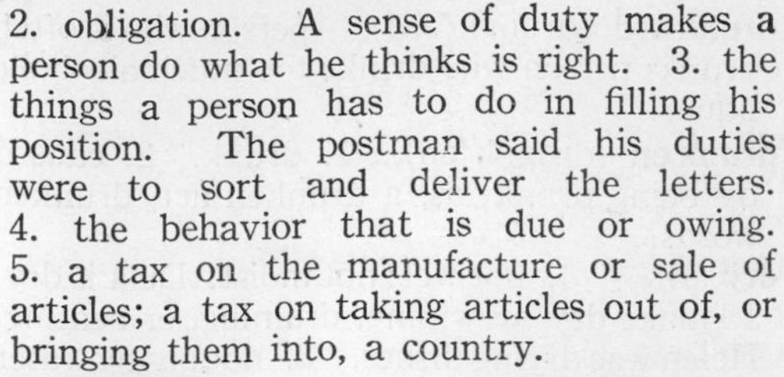

Dunes

dun geon (dun′jən), a strong underground room for prisoners.

dupe (dūp or düp), 1. deceive; trick. The dishonest peddler duped his customers. 2. person easily deceived or tricked.

du pli cate (dū′pli kit or dü′pli kit for 1, 2, and 4, dū′pli kāt or dü′pli kāt for 3), 1. exactly like something else. We have duplicate keys for the front door. 2. one of two things exactly alike; exact copy. He mailed the letter, but kept a duplicate. 3. make an exact copy of; repeat exactly. 4. double.

du ra ble (dūr′ə bəl or dür′ə bəl), lasting a long time; not soon injured or worn out.

du ra tion (dū rā′shən or dü rā′shən), length of time; the time during which anything continues. He enlisted in the army for the duration of the war.

dur ing (dūr′ing or dür′ing). The boys played during the afternoon. Sometime during the day come to see me. During recess means while recess lasts.

durst (dėrst), dared. See **dare.**

dusk (dusk), 1. the time just before dark. 2. shade; gloom. 3. dark-colored; dim.

dusk y (dus′ki), 1. somewhat dark; dark-colored. 2. dim; obscure.

dust (dust), 1. fine, dry earth; any fine powder. Dust lay thick in the street. The old papers had turned to dust. The tomb contains the dust of kings. The bee is covered with yellow dust from the flowers. 2. get dust off; brush or wipe the dust from. The maid dusts the furniture after sweeping. 3. sprinkle with (dust or powder). The nurse dusted powder over the baby. 4. earth; ground.

dust y (dus′ti), 1. covered with dust; filled with dust. 2. like dust; dry and powdery. 3. having the color of dust.

du ties (dū′tiz or dü′tiz), more than one duty.

du ti ful (dū′ti fəl or dü′ti fəl), doing your duty; obedient; as, a dutiful daughter.

du ty (dū′ti or dü′ti), 1. the thing that is right to do; what a person ought to do. 2. obligation. A sense of duty makes a person do what he thinks is right. 3. the things a person has to do in filling his position. The postman said his duties were to sort and deliver the letters. 4. the behavior that is due or owing. 5. a tax on the manufacture or sale of articles; a tax on taking articles out of, or bringing them into, a country.

dwarf (dwôrf), 1. a person, an animal, or a plant much below the usual size for its kind. 2. in fairy tales, an ugly little man with magic power. 3. below the usual size for its kind; stopped in growth. 4. keep from growing large. 5. cause to seem small by comparison or by distance. That tall building dwarfs all those around it.

dwell (dwel), 1. live; make one's home. They dwell in the country. 2. **Dwell on** a thought or a subject means think, speak, or write about it for a long time.

dwell er (dwel′ər), one who dwells or lives. A city dweller lives in cities. A cliff dweller lives on cliffs.

dwell ing (dwel′ing), house; place in which one lives.

dwelling place, a dwelling.

dwelt (dwelt), dwelled. We have dwelt in the country for years.

dwin dle (dwin′dəl), become smaller and smaller; shrink. Our supply of food has dwindled.

dye (dī), 1. to color or stain by dipping into water containing coloring matter; as, to have a dress dyed. 2. a color used for dyeing materials. We bought some blue dye. 3. a color produced by dipping into liquid containing dye. A good dye will not fade. 4. to color or stain. His blood dyed the ground.

dy ing (dī′ing), 1. about to die; ceasing to live; as, a dying man. 2. coming to an end; as, the dying year.

dyke (dīk), dike.

dy na mite (dī′nə mīt), 1. the material most commonly used in blasting rocks. 2. blow up with dynamite.

dy na mo (dī′nə mō), a machine for changing mechanical energy into electric energy. Mr. Day makes his own electricity with a small dynamo that is run by a gasoline engine.

dy nas ty (dī′nəs ti), series of rulers who belong to the same family.

E

E or **E.,** 1. east. 2. eastern.

each (ēch). Each of the six boys had a dog. We gave one bone to each dog. Each cup has a saucer.

ea ger (ē′gər), wanting very much. The child is eager to have the candy.

ea ger ness (ē′gər nis), keen desire.

Eagle (3 ft. from head to tail)

ea gle (ē′gəl), 1. a large bird that can see far and fly strongly. 2. like that of an eagle. The eagle eye of the guide was watching every move. 3. a design or picture shaped like an eagle often used on a flag, a stamp, or a coat of arms. 4. a former gold coin of the United States, worth $10.

ear[1] (ēr), 1. the part of the body by which men and animals hear. 2. something like an ear. 3. the sense of hearing. She has a good ear for music. 4. **Give ear** means listen or attend.

ear[2] (ēr), 1. the part of certain plants that contains the grains. The grains of corn, wheat, oats, barley, and rye are formed on ears. 2. grow ears. Soon the corn will ear.

Ear of corn

earl (ėrl), an English noble, below a marquis but above a viscount. The wife of an earl is called a countess.

ear ly (ėr′li), 1. In his early years he liked ships. 2. The sun is not hot early in the day. Please come early before the others come. Clara came earlier than Mary; Jane was the earliest of all.

earn (ėrn), 1. get in return for work or service; be paid. Mary gives her mother half of what she earns. 2. do enough work for; do good enough work for. Donald is paid more than he really earns.

ear nest (ėr′nist), 1. putting one's whole self into it. An earnest pupil has his mind on his work. 2. **In earnest** means determined or sincere.

ear nest ness (ėr′nist nis), seriousness of purpose; being earnest.

earn ings (ėr′ningz), money earned; wages; profits.

ear ring (ēr′ring′), ornament for the ear.

ear shot (ēr′shot′), range of hearing. We shouted, but he was out of earshot.

earth (ėrth), 1. the globe on which we live. The earth is a great ball that moves around the sun. China is on the other side of the earth. 2. ground. The earth in his garden is good soft soil.

earth en (ėr′thən), 1. made of earth. 2. made of baked clay.

earth en ware (ėr′thən wãr′), dishes or containers made of baked clay; crockery or pottery of the coarser kinds.

earth ly (ėrth′li), having to do with the earth, not with heaven.

earth quake (ėrth′kwāk′), a shaking or sliding of the ground, caused by changes far beneath the surface. Earthquakes sometimes destroy whole cities.

earth work (ėrth′wėrk′), a bank of earth piled up for a fortification.

earth worm (ėrth′wėrm′), the commonest worm that lives in the earth. It helps in loosening the soil.

Earthworm

ease (ēz), 1. freedom from pain or trouble. 2. make free from pain or trouble. 3. freedom from trying hard. **With ease** means without trying hard. 4. make less; lighten. Some medicines ease pain. 5. make easy; loosen. The belt is too tight; ease it a little. 6. move slowly and carefully. He eased the big box through the narrow door.

ea sel (ē′zəl), a support for a picture, blackboard, etc. See the picture.

Easel

eas i er (ēz′i ər), not so hard; less difficult; more easy.

eas i ly (ēz′i li), 1. in an easy manner. 2. without trying hard; with little effort. 3. without pain or trouble; comfortably. 4. smoothly. The cowboy rode his pony easily. 5. surely. She is easily the best singer in the choir. 6. probably. A war may easily happen.

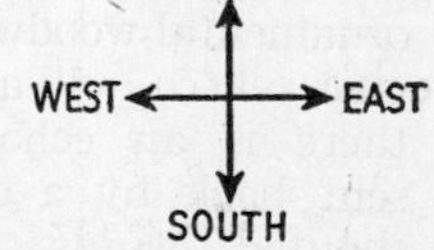

east (ēst), 1. the direction of the sunrise. 2. toward the east; farther toward the east. Walk east to find the road. 3. from the east; as, an east wind. 4. the part of any country toward the east.

Easter (ēs′tər), 1. the day for celebrating Christ's rising from the dead; a yearly church holiday that comes on a Sunday between March 21 and April 26. 2. of Easter; for Easter; as, Easter music.

eastern (ēs′tərn), 1. toward the east; as, an Eastern trip. 2. from the east; as, Eastern tourists. 3. of the east; in the east; as, Eastern schools.

eastward (ēst′wərd), toward the east; east. He walked eastward. The orchard is on the eastward slope of the hill.

easy (ēz′i), 1. not hard to do or get; as, an easy lesson. 2. not hard to bear; as, easy terms, an easy life. 3. giving comfort or rest; as, an easy chair. 4. not strict or harsh; not hard to get on with; kindly. 5. smooth and pleasant; as, easy manners, an easy way of speaking. **easier** and **easiest** are formed from **easy.**

eat (ēt), 1. chew and swallow (food). Cows eat grass and grain. 2. have a meal. Where shall we eat? 3. destroy as if by eating. The flames ate up the wood. Acid eats metal. **ate** and **eaten** are formed from **eat.**

eatable (ēt′ə bəl), 1. fit to eat. 2. **Eatables** means food.

eaten (ēt′ən). See **eat.** Have you eaten your dinner?

eater (ēt′ər), person or animal that eats.

EAVES

eaves (ēvz), the lower edge of a roof that stands out a little from the building.

ebb (eb), 1. a flowing of the tide away from the shore; fall of the tide. 2. flow out; fall. We waded farther out as the tide ebbed. 3. a growing less or weaker; decline. His fortunes were at an ebb. 4. grow less or weaker; decline. His courage began to ebb as he neared the haunted house.

ebony (eb′ən i), a hard, black wood, used for the black keys of a piano, brushes, and ornamental woodwork.

echo (ek′ō), 1. a sounding again. We say there is an echo when sound waves are sent back by a cliff or a hillside, so that shouted words are heard again as if from a distance. The echoes from Echo Hill are very clear. 2. repeat; be heard again. 3. say always what another says.

eclipse (i klips′), 1. passing from sight because light is cut off. In an eclipse of the sun, the moon is between us and the sun, so that from any point within the moon's shadow on the earth the sun is invisible. 2. cut off the light from, and so make invisible; darken. 3. shine much more brightly than; cast into the shade. In sports he quite eclipsed his older brother.

Sun showing almost entire eclipse

economical (ē′kə nom′i kəl), avoiding waste; thrifty; saving.

economy (i kon′ə mi), making the most of what one has; thrift; freedom from waste in the use of anything.

ecru (ek′rü), pale brown; light tan.

ecstasy (ek′stə si), rapture; a state of very great joy; strong feeling that thrills the heart. She was in ecstasies over her first Christmas tree.

eddied (ed′id), made eddies; whirled.

eddy (ed′i), 1. a small whirlpool or whirlwind; water, air, or smoke whirling around. 2. whirl.

Eden (ē′dən), 1. the garden where Adam and Eve lived. 2. delightful spot; a paradise.

edge (ej), 1. the part that is farthest from the middle; the side; as, the edge of the paper. 2. the thin side that cuts. The knife had a very sharp edge. 3. move side first. She edges her way through the crowd. 4. move little by little. He edged his chair nearer to the fire.

edible (ed′i bəl), 1. fit to eat. 2. thing fit to eat.

edict (ē′dikt), a decree; an order by some authority.

edifice (ed′i fis), a building, especially a large or imposing one.

edition (i dish′ən), 1. all the copies of a book, newspaper, etc., printed just alike and at or near the same time. The first edition of *Robinson Crusoe* was printed in 1719. 2. the form in which a book is printed. The new edition of *Mother Goose* has better pictures than the older editions.

educate (ej′ů kāt), teach; send to school.

education (ej′ů kā′shən), 1. schooling; teaching; changing a person's nature. In the United States, public schools offer an education to all children. 2. the knowledge and abilities gained through training.

ed u ca tion al (ej′ů kā′shən əl), 1. giving education; as, an educational moving picture. 2. having something to do with education; as, an educational association.

eel (ēl), a long, slippery fish shaped like a snake. An eel is hard to hold; so we say "as slippery as an eel."

Eel (2½ ft. long)

e'en (ēn), even.

e'er (ãr), ever.

ef face (i fās′), 1. rub out; blot out; do away with; destroy; wipe out. It takes many years to efface the unpleasant memories of a war. 2. keep (oneself) from being noticed. The shy boy effaced himself by staying in the background.

ef fect (i fekt′), 1. bring about; make happen. The war effected changes all over the world. 2. result; what is caused. The effect of the gale was to overturn several boats. 3. Some special meanings are:

effects, goods; belongings.

for effect, for show; to impress others.

give effect to, put in operation.

take effect, operate; become active.

ef fec tive (i fek′tiv), 1. able to cause something. 2. able to cause some desired result. 3. in operation; active.

ef fec tu al (i fek′chü əl), producing the effect desired; capable of producing the effect desired. Quinine is an effectual preventive of malaria.

ef fec tu al ly (i fek′chü əl i), with a desired effect; thoroughly.

ef fi ca cy (ef′i kə si), power to produce a desired result.

ef fi cien cy (i fish′ən si), ability to do things without waste; activity that counts toward a purpose.

ef fi cient (i fish′ənt), capable; doing things without waste. An efficient cook receives good pay.

ef fort (ef′ərt), 1. use of energy and strength to do something; trying hard. Climbing a steep hill takes effort. 2. hard try; strong attempt. 3. result of effort; thing done with effort. Works of art are artistic efforts.

ef fu sion (i fū′zhən), 1. pouring out; as, the effusion of blood. 2. unrestrained expression of feeling, etc., in talking or writing.

eft (eft), 1. a small amphibian with a tail. 2. a small lizard.

egg[1] (eg). Birds' eggs have shells. We eat hens' eggs. Fishes come from eggs. Birds, chickens, snakes, and alligators also come from eggs.

egg[2] (eg), urge. The other boys egged John on to fight.

egg plant (eg′plant′), a plant with large purple fruit shaped somewhat like an egg, used as a vegetable.

Eggplant

eg lan tine (eg′lən tīn), a rose with a tall, prickly stem and single pink flowers. See the picture just below.

eh (ā), an exclamation expressing surprise or doubt, or suggesting "Yes" for an answer. Wasn't it lucky, eh?

Eglantine

ei der (ī′dər), a large sea duck, generally black and white. The soft breast feathers of eiders make a valuable down. See the picture just below.

eight (āt), one more than seven; 8. Four and four make eight.

eight een (ā′tēn′), eight more than ten; 18.

eight eenth (ā′tēnth′), 1. next after the 17th. If you stand eighteenth in your class, there are just seventeen ahead of you. 2. one of 18 equal parts.

Eider (2 ft. long)

eighth (ātth), 1. next after the 7th. August is the eighth month of the year. 2. one of 8 equal parts.

ei ther (ē′ᴛʜər or ī′ᴛʜər), 1. one or the other of two. A door must be either shut or open. Either come in or go out. 2. each of two. On either side of the river lie fields of corn. 3. any more than another. If you do not go, I shall not go either.

e jac u late (i jak′ū lāt), say suddenly and quickly; exclaim.

e ject (i jekt′), throw out; turn out; drive out. The volcano ejected smoke, ashes, and lava.

eke out (ēk′ out′), add to; increase; help. She eked out her income by working in the evenings.

e lab o rate (i lab′ə rit for 1, i lab′ə rāt for 2), 1. worked out with great care; having many details; complicated. Grace's mother wore an elaborate evening gown. 2. work out with great care; add details to. The inventor spent months in elaborating his plans for a new engine.

e lapse (i laps′), pass; slip away; glide by. Hours elapsed while he slept like a log.

e las tic (i las′tik), 1. that can be stretched or pressed together and then return to its own shape. Toy balloons, sponges, and steel springs are elastic. 2. recovering easily. His elastic spirits never let him be discouraged for long. 3. tape woven partly of rubber. 4. a rubber band.

e lat ed (i lāt′id), in high spirits.

el bow (el′bō), 1. the joint between the upper and lower arm. 2. any bend or corner having the same shape as a bent arm. 3. push with the elbow. Don't elbow me off the sidewalk.

Elbow of a stovepipe

eld er (el′dər), 1. older. 2. an older person. Children should respect their elders. 3. an officer in a church.

eld er ly (el′dər li), somewhat old.

eld est (el′dist), oldest.

e lect (i lekt′), 1. choose. 2. choose by vote. Washington was elected president. 3. chosen; selected.

e lec tion (i lek′shən), 1. choice. 2. choosing by vote.

e lec tric (i lek′trik), 1. of electricity; having something to do with electricity. 2. charged with electricity; as, an electric battery. 3. giving an electric shock; as, an electric eel. 4. run by electricity. 5. exciting; thrilling.

e lec tri cal (i lek′tri kəl), electric.

e lec tri cian (i lek′trish′ən), person who repairs or installs electric wiring, lights, motors, etc.

e lec tric i ty (i lek′tris′i ti), 1. form of energy which can give certain metals the power to pull together or push apart from one another, and which can produce light and heat. 2. electric current. Electric refrigerators are run by electricity.

e lec tri fy (i lek′tri fī), 1. charge with electricity. 2. equip for the use of electric power. 3. excite; thrill. The speaker electrified his audience.

el e gance (el′i gəns), refined grace and richness; luxury free from coarseness. We admired the elegance of the lady's clothes.

el e gant (el′i gənt), showing good taste; refined; superior.

el e ment (el′i mənt), 1. a simple substance, one of 92 that cannot yet be separated into simpler parts. Gold, iron, oxygen, carbon, and tin are elements. In ancient times, people thought that there were four elements: earth, water, air, and fire. 2. one of the parts of which anything is made up. Honesty, industry, and kindness are elements of a good character. 3. a simple or necessary part. We learn the elements of arithmetic before the seventh grade. 4. **The elements** sometimes means the forces of the air, especially in bad weather. 5. **Be in one's element** means be where one can succeed.

el e men ta ry (el′i men′tə ri), introductory; dealing with the simpler parts; as, elementary arithmetic.

el e phant (el′i fənt), the largest four-footed animal now living. See the picture.

Elephant
(10 ft. tall; body 8 ft. long; ears 5 ft. across)

el e vate (el′i vāt), raise; lift up. He spoke from an elevated platform. The soldier was elevated to a higher rank for bravery.

el e va tion (el′i vā′shən), 1. raised place; high place. A hill is an elevation. 2. height above the earth's surface. The airplane fell from an elevation of 2000 feet. 3. height above sea level. The elevation of Denver is 5300 feet. 4. elevating; being elevated; as, the elevation of David to be the ruler of the Hebrews.

el e va tor (el′i vā′tər), 1. something that lifts. 2. machine for carrying people up and down in a building or for lifting things. 3. a building for storing grain.

e lev en (i lev′ən), 1. one more than ten; 11. 2. a football or cricket team.

e lev enth (i lev′ənth), 1. next after the 10th. 2. one of 11 equal parts.

elf (elf), a tiny being that is full of mischief; a fairy. Four elves sat on a cabbage leaf.

Elf

e lic it (i lis′it), draw forth; as, to elicit a reply, to elicit applause, to elicit the truth.

el i gi ble (el′i ji bəl), fit to be chosen; desirable; qualified. Pupils must pass in all subjects to be eligible for the team.

e lim i nate (i lim′i nāt), 1. remove; get rid of. Bridges over railroad tracks eliminate danger in crossing. 2. leave out; omit. Eliminate slang from a careful speech.

elk (elk), 1. large deer of Europe and Asia. It has antlers like a moose. 2. large, red deer of North America.

American elk (def. 2) (5 ft. high at the shoulder)

ell (el), a former measure of length, in England just 45 inches. Give him an inch (a little) and he'll take an ell (much).

el lipse (i lips′), oval having both ends alike. See the picture.

Ellipses

elm (elm), 1. a tall, graceful shade tree. 2. its hard, heavy wood.

e lon gate (i lông′gāt), 1. lengthen; extend. A rubber band will elongate easily. 2. lengthened. 3. long and thin; as, the elongate leaf of the willow.

el o quence (el′ə kwəns), 1. a flow of speech that has grace and force. The eloquence of the President moved all hearts. 2. power to win by speaking; the art of speaking so as to stir the feelings.

el o quent (el′ə kwənt), 1. having eloquence. 2. very expressive.

else (els), 1. other; not that one; instead. Will somebody else speak? What else could I say? 2. differently. How else can he act? 3. otherwise; if not. Hurry, else you will be late.

else where (els′hwār), somewhere else; in or to some other place.

e lude (i lüd′), avoid or escape by quickness or cleverness; slip away from. The fox eluded the dogs.

e lu sive (i lü′siv), 1. tending to elude or escape. The elusive enemy got away. 2. hard to express or define. I had an idea that was too elusive to be put in words.

elves (elvz), more than one elf; fairies.

e ma ci at ed (i mā′shi āt′id), thin from loss of flesh.

e man ci pate (i man′si pāt), set free from slavery of any kind; release. Lincoln emancipated the slaves.

em balm (em bäm′), 1. preserve (a dead body) with spices or drugs. 2. keep in memory. 3. fill with sweet scent. Roses embalmed the June air.

em bank ment (em bangk′mənt), a raised bank of earth, stone, etc., used to hold back water, support a roadway, etc.

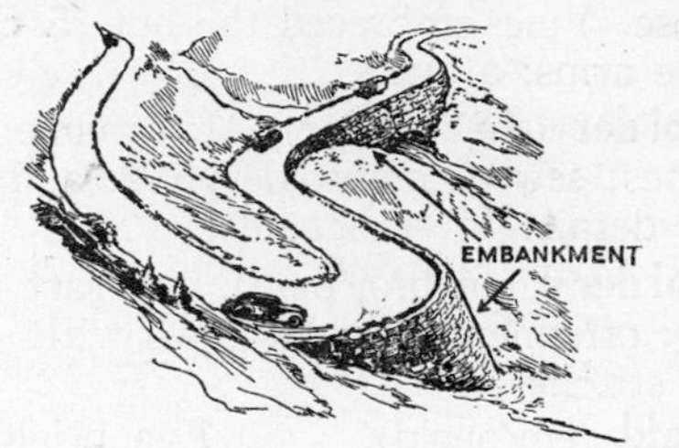

em bark (em bärk′), 1. go on board ship. The troops embarked for France. 2. put on board ship. 3. set out; start. **Embark on** means begin; enter upon.

em bar rass (em bar′əs), 1. disturb (a person); make self-conscious. She embarrassed me by asking me if I really liked her. 2. hinder. His business was embarrassed for a time by lack of ready money.

em bas sy (em′bə si), 1. one or more persons sent, usually to the ruler or government of a country, with authority to make some arrangement. 2. the headquarters of an ambassador.

em bat tled (em bat′əld), 1. drawn up ready for battle; prepared for battle. 2. fortified.

em bed (em bed′), 1. put in a bed. He embedded the bulbs in a box of sand. 2. fix or enclose in a surrounding mass. Precious stones are found embedded in rock.

em ber (em′bər), piece of wood or coal from a fire, still burning a little. **Embers** often means ashes in which there is still some fire.

em bit ter (em bit′ər), make bitter. The unhappy old man was embittered by the loss of his money.

em blem (em′bləm), symbol; sign of an idea; token. The dove is an emblem of peace. The white flag is the emblem of surrender.

em bod y (em bod′i), 1. give a body to; give reality to. A building embodies the idea of the architect. 2. form into a body; include. The Boy Scouts' *Handbook for Boys* embodies the information a boy needs to become a good Scout.

em boss (em bôs′), raise the surface of into a pattern; ornament with a raised pattern. The silver cup is embossed with a design of flowers.

em brace (em brās′), 1. fold in the arms to show love; hold in the arms. A mother embraces her baby. 2. include; contain. The cat family embraces lions and tigers. 3. take up; accept. He eagerly embraced the offer of a trip to Mexico. 4. surround; enclose. Vines embraced the hut. 5. clasping in the arms; a hug.

em broi der (em broi′dər), 1. ornament with stitches; sew at embroidery. 2. add imaginary details to; exaggerate.

em broi der y (em broi′dər i), art needlework; ornamental figures sewn with solid or open stitches.

em er ald (em′ər əld), 1. a bright-green precious stone or jewel. 2. bright green.

e merge (i mėrj′), come out; come up; come into view. The sun emerged from behind a cloud. Many facts emerged as a result of the investigation.

e mer gen cy (i mėr′jən si), sudden need for immediate action. I keep a box of tools in my car for use in an emergency.

em er y (em′ər i), a hard dark mineral which is used for grinding, smoothing, and polishing metals, stones, etc.

em i grant (em′i grənt), one who leaves his own country to settle in another.

em i grate (em′i grāt), leave one's own country to settle in another.

em i gra tion (em′i grā′shən), 1. leaving one's own country to settle in another. There has been much emigration from Italy. 2. body of emigrants. The largest emigration to the United States in a single year was that of 1907.

em i nence (em′i nəns), 1. a high place; a mountain, hill, or other high point of land. 2. high position in affairs; greatness; fame. Edison won eminence as an inventor.

em i nent (em′i nənt), high; above all others. Washington, Grant, and Lee were eminent generals.

em i nent ly (em′i nənt li), so as to be conspicuous and distinguished from others; specially.

em is sar y (em′i sãr′i), 1. person sent on a mission or errand. 2. spy; secret agent.

e mit (i mit′), send out; give off. A volcano emits smoke. The sun emits light. The lion emitted a roar of rage.

e mo tion (i mō′shən), strong feeling of any kind. Joy, grief, fear, hate, love, rage, and excitement are emotions.

e mo tion al (i mō′shən əl), 1. of the emotions. 2. appealing to the emotions. The speaker made an emotional plea for money to help crippled children. 3. easily excited. Emotional people are likely to cry if they hear sad music or read sad stories.

em per or (em′pər ər), the ruler of an empire. Japan has an emperor.

em pha sis (em′fə sis), 1. special force of voice put on particular words or syllables. In reading, put emphasis upon the most important words. 2. stress; importance. That school puts emphasis on arithmetic and reading.

em pha size (em′fə sīz), 1. make emphatic. He emphasized that word by saying it very loudly. 2. call attention to. The great number of automobile accidents emphasizes the need for careful driving.

em phat ic (em fat′ik), said or done with force; meant to stand out; clear; positive; striking; emphasized. Her answer was an emphatic "No!"

em phat i cal ly (em fat′i kəl i), in an emphatic manner; to an emphatic degree.

em pire (em′pīr), 1. a group of nations or states under one head or government. 2. a country ruled by an emperor. 3. power; rule.

em ploy (em ploi′). 1. use. You should employ your time in sensible work and play. 2. give work and pay to. She employs a cook.

em ploy ee (em ploi′ē), person who works for some person or firm for pay.

em ploy er (em ploi′ər), person who employs others.

em ploy ment (em ploi′mənt), 1. work; what one is doing. 2. use.

em pow er (em pou′ər), 1. give power or authority to. The treasurer was empowered to pay certain bills. 2. enable; permit. Man's erect position empowers him to use his hands in many ways.

em press (em′pris), 1. woman who rules over an empire. 2. wife of an emperor.

emp ti ness (emp′ti nis), being empty; lack of contents.

emp ty (emp′ti), 1. with nothing in it. The birds had gone, and their nest was left empty. 2. pour out or take out all that is in (a thing). Billy emptied his glass quickly. 3. flow out. The Mississippi River empties into the Gulf of Mexico.

em u late (em′ū lāt), try to equal or excel. The proverb tells us to emulate the industry of the ant.

em u la tion (em′ū lā′shən), imitation in order to equal or excel; desire to equal or excel.

e mul sion (i mul′shən), a milklike liquid, containing very tiny drops of fat or of some other substance.

en a ble (en ā′bəl), make able; give ability, power, or means to. Airplanes enable people to travel through the air.

en act (en akt′), 1. make into law. 2. act out; play. He enacted the part of an Indian very well.

en am el (en am′əl), 1. glasslike substance melted and then cooled to make a smooth, hard surface. Different colors of enamel are used to cover or decorate metal, pottery, etc. 2. paint or varnish used to make a smooth, hard, glossy surface. 3. smooth, hard, glossy, outer layer of the teeth. 4. any smooth, hard coating or surface that shines. 5. cover or decorate with enamel.

en camp (en kamp′), make camp; settle in tents for a time.

en camp ment (en kamp′mənt), 1. forming a camp. 2. a camp of soldiers.

en chant (en chant′), 1. use magic on; put under a spell. The witch had enchanted the princess. 2. delight greatly; charm. The dance music was enchanting.

en chant ment (en chant′mənt), 1. the use of magic spells; a spell or charm. The Greek witch turned men into pigs by her enchantments. 2. something that gives rapture or delight. We felt the enchantment of the moonlight on the lake.

en chant ress (en chan′tris), 1. woman who enchants; witch. 2. very delightful, charming woman.

en cir cle (en sėr′kəl), 1. form a circle around; surround. Trees encircled the pond. 2. go in a circle around. The moon encircles the earth.

en close (en klōz′), 1. shut in on all sides; surround. 2. put a wall or fence around. 3. put in an envelope along with a letter.

en clo sure (en klō′zhər), 1. act of enclosing. 2. state of being enclosed. 3. an enclosed place. A pen is an enclosure for animals. 4. thing that encloses. A wall or fence is an enclosure. 5. thing enclosed. The envelope contained a letter and $5 as an enclosure.

en com pass (en kum′pəs), go or reach all the way around; encircle. The atmosphere encompasses the earth.

en coun ter (en koun′tər), 1. meet unexpectedly. What if we should encounter a bear? 2. meet as an enemy. 3. a battle. 4. unexpected meeting.

en cour age (en kėr′ij), 1. give hope, courage, or confidence to; urge on. The cheers of Tom's schoolmates encouraged him. 2. give help to; make favoring conditions for. High prices for corn will encourage farming.

en cour age ment (en kėr′ij mənt), 1. an urging on toward success. 2. something that gives hope, courage, or confidence.

en croach (en krōch′), 1. go beyond proper or usual limits. The sea encroached upon the shore and covered the beach. 2. trespass upon the property or rights of another; intrude.

en cum ber (en kum′bər), 1. burden with weight, difficulties, cares, debt, etc. Mother is encumbered with household cares. 2. fill; block up. His yard was encumbered with old carts and other rubbish.

en cum brance (en kum′brəns), burden; something useless or in the way; annoyance; trouble.

en cy clo pe di a or **en cy clo pae di a** (en sī′klō pē′di ə), 1. a book giving information arranged alphabetically on all branches of knowledge. 2. a book treating one subject very thoroughly, with its articles arranged alphabetically.

end (end), 1. last part. He read to the end of the book. 2. the part where a thing begins or where it stops. Every stick has two ends. 3. bring or come to its last part; finish. Let us end this fight. 4. purpose; what is aimed at in doing any piece of work. He had this end in mind—to do his work without a mistake.

en dan ger (en dān′jər), cause danger to. A war endangers millions of lives.

en dear (en dēr′), make dear. Her kindness endeared her to all of us.

en deav or (en dev′ər), 1. try; make an effort; strive. A runner endeavors to win a race. 2. an effort; an attempt.

end ing (en′ding), end; last part.

end less (end′lis), 1. having no end; never stopping; lasting or going on forever. 2. joined in a circle; without ends; as, an endless chain.

en dorse (en dôrs′), 1. write one's name, a comment, etc., on the back of (a check, note, or other document). He had to endorse the check before the bank would cash it. 2. approve; support. Parents heartily endorsed the plan for a school playground.

en dow (en dou′), 1. give money or property to provide an income for. The rich man endowed a college. 2. give from birth. Nature endowed her with both beauty and brains.

en dur ance (en dūr′əns or en dür′əns), 1. ability to last and to withstand hard wear. A man must have great endurance to run 30 miles in a day. Cheap silk has not much endurance. 2. power to stand something without giving out; holding out; bearing up. His endurance of the pain was remarkable.

en dure (en dūr′ or en dür′), 1. last; keep on. A gold ring will endure for a thousand years. 2. undergo; bear; stand. The Indians could endure much pain.

end ways (end′wāz′), 1. on end. 2. with the end forward. 3. lengthwise. 4. end to end.

end wise (end′wīz′), endways.

en e my (en′i mi), 1. one who is on the other side or against; not a friend. Two countries fighting against each other are enemies. 2. anything that will harm. Frost is an enemy of flowers. Farmers used to think that birds were their enemies, but have now learned that they are often good friends.

en er get ic (en′ər jet′ik), full of energy; active; eager to work; full of force. Cool autumn days make us feel energetic.

en er get i cal ly (en′ər jet′i kəl i), with energy; vigorously.

en er gy (en′ər ji), 1. vigor; will to work. He is so full of energy that he cannot keep still. 2. power to work or act; force. All our energies were used in keeping the fire from spreading.

en fee ble (en fē′bəl), make feeble.

en fold (en fōld′), 1. fold in; wrap up. The old lady was enfolded in a shawl. 2. embrace; clasp. The mother enfolded her baby in her arms.

en force (en fōrs′), force obedience to; cause to be carried out. The policeman will enforce the rules of the city.

en force ment (en fōrs′mənt), an enforcing. Strict enforcement of the laws against speeding will reduce automobile accidents.

en gage (en gāj′), 1. promise; bind oneself. I will engage to be there on time. 2. promise to marry. John and Mary are engaged. John is engaged to Mary. 3. keep busy; be active. They engaged in conversation. I cannot call Mr. Smith; he is engaged just now. 4. hire. They engaged a cook for the summer. 5. attract. Bright objects engage a baby's attention. 6. fit into; lock together. The teeth in one gear engage in another. 7. start a battle against; attack. Our soldiers engaged the enemy.

Cog wheels engaged

en gaged (en gājd′), 1. pledged to marry. 2. busy; occupied.

en gage ment (en gāj′mənt), 1. promise; pledge. 2. a promise to marry. 3. a meeting with someone at a certain time; an appointment. 4. a battle.

en gen der (en jen′dər), bring into being; cause; produce. Filth engenders disease.

en gine (en′jən), 1. machine for turning power on to some work, especially a machine that can start others moving. 2. the machine that pulls a railroad train. 3. anything used to bring about a result; machine; instrument. Cannons are engines of war.

Steam engine for providing power

en gi neer (en′jə nēr′), 1. man who makes, takes care of, or runs engines. 2. man who plans and builds machines, roads, bridges, canals, forts, and the like. 3. do the work of an engineer. 4. guide; manage. Mary engineered the whole job from start to finish.

en gi neer ing (en′jə nēr′ing), the science, work, or profession of an engineer. James is studying engineering. Engineering is needed in building railroads, bridges, and dams.

Eng land (ing′glənd), the largest division of Great Britain.

Eng lish (ing′glish), 1. of or having to do with England, its people, or their language. 2. the people of England. 3. the language of England. English is spoken also in Canada, the United States, South Africa, and Australia.

en grave (en grāv′), 1. carve; cut (a mark) deeply in; as, a name engraved on a tombstone. 2. fix in the memory. 3. cut in lines on wood, stone, metal, or glass plates.

en grav ing (en grāv′ing), 1. the art or act of a person who engraves. 2. a copy of a picture made from an engraved plate; a print.

en gross (en grōs′), 1. occupy wholly; fill the mind of. She was engrossed in an interesting story. 2. copy or write in large letters; write a beautiful copy of.

en gulf (en gulf′), swallow up. The waves engulfed the boat.

en hance (en hans′), add to; make greater. Health enhances beauty. The growth of a city often enhances the value of land close to it.

e nig ma (i nig′mə), a riddle; anything puzzling. The girl's habit of eating paper was an enigma to her parents.

en join (en join′), 1. order; direct; urge. The father enjoined good conduct on his son. 2. forbid.

en joy (en joi′), 1. have or use with joy; be happy with; take pleasure in. 2. have as an advantage or benefit. He enjoyed good health. 3. **Enjoy oneself** means be happy; have a good time.

en joy a ble (en joi′ə bəl), giving joy; pleasant.

en joy ment (en joi′mənt), 1. pleasure; joy; delight. 2. possession or use. The son now has the enjoyment of his father's wide lands.

en large (en lärj′), 1. make larger. 2. grow larger. 3. **Enlarge upon a subject** means talk or write more about it.

en large ment (en lärj′mənt), 1. making larger. 2. amount that is added. 3. a photograph or other thing that has been made larger.

en light en (en līt′ən), make clear; give the light of truth and knowledge to; inform; instruct.

en list (en list′), 1. join. 2. join the army or navy. 3. get the support of. The Red Cross seeks to enlist the interest of all citizens.

en liv en (en līv′ən), make lively, active, gay, or bright. Spring enlivens all nature. Bright curtains enliven a dull room.

en mi ty (en′mi ti), the feeling that enemies have for each other; hate.

e nor mous (i nôr′məs), very, very large. Long ago there were enormous beasts in the world.

e nough (i nuf′), 1. as many as needed. Are there enough seats for all? 2. as much as needed. Has Tom had enough to eat? 3. sufficiently; until no more is needed or desired. Have you played enough?

en quire (en kwīr′), inquire.

en quir y (en kwīr′i), inquiry.

en rage (en rāj′), make very angry; make furious; madden.

en rich (en rich′), make rich or richer. An education enriches your mind. You can enrich a food by adding cream or butter. Fertilizer enriches the soil.

en roll or **en rol** (en rōl′), 1. write in a list. 2. have one's name written in a list. 3. make a member. 4. become a member. 5. enlist. Dick enrolled in the Navy.

en sign (en′sīn, also en′sən for 2), 1. a flag or banner. 2. the lowest commissioned officer in the navy. 3. army officer whose duty it was to carry the flag.

en slave (en slāv′), make a slave of; take away freedom from.

en sue (en sü′), 1. follow. The ensuing year means the year following this. 2. happen as a result. In his anger he hit the man, and a fight ensued.

en sure (en shür′), 1. make sure or certain. Careful planning and hard work ensured the success of the party. 2. make sure of getting; secure. A letter of introduction will ensure you an interview. 3. make safe; protect. Proper clothing ensured us against suffering from the cold.

en tail (en tāl′), impose; require; put (a burden, work, etc.) on somebody. Owning an automobile entailed greater expense than he had expected.

en tan gle (en tang′gəl), 1. get mixed and caught. Threads are easily entangled. 2. involve; get into difficulty. Do not entangle my brother with your schemes.

en tan gle ment (en tang′gəl mənt), 1. entangling. 2. being entangled. George Washington warned against entanglements with foreign countries. 3. thing that entangles; snare; something hard to get out of or to get through. The trenches were protected by barbed wire entanglements.

en ter (en′tər), 1. go into; come into. He entered the house. 2. go in; come in. Let them enter. 3. join; become a part or member of. Soldiers enter the army. 4. cause to join or enter. Parents enter their children in school. 5. begin; start. 6. write or print in a book, list, etc. A dictionary enters words in alphabetical order.

en ter prise (en′tər prīz), 1. an important, difficult, or dangerous undertaking. 2. any undertaking; a project. Ben had two enterprises—raising chickens and collecting butterflies. 3. readiness to start projects. Benjamin Franklin showed great enterprise.

en ter pris ing (en′tər prīz′ing), likely to start projects; ready to face difficulties.

en ter tain (en′tər tān′), 1. interest; please; make fun for. A circus entertains children. 2. have as a guest. She entertained ten people at dinner. 3. have guests; provide entertainment for guests. She entertains a great deal. 4. take into the mind; consider. I refuse to entertain such a foolish idea.

en ter tain ment (en′tər tān′mənt), 1. something that interests, pleases, or amuses, such as a show or a circus. 2. food and lodging; a supplying of wants. That hotel is famous for its good entertainment. 3. entertaining; being entertained.

en thrall or **en thral** (en thrôl′), 1. captivate; fascinate; charm. *Treasure Island* is an enthralling story of adventure. 2. make a slave of.

en throne (en thrōn′), 1. set on a throne. 2. place highest of all; exalt. Washington is enthroned in the hearts of his countrymen.

en thu si asm (en thü′zi azm), eager interest; zeal. Hunting and fishing arouse enthusiasm in many boys.

en thu si ast (en thü′zi ast), 1. person who is filled with enthusiasm. 2. person who is carried away by his feelings for a cause.

en thu si as tic (en thü′zi as′tik), full of enthusiasm; eagerly interested.

en thu si as ti cal ly (en thü′zi as′ti kəl i), with enthusiasm.

en tice (en tīs′), attract; lead into something by raising hopes or desires; tempt. The smell of food enticed the hungry children into the hut.

en tire (en tīr′), 1. whole; complete; having all the parts. 2. not broken; in one piece.

en tire ly (en tīr′li), wholly; fully.

en ti tle (en tī′təl), 1. give a claim or right. The one who guesses the answer is entitled to ask the next question. 2. give the title of. The King of England is also entitled Emperor of India.

en trance[1] (en′trəns), 1. act of entering. 2. place by which to enter. 3. right of entering. The prince had entrance to the best society.

en trance[2] (en trans′), 1. put into a trance. 2. delight; carry away with joy.

en treat (en trēt′), keep asking earnestly; beg and pray. The savage entreated Robinson Crusoe not to kill him. Helen entreated her father not to send her away to school.

en treat y (en trēt′i), earnest request. Helen's father gave in to her entreaties.

en trench (en trench′), intrench.

en trust (en trust′), 1. trust; charge with a trust. We entrusted Joe with all the money to pay the fares. 2. give (something or somebody) in trust. She entrusted the children to the care of a nurse. He entrusted his life to his doctor.

en try (en′tri), 1. act of entering. 2. place by which to enter; way to enter. An entrance hall is an entry. 3. thing written or printed in a book, list, etc. Each word explained in a dictionary is an entry. 4. person or thing that takes part in a contest. The potato race had nine entries.

en twine (en twīn′), 1. twine together. 2. twine about. Roses and honeysuckle entwine the little cottage.

e nu mer ate (i nū′mər āt or i nü′mər āt), 1. name one by one; give a list of. He enumerated the 48 States. 2. count.

en vel op (en vel′əp), to wrap, cover, or hide. The baby was so enveloped in blankets that we could hardly see its face.

en ve lope (en′və lōp), 1. a folded and gummed paper cover in which a letter or anything flat may be mailed. 2. a wrapper; a covering.

en vi a ble (en′vi ə bəl), to be envied; desirable. Susan has an enviable school record.

en vied (en′vid). See **envy.**

en vi ous (en′vi əs), 1. wishing to have something which someone else has. 2. disliking someone who has more than oneself. The weak are often envious of the strong.

en vi ron ment (en vī′rən mənt), 1. surrounding. 2. being surrounded. 3. surrounding things, conditions, or influences. A child's character is greatly influenced by his home environment.

en voy (en′voi), 1. messenger. 2. a diplomatic agent next to an ambassador in rank.

en vy (en′vi), 1. discontent or ill will at another's good fortune because one wishes it had been his; dislike for a person who has what one wants. All the boys were filled with envy when they saw Tom's new bicycle. 2. feel envy toward. Some people envy the rich. 3. feel envy because of. James envied his friend's success. 4. the object of such feeling; person who is envied. She was the envy of the younger girls in the school.

e phem er al (i fem′ər əl), lasting only a day or only a very short time.

ep ic (ep′ik), 1. long and noble poem that tells of the adventures of one or more great heroes. 2. grand in style.

ep i dem ic (ep′i dem′ik), 1. rapid spreading of a disease so that many people have it at the same time. All the schools in the city were closed during the epidemic of scarlet fever. 2. widespread.

ep i sode (ep′i sōd), a single happening or group of happenings in real life or a story.

e pis tle (i pis′əl), a letter. In the Bible, the **Epistles** were letters written by the Apostles to various churches and individuals.

ep och (ep′ək), 1. a period of time; an era. 2. a period of time in which striking things happened. The years from 1860 to 1865 were an epoch in the history of our country. 3. the starting point of such a period.

e qual (ē′kwəl), 1. the same in amount, size, number, or value. Ten dimes are equal to one dollar. 2. be the same as. Four times five equals twenty. 3. person or thing that is equal. In spelling she had no equal. 4. make or do something equal to. Our team equaled the other team's score, and the game ended in a tie. 5. **Equal to** sometimes means strong enough for. One horse is not equal to pulling a load of five tons.

e qual i ty (ē kwol′i ti), exact likeness in size, number, value, rank, etc.

e qual ly (ē′kwəl i), in equal shares; in equal manner; to an equal degree. The sun shines equally on all. The two sisters are equally pretty.

e qua tor (ē kwā′tər), an imaginary circle around the middle of the earth, halfway between the North Pole and the South Pole. The United States is north of the equator.

e qui lib ri um (ē′kwi lib′ri əm), balance. The acrobat in the circus maintained equilibrium on a tightrope. Scales are in equilibrium when weights on each side are equal.

e quip (i kwip′), fit out; provide; furnish with all that is needed. The soldiers equipped the fort with guns, powder, and food. Is the ship fully equipped for its voyage?

e quip ment (i kwip′mənt), 1. fitting out; providing. 2. outfit; what one is equipped with; supplies.

eq ui ta ble (ek′wi tə bəl), fair; just.

eq ui ty (ek′wi ti), fairness; justice.

e quiv a lent (i kwiv′ə lənt), 1. equal. 2. something equivalent.

e ra (ēr′ə), 1. an age in history; historical period. 2. period of time starting from some important or significant happening, date, etc. We live in the 20th century of the Christian era.

e rase (i rās′), rub out; scrape out.

e ras er (i rās′ər), thing used to rub out or erase.

ere (ãr), before. He will come ere long.

e rect (i rekt′), 1. straight up; not tipping; not bending. A telegraph pole stands erect. 2. set up; build. That building was erected fifty years ago.

e rec tion (i rek′shən), 1. a setting up; a raising. The erection of the tent took only a few minutes. 2. thing erected; building.

er mine (ėr′min), 1. a weasel that is brown in summer, but white in winter, except for a black tip on its tail. 2. its soft, white fur, used on the robes of English judges and for women's garments. 3. the position, rank, or duties of a judge.

Ermine (length with tail 15 in.)

e ro sion (i rō′zhən), eating away; being worn away. In geography, we study the erosion of the earth by wind and water.

err (ėr), 1. go wrong; make a mistake. 2. be wrong. 3. do wrong; sin.

er rand (er′ənd), 1. a trip to do something. She is gone on an errand. 2. what one is sent to do. She did ten errands in one trip.

er rant (er′ənt), 1. wandering; roving. He was a knight-errant seeking adventures. 2. wrong; mistaken.

er ro ne ous (i rō′ni əs), mistaken; incorrect; wrong.

er ror (er′ər), mistake; something done that is wrong; something that is not the way it ought to be.

e rup tion (i rup′shən), 1. bursting forth. There was an eruption of glowing melted rock from the mountain top. 2. a rash; red spots on the skin. In scarlet fever, there is an eruption on the body.

es cape (es kāp′), 1. get free; get out and away. The soldier escaped from the enemy's prison. 2. keep free or safe from. We all escaped the measles. 3. act of escaping. 4. way of escaping.

es cort (es′kôrt for 1, es kôrt′ for 2), 1. one or more persons going with other persons, or with valuable goods, to see that they keep safe, or to honor them. Her escort to the party was a tall young man. An escort of ten airplanes greeted the famous aviator. 2. go with to keep safe or to honor. Warships escorted the steamer.

Es ki mo (es′ki mō), 1. member of a race that lives on the Arctic shores of North America. Eskimos are short and stocky, and have broad, flat faces, yellowish skin, and black hair. 2. such as Eskimos have; as, an Eskimo dog, an Eskimo house.

Eskimos

es pe cial (es pesh′əl), special; chief; more than others. Your birthday is an especial day for you.

es pe cial ly (es pesh′əl i), particularly; principally; chiefly.

es pied (es pīd′), saw.

es py (es pī′), see; spy. We usually say espy only if the thing is hard to see because it is far away, or small, or hidden.

es say (es′ā for 1, e sā′ for 2), 1. a short composition on a particular subject. 2. try; attempt.

es sence (es′əns), 1. that which makes a thing what it is. Kindness of heart is the essence of politeness. 2. a concentrated preparation; as, essence of peppermint. 3. perfume.

es sen tial (e sen′shəl), 1. needed to make a thing what it is; necessary; very important. Good food and enough rest are essential to good health. 2. absolutely necessary element or quality. Learn the essentials first; then learn the details.

es sen tial ly (e sen′shəl i), in essence; in essentials; in an essential manner.

es tab lish (es tab′lish), 1. set up and keep going for a long time. The English established colonies in America. 2. settle in a position; set up in business. A new doctor has established himself on this street. 3. cause to be accepted and used for a long time. 4. show beyond dispute; prove; as, to establish a fact.

es tab lish ment (es tab′lish mənt), 1. establishing. 2. being established. 3. something established. A household, a large store, a church, or an army can be called an establishment.

es tate (es tāt′), 1. that which a person owns. When the rich man died, he left an estate of two million dollars. Land and buildings are called real estate. 2. a large piece of land. He has a beautiful estate 40 miles from New York with a country house and a swimming pool on it. 3. a class or condition in life. A boy reaches man's estate at the age of 21.

es teem (es tēm′), 1. think highly of. We esteem courage. 2. high regard. Courage is held in esteem. 3. think; consider. I esteem it my duty to fight.

es ti mate (es′ti māt, also es′ti mit for 1), 1. a judgment or opinion as to how much, how many, how good, etc. His estimate of the length of the fish was 15 inches. 2. form a judgment or an opinion. Father estimated that the rug was 9 feet long and 6 feet wide.

es ti ma tion (es′ti mā′shən), 1. opinion; judgment. In my estimation, your plan will not work. 2. esteem; respect.

etc., 1. and so forth; and others. 2. and the like; and other similar things.

et cet er a (et set′ər ə), and so forth; and so on; and the rest; and the like.

e ter nal (i tėr′nəl), 1. without beginning or ending; lasting throughout all time. 2. always and forever the same. 3. seeming to go on forever.

e ter ni ty (i tėr′ni ti), all time; all the past and all the future.

e ther (ē′thər), 1. a drug which produces unconsciousness when it is inhaled. 2. the upper regions of space; the clear sky.

e the re al (i thēr′i əl), 1. light; airy; delicate. 2. not of the earth; heavenly.

et i quette (et′i ket), customary rules for behavior in society. Etiquette requires a man to rise when a woman enters the room.

Eu rope (ūr′əp), a continent east of the

Atlantic Ocean. France, Germany, and Russia are countries in Europe.

Eu ro pe an (ūr′ə pē′ən), 1. of or having to do with Europe or its people. 2. person who was born in or lives in Europe.

e vac u ate (i vak′ū āt), 1. leave empty; withdraw from. The soldiers will evacuate the town today. 2. make empty; as, to evacuate the stomach.

e vade (i vād′), get away from by trickery; avoid by cleverness. Criminals evade the law. When Father asked who broke the window, Dick tried to evade the question.

e vap o rate (i vap′ə rāt), 1. turn into vapor. Boiling water evaporates rapidly. 2. remove water from. Evaporated milk comes in cans. 3. give off moisture. 4. vanish; die. His good resolutions evaporated soon after New Year's.

e vap o ra tion (i vap′ə rā′shən), evaporating. Wet clothes on a line become dry by evaporation.

eve (ēv), 1. the evening or day before some special day; as, Christmas Eve. 2. the time just before; as, on the eve of battle. 3. evening.

Eve (ēv), in the Bible, the first woman, the wife of Adam. A **daughter of Eve** means a woman.

e ven (ē′vən), 1. level; flat; smooth. The country is even, with no high hills. 2. at the same level. The snow is even with the window. 3. keeping about the same; uniform. The car goes with an even motion. This boy has an even temper. 4. equal; no more or less than. They had even shares of the money. 5. make equal or level; as, to even off edges. 6. that can be divided by 2 without a remainder. 2, 4, 6, 8, and 10 are even numbers. 7. without a remainder. 8. just. He went away even as you came. 9. indeed. He is ready, even eager, to fight. 10. Even often gives the idea of something that would not be expected. Some of the expressions are: He wants even more than that. Even young children can understand it. Even the last man arrived on time. I will come even if I am tired. 11. still; yet. You can read even better if you try.

eve ning (ēv′ning), the time between day and night; the time between sunset and bedtime.

e ven ly (ē′vən li), 1. smoothly; at the same level. Spread the frosting evenly on the cake. 2. at about the same speed. 3. equally. Divide the money evenly.

e vent (i vent′), 1. happening; important happening. The discovery of America was a great event. 2. result; outcome. We made careful plans and awaited the event. 3. **In the event of** means in the case of. In the event of rain, the party will be held indoors. 4. item or contest in a program of sports.

e vent ful (i vent′fəl), 1. full of events; having many unusual events. An eventful day for Joe was the one when he lost a tooth, found a dollar, and had a perfect mark in spelling. 2. having important results; important.

e ven tide (ē′vən tīd′), evening.

e ven tu al (i ven′chü əl), coming in the end.

e ven tu al ly (i ven′chü əl i), finally; in the end.

ev er (ev′ər), 1. at any time. Is he ever at home? 2. at all times; always. A mother is ever ready to help her children. 3. by any chance; at all. What did you ever do to make him so angry? 4. **Ever so** means very. The ocean is ever so deep.

ev er green (ev′ər grēn′), 1. having green leaves all the year. 2. evergreen plant. Pine, spruce, cedar, ivy, box, etc., are evergreens. 3. **Evergreens** sometimes means evergreen twigs or branches used for decoration.

A large evergreen tree, the spruce.

ev er last ing (ev′ər las′ting), 1. lasting forever; never stopping. 2. lasting a long time. 3. lasting too long; tiresome.

ev er more (ev′ər mōr′), always; forever.

eve ry (ev′ri). Every word is made of letters. Every boy has a head.

eve ry bod y (ev′ri bod′i), every person.

eve ry day (ev′ri dā′), 1. of every day; daily. Accidents are everyday occurrences. 2. for every ordinary day; not for Sundays or holidays. A person wears everyday clothes to work. 3. usual; not exciting. Nan had only an everyday story to tell.

eve ry one or **every one** (ev′ri wun), each one; everybody.

eve ry thing (ev′ri thing), every thing; all things. Nan does everything she can to help her mother.

ev ery where (ev′ri hwãr), in every place; in all places or lands. A smile is understood everywhere.

ev i dence (ev′i dəns), 1. facts; proof; anything that shows or makes clear. The jam on Bill's face was evidence that he had been in the kitchen. His first day's work gave evidence of his speed. 2. show clearly. His smiles evidenced his pleasure. 3. **In evidence** means easily seen or noticed. A crying baby is much in evidence.

ev i dent (ev′i dənt), easy to see or understand; clear; plain. It is evident that children grow up.

e vil (ē′vəl), 1. bad; wrong; that does harm. 2. something bad; evil quality or act. 3. thing causing harm.

e vince (i vins′), show clearly. The cat evinced fear of the big dog.

e voke (i vōk′), call forth; bring out. A good joke evokes a laugh.

ev o lu tion (ev′ə lü′shən), 1. a gradual development; as, the evolution of the flower from the bud, the evolution of one kind of animal or plant from a simpler kind. 2. the theory of the development of all living things from a few simple forms of life, or from a single form. 3. a movement of dancers. 4. a movement of ships or of soldiers, planned beforehand. 5. a releasing or giving off; as, the evolution of heat from burning coal.

e volve (i volv′), unfold; develop gradually. The boys evolved a plan for earning money during their summer vacation.

ewe (ū), a female sheep.

ex act (eg zakt′), 1. without any error; correct; as, an exact measurement, the exact amount. 2. demand and get. If he does the work, he can exact payment for it.

ex act ing (eg zak′ting), 1. requiring much; hard to please. 2. requiring effort, care, or attention. Flying an airplane is exacting work.

ex act ly (eg zakt′li), 1. without any error; precisely. 2. just so; quite right.

ex ag ger ate (eg zaj′ər āt), make too large; say or think something is greater than it is; go beyond the truth. The little boy exaggerated when he said there were a million cats in the back yard.

ex ag ger a tion (eg zaj′ər ā′shən), 1. an exaggerating. 2. a being exaggerated. 3. an exaggerated statement. It is an exaggeration to say that you would rather die than touch a snake.

ex alt (eg zôlt′), 1. make high in rank, honor, power, character, or quality. We exalt a man when we elect him President of our country. 2. fill with pride or joy or noble feeling. An exalted mood is one in which we think noble thoughts. 3. praise; honor. God shall be exalted.

ex am i na tion (eg zam′i nā′shən), examining; test. The doctor made a careful examination of my eyes. The teacher gave us an examination in arithmetic.

ex am ine (eg zam′in), 1. look at closely and carefully. The doctor examined the wound. 2. test; test the knowledge or ability of; ask questions of.

ex am ple (eg zam′pəl), 1. a sample; one thing taken to show what the others are like. New York is an example of a busy seaport. 2. a model; a pattern. Lincoln is a good example for boys to follow. 3. a problem in arithmetic. 4. warning to others. The captain made an example of the soldiers who shirked by making them clean up the camp.

ex as per ate (eg zas′pər āt), irritate; annoy greatly; make angry. The little boy's noise exasperated his father.

ex ca vate (eks′kə vāt), 1. make hollow; hollow out. 2. make by digging; dig. The tunnel was excavated through solid rock. 3. dig out; scoop out. Big machines excavated the dirt and loaded it into trucks. 4. uncover by digging. They excavated an ancient buried city.

ex ca va tion (eks′kə vā′shən), 1. a digging out; a digging. 2. hole made by digging.

ex ceed (ek sēd′), go beyond; be more or greater than. The sum of 5 and 7 exceeds 10. To lift a heavy trunk exceeds a girl's strength.

ex ceed ing (ek sēd′ing), very great. Helen is a girl of exceeding beauty.

ex ceed ing ly (ek sēd′ing li), very greatly; to an unusual degree; very.

ex cel (ek sel′), 1. be better than; do better than. John excelled his class in spelling. 2. be better than others; do better than others. Solomon excelled in wisdom.

ex cel lence (ek′sə ləns), high quality; being better than others. This state boasts of the excellence of its climate.

ex cel len cy (ek′sə lən si), 1. excellence. 2. a title of honor. A governor is formally spoken of as His Excellency.

ex cel lent (ek′sə lənt), very, very good; better than others. Excellent work deserves high praise.

ex cept (ek sept′), 1. leaving out; other than. He works every day except Sunday. 2. leave out. The teacher excepted John from the examination list.

ex cept ing (ek sep′ting), leaving out; except.

ex cep tion (ek sep′shən), 1. leaving out. She likes all her teachers with the exception of Miss Smith. 2. thing left out. She praised them all, with two exceptions. 3. thing that is different from the rule. 4. objection. **Take exception** means (1) object. (2) be offended.

ex cep tion al (ek sep′shən əl), unusual; out of the ordinary. This warm weather is exceptional for January.

ex cess (ek ses′, also ek′ses for 4), 1. the part that is too much. Pour off the excess. 2. **To excess** means too much. He eats to excess. 3. amount by which one thing is greater than another. The excess of 7 over 5 is 2. **In excess of** means more than. 4. extra. We pay excess fare on some very fast trains.

ex ces sive (ek ses′iv), too much; too great; extreme. Twenty cents is an excessive price for a pound of sugar.

ex change (eks chānj′), 1. change; give and take. You two boys exchange places. 2. giving and taking. Ten pennies for a dime is a fair exchange. 3. central telephone office. 4. a place where men trade.

ex cit a ble (ek sīt′ə bəl), easily excited.

ex cite (ek sīt′), 1. stir up the feelings of. The news of war excited everybody. 2. arouse. Her new dress excited envy. 3. stir to action. Do not excite the dog; let him keep still.

ex cite ment (ek sīt′mənt), 1. excited state. The baby's first step caused great excitement in the family. 2. a cause of being excited.

ex claim (eks klām′), cry out; speak suddenly in surprise, strong feeling, etc. "Here you are at last!" exclaimed Jack's mother.

ex cla ma tion (eks′klə mā′shən), something said suddenly as the result of feeling. Oh! Hurrah! Well! Look! and Listen! are common exclamations.

ex clude (eks klüd′), 1. shut out; keep out. Curtains exclude light. The government excludes immigrants that have certain diseases. 2. drive out and keep out. Perfect faith excludes doubt.

ex clu sion (eks klü′zhən), 1. an excluding. 2. a being excluded. Amy's exclusion from the club hurt her feelings.

ex clu sive (eks klü′siv), 1. shutting out; leaving out. There are 26 days in that month, exclusive of Sundays. 2. shutting out all or most. This school is exclusive; only very bright children can go to it. 3. single; sole; not divided or shared with others. An inventor has an exclusive right for a certain number of years to make what he has invented. 4. very particular about choosing friends, members, patrons, etc. It is hard to get admitted to an exclusive club.

ex clu sive ly (eks klü′siv li), with the exclusion of all others. That selfish girl looks out for herself exclusively.

ex cur sion (eks kėr′zhən), 1. a short journey. 2. a trip taken for interest or pleasure, often by a number of people together; as, an excursion to the seashore.

ex cuse (eks kūz′ for 1, 2, 3, and 4, eks kūs′ for 5 and 6), 1. offer an apology for; try to remove the blame of. **Excuse oneself** means ask to be pardoned. He excused himself for bumping into me by saying that he was in a hurry. 2. be a reason or explanation for. Sickness excuses absence from school. 3. pardon; forgive. Excuse me; I have to go now. 4. let off. You are excused from spelling today. 5. a reason, real or pretended, that is given. He had many excuses for coming late. 6. act of excusing.

ex e cute (ek′si kūt), 1. carry out; do. The nurse executed the doctor's orders. 2. put into effect; enforce. John makes the plans; Dick executes them. 3. put to death according to law. The murderer was executed. 4. make according to a plan or design.

ex e cu tion (ek′si kū′shən), 1. a carrying out; a doing. 2. a putting into effect. 3. a way of carrying out or doing; skill. 4. a putting to death according to law. 5. a making according to a plan or design.

ex e cu tion er (ek′si kū′shən ər), person who kills criminals who are sentenced to death.

ex ec u tive (eg zek′ū tiv), 1. having to do with management. An executive job is a job at managing something. The President is the executive head of the nation. 2. manager; person who carries out what he (or another) has decided should be done.

ex empt (eg zempt′), 1. make free (from). The school exempts good pupils from examinations. 2. freed (from). School property is exempt from all taxes.

ex er cise (ek′sər sīz), 1. use; practice. It is wise to exercise caution in crossing the street. Exercise of the body is good for the health. 2. something that gives practice. Do the exercises on page 50. 3. procedure; activity; performance. The opening exercises in our Sunday school are a song and a prayer.

ex ert (eg zėrt′), use; put into use; use fully. A fighter exerts strength. A ruler exerts authority. **Exert oneself** means make an effort; try hard; strive.

ex er tion (eg zėr′shən), 1. effort. The exertions of the firemen kept the fire from spreading. 2. use; active use; putting into action. Unwise exertion of authority may cause rebellion.

ex hale (eks hāl′), 1. breathe out. We exhale air from our lungs. 2. give off (air, vapor, smoke, odor, etc.). 3. pass off as vapor; rise like vapor. Sweet odors exhale from the flowers.

ex haust (eg zôst′), 1. to empty; as, to exhaust a well. 2. to use up; as, to exhaust the supply of water, to exhaust one's strength or money. 3. tire out; as, to exhaust oneself by hard work. 4. escape of used steam, gasoline, etc., from a machine. 5. means or way for used steam, gasoline, etc., to escape from an engine. 6. used steam, gasoline, etc., that escapes.

ex haust ed (eg zôs′tid), 1. used up. 2. worn out; very tired.

ex haus tion (eg zôs′chən), 1. act of exhausting. 2. being exhausted. 3. extreme fatigue.

ex hib it (eg zib′it), 1. show. The child exhibited a bad temper at an early age. He exhibits interest whenever you talk about dogs. 2. show publicly. You should exhibit your roses in the Flower Show. 3. something shown to the public. Their exhibit of corn products won the prize.

ex hi bi tion (ek′si bish′ən), 1. showing. Such an exhibition of bad manners I never saw before. 2. public show. The art school held an exhibition of paintings. 3. thing or things shown publicly; exhibit.

ex hil a rate (eg zil′ə rāt), cheer; make merry; make lively. The joy of Christmas exhilarates us all. We enjoy an exhilarating swim.

ex ile (eg′zīl or ek′sīl), 1. make (a person) go from home or country, often by law as a punishment; banish. The traitor was exiled from his country for life. 2. person who is banished. He has been an exile for ten years. 3. banishment. He was sent into exile for life.

ex ist (eg zist′), 1. be. The world has existed a long time. 2. be real. Do fairies exist or not? 3. live. A man cannot exist without air. 4. occur. Cases exist of persons who cannot smell anything.

ex ist ence (eg zis′təns), 1. being; as, come into existence. 2. being real. People do not now believe in the existence of ghosts. 3. life. Many aviators lead a dangerous existence.

ex ist ent (eg zis′tənt), 1. existing. 2. existing now.

ex it (eg′zit or ek′sit), 1. way out. The theater had six exits. 2. the departure of a player from the stage. 3. act of going out. When the cat came in the mice made a hasty exit.

ex pand (eks pand′), spread out; open out; unfold; swell; make or grow larger. A balloon expands when it is blown up. Our country has expanded many times. A man may expand his business, his umbrella, or a speech.

ex panse (eks pans′), open or unbroken stretch; a wide, spreading surface. The Pacific Ocean is a vast expanse of water.

ex pan sion (eks pan′shən), 1. an expanding. Heat causes the expansion of gas. 2. a being expanded; increase in size, volume, etc. The expansion of the factory made room for more machines.

ex pect (eks pekt′), look for; think something will come or happen. We expect hot days in summer.

ex pect ant (eks pek′tənt), expecting; looking for; thinking something will come or happen. Mary was expectant of a doll on her birthday.

ex pec ta tion (eks′pek tā′shən), 1. an expecting or being expected; anticipation. 2. thing expected. 3. good reason for expecting something; prospect. He has expectations of money from a rich uncle.

ex pe di ent (eks pē′di ənt), 1. useful; helping to attain some result. It is expedient to make friends if you wish to be elected president of your class. 2. a way of getting something; a means to an end. If you wish a fire and have no matches, you can try such expedients as using flint, steel, and tinder.

ex pe di tion (eks′pi dish′ən), 1. a journey for a special purpose, such as war, discovery, or collecting new plants. 2. the people, ships, etc., making such a journey. 3. speed.

ex pel (eks pel′), 1. drive out with much force. A bullet is expelled from the barrel of a gun. 2. put out. A bad boy may be expelled from a school.

ex pend (eks pend′), spend; use up.

ex pen di ture (eks pen′di chər), 1. a spending; a using up. A large piece of work requires the expenditure of much money, time, and effort. 2. amount of money, etc., spent; expense. Mary's expenditures for Christmas presents were $1.05 and 14 hours of work.

ex pense (eks pens′), 1. paying out money; laying out of money. One expense followed another until Emma's money was all gone. 2. cost. The expenses of the trip were over six dollars.

ex pen sive (eks pen′siv), costly; high-priced. He had a very expensive knife which cost $6.

ex pe ri ence (eks pēr′i əns), 1. what happens to a person; as, a pleasant or sad experience, to know by experience. 2. practice; knowledge gained by doing or seeing things. Have you had any experience in this kind of work? 3. feel; have happen to one; as, to experience very great pain.

ex pe ri enced (eks pēr′i ənst), 1. taught by experience. 2. skillful or wise through experience; as, an experienced teacher, an experienced nurse.

ex per i ment (eks per′i ment for 1, eks per′i-mənt for 2), 1. try in order to find out; make trials or tests. A baby experiments with his hands. That man is experimenting with dyes to get the color he wants. 2. a trial or test to find out something; as, a cooking experiment. Science tests out theories by experiment.

ex per i men tal (eks per′i men′təl), 1. based on experiments. Chemistry is an experimental science. 2. used for experiments. We worked in the experimental room. 3. based on experience, not on theory or authority. 4. testing; trying out. This trip will be only experimental.

ex pert (eks′pėrt, also eks pėrt′ for 2), 1. person who has skill or who knows a great deal about some special thing. Alice is an expert at fancy skating. 2. having skill; knowing a great deal about some special thing. His father is an expert painter.

ex pire (ek spīr′), 1. come to an end. You must obtain a new license when your old one expires. 2. die. 3. breathe out. Used air is expired from the lungs.

ex plain (eks plān′), make plain; tell the meaning of; tell how to do. The teacher explained long division to the class.

ex pla na tion (eks′plə nā′shən), 1. an explaining; clearing up a difficulty or mistake. He did not understand the teacher's explanation of long division. 2. something that explains. We had an explanation and agreed to quarrel no more.

ex plode (eks plōd′), 1. blow up; burst with a loud noise. The building was destroyed when the defective boiler exploded. 2. cause to explode. Many boys explode firecrackers on the Fourth of July. 3. burst forth noisily. The speaker's mistake was so funny the audience exploded with laughter. 4. cause to be rejected. Columbus helped to explode the theory that the earth is flat.

ex ploit (eks ploit′, also eks′ploit for 1), 1. bold, unusual act; daring deed. Old stories tell about the exploits of famous heroes. 2. make use of; turn to practical account. A mine is exploited for its minerals. 3. make unfair use of; use selfishly for one's own advantage. Nations used to exploit their colonies, taking as much wealth out of them as they could.

ex plo ra tion (eks′plə rā′shən), 1. a traveling in little known lands or seas for the purpose of discovery. 2. a going over carefully; a looking into closely; examining.

ex plore (eks plōr′), 1. travel over little known lands or seas for the sake of discovery. Byrd explored around the South Pole. 2. go over carefully; examine. The children explored the new house from attic to cellar.

ex plor er (eks plōr′ər), person who explores.

ex plo sion (eks plō′zhən), 1. a blowing up; a bursting with a loud noise. The explosion of the bomb shook the whole neighborhood. 2. loud noise caused by this. People five miles away heard the explosion. 3. noisy bursting forth; outbreak; as, explosions of anger, an explosion of laughter.

ex plo sive (eks plō′siv), 1. of or for explosion; tending to explode. Gunpowder is explosive. 2. explosive substance. Explosives are used in making fireworks. 3. tending to burst forth noisily. The irritable old man had an explosive temper.

ex port (eks′pōrt, also eks pōrt′ for 1), 1. send out of one country for sale in another. The United States exports many kinds of machinery. 2. act or fact of exporting. 3. article exported. Cotton is the most important export of the Southern States of the United States.

ex pose (eks pōz′), 1. lay open; uncover; leave without protection. Soldiers in an open field are exposed to the enemy's fire. Foolish actions expose a person to ridicule. 2. put in plain sight; display. Goods are exposed for sale in a store. 3. make known; reveal. He exposed the plot to the police. 4. abandon; put out without shelter. 5. allow light to reach and act on (a photographic film or plate).

ex po si tion (eks′pə zish′ən), 1. public show or exhibition. A world's fair is an exposition. 2. explanation.

ex po sure (eks pō′zhər), 1. exposing; laying open; making known. The exposure of the real criminal cleared the innocent man. Anyone would dread public exposure of all his faults. 2. being exposed. Exposure to the weather has spoiled this chair. 3. "This house has a southern exposure" means that the house is exposed to sun and wind from the south. 4. abandoning; putting out without shelter.

ex pound (eks pound′), 1. make clear; explain. The teacher expounds each new rule or principle in arithmetic to the class. 2. set forth in detail.

ex press (eks pres′), 1. put into words. Try to express your idea clearly. **Express oneself** means say what one thinks. 2. show by look, voice, or action. A smile expresses joy. 3. clear and definite. It was his express wish that we should go without him. 4. a company that carries packages, money, etc. 5. a quick means of sending; as, to send it by express. 6. send by some quick means; as, to express a package. 7. by express; specially. Send your trunk express to Boston. 8. quick; as, an express train. 9. press out. Wine is made by expressing the juice from grapes.

ex pres sion (eks presh′ən), 1. putting into words; as, the expression of an idea. 2. a word or words used as a unit. "Swell guy" is a slang expression. 3. showing by look, voice, or action; as, the expression of a feeling. 4. a look that shows feeling; as, a hurt expression. 5. bringing out the meaning or beauty of something read, spoken, sung, or played. Try to read with more expression.

ex pres sive (eks pres′iv), 1. expressing. Alas! is a word expressive of sadness. 2. carrying much feeling. "His skin hung on his bones" is a more expressive sentence than "He was very thin."

ex press ly (eks pres′li), 1. plainly. You are expressly forbidden to touch it. 2. on purpose. I came expressly to bring it to you.

ex pul sion (eks pul′shən), 1. a forcing out; as, expulsion of air from the lungs. 2. being forced out. Expulsion from school is a punishment for bad behavior.

ex qui site (eks′kwi zit), 1. very lovely; delicate; beautifully made. The violet is an exquisite flower. 2. sharp; as, exquisite pain. 3. of highest excellence; most admirable. She has exquisite taste and manners.

ex tend (eks tend′), 1. stretch out; as, to extend your hand, to extend help to the poor, an extended visit, a road that extends to New York. 2. give; grant. Charity extends help to poor people.

ex ten sion (eks ten′shən), 1. stretching out; as, the extension of a road. 2. addition; as, a new extension built on the old school.

ex ten sive (eks ten′siv), far-reaching; large; as, extensive changes, an extensive park.

ex tent (eks tent′), 1. size, space, length, amount, or degree to which a thing extends. Railroads carry people and goods through the whole extent of the country. The extent of a judge's power is limited by law. 2. something extended; extended space; as, a vast extent of prairie.

ex te ri or (eks tēr′i ər), 1. outside. I saw only the exterior of the house, not the interior. The man has a harsh exterior, but a kind heart. 2. outer. Skin is the exterior covering of our bodies. 3. coming from without; happening outside.

ex ter mi nate (eks tėr′mi nāt), destroy completely. This poison will exterminate rats.

ex ter nal (eks tėr′nəl), 1. outer; outside; outside ourselves. 2. outside part. 3. easily seen but not essential. Going to church is an external act of worship.

ex tinct (eks tingkt′), 1. no longer existing. Dinosaurs are extinct. 2. gone out; not burning; as, an extinct volcano.

ex tinc tion (eks tingk′shən), 1. extinguishing. The extinction of the lights left us in total darkness. 2. suppression; wiping out; destruction. Physicians are working for the extinction of diseases.

ex tin guish (eks ting′gwish), 1. put out. 2. wipe out; bring to an end. We can extinguish a fire with water.

ex tol or **ex toll** (eks tōl′), praise highly. The newspapers extolled our brave soldiers.

ex tra (eks′trə), 1. beyond what is usual, expected, or needed; as, extra pay, extra fine quality, extra fare. 2. anything that is extra. Her bill for extras was $30. 3. special edition of a newspaper.

ex tract (eks trakt′ for 1, eks′trakt for 2), 1. draw out, usually with some effort; take out; as, to extract oil from olives or iron from the earth, to extract a tooth, to extract pleasure from a party. 2. something drawn out or taken out. He read several extracts from the poem. Vanilla extract is made from vanilla beans.

ex traor di nar i ly (eks trôr′di nãr′i li), most unusually.

ex traor di nar y (eks trôr′di nãr′i), beyond what is ordinary; very unusual; remarkable; special. Seven feet is an extraordinary height for a man.

ex trav a gance (eks trav′ə gəns), 1. careless and lavish spending; waste. His extravagance kept him always in debt. 2. going beyond the bounds of reason. The extravagance of his story made us doubt him.

ex trav a gant (eks trav′ə gənt), 1. spending much and spending it carelessly; wasteful. 2. costing more than is fit and proper. A dinner for four people at $75.00 is extravagant. 3. beyond the bounds of reason. To call a poodle "the sweetest thing alive" is extravagant.

ex treme (eks trēm′), 1. very great; very strong; as, extreme love for one's country. 2. at the very end; the farthest possible; last. 3. something extreme. Love and hate are two extremes of feeling. **Go to extremes** means to do or say too much.

ex treme ly (eks trēm′li), much more than usual; very.

ex trem i ty (eks trem′i ti), 1. the very end; the tip. 2. **The extremities** are the hands and feet. 3. extreme degree. Perfect bliss is the extremity of happiness. 4. an extreme measure. The soldiers were forced to the extremity of firing to scatter the mob. 5. **In extremity** means in very great danger or need. People on a sinking ship are in extremity.

ex tri cate (eks′tri kāt), release; free from entanglements, difficulties, embarrassing situations, etc. Tom extricated the kitten from the net. The dog got caught in the briars and had trouble in extricating itself.

ex ult (eg zult′), be very glad; rejoice greatly. The winners exulted in their victory.

ex ult ant (eg zul′tənt), exulting; rejoicing greatly; triumphant.

ex ul ta tion (eg′zul tā′shən), great joy; triumph. There was exultation over the army's victory.

eye (ī), 1. the part of the body by which men and animals see. 2. action of the eye; seeing. 3. power of seeing. An artist should have an eye for color. 4. look; glance. 5. to watch; observe. The children eyed the stranger. 6. way of looking. Taking stolen goods is a crime in the eye of the law. 7. regard; view; aim. 8. something like an eye or that suggests an eye. The little spots on potatoes, the hole in a needle, and the loop into which a hook fastens are all called eyes. 9. Some special meanings are:

catch one's eye, attract one's attention.

have an eye to, look out for; pay attention to. Almost everyone has an eye to his own advantage.

keep an eye on, look after; watch carefully. Keep an eye on the baby.

make eyes at, look at with liking or love.

see eye to eye, agree entirely.

set eyes on, see; look at.

eye brow (ī′brou′), 1. arch or strip of hair above the eye. 2. bony ridge that it grows on.

eye glass (ī′glas′), 1. a lens to aid poor vision. 2. **Eyeglasses** means a pair of glass lenses to help vision.

eye lash (ī′lash′), 1. one of the hairs on the edge of the eyelid. 2. fringe of such hairs.

eye let (ī′lit), 1. small, round hole for a lace or cord to go through. 2. metal ring around such a hole to strengthen it.

eye lid (ī′lid′), the cover of skin, upper or lower, by means of which we can shut and open our eyes.

eye piece (ī′pēs′), the lens or lenses in a telescope, microscope, etc., that are nearest the eye of the user.

eye sight (ī′sīt′), sight; power to see.

F

fa ble (fā′bəl), 1. story that is made up to teach a lesson. Fables are often about animals who can talk. 2. story that is not true.

fab ric (fab′rik), 1. cloth; woven or knitted material. Velvet, canvas, linen, and flannel are fabrics. 2. thing that is put together. 3. frame or structure; way in which a thing is put together.

fab u lous (fab′ū ləs), 1. like a fable. 2. too extraordinary to seem possible; incredible; amazing. That antique shop asks fabulous prices. 3. of or belonging to a fable; imaginary. The centaur is a fabulous monster.

face (fās), 1. the front part of the head. Your eyes, nose, and mouth are parts of your face. 2. look; expression. His face was sad. 3. the front part; the right side; surface; as, the face of a clock, the whole face of the earth. 4. outward appearance. This action, on the face of it, looks bad. 5. to front toward. The house faces the street. The picture faces page 60 in my book. 6. meet bravely or boldly. 7. boldness; impudence. Lulu had the face to insult a policeman. 8. cover with a different material. She faced the sleeves with silk. A wooden house is sometimes faced with brick. 9. **In the face of** means (1) in the presence of. (2) in spite of.

fac et (fas′it), one of the polished surfaces of a cut gem.

Cut gem showing facets

fa cil i tate (fə sil′i tāt), make easy; lessen the labor of; help forward; assist. A vacuum cleaner facilitates housework.

fa cil i ty (fə sil′i ti), 1. ease; absence of difficulty. The boy ran and dodged with such facility that no one could catch him. 2. power to do anything easily, quickly, and smoothly. 3. aid; convenience; something which makes an action easy. Ropes, swings, and sand piles are facilities for play.

fact (fakt), 1. thing known to be true; thing known to have happened. 2. what is real; truth. 3. thing said or supposed to be true or to have really happened. We doubted his facts.

fac tor (fak′tər), 1. any one of the causes of a result; one element in a situation. Ability, industry, and health are factors of success in school. 2. any of the numbers or expressions which, when multiplied together, form a product. 2 and 5 are factors of 10. 3. separate into factors. 4. person who does business for another; agent.

fac to ry (fak′tə ri), 1. a building or group of buildings where things are manufactured. A factory usually has machines in it. Hats, shoes, dishes, and chairs are made in factories. 2. a trading post in a foreign country. At the factories on the coast of Africa, cloth, knives, etc., were exchanged for ivory.

fac ul ty (fak′əl ti), 1. power to do some special thing, especially a power of the mind. Nell has a great faculty for arithmetic. Old people sometimes lose their faculties. 2. the teachers of a school, college, or university.

fade (fād), 1. become less bright; lose color. Daylight fades when the sun sets. Colored cloth often fades when it is washed. 2. become weak; die slowly. The sound fades after a train goes by. Flowers fade. 3. cause to fade. Sunlight will fade some dresses.

faer ie or **faer y** (fãr′i), 1. fairyland. 2. fairy.

fag (fag), 1. work hard or until wearied. Tom fagged away at his arithmetic. 2. tire by work. The horse was fagged.

fag got or **fag ot** (fag′ət), a bundle of sticks or twigs tied together for fuel.

Faggot of twigs

fail (fāl), 1. not succeed; come to nothing; not be able to do. He tried hard to learn to sing, but he failed. 2. not do; neglect. He failed to follow our advice. 3. be of no use to when needed. When I wanted his help, he failed me. 4. be missing; be not enough. The wind failed us, so that we could not sail home. 5. grow weak; die away. The sick man's heart was failing. 6. not be able to pay what one owes; as, to fail in business. 7. **Without fail** means surely.

fail ing (fāl′ing), 1. failure. 2. fault; weakness; defect. 3. lacking; in the absence of. Failing good weather, the game will be played indoors.

fail ure (fāl′yər), 1. failing; lack of success. 2. falling short; as, failure of crops. 3. losing strength; becoming weak; as, failure of eyesight. 4. being unable to pay what one owes. 5. person or thing that has failed. The picnic was a failure because it rained.

fain (fān), 1. gladly; willingly; by choice. 2. willing, but far from eager. 3. glad; willing. 4. eager; desirous.

faint (fānt), 1. a condition in which one lies as if dead and does not know what is going on around him. 2. fall into a faint. 3. **Feel faint** means feel ready to faint. 4. weak; dim; not plain; as, a faint voice, faint colors, a faint idea.

fair[1] (fãr), 1. just; honest; as, fair play. 2. average; not bad. There is a fair crop of wheat this year. 3. light; not dark. She had fair hair and skin. 4. clear; sunny; not stormy. The weather will be fair today. 5. beautiful. The fairest of the maidens smiled at him. 6. gentle; civil; courteous; as, fair words. 7. clean. Make a fair copy and throw that dirty one away. 8. plain; easily read; as, fair handwriting. 9. in a fair manner; honestly; as, fair-spoken, to play fair. 10. **Fair game** sometimes means game that it is right to hunt. 11. **Bid fair** means seem likely.

fair[2] (fãr), 1. a showing of products and manufactured goods for the purpose of helping people see what has been done and urging them to buy better seeds, stock, and machinery. 2. a gathering of people for the buying and selling of goods, often held at regular times during the year. 3. an entertainment and sale of articles. The church held a fair to raise money for charity.

fair ly (fãr′li), 1. in a fair manner; justly. 2. not extremely; to a moderate degree; rather. A fairly good pupil is neither bad nor very good.

fair ness (fãr′nis), being fair; justice.

fair y (fãr′i), 1. a tiny being, very lovely and delicate, who could help or harm human beings. Don't you wish you had fairies to help you? 2. of fairies. 3. like a fairy; lovely; delicate.

Fairy

fair y land (fãr′i land′), 1. the place where the fairies live. 2. an enchanting and pleasant place.

faith (fāth), 1. trust; believing without proof. 2. believing in God or in God's promises. 3. what a person believes. 4. religion. 5. being loyal. 6. **Keep faith** means keep one's promise. 7. **In good faith** means honestly; sincerely.

faith ful (fāth′fəl), 1. loyal; worthy of trust; as, a faithful friend, a faithful servant. 2. true to fact; accurate; as, a faithful account of what happened.

faith less (fāth′lis), not true to duty or to one's promises. A traitor is faithless.

fal con (fô′kən), 1. a hawk trained to hunt and kill birds and small game. In the Middle Ages, hunting with falcons was a popular sport. 2. swift-flying hawk having a short, curved bill and long claws and wings.

Falcon (17 in. long)

fall (fôl), 1. drop or come down from a higher place. Snow is falling fast. His hat fell off. Leaves fall from the trees. 2. dropping from a higher place. The fall from his horse hurt him. 3. amount that comes down; as, the fall of rain for a year. 4. distance anything drops or comes down. The fall of the river here is two feet. 5. come down suddenly from a standing position. A baby often falls when learning how to walk. 6. coming down suddenly from a standing position. 7. become bad or worse. He was tempted and fell. 8. becoming bad or worse; ruin; destruction; as, Adam's fall. 9. be taken by any evil. The city has fallen into the power of its enemies. Rome fell. 10. come by lot or chance. The choice falls on you. 11. become lower or less. Prices are falling. The water in the river has fallen two feet. 12. becoming lower or less; as, a fall in prices, the fall of the tide. 13. be divided. His story falls into five parts. 14. to slope. The land falls away here. 15. a slope. 16. season of the year between summer and winter; autumn. 17. way of throwing or being thrown; as, falls in wrestling. 18. Some special meanings are:

fall back, retreat; go toward the rear.

fall back on, 1. go back to for safety. 2. turn to for help or support.

fall in, 1. take a place in line. "Fall in!" said the officer to the soldiers. 2. meet. On our trip we fell in with some interesting people. 3. agree. They fell in with our plans.

fall on, attack.

fall out, 1. leave a place in line. "Fall out!" said the officer to the soldiers. 2. quarrel; stop being friends.

fall upon, attack.

fal la cious (fə lā′shəs), 1. deceptive; misleading. 2. not logical. Faulty reasoning causes fallacious conclusions.

fal la cy (fal′ə si), 1. misleading argument; flaw in reasoning. 2. anything deceptive or false; delusion; error. It is a fallacy to suppose that riches always bring happiness.

fall en (fôl′ən), 1. dropped. 2. face down; down on the ground; down flat. 3. overthrown; ruined. 4. dead. 5. See **fall.** Much rain has fallen.

fal low (fal′ō), 1. plowed but not seeded for a season or more; uncultivated. 2. land left fallow for a season or more. 3. plowing of land without seeding it for a season in order to destroy weeds, improve the soil, etc.

false (fôls), 1. not true; not correct; wrong. A false note is wrong in pitch. A false step is a stumble or a mistake. 2. lying; as, a false witness. 3. disloyal; deceitful; as, a false friend, a man false to his promise. 4. used to deceive; as, false weights, false signals. A ship sails under **false colors** when she raises the flag of another country than her own. 5. not real; artificial; as, false teeth, false diamonds. 6. based on wrong notions. False pride kept the poor man from accepting money from his rich brothers. 7. in a false manner.

false hood (fôls′hu̇d), 1. a lie. 2. a being false; falsity.

false ness (fôls′nis), being false; falsity.

fal si ty (fôl′si ti), 1. quality or condition of being false; false nature. Education shows us the falsity of many superstitions. 2. deceit; treachery.

fal ter (fôl′tər), 1. not go straight on; hesitate; waver; lose courage. The soldiers faltered for a moment as their captain fell. 2. become unsteady in movement; stumble; stagger. 3. speak in hesitating and broken words. Greatly embarrassed, he faltered out his thanks.

fame (fām), 1. having a good deal said about one; fact, state, or condition of being well known; as, the fame of George Washington. 2. what is said about one.

famed (fāmd), made famous; celebrated; well known.

fa mil iar (fə mil′yər), 1. known to all. A knife is a familiar tool. 2. well known. French was as familiar to him as English. 3. well acquainted. He is familiar with French. 4. close; personal; intimate. Familiar friends know each other very well. 5. too friendly; forward. His manner is too familiar. 6. a spirit or demon supposed to serve a person.

fa mil i ar i ty (fə mil′i ar′i ti), 1. close acquaintance. 2. behavior suitable only to friends; lack of formality or ceremony. 3. an instance of such behavior. She dislikes such familiarities as the use of her first name by people that she has just met.

fam i ly (fam′i li), 1. father, mother, and their children. Our town has about a thousand families. 2. children; offspring. She brought up a family. 3. group of people living in the same house. 4. all of a person's relatives. 5. tribe; race; group of related people. 6. group of related animals or plants. Lions, tigers, and leopards belong to the cat family. 7. any group of related or similar things.

fam ine (fam′in), 1. lack of food in a place; a time of starving. Many people died during the famine in India. 2. a very great lack of anything; as, a coal famine. 3. starvation.

fam ish (fam′ish), be very hungry; starve.

fa mous (fā′məs), very well known; noted. A great crowd of people greeted the famous hero.

fan[1] (fan), 1. thing with which to stir the air in order to cool a room or one's face, or to blow dust away. 2. thing that is flat and spread out. 3. stir (the air); blow on; stir up. 4. use a fan on. She fanned herself.

Lady's fan

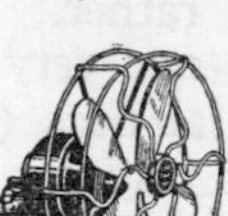
Electric fan

fan[2] (fan), in common talk, a person extremely interested (in baseball, movies, radio, etc.).

fan ci ful (fan′si fəl), 1. showing fancy; quaint; odd; fantastic; as, a fanciful decoration. 2. led by fancy; using fancies. Hans Christian Andersen is a fanciful writer. 3. imaginary; unreal. A story about a trip to the moon is fanciful.

fan cy (fan′si). All the meanings of fancy have something to do with the imagination or play of the mind. 1. picture to oneself; imagine. Can you fancy yourself in fairyland? 2. power to imagine. Dragons, fairies, and giants are creatures of fancy. 3. something imagined. Is it a fancy, or do I hear a sound? 4. like. Nell fancies the idea of having a picnic. 5. liking. He has a fancy for bright ties. 6. arranged especially to please; as, fancy dress, fancy dancing, fancywork. 7. costing extra to please the mind; as, fancy fruits, a fancy price. **fancied, fancying, fancies, fancier,** and **fanciest** are formed from **fancy.**

fane (fān), temple; church.

fang (fang), 1. a long, pointed tooth of a dog or wolf or snake. 2. something like it. The root of a tooth is called a fang.

Fangs of a snake

fan tas tic (fan tas′tik), odd; due to fancy; unreal; strange and wild in shape or manner. Many dreams are fantastic.

fan tas ti cal (fan tas′ti kəl), fantastic.

fan ta sy (fan′tə si), 1. imagination; play of the mind. 2. a picture in the mind. 3. a wild, strange fancy.

far (fär), 1. a long way; a long way off. The moon is far from the earth. 2. more distant. He lives on the far side of the hill. 3. much. It is far better to go by train. 4. Some special meanings are:

far and away, very much.

so far, to this point; to that point.

farther and **farthest** are formed from **far.**

far a way (fär′ə wā′), 1. distant; far away. 2. dreamy. She had a faraway look in her eyes.

farce (färs), 1. a play full of ridiculous or absurd happenings, meant to be very funny. 2. a ridiculous pretense that everybody can see through.

fare (fãr), 1. the money that one pays to ride in a train, car, bus, etc. 2. passenger. 3. food. 4. be fed. We fared very well at Grandmother's. 5. do; get on. He is faring well in school. 6. go; as, to fare forth on a journey.

fare well (fãr′wel′), 1. good luck; good-by. 2. good wishes at parting. 3. parting; as, a farewell kiss.

farm (färm), 1. the land which a person uses to raise crops or animals. 2. raise crops or animals either to eat or to sell. Mary's father farms for a living. 3. cultivate (land). He farms forty acres. 4. let for hire. Mr. Bond farms out the right to pick berries on his land.

farm er (fär′mər), man who owns or works a farm.

farm house (färm′hous′), the dwelling house on a farm.

farm ing (fär′ming), business of raising crops or animals on a farm; agriculture.

farm yard (färm′yärd′), the yard connected with the farm buildings or enclosed by them.

far-off (fär′ôf′), distant; far away.

far-reach ing (fär′rēch′ing), having a wide influence or effect.

far ri er (far′i ər), 1. blacksmith who shoes horses. 2. veterinary; horse doctor.

far-see ing (fär′sē′ing), 1. able to see far. 2. planning wisely for the future.

far ther (fär′ᴛʜər), 1. more far. Three miles is farther than two. We walked farther than we meant to. 2. more; to a greater degree. Do you need farther help? 3. also; in addition.

far thest (fär′ᴛʜist), 1. most distant. 2. to or at the greatest distance. 3. most. 4. longest.

far thing (fär′ᴛʜing), an English coin, a fourth of a penny, worth about half a cent in United States money.

fas ci nate (fas′i nāt), 1. charm. Alice is a fascinating girl. 2. hold motionless by strange power or by terror. Snakes are said to fascinate small birds.

fas ci na tion (fas′i nā′shən), 1. a fascinating. 2. powerful attraction; charm.

fash ion (fash′ən), 1. to make, shape, or form. He fashioned a whistle out of a piece of wood. 2. the way a thing is shaped or made or done. He walks in a peculiar fashion. 3. style. She likes to read about the latest fashions.

fash ion a ble (fash′ən ə bəl), following the fashion; in fashion; stylish.

fast[1] (fast), 1. Airplanes go fast. A fast runner can beat a slow one. The car made a fast trip. 2. When a watch is fast, it shows time ahead of what it really is. 3. Fast sometimes means too gay or wild. He led a fast life, drinking and gambling. 4. firmly fixed. This color is fast and will not wash out. He held fast as the car went on down the hill. The fox was caught fast in the trap. 5. firm. They were fast friends. 6. thoroughly. The baby is fast asleep.

fast[2] (fast), 1. go without food; eat very little. Members of some churches fast on certain days. 2. fasting. 3. a day or time of fasting.

fas ten (fas′ən), tie, lock, or make hold together in any way; as, to fasten a dress, to fasten a door, to fasten two cars together, to fasten one's eyes on something.

fas ten ing (fas′ən ing), thing used to fasten something. Locks, bolts, clasps, hooks, buttons, etc., are all fastenings.

fas tid i ous (fas tid′i əs), hard to please; dainty in taste; easily disgusted.

fast ness (fast′nis), 1. strong, safe place; stronghold. The bandits hid in their mountain fastness. 2. firmness.

fat (fat), 1. a white or yellow oily substance formed in the body of animals. 2. having much of this; as, fat meat. 3. having much flesh; well fed; as, a fat pig. Fred is fatter than Joe; Bill is the fattest of all. 4. Live on **the fat of the land** means have the best of everything. 5. plentiful; full of good things. A fat job pays well. 6. make or become fat.

fa tal (fā′təl), 1. causing death; as, fatal accidents. 2. causing destruction or ruin. The loss of all our money was fatal to our plans. 3. important; fateful. At last the fatal day for the contest arrived.

fate (fāt), 1. a power that is believed to fix what is to happen. He does not believe in fate. 2. what is fixed to happen. 3. one's lot or fortune. In every game it was Mary's fate to get caught.

fat ed (fāt′id), controlled by fate.

fate ful (fāt′fəl), 1. controlled by fate. 2. determining what is to happen; important; decisive. 3. causing death, destruction, or ruin; disastrous.

fa ther (fä′ᴛʜər), 1. male parent. The father of a family tries to take good care of his children. 2. take care of as a father does. 3. man who does important work as a maker or leader. George Washington is called the father of his country. 4. be the cause of; originate. Edison fathered many inventions. 5. priest. 6. God is called **Our Father.**

fa ther-in-law (fä′ᴛʜər in lô′), father of one's husband or wife.

fa ther land (fä′ᴛʜər land′), one's native country.

fa ther ly (fä′ᴛʜər li), 1. of a father. 2. like a father; like a father's. The old gentleman gave the little boy a fatherly smile.

fath om (faᴛʜ′əm), 1. a measure of 6 feet, used mostly in speaking of the depth of water. The ship sank in 10 fathoms. 2. find the depth of. 3. get to the bottom of; understand.

fath om less (faᴛʜ′əm lis), 1. too deep to be measured. 2. that cannot be comprehended; as, the fathomless purposes of God.

fa tigue (fə tēg′), 1. make weary or tired. 2. weariness.

fat ness (fat′nis), amount of fat; state of being fat.

fat ten (fat′ən), 1. make fat. 2. become fat.

fat ty (fat′i), 1. of fat; containing fat. 2. like fat; oily; greasy.

fau cet (fô′sit), a device for controlling the flow of water or other liquid from a pipe or container holding it. See the picture.

Faucet

fault (fôlt), 1. something that is not as it should be. Her dog has two faults; it eats too much, and it howls at night. 2. mistake. **Find fault** means find mistakes; complain. **Find fault with** means object to or criticize.

fault less (fôlt′lis), without a single fault or defect; perfect.

fault y (fôl′ti), having faults; imperfect; defective.

faun (fôn), a Roman god that helped farmers and shepherds. A faun looked like a man, but had the ears, horns, tail, and sometimes the legs of a goat.

Faun

fa vor (fā′vər), 1. kindness. Do me a favor. 2. show kindness to; oblige. Favor us with a song. 3. liking. The king looked on Joseph with favor. 4. prefer. We favor John's plan. 5. give more than is fair to. The teacher favors you. 6. aid; help. **In his favor** means for him; to his benefit. 7. a gift to show fondness. The knight wore his lady's favor on his sleeve. 8. look like. She favors her mother. 9. **In favor of** means (1) on the side of. (2) to the advantage of.

fa vor a ble (fā′vər ə bəl), 1. favoring; approving; as, a favorable answer. 2. being to one's advantage; helping; as, a favorable wind.

fa vor a bly (fā′vər ə bli), with consent or approval; hopefully; kindly.

fa vor ite (fā′vər it), 1. the one liked very much. Bob is a favorite with everybody. 2. liked best. What is your favorite flower?

fawn[1] (fôn), 1. deer less than a year old. 2. light yellowish brown.

Fawn

fawn[2] (fôn), crouch and lick as a dog does; try to get favor or notice by slavish acts. Many flattering relatives fawned on the rich old man.

fe al ty (fē′əl ti), 1. loyalty and duty owed by a vassal to his feudal lord. The nobles swore fealty to the king. 2. loyalty; faithfulness; allegiance.

fear (fēr), 1. a feeling which makes you turn away or run from something, or cover your eyes, or scream, or jump away. 2. have fear. 3. be afraid of. Cats fear big dogs. Monkeys fear big snakes. Babies fear loud noises. 4. have an uneasy feeling or idea. He fears that the children will be sick. I fear that I am late.

fear ful (fēr′fəl), 1. causing fear; terrible; dreadful. 2. feeling fear; frightened. 3. showing fear. 4. easily frightened; timid.

fear less (fēr′lis), afraid of nothing; brave.

fea si ble (fē′zi bəl), that can be done; possible without difficulty or damage. The committee selected the plan that seemed most feasible.

feast (fēst), 1. a rich meal prepared for some special occasion, usually a joyous one. 2. eat many good things. 3. provide a rich meal for. The king feasted his friends. 4. take delight in; delight. We feasted our eyes on the beautiful picture. 5. celebration. Christmas and Easter are the most important Christian feasts.

feat (fēt), great deed; act requiring great skill, strength, or daring.

feath er (feᴛʜ′ər), 1. Birds are covered with feathers which grow out from the skin. Feathers are very light, so that we say "as light as a feather." 2. supply or cover with feathers. 3. **A feather in one's cap** means something to be proud of.

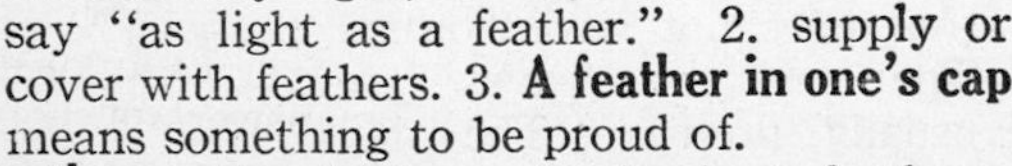

Feathers

feath er y (feᴛʜ′ər i), 1. having feathers; covered with feathers. 2. like feathers; as, feathery snow.

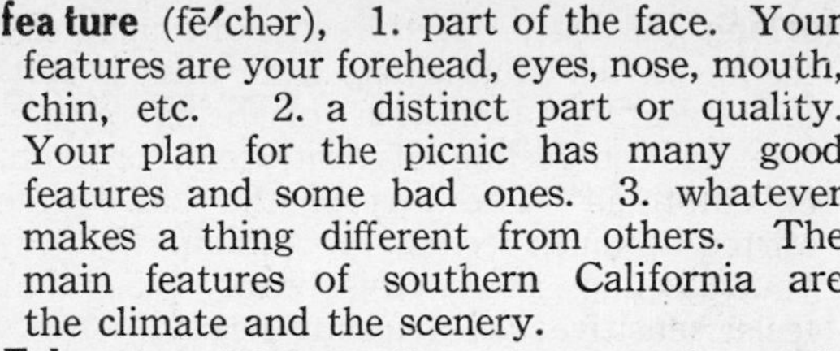

fea ture (fē′chər), 1. part of the face. Your features are your forehead, eyes, nose, mouth, chin, etc. 2. a distinct part or quality. Your plan for the picnic has many good features and some bad ones. 3. whatever makes a thing different from others. The main features of southern California are the climate and the scenery.

Feb ru ar y (feb′rü ãr′i), the second month of the year. It has 28 days except in leap years, when it has 29.

fed (fed). See **feed.** We fed the birds yesterday. Have they been fed today?

fed er al (fed′ər əl), 1. of the central government of the United States, not of any State or city alone. Coining money is a federal power. 2. formed by an agreement of states. The League of Nations is a federal union.

fee (fē), 1. a charge; money paid for some service or privilege. The doctor's fee for a visit will be $3. 2. ownership.

fee ble (fē′bəl), weak; as, a feeble old man, a feeble mind, a feeble cry, a feeble attempt.

fee ble ness (fē′bəl nis), weakness.

feed (fēd). We feed a baby who cannot feed himself. We put cows to feed in the meadow. We fed corn to the chickens. Have you fed the fire? Corn is used as chicken feed. **fed** is formed from **feed.**

feel (fēl), 1. touch. Feel the cloth. 2. try to touch; try to find by touching. He felt in his pocket for a match. 3. find out by touching. Feel how cold my hands are. 4. be aware of. He felt the cool breeze. She felt the heat. 5. be. She feels glad. He feels angry. 6. have the feeling of being. We felt hot. She felt sure. 7. give the feeling of being. The air feels cold. Your dress feels wet. 8. have in one's mind; experience. They feel pity. I felt pain. He felt fear of the thunder. 9. have a feeling. I felt for the poor, lonesome dog. Try to feel more kindly toward her. I feel that Jack will come. 10. feeling. Wet soap has a greasy feel. **felt** is formed from **feel.**

FEELERS

LEGS

feel er (fēl′ər), 1. something that feels. A cat's whiskers are its feelers. The long feelers on the heads of insects help them find their way. 2. a suggestion, remark, hint, or question meant to bring out the plans, opinions, or purposes of others.

feel ing (fē′ing), 1. the sense of touch. By feeling we tell what is hard from what is soft. 2. sensation; condition of being aware. She had no feeling of heat, cold, or pain. 3. emotion. The loss of the ball game stirred up much feeling. 4. opinion. What is your feeling about this idea? 5. that feels; sensitive; as, a feeling heart.

feet (fēt). A dog has four feet. See **foot.**

feign (fān), 1. pretend. Some animals feign death when in danger. 2. make up to deceive; as, to feign an excuse.

feint (fānt), 1. pretense. Jack made a feint of being absorbed in his lessons, but he was listening to the radio. 2. a movement made with the purpose of deceiving; a sham attack or blow. The fighter made a feint at his opponent with his right hand and struck with his left. 3. make a feint.

fe lic i ty (fi lis′i ti), 1. happiness; bliss. 2. good fortune; blessing. 3. pleasing ability in expression.

fell[1] (fel). See **fall.** Snow fell last night.

fell[2] (fel), 1. cause to fall; knock down. One blow felled him to the ground. 2. cut down (a tree). The lumberman will fell these great trees. 3. turn down and stitch one edge of (a seam) over the other.

fell[3] (fel), heavy; terrible; cruel; as, a fell blow, a fell disease, the murderer's fell plans.

fell[4] (fel), the skin or hide of an animal.

fel low (fel′ō), 1. one; a man, boy, dog, etc. Never mind, old fellow. Poor fellow! 2. I or me. Have pity on a fellow. 3. companion; one of the same class; equal. He was cut off from his fellows. 4. the other one of a pair; a match. I have the fellow of your glove. 5. being in the same or a like condition; as, fellow citizens, fellow sufferers, fellow workers.

fel low ship (fel′ō ship), 1. companionship; friendliness. 2. being one of a group; membership; sharing. I have enjoyed my fellowship with you in this club. 3. a group of companions.

fel on[1] (fel′ən), criminal. Murderers and thieves are felons.

fel on[2] (fel′ən), very painful inflammation of a finger or toe near the nail.

felt[1] (felt). See **feel.** He felt the cat's soft fur. Things are felt with the hands.

felt[2] (felt), 1. cloth not woven, but made by rolling and pressing wool, hair, or fur together. 2. made of felt; as, a felt hat.

fe male (fē′māl), 1. woman or girl. 2. of women or girls. Sewing is usually a female occupation. 3. belonging to the sex that brings forth young. Mares and cows are female animals. 4. animal belonging to this sex.

fem i nine (fem′i nin), 1. of women or girls. Jewelry and lace are mostly feminine belongings. 2. like a woman; womanly; weak; gentle.

fen (fen), marsh; swamp; marshland.

fence (fens), 1. something put around a yard, garden, field, farm, etc., to show where it ends or to keep out people or animals. Most fences are made of wood, wire, or metal. A stone fence is a wall. A fence of growing bushes is a hedge. 2. put a fence around. 3. **On the fence** sometimes means not having made up one's mind which side to take. 4. fight with long slender swords or foils. 5. person who buys stolen goods.

fenc er (fen′sər), person who knows how to fight with a sword or foil.

Girls fencing

fenc ing (fen′sing), 1. the art of attack and defense with swords or foils. 2. material for fences. 3. fences.

fend er (fen′dər), thing that protects by being between and keeping something off. A bar in front of an automobile and a screen in front of a fireplace are fenders.

fen nel (fen′əl), a tall plant whose seeds are used in medicine and cookery.

fer ment (fər ment′ for 1 and 4, fėr′ment for 2 and 3), 1. undergo or produce a gradual chemical change, becoming sour or alcoholic and giving off bubbles of gas. Vinegar is formed when cider ferments. 2. substance that causes others to ferment. Yeast is a ferment. 3. tumult; excitement. The school was in a ferment. 4. excite; be excited.

fern (fėrn), a kind of plant that does not have flowers. The feathery leaves are usually pretty. The tiny seeds (called spores) grow in the little brown dots on the backs of the leaves.

Fern

fe ro cious (fi rō′shəs), fierce; savage: very cruel.

fe roc i ty (fi ros′i ti), fierceness; savage behavior; great cruelty.

fer ret (fer′it), 1. a kind of weasel used for killing rats, driving rabbits from their holes, etc. 2. to hunt with ferrets. 3. hunt; search. The detectives ferreted out the criminal.

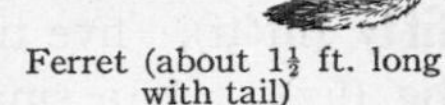
Ferret (about 1⅓ ft. long with tail)

fer ry (fer′i), 1. carry (people and goods) back and forth across a river or narrow stretch of water. 2. the boat that makes the trip. 3. a place where boats carry people and goods across a river or narrow stretch of water. 4. go across in a ferryboat.

fer tile (fėr′til), 1. producing seeds or fruit. 2. able to bear seeds, fruit, or young. Chicks hatch from fertile eggs. 3. producing crops easily; as, fertile soil. 4. producing much of anything.

fer til i ty (fər til′i ti), 1. bearing, or abundant bearing, of seeds, fruits, crops, or young. 2. power to produce. Fertility of the mind means power to produce many ideas.

fer ti li za tion (fėr′ti li zā′shən), 1. fertilizing. 2. being fertilized.

fer ti lize (fėr′ti līz), 1. make fertile. 2. make (a thing) start to grow. 3. make (the soil) richer by adding manure or other fertilizer.

fer ti liz er (fėr′ti līz′ər), manure or any substance spread over the soil to make it richer in plant foods.

fer vent (fėr′vənt), 1. showing warmth of feeling; very earnest. 2. hot; glowing.

fer vid (fėr′vid), burning; ardent; spirited; as, a fervid orator.

fer vor (fėr′vər), great warmth of feeling; enthusiasm; earnestness.

fes tal (fes′təl), of a feast or holiday; gay; festive. A wedding is a festal occasion.

fes ti val (fes′ti vəl), 1. a day or special time of rejoicing or feasting, often in memory of some great happening. Christmas and Easter are two festivals of the Christian church. 2. celebration; entertainment. Every year the city has a music festival during the first week in May. 3. merry-making.

fes tive (fes′tiv), of or suitable for a feast or holiday; gay; merry. Helen's birthday was a festive occasion.

fes tiv i ty (fes tiv′i ti), a rejoicing and feasting; merry party. The wedding festivities were very gay.

fes toon (fes tün′), 1. flowers, leaves, ribbons, etc., hanging in a curve. 2. form into festoons; adorn with festoons. The house was festooned with Christmas decorations.

Festoon

fetch (fech), go and get; bring. Please fetch me my glasses. These eggs will fetch a good price.

fetch ing (fech′ing), charming; attractive. She wore a fetching hat.

fete or **fête** (fāt), 1. festival; party. 2. give parties for; entertain. The bride-to-be was feted by her friends.

fet ter (fet′ər), 1. chain or shackle for the feet. Fetters prevent escape. 2. bind with fetters; chain the feet of. 3. anything that shackles or binds. 4. bind; restrain.

feud (fūd), 1. a long and deadly quarrel between families. 2. bitter hatred between two persons or groups.

fe ver (fē′vər), 1. body temperature that is greater than usual. A sick person may have a fever. 2. any sickness that heats the body and makes the heart beat fast; as, scarlet fever. 3. an excited, restless condition. When gold was discovered the miners were in a fever of excitement.

fe vered (fē′vərd), 1. having fever. 2. excited; restless.

fe ver ish (fē′vər ish), 1. having fever. 2. having some fever but not much. 3. excited; restless. 4. likely to cause fever; infested with fever; as, a feverish swamp.

few (fū), not many. There are few men more than six feet tall. Winter has not many warm days, only a few.

fez (fez), a felt cap, usually red and ornamented with a long black tassel.

Fez

fib (fib), 1. a lie about some small matter. 2. tell such a lie.

fi ber (fī′bər), 1. thread; threadlike part. 2. substance made up of threads or threadlike parts. Hemp fiber can be spun into rope or woven into a coarse cloth. 3. texture; as, cloth of coarse fiber. 4. character; nature. A person of strong moral fiber can resist temptation.

fi bre (fī′bər), fiber.

fi brous (fī′brəs), stringy; made of fibers.

fick le (fik′əl), changing; not constant; likely to change without reason; as, fickle fortune, a fickle lover.

fic tion (fik′shən), something made up; a story that is not fact. Short stories and novels are fiction.

fid dle (fid′əl), 1. violin. 2. play the violin.

fid dler (fid′lər), person who plays the violin.

fi del i ty (fī del′i ti), 1. loyalty; being faithful. 2. accuracy; exactness.

fidg et (fij′it), 1. move about restlessly; be uneasy. A child fidgets if he has to sit still a long time. 2. make uneasy. 3. condition of being restless or uneasy. The long, tiresome speech gave Bob the fidgets.

fie (fī), for shame; shame. Fie upon you!

field (fēld), 1. land with few or no trees. They rode through forest and field. 2. piece of land used for crops or for pasture. 3. piece of land used for some special purpose; as, a baseball field. 4. a battlefield. 5. land yielding some product; as, the coal fields of Pennsylvania, the gold fields of South Africa. 6. flat space. A field of ice surrounds the North Pole. 7. region. 8. range or sphere of activity; as, the field of politics, the field of art, the field of science. 9. in baseball, to stop (a batted ball) and throw it in.

field glass, small telescope.

field gun, cannon mounted on a carriage for use in the field.

Field glasses

fiend (fēnd), 1. devil; an evil spirit. 2. very wicked or cruel person.

fiend ish (fēn′dish), devilish; very cruel.

fierce (fērs), savage; raging; wild; violent; as, a fierce lion, fierce anger, a fierce wind.

fierce ly (fērs′li), in a fierce way; wildly.

fierce ness (fērs′nis), wildness and rage; cruelty.

fi er y (fī′ri), 1. containing fire; burning; flaming. 2. like fire; very hot. 3. full of feeling or spirit; as, a fiery speech. 4. easily aroused or excited; as, a fiery temper.

Man playing a fife

fife (fīf), 1. a small, shrill musical instrument like a flute, played by blowing. Fifes are used with drums in warlike music. 2. play on a fife.

fif teen (fif′tēn′), five more than ten; 15.

fif teenth (fif′tēnth′), 1. next after the 14th. 2. one of 15 equal parts.

fifth (fifth), 1. next after the 4th. 2. one of 5 equal parts. Twenty cents is a fifth of a dollar.

fif ti eth (fif′ti ith), 1. next after the 49th. 2. one of 50 equal parts.

fif ty (fif′ti), five times ten; 50.

fig (fig), 1. a small, soft, sweet fruit that grows in warm regions. Figs are sometimes eaten fresh or canned, but usually are dried like dates and raisins. 2. the tree it grows on. 3. a very small amount. I don't care a fig for your opinion.

Figs

fight (fīt). When boys fight, they hit one another. Soldiers fight by shooting with guns. Countries fight with armies and ships. A fight ends when one side gives up. We speak of fighting disease and other bad conditions. We may fight against our own feelings and desires. **Fight shy of** means keep away from. **fought** is formed from **fight.**

fight er (fīt′ər), one that fights.

fig ure (fig′yər), 1. symbol for a number. 1, 2, 3, 4, etc., are figures. 2. use numbers to find out the answer to some problem. 3. price. His figure for that house is very high. 4. Squares, triangles, cubes, and other shapes are called figures. 5. form or shape. I could see the figure of a woman against the window. 6. Figure is used in telling how a person looks. She was a figure of distress. He cut a poor figure. 7. person; character. George Washington is the best-known figure in American history. 8. be conspicuous; appear. 9. a design or pattern. 10. picture; drawing; diagram; illustration. This book has many figures to help explain words. 11. **Figure out** means think out; understand.

Artist painting a design for a figured glass window

fig ured (fig′yərd), 1. decorated with a design or pattern; not plain. 2. formed; shaped. See the picture of the figured window above.

fil a ment (fil′ə mənt), very fine thread; very slender part that is like a thread. The wire that gives off light in a bulb is a filament.

FILAMENT

file[1] (fīl), 1. place for keeping papers in order. See the picture below. 2. set of papers kept in order. 3. put away in order. 4. a row of persons or things one behind another; as, a file of soldiers, or ships sailing in file. 5. march or move in file.

File for papers

file[2] (fīl), 1. steel tool with many small ridges or teeth on it. Its rough surface is used to smooth or wear away hard substances. See the picture just below. 2. smooth or wear away with a file.

fil i al (fil′i əl), due from a son or daughter toward a mother or father; as, filial affection.

fil ings (fīl′ingz), small pieces removed by a file.

File

fill (fil), 1. put into until there is room for nothing more; make full. Fill this bottle with water. Fill this hole with something. 2. become full. The well filled with water. 3. take up all the space in. Children filled the room. 4. that which fills. 5. as much as there is room for. He ate his fill. 6. supply what is needed for. The druggist filled the doctor's prescription. Can John fill the office of class president? 7. stop up or close by putting something in. After a dentist has taken out the decayed part, he fills the tooth.

fill ing (fil′ing), thing put in to fill something; a filling in a tooth.

fil ly (fil′i), female colt; young mare.

film (film), 1. a very thin surface or coating, often of liquid; as, a film of oil over water. 2. cover or become covered with a film. Tears filmed her eyes. 3. a roll or sheet covered with a coating that is changed by light, used to take pictures. 4. a moving picture. We saw a film about animals. 5. make a moving picture of. They filmed the scene three times. 6. photograph or be photographed for moving pictures.

film y (fil′mi), 1. like film; very thin. 2. covered with a film.

fil ter (fil′tər), 1. a device for passing water or other liquids, or air, through felt, paper, sand, or charcoal, in order to remove impurities. 2. the material a filter is made of. 3. pass or flow slowly through a filter. The water filters slowly through the sand. 4. put through a filter. We filter this water for drinking. 5. act as a filter for. The charcoal filters the water. 6. remove by a filter. Filter out all the solid matter and save it.

filth (filth), nasty dirt.

filth y (fil′thi), very dirty; foul.

fin (fin), 1. one of the movable winglike or fanlike parts at the sides and tail of a fish with which it moves the water in swimming and in balancing itself. The large fins of a flying fish unfold like a fan and can carry it a little way through the air. 2. thing shaped or used like a fin.

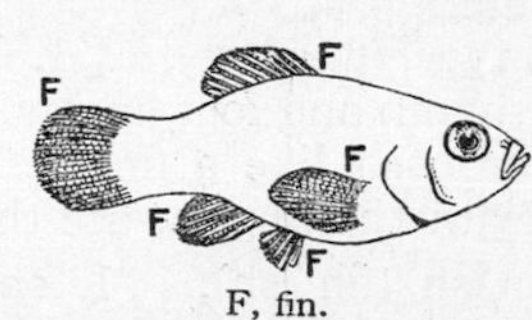

F, fin.

fi nal (fī′nəl), coming last; deciding; closing the question. **Finals** means the last or deciding set in a series of games or examinations.

fi na le (fi nä′li), 1. the concluding part of a piece of music or a play. 2. the end.

fi nal ly (fī′nəl i), 1. at the end; at last. 2. in such a way as to decide or close the question.

fi nance (fi nans′), 1. money matters. The millionaire boasted of his skill in finance. 2. provide money for. His father financed Dick's way through college. 3. **Finances** means money; funds; revenues; financial condition.

fi nan cial (fi nan′shəl), having to do with money matters.

finch (finch), a small songbird. Sparrows, buntings, and canaries are finches.

find (fīnd), 1. meet with; come upon. He found a dollar in the road. They find trouble everywhere. 2. look for and get. Please find my hat for me. 3. reach; arrive at. 4. learn; discover. We found that he could not swim. **Find out** means discover. 5. decide and declare. The jury found the thief guilty. 6. something found. 7. **Find oneself** sometimes means learn one's abilities and how to make good use of them.

fine[1] (fīn), 1. Thread is finer than rope. Sand is finer than gravel. A spider web is fine. 2. excellent. Lee was a fine general. Helen is the finest singer in our class. 3. delicate; refined. 4. clear; as, fine weather.

fine[2] (fīn), 1. a sum of money paid as a punishment for not doing the right thing. 2. make pay such a sum. The judge fined Mr. Vick ten dollars.

fine ly (fīn′li), 1. very well. Our soldiers did finely. 2. in small or thin pieces. 3. with care for details.

fin er y (fīn′ər i), showy clothes, ornaments, etc.

fin ger (fing′gər), 1. Each hand has one thumb and four fingers. 2. anything shaped or used like a finger. 3. touch or handle with the fingers; use the fingers on.

fin ish (fin′ish), 1. end; as, to fight to a finish. 2. complete; bring to an end; reach the end of; as, to finish a dress, to finish one's dinner, to finish a race. 3. the way in which the surface is prepared; as, a smooth finish on furniture. 4. prepare the surface of in some way. 5. perfection; polish; as, the finish of a person's manners. 6. to perfect; to polish.

fiord (fyōrd), a long, narrow bay bordered by steep cliffs.

Fiord

fir (fėr), a tree somewhat like a pine. Small firs are often used for Christmas trees. The leaves have a pleasant smell.

fire (fīr), 1. something burning. 2. a flame. 3. make burn; set on fire. 4. to discharge. He fired his gun four times. 5. the discharge of guns. The enemy's fire sent thousands of bullets against us. 6. arouse; excite; inflame. The soldier fired the children by stories of battles. 7. heat of feeling; readiness to act; excitement. Their hearts and minds were full of fire. 8. Some special meanings are:

Branch of fir with cones

on fire, 1. burning. 2. excited.

under fire, 1. exposed to shooting from the enemy's guns. Soldiers are under fire in a battle. 2. attacked; blamed.

fire arms (fīr′ärmz′), guns, pistols, and other weapons to shoot with, usually such as a man can carry.

fire brand (fīr′brand′), 1. piece of burning wood. 2. person who arouses angry feelings in others.

fire engine, an engine for throwing water to put out fires.

Fire engine

fire fly (fīr′flī′), a small insect flying at night, which shines with a little light.

fire light (fīr′līt′), the light from a fire.

fire man (fīr′mən), 1. man who belongs to a fire company, trained to help put out fires. 2. man who looks after fires in engines, furnaces, etc.

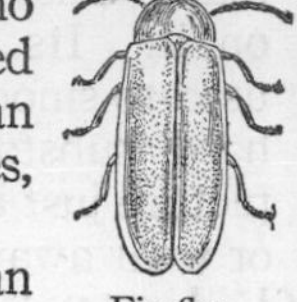
Firefly

fire men (fīr′mən), more than one fireman.

fire place (fīr′plās′), place built to hold a fire. Fireplaces are sometimes made of stones out of doors, but usually of brick or stone in a room, with a chimney leading up from them. Cooking used to be done over the fire in a big fireplace.

Fireplace in a room

fire proof (fīr′prüf′), 1. that will not burn, or will not burn easily; as, a fireproof building. 2. make so that it will not burn, or not burn easily; as, to fireproof a roof, to fireproof a theater curtain.

fire side (fīr′sīd′), 1. space around the fireplace. 2. beside the fire; as, fireside comfort. 3. hearth. 4. home.

fire wood (fīr′wu̇d′), wood to make a fire.

fire works (fīr′wėrks′), rockets, Roman candles, bombs, and other things that make a beautiful fiery display at night.

firm (fėrm), 1. not yielding when pressed; as, firm flesh, firm ground. 2. solid; fixed in place; not easily shaken or moved; as, a tree firm in the earth. We speak also of a firm voice, character, or belief. 3. a company of two or more persons in business together.

fir ma ment (fėr′mə mənt), the sky; the arch of the heavens.

firm ness (fėrm′nis), firm quality or condition. A steel bar has firmness.

first (fėrst), 1. coming before all others.

John is first in his class. 2. what is first; the beginning. At first, John did not like school. 3. before all others; before anything else. We eat first and then feed the cat. 4. rather; sooner. The soldiers said they would never give up their flag, but would die first. 5. for the first time. When first I met her, she was a child.

first-class (fėrst′klas′), 1. of the highest class or best quality; excellent. 2. on a first-class ship, train, etc. We could not afford to travel first-class.

first-hand (fėrst′hand′), direct; from the original source; as, first-hand information.

first-rate (fėrst′rāt′), 1. of the highest class. 2. excellent; very good.

firth (fėrth), narrow arm of the sea.

fish (fish), 1. an animal that lives in the water, is covered with scales, has gills to breathe with, and has a long backbone for support. 2. catch fish; try to catch fish. 3. try for something as if with a hook. Tom fished with a stick for his watch which had fallen through a grating. 4. find and pull. Jim fished the old map out of a box.

fish er (fish′ər), 1. man who fishes; anything that fishes. 2. a kind of marten. See the picture.

Fisher (about 2 ft. long without the tail)

fish er man (fish′ər mən), man who fishes, especially one who makes his living by catching fish.

fish er y (fish′ər i), 1. the occupation of catching fish. 2. place for catching fish.

fish hook (fish′hu̇k′), hook used to catch fish.

fis sure (fish′ər), a split; a crack; long, narrow opening. Water dripped from a fissure in the rock.

fist (fist), the hand closed tightly. He shook his fist at me.

fit[1] (fit), 1. He is now well and fit for work. Grass is a fit food for cows; it is not fit for men. A lace dress is fit for parties. 2. be right, proper, or suitable to. The dress fitted Mary. 3. make right, proper, or suitable. 4. try to make fit; adjust. Father was fitting new springs on our car. 5. to suit; as, to fit the action to the word. 6. the way something fits. The coat was not a very good fit. 7. **Fit out** means supply with everything needed.

fit[2] (fit), 1. a sudden, sharp attack of disease. 2. any sudden, sharp attack; as, a fit of anger. 3. a short period of doing some one thing; as, a fit of laughing.

fit ful (fit′fəl), irregular; going on and then stopping for a while; as, a fitful sleep, a fitful conversation.

fit ness (fit′nis), a being fit; a being right or suitable.

fit ting (fit′ing), proper; suitable; fit.

five (fīv), one more than four; 5.

fix (fiks), 1. make firm; become firm. The man fixed the post in the ground. The boy fixed the spelling lesson in his mind. 2. settle; set; as, to fix a price, to fix an amount to be raised, to fix on a day for a picnic. 3. direct or hold steadily (eyes, attention, etc.); be directed. 4. put or place definitely; as, to fix the blame on someone. 5. make or become stiff or rigid; as, eyes fixed in death. 6. set right; put in order; as, to fix one's hair. 7. mend; repair; as, to fix a watch. 8. position hard to get out of. The boy who cried "Wolf" got himself into a bad fix.

fix ture (fiks′chər), something put in place to stay. A chandelier is a lighting fixture. Mr. Coy is a fixture and will hold his job for many years.

fjord (fyōrd), fiord.

flag[1] (flag), 1. piece of cloth, usually with square corners, on which is the picture or pattern that stands for some country; as, the flag of the United States, the British flag. Flags are hung on poles over buildings, ships, army camps, etc. 2. Other flags mean other things. The white flag of truce means "Stop fighting." Pirate ships carried black flags. Weather flags are flown to let people know what kind of weather is coming. 3. to signal or stop (a person, train, etc.) by waving a flag. The train was flagged at the bridge.

flag[2] (flag), a blue, white, purple, or yellow flower with leaves that have the shape of a sword.

flag[3] (flag), droop; get tired; grow weak. My horse was flagging, but I urged him on.

flag on (flag′ən), 1. a container for liquids, with a handle, spout, and cover. 2. large bottle.

Flagon

flail (flāl), an instrument for threshing grain by hand. A flail consists of a wooden handle with a short, heavy stick fastened at one end by a thong.

flake (flāk), 1. a flat, thin piece, usually not very large, and often rather loosely held together; as, a flake of snow, flakes of rust. 2. come off in flakes; separate into flakes.

flam boy ant (flam boi′ənt), flaming; gorgeous; striking in a showy way.

flame (flām), 1. one of the glowing tongues of light, usually red or yellow, that come when a fire blazes up. 2. blaze; rise up in flames. 3. be or act like a flame. 4. something like flame.

fla min go (flə ming′gō), tropical wading bird with very long legs and neck, and feathers that vary from pink to scarlet.

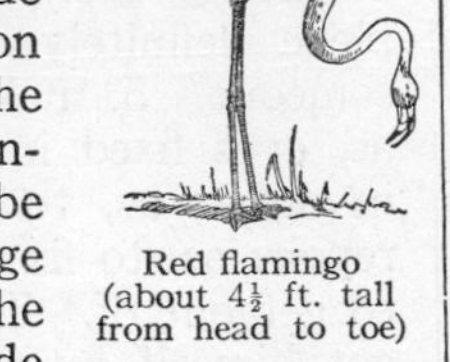
Red flamingo (about 4½ ft. tall from head to toe)

flank (flangk), 1. the side of an animal or a person between the ribs and the hip. 2. the side of a mountain, building, etc. 3. be at the side of. A garage flanked the house. 4. the far right or the far left side of an army, fort, or fleet. 5. get around the side of (an enemy's army). 6. attack from the side.

flan nel (flan′əl), 1. a soft, warm material made of wool. 2. **Flannels** are clothes made of this. 3. made of flannel.

flap (flap), 1. strike noisily with something broad and loose. The sail flapped. 2. a blow from something broad and loose; as, a flap from a whale's tail. 3. move (wings) up and down; fly by flapping the wings. The goose flapped its wings but could not rise from the ground. At last it did rise and flapped heavily away through the air. 4. flapping motion; flapping noise. 5. piece hanging or fastened at one edge only; as, the flap of cloth over the opening to a pocket.

flare (flãr), 1. flame up briefly or unsteadily, sometimes with smoke. A lamp flares when it is turned too high. 2. a blaze; a bright, brief, unsteady flame. The match gave a last flare. 3. burst into sudden action or feeling. 4. spread out in the shape of a bell. This skirt flares at the bottom. 5. spreading out; a bell shape; as, the flare of a skirt. See the picture.

Dress with a flared skirt

flash (flash), 1. a sudden, brief light or flame; as, a flash of lightning. 2. give out such a light or flame. The lighthouse flashes signals twice a minute. 3. come suddenly; pass quickly. A bird flashed across the road. 4. a sudden, short feeling; as, a flash of hope. 5. a very short time. It all happened in a flash. 6. give out or send out like a flash.

flash y (flash′i), 1. flashing; brilliant for a short time. 2. showy; gaudy.

flask (flask), a bottle or can.

Flask

flat[1] (flat), 1. smooth and level; even. A floor is flat. 2. horizontal; at full length; as, lying flat on the ground. 3. the flat part; as, with the flat of the sword. 4. flat land. 5. not very deep or thick; as, a flat dish, flat bone. 6. positive; not to be changed. A flat rate has no extra charges. 7. without much flavor; dull; as, to taste flat. This is the flattest mush I ever ate. 8. below the true pitch; as, to sing flat. 9. a tone one half step below natural pitch; as, music written in B flat. 10. the sign in music (♭) that shows this. 11. flatly. Bill fell flat on the floor. 12. make flat; become flat.

flat[2] (flat), an apartment or set of rooms on one floor.

flat boat (flat′bōt′), a large, flat-bottomed boat used especially for floating goods down a river.

flat fish (flat′fish′), any of a group of fishes having a flat body and swimming on one side. Halibut, flounder, and sole are flatfishes.

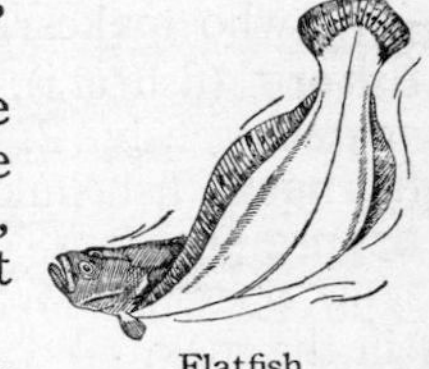
Flatfish

flat ten (flat′ən), make flat; become flat. The silk has been wrinkled, but it will flatten out again if you iron it.

flat ter (flat′ər), 1. praise beyond the truth. 2. show as more beautiful or better looking than is the truth. This picture flatters him. 3. win over or please by praising words, often not true.

flat ter y (flat′ər i), act of flattering; words of praise, usually untrue or exaggerated. Some people use flattery to get favors.

flaunt (flônt), 1. wave proudly; as, banners flaunting in the breeze. 2. show off. She flaunts her riches before her friends.

fla vor (flā′vər), 1. taste; as, the flavor of peppermint. 2. add salt, pepper, or herbs to; to season; give taste to. The onion flavors the whole stew.

fla vor ing (flā′vər ing), something used to

give a particular taste to food or drink; as, chocolate flavoring.

flaw (flô), 1. a crack; slight defect; fault. His nasty temper is the only flaw in his character. 2. to damage; become defective.

flaw less (flô′lis), perfect.

flax (flaks), 1. a slender, upright plant from whose stems linen is made. Flax has small narrow leaves and blue flowers. Linseed oil is made from its seeds. 2. the threadlike parts into which the stems of this plant separate, prepared ready for spinning.

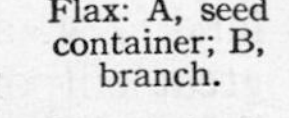

Flax: A, seed container; B, branch.

flax en (flak′sən), 1. made of flax. 2. like flax; pale-yellow; as, flaxen hair.

flay (flā), 1. take the skin off of. 2. scold severely and painfully.

flea (flē), a small, jumping insect without wings. Fleas live in the fur of dogs, cats, and monkeys or under the clothing of human beings, and feed on their blood.

Flea. Line shows actual length.

fleck (flek), 1. spot; mark; speck; spot of color or light. Freckles are brown flecks on the skin. 2. to spot; mark with spots of color or light. The bird's breast is flecked with brown.

fled (fled). See **flee.** The enemy fled when we attacked.

fledg ling or **fledge ling** (flej′ling), 1. a young bird just able to fly. 2. inexperienced person.

flee (flē), 1. run away. The robbers tried to flee, but they were caught. 2. go quickly. The clouds are fleeing before the wind.

fleece (flēs), 1. the wool that covers a sheep. The coat of wool cut off or shorn from one sheep is called a fleece. 2. cut the fleece from. 3. rob; cheat; strip of money or belongings.

fleec y (flēs′i), like a fleece; soft and white. Fleecy clouds floated in the blue sky.

fleet[1] (flēt), 1. ships under one command; ships sailing together; as, the American fleet, a fleet of fishing boats. 2. airplanes, automobiles, or the like, moving or working together. A fleet of trucks carried the soldiers to their camp.

fleet[2] (flēt), fast moving; rapid; as, a fleet horse.

fleet ing (flēt′ing), passing rapidly; soon gone.

flesh (flesh), 1. the softer substance of the body that covers the bones. A fat person has a great deal of flesh. 2. meat. 3. one's family; as, one's own flesh and blood. 4. the soft part of fruits or vegetables; the part of fruits that can be eaten. The flesh of the peach is yellow or white. 5. **In the flesh** means (1) alive. (2) really present, not merely thought of.

flesh y (flesh′i), having much flesh; plump; fat.

flew (flü). See **fly**[2]**.** The bird flew high in the air.

flex (fleks), bend.

flex i ble (flek′si bəl), that can be bent without breaking; not stiff; easily bent in all directions. Leather, rubber, and wire are flexible.

flick (flik), 1. a sudden light blow or stroke. The farmer drove the fly from his horse's head by a flick of his whip. 2. strike lightly with whip or finger. He flicked the dust from his coat sleeve. 3. move with a jerk. The boys flicked wet towels at each other.

flick er[1] (flik′ər), 1. shine with a wavering, unsteady light. The firelight flickered on the walls. 2. a wavering, unsteady flame or light. 3. move lightly and quickly in and out, or back and forth. The tongue of a snake flickers. 4. a flickering movement; as, the flicker of an eyelash.

flick er[2] (flik′ər), a bird common in eastern North America, the golden-winged woodpecker or yellowhammer.

fli er (flī′ər), 1. something that flies, such as a bird or insect. The eagle is a high flier. 2. aviator. 3. very fast train, ship, bus, etc.

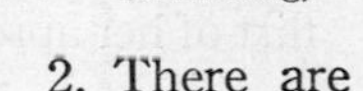

Flicker (about 12 in. long)

flies (flīz), 1. A bird flies. 2. There are many flies on the window.

flight[1] (flīt), 1. act or manner of flying; as, the flight of a bird through the air. 2. distance a bird, bullet, airplane, etc., can fly. 3. group of things flying through the air together; as, a flight of six airplanes. 4. trip in an airplane or airship. 5. a soaring above or beyond the ordinary; as, a flight of fancy. 6. set of stairs or steps from one landing or one story of a building to the next.

flight[2] (flīt), running away; escape. Our soldiers put the enemy to flight. The flight of the prisoners was discovered.

flinch (flinch), 1. draw back from difficulty, danger, or pain; shrink. The baby flinched when he touched the hot radiator. 2. drawing back.

fling (fling), 1. throw; throw with force. 2. rush. 3. a throw. 4. move violently; plunge; kick. 5. a time of doing as one pleases. She had her fling when she was young. 6. a lively Scotch dance. **flung** is formed from **fling.**

flint (flint), 1. a very hard stone, which makes a spark when struck against steel. 2. anything very hard.

flint lock (flint′lok′), 1. gunlock in which a piece of flint striking against steel makes sparks that set fire to the gunpowder. 2. old-fashioned gun with such a lock.

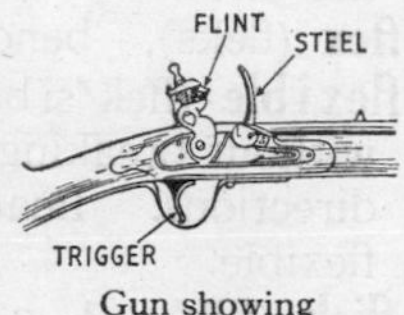

Gun showing flintlock

flint y (flin′ti), 1. made of flint; containing flint. 2. like flint; very, very hard.

flip (flip), 1. move by the snap of a finger and thumb. The man flipped a coin on the counter. 2. move with a jerk or toss. The driver flipped at a fly with his whip. The twig flipped back and scratched his face. 3. a snap; smart tap; sudden jerk. The cat gave the kitten a flip on the ear.

flip pant (flip′ənt), smart or pert in speech; not respectful. She gave him a flippant answer.

flip per (flip′ər), broad, flat limb adapted for swimming. Seals have flippers.

flirt (flėrt), 1. play at making love; make love just for fun. 2. person who makes love without meaning it. 3. move quickly. She flirted her fan. 4. a quick movement; as, a flirt of her apron.

flit (flit), 1. fly lightly and quickly. A hummingbird flitted by. 2. move lightly and quickly. Fairies flitted about on tiptoe.

float (flōt), 1. stay on top of or be held up by air, water, or other liquid. A cork will float, but a stone sinks. 2. anything that stays up or holds up something else in water. A raft is a float. A cork on a fish line is a float. 3. move along without trying; be moved along by the movement of what one is in or on. The boat floated out to sea. 4. a low, flat car that carries something to be shown in a parade.

flock (flok), 1. a group of animals of one kind; as, a flock of sheep, a flock of geese. 2. people of the same church group. 3. go in a flock; keep in groups. Sheep usually flock together. 4. crowd; come crowding. The children flocked around the Christmas tree.

floe (flō), a field or sheet of floating ice.

Floe

flog (flog), beat or whip hard.

flood (flud), 1. fill to overflowing. A wave flooded the holes I had dug in the sand. 2. flow over. The river flooded our fields. 3. a flow of water over what is usually dry land. 4. a large amount of water. 5. a great outpouring of anything; as, a flood of light, a flood of words. 6. fill, cover, or overcome, as if with a flood. The room was flooded with moonlight.

floor (flōr), 1. the part of a room to walk on. The floor of this room is made of hardwood. 2. put a floor in or on. We will floor this room with oak. 3. flat surface at the bottom. They dropped their net to the floor of the ocean. 4. story of a building. Five families live on the fourth floor. 5. knock down. Tom floored Percy with one blow.

flop (flop), 1. move loosely or heavily; flap around clumsily. The fish flopped helplessly on the deck. 2. fall, drop, throw, or move heavily or clumsily. He flopped down into a chair. 3. a flopping. 4. sound made by flopping. 5. change or turn suddenly.

flo ral (flō′rəl), of flowers; as, floral decorations.

flor in (flor′in), a gold or silver coin in use at various times in different countries of Europe.

flo rist (flō′rist), person who raises or sells flowers.

floss (flôs), 1. silky fiber like that in milkweed pods. 2. shiny, silk thread that has not been twisted. Floss is used for embroidery. Waxed floss is used for cleaning between the teeth.

floun der[1] (floun′dər), 1. plunge about; struggle without making much progress. Men and horses were floundering in the deep snow beside the road. 2. be clumsy and make mistakes. The girl was frightened by the audience and floundered through her song.

floun der[2] (floun′dər), a flatfish that has a large mouth.

flour (flour), 1. the fine meal made by grinding grain, especially wheat. 2. cover with flour.

flour ish (flėr′ish), 1. grow in vigor; thrive; be prosperous. Your radishes are flourishing. His newspaper business grew and flourished. 2. wave in the air. John flourished the letter when he saw us. 3. waving about. The donkey gave a flourish of his heels. 4. a display or show. The agent showed us about the house with much flourish. 5. a showy trill or passage in music. 6. an extra ornament or curve in handwriting.

Flourishes in handwriting

flout (flout), 1. mock; scoff at; treat with disdain or contempt. The foolish boy flouted his mother's advice. 2. a mockery; sneer; insult.

flow (flō), 1. run like water. A stream flows past the house. 2. current; stream. There is a constant flow of water from the spring. 3. glide; move easily; as, a flowing movement in a dance, flowing verse. 4. hang loosely; as, flowing robes, a flowing tie. 5. any smooth, steady movement; as, a flow of words. 6. pouring out; as, a flow of blood. 7. the rise of the tide. 8. rate of flowing.

flow er (flou′ər), 1. blossom. The flower is the part of a plant or tree which produces the seed. Flowers are often beautifully colored or shaped. 2. a plant grown for its blossoms. 3. produce flowers; bloom; cover with flowers. 4. the finest part of a thing. The flower of the land would be killed by a war. 5. the time when a thing is at its best. 6. be at its best.

flow er y (flou′ər i), 1. having many flowers. 2. full of fine words and fanciful expressions.

flown (flōn). See **fly**[2]. The bird has flown. The flag is flown on national holidays.

flue (flü), a passage for smoke or hot air, such as there is in a chimney.

fluff (fluf), soft, light, downy particles, such as come from cotton or from new blankets.

fluff y (fluf′i), 1. soft and light like fluff. Whipped cream is fluffy. 2. covered with fluff; as, fluffy baby chicks.

flu id (flü′id), 1. any liquid or gas; something that will flow. Water, mercury, air, and oxygen are fluids. 2. like a liquid. She poured the fluid mass of hot candy into a dish to harden.

flung (flung). See **fling.** The boy flung the ball. The paper was flung away.

flur ry (flėr′i), 1. sudden gust of wind. 2. light fall of rain or snow. 3. sudden commotion. 4. excite; agitate. Noise in the audience flurried the actor so that he forgot his lines.

flush (flush), 1. blush. The girl flushed when they laughed at her. 2. cause to blush. 3. a rosy glow or blush. The flush of sunrise was on the clouds. 4. rush suddenly. 5. a sudden rush; rapid flow. 6. send a sudden rush of water over or through. 7. start up suddenly; cause to start up suddenly. Our dog flushed a partridge in the woods. 8. even; level. Make that shelf just flush with this one. Their edges should be flush. 9. full; full to overflowing. 10. having plenty of money.

flute (flüt), 1. a long, slender, pipelike musical instrument. A flute is played by blowing across a hole on the side near one end. Different notes are made by covering the different holes along the side with the fingers or with keys. 2. play on a flute. 3. sing or whistle so as to sound like a flute.

Man playing a flute

flut ter (flut′ər), 1. wave back and forth quickly and lightly. A flag flutters in the breeze. 2. flap the wings; flap. The young birds fluttered to the ground. 3. come or go with a trembling or wavy motion. 4. move restlessly. 5. tremble. 6. a fluttering. 7. excitement.

fly[1] (flī), 1. an insect with two wings. There are many different kinds of flies. 2. a fishhook with silk, tinsel, etc., on it to suggest a fly.

House fly. Line shows actual length.

fly[2] (flī), 1. move through the air with wings. Birds fly long distances. 2. travel through the air in an airplane or airship. 3. float or wave in the air. Our flag flies every day. 4. cause to fly. The boys are flying kites. 5. move rapidly. The ship flies before the wind. 6. run away. 7. a batted ball going high in the air. **flew** and **flown** are formed from **fly.**

fly er (flī′ər), flier.

fly ing (flī′ing), 1. that flies; moving through the air. 2. floating or waving in the air. 3. swift. 4. short and quick; hasty.

flying fish, tropical sea fish that has fins like wings and can leap through the air. See the picture.

Flying fish of the Atlantic coast (about 8 in. long)

foal (fōl), 1. young horse or donkey. 2. give birth to (a foal).

foam (fōm), 1. a mass of very small bubbles. 2. form foam. 3. break into foam. The stream foams over the rocks.

fo ci (fō′sī), focuses.

fo cus (fō′kəs), 1. a point at which rays of light, heat, etc., meet after being reflected from a mirror or bent by a lens. 2. bring (rays of light, etc.) to a focus. The lens focused the sun's rays on a piece of paper and burned a hole in it. 3. adjust (a lens, the eye, etc.) so that it brings rays of light to the right focus. 4. bring into focus. 5. a central point of attraction, attention, activity, etc. The new baby was the focus of attention.

Rays of light brought to a focus at F by the lens, L.

fod der (fod′ər), coarse food for horses, cattle, etc. Hay and cornstalks with their leaves are fodder.

foe (fō), enemy.

fog (fog), 1. thick mist. 2. to cover with fog. 3. make misty or cloudy. Something fogged six of our photographs.

fog gy (fog′i), having much fog; misty; not clear.

fog horn (fog′hôrn′), horn that warns ships in foggy weather.

foi ble (foi′bəl), weak point.

foil[1] (foil), outwit; prevent from carrying out (plans). The hero foiled the villain.

foil[2] (foil), 1. metal beaten, hammered, or rolled into a very thin sheet. Candy is sometimes wrapped in tin foil to keep it fresh. 2. something which, when placed near a thing, makes it look better by contrast. The green pillow was a foil for Mary's red hair.

foil[3] (foil), long, narrow sword with a knob or button on the point to prevent injury, used in practice.

Foil

fold[1] (fōld), 1. bend or double over on itself. You fold a letter or your napkin. 2. bend till close to the body. You fold your arms. A bird folds its wings. 3. put the arms around and hold tenderly. A mother folds her child to her breast. 4. wrap. He folded the pills in a blue paper. 5. a layer of something folded.

fold[2] (fōld), 1. pen for sheep. 2. a church.

fo li age (fō′li ij), the leaves of a plant.

folk (fōk), 1. people. 2. tribe; nation. 3. **Folks** often means (1) people. (2) relatives. How are all your folks?

fol low (fol′ō), 1. go or come after. Sheep follow a leader. Night follows day. He leads; we follow. 2. result from; result. Misery follows war. If you eat too much candy, a stomach ache will follow. 3. go along (a road, etc.). Follow this road to the corner. 4. use; obey; act according to; take as a guide. Follow her advice. 5. keep the eyes on. I could not follow that bird's flight. 6. keep the mind on. Try to follow the President's speech. 7. be engaged in; be concerned with. Harry expects to follow the profession of lawyer. 8. **Follow up** means pursue closely; act upon with energy.

fol low er (fol′ō ər), 1. person or thing that follows. 2. person who follows the ideas or beliefs of another. 3. member of the household of a king or nobleman.

fol low ing (fol′ō ing), 1. group of followers. 2. that follows; next after. If that was Sunday, then the following day must have been Monday.

fol ly (fol′i), 1. being foolish; lack of sense; unwise conduct. It is folly to eat too much. 2. foolish act, practice, or idea; something silly. "You are too old for such follies," said mother.

fond (fond), 1. loving; liking; as, a fond look. 2. loving unwisely or too much.

fon dle (fon′dəl), pet; caress.

fond ness (fond′nis), affection; liking.

font (font), 1. basin holding water for baptism. 2. basin for holy water. 3. fountain; source.

food (füd). Plants, animals, and people eat or drink food to make them live and grow.

fool (fül), 1. person without sense; person who acts unwisely. 2. a clown formerly kept in a nobleman's house to amuse people. 3. act like a fool for fun; play; joke. 4. make a fool of; deceive; trick.

fool ish (fül′ish), without sense; unwise; like a fool.

fool ish ness (fül′ish nis), foolish behavior; lack of sense.

fool proof (fül′prüf′), so safe that even a fool can use it.

foot (fůt), 1. the part that a person or animal stands on. 2. the lowest part; the base; as, the foot of a column, the foot of a hill, the foot of a page. 3. walk. The boys footed the whole ten miles. 4. pay. Father foots the bill. 5. 12 inches. 6. one of the parts into which a line of poetry is divided. This line has four feet:
"The boy | stood on | the burn | ing deck." |

foot ball (fůt′bôl′), 1. a leather ball used in games where the ball is kicked. 2. a game played with a football which is to be kicked or carried past the goal line at the end of the field.

foot fall (fůt′fôl′), sound of steps coming or going; footstep.

foot hill (fůt′hil′), low hill at the base of a mountain or mountain range.

foot hold (fůt′hōld′), place to put a foot; support for the feet; footing. The man climbed the steep cliff by getting footholds in cracks.

foot ing (fůt′ing), 1. a firm placing or position of the feet. Jim lost his footing and fell down on the ice. 2. a place or support for the feet. The steep cliff gave us no footing. 3. a secure position. 4. condition; position; relationship. We are on a friendly footing with the Smiths.

foot man (fůt′mən), 1. a man servant dressed in a special suit, who answers the bell, waits on table, goes with the carriage or car to open the door, etc. 2. soldier who fights on foot.

foot men (fůt′mən), more than one footman.

foot path (fůt′path′), path for people on foot only.

foot print (fůt′print′), the mark made by a foot.

foot sore (fůt′sōr′), having sore feet from much walking.

foot step (fůt′step′), 1. a person's step. 2. distance covered in one step. 3. the sound of steps coming or going. 4. the mark made by a foot. **Follow in his footsteps** means do as he did.

foot stool (fůt′stül′), low stool on which to place the feet when seated.

Footstool

foot wear (fůt′wãr′), shoes, slippers, stockings, gaiters, etc.

fop (fop), man very fond of clothes.

for (fôr), 1. in place of. He gave me a new book for the old one. 2. in support of. He stands for honest government. 3. in honor of. A party was given for him. 4. in return; in consideration of. These apples are twelve for a dollar. We thanked him for his kindness. 5. with the object or purpose of; as, to go for a walk, to act for advantage, a suit for damages, to seek for happiness. 6. used with; suited to; as, a box for gloves, books for children. 7. with a feeling toward; as, an eye for beauty, to long for home, love for friends. 8. with regard or respect to; as, warm for April, bad for one's health. 9. because of; by reason of; as, to shout for joy, to punish for stealing. 10. as far as. We walked for a mile. 11. as long as. We worked for an hour. 12. as being. They know it for a fact. 13. because. His story of the fight is true, for I saw it myself.

for age (for′ij), 1. hay, grain, or other food for horses, cattle, etc. 2. hunt or search for food. Rabbits forage in our garden. 3. get by hunting or searching about. 4. hunt; search about. The boys foraged for old metal.

for ay (for′ā), 1. raid for plunder. Armed bandits made forays on the villages and took away food and cattle. 2. plunder; lay waste; pillage.

for bade or **for bad** (fôr bad′). See **forbid.** The doctor forbade the sick boy to leave his bed.

for bear (fôr bãr′), 1. hold back; keep from doing, saying, using, etc. Henry forbore to hit back because the other boy was smaller. 2. be patient; control oneself. **forbore** and **forborne** are formed from **forbear.**

for bear ance (fôr bãr′əns), patience; control; not acting against someone when you have a right to do so.

for bid (fôr bid′), not allow; say one must not do; make a rule against. The teacher could forbid us to leave our seats. If my father had known that I was going, he would have forbidden it. **forbade** and **forbidden** are formed from **forbid.**

for bid den (fôr bid′ən), 1. not allowed; against the law or the rules. Eve ate the forbidden fruit. 2. See **forbid.**

for bid ding (fôr bid′ing), causing fear or dislike; looking dangerous or unpleasant. The coast was rocky and forbidding.

for bore (fôr bōr′). See **forbear.** He forbore from showing his anger.

for borne (fôr bōrn′). See **forbear.** We have forborne from vengeance.

force (fōrs), 1. power; strength. 2. strength used against a person or thing; violence. 3. make (a person) act against his will; make do by force. Give it to me at once, or I will force you to. 4. take by force. 5. break through; as, to force a door. 6. press or urge to violent effort. 7. hurry the growth of (flowers, fruits, or a child's mind). 8. group of people who work together; as, an office force. **Forces** sometimes means the army or navy.

force ful (fōrs′fəl), having much force; forcible; effective; vigorous.

for ci ble (fōr′si bəl), 1. made or done by force; using force; as, a forcible entrance into a house. 2. having or showing force; strong; powerful; as, a forcible speaker.

ford (fōrd), 1. place where a river, stream, or other body of water is not too deep to cross by walking through the water. 2. cross (a river, etc.) by walking or driving through the water.

fore (fōr), 1. at the front; toward the beginning or front; forward. 2. the front part.

fore arm[1] (fōr′ärm′), the part of the arm between the elbow and the wrist.

fore arm[2] (fōr ärm′), prepare for trouble ahead of time; arm beforehand.

fore bod ing (fōr bōd′ing), 1. prediction. 2. a feeling that something bad is going to happen.

fore cast (fōr′kast′), 1. prophecy; a statement of what is coming. What is the forecast about the weather for today? 2. prophesy; tell what is coming.

fore cas tle (fōk′səl or fōr′kas′əl), 1. the upper deck in front of the foremast. See the diagram. 2. the sailors' rooms in the forward part of a merchant ship.

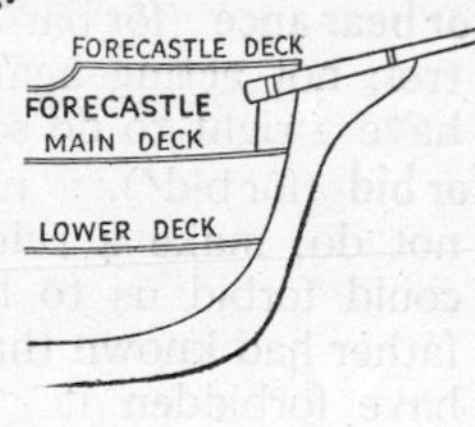

fore fa ther (fōr′fä′ᴛʜər), ancestor.

fore fin ger (fōr′fing′gər), the finger next to the thumb.

fore foot (fōr′fu̇t′), one of the front feet of an animal.

fore go (fōr gō′), do without; give up. Alice decided to forego the movies and do her lessons.

fore go ing (fōr′gō′ing), preceding; going before. There have been many pictures in the foregoing pages.

fore gone (fōr′gôn), previous; that has gone before. A **foregone conclusion** is a fact that was almost surely known beforehand.

fore ground (fōr′ground′), the part of a picture or scene nearest the observer; the part in the front. The cottage stands in the foreground with the mountains in the background.

fore head (for′id), the part of the face above the eyes.

for eign (for′in), 1. outside one's own country. She has traveled much in foreign countries. 2. coming from outside one's own country; as, a foreign ship, a foreign language, foreign money. 3. having to do with other countries; as, foreign trade. 4. not belonging. Sitting still all day is foreign to a healthy boy's nature.

for eign er (for′in ər), person from another country; an outsider.

fore man (fōr′mən), man in charge of a group of workmen; man in charge of the work in some part of a factory.

fore mast (fōr′məst or fōr′mast′), the mast nearest the bow of a ship.

fore most (fōr′mōst), 1. first. He stumbled and fell head foremost. 2. chief; leading.

fore noon (fōr′nün′), 1. the time from about eight o'clock to noon. 2. the part of the day from sunrise to noon.

fore saw (fōr sô′). See **foresee.**

fore see (fōr sē′), see or know beforehand. Mother put up a big picnic lunch, because she foresaw how hungry we would be. Nobody could have foreseen how cold it would be.

fore seen (fōr sēn′). See **foresee.**

fore sight (fōr′sīt′), 1. power to see or know beforehand. 2. careful thought for the future; prudence.

for est (for′ist), 1. thick woods; woodland, often covering many miles. 2. of the forest; as, forest fires. 3. plant with forest trees.

for est er (for′is tər), officer in charge of a forest to guard against fires, look after timber, etc.

for est ry (for′is tri), the science and art of taking care of forests.

fore tell (fōr tel′), tell beforehand; predict; prophesy. Who can foretell what a baby will do next? Our newspaper and radio had foretold the cold wave.

fore told (fōr tōld′). See **foretell.**

for ev er (fôr ev′ər), for ever; without ever coming to an end; always.

for ev er more (fôr ev′ər mōr′), forever.

for feit (fôr′fit), 1. lose or have to give up by one's own act, neglect, or fault. He forfeited his life by his careless driving. 2. thing lost or given up because of some act, neglect, or fault. His health was the forfeit he paid for being careless. 3. lost or given up.

for fei ture (fôr′fi chər), forfeit; loss by forfeiting.

for gave (fôr gāv′). See **forgive.**

forge[1] (fōrj), 1. place with fire where metal is heated very hot and then hammered into shape. A blacksmith uses a forge. 2. blacksmith's shop. 3. heat (metal) very hot and then hammer into shape. The blacksmith forged a bar of iron into a big strong hook. 4. place where iron or other metal is melted and refined. 5. make; shape; form. 6. make or write (something false). 7. sign (a name that is not one's own) falsely to deceive.

Blacksmith's shop with forge

forge[2] (fōrj), move forward slowly but steadily. One runner forged ahead of the others and won the race.

for get (fôr get′), 1. let go out of the mind; fail to remember. 2. fail to think of; fail to do, etc. **forgot** and **forgotten** are formed from **forget.**

for get ful (fôr get′fəl), 1. apt to forget; having a poor memory. 2. heedless.

for get ful ness (fôr get′fəl nis), forgetting; poor memory.

for get-me-not (fôr get′mē not′), a small blue flower; the plant bearing it.

Forget-me-not

for give (fôr giv′), pardon; give up the wish to punish; not have hard feelings at or toward. Please forgive my mistake. She forgave her brother for breaking her doll.

for giv en (fôr giv′ən). See **forgive.** Your mistakes are forgiven.

for give ness (fôr giv′nis), 1. act of forgiving; pardon. 2. willingness to forgive.

for go (fôr gō′), forego; do without; give up. Alice decided to forgo the movies and do her lessons.

for got (fôr got′). See **forget.** Tom was so busy that he forgot to eat his lunch.

for got ten (fôr got′ən). See **forget.** He has forgotten much of what he learned.

fork (fôrk), 1. a handle with two or more long points, with which to lift food. 2. a much larger kind with which to lift hay; a pitchfork. 3. lift with a fork. 4. any branching; as, the fork of a tree or the fork of a road. 5. one of the branches of a fork. 6. have forks; divide into forks. There is a garage where the road forks.

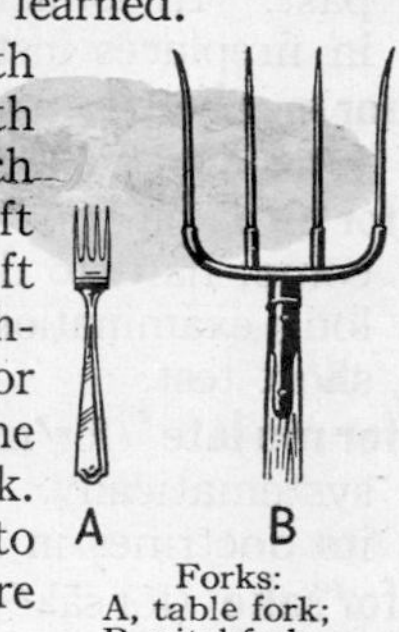

Forks: A, table fork; B, pitchfork.

for lorn (fôr lôrn′), left alone; neglected; miserable; hopeless. The lost kitten, a forlorn little animal, was wet and dirty.

form (fôrm), 1. a shape. Circles and triangles are forms. 2. to shape; make. 3. take shape. Ice formed in the pail. 4. become. Water forms ice when it freezes. 5. develop. Form good habits while you are young. 6. a kind; a sort. Ice, snow, and steam are forms of water. 7. manner; method. Her form in swimming is excellent. 8. formality; ceremony. He said "Good morning" as a matter of form, although he hardly noticed me. 9. arrangement. In what form did he put the list of words? 10. mold; pattern. Ice cream is often made in forms.

for mal (fôr′məl), 1. stiff; not familiar and homelike; as, a formal bow. 2. according to set customs or rules. 3. done with the proper forms; clear and definite. 4. having to do with the form, not the content of a thing.

for mal i ty (fôr mal′i ti), 1. an outward form; a ceremony; something required by custom; as, the formalities of a wedding or a funeral. 2. attention to forms and customs. Visitors at the court of a king are received with formality. 3. stiffness of manner, behavior, or arrangement. The formality of the party made Amy shy.

for mal ly (fôr′məl i), in a formal way; clearly and definitely.

for ma tion (fôr mā′shən), 1. the forming, making, or shaping (of something); as, the formation of a crust on bread as it bakes. 2. the way in which something is arranged; arrangement; order; as, troops in battle formation. 3. thing formed. Clouds are formations of tiny drops of water in the sky.

for mer (fôr′mər), 1. the first of two. Both the pink and the blue dresses are pretty, but I like the former better. 2. earlier; past; long past. In former times, people cooked food in fireplaces instead of stoves.

for mer ly (fôr′mər li), in time past; some time ago.

for mi da ble (fôr′mi də bəl), hard to overcome; hard to deal with; to be dreaded. A long examination is more formidable than a short test.

for mu late (fôr′mū lāt), state definitely or systematically. A church may formulate its doctrines in a creed.

for sake (fôr sāk′), give up; leave; leave alone. Ben ran away, forsaking his home and friends. **forsook** and **forsaken** are formed from **forsake.**

for sak en (fôr sāk′ən), 1. deserted; abandoned; forlorn. 2. given up. See **forsake.** Mary has forsaken her old friends.

for sook (fôr sůk′), gave up; left. See **forsake.**

for sooth (fôr süth′), in truth; indeed.

fort (fōrt), a strong building or castle that can be defended against an enemy.

forth (fōrth), 1. forward. 2. out. The sun came forth from behind the clouds. 3. away. Go forth and seek your fortune.

forth com ing (fōrth′kum′ing), 1. about to appear; approaching. The forthcoming week will be busy. 2. coming forth; ready when wanted. "If you need help, it will be forthcoming," father promised.

forth with (fōrth′wiᴛʜ′), at once; immediately.

for ti fi ca tion (fôr′ti fi kā′shən), 1. making strong; adding strength to. 2. place made strong by building walls and forts. 3. a wall or a fort built to make a place strong.

for ti fy (fôr′ti fī), 1. make strong; add strength to. 2. protect a place against attack; strengthen with forts, walls, etc. 3. build forts, walls, etc.

for ti tude (fôr′ti tūd or fôr′ti tüd), courage in pain, danger, or trouble; firmness of spirit.

fort night (fôrt′nīt), two weeks.

for tress (fôr′tris), fort; a place built with walls and defenses.

for tu nate (fôr′chə nit), 1. lucky; having good luck. 2. bringing good luck; having favorable results.

for tune (fôr′chən), 1. great deal of money or property; riches; wealth. Henry Ford made a fortune. 2. luck; chance; what happens. Fortune was against us; we lost. 3. good luck; success; prosperity. 4. **Tell a person's fortune** means tell what is going to happen to him.

for ty (fôr′ti), four times ten; 40.

for ward (fôr′wərd), 1. onward; ahead. Forward, march! 2. to the front. He brought forward several new ideas. 3. advanced; as, a child forward for his years. 4. help on; as, to forward your friends' plans. 5. send on farther; as, to forward a letter. 6. ready; eager. 7. pert; bold.

for wards (fôr′wərdz), onward; ahead; to the front.

fos sil (fos′il), 1. the hardened remains or trace of an animal or plant. Fossils of ferns are found in coal. 2. very old-fashioned person who is set in his ways. 3. belonging to the outworn past; as, fossil ideas.

fos ter (fos′tər), 1. help the growth or development of; encourage. Our city fosters libraries, parks, and playgrounds. 2. in the same family, but not related by birth. A **foster child** is a child brought up by a person not his parent. A **foster father, foster mother,** and **foster parent** are persons who bring up the child of another.

fought (fôt). See **fight.** He fought bravely yesterday. A battle was fought.

foul (foul), 1. very dirty; nasty; smelly. We opened the windows to let out the foul air. 2. make dirty; become dirty. 3. very wicked; vile. Murder is a foul crime. 4. unfair. 5. in football, basketball, etc., an unfair play. 6. in baseball, a batted ball that does not count because the ball lands outside the base lines. 7. hit against. Their boat fouled ours. 8. hitting against. One boat went foul of the other. 9. get tangled up with. The rope they threw fouled our anchor chain.

found[1] (found). See **find.** We found the treasure. The lost child was found.

found[2] (found), establish. The English founded a colony in the new country.

foun da tion (foun dā′shən), 1. the part on which the rest stands or depends; base. The foundation of a house is built first. 2. founding; establishing. The foundation of the United States began in 1776.

found er[1] (foun′dər), person who founds or establishes.

foun der[2] (foun′dər), 1. fall down; stumble; break down. Cattle foundered in the swamp. 2. fill with water and sink. The ship foundered in the storm.

found ling (found′ling), a baby or little child found deserted.

found ry (foun′dri), place where metal is melted and molded; place where things are made of melted metal.

fount (fount), 1. fountain. 2. source.

foun tain (foun′tən), 1. water flowing or rising into the air in a spray; the pipes through which water is forced and the basin built to receive it. 2. spring of water. 3. place to get a drink; as, a drinking fountain, a soda fountain. 4. source. John found that his father was a fountain of information.

Fountain

four (fōr), one more than three; 4. A dog has four legs.

four fold (fōr′fōld′), 1. four times as much or as many. 2. having four parts.

four score (fōr′skōr′), four twenties; 80.

four teen (fōr′tēn′), four more than ten; 14.

four teenth (fōr′tēnth′), 1. next after the 13th. 2. one of 14 equal parts.

fourth (fōrth), 1. next after the 3rd. 2. a quarter; one of four equal parts. Twenty-five cents is one fourth of a dollar.

fowl (foul), 1. any bird; as, a waterfowl. 2. a common rooster or hen. 3. the flesh of a fowl used for food.

Fowl (def. 2)

fox (foks), 1. a small animal somewhat like a dog. See the picture. In many stories the fox gets the better of other animals by his cunning. 2. its fur. 3. a cunning or crafty person.

Red fox (about 3½ ft. long with the tail)

fox glove (foks′gluv′), plant with tall stalks having many bell-shaped flowers.

fox hound (foks′hound′), dog with a keen sense of smell, trained to hunt foxes.

fox y (fok′si), crafty; like a fox.

frac tion (frak′shən), 1. one or more of the equal parts of a whole. $\frac{1}{2}$, $\frac{1}{4}$, $\frac{3}{4}$, $\frac{1}{3}$, and $\frac{2}{3}$ are fractions. 2. a part broken off; not all of a thing.

frac ture (frak′chər), 1. break; crack. The boy fell from a tree and fractured his arm. 2. a breaking. 3. the breaking of a bone or cartilage.

frag ile (fraj′il), easily broken; delicate; frail. Thin glass is fragile.

frag ment (frag′mənt), a part broken off; piece of something broken. When Ann broke the dish, she tried to put the fragments back together.

fra grance (frā′grəns), sweet smell; pleasing odor.

fra grant (frā′grənt), sweet-smelling. A rose is fragrant.

frail (frāl), 1. weak; slender and not very strong; as, a frail child. 2. easily broken or giving way. Be careful; those branches are a very frail support.

frail ty (frāl′ti), weakness.

frame (frām), 1. support over which something is stretched or built; as, the frame of a house. 2. body; as, a man of heavy frame. 3. the way in which a thing is put together. 4. make; put together; plan. 5. the border in which a thing is set; as, a window frame, a picture frame. 6. put a border around; as, to frame a picture. 7. **Frame of mind** means way one is thinking or feeling; disposition; mood.

Part of the frame of a house

frame work (frām′wėrk′), support or skeleton; the stiff part which gives shape. The bridge had a steel framework.

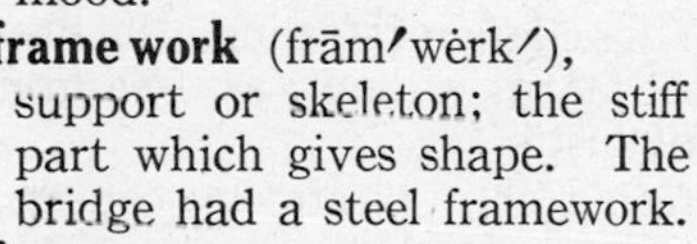

Picture frame

franc (frangk), the unit of money in France and Switzerland. One franc used to be worth about 20 cents.

France (frans), a country in western Europe.

frank (frangk), free to express one's real thoughts and feelings; open; not hiding one's mind; not afraid to say what one thinks.

frank ness (frangk′nis), being frank; saying just what one thinks.

fran tic (fran′tik), very much excited; wild with rage, pain, or grief.

fran ti cal ly (fran′ti kəl i), in a frantic manner; with wild excitement.

fra ter nal (frə tėr′nəl), brotherly.

fra ter ni ty (frə tėr′ni ti), 1. brotherhood. 2. group of men or boys joined together for fellowship or for some other purpose. There are student fraternities in many American colleges. 3. group of men having the same interests, kind of work, etc.

fraud (frôd), 1. dishonest dealing; cheating; trickery. 2. something which is not what it seems to be.

fraught (frôt), loaded; filled. A battlefield is fraught with horror.

fray[1] (frā), a fight; noisy quarrel.

fray[2] (frā), 1. separate into threads; make or become ragged or worn along the edge. Long wear had frayed the collar and cuffs of his old shirt. 2. wear away; rub.

freak (frēk), 1. something very queer or unusual. A green leaf growing in the middle of a rose would be called a freak of nature. 2. sudden change of mind without reason; odd notion or fancy.

freck le (frek′əl), 1. one of the small light-brown spots that some people have on the skin. 2. make freckles on. 3. become marked with freckles.

free (frē), 1. loose; not fastened or shut up. 2. not held back from action or thought by law or by persons. This is one of the freest nations in the world. 3. not bound to any country, person, or thing. 4. without anything to pay. These tickets are free. 5. let go; let loose. 6. make free; relieve from any kind of burden, bondage, or slavery. Lincoln freed the slaves. 7. to clear. He will have to free himself of this charge of stealing. 8. **Free from** or **free of** means without; as, free from fear, air free of dust.

free boot er (frē′büt′ər), pirate; buccaneer.

free dom (frē′dəm), 1. being free. 2. liberty; power of choosing what one will do. 3. free use. We give a guest the freedom of the house. 4. too great liberty. We did not like the freedom of his manner. 5. ease of movement or action.

free man (frē′mən), man not a slave nor a serf; man who could own land.

fre er (frē′ər), more free.

fre est (frē′ist), most free.

freeze (frēz), 1. turn into ice; harden by cold. 2. make very cold. 3. become very cold. 4. kill or injure by frost. 5. cover or become covered with ice. 6. a freezing. 7. being frozen. 8. make or become stiff and unfriendly. 9. chill or be chilled with fear, etc. 10. become motionless. The baby rabbit learned to freeze at a strange sound. **froze** and **frozen** are formed from **freeze.**

freight (frāt), 1. the goods that a ship or a train carries. 2. the price paid for carrying. 3. a freight train or ship. He sent the box by freight.

French (french), 1. of or having to do with France, its people, or their language. 2. the people of France. 3. the language of France.

fren zied (fren′zid), frantic; wild; very much excited.

fren zy (fren′zi), brief fury; almost madness; very great excitement.

fre quen cy (frē′kwən si), 1. frequent occurrence. 2. rate of occurrence. The flashes of light came with a frequency of three per minute.

fre quent (frē′kwənt for 1, fri kwent′ for 2), 1. happening often, near together, or every little while. Storms are frequent in March. 2. be often in; go to often. Frogs frequent ponds, streams, and marshes.

fre quent ly (frē′kwənt li), often.

fresh (fresh), 1. newly made, grown, or gathered. These are fresh vegetables. 2. new. Is there any fresh news from home? 3. not salty. Rivers are usually fresh water. 4. not spoiled. 5. not tired out. Put in fresh horses. 6. healthy-looking. 7. pure; cool; as, a fresh breeze.

fresh en (fresh′ən), 1. make fresh. 2. become fresh.

fresh et (fresh′it), a rush of water caused by heavy rains or melted snow.

fresh ness (fresh′nis), fresh condition; being fresh.

fresh-wa ter (fresh′wô′tər), of or living in water that is not salty. The catfish is a fresh-water fish.

fret (fret), 1. to worry; be peevish; be discontented. Baby frets in hot weather. 2. make peevish; make discontented. Lola's failures fretted her. 3. condition of worry or discontent. She is in a fret about her examinations.

fret ful (fret′fəl), peevish; discontented; ready to fret. Babies are fretful when cutting their teeth.

fri ar (frī′ər), man who belongs to one of certain religious brotherhoods of the Roman Catholic Church.

fric tion (frik′shən), 1. the rubbing of one thing against another, such as skates on ice, hand against hand, a brush on shoes. Matches are lighted by friction. 2. resistance to motion of surfaces in contact. Oil reduces friction. 3. clash; conflict; as, friction between England and Germany.

Fri day (frī′di), the sixth day of the week.

fried (frīd), 1. cooked in hot fat. 2. See **fry.** I fried the ham. Are the potatoes fried?

friend (frend), 1. person who knows and likes another. 2. person who favors and supports. Our church has many friends.

friend less (frend′lis), without friends.

friend li ness (frend′li nis), friendly nature; friendly action.

friend ly (frend′li), 1. of a friend. 2. like a friend; like a friend's. 3. on good terms; as, friendly relations between countries. 4. wanting to be a friend; as, a friendly dog.

friend ship (frend′ship), 1. state of being friends. 2. a liking between friends. 3. friendly feeling or behavior.

frieze (frēz), a band or ornament on a wall.

Frieze

frig ate (frig′it), fast, three-masted sailing warship of medium size. Frigates were much used from 1750 to 1850. See the picture.

fright (frīt), 1. sudden fear; sudden terror. 2. person or thing that is ugly, shocking, or ridiculous. 3. frighten.

fright en (frīt′ən), make afraid.

fright ful (frīt′fəl), that would frighten; dreadful.

frig id (frij′id), 1. very cold; as, a frigid climate. 2. cold in feeling or manner; stiff; as, a frigid bow, a frigid stare, frigid conversation.

Frigate

frill (fril), 1. a ruffle. 2. thing added merely for show; useless ornament.

fringe (frinj), 1. border or trimming made of threads, cords, etc., either loose or tied together in small bunches. 2. anything like this; a border. A fringe of hair hung over her forehead. 3. make a fringe for. 4. be a fringe for. Bushes fringed the road.

Fringes

frisk (frisk), frolic about joyously; dance and skip in play. A lively puppy frisks all over the house.

frisk y (fris′ki), playful; lively.

friv o lous (friv′ə ləs), 1. lacking in seriousness or sense; silly. Frivolous behavior is out of place in church. 2. of little worth or importance. He wasted his time on frivolous matters.

fro (frō). **To and fro** means first one way and then back again; back and forth.

Frog

frock (frok), 1. gown; dress. 2. loose outer garment. 3. robe worn by a clergyman.

frog (frog), 1. a small, leaping animal that lives in or near water. Frogs hatch from eggs as tadpoles, which live in the water until they grow legs. Some frogs live in trees. See the picture above. 2. a long, covered button and the fancy loop that goes over it, used to fasten cloaks, etc.

F, frogs on a cloak.

frol ic (frol′ik), 1. a joyous game or party; play; fun. 2. play about joyously; have fun together. **frolicked** and **frolicking** are formed from **frolic.**

from (from). This book came from New York. Five miles from here is another school. Three weeks from today is a holiday. Steel is made from iron. He took a book from the table. Dick is suffering from a cold. Anyone can tell apples from oranges. A child can count from 1 to 10.

front (frunt), 1. first part. 2. part that faces forward. 3. thing fastened or worn on the front. 4. place where fighting is going on. 5. land facing a street, river, etc. 6. on the front; at the front. 7. have the front toward; face. Helen's house fronts the park.

fron tier (frun tēr′), 1. the last edge of settled country, where the wilds begin. 2. part of one country that touches the edge of another; boundary line between two countries.

frost (frôst), 1. freezing. 2. cold weather. 3. moisture frozen on or in a solid surface. 4. frozen dew or vapor. On cold fall mornings there is frost on the grass. 5. kill by freezing. 6. cover with frost. 7. cover with anything that suggests frost; as, to frost a cake with sugar and white of egg mixed together.

frost ing (frôst′ing), 1. a mixture of sugar and some liquid for covering cake. 2. a dull finish of glass or metal.

frost y (frôs′ti), 1. cold enough for frost; as, a frosty morning. 2. covered with frost. The glass is frosty. 3. cold and unfriendly; with no warmth of feeling; as, a frosty manner.

froth (frôth), 1. foam. There was froth on the mad dog's lips. 2. to foam; cover with foam. 3. cause to foam by beating, pouring, etc. 4. something light and trifling; unimportant talk.

frown (froun), 1. a drawing together of the brows, usually in deep thought or in strong feeling. 2. draw the brows together; look with disapproval. You may frown when you are angry or not pleased. 3. look displeased or angry.

froze (frōz). See **freeze.** The water in the pond froze last week.

fro zen (frō′zən), 1. hardened with cold; turned into ice; as, a river frozen over, frozen pudding. 2. killed with cold; as, frozen to death. 3. cold and unfeeling; as, a frozen heart. 4. too frightened or stiff to move; as, frozen to the spot in horror. 5. See **freeze.** The water has frozen to ice.

fru gal (frü′gəl), 1. without waste; not wasteful; saving; using things well. A frugal housekeeper buys and uses food carefully. 2. costing little. He ate a frugal supper of bread and milk.

fru gal i ty (frü gal′i ti), being frugal; thrift.

fruit (früt), 1. Apples, pears, oranges, bananas, peaches, and plums are fruit. 2. the part of the plant in which the seeds are. 3. useful product of plant growth; as, fruits of the earth. 4. the result of anything. His invention was the fruit of much effort. 5. produce fruit.

fruit ful (früt′fəl), 1. producing much fruit. 2. producing much of anything. 3. having good results; bringing benefit or profit. A successful plan is fruitful.

fruit less (früt′lis), 1. having no results; useless; unsuccessful. 2. producing no fruit.

fruit y (früt′i), tasting or smelling like fruit.

frus trate (frus′trāt), foil; bring to nothing; defeat; baffle. Heavy rain frustrated our plans for a picnic.

fry (frī), 1. cook in fat, in a deep or shallow pan. Mary is frying potatoes. 2. something fried.

ft., 1. foot. 2. feet. 3. fort.

fu el (fū′əl), 1. anything that can be burned to make a useful fire. Coal, wood, and oil are fuels. 2. anything that keeps up or increases a feeling. Her insults were fuel to his hatred.

fu gi tive (fū′ji tiv), 1. person who is running away. The murderer became a fugitive from justice. 2. running away; as, a fugitive slave. 3. lasting a very short time; passing rapidly.

ful crum (ful′krəm), support on which a lever turns or is supported in moving or lifting something.

ful fill or **ful fil** (fu̇l fil′), 1. carry out (a promise, prophecy, etc.). 2. perform or do (a duty, command, etc.). Ruth fulfilled all our requests. 3. satisfy (requirements, etc.); answer (a purpose).

ful fill ment or **ful fil ment** (fu̇l fil′mənt), fulfilling; accomplishment.

full (fu̇l), 1. that can hold no more. Anything is full when it holds all that it is intended to hold. **Full of** means filled with. 2. complete; entire; as, a full supply of clothes. 3. completely. Fill the pail full. 4. completeness; greatest degree. He satisfied his ambition to the full. 5. plump; well filled out; as, a full face. 6. having wide folds; as, a full skirt.

full-grown (fu̇l′grōn′), fully grown; mature.

full ness or **ful ness** (fu̇l′nis), being full. The bag bulged because of its fullness.

ful ly (fu̇l′i), 1. completely; entirely. Was he fully satisfied? 2. abundantly. 3. quite.

fum ble (fum′bəl), 1. grope awkwardly. He fumbled in the darkness for the doorknob. 2. handle awkwardly; let drop instead of catching and holding. The first baseman fumbled the ball, and two runs were scored. 3. an awkward attempt to find or handle something.

fume (fūm), 1. vapor, gas, or smoke. 2. give off vapor, gas, or smoke. The candle fumed, sputtered, and went out. 3. let off one's rage in angry complaints. He fumed about the slowness of the train.

fun (fun), 1. playfulness; merry play; amusement; joking. 2. **Make fun of** means laugh at; ridicule.

func tion (fungk′shən), 1. proper work; purpose; use. The function of the stomach is to help digest food. 2. to work; be used; act. Mary functioned as teacher. This old fountain pen does not function very well. 3. a formal public or social gathering for some purpose, such as a wedding.

fund (fund), 1. a stock or store ready for use. There is a fund of knowledge in a dictionary. 2. a sum of money set aside for a special purpose. Our school has a fund of $1000 to buy books with. 3. **Funds** sometimes means money.

fun da men tal (fun′də men′təl), forming a basis; essential.

fu ner al (fū′nər əl), 1. things that are done at the burial or burning of a dead body. A funeral includes a religious service and taking the body from the church or house to the graveyard. 2. of a funeral; suitable for a funeral. A funeral march is very slow.

Fungi growing on a tree

fun gi (fun′jī), funguses.

fun gus (fung′gəs), plant without flowers, leaves, or green coloring matter. Mushrooms, toadstools, molds, and mildews are funguses.

fun nel (fun′əl), 1. an open vessel ending at the bottom in a tube. See picture A. If a funnel is used, anything such as a liquid, powder, or grain, may be poured into a small opening without spilling. 2. the smokestack or chimney on a steamship or steam engine. See picture B.

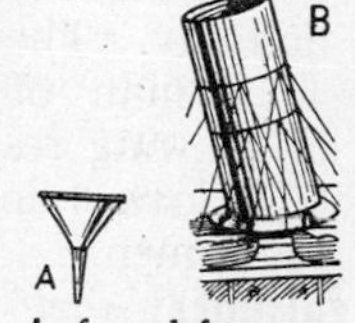

A, funnel for pouring; B, funnel for smoke.

fun ny (fun′i), 1. causing laughter. 2. In free and easy talk, funny sometimes means strange or queer. **funnier** and **funniest** are formed from **funny.**

fur (fėr), 1. the soft coat of hair that covers many animals. 2. clothes made of fur. Furs keep you warm.

fu ri ous (fūr′i əs), 1. raging; violent. 2. full of wild, fierce anger.

furl (fėrl), roll up; fold up; as, to furl a sail, to furl a flag. Birds furl their wings. In the morning, the boys broke up camp and furled the tent.

fur long (fėr′lông), a measure of distance, $\frac{1}{8}$ of a mile.

fur nace (fėr′nis), something to make a hot fire in, in order to melt iron, make glass, or heat a building. A furnace has an enclosed chamber or box for the fire.

fur nish (fėr′nish), 1. supply; provide; as, to furnish an army with blankets. 2. supply with beds, chairs, tables, etc.; as, to furnish a bedroom.

fur ni ture (fėr′ni chər), 1. articles needed. 2. articles needed in a house or room, such as chairs, tables, beds, desks, etc.

furred (fėrd), 1. having fur. 2. made covered, trimmed, or lined with fur.

fur row (fėr′ō), 1. the long, narrow track in the earth cut by a plow. 2. cut furrows in. 3. a wrinkle. 4. make wrinkles in.

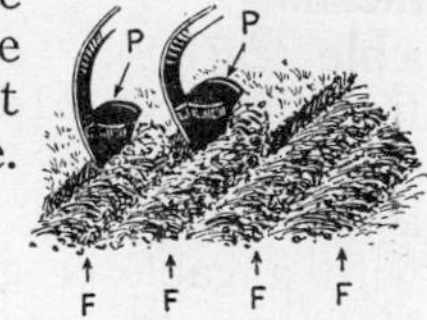

F, furrow; P, plow.

fur ry (fėr′i), covered with fur; soft like fur.

fur ther (fėr′ᴛʜər), 1. farther. 2. more. Do you need further help? 3. help forward. Mother furthered our plans.

fur ther more (fėr′ᴛʜər mōr), moreover; also; besides.

fur ther most (fėr′ᴛʜər mōst), farthest.

fur thest (fėr′ᴛʜist), farthest.

fur tive (fėr′tiv), done by stealth; secret; sly; stealthy; as, a furtive snatch at the candy, a furtive glance into the forbidden room, a furtive manner.

fu ry (fūr′i), 1. rage; a storm of anger. 2. violence. 3. a raging or violent person.

fuse[1] (fūz), 1. part of an electric circuit that melts and breaks the circuit if the current becomes dangerously strong. 2. the wick in a firecracker; a longer wick used to set off a bomb or a blast of gunpowder, so that one may have time to get away after lighting it.

fuse[2] (fūz), 1. melt; join together by melting. 2. blend; unite.

fu se lage (fū′zə lij or fū′zə läzh′), body of an airplane. The wings and tail are fastened to it. The fuselage holds the passengers, cargo, etc. See the picture of **airplane.**

fuss (fus), 1. much bother about small matters; useless talk and worry; attention given to something not worth it. 2. make a fuss. She fussed about with her work in a nervous manner.

fu tile (fū′til), useless; not successful. Many persons have made futile attempts to swim from England to France.

fu ture (fū′chər), 1. the time not yet come; what is to come. 2. coming; that will be. We hope your future years will all be happy.

G

gab ar dine or **gab er dine** (gab′ər dēn), 1. long, loose cloak or frock. 2. kind of loosely woven cloth, used for raincoats, suits, etc.

gab ble (gab′əl), 1. talk rapidly with little or no meaning. 2. rapid talk with little or no meaning.

ga ble (gā′bəl), end of a ridged roof, with the three-cornered piece of wall that it covers.

ga bled (gā′bəld), built with a gable or gables; having or forming gables.

GABLE GABLE

gad (gad), move about restlessly; go about looking for pleasure or excitement. They were gadding all around the town.

gad fly (gad′flī′), a fly that stings cattle and other animals.

gag (gag), 1. something put in the mouth to silence a person. 2. stop up the mouth of with a gag. 3. to strain in an effort to vomit.

gage[1] (gāj), 1. a glove thrown down as a challenge to combat; a challenge. 2. pledge; security. The knight left a diamond as gage for the horse and armor.

gage[2] (gāj), gauge.

gai e ty (gā′i ti), 1. being gay. Her gaiety helped the party. 2. bright appearance.

gai ly (gā′li), 1. as if gay; merrily; happily. 2. brightly. Nell was gaily dressed.

gain (gān), 1. get; obtain; secure. The king gained possession of more lands. 2. profit. How much did I gain by that? 3. win. We will gain the battle. 4. arrive at. The swimmer gained the shore. 5. make progress. The sick child is gaining. 6. advance. One boat is gaining on another. 7. advantage; what one gains. 8. **Gains** sometimes means profits; earnings; winnings.

gain say (gān′sā′), deny; contradict, dispute.

gainst or **'gainst** (genst), against.

gait (gāt), the kind of steps used in going along; manner of walking; as, a slow gait, a lame gait.

gai ter (gā′tər), 1. an outer covering of cloth or leather for the leg below the knee or for the ankle, for outdoor wear. 2. cloth or leather shoe with an elastic strip in each side.

Gaiters (def. 1)

ga la (gā′lə), festive. Christmas and the Fourth of July are gala days.

gale (gāl), 1. very strong wind. 2. noisy outburst; as, gales of laughter.

gall[1] (gôl), 1. a bitter liquid made in the liver. 2. anything very bitter. 3. bitterness; hate.

gall[2] (gôl), 1. a sore spot on the skin caused by rubbing. 2. make sore by rubbing. The rough strap galled the horse's skin. 3. annoy; irritate. The child was galled by being scolded so much.

gall[3] (gôl), a lump or ball that swells up on the leaves, stems, or roots of plants where they have been injured by insects.

Galls on a leaf

gal lant (gal′ənt), 1. noble in spirit or in looks; brave. King Arthur was a gallant knight. 2. grand; fine; stately. A ship with all of its sails spread is a gallant sight. 3. looking dressed up and gay. The garden made a gallant show. 4. a man of fashion; a fine gentleman. 5. showing respect and courtesy to women. 6. a man who is very polite and attentive to women.

gal lant ry (gal′ən tri), 1. bravery; dashing courage. 2. respect and courtesy to women. 3. gallant act or speech.

gal ler y (gal′ər i), 1. a hall or long narrow passage. 2. a balcony looking down into a large hall or room. 3. the highest balcony of a theater. 4. people who sit there. 5. a building or room used to show collections of pictures and statues. We visited picture galleries in New York.

gal ley (gal′i), 1. long, narrow ship of former times having oars and sails. Galleys were often rowed by slaves or prisoners. 2. a large rowboat. 3. the kitchen of a ship.

Galley (def. 1)

gal lon (gal′ən), the amount of 4 quarts of liquid.

gal lop (gal′əp), 1. the fastest gait of a horse or other four-footed animal. In a gallop, all four feet are off the ground together at each leap. 2. ride at a gallop. 3. go at a gallop. 4. cause to go at a gallop. John galloped his horse down the road. 5. go very fast; hurry.

gal lows (gal′ōz), 1. wooden frame made of a crossbar on two upright posts, used for hanging criminals. 2. hanging as a punishment.

Gallows

gam ble (gam′bəl), 1. play games of chance for money. 2. take great risks in business. 3. bet; wager.

gam bler (gam′blər), 1. person who gambles. 2. person who gambles a great deal.

gam bol (gam′bəl), 1. a frolic; running and jumping about in play. 2. to frolic; run and jump about; play. Lambs gamboled in the meadow.

game (gām), 1. a way of playing; as, a game with bat and ball, a game of tag. 2. the things needed for a game. This store sells games. 3. contest with certain rules. One person or side tries to win it. 4. the score in a game. 5. scheme; plan. 6. animals and birds that are hunted. 7. the flesh of wild animals and birds when used for food. 8. having to do with game and hunting; as, game laws. 9. brave; plucky; daring to do a thing. Are you game to swim across the river? 10. gamble. 11. **Make game of** means make fun of; laugh at.

gan der (gan′dər), male goose.

gang (gang), 1. group of people acting or going around together. Criminals often form gangs. 2. group of people working together under one foreman. Two gangs of workmen were mending the road.

gang plank (gang′plangk′), a movable bridge used in passing on and off a ship.

gang way (gang′wā′), 1. a passageway. 2. a passageway on a ship. This ship has a gangway between the rail and the cabins. 3. gangplank. 4. Get out of the way! Stand aside and make room!

Gangplank

gaol (jāl), jail.

gaol er (jāl′ər), jailer.

gap (gap), 1. break or opening; as, a gap in a fence or wall. 2. unfilled space; a blank. The record is not complete; there are several gaps in it. 3. a pass through mountains.

gape (gāp), 1. open wide. A deep hole in the earth gaped before us. 2. wide opening. 3. open the mouth wide; yawn. 4. act of opening the mouth wide; a yawning. 5. stare with the mouth open. The savages gaped when they saw an airplane for the first time.

ga rage (gə räzh′), place for keeping automobiles; shop for repairing automobiles.

garb (gärb), 1. the way one is dressed. 2. clothing. 3. clothe.

gar bage (gär′bij), waste food from the kitchen or dining room; scraps of food to be thrown away.

gar den (gär′dən), 1. ground used for growing vegetables, flowers, or fruits. 2. take care of a garden. He liked to garden, for it kept him out of doors.

gar den er (gärd′nər), 1. person hired to take care of a garden. 2. person who makes a garden or works in a garden.

gar land (gär′lənd), 1. wreath of flowers, leaves, etc. 2. decorate with garlands.

gar lic (gär′lik), a plant like an onion, used in cooking. Its flavor is stronger than that of an onion.

gar ment (gär′mənt), any article of clothing.

gar ner (gär′nər), gather and store away. Wheat is cut and garnered at harvest time.

gar net (gär′nit), 1. a deep-red precious stone. 2. deep red.

gar nish (gär′nish), 1. something laid on or around a dish as a decoration. The turkey was served with a garnish of cranberries and parsley. 2. decorate (food). 3. decoration; trimming. 4. decorate; trim.

gar ret (gar′it), space in a house just below a sloping roof; attic.

gar ri son (gar′i sən), 1. the soldiers stationed in a fort, town, etc., to defend it. 2. place that has a garrison. 3. station soldiers in (a fort, town, etc.) to defend it. 4. occupy (a fort, town, etc.) as a garrison.

gar ter (gär′tər), 1. band or strap to hold up a stocking or sock. It is usually elastic. 2. fasten with a garter.

gas (gas), 1. vapor; not a solid or liquid; any substance when it is like air in form. Oxygen and hydrogen are gases. 2. a gas obtained from coal and other substances. Gas was once much used for lighting and is now used for cooking and heating. 3. gasoline. 4. kill or injure by poisonous gas.

gas e ous (gas′i əs), in the form of gas; of gas; like gas. Steam is water in a gaseous condition.

gash (gash), 1. a long, deep cut or wound. 2. make a long, deep cut in.

gas o line or **gas o lene** (gas′ə lēn), a colorless liquid made from petroleum. It evaporates and burns very easily. Gasoline is used to make automobiles go.

gasp (gasp), 1. a short, quick breath with open mouth. 2. pant with open mouth; breathe with gasps. 3. utter with gasps. "Help! Help!" gasped the drowning man.

gate (gāt), 1. an opening in a wall or fence, usually fitted with a door. 2. a door in a wall or fence. 3. door, valve, etc., to stop or control the flow of water in a pipe, dam, canal, lock, etc.

gate way (gāt′wā′), 1. an opening in a wall or fence where a gate is. 2. way to go in or out; way to get to something.

gath er (gaTH′ər), 1. collect; bring into one place. 2. come together. 3. pick; glean or pluck. Farmers gather their crops. 4. put together in the mind. I gathered from his words that he was really much upset. 5. pull together in folds. 6. one of the little folds between the stitches when cloth is gathered.

gath er ing (gaTH′ər ing), 1. an assembly; a meeting. 2. a swelling that comes to a head. A boil is a painful gathering.

gaud y (gôd′i), too bright and gay to be in good taste; cheap and showy.

gauge (gāj), 1. standard measure; measure. There are gauges of the capacity of a barrel, the thickness of sheet iron, the diameter of a shotgun bore, wire, etc. 2. instrument for measuring. A steam gauge measures the pressure of steam. 3. measure exactly. 4. estimate; judge. It is difficult to gauge the character of a stranger. 5. distance between the rails of a railroad.

Gauge for measuring wire

gaunt (gônt), 1. thin and bony; hollow-eyed and starved-looking. 2. looking bare and gloomy; desolate.

gaunt let[1] (gônt′lit), 1. an iron glove which was part of a knight's armor. 2. a stout, heavy glove with a deep, flaring cuff. 3. **Throw down the gauntlet** means give a challenge.

Iron gauntlet

gaunt let[2] (gônt′lit). **Run the gauntlet** means pass between two rows of men each of whom strikes the victim as he passes.

gauze (gôz), a very thin, light cloth, easily seen through.

gave (gāv). See **give.** He gave me some of his candy.

gay (gā), 1. happy and full of fun; merry. 2. bright-colored.

gay e ty (gā′i ti), gaiety.

gay ly (gā′li), gaily.

gaze (gāz), 1. look long and steadily. 2. a long, steady look.

ga zelle (gə zel′), small, graceful kind of antelope with large, soft eyes.

Gazelle (about 2 ft. high at the shoulder)

gear (gēr), 1. an arrangement of parts for some purpose, such as harness, tools, machinery, clothing, or household goods. 2. a wheel having teeth that fit into teeth in another wheel; wheels turning one another by teeth. 3. **In gear** means connected with the motor. **Out of gear** means not connected with the motor. An automobile in low gear moves slowly, but strongly. 4. provide with gear. 5. come into gear or be in gear.

Wheels in gear

geese (gēs), more than one goose.

gel a tin or **gel a tine** (jel′ə tin), a substance like glue or jelly obtained by boiling the bones, hoofs, and other waste parts of animals. Gelatin is used in making glue and desserts.

gem (jem), 1. a precious stone; jewel. Diamonds and rubies are gems. 2. anything that is very beautiful. 3. the most precious thing. The gem of his collection was a rare Persian stamp. 4. set with gems. Stars gemmed the sky. 5. muffin.

gen darme (zhän′därm), a French soldier who has the duties of a policeman.

gen er al (jen′ər əl), 1. of all; for all; from all. 2. widespread; not limited to a few; for many; from many. There is a general interest in radio. 3. not detailed. He made only a general plan. 4. not special; as, a general store, a general magazine. 5. chief; as, attorney general, postmaster general. 6. a high officer in command of many men in an army. 7. **In general** means usually; commonly.

gen er al ly (jen′ər əl i), 1. for the most part; usually. 2. in a general way; not specially. I bought a suit that will be generally useful.

gen er ate (jen′ər āt), produce; cause to be. Burning coal can generate steam. The steam can generate electricity.

gen er a tion (jen′ər ā′shən), 1. the people born in the same period; as, our grandmother's generation, the coming generation. 2. about thirty years. 3. one step or degree in a family. The picture showed four generations—great-grandmother, grandmother, mother, and baby. 4. act or process of producing; as, the generation of steam in a boiler.

gen er os i ty (jen′ər os′i ti), 1. being generous; unselfishness; willingness to share with others. 2. noble character; freedom from meanness. 3. generous behavior.

gen er ous (jen′ər əs), 1. unselfish; willing to share with others. 2. noble and forgiving; not mean. 3. large; plentiful. A quarter of a pie is a generous piece.

gen ial (jēn′yəl), 1. smiling and pleasant; cheerful and friendly; kindly; as, a genial welcome, the genial village blacksmith. 2. helping growth; giving warmth or comfort; as, genial sunshine.

ge nie (jē′ni), a powerful spirit. When Aladdin rubbed his lamp, the genie came and did what Aladdin asked.

gen ius (jēn′yəs), 1. very great natural power of mind. 2. a person having such power. 3. great natural ability. A great actor has a genius for acting.

gen tian (jen′shən), a plant with flowers (usually blue), growing mostly in hilly regions.

Gentian

gen tile or **Gen tile** (jen′til), 1. person who is not a Jew. 2. not Jewish.

gen til i ty (jen til′i ti), 1. gentle birth; membership in the aristocracy or class of gentlemen and gentlewomen. 2. good manners. 3. refinement.

gen tle (jen′təl), 1. mild; not rough; as, a gentle tap. 2. soft; low; as, a gentle sound. 3. moderate; as, gentle heat, a gentle slope. 4. kindly; friendly; as, a gentle disposition. 5. easy to manage; as, a gentle dog. 6. of good family and social position; wellborn. 7. refined; polite.

gen tle man (jen′təl mən), 1. man of good family and social position. 2. man who is honorable and well-bred. 3. polite term for any man.

gen tle man ly (jen′təl mən li), like a gentleman; well-bred; polite.

gen tle men (jen′təl mən), more than one gentleman.

gen tle ness (jen′təl nis), being gentle; softness in voice, touch, and manner.

gen tle wom an (jen′təl wu̇m′ən), 1. woman of good family and social position. 2. well-bred woman; lady. 3. woman attendant of a lady of rank.

gen tly (jen′tli), 1. in a gentle way; tenderly; softly. 2. gradually; as, a gently sloping hillside.

gen try (jen′tri), 1. the class of wellborn and well-bred people. 2. in England, the class next below the nobility. 3. people of any particular class.

gen u ine (jen′ū in), 1. real; true; as, genuine leather, a genuine diamond. 2. frank; sincere; as, genuine sorrow.

ge o graph i cal (jē′ə graf′i kəl), of geography; having something to do with geography.

ge og ra phy (ji og′rə fi), 1. study of the earth's surface, climate, continents, countries, peoples, industries, and products. 2. surface features of a place or region. 3. book about geography. Nan owns four geographies.

ge ol o gy (ji ol′ə ji), the science that deals with the earth's crust, the layers of which it is composed, and their history.

ge om e try (ji om′i tri), the study that measures and compares lines, angles, surfaces, and solids; the mathematics of space.

ge ra ni um (ji rā′ni əm), 1. a house or garden plant with showy flowers of scarlet, pink, or white. 2. a wild plant with pink or purple flowers.

Garden geranium

germ (jėrm), 1. a simple animal or plant, too small to be seen, which causes disease; as, the germ of scarlet fever. 2. a seed or bud. 3. the beginning of anything. Counting was the germ of arithmetic.

Ger man (jėr′mən), 1. of Germany, its people, or their language. 2. person born in Germany, living there, or having German parents. 3. the language of Germany.

Ger ma ny (jėr′mə ni), a country in Central Europe.

ger mi nate (jėr′mi nāt), 1. begin to grow; develop; sprout. Seeds germinate in the spring. 2. cause to grow. You can germinate beans by soaking them in water and planting them in damp sawdust.

ges ture (jes′chər), 1. a motion of the body used instead of words or with words to help express an idea or a feeling. 2. any action for effect or to impress others. Her refusal was merely a gesture; she really wanted to go. 3. make gestures; use gestures.

get (get), 1. obtain. 2. become. It is getting colder. 3. persuade; influence. Try to get Jack to come, too. 4. cause to be or do. Get the windows open. Mary got her work done. 5. Some special meanings are:

Gibbon (about 30 in. tall)

get away, 1. go away. 2. escape.

get in, 1. go in. 2. put in. 3. arrive.

get off, 1. come down from or out of. 2. take off. 3. escape. 4. start.

get on, 1. go up on or into. 2. put on. 3. advance. 4. succeed. 5. agree.

get out, 1. go out. 2. take out. 3. go away. 4. escape. 5. help to escape. 6. become known.

get over, recover from.

get together, 1. bring together. 2. meet.

get up, 1. arise. He got up at six o'clock. 2. stand up. 3. prepare.

getting, got, and **gotten** are formed from **get.**

gey ser (gī′zər), a hot spring that sends up fountains or jets of hot water or steam.

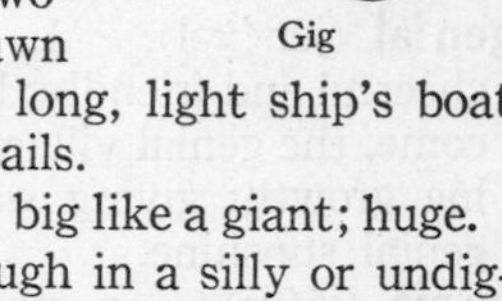
Geyser

ghast ly (gast′li), 1. horrible. Murder is a ghastly crime. 2. like a dead person or ghost; deathly pale. A very sick person looks ghastly. 3. in a ghastly manner.

ghost (gōst), the spirit of one who is dead appearing to the living. The ghost of the murdered man haunted the house.

ghost ly (gōst′li), 1. like a ghost. A ghostly form walked across the stage. 2. spiritual.

gi ant (jī′ənt), 1. a man of great size or very great power. 2. huge; as, a giant potato.

gib bet (jib′it), 1. an upright post with a projecting arm at the top, from which the bodies of criminals were hung after they were killed. 2. hang on a gibbet. 3. gallows.

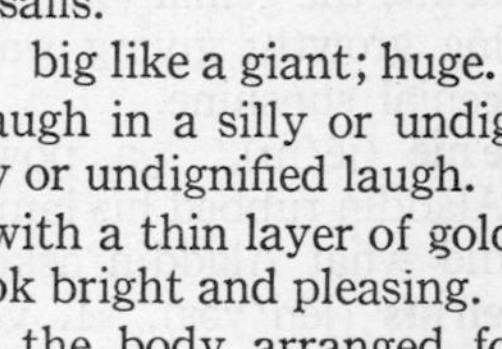
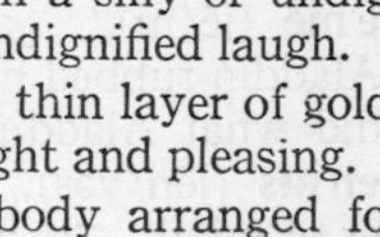
Gibbet

gib bon (gib′ən), a small, long-armed ape of southeastern Asia and the East Indies that lives in trees. See the picture in the first column.

gibe (jīb), jeer; scoff; sneer.

gid dy (gid′i), 1. dizzy; having a whirling in the head. It makes me giddy to go on a merry-go-round. 2. making dizzy; as, a giddy dance. 3. never serious; living for the pleasure of the moment; in a whirl. Nobody can tell what the giddy girl will do next.

gift (gift), 1. something given; a present; as, the gift of a thousand dollars to a church. 2. giving. The house came to him by gift from an uncle. 3. natural talent; special ability; as, a gift for painting.

gift ed (gif′tid), very able; having special ability. Beethoven was gifted in music.

gig (gig), 1. a light, two-wheeled carriage drawn by one horse. 2. a long, light ship's boat moved by oars or by sails.

Gig

gi gan tic (jī gan′tik), big like a giant; huge.

gig gle (gig′əl), 1. laugh in a silly or undignified way. 2. a silly or undignified laugh.

gild (gild), 1. cover with a thin layer of gold. 2. make (a thing) look bright and pleasing.

gill[1] (gil), a part of the body arranged for breathing in water. Fish, tadpoles, and crabs have gills.

gill[2] (jil), a small liquid measure, one quarter of a pint. A gill is about half a cup.

gilt (gilt), 1. gilded. 2. material with which a surface is gilded. The gilt is coming off from this frame.

gin[1] (jin), strong alcoholic drink, usually flavored with juniper berries.

gin[2] (jin), 1. a machine for separating cotton from its seeds. 2. separate (cotton) from its seeds.

gin ger (jin′jər), 1. spice made from the root of a tropical plant. It is used for flavoring and in medicine. 2. the root. Ginger is often preserved in syrup or candied. 3. the plant. 4. liveliness; energy.

gin ger bread (jin′jər bred′), 1. a kind of cake flavored with ginger. Gingerbread is often made in fancy shapes to please children. 2. showy; gaudy. The porch of that old house has too much gingerbread ornament.

ging ham (ging′əm), a cotton cloth made from colored threads. The patterns are usually in stripes, plaids, and checks.

gip sy (jip′si), gypsy.

gi raffe (jiraf′), a large African animal with a very long neck and legs and a spotted skin. Giraffes are the tallest living animals.

Giraffe (about 18 ft. tall)

gird (gėrd), 1. put a belt around. 2. fasten with a belt or girdle; as, to gird up one's clothes. 3. get ready. The soldiers girded themselves for battle.

gir dle (gėr′dəl), 1. belt. 2. a kind of elastic corset. 3. anything that surrounds; as, a girdle of trees around a pond. 4. put a girdle on or around.

girl (gėrl), 1. female child. 2. young, unmarried woman. 3. female servant. 4. sweetheart.

girl hood (gėrl′hůd), 1. the time of being a girl. 2. girls; as, the girlhood of the nation.

girl ish (gėr′lish), 1. of a girl. 2. like that of a girl. 3. proper for girls.

Girl Scouts, organization for girls that seeks to develop health, character, and a knowledge of homemaking.

girt (gėrt), girded. The knight girt himself for battle.

girth (gėrth), 1. the measure around anything; as, a man of large girth, the girth of a tree. 2. the strap or band that keeps the saddle in place on a horse.

give (giv), 1. hand over as a present without pay. He likes to give books to his friends. 2. pay. He can give as much as three dollars for the wagon. 3. cause by some action of the body. Some boys give hard blows, even in play. 4. produce. This farm gives large crops. Reading gives knowledge. 5. present; offer. This newspaper gives a full story of the game. 6. put forth; utter. He gave a cry of pain. 7. cause; make. Don't give the teacher any trouble. 8. yield to force. The lock gave under hard pushing. 9. a yielding to force. 10. Some special meanings are:

give in, 1. stop fighting and admit defeat. 2. hand in.

give out, 1. send out; put forth. 2. distribute. 3. make known. 4. become used up or worn out.

give up, 1. hand over; surrender. 2. stop having or doing. 3. stop trying. 4. have no more hope for. 5. devote entirely.

gave and **given** are formed from **give.**

giv en (giv′ən), 1. stated. At the given time she arrived. 2. inclined; disposed; as, given to boasting. 3. See **give.** That book was given to me.

giv er (giv′ər), person who gives.

giz zard (giz′ərd), a bird's second stomach, where the food from the first stomach is ground up fine.

gla cial (glā′shəl), icy; of ice; having much ice. During the glacial period, much of the northern hemisphere was covered with great ice sheets.

gla cier (glā′shər), a large mass of ice formed from the snow on high ground and moving very slowly down a mountain side or along a valley.

glad (glad). She is glad to be well again. The glad news made her happy.

glad den (glad′ən), make glad; become glad.

glade (glād), a little open space in a wood or forest.

glad i a tor (glad′i ā′tər), a slave, captive, or paid fighter who fought at the public shows in ancient Rome.

glad i o li (glad′i ō′lī), gladioluses.

glad i o lus (glad′i ō′ləs), a plant with spikes of large, handsome flowers in various colors.

Gladiolus

glad ness (glad′nis), glad feeling; happiness; joy.

glam our or **glam or** (glam′ər), magic; charm. The moon cast a glamour over the garden.

glance (glans), 1. a quick look. 2. look quickly. 3. a flash of light; gleam. 4. hit and go off at a slant. The spear glanced against the wall and missed him by a few inches.

gland (gland), an organ in the body which makes and gives out some substance. Glands make the liquid which moistens the mouth. A cow has glands which make milk.

glare (glãr), 1. a strong, unpleasant light; a light that shines so brightly that it hurts the eyes. 2. shine strongly or unpleasantly; shine so as to hurt the eyes. 3. a fierce, angry stare. 4. stare fiercely and with anger.

glar ing (glãr′ing), 1. very bright; shining so brightly that it hurts the eyes; dazzling. 2. staring fiercely and angrily. 3. too bright and showy. 4. very easily seen; conspicuous.

glass (glas), 1. a hard substance that breaks easily and can usually be seen through. Windows are made of glass. 2. thing or things made of glass. This shop sells china and glass. 3. something to drink from made of glass. 4. the amount a glass can hold. Drink a glass of water. 5. mirror. Look at yourself in the glass. 6. **Glasses** often means eyeglasses. 7. made of glass; as, a glass dish. 8. cover or protect with glass.

glass y (glas′i), 1. like glass; smooth; easily seen through. 2. having a fixed, stupid stare.

glaze (glāz), 1. put glass in; cover with glass; as, to glaze a window or a picture. 2. a smooth, glossy surface or coating; as, the glaze on a china cup, a glaze of ice on the walk. 3. make a glossy or glassy surface on (vases, dishes, foods, etc.). 4. become glossy or glassy. The man's eyes were glazed in death.

gleam (glēm), 1. a flash or beam of light. 2. send forth a gleam; shine. 3. short appearance. After one gleam of hope, all was discouraging and dark.

glean (glēn), 1. gather stalks of grain left on the field by reapers. 2. gather little by little.

glee (glē), 1. joy; delight; mirth. 2. a song for three or more voices carrying different parts.

glee ful (glē′fəl), merry; joyous.

glen (glen), a small, narrow valley.

glib (glib), 1. speaking or spoken smoothly and easily. A glib salesman sold her a set of dishes that she did not want. 2. speaking or spoken too smoothly and easily to be sincere. No one believed his glib excuses.

glide (glīd), 1. move along smoothly, evenly, and easily. Birds, ships, dancers, and skaters glide. 2. smooth, even, easy movement.

glid er (glīd′ər), airplane without a motor. Rising air currents keep a glider up in the air.

glim mer (glim′ər), 1. faint, unsteady light. 2. shine with a faint, unsteady light. The match glimmered and went out. 3. faint glimpse. The doctor's report gave us only a glimmer of hope.

glimpse (glimps), 1. a very brief view; a short look. I got a glimpse of the falls as our train went by. 2. catch a brief view of. I glimpsed her dress as she went by.

glint (glint), gleam; flash.

glis ten (glis′ən), sparkle; glitter; shine.

glit ter (glit′ər), 1. sparkle; seem to have shining bits in it. 2. shine with a bright, sparkling light. Jewels and new coins glitter. 3. bright, sparkling light. 4. be bright and showy. 5. brightness; bright display.

gloat (glōt), gaze or think about intently and with satisfaction. The miser gloated over his gold.

globe (glōb), 1. anything that is round like a ball. 2. the earth; world. 3. a sphere with a map of the earth on it.

Globe (def. 3)

gloom (glüm), 1. darkness; deep shadow; dim light. 2. dark thoughts and feelings; low spirits; sadness.

gloom y (glüm′i), 1. dark; dim. 2. sad; melancholy. 3. dismal; causing gloom. A rainy night is gloomier than a sunny day.

glo ri fy (glō′ri fī), 1. give glory to; make glorious. 2. to worship; to praise. We sing hymns to glorify God. 3. make more beautiful or splendid. Sunset glorified the valley.

glo ri ous (glō′ri əs), 1. having or deserving glory. 2. giving glory. 3. magnificent; splendid.

glo ry (glō′ri), 1. great praise and honor; fame. 2. something that brings praise and honor. 3. be proud; rejoice. 4. brightness; splendor. 5. condition of magnificence, splendor, or greatest prosperity. 6. heaven. **glories, gloried,** and **glorying** are formed from **glory.**

gloss (glôs), 1. a smooth, shiny surface on anything. Varnished furniture has a gloss. 2. put a smooth, shiny surface on. 3. **Gloss** (a thing) **over** means smooth it over or make it seem right even though it is really wrong.

gloss y (glôs′i), smooth and shiny.

glove (gluv), 1. a covering for the hand with separate places for each finger. 2. cover with a glove.

glow (glō), 1. the shine from something that is red-hot or white-hot; a similar shine without heat. 2. shine as if red-hot or white-hot. 3. a bright, warm color; as, the glow of sunset. 4. the warm feeling or color of the body; as, the glow of health on his cheeks. 5. show a warm color; look warm. 6. look eager. His face glowed at the idea.

glow er (glou′ər), stare; scowl. The sullen boy glowered at his father.

glue (glü), 1. substance made from the hoofs of animals and used to stick pieces of wood together. 2. any similar substance. Glues are stronger than pastes. 3. stick together with glue. 4. fasten tightly. He glued his eyes to the windows.

glum (glum), gloomy; dismal; sullen.

glut ton (glut′ən), greedy eater.

gnash (nash), strike together. Angry animals often gnash their teeth.

gnat (nat), a small, two-winged insect or fly. Most gnats make bites that itch.

Gnat. Line shows actual length.

gnaw (nô), bite at and wear away. A mouse has gnawed right through the cover of this box.

go (gō). Cars go on the road. The wheels go round. Does your watch go well? His work is going well. We will go over the lesson. Summer had gone. All my money is gone. Bacon and eggs go together. Let the poor kid go. Let go. I go by what the book says. **gone** is formed from **go.**

goad (gōd), 1. stick for driving cattle that has a point on the end. 2. anything that drives or urges one on. 3. drive or urge on; act as a goad to. Hunger goaded him to steal a loaf of bread.

goal (gōl), 1. place reached at the end of a race. 2. something desired. The goal of his ambition was to be captain of the ball team. 3. place which players try to reach in games. 4. points won by reaching this place.

goat (gōt), a small lively animal with horns. Goats are stronger, less timid, and more active than sheep.

Goat

gob ble[1] (gob′əl), eat fast and greedily.

gob ble[2] (gob′əl), 1. the noise a turkey makes. 2. make this noise or one like it.

gob bler (gob′lər), a male turkey.

go-be tween (gō′bi twēn′), person who goes back and forth between others with messages, proposals, suggestions, etc.

gob let (gob′lit), a drinking glass that stands high above its base on a stem, and has no handle.

Goblet

gob lin (gob′lin), a mischievous spirit or elf in the form of an ugly-looking little man.

God (god), the maker and ruler of the world; a being that loves and helps man.

god (god), a being with greater powers than any man has.

god dess (god′is), 1. a female god. 2. a very beautiful or wonderful woman.

god fa ther (god′fä′ᴛʜər), man who takes vows for a child when it is baptized. The godfather promises to help the child to be a good Christian.

god like (god′līk′), 1. like God or a god. 2. suitable for God or a god.

god ly (god′li), religious; pious; obeying, loving, and fearing God.

god moth er (god′muᴛʜ′ər), woman who takes vows for a child when it is baptized.

goes (gōz). See **go.** He goes to school.

go ing (gō′ing), 1. leaving. His going was very sudden. 2. moving; in action. Set the clock going. 3. condition of the roads. The going is bad through this muddy road. 4. that goes; that can or will go.

gold (gōld), 1. a heavy, bright-yellow, precious metal. Gold is used in making coins, watches, and rings. 2. money in large sums. 3. made of gold. 4. bright yellow.

gold en (gōl′dən), 1. made of gold; as, golden dishes. 2. containing gold. 3. shining like gold; bright-yellow; as, golden hair. 4. very good; as, a golden age, golden deeds. 5. very happy; flourishing.

gold en rod (gōl′dən rod′), a common fall plant with tall stalks of small yellow flowers.

Goldenrod

gold smith (gōld′smith′), man who makes articles of gold.

golf (golf), 1. an outdoor game played by hitting a small, hard ball with certain kinds of clubs or sticks. The player tries to drive the ball into a number of holes with as few strokes as possible. 2. play this game.

gon do la (gon′də lə), 1. a long, narrow boat with a high peak at each end, used on the canals of Venice. 2. freight car that has low sides and no top. 3. car that hangs under a dirigible and holds the motors, passengers, etc.

Gondola

gone (gôn), 1. moved away; left. 2. lost. 3. dead. 4. used up; consumed. 5. failed. 6. weak; faint. 7. See **go.**

gong (gông), piece of metal shaped like a bowl or a saucer which makes a loud noise when struck. A gong is a kind of bell.

good (gu̇d), 1. excellent. 2. behaving well. 3. right; as it ought to be. 4. desirable. 5. satisfying. 6. pleasant. 7. kind; friendly. Say a good word for me. 8. real; genuine. 9. that which is good. 10. benefit. What good will it do? 11. Some special meanings are:

as good as, almost; practically.

for good, forever; finally; permanently.

make good, 1. make up for; pay for. 2. fulfill; carry out. 3. succeed.

good-by or **good-bye** (gu̇d′bī′), farewell. We say "Good-by" to a friend when he goes away.

good day, words of greeting or farewell.

Good Friday, the Friday before Easter.

good ly (gu̇d′li), 1. pleasant; as, a goodly land. 2. good-looking; as, a goodly youth. 3. considerable; as, a goodly quantity.

good-na tured (gu̇d′nā′chərd), pleasant; kindly; obliging; cheerful.

good ness (gu̇d′nis), 1. being good; kindness. 2. **Goodness me** and **Goodness gracious** are used to express surprise.

goods (gu̇dz), 1. belongings. He gave half of his goods to the poor. 2. wares; thing or things for sale.

good-sized (gu̇d′sīzd′), large; somewhat large.

good-tem pered (gu̇d′tem′pərd), easy to get along with; cheerful; agreeable.

good will, 1. kindly feeling; friendly attitude. 2. the standing a business has with its customers.

Wild goose

good y (gu̇d′i), 1. something very good to eat; a piece of candy or cake. 2. an exclamation of pleasure. Are we going? Oh, goody!

goose (güs), 1. a tame or wild bird like a duck, but larger and with a longer neck. See the picture above. 2. female goose. 3. flesh of a goose used for food. 4. silly person.

Gooseberries

goose ber ry (güz′ber′i), 1. small, sour berry somewhat like a currant but larger. Gooseberries are used to make pies, tarts, jam, etc. 2. a thorny bush that it grows on.

go pher (gō′fər), 1. a ratlike animal of North America with large cheek pouches. Gophers dig holes in the ground. See the picture below. 2. a ground squirrel.

gore[1] (gōr), blood that is spilled; thick blood. The battlefield was covered with gore.

gore[2] (gōr), wound with a horn or tusk. The savage bull gored the farmer to death.

Gopher (about 9 in. long with the tail)

gore[3] (gōr), 1. a long, three-sided piece in a skirt, sail, etc. 2. piece that tapers.

gorge (gôrj), 1. a deep, narrow valley, usually steep and rocky. 2. eat greedily until full. Don't gorge yourself.

Gorge

gor geous (gôr′jəs), richly colored; splendid. The peacock spread his gorgeous tail. The gorgeous sunset thrilled us all.

Gor gon (gôr′gən), one of three horrible sisters who had snakes for hair, and whose look turned the beholder to stone.

go ril la (gə ril′ə), the largest kind of ape.

gor y (gōr′i), bloody.

gos ling (goz′ling), a young goose.

Gorilla (standing height of male 6 ft.)

gos pel (gos′pəl), 1. teachings of Jesus and the apostles. 2. anything earnestly believed. Drink plenty of water; that is my gospel. 3. absolute truth. They take her words for gospel.

gos sa mer (gos′ə mər), 1. film or thread of cobweb. 2. any very thin, light cloth or substance. 3. thin and light.

gos sip (gos′ip), 1. idle talk, not always true, about other people and their affairs. 2. repeat what one knows or hears about other people and their affairs. 3. person who gossips a good deal.

got (got). See **get.** We got the letter yesterday. We had got tired of waiting for it.

got ten (got′ən). See **get.** It has gotten to be quite late.

Gouge

gouge (gouj), 1. chisel with a curved blade. 2. cut with a gouge; dig out. 3. groove or hole made by gouging.

gourd (gōrd), 1. the fruit of a plant whose dried shell is used for bottles, bowls, etc. 2. the plant itself. 3. a bottle, bowl, etc., made from such a dried shell.

gov ern (guv′ərn), rule; control; manage.

gov ern a ble (guv′ər nə bəl), that can be governed.

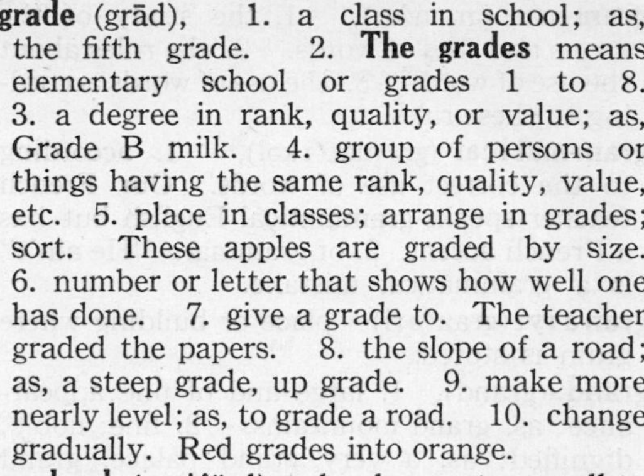

Gourds

gov ern ess (guv′ər nis), woman who teaches children in a private home.

gov ern ment (guv′ərn mənt), 1. the ruling of a country. 2. the person or persons ruling a country at any time. 3. system of ruling. 4. rule; control.

gov er nor (guv′ər nər), 1. man who rules. 2. ruler of a State or province. 3. the executive head of a State. The Governor of New York carries out the laws made by the State legislature. 4. a device arranged to keep a machine going at an even speed.

gown (goun), 1. woman's dress. 2. a loose outer robe worn by college graduates, lawyers, and others. 3. nightgown.

Gown of college graduate

grab (grab), 1. snatch; seize suddenly. The dog grabbed the meat and ran. 2. a snatching; a sudden seizing.

grace (grās), 1. pleasing or agreeable quality; beauty of form or movement. 2. willingness; as, to obey with good grace or bad grace. 3. favor; as, to be in a person's good graces or bad graces. 4. favor and love of God. 5. a short prayer of thanks given before or after a meal. 6. behavior put on to seem attractive. Mary came home from boarding school with little airs and graces. 7. a title of a duke, duchess, or archbishop. May I assist **Your Grace?** 8. give grace or honor to. Will you grace our party with your presence?

grace ful (grās′fəl), beautiful in form or movement; pleasing; agreeable; as, a graceful white birch tree, the graceful turn of a swan's neck, a graceful dance, a graceful speech of thanks.

gra cious (grā′shəs), 1. pleasant and kindly. Mrs. Brown received her guests in a gracious manner which made them feel at ease. 2. pleasant and kindly to people of lower social position. The queen greeted her with a gracious smile.

grade (grād), 1. a class in school; as, the fifth grade. 2. **The grades** means elementary school or grades 1 to 8. 3. a degree in rank, quality, or value; as, Grade B milk. 4. group of persons or things having the same rank, quality, value, etc. 5. place in classes; arrange in grades; sort. These apples are graded by size. 6. number or letter that shows how well one has done. 7. give a grade to. The teacher graded the papers. 8. the slope of a road; as, a steep grade, up grade. 9. make more nearly level; as, to grade a road. 10. change gradually. Red grades into orange.

grad u al (graj′ü əl), by degrees too small to be separately noticed; little by little.

grad u al ly (graj′ü əl i), by degrees; little by little.

grad u ate (graj′ü āt), 1. finish the course of a school or college and be given a diploma or paper saying so. 2. person who has graduated and has a diploma. 3. mark out in equal spaces. A ruler is graduated in inches. A measuring cup is graduated in quarters and thirds.

grad u a tion (graj′ü ā′shən), 1. graduating from a school or college. 2. graduating exercises.

graft (graft), 1. a shoot from one tree or plant fixed in a slit in another tree or plant, to grow there as a part of it. A graft from a fine apple tree may be put on a worthless one to improve it. 2. make a graft; put (a shoot) from one plant into another.

Grafting

gra ham (grā′əm), made from wheat flour that has not been sifted; as, graham crackers.

Grail (grāl), the cup supposed to have been used by Christ at the Last Supper, and to contain the last drop of blood from Christ's body on the cross.

grain (grān), 1. the seed of plants like wheat, oats, and corn. 2. one of the tiny bits of which sand, sugar, salt, etc., are made up. 3. a very small weight. A pound equals 7000 grains. 4. the little lines and markings in wood, marble, etc. 5. the arrangement of the particles of anything. Mahogany has a fine grain. 6. character. **Against the grain** means contrary to nature.

gram or **gramme** (gram), a unit of weight in the metric system. Twenty-eight grams weigh about one ounce.

gram mar (gram′ər), 1. the study of the forms and uses of words. 2. the rules about the use of words. 3. the use of words according to these rules.

gram mat i cal (grə mat′i kəl), 1. according to the correct use of words. Our French teacher speaks grammatical English but has a French accent. 2. of grammar. "He ain't" is a grammatical mistake.

gran a ry (gran′ə ri) place or building where grain is stored.

grand (grand), 1. large and of fine appearance; as, grand mountains. 2. fine; noble; dignified; as, a very grand palace, grand music, a grand old man. 3. highest or very high in rank; chief; as, a grand duke. 4. great; important; main; as, the grand staircase. 5. complete; comprehensive; as, grand total. 6. very satisfactory.

grand child (grand′chīld′), child of one's son or daughter.

grand chil dren (grand′chil′drən), more than one grandchild.

grand daugh ter (grand′dô′tər), daughter of one's son or daughter.

gran deur (gran′jər), greatness; majesty; nobility; dignity; splendor. The grandeur of Niagara Falls is famous.

grand fa ther (grand′fä′ᴛʜər), 1. father of one's father or mother. 2. any forefather.

grand ma (grand′mä′), grandmother.

grand moth er (grand′muᴛʜ′ər), mother of one's mother or father.

grand pa (grand′pä′), grandfather.

grand par ent (grand′pãr′ənt), grandfather or grandmother.

grand son (grand′sun′), son of one's son or daughter.

grange (grānj), 1. farm with its buildings. 2. an association of farmers.

gran ite (gran′it), a very hard rock, used for buildings, monuments, etc. Granite is usually gray.

gran ny (gran′i), 1. grandmother. 2. old woman.

grant (grant), 1. allow; give what is asked; as, to grant a request. 2. admit. I grant that you are right so far. 3. **Take for granted** means accept as agreed to. 4. a gift; especially, land or rights given by the government.

grape (grāp), 1. a small, round fruit, red, purple, or pale-green, that grows in bunches on a vine. Grapes are eaten, or made into raisins or wine. 2. grapevine.

grape fruit (grāp′früt′), a pale-yellow fruit like an orange, but larger and sourer.

grape vine (grāp′vīn′), vine that bears grapes.

Grapes

graph ic (graf′ik), 1. lifelike; vivid. The returned soldier gave a graphic account of a battle. 2. of or about diagrams and their use; as, a graphic record of school attendance for a month. 3. of or about drawing, painting, engraving, etc.; as, the graphic arts.

graph ite (graf′īt), a soft, black form of carbon used for lead in pencils and for greasing machinery.

Grappling iron

grap ple (grap′əl), 1. seize and hold fast; grip or hold firmly. 2. a seizing and holding fast; firm grip or hold. 3. struggle; fight. 4. A **grappling iron** is an iron bar with hooks at one end for seizing and holding something.

grasp (grasp), 1. seize; hold fast by closing the fingers around. 2. seizing and holding tightly; clasp of the hand. 3. **Grasp at** means try to grasp; try to take hold of. 4. power of seizing and holding; reach. 5. control; possession. 6. understand. 7. understanding. She has a good grasp of arithmetic.

grass (gras), 1. the green blades that cover fields and lawns. 2. land covered with grass; pasture. 3. a plant that has jointed stems and long, narrow leaves. Wheat, corn, and sugar cane are grasses.

grass hop per (gras′hop′ər), an insect with strong legs and wings for jumping.

Grasshopper (2 to 3 in. long)

grass y (gras′i), 1. covered with grass; having much grass. 2. of grass. 3. like grass.

grate[1] (grāt), 1. a framework of iron to hold a fire. 2. iron bars, such as those over a prison window. 3. furnish with iron bars.

Grate for an open fire

grate[2] (grāt), 1. have an annoying or unpleasant effect. Her manners grate on me. 2. rub with a harsh sound. The door grated on its old hinges. 3. wear down or grind off in small pieces; as, to grate cheese.

grate ful (grāt′fəl), 1. feeling gratitude; thankful. Dogs seem more grateful than cats. 2. pleasing; welcome. A breeze is grateful on a hot day, a fire on a cold one.

grate ful ly (grāt′fəl i), with gratitude; with thanks.

grat i fi ca tion (grat′i fi kā′shən), 1. gratifying. The gratification of every wish of every person is not possible. 2. something that pleases or satisfies. John's success was a great gratification to his parents.

grat i fy (grat′i fī), 1. please; give pleasure to. Praise gratifies most people. 2. give satisfaction to. A drunkard gratifies his craving for liquor.

grat ing[1] (grāt′ing), grate; a framework of parallel or crossed bars.

Grating

grat ing[2] (grāt′ing), 1. irritating; unpleasant. 2. harsh or jarring in sound.

grat i tude (grat′i tūd or grat′i tüd), thankfulness; kindly feeling because of a favor received; desire to do a favor in return.

grave[1] (grāv), 1. hole dug in the ground where a dead body is to be buried. 2. any place of burial; as, a watery grave. 3. death.

grave[2] (grāv), 1. earnest; thoughtful; serious; as, grave words, a grave situation. 2. dignified; slow-moving; not gay; as, grave music. 3. important; as, a grave decision.

grav el (grav′əl), 1. pebbles and rock fragments coarser than sand. Gravel is much used for roads and walks. 2. cover with gravel.

grav i ty (grav′i ti), 1. natural force that causes objects to move or tend to move toward the center of the earth. 2. natural force that makes objects move or tend to move toward each other. 3. heaviness; weight. He balanced the long pole at its center of gravity. 4. seriousness. The gravity of the child playing nurse was amusing in one so small. 5. importance. The gravity of the situation was greatly increased by threats of war.

gra vy (grā′vi), 1. the juice that comes out of meat in cooking. 2. a sauce for meat, potatoes, etc., made from this juice.

gray (grā), 1. any shade obtained by mixing black and white. 2. having a shade between black and white. Ashes, lead, and hair getting white with age are gray. 3. become gray; make gray.

graze[1] (grāz), 1. feed on growing grass. Cattle were grazing in the field. 2. put (cattle, sheep, etc.) to feed on growing grass.

graze[2] (grāz), 1. touch lightly in passing; rub lightly against. The car grazed the garage door. 2. scrape the skin from. The bullet grazed his shoulder. 3. a grazing.

grease (grēs), 1. soft animal fat. 2. any thick, oily substance. 3. rub grease on. 4. put grease or oil on. Indians greased their bodies.

greas y (grēs′i), 1. containing much grease; oily. 2. having grease on it. 3. like grease; smooth; slippery.

great (grāt), 1. big; large. 2. much; more than is usual; as, great pain, great kindness. 3. important; high in rank; remarkable; as, a great singer, a great event, a great picture.

Great Brit ain (grāt′ brit′ən), England, Scotland, and Wales.

great coat (grāt′kōt′), heavy overcoat.

great ly (grāt′li), 1. in a great manner. Solomon ruled greatly and wisely. 2. much; as, greatly feared.

great ness (grāt′nis), 1. being great; bigness. 2. high place or power. 3. great mind or character.

Greece (grēs), a small country in southeastern Europe.

greed (grēd), wanting more than one's share; as, a miser's greed for money.

greed i ly (grēd′i li), in a greedy manner; like a pig.

greed y (grēd′i), 1. wanting to get more than one's share. 2. wanting to get a great deal. 3. wanting to eat a great deal in a hurry.

Greek (grēk), 1. person born in Greece, living there, or having Greek parents. 2. the language of Greece. 3. of Greece, its people, or their language.

green (grēn), 1. the color of most growing plants, grass, and the leaves of trees in summer. 2. having this color; of this color. 3. not ripe; not fully grown. Green fruit is not good to eat. 4. not trained. He was a green boy in business. 5. ground covered with grass. 6. **Greens** sometimes means (1) green leaves and branches used for decoration. (2) leaves and stems of plants used for food.

green horn (grēn′hôrn′), 1. person without experience. 2. person easy to trick or cheat.

green house (grēn′hous′), building with a glass roof and glass sides kept warm for growing plants; hothouse.

green ish (grēn′ish), somewhat green.

green sward (grēn′swôrd′), green grass; turf.

green wood (grēn′wu̇d′), forest in spring and summer when the trees are green with leaves.

greet (grēt), 1. say "Hello," "How do you do," "Welcome," etc., to; address in welcome; hail. 2. respond to. His speech was greeted with cheers. 3. meet; present itself to. When she opened the door, a strange sight greeted her eyes.

greet ing (grēt′ing), the act or words of a person who greets somebody; welcome.

Grenadier of the 18th century blowing fuse to light a grenade

gre nade (gri nād′), a small bomb. The soldiers threw grenades into the enemy's trenches.

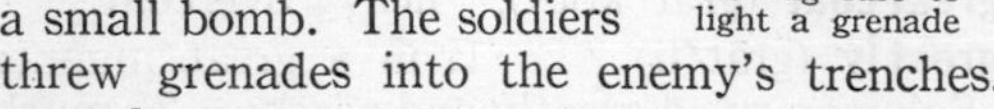

gren a dier (gren′ə dēr′), 1. a soldier who threw grenades. See the picture above. 2. a very tall soldier who fought on foot.

grew (grü). See **grow.** It grew cold last night.

grey (grā), gray.

Greyhound (about 28 in. high at the shoulder)

grey hound (grā′hound′), a tall, slender hunting dog with a long nose. Greyhounds can run very fast.

grid dle (grid′əl), a heavy, flat plate on which to cook buckwheat cakes, etc.

grid i ron (grid′ī′ərn), a utensil with parallel bars for broiling.

Gridiron

grief (grēf), heavy sorrow; deep sorrow; that which causes sorrow. **Come to grief** means have trouble; fail.

griev ance (grēv′əns), a real or imagined wrong; reason for being annoyed or angry. The captain told his men to report any grievances to him.

grieve (grēv), 1. feel grief; be very sad. 2. cause to feel grief; make sad.

griev ous (grēv′əs), 1. hard to bear; causing great pain or suffering; severe; as, grievous cruelty. 2. outrageous. Wasting food when people are starving is a grievous wrong. 3. causing grief. 4. full of grief; showing grief; as, a grievous cry.

grill (gril), 1. gridiron. 2. to broil; cook by holding near the fire. 3. a dish of broiled meat, fish, etc. 4. a dining room in a hotel or restaurant, especially one specializing in serving broiled meat, fish, etc. 5. to torture with heat. 6. question severely and persistently. The detectives grilled the prisoner until he finally confessed.

grim (grim), 1. stern; harsh; fierce; without mercy. 2. not yielding; not relenting. 3. looking stern, fierce, or harsh. Father was grim when he heard about the six broken windows. 4. horrible; frightful; ghastly. He made grim jokes about death and ghosts.

gri mace (gri mās′), 1. a twisting of the face; an ugly or funny smile. 2. make faces. The clown grimaced at the children.

grime (grīm), 1. dirt rubbed deeply and firmly into a surface; as, the grime on a coal miner's hands. 2. make very dirty.

grim y (grīm′i), covered with grime; very dirty.

grin (grin), 1. smile broadly. 2. broad smile. 3. draw back the lips and show the teeth.

grind (grīnd), 1. crush into bits, into meal, or into powder. A mill grinds corn. Our teeth grind meat. 2. crush by harsh rule. The slaves were ground down by their masters. 3. sharpen or smooth by rubbing on something rough. He ground the ax on the grindstone. 4. work by turning a handle. He grinds out music from a street organ. 5. rub harshly together; as, to grind one's heel into the earth, to grind one's teeth. **ground**[2] is formed from **grind.**

grind stone (grīnd′stōn′), flat, round stone set in a frame and turned by hand, foot, or a motor. It is used to sharpen tools, or to smooth and polish things.

Man using a grindstone

grip (grip), 1. seizing and holding tight; a tight grasp; a firm hold. 2. seize and hold tight; take a firm hold on. The dog gripped the stick. 3. a certain way of gripping the hand as a sign of belonging to some secret society. 4. a handle. 5. a small suitcase or handbag. 6. control. 7. understanding.

grist (grist), 1. grain to be ground. 2. grain that has been ground; meal or flour.

grit (grit), 1. very fine gravel or sand. 2. coarse sandstone. 3. pluck; endurance; courage. 4. grind; make a grating sound by holding closed and rubbing. He grits his teeth.

griz zled (griz′əld), grayish; gray.

griz zly (griz′li), 1. gray. 2. a large, fierce bear of western North America.

groan (grōn), 1. a sound made down in the throat that expresses grief, pain, or disapproval; a deep, short moan. 2. give a groan or groans. 3. be loaded or burdened. The table groaned with food.

Grizzly bear (about 8 ft. long)

gro cer (grō′sər), person who sells tea, coffee, sugar, flour, fruits, spices, and other articles of food.

gro cer y (grō′sər i), 1. grocer's shop. 2. **Groceries** sometimes means articles of food sold by a grocer.

groom (grüm), 1. man who is a servant; man or boy who has charge of horses. 2. feed and take care of (horses); rub down and brush. 3. take care of the appearance of; make neat and tidy; as, a well-groomed person. 4. bridegroom.

groove (grüv), 1. a long, narrow channel or furrow cut by a tool. My desk has a groove for pencils. The plate rests in a groove on the rack. 2. any similar channel; a rut. Wheels leave grooves in a dirt road. 3. make a groove in. The sink shelf is grooved so that the water will run off. 4. fixed way of doing things. It is hard to get out of a groove.

grope (grōp), 1. feel about with the hands. He groped for a match when the lights went out. 2. search here and there rather blindly. The detectives groped for some clue to the murder. 3. find by feeling about with the hands; feel (one's way) slowly. The blind man groped his way to the door.

gross (grōs), 1. whole; entire; with nothing taken out; total. Gross receipts are all the money taken in. 2. the total amount. 3. twelve dozen; 144. 4. very bad; easy to see. She makes gross errors in pronouncing words. 5. coarse; vulgar. Her manners are too gross for a lady. 6. too big; too fat; fed too much. 7. thick; heavy; dense; as, the gross growth of a jungle.

gro tesque (grō tesk′), 1. queer; odd or unnatural in shape, appearance, manner, etc. The book had pictures of hideous dragons and other grotesque monsters. 2. ridiculous; absurd. The monkey's grotesque antics made the children laugh.

grot to (grot′ō), 1. cave. 2. an artificial cave made for coolness or pleasure.

ground[1] (ground), 1. the surface of the earth; soil. 2. any piece of land or region used for some purpose. The West was his favorite hunting ground. 3. of the ground; on the ground; as, the ground floor of a building. 4. put on the ground; cause to touch the ground. 5. run aground. The ship was grounded in shallow water. 6. foundation for what is said or done; basis; reason. There is no ground for complaining of his conduct. On what ground do you say that is true? 7. fix firmly; establish. This class is well grounded in arithmetic. 8. background. The pattern was red on a gray ground. 9. connect (an electric wire) with the ground. 10. Some special meanings are:

give ground, retreat; yield.

grounds, 1. land, lawns, and gardens around a house. 2. small bits that sink to the bottom of a drink such as coffee or tea; sediment.

lose ground, retreat; lose influence.

ground[2] (ground). See **grind.** Wheat is ground to make flour.

ground hog, a woodchuck.

group (grüp), 1. a number of persons or things together. A group of children were playing tag. The statue will be a group of three figures. 2. number of persons or things belonging or classed together. Wheat, rye, and oats belong to the grain group. 3. form into a group. The children grouped themselves in front of the monkey's cage. 4. put in a group.

grouse (grous), game bird with feathered legs. See the picture.

grove (grōv), group of trees standing together. An orange grove is an orchard of orange trees.

Ruffed grouse (about 1½ ft. long)

grov el (gruv′əl), lie face downward; crawl at someone's feet; humble oneself. The dog groveled before his master when he saw the whip.

grow (grō), 1. become bigger; increase. Plants and animals grow by taking in food. His business has grown fast. 2. become. It grew cold. 3. cause to develop; raise. We grow cotton in many parts of the United States. **grew** and **grown** are formed from **grow.**

growl (groul), 1. sound like that made by a fierce dog; a deep, warning snarl. 2. make such a sound. The dog growled at the tramp. 3. grumble; complain about things.

grown (grōn), 1. arrived at full growth. A grown man is an adult. 2. See **grow.** Tom has grown very tall.

grown-up (grōn′up′), 1. arrived at full growth. 2. adult.

growth (grōth), 1. growing; development. 2. amount grown; increase; progress; as, one year's growth. 3. what has grown or is growing; as, a thick growth of bushes.

grub (grub), 1. dig; dig up; root out of the ground. Pigs grub for roots. 2. a smooth, thick, wormlike larva of an insect, especially that of a beetle. 3. to toil. 4. food.

grudge (gruj), 1. ill will; a sullen feeling against; a dislike of long standing. 2. feel ill will at. Bill grudged Dick his prize even though he had won a better prize himself. 3. give unwillingly. The mean man grudged the food his horse ate.

grudg ing ly (gruj′ing li), unwillingly.

gru el (grü′əl), a thin, almost liquid food made by boiling oatmeal, etc., in water or milk. Gruel is often made for persons who are sick or old.

gruff (gruf), rough or harsh in voice or manner; rude.

grum ble (grum′bəl), 1. complain in a rather sullen way; mutter in discontent; find fault. 2. a mutter of discontent; bad-tempered complaint. 3. make a low, heavy sound like far-off thunder.

grunt (grunt), 1. deep, hoarse sound that a hog makes. 2. a sound like this. The old man got out of his chair with a grunt. 3. make this sound. 4. say with this sound. The sullen boy grunted his apology.

guar an tee (gar′ən tē′), 1. a promise to pay or do something if another fails to do it; pledge to replace goods if they are not as represented. 2. person who so promises. 3. stand back of; give a guarantee for. This company guarantees its clocks for a year. 4. undertake to secure for another. He will guarantee us possession of the house by May. 5. secure (against or from). His insurance guaranteed him against money loss in case of fire. 6. pledge to do (something); promise (that) something has been or will be. I will guarantee to prove every statement I made.

guard (gärd), 1. watch over; take care of; keep safe; defend. 2. keep from escaping. 3. that which guards; person who guards; any arrangement to give safety. 4. a position in which one is ready to defend in fencing, boxing, and in some games. 5. careful watch; as, keep guard. **On guard** means ready to defend or protect; watchful. 6. a picked body of soldiers. 7. man who opens and closes the gates or doors on a train. 8. player at either side of the center in football. 9. either of two players defending the goal in basketball.

guard i an (gär′di ən), 1. person who takes care of another or of some special thing. 2. person appointed by law to take care of the affairs of someone who is young or cannot take care of them himself. 3. protecting. My guardian angel must have looked after me then.

guess (ges), 1. an opinion formed without really knowing. My guess is that it will rain tomorrow. 2. form an opinion when one does not know exactly. Let us guess at the height of the tree. 3. get right by guessing; as, to guess a riddle. 4. think; believe; suppose. I guess he is really sick after all.

guest (gest), 1. visitor; person who is received and entertained at another's house or table. 2. person who is living at a hotel, etc.

guid ance (gīd′əns), guiding; direction; leadership. Under her mother's guidance, Nan learned how to cook.

guide (gīd), 1. show the way; lead; direct. 2. person or thing that shows the way. Tourists and hunters sometimes hire guides. Your feelings are often a poor guide for actions and beliefs. 3. guidebook.

guide book (gīd′bu̇k′), book of directions and information for travelers.

guild (gild), 1. society for mutual aid or for some common purpose; as, the Ladies' Auxiliary Guild of a church. 2. a union of the men in one trade to keep standards high, and to look out for the interests of their trade.

guile (gīl), crafty deceit; cunning; crafty behavior; sly tricks. By guile the fox got the cheese from the crow.

guil lo tine (gil′ə tēn), machine for cutting off people's heads by a heavy blade that slides up and down in grooves made in two posts.

Guillotine

guilt (gilt), fact or state of having done wrong; being guilty; being to blame.

guilt less (gilt′lis), not guilty; innocent.

guilt y (gil′ti), 1. having done wrong; deserving to be blamed and punished. The jury pronounced the prisoner guilty of murder. 2. knowing or showing that one has done wrong. The one who did the crime had a guilty conscience and a guilty look.

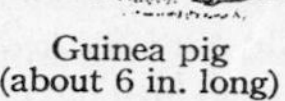

Guinea pig (about 6 in. long)

guin ea pig (gin′i pig′), a short-eared, short-tailed animal like a big, fat, harmless rat.

guise (gīz), 1. style of dress; garb. The soldier went in the guise of a monk and was not recognized. 2. appearance. 3. feigned appearance. Fred deceived the enemy by his guise of ignorance and dullness.

gui tar (gi tär′), a musical instrument with six strings, played with the fingers.

Man playing a guitar

gulch (gulch), a very deep, narrow valley.

gulf (gulf), 1. a large bay; an arm of water extending into the land. The Gulf of Mexico is between Florida and Mexico. 2. a very deep break or cut in the earth. 3. wide separation. The quarrel created a gulf between the old friends.

gull[1] (gul), graceful gray-and-white bird living on or near large bodies of water. A gull has long wings, webbed feet, and a thick, strong beak.

Gull (about 18 in. long)

gull[2] (gul), 1. deceive; cheat. 2. person who is easily deceived or cheated.

gul ly (gul′i), narrow gorge; little steep valley; ditch made by heavy rains.

gulp (gulp), 1. swallow eagerly or greedily. 2. act of swallowing. 3. amount swallowed at one time; mouthful. 4. keep in; choke back; repress. The disappointed boy gulped down a sob. 5. gasp; choke.

gum[1] (gum), 1. the sticky juice of trees which is used for sticking paper and other things together. 2. a tree that yields gum. 3. gum prepared for chewing. 4. stick together with gum. 5. become sticky. Jack's pocket is all gummed up with candy.

gum[2] (gum), the flesh around the teeth.

gun (gun), 1. weapon with a metal tube for shooting bullets, shot, etc. A rifle or cannon is a gun. Pistols and revolvers are called guns in ordinary talk. 2. anything resembling a gun in use or shape. 3. shooting of a gun as a signal or salute. The President gets twenty-one guns as a salute. 4. shoot with a gun: hunt with a gun. Bill went gunning for rabbits.

gun boat (gun′bōt′), small warship that can be used in shallow water.

gun lock (gun′lok′), the part of a gun that controls the hammer and fires the charge.

gun ner (gun′ər), 1. man trained to fire artillery; soldier who handles and fires cannon. 2. navy officer in charge of a ship's guns. 3. person who hunts with a gun.

gun pow der (gun′pou′dər), a powder that goes off with noise and force when touched with fire. Gunpowder is used in firearms, blasting, and fireworks.

gun wale (gun′əl), the upper edge of a ship's or boat's side.

GUNWALE

gur gle (gėr′gəl), 1. flow or run with a bubbling sound. Water gurgles when it is poured out of a bottle or flows among stones. 2. a bubbling sound. 3. make a bubbling sound. The baby gurgled happily.

gush (gush), 1. a rush of water or other liquid from an enclosed space. If you get a deep cut, there usually is a gush of blood. 2. rush out suddenly; pour out. 3. give out a rush of soft or silly talk.

gust (gust), 1. a sudden rush of wind, often whirling. 2. an outburst of anger or other feeling. Gusts of laughter greeted the clown.

gut ter (gut′ər), 1. channel or ditch along the side of a street or road to carry off water; low part of a street beside the sidewalk. 2. channel or trough along the lower edge of a roof to carry off rain water. 3. flow or melt in streams. A candle gutters when the melted wax runs down its sides.

guy (gī), 1. a rope or chain attached to something to steady it. 2. to guide, steady, or secure with a guy or guys. The mast was guyed by four ropes.

gym na si um (jim nā′zi əm), room, building, etc., fitted up for physical exercise or training and for indoor athletic sports.

gyp sy (jip′si), 1. person belonging to a wandering race of dark-skinned, dark-eyed people who probably came from India long ago. 2. person who looks or lives like a gypsy. 3. of the gypsies; as, a gypsy girl. Also spelled **gipsy.**

H

ha (hä), 1. an exclamation of surprise, joy, or triumph. "Ha! I've caught you!" cried the giant to Jack. 2. sound of a laugh. "Ha! ha! ha!" laughed the boys.

hab it (hab′it), 1. custom; practice. Form the habit of brushing your teeth twice a day. 2. condition of body or mind. The runner was of lean habit. 3. the dress of persons belonging to a religious order; as, a nun's habit. 4. a woman's riding dress. The lady on the white horse wore a black habit.

hab it a ble (hab′i tə bəl), fit to live in.

hab i tat (hab′i tat), 1. place where an animal or plant naturally lives or grows. The jungle is the habitat of tigers. 2. dwelling place.

hab i ta tion (hab′i tā′shən), 1. a place or building to live in. 2. living in. Is the house fit for habitation?

ha bit u al (hə bich′ü əl), 1. done by habit; as, a habitual smile, habitual courtesy. 2. regular; steady. A habitual reader reads a great deal. 3. usual; customary. Ice and snow are a habitual sight in arctic regions.

ha bit u al ly (hə bich′ü əl i), as a habit; regularly; commonly.

hack[1] (hak), 1. cut roughly. Tom hacked the box apart with the dull ax. 2. a rough cut. 3. give short, dry coughs.

hack[2] (hak), 1. a carriage for hire. Hacks were waiting at the railroad station. 2. a horse for hire. 3. a riding horse for common use. 4. person who does tedious work; a drudge. 5. drudging. Hack work is work done just for money.

had (had). See **have.** She had a party. A fine time was had by all who came.

had n't (had′ənt), had not.

hadst (hadst), an old form meaning **had.** "Thou hadst" means "you had."

haft (haft), handle of a knife, sword, etc.

hag (hag), 1. a very ugly old woman. 2. witch.

hag gard (hag′ərd), looking wild from pain, fatigue, worry, hunger, etc.; careworn.

hag gle (hag′əl), dispute, especially about a price. The cook and the grocer haggled over the price of eggs.

hail[1] (hāl), 1. frozen rain. Hail fell with such violence that it broke windows. 2. fall in hail. Sometimes it hails during a summer shower. 3. shower like hail. A hail of bullets met the soldiers. 4. pour down in a shower like hail. The angry mob hailed blows on the thief.

hail[2] (hāl), 1. greet; cheer. The crowd hailed the victor. 2. Greetings! Welcome! a greeting. Hail to the chief! 3. call loudly to; shout. The boys hailed passing cars to beg a ride. 4. loud call; shout. The ship moved on without heeding our hails. 5. **Hail from** means come from. The ship hails from Boston.

hail stone (hāl′stōn′), frozen drop of rain. Hailstones are usually very small, but sometimes they are as big as marbles.

hair (hãr). The hair on her head was yellow and silky. The hairs on a plant are fine like threads.

hair i ness (hãr′i nis), hairy condition.

hair less (hãr′lis), without hair.

hair y (hãr′i), 1. covered with hair; having much hair; as, hairy hands, a hairy ape. 2. like hair.

hal cy on (hal′si ən), happy; calm; peaceful.

hale[1] (hāl), strong and well.

hale[2] (hāl), drag by force.

half (haf), 1. one of two equal parts. A half of 4 is 2. Two halves make a whole. 2. making a half of; needing as much more to make a whole; as, a half pound, a half barrel. 3. to a half of the full amount or degree; as, half cooked. 4. partly. She spoke half aloud. 5. **Not half bad** means fairly good.

half-breed (haf′brēd′), child whose parents are of different races.

half brother, brother by one parent only.

half-heart ed (haf′här′tid), lacking courage, interest, or enthusiasm.

half sister, sister by one parent only.

half way (haf′wā′), 1. half over the way; as, a rope reaching only halfway. **Meet** (someone) **halfway** means do one's share to agree or be friendly with. 2. one half. The lesson is halfway finished. 3. midway; as, a halfway house between two towns. 4. incomplete; not going far enough; as, halfway prevention of fires.

hal i but (hal′i bət), very large flatfish, much used for food. Halibuts sometimes weigh several hundred pounds.

hall (hôl), 1. a way to go through a building. A hall ran the length of the upper floor of the house. 2. a passage or room at the entrance of a building. Leave your umbrella in the hall. 3. a large room for holding meetings, parties, banquets, etc. No hall in town was large enough for the crowd gathered to hear the famous singer. 4. a building for public business, assemblies, etc. The town hall contains several offices and a big assembly room. 5. the house of an English lord, squire, or owner of a big estate. 6. a building of a school or college.

hal le lu jah or **hal le lu iah** (hal′i lü′yə), 1. Praise ye the Lord! 2. a song of praise.

hal loa (hə lō′), hello.

hal loo (hə lü′), hello.

hal low (hal′ō), make holy or sacred. "Hallowed be Thy name."

Hal low een or **Hal low e'en** (hal′ō ēn′), the evening of October 31.

hall way (hôl′wā′), hall; a passage in a building.

ha lo (hā′lō), 1. ring of light. 2. glory; glamour. A halo of romance surrounds King Arthur and his knights.

Halo about the head of Joan of Arc

halt[1] (hôlt), stop. The soldiers halted for a short rest.

halt[2] (hôlt), 1. hesitate. Shyness made the boy speak in a halting manner. 2. limp. 3. lame; crippled.

hal ter (hôl′tər), 1. a rope or strap for leading or tying an animal. 2. a rope for hanging a person.

Halter

halve (hav), 1. divide into two equal parts; share equally. The knight halved his bread with the beggar. 2. reduce to half. The new machine halves the time of doing the work.

halves (havz), more than one half. Two halves make one whole.

hal yard (hal′yərd), a rope used to raise or lower a sail, yard, or flag.

ham (ham), 1. salted and smoked meat from the upper part of a hog's hind leg. 2. the back of the thigh; the thigh and buttock.

ham let (ham′lit), small village; little group of houses in the country.

ham mer (ham′ər), 1. a tool with a metal head and a handle, used for driving nails, etc. 2. something shaped or used like a hammer. The hammer of a gun explodes the charge. 3. drive, hit, or work with a hammer. 4. beat into shape with a hammer. Metal is hammered into ornaments. 5. fasten by using a hammer. 6. force by many efforts. Arithmetic has to be hammered into that dull boy's head.

Hammer (def. 1)

ham mock (ham′ək), hanging bed or couch made of canvas, netted cord, etc.

Hammock

ham per[1] (ham′pər), get in the way of; hinder. Clothes hamper a swimmer. Poor health hampers him.

ham per[2] (ham′pər), a large basket with a cover.

hand (hand), 1. the end part of the arm, which takes and holds objects. Each hand has four fingers and a thumb. 2. thing like a hand; as, the hands of a watch. 3. a hired worker who uses his hands; as, a farm hand, a factory hand. 4. give with the hand. Please hand me a spoon. 5. help with the hand. He handed the lady into her car. 6. possession; control. This property is no longer in my hands. 7. part or share in doing something. He had no hand in the matter. 8. side. At her left hand stood two men. On the other hand, it costs more than I wish to pay. 9. source. She heard the story at second hand. 10. style of handwriting. He writes in a clear hand. 11. skill; ability. This painting shows the hand of a master. 12. promise of marriage. 13. the breadth of a hand, 4 inches. This horse is 18 hands high. 14. the cards held by a player. 15. a single round in a card game. 16. a player in a card game. 17. Some special meanings are:

from hand to mouth, without providing for the future.

hand to hand, close together; as, to fight hand to hand.

hand bag (hand′bag′), 1. a woman's small bag for money, toilet articles, etc. 2. a small traveling bag to hold clothes, etc.

hand ball (hand′bôl′), 1. a game in which a small ball is batted against a wall with the hand. 2. the ball used in this game.

hand cuff (hand′kuf′), 1. a device to keep a person from using his hands, usually one of two steel bracelets joined by a short chain. 2. put handcuffs on.

Handcuffs and key

hand ful (hand′fụl), 1. as much or as many as the hand can hold; as, a handful of candy. 2. a small number; as, a handful of men.

hand i cap (han′di kap), 1. a race, contest, or game in which some are given special advantages and some are given special disadvantages. 2. the advantage or disadvantage given in such a race, contest, or game. 3. give a handicap to. 4. an extra burden or task; hindrance. A sore throat is a handicap to a singer. 5. hinder; give an extra burden to. A lame arm handicapped the baseball player.

hand ker chief (hang′kər chif), a soft square of cloth used for wiping the nose, face, hands, etc. Large handkerchiefs are sometimes worn about the neck.

han dle (han′dəl), 1. a part of a thing made to be grasped by the hand. Spoons, pitchers, hammers, and pails have handles. 2. to touch, feel, or use with the hand. Don't handle that book until you wash your hands. 3. manage; direct. The captain handles his men well. 4. behave or act when handled. This car handles easily. 5. treat. The poor cat had been roughly handled by the cruel boys. 6. deal in. This shop handles meat and groceries.

han dle bar (han′dəl bär′), the part of a bicycle, motorcycle, etc., that the rider holds and steers by.

hand maid (hand′mād′), female servant.

hand maid en (hand′mād′ən), female servant.

hand some (han′səm), 1. good-looking; pleasing in appearance. We usually say that a man is handsome, but that a woman is pretty or beautiful. 2. fairly large; considerable. Ten thousand dollars is a handsome sum of money. 3. generous. He gave each servant a handsome gift of one hundred dollars.

hand spring (hand′spring′), a spring or leap in which a person turns his heels over his head while balancing on one or both hands.

hand-to-hand (hand′tu̇ hand′), close together; at close quarters; as, a hand-to-hand fight.

hand writ ing (hand′rīt′ing), 1. writing by hand; writing with pen, pencil, etc. 2. manner or style of writing. He recognized his mother's handwriting on the envelope.

hand y (han′di), 1. easy to reach or use; saving work; useful. There were handy shelves near the kitchen sink. 2. skillful with the hands. Tom is handy with tools.

hang (hang), 1. fasten or be fastened to something above. Hang your cap on the hook. The swing hangs from a tree. 2. fasten so as to leave swinging freely; as, to hang a door on its hinges. 3. put to death by hanging with a rope around the neck. 4. droop; bend down. She hung her head in shame. 5. to cover or decorate with things that are fastened to something above. All the walls were hung with pictures. 6. the way in which a thing hangs; as, the hang of a skirt. 7. meaning; way of using or doing. I can't get the hang of this problem. **hung** is formed from **hang.**

han gar (hang′ər), a shed for airships or airplanes.

hang ing (hang′ing), 1. death by hanging with a rope around the neck. 2. thing that hangs from a wall, bed, etc. Curtains and draperies are hangings. 3. that hangs.

hank (hangk), coil; skein.

hap (hap), 1. chance; luck. 2. happen.

hap haz ard (hap′haz′ərd), 1. chance. 2. random; not planned. Haphazard answers are usually wrong. 3. by chance; at random.

hap less (hap′lis), unlucky; unfortunate.

hap ly (hap′li), perhaps; by chance.

hap pen (hap′ən), 1. take place; occur. Nothing happened while we were there. 2. be or take place by chance. Accidents will happen. 3. have the fortune (to). I happened to sit beside Mary. 4. be done (to). Something has happened to this lock; the key won't turn. 5. **Happen on** means (1) meet. (2) find.

hap pen ing (hap′ən ing), 1. event. 2. thing that happens.

hap pi ly (hap′i li), 1. in a happy manner. She lives happily. 2. by luck; with good fortune. Happily I saved you from falling.

hap pi ness (hap′i nis), 1. being happy; gladness. 2. good luck.

hap py (hap′i), 1. feeling as you do when you are well and are having a good time; contented. 2. showing that one is glad; as, a happy smile, a happy look. 3. lucky. By a happy chance we found the watch just where I left it. 4. fit; successful; fortunate; as, a happy way of expressing an idea. **happier** and **happiest** are formed from **happy.**

har ass (har′əs or hə ras′), 1. trouble by repeated attacks. The pirates harassed the villages along the coast. 2. disturb; worry.

har bor (här′bər), 1. place of shelter for ships. 2. any place of shelter. 3. give shelter to. The shaggy dog harbors fleas. Don't harbor unkind thoughts.

hard (härd), 1. like steel, glass, and rock; not soft; not yielding to touch. 2. firm; solid. 3. firmly; solidly. 4. not yielding to influence; stern. He was a hard father. 5. needing much ability, effort, or time; as, a hard job, a hard lesson, a hard man to get on with. 6. with effort; with vigor. Try hard to lift this log. It is raining hard. 7. severe; causing much pain, trouble, care, etc. Last winter was a hard winter. When our father was out of work, we had a hard time. 8. severely; badly. It will go hard with him if he is caught. 9. not pleasant; harsh; ugly. That man has a hard face. 10. near. The house stands hard by the bridge. 11. **Hard of hearing** means somewhat deaf. 12. **Hard water** contains substances that hinder the action of soap.

hard en (här′dən), make hard; become hard.

hard-head ed (härd′hed′id), not easily excited or deceived; practical; shrewd.

hard-heart ed (härd′här′tid), without pity; cruel.

har di hood (här′di hůd), boldness; daring.

har di ly (här′di li), boldly.

hard ly (härd′li), 1. barely; only just. We hardly had time to eat breakfast. 2. not quite. His story is hardly true. 3. probably not. They will hardly come in all this rain. 4. with trouble or effort; as, a hardly fought game. 5. in a hard manner; harshly; severely. Cinderella's sisters treated her hardly.

hard ness (härd′nis), being hard.

hard ship (härd′ship), something hard to bear. Hunger, cold, and sickness are hardships.

hard ware (härd′wãr′), articles made from metal. Locks, hinges, nails, screws, knives, etc., are hardware.

hard wood (härd′wůd′), hard, compact wood. Oak, cherry, maple, ebony, and mahogany are hardwoods.

har dy (här′di), 1. able to bear hard treatment. Cold weather does not kill hardy plants. 2. bold; daring.

hare (hãr), an animal with long ears, a divided upper lip, a short tail, and long hind legs. A hare is very much like a rabbit, but larger.

Hare (about 2 ft. long)

hare bell (hãr′bel′), a slender plant with blue, bell-shaped flowers; the bluebell.

hark (härk), listen.

hark en (här′kən), hearken; listen.

harm (härm), hurt; damage.

harm ful (härm′fəl), injurious; hurtful.

harm less (härm′lis), doing no harm; not harmful; such as would not harm anyone or anything.

har mon i ca (här mon′i kə), a small musical instrument played by the mouth. See the picture.

Harmonica

har mo ni ous (här mō′ni əs), 1. getting on well together; not disturbed by disagreement. The children played in a harmonious group. 2. going well together; as, harmonious sounds. 3. sweet-sounding; musical.

har mo nize (här′mə nīz), 1. be in harmony. 2. bring into harmony; make harmonious.

har mo ny (här′mə ni), 1. getting on well together. There was perfect harmony between the two brothers. 2. going well together. His plans are in harmony with mine. 3. sweet or musical sound. 4. the sounding together of musical notes in a chord.

har ness (här′nis), 1. leather fittings for a horse, which connect him to a carriage, plow, etc., or are used in riding. Reins, collar, and bridle are parts of a horse's harness. 2. put harness on. Harness the horse. 3. control and put to work. We harness streams by dams and machinery. 4. **In harness** means in one's regular work. 5. the armor of a knight or warrior.

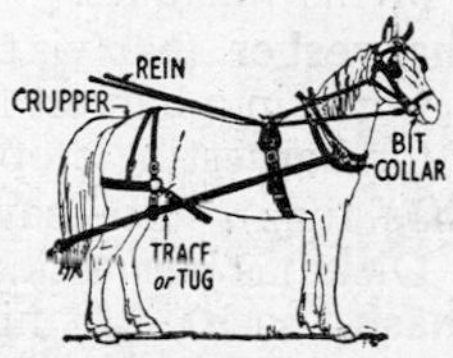

Horse's harness

harp (härp), 1. a large stringed musical instrument played with the fingers. 2. **Harp on** a subject means talk about it very much or too much. 3. play on the harp.

Woman playing a harp

harp er (här′pər), person who plays a harp.

harp ist (här′pist), harper.

har poon (här pün′), 1. a spear with a rope tied to it. It is used for catching whales and other sea animals. 2. strike, catch, or kill with a harpoon.

har row (har′ō), 1. a heavy frame with iron teeth or upright disks. Harrows are used by farmers to break up plowed ground into finer pieces, or to cover seed with earth. 2. draw a harrow over. 3. to hurt; wound. 4. arouse uncomfortable feelings in. He told a harrowing tale of ghosts.

Harrow

har ry (har′i), 1. raid and rob with violence. The pirates harried the towns along the coast. 2. keep troubling; worry; torment. Fear of losing his job harried the clerk.

harsh (härsh), 1. rough to the touch, taste, eye, or ear; as, a harsh voice, a harsh climate. 2. cruel; unfeeling; as, a harsh man.

hart (härt), a male deer, especially of the red deer after its fifth year.

har vest (här′vist), 1. reaping and gathering in grain and other food crops, usually in the fall. 2. the time or season of the harvest. 3. gather in and bring home for use; as, to harvest wheat. 4. one season's yield of any natural product; crop. The oyster harvest was small this year. 5. result; consequences. He is reaping the harvest of his mistakes.

har vest er (här′vis tər), 1. person who works in a harvest field; reaper. 2. machine for harvesting crops, especially grain.

has (haz). See **have.** Who has my book? Dick has been sick.

hash (hash), 1. mixture of cooked meat, potatoes, etc., chopped into small pieces and fried or baked. 2. chop into small pieces. 3. mixture. 4. a mess; muddle. A falling tree made a hash of my garden.

has n't (haz′ənt), has not.

hast (hast), an old form meaning **have.** "Thou hast" means "you have."

haste (hāst), 1. a hurry; trying to be quick. Bring the doctor in haste. All his haste was of no use. **Make haste** means hurry; be quick. 2. hasten.

has ten (hās′ən), 1. hurry; cause to be quick; speed. 2. be quick; go fast.

hast i ly (hās′ti li), 1. in a hurried way; quickly and not very carefully. 2. rashly. 3. in a quick-tempered way.

hast y (hās′ti), 1. quick; hurried; as, a hasty glance, a hasty trip to town. 2. rash; not well thought out; as, a hasty decision. 3. easily angered; quick-tempered; as, a hasty old gentleman.

hat (hat), 1. a covering for the head when outdoors. A hat usually has a crown and a brim. 2. provide with a hat; put a hat on. The lady was beautifully gowned and hatted.

hatch[1] (hach), 1. bring forth (young) from an egg or eggs. A hen hatches chickens. 2. keep (an egg or eggs) warm until the young come out. It takes three weeks to hatch hens' eggs. 3. come out from the egg. Three of the chickens hatched today. 4. grow to be young animals. Will these eggs hatch? 5. a brood. There are twelve chickens in this hatch. 6. arrange; plan. 7. plan secretly; plot. The robbers were hatching an evil scheme.

hatch[2] (hach), 1. an opening in a ship's deck through which the cargo is put in. 2. opening in the floor or roof of a building, etc. 3. the trap door covering this opening.

Hatch (def. 1)

hatch et (hach′it), a small ax with a handle about a foot long.

hate (hāt). Cats usually hate dogs. God hates sin. She felt a very strong dislike or hate of snakes. Her hate for lies would not let her be friends with any girl who lied.

Hatchet

hate ful (hāt′fəl), 1. causing hate. 2. feeling hate; showing hate.

hat er (hāt′ər), one who hates.

hath (hath), an old form meaning **has.**

ha tred (hā′trid), very strong dislike; hate.

haugh ty (hô′ti), 1. too proud of oneself and too scornful of others; as, a haughty girl. 2. showing too great pride of oneself and scorn for others; as, a haughty glance, haughty words.

haul (hôl), 1. pull or drag with force. The logs were hauled to the mill by horses. 2. act of hauling; hard pull. 3. load hauled. Powerful trucks are used for heavy hauls. 4. distance that a load is hauled. 5. amount won, taken, etc., at one time; catch. The fishing boats made a good haul today. 6. change the course of (a ship).

haunch (hônch), 1. the part of the body around the hips. A dog sits on his haunches. 2. the leg and loin of an animal, used for food; as, a haunch of venison.

haunt (hônt), 1. go often to; visit frequently. People say ghosts haunt that old house. 2. place visited often. The swimming pool was a favorite haunt of the boys in the summer. 3. be often with. Memories of his youth haunted the old man.

haunt ed (hôn′tid), visited by ghosts.

have (hav), 1. hold. I have a club in my hand. 2. possess; own. He has a big house and farm. A house has windows. She has no news of her brother. 3. know; understand. She has your idea. 4. be forced; be compelled. All animals have to sleep. He will have to go now because his work begins. 5. cause (somebody to do something or something to be done). Please have the boy bring my mail. She will have the car washed for me. 6. get; take. You need to have a rest. 7. experience. Have a pleasant time. They had trouble with this engine. 8. allow; permit. Ann won't have any noise while she is reading. 9. Have is used with words like *asked, been, broken, done,* or *called* to express completed action. He has eaten. She had gone before. I have called her. They will have seen her by Sunday. **has** and **had** are formed from **have.**

ha ven (hā′vən), 1. harbor, especially one for shelter from a storm. 2. place of shelter and safety. The old cabin was a haven from the storm.

have n't (hav′ənt), have not.

hav oc (hav′ək), very great destruction or injury. Tornadoes, severe earthquakes, and plagues create widespread havoc.

hawk[1] (hôk), 1. a bird of prey with a strong, hooked beak, and large curved claws. Long ago hawks were trained to hunt and kill other birds. 2. hunt with trained hawks.

Red-tailed hawk (about 2 ft. long)

hawk[2] (hôk), carry (goods) about for sale, as a street peddler does.

haw ser (hô′zər), large rope or small cable. Hawsers are used for mooring or towing ships.

haw thorn (hô′thôrn), a shrub or small tree with many thorns and clusters of fragrant flowers and red berries.

hay (hā), 1. grass cut and dried as food for cattle and horses. 2. cut and dry grass for hay.

Haycock

hay cock (hā′kok′), a small pile of hay in a field.

hay mow (hā′mou′), 1. place in a barn for storing hay. 2. hay stored in a barn.

hay rick (hā′rik′), haystack.

hay stack (hā′stak′), a large pile of hay outdoors.

haz ard (haz′ərd), 1. risk; danger. The life of an aviator is full of hazards. 2. to risk; take a chance with. I would hazard my life on his honesty.

haz ard ous (haz′ər dəs), dangerous; risky; perilous.

haze[1] (hāz), 1. a small amount of mist or smoke in the air. A thin haze veiled the distant hills. 2. vague condition of the mind; slight confusion.

haze[2] (hāz), force to do unnecessary or ridiculous tasks.

ha zel (hā′zəl), 1. a shrub or small tree whose light-brown nuts are good to eat. 2. light brown.

Hazel leaves and nuts

ha zy (hā′zi), 1. misty; smoky; dim; as, a hazy sky. 2. not distinct; obscure; as, a hazy idea.

he (hē), 1. the boy, man, or male animal spoken about. He works hard, but his work pays him well. 2. male.

head (hed), 1. the top part of the human body where the eyes and mouth are. 2. the front of an animal where the eyes and mouth are. 3. the top part of anything; as, the head of a pin, a cabbage, a crane, a drum, or a barrel. 4. the front or face part of anything; as, the head of a procession, or the head of a street. 5. at the front or top. 6. be at the front or the top of. 7. coming from in front; as, a head wind, a head sea. 8. move toward, face toward. You are heading north. 9. chief person; leader. 10. chief; leading. 11. be the head or chief of; lead. 12. one or ones; an individual. Ten cows are ten head of cattle. 13. the striking part of a tool or implement; as, the head of a hammer, the head of a golf club. 14. mind; understanding; intelligence. He has a good head for figures. 15. topic. He arranged his speech under four heads. 16. crisis; conclusion. His sudden refusal brought matters to a head. 17. pressure; as, a head of steam. 18. source; as, the head of a brook. 19. **Head off** means get in front of; check. 20. **Over one's head** means too hard for one to understand. 21. **Out of one's head** means crazy.

head ache (hed′āk′), a pain in the head.

[head dres]s (hed′dres′), a covering or [decorat]ion for the head. See the picture.

[head fi]rst (hed′fėrst′), [1.] with the head first. [2.] hastily; rashly.

head land (hed′lənd), cape; point of land running out into water.

head light (hed′līt′), a bright light at the front of an automobile, a streetcar, a train, etc.

Headdress worn 500 years ago

head line (hed′līn′), a title line over an article in a newspaper or at the top of a page in a book or magazine.

head long (hed′lông), 1. headfirst; as, to plunge headlong into the sea. 2. with great haste and force; as, to rush headlong into the crowd. 3. in too great a rush; without stopping to think.

head quar ters (hed′kwôr′tərz), 1. in an army, the place where the commander in chief or the officer in charge lives or has his office; the place from which orders are sent out. 2. the main office; the center of operations or of authority. The headquarters of the Red Cross is in Washington.

head strong (hed′strông′), rashly or foolishly determined to have one's own way; hard to control or manage; obstinate.

head way (hed′wā′), 1. motion forward. The ship could make no headway against the strong wind and tide. 2. progress with work, etc. 3. clear space, such as in a doorway or under an arch.

heal (hēl), 1. cure; make well; bring back to health. 2. grow well; become well.

health (helth), 1. being well or not sick; freedom from illness of any kind. 2. condition of the body; as, good health, poor health. 3. **Drink a health** to (someone) means drink in honor of (someone) and wish (him) well.

health ful (helth′fəl), giving health; good for the health; as, a healthful diet.

health y (hel′thi), 1. having good health; as, a healthy baby. 2. giving health; good for the health.

heap (hēp), 1. pile of many things thrown or lying together; as, a heap of stones, a sand heap. 2. form into a heap; gather in heaps. 3. give generously or in large amounts. 4. fill full or more than full; as, to heap a plate with food.

hear (hēr). We hear with our ears. You must hear what he has to say. Have you heard from your friends in China?

heard (hėrd). See **hear.** I heard the noise. The gun was heard a mile away.

hear er (hēr′ər), person who hears or listens.

hear ing (hēr′ing), 1. power to hear; the sense by which sound is perceived. The old man's hearing is poor. 2. act or process of perceiving sound. Hearing the good news made him happy. 3. chance to be heard. The judge gave both sides a hearing. 4. the distance that a sound can be heard. Mother stays within hearing of the baby.

heark en (här′kən), listen.

hearse (hėrs), a carriage or car to carry a dead person to his grave.

heart (härt), 1. the part of the body that pumps the blood. 2. feelings; mind; soul. She has a kind heart. 3. the part that feels, loves, hates, and desires; as, to give one's heart. 4. kindness; sympathy. 5. courage; enthusiasm. 6. middle; center; as, the heart of the forest. 7. main part; most important part. 8. figure shaped somewhat like the picture. 9. Some special meanings are:

at heart, in one's deepest thoughts or feelings.

learn by heart, memorize.

take heart, be encouraged.

take to heart, think seriously about.

heart bro ken (härt′brō′kən), crushed by sorrow or grief.

heart en (här′tən), cheer; cheer up; encourage. Good news heartens you.

heart felt (härt′felt′), sincere; genuine; as, heartfelt sympathy.

hearth (härth), 1. the floor of a fireplace. 2. fireside; home. The soldiers longed for their own hearths.

hearth stone (härth′stōn′), 1. a stone forming a hearth. 2. fireside; home.

heart i ly (här′ti li), 1. with sincere feeling. Mary welcomed her cousins heartily. 2. with a good will; in good spirits for what one is doing; as, to set to work heartily. 3. with a good appetite; as, to eat heartily. 4. very; completely. My mother was heartily tired of so much housework.

heart i ness (här′ti nis), 1. sincerity. 2. warmth. 3. vigor.

heart less (härt′lis), without a heart; unfeeling; cruel.

heart y (här′ti), 1. cheerful; friendly; eager; full of feeling; sincere; as, a hearty laugh, a hearty greeting, hearty wishes for a happy birthday. We bade them a hearty good-by. 2. strong and well; vigorous; as, to be hale and hearty at sixty. 3. abundant; heavy; as, a hearty meal.

heat (hēt), 1. the condition that makes anything hot. 2. warmth; as, the heat of a fire. 3. make warm or hot. The stove heats the room. 4. hot weather. 5. hottest point; most violent stage. In the heat of the fight he lost his temper. 6. one trial in a race. He won the first heat, but lost the final race.

heat er (hēt′ər), something that gives heat or warmth, such as a stove, furnace, or radiator.

heath (hēth), 1. open, waste land with heather or low bushes growing on it; moor. A heath has few or no trees. 2. low bush growing on such land. Heather is a kind of heath.

American heath

hea then (hē′ᴛʜən), 1. person who does not believe in the God of the Bible; person who is not a Christian, Jew, or Mohammedan. The wild savages of Africa are heathens. 2. people who are heathen. 3. of heathens.

heath er (heᴛʜ′ər), a low shrub which covers waste lands in Scotland and northern England.

heave (hēv), 1. lift with force or effort. He heaved the heavy box into the wagon. 2. lift and throw. The sailors heaved the anchor overboard. 3. pull with force or effort; haul. They heaved on the rope. 4. give (a sigh, groan, etc.) with a deep, heavy breath. 5. rise and fall alternately. Waves heave in a storm. 6. breathe hard; pant. 7. rise; swell; bulge; as, heaving waves. 8. a heaving; a throw. With a mighty heave Tom pushed the boat into the water. 9. **Heave in sight** means come into view. 10. **Heave to** means stop a ship; stop.

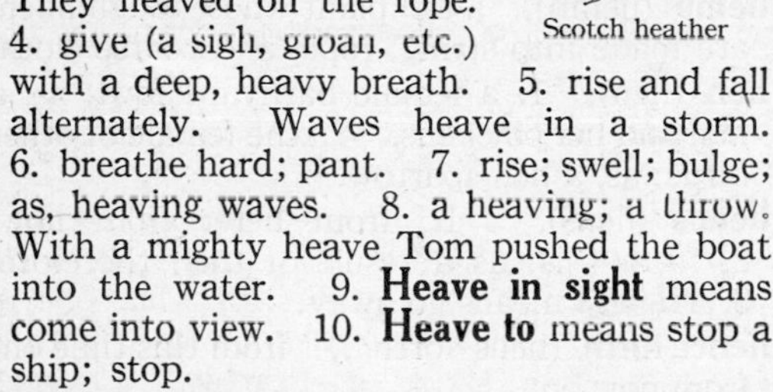

Scotch heather

heav en (hev′ən), 1. place where God and His angels live. 2. God; Providence. It was the will of Heaven. 3. place or condition of greatest happiness. 4. upper air in which clouds float, winds blow, and birds fly; the sky. We usually say heavens.

heav en ly (hev′ən li), 1. of or in heaven. God is our heavenly Father. 2. like heaven; suited to heaven; as, a heavenly spot, heavenly peace. 3. very, very excellent. 4. of or in the heavens. The sun, moon, and the stars are heavenly bodies.

heav i ly (hev′i li), in a heavy way or manner.

heav i ness (hev′i nis), 1. being heavy; great weight. 2. sadness.

heav y (hev′i), 1. hard to lift or carry; having much weight. Iron is heavy and feathers are light. 2. of more than usual weight for its kind; as, heavy silk, heavy bread. 3. large; greater than usual; as, a heavy rain, a heavy crop, a heavy meal, a heavy vote, a heavy sea, a heavy sleep. 4. weighted down; laden; as, air heavy with moisture, eyes heavy with sleep. A heavy heart is full of sorrow. 5. hard to bear or endure. Her troubles became heavier and heavier. 6. hard to deal with. A heavy road is muddy or sandy, so that a load is hard to draw. Heavy food is hard to digest.

He brew (hē′brü), 1. a Jew; a descendant of one of the desert tribes led by Moses who settled in Palestine. 2. Jewish. 3. the ancient language of the Jews.

hec tic (hek′tik), 1. very exciting; feverish. 2. showing the signs of tuberculosis; having flushed cheeks, hot skin, and loss of flesh.

he'd (hēd), 1. he had. 2. he would.

hedge (hej), 1. a thick row of bushes or low trees planted as a fence. 2. put a hedge around; as, to hedge a garden. 3. **Hedge in** means hem in; surround on all sides. 4. bet on both sides in order to reduce one's possible losses. 5. avoid giving a direct answer; evade questions.

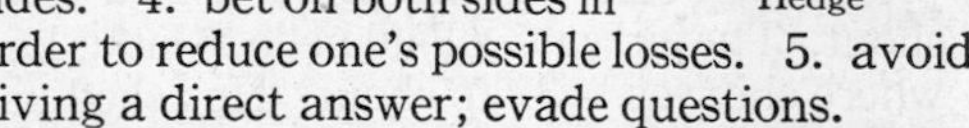

Hedge

hedge hog (hej′hog′), 1. a small animal of the Old World with spines on its back. When attacked, hedgehogs roll up into a bristling ball. 2. the porcupine of North America.

European hedgehog (about 10 in. long)

hedge row (hej′rō′), a thick row of bushes or small trees forming a hedge.

heed (hēd), 1. give careful attention to; take notice of. Now heed what I say. 2. careful attention. She pays heed to her clothes.

heed less (hēd′lis), careless; thoughtless.

), 1. the back part of the human ...low the ankle. 2. the part of a stock- ...shoe that covers the heel. 3. the part ...shoe or boot that is under the heel or raises ...e heel. 4. anything shaped or used like a ...eel.

heel[2] (hēl), lean over to one side.

heif er (hef′ər), a young cow that has not had a calf.

height (hīt), 1. how tall a person is; how high anything is; how far up a thing goes; as, the height of a mountain. 2. a rather great distance up; as, rising at a height above the valley. 3. a high point or place; as, on the mountain heights. 4. highest part; top. 5. highest point; greatest degree. Playing with loaded guns is the height of folly.

height en (hīt′ən), 1. make or become higher. 2. increase; make stronger.

heir (ãr), person who has the right to somebody's property after that one dies. The rich man adopted the boy and made him his heir.

heir ess (ãr′is), 1. heir who is a woman or girl. 2. woman or girl inheriting great wealth.

heir loom (ãr′lüm′), a possession handed down from generation to generation. This clock is a family heirloom.

held (held). See **hold**[1]. Mary held the baby. The swing is held by strong ropes.

he li o trope (hē′li ə trōp), 1. a plant with small, sweet-smelling, purple or white flowers. 2. light purple.

hell (hel), 1. the place where wicked persons are punished after death. 2. any very bad place or condition.

he'll (hēl), 1. he will. 2. he shall.

hel lo (he lō′), 1. a call of greeting or surprise. Tom said, "Hello! Bill." 2. a call or shout. The girl gave a loud hello to let us know where she was. 3. to shout. He asked us to hello until somebody came.

helm[1] (helm), 1. the handle or wheel by which a ship is steered. 2. position of control or guidance.

helm[2] (helm), helmet.

Modern Medieval
Soldiers' helmets

hel met (hel′mit), a covering to protect the head. Knights wore helmets as part of their armor. Soldiers wear steel helmets; firemen often wear leather helmets.

helms man (helmz′mən), man who steers a ship.

help (help), 1. Please give me some help. A sewing machine is a help in making clothes. Mother helps us. 2. means of making better. The medicine was a help. 3. make better. The doctor helped my sore throat. 4. give food to; serve with food. Help yourself to milk and sugar. 5. avoid; keep from. He cannot help going to sleep. 6. a helping.

help er (hel′pər), person that helps.

help ful (help′fəl), useful.

help less (help′lis), 1. not able to help oneself. A little baby is helpless. 2. without help.

help less ness (help′lis nis), being helpless; as, the helplessness of a little baby.

hem[1] (hem), 1. a border or edge on a garment; the edge made by folding over the cloth and sewing it down. 2. fold over and sew down the edge of (cloth). Amy hemmed six napkins. 3. **Hem in, hem around,** or **hem about** means surround and not let out.

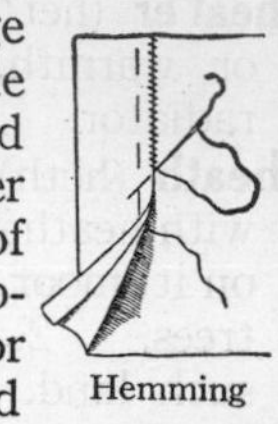

Hemming

hem[2] (hem), 1. a sound like clearing the throat, used to attract attention or show doubt or hesitation. 2. make this sound.

hem i sphere (hem′i sfēr), 1. half of a sphere or globe. 2. half of the earth's surface. North and South America are in the Western Hemisphere; Europe, Asia, and Africa are in the Eastern Hemisphere. All the countries north of the equator are in the Northern Hemisphere.

hem lock (hem′lok), 1. a poisonous plant with spotted stems, finely divided leaves, and small white flowers. 2. a poisonous drink made of hemlock. 3. an evergreen tree, a kind of spruce. Hemlock bark is used in tanning. 4. its wood.

hemp (hemp), a tall plant whose tough fibers are made into string, rope, and coarse cloth.

hen (hen), 1. a female barnyard fowl; as, a hen and her chickens. 2. the female of other birds; as, a hen sparrow.

hence (hens), 1. from here; from now. 2. from this; as a result of this; therefore. 3. **Hence!** means go away.

hence forth (hens′fōrth′), from this time on; from now on.

hen coop (hen′küp′), coop for hens.

her (hėr), 1. She is not here. Have you seen her? Find her. *She* and *her* mean the girl or woman or female animal spoken about. 2. of her; belonging to her. She has left her book. The cat won't let you touch her kittens.

her ald (her′əld), 1. person who carries messages and makes announcements. The king sent two heralds to the duke. 2. bring news of; announce. The newspapers heralded the arrival of the army.

herb (ėrb or hėrb), a plant with leaves that are used for medicine, seasoning, or food. Sage, mint, and lavender are herbs.

herb age (ėr′bij or hėr′bij), herbs; grass.

Her cu les (hėr′kū lēz), a hero of Greek mythology famous for his great strength and for the twelve tasks he performed.

herd (hėrd), 1. a number of animals together; as, a herd of cows, a herd of horses, a herd of elephants. The animals in a herd are usually large and all of one kind. 2. person who takes care of a herd. A cowherd takes care of a herd of cows. 3. a large number of people. 4. common people. 5. join together; flock together. 6. form into a flock, herd, or group. 7. tend or take care of (cattle or sheep).

herd er (hėr′dər), herdsman; person who takes care of a herd.

herds man (hėrdz′mən), man who tends a herd.

here (hēr), 1. in this place; at this place. We live here in the summer. We will stop here. 2. to this place. Bring the children here for their lesson. 3. this place. 4. In answering a roll call, **Here!** means "I am present!" 5. Here is sometimes used in calling attention to a person or thing. My friend here can help you.

here a bout (hēr′ə bout′), about this place; around here; near here.

here a bouts (hēr′ə bouts′), hereabout.

here af ter (hēr af′tər), 1. after this; after now. 2. **The hereafter** means the life or time after death.

here by (hēr bī′), by this; by this means. The license said, "You are hereby given the right to hunt and fish in Dover County."

here in (hēr in′), in this.

here's (hērz), here is.

her e sy (her′ə si), 1. a belief different from the accepted belief of a church, school, or profession. 2. the holding of such a belief.

her e tic (her′ə tik), person who holds a belief that is different from the accepted belief of his church, school, or profession.

here to fore (hēr′tü fōr′), before this time; until now.

here up on (hēr′ə pon′), 1. upon this. 2. immediately after this.

here with (hēr wiŦH′), with this. I am sending ten cents in stamps herewith.

her it age (her′i tij), what is or may be handed on to a person from his ancestors; inheritance.

her mit (hėr′mit), person who goes away from other people and lives by himself. A hermit often lives a religious life.

her mit age (hėr′mi tij), the home of a hermit.

he ro (hēr′ō), 1. very brave boy or man. 2. the most important male person in a story or play. David is one of the heroes in the Bible.

he ro ic (hi rō′ik), 1. like a hero; very brave; noble. 2. of or about heroes. 3. bold; daring. The doctor used a heroic treatment.

he ro ics (hi rō′iks), language that sounds too grand and noble.

her o ine (her′ō in), 1. very brave girl or woman. 2. the most important female person in a story or play.

her o ism (her′ō izm), 1. great courage. 2. doing something noble at great cost to oneself.

her on (her′ən), a wading bird with long legs, a long neck, and a long bill.

Great blue heron (about 5 ft. tall)

her ring (her′ing), a food fish of the northern Atlantic Ocean. Herring come near the shore to lay their eggs.

hers (hėrz), 1. of her; belonging to her. This money is hers. 2. the one or ones belonging to her. Your problems are wrong; hers are right.

Herring (about 7 in. long)

her self (hėr self′), 1. Herself is used to make a statement stronger. Mary herself brought the book. 2. Herself is used instead of she or her in cases like: She hurt herself. Mary did it by herself. 3. her self. The cat saw herself in the glass. 4. her real or true self. In those fits she is not herself.

he's (hēz), he is.

hes i tate (hez′i tāt), 1. hold back; feel doubtful; be undecided; show that one has not yet made up one's mind. 2. to stop an instant; pause. 3. speak in a hesitating way. 4. feel that perhaps one shouldn't; not wish to. She hesitated to hurt the child's feelings.

hes i ta tion (hez′i tā′shən), 1. act of hesitating; doubt. 2. a slight stopping. Grace has a hesitation in her speech.

hew (hū), cut; chop. They hewed the logs into beams.

hewn (hūn), hewed. See **hew.**

hey (hā), a sound made to attract attention, express surprise or other feeling, or ask a question. Hey! stop! Hey! here's Charles. Hey? what did you say?

hi ber nate (hī′bər nāt), spend the winter in sleep, as bears and some other wild animals do.

hick o ry (hik′ə ri), 1. a tree whose nuts are good to eat. 2. its tough, hard wood.

BRANCH NUT
Hickory

hid (hid). See **hide**[1]. The dog hid his bone. The money was hid in a safe place.

hid den (hid′ən), 1. put or kept out of sight; secret; not clear. The story is about hidden treasure. 2. See **hide**[1]. The moon was hidden behind a dark cloud.

hide[1] (hīd), 1. put out of sight; keep out of sight. Hide it where no one else will know of it or know where it is. 2. shut off from sight; be in front of. Clouds hide the sun. 3. keep secret. Amy hid her anxiety. 4. hide oneself. I'll hide, and you find me. **hid** and **hidden** are formed from **hide.**

hide[2] (hīd), 1. an animal's skin, raw or tanned. 2. a person's skin. He tried to save his own hide.

hid e ous (hid′i əs), ugly; frightful; horrible.

hie (hī), go quickly.

high (hī), 1. up above the ground; as, a high jump. 2. up above others. A general has high rank. Washington was a man of high character. 3. great; greater or stronger than others; as, a high price, a high wind. 4. chief; main; as, the high altar. 5. at or to a high point, place, rank, amount, degree, price, etc. The eagle flies high. Strawberries come high in winter. Gamblers play high. 6. shrill; sharp. 7. Some special meanings are:

high and dry, 1. up out of water. 2. alone; without help.

high seas, the open ocean.

high spirits, cheerfulness; gaiety.

high tide, the time when the ocean comes up highest on the shore.

high time, the time just before it is too late.

high words, angry words.

high land (hī′lənd), country that is mostly hills and mountains; land high above sea level.

high ly (hī′li), 1. in a high degree; very; very much; as, highly amusing, highly recommended. 2. very favorably; as, to speak highly of your best friend. 3. at a high price; as, highly paid.

high ness (hī′nis), being high; height.

High ness (hī′nis), title of honor given to members of royal families.

high road (hī′rōd′), main road.

high school, a school attended after the elementary school.

hight (hīt), named; called. The knight was hight Gawain.

high way (hī′wā′), 1. public road. 2. a main road or route.

high way man (hī′wā′mən), man who robs travelers on the public road.

hike (hīk), 1. take a long walk; march. 2. a tramp or march.

hi lar i ous (hi lãr′i əs), very merry; noisily gay.

hill (hil), 1. a raised part of the earth's surface, not so big as a mountain. 2. a heap of any kind; as, an ant hill. 3. plant with a little heap of soil over and around its roots; as, a hill of corn.

hill ock (hil′ək), little hill.

hill side (hil′sīd′), side of a hill.

hill top (hil′top′), the top of a hill.

hill y (hil′i), having many hills; as, hilly country.

hilt (hilt), handle of a sword or dagger.

HILT
Hilt of a sword

him (him). Don't hit him hard. Give him a drink. Go to him. He and him mean the boy or man or male animal spoken about.

him self (him self′), 1. Himself is used to make a statement stronger. Did you see John himself? 2. *Himself* is used instead of *he* or *him* in cases like: He cut himself. John asked himself what he really wanted. He kept the toy for himself. He cared more for himself than for anything else. 3. his real self. He feels like himself again.

hind[1] (hīnd), back; rear.

hind[2] (hīnd), a female deer, especially after its third year.

hind[3] (hīnd), farm worker.

hin der (hin′dər), hold back; be in the way of; stop; make hard to do. Deep mud hindered travel.

hin drance (hin′drəns), 1. person or thing that hinders; obstacle. Heavy clothes are a hindrance to swimming. 2. a hindering.

hinge (hinj), 1. a joint on which a door, gate, cover, lid, etc., moves back and forth. See the picture. 2. furnish with hinges; attach by hinges. 3. hang or turn on a hinge. 4. depend. The success of the picnic hinges on the kind of weather we will have.

Hinge on a door

hint (hint), 1. slight sign; indirect suggestion. A small black cloud gave a hint of a coming storm. 2. suggest slightly; show in an indirect way. Nell hinted that she wanted to go to bed by saying, "Do you often stay up this late?"

hip (hip), 1. the part that sticks out on each side of the body below a person's waist. 2. a similar part in animals, where the hind leg joins the body.

hip po pot a mus (hip′ə pot′ə məs), a huge animal found near the rivers of Africa. It lives on plants and can stay under water for a considerable time.

Hippopotamus (about 13 ft. long)

hire (hīr), 1. pay for the use of. He hired a car and a man to drive it. 2. employ. The storekeeper hired ten girls for the Christmas rush. 3. wages. Some men fight for glory; some fight for hire.

his (hiz), 1. of him; belonging to him. His name is Bill. 2. the one or ones belonging to him. My books are new; his are old.

hiss (his), 1. make a sound like *ss*, or like a drop of water on a hot stove. Geese and snakes hiss. 2. a sound like *ss*. Hisses were heard from many who disliked what the speaker was saying.

hist (hist), be still! listen!

his to ri an (his tō′ri ən), person who writes about history.

his tor ic (his tor′ik), 1. famous in history. Plymouth Rock and Bunker Hill are historic spots. 2. historical.

his tor i cal (his tor′i kəl), 1. of history; having something to do with history; as, a historical town. 2. according to history; based on history; as, a historical novel. 3. known to be real or true; in history, not in legend; as, historical facts.

his to ry (his′tə ri), 1. a statement of what has happened. 2. the story of a man or a nation. 3. a known past. This knife has a history.

hit (hit), 1. When boys fight, they hit each other. He hit the ball with a bat. He hit his head against the shelf. The man hit out at the thieves who attacked him. 2. come upon; meet with; find. We hit the right road in the dark. The boys hit upon a plan for making money. 3. have a painful effect on; influence in a bad way. 4. a blow; a stroke. 5. successful attempt or performance. The new play is the hit of the season.

hitch (hich), 1. move or pull with a jerk. He hitched his chair nearer to the fire. 2. short, sudden pull or jerk. The sailor gave his trousers a hitch. 3. fasten with a hook, ring, rope, strap, etc. He hitched his horse to a post. 4. fasten; catch; become fastened or caught. A knot made the rope hitch. 5. obstacle; stopping. A hitch in their plans made them miss the train. 6. kind of knot used for temporary fastening.

hith er (hiᴛʜ′ər), 1. here; to this place. 2. on this side; nearer. 3. **Hither and thither** means here and there.

hith er to (hiᴛʜ′ər tü′), up to this time; until now.

hith er ward (hiᴛʜ′ər wərd), toward this place; hither.

hive (hīv), 1. a house for bees to live in. 2. a large number of bees living together. The whole hive was busy. 3. put (bees) in a hive. 4. enter a hive. 5. live close together as bees do. 6. a busy place full of people or animals.

Beehives

ho (hō), 1. an exclamation of surprise, joy, or scornful laughter. 2. an exclamation to get attention. The captain said, "Ho, men! Listen to me."

hoar (hōr), hoary.

hoard (hōrd), 1. save and store up. The squirrel hoards nuts for the winter. A miser hoards money. 2. things stored. The squirrel keeps his hoard in a tree.

hoar frost (hōr′frôst′), white frost.

hoarse (hōrs), 1. sounding rough and deep; as, the hoarse sound of the bullfrog. 2. having a rough voice. A bad cold often makes a person hoarse.

hoar y (hōr′i), 1. white or gray. 2. white or gray with age; as, hoary hair. 3. old; as, hoary ruins.

hob ble (hob′əl), 1. walk awkwardly; limp. The wounded man hobbled away. 2. a limping walk. 3. tie the legs of (a horse, etc.) together. 4. a rope or strap used to hobble an animal.

hob by (hob′i), something a person especially likes to work at or to study which is not his main business. Growing roses is our doctor's hobby.

hob gob lin (hob′gob′lin), 1. goblin; elf. 2. ghost.

hob nail (hob′nāl′), short nail with a large head to protect the soles of heavy shoes.

hock ey (hok′i), game played by two teams on ice or on a field. The players hit a rubber disk or ball with curved sticks to drive it across a goal.

hod (hod), 1. a trough at the top of a long straight handle, used by builders for carrying bricks, mortar, etc., on the shoulder. 2. a pail for carrying coal.

Hod for mortar

hoe (hō), 1. a tool with a small blade at the end of a long handle, used for loosening soil, cutting small weeds, etc. 2. loosen, dig, or cut with a hoe. 3. use a hoe.

Hoe

hog (hog), 1. pig. See the picture just below. 2. full-grown pig.

hogs head (hogz′hed), 1. a large barrel containing from 100 to 140 gallons. 2. a liquid measure equal to 63 gallons.

hoist (hoist), 1. raise on high; lift up, often with ropes and pulleys; as, to hoist a flag, to hoist sails, to hoist blocks of stone in building. 2. a hoisting; a lift. He gave me a hoist up the wall. 3. elevator.

Hog

hold[1] (hōld), 1. grasp and keep. Please hold my hat. Hold my watch while I play this game. 2. a grasp or grip. Take a good hold of this rope. 3. thing to hold by. 4. keep in some place or position. Hold the dish level. He will hold the paper steady while you draw. 5. keep. Hold the fort. 6. place to be kept; fort; stronghold. 7. keep in; contain. This cup will hold water. How much will it hold? This theater will hold a thousand people. 8. have. Shall we hold a meeting of the club? He holds much property in the city. That man holds two offices in our town. He holds a high opinion of you. 9. be true. Will this rule hold in all cases? 10. be faithful. He held to his promise. 11. consider; think. People once held that the world was flat. 12. keep the same; continue. Will the weather hold warm? 13. keep from acting; keep back; as, to hold one's tongue, to hold one's breath. 14. Some special meanings are:

hold forth, 1. talk; preach. 2. offer.

hold in, restrain oneself.

hold out, 1. continue; last. 2. keep resisting; not give in.

hold over, 1. postpone. 2. stay in office beyond the regular term.

hold up, 1. keep from falling. 2. show; display. 3. continue; last; endure. 4. stop. 5. stop by force and rob.

hold with, 1. agree with. 2. approve of.

lay hold of, seize; grasp.

held is formed from **hold.**

hold[2] (hōld), the lowest part of a ship's interior. A ship's cargo is carried in its hold.

hold er (hōl′dər), 1. person who holds something. An owner or possessor of property is a holder. 2. thing to hold something else with. Pads of cloth are used as holders for lifting hot dishes.

hole (hōl), 1. open place; as, a hole in a stocking. 2. a hollow place in something solid. This cheese has holes in it. 3. place which is lower than the parts around it; as, a hole in the road. 4. a small, dark, mean place. 5. put in a hole. Bears hole themselves up during the winter.

hol i day (hol′i dā), 1. a day when one does not work; a day of enjoyment. Christmas is a holiday for everyone. 2. vacation.

ho li ness (hō′li nis), 1. being holy or sacred. 2. **His Holiness** is a title of the Pope.

hol low (hol′ō), 1. having nothing, or only air, inside; empty; with a hole inside; not solid. A tube or pipe is hollow. Most rubber balls are hollow. 2. shaped like a bowl or cup; as, a hollow dish for vegetables. 3. a hollow place; a hole; as, a hollow in the road. 4. bend or dig out to a hollow shape. He hollowed a whistle out of the piece of wood. 5. a valley; as, Sleepy Hollow. 6. dull; as if coming from something hollow; as, a hollow voice or groan, the hollow boom of a foghorn. 7. not real or sincere; false; as, hollow promises, hollow joys. 8. hungry. By twelve o'clock we feel rather hollow.

hol ly (hol′i), an evergreen shrub with shiny, sharp-pointed leaves and bright red berries, used especially as Christmas decorations.

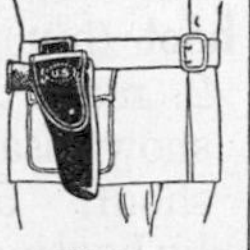
Holly

hol ly hock (hol′i hok), a tall plant with clusters of large, showy flowers of various colors.

hol ster (hōl′stər), a leather case for a pistol, worn on the belt or attached to a horseman's saddle. See the picture just below.

Holster

ho ly (hō′li), 1. given or belonging to God; set apart for God's service; coming from God; sacred; as, the Holy Bible, Holy Communion. 2. like a saint; spiritually perfect; very good; pure in heart; as, a holy man. 3. worthy of reverence. The grave of the unknown soldier is a holy place. 4. The **holy of holies** means the most sacred place.

Holy Land, Palestine.

Holy Week, the week before Easter.

Holy Writ, the Bible.

hom age (hom′ij), 1. respect; reverence; honor. 2. formal acknowledgment by a vassal that he owed faith and service to his lord.

home (hōm), 1. the place where one lives. Her home is at 25 South Street. 2. the town or country where one was born. His home is New York. 3. place where one can rest and be safe. 4. place where people who are homeless, poor, old, sick, blind, etc., may live. 5. place where a thing is specially common. Alaska is the home of the fur seal. 6. having something to do with one's home or country. Write me all the home events. 7. at or to one's home or country. I want to go home. 8. the goal in many games. 9. to its goal; to the place where it belongs. The spear struck home to the tiger's heart. 10. to the heart or center; deep in.

home less (hōm′lis), without a home.

home like (hōm′līk′), like home; friendly; familiar; comfortable.

home ly (hōm′li), 1. suited to home life; simple; everyday; as, homely pleasures, homely food. 2. ugly; plain; not good-looking.

home made (hōm′mād′), made at home.

home sick (hōm′sik′), overcome by sadness because home is far away; ill with longing for home.

home sick ness (hōm′sik′nis), longing for home.

home spun (hōm′spun′), 1. spun or made at home. 2. cloth made of homespun yarn. 3. loose, but strong, cloth that looks like homespun. 4. plain; simple; as, homespun manners.

home stead (hōm′sted), 1. a house with its buildings and grounds; a farm with its buildings. 2. land granted to a settler under certain conditions by the United States government.

home ward (hōm′wərd), toward home. We turned homeward. The ship is on her homeward course.

home wards (hōm′wərdz), homeward.

home work (hōm′wėrk′), 1. work done at home. 2. lesson to be studied or prepared outside the classroom.

hon est (on′ist), 1. fair and upright; truthful; not lying, cheating, or stealing. Job was an honest man. 2. without lying, cheating, or stealing. He lived an honest life. 3. frank; open; not hiding one's real nature. Mary has an honest face. 4. genuine; pure; not mixed with something of less value. Stores should sell honest goods.

hon es ty (on′is ti), honest behavior; honest nature; honest quality.

hon ey (hun′i), 1. a thick, sweet, yellow liquid, good to eat, that bees make out of the drops they collect from flowers. 2. the drop of sweet liquid found in many flowers, that draws bees to them. 3. sweetness. 4. darling.

hon ey comb (hun′i kōm′), 1. a structure of wax containing rows of six-sided cells formed by bees to hold honey and their eggs. 2. thing like this. 3. like a honeycomb; as, a honeycomb weave of cloth, a honeycomb pattern in knitting. 4. pierce with many holes. The rock was honeycombed with passages.

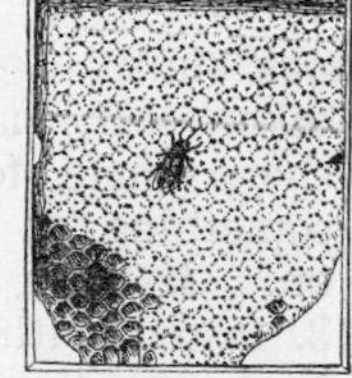
Honeycomb

hon ey moon (hun′i mün′), 1. the holiday spent together by a newly married couple. 2. spend or have a honeymoon.

hon ey suck le (hun′i suk′əl), a climbing shrub with fragrant flowers.

honk (hongk), 1. the cry of a wild goose. 2. any similar sound; as, the honk of an auto horn. 3. make such a sound.

hon or (on′ər), 1. glory; fame; renown. 2. good name; credit for acting well. It was greatly to his honor that he refused the reward. 3. a source of credit; person or thing that reflects honor; as, to be an honor to one's family or one's school. 4. nobility of mind; a nice sense of what is right or proper. 5. great respect; high regard. George Washington is held in honor. 6. an act that shows respect or high regard; as, funeral honors, military honors. The **honors of war** means favors shown to brave foes, such as keeping their flag flying. 7. respect highly; think highly of. 8. show respect to.

hon or a ble (on′ər ə bəl), 1. honest; upright; showing honor. It is not honorable to steal. 2. bringing honor or honors to somebody; as, honorable wounds. 3. noble; worthy of honor; as, an honorable name, to perform honorable deeds. 4. having a title, rank, or position of honor.

hon or ar y (on′ər ãr′i), 1. given or done as an honor. 2. as an honor only, without pay or regular duties. Some associations have honorary secretaries as well as regular paid secretaries.

hood (hu̇d), 1. a soft covering for the head and neck, either separate or as part of a cloak. My raincoat has a hood. 2. anything like a hood in shape or use. 3. the metal covering over the engine of an automobile. 4. to cover with a hood.

hoof (hüf), 1. the hard, horny covering of the foot of a horse, cow, sheep, pig, and some other animals. 2. the whole foot of such animals. 3. The human foot is sometimes called a hoof in fun.

hoofed (hüft), having hoofs.

hook (hu̇k), 1. piece of metal, wood, or other stiff material, curved or having a sharp angle, for catching hold of something or for hanging things on. 2. catch hold of with a hook. 3. fasten with hooks. Will you hook my dress for me? 4. bent piece of wire, usually with a backward bend at the end, for catching fish. 5. catch (fish) with a hook. 6. A reaping hook is a large curved knife for cutting down grass or grain. 7. a sharp bend; as, a hook in a river. 8. **By hook or by crook** means by fair means or foul.

Coat-hook

hook worm (hu̇k′wėrm′), 1. a worm that gets into the intestines and causes a disease with weakness and apparent laziness. 2. this disease.

hoop (hüp), 1. a ring or a flat band in the form of a circle; as, a hoop for holding together the staves of a barrel. 2. fasten together with hoops. 3. a large wooden or iron circle to be rolled along the ground by a child. 4. a circular frame formerly used to hold out a woman's skirt. See the picture. 5. an iron arch used in the game of croquet.

Hoop skirt

hoot (hüt), 1. sound that an owl makes. 2. make this sound or one like it. 3. shout to show disapproval or scorn. 4. make such a shout. 5. show disapproval of, or scorn for, by hooting. The audience hooted the speaker's plan. 6. force or drive by hooting. They hooted him off the platform.

hop[1] (hop), 1. spring, or move by springing, on one foot. How far can you hop on your right foot? Tom hopped fifty yards. 2. spring, or move by springing, with all feet at once. Many birds hop. A kangaroo hops. 3. hop over; as, to hop a ditch.

hop[2] (hop), 1. vine having flower clusters that look like small, yellow pine cones. 2. **Hops** are the dried, ripe, flower clusters of the hop vine, used to flavor beer and other malt drinks.

Hops

hope (hōp), 1. a feeling that what you desire will happen. His words gave me hope. 2. wish and expect. You hope to do well in school this year. 3. thing hoped for. 4. a cause of hope. He is the hope of the family.

hope ful (hōp′fəl), 1. feeling hope. 2. giving hope; likely to succeed.

hope less (hōp′lis), 1. feeling no hope. 2. giving no hope; as, a hopeless illness.

hop per (hop′ər), 1. one that hops. 2. a grasshopper or other hopping insect. 3. the receiver of grain in a mill; the receiver in various machines, larger at the top than at the bottom, which feeds material into the machine.

Hopper (def. 3)

horde (hōrd), multitude; crowd; swarm; as, hordes of grasshoppers.

ho ri zon (hə rī′zən), 1. the line where earth and sky appear to meet. You cannot see beyond the horizon. 2. the limit of one's thinking, experience, or interest.

hor i zon tal (hor′i zon′təl), 1. parallel to the horizon; at right angles to a vertical line. 2. flat; level.

—VERTICAL

HORIZONTAL

horn (hôrn), 1. a hard growth, often curved and pointed, on the heads of cattle, sheep, goats, and some other animals. 2. anything that sticks up on the head of an animal; as, a snail's horns, an insect's horns. 3. the substance or material of horns. 4. a container made by hollowing out a horn; as, a drinking horn, a powder horn. 5. a musical instrument sounded by blowing; as, a hunting horn, a French horn, an English horn. 6. the tip of the new moon, or of some crescent.

Powder horn

Horn

hor net (hôr′nit), a large insect like a wasp, that can give a very painful sting. See the picture just below.

horn y (hôr′ni), 1. made of horn or a substance like it. 2. hard like horn. A farmer's hands are horny from work.

hor ri ble (hor′i bəl), frightful; shocking; terrible.

hor rid (hor′id), terrible; frightful.

Hornet (about 1 in. long)

hor ri fy (hor′i fī), 1. cause to feel horror. 2. shock very much. We were horrified by the wreck.

hor ror (hor′ər), 1. a shivering, shaking terror. 2. very strong dislike. Little girls sometimes have a horror of snakes or spiders. 3. thing that causes great fear.

horse (hôrs), 1. See the picture. Horses are used for riding and for carrying and pulling loads. 2. soldiers on horses; cavalry. 3. a supporting frame. Five boards laid on two horses made our picnic table.

Horse

horse back (hôrs′bak′), 1. the back of a horse. 2. on the back of a horse; as, to ride horseback.

horse chestnut, 1. a shade tree with spreading branches, large leaves, clusters of showy white flowers, and glossy brown nuts. 2. the nut.

horse fly (hôrs′flī′), fly that bites horses.

horse hair (hôrs′hãr′), 1. hair from the mane or tail of a horse. 2. made of horsehair; stuffed with horsehair.

Horsefly (somewhat over life size)

horse man (hôrs′mən), 1. man who rides on horseback. 2. man who is skilled in managing horses.

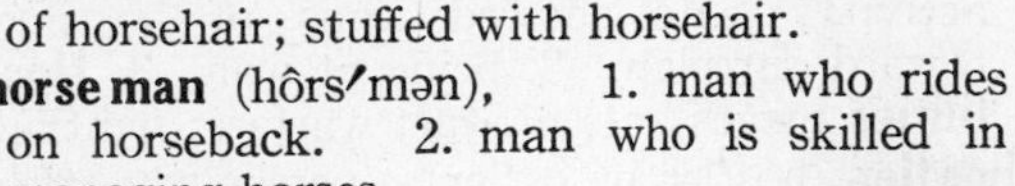

horse shoe (hôrs′shü′), 1. a U-shaped metal plate nailed to a horse's hoof to protect it. 2. thing shaped like a horseshoe.

Horseshoe

hose (hōz), 1. stockings. 2. a tube of rubber or something else that will bend, for carrying any liquid for short distances. A hose is used in pumping gasoline into automobiles. 3. long, tight breeches worn by men in olden times.

Rubber hose for sprinkling

ho sier y (hō′zhər i), stockings.

hos pice (hos′pis), a house for travelers to rest in.

hos pi ta ble (hos′pi tə bəl), 1. giving or liking to give a welcome, food and shelter, and friendly treatment to guests or strangers; as, a hospitable family. 2. willing and ready to entertain; as, a person hospitable to new ideas.

hos pi ta bly (hos′pi tə bli), in a hospitable manner.

hos pi tal (hos′pi təl), a place for the care of the sick or wounded. The doctor removed Joe's tonsils at the hospital.

hos pi tal i ty (hos′pi tal′i ti), friendly reception; generous treatment of guests or strangers.

host[1] (hōst), 1. one who receives another person at his house as his guest. 2. the keeper of an inn or hotel.

host[2] (hōst), a large number. As it grew dark, a few stars appeared, then a host.

hos tage (hos′tij), 1. person given to another or to an enemy as a pledge. The hostage will be kept safe and will be returned when the promises or agreements have been carried out. 2. pledge; security.

hos tel (hos′təl), inn; hotel.

host ess (hōs′tis), 1. woman who receives another person as her guest. 2. woman who keeps an inn or hotel, or helps her husband to do so.

hos tile (hos′til), 1. of an enemy or enemies; as, the hostile army. 2. unfriendly; unfavorable; as, a hostile look.

hos til i ty (hos til′i ti), 1. the feeling that an enemy has; hostile nature; hostile activity. He showed signs of hostility toward our plan. 2. being at war. 3. **Hostilities** means acts of war; warfare; fighting.

hos tler (hos′lər or os′lər), person who takes care of horses.

hot (hot), 1. having much heat. Fire is hot. The sun is hot. That long run has made me hot. 2. tasting sharp, as pepper and mustard do. 3. fiery; eager. The boys were hot after the treasure. 4. new; fresh; as, a hot scent or trail. **hotter** and **hottest** are formed from **hot.**

ho tel (hō tel′), house that supplies rooms and food for pay. Hotels in cities are often large buildings with many comforts and luxuries.

hot house (hot′hous′), a building with a glass roof and sides, kept warm for growing plants.

Hothouse

hound (hound), 1. dog of any of various breeds, most of which hunt by scent and have large, drooping ears and short hair. 2. any dog. 3. hunt; chase. 4. urge (on).

hour (our), 1. 60 minutes make an hour. 24 hours make a day. It is 12 hours from noon to midnight. 2. the time of day. This clock strikes the hours and the half hours. 3. the time for anything. Our breakfast hour is at eight. Our school hours are 9 to 12 and 1 to 4.

hour ly (our′li), 1. every hour. Give two doses hourly. 2. done, happening, or counted every hour; as, to give hourly doses of a medicine. 3. very often; frequently. Messages were coming from the front hourly. 4. frequent; as, hourly messages from the front.

house (hous for 1, 2, 3, 5, and 6, houz for 4), 1. a building in which people live. 2. building for any purpose; as, a storehouse, a henhouse, a schoolhouse. 3. a family; especially, a noble family. He was a prince of the house of David. 4. take or put into a house; shelter. Where can we house all these children? 5. business firm. 6. audience. The singer sang to a large house.

house hold (hous′hōld), 1. all the people living in a house; family; family and servants. 2. a home and its affairs. 3. of a household; having to do with a household; domestic; as, household expenses, household cares.

house hold er (hous′hōl′dər), 1. person who owns or lives in a house. 2. head of a family.

house keep er (hous′kēp′ər), 1. woman who manages a home and its affairs and does the housework. 2. woman who directs the servants that do the housework.

house keep ing (hous′kēp′ing), 1. management of a home and its affairs. 2. housework.

house top (hous′top′), top of a house; roof.

house wife (hous′wīf′), 1. woman who manages a home and its affairs. A housewife plans the housework and usually does the buying for the family. 2. woman who is the head of a household.

house work (hous′wėrk′), washing, ironing, cleaning, sweeping, cooking, etc.

hous ing (houz′ing), 1. sheltering; providing shelter. 2. houses. The housing of that city is not enough for the people who will be there next year.

hove (hōv), heaved. See **heave.** The sailors hove at the ropes.

hov el (huv′əl), a house that is small, mean, and unpleasant to live in.

hov er (huv′ər), 1. stay in or near one place in the air. The two birds hovered over their nest. 2. stay in or near one place. The dogs hovered around the meat truck. 3. be in an uncertain condition; waver. The sick man hovered between life and death.

how (hou), 1. in what way. I wonder how you go there? How can it be done? How did it happen? 2. to what degree or amount. How tall are you? How hot is it? How much shall I bring you? 3. in what condition. How is your health? Tell me how Mrs. Jones is. How do I look? 4. for what reason; why. How is it you don't like candy?

how e'er (hou ãr′), however.

how ev er (hou ev′ər), 1. nevertheless. We were very late for dinner; however, there was plenty left for us. 2. to whatever degree or amount. I'll come however busy I am. 3. in whatever way; by whatever means. However did you get so dirty?

howl (houl), 1. give a long, loud, mournful cry. Dogs often howl at night. 2. a long, loud, mournful cry; as, the howl of a wolf. 3. give a long, loud cry of pain or rage. 4. a loud cry of pain or rage. 5. yell; shout. It was so funny that we howled with laughter. 6. force or drive by howling. The angry mob howled the speaker off the platform.

hub (hub), 1. the central part of a wheel. 2. center of activity, etc. London is the hub of English life.

SPOKE HUB AXLE FELLOE

Hub

hub bub (hub′ub), loud, confused noise; uproar. The crowd of boys was in a hubbub.

huck le ber ry (huk′əl ber′i), 1. a small berry like a blueberry, but darker in color. 2. the shrub it grows on.

hud dle (hud′əl), 1. to crowd close. The sheep huddled together in a corner. 2. put close together. She huddled all four boys into one bed. 3. a confused heap, mass, or crowd. Your books and papers are in a huddle; put them in better order at once.

Huckleberry

hue (hū), color; tint. The girls' dresses showed almost all the hues of the rainbow.

hug (hug), 1. put the arms around and hold close. The girl hugs her big doll. 2. a tight clasp with the arms. Give mother a hug. 3. cling firmly or fondly to; as, to hug an opinion. 4. keep close to. The boat hugged the shore.

huge (hūj), very, very large. Whales and elephants are huge animals.

hulk (hulk), 1. the body of an old or worn-out ship. 2. a big, clumsy person. 3. anything large and hard to manage.

hulk ing (hul′king), big and clumsy.

hull (hul), 1. body or frame of a ship. Masts, sails, and rigging are not part of the hull. 2. main body or frame of a seaplane, airship, etc. 3. outer covering of a seed. 4. calyx of some fruits. We call the green frill of a strawberry its hull. 5. remove the hull or hulls from.

HULL

Strawberry

hum (hum), 1. make a continuous murmuring sound like that of a bee or of a spinning top. The sewing machine hums as it runs. 2. a continuous, murmuring sound; as, the hum of bees, the hum of the city streets. 3. sing with closed lips, not sounding words. She was humming a tune. 4. be busy and active.

hu man (hū′mən), of man; like a man. Men, women, and children are human beings. Some monkeys look almost human.

hu mane (hū mān′), kind; not cruel or brutal.

hu man i ty (hū man′i ti), 1. people. All humanity will be helped by advances in medical sciences. 2. the nature of man. Humanity is a mixture of good and bad qualities. 3. kindness. Treat animals with humanity.

hum ble (hum′bəl), 1. low in position or condition; not important; not grand. He held a humble position with a very small salary. We live in a humble cottage of one room. 2. modest; not proud. 3. make humble; make lower in position, condition, or pride.

hum bly (hum′bli), in a humble manner.

hum bug (hum′bug′), 1. a cheat; a sham. 2. to cheat; deceive with a sham.

hu mid (hū′mid), moist; damp. The air is very humid near the sea.

hu mid i ty (hū mid′i ti), 1. moistness; dampness. The humidity today is worse than the heat. 2. amount of moisture in the air.

hu mil i ate (hū mil′i āt), lower the pride, dignity, or self-respect of. John felt humiliated by his failure. A child who behaves badly when guests are present humiliates his parents.

hu mil i a tion (hū mil′i ā′shən), a lowering of pride, dignity, or self-respect.

hu mil i ty (hū mil′i ti), humbleness; lack of pride; meekness.

hum ming bird (hum′ing bėrd′), a very small, brightly colored American bird with a long, narrow bill and narrow wings that make a humming sound.

Hummingbird (about $3\frac{3}{4}$ in. long)

hum mock (hum′ək), 1. a very small, rounded hill; knoll; hillock. 2. a bump or ridge in a field of ice.

hu mor (hū′mər), 1. funny quality. I see no humor in your tricks. 2. ability to find fun and amusement in things. 3. state of mind; mood; temper. Is the teacher in a good humor this morning? I feel in the humor for working. **Out of humor** means cross; in a bad mood. 4. fancy; whim. 5. give in to (a person); agree with. A sick child has to be humored.

hu mor ist (hū′mər ist), 1. person with a strong sense of humor. 2. humorous talker; writer of jokes and funny stories.

hu mor ous (hū′mər əs), full of humor; funny; amusing.

hump (hump), 1. a rounded lump that sticks out. Some camels have two humps on their backs. 2. raise or bend up into a lump. The cat humped her back when she saw the dog.

hump backed (hump′bakt′), having a back with a hump on it.

humph (həm), an exclamation expressing doubt, disgust, contempt, etc.

hu mus (hū′məs), soil made from dead leaves and other vegetable matter.

hunch (hunch), 1. hump. 2. draw, bend, or form into a hump. He sat hunched up with his chin on his knees. 3. move, push, or shove by jerks. 4. an expectation that you don't know the reason for.

hunch back (hunch′bak′), person with a hump on his back.

hunch backed (hunch′bakt′), humpbacked.

hun dred (hun′drəd), ten times ten; 100. There are one hundred cents in a dollar.

hun dred fold (hun′drəd fōld′), a hundred times as much or as many.

hun dredth (hun′drədth), 1. next after the 99th. 2. one of 100 equal parts.

hung (hung). See **hang.** He hung up his cap. Your dress has hung here all day.

hun ger (hung′gər), 1. painful feeling caused by having nothing to eat. The little boy who ran away from home soon felt hunger. 2. desire or need for food. 3. feel hunger; be hungry. 4. strong desire; as, a hunger for books. 5. have a strong desire. The lonely girl hungered for friends.

hun gri ly (hung′gri li), in a hungry manner.

hun gry (hung′gri), 1. feeling a desire or need for food. 2. showing hunger. The cook saw a hungry look on the beggar's face. 3. eager. Jean is hungry for books.

hunk (hungk), a big lump or piece.

hunt (hunt), 1. chase (game and other wild animals) for food or for fun. 2. hunting. 3. a group of people hunting together. 4. search; seek; look; as, to hunt for a lost book. 5. a search; an attempt to find something. 6. drive; chase; as, to hunt a neighbor's chickens out of our yard.

hunt er (hun′tər), 1. person who hunts. 2. a horse or dog for hunting.

hunt ress (hun′tris), woman who hunts.

hunts man (hunts′mən), 1. hunter. 2. manager of a hunt.

hur dle (hėr′dəl), 1. barrier for people or horses to jump over in a race. 2. jump over. Joe hurdled the fence. 3. obstacle, difficulty, etc. 4. overcome (an obstacle, difficulty, etc.). 5. frame made of sticks and used as a fence.

Hurdles for racing

hur dy-gur dy (hėr′di gėr′di), a hand organ or street piano played by turning a handle.

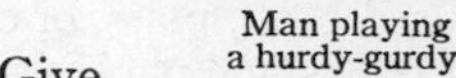

Man playing a hurdy-gurdy

hurl (hėrl), throw with much force. The man hurled his spear at one bear, and the dogs hurled themselves at the other.

hur rah (hu̇ rä′). Give a hurrah for the hero! We hurrah when we see the soldiers go by.

hur ray (hu̇ rā′), hurrah.

hur ri cane (hėr′i kān), 1. tropical cyclone; storm with violent wind and, usually, very heavy rain. The wind in a hurricane blows from 70 to 100 miles per hour. 2. sudden, violent outburst.

hur ried (hėr′id), 1. forced to hurry. 2. done or made in a hurry; hasty.

hur ried ly (hėr′id li), in a hurry; hastily. She packed her bags hurriedly so as to catch the train.

hur ry (hėr′i), 1. to drive, carry, send, or move quickly. They hurried the sick child to the doctor. He hurried his book out of sight when the teacher appeared. 2. move or act with more than an easy or natural speed. If you hurry, your work may be poor. He hurried to get the doctor. 3. hurried movement or action. In her hurry she dropped the eggs. 4. eagerness to have quickly or do quickly. She was in a hurry to see her father. 5. urge to great speed or to too great speed. 6. hasten; make go on or occur more quickly. Please hurry dinner.

hurt (hėrt), 1. cause pain or injury to. The stone hurt his foot badly. 2. a cut or bruise; the breaking of a bone; any wound or injury.

3. suffer pain. My hand hurts. 4. have a bad effect on; do damage or harm to. Will it hurt this hat if it gets wet? 5. harm; wrong. It would do no hurt to get the house painted this summer.

hurt ful (hėrt′fəl), causing hurt, harm, or damage.

hur tle (hėr′təl), 1. dash violently; rush violently. Spears hurtled against shields. 2. hurtling; a clash.

hus band (huz′bənd), 1. man who has a wife. 2. manage carefully; be saving of. A man must husband his strength when he is ill.

hus band man (huz′bənd mən), farmer.

hus band ry (huz′bənd ri), 1. farming. 2. management of one's affairs. To let a roof leak would be bad husbandry. 3. careful management; thrift.

hush (hush), 1. stop making a noise. Hush! Hush! The wind has hushed. 2. stillness.

husk (husk), 1. the dry outer covering of certain seeds or fruits. An ear of corn has a husk. 2. dry or worthless outer covering of anything. 3. remove the husk from. Husk the corn.

Husk on an ear of corn

husk i ness (hus′ki nis), hoarseness or roughness of voice.

husking bee, a gathering of neighbors and friends to husk corn.

husk y[1] (hus′ki), 1. dry in the throat; hoarse; rough of voice; as, a husky cough. 2. big and strong.

Husk y or **husk y**[2] (hus′ki), Eskimo dog.

hus tle (hus′əl), 1. hurry. Mother hustled baby to bed. 2. rush roughly; push one's way; as, to hustle along through the crowd. 3. push or shove roughly. The other boys hustled Ned along the street. 4. go or work quickly or with energy. 5. hustling. It was done with much hustle and bustle. It was a hustle to get the dishes washed by seven o'clock.

hut (hut), a small, roughly made house; a small cabin. The boys built a hut in the woods.

Hyacinth

huz za (hu zä′), hurrah.

hy a cinth (hī′ə sinth), a spring plant that grows from a bulb and has a spike of small, fragrant, bell-shaped flowers.

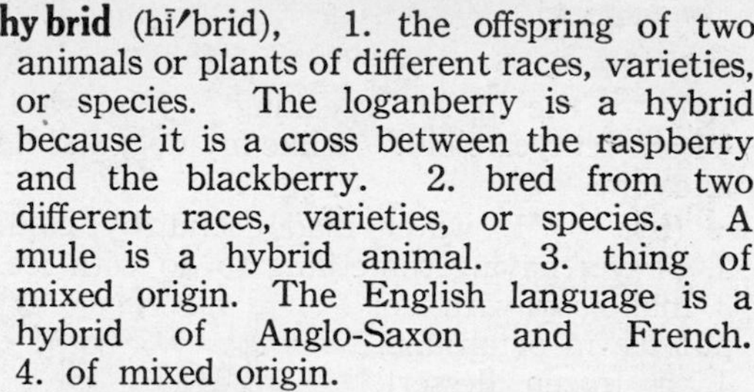

hy brid (hī′brid), 1. the offspring of two animals or plants of different races, varieties, or species. The loganberry is a hybrid because it is a cross between the raspberry and the blackberry. 2. bred from two different races, varieties, or species. A mule is a hybrid animal. 3. thing of mixed origin. The English language is a hybrid of Anglo-Saxon and French. 4. of mixed origin.

hy dran gea (hī drān′jə), a shrub with large, showy flower clusters, white, pink, or bluish in color.

hy drant (hī′drənt), a large pipe with a valve for drawing water; a hose connection. Hydrants are used to get water to put out fires and to wash the streets.

Hydrant

hy dro gen (hī′drə jən), a colorless gas that burns easily. Hydrogen weighs less than any other known substance.

hy dro pho bi a (hī′drə fō′bi ə), the disease a mad dog has. If bitten by a mad dog, a person may get the disease.

hy dro plane (hī′drə plān), 1. motorboat that glides on the surface of water. 2. seaplane; airplane provided with floats or something like a boat so that it can alight upon and ascend from water.

hy e na (hī ē′nə), a wild animal much like a large dog in shape and size. Most hyenas are cowardly, but utter terrifying yells.

Striped hyena (about 2 ft. high at the shoulder)

hy giene (hī′jēn), the rules of health; the science of keeping well.

hymn (him), 1. song in praise or honor of God. 2. any song of praise.

hym nal (him′nəl), a book of hymns.

hy phen (hī′fən), a mark (-) used to connect the parts of a compound word, or the parts of a word divided at the end of a line.

hy poc ri sy (hi pok′ri si), 1. putting on a false appearance of goodness or religion. 2. pretending to be what one is not; pretense.

hyp o crite (hip′ə krit), person who puts on a false appearance of goodness or religion.

hys te ri a (his tēr′i ə), 1. senseless excitement. 2. nervous disorder that causes sham illnesses, etc.

I

I (ī), the person speaking. John said, "I am ten years old." I like my dog, and he likes me.

ice (īs), 1. water made solid by cold. 2. of ice; having something to do with ice. 3. make cool with ice; put ice in or around. 4. a frozen dessert, usually one made of sweetened fruit juice.

ice berg (īs′bėrg′), a large mass of ice floating in the sea. A ship may be wrecked on an iceberg. See the picture just above.

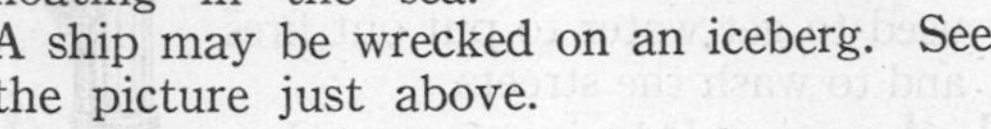

Iceberg

ice cream, a dessert made of cream or custard sweetened, flavored, and frozen.

i ci cle (ī′si kəl), a pointed, hanging stick of ice formed by the freezing of dripping water.

Icicle

i ci ly (ī′si li), very coldly.

i cy (ī′si), 1. like ice; very cold; slippery. 2. having much ice; covered with ice. 3. of ice. 4. without warm feeling; cold and unfriendly.

I'd (īd), 1. I should; I would. 2. I had.

i de a (ī dē′ə), 1. a plan, picture, or belief of the mind. Candy and toys are a child's ideas of happiness. 2. thought; fancy; opinion. John had no idea that work at school was so hard.

i de al (ī dē′əl), 1. a perfect type; a model to be imitated. Ruth's mother is her ideal. The Christian religion holds up high ideals. 2. perfect; just as one would wish. A clear, warm day is ideal for a picnic.

i den ti cal (ī den′ti kəl), 1. the same. That is the identical pen I lost. 2. exactly alike. The two boys took identical trips last summer.

i den ti fy (ī den′ti fī), 1. recognize as being a particular person or thing; prove to be the same. Fred identified the bag as his by telling what it contained. 2. make the same; treat as the same. A good king identifies the interest of his people with his own prosperity.

i den ti ty (ī den′ti ti), 1. individuality; who a person is; what a thing is. The writer concealed his identity by signing his stories with a false name. 2. exact likeness The identity of the crimes led the police to think that the same person committed them.

id i ot (id′i ət), 1. person so stupid that he can never learn to read or to count; a born fool. 2. very stupid or foolish person. What an idiot I was to forget my bag!

id i ot ic (id′i ot′ik), very stupid or foolish.

i dle (ī′dəl), 1. not doing anything; not busy; as, idle hours of a holiday. 2. lazy; not willing to do things. The idle boy would not study. 3. useless. It is idle for a girl to wish to be a boy. 4. without any good reason or cause; as, idle fears, idle rumors. 5. be idle; do nothing. 6. waste (time); spend. Jane idled away many hours lying in the hammock. 7. run slowly without transmitting power. A motor idles when it is out of gear and running slowly.

i dle ness (ī′dəl nis), 1. having nothing to do. The closing of the large factory made many workers live in idleness. 2. tendency to avoid work; being lazy. Idleness may be caused by poor health.

i dler (ī′dlər), a lazy person.

i dly (ī′dli), in an idle manner; doing nothing.

i dol (ī′dəl), 1. a thing, usually an image, that is worshiped. 2. person or thing that is loved very, very much. Little Mary was the idol of her family.

Idol

if (if). Come if you can. If it rains tomorrow, we shall stay at home. I do not know if he is rich or poor.

ig loo (ig′lü), an Eskimo hut that is often shaped like a dome, and built of blocks of hard snow.

Igloo

ig nite (ig nīt′), 1. set on fire. You ignite a match by scratching it. 2. take fire; begin to burn. Gasoline ignites easily.

ig no ble (ig nō′bəl), 1. mean; base; without honor. To betray a friend is ignoble. 2. of low birth. Some very great men have come from ignoble families.

ig no rance (ig′nə rəns), lack of knowledge; being ignorant.

ig no rant (ig′nə rənt), knowing little or nothing. Nell is ignorant of farm life. This boy is not stupid, but he has never been to school or had much chance to learn; so he is very ignorant.

ig nore (ig nōr′), pay no attention to; disregard. When you bump your head, it is better to ignore the pain than to cry.

ill (il), 1. not well; having some disease; as, ill with a fever. 2. sickness; disease. She told us about all the ills she had. 3. bad; evil; as, to do a person an ill turn. 4. badly; as, work ill done. 5. an evil; a harm. Many ills happened to Job.

I'll (īl), 1. I shall. 2. I will.

il le gal (i lē′gəl), not lawful; against the law.

ill ness (il′nis), sickness; poor health. Scarlet fever is a serious illness.

il log i cal (i loj′i kəl), 1. not logical. 2. not reasonable.

ill-treat (il′trēt′), treat cruelly; treat badly; do harm to.

il lu mi nate (i lü′mi nāt), 1. light up; make bright. The room was illuminated by four large lamps. 2. throw a strong light on. The big searchlight illuminates a spot a mile away. 3. make clear; explain. Our interesting teacher could illuminate almost any subject we studied.

il lu mi na tion (i lü′mi nā′shən), 1. lighting; lights. 2. the light supplied. 3. making clear.

il lu mine (i lü′min), light up; make bright. Electric lights illumine our houses. A smile often illumines a homely face.

ill-use (il′ūz′), treat badly.

il lu sion (i lü′zhən), 1. an appearance which is not real. That slender snow-covered bush at the gate gave me an illusion of a woman waiting there. 2. a false idea. Many people have the illusion that wealth is the chief cause of happiness.

il lus trate (il′əs trāt or i lus′trāt), 1. make clear or explain by stories, examples, comparisons, etc. The way that a pump works is used to illustrate how the heart sends blood around the body. 2. provide with pictures, diagrams, maps, etc., that explain or decorate. This book is well illustrated.

il lus tra tion (il′əs trā′shən), 1. picture, diagram, map, etc., used to explain or decorate something. 2. story, example, comparison, etc., used to make clear or explain something. The teacher cut an apple into four equal pieces as an illustration of what $\frac{1}{4}$ means. 3. act or process of illustrating. Illustration is used in teaching children.

il lus tri ous (i lus′tri əs), very famous. Washington and Lincoln are illustrious Americans.

ill will, unfriendly feeling.

I'm (īm), I am.

im age (im′ij), 1. a likeness or copy. You see your image in the mirror. She is almost the exact image of her mother. I can shut my eyes and see images of things and persons. 2. a likeness made of stone, wood, or some other material; statue. The shelf was full of little images of all sorts of animals. 3. make an image of. 4. reflect as a mirror does. The clouds were imaged in the still waters of the lake. 5. a comparison used to add force or beauty. Some poems contain many images.

i mag i na ble (i maj′i nə bəl), that can be imagined. Cinderella was dressed with the greatest splendor imaginable.

i mag i nar y (i maj′i nãr′i), existing only in the imagination; not real. Fairies are imaginary. The equator is an imaginary line.

i mag i na tion (i maj′i nā′shən), 1. imagining; the power of forming pictures in the mind of things not present to the senses. The child's imagination filled the woods with strange animals and fairies. 2. ability to create new things or ideas or to combine old ones in new forms. Poets, artists, and inventors need imagination. 3. a creation of the mind; a fancy.

i mag i na tive (i maj′i nā′tiv), 1. able to imagine well. The imaginative child made up fairy stories. 2. of imagination. 3. showing imagination.

i mag ine (i maj′in), form a picture of in the mind; have an idea. Charles likes to imagine himself a knight. We can hardly imagine life as it was two hundred years ago.

im be cile (im′bi sil), 1. weak in mind; very stupid. 2. person who has a very weak mind. An imbecile is almost an idiot.

im i tate (im′i tāt), 1. try to be like; follow the example of. The boy imitates his older brother. 2. make or do something like; copy. The parrot imitates the sounds he hears. 3. act like. John amused the class by imitating a baby, an old man, and a bear. 4. be like; look like. Wood is sometimes painted to imitate stone.

im i ta tion (im′i tā′shən), 1. imitating. We learn many things by imitation. 2. copy. Give as good an imitation as you can of a rooster crowing. 3. not real. You can buy imitation pearls in the ten-cent stores.

im mac u late (i mak′ū lit), 1. without a spot or stain. 2. pure; without sin.

im ma ture (im′ə tūr′ or im′ə tür′), not mature; not ripe; not full-grown.

im meas ur a ble (i mezh′ər ə bəl), that cannot be measured.

im me di ate (i mē′di it), 1. coming at once; without delay. Please send an immediate reply. 2. nearest; with nothing between. My immediate neighbor is Mrs. Jones.

im me di ate ly (i mē′di it li), 1. at once; without delay. I answered his letter immediately. 2. next; with nothing between.

im me mo ri al (im′i mō′ri əl), extending back beyond the bounds of memory; very, very old.

im mense (i mens′), very, very large; huge; vast.

im mense ly (i mens′li), very greatly.

im men si ty (i men′si ti), vastness; boundless or vast extent; as, the ocean's immensity.

im merse (i mėrs′), 1. plunge into (a liquid). 2. baptize by dipping (a person) under water. 3. absorb; involve deeply; as, immersed in thought, immersed in debts.

im mi grant (im′i grənt), person who comes into a country or region to live. Canada has many immigrants from Europe. California has many immigrants from other States.

im mi grate (im′i grāt), come into a country or region to live there.

im mi gra tion (im′i grā′shən), 1. coming into a country or region to live. There was immigration to America from all the countries of Europe. 2. the persons who immigrate. The immigration of 1910 included many people from Italy.

im mi nent (im′i nənt), likely to happen soon; about to occur. Black clouds, thunder, and lightning show that a storm is imminent.

im mor al (i mor′əl), morally wrong; wicked. Lying and stealing are immoral.

im mor tal (i môr′təl), living forever; never dying; everlasting. A man's body dies, but his soul may be immortal.

im mor tal i ty (im′ôr tal′i ti), 1. endless life; living forever. 2. fame that lasts forever.

im mov a ble (i müv′ə bəl), that cannot be moved; fixed; firm; steadfast; as, immovable mountains, an immovable purpose.

imp (imp), 1. a child of the devil; little devil. 2. mischievous child.

Imp

im pact (im′pakt), striking of one thing against another. The impact of the two swords broke both of them.

im pair (im pãr′), make worse; damage; harm; weaken. Poor food impaired his health.

im part (im pärt′), give a share in; give; communicate; tell. A teacher imparts knowledge to her pupils. I will impart a secret to you.

im par tial (im pär′shəl), fair; just; showing no more favor to one side than to the other.

im pass a ble (im pas′ə bəl), not passable; so that one cannot go through. The muddy road was impassable.

im pas sioned (im pash′ənd), emotional; full of strong feeling; ardent. The general made an impassioned speech to his soldiers.

im pa tience (im pā′shəns), 1. lack of patience; being impatient. 2. uneasiness and eagerness.

im pa tient (im pā′shənt), 1. not patient; not willing to bear delay, pain, bother, etc. Jim is impatient with his little sister. 2. restless. The horses were impatient to start in the race. 3. showing lack of patience; as, an impatient answer.

im pede (im pēd′), hinder; obstruct. The deep snow impeded travel.

im ped i ment (im ped′i mənt), 1. hindrance; obstacle. 2. defect in speech.

im pel (im pel′), 1. drive; force; cause. Hunger impels me to eat. 2. push forward; drive on. A strong tide impelled the boat toward the island.

im pen e tra ble (im pen′i trə bəl), 1. that cannot be entered, pierced, or passed. The thorny branches made a thick, impenetrable hedge. A thick sheet of steel is impenetrable by an ordinary bullet. 2. that cannot be seen into or understood.

im per a tive (im per′ə tiv), 1. urgent; not to be avoided; necessary. It is imperative that a very sick child should stay in bed. 2. command. The great imperative is "Love thy neighbor as thyself."

im per cep ti ble (im′pər sep′ti bəl), that cannot be perceived or felt; very slight.

im per fect (im pėr′fikt), 1. not perfect; having some defect or fault. A crack in the cup made it imperfect. 2. not complete.

im per fec tion (im′pər fek′shən), 1. lack of perfection; imperfect condition or character. 2. fault; defect.

im pe ri al (im pēr′i əl), 1. of an empire or its ruler. 2. having the rank of an emperor. 3. supreme; majestic; magnificent. 4. a very small beard left growing beneath the lower lip.

Man wearing an imperial

im per il (im per′il), put in danger.

im pe ri ous (im pēr′i əs), 1. haughty; arrogant; domineering; overbearing. 2. not to be avoided; urgent; necessary. They worked to satisfy the imperious demands of hunger.

im per son al (im pėr′sən əl), referring to all or any persons, not to any special one. "First come, first served" is an impersonal remark.

im per ti nent (im pėr′ti nənt), saucy; impudent; insolent; rude.

im pet u ous (im pech′ü əs), 1. moving with great force; as, the impetuous rush of water over Niagara Falls. 2. acting hastily, rashly, or with sudden feeling. Boys are more impetuous than old men.

im pe tus (im′pi təs), 1. the force with which an object moves. Anything that you can stop easily has little impetus. 2. driving force. Ambition is an impetus to work.

im pi ous (im′pi əs), not pious; not having reverence for God; wicked.

im ple ment (im′pli mənt), useful article of equipment; tool; instrument; utensil. A broom, a pail, a shovel, or an ax is an implement.

im plore (im plōr′), 1. beg earnestly for. The prisoner implored pardon. 2. beg (a person) to do something. He implored the judge to spare his life.

im ply (im plī′), mean (a thing) without saying it outright; express in an indirect way. Silence often implies consent. The teacher's smile implied that she had forgiven us.

im port (im pōrt′ for 1 and 3, im′pōrt for 2, 4, and 5), 1. bring in from a foreign country. The United States imports sugar from Cuba. 2. an article brought into a country. Rubber is a useful import. 3. mean; make known. What does this message import? 4. meaning. 5. importance.

im por tance (im pôr′təns), being important; consequence; value. Anybody can see the importance of good health.

im por tant (im pôr′tənt), 1. meaning much; having value or influence; as, important business, an important occasion. 2. acting as if important; seeming to have influence. An important little man rushed around giving orders.

im por ta tion (im′pōr tā′shən), 1. bringing in merchandise from foreign countries. 2. something brought in. Her shawl is a recent importation from Mexico.

im pose (im pōz′), 1. put (a burden, tax, or punishment) on. The judge imposed a fine of $500 on the guilty man. Do not let the children impose on you. 2. **Impose on** or **upon** sometimes means (1) use selfishly. (2) deceive.

im pos ing (im pōz′ing), impressive because of size, appearance, dignity, etc. The Capitol at Washington, D. C., is an imposing building.

im pos si bil i ty (im pos′i bil′i ti), 1. being impossible. We all realize the impossibility of living long without food. 2. something impossible.

im pos si ble (im pos′i bəl), 1. that cannot be or happen. It is impossible for two and two to make six. 2. not possible to use; not to be done; not possible to endure. Tom said a summer without swimming would be impossible.

im pos tor (im pos′tər), 1. person who assumes a false name or character. 2. deceiver; cheat.

im po tent (im′pə tənt), not having power; helpless. Without guns and ammunition the soldiers were impotent. The cripple fell back in an impotent rage.

im pov er ish (im pov′ər ish), 1. make very poor. 2. exhaust the strength or richness of; as, to impoverish the soil, the blood, or the mind.

im prac ti ca ble (im prak′ti kə bəl), not working well in practice; that cannot be used.

im pre ca tion (im′pri kā′shən), 1. act of calling down evil on a person; cursing. 2. a curse. The beggar shouted imprecations after the traveler.

im preg na ble (im preg′nə bəl), not to be taken by force; able to resist attack; as, an impregnable fortress, an impregnable argument.

im press (im pres′ for 1, 2, 4, and 5, im′pres for 3 and 6), 1. make marks on by pressing or stamping. We can impress wax with a seal. 2. to imprint; to stamp. 3. impression; mark; a stamp. An author leaves the impress of his personality on what he writes. 4. have a strong effect on the mind or feelings of. A hero impresses us with his courage. 5. fix in the mind. She repeated the words to impress them in her memory. 6. act of impressing.

im pres sion (im presh′ən), 1. effect produced on a person. Punishment seemed to make little impression on the child. 2. idea; notion. I have a vague impression that I left the house unlocked. 3. something made by pressure, such as a mark, stamp, or print. The thief had left an impression of his foot in the garden.

im pres sive (im pres′iv), able to impress the mind, feelings, conscience, etc.; as, an impressive sermon, an impressive storm, an impressive ceremony.

im print (im′print for 1 and 2, im print′ for 3), 1. mark made by pressure; print; as, the imprint of a foot in the sand. 2. impression; mark; as, the imprint of suffering on her face. 3. press or impress; as, to imprint a kiss on someone's cheek, a scene imprinted on my memory.

im pris on (im priz′ən), 1. put in prison; keep in prison. 2. confine closely.

im pris on ment (im priz′ən mənt), 1. an imprisoning. 2. a being imprisoned.

im prob a ble (im prob′ə bəl), not probable; not likely to happen; not likely to be true.

im prop er (im prop′ər), 1. wrong; not correct. "We ain't" is improper speech. 2. not suitable. A bright dress is improper for a funeral. 3. not decent. 4. An **improper fraction** is a fraction greater than 1. $\frac{3}{2}$, $\frac{5}{3}$, $\frac{7}{4}$, $\frac{21}{12}$, and $\frac{8}{5}$ are improper fractions.

im prove (im prüv′), 1. make better. You could improve your handwriting if you tried. 2. become better; as, to improve in health. 3. use well. We had two hours to wait and improved the time by seeing the city.

im prove ment (im prüv′mənt), 1. making better; becoming better. Will's schoolwork shows much improvement since last term. 2. anything that adds value. The improvements in his house cost over a thousand dollars. 3. better condition; a gain; advance. Automobiles are an improvement over horses.

im pru dent (im prü′dənt), not prudent; rash; not discreet.

im pu dence (im′pū dəns), lack of shame or modesty; rude boldness.

im pu dent (im′pū dənt), without shame or modesty; forward; rudely bold. The impudent boy made faces at the teacher.

im pulse (im′puls), 1. driving on; thrust; push; as, the impulse of a wave, the impulse of pity, of hunger, of curiosity. 2. a sudden inclination or tendency to act. A mob is influenced more by impulse than by reason.

im pul sive (im pul′siv), 1. pushing; driving onward; impelling. 2. acting upon impulse; easily moved. The impulsive child gave all his money to the beggar.

im pu ni ty (im pū′ni ti), freedom from punishment or bad consequences. You cannot pull a tiger's tail with impunity.

im pure (im pūr′), 1. not pure; dirty. The air in cities is often impure. 2. mixed with foreign matter. The salt we use is slightly impure. 3. bad; corrupt. Avoid impure talk, thoughts, acts, and people.

im pu ri ty (im pūr′i ti), 1. lack of purity; being impure. 2. impure thing or element; thing that makes something else impure. Filtering the water removed some of its impurities.

in (in). We live in the country in the summer. You can do this in an hour. He is in business for himself. She is dressed in white. The child was in tears. The party is in honor of Mary's birthday. The board broke in two. Come in. Lock the dog in. Mrs. Smith is in. A sheepskin coat has the woolly side in. In has many special meanings in connection with other words. Most of them are well known. The **ins** means those that are in office. **Ins and outs** means the different parts; the twists and turns. **In with** means (1) friendly with. (2) partners with.

in., inch; inches.

in a bil i ty (in′ə bil′i ti), lack of ability, means, or power.

in ac ces si ble (in′ak ses′i bəl), 1. that cannot be reached easily. A fort on top of a steep hill is inaccessible. 2. that cannot be reached at all.

in ac tive (in ak′tiv), not active; idle; sluggish.

in ad e quate (in ad′i kwit), not adequate; not enough; not so much as is required.

in ane (in ān′), 1. silly. 2. empty.

in as much (in′əz much′). **Inasmuch as**

means (1) in so far as. (2) because. Bob was given a start in the race, inasmuch as he was smaller than the others.

in au gu rate (in ô′gū rāt), 1. install in office with a ceremony. A President of the United States is inaugurated every four years. 2. make a formal beginning of; begin. The invention of the airplane inaugurated a new era in transportation. 3. begin public use of with a ceremony or celebration.

in born (in′bôrn′), born in a person; as, an inborn love of rhythm, inborn talent for art.

in ca pa ble (in kā′pə bəl), 1. not capable. A foreigner is incapable of becoming President of the United States. Gold is almost incapable of rusting. 2. not able; having very little ability. An idiot is very incapable.

in cense[1] (in′sens), 1. a substance giving off a sweet smell when burned. 2. the perfume or smoke from it. 3. something sweet like incense; as, the incense of flowers, the incense of flattery, the incense of praise, etc.

in cense[2] (in sens′), make very angry. Cruelty incenses kind people.

in cen tive (in sen′tiv), motive; stimulus. The fun of playing the game was a greater incentive than the prize.

in ces sant (in ses′ənt), never stopping; continual. The roar of Niagara Falls is incessant. The incessant noise of whistles kept me awake all night.

inch (inch), 1. a measure of length, $\frac{1}{12}$ of a foot. An inch of rainfall is the amount of water that would cover a surface to the depth of one inch. 2. move by inches or little by little. The worm inched along.

in ci dent (in′si dənt), 1. a happening; an event. 2. an unimportant event. 3. liable to happen; belonging. Hardships are incident to the life of an explorer.

in ci den tal (in′si den′təl), 1. happening or likely to happen in connection with something else. Certain discomforts are incidental to camping out. 2. occurring by chance. 3. something incidental. On our trip we spent $52 for meals, room, and railroad fare, and $1.50 for incidentals, such as candy, magazines, and stamps.

in ci den tal ly (in′si den′təl i), 1. as an incident along with something else; by the way. Fred said, incidentally, that he had had no dinner. 2. accidentally.

in cip i ent (in sip′i ənt), just beginning; in an early stage.

in cite (in sīt′), urge on; stir up; rouse. Their captain's example incited the men to bravery.

in clem ent (in klem′ənt), 1. rough; stormy. 2. severe; harsh; as, an inclement ruler.

in cli na tion (in′kli nā′shən), 1. tendency. 2. preference; liking. Most boys have a strong inclination for sports. 3. a leaning; a bending; a bowing. A nod is an inclination of the head. 4. slope; slant; as, the inclination of a roof.

in cline (in klīn′ for 1, 2, 3, and 5, in′klīn or in klīn′ for 4), 1. be favorable; be willing; tend. Dogs incline to eat meat as a food. 2. make favorable; make willing; influence. Incline your hearts to obey God's laws. 3. slope; slant. 4. sloping surface. The side of a hill is an incline. 5. lean; bend; bow.

Man pushing a wheelbarrow up an inclined plank

in clined (in klīnd′), 1. favorable; willing; tending. 2. sloping; slanting.

in close (in klōz′), enclose.

in clo sure (in klō′zhər), enclosure.

in clude (in klüd′), hold or enclose within limits; contain. The price includes both house and furniture. Their farm includes 160 acres.

in come (in′kum), what comes in from property, business, labor, etc.; money that comes in; receipts; returns. The grocer's store brings in an income of $5000.

in com pa ra ble (in kom′pə rə bəl), without an equal; matchless.

in com pe tent (in kom′pi tənt), 1. not competent; without ability or qualifications. 2. person who is without ability.

in com plete (in′kəm plēt′), not complete; lacking some part; unfinished.

in com pre hen si ble (in′kom pri hen′si bəl), impossible to understand.

in con ceiv a ble (in′kən sēv′ə bəl), impossible to imagine; unthinkable. A circle without a center is inconceivable.

in con sist ent (in′kən sis′tənt), not consistent; not in agreement with itself or with something else. The policeman's failure to arrest the thief was inconsistent with his duty.

in con spic u ous (in′kən spik′ū əs), not conspicuous; attracting little or no attention. The woman's dress was an inconspicuous gray.

in con stant (in kon′stənt), not constant; changeable; fickle.

in con ven ience (in′kən vēn′yəns), 1. trouble; bother; lack of convenience or ease. 2. cause of trouble, difficulty, or bother. 3. to cause trouble, difficulty, or bother to. Will it inconvenience you to carry this package to your mother?

in con ven ient (in′kən vēn′yənt), not convenient; troublesome; causing bother, difficulty, or discomfort.

in cor po rate (in kôr′pə rāt), 1. make (something) a part of something else; join or unite (something) with something else. We will incorporate your suggestion in this new plan. 2. form into a corporation. When Mr. Smith's business became large, he incorporated it.

in cor rect (in′kə rekt′), 1. not correct; wrong; faulty. 2. not proper.

in crease (in krēs′ for 1, 2, and 3, in′krēs for 4 and 5), 1. make greater, more numerous, richer, more powerful, etc. The driver increased the speed of the car. 2. become greater; grow in numbers. His weight has increased ten pounds. These flowers will increase every year. 3. gain in size, numbers, etc.; growth. 4. addition; the amount added; the result of increasing. 5. **On the increase** means increasing.

in creas ing ly (in krēs′ing li), more and more. As we traveled south, it became increasingly harder to keep cool.

in cred i ble (in kred′i bəl), beyond belief; seeming too extraordinary to be possible. The hero fought with incredible bravery. Some old beliefs seem incredible to educated people.

in cred i bly (in kred′i bli), beyond belief; so as to be incredible; as, an incredibly swift flight.

in cred u lous (in krej′ů ləs), 1. not ready to believe. People nowadays are incredulous about ghosts and witches. 2. showing a lack of belief. Father heard the tramp's story with an incredulous smile.

in cum ber (in kum′bər), encumber.

in cum brance (in kum′brəns), encumbrance.

in cur (in kėr′), run or fall into (something unpleasant); bring (blame, punishment, etc.) on oneself. The hunter incurred great danger in killing the tiger.

in cur a ble (in kūr′ə bəl), 1. that cannot be cured; as, an incurable invalid, an incurable disease. 2. person suffering from an incurable disease. That building is a home for incurables.

in debt ed (in det′id), owing money or gratitude; in debt; obliged. We are indebted to science for many of our comforts.

in deed (in dēd′), 1. in fact; in truth; really. She is hungry; indeed, she is almost starving. War is indeed terrible. 2. expression of surprise or contempt. Indeed! I never would have thought it.

in de fat i ga ble (in′di fat′i gə bəl), tireless; untiring.

in def i nite (in def′i nit), 1. not clearly defined; not precise; vague. "Maybe" is a very indefinite answer. 2. not limited. We have an indefinite time to finish this work.

in del i ble (in del′i bəl), 1. that cannot be erased or removed; permanent; as, indelible ink, an indelible disgrace. 2. making an indelible mark; as, an indelible pencil.

in de pend ence (in′di pen′dəns), freedom from the control, support, or influence of others. The American colonies won independence from England.

in de pend ent (in′di pen′dənt), 1. needing, wishing, or getting no help from others; as, independent work, independent thinking. 2. acting, working, or, especially, voting by one's own ideas, not as the crowd does. 3. guiding, ruling, or governing one's self; not under another's rule. The American colonies became independent of England. 4. not depending on others. Miss Jones has an independent fortune. 5. person who votes without regard to party.

in de scrib a ble (in′di skrīb′ə bəl), that cannot be described; beyond description.

in dex (in′deks), 1. list of what is in a book, telling on what pages to find each thing, usually put at the end of the book and arranged in alphabetical order. 2. make an index of. 3. thing that points out or shows; sign. A person's face is often an index of his character. 4. finger next to the thumb; forefinger. 5. pointer. A dial or scale usually has an index.

In di a (in′di ə), a country in southern Asia. Most of it is under British control.

In di an (in′di ən), 1. one of the so-called red people living in America before the white people came; an American Indian. 2. of or having to do with American Indians; as, an Indian camp, Indian blankets, an Indian language. 3. made of Indian corn or maize; as, Indian pudding. 4. of India; as, Indian elephants, Indian temples, Indian costumes. 5. a native of India.

in di cate (in′di kāt), 1. point out; show; make known. The arrow on a sign indicates the way to go. A dog indicates his feelings by growling, whining, barking, and wagging his tail. 2. be a sign of. Fever indicates illness.

in di ca tion (in′di kā′shən), thing that indicates; sign.

in di ca tor (in′di kā′tər), 1. person or thing that indicates. 2. a pointer on a dial that shows the amount of heat, pressure, speed, etc. 3. any recording apparatus.

in dif fer ence (in dif′ər əns), 1. not caring; lack of interest or attention. The boy's indifference to his lessons worried his parents. 2. lack of importance. It was a matter of indifference to Tom whether his hands were clean or dirty.

in dif fer ent (in dif′ər ənt), 1. not caring one way or the other. 2. unimportant; not mattering much. The time for starting is indifferent to me. 3. having or showing no interest. Mary enjoyed the trip, but Ann was indifferent. 4. neither good nor bad; just fair; as, an indifferent singer.

in dif fer ent ly (in dif′ər ənt li), 1. with indifference. 2. neither very well nor very badly. 3. poorly; badly.

in dig e nous (in dij′i nəs), native; originating in the region or country where found. Lions are indigenous to Africa.

in di ges tion (in′di jes′chən), inability to digest food; difficulty in digesting food.

in dig nant (in dig′nənt), angry at something unworthy, unfair, or mean. She was indignant at the man who beat his horse.

in dig na tion (in′dig nā′shən), anger at something unworthy, unfair, or mean. Cheating should arouse indignation.

in dig ni ty (in dig′ni ti), an injury to dignity; an insult. Bill felt that being called "Willie, dear" was an indignity.

in di go (in′di gō), 1. a blue dye obtained from various plants. 2. a plant yielding it. 3. deep violet-blue.

in di rect (in′di rekt′), 1. not direct; not straight. We walk to town by a road that is indirect, but very pleasant. 2. not directly connected. Happiness is an indirect result of doing one's work well. 3. not straightforward and to the point. She would not say yes or no, but gave an indirect answer to my question.

in dis creet (in′dis krēt′), not discreet; not wise and judicious. The indiscreet girl often talked with strangers.

in dis cre tion (in′dis kresh′ən), 1. lack of good judgment. 2. an indiscreet act.

in dis pens a ble (in′dis pen′sə bəl), absolutely necessary. Air is indispensable to life.

in dis tinct (in′dis tingkt′), not distinct; not clear to the eye, ear, or mind; confused; as, an indistinct picture, an indistinct roar from the distant ocean.

in di vid u al (in′di vij′ü əl), 1. a person. Robert is a tall individual. 2. a single person, animal, or thing. 3. single; separate; for one only. Benches are for several people; chairs are individual seats. Washbowls are for general use; toothbrushes are for individual use. 4. belonging to or marking off one person or thing specially. Alice has an individual style of arranging her hair.

in di vid u al i ty (in′di vij′ü al′i ti), 1. the character or sum of the qualities which distinguish one person or thing from another. 2. being individual; existence as an individual.

in di vid u al ly (in′di vij′ü əl i), personally; one at a time; as individuals. Sometimes our teacher helps us individually.

in di vis i ble (in′di viz′i bəl), that cannot be divided.

in do lence (in′də ləns), laziness.

in do lent (in′də lənt), lazy.

in dom i ta ble (in dom′i tə bəl), that cannot be conquered.

in door (in′dōr′), in a building.

in doors (in′dōrz′), in or into a building.

in dorse (in dôrs′), endorse.

in duce (in dūs′ or in düs′), 1. influence; persuade. Advertisements induce people to buy. 2. cause. The doctor says that this medicine will induce sleep.

in duce ment (in dūs′mənt or in düs′mənt), something that influences or persuades. Prizes are inducements to work.

in dulge (in dulj′), 1. yield to the wishes of; humor; as, to indulge a child, to indulge the fancies of a sick person. 2. give way to one's pleasure; allow oneself something desired; as, to indulge in tobacco, to indulge in a fit of temper, to indulge in a new hat.

in dul gence (in dul′jəns), 1. an indulging. 2. thing indulged in. 3. favor; privilege.

in dul gent (in dul′jənt), 1. indulging; kind; almost too kind. The indulgent mother bought her boy everything he wanted. 2. lenient; not critical. Our indulgent teacher praised every poem we wrote.

in dus tri al (in dus′tri əl), 1. of industry; having something to do with industry. Industrial workers work at trades or in factories. An industrial school teaches trades. 2. of or having something to do with the workers in industries.

in dus tri ous (in dus′tri əs), hard-working.

in dus try (in′dəs tri), 1. steady effort; busy application. Industry and thrift bring success. 2. any branch of business, trade, or manufacture; as, the automobile industry. Industries dealing with steel, copper, coal, and oil employ millions of men.

in ed i ble (in ed′i bəl), not fit to eat.

in ef fi cient (in′i fish′ənt), 1. not efficient; not able to produce an effect without waste of time or energy. A machine that uses too much power is inefficient. 2. not able to get things done.

in ept (in ept′), 1. not suitable. 2. foolish.

in e qual i ty (in′ē kwol′i ti), 1. lack of equality; a being unequal in amount, size, value, rank, etc. 2. lack of evenness, regularity, or uniformity. There are many inequalities in the surface of this old road.

in ert (in ėrt′), 1. lifeless; having no power to move or act. A stone is inert. 2. inactive; sluggish.

in es ti ma ble (in es′ti mə bəl), of too great worth or value to be measured. Freedom is an inestimable privilege.

in ev i ta ble (in ev′i tə bəl), sure to happen. Death is inevitable.

in ex haust i ble (in′eg zôs′ti bəl), 1. that cannot be exhausted; very abundant. 2. tireless.

in ex o ra ble (in ek′sə rə bəl), relentless; unyielding; not influenced by prayers or entreaties.

in ex pen sive (in′eks pen′siv), 1. not expensive. 2. cheap.

in ex pe ri enced (in′eks pēr′i ənst), without experience or practice.

in ex pli ca ble (in eks′pli kə bəl), mysterious; that cannot be explained.

in fal li ble (in fal′i bəl), 1. free from error; that cannot be mistaken; as, an infallible rule. 2. absolutely reliable; sure; as, infallible obedience.

in fa mous (in′fə məs), 1. very wicked; so bad as to deserve public disgrace. 2. having a very bad reputation. A traitor's name is infamous.

in fa my (in′fə mi), 1. very bad reputation; public disgrace. Traitors are held up to infamy. 2. extreme wickedness.

in fan cy (in′fən si), 1. babyhood; early childhood. 2. an early stage of anything.

in fant (in′fənt), 1. baby; very young child. 2. of or for an infant; as, an infant class, infant food. 3. just beginning to develop; as, an infant industry.

in fan try (in′fən tri), soldiers who fight on foot.

in fect (in fekt′), 1. cause disease in by introducing germs. Anyone with a bad cold may infect the people around him. 2. influence in a bad way. One bad boy may infect a whole class. 3. influence by spreading. The captain's courage infected his men.

in fec tion (in fek′shən), 1. a causing of disease in people, animals, and plants by the introduction of germs. Air, water, clothing, and insects are all means of infection. 2. disease that can spread from one person to another. Measles is an infection. 3. influence, feeling, or idea spreading from one to another.

in fec tious (in fek′shəs), 1. spread by infection. Measles is an infectious disease. 2. causing infection. 3. apt to spread. He has a jolly, infectious laugh.

in fer (in fėr′), 1. conclude; find out by reasoning. People inferred that so able a governor would make a good president. 2. indicate; imply. Ragged clothing infers poverty.

in fer ence (in′fər əns), 1. the process of inferring. 2. that which is inferred; conclusion. When they saw the pile of paper on the teacher's desk, the class made the inference that they would have written work.

in fe ri or (in fēr′i ər), 1. lower in position or rank. A lieutenant is inferior to a captain. 2. lower in quality; not so good; worse. A wolf is inferior to a lion. This cloth is inferior to real silk. 3. below the average; as, an inferior paper, an inferior grade of coffee. 4. person who is lower in rank or station. A good leader gets on well with inferiors.

in fe ri or i ty (in fēr′i or′i ti), inferior nature or condition; quality of being inferior.

in fer nal (in fėr′nəl), 1. of the lower world; of hell. 2. fit to have come from hell. The heartless conqueror showed infernal cruelty.

in fest (in fest′), trouble or disturb in large numbers. Mosquitoes infest swamps. The mountains were infested by robbers.

in fi del (in′fi dəl), 1. person who does not believe in religion. 2. person who does not accept a particular faith. Mohammedans call Christians infidels. 3. person who does not accept Christianity.

in fi nite (in′fi nit), 1. without limits. 2. very, very great. 3. that which is infinite.

in fi nite ly (in′fi nit li), to an infinite degree. "I am infinitely pleased to see you," said the flatterer.

in firm (in fėrm′), weak. Grandmother was old and infirm.

in fir mi ty (in fėr′mi ti), weakness.

in flame (in flām′), 1. excite. His stirring speech inflamed the crowd. 2. make unnaturally hot, red, sore, or swollen. The smoke had inflamed the fireman's eyes.

in flam ma ble (in flam′ə bəl), 1. easily set on fire. Paper is inflammable. 2. easily excited or aroused; excitable. Tom had an inflammable temper.

in flam ma tion (in′flə mā′shən), 1. a diseased condition of some part of the body, causing heat, redness, swelling, and pain. 2. an inflaming; being inflamed.

in flate (in flāt′), 1. blow out or swell with air or gas; as, to inflate a balloon. 2. swell or puff out; as, to inflate with pride. 3. increase beyond the normal amount.

in flex i ble (in flek′si bəl), 1. stiff; rigid. 2. firm; unyielding.

in flict (in flikt′), 1. give or cause (a stroke, blow, or wound). 2. impose (suffering, punishment, something unwelcome, etc.). Only cruel people like to inflict pain. Disagreeable Mrs. Jones has inflicted herself upon her relatives for a long visit.

in flu ence (in′flü əns), 1. power of persons or things to act on others. Use your influence to persuade your friends to join the club. 2. have power over. The moon influences the tides. What we read influences our thinking. 3. person or thing that has power. Jane was a good influence in our club.

in flu en tial (in′flü en′shəl), 1. having influence. Influential friends helped John to get a good job. 2. using influence; producing results.

in fold (in fōld′), enfold.

in form (in fôrm′), 1. tell; supply with knowledge. Please inform us how to find Dr. Brown's house. 2. tell tales about; accuse. The thief who was caught informed on the others.

in for mal (in fôr′məl), not formal; without ceremony.

in form ant (in fôr′mənt), person who gives information. My informant saw the thing with his own eyes.

in for ma tion (in′fər mā′shən), 1. knowledge; facts; news. A dictionary contains much information. The general sent the people information of his victory. 2. informing. This book is for the information of travelers.

in fre quent (in frē′kwənt), rare; scarce.

in fringe (in frinj′), 1. violate. A false label infringes the food and drug law. 2. trespass. Do not infringe upon the rights of others.

in fu ri ate (in fūr′i āt), make furious; enrage.

in fuse (in fūz′), 1. put in. The captain infused his own courage into his soldiers. 2. inspire. The soldiers were infused with his courage. 3. steep in a liquid. Tea leaves are infused in hot water to make tea.

in gen ious (in jēn′yəs), 1. clever; skillful in making; good at inventing. The ingenious boy made a radio set for himself. 2. cleverly planned and made. This trap is an ingenious device.

in ge nu i ty (in′ji nū′i ti or in′ji nü′i ti), cleverness; skill in planning or inventing. The boy showed ingenuity in making toys.

in grat i tude (in grat′i tūd or in grat′i tüd), lack of thankfulness; being ungrateful.

in gre di ent (in grē′di ənt), one of the parts of a mixture. The ingredients of sponge cake are eggs, sugar, flour, and flavoring.

in hab it (in hab′it), live in. Fish inhabit the sea. Thoughts inhabit the mind.

in hab it ant (in hab′i tənt), a person or animal that lives in a place.

in hale (in hāl′), draw into the lungs; breathe in (air, gas, fragrance, tobacco smoke, etc.).

in her ent (in hēr′ənt), belonging to a person or thing as a quality. In spite of flattery, she kept her inherent modesty.

in her it (in her′it), 1. receive as an heir. Mr. Jones's widow inherited his farm. 2. get from one's ancestors. Mary inherits her father's blue eyes.

in her it ance (in her′i tәns), 1. inheriting. Mr. Jones received his house by inheritance from an aunt. 2. thing inherited. Good health is a fine inheritance.

in hos pi ta ble (in hos′pi tә bәl), not making visitors comfortable. The inhospitable savages would not give us food or water.

in hu man (in hū′mәn), brutal; cruel.

in iq ui ty (in ik′wi ti), 1. very great injustice. 2. a wicked and unjust act.

i ni tial (i nish′әl), 1. first; earliest; occurring at the beginning. Tom's initial effort at skating was a failure. 2. the first letter of a word. The initials U. S. stand for United States. 3. to mark or sign with initials. Mr. John A. Smith initialed the note J. A. S.

i ni ti ate (i nish′i āt), 1. begin; be the one to start; set going. This year we shall initiate a series of free concerts. 2. admit (a person) with formal ceremonies into a group or society. 3. introduce into the knowledge of some art or subject; as, to initiate a person into business methods. 4. person who is initiated.

i ni ti a tion (i nish′i ā′shәn), 1. initiating. 2. being initiated. 3. formal admission into a group or society. 4. ceremonies by which one is admitted to a group or society.

i ni ti a tive (i nish′i ә tiv), 1. active part in taking the first steps in any undertaking; the lead. Charles is shy and does not take the initiative in making acquaintances. 2. readiness and ability to be the one to start a thing. A leader must have initiative.

in ject (in jekt′), 1. force in; as, to inject a drug into the body. 2. throw in; as, to inject a remark into the conversation.

in junc tion (in jungk′shәn), command; order. John obeyed his mother's injunction to hurry straight home.

in jure (in′jәr), 1. do damage to; harm; hurt. Do not break or injure the bushes in the park. 2. do wrong to.

in ju ri ous (in jür′i әs), doing harm; hurtful.

in ju ry (in′jәr i), 1. harm; hurt; damage. Mr. Smith escaped from the train wreck without injury. His trunks received many injuries. The accident will be an injury to the reputation of the railroad. 2. a wrong. The saint never did injury to any man.

in jus tice (in jus′tis), 1. lack of justice. 2. an unjust act.

ink (ingk), 1. a liquid used for writing or printing. 2. put ink on; mark or stain with ink.

ink y (ingk′i), 1. like ink; dark; black. 2. covered with ink.

in laid (in′lād′ or in lād′), 1. set in the surface as a decoration or design. The desk had an inlaid design of light wood in dark. 2. decorated with a design or material set in the surface. The box had an inlaid cover.

in land (in′lәnd), 1. away from the coast or the border; in the interior; as, an inland sea. 2. the interior of a country; land away from the border or the coast. 3. in or toward the interior.

in let (in′let), 1. a narrow strip of water running from a larger body of water into the land or between islands. The fishing village was on a small inlet of the sea. 2. entrance.

in mate (in′māt), 1. occupant; inhabitant. 2. person confined in a prison, asylum, hospital, etc.

in most (in′mōst), 1. farthest in; deepest. We went to the inmost depths of the mine. 2. most secret. Her inmost desire was to be an actress.

inn (in), a public house for lodging and caring for travelers. Hotels have taken the place of the old inns.

in ner (in′әr), 1. farther in; inside; as, an inner room. 2. more private; more secret. She kept her inner thoughts to herself.

in ner most (in′әr mōst), farthest in; inmost.

in ning (in′ing), 1. the turn of one side in a game; chance to play. 2. the time a person or party is in power; chance for action.

inn keep er (in′kēp′әr), person who keeps an inn.

in no cence (in′ә sәns), 1. freedom from sin, wrong, or guilt. The accused man proved his innocence of the crime. 2. simplicity; lack of guile; as, the innocence of a little child.

in no cent (in′ә sәnt), 1. doing no wrong or evil; free from sin or wrong; not guilty. An innocent boy was hurt in the quarrel. 2. without knowledge of evil. A baby is innocent. 3. doing no harm; as, innocent amusements. 4. an innocent person.

in noc u ous (i nok′ū әs), harmless.

in no vate (in′ō vāt), make changes.

in no va tion (in′ō vā′shәn), 1. change made in the accustomed way of doing things. The new teacher made many innovations. 2. making changes; bringing in new things or new ways of doing things.

in nu mer a ble (i nū′mәr ә bәl or i nü′mәr ә-bәl), too many to count; very, very many.

in oc u late (in ok′ū lāt), infect (a person or an animal) with germs that will cause a mild form of a disease, so that the individual will not take the regular disease.

in of fen sive (in′ə fen′siv), not offensive; harmless; not arousing objections.

in quire (in kwīr′), 1. ask; try to find out by questions; as, to inquire a person's name or business, to inquire about a room. 2. search for information, knowledge, or truth.

in quir y (in kwīr′i), 1. a question. The guide answered all our inquiries. 2. a search for truth, information, or knowledge. 3. act of inquiring.

in quis i tive (in kwiz′i tiv), 1. curious; asking many questions. 2. too curious; prying into other people's affairs.

in road (in′rōd′), raid; attack. The expenses of her illness made inroads upon the money she had saved.

in rush (in′rush′), a rushing in. The inrush of water soon filled the pool.

in sane (in sān′), not sane; crazy. Insane people are kept in asylums.

in san i ty (in san′i ti), condition of being insane; mental disease.

in sa tia ble (in sā′shə bəl), that cannot be satisfied; very greedy.

in scribe (in skrīb′), 1. write or mark (words, letters, etc.) on paper, metal, stone, etc. 2. mark (with words, letters, etc.). His tombstone was inscribed with his name and the date of his death. 3. impress deeply. My father's words are inscribed on my memory.

in scrip tion (in skrip′shən), something inscribed; as, the inscription on a monument, on a coin, or on an old temple.

Inscription on a coin

in scru ta ble (in skrü′tə bəl), that cannot be understood; so mysterious or obscure that one cannot make out its meaning.

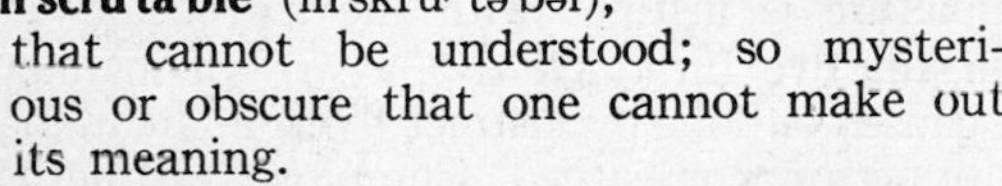

in sect (in′sekt), a small creature with body divided into three parts and with three pairs of legs. Flies, mosquitoes, gnats, and bees are insects.

Parts of an insect

in sen si ble (in sen′si bəl), 1. not able to feel. A blind man is insensible to colors. 2. not aware. The boys in the boat were insensible of the danger. 3. not able to feel anything; unconscious. He was hit by a truck and was insensible for four hours. 4. not easily felt. The room grew cold by insensible degrees.

in sep a ra ble (in sep′ə rə bəl), that cannot be separated.

in sert (in sėrt′ for 1, in′sėrt for 2), 1. put in; set in; as, to insert a key into a lock, to insert a letter into a word, to insert an advertisement into a newspaper. 2. something put in or set in. The book contained an insert of several pages of pictures.

in ser tion (in sėr′shən), 1. act of inserting. The insertion of one word can change the meaning of a whole sentence. 2. something inserted.

in side (in′sīd′ for 1, 2, 3, and 4, in′sīd′ for 5 and 6), 1. the part within; the inner surface. The inside of the box was lined with colored paper. 2. the contents. The inside of the book was more interesting than the cover. 3. being on the inside; covered up; as, inside layers. 4. secret. I have inside information of their plans. 5. within. Please step inside. 6. in. The nut is inside the shell.

in sid i ous (in sid′i əs), 1. crafty; sly; tricky. 2. working secretly or subtly; as, an insidious disease.

in sight (in′sīt′), 1. a view of the inside with understanding. Take the machine apart and get an insight into how it works. 2. wisdom and understanding in dealing with people or with facts. We study science to gain insight into the world we live in.

in sig ni a (in sig′ni ə), medals; badges; distinguishing marks of office or of honor. The crown and the scepter are the insignia of kings.

Naval aviation corps insignia

in sig nif i cant (in′sig nif′i kənt), having little meaning, use, or importance; as, insignificant chatter, an insignificant person. A tenth of a cent is an insignificant amount of money.

in sin u ate (in sin′ū āt), 1. push in or get in by an indirect, twisting way. The stray cat insinuated herself into our kitchen. Laura insinuated herself into Ann's friendship. 2. hint; suggest in an indirect way. To say "Fred can't do it; no coward can" is to insinuate that Fred is a coward.

in sist (in sist′), keep firmly to some demand, statement, or position. John insists that he had a right to use his brother's tools. Mother insists that we wash our hands before eating.

in sist ence (in sis′tən s), 1. act of insisting; as, mother's insistence that we comb our hair. 2. being insistent.

in sist ent (in sis′tənt), 1. insisting. In spite of the rain he was insistent on going out. 2. compelling attention or notice; pressing; urgent. We heard insistent calls of "Help! Help!"

in so lence (in′sə ləns), bold rudeness; insulting behavior or speech.

in so lent (in′sə lənt), boldly rude; insulting. "Shut up!" the insolent boy said to his father.

in sol u ble (in sol′ū bəl), 1. that cannot be dissolved. A diamond is insoluble. 2. that cannot be solved; as, an insoluble mystery.

in spect (in spekt′), 1. look at carefully; examine. A dentist inspects the pupils' teeth twice a year. 2. examine formally or officially.

in spec tion (in spek′shən), 1. an inspecting. An inspection of the roof showed no leaks. 2. formal or official examination. The soldiers lined up for their daily inspection by their officers.

in spec tor (in spek′tər), 1. person who inspects. 2. an officer appointed to inspect; as, a milk inspector. 3. a police officer ranking next below a superintendent.

in spi ra tion (in′spi rā′shən), 1. influence of thought and strong feelings on actions, especially on good actions. Some people get inspiration from sermons; some, from nature. 2. any influence that arouses effort to do well. A brave leader is an inspiration to his followers. 3. idea that is inspired; a sudden brilliant idea. 4. act of drawing air into the lungs.

in spire (in spīr′), 1. put thought, feeling, life, or force into. The speaker inspired the boys with courage. 2. cause (thought or feeling). The leader's courage inspired confidence in others. 3. influence with a thought or feeling. His sly ways inspire me with distrust. 4. suggest; cause to be told or written. His enemies inspired false stories about him. 5. breathe in; draw air into the lungs.

in stall (in stôl′), 1. place (a person) in office with ceremonies. The new judge was installed without delay. 2. establish in a place. The cat installed itself in the easy chair. 3. put in position for use. The new owner of the house had electric lights installed at once.

in stance (in′stəns), 1. example. Lincoln is an instance of a poor boy who became famous. 2. refer to as an example. He instanced the fly as a dirty insect. 3. occasion. I went in the first instance because I was asked to go. 4. request; suggestion. At the instance of the losing team we agreed to play them again next week.

in stant (in′stənt), 1. a moment of time. Stop talking this instant! 2. immediate. The medicine gave instant relief. 3. pressing; urgent; as, instant need for action. 4. present; of the present month. The 10th instant means the tenth day of the present month.

in stan ta ne ous (in′stən tā′ni əs), occurring, done, or made in an instant. A flash of lightning is instantaneous.

in stant ly (in′stənt li), at once.

in stead (in sted′), 1. in place (of). Instead of studying, Grace read a story. 2. in (my, your, her, etc.) place. Ruth stayed home, and her sister went riding instead.

in step (in′step), 1. the upper surface of the human foot between the toes and the ankle. 2. the part of a shoe, stocking, etc., over the instep.

in still or **in stil** (in stil′), put in little by little. Reading good books instills a feeling for really fine literature.

in stinct (in′stingkt for 1 and 2, in stingkt′ for 3), 1. an inborn tendency or power. An instinct leads birds to fly. 2. a natural bent, tendency, or gift. Dorothy has such an instinct for color that she should study art. 3. charged or filled with something. The picture is instinct with life and beauty.

in stinc tive (in stingk′tiv), of instinct; caused or done by instinct; born in an animal or person, not learned. Climbing is instinctive in monkeys.

in sti tute (in′sti tūt or in′sti tüt), 1. set up; establish; begin. The Pilgrims instituted Thanksgiving. After the accident the police instituted an inquiry into its causes. 2. organization or society for some special purpose. An art institute teaches or displays art. A technical school is often called an institute. 3. building used by such an organization or society. We spent the afternoon in the Art Institute.

in sti tu tion (in′sti tū′shən or in′sti tü′shən), 1. something established, such as a law, custom, society, club, college, or any organization. A church, school, college, hospital, asylum, or prison is an institution. Giving presents on Christmas is an institution. 2. a building used for the work of an institution. 3. beginning; starting; establishing; providing for. We hope for the institution of hot lunches at school this winter.

in struct (in strukt′), 1. teach. 2. direct. The owner of the house instructed his agent to sell it. 3. inform. My lawyer instructs me that your last payment on the house is due March first.

in struc tion (in struk′shən), 1. teaching; education; knowledge. 2. **Instructions** often means directions or orders.

in struc tive (in struk′tiv), instructing; useful for instruction; giving information. A trip around the world is an instructive experience.

in struc tor (in struk′tər), teacher.

in stru ment (in′strů mənt), 1. thing with or by which something is done; person made use of by another; means. 2. tool; mechanical device; as, a dentist's instruments. 3. device for producing musical sounds; as, wind instruments, stringed instruments. 4. a formal legal document.

in stru men tal (in′strů men′təl), 1. acting as an instrument; useful; helpful. Mr. Beal was instrumental in finding a job for George. 2. played on or written for musical instruments. An orchestra provided instrumental music to accompany the singing.

in suf fer a ble (in suf′ər ə bəl), unbearable. His insufferable insolence cost him many friends.

in suf fi cient (in′sə fish′ənt), not enough.

in su late (in′sə lāt), 1. protect from losing heat or electricity. Telephone wires are insulated by a covering of rubber or paper. 2. set apart; separate from other things.

in sult (in sult′ for 1, in′sult for 2), 1. treat with scorn, abuse, or great rudeness. They insulted the flag by throwing mud on it. 2. an insulting speech or action.

in sur ance (in shür′əns), 1. an insuring of property, person, or life. Fire insurance, burglary insurance, accident insurance, life insurance, and health insurance are some of the many kinds. 2. the business of insuring property, life, etc. 3. amount of money for which a person or thing is insured. He has $10,000 insurance, which his wife will receive when he dies.

in sure (in shür′), 1. make sure or certain. Check your work to insure its accuracy. 2. make safe; protect. More care will insure you against making so many mistakes. 3. arrange for money payment in case of loss, accident, or death. An insurance company will insure your house against fire. 4. make safe against loss by paying money to an insurance company. He insured his car against theft.

in sur gent (in sėr′jənt), 1. rising in revolt. The insurgent slaves burned their masters' houses. 2. a rebel.

in sur rec tion (in′sə rek′shən), revolt; rebellion.

in tact (in takt′), untouched; uninjured; whole; with no part missing. The money was returned intact by the boy who found it.

in teg ri ty (in teg′ri ti), 1. honesty; sincerity; uprightness. A man of integrity is respected. 2. completeness. 3. perfect condition.

in tel lect (in′tə lekt), 1. the power of knowing; the understanding. Our actions are influenced by our intellect, will, and feelings. 2. intelligence; high mental ability. 3. person of high mental ability.

in tel lec tu al (in′tə lek′chü əl), 1. of the intellect. 2. needing or using intelligence. Teaching is a more intellectual occupation than sweeping. 3. showing intelligence; as, an intellectual book, an intellectual face. 4. person who is well informed and intelligent.

in tel li gence (in tel′i jəns), 1. ability to learn and know; understanding; mind. A dog has more intelligence than a worm. Intelligence tests are given in many schools. 2. knowledge; news; information. The general had secret intelligence of the plans of the enemy.

in tel li gent (in tel′i jənt), having or showing understanding; able to learn and know; quick at learning. Elephants are intelligent animals.

in tel li gi ble (in tel′i ji bəl), that can be understood.

in tend (in tend′), mean; plan. We intend to go home soon. Mr. Smith intends that his sons shall go to college. No insult was intended by Dick's remark.

in tense (in tens′), 1. very much; very great; very strong; as, intense happiness, intense pain, intense light. 2. An intense person is one who feels things very deeply and is likely to be extreme in action.

in ten si fy (in ten′si fī), 1. make more intense. Blowing on a fire intensifies the heat. 2. become more intense.

in ten si ty (in ten′si ti), 1. quality of being intense. 2. extreme degree; great vigor; violence; as, intensity of thought, intensity of feeling. 3. amount or degree of strength of electricity, heat, light, sound, etc., per unit of area, volume, etc.

in tent (in tent′), 1. purpose; intention. The thief shot with intent to kill. 2. meaning. What is the intent of that sentence? **To all intents and purposes** means in almost every way; almost; practically. 3. very attentive; having the eyes or thoughts earnestly fixed on something; earnest; as, an intent look, intent on a task. 4. much interested. She is intent on doing her best.

in ten tion (in ten′shən), 1. intending; purpose; design. Our intention is to travel next summer. 2. meaning.

in ten tion al (in ten′shən əl), done on purpose; intended. His insult was intentional; he wanted to hurt your feelings.

in ten tion al ly (in ten′shən əl i), with intention; on purpose.

in ter (in tėr′), put (a dead body) into a grave or tomb.

in ter cede (in′tər sēd′), plead for another; ask a favor from one person for another. Dan did not dare ask the teacher himself; so Will interceded with her for Dan.

in ter cept (in′tər sept′), 1. take or seize on the way from one place to another; as, to intercept a letter, to intercept a messenger. 2. cut off (light, water, etc.). 3. check; stop; as, to intercept the flight of a criminal.

in ter change (in′tər chānj′ for 1 and 3, in′tər chānj′ for 2 and 4), 1. put each of (two persons or things) in the place of the other. Mary and Alice interchanged hats. 2. putting each of two persons or things in the other's place. The word *team* becomes *meat* by the interchange of the end letters. 3. make an exchange. Tom and Dick interchange things when Tom trades his knife for Dick's ball. 4. exchange.

in ter change a ble (in′tər chān′jə bəl), 1. capable of being used in place of each other. 2. able to change places.

in ter course (in′tər kōrs), communication; dealings between people; exchange of thoughts, services, and feelings. Roads, railroads, and telephones make intercourse easier.

in ter est (in′tər est), 1. a feeling of wanting to know, do, own, or share in. Bob has an interest in reading and in collecting stamps. 2. stir up such a feeling in. A good story interests us. 3. the power to excite such feelings. Your plan has no interest for the others. 4. advantage; profit; benefit. Mother and father look after the interests of the family. 5. a share in property and actions. Father has a half interest in that farm. 6. cause to take a share in; engage or excite the concern, curiosity, or attention of. The agent tried to interest us in buying a car. We were interested in the results of the election. 7. group of people concerned in one sort of thing; as, the business interests of the town. 8. money paid for the use of money. This bank pays 2 per cent interest.

in ter est ed (in′tər es tid), 1. feeling or showing interest. 2. having a share.

in ter est ing (in′tər es ting), arousing interest; holding one's attention. *Black Beauty* is an interesting book for children.

in ter fere (in′tər fēr′), 1. clash; come into opposition with. The two plans interfered. He will come Saturday if nothing interferes. 2. meddle. That woman is always interfering in other people's affairs.

in ter fer ence (in′tər fēr′əns), act or fact of interfering. Lulu's interference spoiled our game.

in te ri or (in tēr′i ər), 1. inside; inner surface or part. The interior of the house was beautifully decorated. 2. inner; on the inside. 3. part of a region or country away from the coast or border. 4. away from the coast or border. 5. affairs within a country. The United States has a Department of the Interior.

in ter jec tion (in′tər jek′shən), 1. an exclamation regarded as a part of speech. *Oh! ah! alas!* and *hurrah!* are interjections. 2. remark; exclamation.

in ter lace (in′tər lās′), 1. arrange (threads, strips, or branches) so that they go over and under each other. We interlace reeds or fibers to make a basket. 2. cross each other over and under; mingle together. The branches of the trees interlaced above the path.

in ter lock (in′tər lok′), lock or join with one another. The two stags were fighting with their horns interlocked. The puzzle consisted of interlocking rings.

in ter lop er (in′tər lōp′ər), intruder; person who forces himself in where he has no right to be.

in ter lude (in′tər lüd), anything that is thought of as filling the time between two things. There was an interlude of sunshine between two showers.

in ter me di ate (in′tər mē′di it), 1. being or occurring between. The intermediate department of the Sunday School is between the primary and the adult departments. Gray is intermediate between black and white. 2. something between.

in ter mi na ble (in tėr′mi nə bəl), endless; so long as to seem endless.

in ter min gle (in′tər ming′gəl), mix together.

in ter mis sion (in′tər mish′ən), 1. pause; time between periods of activity. The band played from eight to twelve with a short intermission at ten. 2. stopping for a time; interruption. The rain continued all day without intermission.

in ter mit tent (in′tər mit′ənt), stopping and beginning again. The intermittent noise of the railroad trains kept me awake.

in ter nal (in tėr′nəl), 1. inner; inside; as, the internal organs of the body, medicine for internal use. 2. existing within a country; domestic; as, internal disturbances.

in ter nal ly (in tėr′nəl i), 1. inside. 2. inside the body. This ointment must not be taken internally.

in ter na tion al (in′tər nash′ən əl), 1. between or among nations. A treaty is an international agreement. 2. having something to do with the relations between nations; as, international law.

in ter pose (in′tər pōz′), 1. put between. 2. come between. 3. put in. He interposed an objection at this point. 4. interfere in order to help. Mother interposed in the dispute.

in ter pret (in tėr′prit), 1. explain the meaning of; as, to interpret a hard passage in a book, to interpret a dream. 2. bring out the meaning of. The actor interpreted the part of the soldier with wonderful skill. 3. understand. We interpret your silence as consent. 4. translate.

in ter pre ta tion (in tėr′pri tā′shən), 1. interpreting; explanation. What is your interpretation of Jack's queer behavior? 2. bringing out the meaning of a dramatic part, music, etc. The actor's interpretations were praised by most of the newspapers.

in ter pret er (in tėr′pri tər), 1. person who interprets. 2. person whose business it is to translate words spoken in a foreign language.

in ter rupt (in′tə rupt′), break in on; hinder; stop. A fire drill interrupted the lesson. It is not polite to interrupt a speaker.

in ter rup tion (in′tə rup′shən), breaking in on; break; stopping. The rain continued without interruption all day.

in ter sect (in′tər sekt′), 1. cut or divide by passing through or crossing. A path intersects the field. 2. cross each other. Streets usually intersect at right angles.

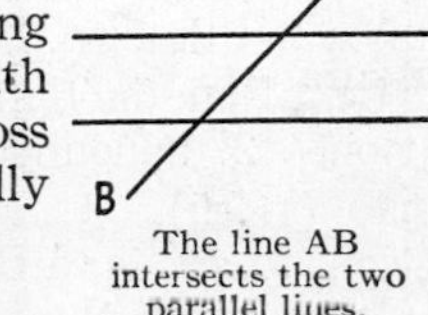

The line AB intersects the two parallel lines.

in ter sec tion (in′tər sek′shən), 1. the place where one thing crosses another. In the diagram above, there are two intersections where the line AB crosses the parallel lines. 2. an intersecting. Bridges are used to avoid the intersection of a railroad and a highway.

in ter sperse (in′tər spėrs′), 1. scatter here and there among other things. Bushes were interspersed among the trees. 2. vary with something put here and there. The grass is interspersed with beds of flowers.

in ter state (in′tər stāt′), between persons or organizations in different states. The federal government regulates interstate commerce.

in ter val (in′tər vəl), 1. time or space between. There is an interval of a week between Christmas and New Year's Day. She has intervals of freedom from pain. There are trees at intervals of twenty feet. 2. in music, the difference in pitch between two tones. 3. **At intervals** means with time or space between.

in ter vene (in′tər vēn′), 1. come between; be between. A week intervenes between Christmas and New Year's Day. 2. come in to help settle a dispute. The President was asked to intervene in the coal strike.

in ter ven tion (in′tər ven′shən), 1. intervening. The strike was settled by the intervention of the President. 2. interference by one nation in the affairs of another; interference.

in ter view (in′tər vū), 1. a meeting, generally of two people, to talk over something special. Father had an interview with the teacher about John's work. 2. visit and talk with. The reporters from *The Daily News* interviewed the returning explorers.

in ter wo ven (in′tər wō′vən), 1. woven together. 2. mixed together; mingled.

in tes tine (in tes′tin), a part of the bowels. **The intestines** means the bowels. See the diagram under **liver.**

in ti ma cy (in′ti mə si), closeness; close acquaintance.

in ti mate[1] (in′ti mit), 1. very familiar; known very well; closely acquainted. 2. a close friend. 3. far within; inmost.

in ti mate[2] (in′ti māt), 1. hint; suggest. 2. make known.

in ti ma tion (in′ti mā′shən), 1. hint; suggestion. 2. announcement.

in to (in′tü), 1. Into shows motion or direction to or toward a place within a thing. Come into the house. Look into the matter of his mistakes. 2. Into also shows a change. Divide the apple into three parts. Cold weather turns water into ice.

in tol er a ble (in tol′ər ə bəl), unbearable; too hard to be endured. The pain from the toothache was intolerable.

in tol er ant (in tol′ər ənt), 1. not tolerant; not willing to let others think as they choose, especially in matters of religion. 2. **Intolerant of** means not able to endure; unwilling to endure.

in tox i cate (in tok′si kāt), 1. make drunk. Alcohol intoxicates people. 2. excite beyond self-control. The joy of victory so intoxicated him that he jumped and sang and behaved like a crazy man.

in tox i cat ing (in tok′si kāt′ing), 1. making drunk. Whiskey is an intoxicating liquor. 2. very exciting.

in tox i ca tion (in tok′si kā′shən), 1. intoxicated condition; drunkenness. 2. great excitement. 3. in medicine, poisoning.

in treat (in trēt′), entreat.

in trench (in trench′), 1. surround with a trench; fortify with trenches. Our soldiers were intrenched opposite the enemy. 2. establish firmly. Exchanging gifts at Christmas is a custom intrenched in many countries. 3. trespass; infringe. Do not intrench upon the rights of another.

in trench ment (in trench′mənt), 1. an intrenching. 2. an intrenched position. 3. a defense consisting of a trench and a rampart of earth or stone.

Intrenchment

in trep id (in trep′id), fearless; dauntless; very brave. A policeman or soldier must be intrepid.

in tri cate (in′tri kit), 1. with many twists and turns; perplexing; complicated; as, an intricate knot, an intricate maze, an intricate plot. 2. very hard to understand; as, an intricate design, intricate directions.

in trigue (in trēg′), 1. secret plotting; crafty dealings. The royal palace was filled with intrigue. 2. form and carry out plans, plots, love affairs, etc., in a secret or sly way. He will fight openly, but he will not intrigue against you. 3. excite the curiosity and interest of.

in tro duce (in′trə dūs′ or in′trə düs′), 1. bring in; as, to introduce a story into the conversation. 2. put in; insert. The doctor introduced a tube down the sick man's throat. 3. bring into use, notice, or knowledge; as, to introduce a new fashion, a new food, or a reform. 4. make known; bring into acquaintance with. Mrs. Brown, may I introduce Mr. Smith? The principal introduced the speaker to the students. I introduced a country cousin to the city. 5. bring forward; as, to introduce a question for debate. 6. begin. John introduced his speech by telling a joke.

in tro duc tion (in′trə duk′shən), 1. an introducing. The introduction of steel made tall buildings easy to build. 2. the beginning of a speech, a piece of music, or a book. 3. being introduced. Mary was shy at her introduction to the company. 4. thing made known; the thing brought into use. Radios are a later introduction than telephones.

in tro duc to ry (in′trə duk′tə ri), used for introducing; preliminary.

in trude (in trüd′), 1. thrust in; force in. Do not intrude your opinions on others. 2. thrust oneself in; come where you aren't wanted.

in trud er (in trüd′ər), one that intrudes.

in tru sion (in trü′zhən), act of intruding.

in trust (in trust′), 1. trust. We intrusted Joe with all the money to pay the fares. 2. give (something or somebody) in trust; as, to intrust children to the care of a nurse, to intrust one's life to a doctor.

in vade (in vād′), 1. enter with force or as an enemy; attack. Grasshoppers invade fields and eat the crops. Disease invades the body. 2. enter as if to take possession. Tourists invaded the city. Night invades the sky. 3. interfere with; violate. The law punishes people who invade the rights of others.

in vad er (in vād′ər), person or thing that invades.

in va lid[1] (in′və lid), 1. a sick, weak person not able to get about and do things. 2. not well; weak and sick. 3. for the use of invalids; as, an invalid chair. 4. remove from active service because of sickness or injury. The wounded soldier was invalided and sent home.

in val id[2] (in val′id), without force; without value.

in val u a ble (in val′ū ə bəl), priceless.

in var i a ble (in vãr′i ə bəl), always the same.

in var i a bly (in vãr′i ə bli), 1. without change. 2. without exception. Spring invariably follows winter.

in va sion (in vā′zhən), act or fact of invading; an entering by force.

in vent (in vent′), 1. make or think out (something new); as, to invent a method, a machine, or a name. 2. make up; as, to invent an excuse.

in ven tion (in ven′shən), 1. making something new; as, the invention of gunpowder. 2. the thing invented. The radio was a wonderful invention. 3. the power of inventing. To be a good writer of stories a person needs invention. 4. made-up story. 5. false statement.

in ven tive (in ven′tiv), good at inventing. An inventive person thinks up ways to save time, money, and work.

in ven tor (in ven′tər), person who invents. Edison was a great inventor.

in vert (in vėrt′), 1. turn upside down; as, to invert a glass. 2. turn around or reverse in position, direction, or order. If you invert "I can," you have "Can I?"

in vest (in vest′), 1. use money to buy something which will produce a profit or an income or both. 2. clothe. The castle was invested with mystery and romance. 3. give power, authority, or right to. He invested his lawyer with complete power to act for him. 4. surround with troops; besiege. The enemy invested the city and cut it off from our army.

in ves ti gate (in ves′ti gāt), search into; examine closely. Detectives investigate crimes. Scientists investigate nature.

in ves ti ga tion (in ves′ti gā′shən), a careful search; a detailed or careful examination.

in ves ti ga tor (in ves′ti gā′tər), person who investigates.

in vest ment (in vest′mənt), 1. investing. Getting an education is a wise investment of time and money. 2. something bought which is expected to yield money as interest or profit or both. United States bonds are a safe investment.

in ves tor (in ves′tər), person who invests money.

in vig or ate (in vig′ər āt), give vigor to; fill with life and energy.

in vin ci ble (in vin′si bəl), unconquerable; not to be overcome.

in vis i ble (in viz′i bəl), not visible; not capable of being seen. Thought is invisible. The queen kept herself invisible in her palace. Germs are invisible to the naked eye.

in vi ta tion (in′vi tā′shən), 1. a request to come to some place or to do something. The children received invitations to the party. 2. act of inviting.

in vite (in vīt′), 1. ask (someone) politely to come to some place or to do something. We invited Helen to join our club. 2. make a polite request for. Alice invited our opinion of her story. 3. give occasion for. The letter invites some questions. 4. attract; tempt. The calm water invited us to swim.

in vit ing (in vīt′ing), attractive; tempting.

in voke (in vōk′), 1. call on (God or another divine being) in prayer; appeal to for aid or protection. 2. ask earnestly for. The condemned murderer invoked the judge's mercy. 3. call forth by magic.

in vol un tar i ly (in vol′ən tãr′i li), 1. without intention. 2. against one's will.

in vol un tar y (in vol′ən tãr′i), 1. not intended; not done on purpose; as, an involuntary injury. 2. not controlled by the will. Breathing is mainly involuntary. 3. unwilling. John was threatened until he gave involuntary consent to the plan.

in volve (in volv′), 1. have as a necessary part; take in; include. Housework involves cooking, washing dishes, sweeping, and cleaning. 2. bring (into difficulty, danger, etc.). One foolish mistake can involve you in a good deal of trouble. 3. entangle; complicate. Long involved sentences are hard to understand. 4. take up the attention of; occupy. She was involved in working out a puzzle. 5. wrap; enfold. Clouds involved the mountain top. The outcome of the contest is involved in doubt.

in ward (in′wərd), 1. toward the inside; as, a passage leading inward. 2. placed within; as, the inward parts of the body. 3. into the mind or soul. Turn your thoughts inward. 4. in the mind or soul; as, inward peace.

in ward ly (in′wərd li), 1. on the inside; within. 2. toward the inside. 3. in the mind or soul. 4. not aloud or openly.

i o din (ī′ə din), iodine.

i o dine (ī′ə dīn), a substance used in medicine, in photography, and in making dyes. Iodine is put on cuts and wounds to kill disease germs and prevent infection.

ire (īr), anger.

Ire land (īr′lənd), one of the British Isles.

Iris

i ris (ī′ris), 1. a plant with beautiful flowers and leaves shaped like swords. 2. the flower. 3. the colored part of the eye around the pupil. 4. the rainbow.

I rish (ī′rish), 1. of or having to do with Ireland, its people, or their language. 2. the people of Ireland. 3. their language. 4. English as spoken by the Irish.

irk some (ėrk′səm), tiresome; tedious. Washing dishes all day would be an irksome task.

i ron (ī′ərn), 1. the strong, cheap metal from which steel is made. 2. something made of iron. 3. made of iron; as, an iron fence. 4. like iron; hard; strong; as, an iron constitution. 5. **Irons** means chains or bands of iron; handcuffs; shackles. 6. an implement to press clothing. 7. to press with an iron.

i ro ny (ī′rə ni), 1. a way of speaking or writing in which the ordinary meaning of the words is the opposite of the thought in the speaker's mind. The boys called the very thin boy "Fatty" in irony. 2. a tendency to turn what would normally have been good into harm. By the irony of fate the farmers had rain when they needed sun, and sun when they needed rain.

ir reg u lar (i reg′ū lər), 1. not regular; not according to rule. It would be quite irregular for a child of fourteen to drive a car. 2. not even; not smooth; not straight. New England has a very irregular coastline.

ir reg u lar i ty (i reg′ū lar′i ti), 1. lack of regularity. 2. something irregular.

ir re sist i ble (ir′i zis′ti bəl), that cannot be resisted; too great to be withstood.

ir res o lute (i rez′ə lüt), not resolute; unable to make up one's mind; not sure of what one wants. Irresolute persons make poor leaders.

ir rev er ent (i rev′ər ənt), not reverent; disrespectful.

ir ri gate (ir′i gāt), 1. supply (land) with water by means of ditches. 2. supply some part of the body with a flow of some liquid. The doctor showed Amy how to irrigate her nose and throat with hot water.

ir ri ta ble (ir′i tə bəl), 1. easily made angry; as, an irritable temper. 2. more sensitive than is natural or normal.

ir ri tate (ir′i tāt), 1. annoy; vex; arouse to impatience or anger. Flies irritate horses. The boy's foolish questions irritated his mother. 2. make (a part of the body) more sensitive than is natural or normal. Sunburn irritates the skin.

ir ri ta tion (ir′i tā′shən), 1. annoyance; vexation. 2. irritating; being irritated. Irritation of your nose makes you sneeze.

is (iz). The earth is round. He is at school. A child is loved by its mother.

is land (ī′lənd), 1. a body of land surrounded by water. To reach the island you go on a boat. 2. something that suggests a piece of land surrounded by water. Platforms in the middle of crowded streets are safety islands.

is land er (ī′lən dər), 1. one born on an island. 2. one living on an island.

isle (īl), island; small island.

is let (ī′lit), little island.

is n't (iz′ənt), is not.

i so late (ī′sə lāt or is′ə lāt), separate from others. People with contagious diseases should be isolated.

i so la tion (ī′sə lā′shən or is′ə lā′shən), 1. setting apart. 2. being set apart. 3. complete separation.

is sue (ish′ü), 1. send out. This magazine is issued every week. 2. something sent out.

Did you read the last issue of our weekly paper? 3. sending out. 4. come out; go out. Smoke issues from the chimney. 5. a coming forth; discharge. Nosebleed is an issue of blood from the nose. 6. way out; outlet. 7. result; as, the issue of the battle. 8. to result. The game issued in a tie. 9. point to be debated. 10. problem. 11. **At issue** means in question. 12. **Take issue** means disagree. 13. children. **Without issue** means without children.

isth mus (is′məs), a narrow strip of land, with water on both sides of it, connecting two larger bodies of land. The Isthmus of Panama connects North America and South America.

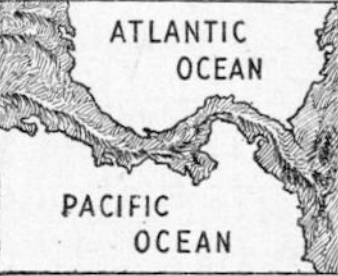

Isthmus of Panama

it (it), the thing, part, animal, or person spoken about. Here is your paper; read it. Look at it carefully. He said, "It is I. What is it you want?" It snows in winter. It is now my turn.

I tal ian (i tal′yən), 1. of Italy, its people, or their language. 2. a native or inhabitant of Italy. 3. the language of Italy.

i tal ic (i tal′ik), of or in type whose letters slant to the right. *These words are in italic type.*

It a ly (it′ə li), a country in southern Europe.

itch (ich), 1. a prickling feeling in the skin that makes one restless, and want to scratch. 2. a disease causing this feeling. 3. cause this feeling. Mosquito bites itch. 4. feel this way in the skin. 5. a restless, uneasy longing or desire for anything; as, an itch to get away and explore. 6. be restless with any desire. John itched to find out their secret.

i tem (ī′təm), 1. separate thing or article. The list had twelve items. 2. piece of news.

its (its), of it; belonging to it. The cat chased its tail. This chair has lost one of its legs.

it's (its), it is.

it self (it self′), 1. *Itself* is used to make a statement stronger. The land itself is worth the money, without the house. 2. *Itself* is used instead of it, him, or her in cases like: The baby hurt itself. 3. its self. The dog saw itself in the glass.

Ivy: A, English ivy; B, poison ivy.

I've (īv), I have.

i vo ry (ī′və ri), 1. the hard, white substance composing the tusks of elephants, walruses, etc. Ivory is used for piano keys and ornaments. 2. substance like ivory. 3. made of ivory. 4. of or like ivory. 5. creamy white.

i vy (ī′vi), a climbing plant with evergreen leaves. See the picture just above.

J

jab (jab), poke; thrust with something pointed. He jabbed his fork into the potato.

jab ber (jab′ər), talk very fast in a confused, senseless way; chatter.

jack (jak), 1. a man or fellow. A **jack of all trades** is a person who can do many different kinds of work. 2. tool or machine for lifting or pushing up heavy weights small distances. We raise or lift the axle off the ground with a jack to change a tire. 3. To **jack** or to **jack up** means to lift or push up with a jack. 4. a device for turning meat roasting before the fire. 5. a ship's flag, smaller than usual, especially one used to show nationality or as a signal.

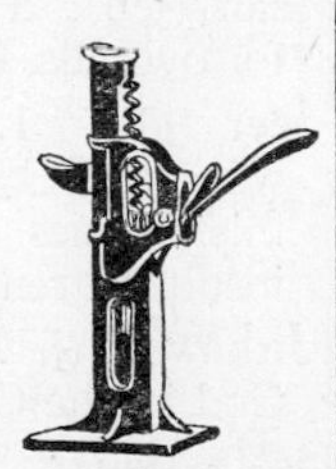
Jack for lifting

jack al (jak′ôl), a wild dog supposed to hunt prey for the lion and eat what the lion left. See the picture below.

jack daw (jak′dô′), European crow.

jack et (jak′it), 1. short coat. 2. outer covering, such as the paper cover for protecting a book, a covering around a steam pipe, or the skin of a potato.

Jackal (about 15 in. high at the shoulder)

jack knife (jak′nīf′), a large, strong pocketknife. Bill has two jackknives.

jack-o'-lan tern (jak′ə lan′tərn), a pumpkin hollowed out and cut to look like a face, used as a lantern at Halloween.

jade[1] (jād), a hard green stone used for jewelry.

jade[2] (jād), 1. inferior or worn-out horse. 2. a woman. 3. to tire; to weary; as, a jaded horse.

jag ged (jag′id), with points sticking out; notched. We cut our bare feet on the jagged rocks.

jag uar (jag′wär), fierce animal much like a leopard, but larger. It lives in forests in the warmer parts of America.

Jaguar (about 6 ft. long with the tail)

jail (jāl), 1. a prison. 2. put in jail; keep in jail.

jail er or **jail or** (jāl′ər), the keeper of a jail.

jam[1] (jam), 1. squeeze between surfaces. The ship was jammed between two rocks. 2. bruise or crush by squeezing; as, to jam your fingers in the door. 3. squeeze (things or people) tight together. A crowd jammed into the streetcar. 4. push (a thing) hard (into a place); as, to jam a fist into a fellow's face. 5. cause (part of a machine) to become caught so that it cannot work; stick fast. 6. fill or block up by crowding. The river was jammed with logs. 7. a crush or squeeze; stoppage of a machine due to jamming; crowded mass. She was delayed by the traffic jam.

jam[2] (jam), a preserve of fruit boiled thick with sugar.

jan gle (jang′gəl), 1. sound harshly. 2. a harsh sound.

jan i tor (jan′i tər), person hired to take care of a building or offices.

Jan u ar y (jan′ū ãr′i), the first month of the year. It has 31 days.

Ja pan (jə pan′), an island empire east of Asia.

Jap a nese (jap′ə nēz′), 1. of Japan, its people, or their language; as, Japanese art, writings, customs, etc. 2. a native of Japan. 3. the language of Japan.

jar[1] (jär), deep container made of earthenware, stone, or glass, with a wide mouth.

Glass jar

jar[2] (jär), 1. shake; rattle. Your heavy footsteps jar my table. 2. make a harsh, grating noise. 3. a harsh, grating noise. 4. have a harsh, unpleasant effect on; send a shock through (your ears, nerves, feelings, etc.). The children's screams jar my nerves. 5. a slight shock to the ears, nerves, feelings, etc. 6. clash; quarrel. We did not get on well together, for our opinions always jarred.

jas per (jas′pər), 1. a colored quartz, usually red or brown. 2. among the ancients, a more valuable stone, green in color.

jaunt (jônt), a short journey or excursion, especially for pleasure.

jaun ty (jôn′ti), easy and lively. When you are well and happy, you usually feel jaunty. He walks with a jaunty step.

jave lin (jav′lin), light spear to be thrown.

jaw (jô), 1. the lower part of the face. 2. The upper and lower **jaws** are two bones or sets of bones that form the framework of the mouth. 3. The **jaws** may mean the mouth of a narrow valley, a pass, or a channel. 4. The **jaws** of a tool or machine are the parts that bite or grasp.

jay (jā), 1. noisy American bird with blue feathers; bluejay. 2. noisy European bird with a crest.

European jay (about 1 ft. long)

jazz (jaz), noisy dance music with the accents falling at unusual places.

jeal ous (jel′əs), 1. feeling as you do when people who usually pay attention to you neglect you and pay much attention to somebody else; fearful that one you love may love someone else better, or may prefer someone else to you. When Tommy sees his mother pet Baby, he becomes jealous. 2. envious; full of envy; as, to be jealous of John's bicycle, or of Amy's new dress. 3. watchful in keeping or guarding something. 4. close; watchful; suspicious. The dog was such a jealous guardian of the child that he would not let him cross the street.

jeal ous y (jel′əs i), dislike or fear of rivals; envy. Jealousy made Pearl unhappy when people praised Kate.

jean (jēn), a stout, heavy cotton cloth used for overalls, etc. **Jeans** often means overalls.

jeer (jēr), 1. make fun in a rude or unkind way; scoff. Do not jeer at the mistakes or misfortunes of others. 2. a mocking or insulting remark.

Je ho vah (ji hō′və), one of the names of God in the Old Testament.

jel ly (jel′i), 1. a food, soft when hot, but firm and partly transparent when cold. Jelly can be made by boiling fruit juice and sugar together, or by cooking meat juice, or by using some stiffening preparation like gelatin.

2. a substance that resembles jelly. 3. become jelly; turn into jelly. Strong soup will jelly as it cools.

jel ly fish (jel′i fish′), a sea animal like a lump of jelly.

Jellyfish

jeop ard ize (jep′ər dīz), risk; endanger. Soldiers jeopardize their lives in war.

jeop ard y (jep′ər di), danger. The man's life was in jeopardy as the tree fell.

jerk[1] (jėrk), 1. a sudden, sharp pull or twist. His old car started with a jerk. 2. pull or twist suddenly. If the water is unexpectedly hot, you jerk your hand out. 3. move with a jerk. The old wagon jerked along.

jerk[2] (jėrk), dry (meat) by cutting it in slices and exposing it to the sun.

jer kin (jėr′kin), short coat or jacket, sometimes without sleeves. Men wore tight leather jerkins in the 16th and 17th centuries.

Jerkin

jerk y (jėr′ki), starting suddenly; with jerks.

jer sey (jėr′zi), 1. close-fitting sweater that is pulled on over the head. 2. knitted cloth made by a machine.

jest (jest), 1. joke. 2. fun. **Spoken in jest** means spoken in fun, not seriously. 3. poke fun; as, to jest at another person's ideals. 4. act of poking fun at; mockery. 5. thing to be mocked or laughed at.

jest er (jes′tər), person who jests. Princes and nobles used to keep jesters to amuse them.

Je sus (jē′zəs), the founder of the Christian religion. The name means "God is salvation."

jet[1] (jet), 1. a stream of water, steam, gas, or any liquid, sent with force, especially from a small opening. A fountain sends up a jet of water. 2. a spout or nozzle for sending out a jet. 3. shoot forth in a jet or forceful stream; gush out. Water jetted from the broken pipe.

Gas jet

jet[2] (jet), 1. a hard black mineral, shining when polished, used for beads and other ornaments. 2. made of jet. 3. deep, shining black; as, hair of jet.

jet ty (jet′i), 1. a structure of stones, timbers, etc., projecting out from the shore to break the force of current or waves; breakwater. 2. landing place; pier.

Jetty or breakwater

Jew (jü), Hebrew; member of a race that once lived in Palestine, but now lives in many countries.

jew el (jü′əl), 1. precious stone; gem. Jewels are used in the works of watches, as well as worn in pins and other ornaments. 2. a valuable ornament to be worn, set with precious stones. 3. person or thing that is very precious. 4. set or adorn with jewels; as, a jeweled comb, a sky jeweled with stars.

jew el er or **jew el ler** (jü′əl ər), person who makes or sells jewels.

jew el ry or **jew el ler y** (jü′əl ri), jewels.

Jew ish (jü′ish), of the Jews; belonging to the Jews; characteristic of the Jews; as, Jewish customs.

jib (jib), a triangular sail set in front of the foremast.

JIB

jif fy (jif′i), a second; a very short time.

jig (jig), 1. a lively dance. 2. music for it. 3. dance a jig.

jin gle (jing′gəl), 1. a sound like that of little bells, or of coins or keys striking together. 2. make such a sound. Sleigh bells jingle. 3. cause (something) to jingle; as, to jingle one's money. 4. a verse that has a jingling sound. Mother Goose rhymes are jingles.

job[1] (job), 1. piece of work. Dick had the job of painting the boat. 2. work done regularly. Washing the supper dishes is Helen's job. 3. work done for pay. Mary's brother is hunting for a job.

Job[2] (jōb), 1. a very patient man in the Bible. 2. the book of the Old Testament which tells about him.

jock ey (jok′i), 1. boy or man who rides horses in races as an occupation. 2. to trick; cheat. Mr. Smith was jockeyed into putting his money into oil stock. 3. maneuver so as to get advantage. The crews were jockeying their boats to get into the best position for the race.

joc und (jok′ənd), cheerful; merry; gay.

jog[1] (jog), 1. shake with a push or jerk. You may jog a person's elbow to get his attention. 2. a shake, push, or nudge. 3. stir up (your own or another person's memory). 4. an urge; a hint or reminder; as, to give your memory a jog. 5. move up or down with a jerk or a shaking motion. The old horse jogged along, and jogged me up and down on his back. 6. go forward heavily and slowly. The tired boys jogged home. 7. slow walk or trot.

jog[2] (jog), part that sticks out or in. We hid behind a jog in the wall.

join (join), 1. bring or put together; connect, fasten, or clasp together; as, to join hands, to join an island to the mainland by a bridge, to join two points. 2. unite; make one; become one; as, to join in marriage. 3. take part with others; as, to join in a song. 4. unite with; come together with. Join us as soon as you can. The stream joins the river just below the mill. 5. take or return to one's place in; as, to join one's ship or one's regiment.

joint (joint), 1. the place at which two things are joined together. 2. the way parts are joined. 3. connect by a joint or joints. 4. in an animal, the parts where two bones move on one another, and the way those parts are put together. **Out of joint** means moved out of place at the joint. 5. one of the parts of which a jointed thing is made up; as, the middle joint of the finger. 6. piece of meat cut for cooking. 7. owned together; owned by, held by, or done by two or more persons. By our joint efforts we managed to push the car back on the road. 8. sharing. My brother and I are joint owners of this dog.

Finger joints: J, joints; K, knuckles and their joints.

joint ly (joint′li), together; as partners. The two boys owned the boat jointly.

joist (joist), one of the parallel pieces of timber to which the boards of a floor or of a ceiling are fastened.

joke (jōk), 1. something said or done to make somebody laugh; something funny. 2. make jokes. 3. person or thing laughed at.

jol li ty (jol′i ti), fun; merriment.

jol ly (jol′i), 1. merry; very cheerful; full of fun. 2. pleasant.

jolt (jōlt), 1. to jar; shake up; move with a shock or jerk. The wagon jolted us when it went over the rocks. 2. a jar; a shock; a jerk. He put his brakes on suddenly, and the car stopped with a jolt. 3. move with a shock or jerk. The car jolted across the rough ground.

jon quil (jong′kwil), a yellow flower much like a daffodil.

Jonquil

jos tle (jos′əl), strike or push against; elbow roughly. We were jostled by the big crowd at the entrance to the circus.

jot (jot), 1. little bit; very small amount. I do not care a jot. 2. write briefly or in haste. The clerk jotted down the order.

jounce (jouns), bounce; bump; jolt.

jour nal (jėr′nəl), 1. a daily record. 2. an account of what happens, or of what one thinks, feels, or notices, such as a diary, a ship's log, the written account of what happens at each meeting of a society or a town meeting. 3. a newspaper or magazine.

jour ney (jėr′ni), 1. a trip; as, a journey around the world. Grace has made four journeys to New York. 2. to travel; take a trip.

jour ney man (jėr′ni mən), qualified workman who works for another person.

joust (just), 1. a combat between two knights on horseback, armed with lances. 2. fight with lances on horseback. Knights used to joust with each other for sport.

Joust

Jove (jōv), the Roman god Jupiter, king of gods and men.

jo vi al (jō′vi əl), kindly and full of fun; good-natured and merry. Santa Claus is a jovial old fellow.

jowl (joul), 1. the jaw, especially the under jaw. 2. the cheek.

joy (joi). Mary felt joy at her new dress. Dick jumped for joy when he saw the circus. On a hot day, a cool swim is a joy. Sometimes joy means be glad or make glad.

joy ful (joi′fəl), 1. glad; happy; as, a joyful heart. 2. causing joy; as, joyful news.

joy ous (joi′əs), joyful; glad; gay.

ju bi lant (jü′bi lənt), rejoicing; exulting.

ju bi lee (jü′bi lē), 1. time of rejoicing; as, to hold a jubilee over a victory. 2. great joy; as, a day of jubilee. 3. an anniversary thought of as a time of rejoicing.

judge (juj), 1. a public officer appointed or elected to hear and decide cases in a law court. 2. act as a judge; hear and decide (cases). 3. person chosen to settle a dispute or to decide who wins a race, etc. 4. settle (a dispute); decide on the winner in a race, a debate, etc. 5. person who can decide on how good a thing is; as, a good judge of dogs, of marbles, of character. 6. form an opinion (about). 7. consider and blame. "Judge not, that ye be not judged." 8. think; suppose; conclude. I judged that you had forgotten to come.

judg ment (juj′mənt), 1. opinion; estimate. In my judgment Helen is prettier than Grace. 2. power to judge well; good sense. Since she has judgment in such matters, we will ask her. 3. act of judging. 4. decision made by anybody who judges. **Pass judgment on** often means make an unfavorable decision about.

ju di cious (jü dish′əs), wise; sensible; having, using, or showing good judgment. A judicious parent encourages his children to decide many things for themselves.

jug (jug), a container for holding liquids. A jug usually has a spout or a narrow neck and a handle.

Jug

jug gle (jug′əl), 1. perform tricks by the skill of hand or eye. He juggled with knives by balancing them on his nose. 2. perform tricks. 3. perform tricks with. The dishonest cashier juggled the accounts to hide his theft. 4. deceive. 5. trick; fraud.

jug gler (jug′lər), one who juggles.

juice (jüs), the liquid part of fruits and vegetables, or of animal bodies; as, the juice of a lemon, meat juice, the juices of the body.

juic y (jüs′i), full of juice; having much juice.

Ju ly (jü lī′), the seventh month of the year. It has 31 days.

jum ble (jum′bəl), 1. mix or confuse. It is easy to jumble up everything in your drawer when you are hunting for something. 2. a muddle; mixed-up mess; state of confusion.

jump (jump), 1. to spring from the ground; to leap; to bound. Our cat can jump to the table, off the table, across the path, etc. 2. a spring from the ground; a leap; a bound. 3. cause to jump; as, to jump a horse over a fence, to jump a child up and down. 4. give a sudden start or jerk. We often jump when a sudden sight, noise, or touch startles us. 5. a sudden, nervous start. 6. **Jump at** (a chance, an offer, a bargain) means accept it eagerly and at once.

jump er[1] (jump′ər), one that jumps.

jump er[2] (jump′ər), 1. loose jacket. Workmen and sailors often wear jumpers to protect their clothes. 2. loose blouse reaching to the hips.

junc tion (jungk′shən), 1. joining or being joined; as, the junction of two rivers. 2. place of joining or meeting; station where railroad lines meet or cross.

junc ture (jungk′chər), 1. joining. 2. being joined. 3. a point or line where two things join; joint.

June (jün), the sixth month of the year. It has 30 days.

jun gle (jung′gəl), wild land thickly overgrown with bushes, vines, trees, etc. They cut a path through the jungle.

jun ior (jün′yər), 1. the younger (used of a son having the same name as his father). John Parker, Junior, is the son of John Parker, Senior. 2. younger person. Tom is his brother's junior by two years. 3. of lower position; of less standing than some others; as, the junior partner, a junior officer. 4. person of lower standing. 5. student during the third year of a high-school or college course. 6. of the third-year students; as, the Junior class, a Junior dance.

Branch of juniper

ju ni per (jü′ni pər), an evergreen shrub with purple berries. See the picture just above.

junk[1] (jungk), old newspapers, metal, and other rubbish; trash.

Junk

junk[2] (jungk), Chinese sailing ship. See the picture just above.

Ju pi ter (jü′pi tər), 1. a Roman god, the ruler of gods and men. 2. the largest planet.

ju ror (jür′ər), member of a jury.

ju ry (jür′i), 1. a group of persons sworn to give a true answer to the question put before them in a law court, that is, "Is the prisoner guilty or not?" 2. any group of persons chosen to give a judgment or to decide who is the winner. The jury gave Helen's poem the first prize.

just (just), 1. right; fair; as, a just reward, a just opinion, a just price. 2. righteous; as, a just person, a just life. 3. exact; as, a just scale. 4. exactly. That is just right. 5. only; merely. He is just an ordinary man. 6. a very little while ago. He just left me. 7. barely. I just caught the train.

jus tice (jus′tis), 1. fairness; rightness; being just; as, the justice of a claim. Justice consists in giving every man what he deserves. 2. just conduct; fair dealing. 3. **Do justice to** means (1) treat fairly. (2) see the good points of; show proper appreciation for. 4. **Not do oneself justice** means not do so well as one really can do.

jus ti fi a ble (jus′ti fī′ə bəl), capable of being justified; proper. An act is justifiable if it can be shown to be just or right.

jus ti fi ca tion (jus′ti fi kā′shən), 1. justifying. 2. being justified. 3. a fact or circumstance that justifies; a good reason or excuse. What is your justification for being so late?

jus ti fy (jus′ti fī), 1. give a good reason for. The fine quality of this cloth justifies its high cost. 2. show to be just or right. Can you justify your act? 3. clear from blame. You are justified in shooting a man in self-defense.

jut (jut), 1. stick out; project; stand out. The pier jutted out from the shore into the water. 2. a part that sticks out or projects.

jute (jüt), a strong fiber used for making coarse fabrics, rope, etc. Jute is obtained from two tropical plants.

ju ve nile (jü′və nil or jü′və nīl), 1. young; youthful. 2. young person. 3. of or for boys and girls; as, juvenile books. 4. book for boys and girls. 5. actor who plays youthful parts.

K

kai ak (kī′ak), kayak.

kale or **kail** (kāl), a kind of cabbage with curled leaves not forming a head. Kale looks somewhat like spinach.

ka lei do scope (kə lī′də skōp), tube containing bits of colored glass and two mirrors. As it is turned, it reflects continually changing patterns.

kan ga roo (kang′gə-rü′), an animal that lives in Australia. It has small forelegs and very strong hind legs, which give it great leaping power. The mother kangaroo has a pouch in front in which she carries her young.

Kangaroo (about 8 ft. long with the tail)

ka ty did (kā′ti did), a large green insect that makes a shrill noise like "Katy did, Katy didn't."

Katydid (about ⅓ life size)

kay ak (kī′ak), an Eskimo canoe made of skins stretched over a light frame of wood or bone with an opening in the middle for a person. See the picture in the next column.

keel (kēl), 1. the main timber or steel piece that extends the whole length of the bottom of a ship or boat. The whole ship is built up on the keel. See the picture just below. 2. part in an airplane or airship that is like a ship's keel. 3. **Keel** or **keel over** means turn or become turned keel up; turn upside down; upset; fall over suddenly. Maud keeled over when she fainted.

Kayak

keel son (kel′sən or kēl′sən), beam or line of timbers or iron plates fastened along the top of a ship's keel to strengthen it.

KEEL

keen (kēn), 1. so shaped as to cut well; sharp; cutting; as, a keen blade, keen wit, keen pain. 2. eager; as, a keen player. 3. able to do its work quickly and exactly; as, a keen mind, a keen sense of smell.

keen ness (kēn′nis), keen or cutting quality; sharpness. The keenness of Ben's appetite was dulled by four large buns.

keep (kēp), 1. have for a long while or forever. You may keep this book. 2. have and not let go. They were kept in prison. Can she keep a secret? 3. have and take care of. She keeps chickens. My aunt keeps two boarders. 4. take care of and protect. The bank keeps money for people. 5. have; hold. Keep this in mind. 6. continue; stay as one is. Keep along this road for two miles. This milk kept sweet for five days. 7. do the right thing with; observe. Good Christians keep the Sabbath. 8. food and a place to sleep. The money he earns would not pay for his keep. 9. the main part of a fortress; a stronghold. See the picture.

KEEP

kept is formed from **keep.**

keep er (kēp′ər), one that watches, guards, or takes care of persons or things.

keep ing (kēp′ing), 1. care; charge; as, money in safe keeping. 2. observance; as, the keeping of Christmas. 3. agreement; harmony. His actions are in keeping with his promises.

keep sake (kēp′sāk′), thing kept in memory of the giver. My friend gave me his picture as a keepsake when he went away.

keg (keg), small barrel, usually holding less than ten gallons.

kelp (kelp), 1. a large, tough, brown seaweed. 2. ashes of seaweed.

ken (ken), 1. range of sight. 2. range of knowledge. What happens on the moon is beyond our ken. 3. know.

ken nel (ken′əl), 1. house for a dog or dogs. 2. place where dogs are bred.

kept (kept). See **keep.** I gave him the book and he kept it. The milk was kept in bottles.

ker chief (kėr′chif), 1. piece of cloth worn over the head or around the neck. 2. handkerchief.

Kerchief

ker nel (kėr′nəl), 1. the softer part inside the hard shell of a nut or inside the stone of a fruit. 2. a grain or seed like that of wheat or corn. 3. the central or important part of anything around which it is formed or built up.

Kernel and shell of a nut

ker o sene (ker′ə sēn), a thin oil made from petroleum, used in lamps and stoves.

ketch (kech), a small, strongly built sailing ship with two masts, and with its sails set lengthwise.

ket tle (ket′əl), 1. any metal container for boiling liquids, cooking fruit, etc. 2. a metal container with a handle and spout for heating water.

key[1] (kē), 1. a small metal instrument for locking and unlocking the lock of a door, a padlock, or any other thing. 2. a place that commands or gives control of a sea, a district, etc., because of its position. 3. the answer to a puzzle or problem. The key to this puzzle will be published next week. 4. a sheet or book of answers. 5. in studying languages, a book that gives the translation one is working out. 6. one of a set of parts pressed in playing a piano, and in operating a typewriter or other instruments. Don't hit the keys so hard. 7. a scale or system of notes in music related to one another in a special way and based on a particular note; as, a song written in the key of B flat. 8. tone of voice; style of thought or expression. The widow wrote in a sorrowful key. 9. regulate the pitch of; as, to key a piano up to concert pitch. 10. **Key** (a person) **up** means raise his courage or nerve. I keyed myself up to ask for a higher salary.

Door key

key[2] (kē), a low island or reef. There are keys near the coast of Florida.

key board (kē′bōrd′), the set of keys in a piano, organ, typewriter, etc.

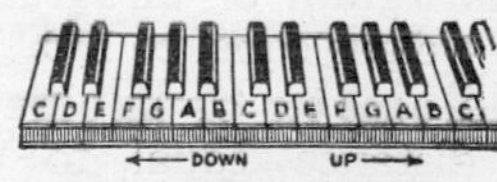

Part of the keyboard of a piano

key note (kē′nōt′), 1. in music, the note on which a scale or system of tones is based. 2. main idea; guiding principle. World peace was the keynote of his speech.

KEYSTONE

key stone (kē′stōn′), middle stone at the top of an arch, holding the other pieces in place. See the picture.

kha ki (kä′ki), 1. the color of dust; dull yellowish-brown. 2. heavy cloth of this color, much used for uniforms of soldiers.

kick (kik). The bad man kicked my dog. This horse kicks. One of his kicks knocked a boy down. The boy kicked the football. Kick off your shoes. Don't kick up so much dust. The blow given to a person's shoulder by a gun when it is fired is called a kick. This old gun kicks. *Kick* is used in free and easy talk to mean (1) grumble or find fault. (2) excitement or thrill.

kid (kid), 1. a baby goat. 2. the leather made from the skin of a young goat, used for gloves and shoes. 3. child.

kid nap (kid′nap), steal (a child); carry off (anyone) by force. Four men kidnaped Mr. Lane's son, but the police soon caught them and rescued him.

kid ney (kid′ni), 1. one of the pair of organs that separate waste matter and water from the blood and pass it off through the bladder in liquid form. 2. kidney or kidneys of an animal, cooked for food. 3. nature; disposition. 4. kind; sort. We don't like cowards, sneaks, tattletales, or any persons of that kidney.

kill (kil), 1. put to death. 2. put an end to; get rid of. 3. act of killing. 4. animal killed.

kill er (kil′ər), person, animal, or thing that kills.

kiln (kil or kiln), furnace or oven for burning, baking, or drying something. Limestone is burned in a kiln to make lime. Bricks are baked in a kiln.

ki lo (kē′lō), kilogram.

kil o gram or **kil o gramme** (kil′ə gram), a weight equal to 1000 grams or $2\frac{1}{5}$ pounds.

kil o me ter or **kil o me tre** (kil′ə mē′tər), distance equal to 1000 meters or 3281 feet.

kilt (kilt), pleated skirt, reaching to the knees, worn by men in parts of Scotland.

Man wearing a kilt

ki mo no (ki mō′nə), 1. the loose, outer garment worn by both men and women in Japan. 2. a woman's loose dressing gown.

kin (kin), 1. family or relatives. All our kin came to the family reunion. 2. family relationship. What kin is she to you? **Near of kin** means closely related. 3. related. My cousin Ann is kin to me.

kind[1] (kīnd). A kind girl tries to help people and make them happy. Taking a blind man across a street is a kind act.

kind[2] (kīnd). All kinds of animals were in the ark. What kind of cake do you like best?

kin der gar ten (kin′dər gär′tən), a school for children from 3 to 6 years old that educates them by games, toys, and pleasant occupations.

kind-heart ed (kīnd′här′tid), having or showing a kind heart; kindly; sympathetic.

kin dle (kin′dəl), 1. set on fire. Light the paper with a match to kindle the wood. 2. catch fire. This damp wood will never kindle. 3. stir up; arouse. His cruelty kindled our anger. 4. become bright or excited. The boy's face kindled as he told about the circus.

kind li ness (kīnd′li nis), 1. kindly feeling or quality. 2. a kindly act.

kin dling (kin′dling), small pieces of wood for starting a fire.

kind ly (kīnd′li), 1. kind; friendly. 2. pleasant; agreeable. 3. in a kind or friendly way. 4. with pleasure. The cat took kindly to her warm bed.

kind ness (kīnd′nis), 1. kind nature; being kind. We admire his kindness. 2. kind treatment. Thank you for your kindness. 3. a kind act. He showed me many kindnesses.

kin dred (kin′drid), 1. a person's family or relatives. 2. family relationship. Does he claim kindred with you? 3. related; as, kindred tribes. 4. being alike; resemblance. There is kindred among the words *receive*, *receipt*, and *reception*. 5. like; similar; connected. She learned about dew, frost, and kindred facts of nature.

kine (kīn), cows; cattle.

king (king), 1. the man who rules a country and its people. Richard the Lion-Hearted was king of England. 2. a man with the title of ruler, but with limited power to rule. The kings of England really do not rule England now. 3. person who has power such as kings used to have; very important person. 4. an important piece in the game of chess or checkers.

king bird (king′bėrd′), quarrelsome bird that catches and eats insects as it flies.

king dom (king′dəm), 1. a country that is governed by a king or a queen; the land or territory ruled by one king. 2. a realm, domain, or province. The mind is the kingdom of thought. 3. one of the three divisions of the natural world: the animal kingdom, the vegetable kingdom, and the mineral kingdom.

king fish er (king′fish′ər), a bright-colored bird. One kind of kingfisher eats fish; the other eats insects.

Belted kingfisher (about 1 ft. long)

king ly (king′li), 1. of a king or kings; of royal rank. 2. fit for a king; as, a kingly crown. 3. like a king; royal; noble. 4. as a king does.

king ship (king′ship), 1. position, rank, or dignity of a king. 2. rule of a king; government by a king.

kink (kingk), 1. a twist or curl in thread, rope, hair, etc. 2. form a kink; make kinks in. 3. mental twist; queer idea.

kins folk (kinz′fōk′), family; relatives.

kin ship (kin′ship), being kin; family relationship. Sam's kinship with the owner of the factory helped him to get a job.

kins man (kinz′mən), male relative. Brothers and uncles are kinsmen.

kirk (kėrk), Scottish word meaning church.

kiss (kis), 1. to touch with the lips as a sign of love, greeting, or respect. 2. a touch with the lips as a sign of love, greeting, or respect. 3. touch gently. A soft wind kisses the tree tops. 4. gentle touch. 5. a kind of candy. 6. a small fancy cake made of sugar and white of egg.

Boy flying a kite

kit (kit), 1. the equipment that a soldier carries with him. 2. any person's equipment packed for traveling. 3. workman's outfit of tools; as, a shoemaker's kit. 4. small wooden tub, pail, etc.

kitch en (kich′ən), room where food is cooked.

kite (kīt), 1. a light wooden frame covered with paper or cloth. Kites are flown in the air on the end of a long string. See the picture just above. 2. a hawk with long, pointed wings.

Kite (about 2 ft. long)

kith (kith), friends; acquaintances. **Kith and kin** means friends and relatives.

kit ten (kit′ən), a young cat.

kit ty (kit′i), pet name for a kitten.

knack (nak), special skill; power to do something easily. A clown has a knack of doing very funny things.

knap sack (nap′sak′), a soldier's leather or canvas bag for clothes, etc., carried on the back; any similar bag or sack.

Knapsack

knave (nāv), a tricky or dishonest man.

knav er y (nāv′ər i), 1. trickery; dishonesty; the behavior of a knave or rascal. 2. a knavish act.

knav ish (nāv′ish), tricky; dishonest.

knead (nēd), 1. work over or work up (moist flour or clay) with the hands into dough or paste. Machines have been invented to knead bread dough. 2. make or shape by kneading. 3. work over with the hands as if kneading; massage. The trainer kneaded the lame muscles of the runner.

knee (nē), 1. the joint between the thigh and the lower leg. 2. anything like a bent knee in shape or position.

kneel (nēl), 1. go down on one's knee or knees. She knelt down to pull a weed from the flower bed. 2. remain on the knees. They knelt in prayer for half an hour.

knell (nel), 1. the sound of a bell rung slowly after a death or at a funeral. 2. ring slowly. 3. something regarded as a sign of death or as telling of a death. Their refusal rang the knell of our hopes. 4. sound sadly; give a warning sound.

knelt (nelt). See **kneel.** She knelt and prayed.

knew (nū or nü). See **know.** Jane knew the right answer.

knick er bock ers (nik′ər bok′ərz), short, loose trousers gathered in at or just below the knee.

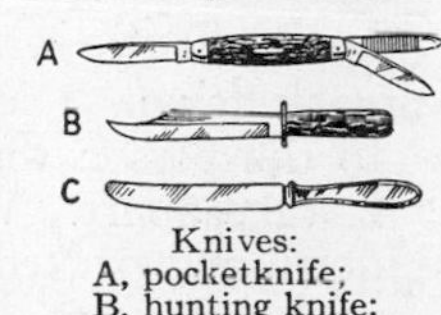

Knives: A, pocketknife; B, hunting knife; C, table knife.

knife (nīf), 1. a flat piece of steel, silver, etc., with a sharp edge, fastened in a handle so that it can be used to cut. A table knife is stiff, with no joint; a pocketknife has a joint so that the sharp edge can be folded inside the handle. 2. a sharp blade forming part of a tool or machine; as, the knives of a lawn mower. 3. cut or stab with a knife.

knight (nīt), 1. in the Middle Ages, a man raised to an honorable military rank and bound to do good deeds. After serving as a page and squire, a man was made a knight by the king or a lord. 2. in modern times, a man raised to an honorable rank because of personal greatness. A knight has the title *Sir* before his name. 3. raise to the rank of knight. He was knighted by the king.

knight-er rant (nīt′er′ənt), knight traveling in search of adventure.

knight-er rant ry (nīt′er′ən tri), 1. conduct or action characteristic of a knight-errant. 2. exaggerated or unwise chivalry.

knight hood (nīt′hu̇d), 1. the rank of a knight. 2. the profession or occupation of a knight. 3. the character or qualities of a knight. 4. knights; as, all the knighthood of France.

knight ly (nīt′li), 1. of a knight; brave; generous; courteous. 2. bravely; generously; as a knight should do.

knit (nit), 1. make with long needles out of wool yarn, or out of silk or cotton thread. Lucy is knitting a sweater. Jersey is knitted cloth. 2. join closely and firmly together. Athletes often have well-knit bodies. 3. grow together. The doctor fixed Tom's arm so that the broken bone would knit. 4. draw (the brows) together in wrinkles. She knits her brows when she frowns.

Knitting

knives (nīvz), more than one knife.

knob (nob), 1. a rounded lump. 2. the handle of a door or of a drawer.

knock (nok), 1. Bill ran against another boy and knocked him down. She knocked on the door. He knocked the dish off the table. She knocked her head against the wall. The hard knock made her cry. 2. Some special meanings are:

knock about, wander.

knock down, 1. sell (an article at an auction) to the person who offers the highest price. 2. take apart. We knocked the bookcases down and packed them in the car.

knock out, hit so hard as to make helpless or unconscious.

knock together, make or put together hastily. The boys knocked together a sort of raft out of old boards.

knock er (nok′ər), 1. one that knocks. 2. a hinged knob, ring, or the like, fastened on a door for use in knocking.

knoll (nōl), a small hill; a mound.

knot (not), 1. a tying or twining together of parts of one or more ropes, strings, etc., to fasten them together; as, a square knot, a slip knot. 2. to tie in a knot. 3. a bow (of ribbon); ribbon made up into an ornament to be put on a dress, etc.; as, a shoulder knot. 4. measure of speed used on ships; one nautical mile ($6080\frac{1}{4}$ ft.) per hour. This ship's usual speed is about 18 knots. 5. the hard mass formed in a tree where a branch grows out, which shows as a round, cross-grained piece in a board. 6. a joint where leaves grow out on the stem of a plant. 7. a group or cluster of persons or things. There was a knot of children around each sailor. 8. a difficulty or problem. 9. unite closely in a way that is hard to undo. 10. tangle. My thread has knotted.

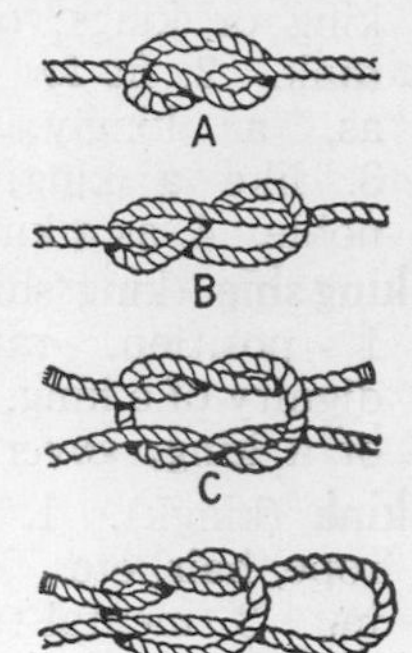

Knots: A, overhand; B, figure-of-eight; C, square; D, slip.

knot hole (not′hōl′), a hole in a board formed where a knot has fallen out.

knot ty (not′i), 1. full of knots; as, knotty wood. 2. difficult; puzzling; as, a knotty problem.

know (nō). We know that 2 and 2 make 4. Doctor Jones does not guess; he knows. Do you know that girl? Do you know where she lives? How many kinds of birds do you know? **knew** and **known** are formed from **know.**

know ing (nō′ing), 1. having knowledge. 2. clever; shrewd. 3. suggesting shrewd or secret understanding; as, a knowing glance.

know ing ly (nō′ing li), 1. in a knowing way. 2. to one's own knowledge. He would not knowingly hurt any living thing.

knowl edge (nol′ij), 1. what one knows. 2. all that is known or can be learned. 3. the fact of knowing. The knowledge of our victory caused great joy. 4. the act of knowing.

known (nōn). See **know.** Washington is known as a general.

knuck le (nuk′əl), 1. a joint in a finger, especially one of the joints at the roots of the fingers. 2. the knee of an animal used as meat; as, pigs' knuckles. 3. **Knuckle down** means (1) submit. (2) work hard.

L

la bel (lā′bəl), 1. a slip of paper or other material attached to anything and marked to show what or whose it is, or where it is to go. Can you read the label on the box? 2. put or write a label on. The bottle is labeled "Poison." 3. put in a class; call; name; as, to label a man a liar.

la bor (lā′bər), 1. work; toil. 2. workers. 3. move slowly and heavily. The ship labored in the heavy seas.

lab o ra to ry (lab′ə rə tō′ri), place where scientific work is done; as, a chemical laboratory.

la bor er (lā′bər ər), 1. worker. 2. person who does work that requires strength rather than skill and training.

la bo ri ous (lə bō′ri əs), 1. requiring much work; requiring hard work. Climbing a mountain is laborious. 2. hard-working. Ants and bees are laborious insects. 3. showing signs of effort; not easy.

labor union, an association of workers to protect and promote their interests.

lab y rinth (lab′i rinth), maze; place through which it is hard to find one's way.

lace (lās), 1. an open weaving or net of fine thread in an ornamental pattern. 2. trim with lace. 3. a cord, string, or leather strip for pulling or holding together. These shoes need new laces. 4. put laces through; pull or hold together with a lace or laces; as, to lace up your shoes.

Lace (def. 1)

lac er ate (las′ər āt), tear roughly; mangle. The bear's claws lacerated the hunter's flesh. Your sharp words lacerated my feelings.

lack (lak), 1. a being without. Lack of food made him hungry; lack of fire made him cold. 2. have no; be without. Guinea pigs lack tails. A coward lacks courage.

lack ey (lak′i), 1. male servant; footman. 2. a completely obedient servant.

lack ing (lak′ing), 1. absent; not here. Water is lacking because the pipe is broken. 2. without; not having. Lacking anything better, we must use what we have.

lac quer (lak′ər), 1. a varnish consisting of shellac dissolved in alcohol, used for coating brass, etc. 2. a natural varnish obtained from the resin of a sumac tree of southeastern Asia. It is used for producing a highly polished surface on wood. 3. to coat with lacquer. 4. articles coated with lacquer.

lac y (lās′i), 1. of lace. 2. like lace.

lad (lad), boy.

lad der (lad′ər), 1. a set of rungs or steps fastened into two long sidepieces of wood, metal, or rope, for use in climbing up and down. 2. a means of climbing higher. Hard work is a ladder to success.

Wooden ladder

lad en (lād′ən), loaded; burdened. The camels were laden with bundles of silk.

la dies (lā′diz), more than one lady.

la dle (lā′dəl), 1. deep, cup-shaped spoon with a long handle, for dipping out liquids. 2. dip out.

Ladle

la dy (lā′di), 1. the mistress of a house. 2. well-bred woman. 3. woman of high social standing. 4. in Great Britain, **Lady** is a title given to women of certain ranks. 5. **Our Lady** is a title of the Virgin Mary.

la dy bird (lā′di bėrd′), ladybug.

la dy bug (lā′di bug′), a small, roundish beetle, reddish with black spots.

lag (lag), 1. move too slowly; fall behind. The child lagged because he was tired. 2. falling behind.

la goon (lə gün′), 1. small pond connected with a larger body of water. 2. shallow water separated from the sea by low ridges of sand. 3. the water within a ring-shaped coral island.

laid (lād). See **lay**[1]. He laid down the heavy bundle. Those eggs were laid this morning.

lain (lān). See **lie**[2]. The snow has lain on the ground a week.

lair (lãr), the den or resting place of a wild animal.

laird (lãrd), a Scottish word meaning an owner of land.

lake (lāk), body of water surrounded by land. A lake is larger than a pond.

lamb (lam), 1. a baby sheep. 2. meat from a lamb; as, roast lamb. 3. give birth to a lamb or lambs. 4. a young, innocent, or dear person.

Lamb

lamb kin (lam′kin), little lamb.

lame (lām), 1. stiff and sore. His arm is lame from playing ball. 2. not able to walk properly; having a hurt leg. 3. make lame; cripple. The accident lamed him for life. 4. poor; not very good. Stopping to play is a lame excuse for being late to school.

lame ness (lām′nis), being lame. Fred's lameness kept him from playing ball.

la ment (lə ment′), 1. sorrow for; mourn. 2. weep; sorrow. 3. a wail; an expression of grief or sorrow. 4. a poem, song, or tune that expresses grief.

lam en ta ble (lam′ən tə bəl), 1. to be regretted or pitied; as, a lamentable accident, a lamentable failure. 2. sorrowful; mournful.

lam en ta tion (lam′ən tā′shən), loud grief; mourning; wailing; cries of sorrow.

lamp (lamp), 1. a vessel for giving light. Oil lamps hold oil and a wick by which the oil is burned. 2. a gas or electric light, especially when covered with a glass globe or other shade. 3. anything that gives light.

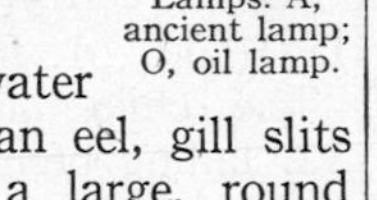

Lamps: A, ancient lamp; O, oil lamp.

lam prey (lam′pri), water animal having a body like an eel, gill slits like a fish, no jaws, and a large, round mouth.

lance (lans), 1. a long wooden spear with a sharp iron or steel head. Knights carried lances. 2. soldier who carries a lance. 3. pierce with a lance. 4. cut open with a surgeon's knife; as, to lance the gum where a new tooth has difficulty in coming through. 5. hurl. The knights lanced themselves against the foe.

land (land), 1. the solid part of the earth's surface. 2. ground; soil. This is good land for a garden. 3. a country and its people. 4. come to land; bring to land. The ship landed at the pier. The pilot landed the airplane in a field. 5. put on shore from a ship or boat. The ship landed its passengers. 6. go on shore from a ship or boat. The passengers landed. 7. arrive. The thief landed in jail. 8. catch; get.

land ing (lan′ding), 1. coming to land; as, the landing of our soldiers in France. 2. place where persons or goods are landed from a ship; as, the steamboat landing. 3. platform between flights of stairs.

land la dy (land′lā′di), 1. woman who owns buildings or lands that she rents to others. 2. mistress of an inn, lodging house, or boarding house.

land lord (land′lôrd′), 1. person who owns buildings or lands that he rents to others. 2. the keeper of an inn, lodging house, or boarding house.

land mark (land′märk′), 1. something familiar or easily seen, used as a guide. 2. any important fact or event; any happening that stands out above others. The telegraph, telephone, and radio are landmarks in the progress of communication.

land own er (land′ōn′ər), person who owns land.

land scape (land′skāp), 1. land scene; a view of scenery on land. The two hills with the valley formed a beautiful landscape. 2. picture showing a land scene. 3. make (land) more pleasant to look at by arranging trees, shrubs, flowers, etc. A park is landscaped.

lane (lān), 1. path between hedges, walls, or fences; a narrow or short grassy road in the country. 2. an alley between buildings. 3. the course or route used by ships or airplanes going in the same direction. 4. any narrow way. The six generals walked down a lane formed by two lines of soldiers and sailors.

lan guage (lang′gwij), 1. human speech, spoken or written. 2. the speech of one nation or race; as, the French language. 3. form, style, or kind of language; as, Shakespeare's language, the language of chemistry. 4. wording; words; as, in the language of the Lord's Prayer. 5. any means of expressing thoughts or feelings; as, a dog's language, the language of the eyes.

lan guid (lang′gwid), feeling weak; without energy; drooping. A hot, sticky day makes a person feel languid.

lan guish (lang′gwish), 1. grow weak; droop. The flowers languish from lack of water. 2. droop with longing. She languished for home.

lank (langk), 1. long and thin; lean; as, a lank boy. 2. long and slender; as, lank grasses. 3. straight and flat; as, lank locks of hair.

lan tern (lan′tərn), a case to protect a light from wind or rain. A lantern has sides of glass, paper, or some other material through which light can shine.

Lantern

lap[1] (lap), 1. the part from the waist to the knees of a person sitting down, with the clothing. Mother holds the baby on her lap. 2. place where anything rests or is cared for.

lap[2] (lap), 1. to wind or wrap round; fold over or about something. Lap this edge over that. 2. enfold or wrap in; surround. 3. lie together, one partly over or beside another. The pieces lapped over each other. 4. act of lapping. 5. the part that laps over. 6. one time around a race track; as, the first lap of the race.

lap[3] (lap), 1. drink as a dog does, by lifting up with the tongue; lick. 2. move or beat gently with a lapping sound. The waves lapping against the shore put me to sleep. 3. act of lapping; as, one lap of the tongue. 4. the sound of little waves on the beach.

lapse (laps), 1. a moment's forgetfulness; a slip of the tongue or pen; a slip away from right conduct. 2. slip back; sink down. The house lapsed into ruin. He sometimes lapses from good behavior. 3. the slipping by of time. 4. slip by; pass away. The boy's interest soon lapsed. 5. the ending of a right, privilege, etc., because not renewed, not used, or not attended to. 6. to end. A claim lapses after a certain time.

lar board (lär′bərd), 1. the left or port side of a ship. See the picture under **aft.** 2. on the left side of a ship.

larch (lärch), 1. a tree with small cones and needles that fall off in the autumn. 2. the wood of this tree.

Branch of larch

lard (lärd), 1. the fat of pigs or hogs, melted down and made clear for use in cooking. 2. put strips of bacon or pork in (meat) before cooking. 3. enrich by inserts; trim. The mayor larded his speech with jokes and stories.

lar der (lär′dər), 1. pantry; place where food is kept. 2. stock of food. The hunters' larder included flour, bacon, and what they shot or caught.

large (lärj). A horse is a large animal. America is larger than England. A very large man is called a giant. **At large** means (1) free. Is the prisoner still at large? (2) in general. The people at large wanted peace.

large ly (lärj′li), much; to a great extent.

lar i at (lar′i ət), 1. lasso; a long rope with a noose for catching horses, cattle, etc. A cowboy throws a lariat at horses or cattle to catch them. 2. a rope for fastening horses, mules, etc., while they graze.

lark[1] (lärk), 1. a small songbird of Europe that soars and sings while in the air. 2. a similar bird in America.

lark[2] (lärk), 1. something that is good fun; joke. 2. have fun; play tricks.

lar va (lär′və), early form of an insect from the time it leaves the egg until it becomes a pupa. A caterpillar is the larva of a butterfly or moth. A grub is the larva of a beetle. Maggots are the larvae of flies.

Larva of a butterfly

lash (lash), 1. the part of a whip that is not the handle. 2. a stroke or blow with a whip, etc. 3. strike with a whip. The driver of the team lashed his horses on. 4. beat back and forth. A lion lashes his tail. The wind lashes the sails. 5. hurt severely by words. 6. hit. 7. tie or fasten with a rope or cord; as, a body lashed to a mast. 8. one of the little hairs on the edge of the eyelid.

lass (las), girl; young girl.

las sie (las′i), girl.

las so (las′ō), 1. long rope with a running noose at the end, used for catching horses and cattle. 2. to catch with a lasso.

Cowboy using a lasso

last[1] (last). *Z* is the last letter; *A* is the first. Ned came last in the line. It rained last night. When did you see him last? **At last** means finally.

last[2] (last), hold out; continue; continue in good condition. How long will our money last? I hope these shoes last a year.

last[3] (last), block shaped like the human foot, on which shoes and boots are formed or mended.

last ing (las′ting), that lasts; that will last; that will last a long time.

last ly (last′li), finally; in the last place.

latch (lach), 1. a catch for fastening a door, gate, or window, often one not needing a key. 2. fasten with a latch.

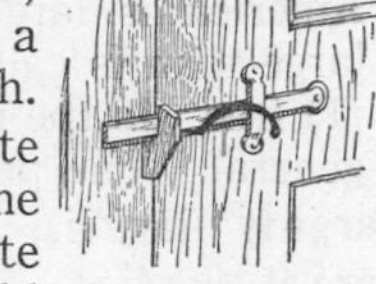
Latch on a door

late (lāt), 1. We had a late supper because father came home late. 2. It was late in the evening. You should not sit up too late at night. 3. recent. The late storm did much harm. 4. recently dead or gone out of office. The late Mr. Smith was a good citizen. The late president is still working actively. 5. **Of late** means lately; a short time ago.

late ly (lāt′li), a little while ago; not long ago.

la tent (lā′tənt), hidden; concealed; present but not active. The power of a grain of wheat to grow into a plant remains latent if it is not planted.

lat er al (lat′ər əl), of the side; at the side; from the side; toward the side.

lath (lath), 1. a thin, narrow strip of wood, used with others like it to form a support for plaster or to make a lattice. 2. cover or line with laths.

lathe (lāTH), a machine for holding articles of wood, metal, etc., and turning them rapidly against a tool used to shape them.

lath er (laTH′ər), 1. foam made from soap and water. 2. put lather on. He lathers his face before shaving. 3. form a lather. This soap lathers well. 4. foam formed in sweating. 5. become covered with lather. The horse lathered from his hard gallop.

lat i tude (lat′i tūd or lat′i tüd), 1. distance north or south of the equator, measured in degrees. 2. place or region having a certain latitude. 3. room to act; freedom from narrow rules. You are allowed much latitude in this work.

lat ter (lat′ər), 1. the second of two. Canada and the United States are in North America; the former lies north of the latter. 2. more recent; later; toward the end; as, the latter part of the week, the old man's latter days.

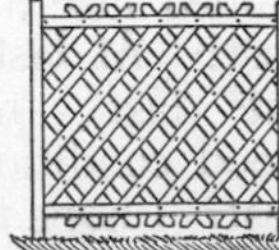
Lattice

lat tice (lat′is), 1. wooden or metal strips crossed with open spaces between them. 2. form into a lattice. 3. furnish with a lattice.

laud (lôd), praise; extol.

laugh (laf), 1. You laugh when you hear a good joke. 2. the sound made when a person laughs. 3. be gay or lively. The little brook laughed. 4. **Laugh at** means make fun of.

laugh a ble (laf′ə bəl), amusing; funny.

laugh ter (laf′tər), 1. the action of laughing. 2. the sound of laughing.

launch[1] (lônch), 1. the largest boat carried by a warship. 2. a rather small open motorboat for pleasure trips.

launch[2] (lônch), 1. cause to slide into the water; set afloat. A new ship is launched from the supports on which it was built. 2. start; set going; set out. His friends launched him in business by lending him money. He used the money to launch into a new business. 3. throw; hurl; send out. A bow launches arrows into the air. An angry person launches threats against his enemies.

laun der (lôn′dər), wash and iron clothes.

laun dress (lôn′dris), woman who washes and irons clothes.

laun dry (lôn′dri), 1. a room or building where clothes are washed and ironed. 2. clothes that are washed.

lau rel (lô′rəl), 1. a small evergreen tree with smooth, shiny leaves. 2. any tree or shrub like this. The mountain laurel has beautiful pale-pink clusters of blossoms. 3. **Laurels** sometimes means (1) victory. (2) high honor.

Laurel leaves (def. 1)

la va (lä′və), 1. hot melted rock flowing from a volcano. 2. rock formed by the cooling of this melted rock. Some lavas are hard and glassy; others are light and porous.

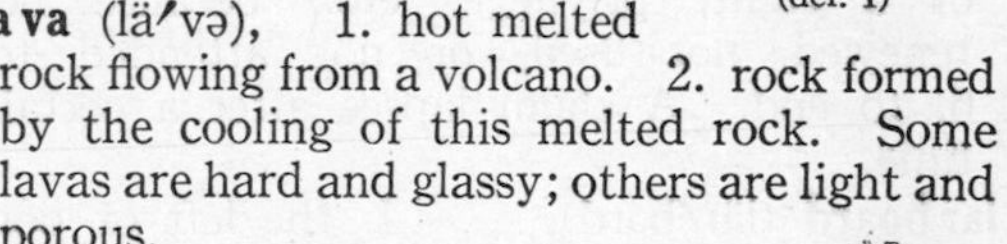

lav en der (lav′ən dər), 1. pale purple. 2. a small shrub with spikes of fragrant, pale-purple flowers, yielding an oil much used in perfumes. 3. its dried flowers, leaves, and stalks used to scent or preserve linen.

Lavender

lav ish (lav′ish), 1. very abundant; too abundant; more than is needed; as, a lavish helping of pudding. 2. liberal; too free; as, lavish with his money. 3. pour out wastefully; as, to lavish affection on a naughty, cruel child.

law (lô), 1. a rule made by a country, state, king, etc. Good citizens obey the laws. There is a law against spitting in streetcars. 2. any rule. Science studies the laws of nature. The laws of a game tell how to play it. 3. a system of rules formed to protect society. English law is not like French law. 4. the study of such a system of rules; the profession of a lawyer. This young man is studying law.

law ful (lô′fəl), according to law; done as the law directs; allowed by law; rightful.

law less (lô′lis), 1. paying no attention to the law; breaking the law. 2. hard to control; disorderly. 3. having no laws.

law mak er (lô′māk′ər), person who helps make the laws of a country.

lawn[1] (lôn), piece of land covered with grass kept closely cut.

lawn[2] (lôn), a kind of thin linen or cotton cloth.

law suit (lô′süt′), a case in a law court; an application to a court for justice. Sometimes a lawsuit is necessary to get what belongs to you.

law yer (lô′yər), person who knows the laws and gives advice about matters of law or acts for another person in court.

lax (laks), 1. loose; slack; not firm; as, a lax cord. 2. not strict; careless; loose in morals. People sometimes become lax when they go away from home. 3. not exact; vague.

lax i ty (lak′si ti), lax condition or quality; lax conduct.

lay[1] (lā), 1. beat down; as, crops laid low by a storm. 2. put down; keep down. Lay your hat on the table. This shower has laid the dust. 3. make quiet or make disappear; as, to lay a ghost. 4. place in a lying-down position. Lay the baby down gently. 5. place or set; as, to lay one's hand on one's heart, to lay a tax on tea. The scene of the story is laid in New York. 6. put. Lay aside that book for me. The horse laid his ears back. 7. put in place; as, to lay bricks. They laid the carpet on the floor. 8. put into a certain state; as, to lay a wound open. 9. put down as a bet; offer as a bet. I lay $5 he will not come. 10. Of a hen, to lay means to give an egg or eggs. 11. way, position, or direction in which something lies. Spies were sent to find out the lay of the land. 12. Some special meanings are:

lay about, hit out on all sides.

lay away or **lay by** (money), save.

lay off, 1. put aside. 2. put out of work. 3. mark off.

lay of the land, the nature of the place; the position of hills, water, woods, etc.

lay oneself out, take great pains.

lay up, 1. save. 2. cause to stay in bed because of illness.

laid is formed from **lay**[1].

lay[2] (lā). See **lie**[2]. An hour ago I lay down for a rest.

lay[3] (lā), of a layman.

lay[4] (lā), 1. a short poem meant to be sung. 2. any song or poem. The blackbird whistles his merry lay.

lay er (lā′ər), 1. person or thing that lays; as, a bricklayer. 2. one thickness or fold; as, the layer of clothing next the skin, a layer of clay between two layers of sand. A layer cake is one made of two or more layers put together.

lay man (lā′mən), person outside of any particular profession, especially one not belonging to the clergy. It is hard for a layman to understand a medical journal.

la zi ness (lā′zi nis), dislike of work; unwillingness to work or be active.

la zy (lā′zi), 1. not willing to work or be active. 2. moving slowly; not very active. A lazy stream winds through the meadows.

lb., pound; pounds. **lbs.,** pounds.

lea (lē), meadow; grassy field; pasture.

lead[1] (lēd), 1. show the way by going along with or in front of. He leads the horses to water. 2. be first among. She leads the class in spelling. 3. be a way or road. Hard work leads to success. 4. pass or spend (time) in some special way. He leads a quiet life in the country. 5. go first; begin a game. You may lead this time. 6. place of leader; place in front. He always takes the lead when we plan to do anything. 7. right to play first. It is your lead this time. 8. amount that one is ahead. He had a lead of 3 yards in the race. **led** is formed from **lead**[1].

lead[2] (led), 1. a heavy, easily melted, bluish-gray metal, used to make pipe, etc. 2. made of lead. 3. a long thin piece of a soft black substance used in pencils. 4. a weight on a line used to find out the depth of water.

lead en (led′ən), 1. made of lead; as, a leaden casket. 2. heavy; hard to lift or move; as, leaden arms tired from working. 3. bluish-gray; as, leaden clouds.

lead er (lēd′ər), one who leads, or is well fitted to lead.

lead er ship (lēd′ər ship), 1. being a leader. 2. ability to lead.

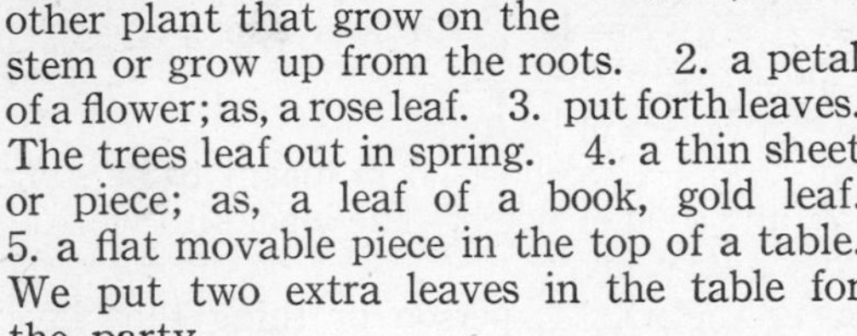

Leaves (def. 1)

leaf (lēf), 1. one of the thin, flat, green parts of a tree or other plant that grow on the stem or grow up from the roots. 2. a petal of a flower; as, a rose leaf. 3. put forth leaves. The trees leaf out in spring. 4. a thin sheet or piece; as, a leaf of a book, gold leaf. 5. a flat movable piece in the top of a table. We put two extra leaves in the table for the party.

leaf less (lēf′lis), having no leaves.

leaf let (lēf′lit), 1. a small or young leaf. 2. a small flat or folded sheet of printed matter; as, leaflets containing the Sunday-school lessons, advertising leaflets.

leaf y (lēf′i), having many leaves; covered with leaves.

league[1] (lēg), 1. a union of persons, parties, or nations to help one another. 2. unite in a league; form a union.

league[2] (lēg), a measure of distance, usually about 3 miles.

leak (lēk), 1. a hole or crack not meant to be there that lets something in or out; as, a leak in a paper bag which lets the sugar run out, a leak in the roof. 2. let something in or out which is meant to stay where it is. My boat leaks and lets water in. That pipe leaks gas. 3. go in or out through a hole or crack, or in ways suggesting a hole or crack. Spies leaked into the city. The gas leaked out. The news leaked out.

lean[1] (lēn), 1. bend; stand slanting, not upright. A small tree leans over in the wind. 2. rest sloping or slanting. Lean against me. 3. set or put in a leaning position. Lean the picture against the wall till I am ready for it. 4. depend; as, to lean on a friend's advice. 5. bend or turn a little; as, to lean toward mercy.

lean[2] (lēn), 1. not fat; thin. 2. meat having little fat. 3. producing little; as, a lean harvest.

leant (lent), leaned.

lean-to (lēn′tü′), a small building with a roof sloping downward from the side of a larger building.

leap (lēp), 1. a jump or spring. 2. to jump. A frog leaps. 3. to jump over. Jack leaped the wall.

Boys playing leapfrog

leap frog (lēp′frog′), game in which one player leaps over another who is bending over.

leapt (lept or lēpt), leaped.

learn (lėrn). In school we learn to read. He learned that $\frac{1}{4}+\frac{1}{4}=\frac{1}{2}$. She is learning history and geography. Some children learn slowly.

learn ed (lėr′nid), scholarly; showing or requiring knowledge.

learn ing (lėr′ning), 1. gaining knowledge or skill. 2. possession of knowledge gained by study; scholarship.

learnt (lėrnt), learned.

lease (lēs), 1. the right to use property for a certain length of time by paying rent for it. 2. a written statement saying for how long a certain property is rented and how much money shall be paid for it. 3. to rent. We have leased an apartment for one year.

leash (lēsh), 1. a strap or line for holding an animal in check. The boy leads the dog on a leash. **Hold in leash** means control. 2. hold in with a leash; control.

least (lēst), 1. smallest. A dime is a little money; five cents is less; one cent is least. 2. smallest amount; smallest thing. The least you can do is to thank him. 3. to the smallest extent or degree. Helen was the least angry girl in the club.

leath er (leᴛʜ′ər), 1. a material made from the skin of animals by removing the hair and then tanning it. Shoes are made of leather. 2. made of leather; as, leather gloves.

leath ern (leᴛʜ′ərn), made of leather.

leath er y (leᴛʜ′ər i), like leather; tough.

leave[1] (lēv), 1. go away. We leave tonight. 2. go away from. They left the room. He has left his home and friends and gone to sea. 3. stop living in, belonging to, or working at or for; as, to leave the country, to leave the Boy Scouts, to leave one's job. 4. go without taking; let stay behind; as, to leave a book on the table. 5. let stay (in a certain condition); as, to leave unsaid or undone. I was left alone as before. The story left him unmoved. 6. let alone. Then the potatoes must be left to boil for half an hour. 7. give (to family, friends, charity) when one dies. He left a large fortune to his two sons. 8. give or hand over (to someone else) to do. I left the cooking to my sister. 9. not attend to. I shall leave my homework till tomorrow. 10. **Leave off** means stop. He left off smoking. 11. **Leave out** means not say, do, or put in. Alice left out two words when she read the sentence.

leave[2] (lēv), 1. consent; permission. Have I your leave to go? 2. **Leave of absence** means permission to stay away (from the army, navy, one's work, or school). 3. length of time for which one has leave of absence. Our annual leave is thirty days. 4. **Take leave of** means say good-by to.

leave[3] (lēv), put forth leaves. Trees leave in the spring.

leaves (lēvz), 1. more than one leaf. 2. goes away.

lec ture (lek′chər), 1. speech; a planned talk on a chosen subject; such a talk written down or printed. 2. give a lecture. 3. a scolding. My mother gives me a lecture when I come home late. 4. scold.

lec tur er (lek′chər ər), person who gives a lecture.

led (led). See **lead**[1]. The policeman led the children across the street. That blind man is led by his dog.

ledge (lej), 1. narrow shelf; as, a window ledge. 2. a shelf or ridge of rock.

lee (lē), 1. side or part sheltered from the wind. The wind was so fierce that we ran to the lee of the house. 2. sheltered from the wind; as, the lee side of a ship. 3. A **lee shore** means a shore toward which the wind is blowing.

leech (lēch), 1. worm living in ponds and streams that sucks the blood of animals. Doctors used to use leeches to suck blood from sick people. 2. person who tries persistently to get what he can out of others. 3. doctor.

leer (lēr), 1. a sly, nasty look to the side; evil glance. 2. give a sly, evil glance.

lee ward (lü′ərd), 1. on the side away from the wind. 2. the side away from the wind. 3. in the direction toward which the wind is blowing.

left[1] (left). A man has a right hand and a left hand. Your left side is toward the west when you face north. Take the left road. He sat at my left.

left[2] (left). See **leave**[1]. He left his hat in the hall. Milk is left at our door. Helen left at four o'clock.

left-hand (left′hand′), 1. on or to the left. 2. of, for, or with the left hand.

leg (leg), 1. Dogs stand on their four legs. A man uses his two legs in walking and running. 2. anything shaped or used like a leg; any support that is much longer than it is wide; as, a table leg.

leg a cy (leg′ə si), 1. money or other property left to a person by the will of someone who has died. 2. something that has come down from an ancestor.

le gal (lē′gəl), 1. of law; as, legal knowledge. 2. of lawyers; as, the legal profession. 3. lawful.

leg end (lej′ənd), 1. a story coming down from the past, which many people have believed. The stories about Robin Hood are legends. 2. such stories as a group. 3. what is written on a coin or medal or below a picture. Read the legend on a five-cent piece.

leg gings (leg′ingz), extra outer coverings of cloth or leather for the legs, for use out of doors.

Child wearing leggings

leg i ble (lej′i bəl), 1. that can be read. 2. easy to read; plain and clear. Her handwriting is beautiful and legible.

le gion (lē′jən), 1. a division in the ancient Roman army containing several thousand foot soldiers and several hundred horsemen. 2. a body of soldiers; army. 3. a great many; a very large number. Legions of grasshoppers destroyed the crops.

leg is late (lej′is lāt), make laws. Congress legislates for the United States.

leg is la tion (lej′is lā′shən), 1. making laws. Congress has the power of legislation. 2. the laws made.

leg is la tive (lej′is lā′tiv), 1. having to do with making laws. 2. having the duty and power of making laws. 3. ordered by law; made to be as it is by law.

leg is la tor (lej′is lā′tər), person who makes laws; member of a group that makes laws.

leg is la ture (lej′is lā′chər), group of persons that has the duty and power of making laws for a State or country. Each State of the United States has a legislature.

le git i mate (li jit′i mit), rightful; lawful; allowed. Sickness is a legitimate reason for a child's being absent from school.

lei sure (lē′zhər), 1. time free from required work in which a person may rest, amuse himself, and do the things he likes to do. A busy man hasn't much leisure to read. 2. free; not busy; as, leisure hours.

lei sure ly (lē′zhər li), without hurry; taking plenty of time. A person, a movement, a performance, or one's manner may be leisurely. He walked leisurely across the street.

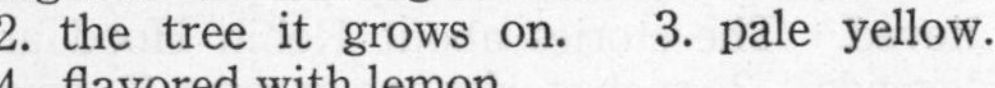

Lemons

lem on (lem′ən), 1. sour, light-yellow fruit that grows in warm climates. The juice of lemons is much used for flavoring and for making lemonade. 2. the tree it grows on. 3. pale yellow. 4. flavored with lemon.

lem on ade (lem′ən ād′), a drink made of lemon juice, sugar, and water.

lend (lend), 1. let another have or use for a time. Will you lend me your bicycle for an hour? 2. make a loan or loans. Nell often lends to Kate. A person who borrows should be willing to lend. 3. give; give (help, etc.) for a time. A becoming dress lends charm to a girl. **lent** is formed from **lend.**

length (length), 1. The length of your arm is how long it is. The length of this stick is 8 inches. The length of a room is the longest way it can be measured. The length of a speech is how long it lasts. The length of a race is the distance run. 2. **At length** means for a long time; fully; at last. 3. long stretch or extent. 4. piece of cloth, etc., of a given length; as, a dress length of silk.

length en (leng′thən), 1. make longer. 2. become or grow longer.

length wise (length′wīz), in the direction of the length. He cut the cloth lengthwise.

length y (leng′thi), long; too long.

le ni ent (lē′ni ənt), mild; gentle; merciful.

lens (lenz), piece of glass, or something like glass, that will bring closer together or send wider apart the rays of light passing through it. The lens of the eye and the lens of a camera make pictures. The lenses of a telescope make things look larger and nearer.

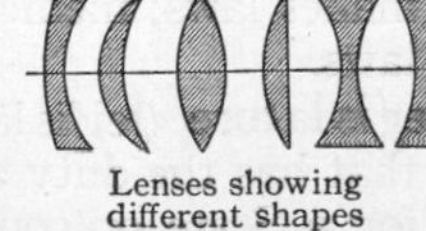

Lenses showing different shapes

lent[1] (lent). See **lend.** I lent you my pencils. He had lent me his knife.

Lent[2] (lent), the forty weekdays before Easter, kept as a time for fasting and repenting of sins.

len til (len′təl), a vegetable much like a bean.

leop ard (lep′ərd), 1. a fierce animal of Africa and Asia, having a dull-yellowish skin spotted with black. 2. The jaguar is sometimes called the American leopard.

Leopard (length about 7 ft. to tip of tail)

lep er (lep′ər), person who has leprosy.

lep ro sy (lep′rə si), a loathsome infectious disease that causes open sores and white scaly scabs, and eats away the body.

less (les), 1. smaller; as, of less width, less importance. 2. not so much; not so much of; as, to have less rain, to put on less butter, to eat less meat. 3. smaller amount; as, could do no less, weigh less than before, refuse to take less than $5. 4. with (something) taken away; without; as, five less two, a coat less one sleeve. 5. not so; not so much; not so well; as, less bright, less important, less known, less talked of.

less en (les′ən), 1. grow less. 2. make less.

less er (les′ər), 1. less; smaller. 2. the less important of two.

les son (les′ən), 1. something to be learned or taught; something that has been learned or taught. Children study many different lessons in school. 2. unit of teaching or learning; what is to be studied or taught at one time. Tomorrow we take the tenth lesson. 3. a selection from the Bible, read as part of a church service.

lest (lest), 1. for fear that; that . . . not; in order that . . . not. Be careful lest you fall from that tree. 2. After words meaning fear, danger, etc., lest means that. I was afraid lest he should come too late to save us.

let[1] (let), 1. allow; permit. Let the dog have a bone. 2. allow to run out. Doctors used to let some of the blood of their fever patients. 3. rent; hire out. Mrs. Bacon lets rooms to students. 4. Let also means allowed; allowed to go out; rented. 5. Let is used in giving suggestions and commands. "Let's go fishing" means "I suggest that we go fishing." Let every man do his duty.

6. suppose. Let the two lines be parallel. 7. Some special meanings are:

let down, 1. lower. He let the box down from the roof. 2. slow up. 3. disappoint.

let in, admit; permit to enter.

let know, tell; inform.

let off, let go free.

let out, 1. let go out. 2. make larger. 3. rent.

let[2] (let), an old word meaning prevent or prevention. **Without let or hindrance** means with nothing to prevent, hinder, or obstruct.

let's (lets), let us.

let ter (let′ər), 1. a mark or sign that stands for any one of the sounds that make up words. There are 26 letters in our alphabet. 2. mark with letters. 3. make letters (on). 4. **To the letter** means very exactly; just as one has been told. I carried out your orders to the letter. **Letter-perfect** means knowing one's part or lesson perfectly. 5. a written message. Put a stamp on that letter before you mail it.

let tuce (let′is), a garden plant with large, crisp, green leaves that are used for salad.

lev ee[1] (lev′i), 1. a bank built to keep a river from overflowing. There are levees in many places along the Mississippi River. 2. landing place for ships.

lev ee[2] (lev′i), reception.

lev el (lev′əl), 1. flat; even; having just the same height everywhere; as, a level floor. 2. something that is level. 3. an instrument for showing whether a surface is level. 4. height. The flood rose to a level of 60 feet. 5. make level or the same level. 6. raise and hold level for shooting; aim.

lev er (lev′ər), 1. a bar for raising or moving a weight at one end by pushing down at the other end. It must be supported at a point in between. 2. any bar working on an axis or support.

LEVER

FULCRUM

Man lifting a stone with a lever

lev y (lev′i), 1. order to be paid. The government levies taxes for national expenses. 2. collect (men) for an army. Troops are levied in time of war. 3. men collected for an army. 4. **Levy war on** means make war on. 5. act of levying. 6. money collected by a levy.

li a ble (lī′ə bəl), 1. likely; unpleasantly likely. Glass is liable to break. You are liable to slip on ice. 2. in danger of having, doing, etc. We are all liable to diseases. 3. responsible; under obligation; bound by law to pay. The Post Office Department is not liable for damage to a parcel sent by mail unless the parcel is insured.

li ar (lī′ər), person who tells lies; one who says what is not true.

lib er al (lib′ər əl), 1. generous. A liberal giver gives much. 2. plentiful; abundant. He put in a liberal supply of coal for the winter. 3. tolerant; not narrow in one's ideas. 4. person favorable to progress and reforms.

lib er al i ty (lib′ər al′i ti), 1. generosity; generous act or behavior. 2. tolerant and progressive nature.

lib er ate (lib′ər āt), set free. Lincoln liberated the slaves.

lib er ty (lib′ər ti), 1. freedom. 2. right or power to do as one pleases; power or opportunity to do something. 3. permission granted to a sailor to go ashore. 4. too great freedom; as, to take liberties with mother's sewing basket. 5. **At liberty** means (1) free. (2) permitted. You are at liberty to make any choice you please. (3) not busy. Mr. Brown will see us as soon as he is at liberty.

li brar i an (lī brãr′i ən), person in charge of a library.

li brar y (lī′brãr′i), 1. a collection of books. Helen and Jean have libraries all their own. 2. room or building in which a collection of books is kept. Jack goes to the library every Saturday.

lice (līs), more than one louse.

li cense or **li cence** (lī′səns), 1. being allowed to do something. 2. permission given by law to do something; as, a license to run an automobile. 3. the paper, card, plate, etc., that gives such permission. 4. permit by law. A doctor is licensed to practice medicine. 5. too much liberty of action; lack of proper control; abuse of freedom.

li chen (lī′kən), a dry-looking plant without flowers that grows like a patch of skin on rocks, trees, and other surfaces. Lichens are gray, yellow, brown, black, or greenish in color.

Lichens growing on a tree

lick (lik), 1. lap up with the tongue. 2. pass about or play over like a tongue. The flames were licking our house. 3. a stroke of the tongue over something. 4. small quantity. 5. a brief stroke of activity or effort. 6. a blow. Jim gave his horse a few gentle licks with his hand. 7. beat or thrash. *Meanings* 5, 6, *and* 7 *are used only in free and easy talk.*

lid (lid), 1. movable cover; top; as, the lid of a box, a stove lid. 2. the cover of skin that is moved in opening and shutting the eye; eyelid.

lie[1] (lī), 1. something said that is not true; something that is not true said to deceive. 2. speak falsely; tell a lie. He says that he has never lied, but I think he is lying when he says it.

lie[2] (lī), 1. have one's body in a flat position along the ground or other surface; as, to lie on the grass, to lie in bed. 2. be kept or stay in a given state; as, to lie idle, to lie hidden, to lie unused. 3. rest (on a surface). The book was lying on the table. 4. be; be placed; as, land that lies high, a lake that lies to the south of us, a road that lies among trees, a ship lying offshore at anchor. 5. exist; be found to be. The cure lies in education. 6. **Lie over** means be left waiting (till another time). 7. **Lie to** means come almost to a stop, facing the wind. **lay**[2] and **lain** are formed from **lie**[2].

liege (lēj), the relation between a lord and his vassals in the Middle Ages. He was their liege lord, or liege, and had a right to their loyal service; they were his lieges, or liegemen, whom he protected.

liege man (lēj′mən), vassal; faithful follower.

lieu (lü). **In lieu of** means in place of or instead of.

lieu ten ant (lü ten′ənt), 1. person who acts in the place of someone above him. The scoutmaster used Jack and Tom as his lieutenants. 2. in the army, an officer next below a captain. 3. in the navy, an officer ranking much below a captain. In the navy the order is captain, commander, lieutenant commander, lieutenant, lieutenant of junior grade, ensign.

life (līf), 1. People, animals, and plants have life; rocks and metals do not. Life or being alive is shown by growing and producing. 2. Each person has his own life or existence. 3. a living being; person. Five lives were lost. 4. living beings. The desert island had almost no animal or vegetable life. 5. period of existence. The life of that government was very short. 6. way of living; as, a country life, a dull life. 7. account of a person's life. Several lives of Lincoln have been written. 8. spirit; vigor. Put more life into your work.

life belt, life preserver.

life boat (līf′bōt′), a strong boat specially built for saving lives at sea or along a coast.

life buoy, life preserver.

life guard (līf′gärd′), man employed on a bathing beach to help in case of accident or danger to bathers.

life insurance, 1. a system by which a person pays a small sum yearly to have a large sum paid to his family if he dies. 2. the sum paid by the insurance company at death. 3. the payments made to the insurance company.

life less (līf′lis), 1. not living. My doll, poor lifeless thing, was no comfort. 2. dead. The lifeless body floated ashore. 3. dull. It was a lifeless party until Marion came.

life like (līf′līk′), like life; looking as if alive; like the real thing.

life long (līf′lông′), lasting all one's life.

life preserver, a wide belt, usually made of cloth and cork, to keep a person afloat in the water; something to keep a person afloat until rescued.

Boy wearing a life preserver

life time (līf′tīm′), the time over which a life lasts. Grandfather has seen many changes during his lifetime.

lift (lift), 1. raise; raise up higher; raise into the air; take up; pick up. Mother lifts the baby from the bed. 2. go up; be raised. This window will not lift. 3. go. The darkness lifts. 4. act of lifting. 5. the distance through which a thing is lifted. 6. helping hand. Give me a lift with this job. 7. free ride.

light[1] (līt), 1. that by which we see. The sun gives light to the earth. 2. thing that gives light. We saw the lights of the city. Bring a light quickly. 3. bright; clear. It was light as day. 4. brightness; clearness. 5. daytime. The workman gets up before light. 6. knowledge; information. We need more light on this subject. 7. open view. Many facts were brought to light. 8. aspect. Look at the matter in the right light. 9. means of letting in light; window or part of a window. 10. model; example; famous person. George Washington is one of the lights of history. 11. bright part; as, light and shade in a painting. 12. pale in color; approaching white; as, light hair, light blue. 13. give light to; fill with light. The room is lighted by six windows. 14. set fire to; as, to light the fire, to light the candles. 15. take fire. Matches light when you scratch them. 16. make bright or clear; as, a face lit up by a smile. 17. become light. The sky lights up at sunset.

light[2] (līt), 1. easy to carry; not heavy; as, a light load. 2. not looking heavy; graceful; delicate; as, a light bridge, light carving. 3. of little weight for its size. Feathers are light. 4. of less than usual weight; as, light clothing. 5. not hard to bear or do; as, light punishment, a light task. 6. moving easily; as, a light step. 7. lightly armed or equipped; as, light infantry. 8. less than usual in amount, force, etc.; as, a light rain, a light sleep, a light meal, a light wine. 9. not important. **Make light of** (a thing) means treat it as of little importance. 10. happy; gay. 11. cheerfully careless. 12. not serious enough; as, a light mind, light of purpose. 13. sandy; as, light soil. 14. **Light in the head** means (1) dizzy. (2) silly; foolish.

light[3] (lit), 1. come down to the ground; alight. 2. come down from flight. A bird lighted on the branch. 3. come by chance. His eye lighted upon a stain on the rug. 4. fall suddenly. The blow lit on his head.

light-col ored (līt′kul′ərd), light in color; not dark.

light en[1] (līt′ən), 1. brighten; become brighter. The sky lightens before the dawn. 2. flash with lightning. It thundered and lightened outside.

light en[2] (līt′ən), 1. reduce the load of; make or become lighter. 2. make or become more cheerful. The good news lightened our hearts.

light-head ed (līt′hed′id), 1. empty-headed; thoughtless. 2. dizzy; giddy; out of one's head; as, to be light-headed from fever.

light-heart ed (līt′här′tid), carefree; cheerful; gay.

light house (līt′hous′), tower or framework built to hold a bright light which shines over the sea to warn and guide ships.

Lighthouse

light ness[1] (līt′nis), 1. brightness; clearness. 2. paleness; light color. 3. the amount of light. The lightness of the sky showed that the rain was really over.

light ness[2] (līt′nis), 1. being light; not being heavy. The lightness of this load is a relief after the heavy one I was carrying. 2. being gay or cheerful; as, lightness of spirits. 3. lack of proper seriousness. Such lightness of conduct is not to be permitted in church.

light ning (līt′ning), a flash of electricity in the sky. The sound that it makes is thunder.

lightning rod, a metal rod fixed on a building or ship to conduct lightning into the earth or water.

light some (līt′səm), 1. bright; light; as, a lightsome face. 2. nimble; as, lightsome feet. 3. gay; as, a lightsome heart.

lik a ble (līk′ə bəl), pleasing; popular.

like[1] (līk), 1. Mary is like her sister. She can sing like a bird. We shall not see his like again. John's uncle promised him $10 if he could earn a like sum. 2. such as one would expect of. Isn't that just like a boy! 3. in the right condition for. He feels like working. 4. **And the like** means and other like things. We went to the zoo and saw elephants, tigers, lions, bears, and the like. 5. likely. The king is sick and like to die.

like[2] (līk). Boys like to play. Baby likes milk. Mother knows all my likes and dislikes.

like li hood (līk′li hůd), probability. Is there any great likelihood of rain this afternoon?

like ly (līk′li), 1. probable. One likely result of this heavy rain is the rising of the river. 2. probably. I shall very likely be at home all day. 3. to be expected. It is likely to be hot in August. 4. promising; suitable. Is this a likely place to fish?

lik en (līk′ən), compare; represent as like.

like ness (līk′nis), 1. resembling; being like; as, a boy's likeness to his father. 2. something that is like; picture; as, to have one's likeness painted. 3. appearance; shape. His fairy godmother came to him in the likeness of a bird.

like wise (līk′wīz′), 1. the same. See what I do. Now you do likewise. 2. also; moreover; too. Mary must go home now, and Nell likewise.

lik ing (līk′ing), preference; kindly feeling; fondness; as, a liking for apples, a liking for children.

li lac (lī′lək), 1. a shrub with clusters of fragrant, pale pinkish-purple or white blossoms. 2. pale pinkish-purple. She wore a lilac gown.

Lilac

lil y (lil′i), 1. a plant that grows from a bulb. Its flowers are usually large, bell-shaped, and beautiful, and are often divided into six parts as shown in the picture. 2. the flower of any lily plant. Grace put four lilies in a vase. 3. like a white lily; pure and lovely.

Tiger lily

limb (lim), 1. Legs, arms, and wings are limbs. 2. large branch; as, the limb of a tree.

lime[1] (līm), 1. a white substance obtained by burning limestone, shells, bone, etc. Lime is used in making mortar and on fields to improve the soil. 2. put lime on. He drained the land and limed it.

lime[2] (līm), 1. juicy fruit much like a lemon. A lime is smaller, greener, and sourer than a lemon; its juice is used for flavoring and in medicine. 2. the tree it grows on.

lime[3] (līm), the linden tree, often used for shade and ornament.

lime stone (līm′stōn′), a rock used for building and for making lime. Marble is a kind of limestone.

lim it (lim′it), 1. the farthest edge or boundary; where something ends or must end. Keep within the limits of the school grounds. 2. set a limit to; restrict. We must limit the expense to $10. Her food was limited to bread and water.

lim it ed (lim′i tid), kept within limits. A limited train is limited in the number of stops, the class of passengers, the time taken, etc.

limp[1] (limp), 1. a lame step or walk. 2. to walk with a limp.

limp[2] (limp), not at all stiff; ready to bend or droop. This starched collar soon gets limp in hot weather. I feel as limp as a rag.

lim pet (lim′pit), a small shellfish that sticks to rocks.

lim pid (lim′pid), clear; transparent; as, a spring of limpid water, limpid eyes.

lin den (lin′dən), a shade tree with heart-shaped leaves and clusters of small, sweet-smelling, greenish-yellow flowers.

Linden leaves and flowers

line[1] (līn), 1. piece of rope, cord, or wire; as, a clothesline, a fish line, a telegraph line. Reins are sometimes called lines. 2. a cord for measuring, making level, etc. 3. a long narrow mark. Draw two lines here. 4. mark with lines. 5. cover with lines. 6. anything that is like a long narrow mark; as, the lines in your face. 7. an edge or boundary. 8. straight line. The lower edges of the two pictures are about on a line. 9. the equator. 10. a row of persons or things; as, a line of chairs. 11. arrange in line. Cars were lined up along the road for a mile. 12. a row of words on a page or in a newspaper column. 13. a single verse of poetry. 14. a connected set or series of persons or things; as, to trace back one's family line. 15. a course, track, or direction; as, the line of march of an army, a railroad line. 16. a row of trenches or other defenses. 17. Some special meanings are:

all along the line, at every point.

in line with, in agreement with.

line up, form a line; form into a line.

read between the lines, get from what one is reading more than the words themselves say.

line[2] (līn), 1. put a layer of paper, cloth, felt, etc., inside of (a dress, hat, box, bag, etc.). 2. serve the purpose of lining. This piece of silk would line your coat very nicely. 3. **Line one's purse or pocket** means fill it with money. He lined his purse by taking bribes.

lin e age (lin′i ij), 1. descent in a direct line from an ancestor. 2. family; race.

lin en (lin′in), 1. cloth or thread made from flax. 2. articles made of linen. Tablecloths, napkins, sheets, towels, shirts, and collars may be called linen even when they are made of some substitute. 3. made of linen.

lin er (līn′ər), 1. ship or airplane belonging to a transportation system. 2. person or thing that makes lines.

lin ger (ling′gər), stay on; go slowly, as if unwilling to leave. Daylight lingers long in the summertime.

lin ing (līn′ing), inside layer; as, the lining of a coat, the lining of a stove.

link (lingk), 1. one ring or loop of a chain. 2. anything that joins as a link joins. 3. join as a link does; unite or connect. Your story links up with what Joe told us.

lin net (lin′it), a small songbird of Europe, Asia, and Africa.

Linnet (about 6 in. long)

lin seed (lin′sēd′), the seed of flax.

lint (lint), 1. the soft down or fleecy material obtained by scraping linen. Lint was formerly much used for putting on wounds. 2. tiny bits of thread. Lint collects on the carpet.

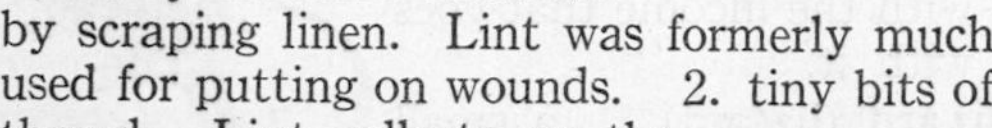

lin tel (lin′təl), a horizontal beam or stone above a door or window.

LINTEL
SILL

li on (lī′ən), 1. a large, strong animal of Africa and southern Asia that has a dull-yellowish skin. 2. person who is very brave and strong. 3. famous man.

li on ess (lī′ən is), female lion.

Lion and lioness (about 3 ft. high at the shoulder)

lip (lip), 1. either one of the two fleshy, movable edges of the mouth. 2. the folding or bent-out edge of any opening; as, the lip of a pitcher. 3. not heartfelt or deep, but just on the surface. The hypocrite gave lip service to the church.

liq uid (lik′wid), 1. a substance that is not a solid or a gas; a substance that flows freely like water. 2. in the form of a liquid; melted; as, liquid soap, butter heated until it is liquid. 3. clear and bright like water. 4. clear and smooth-flowing in sound; as, the liquid notes of a bird.

liq uor (lik′ər), 1. a drink, such as brandy or whiskey, that can make a person drunk. 2. anything liquid. Pickles are put up in a salty liquor.

lisle (līl), 1. a fine, hard-twisted cotton or linen thread. 2. made of lisle; as, lisle stockings.

lisp (lisp), 1. say *th* instead of *s* or *z* in speaking. She lisped and said, "Thing a thong" for "Sing a song." 2. the act of saying a *th* sound for *s* and *z*. Percy spoke with a lisp. 3. speak imperfectly. Babies lisp.

list[1] (list), 1. series of names, numbers, words, or phrases. 2. make a list of. I shall list my errands on a card.

list[2] (list), 1. tipping a ship to one side; a tilt. 2. of ships, to tip to one side; to tilt.

list[3] (list), listen.

lis ten (lis′ən), 1. try to hear; attend with the ears so as to hear. The mother listens for her baby's cry. I like to listen to music. 2. **Listen in** means (1) listen to others talking on a telephone. (2) listen to the radio.

lis ten er (lis′nər), person listening.

list less (list′lis), seeming too tired to care about anything; not interested in things; not caring to be active.

lists (lists), field where knights fought in tournaments.

lit (lit), lighted. Have you lit the candles? Two birds lit on my window sill.

lit er al ly (lit′ər əl i), word for word; without exaggeration; without imagination.

lit er ar y (lit′ər ãr′i), 1. having to do with literature. 2. knowing much about literature.

lit er a ture (lit′ər ə chər), 1. writings of a period or of a country, especially those kept alive by their beauty of style or thought. Shakespeare is the greatest name in English literature. 2. all the books on a subject; as, the literature of stamp collecting.

lithe (līᴛʜ), bending easily; supple.

lit ter (lit′ər), 1. little bits left about in disorder; things scattered about. Children should pick up their own litter. 2. scatter things about; leave odds and ends lying around; make untidy. You have littered the room with your papers. 3. the young animals produced at one time; as, a litter of puppies. 4. straw, hay, etc., used as bedding for animals. 5. a stretcher for carrying a sick or wounded person. 6. a framework to be carried on men's shoulders, or by beasts of burden, with a couch usually enclosed by curtains.

Litter (def. 6)

lit tle (lit′əl), 1. A grain of sand or the head of a pin is little. 2. Wait a little while, and I'll go a little way with you. 3. A very sick child has little strength and eats little food. 4. Mr. Skinflint has a mean little soul. 5. George had a big box of candy but gave his sister only a little. 6. Rest a little. After a little you will feel better. 7. They live in a little known town called Dracut. 8. A coward is little liked. 9. **Not a little** sometimes means much. 10. **Make little of** means treat as of little importance.

live[1] (liv), 1. have life. 2. remain alive. 3. last; endure. 4. keep up life. Most men live by working. 5. feed. Lions live upon other animals. 6. pass life; as, to live well, to live in peace. 7. dwell. Who lives in this house? 8. keep up (life); as, to live a life of ease. 9. carry out in life; as, to live one's religion.

live[2] (līv), 1. having life; as, a live dog. 2. burning or glowing; as, live coals. 3. loaded; as, a live cartridge. 4. carrying an electric current; as, a live wire. 5. full of energy or activity; up-to-date; as, a live person, a live question.

live li hood (līv′li hůd), means of living. John earned his livelihood by working for a farmer.

live li ness (līv′li nis), vigor; activity; gaiety.

live long (liv′lông′), the whole length of.

live ly (līv′li), 1. full of life and spirit; active. 2. exciting. 3. full of cheer; bright. 4. in a lively manner.

liv er (liv′ər), the large, reddish-brown organ in people and animals that makes bile and aids in the absorption of food. Calf's liver is used as a food.

liv er ied (liv′ər id), clothed in livery.

liv er y (liv′ər i), 1. any special uniform provided for the servants of a household, or adopted by any other group or profession. A nurse's livery is often white. 2. the feeding, stabling, and care of horses for pay; the hiring out of horses and carriages. 3. stable where horses are cared for or hired out for pay.

live stock (līv′stok′), farm animals. Cows, horses, sheep, and pigs are livestock.

liv id (liv′id), 1. having a dull-bluish or grayish color; as, the livid face of a dead man. 2. discolored by a bruise; as, the livid marks of blows on his arm.

liv ing (liv′ing), 1. being alive. The sick man is tired of living. 2. a means of keeping alive; livelihood. Mr. Meyer earned his living as a grocer. 3. manner of life. The preacher urged the importance of right living. 4. vigorous; strong; active; as, a living faith. 5. in actual existence; still in use; alive; as, living languages. 6. true to life; vivid; as, a picture which is the living image of a person. 7. of life; for living in; as, living conditions, a living room. 8. sufficient to live on; as, a living wage. 9. a position in the church with the income that goes with it.

liz ard (liz′ərd), a small animal somewhat like a snake, but having four legs.

European green lizard (about 11 in. long)

lla ma (lä′mə), a South American animal somewhat like a camel, but smaller and without a hump. See the picture below.

lla no (lä′nō), a large treeless plain.

lo (lō), look! see! behold!

load (lōd), 1. what one is carrying. The cart has a load of hay. The nurse bears a load of anxiety. 2. put in or put on whatever is to be carried; as, to load a ship. 3. one charge of powder and shot for a gun. 4. put a charge in (a gun).

Llama (about 3 ft. high at the shoulder)

loaf[1] (lōf), 1. bread baked as one piece. A loaf comes apart easily from the loaves it is baked with. 2. A loaf of cake is a rather large cake, often baked in the shape of a loaf of bread. 3. food shaped like a loaf of bread. Meat loaf is meat chopped and mixed with other things and then baked.

loaf[2] (lōf), spend time idly; do nothing. Now that vacation has come, I shall loaf for a few days.

loam (lōm), rich, fertile earth; earth in which decaying leaves, etc., are mixed with clay and sand.

loan (lōn), 1. a lending. 2. anything that is lent, especially money. 3. make a loan; lend.

loath (lōth), unwilling. The little girl was loath to leave her mother.

loathe (lōŦH), feel disgust for; abhor; hate. We loathe rotten food or a nasty smell.

loath ing (lōŦH′ing), strong dislike and disgust; intense aversion.

loath some (lōŦH′səm), disgusting; making one feel sick. A dead cat's decaying body is loathsome.

loaves (lōvz), more than one loaf.

lob by (lob′i), 1. entrance hall; passage; as, the lobby of a theater, the lobby of a hotel. 2. person or persons that try to influence members of a legislative body. 3. try to influence the members of a legislative body.

lob ster (lob′stər), a sea animal about a foot long with two big claws in front and eight legs. Lobsters are used for food. Their shells turn a light bright red when boiled.

Lobster (about 1 ft. long with the claws)

lo cal (lō′kəl), 1. of a place; having something to do with a certain place or places; as, the local doctor, local news. 2. of just one part of the body; as, a local pain, local disease, local application of a remedy. 3. making all, or almost all, stops; as, a local train.

lo cal i ty (lō kal′i ti), place; region; one place and the places near it.

lo cate (lō′kāt), 1. establish in a place. He located his new store on Main Street. 2. establish oneself in a place. Early settlers located where there was water. 3. find out the exact position of. The general tried to locate the enemy's camp. 4. state or show the position of. Can you locate America and Africa on the globe? 5. **Be located** means lie or be situated.

lo ca tion (lō kā′shən), 1. a locating. The Scouts disputed about the location of the camp. 2. a being located. 3. position or place. 4. lot; plot of ground marked out by boundaries.

loch (lok), 1. lake. 2. an arm of the sea partly shut in by land.

lock[1] (lok), 1. a means of fastening (doors, boxes, etc.), usually needing a key of special shape to open it. 2. fasten with a lock. 3. shut (something in or out or up). We lock up jewels in a safe. 4. join, fit, jam, or link together. They lock arms. Two cars locked together in passing. 5. the part of a canal or dock in which the level of the water can be changed by letting water in or out, to raise or lower ships. 6. the part of a gun by means of which it is fired.

Locks in a canal

lock[2] (lok), 1. curl of hair. 2. portion of hair, wool, etc.

lock er (lok′ər), a chest, small closet, or cupboard.

lock et (lok′it), a little ornamental case of gold, silver, etc., for holding a picture of someone or a lock of hair. A locket is usually worn around the neck on a chain.

Locket

lo co mo tion (lō′kə mō′shən), act or power of moving from place to place. Walking, swimming, and flying are common forms of locomotion.

Railroad locomotive

lo co mo tive (lō′kə mō′tiv), 1. railroad engine. 2. any engine that goes from place to place on its own power.

lo cust (lō′kəst), 1. a kind of grasshopper. Sometimes locusts come in great swarms, destroying the crops. 2. a tree with small rounded leaflets and clusters of sweet-smelling white flowers.

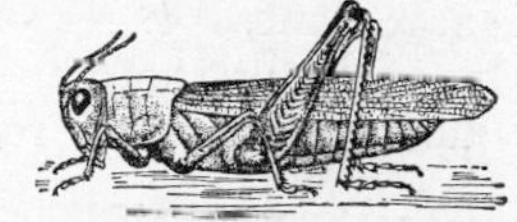
Locust ($1\frac{1}{4}$ to 3 in. long)

lode (lōd), a vein of metal ore. The miners struck a rich lode of copper.

lodge (loj), 1. live in a place for a time. 2. supply with a place to sleep or live in for a time. 3. a place to live in; a house, especially a small or temporary house. 4. live in a rented room in another's house. We are merely lodging at present. 5. get caught or stay in a place without falling or going farther. The boy's kite lodged in the branches of a big tree. 6. fix; put into a particular place. The hunter lodged a bullet in the lion's heart. 7. lay before some authority. We lodged a complaint with the police. 8. one of the branches of certain secret societies. 9. the place where it meets.

lodg er (loj′ər), person who lives in a rented room in another's house.

lodg ing (loj′ing), place where one is living only for a time. **Lodgings** means a rented room or rooms in a house, not in a hotel.

loft (lôft), 1. attic. 2. the room under the roof of a barn. This loft is full of hay. 3. a gallery in a church or hall. 4. upper floor of a business building or storehouse.

loft y (lôf′ti), 1. very high. 2. proud; haughty. 3. exalted; dignified; grand.

Log cabin

log (lôg), 1. a length of wood just as it comes from the tree. 2. made of logs; as, a log house. 3. cut down trees, cut them into logs, and get them out of the forest. 4. the daily record of a ship's voyage. 5. a float for measuring the speed of a ship.

lo gan ber ry (lō′gən ber′i), a large purplish-red berry. The loganberry is a cross between the blackberry and the red raspberry.

log ging (lôg′ing), the work of cutting trees down, sawing them into logs, and moving the logs out from the forest.

log ic (loj′ik), 1. the science of proof. 2. science of reasoning. 3. reasoning; use of argument. 4. reason; sound sense.

log i cal (loj′i kəl), 1. having something to do with logic. 2. reasonable. 3. reasoning correctly.

loin (loin), 1. the part of the body of an animal or man between the ribs and the hip-bones. The loins are on both sides of the backbone and nearer to it than the flanks. 2. a piece of meat from this part of an animal.

loi ter (loi′tər), 1. linger idly; stop and play along the way. Mary loitered along the street, looking into all the shopwindows. 2. spend idly; as, to loiter the hours away.

loll (lol), 1. recline or lean in a lazy manner; as, to loll on a sofa. 2. hang loosely or droop. A dog's tongue lolls out. 3. allow to hang or droop. A dog lolls out his tongue.

lone (lōn), alone; single; lonely. The lone traveler was glad to reach home.

lone li ness (lōn′li nis), being lonely; solitude.

lone ly (lōn′li), 1. alone. 2. without many people; as, a lonely road. 3. feeling oneself alone and longing for company. Little Jack was lonely while his brother was away.

lone some (lōn′səm), 1. feeling lonely. 2. making one feel lonely.

long[1] (lông), 1. An inch is short; a mile is long. A year is a long time. He told a long story. We call anything long if it has a large measure from end to end. 2. in length. My table is three feet long. 3. having a long, narrow shape; as, a long board. 4. a long time. Summer will come before long. 5. **All day long** means through all the day. 6. **As long as** means since; if only.

long[2] (lông), wish very much; desire greatly. He longed for his mother. She longed to see him.

long ing (lông′ing), 1. earnest desire; as, a longing for home. 2. having or showing earnest desire; as, a child's longing look at a window full of toys.

lon gi tude (lon′ji tūd or lon′ji tüd), distance east or west on the earth's surface, measured in degrees.

lon gi tu di nal (lon′ji tū′di nəl or lon′ji tü′di-nəl), 1. of length; in length. 2. running lengthwise. Our flag has longitudinal stripes.

look (luk), 1. see; try to see; turn the eyes. Look at the pictures. 2. look hard; stare. 3. search. 4. a glance; seeing. 5. to face. The house looks to the south. 6. seem; appear. Flowers look pretty. 7. show how one feels by one's appearance. 8. appearance. Good looks means a good appearance. 9. Some special meanings are:

look after, attend to; take care of.

look alive, hurry.

look down on, despise.

look for, expect.

look forward to, expect with pleasure.

look in, make a short visit.

look into, examine; investigate.

look on, 1. watch without taking part. 2. regard; consider.

look oneself, seem like oneself; seem well.

look out, be careful; watch out.

look over, examine; inspect.

look to, 1. attend to; take care of. 2. turn to for help.

look up, hunt up.

look up to, respect.

looking glass, mirror.

look out (luk′out′), 1. a sharp watch for someone to come or for something to happen. Keep a good lookout for Mother. 2. place from which to watch. 3. the person who has the duty of watching.

loom[1] (lüm), machine for weaving cloth.

loom[2] (lüm), appear dimly or vaguely; appear as large or dangerous. A large iceberg loomed through the thick gray fog.

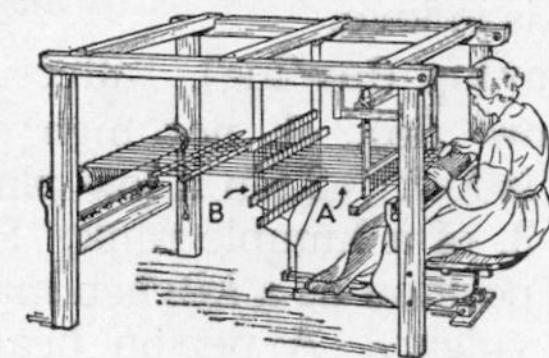

Loom: A, warp; B, woof.

loon[1] (lün), a large diving bird. Loons have a loud, wild cry. See the picture below.

loon[2] (lün), worthless, stupid person.

loop (lüp), 1. the shape of a curved string, ribbon, bent wire, etc., that crosses itself. In writing, *b* and *g* and *h* and *l* have loops. See the picture just below. 2. a fastening or ornament formed of cord, etc., bent and crossed. 3. make a loop of. 4. make loops in. 5. fasten with a loop. 6. form a loop or loops.

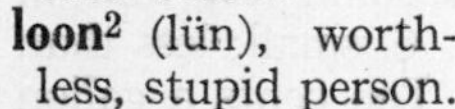

Loops (def. 1)

loop hole (lüp′hōl′), 1. a small opening in a wall for looking through, for letting in air, or for firing through at an enemy outside. 2. a means of escape. The clever lawyer found a loophole in the law to save the prisoner.

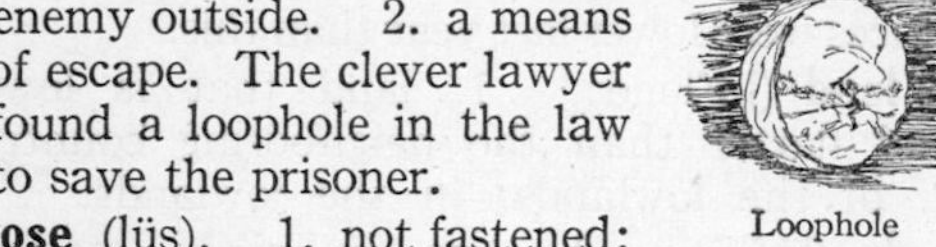

Loophole

loose (lüs), 1. not fastened; as, a loose thread. 2. not tight; as, loose clothing. 3. not firmly set or fastened in; as, a loose tooth. 4. not bound together; as, loose papers. 5. not put up in a box, can, etc.; as, loose coffee. 6. free; not shut in or up. We leave the dog loose at night. 7. not pressed close together; as, loose earth, cloth with a loose weave. 8. not strict, close, or exact; as, a loose account of the accident. 9. careless about morals or conduct; as, a loose character. 10. set free; let go; unbind; make loose.

Loon (about 32 in. long)

loos en (lüs′ən), 1. make loose or looser; untie; unfasten. 2. become loose or looser.

loot (lüt), 1. spoils; plunder; booty; as, loot taken by soldiers from a captured town, burglar's loot. 2. to plunder; rob.

lop[1] (lop), 1. cut; cut off. 2. cut branches from.

lop[2] (lop), 1. hang loosely; droop. 2. flop.

lope (lōp), 1. to run with a long, easy stride. 2. a long, easy stride.

lord (lôrd), 1. owner, ruler, or master; person who has the power. 2. in Great Britain, a man of high rank. 3. rule proudly or absolutely. Philip was the oldest and lorded it over the rest of us.

Lord (lôrd), 1. God. 2. Christ. 3. a title given to men of certain ranks in Great Britain.

lord ly (lôrd′li), 1. like a lord; suitable for a lord; grand; magnificent. 2. haughty; insolent; scornful. The spoiled child treated his friends with lordly contempt.

lord ship (lôrd′ship), 1. the title given to a lord. Yes, Your Lordship. 2. rule; ownership.

lore (lōr), 1. the facts and tales about a certain subject; as, fairy lore, bird lore, Greek lore. 2. learning; knowledge.

lor ry (lor′i), 1. automobile truck. 2. long, flat wagon without sides.

Lorry (def. 2)

lose (lüz), 1. not have any longer; have taken away from one by accident, carelessness, parting, death, etc.; as, to lose a dollar, lose one's life, lose a limb, a father, a friend. 2. fail to keep; as, to lose your patience or your temper. 3. be or become worse off in money, in numbers, etc. The army lost heavily in yesterday's battle. 4. become unable to find; as, to lose a book. 5. waste; spend or let go by without any result; as, to lose time waiting, to lose one's trouble, to lose a chance. 6. miss; fail to get, catch, see, or hear; as, to lose a train, to lose a few words of what was said. 7. not to win; be defeated; as, to lose a bet or a game. 8. cause one to lose. That one act lost him his job. 9. **Be lost in** (something) means be so busy with it that one fails to notice anything else. **lost** is formed from **lose.**

los er (lüz′ər), 1. one who loses something. 2. one who is beaten in a game or battle.

loss (lôs), 1. losing or having lost something. The loss of health is serious, but the loss of a pencil is not. 2. that which is lost. The loss from the fire was $10,000. 3. defeat. Our team had two losses and one tie out of ten games played. 4. **At a loss** means puzzled.

lost (lôst), 1. See **lose.** I lost my new pencil. My ruler is lost, too. 2. destroyed; ruined; as, a lost soul. 3. no longer possessed; as, a lost friend. 4. missing; not found. 5. not won; as, a lost battle, a lost prize. 6. A **lost cause** is one defeated already or sure to be defeated. 7. insensible. The deserting soldier was lost to all sense of duty to his country.

lot (lot), 1. one of a set of objects, such as bits of paper, wood, etc., used to decide something by chance. We drew lots to see who should be captain. 2. such a method of deciding. It was settled by lot. 3. choice made by lot. The lot fell to me. 4. what one gets by lot; one's share. 5. one's fate or fortune. It was his lot later to become president. 6. a plot of ground. Fred's house is between two empty lots. 7. a portion or part. He divided the fruit into ten lots. 8. a number of persons or things considered as a group; collection. This lot of oranges was not so good as the last. 9. great many.

loth (lōth), unwilling. The little girl was loth to leave her mother.

lot ter y (lot′ər i), a scheme for distributing prizes by lot or chance. In a lottery a large number of tickets are sold, some of which draw prizes.

loud (loud), 1. not quiet or soft; making a great sound. A gun goes off with a loud noise. 2. in a loud manner. He called loud and long. 3. showy in dress or manner; too bright; as, loud clothes.

loud ly (loud′li), with much noise; in a loud voice.

lounge (lounj), 1. stand, stroll, sit, or lie at ease in a lazy way. 2. a comfortable and informal room in which one can lounge and be at ease. 3. a couch.

louse (lous), 1. small, wingless insect that infests the hair or the bodies of people. 2. any of similar insects that infest animals or plants. We spray plants to kill the lice.

Louse (def. 1)

lout (lout), awkward, stupid fellow.

lov a ble (luv′ə bəl), worthy of being loved; endearing. She was a most lovable person, always kind and thoughtful.

love (luv), 1. a fond, deep, tender feeling. 2. have such a feeling for. She loves her mother. 3. person who is loved. 4. warm liking. 5. like very much. He loves music.

love li ness (luv′li nis), beauty.

love ly (luv′li), beautiful; beautiful in mind or character; lovable. Ruth is one of the loveliest girls we know.

lov er (luv′ər), person who loves; man who is in love.

lov ing (luv′ing), affectionate; fond.

low[1] (lō), 1. not high or tall. A footstool is low. 2. in a low place; near the ground. 3. of a humble rank. She had a rather low position as a kitchen maid. 4. mean; coarse; vulgar. A person hears some low talk in saloons. 5. poor; poorly. 6. small; less than usual; at a small price. Ten cents a gallon for gasoline is very low. 7. nearly used up. Our coal is low. 8. not high in the musical scale. 9. not loud; not loudly. 10. feeble; weak. The lights were low. 11. **Low spirits** means a condition with little energy or joy. 12. **Low tide** is the time when the ocean is lowest on the shore.

low[2] (lō), 1. make the sound of a cow; moo. 2. the sound a cow makes.

low er (lō′ər), 1. let down or haul down. We lower the flag at night. 2. make lower. 3. sink or become lower. 4. more low. Prices were lower last year than this.

low land (lō′lənd), 1. land that is lower and flatter than the neighboring country. 2. of the lowlands; in the lowlands.

low ly (lō′li), 1. low in rank, station, position, or development. 2. humble; meek; modest in feeling, behavior, or condition. 3. humbly; meekly.

loy al (loi′əl), 1. true and faithful to love, promise, or duty. 2. faithful to one's king, one's government, or one's country.

loy al ty (loi′əl ti), loyal feeling or behavior; faithfulness.

lu bri cant (lü′bri kənt), oil, grease, etc., for putting on parts of machines that slide or move against one another, to make them smooth and slippery so that they will work easily.

lu bri cate (lü′bri kāt), make machinery smooth, slippery, and easy to work by putting on oil or grease.

lu cid (lü′sid), 1. shining; bright. 2. clear; easy to follow or understand. A good explanation is lucid. 3. sane. An insane person sometimes has lucid intervals.

luck (luk), 1. that which seems to happen or come to one by chance; fortune; chance. Luck favored me, and I won. 2. good luck. I am in luck. She gave me a penny for luck.

luck i ly (luk′i li), by good luck; fortunately.

luck less (luk′lis), having bad luck; bringing bad luck. That Friday was a luckless day for me.

luck y (luk′i), having or bringing good luck.

lu di crous (lü′di krəs), ridiculous; absurd but amusing; as, the ludicrous acts of a clown.

lug (lug), pull along or carry with effort; drag. The children lugged home a big Christmas tree.

lug gage (lug′ij), baggage.

luke warm (lük′wôrm′), 1. neither hot nor cold. 2. half-hearted; showing little enthusiasm.

lull (lul), 1. to hush to sleep. The mother lulled the crying baby. 2. to quiet; become calm or more nearly calm. The captain lulled our fears. The wind lulled. 3. period of less noise or violence; brief calm. We ran home during a lull in the storm.

lul la by (lul′ə bī′), song for singing to a child in a cradle; soft song to put a baby to sleep.

lum ber[1] (lum′bər), 1. timber, logs, beams, boards, etc., roughly cut and prepared for use. 2. cut and prepare lumber. 3. household articles no longer in use, old furniture, and other useless things that take up room. 4. fill up or obstruct by taking space which is wanted for something else. Do not lumber up my shelf with your collection of stones and insects.

lum ber[2] (lum′bər), move along heavily and noisily; roll along with difficulty. The old stagecoaches were lumbering means of travel.

lum ber man (lum′bər mən), 1. man who works at cutting down trees and getting out the logs. 2. person who prepares lumber or buys and sells lumber.

lu mi nous (lü′mi nəs), 1. bright; shining by its own light; full of light. The sun and stars are luminous bodies. 2. clear; easily understood.

lump (lump), 1. a small mass of no particular shape. 2. a swelling; a bump. There is a lump on my head where I bumped it. 3. put together. We will lump all our expenses. 4. form into a lump or lumps. Cornstarch will lump if cooked too fast. 5. in lumps; in a lump; including a number of items. The girls were given a lump sum of $6.00 to pay all their expenses.

lu na tic (lü′nə tik), 1. crazy person. 2. insane. 3. extremely foolish.

lunch (lunch), 1. light meal. 2. a light meal between breakfast and dinner. 3. eat a light meal.

lunch eon (lun′chən), 1. lunch. 2. a formal lunch.

lung (lung), either one of the pair of breathing organs found in the chest of man and of other animals with backbones.

lunge (lunj), 1. a thrust; any sudden forward movement. 2. to thrust; make a lunge.

lurch (lėrch), 1. a sudden leaning or roll to one side, like that of a ship, a car, or a staggering person. The car gave a lurch and upset. 2. make a lurch; stagger. The wounded man lurched forward.

lure (lür), 1. lead (away or into something) by arousing desire. 2. attraction. Many people feel the lure of the sea. 3. attract with a bait. We lured the fox into a trap. 4. a decoy; bait.

lu rid (lür′id), 1. lighted up with a red or fiery glare. The sky was lurid with the flames and smoke of the burning city. 2. terrible; sensational; startling. The detective told some lurid stories.

lurk (lėrk), stay about without arousing attention; wait out of sight; be hidden. A tiger was lurking in the jungle outside the village.

lus cious (lush′əs), 1. delicious; richly sweet; as, a luscious peach. 2. very pleasing to taste, smell, hear, see, or feel.

lust (lust), 1. strong desire. 2. have a strong desire. A miser lusts after gold. 3. a bad desire or appetite.

lus ter or **lus tre** (lus′tər), 1. a bright shine on the surface; as, the luster of pearls. 2. brightness. Her eyes lost their luster. 3. fame; glory; brilliance. The deeds of heroes add luster to a nation's history.

lus trous (lus′trəs), having luster; shining; glossy; as, lustrous pearls.

lust y (lus′ti), strong and healthy; full of vigor; as, a lusty boy.

lute (lüt), a stringed instrument of former times that was somewhat like a banjo.

Woman playing a lute

lux u ri ant (lug zhür′i ənt), 1. growing thick and green. 2. producing abundantly. 3. rich in ornament.

lux u ri ous (lug zhür′i əs), 1. fond of luxury; tending toward luxury; self-indulgent. 2. giving luxury; very comfortable and beautiful. Some theaters are luxurious.

Lynx (about 3 ft. long with the tail)

lux u ry (luk′shə ri), 1. the comforts and beauties of life beyond what are really necessary. 2. use of the best and most costly food, clothes, houses, furniture, and amusements. 3. thing that one enjoys, usually something choice and costly. A new car every year is a luxury that few people can afford. 4. thing pleasant but not necessary.

lye (lī), liquid used in cleaning and in making soap.

ly ing[1] (lī′ing), 1. telling a lie; habit of telling lies. 2. false; not truthful.

ly ing[2] (lī′ing). See **lie**[2]. He was lying on the ground.

lynch (linch), put (an accused person) to death without a lawful trial.

lynx (lingks), a wildcat common in the northern United States and Canada. See the picture on this page.

Lyre

lyre (līr), ancient stringed musical instrument somewhat like a small harp.

lyr ic (lir′ik), 1. a short poem expressing personal emotion. A love poem, a lament, and a hymn might all be lyrics. 2. having something to do with such poems. 3. lyrical.

lyr i cal (lir′i kəl), 1. of lyrics. 2. expressed in song; suitable for song. 3. using song; expressing oneself in song. Ann became almost lyrical when she described the scenery.

M

ma (mä), mamma; mother.

ma'am (mam), madam.

mac a ro ni (mak′ə rō′ni), flour paste dried in the form of long, hollow tubes to be cooked for food.

ma chine (mə shēn′), 1. an arrangement of parts, usually metal parts, for doing work, each part having some special thing to do. Sewing machines and washing machines make housework easier. 2. a device for applying power. Levers and pulleys are machines. 3. an automobile. 4. airplane.

machine gun, gun for keeping up a rapid fire of bullets. See the picture below.

ma chin er y (mə shēn′ər i), 1. machines. A factory contains much machinery. 2. the parts or works of a machine. Machinery is oiled to keep it running smoothly. 3. any combination of things or persons by which something is kept going or something is done. Policemen, judges, courts, and prisons are the machinery of the law.

Machine gun

ma chin ist (mə shēn′ist), 1. skilled worker with machine tools. 2. person who runs a machine. 3. man who makes and repairs machinery.

mack er el (mak′ər əl), a salt-water fish, much used for food. See the picture below.

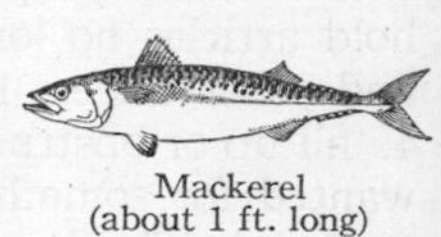
Mackerel (about 1 ft. long)

mack i naw (mak′i nô), 1. a kind of thick blanket, often woven with bars of color, used in the northern and western United States by Indians, lumbermen, etc. 2. a short jacket of thick plaid wool.

mack in tosh (mak′in tosh), 1. waterproof coat; raincoat. 2. waterproof cloth.

mad (mad), 1. out of one's head; crazy; insane. A man must be mad to do a mad thing like cutting himself on purpose. 2. much excited; foolish; wild. The dog made mad efforts to catch up with the automobile. 3. blindly and unreasonably fond. Some girls are mad about going to dances. 4. **Like mad** means furiously; very hard. I ran like mad to catch the train. 5. very angry. The insult made him mad. 6. having hydrophobia. A mad dog foams at the mouth and may bite people.

mad am or **mad ame** (mad′əm), a polite title used in speaking of a lady or to a lady. Madam, will you take my seat?

mad den (mad′ən), make mad; drive mad; become mad.

made (mād), 1. built; constructed; formed; prepared. 2. See **make.** The cook made the cake. It was made for Nan's birthday.

mad e moi selle (mad′ə mə zel′), a French word meaning Miss.

mad ly (mad′li), 1. insanely. 2. furiously. 3. foolishly.

mad man (mad′man′), man who is crazy.

mad ness (mad′nis), 1. being crazy; loss of one's mind. 2. great rage; fury. In his madness he tried to kill his best friend. 3. folly. It would be madness to try to sail a boat in this storm.

Ma don na (mə don′ə), 1. Mary, the mother of Jesus. 2. picture or statue of her.

mad ras (mad′rəs), closely woven cotton cloth, used for shirts.

mag a zine (mag′ə zēn′), 1. a publication appearing weekly or monthly, containing stories and articles by different writers. 2. room in a fort or warship for keeping gunpowder and other dangerous substances that might explode. 3. building for storing gunpowder, guns, food, and other supplies in time of war. 4. place for cartridges in a repeating gun. 5. place for film in a camera.

MAGAZINE
Magazine of a gun

ma gen ta (mə jen′tə), 1. purplish-red dye. 2. purplish red.

mag got (mag′ət), an insect in the earliest, legless stage just after leaving the egg. Maggots usually live in decaying matter.

MAGGOT ADULT
Fly. Lines show actual length.

mag ic (maj′ik), 1. the art of making things happen by secret charms and sayings. The fairy's magic changed the brothers into swans. 2. something that produces results as if by magic. The magic of her voice charmed the audience. 3. done by magic or as if by magic. A magic palace stood in place of their hut.

mag i cal (maj′i kəl), 1. of magic. 2. done by magic or as if by magic.

ma gi cian (mə jish′ən), person who can use magic. The wicked magician cast a spell over the princess.

mag is trate (maj′is trāt), 1. an officer of the government who has power to apply the law and put it in force. The President is the chief magistrate of the United States. 2. a judge.

mag ne si um (mag nē′shi əm), a light, silver-white metal that burns with a dazzling white light.

mag net (mag′nit), 1. a stone or piece of iron or steel that attracts or draws to it bits of iron or steel. 2. anything that attracts. The kittens and rabbits in our back yard were a magnet which attracted all the children.

Magnet attracting nails

mag net ic (mag net′ik), 1. having the properties of a magnet. 2. having something to do with magnetism. 3. very attractive; as, a magnetic personality.

mag net ism (mag′ni tizm), 1. the properties or qualities of a magnet; the showing of magnetic properties. 2. power to attract or charm. If John had magnetism, he would be a leader among his schoolmates.

mag nif i cence (mag nif′i səns), splendor; grand beauty; richness of material, color, and ornament. We may speak of the magnificence of mountain scenery, of kings, or of furniture.

mag nif i cent (mag nif′i sənt), grand; stately; splendid; richly ornamented; as, the magnificent palace of a king, the magnificent jewels of a queen, a magnificent view of the mountains.

mag ni fy (mag′ni fī), 1. cause to look larger than it really is. A microscope is a magnifying glass. 2. make too much of; go beyond the truth in telling. Do not magnify the faults of your friends.

mag ni tude (mag′ni tūd or mag′ni tüd), 1. size. 2. importance. The voters were impressed by the magnitude of the nation's problems.

Magnolia flower

mag no li a (mag nō′li ə), a North American tree with large white, pink, or purplish flowers. There are several kinds. See the picture just above.

mag pie (mag′pī), 1. a black-and-white bird that chatters a great deal. 2. person who chatters.

American magpie (15 to 20 in. long)

ma hog a ny (mə hog′ə ni), 1. a tree that grows in tropical America. 2. the dark reddish-brown wood of this tree, which is very hard and takes a high polish. It is much used for furniture. 3. dark reddish brown.

maid (mād), 1. girl; young unmarried woman. 2. unmarried woman. 3. female servant. 4. A **maid of honor** is (1) an unmarried woman who is the chief attendant of the bride at a wedding. (2) an unmarried lady who attends a queen or a princess.

maid en (mād′ən), 1. girl; young unmarried woman; maid. 2. of a maiden; as, maiden grace. 3. new; untried; unused. 4. first. It was the ship's maiden voyage.

mail[1] (māl), 1. letters to be sent by post. 2. the system by which letters are sent, run by the Post Office Department. 3. all that comes by one post or delivery. 4. train, boat, etc., that carries mail. 5. send by mail; put in a mailbox.

mail[2] (māl), 1. armor; metal garments made of rings, small loops of chain linked together, or plates, for protecting the body against the enemy's arrows, spears, etc. 2. clothe with armor or as if with armor. The **mailed fist** means armed force.

Coat of mail

maim (mām), cut off or hurt an arm, leg, ear, etc.; cripple or disable. He lost two toes by the accident, but we were glad that he was not more seriously maimed.

main (mān), 1. most important; largest; as, the main dish at dinner, the main line of a railway. 2. a large pipe for water, gas, etc. When the water main broke, our cellar was flooded. 3. the open sea. Our daring fleet shall sail the main. 4. **In the main** means for the most part. 5. **By main strength** means by using full strength. 6. **With might and main** means with all one's force.

main land (mān′land′), land that is not a small island; the main part of a continent.

main ly (mān′li), chiefly; mostly; for the most part. Jim is interested mainly in sports and neglects his school work.

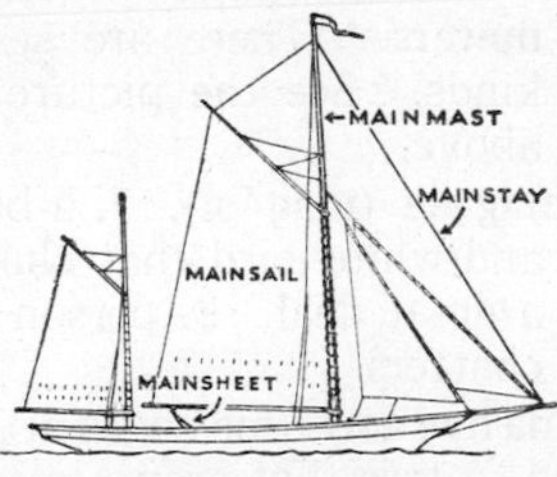

main mast (mān′məst or mān′mast′), the principal mast in a ship. In a ship with three masts, the middle mast is the mainmast.

main sail (mān′səl or mān′sāl′), largest sail of a ship. See the picture.

main stay (mān′stā′), 1. rope supporting the mainmast. 2. main support. Loyal friends are a person's mainstay in time of trouble.

main tain (mān tān′), keep; keep up; carry on; uphold. One may maintain one's hold on a rope, maintain a family or a household, maintain war, or maintain an opinion.

main te nance (mān′ti nəns), 1. a maintaining. Maintenance of quiet is necessary in a hospital. 2. a being maintained; support. A government collects taxes to pay for its maintenance. 3. enough to support life; means of living. His small farm provides a maintenance, but not much more.

Maize

maize (māz), 1. a plant whose grain grows on large ears; corn. 2. the color of ripe corn; yellow.

ma jes tic (mə jes′tik), grand; noble; dignified; stately; kingly.

ma jes ti cal ly (mə jes′ti kəl i), grandly; in a majestic manner.

maj es ty (maj′is ti), 1. stately appearance; royal dignity; nobility. 2. **Your Majesty** or **His Majesty** is a title given to kings, emperors, and the like.

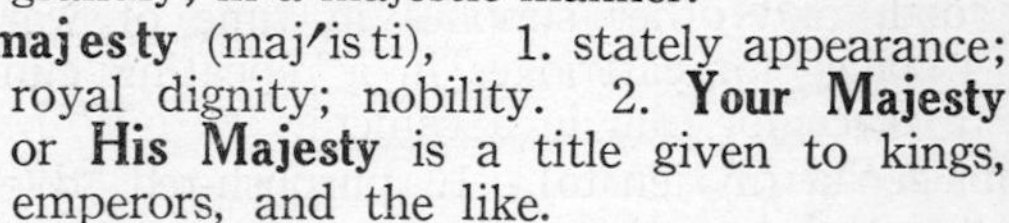

ma jor (mā′jər), 1. an officer in the army, ranking next above a captain. 2. greater. The major part of a little baby's life is spent in sleeping.

ma jor i ty (mə jor′i ti), 1. the greater number or part; more than half. A majority of the children chose red covers for the books they made. 2. the number by which the votes on one side are more than those on the other. John had 18 votes, and James had 12; so John had a majority of 6.

make (māk), 1. bring into being; build; form or shape; as, to make a rag rug, a poem, a boat, a medicine. 2. style; build; character. Do you like the make of that coat? 3. kind; brand. What make of car is this? 4. put into condition for use; arrange; as, to make the beds. 5. get (a thing) started; as, to make a fire. 6. cause; bring about; as, to make a noise, to make peace. 7. give; as, make room for me. 8. pass (a law); decide that there shall be (such a law, rule, etc.). 9. come to have; as, to make a new friend. 10. cause to be or become; as, to make a room warm, make a fool of oneself. 11. become; turn out to be. She will make a good teacher. 12. come to; amount to. 2 and 3 make 5. That makes 40 cents you owe me. 13. count as; be counted as. This makes twice I have been in New York. I made it 47. 14. be; be the whole of. Bread and milk will make a supper for us. 15. earn; gain; as, to make good marks, to make one's living. 16. cause the success of. 17. force to. Make brother stop hitting me. 18. do; perform; as, to make a journey, make an attempt, make a mistake. 19. reach; arrive at. Will the ship make harbor? 20. reach or keep up a speed of. Some airplanes can make more than 200 miles an hour. 21. Some special meanings are:

make away with, 1. get rid of. 2. kill. 3. steal.

make believe, pretend.

make out, 1. write out. 2. prove; try to prove. 3. understand. 4. see with difficulty. I can barely make out what these letters are. 5. complete; fill out. We need two more eggs to make out a dozen. 6. get along; manage. We must try to make out with what we have.

make over, alter; make different; as, to make over a dress.

make up, 1. put together; as, to make up cloth into a dress. 2. arrange; set up; as, to make up a page of type. 3. invent; as, to make up a story. 4. put paint, powder, etc., on the face. 5. become friends again after a quarrel. 6. give or do in place of; as, to make up for lost time. 7. decide; as, to make up one's mind. **made** is formed from **make.**

mak er (māk′ər), person or thing that makes.

make shift (māk′shift′), something made to use for a time instead of the right thing. Spools, bottles, and buttons were the child's makeshifts for toys.

make-up (māk′up′), the way in which a thing is made up or put together; composition; nature; constitution. People of a nervous make-up are excitable. The make-up of an actor is the way he is dressed and painted in order to look his part. The make-up of a paper or magazine is the arrangement of type, illustrations, etc., or the kind of articles, stories, etc., used.

mal a dy (mal′ə di), sickness; illness; disease.

ma lar i a (mə lãr′i ə), a disease that causes chills, fever, and sweating. Malaria is transmitted by the bite of certain mosquitoes.

male (māl). Boys and men are males. A bull, a rooster, and a he-goat are all males.

mal ice (mal′is), active ill will; spite; a wish to hurt or make suffer. Lincoln asked the people of the North to act "with malice toward none, with charity for all."

ma li cious (mə lish′əs), spiteful; showing ill will; wishing to hurt or make suffer. No one likes a malicious telltale.

ma lign (mə līn′), 1. speak evil of; slander. You malign Mr. Jones when you call him stingy, for he gives all he can afford to give. 2. evil; injurious. Gambling often has a malign influence. 3. hateful; malicious.

ma lig nant (mə lig′nənt), 1. very evil; very hateful; very malicious. 2. very harmful; causing death. Cancer is a malignant disease.

mal le a ble (mal′i ə bəl), 1. that can be hammered or pressed into various shapes without breaking. Gold, silver, copper, and tin are malleable and can be beaten into thin sheets. 2. adaptable; yielding.

mal let (mal′it), wooden hammer. Specially shaped mallets are used to play croquet and polo.

Mallet for pounding

malt (môlt), 1. grain, usually barley, soaked in water until it has sprouted and tastes sweet. Malt is used in making beer and ale. 2. make into malt. 3. prepare with malt. Malted milk is a food.

mal treat (mal trēt′), treat roughly or cruelly; abuse. Only very mean children maltreat animals.

ma ma (mä′mə), mother.

mam ma (mä′mə), mother.

mam mal (mam′əl), an animal that gives milk to its young. Human beings, horses, cattle, dogs, and cats are mammals.

mam moth (mam′əth), 1. a very large kind of elephant with a hairy skin and long curved tusks. The last mammoth died thousands of years ago. 2. huge; gigantic. Digging the Panama Canal was a mammoth undertaking.

Mammoth (about 9 ft. tall)

mam my (mam′i), 1. a childish word for mother. 2. a colored woman in charge of white children; an old Negro woman.

man (man), 1. A man is a boy grown up. 2. human being; person. 3. the human race. Man likes company. Man has existed for thousands of years. 4. a male follower, servant, or employee; as, Robin Hood and his merry men. 5. supply with men. We can man ten ships. 6. **To a man** means every one of them. **men** is formed from **man.**

man age (man′ij), 1. control; conduct; handle. A good rider manages his horse well. They hired a man to manage the business. 2. succeed in doing something. I shall manage to keep warm.

man age ment (man′ij mənt), 1. handling; control. Bad management caused the failure. 2. the persons that manage a business or an institution. The management of the store decided to use red wrapping paper at Christmas time.

man ag er (man′ij ər), person who manages.

man date (man′dāt), 1. a command, especially a legal order from a source superior to oneself. 2. the expressed will of voters to their representative.

man do lin (man′də lin), a stringed musical instrument.

Man playing a mandolin

mane (mān), the long heavy hair on the neck of a horse, a lion, etc.

ma neu ver (mə nü′vər), 1. a planned movement of troops or warships. Every year the army and navy hold maneuvers for practice. 2. perform maneuvers; cause troops to perform maneuvers. 3. manipulate skillfully. 4. a skillful plan; a clever series of moves. He forced us to support him by a series of maneuvers. 5. to scheme; use methods that the other fellow cannot follow. That shrewd boy is maneuvering for some advantage. 6. to force or drive (a person or thing) by some scheme. She maneuvered her mother out of the kitchen.

Two stalls with mangers

man ful (man′fəl), manly; brave.

man ga nese (mang′gə nēs), a hard, brittle, grayish-white metal.

man ger (mān′jər), box in a barn or stable built against the wall at the right height for horses and cows to eat from. See the picture just above.

man gle¹ (mang′gəl), 1. cut or tear roughly. The two cats bit and clawed until both were much mangled. 2. spoil. The music was too difficult for little Edith to play and she mangled it badly.

man gle² (mang′gəl), 1. machine with rollers for ironing sheets, towels, etc. 2. to press or smooth in a mangle.

man go (man′gō), 1. the oblong, slightly sour fruit of a tropical tree. Mangoes are eaten ripe or pickled when green. 2. the tree itself.

man hood (man′hu̇d), 1. condition or time of being a man. 2. courage; manliness. 3. men; as, the manhood of our city.

ma ni a (mā′ni ə), 1. a kind of insanity characterized by great excitement. 2. a craze; an unreasonable desire. She has a mania for dancing and going to parties. He has a mania for collecting old bottles.

man i fest (man′i fest), 1. clear; apparent to the eye or to the mind; plain. 2. show plainly. 3. show; prove. 4. a list of a ship's cargo.

man i fes ta tion (man′i fes tā′shən), a showing; a making manifest; an act that shows or proves. Entering a burning building is a manifestation of courage.

man i fold (man′i fōld), 1. having many parts or forms. 2. many and various.

ma nip u late (mə nip′ū lāt), 1. handle or treat, especially with skill. She watched him manipulate all the handles and gears in his automobile until she thought she could run it herself. 2. manage by clever use of influence, especially unfair influence. 3. treat unfairly; change for one's own purpose or advantage. That clerk stole money from the firm and manipulated the accounts to conceal his theft.

man kind (man′kīnd′ for 1, man′kīnd′ for 2), 1. the human race; all human beings. 2. men; the male sex. Mankind and womankind both like praise.

man li ness (man′li nis), manly quality; manly behavior.

man ly (man′li), 1. like a man; as a man should be; strong, frank, brave, noble, independent, and honorable. After Jim's father died, Jim set to work in a very manly way. 2. suitable for a man.

man ner (man′ər), 1. way; way of doing or happening; person's way of acting or behaving; style; fashion. 2. **Manners** means ways or customs. 3. **Manners** sometimes means good manners. 4. kind or kinds. We saw all manner of birds in the forest.

man-of-war (man′əv wôr′), warship.

man or (man′ər), 1. a large estate, part of which was set aside for the lord of the manor and the rest divided among his peasants, who paid the owner rent in goods, services, or money. 2. a large estate.

man sion (man′shən), large house; stately residence.

man tel (man′təl), shelf above a fireplace with its supports.

Mantel

man tel piece (man′təl pēs′), 1. a shelf above a fireplace. 2. mantel.

man tle (man′təl), 1. a loose cloak without sleeves. 2. anything that covers like a mantle. The ground had a mantle of snow. 3. clothe with a mantle. 4. flush; glow with a blush. Her cheek mantled. 5. a light, lacelike tube fixed around a flame, which gets so hot that it glows and gives light.

Mantle

man u al (man′ū əl), 1. a small book that is easy to understand and use. A cookbook is a manual. 2. of the hands; done with the hands; as, manual labor.

man u fac tor y (man′ū fak′tər i), a building in which things are made; a factory.

man u fac ture (man′ū fak′chər), 1. making of articles by hand or by machine, especially in large quantities. 2. make, especially with division of the labor among different persons and with machines. 3. the thing manufactured. 4. make into useful articles.

man u fac tur er (man′ū fak′chər ər), 1. person who manufactures. 2. person who employs a number of people in making things.

ma nure (mə nūr′ or mə nür′), 1. any substance put in or on the soil to make it rich. 2. put manure in or on.

man u script (man′ū skript), a book or paper written by hand or with a typewriter.

man y (men′i). There are many children in the city. Do you know many? He counted how many days it was until Christmas.

map (map), 1. a flat drawing of the earth's surface or of part of it, showing countries, towns, rivers, seas, mountains, etc. 2. a flat drawing of the sky, showing the positions of the stars, etc. 3. make a map of. 4. plan; arrange in detail. Each Monday we mapped out the week's work.

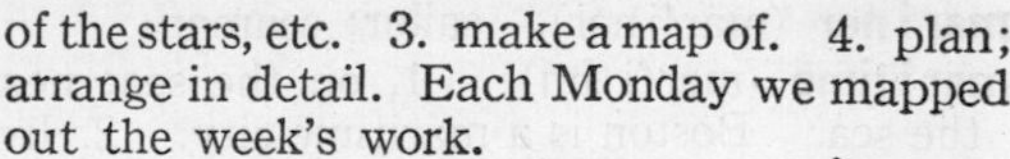

ma ple (mā′pəl), 1. a tree grown for shade, ornament, wood, or sugar. There are many kinds of maples. 2. the wood of the maple.

Maple leaf

mar (mär), injure; spoil the beauty of; ruin. Weeds mar a garden. The nails in the workmen's shoes have marred our floors.

ma raud er (mə rôd′ər), person or animal that goes about in search of plunder. Tigers are night marauders of the jungle.

mar ble (mär′bəl), 1. hard limestone, white or colored, that will take a beautiful polish. Marble is much used for statues and in buildings. 2. made of marble. 3. like marble; hard; unfeeling; as, a marble heart. 4. to color in imitation of the patterns in marble. Some books have marbled edges. 5. a small ball of marble, clay, glass, etc., used in games.

march[1] (märch), 1. to walk as soldiers do, in time and with steps of the same length. 2. marching. The news of the enemy's march made whole villages flee. 3. music meant for marching. 4. distance marched; a long, hard walk. 5. progress; as, the march of events. 6. to cause to march. His mother marched him right off home with her. 7. **Steal a march** means gain an advantage without being noticed.

March[2] (märch), the third month of the year. It has 31 days.

mare (mãr), a female horse, donkey, etc.

mar gin (mär′jin), 1. edge; border; as, the margin of the lake. 2. the space around a page that has no writing or printing on it. 3. extra amount; amount beyond what is necessary; difference. We allow a margin of 15 minutes in catching a train.

mar i gold (mar′i gōld), a plant with yellow, orange, or red flowers.

ma rine (mə rēn′), 1. of the sea; found in the sea; produced by the sea. Seals and whales are marine animals. 2. shipping; fleet; as, our merchant marine. 3. of shipping; of the navy; for use at sea; as, marine supplies. 4. a soldier serving at sea.

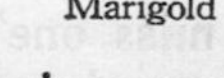

Marigold

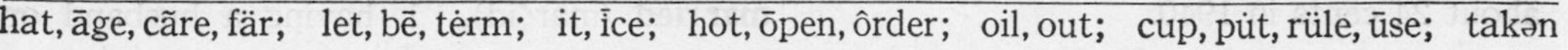

mar i ner (mar′i nər), sailor; seaman.

mar i time (mar′i tīm), 1. on the sea; near the sea. Boston is a maritime city. 2. living near the sea. Many maritime peoples are fishermen. 3. of the sea; having something to do with shipping and sailing. Ships and sailors are governed by maritime law.

mark[1] (märk), 1. something to be aimed at. Standing there, the lion was an easy mark. 2. target for scorn, etc. 3. sign; something that shows what a thing is. Courtesy is a mark of good breeding. 4. make a mark on or put one's name on to show whose a thing is. 5. tag with a mark on it. Take the price mark off from your new suit. 6. put a price mark on; tag. 7. a cross or sign made by a person who cannot write, instead of signing his name. Make your mark here. 8. written stroke or sign. She took up her pen and made a few marks on the paper. 9. make a mark on by stamping, cutting, writing, etc. 10. a grade; a letter or number to show how well one has done. My mark in arithmetic was B. 11. a line to show position. This mark shows how far you jumped. 12. put in a pin, make a line, etc., to show where a place is. Mark all the large cities on this map. 13. a standard; what is usual or proper or expected. Helen does not feel up to the mark. 14. a spot, stain, or scar; as, the mark of an old wound. 15. importance; fame; as, a man of mark. 16. see; notice; give attention to. Mark how carefully he moves. Mark well my words. 17. Some special meanings are:

beside the mark, 1. not hitting it, hitting far to one side, above or below. 2. having nothing to do with the subject; not appropriate.

hit one's mark, succeed in something one tries to do.

make one's mark, become well known.

mark off or **mark out,** make lines, etc., to show the position of or to separate. We marked out a tennis court. The hedge marks off one yard from another.

mark out for, set aside for; select for. He seemed marked out for trouble.

mark time, move the feet as in marching, but without going forward.

miss one's mark, fail in something one tried to do.

mark[2] (märk), German unit of money, worth about 24 cents in 1940.

marked (märkt), 1. having a mark or marks on it. 2. very noticeable; very plain. There are marked differences between apples and oranges.

mar ket (mär′kit), 1. a meeting of people for buying and selling. 2. the people at such a meeting. Excitement stirred the market. 3. an open space or covered building where food, cattle, etc., are shown for sale. 4. a store for the sale of food; as, a meat market. 5. the demand for something; price offered. 6. chance to buy or sell. There is always a market for wheat. 7. region in which goods may be sold. South America is a market for American automobiles. 8. buy or sell in a market. 9. sell.

marks man (märks′mən), 1. person who shoots well. 2. person who shoots. Some marksmen shoot badly.

mar ma lade (mär′mə lād), a preserve similar to jam, made of oranges or of other fruit. The peel is usually sliced up and boiled with the fruit.

Marmoset (length, with the tail, 16 in.)

mar mo set (mär′mə zet), a very small monkey in South and Central America with soft thick fur. See the picture just above.

mar mot (mär′mət), an animal with a bushy tail, somewhat like rats and rabbits. Woodchucks and prairie dogs are marmots.

Marmot (length, with the tail, 2½ ft.)

ma roon[1] (mə rün′), 1. put (a person) ashore and leave (him) on a desert island or in a desolate place. Pirates used to maroon people on desert islands. 2. leave in a lonely, helpless position. We were marooned in a cabin ten miles from any town, with the snow six feet deep and still falling.

ma roon[2] (mə rün′), very dark red.

mar quess (mär′kwis), marquis.

mar quis (mär′kwis), nobleman ranking below a duke and above an earl or count.

mar riage (mar′ij), 1. act of marrying. 2. the ceremony of being married; a wedding. 3. living together as husband and wife; married life. 4. a close union.

mar ried (mar′id), 1. having a husband or

wife. 2. of husband and wife. Married life has many duties.

mar row (mar′ō), 1. a soft substance that fills the hollow central part of most bones. 2. the inmost or important part. The icy wind chilled me to the marrow. The marrow of the plot was that the prince should kill his own father.

mar ry (mar′i), 1. join as husband and wife. The minister married them. 2. take as husband or wife. John marries Grace. 3. become married. She married late in life. 4. give in marriage. She has married all her daughters.

Mars (märz), 1. the Roman god of war. 2. the planet nearest the earth. Some people think Mars is inhabited.

marsh (märsh), swamp; soft wet land; lowland covered at times by water.

mar shal (mär′shəl), 1. officer of various kinds, especially a police officer. A United States marshal is an officer of a Federal court whose duties are like those of a sheriff. 2. a high officer in an army. A Marshal of France is a general of the highest rank in the French Army. 3. person in charge of events. 4. arrange in proper order. He won the argument because he marshaled his facts well. 5. conduct with ceremony; as, to marshal a foreign visitor into the presence of the king.

marsh y (mär′shi), soft and wet like a marsh.

mart (märt), market; center of trade. New York and London are the great marts of the world.

mar ten (mär′tən), 1. a slender animal like a weasel, valued for its fur. 2. the fur.

Marten (length, with the tail, about 2½ ft.)

mar tial (mär′shəl), 1. of war; warlike; as, martial music. 2. brave; fond of fighting; as, a boy of martial spirit.

mar tin (mär′tin), a bird somewhat like a swallow. There are several kinds.

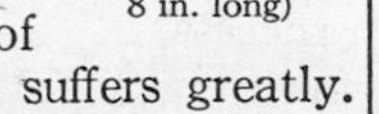
Purple martin (about 8 in. long)

mar tyr (mär′tər), 1. person who is put to death or is made to suffer greatly because of his religion or other beliefs. 2. put (a person) to death because of his beliefs. 3. person who suffers greatly. 4. cause to suffer greatly; torture.

mar tyr dom (mär′tər dəm), 1. the suffering or death of a martyr. 2. torment; suffering.

mar vel (mär′vəl), 1. wonderful thing. The airplane and the radio are among the marvels of science. 2. to wonder.

mar vel ous or **mar vel lous** (mär′vəl əs), 1. wonderful; extraordinary. 2. improbable. Children like tales of marvelous events.

mas cu line (mas′kū lin), 1. of men; male. 2. like a man; manly; strong; vigorous.

mash (mash), 1. a soft mixture; a soft mass. 2. beat into a soft mass; crush to a uniform mass. I'll mash the potatoes. 3. a warm mixture of bran, meal, and water for horses and other animals.

mask (mask), 1. a covering to hide or protect the face. The burglar wore a mask. 2. to cover the face with a mask. 3. a clay or wax likeness of a person's face. 4. a disguise. He hid his evil plans under a mask of friendship. 5. to hide or disguise. At a masked ball the guests wear masks. 6. a masked person.

Mask to hide the face

masked ball, dance at which masks are worn.

ma son (mā′sən), man whose work is building with stone or brick.

ma son ry (mā′sən ri), 1. work built by a mason; walls, chimneys, etc., made of stone or brick. 2. the trade or skill of a mason.

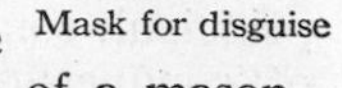
Mask for disguise

masque (mask), 1. an amateur dramatic entertainment, with fine costumes and scenery. 2. masked ball; masquerade.

mas quer ade (mas′kər ād′), 1. party or dance at which masks and fancy costumes are worn. 2. take part in a masquerade. 3. a disguise; a false pretense. 4. disguise oneself; go about under false pretenses. The thief masqueraded as a peddler.

mass (mas), 1. a lump; as, a mass of dough. 2. a large quantity together; as, a mass of treasure. 3. form or collect into a mass. It would look better to mass the peonies behind the roses than to mix them. 4. majority; greater part. The great mass of men consider themselves healthy. 5. bulk; size. 6. **The masses** sometimes means the common people; working people; lower classes of society. 7. the quantity of matter anything contains. The mass of a piece of lead is not changed by melting it.

mas sa cre (mas′ə kər), 1. a wholesale, pitiless slaughter of people or animals. 2. kill (the helpless) in large numbers.

mas sage (mə säzh′), 1. rubbing and kneading the muscles and joints to stimulate their circulation and to make them work better. A thorough massage feels good when you are tired. 2. give a massage to. Let me massage your back for you.

mas sive (mas′iv), large and heavy; large and solid.

mass y (mas′i), massive.

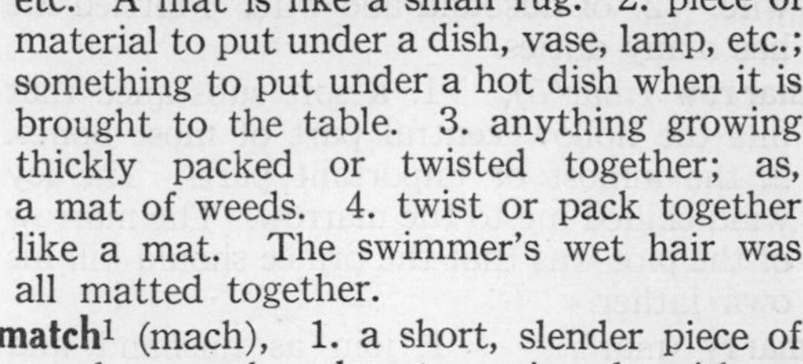

mast (mast), 1. long pole of wood or steel set up on a ship to hold the sails and rigging. 2. any tall upright pole. 3. **Before the mast** sometimes means as a common sailor, because the sailors slept in the forward part of the ship.

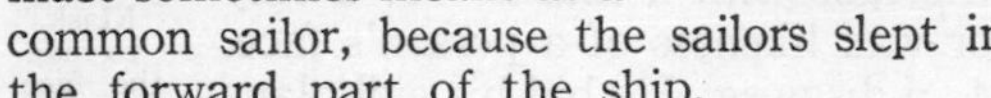

mas ter (mas′tər), 1. person who rules or commands people or things; director; employer; head of a household, school, ship, etc.; the one in control; the owner. 2. male teacher. 3. title of respect for a boy. First prize goes to Master Henry Adams. 4. an expert, such as a great artist or skilled workman; person who knows all there is to know about his work. 5. picture by a great artist. 6. being master; of a master; principal; controlling. 7. become the master of; conquer; control. She learned to master her anger. 8. become master of; become skillful at. He has mastered long division.

mas ter ful (mas′tər fəl), 1. fond of power or authority; domineering. 2. masterly; showing mastery.

mas ter ly (mas′tər li), 1. expert; skillful. 2. in an expert or skillful way.

mas ter piece (mas′tər pēs′), 1. anything done or made with wonderful skill; perfect piece of workmanship. 2. a person's greatest piece of work.

mas ter y (mas′tər i), 1. power such as a master has; rule; control. 2. the upper hand; victory. 3. very great skill or knowledge.

mas tiff (mas′tif), a large, strong dog with drooping ears and hanging lips.

Mastiff (about 28 in. high at the shoulder)

mat (mat), 1. piece of fabric made of woven rushes, straw, rope, fiber, etc., used for floor covering, for wiping mud from the shoes, etc. A mat is like a small rug. 2. piece of material to put under a dish, vase, lamp, etc.; something to put under a hot dish when it is brought to the table. 3. anything growing thickly packed or twisted together; as, a mat of weeds. 4. twist or pack together like a mat. The swimmer's wet hair was all matted together.

match[1] (mach), 1. a short, slender piece of wood, pasteboard, etc., tipped with a mixture that takes fire when rubbed on a rough or specially prepared surface. 2. a wick or cord prepared to burn at a uniform rate, for firing guns and cannon.

match[2] (mach), 1. person or thing equal to another or much like another; an equal; a mate. A boy is not a match for a man. 2. a pair that fit. Those two horses make a good match. 3. find the equal of or one exactly like; as, to match a vase so as to have a pair. 4. be similar; go well together. The rugs and the wallpaper match. 5. the coming together of two sides for a contest, game, etc.; as, a baseball match. 6. be equal to in a contest. No one could match the unknown archer. 7. try (one's skill). Tom matched his strength against Bob's. 8. marriage. Paul and Ellen made a match of it. 9. person considered as a possible husband or wife. That young man is a good match. 10. marry. The duke matched his daughter with the king's son.

match less (mach′lis), so great or wonderful that it cannot be equaled.

mate (māt), 1. one of a pair. The eagle mourned his dead mate. Where is the mate to this glove? 2. join in a pair. Birds mate in the spring. 3. husband or wife. 4. marry. 5. companion or fellow worker. Hand me that hammer, mate. 6. officer of a ship next under the captain. 7. assistant; as, cook's mate.

ma te ri al (mə tēr′i əl), 1. what a thing is made from or done with; as, dress material, building materials, writing materials, the material of which history is made. 2. of matter or things; as, the material world. 3. of the body. Food and shelter are material comforts. 4. that matters; important. The baking is a material factor in making cake. Hard work is a material factor in success.

ma te ri al ly (mə tēr′i əl i), 1. physically. He improved materially and morally. 2. considerably; substantially. The tide helped the progress of the boat materially.

ma ter nal (mə tėr′nəl), 1. motherly; of or like a mother. 2. related on the mother's side of the family. Everyone has two paternal grandparents and two maternal grandparents.

math e mat i cal (math′i mat′i kəl), 1. of mathematics; having something to do with mathematics; as, mathematical problems. 2. exact; accurate.

math e ma ti cian (math′i mə tish′ən), person skilled in mathematics.

math e mat ics (math′i mat′iks), the study of number, measurements, and space. Arithmetic is one part of mathematics.

mat ri mo ny (mat′ri mō′ni), marriage.

ma tron (mā′trən), 1. wife or widow, especially an older married woman. 2. woman who manages the household matters of a school, hospital, dormitory, or other institution. A police matron has charge of the women in a jail.

mat ter (mat′ər), 1. what things are made of; material; substance. Matter occupies space. 2. the substance of the material world. 3. what is said or written, thought of apart from the way in which it is said or written. 4. grounds; cause; basis. You have no matter for complaint in that. 5. thing; things; as, a matter of fact, a matter of record, a matter of accident. 6. things written or printed; as, reading matter. 7. amount; quantity; as, a matter of two days, a matter of ten minutes. 8. importance. Let it go since it is of no matter. 9. be important. Nothing seems to matter when you are very sick. 10. affair; as, business matters, a matter of life and death. 11. pus; to form or discharge pus. 12. Some special meanings are:

as a matter of fact, in truth; in reality.

for that matter, so far as that is concerned.

matter of course, something that is to be expected.

mat ter-of-fact (mat′ər əv fakt′), sticking to facts; not imaginative or fanciful.

mat tress (mat′ris), 1. covering of strong cloth stuffed with hair, cotton, straw, etc. It is used on a bed or as a bed. 2. A spring mattress is made of wire spring stretched on a frame. It is used as a support for a mattress and bedding.

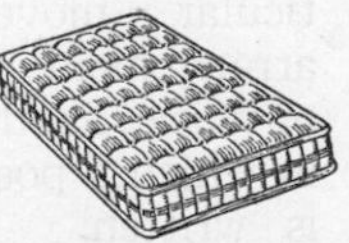
Mattress (def. 1)

ma ture (mə tūr′ or mə tür′), 1. ripen; come to full growth. These apples are maturing fast. 2. ripe; full-grown. Fifty is a mature age. 3. work out carefully. He matured his plans for the long trip. 4. fully worked out; carefully thought out; fully developed; as, mature plans. 5. become due.

ma tu ri ty (mə tūr′i ti or mə tür′i ti), 1. ripeness; full development. He reached maturity at twenty years. 2. being completed or ready. 3. the time a note or debt is payable.

maul (môl), 1. a very heavy hammer or mallet. 2. beat and pull about; handle roughly. Don't maul the cat.

mau so le um (mô′sə lē′əm), a large, magnificent tomb.

mauve (mōv), delicate, pale purple.

maw (mô), 1. mouth. 2. throat. 3. stomach.

max im (mak′sim), rule of conduct; proverb. "A stitch in time saves nine" and "Look before you leap" are maxims.

max i mum (mak′si məm), 1. greatest amount; greatest possible amount. Sixteen miles in a day was the maximum that any of our club walked last summer. 2. greatest; greatest possible. The maximum score in this test is 100.

may[1] (mā), 1. May I have an apple? May I go now? 2. It may rain tomorrow. The train may be late. 3. Good luck! May you be very happy. 4. *May* is sometimes used instead of *can*.

May[2] (mā), the fifth month of the year. It has 31 days.

may be (mā′bi), possibly; perhaps; it may be.

May Day, the first day of May, celebrated by hanging May baskets, crowning the queen of the May, dancing around a pole decorated with flowers, or ribbons, etc.

may hap (mā′hap′), perhaps.

may or (mā′ər), the man at the head of a city government.

mayst (māst), an old form meaning **may.** "Thou mayst" means "you may."

maze (māz), 1. a network of paths through which it is difficult to find one's way. A guide led us through the maze of caves. 2. confusion of thought. He was in such a maze that he couldn't speak.

M.D., doctor of medicine.

me (mē). *I* and *me* mean the person speaking. Mary said, "Give the dog to me. I like it and it likes me."

mead[1] (mēd), meadow.

mead[2] (mēd), an intoxicating drink made from honey and water.

mead ow (med′ō), 1. piece of grassy land, especially one used for raising hay. 2. low grassy land by the bank of a stream.

mea ger or **mea gre** (mē′gər), 1. poor; scanty; as, a meager meal. 2. thin; lean; as, a meager face.

meal[1] (mēl), 1. breakfast, lunch, dinner, or supper. 2. the food eaten or served at any one time.

meal[2] (mēl), 1. grain ground up; as, corn meal. 2. anything ground to a powder.

mean[1] (mēn), 1. intend; have as a purpose; have in mind. Do you think they mean to fight us? Do you mean to use the chops for dinner? He was meant for a soldier. **Mean well by** means have kindly feelings toward. 2. have as its thought; intend to say. Can you make out what this sentence means? **meant** is formed from **mean**[1].

mean[2] (mēn), 1. of low quality or grade. "He is no mean scholar" means "he is a good scholar." 2. low in social position or rank; humble. A peasant is of mean birth; a king is of noble birth. 3. of poor appearance; shabby. The poor widow lived in a mean hut. 4. not noble; petty; unkind. It is mean to spread gossip about your friends. 5. stingy; selfish.

mean[3] (mēn), 1. halfway between two extremes; average. 6 is the mean number between 3 and 9. 2. a condition, quality, or course of action part way between two opposites. Eight hours is a happy mean between too much sleep and too little. 3. A **means** is that or those by which something is brought about. We won the game by fair means. That was the means of saving his life. 4. **By means of** means by the use of; through. I found my dog by means of a notice in the paper. 5. **By all means** means certainly; in any possible way; at any cost. 6. **By no means** means certainly not; in no way. 7. **Means** sometimes means wealth; as, a man of means.

me an der (mi an′dər), 1. to wind about; as, a river which meanders. 2. a winding path or course; as, the meanders of a brook. 3. to wander aimlessly. We were meandering through the park. 4. an aimless wandering.

mean ing (mēn′ing), 1. that which is meant or intended. 2. that means something; expressive; as, a meaning look.

meant (ment). See **mean**[1]. He explained what he meant. That sign was meant as a warning.

mean time (mēn′tīm′), 1. time between. 2. in the time between. 3. at the same time.

mean while (mēn′hwīl′), meantime.

mea sles (mē′zəlz), 1. an infectious disease characterized by a bad cold, fever, and a breaking out of small red spots on the skin. Measles is a disease which children have much more commonly than grown-ups do. 2. **German measles** is a less severe disease with a similar breaking out.

meas ure (mezh′ər), 1. find the size or amount of (anything); find how long, wide, deep, large, much, etc., (a thing) is. We measured the room and found it was 20 feet long and 15 feet wide. We measured the pail by finding out how many quarts of water it would hold. 2. mark off or out (in inches, feet, quarts, etc.). Measure off 2 yards of this silk. 3. compare with a standard or with some other person or thing by estimating, judging, or acting. The soldier measured his strength with that of his enemy in a hand-to-hand fight. 4. be of a certain size or amount. Buy some paper that measures 8 by 10 inches. The party did not measure up to her expectations. 5. find out size or amount. Can he measure exactly? 6. Size or amount; as, one's waist measure. **Short measure** means less than it should be; **full measure** means all it should be. 7. something with which to measure. A foot rule, a yardstick, and a quart dipper are common measures. 8. a unit or standard of measure, such as an inch, mile, acre, peck, quart, gallon, etc. 9. system of measurement; as, liquid measure, dry measure, square measure. 10. limit; bound. "Her joy knew no measure" or "was beyond measure" means it was very, very great. 11. quantity, degree, or proportion. Being drunk and carelessness are in large measure responsible for automobile accidents. 12. particular movement or arrangement in poetry or music; as, the measure in which a poem or song is written. 13. a bar of music. 14. a dance movement. 15. action meant as means to an end. What measures shall we take to find out the thief? 16. a proposed law; a law.

Measure (def. 13)

meas ure ment (mezh′ər mənt), 1. way of measuring; way of finding the size, quantity, or amount. Clocks give us a measurement of time. 2. measuring; finding the size, quantity, or amount. The measurement of length by a yardstick is easy. 3. size, quantity, or amount as measured. The measurements of the room are 10 by 15 feet. 4. system of measuring or of measures.

meat (mēt), 1. animal flesh used for food. Fish and poultry are usually not called meat. 2. food; as, meat and drink. 3. part that can be eaten; as, the meat of a nut.

meat y (mēt′i), 1. of meat. 2. like meat. 3. full of meat. 4. full of substance; solid and nourishing. It was a meaty lesson containing many valuable ideas.

me chan ic (mi kan′ik), workman skilled with tools, especially one who makes, repairs, and uses machines.

me chan i cal (mi kan′i kəl), 1. having something to do with machinery. Mechanical problems are more interesting to boys than to girls. 2. made by machinery. 3. without expression. Her reading is very mechanical.

me chan i cal ly (mi kan′i kəl i), 1. in a mechanical manner. He greeted us mechanically. 2. in mechanical respects. That new engine is mechanically perfect. 3. toward mechanics. Boys are more mechanically inclined than girls are.

mech a nism (mek′ə nizm), 1. machine; machinery. 2. a system of parts working together as the parts of a machine do. The bones and muscles are parts of the mechanism of the body. 3. means by which something is done.

med al (med′əl), piece of metal like a coin, with a figure or inscription stamped on it. A medal is often given as an honor to somebody who has done something great. Sometimes medals are given to celebrate some event or to reward someone for doing something well.

Medal

me dal lion (mi dal′yən), 1. large medal. 2. design, ornament, etc., shaped like a medal. A design on a book or a pattern in lace may be called a medallion.

Lace medallion

med dle (med′əl), busy oneself with or in other people's things or affairs. Don't meddle with my books or my toys.

med dler (med′lər), person who interferes or meddles.

med dle some (med′əl səm), meddling; interfering; likely to meddle in other people's affairs.

me di ae val (mē′di ē′vəl), medieval.

me di ate (mē′di āt), 1. be a connecting link between. 2. be a go-between; act in order to bring about an agreement between persons or sides. Mother mediated in the quarrel between Jim and Joe.

med i cal (med′i kəl), having to do with healing or with the science and art of medicine; as, medical advice, medical schools, medical treatment.

me dic i nal (me dis′i nəl), having value as medicine; healing; helping; relieving.

med i cine (med′i sin), 1. substance, drug, or means used to cure disease or improve health. 2. science of curing disease or improving health; skill in healing; doctor's art; treatment of diseases.

me di e val (mē′di ē′vəl), belonging to the Middle Ages (the years from about 500 A.D. to about 1450 A.D.).

med i tate (med′i tāt), 1. think quietly; reflect. Monks and nuns meditate on God for hours. 2. think about; consider; plan. Our general was meditating an attack.

med i ta tion (med′i tā′shən), quiet thought.

Med i ter ra ne an (med′i tə rā′ ni ən), 1. the sea between Europe and Africa. 2. of this sea or the lands around it.

me di um (mē′di əm), 1. having a middle position, quality, or condition. Eggs can be cooked hard, soft, or medium. Five feet eight inches is a medium height for a man. 2. that which is in the middle; neither one extreme nor the other; middle condition. 3. a substance or agent through which anything acts; a means. Radio is a medium of communication. 4. a substance in which something can live. Water is the only medium in which fish can live. 5. person through whom supposed messages from the world of spirits are sent.

med ley (med′li), 1. a mixture of things that do not belong together. 2. piece of music made up of parts of other pieces.

meed (mēd), reward; what one deserves.

meek (mēk), 1. mild; patient; not easily angered. 2. submitting tamely when ordered about or injured by others. Little Tom was as meek as a lamb.

meek ness (mēk′nis), patience under injury or trouble; submitting easily to another's will.

meet[1] (mēt), 1. come face to face with (something or someone coming from the other direction). There is trouble when two cars meet on a very narrow road. 2. come together; join. 3. receive and welcome on arrival. I must go to the station to meet my mother. 4. be introduced to. Have you met my sister? 5. pay (a bill, one's debts, etc.) when due. 6. a meeting; as, an athletic meet. 7. Some special meanings are:

meet in battle, fight against.

meet needs, wishes, demands, etc., satisfy them.

meet the eye or **the ear,** be seen or heard.

meet with, come across, have, or get. We met with rough weather.

met is formed from **meet**[1].

meet[2] (mēt), fit; proper; suitable. It is meet that you should help your friends.

meet ing (mēt′ing), 1. coming together. 2. an assembly of persons for worship; as, a Quaker meeting, a prayer meeting. 3. any assembly.

meeting house, building used for worship; church.

mel an chol y (mel′ən kol i), 1. sadness; low spirits; tendency to be sad. 2. sad; gloomy. A melancholy man is not good company. 3. causing sadness; as, a melancholy scene.

mel low (mel′ō), 1. ripe, soft, and with a good flavor; sweet and juicy; as, a mellow apple. 2. soft and rich; as, a violin with a mellow tone, velvet with a mellow color. 3. softened and made wise by age and experience. 4. make mellow; become mellow. Apples mellow after they have been picked.

me lo di ous (mi lō′di əs), 1. sweet-sounding; musical. 2. producing melody.

mel o dy (mel′ə di), 1. sweet music; any sweet sound. 2. tune; a succession of single tones in music. Anne sang some sweet old melodies. Music has melody, harmony, and rhythm. 3. the chief part in harmony; the air.

Watermelon

mel on (mel′ən), a large juicy fruit of a vinelike plant much like the pumpkin, squash, and cucumber. The most common melons in the United States are the watermelon and the cantaloupe or muskmelon.

melt (melt), 1. change from solid to liquid. The ice melts in the warmth of spring. Great heat melts iron. 2. dissolve. Sugar melts in water. 3. disappear gradually. The clouds melted away, and the sun came out. 4. change very gradually. In the rainbow, the green melts into blue, the blue into violet. 5. soften. Pity melted her heart.

mem ber (mem′bər), 1. one who belongs to a group. Every member of the family came home for Christmas. Our church has over five hundred members. 2. part of an animal, especially a leg or an arm.

mem ber ship (mem′bər ship), 1. being a member. Do you enjoy your membership in the Boy Scouts? 2. the members. The whole membership of the class was present.

mem brane (mem′brān), a thin soft skin, sheet, or layer of animal tissue, lining or covering some part of the body; a similar layer of vegetable tissue.

mem oir (mem′wär), a record of facts or events written from personal knowledge or from special information. The old general wrote his memoirs of army life.

mem o ra ble (mem′ə rə bəl), worth remembering; not to be forgotten; notable.

me mo ri al (mi mō′ri əl), 1. something that is a reminder of some event or person, such as a statue, an arch or column, a book, or a holiday. 2. helping one remember.

Memorial Day is a day for decorating the graves of soldiers and sailors (in most States, May 30).

mem o rize (mem′ə rīz), commit to memory; learn by heart.

mem o ry (mem′ə ri), 1. ability to remember or keep in the mind. Some children have better memories than others. 2. something that is remembered. His mother died when he was small; she is only a memory to him now. 3. **In memory of** means to help in remembering; as a reminder of. I send you this card in memory of our happy summer together.

men (men), 1. Boys grow up to be men. 2. persons in general. Men and animals are alike in some ways.

men ace (men′is), 1. threat. In dry weather forest fires are a menace. 2. threaten. Floods menaced the valley towns with destruction.

me nag er ie (mə naj′ər i), 1. a collection of wild animals kept in cages for exhibition. 2. place where such animals are kept.

mend (mend), 1. repair; set right; improve; as, to mend a road, to mend a broken doll, to mend stockings. 2. place that has been mended. The mend in your dress scarcely shows. 3. get back one's health. The child will soon mend if she drinks plenty of milk.

men folk (men′fōk′), men.

me ni al (mē′ni əl), 1. belonging to or suited to a servant. Cinderella had to do menial tasks. 2. a servant who does the humblest and most unpleasant tasks.

men tal (men′təl), 1. of the mind; as, a mental test. 2. for the mind; done by the mind; as, mental arithmetic.

men tion (men′shən), 1. speak about. Do not mention the accident before the children. 2. a short statement. There was mention of Grace's party in the newspaper.

men tor (men′tər), wise and trusted adviser.

men u (men′ū), 1. list of the food served at a meal. 2. the food served. Everybody enjoyed the fine menu.

me ow (mi ou′), 1. the sound made by a cat or kitten. 2. to make this sound.

mer ce nar y (mėr′sə nãr′i), 1. working for money only; acting with money as the motive. 2. a soldier serving for pay in a foreign army.

mer chan dise (mėr′chən dīz), goods for sale; wares; articles bought and sold.

mer chant (mėr′chənt), 1. person who buys and sells. 2. person who buys and sells wholesale or on a large scale. 3. a trader whose business is especially with foreign countries. 4. trading; having something to do with trade; as, merchant ships.

mer ci ful (mėr′si fəl), having mercy; showing or feeling mercy; full of mercy.

mer ci less (mėr′si lis), without pity; having no mercy; showing no mercy.

mer cu ry (mėr′kū ri), a heavy, silver-white metal that is liquid at ordinary temperatures. Mercury is used in thermometers.

mer cy (mėr′si), 1. more kindness than justice requires; kindness beyond what can be claimed. 2. a blessing; something to be thankful for. We thank the Lord for all his mercies. 3. **At the mercy of** means in the power of.

mere (mēr), nothing else than; only. The cut was a mere scratch. The mere sight of a dog makes him afraid.

mere ly (mēr′li), simply; only; and nothing more; and that is all.

merge (mėrj), 1. swallow up; absorb; combine and absorb; combine. The steel trusts merged various small businesses. 2. become swallowed up or absorbed in something else. The twilight merges into darkness.

me rid i an (mə rid′i ən), 1. a circle passing through any place on the earth's surface and through the North and South poles. All the places on the same meridian have the same longitude. 2. the highest point which the sun or any star reaches in the sky. 3. the highest point.

me ri no (mə rē′nō), 1. a kind of sheep with fine wool. 2. the wool of this sheep. 3. a fine woolen yarn made from it. 4. a thin, soft woolen cloth made from this yarn or some substitute.

mer it (mer′it), 1. goodness; worth; value; that which deserves reward or praise. Each child will get a mark according to the merit of his work. 2. deserve. A hard-working boy merits praise. 3. real fact or quality, good or bad. I will consider your case on its merits.

mer maid (mėr′mād′), a sea maiden in fairy tales, who is a fish from the waist down.

Mermaid

mer man (mėr′man′), a man in fairy tales, who is a fish from the waist down.

mer ri ly (mer′i li), in a merry manner; laughing and gay.

mer ri ment (mer′i mənt), laughter; fun; mirth; merry enjoyment; gaiety.

mer ry (mer′i), joyous; loving fun; full of fun; laughing and gay; as, a merry Christmas, a merry laugh.

mer ry-go-round (mer′i gō round′), 1. a set of animals, etc., that go round and round by machinery. Children ride on them for fun. 2. any whirl or rapid round. The holidays were a merry-go-round of fun.

mer ry mak ing (mer′i māk′ing), 1. laughter and gaiety; fun. 2. gay festival; merry entertainment. 3. gay and full of fun; having a merry time.

Mesa

me sa (mā′sə), a small high plateau with steep sides. See the picture just above.

mesh (mesh), 1. an open space of a net, sieve, or screen. This net has half-inch meshes. 2. **Meshes** sometimes means network. A fish was entangled in the meshes. 3. catch in a net. 4. engage or become engaged. The teeth of the small gear mesh with the teeth of a larger one. 5. **In mesh** means in gear; fitted together.

Gear teeth in mesh

mes quite (mes kēt′), a tree or shrub common in the southwestern United States and Mexico. Cattle eat mesquite pods.

mess (mes), 1. a dirty or untidy mass or group of things; a dirty or untidy condition. Look what a mess you have made of your dress, playing in that dirt. 2. **Mess** or **mess up** means make dirty; spoil; make a failure of. 3. confusion; difficulty. 4. an unpleasant or unsuccessful affair or state of affairs. 5. **Mess about** or **mess around** means busy oneself without seeming to accomplish anything. 6. a group of people who take meals together regularly; especially, such a group in the army or navy. 7. a meal of such a group. He is at mess now. 8. take one's meals (with). 9. a portion of food; a portion of soft food. He caught a mess of fish.

mes sage (mes′ij), words sent from one person to another.

mes sen ger (mes′ən jər), 1. person who carries a message or goes on an errand. 2. any animal or thing thought of as carrying a message. Each bullet was a messenger of death. 3. a herald.

met (met). See **meet**[1]. My father met us this morning at ten o'clock. We were met at the gate by our three dogs.

met al (met′əl), 1. a substance such as iron, gold, silver, copper, lead, and tin. Aluminum, steel, and brass are also metals. 2. made of a metal, or of a mixture of metals. 3. broken stone used for roads. 4. material; substance. Cowards are not made of the same metal as heroes.

me tal lic (mi tal′ik), 1. of metal; as, a metallic substance. 2. like metal; characteristic of metal; as, the metallic luster of a Japanese beetle.

mete (mēt), give to each his share or what is due him. The judges will mete out praise and blame.

me te or (mē′ti ər), shooting star; mass of stone or metal that comes toward the earth from outer space with enormous speed. Meteors become so hot from rushing through the air that they glow and often burn up.

me ter[1] (mē′tər), 1. a measure of length used in many countries. A meter is equal to $39\frac{1}{3}$ inches. 2. any kind of poetic rhythm; the arrangement of beats or accents in a line of poetry. The meter of "Jack and Jill went up the hill" is not the meter of "One, two, buckle my shoe."

me ter[2] (mē′tər), something that measures, or measures and records; as, a gas meter, a water meter.

me thinks (mi thingks′), it seems to me.

meth od (meth′əd), 1. way of doing something; as, a method of teaching music. Roasting is one method of cooking meat. 2. order or system in getting things done or in thinking. If you used more method, you wouldn't waste so much time.

me thod i cal (mi thod′i kəl), done according to a method; arranged or acting according to a method.

Meth od ist (meth′əd ist), 1. member of a church which had its origin in the work of John Wesley. 2. of the Methodists.

me thought (mi thôt′), it seemed to me.

me tre (mē′tər), meter[1].

me trop o lis (mi trop′ə lis), 1. the most important city of a country or region. New York is the metropolis of North America. 2. large city; important center. Chicago is a busy metropolis.

met ro pol i tan (met′rə pol′i tən), 1. of large cities; as, metropolitan newspapers. 2. person who lives in large cities and knows their ways.

met tle (met′əl), disposition; spirit; courage. **On one's mettle** means ready to do one's best.

mew[1] (mū), 1. the sound made by a cat or kitten. 2. cry like a cat; say meow. Our kitten mews when it gets hungry.

mew[2] (mū), a gull.

mewl (mūl), cry like a baby; whimper.

Mex i co (mek′si kō), a country in North America, south of the United States.

mi., mile; miles.

mi ca (mī′kə), a mineral that divides into thin, partly transparent layers. Mica is used in lanterns and stove doors, where the heat might break glass.

mice (mīs), more than one mouse.

mi cro phone (mī′krə fōn), 1. a device for increasing small sounds. 2. a radio device for transmitting sounds.

mi cro scope (mī′krə skōp), an instrument with a lens or combination of lenses for magnifying objects so that one can see clearly things not visible to, or not clearly visible to, the naked eye.

Microscope: 1, screws to adjust eyepiece; 2, eyepiece; 3, screw to adjust focus; 4, platform to hold objects; 5, mirror.

mi cro scop ic (mī′krə skop′-ik), 1. that cannot be seen without using a microscope; tiny; as, microscopic germs. 2. like a microscope; suggesting a microscope; as, a microscopic eye for mistakes. 3. of a microscope; with a microscope. Jean made a microscopic examination of a fly's wing.

mid[1] or **'mid** (mid), amid.

mid[2] (mid), middle.

mid day (mid′dā′), noon.

mid dle (mid′əl), 1. the point or part that is the same distance from each end or side; the center; as, the middle of the road. 2. equally distant from each end; as, the middle house in a row. 3. in between; as, middle size.

mid dle-aged (mid′əl ājd′), neither young nor old; from about 40 to about 60 years of age.

Middle Ages, the period between ancient and modern times (from about 500 A.D. to about 1450 A.D.).

mid dy (mid′i), 1. nickname for a midshipman. 2. a blouse like a sailor's.

midge (mij), a kind of small insect.

Midge. Line shows actual length.

midg et (mij′it), very small person; dwarf.

mid land (mid′lənd), 1. the middle part of a country; the interior. 2. in or of the midland.

mid night (mid′nīt′), 1. twelve o'clock at night; the middle of the night. 2. of or like midnight.

mid ship man (mid′ship′mən), 1. in the United States navy, a young man attending the Naval Academy at Annapolis. 2. in the British navy, a young graduate of a naval school. 3. formerly, a boy who assisted the officers of a ship.

midst[1] (midst), middle. **In the midst of** sometimes means among. **In our midst** means among us.

midst[2] or **'midst** (midst), amidst.

mid stream (mid′strēm′), the middle of the stream.

mid sum mer (mid′sum′ər), 1. the middle of summer. 2. in the middle of summer. 3. the time near June 21.

mid way (mid′wā′), halfway; in the middle.

mid win ter (mid′win′tər), 1. the middle of winter. 2. in the middle of winter. 3. December 22, or the time just before or after.

mien (mēn), how one bears oneself; one's air, appearance, look, manner, or aspect; as, the mien of a soldier.

might[1] (mīt), great power; strength. Work with all your might.

might[2] (mīt). Mother said that we might play in the barn. He might have done it when you were not looking.

might i ly (mīt′ili), 1. in a mighty manner; powerfully; vigorously. Samson strove mightily. 2. very much; greatly. We were mightily pleased at winning.

might y (mīt′i), 1. powerful; strong. 2. very great.

mi gnon ette (min′yən et′), a plant with spikes of small, very fragrant, greenish-white flowers.

Mignonette

mi grate (mī′grāt), 1. move from one place to another. Pioneers from New England migrated to all parts of the United States. 2. go from one region to another with the change in the seasons. Most birds migrate to warmer countries in the winter.

mi gra tion (mī grā′shən), 1. moving from one place to another. 2. a number of people or animals migrating together.

milch (milch), giving milk; kept for the milk it gives; as, a milch cow.

mild (mild), 1. gentle; kind; as, a mild old gentleman. 2. calm; warm; temperate; not severe; as, mild weather. 3. soft or sweet to the senses; not sharp, sour, bitter, or strong in taste; as, mild cheese, a mild cigar.

mil dew (mil′dū or mil′dü), 1. a kind of fungus that appears on plants or on paper, clothes, leather, etc., during damp weather. Mildew killed the rosebuds in our garden. 2. become covered with mildew. A pile of damp clothes in Bill's closet mildewed.

mile (mīl), a distance equal to 5280 feet. A nautical or geographical mile is about 6080 feet.

mile age (mīl′ij), miles covered or traveled.

mile stone (mīl′stōn′), 1. a stone set up on a road to show distance in miles to a certain place. 2. some event which marks a stage in the journey of life.

Milestone

mil i tant (mil′i tənt), 1. fighting; warlike. 2. militant person.

mil i tar y (mil′i tãr′i), 1. of soldiers or war. 2. done by soldiers. 3. fit for soldiers; suitable for war. 4. warlike. 5. the army; soldiers.

mi li tia (mi lish′ə), army of citizens partly trained for war. Every State has a militia called the National Guard.

milk (milk), 1. the white liquid from cows, which we drink and use in cooking. 2. Many other animals produce milk for their young ones. 3. draw milk from (a cow, goat, etc.). 4. the white juice of a plant, tree, or nut.

milk maid (milk′mād′), woman who milks cows or works in a dairy.

milk man (milk′man′), man who sells milk or delivers it to customers.

milk weed (milk′wēd′), a weed with white juice that looks like milk.

milk y (mil′ki), 1. like milk; white as milk. 2. of milk; containing milk.

mill (mil), 1. a machine for grinding corn, wheat, or other substances. 2. the building where such a machine is housed. 3. grind very fine. 4. a building where manufacturing is done. A cotton mill makes thread from cotton. 5. move about in a circle in a confused way. Cattle sometimes mill when they are frightened.

A small mill (def. 2)

mill er (mil′ər), 1. one who owns or runs a mill, especially a flour mill. 2. an insect whose wings look as if they were powdered with flour.

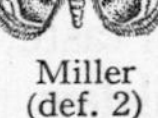
Miller (def. 2)

mil let (mil′it), a grain used for food in Asia and in southern Europe. In the United States, millet is grown chiefly for hay.

mil li ner (mil′i nər), person who makes or sells women's hats.

mil li ner y (mil′i ner′i), 1. women's hats. 2. the business of making, trimming, and selling women's hats.

mil lion (mil′yən), one thousand thousand; 1,000,000.

mil lion aire (mil′yən ãr′), 1. person who has a million dollars. 2. very wealthy person.

mill stone (mil′stōn′), 1. one of a pair of round flat stones for grinding corn, wheat, etc. 2. heavy burden. 3. anything that grinds or crushes.

Woman using millstones to grind corn

mim ic (mim′ik), 1. make fun of by imitating. We like to get John to mimic our old music teacher. 2. person or thing that imitates. 3. copy closely. A parrot can mimic a person's voice. 4. resemble closely. There are insects which mimic leaves. 5. not real, but imitated or pretended for some purpose. The soldiers staged a mimic battle for the visiting general. **mimicked** and **mimicking** are formed from **mimic.**

min a ret (min′ə ret′), a slender, high tower attached to a Mohammedan mosque, from which a crier calls the people to prayer.

Minaret

mince (mins), 1. chop up into very small pieces. 2. put on fine airs in speaking or walking. 3. walk with little short steps.

mind (mīnd), 1. the part of a person that knows and thinks and feels and wishes and chooses. 2. intellect. To learn arithmetic easily you must have a good mind. 3. what one thinks or feels. Speak your mind freely. 4. notice; observe. 5. take care. 6. attend to; take care of. 7. obey. 8. remember. 9. memory. 10. feel bad about; object to. Some people don't mind cold weather. 11. Some special meanings are:

be of one mind, have the same opinion.

have a mind to, intend to; think of doing.

make up one's mind, decide.

mind's eye, imagination.

on one's mind, in one's mind; in one's thoughts.

put in mind, remind.

set one's mind on, want very much.

to my mind, to my way of thinking; in my opinion.

mind ful (mīnd′fəl), 1. thinking; being aware. Mindful of your advice, I went slowly. 2. taking thought; careful. We had to be mindful of every step we took on the slippery sidewalk.

mine[1] (mīn), 1. of me; belonging to me. This book is mine. 2. the one or ones belonging to me. Your shoes are black; mine are brown.

mine[2] (mīn), 1. a large hole or space dug in the earth in order to get out something valuable; as, a coal mine, a gold mine. 2. dig a mine. 3. get from a mine; as, to mine coal, gold, etc. 4. dig in for coal, gold, etc.; as, to mine the earth. 5. a rich or plentiful source. The book proved to be a rich mine of information about radio. 6. an underground passage in which gunpowder is placed to blow up an enemy's forts, etc. 7. make underground passages below. 8. a bomb to be placed just under the surface of the sea, at the entrance to harbors, etc., to blow up an enemy's ships if they should come there. 9. lay mines under; as, to mine the mouth of a harbor.

min er (mīn′ər), man who works in a mine.

min er al (min′ər əl), 1. a substance obtained by mining or digging in the earth. Coal is a mineral. 2. any substance that is neither plant nor animal. 3. containing minerals; as, mineral water.

min gle (ming′gəl), mix. Two rivers which join mingle their waters. He is very shy and does not mingle much with the children at school.

min i a ture (min′i ə chər), 1. anything copied on a small scale. In the museum there is a miniature of the ship *Mayflower*. 2. done on a very small scale; tiny. Mary had miniature furniture for her little doll. 3. a very small painting, usually a portrait.

min i mum (min′i məm), 1. least possible amount; lowest amount. Each of the children had to drink some milk at breakfast; half a glass was the minimum. 2. least possible; lowest. The minimum price is 10 cents.

min ing (mīn′ing), 1. working mines for ores, coal, etc. 2. laying explosive mines.

min ion (min′yən), 1. servant or follower ready to do bad deeds for his master. 2. a darling; a favorite.

min is ter (min′is tər), 1. clergyman serving a church; spiritual guide; pastor. 2. serve as the minister of a church. 3. act as a servant or nurse; be of service or aid; be helpful; as, to minister to a sick man's wants. 4. person who is given charge of a department of the government; as, the Minister of War. 5. person sent to a foreign country to represent his own government; as, the United States Minister to Greece.

min is try (min′is tri), 1. the office, duties, or time of service of a minister. 2. the ministers of a church. 3. the ministers of a government. 4. ministering or serving.

mink (mingk), 1. a furry animal that lives in water part of the time. 2. its valuable brown fur.

Mink (length, with the tail, about 2 ft.)

min now (min′ō), 1. a very small fresh-water fish. 2. any fish when it is very small.

mi nor (mī′nər), 1. smaller. Correct the important errors in your paper, but do not bother with the minor ones. 2. person under the legal age of responsibility. You cannot vote while you are a minor.

mi nor i ty (mi nor′i ti), the smaller number or part; less than half. A minority of the children wanted a party, but the majority chose a picnic.

min strel (min′strəl), 1. a singer or musician in the household of a lord in times long ago. 2. a singer or musician who went about and sang or recited poems, often of his own making. 3. member of a company of actors giving songs, music, and jokes supposed to have come from the Negroes.

mint[1] (mint), 1. a sweet-smelling plant used for flavoring. Peppermint is a well-known kind of mint. 2. piece of candy flavored with mint.

mint[2] (mint), 1. place where money is coined. 2. to coin (money). 3. a large amount. A million dollars is a mint of money.

Dancing the minuet

min u et (min′ū et′), 1. a slow, stately dance. 2. the music for it.

mi nus (mī′nəs), 1. the sign (—) meaning that the quantity following it is to be subtracted. 2. less; decreased by. 12 minus 3 leaves 9.

min ute[1] (min′it), 1. 60 minutes of time make one hour. 2. a short time; an instant. I'll be there in a minute. 3. an exact point of time. The minute you see him coming, please tell me. 4. The **minutes of a meeting** means the account of what happened at the meeting, kept by the secretary.

mi nute[2] (mī nūt′ or mī nüt′), 1. very small; tiny. 2. going into small details. He gave me minute instructions about my work.

minx (mingks), a pert girl.

mir a cle (mir′ə kəl), 1. a wonderful happening that is beyond the known laws of nature. It would be a miracle if the sun should stand still in the heavens for an hour. 2. something marvelous. 3. remarkable example. She must be a miracle of patience to do all that fine hemming.

mi rac u lous (mi rak′ū ləs), 1. going against the known laws of nature. The miraculous tree grew up again an hour after it was cut down. 2. marvelous.

mire (mīr), 1. soft deep mud; slush. 2. get stuck in mire. He mired his horses and had to go for help. 3. to soil with mud or mire.

mir ror (mir′ər), 1. a glass in which you can see yourself; a looking glass; a surface that reflects light. 2. whatever reflects or gives a true description. This book is a mirror of the life of the pioneers. 3. reflect as a mirror does. The water was so still that it mirrored the trees along the bank.

mirth (mėrth), merry fun; laughter.

mirth ful (mėrth′fəl), merry; jolly.

mis ad ven ture (mis′əd ven′chər), bad luck; mishap; unfortunate accident.

mis call (mis kôl′), call by a wrong name.

mis cel la ne ous (mis′ə lā′ni əs), not all of one kind or nature. Fred had a miscellaneous collection of stones, butterflies, marbles, stamps, birds' nests, and many other things.

mis chance (mis chans′), misfortune; bad luck. By some mischance he didn't receive my telegram.

mis chief (mis′chif), 1. harm; injury, usually done by some person. Go away, or I'll do you a mischief. 2. conduct that causes harm or trouble, often without meaning it. Children's mischief may cause serious harm. 3. person who does harm, often just in fun. You little mischief! You have untied my apron. 4. merry teasing. Her eyes were full of mischief.

mis chie vous (mis′chi vəs), 1. harmful; as, a mischievous belief. 2. full of mischief; naughty. 3. full of pranks and teasing fun; as, mischievous fairies.

mis cre ant (mis′kri ənt), 1. having very bad morals; base. 2. a villain.

mis deed (mis dēd′), bad act; wicked deed.

mi ser (mī′zər), person who loves money for its own sake. A miser dislikes to spend money for anything, except to gain more money.

mis er a ble (miz′ər ə bəl), 1. unhappy. A sick child is often miserable. 2. causing trouble or unhappiness. I have a miserable cold. 3. poor; mean; wretched. The ragged child lives in a miserable tenement.

mis er a bly (miz′ər ə bli), in a miserable manner.

mis er y (miz′ər i), 1. a miserable, unhappy state of mind. Think of the misery of having no home or friends. 2. poor, mean, miserable circumstances. The very poor live in misery, without beauty or comfort around them.

mis for tune (mis fôr′chən), bad luck.

mis giv ing (mis giv′ing), a feeling of doubt, suspicion, or anxiety. We started off through the storm with some misgivings.

mis hap (mis hap′), an unlucky accident.

mis judge (mis juj′), judge wrongly or unjustly.

mis lay (mis lā′), 1. put in the wrong place. 2. put in a place and then forget where the place is. **mislaid** is formed from **mislay.**

mis lead (mis lēd′), 1. cause to go in the wrong direction. Our guide misled us in the woods, and we got lost. 2. cause to do wrong. He is a good boy, but he was misled by bad companions. 3. lead to think what is not so; deceive. His lies misled me.

mis lead ing (mis lēd′ing), causing mistakes or wrongdoing.

mis led (mis led′). See **mislead.**

mis man age ment (mis man′ij mənt), bad management.

mis no mer (mis nō′mər), 1. a name that describes wrongly. "Lightning" is a misnomer for a slow, old horse. 2. wrong name.

mis place (mis plās′), 1. put in the wrong place. 2. give (your love or trust) to the wrong person.

miss[1] (mis), 1. fail to hit. Johnny hammers away, but half the time he misses the nail. He fired twice, but both shots missed. 2. a failure to hit or reach; as, to make more misses than hits. 3. fail to find, get, or meet. I set out to meet my father, but in the dark I missed him. 4. let slip by; not seize. I missed the chance of a ride to town. 5. fail to catch; as, to miss the train. 6. leave out; as, to miss a word in reading. 7. fail to hear or understand. What did you say? I missed a word or two. 8. fail to keep, do, or be present at. I missed my music lesson today. 9. notice the absence of; feel the absence of. I did not miss my purse till I got home. I miss my mother when she goes away.

Miss[2] (mis), 1. a title given to a girl or to a woman who is not married; as, Miss Brown, the Misses Brown, the Miss Browns. 2. A **miss** is a girl.

mis shap en (mis shāp′ən), badly shaped; deformed.

mis sile (mis′il), an object that is thrown, hurled, or shot, such as a stone, a bullet, an arrow, or a lance.

miss ing (mis′ing), lacking; wanting; absent; not found; gone. One book is missing.

mis sion (mish′ən), 1. errand. 2. persons sent out on some special business. He was one of a mission sent by our government to France. A mission was sent to Africa by the Baptist Church. 3. the station or headquarters of a religious mission. 4. the business on which a mission is sent. 5. one's business or purpose in life; one's calling. It seemed to be her mission to care for her brother's children.

mis sion ar y (mish′ən ãr′i), 1. person who goes on the work of a religious mission. Missionaries tried to get the Indians to become Christians. 2. of religious missions or missionaries.

mist (mist), 1. a cloud of very fine drops of water in the air; fog. 2. come down in mist; rain in very fine drops. It is misting. 3. a haze or cloud that dims, blurs, or obscures. 4. cover with a mist; put a mist before; make dim. Tears misted her eyes.

mis take (mis tāk′), 1. error; blunder; misunderstanding of a thing's meaning. I used your towel by mistake. 2. make a mistake; misunderstand what is seen or heard; take wrongly. I mistook that stick for a snake. **mistook** and **mistaken** come from **mistake.**

mis tak en (mis tāk′ən), 1. wrong in opinion; having made a mistake. A mistaken person should admit that he was wrong. 2. wrong; wrongly judged; misplaced. It was a mistaken kindness to give that boy more candy, for it will make him sick. 3. See **mistake.**

mis tak en ly (mis tāk′ən li), by mistake.

Mis ter (mis′tər), Mr., a title put before a man's name or the name of his office; as, Mr. Smith, Mr. President. Dr. Jones did not like to be called "mister."

mis tle toe (mis′əl tō), plant with small, white berries, that grows high up in trees. It is used as a Christmas decoration.

Mistletoe growing on a branch of a tree

mis took (mis tůk′). See **mistake.** I mistook you for your sister yesterday.

mis tress (mis′tris), 1. the woman who is at the head of the household. 2. a woman or country who is in control or can rule. England was mistress of the seas. 3. a woman who has a thorough knowledge or mastery. She is complete mistress of the arts of cookery. 4. a woman teaching in a school, or at the head of a school, or giving lessons in a special subject. 5. **Mistress** used to mean Mrs., Madam, or Miss.

mis trust (mis trust′), 1. feel no confidence in; doubt. She mistrusted her ability to learn to swim. 2. lack of trust or confidence.

mist y (mis′ti), 1. of mist. 2. covered with mist. 3. not clearly seen or outlined. 4. as if seen through a mist.

mis un der stand (mis′un dər stand′), understand wrongly; give the wrong meaning to. Kate misunderstood what the teacher said and so did the wrong thing.

mis un der stand ing (mis′un dər stan′ding), 1. understanding wrongly; failure to understand; mistake as to meaning. 2. disagreement.

mis un der stood (mis′un dər stůd′). See **misunderstand.**

mis use (mis ūz′ for 1 and 2, mis ūs′ for 3), 1. to treat badly. He misuses his horses by giving them loads that are too heavy. 2. to use for the wrong purpose. He misuses his knife at the table by lifting food with it. 3. wrong use. I notice a misuse of the word *who* in your letter.

mite (mīt), 1. anything very small; little bit. Though poor, she gave her mite to charity. 2. very small child. What a little mite Dorothy is! 3. a very tiny animal that lives in cheese or on plants or on other animals.

Mite (about 10 times actual length)

mit ten (mit′ən), a kind of winter glove, covering the four fingers together and the thumb separately. See the picture just below.

mix (miks), 1. put together; stir well together. We mix butter, sugar, milk, and flour for a cake. 2. prepare by putting different things together; as, to mix a cake. 3. join; be mixed. Oil and water will not mix. 4. associate together. Some people do not mix well with a group like ours. 5. **Mix up** sometimes means confuse. I was so mixed up that I used the wrong method in that problem.

Mitten

mixed (mikst), 1. formed of different kinds; as, mixed candy, mixed tea. A **mixed number** is a whole number and a fraction; as, $3\frac{5}{8}$ or $28\frac{3}{4}$. A **mixed chorus** has both men and women singers. 2. confused.

mix ture (miks′chər), 1. a mixing. 2. something that has been mixed. Hash is a mixture.

moan (mōn), 1. a long low sound of suffering. 2. any similar sound; as, the moan of the wind. 3. make moans. 4. complain about; grieve for.

moat (mōt), a deep, wide ditch dug around a castle or town as a protection against enemies. Moats were usually kept filled with water.

mob (mob), 1. a large number of people or animals, usually crowded closely together. 2. the common mass of people. 3. a lawless crowd, easily moved to act without thinking. 4. to crowd around in curiosity, anger, etc. The eager children mobbed the candy man the moment he appeared. 5. to attack with violence as a mob does.

mo bile (mō′bil), movable; moving easily; easy to move. The tongue is mobile. A mobile mind is one that is easily moved by ideas or feelings.

moc ca sin (mok′əsin), 1. a soft shoe, often made from the skin of a deer, worn by North American Indians. 2. a poisonous snake found in the southern part of the United States. See the pictures on this page.

mock (mok), 1. laugh at; make fun of. 2. make fun of by copying or imitating. The thoughtless children mocked the queer speech of the new boy. 3. imitate; copy. 4. not real; imitation; as, a mock king, a mock battle, mock modesty. 5. deceive; disappoint. 6. mockery.

mock er y (mok′əri), 1. making fun of. Their mockery of John hurt his feelings. 2. something to be made fun of. Through his foolishness he became a mockery in the village. 3. a bad copy or imitation. The children's housekeeping was a mockery of their elders'.

mock ing bird (mok′ing bėrd′), a songbird that imitates the notes of other birds.

mode (mōd), 1. the manner or way in which a thing is done. Riding on a donkey is a slow mode of travel. 2. the style, fashion, or custom that prevails; the way most people are doing. Bobbed hair became the mode about 1920.

mod el (mod′əl), 1. a small copy; as, a model of a ship or an engine, a model of an island. 2. a figure in clay or wax that is to be copied in marble, bronze, etc.; as, a model for a statue. 3. make, shape, or fashion; design or plan. Model a bird's nest in clay. 4. the way in which a thing is made; the style. I want a dress like yours, for that model is becoming to me. 5. thing or person to be copied or imitated. Make your father your model, and you will become a fine man. 6. follow as a model. Model yourself on your father. 7. just right or perfect, especially in conduct. Lucy is a model child. 8. person who poses for artists. 9. girl in a store who puts on garments in order to show customers how they look.

Moccasin

Water moccasin (about $3\frac{1}{2}$ ft. long)

mod er ate (mod′ər it for 1, 2, and 3, mod′ər āt for 4), 1. kept or keeping within proper bounds; not extreme; as, moderate expenses, moderate styles. 2. calm; not violent; as, moderate in speech or opinion. 3. fair; medium; not very large or good; as, a moderate profit. 4. make less violent; become less extreme. The wind is moderating.

mod er a tion (mod′ər ā′shən), 1. act of moderating. 2. proper restraint; freedom from excess; temperance. It is all right to eat candy in moderation.

mod ern (mod′ərn), 1. of the present time; of times not long past. The radio is a modern invention. 2. person of modern times.

mod est (mod′ist), 1. not thinking too highly of oneself; not vain; humble. 2. bashful; not bold; shy; held back by a sense of what is fit and proper. 3. decent; not calling attention to one's body. 4. not too great; not asking too much; as, a modest request. 5. quiet; not gaudy; humble in appearance; as, a modest little house.

mod es ty (mod′is ti), 1. freedom from vanity; being modest or humble. 2. being shy or bashful. 3. being decent; not calling attention to one's body.

mod i fi ca tion (mod′i fi kā′shən), 1. modifying or being modified; toning down. With the modification of his anger he could think clearly again. 2. partial alteration or change. With some modification your composition will do for the school paper. 3. modified form; variety.

mod i fy (mod′i fī), 1. change somewhat; as, to modify the terms of a lease. 2. make less; tone down; make less severe or strong. He has modified his demands.

Mo ham med (mō ham′id), the founder of a great religion of Asia and Africa.

Mo ham med an (mō ham′i dən), 1. of Mohammed or the religion founded by him. 2. a follower of Mohammed; a believer in his religion.

moist (moist), slightly wet; damp.

moist en (moi′sən), make moist; become moist.

mois ture (mois′chər), slight wetness; water or other liquid spread in very small drops in the air or on a surface. Dew is moisture that collects at night on the grass.

mo las ses (mə las′iz), a sweet syrup. Molasses is obtained in the process of making sugar from sugar cane.

mold[1] (mōld), 1. a hollow shape in which anything is formed or cast; as, the mold into which melted metal is poured to harden into shape, the mold in which jelly is left to stiffen. 2. the shape which is given by a mold. The molds of ice cream were turkeys and pumpkins. 3. the model according to which anything is shaped. 4. make or form into shape; as, to mold dough into loaves to be baked. Children mold figures out of clay.

mold[2] (mōld), 1. a woolly or furry growth, often greenish in color, which appears on food and other animal or vegetable substances when they are left too long in a warm moist place. 2. become covered with mold.

mold[3] (mōld), loose earth; fine, soft, rich soil. Many wild flowers grow in the forest mold.

mold er (mōl′dər), crumble away; break up gradually into dust.

mold ing (mōl′ding), 1. act of shaping; as, the molding of dishes from clay. 2. something molded; a decorative outline used in architecture. 3. a strip, usually of wood, around the upper walls of a room, used to support pictures, to cover electric wires, etc.

mold y (mōl′di), 1. covered with a fuzzy growth of mold; as, a moldy crust of bread, moldy cheese. 2. musty; stale; as, a moldy smell.

mole[1] (mōl), a spot on the skin, usually brown.

mole[2] (mōl), small animal that lives underground most of the time. Moles have velvety fur and very small eyes that cannot see well.

Mole (about 7 in. long, with the tail)

mole[3] (mōl), barrier built of stone to break the force of the waves; a breakwater.

mo lest (mō lest′), meddle with and injure; interfere with and trouble; disturb. We did not molest the big dog, because we were afraid of him.

molt en (mōl′tən), 1. melted. 2. made by melting and casting; as, a molten image.

mo ment (mō′mənt), 1. a very short space of time; an instant. I started the very moment I got your message. 2. importance. The President is busy on a matter of moment.

mo men tar i ly (mō′mən tãr′i li), 1. for a moment. 2. at every moment; from moment to moment. The danger was increasing momentarily. 3. at any moment. We are expecting the postman momentarily.

mo men tar y (mō′mən tãr′i), lasting only a moment.

mo men tous (mō men′təs), very important. Choosing between peace and war is a momentous decision.

mon arch (mon′ərk), king, queen, emperor, etc.; ruler.

mon ar chy (mon′ər ki), 1. government by a monarch. 2. a nation governed by a monarch.

mon as ter y (mon′əs ter′i), a building where monks or nuns live by themselves.

Mon day (mun′di), the second day of the week, the day after Sunday.

mon ey (mun′i), 1. gold, silver, and copper made into coins for use in buying and selling; paper notes which represent gold or silver. Our bank had an exhibit of the moneys of different nations. 2. wealth.

mon grel (mung′grəl), 1. an animal or plant of mixed breed, especially a dog. 2. of mixed breed, race, origin, or nature; as, a mongrel speech which is half Spanish and half Indian.

mon i tor (mon′i tər), 1. pupil in school with special duties, such as helping to keep order and taking attendance. 2. person who gives advice or warning. 3. a low armored warship having one or more turrets for guns.

monk (mungk), man who gives up everything else for religion and enters a monastery to live.

mon key (mung′ki), 1. an animal of the group most like man. Monkeys are very intelligent animals. 2. one of the smaller animals in this group, not a chimpanzee, gorilla, or other large ape. 3. person, especially a child, who is full of mischief. 4. play; fool; trifle.

Small monkey of India (about 2 ft. long, with the tail)

mon o gram (mon′ə gram), a person's initials combined in one design. Monograms are used on note paper, table linen, clothing, jewelry, etc.

Monogram

mon o plane (mon′ə plān), airplane with a single plane. See the picture just below.

mo nop o ly (mə nop′ə li), 1. the exclusive control of a commodity or service. The gas company in our city has a monopoly. 2. such a control granted by a government. An inventor has a monopoly of his invention for a certain number of years. 3. the exclusive possession or control of something. No one country has a monopoly of virtue.

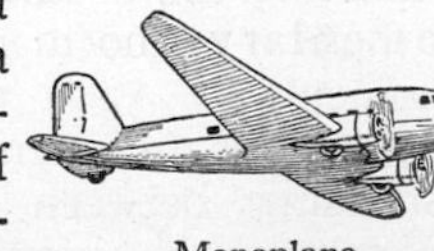

Monoplane

mo not o nous (mə not′ə nəs), 1. continuing in the same tone. 2. not varying; without change. 3. wearying because of its sameness; as, monotonous work.

mo not o ny (mə not′ə ni), 1. sameness of tone or pitch. 2. lack of variety. 3. wearisome sameness.

mon ster (mon′stər), 1. any animal or plant that is very unlike those usually found in nature. A huge sea animal or a cow with two heads is a monster. Imaginary animals having parts of different animals, such as a centaur or mermaid, are monsters. 2. person too wicked to be human. He is a monster of cruelty. 3. huge creature or thing.

mon strous (mon′strəs), 1. huge. 2. wrongly formed or shaped; like a monster. 3. so wrong or absurd as to be almost unheard of. 4. shocking; horrible; dreadful.

month (munth). The year is divided into 12 months. The months I like best are June and October.

month ly (munth′li), 1. of a month; for a month; lasting a month; as, a monthly supply, a monthly salary. 2. done, happening, or paid once a month; as, a monthly meeting, a monthly examination. 3. once a month; every month. Some magazines come monthly. 4. a magazine published once a month.

mon u ment (mon′ū mənt), 1. something set up to keep a person or an event from being forgotten; anything that keeps alive the memory of a person or an event. A monument may be a building, pillar, arch, statue, tomb, or stone. 2. a permanent or prominent instance. The dam in the Grand Canyon is a monument of engineering.

mon u men tal (mon′ū men′təl), 1. of a monument. 2. serving as a monument. 3. like a monument. 4. weighty and lasting; important. A great encyclopedia is a monumental production. 5. very great; as, monumental ignorance.

moo (mü), 1. the sound made by a cow. 2. make this sound.

mood (müd), state of mind or feeling. I am in the mood to play just now; I don't want to study.

mood y (müd′i), 1. likely to have changes of mood. 2. often having gloomy moods. She has been moody ever since she lost her job. 3. gloomy; sullen.

moon (mün), 1. The moon shines in the sky at night. It is a body which revolves around the earth once in 28 days, and looks bright because it reflects the sun's light. 2. A **moon** is about a month or 28 days. The Indians counted time by moons. 3. anything round like the moon. 4. wander about idly; gaze in a dreamy way. Don't moon when you have work to do.

NEW MOON

HALF MOON

FULL MOON

OLD MOON

Phases of the moon

moon beam (mün′bēm′), a ray of moonlight.

moon light (mün′līt′), 1. the light of the moon. 2. having the light of the moon; as, a moonlight night.

moon lit (mün′lit′), lighted by the moon.

moon shine (mün′shīn′), 1. moonlight. 2. foolish talk or ideas; nonsense.

moor[1] (mür), open waste land, especially if heather grows on it.

moor[2] (mür), put or keep (a ship, etc.) in place by means of ropes or chains fastened to the shore or to anchors.

moor ings (mür′ingz), 1. ropes or cables by which a ship is fastened. 2. place where a ship is moored.

moor land (mür′land′), moor; land covered with heather.

moose (müs), an animal like a large deer, living in Canada and the northern part of the United States.

Moose (about 6 ft. high at the shoulder)

mop (mop), 1. a bundle of coarse yarn, rags, or cloth fastened at the end of a stick, for cleaning floors, etc. 2. wash or wipe up; clean with a mop; as, to mop up the floor. 3. wipe tears or sweat from. Joe mopped his brow with his handkerchief. 4. thick head of hair like a mop.

Mop

mope (mōp), 1. give oneself up to being dull, silent, and sad. 2. person who allows himself to be dull, silent, and sad.

mor al (mor′əl), 1. the lesson, inner meaning, or teaching of a fable, a story, or an event. The moral of the story was "Look before you leap." 2. **Morals** means character or behavior. George Washington's morals were excellent. 3. having to do with character, or with the difference between right and wrong. Whether finding should be keeping is a moral question. 4. good in character or conduct; right; just; virtuous according to civilized standards of right and wrong; as, a moral act, a moral man. 5. capable of understanding right and wrong. A little baby is not a moral being. 6. teaching a good lesson; having a good influence.

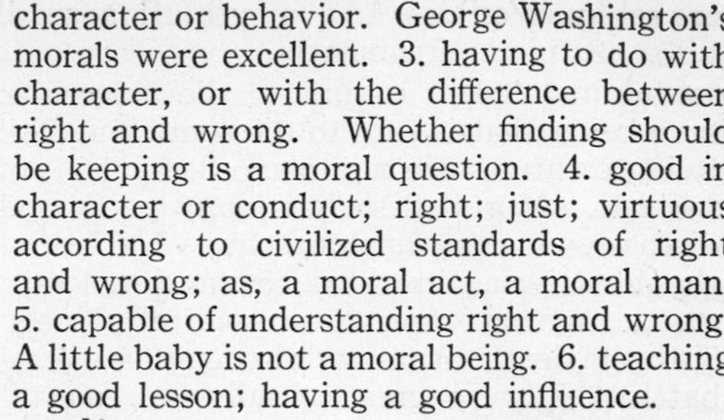

mo ral i ty (mə ral′i ti), 1. the right or wrong of an action. They argued about the morality of dancing on Sunday. 2. doing right; virtue. Dan ranks very high in both intelligence and morality. 3. a system of morals; a set of rules or principles of conduct.

mor al ly (mor′əl i), 1. in a moral manner. 2. in morals; as to morals. Mr. Duke is a good man morally but too stupid for a position of importance. 3. from a moral point of view. 4. practically. I am morally sure that I locked the door.

mo rass (mə ras′), piece of low, soft, wet ground; swamp.

mor bid (môr′bid), 1. unhealthy; sickly; as, morbid fancies, a morbid book, a morbid liking for horrors. 2. caused by disease; characteristic of disease; diseased. Cancer is a morbid growth.

more (mōr), 1. A foot is more than an inch. This plant needs more water. Take one step more. A burn hurts more than a scratch does. The storm grew more and more severe. A horse eats more than a dog does. Tell me more about your farm. 2. We say, "more easily, more truly, more careful, more common." "More common" means commoner. 3. **More or less** means (1) somewhat. Most people are more or less selfish. (2) about. My horse weighs 900 pounds more or less.

more o ver (mōr ō′vər), also; besides. I don't want to go skating. Moreover, the ice is too thin.

Mor mon (môr′mən), 1. member of a church founded in 1830 by Joseph Smith. 2. The sacred book of this church is called the **Book of Mormon.**

morn (môrn), morning.

morn ing (môr′ning), the early part of the day, ending at noon.

mo rose (mə rōs′), gloomy; sullen.

mor row (mor′ō), 1. the following day or time. 2. morning.

mor sel (môr′səl), 1. a mouthful; a small bite. 2. piece; fragment.

mor tal (môr′təl), 1. sure to die sometime. 2. a being that is sure to die sometime. All living creatures are mortals. 3. of man; of mortals. Mortal flesh has many pains and diseases. 4. man; human being. No mortal should strive against God. 5. causing death; as, a mortal wound, a mortal illness. 6. to the death; as, a mortal enemy, a mortal battle. 7. very great; deadly; as, mortal terror. Killing your brother would be a mortal sin.

mor tal ly (môr′təl i), 1. so as to cause death; as, mortally wounded by a bullet. 2. very greatly; bitterly; as, mortally offended.

mor tar (môr′tər), 1. a mixture of lime, sand, and water, for holding bricks or stones together. 2. a very short cannon for shooting shells or fireworks high into the air. 3. a bowl of very hard material, in which substances may be pounded.

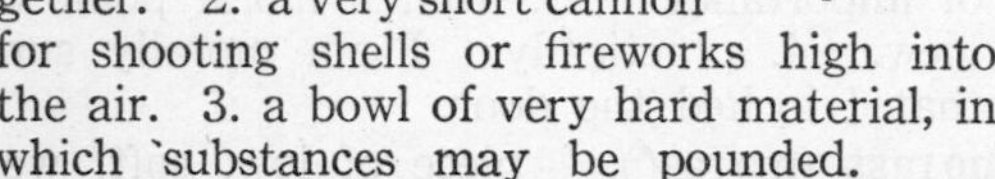

Mortar and pestle

mor ti fi ca tion (môr′ti fi kā′shən), 1. mortifying or being mortified; as, the mortification of the body by fasting. 2. humiliation; cause of humiliation; as, mortification at having spilled food on the table. 3. the death of one part of the body while the rest is alive. The soldier's leg had to be cut off because mortification had set in.

mor ti fy (môr′ti fī), 1. to wound (a person's feelings); make (a person) feel humbled or ashamed. A mother is mortified when her child behaves badly. 2. overcome (bodily desires and feelings) by pain and going without things. The saint mortified his body. 3. die; decay. The injured foot has mortified and must be cut off.

Mosaic design

mo sa ic (mō zā′ik), 1. small pieces of stone, glass, wood, etc., of different colors inlaid to form a design. 2. a picture or design. Mosaics are used in the floors, walls, or ceilings of some fine buildings. 3. anything like a mosaic.

mosque (mosk), a place of worship for followers of Mohammed.

Mosque

mos qui to (məs kē′tō), a small slender insect. The female gives a bite or sting that itches. There are different kinds of mosquitoes; some kinds transmit malaria; some transmit yellow fever.

Mosquito. Line shows actual length.

moss (môs), very small, soft, green plants that grow close together like a carpet on the ground, on rocks, on trees, etc.

moss y (môs′i), 1. covered with moss; as, a mossy bank. 2. like moss; as, mossy green.

most (mōst), 1. You have the most fun on Saturday. The person wins who has most votes. This burn hurts most. That is the most I can do. Most people like ice cream. Most of the toys are broken. 2. We say, "most easily, most truly, most careful, most common." "Most common" means commonest. 3. **For the most part** means mainly; usually. **At most** means not more than.

most ly (mōst′li), mainly; chiefly; almost all.

mote (mōt), a speck of dust.

moth (môth), 1. small winged insect that lays eggs in cloth, fur, etc. Its larvae eat holes in the material. 2. insect very much like a butterfly, but flying mostly at night.

ADULT MOTH

LARVA AT WORK

moth er (muᴛʜ′ər), 1. Mother and father are parents. 2. take care of. Ruth mothers her baby sister. 3. the cause or source of anything. 4. the head of a large community of religious women.

moth er hood (muᴛʜ′ər hu̇d), 1. state of being a mother. The young wife was proud of her motherhood. 2. qualities of a mother. 3. mothers. All the motherhood of the town came to the exhibition of prize babies.

moth er-in-law (muᴛʜ′ər in lô′), the mother of one's husband or wife.

moth er ly (muᴛʜ′ər li), like a mother; like a mother's; kindly.

mo tion (mō′shən), 1. movement; moving; change of position or place; as, the motion of a ship, the motion of one's hand in writing. Anything is in motion which is not at rest. 2. make a movement, as of the hand or head, to show one's meaning; show (a person) what to do by such a motion. He motioned me out. 3. formal suggestion made in a meeting, to be voted on. The motion to adjourn was carried.

mo tion less (mō′shən lis), not moving.

mo tive (mō′tiv), 1. the thought or feeling that makes one act. His motive in going was his wish to please his mother. 2. that makes something move; as, motive power of steam or electricity.

mot ley (mot′li), 1. suit of more than one color worn by clowns. At the party Dick wore motley. 2. of different colors like a clown's suit. 3. a mixture of things that are different. 4. made up of different things; as, a motley collection of old books and toys.

Clown wearing a motley costume

mo tor (mō′tər), 1. engine which makes a thing go; as, an electric motor, a gasoline motor. 2. run by a motor; as, a motor bicycle. 3. an automobile. 4. travel by automobile. 5. having to do with motion. Motor nerves arouse muscles to action.

mo tor boat (mō′tər bōt′), boat that is run by a motor.

mo tor car (mō′tər kär′), automobile.

mo tor cy cle (mō′tər sī′kəl), bicycle run by a motor.

mo tor ist (mō′tər ist), person who travels by automobile, especially one who does it a great deal.

Motorcycle

mot tled (mot′əld), spotted or streaked with different colors.

mot to (mot′ō), 1. a brief sentence adopted as a rule of conduct. "Think before you speak" is a good motto. 2. a sentence, word, or a phrase written or engraved on some object.

mould (mōld), mold.

mould er (mōl′dər), molder.

mould y (mōl′di), moldy.

mound (mound), a bank or heap of earth or stones.

mount[1] (mount), 1. go up; as, to mount a hill or a ladder. 2. get up on; as, to mount a horse, to mount a platform. 3. get on a horse. Paul Revere mounted in haste. 4. put on a horse; furnish with a horse; as, the mounted police. 5. horse for riding. The general had an excellent mount. 6. rise; increase. The cost of living mounts steadily. 7. put in proper position or order for use; fix in a proper setting. We mount photographs on cards. 8. that on which anything is mounted, fixed, supported, or placed; as, the mount for a picture.

mount[2] (mount), mountain; high hill.

moun tain (moun′tən), 1. a very high hill. 2. of mountains; as, mountain air, mountain plants. 3. a very large heap or pile of anything; as, a mountain of rubbish.

moun tain eer (moun′tə nēr′), 1. person who lives in the mountains. 2. person skilled in mountain climbing.

mountain lion, a large American wildcat.

moun tain ous (moun′tə nəs), 1. covered with mountain ranges; as, mountainous country. 2. huge; as, a mountainous wave.

mountain range, a row of mountains; a large group of mountains.

mourn (mōrn), 1. grieve. 2. feel or show sorrow over. Mary mourned her lost doll.

mourn er (mōr′nər), person who mourns, especially at a funeral.

mourn ful (mōrn′fəl), sad; sorrowful.

mourn ing (mōr′ning), 1. wearing of black or some other color to show that a relative has died. 2. draping of buildings, hanging flags down low, etc., as outward signs of sorrow for death. 3. clothes or decorations to show sorrow. 4. of mourning; used in mourning.

mouse (mous for 1, mouz for 2 and 3), 1. a small, gray, gnawing animal. See the picture. The kind that lives in houses is about three or four inches long. Field mice live in the grass. 2. hunt for mice; catch mice for food. Cats and owls go mousing at night. 3. search as a cat does; move about as if searching.

Mouse

mous tache (məs tash′), mustache.

mouth (mouth for 1 and 2, mouтн for 3 and 4), 1. an opening through which an animal takes in food; a space containing tongue and teeth. 2. an opening suggesting a mouth; as, the mouth of a cave, of a river, or of a bottle. 3. utter (words) in an affected, pompous way. I dislike actors who mouth their speeches. 4. seize or rub with the mouth.

mouth ful (mouth′fu̇l), 1. the amount the mouth can easily hold. 2. what is taken in one bite. 3. small amount.

mouth piece (mouth′pēs′), 1. the part of a pipe, horn, etc., that is placed in or at the mouth. 2. person, newspaper, etc., that speaks for others.

mov a ble (müv′ə bəl), 1. that can be moved. Our fingers are movable. 2. that can be carried from place to place as personal belongings can. 3. thing that can be carried from place to place. 4. changing from one date to another in different years. Easter is a movable holy day.

move (müv), 1. put in a different place. Move your chair to the other side of the table. 2. go to another place. 3. change the position of. Do not move your hand. 4. change position. The child moved in his sleep. 5. change one's place of living. We have moved from 96th Street to 110th Street. 6. **Move in** sometimes means to move oneself, one's family, one's belongings, etc., into a new place to live. 7. put or keep in motion; shake; stir. The wind moves the leaves. 8. go. The train moves out slowly. 9. impel; arouse (a person to laughter, anger, pity, etc.). 10. do something about (some matter); act. 11. action taken to bring about some result. Tom's next move was to earn some money. 12. in games, to change to a different square according to rules; as, to move a pawn in chess. 13. the moving of a piece in chess and other games. That was a good move. 14. a player's turn to move. It is your move now. 15. make a move in chess or other games. 16. in a meeting, to bring forward or propose. Mr. President, I move that we have the picnic Friday.

move a ble (müv′ə bəl), movable.

move ment (müv′mənt), 1. moving. We run by movements of the legs. 2. change in the placing of troops or ships. 3. the moving parts (of a machine); a special group of parts that move on each other. The movement of a watch consists of many little wheels. 4. in music, the kind of rhythm and speed a piece has. The movement of a waltz is very different from the movement of a march.

mov er (müv′ər), one that moves.

mov ie (müv′i), moving picture.

mov ing (müv′ing), 1. that moves; as, moving pictures. 2. causing action. John was the moving spirit in planning for the party. 3. touching; pathetic; as, a moving story.

moving picture, picture shown on a screen in which persons or things move.

mow[1] (mō), 1. cut down with a machine or a scythe; as, to mow grass. The men are mowing today. 2. mow the grass or grain from; as, to mow a field. 3. destroy at a sweep or in large numbers, as if by mowing. The firing of the enemy mowed down our men like grass.

mow[2] (mou), 1. the place in the barn where hay, grain, etc., is piled or stored. 2. a pile or stack of hay, grain, etc., in a barn.

mow er (mō′ər), person or thing that mows; as, a lawn mower.

mown (mōn), mowed. New-mown hay is hay that has just been cut.

Mr. or **Mr** (mis′tər), a title put in front of a man's name or the name of his position; as, Mr. Jackson, Mr. Speaker.

Mrs. or **Mrs** (mis′iz), a title put in front of a married woman's name.

Mt., mount; mountain; as, Mt. Whitney.

much (much), 1. There is much water in the sea. A million dollars is much money. Don't eat too much of the cake. How much do you want? 2. We are much pleased when we win. A long rest made her feel much better. 3. Some special meanings are:

make much of, pay much attention to or do much for.

not much of a, not a very good. That is not much of a hat.

too much for, more than a match for.

mu ci lage (mū′si lij), a sticky, gummy substance used to make things stick together.

muck (muk), 1. moist farmyard manure. 2. dirt; filth.

mud (mud), earth so wet that it is soft and sticky; as, mud on the ground after rain, mud at the bottom of a pond.

mud dle (mud′əl), 1. mix up; bring (things) into a mess; as, to muddle a piece of work. 2. think or act in a confused, blundering way; as, to muddle over a problem, to muddle through a difficulty. 3. make confused or stupid. The more you talk, the more you muddle me. 4. a mess; disorder; confusion. When Mother came home, she found the house in a muddle.

mud dy (mud′i), 1. of or like mud; as, muddy footprints on the floor. 2. having much mud; covered with mud; as, a muddy road, muddy shoes. 3. clouded with mud; dull; not pure; as, muddy water, a muddy color. 4. confused; not clear. 5. make muddy; become muddy.

Muff

muff (muf), 1. a covering, usually of fur, into which a woman puts both hands, one at each end, to keep them warm. 2. fail to catch (a ball) when it comes into one's hands. 3. clumsy failure to catch a ball that comes into one's hands. The catcher's muff allowed the runner to score. 4. handle awkwardly.

muf fin (muf′in), a small, round cake made of wheat flour, corn meal, or the like, usually without sugar. Muffins are eaten with butter, and usually served hot.

muf fle (muf′əl), 1. wrap or cover up in order to keep warm and dry. She muffled her throat in a warm scarf. 2. wrap up the head of (a person) in order to keep him from speaking. 3. wrap in something in order to soften or stop the sound. A bell can be muffled with cloth. 4. to dull or deaden (a sound).

muf fler (muf′lər), 1. a wrap or scarf worn for warmth. 2. thing used to deaden sound. An automobile engine has a muffler attached to the exhaust.

mug (mug), 1. a heavy china or metal drinking cup with a handle. 2. amount a mug holds; as, to drink a mug of milk.

Mug

mul ber ry (mul′ber′i), 1. a tree whose leaves are used for feeding silkworms; any of several similar trees. 2. the sweet berry that is the fruit of the mulberry tree. 3. dark purplish red.

Mulberry leaves and berries

mule (mūl), 1. an animal which is half donkey and half horse. See the picture just below. 2. a stupid or stubborn person. 3. a kind of spinning machine.

mu le teer (mū′lə tēr′), a driver of mules.

mul ish (mūl′ish), like a mule; stubborn.

mul let (mul′it), a kind of edible fish. There are red mullets and gray mullets.

mul ti pli ca tion (mul′ti pli-kā′shən), multiplying; being multiplied.

mul ti ply (mul′ti plī), 1. take (a number or quantity) a given number of times. To multiply 6 by 3 means to take 6 three times, making 18. 2. increase in number. As we climbed up the mountain the dangers and difficulties multiplied.

Mule (about 5 ft. high at the shoulder)

mul ti tude (mul′ti tūd or mul′ti tüd), a great number; a crowd.

mum (mum), silent. Keep mum about this; tell no one.

mum ble (mum′bəl), 1. speak indistinctly, as a person does when his lips are partly closed. 2. chew as a person does who has no teeth. The old dog mumbled the crust. 3. act or fact of mumbling; indistinct speech.

mum my (mum′i), a dead body preserved from decay. Egyptian mummies have lasted more than 3000 years.

Egyptian mummy and mummy case

mumps (mumps), a contagious disease that causes swelling of the neck and face and difficulty in swallowing.

munch (munch), chew vigorously and steadily; chew noisily. A horse munches its oats.

mu nic i pal (mū nis′i pəl), 1. of a city or town. The state police assisted the municipal police. 2. having something to do with the affairs of a city, town, or other municipality.

mu nic i pal i ty (mū nis′i pal′i ti), city, town, or other district having local self-government.

mu ni tion (mū nish′ən), 1. material used in war. Munitions are military supplies such as guns, powder, bombs, etc. 2. pertaining to military supplies. A munition plant is a factory for making munitions. 3. provide with military supplies; as, to munition a fort.

mur der (mėr′dər), 1. the unlawful killing of a human being when it is planned beforehand. 2. kill thus. 3. To murder a song or a poem is to give it very badly.

mur der er (mėr′dər ər), one who murders somebody.

mur der ous (mėr′dər əs), 1. able to kill; as, a murderous blow. 2. ready to murder; as, a murderous villain. 3. causing murder; as, a murderous hate.

murk (mėrk), darkness; gloom.

murk y (mėr′ki), dark; gloomy; as, a murky prison.

mur mur (mėr′mər), 1. a soft, low, indistinct sound that rises and falls a little and goes on without breaks; as, the murmur of a stream or of voices in another room. 2. make such a sound. 3. a softly spoken word or speech. 4. say in a murmur. Shy Amy murmured her thanks. 5. a complaint made under the breath, not aloud. 6. complain in this way; grumble.

mus cle (mus′əl), 1. the tissue in the bodies of people and animals which can be tightened or let loose and thus make the body move. 2. a special bundle of such tissue which moves some particular bone or part. You can feel the muscles in your arm. 3. strength.

Frog's legs showing muscles: R, relaxed; C, contracted.

mus cu lar (mus′kū lər), 1. of the muscles; influencing the muscles; as, a muscular strain. 2. having well-developed muscles; strong; as, a muscular arm.

muse (mūz), think; think in a dreamy way.

mu se um (mū zē′əm), the building or rooms in which a collection of objects illustrating science, ancient life, art, or other subjects is kept.

mush (mush), 1. corn meal boiled in water. 2. a soft thick mass. After the heavy rain the old road was a mush.

Mushrooms (stalk 2 to 5 in. high)

mush room (mush′rüm), 1. a small fungus shaped like an umbrella, that grows very fast. Some mushrooms are good to eat; some are poisonous. 2. of or like a mushroom. 3. of very rapid growth; as, a mushroom town.

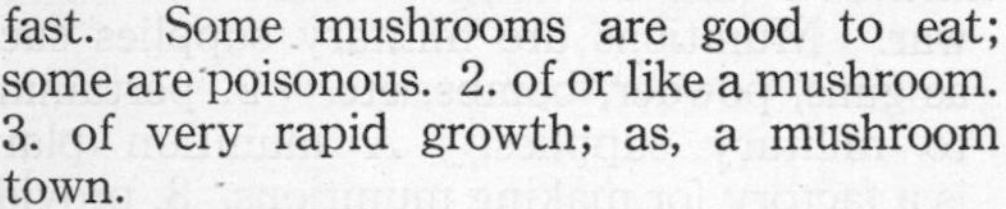

mu sic (mū′zik), 1. the art of making sounds that are beautiful, and putting them together into beautiful arrangements. 2. sounds and compositions made to be beautiful and pleasing to the ear. 3. written or printed signs for tones. Can you read music? **Set to music** means provide (the words of a song) with music. 4. any pleasant sound; as, the music of streams, the music of the wind.

mu si cal (mū′zi kəl), 1. of music; as, musical instruments. 2. sounding beautiful; like music; as, a musical voice. 3. set to music or accompanied by music; as, a musical comedy. 4. fond of music. 5. skilled in music.

musical instrument, piano, violin, or other instrument for producing music.

mu si cal ly (mū′zi kəl i), 1. in a musical manner. 2. in music. She is well educated musically.

mu si cian (mū zish′ən), 1. person skilled in music. 2. person who sings or plays on a musical instrument, especially as a profession or business.

musk (musk), 1. substance with a strong and lasting odor, used in making perfumes. Musk is found in a special gland in one kind of deer. 2. the odor of musk.

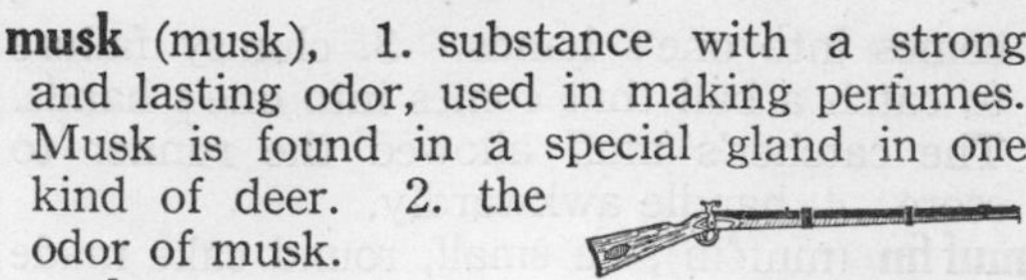

Musket

mus ket (mus′kit), gun used by soldiers before rifles were invented.

mus ket ry (mus′kit ri), 1. muskets. 2. the fire of muskets.

musk mel on (musk′-mel′ən), a kind of sweet, juicy melon. It is also called cantaloupe.

musk ox, arctic animal, somewhat like an ox and even more like a sheep, that has a smell like musk.

Musk ox (about 5 ft. high at the shoulder)

musk rat (musk′rat′), 1. a water animal of North America, like a rat, but larger. 2. its fur. Muskrat is valuable for garments.

Muskrat (length, with the tail, about 20 in.)

mus lin (muz′lin), 1. a thin, fine, cotton cloth, used for dresses, curtains, etc. 2. a heavier cotton cloth, used for sheets, underclothes, etc. 3. made of muslin; as, white muslin curtains.

mus sel (mus′əl), a shellfish having two parts to its shell, living in either salt water or fresh water.

Mussel

must (must), 1. be obliged to; be forced to. All men must die. 2. ought to; should. I must keep my promise. You must read this story. 3. be certain to be, do, etc. The man must be crazy to talk so.

mus tache (məs tash′), 1. hair growing on a man's upper lip. 2. hairs or bristles growing near the mouth of an animal.

mus tang (mus′tang), the small wild or half-wild horse of the American plains.

mus tard (mus′tərd), 1. a plant whose seeds have a sharp hot taste. 2. a powder or paste used for flavoring meats, etc., made from its seeds.

SEED

Mustard

mus ter (mus′tər), 1. assemble; gather together; collect. 2. assembly; collection. 3. summon; as, to muster up courage. 4. bringing together of men or troops for review or service. There was a muster of all the guards.

must n't (mus′ənt), must not.

mus ty (mus′ti), 1. moldy; having a smell or taste suggesting mold or damp; as, a musty room, musty crackers. 2. stale; not used now; as, musty laws about witches.

mute (mūt), 1. silent; not making any sound. The little girl stood mute. 2. dumb; unable to speak. 3. person who cannot speak. 4. a clip or pad put on a musical instrument to soften the sound. 5. put such a clip or pad on. He played the violin with muted strings.

mu ti late (mū′ti lāt), cut, tear, or break off a part of; injure badly by cutting, tearing, or breaking off some part. The victims of the accident were all mutilated; some lost arms, some lost legs.

mu ti neer (mū′ti nēr′), person who takes part in a mutiny.

mu ti nous (mū′ti nəs), rebellious.

mu ti ny (mū′ti ni), 1. open rebellion against lawful authority, especially by sailors or soldiers against their officers. 2. to rebel; take part in a mutiny.

mut ter (mut′ər), 1. speak or utter low and indistinctly, with lips partly closed. 2. complain; grumble. 3. muttered words.

mut ton (mut′ən), meat from a sheep. We had roast mutton for dinner.

mu tu al (mū′chü əl), 1. done, said, felt, etc., by each toward the other; given and received; as, mutual promises, mutual dislike. A family has mutual affection when each person likes the others and is liked by them. 2. each to the other; as, mutual enemies. 3. belonging to each of several; as, our mutual friend.

mu tu al ly (mū′chü əl i), each toward the other.

Muzzle on a dog's head

muz zle (muz′əl), 1. the nose, mouth, and jaws of a four-footed animal. 2. a cover or cage of straps or wires to put over an animal's head to keep it from biting or eating. 3. put such a muzzle on. 4. compel (a person) to keep silent about something. Fear that he might betray his friends muzzled Dick. 5. the open end of a gun, pistol, etc.

my (mī), of me; belonging to me. I learned my lesson.

myr i ad (mir′i əd), a very great number. There are myriads of stars.

myr tle (mėr′təl), 1. an evergreen shrub with shiny leaves and fragrant white flowers. 2. a low, creeping evergreen plant with blue flowers.

Myrtle (def. 1)

my self (mī self′), 1. Myself is used to make a statement stronger. I did it myself. 2. Myself is used instead of I or me in cases like: I can cook for myself. I hurt myself. 3. I don't think much of myself for doing that.

mys te ri ous (mis tēr′i əs), 1. full of mystery; hard to explain. Electricity is mysterious. 2. suggesting mystery.

mys ter y (mis′tər i), 1. a secret; something that is hidden or unknown. 2. secrecy; obscurity. 3. something that is not explained or understood; as, the mystery of God's love.

mys ti fy (mis′ti fī), 1. bewilder purposely; puzzle; perplex. The magician's tricks mystified the audience. 2. make mysterious.

myth (mith), 1. a legend or story, usually one that attempts to account for something in nature. The story of Proserpina is a famous myth to explain summer and winter. 2. any invented story. 3. a made-up person or thing. Amy's wealthy uncle was a myth invented to impress the other girls.

myth i cal (mith′i kəl), 1. of a myth; like a myth; in myths; as, mythical monsters, mythical places. 2. not real; made-up. The Smiths' wealth is merely mythical.

my thol o gy (mi thol′ə ji), 1. myths. 2. the study of myths.

N

N or **N.,** 1. North. 2. Northern.

n., 1. north. 2. northern. 3. noun.

nag[1] (nag), find fault with (a person) all the time; scold; irritate or annoy by peevish complaints. A tired mother sometimes nags her children. When Maud was sick she nagged at everybody.

nag[2] (nag), 1. horse. 2. inferior horse.

nai ad or **Nai ad** (nā′ad), nymph guarding a stream or spring.

nail (nāl), 1. a small, slender piece of metal to be hammered in to hold things together, or to be used as a peg. 2. fasten with a nail or nails. 3. hold or keep fixed; make secure. 4. catch; seize. *Used in common talk.* 5. the hard layer at the end of a finger or toe.

na ked (nā′kid), 1. with no clothes on; bare. A barefoot boy has naked feet. 2. not covered. The **naked truth** is the plain truth without ornament. The **naked eye** is the bare eye not helped by any glass, telescope, or microscope.

na ked ness (nā′kid nis), bareness; naked condition.

name (nām), 1. word or words by which a person, animal, place, or thing is spoken of or to. Our dog's name is Jack. Mary knows all her chickens by name. 2. give a name to. They named the baby Mary. 3. call by name; mention by name. 4. give the right name for. Can you name these flowers? 5. **Know only by name** means know only by hearing about. 6. a word that means any object, or any one of a group of objects. 7. **Call a person names** means call him bad names. 8. reputation; as, to get a bad name, to have a name for honest dealing, to win oneself a name. 9. **In the name of** means (1) acting for. I bought it in my sister's name. (2) for the sake of. 10. mention; give as an instance. She named several cases. 11. appoint; nominate; as, to name Smith for president. 12. choose; settle on.

name less (nām′lis), 1. having no name; as, a nameless grave. 2. not named; as, a book by a nameless writer. 3. that cannot be named or described; as, a strange, nameless longing.

name ly (nām′li), that is to say. Only two pupils got 100 in the test—namely, Arthur and Blanche.

name sake (nām′sāk′), one having the same name as another; especially, one named after another; as, Theodore, namesake of President Theodore Roosevelt.

nap[1] (nap), 1. a short sleep. Baby takes a nap after his dinner. 2. take a short sleep. Grandfather naps in his armchair.

nap[2] (nap), the soft, short, woolly threads or hairs on the surface of cloth; as, the nap on velvet.

nape (nāp), the back of the neck.

naph tha (naf′thə), a liquid made from petroleum, coal tar, etc., used as fuel and to take spots from clothing.

nap kin (nap′kin), 1. piece of cloth used at meals for protecting the clothing or for wiping the lips or fingers; piece of paper used in this way. 2. any similar piece, such as a small towel.

nar cis sus (när sis′əs), a spring flower that grows from a bulb. Jonquils and daffodils are narcissuses.

Narcissus

nar rate (na rāt′), tell the story of.

nar ra tive (nar′ə tiv), 1. story. 2. the telling of stories. 3. that narrates. *Hiawatha* is a narrative poem.

nar row (nar′ō), 1. not wide; having little width. A path a foot wide is narrow. 2. less wide than usual for its kind; as, narrow ribbon. 3. **Narrows** means a narrow part of a river, strait, sound, valley, pass, etc. 4. limited; small. He had only a narrow circle of friends. 5. make narrow; become narrow. 6. not going far from a narrow track; not seeing much beyond a narrow space; as, a narrow mind. 7. close; with a small margin; as, a narrow escape.

na sal (nā′zəl), 1. of the nose; as, nasal bones, a nasal discharge. 2. spoken through the nose. *M*, *n*, and *ng* are nasal sounds or nasals.

na stur tium (nə stėr′shəm), a garden plant with yellow, orange, and red flowers and sharp-tasting seeds and leaves.

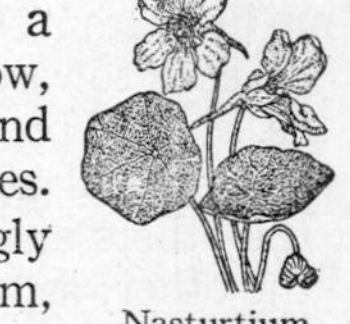
Nasturtium

nas ty (nas′ti), 1. disgustingly dirty; filthy; as, a nasty room, a nasty person, a nasty word or story, a nasty mind. 2. very unpleasant; as, nasty weather, nasty medicines, a nasty cut or fall, a nasty temper.

na tion (nā′shən), 1. a group of people occupying the same country, united under the same independent government, and mostly speaking the same language. 2. a people, race, or tribe; those having the same descent, language, and history; as, the British nation.

na tion al (nash′ən əl), 1. of a nation; belonging to a whole nation; as, national laws, a national disaster. 2. citizen of a nation. Many nationals of Canada visit our country.

na tion al i ty (nash′ən al′i ti), 1. nation. 2. condition of belonging to a nation. Citizens of the same country have the same nationality. 3. condition of being a nation. The Colonies did not attain nationality until they fought with England in 1775-1783.

na tion al ly (nash′ən əl i), as a nation; throughout the nation.

na tive (nā′tiv), 1. person born in a certain country. The natives are the people living in a place, not visitors or foreigners. 2. born in a certain place or country. People born in New York are native sons and daughters of New York. 3. belonging to one because of his birth; as, one's native land. 4. belonging to one because of his country or race; as, one's native language. 5. born in a person; natural; as, native ability, native courtesy. 6. member of an uncivilized race, usually not white. 7. of the natives, especially those not white; as, native customs, native huts. 8. animal or plant that originated in a place. 9. originating, grown, or produced in a certain place. Tobacco is native to America. 10. found in nature; not produced. Native salt is refined for use.

nat u ral (nach′ə rəl), 1. produced by nature; coming in the ordinary course of events. We speak of natural feelings and actions, a natural complexion, natural curls, a natural death, a natural result. 2. belonging to the nature one is born with. It is natural for ducks to swim. 3. in accordance with the facts of some special case; as, a natural conclusion. 4. like nature; as, a natural portrait or natural acting. 5. of or about nature; as, natural history, the natural sciences. 6. in music, not changed in pitch by a sharp or a flat.

nat u ral ist (nach′ə rəl ist), person who makes a study of animals and plants.

nat u ral ly (nach′ə rəl i), 1. in a natural way. Speak naturally; don't try to imitate some actress. 2. by nature; as, a naturally obedient child. 3. as might be expected; of course. She offered me some candy; naturally, I took it.

na ture (nā′chər), 1. the world; all things except those made by man. 2. the regular ways in which things are and act. 3. life without artificial things. 4. quality; character; what a thing really is. It is the nature of robins to fly and to build nests. Women have kinder natures than men. 5. sort; kind. Books of a scientific nature do not interest Helen.

naught (nôt), 1. nothing. 2. zero; 0.

naugh ti ness (nô′ti nis), bad behavior; disobedience; mischief.

naugh ty (nô′ti), bad; not obedient. The naughty child hit his baby sister.

nau se a (nô′shi ə), 1. seasickness. 2. the feeling that one is about to vomit. 3. sick disgust; loathing.

nau ti cal (nô′ti kəl), having something to do with ships, sailors, or navigation.

na val (nā′vəl), 1. of or for warships or the navy; as, naval supplies, a naval officer. 2. having a navy; as, the naval powers.

nav i ga ble (nav′i gə bəl), 1. that ships can travel on. The Mississippi River is deep enough to be navigable. 2. that can be sailed. 3. that can be steered. Without a rudder the ship was not navigable.

nav i gate (nav′i gāt), 1. sail, manage, or steer (a ship, airplane, etc.). 2. sail on or over (a sea or river). 3. sail the seas.

nav i ga tion (nav′i gā′shən), 1. navigating. 2. the art or science of finding a ship's position and course.

nav i ga tor (nav′i gā′tər), 1. one who sails the seas. 2. one who has charge of the navigating of a ship or who is skilled in navigating. 3. an explorer of the seas. The navigator set out on his long voyage. 4. one who finds the position and course of an airship.

na vy (nā′vi), 1. all the ships of war of a country, with their men and the department that manages them. 2. the officers and men of the navy. 3. a fleet of ships.

nay (nā), 1. no. 2. not only that, but also. We are willing, nay, eager to go. 3. vote or voter against something.

near (nēr), 1. at or to a short distance; close; not far; not distant. They searched far and near. Christmas is drawing near. 2. close to; not far from. We live near New York. My birthday is near Christmas. 3. come or draw near to. The vacation was nearing its end. 4. close. It was five o'clock as near as he could guess. 5. **Near at hand** means within easy reach or not far in the future. 6. close in feeling; as, a near friend. 7. short; direct. Take the nearest route. 8. almost; nearly. 9. **Come near doing** means almost do. I came near forgetting. 10. stingy.

near by (nēr′bī′), near; close at hand.

near ly (nēr′li), 1. almost. It is nearly bedtime. 2. closely. This matter concerns you very nearly.

near ness (nēr′nis), being near.

near-sight ed (nēr′sīt′id), not able to see far.

neat (nēt), 1. clean and in order; as, a neat desk, a neat room, a neat dress. 2. able and willing to keep things in order; as, a neat child. 3. well-formed; in proportion; as, a neat design. 4. skillful; clever; as, a neat trick.

neat ness (nēt′nis), being neat.

nec es sar i ly (nes′i sãr′i li), 1. because of necessity. Children are not necessarily naughty. 2. as a necessary result. War necessarily causes misery and waste.

nec es sar y (nes′i sãr′i), 1. that must be. 2. that must be had; that must be done; required. 3. something necessary. Food, clothing, and shelter are necessaries of life.

ne ces si tate (ni ses′i tāt), 1. make necessary. Tom's broken leg necessitated an operation. 2. compel; force.

ne ces si ty (ni ses′i ti), 1. need. We understand the necessity of eating. 2. thing which cannot be done without; necessary thing. Food and water are necessities. 3. that which forces one to act in a certain way. Necessity often drives people to do disagreeable things. 4. poverty. This poor family is in great necessity.

neck (nek), 1. the part of the body that connects the head with the shoulders. 2. the part of a garment that fits the neck; as, the neck of a shirt. 3. narrow part like a neck; as, a neck of land.

neck er chief (nek′ər chif), a cloth worn around the neck.

Necklace

neck lace (nek′lis), string of jewels, gold, silver, beads, etc., worn around the neck as an ornament.

neck tie (nek′tī′), a band or tie worn around the neck and tied in front.

Neckties

nec tar (nek′tər), 1. in Greek stories, the drink of the gods. 2. any delicious drink. 3. a sweet liquid found in many flowers. Bees gather nectar and make it into honey.

need (nēd), 1. something that has to be. **If need be** means if it has to be. **There is no need for it** means it does not have to be. 2. **Have need to** or **need** means must, should, have to, or ought to. I have need to go to town. You need not bother. Why need you go today? Do not stay longer than you need. 3. want; lack. For need of a nail the shoe was lost. 4. be in want of; ought to have; be unable to do without. I need a new hat. 5. thing wanted or lacking; that for which a want is felt. 6. time of need; condition of need. He was a friend in need. He did not fail us in our need. 7. poverty; being poor. This family's need was so great the children did not have shoes.

need ful (nēd′fəl), needed; necessary.

nee dle (nē′dəl), 1. a very slender tool, sharp at one end, and with a hole or eye to pass a thread through, used in sewing. 2. Knitting needles and crochet needles have no eyes. 3. a thin steel pointer on a compass or on electrical machinery. 4. sharp, hollow tool, used for injecting something below the skin. 5. the needle-shaped leaf of a fir tree or pine tree.

A B C

Needles for A, sewing; B, crocheting; C, knitting.

need less (nēd′lis), not needed; unnecessary.

nee dle work (nē′dəl wėrk′), work done with a needle; sewing; embroidery.

need n't (nēd′ənt), need not.

need y (nēd′i), very poor; not having enough to live on; as, a needy family.

ne'er (nãr), never.

neg a tive (neg′ə tiv), 1. saying no. A shake of the head is negative. 2. word or statement that says no or denies. "I won't" is a negative. 3. say no to; deny; vote against. Father negatived our plan. 4. the side that says no or denies in an argument. 5. not positive; consisting in the lack of the opposite. Negative kindness means not being unkind. 6. minus; counting down from zero. Three below zero is a negative quantity. 7. showing the light parts dark and the dark parts light; as, the negative image on a photographic plate. 8. a photographic image in which the lights and shadows are reversed. Prints are made from it.

neg lect (neg lekt′), 1. give too little care or attention to. 2. leave undone. The maid neglected her work. 3. omit; fail. Don't neglect to water the plants. 4. act or fact of neglecting. 5. want of attention to what should be done. 6. being neglected.

neg li gence (neg′li jəns), 1. neglect; lack of proper care or attention. Negligence was the cause of the child's illness. 2. careless conduct; indifference.

neg li gent (neg′li jənt), 1. careless; showing neglect. 2. careless; indifferent.

Ne gro or **ne gro** (nē′grō), 1. person belonging to any of the black races of Africa. 2. a colored person having some black ancestors. Millions of Negroes live in America. 3. of Negroes.

neigh (nā), 1. the sound that a horse makes. 2. make such a sound.

neigh bor (nā′bər), 1. someone who lives in the next house or near by. 2. person or thing near or next to another. The big tree brought down several of its smaller neighbors as it fell. 3. near; neighboring. 4. be near or next to. 5. fellow human being.

neigh bor hood (nā′bər hůd), 1. region near some place or thing. She lives in the neighborhood of the mill. 2. place; district. Is North Street in a good neighborhood? 3. people living near one another; people of a place. The whole neighborhood came to the big party. 4. neighborly feeling or conduct. 5. nearness.

neigh bor ing (nā′bər ing), living or being near; bordering; near. The bird calls from the neighboring woods.

neigh bor ly (nā′bər li), kindly; friendly.

nei ther (nē′ŦHər or nī′ŦHər), 1. not either. 2. nor yet; nor. "They toil not, neither do they spin."

neph ew (nef′ū), son of one's brother or sister; son of one's brother-in-law or sister-in-law.

nerve (nėrv), 1. a fiber or bundle of fibers connecting the brain or spinal cord with the eyes, ears, muscles, glands, etc. 2. mental strength; courage; vigor. It takes nerve to pilot an airplane. 3. arouse strength or courage in. She nerved herself for the struggle. 4. **Strain every nerve** means exert oneself to the utmost.

Human nerves

nerv ous (nėr′vəs), 1. of the nerves. The brain is a part of the nervous system of the human body. 2. having nerves that are weak or out of order; restless or uneasy; easily excited or upset. A person who has been overworking is likely to become nervous. 3. strong; vigorous.

nerv ous ness (nėr′vəs nis), being nervous; being easily upset. Nellie had to overcome her nervousness before she could recite well in school. Nervousness made Bob stutter.

nest (nest), 1. Birds build or choose nests in which to lay eggs and protect their young ones. Some animals and insects make nests in which to live or lay their eggs. Squirrels and wasps have nests. 2. the birds, animals, etc., living in a nest. 3. warm, cozy place; place to sleep. The little girl cuddled down in a nest among the sofa cushions. 4. something suggesting a nest; as, a nest or series of boxes, baskets, or bowls, the smaller fitting within the larger. 5. place that swarms, usually with something bad; as, a nest of thieves. 6. make and use a nest. The bluebirds are nesting here now. 7. place in a nest.

Bird's nest

Wasp's nest

nest egg, 1. egg left in a nest to induce a bird to lay eggs there. 2. money saved.

nes tle (nes′əl), 1. settle oneself or be settled comfortably and cozily; as, to nestle down in a big chair, to nestle close to one's mother, a house nestling among trees. 2. hold closely and comfortably. A mother nestles her baby in her arms.

nest ling (nest′ling), a bird too young to leave the nest.

net[1] (net), 1. string, cord, thread, or hair, knotted together into an open fabric, leaving large or small holes regularly arranged. 2. A fish net is used for catching fish. A mosquito net keeps off mosquitoes. A hair net holds the hair in place. A tennis net is used in the game of tennis. 3. a lacelike cloth. 4. a trap or snare. The guilty boy was caught in the net of his own lies. 5. catch in a net; as, to net fish.

Tennis net

net[2] (net), 1. remaining after deductions; free from deductions. A net gain or profit is the actual gain after all working expenses have been paid. The net weight of a glass jar of candy is the weight of the candy itself. The net price of a book is the real price, from which no deduction can be made. 2. to gain. The sale netted me a good profit.

neth er (neŦH′ər), lower.

net tle (net′əl), 1. a kind of plant having sharp leaf hairs that sting the skin when touched. 2. sting the mind; irritate; make angry; vex.

Nettle

net work (net′wėrk′), 1. netting; net. 2. any system of lines that cross; as, a network of vines, a network of railroads. 3. group of connected radio stations.

neu tral (nū′trəl or nü′trəl), 1. neither one thing nor the other. 2. on neither side in a quarrel or war. 3. a neutral person or country; one not taking part in a war. 4. having little or no color; grayish.

nev er (nev′ər), 1. not ever; at no time. 2. not at all.

nev er more (nev′ər mōr′), never again.

nev er the less (nev′ər ᴛʜə les′), however; none the less; for all that; in spite of it. She was very tired; nevertheless she kept on working.

new (nū or nü), 1. never having been before; now first made, thought out, known or heard of, felt or discovered; as, a new school, a new house, a new idea. 2. lately grown, come, or made; not old; now first used; not worn or used up; as, new potatoes, new cheese, new furniture, new dresses. 3. as if new; fresh; as, to go on with new courage. 4. different; changed; as, to have a new teacher; to feel like a new person. 5. later; modern; recent; as, the new dances, the new woman. 6. not yet used (to). She is still new to the work. 7. beginning again. The new moon is the moon when seen as a thin crescent. 8. newly; as, a newborn babe, new-fallen snow, a new-found friend, new-laid eggs, new-mown hay. 9. anew; again.

new born (nū′bôrn′ or nü′bôrn′), 1. just born; as, a newborn baby. 2. ready to start a new life; born again.

new com er (nū′kum′ər or nü′kum′ər), person who has just come or who came not long ago.

New England, the northeastern part of the United States. Maine, New Hampshire, Vermont, Massachusetts, Rhode Island, and Connecticut are the New England States.

new ly (nū′li or nü′li), lately; recently; as, newly discovered, newly painted.

news (nūz or nüz), something told as having just happened; information about something which has just happened or will soon happen. The news that our teacher was leaving made us sad.

news pa per (nūz′pā′pər or nüz′pā′pər), sheets of paper printed every day or week, telling the news, carrying advertisements, and having stories, poems, jokes, and useful information.

New Testament, the part of the Bible which contains the life and teachings of Christ recorded by His followers, together with their own experiences and teachings.

New World, North and South America.

New Year or **New Year's,** January 1.

New York, 1. an Eastern State of the United States. 2. seaport in southeastern New York State, at the mouth of the Hudson River. It is the largest city in the United States.

next (nekst), 1. nearest. Who is the girl next to Alice? 2. having nothing of the same kind coming in between. The next day after Sunday is Monday. 3. nearest to. We live in the house next the church. 4. in the next place. I am going to do my arithmetic problems next.

Ni ag a ra (nī ag′ə rə), a short river and a great waterfall, on the boundary between the United States and Canada. **Niagara Falls** is one of the great sights of the world.

nib ble (nib′əl), 1. eat away with quick small bites, as a rabbit or a mouse does. 2. bite gently. A fish nibbles at the bait. 3. a nibbling; small bite.

nice (nīs), 1. pleasing; agreeable; satisfactory; as, a nice day, a nice ride, a nice child. 2. very particular; dainty; having a refined or critical taste; as, to be nice in one's habits or dress. 3. very fine; subtle; as, a nice distinction, a nice point or shade of meaning. 4. precise; exact; making very fine distinctions; as, weighed in the nicest scales.

niche (nich), 1. a recess or hollow in a wall for a statue, vase, etc. 2. suitable place or position; place into which a person fits.

Vase in a niche

nick (nik), 1. a place where a small bit has been cut or broken out. She hit a saucer and made a nick in the edge of it. 2. make a nick or nicks in. 3. **In the nick of time** means just at the right moment.

nick el (nik′əl), 1. a metal that looks like silver and is somewhat like iron. Nickel is much used in mixtures with other metals. 2. a coin made of nickel; a United States five-cent piece.

nick name (nik′nām′), 1. a name added to a person's real name, or used instead of it. Ed is a nickname for Edward. 2. give a nickname to. They nicknamed the tall boy "Shorty" as a joke.

niece (nēs), daughter of one's brother or sister; daughter of one's brother-in-law or sister-in-law.

nigh (nī), 1. near. 2. nearly.

night (nīt), 1. the time between evening and morning; the time from sunset to sunrise, especially when it is dark. 2. evening.

night cap (nīt′kap′), a cap to be worn in bed.

night fall (nīt′fôl′), the coming of night.

night in gale (nīt′ən gāl), a small reddish-brown bird of Europe that has a very sweet song.

Nightingale (6 to 7 in. long)

night ly (nīt′li), 1. happening every night. 2. every night. Performances are given nightly except on Sunday. 3. happening at night. 4. at night.

night mare (nīt′mãr′), 1. very distressing dream. 2. very distressing experience. 3. horrible fear or dread.

nim ble (nim′bəl), 1. quick-moving; active and sure-footed; light and quick. Goats are nimble in climbing among the rocks. 2. clever; quick to understand and to reply. The boy had a nimble mind, and could think up excuses as quickly as his mother or teacher could ask for them.

nim bly (nim′bli), quickly without falling or stumbling.

nine (nīn), 1. one more than eight; 9. Six and three make nine. 2. set of nine persons or things.

nine teen (nīn′tēn′), nine more than ten; 19.

nine ty (nīn′ti), nine times ten; 90.

ninth (nīnth), 1. next after the 8th. 2. one of 9 equal parts.

nip[1] (nip), 1. squeeze tight and quickly; pinch; bite. The crab nipped my toe. 2. tight squeeze; pinch; sudden bite. 3. injure; hurt at the tips; spoil. Some of our tomato plants were nipped by frost. **Nip in the bud** means spoil or check at the start. 4. injury caused by frost.

nip[2] (nip), a small drink.

ni tro gen (nī′trə jən), a gas without color, taste, or odor which forms about four fifths of the air.

no (nō), 1. No means the same as shaking your head. Can a cow fly? No. 2. not any. Dogs have no wings. Eat no more. 3. a vote against. The noes won.

no bil i ty (nō bil′i ti), 1. people of noble rank. Earls, counts, princes, and kings belong to the nobility. 2. noble birth; noble rank. 3. noble character.

no ble (nō′bəl), 1. high and great by birth, rank, or title. 2. person high and great by birth, rank, or title. 3. high and great in character; showing greatness of mind; good; as, a noble knight, a noble deed. 4. excellent; fine; splendid; magnificent. Niagara Falls is a noble sight.

no ble man (nō′bəl mən), man of noble rank, title, or birth.

no bly (nō′bli), in a noble manner; as a noble person would do.

no bod y (nō′bod i), 1. no one; no person. 2. person of no importance.

noc tur nal (nok tėr′nəl), 1. of the night. 2. in the night. 3. active in the night. The owl is a nocturnal bird.

nod (nod), 1. bow (the head) slightly and raise it again quickly. 2. say yes by nodding. 3. a nodding of the head. He gave us a nod as he passed. 4. Let the head fall forward and bob about when sleepy or falling asleep. 5. be sleepy; become careless and dull. 6. droop, bend, or sway back and forth; as, nodding plumes.

noise (noiz), 1. a sound that is not musical or pleasant. 2. a sound. 3. tell; spread the news of. It was noised abroad that the king was dying.

noise less (noiz′lis), making no noise; making little noise; as, a noiseless typewriter.

nois i ly (noiz′i li), in a noisy manner.

nois y (noiz′i), 1. making much noise; as, a noisy crowd, a noisy boy, a noisy little clock. 2. full of noise; as, a noisy house, a noisy street, the noisy city. 3. having much noise with it; as, a noisy game, a noisy quarrel.

no mad (nō′mad), member of a tribe which moves from place to place to have food or pasture for its cattle.

nom i nate (nom′i nāt), name as candidate for an office. Three times Bryan was nominated for President, but he was never elected.

nom i na tion (nom′i nā′shən), 1. naming as candidate for office. The nominations for president of the club were written on the blackboard. 2. selection for office; appointment to office. 3. being nominated. Mary's friends were pleased by her nomination.

nom i nee (nom′i nē′), person nominated for an office or to be a candidate for election to an office.

none (nun), 1. not any. 2. no one; not one. 3. no persons. 4. not at all.

non sense (non′sens), words, ideas, or acts without meaning; foolish talk or doings; a plan or suggestion that is foolish. Father says "Nonsense!" when he hears something that cannot be true or is very foolish.

nook (nůk), 1. cozy little corner. 2. hidden spot; sheltered place.

noon (nün), 12 o'clock in the daytime; the middle of the day.

noon day (nün′dā′), noon.

no one or **no-one,** nobody.

noon tide (nün′tīd′), noon.

noose (nüs), 1. loop with a slip knot that tightens as the string or rope is pulled. Nooses are used especially in lassos and snares. 2. a snare or bond; as, the noose of marriage. 3. catch with a noose; snare.

Noose

nor (nôr), 1. and no. There was neither river nor stream in that desert. He had neither food nor drink left. 2. neither. Nor silver nor gold can buy it. 3. and not. I have not gone there, nor will I ever go.

nor mal (nôr′məl), 1. of the usual standard; regular; usual. The normal temperature of the human body is 98.6 degrees. 2. the usual state or level. Tom is ten pounds above normal for his age.

nor mal ly (nôr′məl i), in the normal way; regularly; if things are normal. A child normally begins to lose his first teeth at six years.

north (nôrth), 1. the direction to which a compass needle points; the direction to your right as you face the setting sun. See the diagram. 2. toward the north; farther toward the north. Drive north for the next mile. 3. **North of** means farther north than. Canada is north of the United States. 4. from the north; as, a north wind. 5. in the north; living in the north. 6. the part of any country toward the north. In the United States, **the North** means the States north of Maryland, the Ohio River, and Missouri.

NORTH
WEST EAST
SOUTH

North America, the northern continent of the Western Hemisphere. The United States, Mexico, and Canada are countries in North America.

North American, 1. of or having to do with North America or its people. 2. native or inhabitant of North America.

north east (nôrth′ēst′), 1. halfway between north and east. 2. a northeast direction. 3. a place that is in the northeast part or direction. 4. toward the northeast. At this point the road turns northeast. 5. from the northeast; as, a northeast wind. 6. in the northeast; as, the northeast district.

north east ern (nôrth′ēs′tərn), 1. toward the northeast. 2. from the northeast. 3. of the northeast.

north er ly (nôr′ᴛʜər li), 1. toward the north. The windows face northerly. 2. from the north. 3. of the north.

north ern (nôr′ᴛʜərn), 1. toward the north; as, the northern side of a building. 2. from the north. 3. of the north. He has traveled in northern countries. 4. of the North of the United States; as, a Northern city.

northern lights, streamers and bands of light appearing in the sky in northern regions.

north ern most (nôr′ᴛʜərn mōst), farthest north.

north ward (nôrth′wərd), 1. toward the north; north. He walked northward. The orchard is on the northward slope of the hill. Rocks lay northward of the ship's course. 2. northward part, direction, or point.

north wards (nôrth′wərdz), northward.

north west (nôrth′west′), 1. halfway between north and west. 2. a northwest direction. 3. a place that is the northwest part or direction. 4. toward the northwest. The road from Chicago to Minneapolis runs northwest. 5. from the northwest; as, a northwest wind. 6. in the northwest. The northwest climate was good for wheat.

north west ern (nôrth′wes′tərn), 1. toward the northwest. 2. from the northwest. 3. of the northwest; pertaining to the northwest.

nose (nōz), 1. the part of the face or head just above the mouth. The nose has openings for breathing and smelling. 2. sense of smell. Most dogs have a good nose. A mouse has a good nose for cheese. 3. to smell; discover by smell; smell out. 4. rub with the nose. The cat nosed her kittens. 5. sniff (at). 6. part that stands out, especially the bow of a ship or boat. At last we saw the little steamer's nose poking around the cliff. 7. push (its way) with the nose. The little boat nosed along between the rocks. 8. search (for); pry (into).

nos tril (nos′tril), either of the two openings in the nose. Air is breathed into the lungs, and smells come into the sensitive parts of the nose, through the nostrils.

not (not). Not says "no." Cold is not hot. Six and two do not make ten.

no ta ble (nō′tə bəl), 1. worth noticing; striking; remarkable; important; as, a notable event, a notable man. 2. person who is notable. Many notables came to the President's reception.

no ta bly (nō′tə bli), in a notable manner; to a notable degree.

notch (noch), 1. a V-shaped nick or cut made in an edge or on a curving surface. The Indians cut notches on a stick to keep count of numbers. 2. make a notch or notches in. 3. deep, narrow pass or gap between mountains.

Notches on a stick

note (nōt), 1. a short sentence, phrase, or single word, written down to remind one of what was in a book, a speech, an agreement, etc. Sometimes our teacher has us take notes of what we read. 2. write down as a thing to be remembered. 3. a comment, remark, or piece of information added concerning a word or a passage in a book, often to help pupils in studying the book. Her copy of *Evangeline* has many helpful notes at the back. 4. very short letter. 5. letter from one government to another. 6. a written promise to pay a certain amount of money at a certain time. 7. greatness; fame. Washington is a person of note. 8. observe; notice; give attention to. Now note what I do next. 9. in music, the written sign to show the pitch and the length of a sound. 10. a single musical sound. Sing this note for me. 11. a song or call of a bird. 12. significant sound or way of expression. There was a note of anxiety in her voice. 13. **Take note of** means give attention to or observe.

A B C D

Notes in music: A, whole note; B, half note; C, quarter note; D, eighth note.

note book (nōt′bu̇k′), a book in which to write notes of things to be learned or remembered.

not ed (nōt′id), well-known; specially noticed; famous. Samson was noted for his strength.

note wor thy (nōt′wėr′ᴛʜi), worthy of notice; remarkable. The first flight across the Atlantic was a noteworthy achievement.

noth ing (nuth′ing), 1. not anything. 2. thing of no value or importance. 3. zero. 4. not at all. He was nothing wiser than he was before.

no tice (nō′tis), 1. heed; attention. Take no notice of her. A sudden movement or sound catches one's notice. 2. see; take note of; give attention to. I noticed a hole in my stocking. 3. warning. The driver sounded his horn to give notice that he was going to turn the corner. 4. a written or printed sign; a paper posted in a public place; a large sheet of paper giving information or directions. We saw a notice of today's moving picture outside the theater. 5. a written or printed account in a newspaper. There is a notice in the paper describing Mary's birthday party.

no tice a ble (nō′tis ə bəl), 1. easily seen or noticed. This kitten was noticeable because it was the only one of the five which was yellow. 2. worth noticing.

no ti fy (nō′ti fī), let know; inform; give notice to; announce to. Our teacher notified us that there would be a test on Monday. We have a letter notifying us that Uncle John will visit us soon.

no tion (nō′shən), 1. idea. He has no notion of what I mean. 2. opinion; view; belief. One common notion is that red hair goes with a quick temper. 3. foolish idea or opinion. That silly girl has too many notions. 4. **Notions** sometimes means small useful articles, such as pins, thread, tape, etc.

no to ri ous (nō tō′ri əs), well-known or commonly known, especially because of something bad. That notorious criminal has been sent to prison. Philip is a notorious crybaby.

not with stand ing (not′wiᴛʜ stan′ding), 1. in spite of. Notwithstanding her naughtiness, I love my little girl. 2. in spite of; nevertheless. It is raining; but I shall go, notwithstanding.

nought (nôt), 1. nothing; naught. All my work came to nought. 2. zero; 0. Put two noughts after a six to make six hundred.

noun (noun), a word used as the name of a person, thing, quality, or event. Words like *John*, *table*, *school*, *kindness*, *skill*, and *party* are nouns.

nour ish (nėr′ish), 1. feed; make grow, or keep alive and well, with food. Milk is all we need to nourish a small baby. 2. maintain; foster; as, to nourish a hope.

nour ish ment (nėr′ish mənt), food.

Nov., November.

nov el (nov′əl), 1. new; strange; of a new kind or nature. Flying gives people a novel sensation. 2. a story with characters and a plot, long enough to fill one or more volumes.

nov el ist (nov′əl ist), writer of novels.

nov el ty (nov′əl ti), 1. newness. The novelty of washing dishes soon wore off, and then Mary did not want to do it any more. 2. new or unusual thing. Staying up late was a novelty to the children, and they enjoyed it. **Novelties** are small, unusual articles, toys, cheap jewelry, and the like.

No vem ber (nō vem′bər), the 11th month of the year; the month just before December.

nov ice (nov′is), 1. beginner; one who is new to what he is doing. Novices are likely to make some mistakes. 2. person who is not yet a monk or nun, but is on trial.

now (nou), 1. at this time. We do not believe in ghosts now. 2. by this time. She must have reached the city now. 3. this time; as, by now, until now, from now on. 4. since; now that. Now I am older, I have changed my mind. Now you mention it, I do remember. 5. as things are; as it is. Now I can never believe you again. 6. then; next. 7. Now is used in many sentences where it makes very little difference in the meaning. Now what do you mean? Oh, come now! Now you knew that was wrong. **Now and then** or **now and again** means from time to time; once in a while.

now a days (nou′ə dāz′), at the present day; in these times. Nowadays people travel in automobiles.

no way (nō′wā), in no way; not at all.

no where (nō′hwãr), in no place; at no place; to no place.

no wise (nō′wīz), in no way; not at all.

nox ious (nok′shəs), very harmful; poisonous. Poison ivy is a noxious plant.

noz zle (noz′əl), a tip put on a hose, etc., forming an outlet. See the picture below.

HOSE NOZZLE

nu cle us (nū′kli əs or nü′kli əs), 1. a central part or thing around which other parts or things are collected. 2. a beginning, to which additions are to be made. John's five-dollar bill became the nucleus of a flourishing bank account.

nudge (nuj), 1. push slightly; jog with the elbow to attract attention, etc. 2. a slight push or jog.

nug get (nug′it), lump; valuable lump; as, nuggets of gold, nuggets of wisdom.

nui sance (nū′səns or nü′səns), thing or person that annoys, troubles, offends, or is disagreeable. Flies are a nuisance.

numb (num), 1. having lost the power of feeling or moving. My fingers are numb with cold. 2. make numb. 3. dull the feelings of. When her baby died Mrs. Brown was numbed with grief.

num ber (num′bər), 1. A number tells how many. Two, thirteen, twenty-one, fifty, and one hundred are numbers. Number means the count or sum of a group of things or persons. The number of boys in our class is twenty. 2. a figure or mark that stands for a number. 2, 7, and 9 are numbers. 3. count; find out the number of. 4. give a number to. The pages of this book are numbered. 5. be or amount to a given number. The States in the Union number forty-eight. 6. a large or small quantity. We saw a number of birds. There were numbers who stayed out of school that day. 7. reckon as one of a class or collection. She numbered me among her best friends. 8. amount to; reach the number of. 9. being more; as, to win a battle by force of numbers. 10. an issue of a magazine. The May number of *Boys' Life* is unusually good. 11. limit; fix the number of. 12. in grammar, a word form or ending which shows whether one or more than one is meant. *Boy*, *ox*, and *this* are in the singular number; *boys*, *oxen*, and *these* are in the plural number. 13. **Without number** means too many to count.

num ber less (num′bər lis), very numerous; too many to count. There are numberless fish in the sea.

nu mer al (nū′mər əl or nü′mər əl), 1. a figure or group of figures standing for a number. 7, 25, 463, III, and XIX are numerals. 2. of numbers; standing for a number.

nu mer a tor (nū′mər ā′tər or nü′mər ā′tər), the number above the line in a fraction, which shows how many parts are taken. In $\frac{3}{8}$, 3 is the numerator.

nu mer i cal (nū mer′i kəl or nü mer′i kəl), having to do with number or numbers; in numbers; by numbers.

nu mer ous (nū′mər əs or nü′mər əs), 1. very many. The child asked numerous questions. 2. in great numbers. He has a numerous acquaintance among politicians.

nun (nun), woman who gives up everything else for religion, and with other religious women lives a life of prayer and worship. Some nuns teach; others care for the sick.

nup tial (nup′shəl), 1. of marriage or weddings. 2. **Nuptials** means a wedding.

nurse (nėrs), 1. person who takes care of the sick or the old, or is trained to do this. Hospitals employ nurses. 2. be or act as a nurse for sick people; wait on or try to cure the sick. 3. woman who cares for and brings up the young children or babies of other persons. Mrs. Jones has hired a new nurse. 4. act as a nurse; have charge of or bring up (children). 5. one who feeds and protects. 6. nourish; make grow; protect; treat with special care; as, to nurse a hatred in the heart, to nurse a plant, to nurse a sore arm. 7. hold closely; clasp fondly. 8. give milk to (a baby). 9. suck milk from a mother.

nurse maid (nėrs′mād′), girl or woman employed to care for children.

nurs er y (nėr′sər i), 1. a room set apart for the use of the children of the household. 2. A **day nursery** is a place where babies and small children are cared for during the day. 3. a piece of ground or place where young plants are raised for transplanting or sale.

nur ture (nėr′chər), 1. rear; bring up; care for; foster; train. She nurtured the child as if he had been her own. 2. rearing; bringing up; training; education. The two sisters had received very different nurture, one at home and the other at a convent. 3. nourish. 4. nourishment.

nut (nut), 1. a dry fruit or seed with a hard woody or leathery shell and a kernel inside which is good to eat. 2. the kernel of a nut. 3. a small block, usually of metal, which screws on to a bolt to hold the bolt in place.

BOLT NUT

Bolt with nut screwed on

nut crack er (nut′krak′ər), 1. an instrument for cracking the shells of nuts. 2. a bird of the crow family which feeds on nuts.

Nutcracker

nut meg (nut′meg), a hard spicy seed about as big as a marble, obtained from the fruit of a tree growing in the far East. The seed is grated and used for flavoring food.

nu tri tion (nū trish′ən or nü trish′ən), 1. food; nourishment. 2. process by which food is used in the body.

nu tri tious (nū trish′əs or nü trish′əs), nourishing; valuable as food.

nut ting (nut′ing), gathering nuts.

NW or **N.W.,** northwest.

nymph (nimf), a lesser goddess of nature, who lived in seas, rivers, fountains, hills, woods, or trees.

O

O (ō), 1. O is used before a person's name or title in beginning to speak; as, O King, hear my prayer! 2. O is the same word as **Oh.** O dear me! O joy!

oak (ōk), 1. any of several kinds of trees found in all parts of the world, having leaves like those in the picture and nuts which are called acorns. The wood is very hard and very useful. 2. of an oak; as, oak leaves. 3. the wood of the oak tree. 4. made of oak wood. See the picture on the next page.

oak en (ōk′ən), made of oak wood; as, an oaken chest.

oar (ōr), 1. a long pole with a flat end, used in rowing. Sometimes an oar is used to steer a boat. 2. use an oar; row. 3. person who rows. Dick is the best oar in the crew.

Oar

o a ses (ō ā′sēz), more than one oasis.

o a sis (ō ā′sis), fertile spot in the desert where there is water.

oat (ōt), a plant whose grain is used for food. **Oats** means the grain of the oat plant.

oat en (ōt′ən), 1. made of oats or oatmeal. 2. made of oat straw.

oath (ōth), 1. a solemn promise or statement which God is called on to witness. Mr. Jones made an oath that he would tell the whole truth and nothing but the truth. 2. the name of God used as an exclamation to add force or to express anger. 3. a curse; word used in swearing. The pirate cursed us with fearful oaths.

Oak: leaf and acorn
A, European;
B, American.

oat meal (ōt′mēl′), 1. oats made into meal; ground oats; rolled oats. 2. porridge made from oatmeal.

o be di ence (ō bē′di əns), doing what one is told; submitting to authority or law. Parents desire obedience from their children. Soldiers act in obedience to the orders of their officers.

o be di ent (ō bē′di ənt), doing what one is told; willing to obey. The obedient dog came at his master's whistle.

o bei sance (ō bā′səns), 1. a movement of the body expressing deep respect; deep bow. The men made obeisance to the king. 2. deference; homage.

ob e lisk (ob′ə lisk), a tapering, four-sided shaft of stone with a top shaped like a pyramid.

Obelisk

o bey (ō bā′), 1. do what one is told to do. The dog obeyed and went home. 2. follow the orders of. We obey our father. 3. yield to the control of. A car obeys the driver. A horse obeys the rein.

ob ject (ob′jikt for 1, 2, 3, and 4, əb jekt′ for 5 and 6), 1. thing; something that can be seen or touched. What is that object by the fence? A dark object moved between me and the door. A baby is likely to put any small object into its mouth. 2. person or thing toward which feeling, thought, or action is directed. The blind cripple was an object of charity. Tom was the object of his dog's affection. 3. person or thing that is absurd, funny, or foolish. What an object you are with your hair pulled back that way! 4. thing aimed at; end; purpose. My object in coming here was to get Mary's address. 5. make objections; be opposed; feel dislike. Many people object to loud noise. 6. give as a reason against something. Mother objected that the weather was too wet to play outdoors.

ob jec tion (əb jek′shən), 1. something said in objecting; a reason or argument against something. Mary's objection to the new dress was that it was too long. 2. a feeling of disapproval or dislike.

ob jec tion a ble (əb jek′shən ə bəl), 1. likely to be objected to. 2. unpleasant; disagreeable.

ob jec tive (əb jek′tiv), 1. something aimed at. My objective this summer will be learning to drive a car. 2. real; existing outside the mind as an actual object, and not merely in the mind as an idea.

ob li ga tion (ob′li gā′shən), 1. duty under the law; duty due to a promise or contract; duty on account of social relationship or kindness received. Taxes are an obligation which may fall on everybody. The man is really under obligation to paint our house first. A wife's first obligation is to her husband and children. 2. binding power (of a law, promise, sense of duty, etc.). The one who did the damage is under obligation to pay for it.

o blige (ə blīj′), 1. bind by a promise, contract, or duty; compel; force. The law obliges parents to send their children to school. I am obliged to leave early to catch my train. 2. bind by a favor or service; do a favor to. Kindly oblige me by closing the door. Grace obliged the company with a song.

o blig ing (ə blīj′ing), willing to do favors; helpful.

ob lique (əb lēk′), slanting; not straight up and down; not straight across. AB, CD, EF, and GH are oblique lines. An oblique angle is any angle that is not a right angle. Ann gave an oblique glance to one side.

ob lit er ate (əb lit′ər āt), blot out; remove all traces of; destroy. The heavy rain obliterated all footprints.

ob liv i on (əb liv′i ən), 1. condition of being entirely forgotten. Many ancient cities have long since passed into oblivion. 2. forgetfulness. Grandfather sat by the fire in peaceful oblivion.

ob liv i ous (əb liv′i əs), 1. forgetful; not mindful. The book was so interesting that I was oblivious of my surroundings. 2. bringing forgetfulness; as, an oblivious slumber.

ob long (ob′lông), 1. longer than broad; as, an oblong loaf of bread. 2. a rectangle that is not a square.

Oblong

o boe (ō′bō), a wooden wind instrument in which the tone is produced by a double reed.

ob scure (əb skūr′), 1. not distinct; not clear; as, an obscure shape, obscure sounds. I had only an obscure view of the battle. 2. hidden; not easily discovered; as, an obscure meaning. 3. not well known; attracting no notice; as, an obscure little village, an obscure poet, an obscure job. 4. dark; dim. 5. make obscure; dim; darken; hide from view. Clouds obscure the sun.

Man playing an oboe

ob scu ri ty (əb skūr′i ti), 1. dimness; lack of light. The dog hid in the obscurity of the thick bushes. 2. lack of clearness; difficulty in being understood. The obscurity of the paragraph makes several interpretations possible. 3. being unknown. Lincoln rose from obscurity to fame.

ob serv ance (əb zėr′vəns), 1. act of observing or keeping laws or customs; as, the observance of the Sabbath. 2. act performed as a sign of worship or respect; religious ceremony.

ob serv ant (əb zėr′vənt), 1. observing; quick to notice; watchful. If you are observant in the fields and woods, you will find many flowers that others fail to notice. 2. careful in observing a law, rule, custom, etc. A careful driver is observant of the traffic rules.

ob ser va tion (ob′zər vā′shən), 1. the act, habit, or power of seeing and noting. By his trained observation the doctor knew that the man was not really dead. 2. the fact of being seen; notice; being seen. The tramp avoided observation. 3. something seen and noted. The student of bird life kept a record of his observations. 4. remark. "Haste makes waste," was father's observation as Harry spilled the ice cream.

ob serv a to ry (əb zėr′və tō′ri), 1. a building fitted up for observing the stars and other heavenly bodies, or sometimes for observing other facts and happenings of nature. See the picture just below. 2. high place or building giving a wide view.

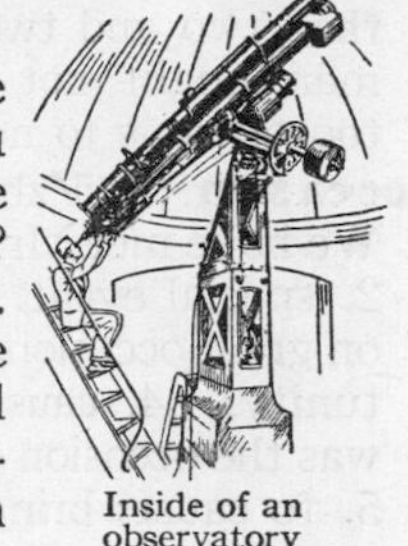
Inside of an observatory

ob serve (əb zėrv′), 1. see and note; notice. Did you observe anything strange in the man's conduct? 2. examine closely; study. An astronomer observes the stars. 3. remark. "Bad weather," the captain observed. 4. keep; follow in practice; as, to observe silence, to observe a rule. 5. show regard for; celebrate; as, to observe Christmas.

ob so lete (ob′sə lēt), no longer in use. Wooden warships are obsolete.

ob sta cle (ob′stə kəl), something that stands in the way or stops progress. A tree fallen across the road was an obstacle to our car. Blindness is an obstacle in most kinds of work.

ob sti na cy (ob′sti nə si), 1. stubborn nature or behavior. Obstinacy sometimes drives us to stick to a thing we have once said, even after we realize that we were mistaken. 2. obstinate act.

ob sti nate (ob′sti nit), 1. stubborn; not giving in. The obstinate girl would go her own way, in spite of all warnings. 2. hard to control or treat; as, an obstinate cough.

ob struct (əb strukt′), 1. block up; make hard to pass through. Fallen trees obstruct the road. 2. be in the way of; hinder. Trees obstruct our view of the ocean. A strike obstructed the work of the factory.

ob struc tion (əb struk′shən), 1. thing that obstructs; something in the way. The soldiers had to get over such obstructions as ditches and barbed wire. Ignorance is an obstruction to progress. 2. blocking; hindering; as, the obstruction of progress by prejudices.

ob tain (əb tān′), 1. get. One may obtain a position one applies for, obtain a prize one has been working for, obtain possession of a house one has rented, obtain knowledge through study, etc. 2. be in use; be customary; prevail. Different rules obtain in different schools.

ob tain a ble (əb tān′ə bəl), that can be obtained.

ob tuse (ob tüs′), 1. blunt. 2. stupid.

ob vi ous (ob′vi əs), plain; easily seen or understood; not to be doubted. It is obvious that two and two make four. That a blind man ought not to drive an automobile is too obvious to need proof.

oc ca sion (ə kā′zhən), 1. a particular time. We have met Mr. Smith on several occasions. 2. special event. The jewels were worn only on great occasions. 3. a good chance; opportunity. 4. cause; a reason. The dog which was the occasion of the quarrel had run away. 5. to cause; bring about.

oc ca sion al (ə kā′zhən əl), 1. happening or coming now and then, or once in a while. We had fine weather all through July except for an occasional thunderstorm. 2. rising out of, or used for, some special time or event. A war calls forth much occasional poetry.

oc ca sion al ly (ə kā′zhən əl i), now and then; once in a while.

oc cu pant (ok′ū pənt), 1. person who occupies. The occupant of the shack stepped out as I approached. 2. person in actual possession of a house, estate, office, etc.

oc cu pa tion (ok′ū pā′shən), 1. business; employment; trade. Teaching is Miss Day's occupation. 2. possession; occupying; being occupied; as, the occupation of a town by the enemy, the occupation of a house by a family.

oc cu py (ok′ū pī), 1. take up; fill. The building occupies an entire block. The lessons occupy the morning. 2. keep busy; engage; employ. Sports occupy Jim's attention. 3. take possession of. The enemy occupied our fort. 4. hold; have in use; live in. A judge occupies an important position. The robins are occupying their former nest.

oc cur (ə kėr′), 1. happen; take place. Storms often occur in winter. Is anything important occurring on Saturday? 2. be found; exist. *E* occurs in print more often than any other letter. 3. come to mind; suggest itself. Has it occurred to you to close the windows?

oc cur rence (ə kėr′əns), 1. an occurring. The occurrence of storms delayed our trip. 2. a happening; an event.

o cean (ō′shən), 1. the great body of salt water that covers almost three fourths of the earth's surface; the sea. 2. any of its five main divisions—the Atlantic, Pacific, Indian, Arctic, or Antarctic oceans.

o' clock (ə klok′), of the clock; by the clock. What o'clock is it? It is one o'clock.

oc tave (ok′tiv or ok′tāv), 1. in music, the interval between a note and another note having twice (or half) as many vibrations. From middle C to the C above it is an octave. 2. the eighth note above (or below) a given tone, having twice (or half) as many vibrations per second. 3. the series of notes or of keys of an instrument filling the interval between a note and its octave. 4. the sounding together of a note and its octave.

Two octaves on the piano (def. 3)

Oc to ber (ok tō′bər), the tenth month of the year. It has 31 days.

oc to pus (ok′tə pəs), 1. a sea animal having a soft body and eight arms with suckers on them. 2. anything like an octopus.

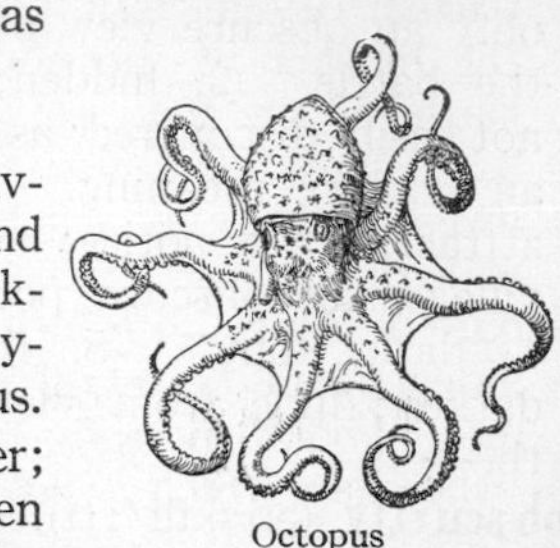
Octopus

odd (od), 1. left over; extra. Here are seven plums for three of you; John may have the odd one. Pay the bill with this money and keep the odd change. We speak of odd jobs, odd moments, and odd numbers or volumes of a magazine. 2. being one of a pair or set of which the rest is missing. There seems to be an odd stocking in the wash. 3. with some extra; as, six hundred odd children in school, thirty odd dollars. 4. leaving a remainder of one when divided by two. Seven is an odd number. 5. strange; peculiar; queer. A corncob makes an odd doll. It seems odd that summer should come in December in South Africa.

odd i ty (od′i ti), 1. strangeness; queerness; peculiarity; as, the oddity of wearing a fur coat over a bathing suit. 2. strange, queer, or peculiar person or thing.

odd ly (od′li), strangely.

odds (odz), 1. difference in favor of one and against another; advantage. The odds are in our favor and we should win. 2. In betting, odds of 3 to 1 means that 3 will be paid if the bet is lost for every 1 that will be received if it is won. 3. In games, odds is an extra allowance given to the weaker side. 4. Some special meanings are:

at odds, quarreling or disagreeing.

odds and ends, remnants; stray bits left over.

ode (ōd), a poem full of noble feeling expressed with dignity.

o di ous (ō′di əs), hateful; very displeasing; offensive.

o dor (ō′dər), 1. smell; as, the odor of roses, the odor of garbage. 2. reputation. Those boys were in bad odor because they were suspected of stealing.

o'er (ōr), over.

of (ov), 1. Of may mean about the same as belonging to; as, the children of the family, a student of the Washington School, a friend of his boyhood, the news of the day, the teacher of our class, the captain of the ship, the mother of the boy who was hurt, the cause of the quarrel, the result of his act. 2. Of may mean about the same as from or away from; as, to be north of Boston, to shoot wide of the mark, to cure of a sickness, to be bare of leaves, to take leave of a friend, to be independent of one's parents. 3. Of may mean about the same as made from, which (who) has, which (who) is, or which (who) is the same as; as, castles of sand, built of brick, a house of six rooms, the name of Mary, that group of trees, the city of New York, to make a fool of me. 4. Of may mean about the same as out of or owing to; as, to come of a good family, to expect much of a new medicine, to wish one joy of a new possession, to be sick of or die of a disease, to be tired of, glad of, proud of, etc. 5. Of may mean about the same as which (who) has as a quality; as, a look of pity, a word of encouragement, an hour of prayer, a person of importance, a woman of good judgment. 6. Of may mean the same as concerning or in regard to; as, to think well of someone, to have heard of it, to take care of, to think of, to feel sure of, to be fond of, to be hard of heart, to be fifteen years of age. 7. Of may mean about the same as among; as, a friend of mine, of late years. His mind is of the quickest. Two of us went, and two of us stayed at home. All five of us went.

off (ôf), 1. away; at a distance; to a distance. He went off in his car. 2. from; away from; far from. He pushed me off my seat. You are off the road. 3. not on; not connected; loose. 4. In some phrases which mean to stop, off is added to the verb. He broke off in the middle of a sentence. 5. wholly; in full. She cleared off her desk. 6. Be **well off** or **comfortably off** means be in a good condition, especially in regard to money. 7. **Off and on** means from time to time; occasionally. 8. straight out from. The boat anchored off the fort. 9. on the right-hand side; as, the off horse of a pair. 10. possible; not very likely. I came on the off chance that I would find you. 11. Be off!

of fence (ə fens′), offense.

of fend (ə fend′), 1. pain; displease; hurt the feelings of; make angry. My friend was offended by my laughter. 2. sin; do wrong. In what have I offended?

of fend er (ə fen′dər), 1. person who offends. 2. person who does wrong or breaks a law. No smoking here; offenders will be fined $5.

of fense (ə fens′), 1. sin; breaking the law; as, an offense against God and man. The punishment for that offense is two years in prison. 2. condition of being offended; hurt feelings; anger. He tried not to cause offense. 3. offending; hurting someone's feelings. No offense was meant. 4. attacking; being the one to attack rather than defend. A gun is a weapon of offense.

give offense, offend.

take offense, be offended.

of fen sive (ə fen′siv), 1. giving offense; unpleasant; disagreeable; disgusting. "Shut up" is an offensive remark. Bad eggs have an offensive odor. 2. used for attack; having to do with attack; as, offensive weapons, an offensive war for conquest. 3. attitude of attack; attack. The army took the offensive.

of fer (ôf′ər), 1. hold out; present; as, to offer one's hand, to offer a gift, to offer help. 2. propose; as, to offer a price, to offer to cure, to offer to go. 3. present in worship; as, to offer sacrifices, to offer prayers. 4. try; attempt. The dog did not offer to hurt Jack, but stopped him if he offered to move. 5. present itself; occur. I will come if opportunity offers. 6. act of offering; as, an offer of money, an offer to sing, an offer of marriage, an offer of $10,000 for a house.

of fer ing (ôf′ər ing), 1. giving something as an act of worship. 2. contribution.

off hand (ôf′hand′), 1. at once; without previous thought or preparation. The carpenter could not tell offhand how much the work would cost. 2. done or made offhand. His offhand remarks were sometimes very wise. 3. careless; informal.

of fice (ôf′is), 1. position, especially a public position; as, to accept or resign an office. The President holds the highest public office in the United States. 2. the duty of one's position; task; job; work. It is my office to open the mail. His office is to decide on applications for aid. 3. the place in which the work of a position is done. His office is on the second floor. The post office is on Main Street. 4. an attention; an act of kindness or unkindness; a service or an injury. Through the good offices of a friend, I was able to get a ticket. 5. a religious ceremony or prayer.

of fi cer (ôf′i sər), 1. person who commands others in the army or navy, such as a major, a general, a captain, or an admiral. 2. person who holds a public, church, or government office; as, a health officer, a police officer. 3. the president, vice-president, secretary, treasurer, etc., of a society or club. 4. furnish with officers. 5. be an officer to; direct; manage. The army was officered by brave men.

of fi cial (ə fish′əl), 1. person who holds a public position or who is in charge of some public work or duty. Postmasters are government officials. 2. officer; person holding office; as, bank officials. 3. of an office. Policemen wear an official uniform. The official title is Superintendent of Playgrounds. 4. having something to do with an office; as, official business. 5. having authority. An official record is kept of the proceedings of Congress. 6. suitable for a person in office; as, the official dignity of a judge.

of fi cial ly (ə fish′əl i), in an official manner; as an official.

off set (ôf′set′ for 1 and 2, ôf′set′ for 3 and 4), 1. make up for; balance. The better roads offset the greater distance. We offset the greater distance by the better roads. 2. set off or balance; as, to offset the better roads against the greater distance. 3. something which makes up for something else; a compensation. In football, John's weight and strength were an offset to his slowness. 4. a short side shoot from a main stem or root which starts a new plant.

off shore (ôf′shōr′), off or away from the shore; as, a wind blowing offshore, offshore fisheries.

off spring (ôf′spring′), what is born from or grows out of something; child or children; descendants. Every one of his offspring had red hair just like his own.

oft (ôft), often.

of ten (ôf′ən), many times.

of ten times (ôf′ən tīmz′), often.

o gre (ō′gər), giant or monster that eats people.

oh or **Oh** (ō), 1. Oh is used before a person's name in beginning to speak. Oh, Mary, have you seen this? 2. Oh is the same word as **O**. Oh, dear me! Oh! joy! Oh, what a pity!

oil (oil), 1. any of several kinds of thick fatty or greasy liquids lighter than water, which will burn easily, and will not mix or dissolve in water but will dissolve in alcohol. Mineral oils are used for fuel; animal and vegetable oils are used in cooking and medicine, and in many other ways. 2. put oil on or in. 3. paint made by grinding coloring matter in oil.

oil cloth (oil′klôth′), 1. cloth made waterproof by coating it with paint. It is used to cover floors, tables, etc. 2. cloth made waterproof by treating it with oil.

oil y (oil′i), 1. of oil. 2. containing oil. 3. covered or soaked with oil; as, oily rags. 4. like oil; slippery. 5. too smooth; smooth in a disagreeable way. Mr. Heep has an oily manner.

oint ment (oint′mənt), a substance made from oil or fat, often containing medicine, used on the skin to heal or to make soft and white. The doctor put an ointment on John's burns.

old (ōld), 1. not young; having been for some time; aged. **The old** often means old people. **Old age** means the last part of one's life when one is very old. 2. that seems old; like an old person in some way. That child has an old face. 3. much worn by age; worn; as, an old coat, old clothes. 4. of age; in age; as, to be ten months old, a four-year-old child. 5. having much experience. The young thief was old in wrongdoing. Tim is an old hand at swimming. 6. belonging to the past; dating far back; ancient; as, old countries. The **old country** means the country an emigrant comes from. 7. not new; not recent; as, an old debt, an old family. 8. former. An old pupil came back to visit his teacher. 9. long known or familiar or dear. Old Rover, I'm glad to see you. 10. the time of long ago; the past; as, the heroes of old.

old en (ōl′dən), old; of old; ancient.

old-fash ioned (ōld′fash′ənd), 1. of an old

fashion; as, an old-fashioned dress. 2. keeping to old ways, ideas, etc.

Old Glory, the flag of the United States; the Stars and Stripes.

Old Testament, the earlier part of the Bible, which contains the religious and social laws of the Hebrews, a record of their history, their important literature, and writings of their prophets.

ol ive (olʹiv), 1. a kind of evergreen tree with gray-green leaves. The olive tree grows in southern Europe and similar climates. 2. the fruit of this tree, with a hard stone and bitter pulp. Olives are eaten as a relish and used to make olive oil. 3. a wreath of olive leaves; olive branch. 4. yellowish green. 5. yellowish brown.

Olives

olive branch, a branch of the olive tree as an emblem of peace.

om e let or **om e lette** (omʹə let), eggs beaten up with milk or water, fried or baked, and then folded over.

o men (ōʹmən), a sign of what is to happen; an object or event that is believed to mean good or bad fortune. Spilling salt is said to be an omen of misfortune.

om i nous (omʹi nəs), unfavorable; threatening. Those clouds look ominous for our picnic.

o mis sion (ō mishʹən), 1. an omitting. 2. a being omitted. 3. thing omitted.

o mit (ō mitʹ), 1. leave out. Dick made many mistakes in spelling by omitting letters. 2. fail to do; neglect. Mary omitted making her bed.

om ni bus (omʹni bus), bus.

on (on), 1. On helps to answer the question, "Where?" Then it means supported by, covering, round about, etc. The book is on the table. His ship is on the ocean. Drop it on the ground. Put the ring on her finger. It hangs on the wall. We put our stockings on. In telling where, on also means close to, touching, in the direction of; as, a house on the shore, to march on Boston, to turn one's back on one's home, to smile on a child, to make an attack on the city. 2. On helps to answer the questions, "How?", "In what way?", "By what means?"; as, to turn on one's heel, to have a thing on good authority, to be on half pay, a story founded on fact, to do it on purpose, to play a piece on the violin, to be on fire, on sale, on the move, on duty, on the watch, or on one's best behavior, to speak on, to turn the gas on. 3. On helps to answer the question, "When?"; as, on Tuesday, on time, on the hour, on arriving, on my return, on looking closely, later on, from that day on. 4. On helps to answer the questions, "Which one?" and "About what?" Then it means about or concerning; as, a tax on tea, interest on one's money, a profit on sales, a book on animals, to have an opinion on the weather. 5. On helps to answer the question, "Why, for what purpose?"; as, to go on an errand. He drew his knife on me. 6. **Be on a committee, a council,** etc., means be a member of it. 7. **On and on** means without stopping.

once (wuns), 1. one time. Read it once more. 2. at some one time in the past; formerly. That big man was once a little baby. 3. if ever. Most boys like to swim, once they have learned how. 4. **At once** means (1) immediately. You must come at once. (2) at the same time. All three boys spoke at once.

one (wun), 1. the number 1. 2. a single. A man has one head and one neck. 3. a single person or thing. I like the ones in that box. 4. some. One day he will get run over. 5. any person, standing for people in general. One does not like to be left out. 6. the same. All face one way. 7. united. The class was one in its approval. 8. a certain. A short speech was made by one Mr. Jones. 9. Some special meanings are:

be at one, agree.

It is all one. It makes no difference.

one by one, one after another.

one ness (wunʹnis), 1. singleness. 2. sameness. 3. unity. 4. agreement.

one self (wunʹselfʹ), one's own self. At the age of seven one ought to dress oneself. **Be oneself** means (1) have full control of one's mind or body. (2) act naturally.

one-sid ed (wunʹsīdʹid), 1. having but one side. 2. having one side larger or more developed than the other. 3. partial; unfair; prejudiced; seeing only one side of a question. The umpire seemed one-sided in his decisions.

Onion bulb

on ion (unʹyən), a vegetable with a root shaped like a bulb, eaten raw and used in cooking. Onions have a sharp, strong smell and taste.

on ly (ōn′li), 1. by itself; one and no more. Water is his only drink. Mary and John are their only children. This was her one and only hope. This is the only road along the shore. 2. just; merely; and no one else; and nothing more; and that is all. It was only the wind. **If only** often means I wish. If only the sun would shine! **Only too glad** means very glad. 3. but then; it must be added that. We had camped right beside a stream, only the water was not fit to drink. 4. except that; if it had not. I could do it, only it would be wrong. He would have started, only it rained. 5. best; finest. Dick is the only boy for me!

on rush (on′rush′), violent forward rush.

on set (on′set′), 1. attack. The onset of the enemy took us by surprise. 2. beginning. The onset of this disease is gradual.

on slaught (on′slôt′), vigorous attack. The Indians made an onslaught on the settlers' fort.

on to (on′tü), on to; to a position on; as, to throw a ball onto the roof, to get onto a horse, a boat driven onto the rocks.

on ward (on′wərd), on; further on; toward the front; forward. The crowd around the store window began to move onward. An onward movement began.

on wards (on′wərdz), onward.

ooze (üz), 1. pass out slowly through small openings; leak out little by little. Blood still oozed from the cut. His courage oozed away as he waited. 2. a slow flow. 3. something that oozes. 4. soft mud or slime, especially at the bottom of a pond or river or on the ocean bottom.

o pal (ō′pəl), a gem that shows beautiful changes of color. The common opal is milky white with colored lights.

o paque (ō pāk′), 1. not letting light through; not transparent. 2. not shining; dark; dull. 3. obscure; hard to understand.

o pen (ō′pən), 1. not shut; not closed; letting (anything or anyone) in or out. Open windows let in the fresh air. 2. not having its gate, door, lid, etc., closed; not shut up; as, an open box, drawer, house, etc. 3. not covered; as, an open fire, an open jar. 4. not closed in; as, the open sea, an open field, an open car. **The open** means open or clear space, open country, open air. 5. not hidden or secret; as, open war. Come **out into the open** with one's plans, etc., means to tell them, not keep them hidden. 6. that may be entered, used, shared, etc., by all, or by a person or persons mentioned; as, an open meeting, an open market. The race is open to boys under 15. 7. free from hindrance; especially, free from ice; as, open water, a river or harbor now open. An **open winter** is one so warm and free from snow that getting about is easy. 8. unfolded; spread out; as, an open flower, letter, or book. 9. frank and sincere; as, an open heart. Please be open with me. 10. make or become open; as, to open a path through the woods. 11. begin; as, to open a debate. School opens in September. To **open fire** means to begin shooting. 12. start or set up; as, to open a new store, an office, an account. 13. spread out or unfold; as, to open a fan, a book, or a letter. 14. come apart or burst open; as, a crack where the earth had opened. The clouds opened, and the sun shone through. 15. Some special meanings are:

keep open house, offer food and shelter to all visitors or to all one's friends.

open a person's eyes, make him see what is really going on.

Give with an **open hand** means give generously.

Have an **open mind** means be ready to listen to new ideas, and to judge them fairly; not to be prejudiced.

Open to arguments, offers, etc., means ready to receive them or listen to them.

open to, into, or **onto,** have an opening or passage. This door opens into the dining room. My window opens to the south.

open up, open a way to; uncover; bring to notice.

the open, empty space that is not closed in.

open air, outdoors.

o pen ing (ō′pən ing), 1. gap; hole; open or clear space; as, an opening in a wall, an opening in the forest. 2. place or position that is open or vacant; as, an opening in a bank, store, or school. 3. favorable chance or opportunity. In talking with your mother, I made an opening to ask her about sending you to camp. As soon as I saw an opening, I landed a blow on his head. 4. the first part; the beginning; as, the opening of his lecture. 5. first; beginning; as, the opening words of his speech. 6. a formal beginning. The opening will be at three o'clock tomorrow afternoon. 7. act of making open. 8. fact of becoming open.

o pen ly (ō′pən li), without secrecy; frankly.

op er a (op′ər ə), a play that is mostly sung, with costumes, scenery, acting, and music to go with the singing.

op er ate (op′ər āt), 1. run; keep working; manage. The machinery operates night and day. The boy operates the elevator. The company operates three factories. 2. work; act; produce an effect. Several causes operated to bring on the war. 3. produce a desired effect. The medicine operated quickly. 4. perform an operation. The doctor operated on the injured man.

op er a tion (op′ər ā′shən), 1. working; action; the way a thing works. The operation of this machine is simple. **In operation** means in action or in use. 2. doing; activity; as, the operation of brushing one's teeth. 3. something done to the body, usually with instruments, to improve health. Taking out the tonsils is a common operation. 4. movement of troops, ships, etc.; as, military and naval operations.

op er a tor (op′ər ā′tər), person who operates; as, a telegraph or telephone operator, the operators of a mine or railroad, an X-ray operator.

op er et ta (op′ər et′ə), a short, amusing opera.

o pin ion (ə pin′yən), 1. what one thinks; belief not so strong as knowledge; judgment. 2. impression; estimate. Everyone has a poor opinion of a coward. 3. formal judgment by an expert; professional advice. Mother wanted the doctor's opinion about the cause of my headache.

o pi um (ō′pi əm), a powerful drug that causes sleep and eases pain. Opium is made from a kind of poppy.

o pos sum (ə pos′əm), a small American animal that lives in trees. When it is caught, it pretends to be dead. The opossum is common in the southern United States. An opossum is often called a **possum.**

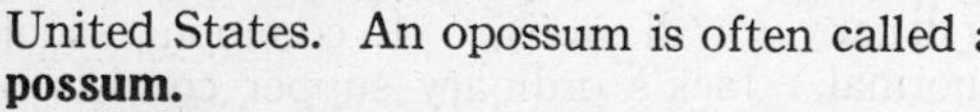
Opossum

op po nent (ə pō′nənt), person who is on the other side in a fight or game or discussion; person fighting, struggling, or speaking against (one). Our opponents won the game because they were quicker than we.

op por tu ni ty (op′ər tū′ni ti or op′ər tü′ni ti), good chance; favorable time; convenient occasion. I had an opportunity to earn some money picking blueberries. I have had no opportunity to give John your message, because I have not seen him.

op pose (ə pōz′), 1. be against; be in the way of; act, fight, or struggle against; try to hinder; resist. A swamp opposed the advance of the army. 2. set up against; place in the way of. Let us oppose good nature to anger, and smiles to cross words. 3. put in contrast. Night is opposed to day. Love is opposed to hate.

op po site (op′ə zit), 1. placed against; as different in direction as can be; face to face; back to back. 2. as different as can be; just contrary. North and south are opposite directions. Sour is opposite to sweet. 3. a thing or person as different as can be. A brave boy is the opposite of a coward.

op po si tion (op′ə zish′ən), 1. action against; resistance. The mob offered opposition to the police. 2. contrast. 3. political party opposed to the party which is in power.

op press (ə pres′), 1. govern harshly; keep down unjustly or by cruelty. A good ruler will not oppress the poor. 2. burden; weigh down; lie heavily on. A sense of trouble ahead oppressed my spirits.

op pres sion (ə presh′ən), 1. oppressing; burdening. The oppression of the people by the nobles caused the war. 2. a being oppressed or burdened. 3. cruel or unjust treatment. 4. a heavy, weary feeling.

op pres sive (ə pres′iv), 1. hard to bear; burdensome. Great heat is oppressive. 2. harsh; severe; unjust.

op pres sor (ə pres′ər), person who is cruel or unjust to people under him.

or (ôr), 1. Or suggests a choice, or a difference, or connects words or groups of words of equal importance in the sentence. Is it sweet or sour? Shall you walk or ride? 2. Or may state the only choice left. Either eat this or go hungry. 3. Or may state what will happen if the first does not happen. Hurry, or you will be late. 4. Or may explain what goes before; as, an igloo or rounded snow house.

or a cle (or′ə kəl), 1. the answer of a god to a question. 2. the place where the god gives answers. 3. the priest, or other means by which the god's answer was given. 4. a high authority; a very wise person.

o ral (ō′rəl), 1. spoken; using speech. An oral agreement is not enough; we must have a written promise. 2. of the mouth. The oral opening in an earthworm is small.

or ange (or′inj), 1. a round, reddish-yellow, juicy fruit. Oranges grow in warm climates. 2. the tree it grows on. 3. reddish yellow.

o ra tion (ō rā′shən), a formal public speech delivered on a special occasion.

or a tor (or′ə tər), 1. person who makes an oration. 2. person who can speak very well in public.

or a to ry[1] (or′ə tō′ri), 1. skill in public speaking; fine speaking. 2. the art of public speaking.

or a to ry[2] (or′ə tō′ri), a small chapel; a room set apart for prayer.

orb (ôrb), 1. sphere; globe. 2. sun, moon, planet, or star. 3. eye.

or bit (ôr′bit), 1. the path of the earth or any one of the planets about the sun. 2. the path of any heavenly body about another heavenly body. 3. the socket in which the eye is placed.

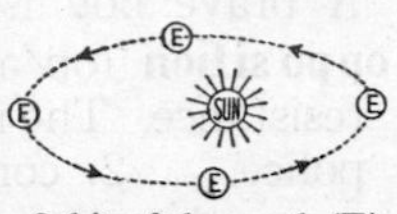

Orbit of the earth (E) around the sun. Arrows show direction.

or chard (ôr′chərd), 1. piece of ground on which fruit trees are grown. 2. the trees in an orchard. The orchard is bearing well this year.

or ches tra (ôr′kis trə), 1. the musicians playing at a concert, an opera, or a play. 2. the violins, cellos, horns, and other instruments played by the musicians together in an orchestra. 3. the part of a theater just in front of the stage, where the musicians sit to play. 4. the main floor of a theater, especially the part near the front. Buy two seats in the orchestra.

or chid (ôr′kid), 1. any of a large group of plants with beautiful flowers that often have strange shapes and colors. 2. the flower. 3. light purple.

or dain (ôr dān′), 1. order; decide; pass as a law. The law ordains that the murderers shall be hanged. 2. officially appoint or consecrate as a minister in a Christian church.

or deal (ôr dēl′), severe test or experience. Jack dreaded the ordeal of a visit to the dentist.

or der (ôr′dər), 1. the way one thing follows another; as, in order of size, in alphabetical order, to copy them in order. 2. a condition in which every part or piece is in its right place; as, to put a room in order. 3. put in proper condition; arrange; as, to order one's affairs. 4. condition; state. We found our room in bad order. 5. the way the world works; the way things happen; as, the order of nature. 6. state or condition of things in which the law is obeyed and there is no trouble; as, to keep order. Order was established. Perfect order reigned throughout the country after the revolution. 7. a command; telling what to do. The orders of the captain must be obeyed. 8. tell what to do; command; bid; give an order. 9. a paper saying that money is to be given or paid, or something handed over; as, a postal money order. 10. a statement or list of things telling a store or tradesman what you wish sent. I gave the grocer an order for two dozen eggs. 11. give (a store, etc.) an order for. A factory orders many tons of coal during the winter. 12. decide; will. The powers that be ordered it so. 13. kind or sort; as, to have ability of a high order. 14. social rank, grade, or class; as, all orders of society. 15. a brotherhood of monks, friars, or knights; as, the Franciscan order. 16. **Order of the day** means the way things are; the way people are doing; the style. 17. **Out of order** means (1) not working rightly. (2) against the rules (of a meeting).

or der ly (ôr′dər li), 1. in order; with regular arrangement, method, or system; as, an orderly arrangement of dishes on shelves, an orderly mind. 2. keeping order; well-behaved or regulated; as, an orderly class. 3. a sergeant, corporal, or private soldier who attends a superior officer to carry orders, etc. 4. a hospital attendant who keeps things clean and in order.

or di nance (ôr′di nəns), a rule or law made by authority. Some cities have ordinances forbidding Sunday amusements.

or di nar i ly (ôr′di nãr′i li), commonly; usually; normally.

or di nar y (ôr′di nãr′i), 1. common; usual; normal. Jack's ordinary supper consists of bread and milk. 2. somewhat below the average. The speaker was ordinary and tiresome.

ord nance (ôrd′nəns), 1. cannon or artillery. 2. military weapons of all kinds.

ore (ōr), rock, sand, or dirt, containing some metal.

or gan (ôr′gən), 1. a musical instrument made of pipes of different lengths, which are sounded by air blown by a bellows and played by keys. Organs are used especially in churches. 2. part of an animal or plant fitted to do certain things in life. The eyes, stomach, heart, and lungs are organs of the body. Stamens and pistils are organs of flowers. 3. a means of action; instrument. A court is an organ of government. 4. a newspaper or magazine which speaks for and gives the views of a political party.

or gan dy or **or gan die** (ôr′gən di), a fine, thin, stiff muslin, used for dresses.

or gan ism (ôr′gən izm), 1. an individual animal or plant. 2. a whole made up of related parts that work together.

or gan ist (ôr′gən ist), person who plays an organ.

or gan i za tion (ôr′gən i zā′shən), 1. grouping and arranging parts to form a whole. The organization of a big picnic takes time and thought. 2. the way in which a thing's parts are arranged to work together. The organization of the human body is very complicated. 3. thing made up of related parts, each having a special duty. A tree is an organization of roots, trunk, branches, leaves, and fruit. 4. group of persons united for some purpose. Churches, clubs, and political parties are organizations.

or gan ize (ôr′gən iz), put into working order; get together and arrange. The explorer organized an expedition to the North Pole.

or gy (ôr′ji), a wild drunken revel.

o ri ent or **O ri ent** (ō′ri ent), 1. the East; eastern countries. China and Japan are important nations of the Orient. **The Orient** usually includes Asia and countries east and southeast of the Mediterranean. 2. to place so as to face the east. 3. to place in the right position. **Orient oneself** means get in the right relations to the things or persons about one.

o ri en tal or **O ri en tal** (ō′ri en′təl), 1. eastern; of the Orient. 2. a native of the East. The Chinese are Orientals.

or i fice (or′i fis), mouth; opening; hole; as, the orifice of a tube or pipe.

or i gin (or′i jin), 1. beginning; starting point; that from which anything comes; as, the origin of the quarrel, the origin of a disease. 2. parentage; birth.

o rig i nal (ə rij′i nəl), 1. first; earliest; belonging to the beginning. The hat has been marked down from its original price. 2. new; fresh; novel. It is hard to plan original games for a party. 3. inventive; able to do, make, or think something new. 4. not copied; not translated. Jean wrote an original poem. 5. thing from which another is copied, imitated, or translated. The original of this picture is in Rome. 6. the language in which a book was first written. Our minister can read the New Testament in the original. 7. an unusual person.

o rig i nal i ty (ə rij′i nal′i ti), 1. ability to do, make, or think up something new. 2. freshness; novelty.

o rig i nal ly (ə rij′i nəl i), 1. by origin; as, a plant originally European. 2. at first; in the first place; as, a house originally small.

o rig i nate (ə rij′i nāt), 1. cause to be; invent. 2. come into being; begin; arise. Where did that story originate?

o ri ole (ō′ri ōl), 1. any of several American birds having yellow-and-black or orange-and-black coloring. 2. any of several European birds having yellow or black coloring.

Baltimore oriole (about 7 in. long)

or na ment (ôr′nə mənt for 1 and 2, ôr′nə ment for 3), 1. something pretty; something to add beauty. Lace, jewels, vases, and statues are ornaments. 2. person or act that adds beauty, grace, or honor. Charming Miss Fair would be an ornament to any society. 3. add beauty to; make more pleasing or attractive; decorate.

or na men tal (ôr′nə men′təl), 1. for ornament; used as an ornament. 2. decorative.

or phan (ôr′fən), 1. a child whose parents are dead. 2. of or for such children; as, an orphan asylum. 3. without a father or mother or both. 4. make an orphan of. The war orphaned me when I was five years old.

or phan age (ôr′fən ij), home for orphans.

or tho dox (ôr′thə doks), 1. generally accepted, especially in religion. 2. having orthodox views or opinions, especially in religion. 3. approved by convention; usual; customary; as, the orthodox Christmas dinner of turkey and plum pudding.

o sier (ō′zhər), a willow whose branches are used in making baskets, etc.

os prey (os′pri), a large hawk that feeds on fish.

Osprey
(about 2 ft. long)

os ten ta tious (os′ten tā′shəs), 1. done for display; intended to attract notice. Tom rode his new bicycle up and down in front of Dick's house in an ostentatious way. 2. showing off; liking to attract notice.

os trich (os′trich), a large bird of Africa and Arabia. Ostriches run fast but cannot fly. They have large feathers or plumes which were much used as ornaments.

Ostrich
(6 to 8 ft. tall)

oth er (uᴛʜ′ər), 1. not the same; different. Come some other day. 2. remaining. John is here, but the other boys are at school. 3. additional. I have no other place to go. 4. other person or thing. 5. in any different way. I could not do other than I did. 6. **Every other** sometimes means every second. We have spelling every other day.

oth er wise (uᴛʜ′ər wīz′), 1. differently; in any other way. I could not act otherwise. 2. different; in a different condition. It might have been otherwise. 3. in other ways. He is noisy, but otherwise a nice boy. 4. or else; if not. Come at once; otherwise you will be too late.

ot ter (ot′ər), 1. a water animal that eats fish. The otter is hunted for its fur. 2. its fur.

Otter (3 to 4 ft. long, with the tail)

ouch (ouch), an exclamation expressing sudden pain.

ought (ôt). Ought expresses the idea of being bound or required: 1. by duty. You ought to obey your parents. 2. by justice. Cruelty and bullying ought not to be allowed. 3. by fitness. You ought to know better. 4. by wisdom. I ought to have washed my hands. 5. by very strong likelihood. It ought to be a fine day tomorrow.

ounce (ouns), 1. a unit of weight, $\frac{1}{16}$ of a pound in ordinary, and $\frac{1}{12}$ of a pound in troy weight. 2. little bit; small amount.

our (our), of us; belonging to us. We need our coats now.

ours (ourz), 1. of us; belonging to us. This garden is ours. 2. the one or ones belonging to us. Ours is a large family. I like ours better than yours.

our self (our self′). Ourself is used by an author, king, judge, etc., meaning myself. "We will ourself reward the victor," said the queen.

our selves (our selvz′), 1. Ourselves is used to make a statement stronger. We ourselves will do the work. 2. Ourselves is used instead of we or us in cases like: We cook for ourselves. We help ourselves. 3. us. We cannot see ourselves as others see us.

oust (oust), push out; drive out. The sparrows have ousted the bluebirds from our birdhouse.

out (out), 1. away; not in or at a place; forth. The water will rush out. Spread the rug out. 2. not at home; away from one's office, work, etc. My mother is out just now. 3. not having power; not in possession; in baseball, not batting. 4. not burning; no longer lighted. The fire (light, etc.) is out. 5. not correct. He was out in his figuring. 6. into the open; made public; make known; into being; so as to be seen. The secret is out now. His new book is out. Many flowers were coming out. A rash broke out on his chest. 7. aloud; plainly. Speak out so that all can hear. 8. **Speak out** also means speak frankly. 9. go out; come out. Murder will out. 10. to or at an end; completely. Let them fight it out. 11. to others; as, to let out rooms, to give out books. 12. from among others. Pick out an apple for me. 13. not friendly. 14. Some special meanings are:

out and away, by far.

Out with him! Put him out!

out-and-out (out′ənd out′), thorough; complete; as, an out-and-out refusal.

out board (out′bōrd′), 1. outside the hull of a ship or boat. 2. away from the middle of a ship or boat.

out break (out′brāk′), 1. a breaking out; as, outbreaks of anger. 2. a riot; a public disturbance.

out build ing (out′bil′ding), a shed or building built against or near a main building.

out burst (out′bėrst′), a bursting forth; as, an outburst of laughter, an outburst of anger.

out cast (out′kast′), 1. cast out from home and friends; homeless; friendless. 2. an outcast person or animal. That kitten was just a little outcast when Tom found it and brought it home.

out come (out′kum′), result; consequence.

out cry (out′krī′), 1. a crying out; sudden cry or scream. 2. a great noise or clamor.

out did (out did′). See **outdo.** The girls outdid the boys in neatness.

out dis tance (out dis′təns), go faster than; leave behind.

out do (out dü′), do more or better than; surpass. Men will outdo boys in most things. **outdid** and **outdone** are formed from **outdo.**

out done (out dun′). See **outdo.** The girls were outdone by the boys in baseball.

out door (out′dōr′), done, used, or living outdoors; as, outdoor games.

out doors (out′dōrz′), 1. out in the open air; not indoors or in the house. 2. the world outside of houses; the open air.

out er (out′ər), on the outside; farther out.

out er most (out′ər mōst), farthest out.

out fit (out′fit), 1. all the articles necessary for any undertaking or purpose; as, a sailor's outfit, the outfit for a camping trip, a bride's outfit. 2. furnish with everything necessary for any purpose; equip. 3. group working together.

out grew (out grü′). See **outgrow.** Tom used to stutter, but he outgrew it.

out grow (out grō′), 1. grow too large for; as, to outgrow one's clothes. 2. grow beyond or away from; get rid of by growing older; as, to outgrow early friends, to outgrow a babyish habit, opinion, fault, etc. 3. grow faster or taller than. This variety of pole bean will outgrow the dwarf kind. By the time he was ten, Tom had outgrown his older brother.

out grown (out grōn′). See **outgrow.** Some of my last year's clothes are outgrown.

out ing (out′ing), a short pleasure trip; a walk or drive; holiday spent outdoors away from home.

out last (out last′), last longer than.

out law (out′lô′), 1. person put outside the protection of the law; an exile; an outcast. 2. a lawless person; a criminal. 3. make or declare (a person) an outlaw. 4. make or declare unlawful. A group of nations agreed to outlaw war.

out lay (out′lā′), 1. expense; laying out money; spending. 2. the amount spent.

out let (out′let), a means or place of letting out or getting out; a way out; as, the outlet of a lake, an outlet for one's energies.

out line (out′līn′), 1. the line that shows the shape of an object. This diagram is the outline of an egg. The outline of Italy suggests a boot. 2. a drawing or style of drawing that gives only outer lines. This is an outline of a house. 3. draw the outer line of anything. Outline a map of America. 4. a brief plan. Make an outline before trying to write a composition. The teacher gave a brief outline of the work planned for the term. 5. give a plan of; sketch; as, to outline a trip abroad.

out live (out liv′), live longer than; last longer than. She outlived her older sister. The idea was good once, but it has outlived its usefulness.

out look (out′lu̇k′), 1. what one sees on looking out; view. The room has a pleasant outlook. 2. what seems likely to happen; prospect. The outlook for our picnic is not very good; it looks as if it would rain. 3. way of thinking about things; attitude of mind; point of view. 4. lookout; tower to watch from.

out ly ing (out′lī′ing), lying outside the boundary; far from the center; remote.

out num ber (out num′bər), be more than; exceed in number. They outnumbered us three to one.

out post (out′pōst′), 1. a guard, or small number of soldiers, placed at some distance from an army or camp, to prevent surprise. 2. place where they are stationed.

out put (out′pu̇t′), 1. the amount produced; the product or yield; as, the daily output of automobiles, of lumber, of shoes. 2. putting forth. With a sudden output of effort John moved the rock.

out rage (out′rāj), 1. a very offensive act; a shameful act of violence. Setting Mr. Brown's house on fire was an outrage. 2. offend greatly; insult; do violence to. 3. break (the law, a rule of morality, etc.) openly; treat as nothing at all. Lulu outraged all rules of politeness by throwing tomatoes at her mother's guests.

out ra geous (out rā′jəs), shocking; very bad or insulting.

out ran (out ran′), ran faster than. See **outrun.**

out right (out′rīt′), 1. altogether; entirely; not gradually. 2. complete; thorough. He would have to be an outright thief to do that. 3. downright; straightforward; direct; as, an outright lie.

out run (out run′), 1. run faster than. Dick can outrun his older sister. 2. leave behind; run beyond; pass the limits of. Dick's story was interesting but it had outrun the facts, and we could not believe it all. **outran** is formed from **outrun.**

out set (out′set′), a setting out; a start; a beginning.

out side (out′sīd′), 1. the side or surface that is out; the outer part; as, the outside of a house, or cup, or watch. 2. on the outside; of or nearer the outside; as, the outside leaves. 3. on or to the outside; outdoors. I feel clean outside and in. Run outside and play. 4. space that is beyond or not inside. 5. out of; beyond the limits of. Stay outside the house. That is outside my plans. 6. the most. I can do it in a week, at the outside. 7. highest; largest; as, an outside estimate, to quote outside prices.

out sid er (out′sīd′ər), person not belonging to a particular group, set, company, party, etc.

out skirts (out′skėrts′), outer parts or edges of a town, district, etc., or of a subject of discussion; outlying parts.

out stand ing (out stan′ding), 1. well-known; important. 2. unpaid; as, outstanding debts. 3. standing out.

out stretched (out′strecht′), stretched out; extended. He welcomed his old friend with outstretched arms.

out strip (out strip′), 1. go faster than; leave behind in a race. A horse can outstrip a man. 2. do better than; excel. Frank can outstrip John both in sports and in studies.

out ward (out′wərd), 1. going toward the outside; turned toward the outside; as, an outward motion. She gave one outward glance. 2. toward the outside; away. 3. outer; as, to all outward appearances. 4. on the outside. 5. that can be seen; on the surface; as, outward behavior.

out ward ly (out′wərd li), on the outside; in appearance. Though frightened, the boy remained outwardly calm.

out wards (out′wərdz), outward.

out weigh (out wā′), 1. weigh more than. 2. exceed in value, importance, influence, etc. The advantages of the plan outweigh its disadvantages.

out wit (out wit′), get the better of; be too clever for. The prisoner outwitted his guards and escaped.

out worn (out′wōrn′), 1. worn out; as, outworn clothes. 2. outgrown; out of date; as, outworn opinions, outworn habits, outworn customs.

o val (ō′vəl), 1. shaped like an egg. 2. shaped like an ellipse. 3. something having an oval shape.

Ovals

o va ry (ō′və ri), 1. the part of an animal in which eggs are produced. 2. the part of a plant enclosing the young seeds.

ov en (uv′ən), 1. a space in a stove or near a fireplace, for baking food. 2. a small furnace for heating or drying.

o ver (ō′vər), 1. above; as, the sky over our heads, a window right over the water. 2. across; so as to get beyond or above; on or to the other side of; as, to jump over the brook, to cross over the road, spoke over her shoulder, payments lasting over several years. 3. moving above; so as to get past. Can you climb over that hill? 4. across a space or distance. Go over to the store for me. 5. out and down (from an edge or from an upright position). If you go too near the edge, you may fall over. 6. out and down from; down from the edge of; as, to lean over the edge. 7. about or upon, so as to cover. Cover the tar over with sand until it has hardened. 8. on; at all or various places on. A smile came over her face. The water ran over the floor. Farms were scattered over the valley. 9. to and fro upon; round about; all through; as, to travel over the United States. He went over everything in his pocket, looking for the letter. 10. from beginning to end; at some length; again. Do that three times over. 11. at an end; done with; settled. The fight is over. 12. about; concerning; in connection with. He is troubled over his health. Don't go to sleep over your work. 13. more than. It cost over ten dollars. 14. too; more; besides; as, to be over careful, not to feel over well, whatever is left over. 15. the other side up; upside down. Turn it over. Roll over and over. 16. higher up; extra; too great. 17. yonder; in the distance; as, over the hill.

o ver alls (ō′vər ôlz′), loose trousers worn over clothes to keep them clean. Overalls usually have a part that covers the chest.

o ver board (ō′vər bōrd′), from a ship into the water. Throw that box overboard.

o ver bold (ō′vər bōld′), too bold.

o ver came (ō′vər kām′). See **overcome.**

o ver cast (ō′vər kast′), 1. cloudy; dark; gloomy. The sky was overcast before the storm. 2. cover (the sky, sun, etc.) with clouds or darkness. 3. fasten by stitching roughly through and over the edges of a seam.

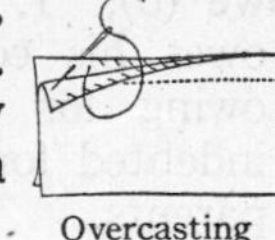
Overcasting

o ver coat (ō′vər kōt′), heavy coat worn over the regular coat.

o ver come (ō′vər kum′), 1. get the better of; conquer; defeat. We can overcome difficulties, enemies, and our own faults. Rage overcame her and she tore her hair. 2. made weak or helpless. The child was overcome by weariness and slept.

o ver crowd (ō′vər kroud′), crowd too much; put in too much or too many.

o ver did (ō′vər did′). See **overdo.**

o ver do (ō′vər dü′), 1. do too much. She overdid and became tired. 2. exaggerate. The funny scenes in the play were overdone. 3. cook too much; as, overdone beef. **overdid** and **overdone** are formed from **overdo.**

o ver flow (ō′vər flō′ for 1, 2, 3, 4, and 5, ō′vər flō′ for 6), 1. flow over (the top). Stop! The milk is overflowing. 2. have the contents flowing over. My cup is overflowing. 3. cover; flood. The river overflowed my garden. 4. extend out beyond; be too many for. The crowd overflowed my little parlor and filled the hall. 5. be very abundant; as, an overflowing harvest, overflowing kindness. 6. overflowing; excess.

o ver grew (ō′vər grü′). See **overgrow.**

o ver grow (ō′vər grō′), 1. grow over. The wall is overgrown with vines. 2. grow too fast; become too big; as, an overgrown boy.

o ver grown (ō′vər grōn′). See **overgrow.**

o ver hang (ō′vər hang′ for 1, ō′vər hang′ for 2 and 3), 1. hang over; project over. Overhanging branches of trees formed an arch across the street. 2. hanging over. 3. something that projects. The overhang of the roof shaded the flower bed beneath.

o ver haul (ō′vər hôl′), 1. examine completely so as to make repairs or changes that are needed. Once a year we overhaul our boat. 2. gain upon; overtake. An automobile can overhaul any horse.

o ver head (ō′vər hed′ for 1, ō′vər hed′ for 2), 1. above; on high; in the sky; on the floor above; as, the flag overhead, the stars overhead, the family overhead. 2. placed above; placed high up. **Overhead expenses** or **overhead** means general expenses for rent, lighting, heating, taxes, repairs, etc.

o ver hear (ō′vər hēr′), hear when one is not meant to hear. They spoke so loud that I could not help overhearing what they said.

o ver hung (ō′vər hung′). See **overhang,** definition 1. A big awning overhung the sidewalk.

o ver joyed (ō′vər joid′), very joyful; filled with joy; delighted.

o ver laid (ō′vər lād′). See **overlay.** The workmen overlaid the dome with gold.

o ver land (ō′vər land′), on land; by land. We traveled overland from New York to Florida.

o ver lap (ō′vər lap′), lap over; cover and extend beyond. Shingles are laid to overlap each other.

o ver lay (ō′vər lā′ for 1, ō′vər lā′ for 2), 1. put a coating over the surface of. The dome is overlaid with gold. 2. something laid over something else; covering; ornamental layer.

o ver load (ō′vər lōd′ for 1, ō′vər lōd′ for 2), 1. load too heavily. 2. too great a load.

o ver look (ō′vər luk′), 1. have a view of from above; be higher than. This high window overlooks half of New York City. 2. fail to see. Here are some letters which you overlooked. 3. excuse; pay no attention to. I will overlook your behavior this time.

o ver night (ō′vər nīt′), 1. during the night; as, to stay overnight with a friend; an overnight stop. 2. for the night. An overnight bag contains articles needed for one night's stay. 3. on the night before. Preparations were made overnight for an early start.

o ver pow er (ō′vər pou′ər), 1. overcome; master; overwhelm. He overpowered all his enemies. I was overpowered by the heat. 2. be much greater or stronger than. The wind brought a horrible smell which overpowered all others. Sudden anger overpowered every other feeling.

o ver ran (ō′vər ran′). See **overrun.**

o ver run (ō′vər run′), 1. spread over and spoil or harm in some way. Weeds had overrun the old garden. 2. spread over. Vines overran the wall. 3. run or go beyond; exceed. The speaker overran the time set for him.

o ver seas (ō′vər sēz′ for 1, ō′vər sēz′ for 2 and 3), 1. across the sea; beyond the sea; abroad. 2. done, used, or serving overseas. 3. of countries across the sea; foreign.

o ver see (ō′vər sē′), look after and direct (work or workers); superintend; manage.

o ver seen (ō′vər sēn′). See **oversee.**

o ver se er (ō′vər sē′ər), one who oversees, superintends, or looks after the work of others.

o ver shad ow (ō′vər shad′ō), 1. be more important than. 2. cast a shadow over.

o ver shoe (ō′vər shü′), a rubber shoe or a felt shoe with a rubber sole, worn over another shoe to keep the foot dry.

o ver sight (ō′vər sīt′), 1. failure to notice or think of something. Through an oversight, the kitten got no supper last night. 2. watchful care. While children are at school they are under their teacher's oversight and direction.

o ver take (ō′vər tāk′), 1. come up with. The blue car overtook ours. 2. come upon suddenly. A storm had overtaken the children.

o ver tak en (ō′vər tāk′ən). See **overtake.**

o ver threw (ō′vər thrü′). See **overthrow.**

o ver throw (ō′vər thrō′ for 1, 2, and 3, ō′vər thrō′ for 4), 1. overturn; upset; knock down. 2. destroy; put an end to. Much of the city was overthrown by the earthquake and a great fire. 3. take away the power of; defeat. The nobles overthrew the king. 4. a defeat; an upset. The overthrow of his plans left him much discouraged.

o ver thrown (ō′vər thrōn′). See **overthrow.**

o ver time (ō′vər tīm′), 1. extra time; time beyond the regular hours. 2. beyond the regular hours.

o ver took (ō′vər tu̇k′). See **overtake.**

o ver ture (ō′vər chər), 1. proposal; offer. The enemy is making overtures for peace. 2. a musical composition played by the orchestra as an introduction to an opera, or other long musical composition.

o ver turn (ō′vər tėrn′ for 1, 2, and 3, ō′vər-tėrn′ for 4), 1. turn upside down. 2. upset; fall down; fall over. The boat overturned. 3. make fall down; overthrow; defeat; destroy the power of. The rebels overturned the government. 4. an overturning.

o ver whelm (ō′vər hwelm′), 1. crush; overcome completely. She was overwhelmed with grief. 2. cover completely as a flood would. A great wave overwhelmed the boat.

o ver work (ō′vər wėrk′), to work too hard or too long.

owe (ō), 1. have to pay; be in debt. William owes his cousin a dollar. He is always owing for something. 2. be obliged or indebted for. We owe a great deal to our parents.

ow ing (ō′ing), 1. that owes; as, a man owing money. 2. due; as, to pay what is owing. 3. **Owing to** sometimes means on account of; because of. Owing to a serious illness, Maud was absent from school for over a month.

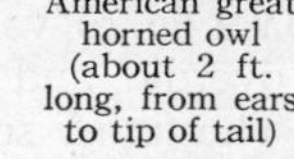
American great horned owl (about 2 ft. long, from ears to tip of tail)

owl (oul), a bird having a big head, big eyes, and a short, hooked beak. See the picture. Owls hunt mice and small birds at night. You can tell an owl by the noise or hoot it makes.

own (ōn), 1. have; possess. I own many books. 2. of one's self. This is my own book. Nell makes her own dresses. 3. admit that one owns or is the father of. His father will not own him. 4. admit. I own you are right. 5. confess. I own to being afraid. 6. Some special meanings are:

come into one's own, 1. get what belongs to one. 2. get the success or credit that one deserves.

hold one's own, keep one's position; not be forced back.

of one's own, belonging to one.

own brother, full brother, not a half brother.

own up, confess. The prisoner owned up.

own er (ōn′ər), one who owns.

own er ship (ōn′ər ship), being an owner; the possessing (of something); right of possession. Ben claimed ownership of a boat that he found drifting down the river.

ox (oks), 1. the full-grown male of domestic cattle when fitted and trained for farm work. 2. any of the group of animals to which cattle, buffaloes, and bison belong.

ox en (ok′sən), more than one ox.

ox ford (oks′fərd), a kind of low shoe.

ox y gen (ok′si jən), a gas without color or odor that forms about one fifth of the air. Animals and plants cannot live without oxygen. Fire will not burn without oxygen.

oys ter (ois′tər), a kind of shellfish much used as food, having a rough irregular shell in two halves. Oysters live in shallow water along seacoasts. See the picture on this page.

P

pa (pä), papa; father.

pace (pās), 1. a step. 2. to walk with regular steps. The tiger paced up and down his cage. 3. the length of a step in walking; about 2½ feet. There were perhaps ten paces between me and the bear. 4. to measure by paces. We paced off the distance and found it to be 69 paces. 5. way of going along. The walk, trot, and gallop are some of the paces of the horse. 6. a particular pace of some horses in which the feet on the same side are lifted and put down together. 7. move thus. Some horses are trained to pace. 8. rate; speed. John sets a fast pace in walking.

Oyster

Pa cif ic (pə sif′ik), the great ocean between Asia and America.

pa cif ic (pə sif′ik), making peace; loving peace; peaceful.

pac i fy (pas′i fī), make calm; quiet down; give peace to. Can't you pacify that screaming baby? We tried to pacify the man we bumped into.

pack (pak), 1. bundle of things wrapped up or tied together for carrying. The soldier carried a pack on his back. 2. put together in a bundle, box, etc. Pack your books in this box. We pack onions in bags. 3. fill with things; put one's things into. Pack your trunk. 4. press or crowd closely together. A hundred men were packed into one small room. 5. set; lot; a number together; as, a pack of thieves, a pack of nonsense, a pack of lies. 6. a number of animals hunting together; a number of dogs kept together for hunting. Lions do not hunt in packs, but alone. 7. a complete set of playing cards, usually 52. 8. a large area of floating pieces of ice pushed together. The ship forced its way through the pack. 9. **Pack** (a person) **off** means send him away. **Send** (a person) **packing** means send him away in a hurry. 10. make tight with something that water, steam, air, etc., cannot leak through.

pack age (pak′ij), bundle of things packed together; parcel; box with things packed in it.

pack animal, animal used for carrying loads or packs.

pack et (pak′it), 1. small package; parcel; as, a packet of letters. 2. A **packet boat** is a mail boat and is sometimes called simply a packet.

Pack animal

pact (pakt), agreement.

pad (pad), 1. cushion; soft mass used for comfort, protection, or stuffing. The baby's carriage has a pad made to fit it. 2. fill with something soft; stuff; as, a padded chair, a padded suit for football. 3. use words just to fill space. 4. number of sheets of paper fastened tightly together; a tablet. 5. a cushionlike part on the bottom of an animal's foot. 6. foot of a dog, fox, etc. 7. large floating leaf of the water lily.

pad dle[1] (pad′əl), 1. short oar with a broad blade at one end or both ends, used without resting it against the boat. 2. move (a boat or a canoe) with a paddle or paddles. 3. act of paddling; a turn at the paddle. 4. one of the broad boards fixed around a water wheel or a paddle wheel to push, or be pushed by, the water. 5. a paddle-shaped piece of wood used for stirring, for mixing, for beating clothes, etc. 6. beat with a paddle.

Paddle

pad dle[2] (pad′əl), move the hands or feet about in water.

pad dock (pad′ək), 1. small field near a stable or house used as a pasture. 2. a pen for horses at a race track.

pad lock (pad′lok′), 1. a lock that can be put on and removed. It hangs by a curved bar, hinged at one end and snapped shut at the other. See the picture. 2. fasten with a padlock.

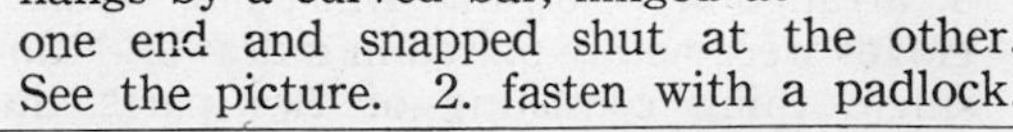

Padlock

pa gan (pā′gən), heathen; not Christian; one who worships false gods. The ancient Greeks were pagans.

page[1] (pāj), 1. one side of a leaf of paper; as, a page in this book. 2. a record; as, the pages of history.

page[2] (pāj), 1. boy servant; errand boy. The pages at hotels usually wear uniforms. 2. try to find (a person) at a hotel, club, etc., by sending someone to call his name. 3. a youth who attends a person of rank. 4. a youth preparing to be a knight.

pag eant (paj′ənt), 1. a show; an elaborate spectacle; a procession in costume; pomp; display. The coronation of the new king was a splendid pageant. 2. a public entertainment that represents scenes from history, legend, or the like. Our school gave a pageant of the coming of the Pilgrims to America.

paid (pād). See **pay.** I have paid my bills. These bills are all paid.

pail (pāl), 1. a round container for carrying liquids, etc.; bucket. 2. the amount a pail holds.

Pail

pain (pān), 1. A cut gives pain; a toothache is a pain. The death of one we love causes us pain. Does your tooth pain you? 2. **Take pains** means be careful. 3. **On pain of death** means with a risk of being killed if something is not done.

pain ful (pān′fəl), hurting; causing pain; unpleasant; as, a painful illness, a painful duty.

pains tak ing (pānz′tāk′ing), very careful.

paint (pānt), 1. solid coloring matter mixed with a liquid, used to color anything. 2. cover or decorate with paint; as, to paint a house. 3. use paint. 4. represent in colors. The artist painted fairies and angels. 5. make pictures. 6. give a vivid description of in words.

paint er[1] (pān′tər), 1. person who paints pictures; an artist. 2. person who paints houses, woodwork, etc.

paint er[2] (pān′tər), a rope fastened to the bow of a boat, for tying it to a ship, pier, etc.

paint ing (pān′ting), picture; something painted.

pair (pãr), 1. a set of two; two that go together; as, a pair of shoes or a pair of horses. 2. arrange or be arranged in pairs. Grace's gloves were neatly paired in a drawer. 3. a single thing consisting of two parts that cannot be used separately; as, a pair of scissors, a pair of trousers. 4. two people who are married or are engaged to be married. 5. join in love and marriage. 6. two animals which are mated. 7. to mate.

pa ja mas (pə jä′məz), garments to sleep in, consisting of a coat and loose trousers fastened at the waist.

Pajamas

pal (pal), comrade; playmate.

pal ace (pal′is), 1. a grand house for a king, a queen, or a bishop to live in. 2. a very fine house or building.

pal ate (pal′it), 1. the roof of the mouth. The bony part in front is the hard palate, and the fleshy part in back is the soft palate. 2. the sense of taste. The new flavor pleased his palate. 3. liking. Lazy Lola had no palate for washing dishes.

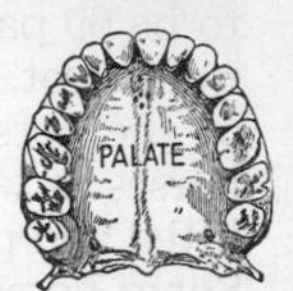

pale[1] (pāl), 1. without much color; whitish. When you have been ill, your face is sometimes pale. 2. not bright; dim. The bright stars are surrounded by hundreds of pale ones. 3. turn pale. Helen paled at the bad news.

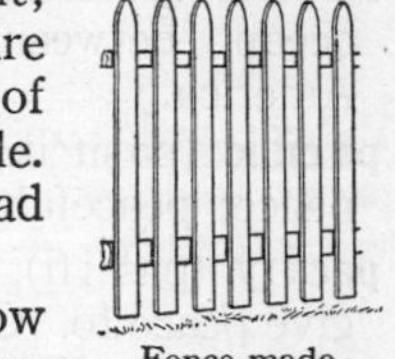

Fence made of pales

pale[2] (pāl), 1. a long, narrow board, pointed at the top, used for fences. 2. a boundary. Murderers are outside the pale of civilized society. 3. enclose with pales.

Pal es tine (pal′is tīn), Canaan; the Holy Land; the home of the Jewish people, in southwestern Asia.

pal frey (pôl′fri), a gentle riding horse, especially one used by ladies.

pal i sade (pal′i sād′), 1. a long, strong, wooden stake pointed at the top end. 2. a fence of stakes set firmly in the ground to enclose or defend. 3. a line of high steep cliffs.

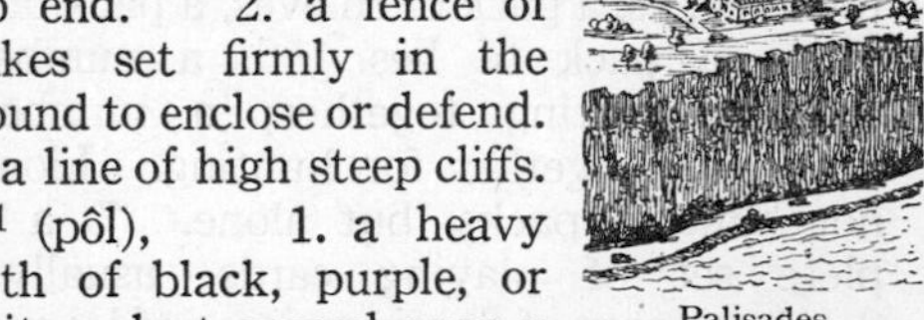

Palisades

pall[1] (pôl), 1. a heavy cloth of black, purple, or white velvet spread over a coffin, a hearse, or a tomb. 2. dark, gloomy covering. A thick pall of smoke shut out the sun from the city.

pall[2] (pôl), become distasteful or very tiresome because there has been too much of it. Fireworks pall on grown-up people after an hour or so.

pal let (pal′it), bed of straw; poor bed.

pal lid (pal′id), pale; lacking color; as, a pallid complexion.

pal lor (pal′ər), paleness; lack of color from fear, illness, death, etc.

palm[1] (päm), 1. the inside of the hand between the wrist and the fingers. 2. the width of a hand; 3 to 4 inches. 3. conceal in the hand. 4. to pass or get accepted (something not good).

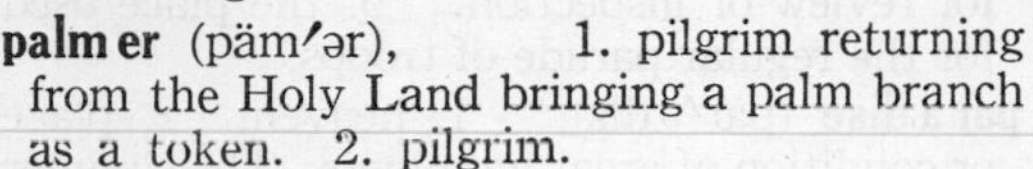
Sentinel palm

palm[2] (päm), 1. any of many kinds of trees growing in warm climates. Most palms are tall and have a bunch of large leaves at the top. 2. a branch or leaf of a palm tree as a symbol of victory or triumph. 3. victory; triumph. He bore off the palm both in tennis and in swimming.

palm er (päm′ər), 1. pilgrim returning from the Holy Land bringing a palm branch as a token. 2. pilgrim.

pal met to (pal met′ō), a kind of palm with fan-shaped leaves, abundant on the southeastern coast of the United States.

Palm Sunday, the Sunday before Easter.

pal sy (pôl′zi), 1. paralysis; loss of power to feel, to move, or to control motion in any part of the body. The man had palsy in his arm. 2. paralyze; afflict with palsy. When Alice was lost in the woods she was almost palsied by fear.

pal try (pôl′tri), trifling; almost worthless; petty; mean. Pay no attention to paltry gossip.

pam pas (pam′pəz), the vast grassy plains of South America, with no trees.

pam per (pam′pər), indulge too much; allow too many privileges. We pamper a dog if we give it fancy food every day.

pam phlet (pam′flit), a booklet in paper covers.

pan (pan), 1. a dish for cooking and other household uses, usually broad, shallow, and with no cover. 2. anything like this. Gold and other metals are sometimes obtained by washing ore in pans. The dishes on a pair of scales are called pans. 3. wash (gravel) in a pan to separate the gold. 4. cook in a pan. 5. **Pan out** means turn out or work out. His scheme panned out well. 6. in old-fashioned guns, the hollow part of the lock that held a little gunpowder to set the gun off.

pan a ma (pan′ə mä), a fine hat plaited from the young leaves of a plant of Central and South America.

pan cake (pan′kāk′), a thin, flat cake made of batter and fried in a pan or on a griddle.

pan da (pan′də), 1. giant panda; bearlike animal of Tibet, mostly white with black legs. 2. reddish-brown animal somewhat like a raccoon, that lives in the mountains of India.

Giant panda (about 6 ft. long)

pane (pān), single sheet of glass in a division of a window, a door, or a sash. Hailstones as big as eggs broke several panes of glass.

pan el (pan′əl), 1. a strip or surface that is different in some way from what is around it. A panel is often sunk below or raised above the rest, and used for a decoration. Panels may be in a door or other woodwork, on large pieces of furniture, or made as parts of a dress. 2. arrange in panels; furnish or decorate with panels. The room was paneled with oak. 3. a picture, photograph, or design much longer than wide. 4. a list of persons called as jurors; the members of a jury.

Panels

pang (pang), 1. a sudden, short, sharp pain; as, the pangs of a toothache. 2. a sudden feeling. A pang of pity moved Ruth's heart.

pan ic (pan′ik), 1. unreasoning fear; a fear spreading through a multitude of people so that they lose control of themselves. When the theater caught fire, there was a panic. When four banks failed in one day, there was a panic among people who had money in banks. 2. caused by panic; showing panic; unreasoning; as, panic terror, panic fear.

pan o ram a (pan′ə ram′ə), 1. a picture of a landscape or other scene often shown as if seen from a central point; a picture unrolled a part at a time and made to pass continuously before the spectators. 2. a continuously passing or changing scene; as, the panorama of city life. 3. a wide, unbroken view of a surrounding region; as, a panorama of beach and sea.

pan sy (pan′zi), a flower somewhat like a violet but much larger and often having several colors.

pant (pant), 1. breathe hard and quickly. 2. a short, quick breath. 3. speak with short, quick breaths. "Come quick. Come quick," panted Joe. 4. be eager; long very much. I am just panting for my turn.

pan ta loon (pan′tə lün′), 1. clown. 2. **Pantaloons** are trousers.

pan ther (pan′thər), 1. a puma or mountain lion. 2. a leopard. 3. the jaguar.

pan to mime (pan′tə mīm), 1. a play without words in which the actors express themselves by gestures. 2. gestures without words.

Panther (def. 1) (about 5 ft. long, without the tail)

pan try (pan′tri), small room in which food, dishes, silver, or table linen is kept.

pants (pants), common name for trousers, slacks, or similar garments.

pap (pap), soft food for infants or invalids.

pa pa (pä′pə), father; daddy.

pa per (pā′pər), 1. a material used for writing, printing, drawing, wrapping packages, and covering walls. This book is made of paper. Paper is made in thin sheets from wood pulp, rags, etc. 2. piece or sheet of paper. 3. document. Important papers were stolen. 4. a newspaper. 5. an article; an essay. Professor Wise read a paper on how to teach English. 6. made of paper; as, paper dolls, paper money. 7. thin; as, almonds with paper shells. 8. wallpaper. 9. to cover with paper.

pa poose or **pap poose** (pa püs′), a North American Indian baby.

Papoose on its mother's back

pap ri ka (pap rē′kə), a kind of red pepper not so strong as the ordinary kind.

par (pär), 1. equality; an equal level. The gains and losses are about on a par. He is quite on a par with his brother in intelligence. 2. an average or normal amount, degree, or condition. Tom has been feeling below par lately. 3. average; normal.

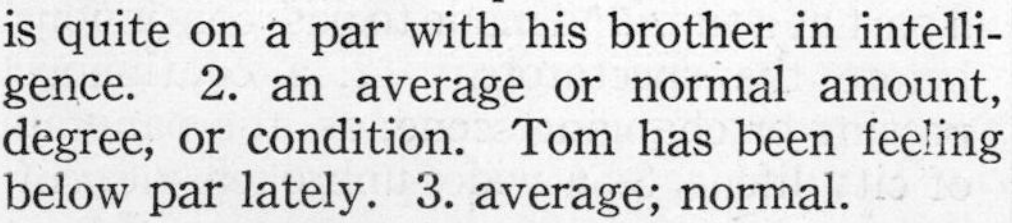

par a ble (par′ə bəl), a short story used to teach some truth or moral lesson. Jesus taught in parables.

par a chute (par′ə shüt), 1. an apparatus used in descending safely through the air from a great height. See the picture. 2. jump with a parachute. The men in the burning plane parachuted safely to the ground.

Man descending with parachute

pa rade (pə rād′), 1. a procession; a march for display. The circus had a parade. 2. to march in a procession; to walk proudly as if in a parade. 3. group of people walking for display or pleasure. 4. place where people walk for pleasure. 5. great show or display. A modest man will not make a parade of his wealth. 6. make a great show of. 7. a military display or review of troops. 8. come together in military order for review or inspection. 9. the place used for the regular parade of troops.

par a dise (par′ə dīs), 1. heaven. 2. place or condition of great happiness. The summer camp was a paradise for Tom.

par a dox (par′ə doks), 1. a statement that may be true but seems to say two opposite things. "More haste, less speed" and "The child is father to the man" are paradoxes. 2. a statement that is false because it says two opposite things.

par af fin (par′ə fin), white tasteless substance like wax. Paraffin is used for making candles and for sealing jars of jelly or jam.

par a gon (par′ə gon), model of excellence or perfection.

par a graph (par′ə graf), 1. group of sentences which belong together; a distinct part of a chapter, letter, or composition. 2. to divide into paragraphs. 3. a separate note or item of news in a newspaper.

par a keet (par′ə kēt), any of various small parrots, most of which have slender bodies and long tails.

par al lel (par′ə lel), 1. at or being the same distance apart everywhere, like the two rails of a railroad track. 2. be at the same distance from. The street parallels the railroad. 3. a parallel line or surface. 4. The parallel circles around the earth, marking degrees of latitude, are called parallels. 5. a comparison to show likeness; as, to draw a parallel between this winter and last winter. 6. find a case which

Three sets of parallel lines

is similar or parallel to. Can you parallel that for friendliness? 7. similar; corresponding.

pa ral y sis (pə ral′i sis), 1. a lessening or loss of the power of motion or sensation in any part of the body. 2. crippling; condition of helpless lack of activity. The war caused a paralysis of trade.

par a lyze or **par a lyse** (par′ə līz), 1. affect with a lessening or loss of the power of motion or feeling. His left arm was paralyzed. 2. cripple; make powerless or inactive. Fear paralyzed my mind.

par a mount (par′ə mount), above others; chief in importance; supreme. Truth is of paramount importance.

par a pet (par′ə pet), 1. low wall to protect soldiers. 2. low wall at the edge of a balcony, roof, bridge, etc.

Parapet of a fort

par a site (par′ə sīt), 1. an animal or plant that lives on another. Lice are parasites on animals. Mistletoe is a parasite on oak trees. 2. person who lives on others without making any useful and fitting return. Beggars and tramps are parasites.

par a sol (par′ə sôl), a light umbrella used as a protection from the sun.

par cel (pär′səl), 1. a bundle of things wrapped or packed together; a box with things packed in it. 2. piece; as, a parcel of land. 3. **Parcel out** means divide into portions or distribute in portions.

parcel post, branch of the postal service which carries parcels.

parch (pärch), 1. dry by heating; roast slightly. The Indians parched corn. 2. make or become hot and dry or thirsty. I am parched with the heat.

parch ment (pärch′mənt), 1. the skin of sheep or goats, prepared for use as a writing material. 2. manuscript or document written on parchment. 3. paper that looks like parchment.

par don (pär′dən), 1. forgiveness. **I beg your pardon** means please excuse me. 2. forgive. Grandmother pardons us when we make mischief. 3. excuse. 4. set free from punishment. The governor pardoned the thief. 5. setting free from punishment.

pare (pãr), 1. cut, trim, or shave off the outer part of; peel; as, to pare an apple. 2. cut away little by little; as, to pare down expenses.

par ent (pãr′ənt), 1. father or mother. 2. source; cause.

par ent age (pãr′ən tij), descent from parents; family line; ancestors.

pa ren tal (pə ren′təl), of a parent; of parents; having something to do with a parent or parents.

pa ren the ses (pə ren′thi sēz), more than one parenthesis. The pronunciations on this page are enclosed in parentheses.

pa ren the sis (pə ren′thi sis), 1. a word, phrase, sentence, etc., inserted within a sentence, to explain or qualify something. 2. either or both of two curved lines ( ) used to set off such an expression.

pa ri ah (pə rī′ə), outcast.

par ish (par′ish), 1. a district that has its own church and clergyman. 2. people of a parish. 3. county in Louisiana.

park (pärk), 1. land set apart for the pleasure of the public. Many cities have beautiful parks. 2. land set apart for wild animals. 3. grounds around a fine house. 4. leave (an automobile, etc.) for a time in a certain place. Park your car here. 5. place to leave an automobile, etc., for a time.

par ley (pär′li), 1. a conference or informal talk to discuss terms or matters in dispute. The general held a parley with the enemy about exchanging prisoners. 2. discuss terms with an enemy.

par lia ment (pär′li mənt), a council or congress that is the highest lawmaking body of a country. The British Parliament consists of the House of Lords and the House of Commons.

par lor (pär′lər), 1. room for receiving or entertaining guests; sitting room. 2. a decorated room used as a shop; a shop; as, a beauty parlor.

parlor car, railroad passenger car for day travel, more luxurious than ordinary cars.

par rot (par′ət), 1. bird with a stout hooked bill and often with bright-colored feathers. Some parrots can imitate sounds and repeat words and sentences. 2. person who repeats words or acts without understanding them.

Gray parrot (about 1 ft. tall)

par ry (par′i), 1. ward off; turn aside; evade. He parried the sword with his dagger. She parried our question by asking us one. 2. act of parrying; avoiding.

pars ley (pärs′li), a garden plant with finely divided fragrant leaves. Parsley is used to flavor food and to trim platters of meat.

pars nip (pärs′nip), 1. vegetable that is the long, tapering whitish root of a plant belonging to the same family as the carrot. See the picture below. 2. the plant.

Parsley

par son (pär′sən), 1. a minister in charge of a parish. 2. any clergyman; minister.

par son age (pär′sən ij), the house provided for a minister by a church.

part (pärt), 1. something less than the whole; fraction. Jack ate part of an apple. A dime is a tenth part of a dollar. 2. thing that helps to make up a whole. A radio has many parts. 3. share. Tom had no part in the mischief. 4. side in a dispute or contest. John always takes his brother's part. 5. character in a play; the words spoken by a character. Jane spoke the part of the fairy in our play. 6. divide into two or more pieces. 7. force apart; divide. The policeman on horseback parted the crowd. 8. go apart; separate. The friends parted in anger. 9. ability; talent. Mr. Bright is a man of parts. 10. one of the voices or instruments in music. The four parts in singing are soprano, alto, tenor, and bass. 11. the music for it. 12. region; district; place. He has traveled much in foreign parts. 13. a dividing line left in combing one's hair. 14. less than the whole; as, part time. 15. partly; in some measure or degree. 16. **Part with** means give up.

Parsnip

par take (pär tāk′), take a share; eat or drink some. Will you partake of our breakfast with us? **partook** and **partaken** are formed from **partake.**

par tak en (pär tāk′ən). See **partake.**

par tial (pär′shəl), 1. not complete; not total. Father has made a partial payment on our new car. The English won a partial victory. 2. inclined to favor one side more than another; favoring unfairly. Our teacher sometimes seems partial to the girls. 3. having a liking for; favorably inclined. She is partial to tomatoes.

par tial ly (pär′shəl i), partly.

par tic i pate (pär tis′i pāt), have a share; take part. The lame boy could not participate in all the games.

par ti cle (pär′ti kəl), a very little bit. I got a particle of dust in my eye.

par tic u lar (pər tik′ū lər), 1. belonging to some one person, thing, group, occasion, etc. Jack's particular task is to care for the dog. A particular characteristic of a skunk is its smell. 2. apart from others; single; considered separately. That particular chair is already sold. 3. different from others; unusual. This vacation was of particular importance to Mary, for she was going to Brazil. Harry is a particular friend of Dick. 4. hard to please; wanting everything to be just right; very careful. Mrs. Brown is so particular about her housework that servants will not work for her. 5. an individual part; item; point. The work is complete in every particular. All the particulars of the accident are now known. 6. **In particular** means especially. We played around, not going anywhere in particular.

par tic u lar ly (pər tik′ū lər li), 1. especially. The teacher praised Ruth particularly. I am particularly fond of Amy. She mentioned that point particularly. 2. in detail; in all its parts. The inspector examined the machine particularly.

part ing (pär′ting), 1. departure; going away; separation. The friends were sad at parting. 2. given, taken, done, etc., at parting; as, a parting request, a parting shot.

par ti san or **par ti zan** (pär′ti zən), 1. strong supporter of a person, party, or cause; one whose support is based on feeling rather than on reasoning. 2. of a partisan; like a partisan.

par ti tion (pär tish′ən), 1. division into parts; as, the partition of a man's wealth when he dies. 2. divide into parts; as, to partition an empire among three brothers, to partition a house into rooms. 3. a wall between rooms.

part ly (pärt′li), in part; in some measure or degree.

part ner (pärt′nər), 1. one who shares. My sister was the partner of my walks. 2. member of a company or firm, sharing the risks and profits of the business. 3. wife or husband. 4. companion in a dance. 5. player on the same side in a game.

part ner ship (pärt′nər ship), being a partner; association; joint interest; as, a business partnership, the partnership of marriage.

par took (pär tu̇k′). See **partake.** He partook of food and drink yesterday.

par tridge (pär′trij), 1. any of several kinds of game birds belonging to the same group as the quail, pheasant, and grouse. 2. in the United States, the ruffed grouse or the quail.

Common gray partridge of Europe (1 ft. from beak to tip of tail)

par ty (pär′ti), 1. a group of people having a good time together. Jean had a party on her birthday. Grace went to ten parties last winter. 2. group of people doing something together; as, a sewing party, a scouting party of three soldiers. 3. group of people thinking alike and wanting the same kind of government or action; as, the Democratic party. 4. of a party; as, party feeling. 5. one who takes part in, aids, or knows about. He was a party to our secret. 6. person. Old Billy Mudd was a queer party. That party in the end seat has fallen asleep.

pass (pas), 1. go by; move past. The parade passed. Many people pass our house every day. 2. move on. The days pass quickly. 3. come to an end; die. King Arthur passed in peace. 4. take place; happen. Mrs. Brown can tell you all that has passed. **Bring to pass** means accomplish. 5. get through or by. The ship passed the channel. Tom passed the examination. The bill passed Congress. 6. go from person to person. Property passes from father to son. Hot words pass when men quarrel. 7. hand around; hand from one to another. Please pass the butter. Dick passed the football quickly. 8. change. Water passes from a liquid to a solid state when it freezes. 9. give a judgment or opinion. Please pass upon this question. A judge passes sentence upon a guilty person. 10. promise; as, to pass one's word. 11. go without notice. Bill was rude, but let that pass. 12. be taken. Ann could pass for twenty. Mr. Crook moved to another city where he passed by the name of Smith. 13. use or spend; as, to pass the days happily. 14. go beyond. Your story passes belief. 15. move. Pass your hand over the velvet and feel how soft it is. 16. in card-playing, to give up a chance or to refuse to play a hand. 17. in fencing, to thrust. 18. a thrust in fencing. 19. narrow road; path. A pass crosses the mountains. 20. written permission; as, a pass to visit the battle front. 21. a free ticket. 22. state; condition. Things have come to a strange pass when children give orders to their parents. 23. motion of the hands. The magician made passes in the air while doing his tricks. 24. be successful in (an examination). 25. act of passing; success in an examination.

pas sage (pas′ij), 1. a hall or way through a building. 2. a means of passing; a way through. "Make passage for the King," they cried. 3. passing; as, the passage of time. 4. piece from a speech or writing; as, a passage from the Bible. 5. going across; voyage. We had a stormy passage across the Atlantic. 6. an exchange of blows; as, a passage of arms.

pas sen ger (pas′ən jər), traveler in a train, bus, boat, etc., usually one that pays a fare.

pass er-by (pas′ər bī′), one that passes by.

pass ing (pas′ing), 1. going by. 2. done or given in passing. 3. allowing one to pass an examination or test. 75 will be a passing mark.

pas sion (pash′ən), 1. very strong feeling. Hate and fear are passions. 2. rage; violent anger. He flew into a passion. 3. love between man and woman. 4. very strong liking. She has a passion for music. 5. thing for which a strong liking is felt. Music is her passion. 6. suffering. **The Passion** means the sufferings of Jesus after the Last Supper.

pas sion ate (pash′ən it), 1. having or showing strong feelings. A tiger is a passionate animal. 2. easily moved by strong feelings. 3. resulting from strong feeling. He made a passionate speech about the sufferings of the poor.

pas sive (pas′iv), 1. not acting in return; being acted on without itself acting; as, a passive mind or disposition. 2. not resisting; yielding or submitting to the will of another. The slaves gave passive obedience to their master.

pass port (pas′pōrt), 1. a paper or book giving one official permission to travel in a foreign country, under the protection of one's own government. 2. anything that gives one admission or acceptance. An interest in gardening was a passport to my aunt's favor.

pass word (pas′wėrd′), secret word that allows a person who says it to pass a guard.

past (past), 1. passed. Summer is past. The past year was full of trouble. For some time past Maud has been ill. 2. past time; what has happened in past time; one's past life. We cannot change the past. 3. the verb form that expresses occurrence in past time. The past of *do* is *did*. 4. beyond; as, half past two, a boy past twelve, to run past the house, hurt past bearing. 5. passing by; by. The cars go past once an hour.

paste (pāst), 1. a mixture that will stick paper together. 2. to stick with paste. 3. a soft mixture. Pottery is made from a paste of clay and water. 4. pie dough. 5. a hard glassy material used in making imitations of precious stones.

paste board (pāst′bōrd′), a stiff material made of sheets of paper pasted together or of paper pulp pressed and dried.

pas teur ize (pas′tər īz), heat hot enough and long enough to kill certain germs. The milk sold in many cities is pasteurized.

pas time (pas′tīm′), pleasant way of passing time. Games and sports are pastimes.

pas tor (pas′tər), minister in charge of a church; spiritual guide.

pas tor al (pas′tər əl), 1. of shepherds or country life. 2. simple or naturally beautiful like the country. 3. of a pastor or his duties.

pas try (pās′tri), 1. food made of baked flour paste, made rich with lard or butter. 2. pies, tarts, and other foods wholly or partly made of rich flour paste.

pas tur age (pas′chər ij), 1. growing grass and other plants for cattle, sheep, or horses to feed on. 2. pasture land.

pas ture (pas′chər), 1. grassy field or hillside; grassy land on which cattle, sheep, or horses can feed. 2. grass and other growing plants. These lands afford good pasture. 3. put (cattle, sheep, etc.) out to pasture. 4. feed on growing grass, etc.

pat (pat), 1. strike or tap lightly with something flat. He patted the dog with his hand. 2. to tap with the hand as a sign of sympathy, approval, or affection; as, to pat a dog. 3. a light stroke or tap with something flat. 4. the sound made by patting. 5. a small mass, especially of butter. 6. apt; suitable; to the point; as, a pat reply. 7. aptly; suitably.

patch (pach), 1. piece put on to mend a hole or a tear. 2. piece of cloth, etc., put over a wound or a sore. 3. pad over a hurt eye to protect it. 4. a small bit of black cloth that ladies used to wear on their faces to show off their fair skin. 5. put patches on; mend; protect or adorn with a patch or patches. 6. to piece together; make hastily; as, to patch up a costume for a play. 7. make right; as, to patch up a quarrel. 8. a small, uneven spot; as, a patch of brown on the skin. 9. piece of ground; as, a garden patch. 10. a scrap or bit of cloth left over.

pate (pāt), the head; the top of the head; as, a bald pate.

pat ent (pat′ənt for 1, 2, 3, 4, and 5, pā′tənt for 6), 1. a government grant to a person by which he is the only one allowed to make or sell a new invention for a certain number of years. 2. given or protected by a patent. 3. get a patent for. 4. an invention that is patented. 5. an official document from a government giving a right or privilege. 6. evident; plain. It is patent that cats dislike dogs.

pat ent leath er (pat′ənt leᴛʜ′ər), leather with a very glossy, smooth surface, usually black.

pa ter nal (pə tėr′nəl), 1. fatherly; of or like a father. 2. related on the father's side of the family. Everyone has two paternal grandparents and two maternal grandparents.

path (path), 1. a way made by people or animals walking. 2. road too narrow for a wagon or automobile. 3. line along which a person or thing moves; as, the path of the moon through the heavens. 4. way of behaving; way of life. Some choose paths of glory; some choose paths of ease.

pa thet ic (pə thet′ik), pitiful; arousing pity. A lost child is pathetic.

path less (path′lis), without paths.

pa thos (pā′thos), the quality in speech, writing, music, events, or a scene that arouses a feeling of pity or sadness.

path way (path′wā′), path.

pa tience (pā′shəns), 1. calm bearing of pain, of waiting, or of anything that annoys, troubles, or hurts. A cat shows patience by watching a mousehole. You need patience when you are having your teeth filled. 2. sticking to a piece of work. 3. a card game.

pa tient (pā′shənt), 1. having patience; showing patience. 2. person who is being treated by a doctor.

pa ti o (pä′ti ō), an inner court or yard open to the sky. Houses in Spanish countries are often built around patios.

Patio

pa tri arch (pā′tri ärk), 1. the father and ruler of a family or tribe. In the Bible, Abraham, Isaac, and Jacob were patriarchs. 2. a venerable old man.

pa tri ot (pā′tri ət), person who loves his country and gives it loyal support.

pa tri ot ic (pā′tri ot′ik), 1. loving one's country. 2. showing love and loyal support of one's own country.

pa tri ot ism (pā′tri ət izm), love and loyal support of one's country.

pa trol (pə trōl′), 1. go the rounds as a watchman or a policeman does. The camp was carefully patrolled. 2. going the rounds to watch or guard. 3. the men who patrol. The patrol was changed at midnight. 4. group of soldiers, ships, or airplanes sent out to find out all they can about the enemy. 5. organized group of eight Boy Scouts or eight Girl Scouts.

pa tron (pā′trən), 1. person who stands back of the work of another, perhaps helps it with money, and gives it the advantage of his approval and his name. 2. person who buys regularly at a given store. 3. guarding; protecting; as, the patron saint of travelers.

pa tron age (pā′trən ij), 1. the favor, encouragement, or support given by a patron. 2. regular business given to a store, hotel, etc., by customers. 3. condescending favor; as, an air of patronage. 4. power to give jobs or favors; as, the patronage of a governor, mayor, or member of Congress.

pa tron ize (pā′trən īz), 1. act as a patron toward; support or protect. People are urged to patronize their neighborhood stores. 2. treat in a condescending way. We dislike to have anybody patronize us.

pat ter[1] (pat′ər), 1. make rapid taps. The rain patters on a windowpane. Bare feet pattered along the hard floor. 2. a series of quick taps or the sound they make; as, the patter of rain, the patter of little feet.

pat ter[2] (pat′ər), 1. talk or say rapidly and easily, without much thought. 2. rapid and easy talk.

pat tern (pat′ərn), 1. a fine example; a model to be followed. Washington was a pattern of manliness. Mary used a paper pattern in cutting out her new dress. 2. make according to a pattern. She patterned herself after her mother. 3. a design; arrangement of forms and colors; as, the patterns of rugs, cloth, jewelry, etc.

pat ty (pat′i), a hollow form of pastry filled with chicken, oysters, etc.

paunch (pônch), belly; stomach.

pau per (pô′pər), very poor person; person supported by charity.

pau per ize (pô′pər īz), make a pauper of.

pause (pôz), stop for a time; wait. He made a short pause and then went on reading. The dog paused when he heard me.

pave (pāv), 1. cover (a street, sidewalk, etc.) with a pavement. 2. prepare; make smooth or easy. He paved the way for me by doing careful work.

pave ment (pāv′mənt), covering or surface for streets, sidewalks, etc., made of stones, bricks, wood, asphalt, etc.

pa vil ion (pə vil′yən), 1. a light building, usually one somewhat open, used for shelter, pleasure, etc.; as, a bathing pavilion. 2. tent; a large tent raised on posts.

Pavilion for dancing

pav ing (pāv′ing), 1. material for pavement. 2. pavement.

paw (pô), 1. the foot of an animal having claws; as, a cat's paw, a dog's paw. 2. strike or scrape with the paws or feet. The cat pawed the mouse she had caught. The horse was pawing the ground, eager to be going again. 3. handle awkwardly or roughly. The big man pawed over the baby's clothes in a helpless way.

pawn[1] (pôn), 1. leave (something) with another person as security that borrowed money will be returned; pledge. She pawned her watch to buy food. 2. something left as security. 3. **In pawn** means being held by someone else as security. Her watch is in pawn.

pawn[2] (pôn), 1. in the game of chess, one of the 16 pieces that are of little value and are often given up to gain some advantage. 2. an unimportant person or thing used by somebody to gain some advantage.

pay (pā), 1. give money for things or work. 2. give money to or for. A good lawyer is highly paid. His uncle paid John's way through college. 3. money given for things or work. Tom gets his pay every Saturday. 4. give what is due. 5. return for favors or hurts. Kate got her pay for being mean. 6. give; offer; as, to pay attention, to pay a compliment. 7. give a profit; be worth while. It pays to be polite.

pay ment (pā′mənt), 1. paying. 2. amount paid; as, a monthly payment of $10. 3. pay. Baby's good health is payment enough for me.

pea (pē), 1. a round seed in the pod of a plant, used as a vegetable; the plant itself. 2. The **sweet pea** is a climbing plant with delicate flowers of many colors.

Pod opened to show peas

peace (pēs), 1. freedom from war or strife; public quiet, order, and security. We had been working for world peace. 2. an agreement to end war; as, the Peace of Paris. 3. quiet; calm; stillness. We enjoy the peace of the country. 4. **Hold one's peace** means keep still.

peace a ble (pēs′ə bəl), 1. liking peace; keeping peace. 2. peaceful.

peace ful (pēs′fəl), 1. quiet; calm; full of peace. 2. liking peace; keeping peace.

peach (pēch), 1. the juicy, nearly round fruit of a tree, having a rough stone or pit in it. 2. the tree it grows on. 3. yellowish pink.

pea cock (pē′kok′), large bird with beautiful green, blue, and gold feathers, and a splendid tail. The tail feathers have spots like eyes on them and can be spread out and held upright like a fan.

Peacock with tail spread out

peak (pēk), 1. the pointed top of a mountain or hill. 2. a mountain that stands alone; as, Pike's Peak. 3. any pointed end or top; as, the peak of a beard, the peak of a roof. 4. the highest point. 5. the front part or the brim of a cap, that stands out. 6. the narrow part of a ship's hold, at either end.

Mountain peak

peal (pēl), 1. a loud, long sound; as, a peal of thunder. 2. loud ringing of bells. 3. a chime; a set of bells. 4. sound out in a peal; ring. The bells pealed forth their message of Christmas joy.

pea nut (pē′nut′), 1. a seed like a nut used for food. 2. the plant it grows on.

pear (pãr), 1. a sweet juicy fruit rounded at one end and smaller toward the stem end. 2. the tree it grows on.

Pear

pearl (pėrl), 1. a white or nearly white gem that has a soft shine like satin. Pearls are found inside the shell of a kind of oyster, or in other similar shellfish. 2. a very fine one of its kind. She is a pearl among women. 3. thing that looks like a pearl, such as a dewdrop, or a tear. 4. very pale, clear, bluish gray.

pearl y (pėr′li), like a pearl in color or luster; as, pearly teeth.

peas ant (pez′ənt), 1. a farmer of the working class in Europe. 2. of peasants; as, peasant labor.

peas ant ry (pez′ənt ri), peasants.

peat (pēt), a kind of sod, used as fuel after being dried. Peat is made of partly rotted moss and plants.

peb ble (peb′əl), a small stone, usually worn and rounded by being rolled about by water.

peb bly (peb′li), having many pebbles; covered with pebbles. The pebbly beach hurt our bare feet.

pe can (pi kän′), 1. a nut that is shaped like an olive, and has a smooth shell. 2. the tree it grows on. Pecans grow in the southern United States.

Pecan: A, branch; B, nuts.

peck[1] (pek), 1. strike at and pick up with the beak. A hen pecks corn. 2. make by striking with the beak. Woodpeckers peck holes in trees. 3. a hole or mark made by pecking. 4. make a pecking motion. 5. a stroke with the beak. The hen gave me a peck. 6. eat only a little, bit by bit. Because she is not feeling well today, she just pecks at her food. 7. a stiff, unwilling kiss.

peck[2] (pek), 1. a unit of dry measure, eight quarts or one fourth of a bushel; as, a peck of beans, a peck of potatoes. 2. a container holding just a peck, to measure with. 3. great deal; as, a peck of trouble.

pe cul iar (pi kūl′yər), 1. strange; odd; unusual. It is peculiar that he has not come today, for he usually appears every Tuesday. A woman's hat on a man's head looks peculiar. What a peculiar thing to say! 2. special; belonging to one person or thing and not to another. This book has a peculiar value because it belonged to George Washington. The Quakers wore a dress peculiar to themselves.

pe cu li ar i ty (pi kū′li ar′i ti), 1. being peculiar; strange or unusual quality. We noticed the peculiarity of his manner at once. 2. some little thing that is strange or odd. One of his peculiarities is that his two eyes are not the same color.

ped al (ped′əl), 1. a lever worked by the foot; the part on which the foot is placed to move any kind of machinery. Organs and pianos have pedals for changing the tone. The two pedals of a bicycle, pushed down one after the other, make it go. 2. work or use the pedals; move by pedals. He pedaled his bicycle slowly up the hill.

ped dle (ped′əl), 1. carry from place to place and sell. 2. sell or deal out in small quantities; as, to peddle candy, to peddle gossip. 3. travel about with things to sell.

ped dler (ped′lər), man who travels about selling things which he carries in a pack or in a cart.

ped es tal (ped′is təl), 1. the base on which a column or a statue stands. 2. the base of a tall vase, lamp, etc.

Pedestal for a statue

pe des tri an (pi des′tri ən), 1. going on foot; walking. 2. person who goes on foot. Pedestrians have to watch for automobiles turning corners.

ped i gree (ped′i grē), 1. list of ancestors; family tree. 2. ancestors; line of descent.

ped lar (ped′lər), peddler.

peek (pēk), 1. look quickly and slyly; peep. You must not peek while you are counting in such games as hide-and-seek. 2. a quick, sly look.

peel (pēl), 1. the rind or outer covering of fruit, etc. 2. strip the skin, rind, or bark from; as, to peel an orange, to peel a potato. 3. strip. The Indians peeled the bark from trees to make canoes. 4. come off. When I was sunburnt, my skin peeled. The paint on my shed is peeling.

peep[1] (pēp), 1. to look through a small or narrow hole or crack. 2. such a look; a little look; as, to take a peep into the pantry. 3. to look when no one knows it. 4. a secret look. 5. look out, as if peeping; come partly out. 6. the first looking or coming out; as, at the peep of day.

peep[2] (pēp), 1. the cry of a young bird or chicken; a sound like a chirp or a squeak. 2. make such a sound; chirp.

peer[1] (pēr), 1. equal. He is so fine a man that it would be hard to find his peer. 2. man who has a title; man who is high and great by birth or rank. A duke, marquis, earl, count, viscount, or baron is a peer.

peer[2] (pēr), 1. look closely to see clearly, as a near-sighted person does. She peered at the tag to read the price. 2. come out slightly; peep out. The sun was peering from behind a cloud.

peer less (pēr′lis), without an equal; matchless. Washington was the peerless leader of our country in his day.

pee vish (pē′vish), cross; fretful; complaining. A peevish child is unhappy and makes others unhappy.

peg (peg), 1. a pin or small bolt of wood or metal used to fasten parts together, to hang things on, to stop a hole, to make fast a rope or string on, to mark the score in a game, etc. 2. fasten or hold with pegs. We must peg down our tent. 3. **Take a person down a peg or two** means humble him. 4. work hard.

pel i can (pel′i kən), a very large, fish-eating water bird with a huge bill and a pouch for storing food.

pel let (pel′it), little ball of mud, paper, hail, snow, food, medicine, etc.; a pill.

Pelican

pell-mell (pel′mel′), 1. in a rushing, tumbling mass or crowd. The children dashed pell-mell down the beach and into the waves. 2. in headlong haste. 3. headlong; tumultuous.

pelt[1] (pelt), 1. throw things at; attack; assail. The boys were pelting the dog with stones. 2. beat heavily. The rain came pelting down. 3. speed. The horse is coming at full pelt.

pelt[2] (pelt), the skin of a sheep, goat, or small fur-bearing animal, before it is tanned.

pen[1] (pen), 1. small yard for cows, sheep, pigs, chickens, etc. 2. shut up in a pen. 3. shut. John had me penned in a corner where I could not escape.

pen[2] (pen), 1. a tool used in writing with ink. 2. write. I shall pen a few words to father today.

pe nal ize (pē′nəl īz), 1. make liable to punishment; set a penalty for by law or by rule. Speeding on city streets is penalized. Fouls are penalized in many games. 2. punish; inflict a penalty on. Our football team was penalized five yards.

pen al ty (pen′əl ti), punishment. The penalty for speeding is a fine of ten dollars.

pen ance (pen′əns), 1. punishment borne to show sorrow for sin, to make up for a wrong done, and to obtain pardon from the church for sin. 2. any act done to show that one is sorry or repents. Grace did penance for hurting her sister by staying home from the circus.

pence (pens), pennies.

pen cil (pen′səl), 1. a pointed tool to write or draw with. 2. mark or write with a pencil.

pend ant (pen′dənt), a hanging ornament, such as a locket.

pend ent (pen′dənt), hanging; as, the pendent branches of willow which touch the water.

Pendant

pend ing (pen′ding), 1. waiting to be decided or settled; as, while the agreement was pending. 2. until; while waiting for. Pending his return, let us get the car all ready. 3. during; as, pending the investigation.

pen du lum (pen′jü ləm), a weight so hung from a fixed point that it is free to swing to and fro. The movement of the works of a tall clock is often timed by a pendulum.

Pendulum. Dotted lines show motion.

pen e trate (pen′i trāt), 1. get into or through. A bullet can penetrate this thin wall, or two inches into that wall. 2. pierce through. Our eyes could not penetrate the darkness. Even where the trees were thickest, the sunshine penetrated. 3. soak through; spread through. The rain penetrated all our clothes. The odor penetrated the whole house. 4. see into; understand. I could not penetrate the mystery.

King penguin (about 3 ft. tall)

pen guin (peng′gwin), a sea bird with flippers for diving and swimming in place of wings for flying.

pen in su la (pən in′sə lə), piece of land almost surrounded by water, or extending far out into the water. Florida is a big peninsula.

pen i tent (pen′i tənt), 1. sorry for doing wrong. The penitent boy promised never to cheat again. 2. one who is sorry for sin, especially one who is doing penance under the direction of the church.

pen knife (pen′nīf′), small pocketknife.

pen nant (pen′ənt), a flag, usually long and narrow, used on ships, in signaling, as a school banner, etc. In some sports, the best team wins a pennant.

Pennant

pen ni less (pen′i lis), without a cent of money; very poor.

pen non (pen′ən), 1. a long triangular flag, originally carried on the lance of a knight. 2. any flag or banner.

pen ny (pen′i), 1. cent; copper coin of the U. S. and Canada. 100 pennies = 1 dollar. 2. an English bronze coin equal to one twelfth of a shilling, or about two cents. 3. It will cost you a **pretty penny** means that it will cost you a large sum of money.

pen sion (pen′shən), 1. a regular payment to a person which is not wages. Pensions are often paid because of long service, special merit, or injuries received. 2. give a pension to.

pen sion er (pen′shən ər), person who receives a pension.

pen sive (pen′siv), thoughtful in a serious or sad way.

pent (pent), penned; closely confined; shut. The princess was pent in the castle all winter. Her pent-up feelings could no longer be restrained, and she burst into tears.

Peony

pe o ny (pē′ə ni), 1. a garden plant with large showy flowers. 2. the flower.

peo ple (pē′pəl), 1. men, women, and children; persons. There were ten people present. 2. race; nation; as, the peoples of Asia, the American people. 3. persons in general; the public. 4. persons of a place, class, or group; as, city people, Southern people, the people here. 5. persons in relation to a superior; as, the king and his people, a pastor and his people. 6. the lower classes. The French nobles oppressed the people. 7. fill with people. Europe very largely peopled America. 8. family. John spends his holidays with his people.

pep per (pep′ər), 1. a seasoning with a hot taste, used for soups, meats, vegetables, etc. Pepper is made by grinding the ripe or unripe berries of black pepper. 2. a hollow red or green vegetable that is baked or fried, and used in pickles. 3. season with pepper; sprinkle with pepper. 4. hit with small objects sent thick and fast. We peppered the enemy's lines with our shot.

pep per mint (pep′ər mint), 1. an herb grown for its oil, used in medicine and in candy. 2. this oil. 3. candy flavored with peppermint oil.

Peppermint

per (pėr), 1. for each; as, a pint of milk per child, ten cents per pound. 2. through; by; by means of. I send this per my son.

per ceive (pər sēv′), 1. be aware of through the senses; see, hear, taste, smell, or feel. Did you perceive a red color or a blue one? 2. take in with the mind; observe. I soon perceived that I could not make him change his mind.

per cent (pər sent′), 1. hundredths. Five per cent of 40 is 2. 2. for each hundred; in each hundred. Seven per cent of the children failed. **Per cent.** and **percent** are other spellings.

per cent age (pər sen′tij), 1. rate or proportion of each hundred; part of each hundred. What percentage of children were absent? 2. part or proportion. A large percentage of schoolbooks now have pictures. 3. the part of arithmetic that deals with numbers expressed in per cents.

per cep ti ble (pər sep′ti bəl), that can be perceived. The other ship was barely perceptible in the fog.

per cep ti bly (pər sep′ti bli), in a perceptible way or amount.

per cep tion (pər sep′shən), 1. act of perceiving. His perception of the change came in a flash. 2. power of perceiving; as, a keen perception. 3. the understanding that is the result of perceiving. Did you have time to get a clear perception of the accident?

perch[1] (pėrch), 1. a bar, branch, or anything else on which a bird can come to rest. 2. alight and rest; sit. A robin perched on our porch railing. 3. high seat. 4. sit rather high. He perched on a stool. 5. to place high up; as, a village perched on a high hill. 6. a measure of length, $5\frac{1}{2}$ yards. A square perch is $30\frac{1}{4}$ square yards.

perch[2] (pėrch), a small fresh-water fish, used for food. See the picture below.

per chance (pər chans′), perhaps.

Perch (about 10 in. long)

per en ni al (pər en′i əl), 1. lasting through the whole year; as, a perennial stream. 2. lasting for a long time; as, the perennial beauty of the hills. 3. living more than two years; as, perennial garden plants. 4. a perennial plant. Roses are perennials.

per fect (pėr′fikt for 1, 3, and 6, pər fekt′ for 2, 4, and 5), 1. having no faults; not spoiled at any point; as, a perfect spelling paper, a perfect apple, a perfect life. 2. remove all faults from; make perfect; add the finishing touches to. The artist was perfecting his picture. 3. whole; having all its parts there. The set was perfect; nothing was missing or broken. 4. carry through; complete; as, to perfect a plan or an invention. 5. raise to the highest point; as, to perfect one's skill. 6. entire; utter; as, a perfect stranger to us.

per fec tion (pər fek′shən), 1. perfect or faultless condition; the highest excellence. 2. perfect person or thing. His work is always perfection. 3. making complete or perfect. Perfection of our plans will take another week.

per fect ly (pėr′fikt li), in a perfect manner; completely; exactly; entirely.

per fo rate (pėr′fə rāt), 1. make a hole or holes through. The target was perforated by bullets. 2. make rows of holes through. Sheets of postage stamps are perforated.

per force (pər fōrs′), by necessity; necessarily. "Perforce I must obey you," said the captive.

per form (pər fôrm′), 1. do. Perform your duty. 2. put into effect; carry out. Perform your promise. 3. act, play, sing, or do tricks in public.

per form ance (pər fôr′məns), 1. carrying out; doing; as, in the performance of one's regular duties. 2. act; deed. The child's kicks and screams made a disgraceful performance. 3. the giving of a play, circus, or other show. The evening performance is at 8 o'clock.

per form er (pər fôr′mər), person who performs; player.

per fume (pėr′fūm for 1 and 2, pər fūm′ for 3), 1. sweet smell; as, the perfume of flowers. 2. liquid having the sweet smell of flowers. 3. fill with sweet odor. Flowers perfumed the air.

per haps (pər haps′), it may be. Perhaps a letter will come to you today.

per il (per′əl), 1. chance of harm; danger. 2. put in danger.

per il ous (per′i ləs), dangerous.

pe ri od (pēr′i əd), 1. a portion of time marked off by events that happen again and again; a time after which the same things begin to happen again. A month, from new moon to new moon, is a period. 2. a certain series of years; as, the period of the World War. 3. portion of time. He visited us for a short period. 4. complete sentence. The orator spoke in stately periods. 5. pause at the end of a sentence. 6. dot (.) marking the end of most sentences or showing an abbreviation, as in Mr. or Dec.

pe ri od i cal ly (pēr′i od′i kəl i), 1. at regular intervals. 2. every now and then.

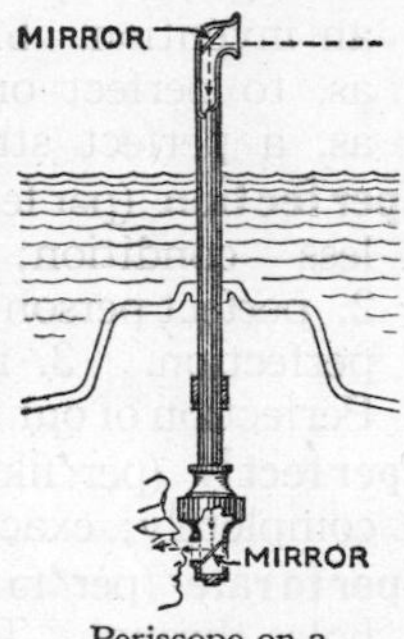

Periscope on a submarine

per i scope (per′i skōp), an instrument that allows those in a submarine or trench to see a view of the surface. It is a tube with an arrangement of prisms or mirrors that reflect light rays down the tube.

per ish (per′ish), die; be destroyed. Flowers perish when frost comes.

per ish a ble (per′ish ə bəl), liable to spoil or decay. Fruit is perishable.

per ma nence (pėr′mə nəns), being permanent; lasting quality or condition; as, the permanence of the sun.

per ma nent (pėr′mə nənt), lasting; intended to last; not for a short time only; as, a permanent filling in a tooth. After doing odd jobs for a week, he got a permanent position as helper in a store.

per me ate (pėr′mi āt), 1. spread through the whole of; pass through; soak through. The smoke permeated the house. 2. penetrate. Water will easily permeate a cotton dress.

per mis sion (pər mish′ən), consent; leave; permitting. He asked the teacher's permission to go early. Father gave me permission to use his car

per mit (pər mit′ for 1, pėr′mit for 2), 1. let; allow. My mother will not permit me to stay up late. Mr. Smith permitted us to swim in his pond. He is permitting it again this summer. 2. a formal written order giving permission to do something. Have you a permit to fish in this lake?

per ni cious (pər nish′əs), 1. that will destroy or ruin; causing great harm or damage. The Japanese beetle is a pernicious insect. Gambling is a pernicious habit. 2. fatal.

per pen dic u lar (pėr′pən dik′ū lər), 1. upright; standing straight up; as, a perpendicular cliff. 2. at right angles. One line is perpendicular to another when it makes a square corner with another. See the diagrams. The floor of a room is perpendicular to the side walls and parallel to the ceiling. 3. a perpendicular line or plane.

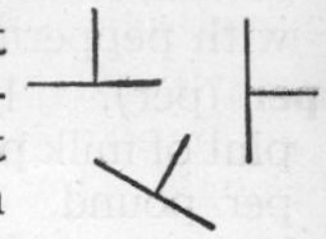

per pet u al (pər pech′ü əl), 1. eternal; lasting forever; as, the perpetual hills. 2. lasting throughout life; as, a perpetual income. 3. continuous; never ceasing; as, a disease that puts a person in perpetual pain.

per pet u al ly (pər pech′ü əl i), forever.

per pet u ate (pər pech′ü āt), make perpetual; keep from being forgotten The Washington Monument was built to perpetuate the memory of a great man.

per plex (pər pleks′), 1. puzzle. This problem is hard enough to perplex even the teacher. 2. trouble with doubt.

per plex i ty (pər plek′si ti), 1. perplexed condition; being puzzled; not knowing what to do or how to act. 2. something that perplexes. Jack's perplexity was so great that he asked many persons for advice.

per se cute (pėr′si kūt), 1. pursue to injure; treat badly; do harm to again and again; oppress. The cruel boy persecuted the kitten by throwing stones at it whenever it came near. 2. punish for religious reasons.

per se cu tion (pėr′si kū′shən), 1. persecuting. The boy's persecution of the kitten was cruel. 2. being persecuted. The kitten's persecution by the boy made it run away.

per se ver ance (pėr′si vēr′əns), sticking to a purpose or an aim; never giving up what one has set out to do. By perseverance the lame boy learned to swim.

per se vere (pėr′si vēr′), persist; continue steadily in doing something hard. To try, try, try again is to persevere.

per sim mon (pər sim′ən), 1. a North American tree with a plumlike fruit. 2. the fruit of this tree, very bitter when green, but sweet and good to eat when very ripe.

per sist (pər sist′), 1. stick to it; refuse to stop or be changed. Johnny persists in reading in bed. 2. last; stay; endure. On the tops of some mountains snow persists throughout the year. 3. say again and again; maintain.

per sist ence (pər sis′təns), 1. being persistent; as, the persistence of a fly buzzing around one's head. 2. continuing existence; as, the persistence of a cough.

per sist ent (pər sis′tənt), 1. persisting; not giving up. That persistent beggar followed me all the way home. 2. lasting; going on; continuing; as, a persistent headache that lasted for three days.

per son (pėr′sən), 1. man, woman, or child. 2. the body; bodily appearance. The person of the king was well guarded.

per son age (pėr′sən ij), 1. person of importance. 2. person. 3. a character in a book or a play.

per son al (pėr′sən əl), 1. belonging to a person; private; as, a personal letter. 2. done in person; directly by oneself, not through others or by letter; as, a personal call. 3. of the body or bodily appearance; as, personal beauty or charms. 4. about or against a person or persons; as, personal remarks, personal abuse.

per son al i ty (pėr′sə nal′i ti), 1. the personal or individual quality that makes one person be different or act differently from another. A baby two weeks old does not have much personality. 2. the qualities of a person. The boy is developing a fine personality. 3. a remark made about or against one particular person. Personalities are not in good taste in general conversation.

per son al ly (pėr′sən əl i), 1. in person; not by the aid of others. The hostess saw to the comfort of her guests personally. 2. as a person. We like Mr. Hart personally, but we dislike his way of earning a living. 3. as far as oneself is concerned. Personally, I like apples better than oranges.

per spi ra tion (pėr′spi rā′shən), 1. sweat. 2. sweating.

per spire (pər spīr′), sweat.

per suade (pər swād′), win over to do or believe; make willing. He persuaded me to go. We persuaded Harry that he was wrong.

per sua sion (pər swā′zhən), 1. persuading. All our persuasion was of no use; she would not come. 2. power of persuading. 3. firm belief. 4. religious belief; religious denomination. Christians are not all of the same persuasion.

per sua sive (pər swā′siv), able to persuade; fitted to persuade. The salesman had a very persuasive way of talking.

pert (pėrt), saucy; bold; too forward or free in speech; as, a pert girl, a pert reply.

per tain (pər tān′), 1. belong. We own the house and the land pertaining to it. 2. refer; be related. "Pertaining to school" means "having something to do with school." 3. be appropriate. We had turkey and everything else that pertains to Thanksgiving Day.

per turb (pər tėrb′), disturb greatly; make uneasy or troubled. Mrs. Smith was much perturbed by her son's illness.

pe ruse (pə rüz′), 1. read thoroughly and carefully. 2. read.

per vade (pər vād′), go or spread throughout; be throughout. The odor of pines pervades the air. He worked so hard that weariness pervaded his whole body.

per verse (pər vėrs′), 1. contrary. The perverse child did just what we told him not to do. 2. wicked. 3. not correct; wrong; as, perverse reasoning.

per vert (pər vėrt′), 1. lead or turn from the right way or from the truth. Reading silly stories perverts our taste. To pervert what a person has said is to give a wrong meaning to it. His enemies perverted his friendly remark and made it into an insult. 2. use for wrong purposes or in a wrong way. A clever criminal perverts his talents.

pest (pest), 1. thing or person that causes trouble, injuries, or destruction; nuisance. Flies and mosquitoes are pests. 2. pestilence.

pes ter (pes′tər), annoy; trouble; vex. Flies pester us. Don't pester me with foolish questions.

pes ti lence (pes′ti ləns), a disease that spreads rapidly, causing many deaths. Smallpox, yellow fever, and the plague are pestilences.

Pestle in a bowl

pes tle (pes′əl), 1. a tool for pounding something to a powder. See the picture just above. 2. pound or crush with a pestle.

pet[1] (pet), 1. an animal kept as a favorite and treated with affection. 2. a darling or favorite; as, teacher's pet. 3. treat as a pet; yield to the wishes of; stroke or pat; touch lovingly and gently. Helen is petting the kitten. 4. treated as a pet. That queer girl has a pet snake.

pet[2] (pet), a fit of being cross or peevish; fretful discontent.

pet al (pet′əl), one of the parts of a flower that are usually colored. A rose has many petals.

pe tite (pə tēt′), small.

pe ti tion (pi tish′ən), 1. formal request. The people on our street signed a petition asking the city council for a new sidewalk. 2. make a formal request to. They petitioned the mayor to use his influence with the city council. 3. prayer. 4. pray.

pet rel (pet′rəl), a small black-and-white sea bird with long, pointed wings.

Stormy petrel (about 5½ in. long)

pet ri fy (pet′ri fī), 1. turn into stone. There is a petrified forest in Arizona. 2. paralyze with fear, horror, or surprise. The bird seemed petrified as the snake came near.

pe tro le um (pi trō′li əm), an oily, dark-colored liquid found in the earth. Gasoline, kerosene, and paraffin are made from petroleum.

pet ti coat (pet′i kōt), 1. a skirt that hangs from the waist or from the shoulders, worn beneath the dress by women, girls, and babies. 2. skirt.

Petunia

pet ty (pet′i), 1. small; having little importance or value. She insisted on telling me all her petty troubles. 2. mean. 3. lower; subordinate.

pet u lant (pech′ů lənt), peevish; likely to have little fits of bad temper; irritable over trifles.

pe tu ni a (pi tū′ni ə or pi tü′ni ə), a plant that has white, pink, and purple flowers shaped like funnels. See the picture just above.

Pews

pew (pū), 1. a fixed bench with a back, in a church. 2. place in a church set apart for the use of a certain family or group of people.

pew ter (pū′tər), 1. alloy of tin with lead, copper, or other metals. 2. dishes or other utensils made of this. Jane polishes the pewter. 3. made of pewter; as, a pewter mug.

phan tom (fan′təm), 1. ghost; an image in the mind which seems to be real; a vague, dim, or shadowy appearance. His fevered brain filled the room with phantoms from the past. 2. like a ghost; unreal; as, a phantom ship.

phase (fāz), 1. one of the changing states or stages of development of a thing. At present Dick's voice is changing; that is a phase all boys go through. 2. one side, part, or view (of a subject). What phase of arithmetic are you studying now?

pheas ant (fez′ənt), a game bird with a long tail and brilliant feathers. Wild pheasants live in many parts of Europe and America.

English pheasant (about 2½ ft. long, with the tail)

phe nom e na (fi nom′i nə), more than one phenomenon.

phe nom e non (fi nom′i non), 1. fact, event, or circumstance that can be observed. Lightning is an electrical phenomenon. Fever and inflammation are phenomena of disease. 2. something extraordinary or remarkable. An eclipse is an interesting phenomenon. The fond parents think their child is a phenomenon.

phi al (fī′əl), vial; small bottle.

phi lan thro pist (fi lan′thrə pist), person who loves mankind and works for its welfare.

phi los o pher (fi los′ə fər), 1. lover of wisdom; person who studies philosophy much. 2. person who has a system of philosophy. 3. person who is calm and reasonable under hard conditions, accepting life and making the best of it.

phil o soph ic (fil′ə sof′ik), 1. of philosophy. 2. wise, calm, and reasonable.

phil o soph i cal (fil′ə sof′i kəl), philosophic.

phi los o phy (fi los′ə fi), 1. the study of the truth or principles of all real knowledge; the study of the most general causes and principles of the universe. 2. an explanation of the world. 3. a system for guiding life. 4. calm and reasonable attitude; accepting things as they are and making the best of them.

phone (fōn), telephone.

pho net ic (fō net′ik), representing sounds

made with the voice. Phonetic symbols are marks used to show pronunciation. We use ᴛʜ as the phonetic symbol for the sound of *th* in *the* or *then*.

pho no graph (fō′nə graf), an instrument that records and reproduces sounds.

REPRODUCING MECHANISM
RECORD
TONE CHAMBER
Phonograph

pho to (fō′tō), photograph.

pho to graph (fō′tə graf), 1. a picture made with a camera. 2. take a photograph of.

pho tog ra pher (fə tog′rə fər), person who takes photographs.

pho tog ra phy (fə tog′rə fi), the taking of photographs.

phrase (frāz), 1. a combination of words. He spoke in simple phrases, so that the children understood him. 2. an expression often used. "Call up" is the common phrase for "get a telephone connection with." 3. a group of words not containing a subject and verb and used as a single word. *In the house, coming by the church,* and *to eat too fast* are phrases. 4. express in a particular way. She phrased her excuse in polite words.

phys ic (fiz′ik), 1. a medicine, especially one that moves the bowels. 2. give medicine to. 3. move the bowels of. 4. the art of healing; the science and practice of medicine.

physicked and **physicking** are formed from **physic.**

phys i cal (fiz′i kəl), 1. of the body; as, physical exercise, physical strength, physical education. 2. of matter; material. His physical force was weak, but his mental and moral force was very great. 3. according to the laws of nature. It is a physical impossibility for the sun to rise in the west. 4. dealing with the natural features of the earth. **Physical geography** teaches about the earth's formation, climate, clouds, and tides.

phys i cal ly (fiz′i kəl i), in a physical manner; in physical respects; as regards the body. After his vacation he was in fine condition both physically and mentally.

phy si cian (fi zish′ən), doctor of medicine.

phys ics (fiz′iks), the science that deals with matter and energy, and the action of different forms of energy. Physics studies force, motion, heat, light, sound, and electricity.

phys i ol o gy (fiz′i ol′ə ji), the science dealing with the normal working of living things or

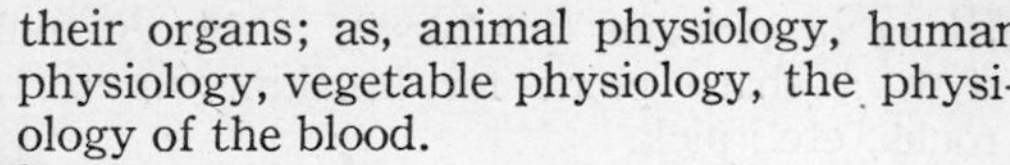

their organs; as, animal physiology, human physiology, vegetable physiology, the physiology of the blood.

phy sique (fi zēk′), body; bodily structure, organization, or development; as, a man of strong physique.

pi an ist (pi an′ist), person who plays the piano.

pi an o (pi an′ō), large musical instrument whose tones come from many wires. The wires are sounded by hammers which are worked by pressing keys on a keyboard.

pi az za (pi az′ə), 1. a large porch along one or more sides of a house. 2. an open public square in Italian towns.

Piazza or porch

Piazza or public square

pick (pik), 1. choose; select. Mr. Sport thinks he can pick a winning horse at a race. 2. choice or selection. This red rose is my pick. 3. the best part. We got a high price for the pick of our peaches. 4. pull away with the fingers; gather; as, to pick fruit or flowers. 5. the amount of a crop picked at one time. 6. a heavy tool with a sharp point for breaking up earth or rock. 7. a sharp-pointed instrument. Ice is broken into pieces with a pick. 8. pierce, dig into, or break up with some pointed tool. 9. use something pointed to remove things from; as, to pick one's teeth, to pick a bone. 10. prepare for use by removing waste parts; as, to pick a chicken. 11. pull apart. The hair in the pillow needs to be picked, as it has matted. 12. use the fingers with a plucking motion. The sick man picked at the blankets. 13. pluck at. The boy picked the banjo. 14. seek and find. Carl picked a quarrel with Dick. 15. eat a bit at a time. The bird picks at the bread. Alice just picked at her food because she did not like it. 16. Some special meanings are:

pick a lock, open it with a pointed instrument, wire, etc.

pick a pocket, steal from a person's pocket.

pick flaws, find fault.

pick off, shoot one by one.

pick up, 1. take up. The boy picked up a stone. 2. get. The woman picks up a bargain. 3. learn without teaching. Jack picks up games easily.

pick ax or **pick axe** (pik′aks′), heavy tool with a sharp point for breaking up dirt, rocks, etc.; pick.

pick er el (pik′ər əl), kind of large fresh-water fish with a long, narrow, pointed head. See the picture just below.

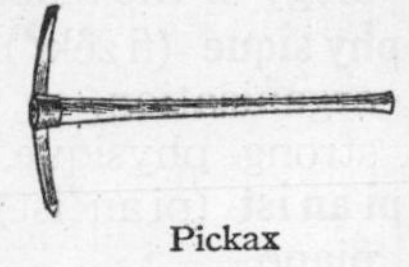
Pickax

pick et (pik′it), 1. a pointed stake or peg driven into the ground to make a fence, to tie a horse to, etc. 2. enclose with pickets. 3. tie to a picket. Picket your horse here. 4. a small body of troops, or a single man, posted at some place to watch for the enemy and guard against surprise. 5. person stationed near a place of work to keep workers from working. 6. station as pickets. 7. station pickets at or near; as, to picket a factory.

Pickerel

pick le (pik′əl), 1. salt water, vinegar, or other liquid in which meat and vegetables can be preserved. 2. a cucumber preserved in pickle. 3. any other vegetable preserved in pickle. 4. preserve in pickle; as, pickled beets. 5. trouble; difficulty. I got in a bad pickle today.

pick pock et (pik′pok′it), person who steals from people's pockets.

pic nic (pik′nik), 1. a trip or pleasure party, with a meal in the open air. 2. go on such a trip. 3. eat in picnic style. **picnicked** and **picnicking** are formed from **picnic.**

pic nick er (pik′nik ər), one who picnics.

pic ture (pik′chər), 1. a drawing, painting, or photograph; a printed copy of any of these. That book contains a good picture of him. 2. scene. The trees and brook make a lovely picture. 3. something beautiful. 4. likeness; image. Mary is the picture of her mother. 5. draw, paint, etc. The artist pictured the saints. 6. form a picture of; imagine. It is hard to picture life a hundred years ago. 7. a vivid description. 8. show by words; describe vividly. The soldier pictured the battle. The speaker pictured the suffering of the poor. 9. moving picture.

pic tur esque (pik′chər esk′), 1. quaint or interesting enough to be used as the subject of a picture; as, a picturesque old mill. 2. making a picture for the mind; vivid.

pie[1] (pī), fruit, meat, etc., enclosed in pastry and baked, such as an apple pie, a chicken pie.

pie[2] (pī), magpie, a black-and-white bird that chatters a great deal.

piece (pēs), 1. bit; scrap; one of the parts into which a thing is divided. The cup broke in pieces. 2. limited part; as, a piece of land containing two acres. **Give a person a piece of one's mind** means scold him. 3. small quantity; as, a piece of bread, a piece of wood. 4. single thing of a set or class. Some pieces of the dinner set have been broken. 5. single composition in an art; as, a piece of poetry, a piece of music. 6. coin. A nickel is a five-cent piece. 7. **Pieces of eight** were dollars used by the Spanish in Spain and America. 8. example; instance. Sleeping with a light in the room is a piece of nonsense. 9. quantity in which goods are put up for the market. The piece of cloth contains ten yards. 10. the amount of work done; as, paid by the piece. 11. gun; cannon. 12. make or repair by adding or joining pieces. Mother pieced a quilt yesterday. 13. join the pieces of.

piece meal (pēs′mēl′), 1. piece by piece; a little at a time; as, work done piecemeal. 2. piece from piece; to pieces; into fragments. The lamb was torn piecemeal by the wolves.

pied (pīd), having patches of two or more colors; many colored.

pier (pēr), 1. a structure built out over the water, and used as a walk or a landing place. 2. breakwater. 3. pillar; one of the solid supports on which the arches of a bridge rest. 4. solid part of a wall between windows, doors, etc.

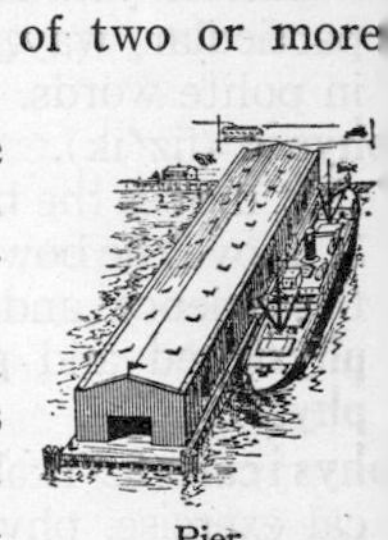
Pier

pierce (pērs), 1. go into; go through. A tunnel pierces the mountain. 2. make a hole in; bore into or through. A nail pierced the tire of our car. 3. force a way through or into. The cold wind pierced our clothes. A sharp cry pierced the air. 4. make a way through with the eye or mind; as, to pierce a disguise, to pierce a mystery.

pi e ty (pī′ə ti), 1. being pious; religious character or conduct; holiness; goodness. 2. dutiful regard for one's parents; as, the piety of the Chinese. 3. pious act.

Pigs

pig (pig), 1. a domestic animal raised for its meat. 2. a young hog. See the picture. 3. person who seems or acts like a pig; one who is greedy, dirty, dull, sullen, or stubborn.

pi geon (pij′ən), a bird with a stout body and short legs; dove. See the picture.

pig ment (pig′mənt), a coloring matter. Paint and dyes are made by mixing pigments with liquid. The color of a person's hair, skin, and eyes is due to pigment in the cells of the body.

Pigeon

pig my (pig′mi), 1. a dwarf. The pigmies living in Africa and Asia are less than five feet high. 2. very small; as, a pigmy mind.

pig sty (pig′stī′), pen for pigs.

pike[1] (pīk), 1. spear; a spear with a long wooden handle which foot soldiers used to carry. 2. point; spike.

pike[2] (pīk), a large fresh-water fish with a long, narrow, pointed head.

pike[3] (pīk), turnpike; a road that has, or used to have, a gate where toll is, or was, paid.

Soldier holding a pike

pile[1] (pīl), 1. many things lying one upon another in a more or less orderly way; as, a pile of wood. 2. a mass like a hill or mound; as, a pile of dirt. 3. make into a pile; heap evenly; heap up. The boys piled the blankets in a corner. 4. gather or rise in piles. Snow piled against the fences. 5. large amount.

pile[2] (pīl), heavy beam driven upright into the ground or the bed of a river to help support a bridge, wharf, etc.

pile[3] (pīl), 1. a soft, thick nap on velvet, plush, and many carpets. The pile of that Chinese rug is almost half an inch long. 2. soft, fine hair or down; wool.

pil fer (pil′fər), steal in small quantities.

pil grim (pil′grim), 1. person who goes on a journey to a sacred or holy place as an act of religious devotion. Long ago many people used to go as pilgrims to Jerusalem and to holy places in Europe. 2. traveler.

pil grim age (pil′gri mij), 1. a journey to some sacred place. 2. a long journey.

pill (pil), 1. medicine made up into a tiny ball to be swallowed whole. 2. a very small ball of anything.

pil lage (pil′ij), 1. to plunder; rob with violence. Pirates pillaged the towns along the coast. 2. plunder; robbery.

pil lar (pil′ər), 1. a slender upright support; a column. Pillars are usually made of stone, wood, or metal and used as supports or ornaments for a building. Sometimes a pillar stands alone as a monument. 2. anything slender and upright like a pillar. 3. an important support.

Pillars around a building

pil lo ry (pil′ə ri), 1. a frame of wood with holes through which a person's head and hands were put. The pillory was formerly used as a punishment, being set up in a public place where the crowd could make fun of the offender. 2. put in the pillory. 3. expose to public ridicule, contempt, or abuse. The newspapers pilloried the cruel father.

Pillory

pil low (pil′ō), 1. a bag or case filled with feathers, down, or other soft material. 2. rest on a pillow.

pi lot (pī′lət), 1. man who steers a ship. 2. man whose business is to steer ships in or out of a harbor or through dangerous waters. A steamer takes on a pilot before coming into a strange harbor. 3. person who steers an airplane, balloon, or airship. 4. act as a pilot of; steer. The aviator pilots his airplane. 5. guide; leader. 6. guide; lead. The manager piloted us through the large factory.

pim ple (pim′pəl), a small, inflamed swelling of the skin.

pin (pin), 1. a short slender piece of wire with a point at one end and a head at the other, for fastening things together. 2. a badge with a pin or clasp to fasten it to the clothing. She wore her class pin. 3. an ornament which has a pin or clasp; brooch. 4. a peg made of wood or metal, used to fasten things together, hold something, or hang things on. 5. fasten with a pin or pins; put a pin through. 6. hold fast in one position. When the tree fell, it pinned his shoulder to the ground.

pin a fore (pin′ə fōr′), a child's apron that covers most of the dress.

pin cers (pin′sərz), 1. a tool for gripping and holding tight, made like scissors but with jaws instead of blades. 2. the large claw with which crabs and lobsters pinch or nip; pair of claws.

pinch (pinch), 1. squeeze between two hard edges; press on so as to hurt; squeeze with thumb and forefinger. He pinched his finger in the door. My new shoes pinch. 2. a squeeze; sharp pressure that hurts; as, the pinch of tight shoes, the pinch of cold, the pinch of hunger. 3. cause to shrink or become thin; as, a face pinched by hunger. 4. as much as can be taken up with the tips of finger and thumb; as, a pinch of salt. 5. be stingy.

pine[1] (pīn), 1. a tree with evergreen leaves shaped like needles. Many pines are of value for lumber, tar, turpentine, etc. 2. the wood of the pine.

Pine leaves and cone

pine[2] (pīn), 1. long eagerly; yearn. 2. waste away with pain, hunger, grief, or desire. The mother was pining to see her son.

pine ap ple (pīn′ap′əl), 1. a large juicy fruit growing in hot climates, that looks somewhat like a big pine cone. 2. the plant with slender stiff leaves on which the pineapple is grown.

Pineapple

pin ion (pin′yən), 1. the last joint of a bird's wing. 2. a wing. 3. any one of the stiff flying feathers of the wing. 4. bind; bind the arms of; bind (to something). The thieves pinioned the man's arms.

pink (pingk), 1. the color obtained by mixing red with white; light or pale red. 2. a garden plant with spicy-smelling flowers of various colors, mostly white, pink, and red. A carnation is one kind of pink. 3. the highest degree or condition. By exercising every day John kept himself in the pink of health.

pin nace (pin′is), 1. a ship's boat. 2. a very small schooner.

pin na cle (pin′ə kəl), 1. a high peak or point of rock. 2. the highest point; as, at the pinnacle of his fame. 3. a slender turret or spire.

piñ on (pin′yon), 1. a kind of pine tree. 2. the large edible seed of this tree.

Pinnacle

pint (pīnt), a unit of measure equal to half a quart.

pin to (pin′tō), 1. spotted in two colors. 2. a pinto horse.

pi o neer (pī′ə nēr′), 1. person who settles in a part of the country that has not been occupied before, except by savage tribes. 2. person who goes first, or does something first, and so prepares a way for others. 3. prepare or open up (a way); take the lead.

pi ous (pī′əs), 1. religious; devoted to a religious life. 2. done under pretense of religion; as, a pious fraud.

pipe (pīp), 1. a tube through which a liquid or gas flows. 2. supply with pipes. Our street is being piped for gas. 3. carry by means of pipes. 4. a musical instrument with a single tube into which the player blows. **Pipes** sometimes means a bagpipe. 5. play music on a pipe. 6. any one of the tubes in an organ. 7. voice, song, or note; as, the pipe of the lark. 8. make a shrill noise; sing in a shrill voice. 9. a tube of clay, wood, etc., with a bowl at one end, for smoking.

pip er (pīp′ər), person who plays on a pipe.

pique (pēk), 1. a little feeling of anger at being slighted; wounded pride. In a pique, she left the party. 2. wound the pride of. 3. arouse; stir up. The boy's curiosity was piqued by the locked trunk.

PETAL
PISTIL

pi ra cy (pī′rə si), robbery on the sea.

pi rate (pī′rit), 1. one who attacks and robs ships when he has no right to do so; robber on the sea. 2. be a pirate.

pis til (pis′til), the seed-bearing part of a flower. See the picture just above.

pis tol (pis′təl), a small short gun held and fired with one hand.

Pistol

pis ton (pis′tən), a short cylinder, or a flat round piece of wood or metal, fitting closely inside a tube or hollow cylinder in which it is moved back and forth by some force (often by steam). A piston receives or transmits motion by means of a rod that is attached to it.

PISTON ROD
PISTON

pit[1] (pit), 1. hole in the ground. 2. hole dug deep into the earth. 3. a hollow on the surface of anything; hole; as, the armpit. 4. a little hole or scar such as is left by smallpox. 5. to mark with small pits or scars. 6. **Pit one person** or **thing against another** means set them to fight one another.

pit[2] (pit), the stone of a cherry, peach, plum, date, etc.

pitch[1] (pich), 1. throw; fling; hurl; toss. The men were pitching horseshoes. 2. in baseball, to throw (a ball) to the man batting. 3. fix firmly in the ground; set up; as, to pitch a tent. 4. fall or plunge forward. The man lost his balance and pitched down the cliff. 5. plunge with the bow rising and then falling. The ship pitched about in the storm. 6. point; position; degree. The poor man has reached the lowest pitch of bad fortune. 7. degree of highness or lowness of a sound. 8. **Pitch into** means attack. 9. **Pitch in** means work hard.

pitch[2] (pich), 1. a black sticky substance made from tar or turpentine, used to cover the seams of ships, to cover roofs, to make pavements, etc. 2. to cover with pitch.

pitch er[1] (pich′ər), 1. a container made of china, glass, silver, etc., with a lip at one side and a handle at the other. Pitchers are used for holding and pouring out water, milk, etc. 2. amount that a pitcher holds.

Pitcher

pitch er[2] (pich′ər), the player on a baseball team who throws the ball for the batter to hit.

pitch fork (pich′fôrk′), a large fork with a long handle for lifting and throwing hay, etc.

Pitchfork

pit e ous (pit′i əs), to be pitied; deserving pity. The starving children are a piteous sight.

pit fall (pit′fôl′), 1. hidden pit to catch animals in. 2. any trap or hidden danger.

pith (pith), 1. the central spongy tissue of plant stems. 2. anything like this tissue; as, the pith of an orange. 3. the important or essential part; as, the pith of a speech. 4. strength; energy.

pit i a ble (pit′i ə bəl), 1. to be pitied; moving the heart; deserving pity. 2. deserving contempt; mean; to be scorned.

pit i ful (pit′i fəl), 1. to be pitied; piteous; deserving pity. The starving children are a very pitiful sight. 2. feeling pity; feeling sorrow for the trouble of others. 3. deserving contempt; mean; to be scorned.

pit i less (pit′i lis), without pity or mercy.

pit y (pit′i), 1. sympathy; sorrow for another's suffering; a feeling for the sorrows of others. 2. feel pity for. Ruth pitied any child who was hurt or hungry. 3. cause for pity or regret. It is a pity to be kept in the house in fine weather.

piv ot (piv′ət), 1. a shaft, pin, or point on which something turns. 2. mount on, attach by, or provide with a pivot. 3. to turn on a pivot; as, to pivot on one's heel. 4. that on which something turns, hinges, or depends; central point. Ed's pitching was the pivot of our hopes.

pix y or **pix ie** (pik′si), fairy.

Pixy sitting on a mushroom

plac ard (plak′ärd), 1. a notice to be posted in a public place; poster. 2. put placards on or in. The circus placarded the city with advertisements.

place (plās), 1. the part of space occupied by a person or thing. 2. a city, town, village, district, island, etc. What place do you come from? 3. house; dwelling. The Smiths have a beautiful place in the country. 4. a building or spot used for some particular purpose. A church is a place of worship. A store or office is a place of business. 5. a part or spot in a body or surface; as, a decayed place in a tooth, a sore place on one's foot. 6. rank; position; way of life. John won first place in the contest. The servant filled his place well. 7. position in time; part of time occupied by an event. The performance went too slowly in several places. 8. right position; usual position. There is a time and place for everything. Each book is in its place on the shelf. 9. a space or seat for a person. We took our places at the table. 10. put in a particular spot, position, or condition. Place the books on the table. The child was placed in a home. We placed an order for hats with this store. The people placed confidence in their leader. 11. duty; business. It is not my place to find fault. 12. work; job; employment. 13. **In place of** means instead of.

plac id (plas′id), calm; peaceful; quiet; as, a placid lake, a placid temper.

plague (plāg), 1. a very dangerous disease that spreads rapidly and often causes death. 2. a punishment thought to be sent by God. 3. thing or person that torments, vexes, annoys, troubles, offends, or is disagreeable. 4. vex; annoy; bother.

plaid (plad), 1. a long piece of woolen cloth, usually having a pattern of checks or stripes in many colors, worn about the shoulders by the Scottish Highlanders. See the picture. 2. any cloth with a pattern of checks or stripes. 3. having a pattern of checks or stripes; as, a plaid dress.

Scottish Highlander's plaid

plain (plān), 1. clear; easy to understand; easily seen or heard. 2. clearly; in a plain manner. 3. without ornament; as, a plain dress. 4. all of one color; as, a plain blue dress. 5. not rich; as, plain food. 6. common; ordinary; simple in manner; as, a plain American boy. 7. not pretty; as, a plain girl. 8. frank; honest; sincere; as, plain speech. 9. flat; level; smooth. 10. a flat stretch of land. Cattle wandered over the plains.

plain-spo ken (plān′spō′kən), plain or frank in speech.

plain tive (plān′tiv), mournful; sad.

plait (plat), 1. a braid. 2. pleat.

plan (plan), 1. think out beforehand how something is to be made or done; decide on methods and materials. I plan to reach New York by train on Tuesday, and stay two days. 2. a way of making or doing something that has been worked out beforehand. Our summer plans were upset by my mother's illness. 3. make a plan of. Have you planned your trip? 4. a drawing or diagram to show how a garden, a floor of a house, a park, etc., is arranged.

Plan of a house

plane[1] (plān), 1. a flat or level surface. 2. flat or level. 3. a level. Keep your work at a high plane. 4. a thin, flat or curved surface that helps to support an airplane. 5. airplane.

plane[2] (plān), 1. a carpenter's tool with a blade for smoothing wood. 2. a machine for smoothing metal. 3. to smooth (wood or metal) with a plane.

Plane for wood

plan et (plan′it), one of the heavenly bodies that move around the sun. Mercury, Venus, the earth, Mars, Jupiter, Saturn, Uranus, Neptune, and Pluto are planets.

plank (plangk), 1. a long, flat piece of sawed timber thicker than a board. 2. to cover with planks. 3. cook on a board; as, planked steak. 4. **Walk the plank** means to be put to death by walking along and off a plank extending from a ship's side over the water.

plant (plant), 1. Trees, bushes, vines, grass, vegetables, and seaweed are all plants. 2. A plant often means a small growth; as, a tomato plant, a house plant. 3. a young growth ready to be set out in another place. The farmer set out 100 cabbage plants. 4. put in the ground to grow. Farmers plant seeds. 5. set firmly; put; place. Columbus planted the flag of Spain in the ground. The boy planted his feet far apart. 6. establish (a colony, city, etc.); settle. 7. put in (ideas, feelings, etc.). Missionaries planted civilization among the savages. 8. the building, machinery, tools, etc., used in manufacturing some article.

plan tain[1] (plan′tin), 1. a kind of large banana. 2. plant that it grows on.

plan tain[2] (plan′tin), a common weed with large spreading leaves close to the ground and long slender spikes carrying flowers and seeds.

plan ta tion (plan tā′shən), 1. a large farm or estate on which such crops as cotton, tobacco, or sugar are grown. The work on a plantation is done by laborers who live there. 2. a large group of trees or other plants that have been planted; as, a rubber plantation. 3. colony.

plant er (plan′tər), 1. man who owns or runs a plantation; as, a cotton planter. 2. a machine for planting; as, a corn planter. 3. person who plants.

plash (plash), splash.

plas ter (plas′tər), 1. a soft mixture of lime, sand, and water that hardens as it dries. Plaster is used for covering walls or ceilings. 2. cover (a wall) with plaster. 3. spread with anything thickly. Dick's shoes were plastered with mud. 4. a medical preparation consisting of some substance spread on cloth, that will stick to the body and protect cuts, relieve pain, etc. Mother put a mustard plaster on my chest when I had a cold.

plas tic (plas′tik), 1. molding or giving shape to material. Sculpture is a plastic art. 2. easily molded or shaped. Clay, wax, and plaster are plastic substances. 3. any of various substances that can be shaped or molded when hot and become hard when cooled. Some plastics are very strong and tough.

plat (plat), 1. a plan; a map. 2. to map. 3. a small piece of ground; plot.

plate (plāt), 1. a dish, usually round, that is almost flat. Our food is served on plates. 2. something having a similar shape. 3. food served to one person at a meal. 4. dishes or utensils of silver or gold. The family plate included a silver pitcher, candlesticks, and the usual knives, forks, and spoons. 5. dishes or utensils coated with gold or silver. 6. cover with a thin layer of gold, silver, or some other metal. 7. a thin, flat sheet or piece of metal. The warship was covered with steel plates. 8. to cover with metal plates for protection. 9. a thin sheet of glass coated with chemicals that are sensitive to light. Plates are used in taking some photographs. 10. in baseball, the home base.

pla teau (pla tō′), a plain in the mountains, or at a height above the sea.

plat form (plat′fôrm), 1. a raised level surface. There usually is a platform beside the track at a railroad station. A hall usually has a platform for speakers. 2. a plan of action or statement of beliefs of a group.

plat i num (plat′i nəm), a heavy metal that looks like silver, but costs much more. Platinum does not tarnish or melt easily. Some watches and rings are made of platinum.

pla toon (plə tün′), 1. a group of soldiers acting as a unit. A platoon is smaller than a company and larger than a squad. 2. small group.

plat ter (plat′ər), a flat dish longer than it is wide.

Platter

plau si ble (plô′zi bəl), 1. appearing true, reasonable, or fair. 2. apparently worthy of confidence but often not really so; as, a plausible liar.

play (plā), 1. fun; sport; action to amuse oneself. All work and no play makes Jack a dull boy. The children are happy at play. 2. have fun; do something in sport; perform. The kitten plays with its tail. Jack played a joke on his sister. 3. take part in (a game). Children play tag and ball. 4. play against. Our team played the sixth-grade team. 5. cause to play. 6. a turn, move, or act in a game. It is your play next. Tom made a good play at checkers. 7. action; as, fair play, foul play. He brought all his strength into play to move the rock. 8. act; as, to play the fool, to play fair. 9. a light, quick movement; as, the play of sunlight on leaves. 10. move lightly. A breeze played on the waters. The poet's fancy played over the old legend and gave it a new form. 11. cause to act or to move. The ship played its light along the coast. 12. freedom for action, motion, etc. The boy gave his fancy full play in telling what he could do with a million dollars. 13. make music on an instrument; make give forth music; produce as music. 14. a story acted on the stage. *Peter Pan* is a charming play. 15. act a part; act the part of. Maude Adams played Peter Pan. 16. make believe; pretend in fun. Let's play the hammock is a boat. 17. act carelessly; do foolish things. Don't play with your pencil. 18. gamble. 19. gambling. The man lost money at play. 20. **Play into the hands of** (a person) means act so as to give him the advantage.

play er (plā′ər), 1. person who plays; as, a ballplayer, a cardplayer. 2. an actor in a theater. 3. thing or device that plays.

play fel low (plā′fel′ō), playmate.

play ful (plā′fəl), 1. full of fun; fond of playing. 2. joking; not serious.

play ground (plā′ground′), piece of ground for play.

play house (plā′hous′), 1. small house for a child to play in. 2. toy house. 3. theater.

playing card, one of a set of cards to play games with.

play mate (plā′māt′), person who plays with another.

play thing (plā′thing′), thing to play with; toy.

pla za (plä′zə), a public square in a city or town.

plea (plē), 1. request; asking. The giant laughed at Jack's plea for pity. 2. excuse; defense. The plea of the man who drove past the red light was that he did not see it.

plead (plēd), 1. offer reasons for or against something; argue. 2. ask earnestly. When the rent was due, the poor man pleaded for more time. 3. offer as an excuse. The woman who stole pleaded poverty.

plead (pled), pleaded.

pleas ant (plez′ənt), 1. that pleases; giving pleasure; as, a pleasant swim on a hot day. 2. easy to get along with; friendly. 3. fair; not stormy.

pleas ant ry (plez′ənt ri), 1. good-natured joke; witty remark. 2. joking.

please (plēz), 1. Toys please children. Sunshine and flowers please most people. 2. Do what you please. 3. Please is a polite way of asking. Come here, please. 4. Mary is a sweet child and tries to please.

pleas ing (plēz′ing), giving pleasure; pleasant.

pleas ure (plezh′ər), 1. the feeling of being pleased; delight; joy. The boy's pleasure in the gift was good to see. 2. something that pleases; a joy; a delight. It would be a pleasure to see you again. 3. anything that amuses; sport; play. He takes his pleasure in riding and hunting. 4. desire; choice. Is it your pleasure to go now?

Girl wearing a dress with a pleated skirt

pleat (plēt), 1. a flat, usually narrow, fold made in cloth by doubling it on itself. 2. fold or arrange in pleats; as, a pleated skirt.

pledge (plej), 1. a promise. The drunkard signed the pledge never to drink again. 2. to promise. We pledge loyalty to our country. 3. security; something that secures or makes safe. The knight left a jewel as pledge of his return. 4. give as security. 5. drink in honor of (someone) and wish (him) well. 6. something given to show favor or love.

plen te ous (plen′ti əs), plentiful.

plen ti ful (plen′ti fəl), more than enough; ample; abundant. Ten gallons of gasoline is a plentiful supply for a seventy-mile trip. Apples are cheap now because they are plentiful.

plen ty (plen′ti), full supply; all that one needs; a large enough number or amount. You have plenty of time to catch the train.

pli a ble (plī′ə bəl), 1. easily bent; flexible; supple. Willow twigs are pliable. 2. easily influenced; yielding. He is too pliable to be a good captain.

pli ant (plī′ənt), 1. bending easily; pliable. 2. easily influenced; yielding.

Pliers

pli ers (plī′ərz), a tool used to hold or turn or bend things.

plight[1] (plīt), condition or state, usually bad. He was in a sad plight when he became ill and had no money.

plight[2] (plīt), pledge; promise. **I plight my troth** means I promise to be faithful.

plod (plod), 1. walk heavily; trudge. The old man plods wearily along the road. 2. proceed in a slow or dull way; work patiently with effort. Dan plodded away at his lessons until he learned them.

plot (plot), 1. secret plan. Two men formed a plot to rob the bank. 2. to plan; plan secretly with others to do something wrong. The traitors plotted against the government. 3. the plan or main story of a play, novel, poem, etc. Boys like plots dealing with adventure and mystery. 4. a small piece of ground; as, a garden plot. 5. divide (land) into plots. The old farm was plotted out into house lots. 6. a map or diagram. 7. make a map or diagram of. 8. mark the position of something on a map or diagram.

plough (plou), plow.

plough man (plou′mən), plowman.

Golden plover (about 11 in. long)

plov er (pluv′ər), a bird with a short tail and a bill like that of a pigeon. See the picture.

plow (plou), 1. a big heavy instrument for cutting the soil and turning it over. 2. turn up (the soil) with a plow. 3. a machine for removing snow, usually called a snowplow. 4. use a plow. 5. move through anything as a plow does. The ship plowed through the waves.

Plow

plow man (plou′mən), 1. man who guides a plow. 2. a farm worker.

plow share (plou′shãr′), the blade of a plow, the part that cuts the soil. See the picture of **plow.**

pluck (pluk), 1. pick; pull off. She plucked flowers in the garden. 2. pull; pull at. Amy plucked her dress. 3. courage. The cat showed pluck in fighting the dog.

pluck y (pluk′i), having or showing courage; as, a plucky dog.

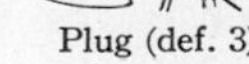
Plug (def. 3)

plug (plug), 1. piece of wood, etc., used to stop up a hole. 2. stop up or fill with a plug. 3. a device for making an electrical connection. There are two wall plugs in our kitchen. 4. a place where a hose can be attached. 5. work steadily. Mary plugged away at the typewriter.

plum (plum), 1. a fruit with a smooth skin. See the picture. Plums are red, green, purple, or yellow. 2. the tree it grows on. 3. raisin. 4. made of raisins. A plum cake has raisins in it. 5. something good. This new job is a fine plum for Mr. Jones.

Plums

plum age (plüm′ij), the feathers of a bird. A parrot has bright plumage.

plumb er (plum′ər), man whose work is putting in and repairing water pipes and fixtures in buildings. When the water pipe froze, we sent for a plumber.

plumb ing (plum′ing), 1. the work or trade of a plumber. 2. the system of pipes for carrying water, etc., in a building; as, bathroom plumbing.

plume (plüm), 1. feather; a large, long feather; a feather ornament. 2. something like a large soft feather; as, a plume of smoke. 3. smooth or arrange the feathers of. The eagle plumed its wing. 4. show pride in (oneself). Mary plumed herself on her skill in dancing. 5. furnish with plumes.

plump[1] (plump), rounded out; fat in an attractive way. A healthy baby has plump cheeks.

plump[2] (plump), 1. fall or drop heavily or suddenly. All out of breath, she plumped down on a chair. 2. a sudden plunge; a heavy fall. 3. heavily or suddenly. The lunch basket fell plump into the pond. He ran plump into me. 4. direct; positive; blunt; as, a plump denial.

plun der (plun′dər), 1. rob; rob by force. The pirates entered the harbor and began to plunder the town. 2. act of robbing by force. During the plunder soldiers came. 3. things stolen. The pirates buried their plunder in a secret place.

plunge (plunj), 1. throw or thrust with force into a liquid or into a place. Plunge your hand into the water. The soldier plunged his sword into the heart of his enemy. 2. throw oneself (into water, danger, a fight, etc.). Dick plunged into the river and saved Tim. 3. rush; dash. 4. a jump or thrust; a dive. 5. pitch suddenly and violently. The ship plunged about in the storm.

plu ral (plür′əl), 1. more than one. 2. the form of a word which shows that it means more than one. *Books* is the plural of *book; men* is the plural of *man; these* is the plural of *this.*

plus (plus), 1. added to. 3 plus 2 equals 5. 2. and also. The work of an engineer requires intelligence plus experience. 3. and more. His mark was B plus. 4. showing addition. The plus sign is +.

plush (plush), a fabric like velvet but thicker and softer.

ply (plī), 1. work with; use. The dressmaker plies her needle. 2. keep up work on; work at or on. The enemy plied our messenger with questions to make him tell his errand. 3. go back and forth regularly between certain places. The bus plies from the station to the hotel. 4. thickness, fold, or twist. Three-ply rope is made up of three twists.

P.M. or **p.m.,** 1. afternoon. 2. the time from noon to midnight. Sam's birthday party lasted till 10 P.M.

pneu mo ni a (nū mō′ni ə or nü mō′ni ə), a disease in which the lungs are inflamed.

poach[1] (pōch), 1. trespass on another's land, especially to hunt or fish. 2. take (game or fish) without any right.

poach[2] (pōch), cook (an egg) by breaking it into boiling water and leaving it there a minute or so.

pock et (pok′it), 1. a small bag sewed into clothing. 2. put in one's pocket. 3. meant to be carried in a pocket; as, a pocket handkerchief. 4. small enough to go in a pocket; as, a pocket camera. 5. **Be out of pocket** means (1) spend or lose money. (2) be a loser. 6. a small bag or pouch. 7. a hollow place. 8. a hole in the earth containing gold or other ore. The miner struck a pocket of silver. 9. shut in; hem in. 10. hold back; suppress; hide. He pocketed his pride and said nothing. 11. take and endure, without doing anything about it. He pocketed the insult. 12. take secretly or dishonestly. 13. any current or condition in the air which causes an airplane to drop suddenly.

pock et book (pok′it bu̇k′), 1. a case for carrying money, papers, etc., in the pocket. 2. woman's purse.

pock et knife (pok′it nīf′), a small knife with one or more blades that fold into the handle.

pod (pod), the shell or case in which plants like beans and peas grow their seeds.

Pod of peas

po em (pō′im), 1. a composition in verse; an arrangement of words in lines with a regularly repeated accent. 2. a composition showing great beauty of language or thought.

po et (pō′it), person who makes poems. Longfellow and Scott were poets.

po et ess (pō′it is), woman poet.

po et ic (pō et′ik), 1. having something to do with poems or poets. 2. suitable for poems or poets. *Alas*, *o'er*, *plenteous*, and *blithe* are poetic words. 3. showing imagination. Alice has such poetic fancies as calling the clouds sheep and the new moon a boat.

po et i cal (pō et′i kəl), poetic.

po et ry (pō′it ri), 1. the art of writing poems. Shakespeare and Milton are masters of English poetry. 2. poems. Have you read much poetry?

point (point), 1. a sharp end; as, the point of a needle. 2. a dot; a punctuation mark. A period is a point. 3. item; small part. The speaker replied to the argument point by point. 4. the main idea or purpose. Your answer is not to the point. I did not get the point of his argument. 5. special quality or feature. Courage and endurance were his good points. 6. piece of land with a sharp end sticking out into the water; cape. 7. place; spot. At this point the cars stopped. 8. a position without length or width. 9. direction. North, northeast, south, southwest, etc., are points of the compass. 10. give a point to; sharpen. The preacher told a story to point his advice. 11. to aim. Don't point your gun at me. 12. show position or direction. 13. **Point out** means show or call attention to. Please point out my mistakes. 14. degree; stage; as, freezing point, boiling point. 15. a unit of scoring. Four points make a game in tennis. 16. **Point of view** means attitude of mind. Farmers and campers have different points of view toward rain.

point ed (poin′tid), 1. having a point or points; as, a pointed roof. 2. sharp; piercing; as, a pointed wit. 3. directed; aimed. 4. emphatic. The prince showed Cinderella pointed attention.

point er (poin′tər), 1. one that points. 2. a long, tapering stick used in pointing things out on a map, blackboard, etc. 3. a short-haired hunting dog. A pointer is trained to show where game is by standing still with his head and body pointing toward it.

Pointer (about 26 in. high at the shoulder)

poise (poiz), balance. She has perfect poise both of mind and body and never seems embarrassed. The athlete poised the weight in the air before throwing it. Poise yourself on your toes.

poi son (poi′zən), 1. a drug or other substance very dangerous to life and health. Strychnine, gas, arsenic, and opium are poisons. 2. kill or harm by poison. 3. put poison in or on.

poison ivy, a climbing plant that looks like ivy, and causes a painful rash on most people if they touch it.

Poison ivy

poi son ous (poi′zən əs), containing poison; very harmful to life and health. The rattlesnake's bite is poisonous.

poke (pōk), 1. push against with something pointed; thrust into; thrust; push. You can poke a person in the ribs with your elbow, or poke a fire. A gossip pokes her nose into other people's business. 2. a poking; a thrust; a push. 3. go in a lazy way; loiter.

pok er[1] (pōk′ər), a metal rod for stirring a fire.

pok er[2] (pōk′ər), a card game.

po lar (pō′lər), 1. near the North or South Pole. It is very cold in the polar regions. 2. having to do with a pole or poles.

pole[1] (pōl), 1. long, slender piece of wood, etc.; as, a telephone pole, a flagpole. 2. make (a boat) go with a pole.

pole[2] (pōl), 1. The North Pole and the South Pole are the ends of the earth's axis. 2. A magnet or a battery has a positive pole and a negative pole.

pole cat (pōl′kat′), 1. small, dark-brown European animal with a very disagreeable odor. 2. a skunk.

Polecat (about 17 in. long; tail about 8 in. long)

pole star (pōl′stär′), a star that is almost directly above the North Pole, and was formerly much used as a guide by sailors.

po lice (pə lēs′), 1. the department of government that keeps order and arrests persons who break the law. 2. the men who do this for a city or state. 3. keep in order; as, to police the camp.

po lice man (pə lēs′mən), member of the police force; police officer.

pol i cy (pol′i si), 1. plan of action; way of management. It is a poor policy to promise more than you can do. The candidates explained their policies. 2. prudence; practical wisdom.

pol ish (pol′ish), 1. make smooth and shiny; as, to polish shoes. 2. smoothness; polished condition. The polish of the furniture reflected our faces like a mirror. Travel with polite people gives polish to a girl's manners. 3. substance used to give smoothness or shine; as, silver polish. 4. become smooth and shiny; take on a polish.

po lite (pə līt′), 1. behaving properly; having or showing good manners. 2. refined; elegant. Helen wished to learn all the customs of polite society.

po lite ness (pə līt′nis), polite nature or behavior. The children were praised for their politeness.

pol i tic (pol′i tik), wise in looking out for one's own interests; prudent. A politic person tries not to offend people.

po lit i cal (pə lit′i kəl), 1. having something to do with citizens or the government. Treason is a political offense. Who shall have the right to vote is a political question. 2. of politicians or their methods.

pol i ti cian (pol′i tish′ən), one who gives much time to political affairs. Politicians are busy near election time.

pol i tics (pol′i tiks), 1. the management of political affairs; the science and art of government. Franklin Roosevelt was engaged in politics for many years. 2. political principles or opinions. My father's politics were strongly against rule by any one man.

pol ka (pōl′kə), 1. a kind of lively dance. 2. music for it.

poll (pōl), 1. the voting at an election. 2. the number of votes cast at an election. 3. list of persons; especially, a list of voters. 4. receive at an election. 5. vote; cast (a vote at an election). 6. take the votes of. 7. the head.

pol len (pol′ən), the fine yellowish powder on flowers. Grains of pollen carried to the pistils of flowers fertilize them.

polls (pōlz), voting place or places.

pol lute (pə lüt′), make dirty; defile. The water at the bathing beach was polluted by garbage from the city.

po lo (pō′lō), a game like hockey played by men on horseback with long-handled mallets and a wooden ball.

Man playing polo

pome gran ate (pom′gran′it), 1. a reddish-yellow fruit with a thick skin, red pulp, and many seeds. The pulp and seeds have a pleasant, slightly sour taste. See the picture just below. 2. the tree it grows on.

pomp (pomp), splendid show or display; magnificence. The king was crowned with great pomp.

pom pous (pom′pəs), fond of display; acting too proudly; trying to seem magnificent. The leader of the band bowed in a pompous manner.

pon cho (pon′chō), a large piece of cloth, often waterproof, with a slit in the middle for the head to go through. Ponchos are worn in South America as cloaks.

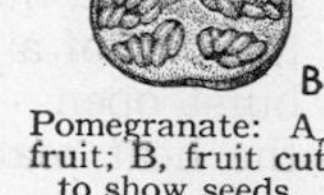

Pomegranate: A, fruit; B, fruit cut to show seeds.

pond (pond), a body of still water, smaller than a lake.

pon der (pon′dər), consider carefully; as, to ponder a problem.

pon der ous (pon′dər əs), 1. very heavy. 2. heavy and clumsy. A hippopotamus is ponderous. 3. dull; tiresome. The speaker talked in a ponderous way.

Poniard

pon iard (pon′yərd), dagger. See the picture just above.

pon toon (pon tün′), 1. a low flat-bottomed boat. 2. such a boat, or some other floating structure, used as one of the supports of a temporary bridge. 3. either of the two parts of an airplane that are like boats, used for landing on or taking off from water. See the picture of **amphibian airplane.**

Bridge supported by pontoons

po ny (pō′ni), a kind of small horse.

poo dle (pü′dəl), a pet dog with thick curly hair. See the picture just below.

Poodle (12 to 15 in. high at the shoulder)

pool[1] (pül), small pond; small body of still water. Our school has a swimming pool.

pool[2] (pül), 1. a game like billards, played with balls on a special table. 2. put (things or money) together for common advantage. The three boys pooled their savings for a year to buy a boat. 3. the things or money put together by different persons.

poor (pür), 1. having few things or nothing. **The poor** are those who have little or nothing. 2. not good in quality; lacking something needed; as, poor soil, a poor crop, poor milk, a poor cook, a poor story, a poor head for figures, poor health. 3. needing pity. This poor child has hurt himself.

poor ly (pür′li), 1. not sufficiently. A desert is poorly supplied with water. 2. badly; not well. Tom did poorly in the test.

pop (pop), 1. make a short, quick, explosive sound. The firecrackers popped in bunches. 2. a short, quick, explosive sound. We heard the pop of a cork. 3. burst open; cause to burst open. When you pop corn, the heat makes the kernels burst open. 4. move, go, or come suddenly or unexpectedly. Our neighbor popped in for a short call. 5. thrust or put suddenly. She popped her head out through the window. 6. shoot; fire a gun or pistol. 7. a soft, bubbling drink; as, strawberry pop.

Lombardy poplar

Pope or **pope** (pōp), the head of the Roman Catholic Church.

pop lar (pop′lər), 1. tree that grows rapidly. The cottonwood is one kind of poplar. 2. its soft wood.

pop py (pop′i), a plant with showy flowers; one of its flowers. Opium is made from one kind of poppy.

Poppy

pop u lace (pop′ū lis), the common people.

pop u lar (pop′ū lər), 1. of the people; by the people; representing the people. The United States has a popular government. 2. suited to the people; as, popular prices, books on popular science. 3. liked by most people; as, a popular song. 4. liked by acquaintances or associates. Fred's good nature makes him the most popular boy in the school.

pop u lar i ty (pop′ū lar′i ti), fact or condition of being liked by most people.

pop u late (pop′ū lāt), 1. inhabit; as, a thickly populated city. 2. furnish with inhabitants. Europeans populated America.

pop u la tion (pop′ū lā′shən), 1. the people of a city, country, or district. 2. the number of people. 3. fact or process of populating.

pop u lous (pop′ū ləs), full of people; having many people per square mile. Rhode Island is the most populous State of the United States.

Porch

por ce lain (pôr′sə lin), very fine earthenware; china. Teacups are often made of porcelain.

porch (pōrch), 1. covered entrance to a building. See the picture just above. 2. veranda.

por cu pine (pôr′kū pīn), an animal covered with spines or quills.

Porcupine (about 3 ft. long, with the tail)

pore[1] (pōr), study long and steadily. Grandfather would rather pore over a book than play.

pore[2] (pōr), a very small opening. Sweat comes through the pores in the skin.

pork (pōrk), the meat of a pig or hog used for food.

po rous (pō′rəs), full of pores or tiny holes. Cloth, blotting paper, and ordinary flowerpots are porous.

por poise (pôr′pəs), a sea animal from five to eight feet long that looks like a small whale. Porpoises eat fish.

por ridge (por′ij), cereal cooked in water or milk.

port[1] (pōrt), 1. harbor; place where ships and boats can be sheltered from storms. 2. the town or city by a harbor. New York City and San Francisco are important ports.

port[2] (pōrt), 1. opening in the side of a ship to let in light and air. 2. opening in a ship through which to shoot.

port[3] (pōrt), 1. the left side of a ship. See the picture under **aft.** 2. on the left side of a ship. 3. turn (the helm) to the left side.

port[4] (pōrt), a strong sweet wine.

port a ble (pōr′tə bəl), capable of being carried or moved. A portable garage can be moved to a new place.

por tage (pōr′tij), 1. carrying boats, provisions, etc., overland from one river, lake, etc., to another. 2. a place over which this is done.

por tal (pōr′təl), gate; door.

port cul lis (pōrt kul′is), strong gate or grating of iron that can be raised or lowered, used to close the gateway of an ancient castle or fortress.

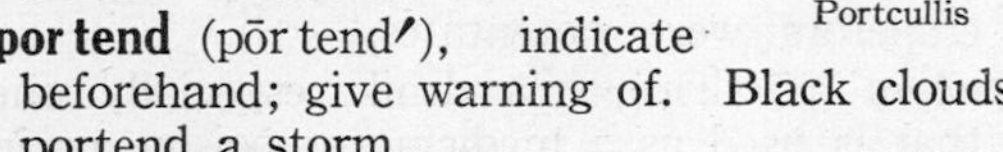

Portcullis

por tend (pōr tend′), indicate beforehand; give warning of. Black clouds portend a storm.

por ter[1] (pōr′tər), 1. man employed to carry burdens or baggage. Give your bags to the porter. 2. attendant in a railroad train.

por ter[2] (pōr′tər), doorkeeper. The porter let them in.

por ter[3] (pōr′tər), a dark-brown beer.

por ti co (pōr′ti kō), a roof supported by columns, forming a porch or a covered walk.

Portico

por tion (pōr′shən), 1. a part or share. Each child has his portion of meat. A portion of each school day is devoted to arithmetic. 2. divide into parts or shares. When Mr. Klein died his money was portioned out among his children.

port ly (pōrt′li), 1. stout; having a large body. 2. stately; dignified.

por trait (pōr′trāt), picture of a person.

por tray (pōr trā′), 1. make a likeness of in a drawing or painting. 2. picture in words; describe. The book *Black Beauty* portrays the life of a horse. 3. represent in a play or movie.

pose (pōz), 1. position of the body; way of holding the body. 2. hold a position. He posed an hour for his portrait. 3. put in a certain position; put. The photographer posed him before taking his picture. 4. an attitude assumed for effect; pretense; affectation. She takes the silly pose of being an invalid when really she is well and strong. 5. take a false position for effect. He posed as a rich man though he owed more than he owned.

po si tion (pə zish′ən), 1. place where a thing or person is. The flowers grew in a sheltered position behind the house. 2. way of being placed. Put the baby in a comfortable position. 3. proper place. Each soldier got into position to defend the fort. 4. job. He lost his position because he was not honest. 5. rank; standing; high standing. He was raised to the position of captain.

pos i tive (poz′i tiv), 1. permitting no question; sure. We have positive knowledge that the earth moves around the sun. 2. too sure. Her positive manner annoys people. 3. definite; emphatic. "No. I will not" is a positive refusal. 4. that surely does something or adds something; practical. Don't just make a negative criticism; give us some positive help. 5. that may be thought of as real and present. Light is a positive thing; darkness is only the absence of light.

pos sess (pə zes′), 1. own; have. Washington possessed great force and wisdom. 2. hold; occupy. 3. control. 4. control by an evil spirit. He fought like one possessed.

pos ses sion (pə zesh′ən), 1. a possessing; a holding. Our soldiers fought hard for the possession of the hilltop. 2. ownership. At his father's death he came into possession of a million dollars. 3. thing possessed; property. Please move your possessions from my room. 4. self-control.

pos ses sor (pə zes′ər), 1. owner. 2. holder.

pos si bil i ty (pos′i bil′i ti), 1. being possible. There is a possibility that the train may be late. 2. a possible thing or event. There are many possibilities. A whole week of rain is a possibility.

pos si ble (pos′i bəl), 1. that can be; that can be done; that can happen. 2. that can be true or a fact.

pos si bly (pos′i bli), 1. by any possibility; no matter what happens. I cannot possibly go. 2. perhaps. Possibly you are right.

pos sum (pos′əm), opossum.

post[1] (pōst), 1. piece of timber, iron, etc., firmly set up, usually to support something else; as, a signpost, a doorpost, a gatepost, the posts of a bed. 2. fasten (a notice) up in a place where it can easily be seen. 3. make public; make known by means of a posted notice. 4. put (a name) in a list that is to be posted up. The steamer *George Washington* is posted as late.

post[2] (pōst), 1. place where a soldier, policeman, etc., is stationed; place where one is supposed to be when one is on duty. When the fire alarm sounds, each man rushes to his post. 2. place where soldiers are stationed; fort. 3. the soldiers in a post. 4. a trading station; as, a post of a fur company. 5. to station at a post. The captain posted guards at the door. 6. job or position.

post[3] (pōst), 1. mail; a single delivery of mail. I shall send the package by post. The post has come. 2. send by mail; put into the mailbox; mail; as, to post a letter. 3. travel with haste; hurry.

post age (pōs′tij), amount paid on anything sent by mail.

post al (pōs′təl), 1. having something to do with mail and post offices. 2. post card; a post card with a postage stamp printed on it.

postal card, post card.

post card, card about $3\frac{1}{2}$ by $5\frac{1}{2}$ inches for sending a message by mail.

post er (pōs′tər), large printed sheet put up in some public place.

pos ter i ty (pos ter′i ti), 1. anyone's children, and their children, and their children, and so on and on. 2. the generations of the future. If we burn up all the coal and oil in the world, what will posterity do?

pos tern (pōs′tərn), 1. a back door or gate. 2. any small door or gate. 3. rear; lesser. The castle had a postern door.

post man (pōst′mən), man who carries and delivers mail for the government.

post mas ter (pōst′mas′tər), person in charge of a post office.

post office, 1. place where mail is handled and postage stamps are sold. 2. the government department that takes charge of mail.

post pone (pōst pōn′), put off till later; put off to a later time; delay. The ball game was postponed because of rain.

post script (pōst′skript), an addition to a letter, written after the writer's name has been signed.

pos ture (pos′chər), 1. position of the body; way of holding the body. Good posture is important to health. 2. take a position. The dancer postured before a mirror.

po sy (pō′zi), 1. flower. 2. a bunch of flowers; bouquet.

pot (pot), 1. a kind of vessel or dish. There are many different kinds and shapes of pots. They are made of iron, tin, earthenware, and other substances. A pot may hold food or drink or contain earth for flowers to grow in. 2. a pot and what is in it; the amount a pot will hold. He had a pot of beans. 3. put into a pot. We bought some potted plants. 4. to shoot. Jim potted four red squirrels.

po ta to (pə tā′tō), a vegetable growing underground. We eat white potatoes and sweet potatoes.

po tent (pō′tənt), powerful; having great power; strong; as, a potent remedy.

po ten tate (pō′tən tāt), 1. person having great power. 2. ruler. Kings, queens, and emperors were potentates.

po tion (pō′shən), a drink, especially one that is used as a medicine or poison, or in magic.

pot tage (pot′ij), a thick soup.

pot ter[1] (pot′ər), person who makes pots and dishes out of clay.

pot ter[2] (pot′ər), keep busy in a rather useless way. She potters about the house all day, but gets very little done.

pot ter y (pot′ər i), 1. pots, dishes, vases, etc., made from clay and hardened by heat. 2. the art or business of making them. 3. a place where such pots, dishes, vases, etc., are made.

Piece of Indian pottery

pouch (pouch), 1. bag or sack; as, a postman's pouch. 2. a fold of skin that is like a bag. Old people often have pouches under their eyes. A kangaroo carries its young in a pouch.

poul try (pōl′tri), chickens, turkeys, geese, ducks, etc.

pounce (pouns), 1. jump suddenly and seize; a sudden swoop or pouncing. The cat pounced upon the mouse. 2. dash suddenly; come suddenly.

pound[1] (pound), 1. a measure of weight; 16 ounces. 2. a unit of troy weight; 12 ounces. 3. a sum of British money worth 20 shillings. In ordinary times a pound is worth about $4.86.

pound[2] (pound), 1. strike or beat heavily again and again. He pounded the door with his fist. After a hard run your heart pounds. 2. crush to powder by beating.

pound[3] (pound), an enclosed place to put stray animals in.

pour (pōr), 1. cause to flow in a steady

stream. I poured the milk from the bottle into the cups. 2. flow in a steady stream. The crowd poured out of the church. The rain poured down. 3. a pouring. 4. a heavy rain.

pout (pout), 1. thrust or push out the lips, as a displeased or sulky child does. 2. a pushing out of the lips when displeased or sulky.

pov er ty (pov′ər ti), 1. condition of being poor. Sickness is one cause of poverty. 2. poor quality. The poverty of the soil makes the crops small. 3. small amount. The dull child's talk shows poverty of ideas.

pow der (pou′dər), 1. a solid reduced to dust by pounding, crushing, or grinding. 2. some special kind of powder. The doctor gave her powders to take after meals. 3. make into powder; become powder. The soil powdered in the heat. 4. sprinkle or cover with powder. 5. sprinkle. The ground was lightly powdered with snow. 6. gunpowder.

pow der y (pou′dər i), 1. of powder. 2. like powder; in the form of powder. 3. covered with powder.

pow er (pou′ər), 1. strength; force; might. 2. ability to do or act. I will give you all the help in my power. The fairy had power to change into different shapes. 3. authority; right; control; influence. Congress has power to declare war. Jack was in the power of the giant. 4. person or thing who has authority or influence; an important nation. Five powers held a peace conference. 5. energy or force that can do work.

pow er ful (pou′ər fəl), strong; having great power or force; mighty; as, a powerful man, a powerful medicine, a powerful sermon, a powerful nation.

pow er less (pou′ər lis), without power; helpless. The mouse was powerless in the cat's claws.

pow wow (pou′wou′), a North American Indian word meaning: 1. priest or medicine man. 2. ceremony. 3. council or conference. 4. hold a powwow.

prac ti ca ble (prak′ti kə bəl), 1. that can be done; capable of being put into practice; as, a practicable idea. 2. that can be used; as, a practicable road.

prac ti cal (prak′ti kəl), 1. having to do with action or practice rather than thought or theory. Earning a living is a practical matter. 2. engaged in actual practice or work. 3. fit for actual practice. 4. useful. 5. having good sense. 6. A **practical joke** is a trick played on someone.

prac ti cal ly (prak′ti kəl i), 1. really; so far as what the results will be. 2. almost; nearly. 3. in a practical way; in a useful way. 4. by actual practice.

prac tice (prak′tis), 1. action done many times over for skill. Practice makes perfect. 2. the skill gained by experience or exercise. He was out of practice at batting. 3. do (some act) again and again to learn to do it well. You can practice pitching a ball, adding, or playing music. Mary practices on the piano every day. 4. do usually; make a custom of. Practice what you preach. 5. follow, observe, or use day after day; as, to practice moderation. 6. the usual way; the custom. It is the practice in our town to blow the whistles at noon. 7. follow as a profession; as, to practice medicine. 8. do something as a habit or profession. That young man is just beginning to practice as a lawyer. 9. the business of a doctor or a lawyer. Dr. Adams sold his practice.

prac ticed or **prac tised** (prak′tist), skilled; expert; as, a practiced musician.

prac tise (prak′tis), practice (definitions 3, 4, 5, 7, 8).

prai rie (prãr′i), a large piece of level or rolling land with grass but few or no trees.

prairie dog, an animal like a woodchuck but smaller. See the picture.

Prairie dog

prairie schooner, large covered wagon used in crossing the plains of North America before the railroads were built. See the picture.

Prairie schooner

praise (prāz), 1. speak well of. 2. saying that a thing or person is good; words which tell the worth or value of a thing or person. 3. worship.

praise wor thy (prāz′wėr′ᴛʜi), worthy of praise; deserving approval.

prance (prans), 1. spring about on the hind legs. Horses prance when they feel lively. 2. move gaily or proudly.

prank (prangk), playful trick; piece of mischief. The fairy Puck liked to play pranks on people.

prate (prāt), 1. talk a great deal in a foolish way. 2. empty or foolish talk.

pray (prā), 1. ask from God; speak to God in worship. 2. ask earnestly. 3. please. Pray come with me.

prayer (prãr), 1. act of praying. 2. thing prayed for. 3. a form of worship. 4. a form of words to be used in praying. The Lord's Prayer begins, "Our Father, who art in heaven." 5. an earnest request.

preach (prēch), 1. speak on a religious subject; deliver (a sermon). 2. give earnest advice. 3. urge; recommend strongly. He was always preaching exercise and fresh air.

preach er (prēch′ər), person who preaches; clergyman; minister.

pre car i ous (pri kãr′i əs), uncertain; not safe; not secure. A soldier leads a precarious life.

pre cau tion (pri kô′shən), 1. care taken beforehand. Locking doors is a precaution against thieves. 2. taking care beforehand.

pre cede (prē sēd′), 1. go before; come before. Mr. Hoover preceded Mr. Roosevelt as President. 2. be higher in rank or importance. A major precedes a captain.

prec e dent (pres′i dənt), action that may serve as an example for later action. Roosevelt's election for a third term established a new precedent.

pre ced ing (prē sēd′ing), going before; coming before; previous.

pre cept (prē′sept), rule or direction. "If at first you don't succeed, try, try again" is a familiar precept.

pre cinct (prē′singkt), 1. the space within a boundary. Do not leave the school precincts during school hours. 2. a part or district of a city. 3. boundary; limit.

pre cious (presh′əs), 1. having great value. Gold and silver are often called the precious metals. Diamonds and rubies are precious stones. 2. dear; much loved.

prec i pice (pres′i pis), very steep place.

pre cip i tate (pri sip′i tāt for 1 and 2, pri sip′i tit for 3), 1. throw down, fling, hurl, send, or plunge in a violent, sudden, or headlong manner; as, to precipitate a rock down a cliff, to precipitate oneself into a struggle. 2. hasten the beginning of; bring about suddenly; as, to precipitate a war. 3. with great haste and force; plunging or rushing; hasty; rash.

pre cip i tous (pri sip′i təs), like a precipice; very steep; as, precipitous cliffs.

pre cise (pri sīs′), 1. exact; accurate; definite. The precise sum was 34½ cents. 2. careful. Alice is precise in her manners. 3. strict. We had precise orders to come home by nine o'clock.

pre cise ly (pri sīs′li), in a precise manner; exactly. Do precisely as the directions say.

pre ci sion (pri sizh′ən), accuracy; being exact; as, the precision of a machine.

pre clude (pri klüd′), shut out; prevent; make impossible.

pre co cious (pri kō′shəs), developed earlier than usual. This very precocious child could read well at the age of four.

pred e ces sor (pred′i ses′ər), person holding a position or office before another. John Adams was Jefferson's predecessor as President.

pre dic a ment (pri dik′ə mənt), an unpleasant, trying, or dangerous situation. Mary was in a predicament when she missed the last train home.

pre dict (pri dikt′), tell beforehand; prophesy. The weather bureau predicts rain for tomorrow.

pre dic tion (pri dik′shən), a prophecy. The official predictions about the weather often come true.

pre dom i nant (pri dom′i nənt), 1. having most power; superior. Will Russia be the predominant nation in Europe? 2. most extensive; most noticeable. Green was the predominant color in the forest.

pre dom i nate (pri dom′i nāt), be greater in power, strength, influence, or numbers.

preen (prēn), 1. smooth or arrange (the feathers) with the beak, as a bird does. 2. dress (oneself) carefully.

pref ace (pref′is), an introduction to a book, writing, or a speech. Has your history book a preface?

pre fer (pri fėr′), 1. like better; choose rather. I will come later, if you prefer. She prefers reading to sewing. 2. put forward; present. In a few words John preferred his claim to the office of captain.

pref er a ble (pref′ər ə bəl), more desirable.

pref er a bly (pref′ər ə bli), by choice. He wants a new job, preferably one in a garage.

pref er ence (pref′ər əns), 1. act of liking better. My preference is for beef rather than lamb. 2. thing preferred; first choice. Helen's preference in reading is a fairy story. 3. the favoring of one above another. A teacher should not show preference for any one of her pupils.

pre fix (prē′fiks for 1, prē fiks′ for 2), 1. a syllable, syllables, or word put at the beginning of a word to make another word, as in *pre*historic, *un*like. 2. put before. We prefix *Mr.* to a man's name.

pre his tor ic (prē′his tor′ik), of or belonging to times before histories were written. We find stone tools made by prehistoric men.

prej u dice (prej′ů dis), 1. an opinion formed without taking time and care to judge fairly; as, a prejudice against doctors. 2. cause a prejudice in; fill with prejudice. That one happening has prejudiced me against all lawyers. 3. harm or injury. I will do nothing to the prejudice of my cousin in this matter. 4. to harm or injure.

prel ate (prel′it), clergyman of high rank, such as a bishop.

pre lim i nar y (pri lim′i nãr′i), 1. coming before the main business; leading to something more important. After the preliminary exercises of prayer and song, the speaker of the day gave an address. 2. a preliminary step; something preparatory. A physical examination is a preliminary to joining the army.

prel ude (prel′ūd), anything serving as an introduction; a preliminary performance; as, the organ prelude to a church service.

pre ma ture (prē′mə tūr′ or prē′mə tür′), before the proper time; too soon.

pre mi er (prē′mi ər for 1, pri mēr′ for 2), 1. first in rank; chief. 2. a chief officer; the head of the British government.

prep a ra tion (prep′ə rā′shən), 1. making ready. 2. being ready. 3. thing done to get ready. 4. a specially made medicine or food or mixture of any kind.

pre par a to ry (pri par′ə tō′ri), 1. making ready. Preparatory schools fit pupils for colleges. 2. as an introduction; preliminary.

pre pare (pri pãr′), 1. make ready; get ready. Bob prepares his lessons while his mother prepares supper. 2. make by a special process.

prep o si tion (prep′ə zish′ən), a word that shows certain relations between other words. *With*, *for*, *by*, and *in* are prepositions in the sentence "A man *with* rugs *for* sale walked *by* our house *in* the morning."

pre pos ter ous (pri pos′tər əs), absurd; senseless; foolish. It would be preposterous to shovel coal with a teaspoon. That the moon is made of green cheese is a preposterous notion.

Pres by te ri an (prez′bi tēr′i ən), 1. the name of a Protestant church or denomination that has no bishops and is the most important church in Scotland. 2. of the Presbyterian church. 3. member of the Presbyterian church.

pre scribe (pri skrīb′), 1. order. Good citizens do what the laws prescribe. 2. order as medicine. The doctor prescribed a complete rest for Ann. 3. give medical advice.

pre scrip tion (pri skrip′shən), 1. an order; a direction. 2. a written direction or order for medicine; as, a prescription for a cough.

pres ence (prez′əns), 1. being present in a place. I knew of his presence in the other room. 2. place where a person is. The messenger was admitted to my presence. 3. **In the presence of** means in the sight or company of. He signed his name in the presence of two witnesses. 4. appearance; bearing; as, a man of noble presence. 5. something present, especially a ghost, spirit, or the like. 6. **Presence of mind** means ability to think calmly and quickly when taken by surprise.

pres ent[1] (prez′ənt), 1. at hand; not absent. Every member of the class was present. 2. **Be present** sometimes means be or exist. Oxygen is present in the air. 3. at this time; being or occurring now; as, the present ruler, present prices. 4. now; this time; this day, year, etc. That is enough for the present. **At present** means now.

pre sent[2] (pri zent′ for 1, 3, 4, 5, and 6, prez′ənt for 2), 1. give. They presented flowers to their teacher. **Present with** sometimes means give to. Our class presented the school with a picture. 2. gift; something given; as, a Christmas present. 3. introduce; make acquainted; bring (a person, etc.) before somebody. Miss Smith, may I present Mr. Brown? 4. offer; set forth in words. The speaker presented arguments for his side. 5. hand in; send in. The grocer presented his bill. 6. point or turn. The soldier presented his face to his enemy.

pres en ta tion (prez′ən tā′shən), 1. introduction; as, the presentation of a lady to the queen. 2. exhibition; showing; as, the presentation of a play or motion picture. 3. act of giving; delivering; as, the presentation of a gift. 4. the gift that is presented.

pres ent ly (prez′ənt li), soon. The clock will strike presently.

pres er va tion (prez′ər vā′shən), 1. preserving; keeping safe. Doctors work for the preservation of health. 2. being preserved; being kept safe.

pre serve (pri zėrv′), 1. keep from harm or change; keep safe; protect. 2. keep up; maintain. 3. keep from spoiling. Ice helps to preserve food. 4. prepare (food) to keep it from spoiling. Boiling with sugar, salting, smoking, and pickling are different ways of preserving food. 5. fruit cooked with sugar and sealed from the air. Mother made some plum preserves. 6. place where wild animals or fish are protected. People are not allowed to hunt on the preserves.

pre serv er (pri zėr′vər), person or thing that saves and protects from danger. Life preservers made like cork vests help to save people from drowning.

pre side (pri zīd′), 1. hold the place of authority; have charge of a meeting. Our principal will preside at our election of school officers. 2. have authority; have control. The manager presides over the business of the store.

pres i den cy (prez′i dən si), 1. office of president. Lucy was elected to the presidency of the Junior Club. 2. time during which a president is in office.

pres i dent (prez′i dənt), chief officer of a company, college, society, club, etc. The highest officer of a modern republic is usually called the President.

pres i den tial (prez′i den′shəl), of or belonging to a president or presidency; having something to do with a president or presidency; as, a presidential election, a presidential candidate.

press[1] (pres), 1. use force or weight steadily in pushing; push; force. Press the button to ring the bell. You press clothes with an iron. Press the orange juice out. 2. hug. Mother pressed the baby to her. 3. urge; keep asking (somebody) earnestly. Because it was so stormy, we pressed our guest to stay all night. 4. keep on pushing one's way; push ahead with eagerness or haste. The boys pressed on in spite of the wind. 5. a push; force; pressure. The press of many duties keeps her busy. 6. crowd. The little boy was lost in the press. 7. a machine for pressing; as, a printing press, an ironing press. 8. the business of printing newspapers and magazines. 9. the newspapers and the people who write for them. Our school picnic was reported by the press.

press[2] (pres), 1. force into service, usually naval or military. Navy officers used to visit towns and ships to press men for the fleet. 2. forcing into service.

press ing (pres′ing), requiring immediate action or attention; persistent.

pres sure (presh′ər), 1. the continued action of a weight or force. The small box was flattened by the pressure of the heavy book on it. The pressure of the wind filled the sails of the boat. 2. force per unit of area. There is a pressure of 20 pounds to the inch on this tire. 3. a state of trouble or strain; as, the pressure of poverty, working under pressure. 4. a compelling influence. Pressure was brought to bear on John to make him do better work.

pres tige (pres tēzh′), reputation, influence, or distinction, based on what is known about one's abilities, achievements, opportunities, associations, etc. Tom's prestige rose when the boys learned that his father was a captain.

pres to (pres′tō), 1. quickly. 2. quick. 3. a quick part of a piece of music.

pre sum a ble (pri züm′ə bəl), that can be taken for granted; probable; likely; as, the presumable time of their arrival.

pre sum a bly (pri züm′ə bli), probably.

pre sume (pri züm′), 1. suppose; take for granted without proving. You'll play out of doors, I presume, if there is sunshine. 2. take upon one's self; venture; dare. May I presume to tell you you are wrong? 3. take an unfair advantage. Don't presume on a person's good nature by borrowing from him every week.

pre sump tion (pri zump′shən), 1. thing taken for granted. As his mouth was sticky, the presumption was that he had eaten the cake. 2. unpleasant boldness. It is presumption to go to a party when one has not been invited. 3. act of presuming.

pre sump tu ous (pri zump′chü əs), forward; too bold; daring too much.

pre tence (pri tens′), pretense.

pre tend (pri tend′), 1. make believe. 2. claim. I don't pretend to be a musician.

3. claim falsely. She pretends to like you, but talks about you behind your back. 4. lay claim. James Stuart pretended to the English throne.

pre tense or **pre tence** (pri tens′), 1. a make-believe; pretending. My anger was all pretense. 2. false appearance. Under pretense of picking up the handkerchief, she took the money. 3. false claim. The girls made a pretense of knowing the boys' secret. 4. claim. 5. display; showing off. Her manner is modest and free from pretense.

pre ten sion (pri ten′shən), 1. a claim. The young prince has pretensions to the throne. 2. a putting forward of a claim; laying claim to. 3. doing things for show or to make a fine appearance; showy display.

pre text (prē′tekst), a misleading excuse; a false reason concealing the real reason; a pretense. He used his sore finger as a pretext for not going to school.

pret ty (prit′i), 1. pleasing; as, a pretty face, a pretty dress, a pretty tune, a pretty story, pretty manners. Pretty is used to describe people and things that are dainty, sweet, charming, etc., but not stately, grand, elegant, or very important. 2. fairly; rather. It is pretty late. 3. brave; bold; strong. Robin Hood was a pretty fellow. **prettier** and **prettiest** are formed from **pretty.**

pre vail (pri vāl′), 1. be the stronger; gain the victory. The knights prevailed against their foe. 2. be the most usual or strongest. Yellow is the prevailing color in her room. Sadness prevailed in our minds. 3. exist in many places; be in general use. The custom still prevails of hanging up stockings the night before Christmas. 4. **Prevail on** or **prevail upon** means persuade. Can't I prevail upon you to stay to dinner?

pre vail ing (pri vāl′ing), 1. that prevails; having superior force or influence. 2. in general use; common. The prevailing summer winds here are from the west.

prev a lence (prev′ə ləns), widespread occurrence; general use; as, the prevalence of complaints about the weather, the prevalence of automobiles.

prev a lent (prev′ə lənt), widespread; in general use; common. Colds are prevalent in winter.

pre vent (pri vent′), 1. keep (from). Illness prevented him from doing his work. 2. keep from happening. Rain prevented the game. 3. hinder. I'll meet you at six if nothing prevents.

pre ven tion (pri ven′shən), 1. preventing; hindering; as, the prevention of fire. 2. something that prevents.

pre ven tive (pri ven′tiv), 1. that prevents or hinders; as, preventive measures against disease. 2. something that prevents. Vaccination is a preventive against smallpox.

pre vi ous (prē′vi əs), 1. coming before; that came before. She did better in the previous lesson. 2. **Previous to** means before. Previous to her departure she gave a big party.

pre vi ous ly (prē′vi əs li), at a previous time; before.

prey (prā), 1. animal hunted or seized for food. Mice and birds are the prey of cats. 2. person or thing injured; victim; as, to be a prey to fear or disease. 3. take plunder; seize prey; hunt. Cats prey upon mice. 4. do harm. Worry preys on her mind. 5. the habit of hunting. Hawks are birds of prey.

price (prīs), 1. the amount for which a thing is sold or can be bought; the cost to the buyer. The price of this hat is $2.98. 2. amount paid for any result. We paid a heavy price for victory, for we lost ten thousand men. 3. find out the price of. Mother is pricing rugs. 4. put a price on; set the price of. 5. **Beyond price** or **without price** means so valuable that it cannot be bought.

price less (prīs′lis), very, very valuable.

prick (prik), 1. sharp point. 2. the little hole or mark a sharp point makes. 3. make a mark on with a sharp point. I pricked the map with a pin to show our route. 4. a pain like that made by a sharp point. 5. cause such a pain. Thorns prick. The cat pricked me with its claws. 6. act of pricking. 7. **Prick up the ears** means (1) point the ears upward. (2) give sudden attention.

prick le (prik′əl), 1. a small sharp point. 2. feel a prickly or smarting sensation. Her skin prickled when she saw the big snake.

prick ly (prik′li), 1. having many sharp points like thorns; as, a prickly rosebush. 2. smarting. Heat sometimes causes a prickly redness of the skin.

pride (prīd), 1. high opinion of one's own worth or possessions. Pride in our city should make us help to keep it clean. 2. too high an opinion of oneself. Pride goes before a fall. 3. something that one is proud of. Her youngest child is her great pride. 4. **Pride oneself on** means be proud of. We pride ourselves on our clean streets.

pried (prīd). See **pry.**

priest (prēst), 1. special servant of a god; as, priests of Apollo. 2. clergyman or minister of a Christian church.

priest hood (prēst′hu̇d), 1. position or rank of priest. He was admitted to the priesthood. 2. priests as a group. The priesthood had great power in Spain.

priest ly (prēst′li), 1. of or pertaining to a priest. 2. like a priest; suitable for a priest.

prim (prim), precise, neat, proper, or formal.

pri ma ry (prī′mãr i), 1. first in time; first in order. Little children go to the primary school. 2. original; from which others are made. The primary colors are red, blue, and yellow. 3. chief; first in importance. Good health and character are primary.

prime[1] (prīm), 1. first in rank; chief. His prime object was to get enough to eat. 2. first in quality; first-rate; excellent; as, prime ribs of beef. 3. best part; best time; best condition. A man of forty is in the prime of life.

prime[2] (prīm), [illegible]oad; prepare by putting something in or [illegible] You prime a pump by putting water in it.

prim er (prim′ər), 1. first book in reading. 2. first book; beginner's book.

pri me val (prī mē′vəl), 1. of or pertaining to the first age or ages. In its primeval state the earth was a fiery glowing ball. 2. ancient; as, primeval forests untouched by the ax.

prim i tive (prim′i tiv), 1. first of the kind; as, primitive Christians. 2. very early; living long ago. Primitive men lived in caves. 3. very simple; such as people had early in human history. A primitive way of making fire is by rubbing two sticks together.

Primrose (def. 1)

prim rose (prim′rōz′), 1. a little plant with pale-yellow flowers. See the picture. 2. a plant like this; as, the evening primrose. 3. pale yellow.

prince (prins), 1. son of a king; son of a king's son. 2. a ruler of a small state or country. 3. man of highest rank; the best; the chief; as, a merchant prince, a prince of artists.

prince ly (prins′li), 1. of a prince or his rank. 2. like a prince; noble. 3. fit for a prince.

prin cess (prin′sis), 1. daughter of a king; daughter of a king's son. 2. wife of a prince.

prin ci pal (prin′si pəl), 1. most important; chief; main. Chicago is the principal city of Illinois. 2. chief person; one who gives orders; as, the principal of a school. 3. person who hires another person to act for him. Smith does the business of renting the houses for Mr. Jones, his principal. 4. a sum of money on which interest is paid.

prin ci pal ly (prin′si pəl i), chiefly; above all; mainly; for the most part.

prin ci ple (prin′si pəl), 1. a rule of science explaining how things act; as, the principle by which a machine works. 2. a truth that is a foundation for other truths; as, the principles of democratic government. 3. a rule of action or conduct. I make it a principle to save some money every month. 4. a fundamental belief; as, religious principles. 5. uprightness; honor. Washington was a man of principle.

print (print), 1. a mark made by pressing or stamping, such as a footprint. 2. words in ink stamped by type. This book has clear print. 3. use type to stamp words on (paper, etc.). 4. cause to be printed; publish. Most newspapers are printed daily. 5. A book is **out of print** when no more printed copies can be bought from the publisher. 6. make letters the way they look in print instead of writing them. 7. to mark (cloth, paper, etc.) with patterns or designs. Machines print the rolls of paper that are used on walls. 8. cloth with a pattern pressed on it. Amy has two dresses made of print. 9. a picture made in a special way; a printed picture or design.

print er (prin′tər), person whose business or work is printing or setting type.

print ing (prin′ting), 1. the producing of books, newspapers, etc., by impression from movable types, plates, etc. 2. printed words. 3. letters made like those in print.

pri or (prī′ər), 1. earlier. I have a prior engagement and so can't go with you. 2. the superior officer in a monastery for men. The monks had to obey their prior.

pri or ess (prī′ər is), woman at the head of a monastery for women.

pri o ry (prī′ə ri), religious house governed by a prior or prioress.

prism (prizm). See the pictures. A six-sided pencil before it is sharpened has the shape of one kind of prism. A three-sided glass prism will separate white light into the colors of the rainbow.

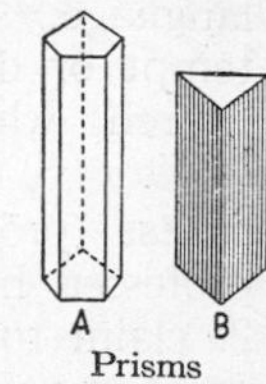

Prisms

pris on (priz′ən), place where one is shut up against his will. Burglars are put in prison. The small apartment was a prison to the big dog and he longed to be back on the farm.

pris on er (priz′ən ər), 1. person who is kept shut up against his will, or who is not free to move. 2. person taken by the enemy in war.

prith ee (priᴛʜ′i). I pray thee; I ask you. Prithee, who art thou?

pri va cy (prī′və si), 1. condition of being private; being away from others. 2. secrecy. He told me his reasons in strict privacy.

pri vate (prī′vit), 1. not for the public; for just a few special people or for one; as, a private road, a private house, a private letter. 2. having no public office; as, a private citizen. 3. a common soldier, not an officer. 4. secret. **In private** means secretly.

pri va teer (prī′və tēr′), 1. an armed ship owned by private persons, holding a government commission to attack and capture enemy ships. 2. commander of a privateer; one of its crew. 3. to cruise as a privateer.

pri vate ly (prī′vit li), in a private manner; not publicly; secretly.

pri va tion (prī vā′shən), 1. lack of the comforts or of the necessities of life. Many children died because of privation during the war. 2. loss; absence; being deprived. Privation of the company of all other human beings is a serious hardship.

priv i lege (priv′ilij), a special right, advantage, or favor. Mr. Hope has given us the privilege of using his radio.

priv i leged (priv′i lijd), having a special advantage or advantages. The nobility in Europe was a privileged class.

priv i ly (priv′i li), secretly.

priv y (priv′i), 1. private. A **privy council** is a body of personal advisers to a ruler. 2. secret. **Privy to** means having secret or private knowledge of.

prize[1] (prīz), 1. a reward worth working for. 2. a reward won after trying against other people. Prizes will be given for the three best stories. 3. something captured from the enemy in war. 4. worthy of a prize; as, prize vegetables. 5. given as a prize.

prize[2] (prīz), value highly. Mother prizes her best china.

pro (prō), 1. in favor of; for. 2. a reason in favor. The pros and cons of a question are the arguments for and against it.

prob a bil i ty (prob′ə bil′i ti), 1. quality of being likely or probable; chance. There is a probability that school will close a week earlier than usual. 2. something likely to happen. A storm is one of the probabilities for tomorrow.

prob a ble (prob′ə bəl), 1. likely to happen. Cooler weather is probable after this shower. 2. likely to be true. Something he ate is the probable cause of his pain.

prob a bly (prob′ə bli), more likely than not.

probe (prōb), 1. search into; examine thoroughly; as, to probe into the causes of a crime, to probe one's thoughts or feelings to find out why one acted as one did. 2. a slender instrument with a rounded end for exploring the depth or direction of a wound, a cavity in the body, etc. 3. examine with a probe.

prob lem (prob′ləm), 1. question; difficult question. 2. a matter of doubt or difficulty.

pro ce dure (prō sē′jər), way of proceeding; method of doing things. What is your procedure in making bread?

pro ceed (prō sēd′), 1. go on after having stopped; move forward. Please proceed with your story. The train proceeded at the same speed as before. 2. carry on any activity. He proceeded to light his pipe. 3. come forth; issue; go out. Heat proceeds from fire.

pro ceeds (prō′sēdz), 1. results. 2. money obtained from a sale, etc. The proceeds from the school play will be used to buy a new curtain for the stage.

proc ess (pros′es), 1. going on; moving forward. In process of time the house will be finished. 2. a set of actions or changes in a special order. By what processes is cloth made from wool? 3. treat or prepare by some special method. This cloth has been processed to make it waterproof.

pro ces sion (prō sesh′ən), something that moves forward; persons marching. A funeral procession filled the street.

pro claim (prō klām′), make known publicly and officially; declare publicly. War was proclaimed. The people proclaimed him king.

proc la ma tion (prok′lə mā′shən), proclaiming; a public and official announcement. Every year the President issues a Thanksgiving proclamation.

pro cure (prō kūr′), 1. obtain by care or effort; get. A friend procured a position in the bank for my big brother. It is hard to procure water in a desert. 2. cause.

prod (prod), 1. poke with something pointed; as, to prod an animal with a stick. 2. stir up; urge on; goad; as, to prod a lazy boy to action by threats and entreaties. 3. a poke; a thrust. That prod in the ribs hurt. 4. a stick with a sharp point; a goad.

prod i gal (prod′i gəl), 1. spending too much; wasting money or other things; wasteful. America has been prodigal of its forests. 2. abundant; lavish. 3. person who wastes. The father welcomed the prodigal back home.

pro di gious (prō dij′əs), 1. huge; vast. 2. wonderful; marvelous.

prod i gy (prod′i ji), a marvel; a wonder. An infant prodigy is a child remarkably brilliant in some respect.

pro duce (prō dūs′ or prō düs′ for 1, 2, and 3, prod′ūs or prod′üs for 4), 1. bring forward; show. Produce your proof. Our class produced a play. 2. to supply; bring forth. Hens produce eggs. 3. make. This factory produces stoves. Hard work produces success. 4. the yield. Vegetables are a garden's produce.

pro duc er (prō dūs′ər or prō düs′ər), one that produces.

prod uct (prod′əkt), 1. that which is produced; a result of work or of growth; as, factory products, farm products. 2. a number or quantity resulting from multiplying. 40 is the product of 5 and 8.

pro duc tion (prō duk′shən), 1. act of producing; manufacture. His business is the production of automobiles. 2. something which is produced. That worthless book is the production of an ignorant author.

pro duc tive (prō duk′tiv), 1. producing; bringing forth. That field is productive only of weeds. Hasty words are productive of quarrels. 2. producing food or other useful articles. Farming is productive labor. 3. fertile; producing much; as, a productive farm, a productive writer.

pro fane (prō fān′), 1. not sacred. 2. with contempt or disregard for God or holy things; as, a profane man using profane language. 3. treat (holy things) with contempt or disregard. Soldiers profaned the church when they stabled their horses in it.

pro fess (prō fes′), 1. declare openly. He professed his loyalty to the United States. 2. claim to have; claim. He professed the greatest respect for the law. I don't profess to be an expert.

pro fes sion (prō fesh′ən), 1. an occupation requiring an education; especially, law, medicine, teaching, or the ministry. 2. the people engaged in such an occupation. The medical profession favors this law. 3. act of professing. I don't believe her profession of friendship for us.

pro fes sion al (prō fesh′ən əl), 1. of or pertaining to a profession. Dr. Smith has a professional gravity very unlike his ordinary joking manner. 2. engaged in a profession. A lawyer or a doctor is a professional man. 3. making a business or trade of something which others do for pleasure; as, professional ballplayers, professional musicians. 4. person who does this.

pro fes sor (prō fes′ər), 1. a teacher of the highest rank in a college or university. 2. teacher.

prof fer (prof′ər), offer. We proffered regrets at having to leave so early. His proffer of advice was accepted.

pro fi cient (prō fish′ənt), advanced in any art, science, or subject; skilled; expert. Anne was very proficient in music.

pro file (prō′fīl), 1. side view. 2. outline.

Profile of Lincoln

prof it (prof′it), 1. the gain from a business; what is left when the cost of goods and of carrying on the business is subtracted from the amount of money taken in. The profits in this business are not large. 2. advantage; benefit. What profit is there in worrying? 3. get advantage; gain; benefit. A wise person profits from his mistakes.

prof it a ble (prof′it ə bəl), bringing gain; useful; yielding profit. We spent a profitable afternoon in the library. The sale held by the Girl Scouts was very profitable.

prof it a bly (prof′it ə bli), with profit.

pro found (prō found′), 1. very deep; as,

a profound sigh, a profound sleep. 2. felt strongly; very great. 3. going far deeper than what is easily understood; having or showing great knowledge or understanding; as, a profound book, a profound thinker, a profound thought.

pro fuse (prō fūs′), 1. very abundant; as, profuse thanks. 2. spending or giving much. He was so profuse with his money that he is now poor.

pro fu sion (prō fū′zhən), 1. great abundance. 2. extravagance.

prog e ny (proj′i ni), children; offspring; descendants. A cat's kittens are her progeny.

pro gram (prō′gram), 1. list of items or events. There are concert programs, theater programs, and programs of a meeting. 2. plan of what is to be done; as, a school program, a business program, a government program. Also spelled **programme.**

pro gress (prō gres′ for 1 and 3, prog′res for 2 and 4), 1. move forward; go ahead. 2. moving forward; going ahead. 3. advance; develop; get better. 4. an advance; growth; development; improvement.

pro gres sive (prō gres′iv), 1. making progress; advancing to something better; improving; as, a progressive nation. 2. favoring progress. 3. person who favors improvement and reform in government, religion, or business. He is a progressive in his beliefs.

pro hib it (prō hib′it), 1. forbid by law or authority. Picking flowers in the park is prohibited. 2. prevent.

pro hi bi tion (prō′i bish′ən), 1. a prohibiting. The prohibition of swimming in the city's reservoirs is sensible. 2. a law or laws against making or selling alcoholic liquors.

proj ect (proj′ekt for 1, prō jekt′ for 2, 3, and 4), 1. a plan. Flying in a heavy machine was once thought an impossible project. 2. to plan; scheme. 3. throw or cast forward; cause to fall on a surface. Moving pictures are projected on the screen. The tree projects a shadow on the grass. 4. stick out. The rocky point projects far into the water.

pro jec tile (prō jek′til), an object that can be thrown, hurled, or shot, such as a stone or bullet.

pro jec tion (prō jek′shən), 1. part that projects or sticks out; as, rocky projections on the face of a cliff. 2. a sticking out. 3. a throwing or casting; as, the projection of a cannon ball from a cannon.

pro lif ic (prō lif′ik), 1. producing many offspring. Rabbits are prolific. 2. producing much; as, a prolific tree, garden, imagination, or writer.

pro long (prō lông′), make longer; extend. Good care may prolong a sick person's life. The dog uttered prolonged howls whenever the family left the house.

prom e nade (prom′i nād′), 1. walk for pleasure or for show. The Easter promenade is well known as a fashion show. He promenaded back and forth on the ship's deck. 2. a public place for such a walk. Atlantic City has a famous promenade along the beach.

prom i nence (prom′i nəns), 1. something that juts out or projects, especially upward. A hill is a prominence. 2. being prominent, distinguished, or conspicuous; as, the prominence of Washington as a leader; the prominence of baseball as a sport.

prom i nent (prom′i nənt), 1. standing out; projecting. Some insects have prominent eyes. 2. easy to see. A single tree in a field is prominent. 3. well-known; important; as, a prominent citizen.

prom ise (prom′is), 1. words said, binding a person to do or not to do something. A man of honor always keeps his promise. 2. give one's word; give a promise. He promised to stay till we came. 3. make a promise of; as, to promise help. 4. that which gives hope of success; as, a pupil of promise in music. 5. give hope; give hope of. The rainbow promises fair weather.

prom is ing (prom′is ing), likely to turn out well; hopeful.

prom on to ry (prom′ən tō′ri), a high point of land extending from the coast into the water; headland.

Promontory

pro mote (prə mōt′), 1. raise in rank or importance. Pupils who pass this test will be promoted to the next grade. 2. help to grow or develop; help to success. A kindly feeling toward other countries will promote peace.

pro mo tion (prə mō′shən), 1. advance in rank or importance. The clerk was given a promotion and an increase in salary. 2. helping along to success. The doctors were busy in the promotion of a health campaign.

prompt (prompt), 1. quick; on time; done at once. Be prompt to obey. 2. cause (someone) to do something. His curiosity prompted him to ask questions. 3. remind of the words or actions needed. Do you know your part in the play or shall I prompt you?

prone (prōn), 1. inclined; liable. We are prone to think evil of people we don't like. 2. lying face down.

prong (prông), one of the pointed ends of a fork, antler, etc.

pro noun (prō′noun), a word used to indicate without naming, such as *you, it, they, him, we, your, whose, this,* or *whoever;* a word used instead of a noun.

pro nounce (prə nouns′), 1. speak; make the sounds of. Pronounce your words clearly. 2. declare solemnly or positively. The judge pronounced sentence on the prisoner.

pro nounced (prə nounst′), strongly marked; emphatic; decided; as, pronounced opinions, pronounced likes and dislikes.

pro nun ci a tion (prə nun′si ā′shən), speaking; making the sounds of words; way of sounding words.

proof (prüf), 1. way or means of showing beyond doubt the truth of something. Is what you say a guess or have you proof? 2. act of testing. That box looks big enough; but let us put it to the proof. 3. of tested value against something; as, proof against being taken by surprise.

prop (prop), 1. hold up by placing a support under or against. Prop the clothesline with a stick. He was propped up in bed with pillows. 2. thing or person used to support another. A son can be the prop of his father's old age.

prop a gan da (prop′ə gan′də), 1. systematic efforts to spread opinions or beliefs. Advertisements are often propaganda. 2. the opinions or beliefs thus spread.

prop a gate (prop′ə gāt), 1. produce young. 2. increase in number. Trees propagate themselves by seeds. 3. cause to increase in number by the production of young. Cows and sheep are propagated on farms. 4. pass on; send further. 5. spread (news or knowledge). Don't propagate unkind reports.

pro pel (prō pel′), drive forward; as, a boat propelled by oars, a person propelled by ambition.

pro pel ler (prō pel′ər), a revolving hub with blades for propelling boats, airships, and airplanes.

pro pen si ty (prō pen′si ti), leaning the mind toward; a natural inclination or bent. Most boys have a propensity for playing with machinery.

prop er (prop′ər), 1. correct; right; fitting. Night is the proper time to sleep, and bed the proper place. 2. belonging to one or a few; not common to all. *John Adams* is a proper name.

prop er ly (prop′ər li), 1. in a proper, correct, or suitable manner. Eat properly. 2. rightly; justly. An honest man is properly indignant at the offer of a bribe.

prop er ty (prop′ər ti), 1. thing or things owned; possessions. This farmhouse is the property of Mr. Jones. Ask for your purse at the lost-property office. 2. ownership. 3. a quality or power belonging specially to something. Soap has the property of removing dirt. Copper has several important properties.

proph e cy (prof′i si), 1. telling what will happen; foretelling future events. 2. thing told about the future.

proph e sy (prof′i sī), 1. tell what will happen; foretell; predict. The sailor prophesied a severe storm. 2. speak when or as if inspired by God.

proph et (prof′it), 1. person who tells what will happen. Don't be a bad-luck prophet. 2. person who preaches what he thinks has been revealed to him. Every religion has its prophets.

pro phet ic (prō fet′ik), 1. belonging to a prophet; such as a prophet has; as, prophetic power. 2. containing prophecy; as, a prophetic saying. 3. giving warning of what is to happen. Thunder is prophetic of showers.

pro pi tious (prō pish′əs), favorable; as, propitious weather for our trip.

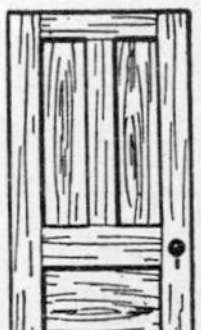

pro por tion (prə pōr′shən), 1. relation of two things in magnitude; a size, number, or amount compared to another. This door is narrow in proportion to its height. Mix water and orange juice in the proportions of three to one by taking three measures of water to every measure of orange juice. 2. proper relation between parts. His short legs were not in proportion to his long body. 3. fit (one thing to another) so that they go together. The designs in that rug are well proportioned. 4. part; share. A large proportion of Nevada is desert.

pro pos al (prə pōz′əl), 1. plan; scheme; suggestion. The club will now hear this member's proposal. 2. an offer of marriage. 3. act of proposing. Proposal is easier than performance.

pro pose (prə pōz′), 1. put forward; suggest. Ruth proposed that we take turns at the swing. 2. make an offer of marriage. 3. present (the name of someone) for an office. I am proposing John for president. 4. intend; plan. She proposes to save half of all she earns.

prop o si tion (prop′ə zish′ən), 1. what is offered to be considered; proposal. The tailor made a proposition to buy out his rival's business. 2. a statement; a statement that is to be proved true. 3. a problem to be solved.

pro pri e tor (prə prī′ə tər), owner.

pro pri e ty (prə prī′ə ti), 1. fitness. 2. proper behavior. She acted with propriety. Propriety demands that a boy tip his hat to a lady whom he knows.

pro sa ic (prō zā′ik), like prose; matter-of-fact; ordinary; not exciting.

prose (prōz), the ordinary form of spoken or written language; plain language not arranged in verses.

pros e cute (pros′i kūt), 1. bring before a court of law. People failing to shovel the snow from their sidewalks will be prosecuted. 2. carry out; follow up. He started an inquiry into the cause of the fire, and prosecuted it for several weeks.

pros e cu tion (pros′i kū′shən), 1. the carrying on of a lawsuit. 2. carrying out; following up. In prosecution of his plan, he stored away a supply of food.

pros pect (pros′pekt), 1. view; scene. The prospect from the mountain was grand. 2. looking forward; expectation. The prospect of a vacation is pleasant. 3. things expected or looked forward to. The prospects from our gardens are good this year. 4. to search or look; as, to prospect for gold.

pro spec tive (prə spek′tiv), 1. probable; expected. 2. looking forward in time; future.

pros pec tor (pros′pek tər), person who explores or examines a region, searching for gold, silver, oil, etc., or estimating the value of some product of the region.

pros per (pros′pər), 1. be successful; flourish; have good fortune. 2. make successful.

pros per i ty (pros per′i ti), success; good fortune; prosperous condition. Peace brings prosperity.

pros per ous (pros′pər əs), 1. successful; thriving; doing well; fortunate. A prosperous person is one who is happy, healthy, paying his way, and getting on well in his work. 2. favorable; helpful; as, prosperous weather for growing wheat.

pros trate (pros′trāt), 1. lay down flat; cast down. The captives prostrated themselves before the conqueror. 2. lying flat or face downward. He was humbly prostrate in prayer. 3. lying flat. 4. make very weak or helpless; exhaust. Sickness often prostrates people. 5. overcome; helpless. She is prostrate with her great grief.

pro tect (prə tekt′), shield from harm or danger; shelter; defend; guard. Protect yourself from danger. Protect the baby's eyes from the sun.

pro tec tion (prə tek′shən), 1. act of protecting; condition of being kept from harm; defense. We have policemen for our protection. 2. thing or person that prevents damage. An apron is a protection when doing dirty work.

pro tec tive (prə tek′tiv), 1. protecting; being a defense; as, the hard protective covering of a turtle. 2. preventing injury to those around; as, a protective device on a machine.

pro tec tor (prə tek′tər), one that protects; defender.

pro test (prō′test for 1, prō test′ for 2, 3, and 4), 1. statement that denies or objects strongly. They yielded only after protest. 2. declare solemnly; assert. The accused man protested his innocence. 3. to object. The boys protested against having girls in the game. 4. object to. John protested the umpire's decision.

Prot es tant (prot′is tənt), 1. member of any of most Christian churches except the Roman Catholic and Greek Catholic. Baptists, Methodists, Quakers, and many others are all Protestants. 2. of Protestants or their religion.

prot es ta tion (prot′es tā′shən), 1. solemn declaration. 2. a protest.

pro trude (prō trüd′), 1. thrust forth; stick out. The saucy child protruded her tongue. 2. be thrust forth; project. Helen's teeth protrude too far.

proud (proud), 1. thinking well of oneself. 2. thinking too well of oneself. 3. **Proud of** means thinking well of or being well satisfied with. 4. very pleasing to one's feelings or one's pride. It was a proud moment for Tom when he shook hands with the President. 5. grand; magnificent. The big ship was a proud sight.

proud ly (proud′li), in a proud manner; with pride; with a good opinion of oneself.

prove (prüv), 1. show that (a thing) is true and right. Prove these answers. 2. turn out; be found to be. The book proved interesting. 3. try; test; as, to prove a new tool. 4. know because of having tested. We have proved John's good temper.

prov en (prüv′ən), proved.

prov en der (prov′ən dər), food; dry food for animals, such as hay or corn.

prov erb (prov′ərb), a short wise saying used for a long time by many people. "Haste makes waste" is a proverb.

pro vide (prə vīd′), 1. take care for the future; as, to provide against accident, to provide for old age. 2. get ready; prepare. Mother provides a good dinner. 3. supply; furnish. Sheep provide us with wool. 4. arrange in advance; state as a condition beforehand. Our club's rules provide that dues must be paid monthly.

pro vid ed (prə vīd′id), on the condition that. She will go provided her friends can go also.

prov i dence (prov′i dəns), 1. God's care; God. Trusting in Providence, the Pilgrims sailed for the unknown world. 2. care for the future. Greater providence on the father's part would have kept the children from poverty.

prov i dent (prov′i dənt), careful in providing for the future; having or showing foresight. Provident men save money for their families.

prov ince (prov′ins), 1. a part of a country at a distance from the capital. 2. a big division of a country. Canada is divided into provinces. 3. a division; a department. 4. proper work or activity. Astronomy is not within the province of Grade 5.

pro vin cial (prə vin′shəl), 1. of a province; as, provincial government. 2. person born or living in a province. 3. having the manners, speech, dress, point of view, etc., of people living in a province.

pro vi sion (prə vizh′ən), 1. that which is made ready; a supply; a stock, especially of food; food. They took plenty of provisions on their trip. 2. to supply with provisions. 3. act of providing; preparation. Mr. Arch made provision for his children's education. 4. statement making a condition. Our library has a provision that hands must be clean before books are taken out.

pro vi sion al (prə vizh′ən əl), for the time being; temporary; as, a provisional agreement, a provisional governor.

prov o ca tion (prov′ə kā′shən), 1. something that stirs one up; cause of anger. Though the other boys' remarks were a provocation, John kept his temper. 2. act of provoking.

pro voke (prə vōk′), 1. make angry; vex. She provoked him by her teasing. 2. stir up; excite. An insult provokes a person to anger. 3. call forth; bring about; cause; start into action. The clown's acts provoked laughter and applause.

PROW

Prow of a ship

prow (prou), 1. the bow or forward pointed part of a ship or boat. 2. something like it; as, the prow of an airship.

prow ess (prou′is), 1. bravery; daring. 2. brave or daring acts. 3. unusual skill or ability. The knights of old were famous for their prowess with the spear.

prowl (proul), 1. go about slowly and secretly hunting for something to eat or steal. Many wild animals prowl at night. 2. wander.

pru dence (prü′dəns), wise thought before acting; good judgment.

pru dent (prü′dənt), planning carefully ahead of time; sensible; discreet. A prudent man saves part of his wages.

prune[1] (prün), a kind of plum that is dried. We had stewed prunes for breakfast.

prune[2] (prün), 1. cut out useless parts from. 2. cut off; cut.

pry[1] (prī), look with curiosity; peep. She is always prying into other people's affairs.

pry[2] (prī), 1. raise or move by force. Pry up that stone with your pickax. 2. a lever for prying. 3. get with much effort. We finally pried the secret out of him.

psalm (säm), a sacred song or poem, especially one from the Bible.

pshaw (shô), an exclamation expressing impatience, contempt, or dislike.

pub lic (pub′lik), 1. of the people; as, public opinion. 2. belonging to the people; as, public buildings. 3. by the people; as, public help for the poor. 4. for the people; serving the people; as, public meetings, public libraries, public schools. 5. known to many or all; not private; as, a matter of public knowledge. 6. all the people.

pub li ca tion (pub′li kā′shən), 1. book, newspaper, or magazine; anything that is published. *Boys' Life* is a publication of the Boy Scouts. 2. the printing and selling of books, newspapers, magazines, etc. 3. act of making known; fact or state of being made known; public announcement. There is prompt publication of any important news over the radio.

pub lic i ty (pub lis′i ti), 1. being public; being seen by or known to everybody; as, in the publicity of the street. 2. being brought to public notice by special effort, through newspapers, signs, radio, etc. 3. public notice; as, the publicity which actors desire.

pub lish (pub′lish), 1. prepare and offer (a book, paper, map, piece of music, etc.) for sale or distribution. 2. make publicly or generally known. Don't publish the faults of your friends.

pub lish er (pub′lish ər), person or company whose business is to print and sell books, magazines, etc.

puck (puk), a mischievous spirit; a goblin.

Puck

puck er (puk′ər), 1. draw into wrinkles or irregular folds; as, to pucker one's brow, to pucker cloth in sewing. A baby puckers his lips before crying. 2. a wrinkle; an irregular fold. This coat does not fit; there are puckers at the shoulders.

pud ding (pu̇d′ing), a soft cooked food, usually sweet, such as rice pudding.

pud dle (pud′əl), a small dirty pool; as, a puddle of rain water, a puddle of ink.

pueb lo (pweb′lō), 1. an Indian village built of adobe and stone. There were many pueblos in the southwestern United States. 2. A **Pueblo** is an Indian living in such a village.

puff (puf), 1. blow with short, quick blasts. The engine puffed. 2. a little short, quick blast. A puff of wind blew away the letter. 3. breathe quick and hard. She puffed as she climbed the stairs. 4. swell with air or pride. He puffed out his cheeks. 5. act of puffing. 6. light pastry filled with whipped cream, jam, etc.; as, a cream puff. 7. praise in exaggerated language. They puffed him to the skies. 8. soft round mass. She wore her hair in three puffs. 9. arrange in puffs; arrange softly and loosely. 10. a small pad for putting powder on the skin, etc.

pug na cious (pug nā′shəs), having the habit of fighting; fond of fighting; quarrelsome.

pull (pu̇l), 1. Baby pulled Nell's hair. Pull the trigger of the gun. He pulled my tooth out. We will pull the sled. Baby pulled the flower to pieces. Pull toward the shore, sailor. The train pulled out from the station. **Pull through** means get through a difficult or dangerous situation. **Pull oneself together** means get control of one's mind, energies, etc. 2. act of pulling. The boy gave a pull at the rope. 3. force exerted in pulling; effort. It was a hard pull to get up the hill. 4. a handle to pull by.

pul let (pu̇l′it), young hen, usually one less than a year old.

pul ley (pu̇l′i), a wheel with a hollowed rim in which a rope can run, and so lift weights, or change the direction of the pull. Our flag is raised to the top of a pole by a rope and two pulleys.

PULLEY

pulp (pulp), 1. the soft fleshy part of any fruit. 2. the soft inner part of a tooth. 3. any soft wet mass. Paper is made from wood ground to a pulp.

pul pit (pu̇l′pit), 1. a platform in a church from which the minister preaches. 2. preachers or preaching. The pulpit is against Sunday movies.

Pulpit

pul sate (pul′sāt), 1. beat; throb. 2. vibrate; quiver.

pulse (puls), 1. the beating of the heart; the changing flow of blood in the arteries caused by the beating of the heart. 2. any regular, measured beat; as, the pulse in music, the pulse of an engine. 3. beat; throb; vibrate. His heart pulsed with excitement.

pul ver ize (pul′vər īz), grind to powder; become dust.

pu ma (pū′mə), a large American wildcat. The mountain lion is also a common name for it.

Puma (4 or 5 ft. long, without the tail)

pum ice (pum′is), light spongy stone thrown up from volcanoes. Pumice is used for cleaning and polishing. Rub your hands with pumice to remove ink.

pump[1] (pump), 1. a machine for forcing liquids, air, or gas into or out of things; as, a water pump, an oil pump. 2. move (liquids, air, etc.) by a pump. Pump water from the well into the pail. Pump up the car's tires. 3. get information out of. Don't let him pump you.

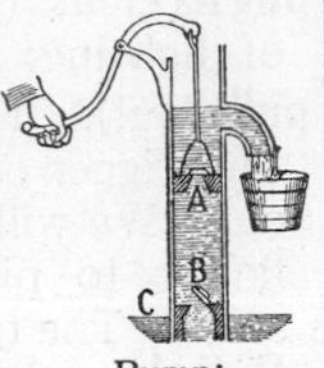

Pump: A and B, valves; C, water.

pump[2] (pump), a low shoe with a thin sole and no laces, straps, or buttons to hold it on.

pump kin (pump′kin or pung′kin), a large orange-yellow fruit of a trailing vine, much like a squash; the vine itself.

Pumpkin

punch[1] (punch), 1. hit with the fists. Boys punch; girls often slap. 2. a quick thrust or blow. 3. a tool for making holes. See the picture below. 4. pierce a hole in. The train conductor punches the tickets.

punch[2] (punch), a drink made of different liquids mixed together.

Punch

punc tu al (pungk′chü əl), prompt; on time. He is punctual to the minute.

punc tu a tion (pungk′chü ā′shən), use of periods, commas, and other marks to help make the meaning clear. Punctuation does for writing or printing what pauses and change of voice do for speech.

punc ture (pungk′chər), 1. hole made by something pointed. 2. make such a hole in. 3. have or get a puncture. 4. act or process of puncturing.

pun gent (pun′jənt), sharp; biting; as, a pungent pickle, the pungent smell of burning leaves, pungent criticism, a pungent wit.

pun ish (pun′ish), 1. cause pain, loss, or discomfort to (an offender). Father sometimes punishes us when we do wrong. 2. give punishment for. The law punishes crime.

pun ish a ble (pun′ish ə bəl), 1. liable to punishment. 2. deserving punishment.

pun ish ment (pun′ish mənt), 1. punishing; being punished. 2. pain, suffering, or loss. Her punishment for stealing was a year in prison.

pu ny (pū′ni), weak; of less than usual size, strength, or importance.

pup (pup), a young dog; puppy. The young of foxes, wolves, and other animals are also called pups.

pu pa (pū′pə), a stage in the life of an insect when it is in a case; an insect in this stage. It comes between the larva (caterpillar) and the winged adult stage.

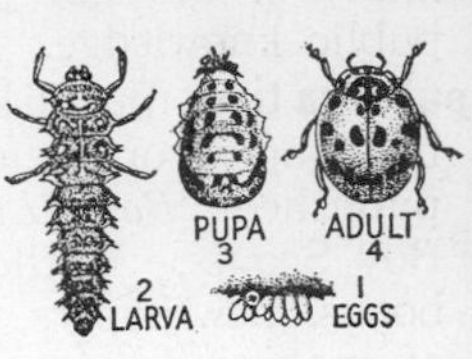

pu pil (pū′pəl), 1. one who is learning in school or being taught by someone. The music teacher takes private pupils. 2. the black center of the eye.

pup pet (pup′it), 1. small doll. In a puppet show the puppets are often moved by wires. 2. anybody who is not independent, waits to be told how to act, and does what somebody else says.

Puppet show

pup py (pup′i), 1. a young dog. Brownie had four puppies. 2. a silly, conceited young man.

pur chase (pėr′chəs), 1. buy; get by paying a price. 2. get in return for something; as, to purchase safety at the cost of happiness. 3. act of buying. 4. thing bought. That hat was a good purchase. 5. a firm hold to help move something, or to keep from slipping. Wind the rope twice around that tree for a better purchase.

pur chas er (pėr′chəs ər), buyer.

pure (pūr), 1. clean; clear; genuine; without defects. 2. not mixed with anything else; as, pure fun, pure gold. 3. with no evil; without sin; as, a pure mind.

pure ly (pūr′li), 1. in a pure manner. 2. entirely. 3. merely. 4. innocently.

purge (pėrj), wash away all that is not clean; make clean. King Arthur tried to purge his land from sin.

pu ri fi ca tion (pūr′i fi kā′shən), purifying.

pu ri fy (pūr′i fī), make pure. Filters are used to purify water. Gold is purified by fire.

pu ri tan (pūr′i tən), person who is strict in morals and religion.

pu ri ty (pūr′i ti), 1. freedom from dirt or mixture; clearness; cleanness. 2. freedom from evil; innocence. 3. careful correctness; as, purity of language.

pur loin (pėr loin′), steal.

pur ple (pėr′pəl), a dark color made by mixing red and blue. **Born to the purple** means born in a very grand family.

pur plish (pėr′plish), somewhat purple.

pur port (pėr′pōrt for 1, pėr pōrt′ for 2 and 3), 1. meaning; as, the purport of a letter. 2. to mean; have as its main idea. 3. to claim. The letter purported to be from the governor.

pur pose (pėr′pəs), 1. plan; aim; intention; something one has in mind to get or do. 2. to plan; to aim; to intend. 3. **On purpose** means with a purpose; not by accident.

pur pose ful (pėr′pəs fəl), having a purpose.

pur pose ly (pėr′pəs li), on purpose. Did you leave the door open purposely?

purr (pėr), 1. low murmuring sound such as a cat makes when pleased. 2. make this sound.

Pocket purse

purse (pėrs), 1. little bag or case for carrying money around with one. 2. a sum of money. A purse was made up for the victims of the fire. 3. draw together; press into folds or wrinkles. Grace pursed her lips and frowned.

pur sue (pər sü′), 1. follow to catch or kill; chase. The policeman pursued the robbers. 2. follow closely and annoy. The boy pursued his father with questions. 3. strive for; try to get. 4. carry on; keep on with. She pursued the study of music for four years.

pur su er (pər sü′ər), one who pursues.

pur suit (pər süt′), 1. act of pursuing; chase. The dog is in pursuit of the cat. 2. occupation. Fishing is his favorite pursuit; reading is mine.

pus (pus), a thick yellowish-white fluid found in sores.

push (pu̇sh), 1. move (something) away by pressing against it. Push the door; don't pull. 2. press hard. We pushed with all our strength. 3. go forward by force. We pushed through the crowd. 4. urge; make go forward. He pushed his plans strongly. Please push this job and get it done this week. 5. act of pushing. 6. force; power to succeed. She has plenty of push.

puss (pu̇s), 1. cat. 2. hare.

puss y (pu̇s′i), 1. cat. 2. catkin.

pussy willow, a small willow with silky catkins. See the picture just below.

Pussy willow

put (pu̇t), 1. place; lay; set; cause to be in some place or position. I put sugar in my tea. Put away your toys. Nell is putting on her hat. 2. cause to be in some condition or relation. Put your room in order. Put the question in writing. The murderer was put to death. 3. express. The teacher puts things plainly. 4. Some special meanings are: A ship **puts out** to sea, **puts in** to port, **puts about** to change its direction.

put off, 1. lay aside; make wait. 2. go away; start out.

put out, 1. extinguish; make an end to; destroy; as, to put out a fire, to put out one's eye. 2. provoked; offended.

put through, carry out with success.

put up, 1. lay aside (work). 2. pack up or preserve (fruit). 3. build. 4. offer; offer for sale. 5. give lodging or food to. 6. get (a person) to do.

One of the huge stone pyramids of Egypt

put up with, bear with patience; endure.

pu trid (pū′trid), rotten; foul.

puz zle (puz′əl), 1. hard problem. How to get all my things into one trunk is a puzzle. 2. a problem or task to be done for fun. A famous Chinese puzzle has seven pieces of wood to fit together. 3. perplex. How the cat got out puzzled us. 4. be perplexed; exercise (one's mind) on something hard. They puzzled over their arithmetic for an hour.

Pyramids

pyg my (pig′mi), 1. a dwarf. The pygmies living in Africa and Asia are less than five feet high. 2. very small; as, a pygmy mind.

pyr a mid (pir′ə mid), a solid having triangular sides meeting in a point. See the pictures above.

Python

py thon (pī′thon), a large snake that crushes its prey. Pythons usually live in trees.

Q

quack[1] (kwak), 1. the sound a duck makes. 2. make such a sound.

quack[2] (kwak), 1. a dishonest person who pretends to be a doctor. 2. an ignorant pretender to knowledge or skill of any sort. Don't pay a quack to tell your fortune. 3. used by quacks. 4. not genuine.

quad ru ped (kwod′rů ped), an animal that has four feet.

quaff (kwäf or kwaf), drink in large swallows; drink much of.

quail[1] (kwāl), a game bird about ten inches long, especially the bobwhite. See the picture.

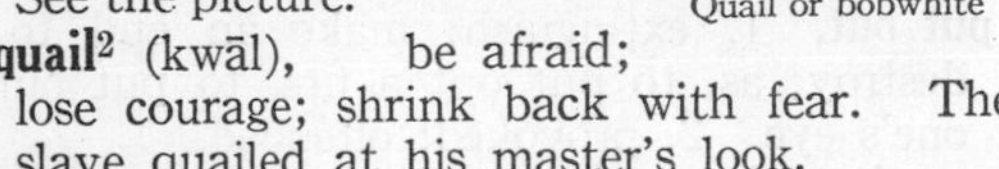
Quail or bobwhite

quail[2] (kwāl), be afraid; lose courage; shrink back with fear. The slave quailed at his master's look.

quaint (kwānt), strange or odd in an interesting, pleasing, or amusing way. Old photographs seem quaint to us today.

quake (kwāk), 1. shake; tremble. She quaked with fear. 2. a shaking; a trembling. 3. an earthquake.

Quak er (kwāk′ər), member of a Christian group called the Society of Friends. Quakers are opposed to war and favor simple clothes and manners.

qual i fi ca tion (kwol′i fi kā′shən), 1. that which makes a person fit for a job, task, office, etc. To know the way is one qualification for a guide. 2. that which limits or changes, and makes less free and full.

qual i fied (kwol′i fīd), 1. fitted; competent. 2. limited; modified.

qual i fy (kwol′i fī), 1. make fit or competent. 2. become fit; show oneself fit. Can you qualify for the Boy Scouts? 3. limit; make less strong; change somewhat. Qualify your statement that dogs are loyal by adding "usually."

qual i ty (kwol′i ti), 1. the kind that anything is. That is a poor quality of cloth. 2. something special about a person or object. One quality of iron is hardness; one quality of sugar is sweetness. Ruth had many good qualities. 3. merit; excellence. Look for quality rather than quantity.

qualm (kwäm), 1. sudden disturbing feeling in the mind; uneasiness; a misgiving or doubt. I tried the test with some qualms. 2. disturbance or scruple of conscience. Kate felt some qualms at staying away from church. 3. feeling of faintness or sickness, especially of nausea, that lasts for just a moment.

quan ti ty (kwon′ti ti), 1. amount. Use equal quantities of nuts and raisins in the cake. 2. large amount; large number. The baker buys flour in quantity. She owns quantities of books.

quar rel (kwor′əl), 1. an angry dispute; a fight with words. The children had a quarrel over the division of the candy. 2. fight with words; dispute; disagree. 3. cause for dispute. An honest man has no quarrel with the laws. A bully likes to pick quarrels. The knight took up the poor man's quarrel and fought his oppressor. 4. breaking off of friendship. Ruth and May have had a quarrel and don't speak to each other. 5. stop being friends. 6. find fault. It is useless to quarrel with fate.

quar rel some (kwor′əl səm), too ready to quarrel; fond of fighting and disputing. A quarrelsome child has few friends.

quar ry[1] (kwor′i), 1. place where stone is dug, cut, or blasted out for use in building. 2. obtain from a quarry. We watched the workmen quarry out a huge block of stone.

quar ry[2] (kwor′i), animal chased in a hunt; game; prey. The fox hunters chased their quarry for hours.

quart (kwôrt), 1. a measure for liquids, equal to one fourth of a gallon. 2. a measure for dry things, equal to one eighth of a peck.

quar ter (kwôr′tər), 1. one of four equal parts; half of a half; one fourth; as, a quarter of an apple, a quarter of lamb. A quarter of an hour is 15 minutes. A quarter of a dollar is 25 cents. 2. divide into fourths. She quartered the apple. 3. direction. From what quarter did the wind blow? 4. region; section; place. The quarter where they live is near the railroad. 5. **At close quarters** means very close together; almost touching. 6. **Quarters** sometimes means a place to live or stay in. The servants have quarters in a cottage. 7. give a place to live. Troops were quartered in the conquered town. 8. mercy to an enemy. The Indians gave no quarter.

One quarter of this circle is shaded.

quar ter ly (kwôr′tər li), 1. four times a year; as, to make quarterly payments on one's insurance. 2. once each quarter of a year. Father pays his income tax quarterly.

quar ter staff (kwôr′tər staf′), old weapon consisting of a stout pole 6 to 8 feet long, tipped with iron.

quar tet or **quar tette** (kwôr tet′), 1. four singers or players. 2. piece of music for four voices or instruments. 3. any group of four.

quartz (kwôrts), a very hard kind of rock. Agate, amethyst, jasper, and many other stones are quartz.

qua′ver (kwā′vər), 1. shake; tremble. The old man's voice quavered. 2. sing or say in trembling tones. 3. a trembling of the voice.

quay (kē), solid landing place for ships, often built of stone.

Quay

queen (kwēn), 1. wife of a king. 2. woman ruler. 3. the most important woman or girl; as, the queen of society, the queen of the May. 4. act like a queen.

queer (kwēr), 1. strange; odd; peculiar. 2. not well; faint; giddy.

quell (kwel), overcome; subdue.

quench (kwench), 1. drown out; put out. Water will quench a fire. 2. put an end to; stop; as, to quench a thirst.

que ry (kwēr′i), 1. a question. 2. the sign (?) put after a question. 3. ask; ask about; inquire into. 4. express doubt about.

quest (kwest), 1. a search; a hunt. Mary went to the library in quest of something to read. 2. to search; to seek. 3. expedition of knights. There are many stories about the quest of the Holy Grail.

ques tion (kwes′chən), 1. ask in order to find out. 2. the thing asked. 3. a matter to be talked over. What is the question you have raised? 4. matter to be voted upon. The president asked if the club members were ready for the question. 5. to doubt; to dispute. I question the truth of many fish stories. 6. A matter is **out of the question** when it is not to be considered. It is **beyond question** or **without question** when there is no doubt about it.

ques tion a ble (kwes′chən ə bəl), open to question; doubtful; uncertain. Whether your statement is true is questionable.

queue (kū), 1. braid of hair hanging down the back. 2. line of persons, automobiles, etc.

Queue

quick (kwik), 1. fast and sudden. The cat made a quick jump. Many weeds have a quick growth. 2. lively; ready; active; as, a quick wit, a quick ear. 3. coming soon; prompt; as, a quick reply. 4. not patient; hasty; as, a quick temper. 5. living; as, the quick and the dead. 6. the tender, sensitive part. The child bit his nails down to the quick. The boy's pride was cut to the quick by the words of blame. 7. quickly.

quick en (kwik′ən), 1. move more quickly; hasten. Quicken your pace. 2. stir up; make alive. He quickened the hot ashes into flames. 3. become more active or alive.

quick ly (kwik′li), with haste; very soon.

quick ness (kwik′nis), 1. speed. 2. the quality of understanding things easily.

quick sand (kwik′sand′), soft wet sand, very deep, that will not hold up one's weight. A quicksand may swallow up men, animals, etc.

quick sil ver (kwik′sil′vər), mercury.

qui et (kwī′ət), 1. making no sound; without noise; as, quiet footsteps, a quiet room. 2. still; moving very little; as, a quiet river. 3. at rest; not busy; as, a quiet evening at home. 4. peaceful; with nothing to fear; as, a quiet mind. 5. gentle; not offending others; as, a quiet girl. 6. not loud; not showy and bright. Gray is a quiet color. 7. make quiet. Mother quieted the frightened child. 8. become quiet. The wind quieted down. 9. state of rest; stillness; no noise; peace; as, to read in quiet.

Quill (def. 1)

quill (kwil), 1. large stiff feather. 2. pen made from a feather. 3. a stiff sharp hair or spine like the end of a feather. A porcupine has quills.

quilt (kwilt), 1. a bedcover; a bedcover made of two pieces of cloth with a soft pad between, held in place by lines of stitching. 2. to make quilts. 3. to stitch as in a quilt. She made a quilted jacket.

Quince

quince (kwins), 1. a hard, yellowish fruit, used for preserves. See the picture on p. 463. 2. the tree it grows on.

qui nine (kwī′nīn), a bitter medicine used for colds and malaria.

quit (kwit), 1. stop. The men quit work when the whistle blew. 2. leave. Jim's big brother is quitting school this June. 3. rid; free; clear. I gave him money to be quit of him. 4. behave. "Quit yourselves like brave men" means act bravely.

quite (kwīt), 1. completely; entirely. I am quite alone. 2. really; truly. Jean is quite the best reader in the class. 3. very; rather; somewhat. It is quite hot.

quiv er[1] (kwiv′ər), shake; shiver; tremble. The dog quivered with excitement.

Quiver

quiv er[2] (kwiv′ər), case to hold arrows.

quiz (kwiz), 1. examine by questions; test the knowledge of. 2. a test; as, to have a quiz in geography. 3. make fun of. 4. person who makes fun of others.

quoit (kwoit), 1. a heavy ring thrown to encircle a peg stuck in the ground or to come as close to it as possible. 2. **Quoits** is the game so played. The game of quoits is often played with horseshoes.

Quoit

quo ta (kwō′tə), the share of a total due from or to a particular district, State, person, etc.

quo ta tion (kwō tā′shən), somebody's words repeated exactly by another person; passage quoted from a book, speech, etc.

quote (kwōt), 1. repeat exactly the words of another or a passage from a book. She often quotes her husband. The minister quoted from the Bible. 2. a quotation.

quoth (kwōth), said. "Come hither," quoth the prince.

R

rab bi (rab′ī), teacher of the Jewish law; pastor of a Jewish church.

rab bit (rab′it), an animal about as big as a cat, with soft fur and long ears. A rabbit can make long jumps.

Rabbit

rab ble (rab′əl), 1. a disorderly crowd; a mob. 2. the rude lower class of persons. The nobles scorned the rabble.

rac coon (ra kün′), 1. a small, grayish animal with a bushy ringed tail, that eats flesh, lives mostly in trees, and is active at night. 2. its fur.

Raccoon (about 22 in. long without the tail)

race[1] (rās), 1. a run. 2. a run to see who will do best. 3. run; move fast. 4. make go fast. 5. run a race with. 6. a strong or rapid current of water.

race[2] (rās), 1. a group of persons, animals, or plants having the same ancestors, far back in the past; as, the white race, the race of fishes. 2. a group of people of the same kind; as, the brave race of seamen.

race track, ground laid out for racing.

rack (rak), 1. frame with bars, shelves, or pegs to hold, arrange, or keep things on, such as a hat rack, tool rack, or baggage rack. 2. a frame of bars to hold hay and other food for cattle. 3. a framework set on a wagon for carrying hay, straw, etc. 4. an instrument once used for torturing people by stretching them. 5. hurt very much; as, racked with grief, a racking earache. 6. stretch; strain. 7. a bar with pegs or teeth on one edge, into which teeth on the rim of a wheel may fit. See the picture just below.

Rack for holding hay

Towel rack

WHEEL

RACK

Rack (def. 7)

rack et[1] (rak′it), 1. loud noise; din; loud talk. Don't make a racket when others are reading. 2. a time of gay parties and social excitement. She is tired after all the racket.

rack et[2] (rak′it), a light wide bat made of network stretched on a frame, used for games like tennis.

Tennis racket

ra coon (ra kün′), raccoon.

ra di ance (rā′di əns), brightness; as, the radiance of the sun, of electric lights, or of a person's smile.

ra di ant (rā′di ənt), 1. shining; bright; beaming; as, radiant sunshine, a radiant smile. 2. sent off in rays from some source; radiated. We get radiant heat from the sun.

ra di ate (rā′di āt), 1. give out rays of. The sun radiates light and heat. 2. issue in rays. Heat radiates from hot steam pipes. 3. spread out from a center. Roads radiate from the city in every direction. 4. give out; send forth. His face radiates joy.

Radiator

ra di a tor (rā′di ā′tər), set of pipes that give off heat. The radiator of an automobile gives off heat very fast and so cools the water inside it.

rad i cal (rad′i kəl), 1. going to the root; fundamental. If she wants to grow thin, she must make radical changes in her diet. 2. extreme; favoring extreme changes or reforms. 3. person with extreme opinions.

ra di o (rā′di ō), 1. wireless telegraph or telephone; a way of sending and receiving words, music, etc., by electric waves without wires. We can listen to music broadcast by radio. 2. of radio; used in radio; sent by radio; as, a radio set, radio speeches. 3. transmit or send out by radio. They radioed a call for help.

Radish

rad ish (rad′ish), a small crisp root with a red or white skin, used as a relish and in salads.

ra di um (rā′di əm), a rare metal that gives off powerful rays.

ra di us (rā′di əs), 1. any line going straight from the center to the outside of a circle or a sphere. Any spoke of a wheel is a radius. 2. circular area measured by the length of its radius. The explosion could be heard within a radius of ten miles.

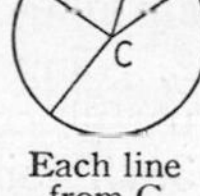

Each line from C (center) is a radius.

raft (raft), logs or boards fastened together to make a floating platform. We had no boat; so we crossed the stream on a raft.

Raft

raft er (raf′tər), slanting beam of a roof. See the picture in the next column.

rag (rag), 1. a small cloth. A washrag is a washcloth. 2. a torn or waste piece of cloth. Use clean rags to rub this mirror bright. His clothes were in rags. 3. small piece of anything of no value. The meat was boiled to rags. 4. made from rags; as, a rag doll, a rag rug.

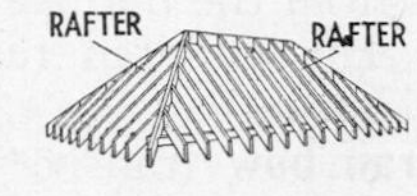

rage (rāj), 1. violent anger; passion. Mad with rage, Dick dashed into the fight. 2. talk or act violently; storm. Keep your temper; don't rage. The wind rages wildly. 3. what everybody wants for a short time; the fashion. Red ties are all the rage this season.

rag ged (rag′id), 1. worn or torn into rags; as, ragged clothing. 2. wearing ragged clothes. 3. rough; not smooth and tidy; as, an old dog's ragged coat, a ragged garden. 4. having loose shreds or bits; as, a ragged wound.

raid (rād), 1. an attack; a sudden attack. 2. attack suddenly. 3. an entering and seizing what is inside. The hungry boys made a raid on the pantry. 4. force a way into; enter and seize what is in. The police raided the house where the thieves had hidden the jewels.

Rail fence

rail[1] (rāl), 1. bar of wood or of metal. There are stair rails, fence rails, rails protecting monuments, etc. Bars laid along the ground for a car or railroad track are called rails. 2. a railroad. We travel by rail and by boat. 3. **Rail in** means shut in with bars. **Rail off** means shut off or separate with bars. They railed off a space for the horses.

rail[2] (rāl), complain bitterly; use violent and reproachful language. He railed at his hard luck.

rail ing[1] (rāl′ing), 1. a fence of rails. 2. material for rails. 3. rails.

rail ing[2] (rāl′ing), violent complaints or reproaches; jeers.

rail road (rāl′rōd′), 1. road or track with parallel steel rails on which the wheels of cars may go. Engines pull trains on the railroad. 2. the tracks, stations, trains, and the people who manage them. 3. to work on a railroad.

rail way (rāl′wā′), 1. railroad. 2. track made of rails.

rai ment (rā′mənt), clothes.

rain (rān), 1. water falling in drops from the clouds. The rain wet the windows. 2. the fall of such drops. 3. a thick, fast fall of anything; as, a rain of bullets. 4. to fall in drops of water. It rained all day. 5. to fall like rain. Sparks rained down from the burning building. 6. send like rain. The children rained flowers on the May queen.

rain bow (rān′bō′), 1. a bow or arch of seven colors seen sometimes in the sky, or in mist or spray, when the sun shines on it from behind one. The colors of the rainbow are violet, indigo, blue, green, yellow, orange, and red. 2. having many colors like a rainbow.

rain coat (rān′kōt′), coat for protection from rain.

rain drop (rān′drop′), drop of rain.

rain fall (rān′fôl′), 1. shower of rain. 2. the amount of water falling in a given time. The yearly rainfall in New York is much greater than that in Arizona.

rain y (rān′i), 1. having rain; having much rain. 2. bringing rain. April is a rainy month. 3. wet with rain.

raise (rāz), 1. lift up; put up. The soldiers raised a white flag. Children in school raise their hands to answer. 2. build; build up; set up. People raise monuments to soldiers who have died for their country. 3. cause to rise. The automobiles raise a dust. Bread is raised by yeast. 4. make higher or larger; increase in degree, amount, etc.; as, to raise prices, to raise the rent, to raise one's courage. 5. rouse; stir up. The dogs had raised a rabbit and were chasing it. 6. bring up; make grow; help to grow. The farmer raises chickens and corn. 7. cause; bring about. The child's remark raised a smile. 8. bring together; get together; gather. The leader raised an army. 9. lift up in mind, morals, rank, position, etc. The boy raised himself by hard study to be a great lawyer. 10. utter in a loud voice; cause to be heard. The boys raised a shout. 11. end; as, to raise a blockade, to raise a siege. 12. an increase in amount; as, a raise in pay. 13. **Raise the dead** means bring them to life.

rai sin (rā′zən), a sweet dried grape.

ra jah or **ra ja** (rä′jə), ruler or chief in India, and in some other Eastern countries.

rake (rāk), 1. a long-handled tool having a bar at one end with teeth in it. A rake is used for smoothing the soil or gathering together loose leaves, hay, straw, etc. 2. move with a rake. Rake the leaves off the grass. 3. use a rake. I like to rake. 4. gather; gather together. 5. search carefully. He raked the newspapers for descriptions of the accident. 6. fire guns along the length of (a ship or a line of soldiers).

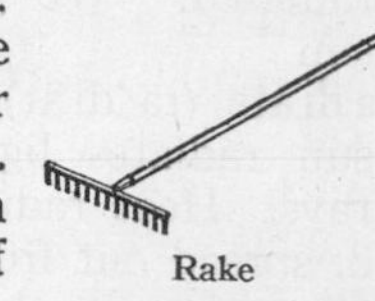
Rake

ral ly[1] (ral′i), 1. bring together; bring together again; get in order again. The commander was able to rally the fleeing troops. 2. come together for a common purpose. The girls at the camp rallied to do the housework when the servants were sick. 3. come to help. Bob rallied to the side of his frightened sister. 4. recover health and strength. The sick man may rally now. 5. coming together; meeting of many people; as, a political rally.

ral ly[2] (ral′i), tease; make fun of. The boys rallied John on his short haircut.

ram (ram), 1. male sheep. 2. butt against; strike head on; strike violently. One ship rammed the other ship. I rammed my head against the door in the dark. 3. push hard; drive down or in by heavy blows. 4. a machine or part of a machine that strikes heavy blows. A battering ram knocks walls down.

Ram

ram ble (ram′bəl), 1. wander about. We rambled here and there through the woods. 2. a walk for pleasure, not to go to any special place. 3. talk about first one thing and then another with no useful connections.

ram bling (ram′bling), 1. wandering about. 2. going from one thing to another with no useful connections; as, a rambling speech. 3. climbing; as, rambling roses. 4. extending in irregular ways in various directions; not planned in an orderly way; as, a rambling old farmhouse.

ramp ant (ram′pənt), 1. not checked; growing without any check. The vines were rampant over the fence. 2. angry; excited; violent.

PARAPET→ RAMPART DITCH

ram part (ram′pärt), a wide bank of earth, often with a wall on top, built around a fort to help defend it. See the picture.

ram rod (ram′rod′), 1. a rod for ramming down the charge in a gun that is loaded from the muzzle. 2. rod for cleaning the barrel of a gun.

ran (ran). See **run.** The dog ran after the cat.

ranch (ranch), 1. a very large farm. Many ranches are used for raising cattle. 2. a farm; as, a chicken ranch, a fruit ranch. 3. to work on a ranch; manage a ranch.

ran dom (ran′dəm), by chance; with no plan. John was not listening and made a random answer when called upon to recite. **At random** means by chance. Alice took a book at random from the shelf.

rang (rang). See **ring**[2]. The telephone rang.

range (rānj), 1. a row or line; as, a range of mountains. 2. put in a row or rows. Range the books by size. 3. put in groups or classes. 4. put in line on someone's side. Loyal citizens ranged themselves with the king. 5. land for grazing. 6. district in which certain plants or animals live. 7. distance between any limits; extent; as, a range of colors to choose from, a range of prices from 5 cents to 25 dollars, the range of hearing. 8. distance a gun can shoot. 9. place to practice shooting; as, a rifle range. 10. wander; rove; roam. Buffaloes ranged the plains. Our talk ranged over all that had happened on vacation. 11. extend; be found; occur; as, a boundary ranging east and west, a plant ranging from Canada to Mexico. 12. a stove for cooking.

rang er (rān′jər), 1. person employed to guard a tract of forest. 2. one of a body of armed men employed in ranging over a region to police it. 3. one that ranges; rover.

rank[1] (rangk), 1. a row or line, usually of soldiers, placed side by side. 2. Common soldiers or ordinary people are said to be in **the ranks** or to be **the rank and file.** 3. position; grade; class. New York is a city of first rank. 4. high position. A duke is a man of rank. 5. arrange in a row or line. 6. put in some special order in a list. Rank the states for area. 7. have a certain rank. Bill ranked low in the test.

rank[2] (rangk), 1. large and coarse; as, rank grass. 2. growing thickly. 3. producing a dense but coarse growth; as, rank swamp land. 4. having a bad, strong taste or smell; as, rank meat, rank tobacco. 5. strongly marked; extreme; as, rank ingratitude, rank nonsense.

ran kle (rang′kəl), be sore; cause soreness; give pain. The memory of the insult rankled in his mind.

ran sack (ran′sak), 1. search thoroughly through. The thief ransacked the house for jewelry. 2. rob; plunder.

ran som (ran′səm), 1. price paid or demanded before a captive is set free. The robber chief held the travelers in hope of a ransom. 2. obtain the release of (captives) by paying a price. 3. redeem.

rap (rap), 1. a quick light blow; a light sharp knock; as, a rap on the door. 2. knock sharply; tap. The chairman rapped on the table for order. 3. say sharply; as, to rap out an answer.

rap id (rap′id), 1. very quick; swift; as, a rapid walk. 2. **Rapids** are a part of a river where the water rushes very swiftly.

ra pid i ty (rə pid′i ti), quickness; swiftness; speed.

rap id ly (rap′id li), at a rapid rate; fast.

ra pi er (rā′pi ər), a long and light sword used for thrusting.

Rapier

rapt (rapt), 1. lost in delight. 2. so busy thinking of or enjoying one thing that one does not know what else is happening. The children listened to the story with rapt minds. 3. showing that a person is rapt; as, a rapt smile.

rap ture (rap′chər), strong feeling that absorbs the mind; very great joy. The mother gazed with rapture at her long-lost son.

rap tur ous (rap′chər əs), full of rapture; feeling rapture; expressing rapture.

rare[1] (rãr), 1. not usually found; few; not happening often. Storks and peacocks are rare birds in the United States. 2. unusually good. Edison had rare powers as an inventor. 3. thin; not dense. The higher we go above the earth, the rarer the air is.

rare[2] (rãr), not cooked much; as, a rare piece of steak.

rare ly (rãr′li), 1. seldom; not often. 2. unusually; unusually well.

rar i ty (rãr′i ti), 1. something rare. A man a hundred years old is a rarity. 2. scarcity. 3. rare or thin condition; as, the rarity of the air on high mountains.

ras cal (ras′kəl), bad, dishonest person. Sometimes *rascal* is used in a joking way, as when one calls a child a little rascal.

ras cal ly (ras′kəl i), mean; dishonest; bad. To steal the poor boy's lunch was a rascally trick.

rash[1] (rash), too hasty; careless; taking too much risk. It is rash to cross the street without looking both ways.

rash[2] (rash), a breaking out with many small red spots on the skin. Scarlet fever causes a rash.

Rasp (def. 5)

rasp (rasp), 1. make a harsh, grating sound. The file rasped as he worked. 2. a harsh, grating sound; as, the rasp of crickets, a rasp in a person's voice. 3. grate on; irritate. Her feelings were rasped and exploded into anger. 4. scrape with a rough instrument. 5. a coarse file with pointed teeth.

Raspberries and leaves

rasp ber ry (raz′ber′i), 1. a small fruit that grows on bushes. It is usually red or black, but some kinds are white or yellow. 2. the bush it grows on.

rat (rat), a gnawing animal like a mouse, but larger. Rats are gray, black, brown, or white.

rate[1] (rāt), 1. quantity, amount, or degree, measured in proportion to something else. The rate of interest is 6 cents on the dollar. The railroad rate is 3 cents a mile. The parcel-post rate is 10 cents for the first pound. The car was going at the rate of 40 miles an hour. 2. price. We pay the regular rate. 3. put a value on. We rated the house as worth $10,000. 4. rank; estimate. He was rated one of the richest men in town. 5. class; grade; as, first rate, second rate. 6. **At any rate** means anyway; in any case.

rate[2] (rāt), scold.

rath er (raᴛʜ′ər), 1. more willingly. I would rather go today than tomorrow. **Had rather** means would prefer to. Mary had rather play than rest. 2. more truly; with better reason. This is rather for father to decide than for you. 3. somewhat; to some extent. After working so long he was rather tired.

rat i fi ca tion (rat′i fi kā′shən), confirmation; approval.

rat i fy (rat′i fī), confirm; approve.

ra tio (rā′shō), the relation between two numbers or quantities meant when we say *times as many* or *times as much.* "He has sheep and cows in the ratio of 10 to 3" means that he has ten sheep for every three cows, or $3\frac{1}{3}$ times as many sheep as cows. The ratio between two quantities is the number of times one contains the other.

ra tion (rā′shən or rash′ən), 1. a fixed allowance of food; the daily allowance of a soldier, a sailor, or a horse. 2. portion of anything dealt out; as, rations of sugar, of coal, etc. 3. supply with rations; as, to ration an army. 4. allow only certain amounts to; as, to ration citizens when supplies are scarce. 5. distribute in limited amounts; as, to ration food to the public in wartime.

ra tion al (rash′ən əl), 1. sensible; reasonable; reasoned out. When very angry, people seldom act in a rational way. 2. able to think and reason clearly. 3. of reason; based on reasoning.

Rattlesnake (from 2 to 8 ft. long, according to the kind)

rat tle (rat′əl), 1. make a number of short sharp sounds. The window rattled in the wind. 2. cause to rattle. She rattled the dishes. 3. a number of short sharp sounds. We hear the rattle of the milk bottles in the morning. 4. a toy or instrument that makes a noise when it is shaken. The baby shakes his rattle. 5. talk or say quickly, on and on. In free and easy talk, rattle sometimes means confuse.

Rattlesnake's tail

rat tler (rat′lər), rattlesnake.

rat tle snake (rat′əl snāk′), a poisonous snake that makes a rattling noise with its tail. See the pictures.

rav age (rav′ij), 1. destroy; lay waste; damage greatly. The forest fire ravaged many miles of country. 2. violence; destruction; great damage.

Raven (about 2 ft. long)

rave (rāv), 1. talk wildly. An excited, angry person raves; so does a madman. 2. talk with too much enthusiasm. She raved about her food. 3. howl; roar; rage. The wind raved about the lighthouse.

ra ven (rā′vən), 1. a large black bird like a crow. See the picture. 2. deep glossy black.

rav en ous (rav′ən əs), 1. very hungry. 2. greedy.

ra vine (rə vēn′), a long, deep, narrow valley. The river had worn a ravine between the two hills.

rav ish (rav′ish), 1. fill with delight. The prince was ravished by Cinderella's beauty. 2. carry off by force. The wolf ravished the lamb from the flock.

rav ish ing (rav′ish ing), very delightful; enchanting; as, jewels of ravishing beauty.

raw (rô), 1. not cooked; as, raw meat. 2. in the natural state; not manufactured, treated, or prepared; as, raw materials, raw hides. 3. not experienced; not trained; as, a raw soldier in the army. 4. damp and cold; as, a raw wind. 5. with the skin off; sore; as, a raw spot on a horse where the harness rubbed.

raw hide (rô′hīd′), 1. a hide that has not been tanned. 2. a rope or whip made of this.

raw material, 1. stuff that comes from mines, farms, etc., and can be used to make articles in factories, etc. Coffee, steel, wool, and cotton are raw materials. 2. stuff before much labor has been spent on it. Those boys are the raw material for a fine army.

ray[1] (rā), 1. a line or beam of light; as, rays of the sun. 2. a line or stream of heat or electricity or energy; as, X rays. 3. a thin line like a ray coming out from a center. 4. something bright or light; a gleam; as, a ray of hope, a ray of intelligence. 5. send out rays.

ray[2] (rā), a kind of broad flat fish. See the picture.

Eagle ray (about 5 ft. long)

ray on (rā′on), a fiber stiffer than silk but not so strong.

raze (rāz), tear down; destroy completely. The old school was razed to the ground, and a new one was built.

ra zor (rā′zər), a tool with a sharp blade to shave with. See the picture below.

reach (rēch), 1. get to; arrive at; come to. Your letter reached me yesterday. 2. stretch out; hold out. A hand reached from the dark and seized Jack. 3. hold out to be taken; give or pass by handing. 4. move to touch or seize something; try to get. The man reached for his gun. 5. stretch; extend. The United States reaches from ocean to ocean. 6. touch; put a hand on. 7. get at; influence. Men are reached by flattery. The speaker reached the hearts of his hearers. 8. amount to; be equal to. The cost of the war reached billions. 9. reaching; stretching out. By a long reach the drowning man grasped the rope. 10. the extent or distance of reaching. Food and water were left within reach of the sick dog. 11. range; power; capacity. Philosophy is beyond a child's reach; he cannot understand it. 12. a long stretch or extent; as, a reach of water.

A, ordinary razor used by barbers; B, safety razor.

re act (ri akt′), 1. act back; have an effect on the one that is acting. Unkindness often reacts on the unkind person and makes him unhappy. 2. act in response. Dogs react to kindness by showing affection. 3. **React against** means act unfavorably toward or take an unfavorable attitude toward.

re ac tion (ri ak′shən), action in response to some influence. Our reaction to a joke is to laugh.

read[1] (rēd), 1. get the meaning of writing or print. We read books. 2. speak out loud the words of writing or print. Please read it to me. 3. get the meaning of other things; understand. God reads men's hearts. The prophet reads the future. 4. get the meaning of by the use of the finger tips. The blind girl reads special raised print by touching it. 5. study. John is reading law. 6. learn from writing or print. We read of heroes of other days. 7. show by figures, letters, signs, etc. The thermometer reads 70 degrees. The ticket reads "From New York to Boston." 8. give the meaning of; interpret. Silence is not always to be read as consent.

read[2] (red), 1. having knowledge gained by reading; informed; as, a well-read man. 2. See **read.** I read that book last year. Joe has read it too.

read er (rēd′ər), 1. person who reads. 2. a book for learning to read.

read i ly (red′i li), 1. quickly. A bright boy answers readily when called on. 2. easily. 3. willingly.

read i ness (red′i nis), 1. being ready; preparedness. Everything is in readiness for the party. 2. quickness; promptness. 3. ease. 4. willingness.

read ing (rēd′ing), 1. getting the meaning of written or printed words. 2. speaking out loud written or printed words; public recital. 3. study of books. 4. written or printed matter read or to be read. 5. the amount shown on the scale of an instrument. The reading of the thermometer was 96 degrees.

read y (red′i), 1. prepared for action or use at once; prepared. The soldiers are ready for battle. Dinner is ready. We were ready to start at nine. 2. willing. The soldiers were ready to die for their country. Mary is ready to forgive. 3. likely; liable. Kate is too ready to find fault. 4. quick; prompt. The speaker has a ready wit. A kind man gave ready help to the children. 5. easy to get at; easy to reach; as, ready money.

read y-made (red′i mād′), ready for immediate use; made for anybody who will buy. Department stores sell ready-made clothes.

re al (rē′əl), actual; existing as a fact; true; not imagined; not made up; as, the real thing, real diamonds, real pleasure, the real reason.

real estate, land together with the buildings, fences, trees, water, and minerals which belong to it.

re al i ty (ri al′i ti), 1. actual existence; the true state of affairs. I doubted the reality of what he had seen, and thought he must have dreamed it. 2. **In reality** means really; in fact. We thought he was joking, but in reality he was serious. 3. real thing or fact. Slaughter and destruction are the terrible realities of war.

re al i za tion (rē′əl i zā′shən), 1. a making real or the being made real of something imagined or planned. The realization of her hope to be an actress made her happy. 2. understanding. The explorers had a full realization of the dangers they would face.

re al ize (rē′əl īz), 1. understand. The teacher realizes now how hard you worked. 2. make real. Her uncle's present made it possible for her to realize the dream of going to college.

re al ly (rē′əl i), 1. actually; truly; in fact. 2. indeed.

realm (relm), 1. kingdom. 2. region.

reap (rēp), 1. cut (grain). 2. gather (a crop). 3. cut grain or gather a crop from. The farmer reaps his fields. 4. get as a return or reward. Kind acts reap happy smiles.

reap er (rēp′ər), person or machine that cuts grain.

re ap pear (rē′ə pēr′), come into sight again.

rear[1] (rēr), 1. back part; the back. The kitchen is in the rear of the house. **In the rear** often means behind. 2. back; at the back. Leave by the rear door of the car. 3. the last part of an army, fleet, etc.

rear[2] (rēr), 1. make grow; help to grow; bring up. The mother was very careful in rearing her children. 2. set up; build. The men of old reared altars to their gods. The pioneers soon reared churches in their settlements. 3. raise; lift up. 4. rise on the hind legs. The horse reared as the fire engine dashed past.

rear admiral, naval officer next in rank above a captain.

rear guard, part of an army that protects the rear.

re ar range (rē′ə rānj′), 1. arrange in a new way. 2. arrange again.

rea son (rē′zən), 1. cause; motive; explanation. Sickness is the reason for Mary's absence. Tell me your reasons for not liking him. 2. think things out; solve new problems. An idiot cannot reason. 3. power to think. That poor old man has lost his reason. 4. right thinking; common sense. The stubborn child was at last brought to reason. **It stands to reason** means it is reasonable and sensible. 5. argue. Reason with Helen and try to make her change her mind.

rea son a ble (rē′zən ə bəl), 1. according to reason; sensible. 2. able to reason. 3. moderate; fair; as, a reasonable price.

rea son a bly (rē′zən ə bli), in a reasonable manner; with reason.

rea son ing (rē′zən ing), 1. the process of drawing conclusions from facts. 2. reasons; arguments.

re as sure (rē′ə shür′), 1. assure again or anew. 2. restore to confidence. The teacher's calm behavior during the storm reassured the children.

reb el (reb′əl for 1 and 2, ri bel′ for 3 and 4), 1. person who resists or fights against authority instead of obeying. The rebels armed themselves against the government. 2. defying law or authority; as, the rebel army. 3. resist or fight against law or authority. 4. feel a great dislike or opposition. We rebelled at having to stay in on so fine a day.

re bel lion (ri bel′yən), a fight against government; revolt; rebelling. The slaves rose in rebellion against their masters.

re bel lious (ri bel′yəs), defying authority; acting like a rebel. The rebellious boy would not obey the school rules.

re bound (ri bound′ for 1, rē′bound′ for 2), 1. spring back. 2. a springing back. You hit the ball on the rebound in handball.

re buff (ri buf′), 1. a blunt or sudden check to a person who makes advances, offers help, makes a request, etc. We tried to be friendly, but his rebuff made us think he wanted to be left alone. 2. give a rebuff to. The friendly dog was rebuffed by a kick.

re build (rē bild′), build again or anew.

re built (rē bilt′), built again.

re buke (ri būk′), 1. find fault with; reprove. The teacher rebuked the child for throwing paper on the floor. 2. finding fault; scolding. The child feared the teacher's rebukes.

re call (ri kôl′), 1. call back to mind; remember. I can recall stories that my mother told me years ago. 2. call back; order back. The captain was recalled from the front line. 3. take back; withdraw. I shall recall my order for a new coat because I have had one given me. 4. act of calling back; fact of being called back.

re cap ture (rē kap′chər), capture again.

re cede (ri sēd′), 1. go back; move back. Houses and trees seem to recede as you ride past in a train. 2. slope backward. This boy has a receding chin.

re ceipt (ri sēt′), 1. written statement that money, a package, a letter, etc., has been received. Sign the receipt for this parcel. 2. write on (a bill, etc.) that something has been received or paid for. Pay the bill and ask the grocer to receipt it. 3. **Receipts** means money received. Our expenses were less than our receipts. 4. receiving; being received. On receipt of the news he went home.

re ceive (ri sēv′), 1. take (something offered or sent); as, to receive presents. 2. take or let into the mind; accept; as, to receive new ideas, news, an education. 3. let into one's house, society, etc. The ladies of the town would not receive Mrs. Loud. 4. be at home to friends. Mrs. Rich receives on Tuesdays. 5. be given; experience; suffer; as, to receive blows, insult, or punishment. 6. take in; support; bear; hold. The boat received a heavy load. A basin receives the water from the fountain.

re ceiv er (ri sēv′ər), 1. person who receives. The receiver of a gift should thank the giver. 2. thing that receives; as, an ash receiver, a telephone receiver.

re cent (rē′sənt), done or made not long ago.

re cent ly (rē′sənt li), lately; not long ago.

re cep ta cle (ri sep′tə kəl), any container or place used to put things in. Bags, baskets, and vaults are all receptacles.

re cep tion (ri sep′shən), 1. act of receiving. Her calm reception of the bad news surprised us. 2. being received. Helen's reception as a club member pleased her. 3. manner of receiving. We were given a warm reception on returning home. 4. party; entertainment. Our school gave a reception to our new principal.

re cess (ri ses′), 1. time during which work stops. Our school has an hour's recess at noon. 2. take a recess. The committee recessed for lunch. 3. a part in a wall, set back from the rest. This long seat will fit nicely in that recess. 4. inner place or part; as, the recesses of a cave, the recesses of one's secret thoughts.

rec i pe (res′i pi), 1. directions for preparing something to eat. Please give me your recipe for cookies. 2. directions for preparing any thing or result.

re cit al (ri sīt′əl), 1. reciting; telling facts in detail. Her recital of her experiences in the hospital bored her hearers. 2. story; account. 3. musical entertainment. My music teacher will give a recital Tuesday afternoon.

rec i ta tion (res′i tā′shən), 1. reciting; reciting a prepared lesson by pupils before a teacher. 2. repeating something from memory before an audience. 3. piece repeated in this way.

re cite (ri sīt′), 1. say over; repeat. Pupils recite their lessons. He can recite that poem from memory. 2. tell one by one. Will you recite the names of the pupils who have not been absent this term?

reck (rek), care; heed. The brave soldier recked little of danger.

reck less (rek′lis), rash; heedless; careless. Reckless of danger, the boy played with a loaded gun. Reckless driving causes many automobile accidents.

reck on (rek′ən), 1. count; find the number or value of. Reckon the cost before you decide. 2. consider; judge. He is reckoned the best player on the team. 3. depend; rely. Can we reckon on your help?

reck on ing (rek′ən ing), 1. count; calculation. By my reckoning we are miles from home. 2. rendering or settling an account; as, a day of reckoning. 3. a bill, especially at an inn or tavern. 4. the calculation of the position of a ship.

re claim (ri klām′), 1. bring back to a useful, good condition. Some farmers reclaim waste land. The church reclaims a bad man by helping him to be good. 2. demand the return of. He had no right to take your book away; so reclaim it.

rec la ma tion (rek′lə mā′shən), restoration to a useful, good condition; as, the reclamation of deserts by irrigation.

re cline (ri klīn′), lean back; lie down. The tired woman reclined on the couch.

re cluse (ri klüs′), person who lives shut up or withdrawn from the world.

rec og ni tion (rek′əg nish′ən), 1. knowing again; recognizing. 2. being recognized. By a good disguise he escaped recognition. 3. acknowledgment. We insisted on complete recognition of our rights. 4. attention; favorable notice. The actor soon won recognition from the public.

rec og nize (rek′əg nīz), 1. know again. You have grown so that I scarcely recognized you. 2. acknowledge; accept; admit. I recognize your right to ask that question.

re coil (ri koil′), 1. draw back; shrink back. Most people would recoil at seeing a snake in the path. 2. spring back. A gun recoils after being fired. 3. a springing back.

rec ol lect (rek′ə lekt′), remember.

rec ol lec tion (rek′ə lek′shən), 1. act or power of recalling to mind. 2. memory; remembrance. This has been the hottest summer within my recollection. 3. thing remembered.

rec om mend (rek′ə mend′), 1. speak in favor of; suggest favorably. Can you recommend a good story of adventure? 2. advise. 3. make pleasing or attractive. The position of the camp recommends it as a summer home. 4. hand over for safekeeping. He recommended his soul to God.

rec om men da tion (rek′ə men dā′shən), 1. a recommending. 2. anything that recommends a person or thing. 3. words of advice or praise.

rec om pense (rek′əm pens), 1. to reward; pay back. The travelers recompensed the man who so carefully directed them. 2. make a fair return for (anything lost, damage done, hurt received, etc.). 3. payment; reward; return.

rec on cile (rek′ən sīl), 1. make friends again. The children had quarreled but were soon reconciled. 2. settle (quarrels or differences). The teacher had to reconcile disputes among her pupils. 3. make satisfied. It is hard to reconcile oneself to being sick a long time. 4. make agree; bring into harmony. It is impossible to reconcile his story with the facts.

rec on cil i a tion (rek′ən sil′i ā′shən), 1. bringing together again in friendship. 2. settlement or adjustment of disagreements, differences, etc.

rec on noi ter or **rec on noi tre** (rek′ə noi′tər), 1. approach and examine or observe in order to learn something. Our scouts will reconnoiter the enemy's position before we attack. 2. approach a place and make a first survey of it. It seemed wise to reconnoiter before entering the town.

re con struct (rē′kən strukt′), construct again; make over.

re cord (ri kôrd′ for 1 and 2, rek′ərd for 3, 4, 5, 6, and 7), 1. set down in writing so as to keep for future use. Listen to the speaker and record what he says. 2. put in some permanent form; keep for remembrance. We record music on a phonograph; we record history in books. 3. the thing written or kept. 4. an official account. A secretary keeps a record of what is done at a meeting. 5. a disk or cylinder used on a phonograph. 6. the known facts about what a person, animal, ship, etc., has done. John has a fine record at school. 7. the best yet done; the best amount, rate, speed, etc., yet attained. Who holds the record for the high jump? **Break a record** means make a better record.

re count[1] (ri kount′), tell; give an account of. He recounted the events of the day.

re count[2] or **re-count** (rē kount′ for 1, rē′kount′ for 2), 1. count again. 2. a second count.

re course (ri kōrs′), 1. an appealing; a turning for help or protection. Our recourse in illness is to a doctor. **Have recourse to** means turn to for help. When we do not know what a word means, we have recourse to a dictionary. 2. person or thing resorted to for help or protection. A child's great recourse in trouble is its mother.

re cov er (ri kuv′ər), 1. get back (something lost, taken away, or stolen); as, to recover one's temper or health, to recover a purse. 2. make up for (something lost or damaged); as, to recover lost time. 3. get well; get back to a normal condition. Amy is recovering from scarlet fever. 4. **Recover oneself** means get back to a proper position or condition.

re cov er y (ri kuv′ər i), 1. coming back to health or normal condition. We heard of your recovery from fever. 2. getting back something that was lost, taken away, or stolen. 3. getting back to a proper position or condition. He started to fall, but made a good recovery.

rec re ant (rek′ri ənt), 1. cowardly. 2. coward. 3. unfaithful; false. 4. traitor.

rec re a tion (rek′ri ā′shən), play; amusement. Walking, gardening, and reading are quiet forms of recreation.

re cross (rē krôs′), cross again.

re cruit (ri krüt′), 1. a newly enlisted soldier or sailor. 2. get (men) to join an army or navy. 3. new member of any group or class. The Nature Club needs recruits. 4. get (people) to join. 5. increase the number of.

rec tan gle (rek′tang′gəl), a four-sided figure with four right angles.

Rectangles

rec tan gu lar (rek tang′gū lər), shaped like a rectangle.

rec ti fy (rek′ti fī), make right; put right; adjust; remedy. The storekeeper admitted his mistake and was willing to rectify it.

rec tor (rek′tər), clergyman who has certain privileges and duties.

re cur (ri kėr′), 1. come up again; occur again; be repeated. Leap year recurs every four years. 2. return in thought or speech. He recurred to the matter of cost. Old memories often recurred to him.

red (red), 1. the color of blood or of the lips. 2. having the color of blood or of the lips. 3. being like or suggesting the color of blood; as, red hair, a red cent, red fox, red clover. 4. violent; favoring revolution. 5. **See red** means become very angry.

Red Cross, an international organization to care for the sick and wounded in war, and to relieve suffering caused by floods, fire, diseases, and other disasters. Its badge is a red cross on a white background.

red den (red′ən), 1. make red. 2. become red. 3. blush.

red dish (red′ish), somewhat red.

re deem (ri dēm′), 1. buy back. Property on which money has been lent is redeemed when the loan is paid back. 2. pay off. He redeemed the debt. 3. fulfill; carry out; make good. We redeem a promise by doing what we said we would. 4. set free; rescue; save; as, redeemed from sin.

re demp tion (ri demp′shən), 1. buying back; paying off. 2. ransom. 3. deliverance; rescue. 4. salvation.

red-hot (red′hot′), 1. red with heat; very hot; as, red-hot iron. 2. very enthusiastic; excited; violent.

re dou ble (rē dub′əl), 1. double again. 2. double; increase greatly. When he saw land ahead, the swimmer redoubled his speed.

re doubt a ble (ri dout′ə bəl), that should be feared or dreaded; as, a redoubtable warrior, a redoubtable opponent.

re dress (ri dres′), 1. set right; repair; remedy. King Arthur tried to redress wrongs in his kingdom. 2. reparation; setting right. Any man deserves redress if he has been injured unfairly.

red skin (red′skin′), a North American Indian.

re duce (ri dūs′ or ri düs′), 1. decrease; make less; make smaller. We have reduced expenses this year. She is trying to reduce her weight. 2. bring down; lower. That poor woman is reduced to begging. She was reduced to tears by the cruel words. 3. change to another form. The chalk was reduced to powder. Reduce that statement to writing. 4. bring to a different condition; change. The teacher soon reduced the noisy class to order. 5. conquer.

re duc tion (ri duk′shən), 1. a reducing or being reduced; as, a reduction of ten pounds in weight. 2. change of form or condition. 3. amount by which a thing is reduced. The reduction in cost was $5. 4. copy of something on a smaller scale.

red wood (red′wu̇d′), 1. a California evergreen tree. Redwoods sometimes grow to a height of 300 feet. 2. the brownish-red wood of this tree.

Redwood

reed (rēd), 1. a kind of tall grass with a hollow stalk that grows in wet places. 2. anything made from the stalk of a reed, such as a pipe to blow on or an arrow. 3. thin piece of wood or metal in a musical instrument that produces sound when a current of air moves it.

reef[1] (rēf), a narrow ridge of rocks or sand at or near the surface of the water. The ship was wrecked on the hidden reef.

Reefed sail

reef[2] (rēf), 1. the part of a sail that is taken in or let out. 2. reduce the size of (a sail) by rolling or folding up a part of it.

reek (rēk), 1. vapor; unpleasant smell. We noticed the reek of cooking cabbage as we entered the hall. 2. send out vapor or an unpleasant smell. She reeked with cheap perfume. 3. be wet with sweat or blood.

Reel for a hose

reel[1] (rēl), 1. a frame like a spool, for winding thread, yarn, a fish line, rope, wire, etc. 2. spool; roller. 3. something wound on a reel; as, two reels of moving-picture film. 4. to wind on a reel. 5. draw with a reel or by winding. He reels in a fish. 6. **Reel off** means say, write, or make in a quick, easy way. He can reel off stories by the hour.

reel[2] (rēl), 1. be in a whirl; be dizzy. 2. sway, swing, or rock under a blow or shock. 3. sway in standing or walking.

reel[3] (rēl), 1. a lively dance. Two kinds are the Highland reel and the Virginia reel. 2. music for it.

re ë lect (rē′i lekt′), elect again.

re ën force (rē′en fōrs′), reinforce.

re ën force ment (rē′en fōrs′mənt), reinforcement.

re ën ter (rē en′tər), enter again; go in again.

re ës tab lish (rē′es tab′lish), establish again; restore.

re fer (ri fėr′), 1. hand over; send or direct for information or help or action. Let's refer our disputes to Mother. Our teacher is referring us to many good books. 2. turn for information or help. A person refers to a dictionary to find the meaning of words. 3. **Refer to** may mean (1) direct attention to or speak about. The preacher often referred to the Bible. (2) assign to or think of as caused by. Some people refer all their troubles to bad luck instead of to lack of ability.

ref er ence (ref′ər əns), 1. direction of the attention. This history contains many references to larger histories. 2. statement referred to. You will find that reference on page 16. 3. use for information or help. A dictionary is a book of reference. 4. mention. Do not make any reference to his lameness. 5. person who can give information about another person's character or ability. Tom gave his principal as a reference. 6. a statement about someone's character or ability. The boy had excellent references from men for whom he had worked.

re fine (ri fīn′), 1. make pure; become pure. Sugar, oil, and metals are refined before they are used. 2. make or become fine, polished, or cultivated. Reading good books helps to refine one's speech.

re fined (ri fīnd′), 1. freed from impurities; as, refined sugar. 2. free from coarseness or vulgarity; well-bred; as, refined tastes, refined manners, a refined voice.

re fine ment (ri fīn′mənt), 1. fine quality of feeling, taste, manners, or language. Good manners and correct speech are marks of refinement. 2. act or result of refining.

re fit (rē fit′), fit, prepare, or equip for use again; as, to refit a ship for a voyage.

re flect (ri flekt′), 1. throw back (light, heat, sound, etc.). The sidewalks reflect heat on a hot day. 2. give back an image of. The mirror reflects my face. The stage reflects the customs of the time. 3. cast blame, reproach, or discredit. That child's bad behavior reflects on his home training. 4. think carefully. Take time to reflect on important things.

re flec tion (ri flek′shən), 1. act of reflecting. 2. something reflected; image. See the reflection of the tree in this still water. 3. thinking; careful thinking. On reflection, we thought the plan too dangerous. 4. thought;

idea. 5. expression of unfavorable opinion; blame.

re form (ri fôrm′), 1. make better. Prisons should try to reform wrongdoers. 2. become better. The boy promised to reform if given another chance. 3. improvement. Let us see what reforms are needed.

ref or ma tion (ref′ər mā′shən), change for the better; improvement.

re form er (ri fôr′mər), person who reforms, or tries to reform, some state of affairs, custom, etc.

re frain[1] (ri frān′), hold back. Refrain from wrongdoing.

re frain[2] (ri frān′), a phrase or verse repeated regularly in a song or poem. In "The Star-Spangled Banner" the refrain is "O'er the land of the free and the home of the brave."

re fresh (ri fresh′), 1. make fresh again; renew. His bath refreshed him. Cool drinks are refreshing on a warm day. She refreshed herself with a cup of tea. He refreshed his memory by a glance at the book. 2. become fresh again.

re fresh ing (ri fresh′ing), 1. that refreshes. 2. welcome as a pleasing change.

re fresh ment (ri fresh′mənt), 1. refreshing; being refreshed. 2. thing that refreshes. 3. food or drink. Cake and lemonade were the refreshments at our party.

re frig er a tor (ri frij′ər ā′tər), something that keeps things cool. An electric refrigerator keeps things cool without ice.

ref uge (ref′ūj), shelter; protection. The cat took refuge in a tree.

ref u gee (ref′ū jē′), person who flees for refuge or safety. Many refugees came from Europe to America.

re fund (ri fund′ for 1, rē′fund for 2), 1. pay back. If these shoes do not wear well, the shop will refund your money. 2. return of money paid.

re fus al (ri fūz′əl), 1. act of refusing. His refusal to play the game provoked the other boys. 2. the right to refuse or take a thing before it is offered to others. Give me the refusal of the car till tomorrow.

re fuse[1] (ri fūz′), 1. say "no." 2. say "no" to. He refuses the offer. She refused him when he begged her to marry him. 3. say one will not do it, give it, etc. He refuses to obey.

ref use[2] (ref′ūs), useless stuff; waste; rubbish. The street-cleaning department takes away all refuse from the streets.

re fute (ri fūt′), prove (a claim, opinion, or argument) to be false or incorrect. How would you refute the statement that the cow jumped over the moon?

re gain (ri gān′), 1. get again; as, to regain health. 2. get back to; reach again; as, to regain the main road.

re gal (rē′gəl), 1. belonging to a king; royal. The regal power descends from father to son. 2. such as kings have; fit for a king. It was a regal banquet.

re gale (ri gāl′), 1. entertain very well; delight with something pleasing. The old sailor regaled the boys with sea stories. 2. feast. The rabbits regaled themselves with the young lettuce.

re gard (ri gärd′), 1. look at; look closely at; watch. The cat regarded me anxiously when I picked up her kittens. 2. a look; a steady look. The man's regard seemed fixed upon some distant object. 3. consider; think of. He is regarded as the best doctor in town. 4. care for; respect. She always regards her parents' wishes. 5. consideration; thought; care. Have regard for the feelings of others. 6. esteem; favor; good opinion. The teacher has high regard for John's ability. 7. **Regards** means good wishes or an expression of esteem. He sends his regards. 8. to concern; relate to. As regards money, I have enough. 9. **In regard to** or **with regard to** means concerning.

re gard ing (ri gär′ding), concerning; about. A letter regarding the boy's conduct was sent to his father.

re gard less (ri gärd′lis), with no heed; careless. Regardless of grammar, he said, "Him and I have went."

re gent (rē′jənt), person who rules when the regular ruler is absent or unfit. The queen will be the regent till her son grows up.

re gime or **ré gime** (rā zhēm′), 1. system of government or rule. Under the old regime women could not vote. 2. system of living. Baby's regime includes two naps a day.

reg i ment (rej′i mənt for 1 and 2, rej′i ment for 3), 1. several companies of soldiers organized into one large group, commanded by a colonel. 2. large number. 3. form into a regiment or organized group.

re gion (rē′jən), 1. space; place; part of the world; as, the region of the equator, a mountainous region. 2. part of the body; as, the region of the heart.

reg is ter (rej′is tər), 1. a list; record. A register of attendance is kept in our school. 2. a book in which a list is kept. Look up Tom's record in the register. 3. write in a list. Register the names of the new pupils. 4. have one's name written in a list. You must register if you intend to vote. 5. thing that records. A cash register shows the amount of money taken in. 6. indicate; record. The thermometer registers 90 degrees. 7. have recorded in the post office. Register this letter. 8. show (surprise, joy, anger, etc.) by the expression on one's face or by actions. 9. the range of a voice or an instrument.

reg is tra tion (rej′is trā′shən), 1. registering. 2. an entry in a register. 3. number of people registered.

re gret (ri gret′), 1. the feeling of being sorry; sorrow; sense of loss. 2. feel sorry. Jim wrote, regretting that he could not visit us. 3. feel sorry for. We regretted his absence. 4. **Regrets** sometimes means a polite reply declining an invitation. She could not come but sent regrets.

reg u lar (reg′ū lər), 1. usual; fixed by custom or rule. Our regular sleeping place is in a bedroom. 2. coming again and again at the same time. Saturday is a regular holiday. 3. well-balanced; even in size, spacing, or speed; as, regular teeth, regular breathing. 4. following some rule or principle; according to rule. A period is the regular ending for a sentence. 5. orderly; methodical. He leads a regular life. 6. properly fitted or trained. 7. member of a regularly paid group of any kind. The army was made up of regulars and volunteers.

reg u lar i ty (reg′ū lar′i ti), order; system; steadiness; being regular.

reg u lar ly (reg′ū lər li), 1. in a regular manner. 2. at regular times.

reg u late (reg′ū lāt), 1. control by rule, principle, or system. Accidents happen even in the best regulated families. 2. keep at some standard. This instrument regulates the temperature of the room.

reg u la tion (reg′ū lā′shən), 1. control by rule, principle, or system. 2. law; ruie; as, traffic regulations. 3. regular; required by some regulation. Soldiers wear a regulation uniform. 4. usual; ordinary.

re hears al (ri hėr′səl), rehearsing; performance beforehand for practice or drill.

re hearse (ri hėrs′), 1. practice for a public performance. We rehearsed our parts for the school play. 2. repeat. The child rehearsed the happenings of the day to his father in the evening.

reign (rān), 1. act of ruling; royal power. 2. the period of power of a ruler. 3. to rule. A king reigns over his kingdom. 4. prevail. On a still night silence reigns.

rein (rān), 1. a long, narrow strap or line fastened to a bridle, by which to guide and control an animal. A driver or rider of a horse holds the reins in his hands. See the diagram under **harness.** 2. a means of control and direction. President Roosevelt held the reins of government. 3. to guide and control. He reined his horse well. Rein your tongue. 4. **Give rein to** anything means leave it free to go without guiding.

rein deer (rān′dēr′), a kind of large deer, with branching horns, found in the north. Santa Claus's sleigh is drawn by reindeer.

Reindeer (about 4½ ft. high at the shoulder)

re in force (rē′in fōrs′), 1. strengthen with new force or materials; as, to reinforce an army or a fleet, to reinforce a garment with an extra thickness of cloth, to reinforce a wall or a bridge. 2. strengthen; as, to reinforce an argument, a plea, an effect, a stock, a supply, etc.

re in force ment (rē′in fōrs′mənt), 1. strengthening; being strengthened. 2. something that strengthens. **Reinforcements** means extra soldiers or warships. Reinforcements were sent to the battle front.

re it er ate (rē it′ər āt), repeat again; say or do several times. The boy did not move though the teacher reiterated her command.

re ject (ri jekt′), 1. refuse to take. He rejected our help. He tried to join the army but was rejected. 2. throw away. Reject all spotted apples.

re jec tion (ri jek′shən), 1. rejecting. 2. being rejected. 3. thing rejected.

re joice (ri jois′), 1. be glad. Mother rejoiced at our success. 2. make glad.

re join (rē join′ for 1, ri join′ for 2), 1. join again; unite again. The sailor will rejoin his comrades. 2. answer; reply. "Not on your life," rejoined Dick.

re lapse (ri laps′), 1. fall or slip back into a former state or way of acting. After one cry of surprise she relapsed into silence. 2. falling or slipping back. He seemed to be getting over his illness but had a relapse.

re late (ri lāt′), 1. tell; give an account of. The traveler related his adventures. 2. connect in thought or meaning. *Better* and *best* are related to *good*. 3. **Be related** sometimes means belong to the same family. Cousins are related.

re la tion (ri lā′shən), 1. act of telling; account. We were interested by his relation of his adventures. 2. connection. The relation between master and servant has changed greatly during the last century. Our firm has business relations with his firm. Part of your answer has no relation to the question. The relation of mother and child is the closest in the world. 3. reference; regard. We must plan with relation to the future. 4. father, brother, aunt, nephew, cousin, etc.

re la tion ship (ri lā′shən ship), connection. What is the relationship of clouds to rain?

rel a tive (rel′ə tiv), 1. father, brother, aunt, nephew, cousin, etc. 2. having relation or connection with each other. Before ordering our dinner, we considered the relative merits of chicken and roast beef. 3. depending for meaning on a relation to something else. East is a relative term; for example, Chicago is east of California but west of New York.

rel a tive ly (rel′ə tiv li), 1. comparatively. One inch is a relatively small difference in a man's height. 2. **Relatively to** means in comparison with; in proportion to; for. Tom is strong relatively to his size. A scow is broad relatively to its length.

re lax (ri laks′), 1. loosen up; become less stiff or firm. Relax your muscles to rest them. Relax when you dance. 2. make or become less strict or severe. Discipline is relaxed on the last day of school. 3. weaken. Pupils often relax their efforts after the examinations are over.

re lay (rē′lā for 1, ri lā′ for 2), 1. a fresh supply. New relays of men were sent to the battle front. 2. take and carry farther. Messengers will relay your message.

re lease (ri lēs′), 1. let go. Release the catch and the box will open. 2. let loose; set free. She released him from his promise. 3. free; relieve. The nurse is released from duty at seven o'clock. 4. setting free. Lincoln proclaimed the release of the slaves. 5. freedom; relief. This medicine will give you a release from pain.

re lent (ri lent′), become less harsh; be more tender and merciful. After hours of cruel treatment of the prisoners, the soldiers relented.

re lent less (ri lent′lis), not relenting; harsh; without pity. The storm raged with relentless fury.

re li a ble (ri lī′ə bəl), worthy of trust; that can be depended on. Send Joe to the bank for the money; he is a reliable boy.

re li ance (ri lī′əns), 1. trust; dependence. A child has reliance on his mother. 2. confidence. 3. thing on which one depends.

rel ic (rel′ik), 1. thing or piece left from the past. This ruined bridge is a relic that reminds us of the war. 2. something belonging to a holy person, kept as a sacred memorial.

re lied (ri līd′), depended. See **rely.**

re lief (ri lēf′), 1. aid; help; something that lessens or frees from pain, burden, difficulty, etc. Relief was quickly sent to the sufferers from the great fire. 2. the lessening of, or freeing from, a pain, burden, difficulty, etc. 3. **On relief** sometimes means receiving a dole from public funds. 4. freedom from a post of duty. This nurse is on duty from seven in the morning until seven at night, with only two hours' relief. 5. change of persons on duty. 6. persons who relieve others from duty. 7. projection of figures and designs from a surface in sculpture, etc.

re lieve (ri lēv′), 1. make less; make easier; reduce the pain or trouble of. What will relieve a headache? We telephoned to relieve our mother's uneasiness. 2. set free. Your coming relieves me of the bother of writing a long letter. 3. free (a person on duty) by taking his place. 4. bring aid to; help. Soldiers were sent to relieve the fort. 5. give variety to. The black dress was relieved by red trimming.

re li gion (ri lij′ən), 1. belief in God or gods. 2. worship of God or gods.

re li gious (ri lij′əs), 1. of religion; connected with religion; as, religious meetings, religious books, religious differences. 2. much interested in religion; devoted to the worship of God or gods. She is very religious and goes to church every day. 3. strict; done with care. Grace gave religious attention to her hair and complexion. 4. monk or nun; member of a religious order. There are sixty religious in one town.

re lin quish (ri ling′kwish), give up; let go. The small dog relinquished his bone to the big dog. She has relinquished all hope of going to Europe this year.

rel ish (rel′ish), 1. pleasant taste; good flavor. Hunger gives relish to simple food. 2. something to add flavor to food. Olives and pickles are relishes. 3. liking; appetite. The hungry boy ate with a great relish. The teacher has no relish for John's jokes. 4. like the taste of; like. A cat relishes cream. Dick did not relish the prospect of staying after school.

re load (rē lōd′), load again.

re luc tance (ri luk′təns), unwillingness; slowness in action because of unwillingness. She agreed with reluctance to take part in the game.

re luc tant (ri luk′tənt), unwilling; slow to act because unwilling. The policeman led the reluctant boy to the principal. I am reluctant to see the summer end.

re ly (ri lī′), depend; trust. Rely on your own efforts. I relied upon your promise absolutely.

re main (ri mān′), 1. stay. We shall remain at the seashore till October. 2. continue; last; keep on. The town remains the same year after year. 3. be left. A few apples remain on the tree. If you take 2 from 5, 3 remains.

re main der (ri mān′dər), the part left over; the rest. If you take 2 from 9, the remainder is 7. After studying an hour, Alice spent the remainder of the afternoon in play.

re mains (ri mānz′), 1. what is left. The remains of the meal were fed to the dog. 2. dead body. Washington's remains are buried at Mount Vernon.

re mark (ri märk′), 1. say; speak; comment. Mother remarked that Bill's hands would be better for a wash. 2. something said in a few words; short statement. The president made a few remarks. 3. to notice; observe. Did you remark that queer cloud?

re mark a ble (ri mär′kə bəl), worthy of notice; unusual. He has a remarkable memory.

re mark a bly (ri mär′kə bli), notably; unusually.

rem e dy (rem′i di), 1. a cure; a means of removing or relieving diseases or any bad condition. 2. to cure; put right; make right. A thorough cleaning remedied the trouble.

re mem ber (ri mem′bər), 1. call back to mind. I can't remember that man's name. 2. keep in mind; take care not to forget. Remember me when I am gone. 3. have (something) return to the mind. 4. keep in mind as deserving a reward, gift, etc. My dead uncle remembered me in his will. 5. mention as sending greetings. Ruth asked to be remembered to Ann's sister.

re mem brance (ri mem′brəns), 1. memory; act of remembering. It comes to my remembrance. 2. keepsake; any thing or action that makes one remember a person.

re mind (ri mīnd′), make (one) think or remember. This picture reminds me of a story I heard.

re mind er (ri mīn′dər), something to help one remember.

re mit (ri mit′), 1. send money to a person or place. Enclosed is our bill; please remit. 2. refrain from carrying out. The king is remitting the prisoner's punishment. 3. pardon; forgive. Christ gave His disciples power to remit sins. 4. decrease; make less. After we had rowed the boat into calm water, we remitted our efforts.

rem nant (rem′nənt), small part left. She bought a remnant of silk at a bargain. This town has only a remnant of its former population.

re mod el (rē mod′əl), 1. model again. 2. make over. They are remodeling the old barn into a house.

re mon strance (ri mon′strəns), protest; complaint.

re mon strate (ri mon′strāt), object; protest. The teacher remonstrated with the boy about his poor work.

re morse (ri môrs′), deep, painful regret for having done wrong. The thief felt remorse for his crime and confessed.

re morse less (ri môrs′lis), 1. without remorse. 2. pitiless; cruel.

re mote (ri mōt′), 1. far away; far off. The North Pole is a remote part of the world.

Those queer animals, the dinosaurs, lived in remote ages. This remote village is so out of the way that mail comes only once a week. 2. distant. He is a remote relative. 3. slight. I haven't the remotest idea what you mean.

re mov al (ri müv′əl), 1. taking away. After the removal of the soup, fish was served. 2. change of place. The store announces its removal to larger quarters. 3. dismissal from an office or position.

re move (ri müv′), 1. move from a place or position; take off; take away. People remove their hats in a theater. The governor removed the mayor for failing to do his duty. 2. get rid of; put an end to. 3. go away; move away. 4. moving away. 5. step or degree of distance. At every remove the mountain seemed smaller.

rend (rend), 1. tear; pull apart violently; split. Wolves will rend a lamb in pieces. 2. split. Lightning rent the tree. 3. disturb violently. John was rent by a wish to keep the money he found and the knowledge that he ought to return it. **rent**[2] is formed from **rend.**

ren der (ren′dər), 1. cause to become; make. An accident has rendered him helpless. 2. give; do. Can I render any aid? What service has he rendered to the school? 3. hand in; report. The committee rendered an account of all the money spent. 4. give in return. Render thanks for your blessings. 5. pay as due. The conquered rendered tribute to the conqueror. 6. represent; bring out the meaning of. The actor rendered the part of the villain well. 7. play or sing (music).

ren dez vous (rän′də vü), 1. an appointment to meet at a fixed place or time; meeting by agreement. 2. meeting place; gathering place. The family had two favorite rendezvous, the library and the garden.

ren e gade (ren′i gād), traitor.

re new (ri nū′ or ri nü′), 1. make new again; make like new; restore. 2. begin again. He renewed his efforts to open the window. 3. replace by new material or a new thing of the same sort; fill again. She renewed the sleeves of her dress. The well renews itself no matter how much water is taken away. 4. give or get for a new period.

re new al (ri nū′əl or ri nü′əl), renewing; being renewed. Next summer there will be a renewal of swimming.

re nounce (ri nouns′), 1. give up; give up entirely; declare that one gives up. He renounces his claim to the money. 2. cast off; refuse to recognize as one's own. The sad father renounced his wicked son.

re nown (ri noun′), fame. A hero in war wins renown.

re nowned (ri nound′), famous.

rent[1] (rent), 1. a regular payment for the use of property. 2. to pay for the use of (property). We rent a house from Mr. Smith. 3. take pay for the use of (property). He rents several other houses. 4. be rented. This farm rents for $500 a year.

rent[2] (rent), 1. a tear; a torn place; a split. 2. torn; split. See **rend.** The tree was rent by the wind.

rent al (ren′təl), amount received or paid as rent.

re o pen (rē ō′pən), open again. School will reopen in September.

re paid (ri pād′). See **repay.** He repaid the money he had borrowed. All debts should be repaid.

re pair[1] (ri pãr′), 1. mend; put in good condition again. He repairs shoes. 2. act or work of repairing. Repairs on the school building are made during the summer. 3. condition fit to be used. The State keeps the roads in repair. 4. condition for use. They used to be in very bad repair. 5. make up for. How can I repair the harm done?

re pair[2] (ri pãr′), go (to a place). After dinner we repaired to the porch.

rep a ra tion (rep′ə rā′shən), 1. compensation for wrong or injury. 2. giving satisfaction or compensation for wrong or injury done.

re past (ri past′), meal; food. Breakfast at our house is a light repast.

re pay (ri pā′), 1. pay back. He repaid the money he had borrowed. 2. make return for. No thanks can repay such kindness. 3. make return to. The boy's success repaid the teacher for her efforts.

re peal (ri pēl′), 1. take back; withdraw. 2. act of repealing; withdrawal; abolition. He voted for the repeal of that law.

re peat (ri pēt′), 1. do again. 2. say again. 3. say over; recite. Mary can repeat many poems from memory.

re peat ed ly (ri pēt′id li), again and again; more than once.

re pel (ri pel′), 1. force back; drive back; drive away. They repelled the enemy. We can repel bad thoughts. 2. be displeasing to; cause dislike in. Spiders and worms repel me.

re pent (ri pent′), 1. feel sorry for sin and seek forgiveness. He had done wrong, but repented. 2. feel sorry for; regret. She bought the red hat and has repented her choice.

re pent ance (ri pen′təns), sorrow for wrongdoing; regret.

re pent ant (ri pen′tənt), feeling regret; sorry for wrongdoing.

rep e ti tion (rep′i tish′ən), 1. repeating; doing again; saying again. Repetition helps learning. Any repetition of the offense will be punished. 2. repeated occurrence; thing repeated.

re pine (ri pīn′), be discontented; fret; complain.

re place (ri plās′), 1. fill or take the place of. Tom replaced Will as captain. 2. get another in place of. I will replace the cup I broke. 3. put back; put in place again. Replace the books on the shelves.

re plen ish (ri plen′ish), fill again; provide a new supply for. Her supply of towels needs replenishing. You had better replenish the fire.

re ply (ri plī′), answer. **replies, replied,** and **replying** are formed from **reply.**

re port (ri pōrt′), 1. an account of something seen, heard, or read about. 2. anything formally expressed, generally in writing; as, a school report. 3. give or bring an account of; make a report of; state formally. Our treasurer reports that all dues are paid up. 4. describe; tell. 5. present oneself. Report for work at eight o'clock. 6. the sound of an explosion; as, the report of a gun.

re port er (ri pōr′tər), 1. person who reports. 2. person who gathers news for a newspaper.

re pose[1] (ri pōz′), 1. rest; sleep. Do not disturb her repose. 2. lie at rest. The cat reposed upon the cushion. 3. lay to rest. Repose yourself in the hammock. 4. quietness; ease. She has repose of manner.

re pose[2] (ri pōz′), put; place. We repose entire confidence in his honesty.

rep re sent (rep′ri zent′), 1. stand for; be a sign of. The stars in our flag represent the States. A policeman represents the power of the law. 2. act in place of; speak and act for. We chose a committee to represent us. 3. act the part of. Each child will represent an animal at the party. 4. describe; show. He represented the plan as safe, but it was not. 5. bring before the mind; make one think of. Images in the mind represent real objects.

rep re sen ta tion (rep′ri zen tā′shən), 1. act of representing. 2. condition or fact of being represented. "Taxation without representation is tyranny." 3. picture, model, play, etc.; presentation. A representation of the story of Rip Van Winkle will be given in the school assembly today.

rep re sent a tive (rep′ri zen′tə tiv), 1. person appointed to act or speak for others. Who is your Representative in Congress? 2. having its citizens represented by chosen persons; as, a representative government. 3. representing. Images representative of animals were made by the children. 4. example; type. The tiger is a common representative of the cat family. 5. enough like all those of its kind to stand for all the rest. Balls, blocks, and trains are representative toys.

re press (ri pres′), 1. prevent from acting; check. She repressed an impulse to cough. 2. keep down; put down. The government repressed a revolt.

re pres sion (ri presh′ən), 1. repressing. The repression of a laugh made Jim choke. 2. being repressed. Repression made Lulu behave worse.

re proach (ri prōch′), 1. blame. Bad people bring reproach on their families. Father reproached me for being late. 2. a cause of blame or disgrace. A coward is a reproach to an army.

re proach ful (ri prōch′fəl), full of reproach; expressing reproach.

re pro duce (rē′prə dūs′ or rē′prə düs′), 1. produce again. A radio reproduces sounds. 2. make a copy of. A camera will reproduce a picture. 3. produce offspring. Most plants reproduce by seeds.

re pro duc tion (rē′prə duk′shən), 1. reproducing; being reproduced; as, the reproduction of sounds. 2. copy. 3. the production of offspring.

re proof (ri prüf′), blame; words of blame or disapproval.

re prove (ri prüv′), find fault with; blame; disapprove. Reprove the boy for teasing the cat.

rep tile (rep′til), a cold-blooded animal that creeps or crawls. Snakes, lizards, turtles, alligators, and crocodiles are reptiles.

re pub lic (ri pub′lik), nation in which the citizens elect representatives to manage the government.

re pub li can (ri pub′li kən), 1. of a republic; like that of a republic. Many countries have a republican form of government. 2. person who favors a republic. 3. The **Republican Party** is one of the two main political parties in the United States. 4. Its members are called **Republicans.** 5. of the Republican Party.

re pu di ate (ri pū′di āt), 1. cast off; disown; as, to repudiate a son. 2. refuse to accept; reject; as, to repudiate a doctrine. 3. refuse to acknowledge or pay; as, to repudiate a debt.

re pulse (ri puls′), 1. drive back; repel. Our soldiers repulsed the enemy. 2. driving back; being driven back. After the second repulse, the enemy surrendered. 3. refuse to accept; reject. She coldly repulsed him. 4. refusal; rejection.

re pul sive (ri pul′siv), causing disgust or strong dislike; as, a repulsive snake.

rep u ta ble (rep′ū tə bəl), having a good reputation; well thought of.

rep u ta tion (rep′ū tā′shən), 1. what people think and say the character of a person or thing is; character in the opinion of others. This store has an excellent reputation for fair dealing. 2. good name; good reputation. 3. fame.

re pute (ri pūt′), 1. reputation. This is a district of bad repute on account of many robberies. 2. consider; suppose; suppose to be. He is reputed the richest man in the State.

re put ed (ri pūt′id), supposed.

re quest (ri kwest′), 1. ask for; ask; ask as a favor. He requested a loan from the bank. 2. act of asking. Your request for a ticket was made too late. 3. what is asked for. The king granted his request. 4. state of being desired or sought after. She is such a good dancer that she is in great request.

re quire (ri kwīr′), 1. need. We require more spoons for our party. 2. demand; order; command. The rules required us all to be present.

re quire ment (ri kwīr′mənt), 1. a need; thing needed. Patience is a requirement in teaching. 2. a demand; thing demanded; as, requirements for graduation.

req ui site (rek′wi zit), 1. required by circumstances; needed; necessary; as, the number of votes requisite for election. 2. requirement; thing needed. Food and air are requisites for life.

req ui si tion (rek′wi zish′ən), 1. act of requiring. 2. a demand made, especially a formal written demand; as, the requisition of supplies for troops. 3. demand or take by authority; as, to requisition supplies, horses, or labor.

re quite (ri kwīt′), 1. pay back; make return for. The Bible says to requite evil with good. 2. make return to. The knight requited the boy for his warning.

res cue (res′kū), 1. save from danger or harm; free; deliver. The dog rescued the child from drowning. 2. saving or freeing from harm or danger. The fireman was praised for his brave rescue of the children in the burning house. A dog was chasing our cat when Mary came to the rescue.

res cu er (res′kū ər), one that rescues.

re search (ri sėrch′), a careful hunting for facts or truth; inquiry; investigation. The researches of men of science have done much to lessen disease.

re sem blance (ri zem′bləns), likeness; similar appearance. Twins often show great resemblance.

re sem ble (ri zem′bəl), be like. An orange resembles a grapefruit.

re sent (ri zent′), feel injured and angry at; feel indignation at. Grace resented being called a baby. Our cat resents having anyone sit in its chair.

re sent ful (ri zent′fəl), feeling resentment; injured and angry; showing resentment.

re sent ment (ri zent′mənt), the feeling that one has at being injured or insulted; indignation. Everyone feels resentment at being treated unfairly.

res er va tion (rez′ər vā′shən), 1. keeping back; hiding in part; something not expressed. She outwardly approved of the plan with the mental reservation of changing things to suit herself. 2. limiting condition. The United States accepted the plan with reservations plainly stated. 3. land set aside for a special purpose. The government has set apart Indian reservations. 4. arrangement to keep a thing for a person; the securing of accommodations, etc. We make reservations of rooms at a hotel, seats in a parlor car, and passage on a steamship.

re serve (ri zėrv′), 1. keep back; hold back; set apart; save for use later. Reserve enough money for your fare home. 2. something kept back for future use; store. Banks must keep a reserve of money. Reserves will be sent to help the men fighting at the front. 3. public land set apart for a special purpose; as, a forest reserve. 4. keeping back; holding back; reservation. You may speak before her without reserve. 5. self-restraint in action or speech. 6. a silent manner that keeps people from making friends easily.

re served (ri zėrvd′), 1. kept in reserve. 2. set apart. 3. having or showing self-restraint. 4. disposed to keep to one's self. A reserved boy does not make friends easily.

res er voir (rez′ər vwär), 1. place where water is collected and stored for use. This reservoir supplies the entire city. 2. anything to hold a liquid. A fountain pen has an ink reservoir. 3. place where anything is collected and stored. His mind was a reservoir of facts. 4. a great supply.

Reservoir for water

re side (ri zīd′), 1. dwell; live (in or at) for a long time. This family has resided in our town for 100 years. 2. be (in); exist (in). Her charm resides in her happy smile.

res i dence (rez′i dəns), 1. house; home; abode. 2. residing. Long residence in Russia made Mr. Pares very fond of the Russian people.

res i dent (rez′i dənt), 1. person living in a place, not a visitor. The residents of the town are proud of its new library. 2. staying; dwelling in a place. Dr. Jones is a resident physician at the hospital.

res i due (rez′i dū or rez′i dü), remainder; what remains after a part is taken. The syrup had dried up, leaving a sticky residue.

re sign (ri zīn′), 1. give up; give up a job, office, etc. John resigned his position on the school paper. 2. yield; submit. Jim had to resign himself to a week in bed when he hurt his back.

res ig na tion (rez′ig nā′shən), 1. act of resigning. There have been so many resignations from the committee that a new one must be formed. 2. written statement giving notice that one resigns. 3. patient acceptance; quiet submission. She bore the pain with resignation.

res in (rez′in), sticky substance that flows from some trees. Resin is used in medicine, varnishes, etc. Pine resin is much used and is often called rosin.

res in ous (rez′i nəs), 1. of resin. 2. like resin. 3. containing resin; full of resin.

re sist (ri zist′), 1. act against; strive against; oppose. The window resisted his efforts to open it. 2. strive successfully against; keep from; withstand. I could not resist laughing.

re sist ance (ri zis′təns), 1. act of resisting. The bank clerk made no resistance to the robbers. 2. power to resist. She has little resistance to germs and so is often ili. 3. opposition; opposing force; thing or act that resists. An airplane can overcome the resistance of the air and go in the desired direction, but an ordinary balloon simply drifts.

re sist ant (ri zis′tənt), resisting.

res o lute (rez′ə lüt), determined; firm; bold. He was resolute in his attempt to climb to the top of the mountain. A soldier must be resolute in battle. The captain's resolute words cheered the team.

res o lu tion (rez′ə lü′shən), 1. thing decided on; thing determined. He made a resolution to get up early. 2. power of holding firmly to a purpose.

re solve (ri zolv′), 1. make up one's mind; determine; decide. He resolved to do better work in the future. 2. thing determined on; thing decided. He kept his resolve to do better. 3. firmness in carrying out a purpose; determination. Washington was a man of great resolve. 4. decide by vote. It was resolved that our school have a lunchroom. 5. break into parts. 6. solve; answer and explain. His letter resolved all our doubts.

re solved (ri zolvd′), determined; firm; resolute.

res o nant (rez′ə nənt), 1. resounding; continuing to sound. 2. tending to increase or prolong sounds.

re sort (ri zôrt′), 1. go; go often. Many people resort to the beaches in hot weather. 2. place people go to. There are many summer resorts in the mountains. 3. **Resort to** sometimes means seek help from or make use of. The mother resorted to punishment to make the child obey. 4. act of turning to for help. The resort to force is forbidden in this school. 5. person or thing turned to for help. Books are her resort when she is lonely. Friends are the best resort in trouble.

re sound (ri zound′), 1. echo; give back sound. The hills resounded when we shouted. 2. sound loudly. Radios resound from every house. 3. be filled with sound. The room resounded with the children's shouts.

re source (ri sōrs′), 1. any supply that will meet a need. We have resources of money, of knowledge, and of strength. 2. any means of getting success or getting out of trouble. Climbing a tree is a cat's resource when chased by a dog. 3. skill in meeting difficulties, getting out of trouble, etc.

re source ful (ri sōrs′fəl), good at thinking of ways to do things.

re spect (ri spekt′), 1. honor; esteem. Children should show respect to those who are older and wiser. 2. feel or show honor or esteem for. We respect an honest person. 3. **Respects** means expressions of respect; regards. Give her my respects. We must pay our respects to the governor. 4. care; consideration. We should show respect for school buildings, parks, and other public property. 5. to care for; show consideration for. Respect the ideas of others. 6. relation; reference. We must plan with respect to the future. 7. feature; point; matter; detail. Giving to beggars is unwise in many respects.

re spect a ble (ri spek′tə bəl), 1. worthy of respect; having a good reputation. Respectable citizens obey the laws. 2. fairly good; moderate in size or quality. John's record in school was always respectable, if never brilliant. 3. good enough to use; fit to be seen. That dirty dress is not respectable.

re spect ful (ri spekt′fəl), showing respect; polite. He was always respectful to older people.

re spect ing (ri spek′ting), regarding; about; concerning. A discussion arose respecting the merits of different automobiles.

re spec tive (ri spek′tiv), belonging to each; particular; individual. The classes went to their respective rooms.

re spec tive ly (ri spek′tiv li), as regards each one in his turn or in the order mentioned. Bob, Dick, and Tom are 6, 8, and 10 years old, respectively.

res pi ra tion (res′pi rā′shən), breathing. A bad cold hinders respiration.

res pite (res′pit), time of relief and rest; lull. A big cloud brought a respite from the glare of the sun.

re splend ent (ri splen′dənt), very bright; shining; splendid. The queen was resplendent with jewels.

re spond (ri spond′), 1. answer; reply. He responded briefly to the question. 2. act in answer; react. A dog responds to kind treatment by loving its master. Mary responded quickly to the medicine and was well in a few days.

re sponse (ri spons′), 1. an answer by word or act. Her response to my letter was prompt. Mary stuck out her tongue in response to Tom's teasing. 2. words said or sung by the congregation or choir in answer to the minister.

re spon si bil i ty (ri spon′si bil′i ti), 1. being responsible; obligation. A little child does not feel much responsibility. 2. thing for which one is responsible. A task, a debt, and little children to care for are all responsibilities.

re spon si ble (ri spon′si bəl), 1. obliged or expected to account (for). Each pupil is responsible for the care of the books given him. 2. deserving credit or blame. The bad weather is responsible for the small attendance. 3. trustworthy; reliable. The class should choose a responsible pupil to take care of its money. 4. involving obligation or duties.

re spon sive (ri spon′siv), 1. making answer; responding; as, a responsive glance. 2. easily moved; responding readily. Dogs are responsive to kindness. 3. using or containing responses.

rest[1] (rest), 1. sleep. The children had a good night's rest. 2. quiet; freedom from anything that tires, troubles, disturbs, or pains. The medicine gave the sick man a short rest from pain. 3. ease after work or effort. The workmen were allowed an hour for rest. 4. absence of motion; stillness. The driver brought the car to rest. The lake was at rest. 5. in music or reading, a pause. 6. a mark to show such a pause. 7. be still or quiet. My mother rests for an hour every afternoon. 8. be free from work, effort, care, trouble, etc. Schoolteachers can rest in the summer. 9. be at ease. Don't let Mrs. White rest till she promises to visit us. 10. lie in death or the grave. The old man rests with his forefathers. 11. give rest to; refresh by rest. Stop and rest your horse. It rests one's feet to take off one's shoes. 12. to look; be fixed. Our eyes rested on the open book. 13. a support; something to lean on; as, a footrest. 14. lean; lie; be supported. The ladder rested against the walls. The roof rests on columns. 15. depend. Our hope rests on you. 16. lie; be found; be present. In a democracy, government rests with the people. A smile rested on the girl's lips.

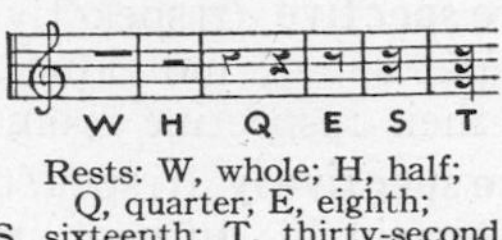

Rests: W, whole; H, half; Q, quarter; E, eighth; S, sixteenth; T, thirty-second.

rest[2] (rest), 1. what is left; those that are left. 2. continue to be; remain. The final decision rests with father.

res tau rant (res′tə rənt), place to buy and eat a meal.

rest ful (rest′fəl), 1. full of rest; giving rest. She had a restful nap. 2. quiet; peaceful.

rest less (rest′lis), 1. unable to rest; uneasy. The dog seemed restless, as if he sensed some danger. 2. without rest or sleep; not restful. The sick child passed a restless night. 3. never still or quiet. That nervous boy is very restless.

res to ra tion (res′tə rā′shən), 1. restoring or being restored; bringing back to a former condition; as, the restoration of health, the restoration of a king. 2. something restored. The house we slept in was a restoration of a Colonial mansion.

re store (ri stōr′), 1. bring back; establish again. 2. bring back to a former condition or to a normal condition. The old house has been restored. He is completely restored to health. 3. give back; put back. He was obliged to restore the money to its owner.

re strain (ri strān′), hold back; keep down; keep in check; keep within limits. She could not restrain her curiosity to see what was in the box.

re straint (ri strānt′), 1. restraining or being restrained. Noisy children sometimes need restraint. 2. a means of restraining. 3. tendency to restrain natural feeling. Joe was very angry, but he spoke with restraint.

re strict (ri strikt′), keep within limits; confine. Our club membership is restricted to twelve.

re stric tion (ri strik′shən), 1. something that restricts; a limiting condition or rule. The restrictions on the use of the playground are: No fighting. No damaging property. 2. a restricting or being restricted. This park is open to the public without restriction.

re sult (ri zult′), 1. that which happens because of something; what is caused. The result of his fall was a broken leg. 2. good or useful result. We want results, not talk. 3. be a result; follow as a consequence. Sickness often results from eating too much. 4. end. **Result in** means have as a result. Eating too much often results in sickness.

re sume (ri züm′), 1. begin again; go on. Resume reading where we left off. 2. take again. Those standing may resume their seats.

res ur rec tion (rez′ə rek′shən), 1. coming to life again; rising from the dead. **The Resurrection** is the rising again of Christ after His death and burial. 2. being alive again after death.

re tail (rē′tāl), 1. sale of goods in small quantities at a time. He buys at wholesale and sells at retail. 2. in small lots or quantities. The wholesale price of this coat is $20; the retail price is $30. 3. selling in small quantities; as, a retail merchant, the retail trade. 4. sell in small quantities. 5. tell over again. She retails everything she hears about her acquaintances.

re tail er (rē′tāl ər), retail merchant.

re tain (ri tān′), 1. keep. China dishes retain heat longer than metal pans do. The old lady has retained all her interest in life. 2. keep in mind; remember. She retained the tune but not the words of the song.

re tain er (ri tān′ər), one who serves a person

of rank; vassal; attendant; follower.

re tal i ate (ri tal′i āt), pay back a wrong or injury; to return like for like, usually to return evil for evil. If we insult people, they will retaliate.

re tard (ri tärd′), make slow; delay the progress of; keep back; hinder. Lack of education retards progress. Bad roads retard the car.

ret i nue (ret′i nū or ret′i nü), a group of attendants or followers. The King's retinue accompanied him on the journey.

re tire (ri tīr′), 1. withdraw; draw back; send back. The government retires worn or torn dollar bills from use. 2. go back; retreat. 3. go away to be quiet. She retired to a convent. 4. give up an office, occupation, etc. Our teachers retire at 70. 5. remove from an office, occupation, etc. 6. go to bed. We retire early.

re tired (ri tīrd′), 1. withdrawn from one's occupation; as, a retired captain, a retired teacher. 2. reserved; retiring. She has a shy, retired nature. 3. secluded; shut off; hidden; as, a retired spot.

re tire ment (ri tīr′mənt), 1. withdrawing or being withdrawn. The teacher's retirement from teaching was regretted by the school. 2. a quiet way or place of living. She lives in retirement, neither making nor receiving visits.

re tir ing (ri tīr′ing), shrinking from society or publicity; shy.

re tort (ri tôrt′), 1. reply quickly or sharply. "It's none of your business," he retorted. 2. a sharp or witty reply. "Why are your teeth so sharp?" asked Red Ridinghood. "The better to eat you with" was the wolf's retort.

re trace (ri trās′), go back over. We retraced our steps to where we started.

re tract (ri trakt′), 1. draw back or in. The dog snarled and retracted his lips. 2. withdraw; take back; as, to retract an offer or an opinion.

re treat (ri trēt′), 1. go back; withdraw. The enemy retreated before the advance of our soldiers. Seeing the big dog, the tramp retreated rapidly. 2. act of going back or withdrawing. The army's retreat was orderly. 3. signal for retreat. The drums beat a retreat. 4. a safe, quiet place; place of rest or refuge.

re trieve (ri trēv′), 1. get again; recover; as, to retrieve a lost pocketbook. 2. restore; bring back to a former or better condition; as, to retrieve one's fortunes. 3. make good. A person can retrieve a mistake, a loss, or a defeat. 4. find and bring to a person. Some dogs can be trained to retrieve game.

re turn (ri tėrn′), 1. bring back; give back; send back; put back; pay back. Return that book to the library. You took his cap; return it at once. Return good for evil. 2. bringing back; giving back; sending back; putting back; paying back. Dick's bad behavior was a poor return for his uncle's kindness. 3. go back; come back. Return home for your report card. Your mother will return in a moment. We'll return to this hard example after doing the easy ones. 4. going back; coming back. We look forward all winter to our return to the country. We wish you many happy returns of your birthday. 5. reply; answer. "Not I," he returned crossly. 6. report; account. I must send in my return today. The election returns are all in. 7. profit. The returns from the sale were more than a hundred dollars. 8. having something to do with a return; as, a return ticket. 9. sent, given, or done in return; as, a return game.

re un ion (rē ūn′yən), coming together again. We have a family reunion every Thanksgiving Day.

re u nite (rē′ū nīt′), bring together again; come together again. Mother and child were reunited after years of separation.

re veal (ri vēl′), 1. make known. Promise never to reveal my secret. 2. display; show. Her laugh revealed her even teeth.

rev eil le (rev′ə li), a signal on a bugle or drum to waken soldiers or sailors in the morning. The bugler blows reveille.

rev el (rev′əl), 1. take great pleasure. The children revel in country life. 2. a merrymaking; a noisy good time. Christmas revels with feasting and dancing were common in England. 3. make merry.

rev e la tion (rev′ə lā′shən), 1. act of making known. The revelation of the thieves' hiding place caused their capture. 2. the thing made known. Her true nature was a revelation to me.

rev el ry (rev′əl ri), boisterous reveling or festivity; wild merrymaking.

re venge (ri venj′), 1. harm done in return for a wrong; vengeance; returning evil for evil; as, a blow struck in revenge. 2. desire for vengeance. 3. to do harm in return for. I will revenge that insult. 4. **Revenge oneself on** a person means pay back the injury that person did to one. The cat revenged herself on John by scratching him. 5. **Be revenged** means have the person who hurt you get hurt in return.

re venge ful (ri venj′fəl), feeling or showing a strong desire for revenge.

rev e nue (rev′ə nū or rev′ə nü), money coming in; income. The government gets revenue from taxes.

re vere (ri vēr′), love and respect deeply; honor greatly; show reverence for. We revere noble, saintly men.

rev er ence (rev′ər əns), 1. a feeling of deep respect, mixed with wonder, fear, and love. 2. revere; regard with reverence. We reverence men of noble lives. 3. a deep bow.

rev er end (rev′ər ənd), 1. worthy of great respect. 2. a title for clergymen; as, the Reverend Thomas A. Johnson.

rev er ent (rev′ər ənt), feeling reverence; showing reverence. He gave reverent attention to the sermon.

rev er ie or **rev er y** (rev′ər i), dreamy thoughts; dreamy thinking of pleasant things. She was so lost in reverie that she did not hear the bell ring. He loved to indulge in reveries about his future.

re verse (ri vėrs′), 1. turned backward; opposite or contrary in position or direction. Play the reverse side of that record. 2. the opposite or contrary. She did the reverse of what I ordered. 3. the back. His name is on the reverse of the medal. 4. a change to bad fortune; check or defeat. He used to be rich, but he met with reverses. 5. to turn the other way; turn inside out; turn upside down. Reverse that gun; don't point it at me. 6. to change to the opposite; repeal.

re vert (ri vėrt′), go back; return. After the settlers left, the natives reverted to their savage customs. My thoughts reverted to the last time that I had seen her.

re view (ri vū′), 1. study again; look at again. Review today's lesson for tomorrow. 2. studying again. Before the examinations we have a review of the term's work. 3. look back on. Before falling asleep. Helen reviewed the day's happenings. 4. a looking back on. A review of the trip was pleasant. 5. look at with care; examine. 6. examination; inspection. A review of the troops will be held during the general's visit to camp. 7. inspect formally. The President reviewed the fleet.

re vile (ri vīl′), call bad names; abuse with words. The tramp reviled the man who drove him off.

re vise (ri vīz′), read carefully in order to correct; look over and change; examine and improve. Jean has revised the poem she wrote.

re viv al (ri vīv′əl), 1. bringing or coming back to life or consciousness. 2. restoration to vigor or health. 3. bringing or coming back to style or use; as, the revival of a play of years ago. 4. an awakening or increase of interest in religion.

re vive (ri vīv′), 1. bring back or come back to life or consciousness. Tom was nearly drowned, but we revived him. 2. come back to a fresh, lively condition. The flowers revived in water. 3. restore; make fresh. Hot coffee revives a cold tired man. 4. bring back or come back to notice, use, fashion, memory, activity, etc.

re volt (ri vōlt′), 1. turn away from and fight against a leader; rise against the government's authority. The people revolted against the king. 2. act or state of rebelling. The town is in revolt. 3. turn away with disgust; as, to revolt at a bad smell. 4. to cause to feel disgust. A dirty house revolts mother.

rev o lu tion (rev′ə lü′shən), 1. a complete change in government. 2. complete change. The automobile caused a revolution in ways of traveling. 3. a moving round some point in a circle or curve. One revolution of the earth around the sun takes a year. 4. turning round. The revolution of the earth causes day and night.

rev o lu tion ar y (rev′ə lü′shən ãr′i), 1. of a revolution; connected with a revolution. 2. bringing or causing great changes.

rev o lu tion ize (rev′ə lü′shən īz), change completely; produce a very great change in. The automobile and radio revolutionized country life. The new chief of police says he will revolutionize that department.

re volve (ri volv′), 1. move in a circle; move in a curve round a point. The moon revolves around the earth. 2. turn round. The wheels of a moving car revolve. 3. turn over in the mind; consider from many points of view. He wishes to revolve the problem before giving an answer.

re volv er (ri vol′vər), a pistol that can be fired several times without loading it again.

Revolver

re ward (ri wôrd′), 1. return made for something done. 2. money payment given or offered. Rewards are given for the capture of criminals, the return of lost property, etc. 3. give a reward to. 4. give a reward for.

rheu ma tism (rü′mə tizm), a disease with inflammation, swelling, and stiffness of the joints.

rhi noc er os (rī nos′ər əs), large, thick-skinned animal of Africa and Asia with one or two upright horns on the snout.

Rhinoceros (5 ft. high; 10 ft. long)

rhu barb (rü′bärb), 1. a garden plant with very large leaves, whose sour stalks are used for making sauce, pies, etc. 2. the stalks. 3. sauce made of them.

Rhubarb

rhyme (rīm), 1. sound alike in the last part. *Long* and *song* rhyme. *Go to bed* rhymes with *sleepy head.* 2. a word or line having the same last sound as another. *Cat* is a rhyme for *mat.* "Hey! diddle, diddle" and "The cat and the fiddle" are rhymes. 3. verses or poetry with a regular return of similar sounds. 4. agreement in the final sounds of words or lines. 5. make rhymes. Also spelled **rime.**

rhythm (riᴛʜm), movement with a regular repetition of a beat, accent, rise and fall, or the like; as, the rhythm of dancing, or the rhythm of the tides.

rib (rib), 1. one of the curved bones extending round the chest from the backbone to the front of the body. 2. something like a rib. The curved timbers in a ship's frame are called ribs. The thick vein of a leaf is also called a rib.

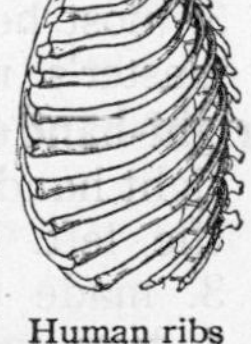

Human ribs

rib bon (rib′ən), 1. a strip or band of silk, satin, velvet, etc. Bows for the hair, belts, and badges are often made of ribbon. 2. anything like such a strip; as, a typewriter ribbon. Her dress was torn to ribbons by the thorns and briers she had come through.

rice (rīs), 1. the seeds or grain of a certain plant grown in warm climates. Rice is an important food in India, China, and Japan. 2. the plant itself.

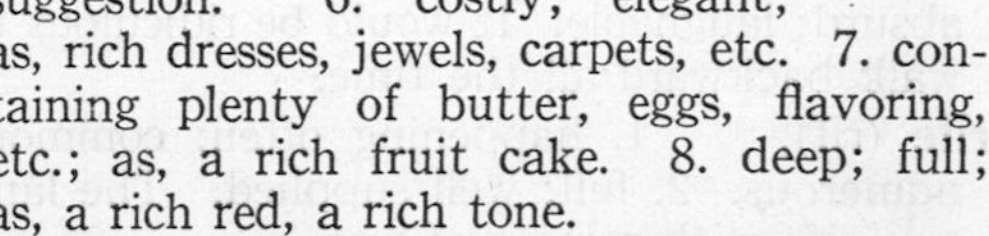

Rice

rich (rich), 1. having much money, land, goods, etc. 2. rich people. 3. abounding; well supplied. The United States is rich in oil and coal. 4. fertile; producing much; as, a rich soil, a rich mine. 5. valuable; worthy; as, a rich harvest, a rich suggestion. 6. costly; elegant; as, rich dresses, jewels, carpets, etc. 7. containing plenty of butter, eggs, flavoring, etc.; as, a rich fruit cake. 8. deep; full; as, a rich red, a rich tone.

rich es (rich′iz), wealth; abundance of property; much money, land, goods, etc.

rich ness (rich′nis), rich condition or quality. The richness of the soil favored the growth of crops.

rick et y (rik′i ti), 1. weak; liable to fall or break down; shaky; as, a rickety chair. 2. feeble in the joints.

rid (rid), make free. What will rid a house of rats? **Get rid of** means get free from. I can't get rid of this cold.

rid den (rid′ən). See **ride.** The horseman had ridden all day.

rid dle[1] (rid′əl), a puzzling question, statement, problem, etc. *Example:* When is a door not a door? *Answer:* When it is ajar.

rid dle[2] (rid′əl), 1. make many holes in. The door of the fort was riddled with shot. 2. a coarse sieve. 3. sift; as, to riddle gravel.

ride (rīd), 1. sit on a horse and make it go. 2. sit on something and make it go; as, to ride a camel, to ride a bicycle. 3. manage; control. 4. be carried along; as, to ride on a train, to ride in a car. 5. move or float on the water. The ship rides at anchor. 6. a trip on horseback, in an automobile, on a train, etc. **rode** and **ridden** are formed from **ride.**

rid er (rīd′ər), 1. person who rides. The West is famous for its riders. 2. anything added to a record, document, or statement after it was supposed to be complete.

ridge (rij), 1. the long and narrow upper part of something; as, the ridge of an animal's back. 2. the line where two sloping surfaces meet; as, the ridge of a roof. 3. a long narrow chain of hills or mountains. 4. any raised narrow strip; as, the ridges in plowed ground, the ridges on corduroy cloth. 5. make into ridges; form into ridges. 6. cover with ridges.

ridge pole (rij′pōl′), the horizontal timber along the top of a roof or tent.

rid i cule (rid′i kūl), 1. laugh at; make fun of. 2. laughter in mockery; words or actions that make fun of somebody or something. Percy's curls made him an object of ridicule.

ri dic u lous (ri dik′ū ləs), deserving ridicule; absurd; laughable. It would be ridiculous to walk backward all the time.

rife (rīf), 1. happening often; common; numerous. 2. full; well supplied. The land was rife with rumors of war.

ri fle[1] (rī′fəl), 1. gun with spiral grooves in its barrel which spin or twist the bullet as it is shot. 2. cut such grooves in.

ri fle[2] (rī′fəl), 1. search and rob; ransack and rob. 2. steal; take away. 3. strip bare. The bad boys rifled the apple tree.

ri fle man (rī′fəl mən), 1. soldier armed with a rifle. 2. man skilled in the use of the rifle.

rift (rift), split; cleft; break; crack. There's a rift in the clouds; perhaps the sun will come out soon.

rig (rig), 1. fit (a ship) with masts and sails; fit out. The sailor rigged a toy boat for the little boy. 2. the arrangement of masts, sails, etc., on a ship. The rig of a schooner is not the same as the rig of a brig. 3. dress. On Halloween the children rig themselves up in queer clothes. John's rig consisted of a silk hat and overalls.

rig ging (rig′ing), 1. the ropes, chains, etc., used to support and work the masts, yards, sails, etc., on a ship. 2. tackle; equipment. Do you need all that rigging for a trip of only two days?

right (rīt), 1. good; just; lawful. Jack did the right thing when he told the truth. 2. in a way that is good, just, or lawful. 3. correct; true; as, the right answer. 4. that which is right, just, good, true. Do right, not wrong. 5. a just claim; something that is due to a person. Each member of the club has a right to vote. He demanded his rights. A **right of way** is the right to pass over another's land. 6. correctly. I guessed right. **By rights** or **by right** means rightly; properly; correctly. 7. fitting; suitable; proper. Learn to say the right thing at the right time. 8. properly; well. It serves you right to lose if you cheat. 9. well; healthy; in good condition. Tommy was thin and pale, but he looks all right now. 10. meant to be seen; most important; as, the right side of cloth. 11. make correct; set right; as, to right a wrong. 12. to put right; get into the proper position. The boys righted the boat. The ship righted after the big wave passed. 13. You have a right hand and a left hand. Your right side is toward the east when you face north. Most people eat, write, and work with their right hands. 14. the right-hand side; as, turn to your right, the school on the right. 15. to the right hand; as, turn right. 16. exactly. Your cap is right where you left it. 17. at once; immediately. Stop playing right now. 18. very; as, right honorable. 19. in a straight line; directly. Dick looked the man right in the eye. 20. straight.

right angle, an angle that is formed by a line perpendicular to another line, as shown in the diagram. The angles in a square or in the capital letters F, L, and T are right angles. ⊥

right eous (rī′chəs), 1. doing right; virtuous; behaving justly. 2. proper; just; right; as, righteous anger.

right eous ness (rī′chəs nis), upright conduct; virtue; being right and just.

right ful (rīt′fəl), 1. according to law; by rights; as, the rightful owner of this dog. 2. just and right; proper.

right ful ly (rīt′fəl i), 1. according to right, law, or justice. 2. properly.

right-hand (rīt′hand′), 1. situated on the right. 2. of, for, or with the right hand. 3. most helpful or useful. Ben is the scoutmaster's right-hand man.

right-hand ed (rīt′han′did), 1. using the right hand more easily and more readily than the left. 2. done with the right hand. 3. made to be used with the right hand. 4. turning from left to right.

right ly (rīt′li), 1. justly; fairly. 2. correctly. He rightly guessed that I was safe. 3. properly; in a suitable manner.

rig id (rij′id), 1. stiff; firm; not bending.

Hold your arm rigid. 2. strict; not changing. In our home, it is a rigid rule to wash one's hands before eating.

rig or (rig′ər), strictness; severity; as, the rigor of a long, cold winter.

rig or ous (rig′ər əs), 1. very severe; harsh; strict; as, the rigorous discipline in a prison. 2. exact; thoroughly logical and scientific.

rill (ril), tiny stream; little brook.

rim (rim), 1. an edge, border, or margin on or around anything; as, the rim of a wheel, the rim of a cup. 2. form a rim around. Wild flowers and grasses rimmed the little pool.

rime[1] (rīm), rhyme.

rime[2] (rīm), white frost; hoarfrost.

rind (rīnd), firm outer covering. We do not eat the rind of oranges, melons, and cheese. The bark of a tree or plant may be called the rind.

ring[1] (ring), 1. circle. The fairies danced in a ring. You can tell the age of a tree by the number of rings in the wood. 2. thin circle of metal, etc.; as, a wedding ring, a key ring, a napkin ring. 3. put a ring around; enclose; form a circle around. 4. enclosed space (for races or games); as, a circus ring, a ring for a fight.

Finger rings

ring[2] (ring), 1. sound or cause to sound. Did the telephone ring? Ring the doorbell. His words ring true. Ring the coin on the counter to find out if it is good money. 2. echo; give back sound. The woods rang with their shouts. 3. sound of a bell. Did you hear a ring? 4. a sound like that of a bell. On a cold night we can hear the ring of the skates on ice. **rang** and **rung** are formed from **ring**[2].

ring let (ring′lit), 1. little ring. Drops of rain made ringlets in the pond. 2. curl. She wears her hair in ringlets.

rink (ringk), 1. a sheet of ice for skating. 2. a smooth floor for roller skating.

rinse (rins), 1. wash with clean water. Rinse all the soap out of your hair after you wash it. Give it a last rinse in cold water. 2. wash lightly. Rinse your mouth with water and soda. 3. a rinsing.

ri ot (rī′ət), 1. disturbance; confusion; disorder; a wild, violent public disturbance. The police stopped several riots on election night. 2. behave in a wild, disorderly way. 3. revel.

run riot, 1. act without restraint. 2. grow wildly.

ri ot ous (rī′ət əs), taking part in a riot; boisterous; disorderly. He was expelled from college for riotous conduct. Sounds of riotous glee came from the playhouse.

rip (rip), 1. cut roughly; tear apart; tear off. Rip the cover off this box. 2. cut or pull out (the threads in the seams of a garment). 3. torn place; a seam burst in a garment. Please sew up this rip in my sleeve.

ripe (rīp), 1. full-grown and ready to be gathered and eaten; as, ripe fruit, ripe grain, ripe vegetables. 2. fully developed and fit to use; as, ripe knowledge. 3. ready; as, ripe for mischief.

rip en (rīp′ən), become ripe; make ripe.

rip ple (rip′əl), 1. a very little wave. Throw a stone into still water and watch the ripples spread in rings. 2. anything that seems like a tiny wave; as, ripples in hair. 3. a sound that reminds one of little waves; as, a ripple of laughter in the crowd. 4. make little ripples on. A breeze rippled the quiet waters.

rise (rīz), 1. stand up; get up. Rise when you recite. The slaves rose in rebellion against their masters. 2. go up; come up. The kite rises in the air. Bread rises. Mercury rises in a thermometer on a hot day. Fish rise to the surface. 3. go higher; increase. The wind rose rapidly. His anger rose at that remark. Butter rose five cents in price. 4. going up; increase. We watched the rise of the balloon. There had been a great rise in prices since the war. 5. slope upward. Hills rise in the distance. 6. start; begin. The river rises from a spring. Quarrels often rise from trifles. 7. origin; beginning. Mr. Gotto's queer behavior gave rise to the fear that he was becoming insane. 8. upward slope. The rise of the hill is gradual. The house is situated on a rise. **rose** and **risen** are formed from **rise.**

ris en (riz′ən). See **rise.** The sun had risen long before I woke up.

ris ing (rīz′ing), 1. act of that which rises; as, the rising of the sun. Seven o'clock is my hour for rising. 2. a fight against the government; revolt. 3. that rises; advancing in power, influence, etc.; growing.

risk (risk), 1. chance of harm or loss; danger. He rescued the dog at the risk of his own life. If you drive carefully, there is no risk of being fined. 2. expose to the chance of harm or loss. Don't risk any money in oil stock. You risk your neck trying to climb that tree. 3. take the risk of. They risked defeat in fighting the larger army.

risk y (ris′ki), full of risk; dangerous.

rite (rīt), solemn ceremony. The church has rites for baptism, marriage, and burial. Secret societies have their special rites.

ri val (rī′vəl), 1. person who wants the same thing as another; one who tries to equal or do better than another. The two boys were rivals for the same class office. They were also rivals in sports. 2. wanting the same thing as another; being a rival. A rival store tried to get our grocer's trade. 3. try to equal or outdo. The stores rival each other in beautiful window displays. 4. equal; match. The sunset rivaled the sunrise in beauty.

ri val ry (rī′vəl ri), competition; effort to obtain something another person wants.

riv en (riv′ən), torn apart; split.

riv er (riv′ər), large stream of water.

riv er side (riv′ər sīd′), 1. the bank of a river. We walked along the riverside. 2. beside a river. The riverside path is much used.

riv et (riv′it), 1. metal bolt with each end hammered into a head. Rivets fasten heavy steel beams together. 2. fasten with rivets. 3. fasten firmly; fix firmly. Their eyes were riveted on the speaker.

riv u let (riv′ū lit), very small stream.

road (rōd), 1. a way between places; as, the road from New York to Boston. Our road went through the woods. 2. a way; as, the road to ruin, a road to peace. 3. a place near the shore where ships may anchor.

road side (rōd′sīd′), 1. the side of a road. Flowers grew along the roadside. 2. beside a road; as, a roadside inn.

road way (rōd′wā′), 1. road. 2. the part of a road used by wheeled vehicles. Walk on the path, not in the roadway.

roam (rōm), wander; go about with no special plan or aim; as, to roam through the fields.

roan (rōn), 1. yellowish or reddish brown sprinkled with gray or white. 2. a roan horse.

roar (rōr), 1. make a loud deep sound; make a loud noise. The bull roared with anger. The wind roared at the windows. 2. a loud deep sound; loud noise; as, the roar of the cannon, a roar of laughter.

roast (rōst), 1. bake; cook by dry heat. We roasted meat and potatoes. 2. piece of baked meat; piece of meat to be roasted. 3. roasted; as, roast beef, roast pork. 4. prepare by heating; as, to roast coffee, to roast a metal ore. 5. make or become very hot.

rob (rob), take away from by force; steal. Thieves robbed the bank of thousands of dollars. Some boys robbed the orchard. They said they would not rob again.

rob ber (rob′ər), person who robs; thief.

rob ber y (rob′ər i), robbing; theft; stealing.

robe (rōb), 1. long, loose, outer garment. The priests wore robes. John has a bathrobe. 2. garment that shows rank, office, etc.; as, a judge's robe, the king's robes of state. 3. covering or wrap. Put a robe over you if you go for a ride on a cold day. 4. put a robe on; dress.

rob in (rob′in), 1. a large American thrush with a reddish breast. 2. a small European bird with a yellowish-red breast.

American robin

Rob in Hood (rob′in hu̇d′), in English legend, an outlaw who robbed the rich but gave money to the poor.

ro bust (rō bust′), strong and healthy, sturdy.

rock[1] (rok), 1. large mass of stone. The ship was wrecked on the rocks. 2. stone. The earth's crust is made up of rock under a layer of soil. 3. made of rock. 4. something firm like a rock; support; defense. Christ is called the Rock of Ages.

rock[2] (rok), 1. move backward and forward, or from side to side. My chair rocks. The waves rocked the ship. The earthquake rocked the houses. Mother rocked the baby to sleep. 2. a rocking.

rock er (rok′ər), 1. one of the curved pieces on which a cradle, rocking chair, etc., rocks. See the picture under **rocking chair.** 2. rocking chair.

Rocket

rock et (rok′it), 1. a firework that shoots up high in the air and bursts into a shower of sparks or stars. Rockets are used by ships as signals of distress. 2. go like a rocket.

rocking chair, chair mounted on rockers, or on springs, so that it can rock back and forth.

rock y[1] (rok′i), 1. full of rocks. 2. made of rock. 3. like rock; hard; firm.

rock y[2] (rok′i), shaky; likely to rock. That table is a bit rocky; put a piece of wood under the short leg.

ROCKERS

Rocking chair

rod (rod), 1. a thin straight bar of metal or wood. 2. a thin straight stick, either growing or cut off. 3. a stick used to beat or punish; punishment. 4. a long light pole; a fishing pole. 5. a measure, $5\frac{1}{2}$ yards or $16\frac{1}{2}$ feet. A square rod is $30\frac{1}{4}$ square yards or $272\frac{1}{4}$ square feet.

rode (rōd). See **ride.** We rode ten miles yesterday.

ro dent (rō′dənt), 1. an animal that gnaws. Rats, mice, squirrels, hares, and rabbits are rodents. 2. gnawing.

ro de o (rō dā′ō or rō′di ō), 1. a contest or exhibition of skill in roping cattle, riding horses, etc. 2. the driving of cattle together.

roe[1] (rō), fish eggs.

roe[2] (rō), a small deer of Europe and Asia.

rogue (rōg), 1. tricky, dishonest, or worthless person; rascal. The **rogues' gallery** is a collection of photographs of known criminals. 2. Rogue is used playfully to mean a mischievous person. The little rogue has his grandpa's glasses on. 3. an animal with a savage nature that lives apart from the herd. A rogue elephant is very dangerous.

rôle or **role** (rōl), 1. an actor's part in a play. Helen wished to play the leading rôle. 2. a part played in real life. A mother's rôle is to comfort and console.

roll (rōl), 1. move along by turning over and over. Wheels roll. A ball rolls. The child rolls a hoop. 2. turn round and round on itself or on something else; wrap; be wrapped round. She rolled the string into a ball. The boy rolled himself up in a blanket. 3. move on wheels. The nurse rolls the baby carriage. The automobile rolls along. 4. move smoothly; sweep along. Waves roll in on the beach. The years roll on. 5. make flat or smooth with a roller; spread out with a rolling pin, etc. Rolling the grass makes a smooth lawn. Mother rolls the dough for cookies. 6. move with a side-to-side motion. The ship rolls in the waves. The girl rolled her eyes. 7. the act of rolling; motion from side to side. The ship's roll made many people sick. 8. rise and fall again and again; as, rolling country, rolling waves. 9. trill; as, to roll your r's. 10. make deep, loud sounds. Thunder rolls. 11. a deep, loud sound. 12. pile (up); increase. Bills roll up fast. 13. anything rolled up; as, a roll of carpet, a roll of paper. 14. a list of names; list. I will call the roll to find out who are absent. 15. a rounded or rolled-up mass; as, a roll of butter. 16. a kind of bread or cake; as, a sweet roll.

roll er (rōl′ər), 1. thing that rolls; cylinder on which something is rolled along or rolled up. 2. a cylinder of metal, stone, wood, etc., used for smoothing, pressing, crushing, etc. A steam roller is used in making and repairing roads. A wet garment is put between the rollers of a clothes wringer to squeeze out the water in it. 3. a long, swelling wave. Huge rollers broke on the rocky shore. 4. person who rolls something.

Steam roller

roller skate, a skate with small wheels instead of a runner, for use on a floor or sidewalk.

Roller skate

rolling pin, a cylinder of wood or glass about a foot long for rolling out dough. See the picture just below.

Ro man Cath o lic (rō′mən kath′ə lik), 1. of, pertaining to, or belonging to the Christian church that recognizes the Pope as the supreme head. 2. member of this church.

Rolling pin

ro mance (rō mans′), 1. a story or poem telling of heroes. 2. a story of adventure. 3. a love story; a love affair. 4. interest in adventure and love. 5. a made-up story. Nobody believes her romances about the wonderful things that have happened to her. 6. make up romances; think or talk in a romantic way. Some children romance because of their lively imaginations.

ro man tic (rō man′tik), 1. characteristic of romances or romance; appealing to fancy and the imagination. She likes romantic tales of love and war. May thinks it would be romantic to be an actress. 2. having ideas or feelings suited to romance. The romantic schoolgirl's mind was full of handsome heroes, jewels, balls, and fine clothes. 3. suited to a romance. What a romantic wood! Fairies might live here!

romp (romp), 1. to play in a rough, boisterous way; rush, tumble, and punch in play. 2. rough, lively play or frolic. A pillow fight is a romp. 3. a girl or boy who likes to romp.

roof (rüf), 1. the top covering of a building. 2. something like it; as, the roof of a cave, the roof of a car, the roof of the mouth. 3. to cover with a roof; form a roof over. The trees roofed the glade where we camped.

roof tree (rüf′trē′), the horizontal timber along the top of a roof.

Rook (about 19 in. long)

rook (rük), a European crow that nests in trees near buildings.

room (rüm), 1. a part of a house, or other building, with walls of its own; as, a dining room, a schoolroom. 2. people in a room. The whole room laughed. 3. space. The street was so crowded that the cars did not have room to move. There is room for one more in the automobile. 4. opportunity. There is room for improvement in John's work. 5. occupy a room; live in a room. Mr. Smith rooms in the gray house. Ethel rooms with Edith in the college dormitory.

room i ness (rüm′i nis), ample space.

room mate (rüm′māt′), person who shares a room with another.

room y (rüm′i), large; spacious; having plenty of room.

roost (rüst), 1. a bar, pole, or perch on which birds rest or sleep. 2. sit as birds do on a roost; settle for the night. 3. place for birds to roost in. 4. a place to rest or stay in; as, a robber's roost in the mountains.

Rooster

roost er (rüs′tər), male domestic fowl. See the picture just above.

root[1] (rüt), 1. the part of a plant that grows down into the soil, holds it in place, and feeds it. 2. any underground part of a plant. 3. something like a root in shape, position, use, etc.; as, the root of a tooth, the roots of the hair. 4. a part from which other things grow and develop; a cause; source. "The love of money is the root of all evil." 5. become fixed in the ground; send out roots and begin to grow. Some plants root more quickly than others. 6. fix firmly. He was rooted to the spot by surprise. 7. **Root out** means get completely rid of.

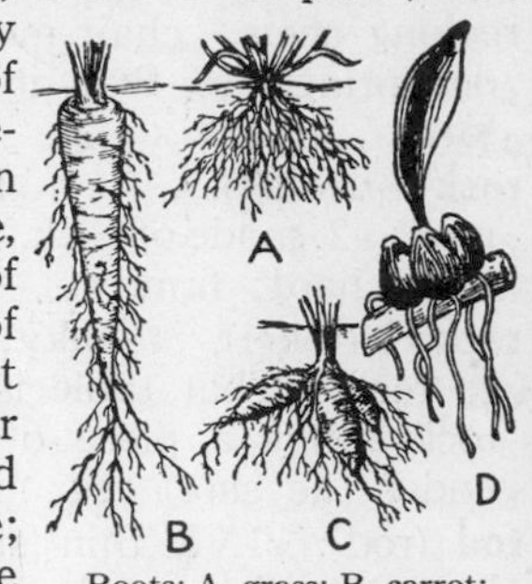

Roots: A, grass; B, carrot; C, sweet potato; D, orchid.

root[2] (rüt), dig with the snout. The pigs rooted up the garden.

rope (rōp), 1. a strong thick line or cord made by twisting smaller cords together. 2. a number of things twisted or strung together; as, a rope of onions, a rope of pearls. 3. to tie, bind, or fasten with rope. 4. enclose or mark off with a rope. 5. catch with a lasso. 6. a sticky, stringy mass; as, a rope of molasses candy. 7. **Know the ropes** means (1) know the various ropes of a ship. (2) know about a business or activity.

Rope (def. 1)

ro sa ry (rō′zə ri), 1. a series of prayers. 2. a string of beads for keeping count in saying these prayers. 3. rose garden.

rose[1] (rōz), 1. a flower that grows on a bush with thorny stems. Roses are red, pink, white, or yellow. They usually smell very sweet. 2. pinkish red; rose-pink. Her dress was rose. 3. something shaped like a rose, or suggesting a rose.

rose[2] (rōz). See **rise.** The cat rose and stretched itself.

rose bud (rōz′bud′), the bud of a rose.

ro sette (rō zet′), an ornament shaped like a rose. Rosettes are often made of ribbon.

ros in (roz′in), a hard, yellow substance made from turpentine gum. Rosin is rubbed on violin bows, and on the shoes of circus performers to keep them from slipping.

ros y (rōz′i), 1. like a rose; rose-red; pinkish-red. 2. bright; cheerful; as, a rosy future.

rot (rot), 1. decay; spoil. So much rain will make the fruit rot. 2. process of rotting; decay. 3. a disease of plants and animals, especially sheep.

ro tate (rō′tāt), 1. move around a center or axis; turn in a circle; revolve. Wheels, tops, and the earth rotate. 2. change in a fixed order; cause to take turns; as, to rotate crops in a field.

ro ta tion (rō tā′shən), 1. a turning round; as, the rotation of a top. The earth's rotation causes night and day. 2. **In rotation** means in turn; in regular succession. 3. **Rota-tion of crops** means varying the crops grown in the same field.

rot ten (rot′ən), 1. decayed; spoiled. 2. foul; bad-smelling; as, rotten air. 3. not in good condition; unsound; weak. The rotten ice gave way, and John fell into the water. 4. corrupt; dishonest.

rouge (rüzh), 1. a red powder or paste for coloring the cheeks or lips. 2. to color with rouge.

rough (ruf), 1. not smooth; not level; as, a rough, rocky hill. 2. stormy; as, rough weather. 3. harsh; rude; not gentle; likely to hurt others; as, rough manners. 4. without luxury and ease; as, rough life in camp. **Rough it** means live without comforts and conveniences. 5. without polish or fine finish; as, rough diamonds. 6. not completed; done as a first try; without details; as, a rough drawing, a rough idea. 7. coarse and tangled; as, rough fur, a rough coat of hair. 8. a coarse, violent person. 9. make rough; roughen. 10. roughly.

rough en (ruf′ən), 1. make rough. 2. become rough.

rough ly (ruf′li), 1. in a rough manner. 2. approximately. From New York to Los Angeles is roughly three thousand miles.

rough ness (ruf′nis), 1. the state or quality of being rough. 2. a rough part or place.

round (round), 1. shaped like a ball. 2. shaped like a ring or circle. 3. shaped like the trunk of a tree. 4. full; complete; large; as, a round dozen, a good round sum of money. 5. plain-spoken; frank; plainly expressed. Dan's father scolded him in good round terms. 6. with a full tone; as, a mellow, round voice. 7. vigorous; brisk; quick; as, a round trot. 8. spoken with the lips curved. *O* is a round vowel. 9. anything shaped like a ball or circle or tree trunk; as, the rounds of a ladder. 10. a fixed course ending where it begins. The watchman makes his rounds every hour. 11. movement in a circle or about an axis; as, the earth's yearly round. 12. a cut of beef just above the leg. 13. a dance in which the dancers move in a circle. 14. a series (of duties, events, etc.); routine; as, a round of pleasures, a round of duties. 15. a section of a game or sport; as, a round in a fight, a round of cards. 16. the distance between any limits; range; circuit; as, the round of human knowledge. 17. an act which a number of people do together; as, a round of applause, a round of cheers. 18. a short song sung by several persons or groups beginning one after another. "Three Blind Mice" is a round. 19. a discharge of guns by a group of soldiers all together. 20. powder, bullets, etc., for one such discharge. Only three rounds of ammunition were left. 21. make or become round. We round our lips to say *oo*. 22. go round; make a turn to the other side of; as, to round a corner, to round Cape Horn. 23. to fill (out); complete; as, to round out a paragraph, to round out a career. 24. **Round up** means drive or bring (cattle, etc.) together. 25. on all sides; around. The travelers were compassed round by dangers. 26. in a circle; with a whirling motion. Wheels go round. 27. in circumference; the distance around. The pumpkin measures 50 inches round. 28. from one to another. A report is going round that the schools will close early. 29. through a round of time. Summer will soon come round again. In the tropics it is warm all the year round. 30. by a longer road or way. 31. on all sides of; so as to make a turn to the other side of. 32. about; around. 33. in all directions from; to all parts of.

round a bout (round′ə bout′), indirect; as, a roundabout route, to hear in a roundabout way.

round ish (roun′dish), somewhat round.

round ly (round′li), 1. in a round manner; in a circle. 2. plainly; bluntly; severely; as, to refuse roundly, to scold roundly. 3. fully; completely.

round-shoul dered (round′shōl′dərd), having the shoulders bent forward.

round trip, a trip to a place and back again.

round up (round′up′), 1. act of driving or bringing cattle together from long distances. 2. the men and horses who round up cattle. 3. any similar gathering; as, a roundup of old friends.

rouse (rouz), wake up; stir up; excite. I was roused by the telephone bell. The dogs roused a deer from the bushes. He was roused to anger by the insult.

rout[1] (rout), 1. flight of a defeated army in disorder; complete defeat. 2. put to flight; defeat completely. Our soldiers routed the enemy.

rout[2] (rout), 1. dig (out); get by searching. 2. put (out); force (out). The farmer routed his sons out of bed at five o'clock. 3. dig with the snout. The pigs were routing for nuts under the trees.

route (rüt or rout), 1. way to go; road. Shall you go to the coast by the northern route? 2. arrange the way for. 3. send by a certain route.

rou tine (rü tēn′), 1. a fixed, regular method of doing things; habitual doing of the same things in the same way. Getting up and going to bed are parts of your daily routine. 2. using routine; as, routine methods, routine workers.

rove (rōv), wander; wander about; roam. He roved over the fields and woods.

rov er (rōv′ər), 1. wanderer. 2. pirate. 3. pirate ship.

row[1] (rō), line; rank. The children stood in a row in front of the row of chairs. Corn is planted in rows.

row[2] (rō), 1. use oars. 2. move by oars. Row us to the island. 3. trip in a rowboat. It's only a short row.

Boy rowing a rowboat

row[3] (rou), noisy quarrel; noise. The children had a row over the bicycle. What's all this row about?

row boat (rō′bōt′), boat moved by oars. See the picture just above.

roy al (roi′əl), 1. of kings and queens; as, the royal family. 2. belonging to a king or queen; as, royal power, a royal palace. 3. from or by a king or queen; as, a royal command. 4. of a kingdom. 5. appropriate for a king; splendid; as, a royal welcome, a royal feast. 6. like a king. The lion is a royal beast.

roy al ly (roi′əl i), in a royal manner; grandly; richly.

roy al ty (roi′əl ti), 1. a royal person; royal persons. Kings, queens, princes, and princesses are royalty. A box in the theater was reserved for royalty. 2. the rank or dignity of a king or queen; royal power. The crown is the symbol of royalty. 3. kingly nature; royal quality; nobility.

rub (rub), 1. move one thing back and forth against another. He rubs his hands with soap. 2. to clean, smooth, or polish by moving one thing firmly against another. Rub out your work with an eraser and do it over again. 3. push and press along the surface of. The nurse rubbed Dick's lame back. That door rubs on the floor. 4. act of rubbing. Give the silver a rub with the polish. 5. thing that rubs or hurts the feelings. He didn't like her mean rub at his slowness. 6. difficulty. The rub came when both boys wanted to sit with the driver.

rub ber (rub′ər), 1. person or thing that rubs. 2. an elastic substance made from the juice of certain tropical plants. Rubber will not let water through. 3. made of rubber. 4. something made from this substance. I need a strong rubber to hold these papers together. We wear rubbers on our feet when it rains. Pencils often have rubbers for erasing pencil marks.

rub bish (rub′ish), 1. waste stuff of no use; trash. Pick up the rubbish and burn it. 2. nonsense; silly words and thoughts.

ru by (rü′bi), 1. a precious stone, red in color, clear, and hard. Real rubies are very rare. 2. red; as, ruby lips, ruby wine.

rud der (rud′ər), 1. a movable flat piece at the rear end of a boat or ship by which it is steered. See the picture. 2. a similar piece in an airplane. See the diagram of **airplane.**

Rudder of a boat

rud dy (rud′i), 1. red. 2. healthy red; as, ruddy cheeks.

rude (rüd), 1. coarse; rough; without finish or polish. He made a rude bed from the branches of evergreen trees. The savage made rude ornaments from shells and pebbles. 2. rough in manners or behavior; violent. Rude hands seized the child and threw him into the car. John had a rude shock when the other boys poured a pail of water on him. 3. not polite; not courteous. It is rude to stare at people or to point. 4. not having learned much; rather wild; barbarous. Life is rude in tribes that have few tools.

rude ness (rüd′nis), roughness; coarseness; bad manners; violence. His rudeness is inexcusable.

ru di ment (rü′di mənt), 1. part to be learned first; beginning; as, the rudiments of arithmetic. 2. something in an early stage; as, the rudiments of wings on a baby chick.

ru di men ta ry (rü′di men′tə ri), 1. to be learned or studied first; elementary. 2. in an early stage of development.

rue (rü), be sorry for; repent; regret. She will rue the day she insulted your mother.

rue ful (rü′fəl), 1. sorrowful; unhappy; mournful; as, a rueful expression. 2. causing sorrow or pity; as, a rueful sight.

Ruff

ruff (ruf), 1. a deep frill stiff enough to stand out, worn around the neck by men and women in the 16th century. 2. a collar of specially marked feathers or hairs on the neck of a bird or other animal.

ruf fi an (ruf′i ən), 1. a rough, brutal, or cruel fellow. 2. rough; cruel.

ruf fle (ruf′əl), 1. to wrinkle; make rough or uneven. A breeze ruffled the lake. The hen ruffled her feathers at the sight of the dog. 2. a strip of cloth, ribbon, or lace gathered along one edge and used for trimming. Ruffles used to be much worn; even men had ruffled shirts. 3. gather into a ruffle. 4. disturb; annoy. Nothing can ruffle her calm temper.

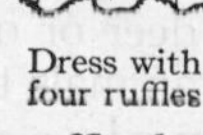

Dress with four ruffles

rug (rug), 1. a heavy floor covering. We have rag rugs, a fur rug, and a grass rug. 2. a thick warm cloth used as covering. He wrapped his woolen rug around him.

rug ged (rug′id), 1. rough; wrinkled. 2. harsh; stern; severe. The early settlers led rugged lives. 3. strong; vigorous.

ru in (rü′in), 1. a building, wall, etc., that has fallen to pieces. That ruin was once a famous castle. 2. destruction; very great damage; overthrow. The ruin of property caused by the earthquake was enormous. They planned the duke's ruin. 3. a fallen or decayed condition. The house had gone to ruin from neglect. 4. cause of destruction, decay, or downfall. Gambling was his ruin. 5. destroy; spoil; bring to ruin. The rain has ruined my new dress.

ru in ous (rü′i nəs), 1. causing ruin. 2. fallen into ruins.

rule (rül), 1. a principle governing conduct, action, etc.; statement of what to do and what not to do. Learn the rules of the game. 2. set of rules; as, the rule of Saint Benedict. 3. decide; make a rule. 4. to control; govern. The majority rules in a democracy. 5. control; government. Democracy means the rule of the people. 6. regular method; thing that usually happens; what is usually true. Fair weather is the rule in June. **As a rule** means usually. 7. straight strip of wood, metal, etc., used to measure or as a guide in drawing. 8. to mark with lines. He used a ruler to rule the paper. 9. mark off.

Rule or ruler

rul er (rül′ər), 1. person who rules. 2. a straight strip of wood, metal, etc., used in drawing lines. See the picture above.

rum (rum), 1. alcoholic liquor made from sugar cane, molasses, etc. 2. alcoholic liquor.

rum ble (rum′bəl), 1. make a deep, heavy, continuous sound. 2. a deep, heavy, continuous sound. We hear the far-off rumble of thunder. 3. move with such a sound. 4. the rear part of an automobile or carriage containing an extra seat or a place for baggage.

rum mage (rum′ij), 1. search thoroughly by moving things about. I rummaged three drawers before I found my gloves. 2. search in a disorderly way. I rummaged in my drawer for a pair of gloves. 3. pull from among other things. 4. a rummaging search.

ru mor (rü′mər), 1. a story or statement talked of as news without any proof that it is true. The rumor spread that a new school would be built here. 2. vague, general talk. Rumor said that Italy would quarrel with France. 3. tell or spread by rumor.

rump (rump), the hind part of the body of an animal, where the legs join the back. A rump steak is a cut of beef from this part.

rum ple (rum′pəl), crumple; crush; wrinkle. Don't play in your best dress; you'll rumple it.

run (run), 1. move the legs quickly; go faster than walking. A horse can run faster than a man. 2. go; move; keep going. This train runs from Kansas City to St. Louis. Does your watch run well? 3. creep; grow; climb. Vines run along the sides of the road. 4. flow. Blood runs from a cut. The child's nose runs. The boy has a running sore. 5. spread. The color of the dress ran when it was washed. 6. extend; stretch. Shelves ran around the walls. The man ran a fence across the lot. 7. get; become. The well ran dry in summer. Never run into debt. 8. occur; be in action. A thought ran through my mind. 9. sew by passing a needle in and out with even stitches in a line. 10. get past or through; as, to run a blockade. 11. expose oneself to; as, to run a risk of taking cold. 12. be a candidate for election. Mr. Smith will run for president. 13. make run; as, to run a horse. 14. make go; force; thrust. Tom ran his nose against a post. He ran a splinter into his hand. 15. shape by melting; as, to run bullets in a mold. 16. act of running. The dog came on the run. 17. course; direction; trend; as, the run of events. 18. free use; as, to give a person the run of a house. 19. a trip. The train makes a run of one hundred miles in two hours. 20. drop stitches. Cheap, thin stockings often run. 21. place where stitches have slipped out or become undone; as, a run in a stocking. 22. time; period; spell; as, a run of good luck, a run of wet weather. 23. a sudden demand or call; as, a run on a bank to draw out money. 24. series of performances. This play had a run of 200 nights. 25. kind; class; as, the common run of mankind. 26. number of fish moving together; as, a run of salmon. 27. a stretch of ground or an enclosed place for animals; as, a cattle run, a chicken run. 28. a unit of score in baseball or cricket. 29. Some special meanings are:

in the long run, on the whole; in the end.

run down, 1. stop going or working. The clock has run down. 2. chase till caught. 3. speak evil against. 4. make tired or ill. She is run down from working too hard.

run out, come to an end.

run out of, use up; have no more.

run through, 1. spend rapidly and foolishly. 2. pierce.

ran and **running** are formed from **run.**

run a way (run′ə wā′), 1. person, horse, etc., that runs away. 2. running away. 3. running with nobody to guide or stop it; out of control; as, a runaway horse, a runaway car. 4. done by runaways; as, a runaway marriage.

rung[1] (rung). See **ring**[2]. The bell has rung.

rung[2] (rung), 1. round rod or bar used as a step of a ladder. 2. crosspiece set between the legs of a chair or as part of the back or arm of a chair. 3. spoke of a wheel.

R, rungs.

R, rungs.

run ner (run′ər), 1. person or animal that runs; messenger. 2. either of the narrow pieces on which a sleigh or sled slides; the blade of a skate. 3. a slender stem that takes root along the ground, thus producing new plants. See the picture just below. 4. a ship that tries to evade somebody; smuggler; as, a blockade runner. 5. a long narrow strip. We have a runner of carpet in our hall, and runners of linen and lace on bureaus.

Runner of a strawberry plant

run ning (run′ing), 1. act of one that runs. 2. flow of liquids; as, a running of the nose in a cold. 3. that runs. Running handwriting joins all letters of a word together. A running sore discharges pus.

run way (run′wā′), 1. a way, track, groove, trough, or the like, along which something moves, slides, etc. 2. the beaten track of deer or other animals. 3. enclosed place for animals to run in.

ru ral (rür′əl), in the country; belonging to the country; like that of the country. Rural life is healthful and quiet.

ruse (rüz), trick; stratagem.

rush[1] (rush), 1. move, go, or send with speed and force. The river rushed past. Rush this order, please. 2. go or act with great haste. He rushes into things without knowing anything about them. 3. to attack with much speed and force. The soldiers rushed the enemy's trenches. 4. act of rushing; dash. The rush of the flood swept everything before it. 5. hurry. What is your rush? Wait a minute. 6. pressure; eager demand; effort of many people to go somewhere or get something. The Christmas rush is hard for clerks.

rush[2] (rush), a plant with a hollow stem

that grows in wet soil or marshy places. The seats of chairs are sometimes made of rushes.

rus set (rus′it), 1. yellowish brown; reddish brown. The leaves in the fall are scarlet, yellow, and russet. 2. a coarse, russet-colored cloth. The peasants used to make and wear russet. 3. a kind of apple with a rough brownish skin.

Rus sia (rush′ə), country in eastern Europe and northwestern Asia. Before the revolution in 1917, it was an empire ruled by a czar. It is now a large part of the Union of Soviet Socialist Republics.

Rus sian (rush′ən), 1. of or pertaining to Russia, its people, or their language. 2. a native or inhabitant of Russia. 3. the language of Russia.

rust (rust), 1. the reddish-brown or orange coating that forms on iron or steel when exposed to air or moisture. 2. become covered with this. Don't let your tools or machines rust. 3. become spoiled by not being used. Don't let your mind rust during the vacation. 4. a plant disease that spots leaves and stems.

rus tic (rus′tik), 1. belonging to the country; rural; suitable for the country. 2. simple; like those of country people. His rustic ways made him uncomfortable in the city. 3. rough; awkward. 4. country person. The rustics had gathered at the county fair.

rus tle (rus′əl), 1. sound that leaves make when moved by the wind; sound like this. 2. move so as to make such a sound. Leaves rustle in the breeze. 3. move or stir (something) so that it makes such a sound; as, to rustle the papers. 4. steal (cattle, etc.).

rust y (rus′ti), 1. rusted; covered with rust; as, a rusty knife. 2. made by rust; as, a rusty spot. 3. colored like rust. 4. faded; as, a rusty black. 5. damaged by lack of use. Mother's arithmetic is rusty, she says.

rut (rut), 1. a track made in the ground by wheels. 2. make ruts in. 3. fixed or established way of acting; groove.

ruth less (rüth′lis), cruel; having no pity; showing no mercy.

Rye

rye (rī), 1. a grain that is made into a kind of flour. Peasants in Germany and Russia eat a great deal of almost black rye bread. 2. the plant rye grows on. See the picture.

S

Sab bath (sab′əth), 1. the day of the week used for rest and worship. Sunday is the Christian Sabbath. Saturday is the Jewish Sabbath. 2. of or belonging to the Sabbath.

sa ber or **sa bre** (sā′bər), a heavy, curved sword with a sharp edge, used by cavalry.

Saber

sa ble (sā′bəl), 1. a small animal valued for its dark, glossy fur. 2. its fur. Sable is one of the most costly furs. 3. black. The widow's sable garments showed that she was in mourning.

Sable (about 1½ ft. long without the tail)

sack[1] (sak), 1. large bag made of coarse cloth or strong paper. Sacks are used for holding grain, flour, potatoes, and coal. 2. such a bag with what is in it. He bought two sacks of corn. 3. any bag with what is in it; as, a sack of candy. 4. put into a sack. 5. loose coat; as, a knitted sack for a baby.

sack[2] (sak), 1. plunder (a captured city). The soldiers sacked the town. 2. a plundering (of a captured city).

sac ra ment (sak′rə mənt), a solemn religious ceremony of the Christian church. Baptism is a sacrament.

sa cred (sā′krid), 1. belonging to God; holy. A church is a sacred building. 2. connected with religion; religious. Prayer is a sacred duty. 3. worthy of reverence. Washington is a sacred name. 4. that must not be injured. He made a sacred promise.

sac ri fice (sak′ri fīs), 1. act of offering to a god; thing offered. The ancient Hebrews killed animals on the altars as sacrifices to God. 2. give or offer to a god. They sacrificed oxen, sheep, and doves. 3. giving up one thing for another. Our teacher does not approve of any sacrifice of studies to sports. 4. give up. A mother will sacrifice her life for her children. 5. loss. He will sell his house at a sacrifice because he needs money. 6. sell at a loss.

sad (sad), 1. You feel sad if your best friend goes away. Mary was sad because she lost her money. 2. causing sorrow. The death of a pet is a sad loss. **sadder** and **saddest** are formed from **sad.**

sad den (sad′ən), make sad; become sad.

sad dle (sad′əl), 1. seat for a rider on a horse's back, on a bicycle, etc. **In the saddle** sometimes means in a position of control. 2. thing shaped like a saddle. A ridge between two mountain peaks is called a saddle. 3. put a saddle on. Saddle the horse. 4. to burden. Mr. Brown is saddled with a big house which he does not need or want.

Saddle on a horse

sad ness (sad′nis), sorrow; grief.

safe (sāf), 1. free from harm or danger. The package came safe and sound. The cat in the tree is safe from the dog. Keep money in a safe place. 2. not causing harm or danger. Is it safe to leave the house unlocked? A soft rubber ball is a safe plaything. 3. careful; as, a safe guess, a safe move. 4. that can be depended on; as, a safe guide. 5. a place or container for keeping things safe.

Safe (def. 5)

safe guard (sāf′gärd′), 1. keep safe; guard against hurt or danger; protect. Pure food laws safeguard our health. 2. protection; defense. Keeping clean is a safeguard against disease.

safe ty (sāf′ti), 1. freedom from harm or danger. A bank assures safety for your money. You can cross the street in safety when the policeman holds up his hand. 2. bringing no harm or danger; preventing harm; as, a safety pin, a safety match, a safety razor.

saf fron (saf′rən), 1. an orange-yellow coloring matter obtained from a kind of crocus. Saffron is used to color and flavor candy, drinks, etc. 2. orange yellow.

sag (sag), 1. sink under weight or pressure; bend down in the middle. 2. hang down unevenly. Your dress sags in the back. 3. become less firm or elastic; droop; sink. Our courage sagged. 4. a sagging.

sa ga cious (sə gā′shəs), shrewd; wise in a keen, practical way.

sa gac i ty (sə gas′i ti), shrewdness; keen, sound judgment. Lincoln was a man of great sagacity.

sage[1] (sāj), 1. wise. 2. wise-looking. Owls are sage birds. 3. wise man. The sage gave sage advice to his followers.

sage[2] (sāj), a plant whose leaves are used in cooking and in medicine. The turkey stuffing is seasoned with sage.

said (sed), 1. See **say.** He said he would come. She had said "No" every time. 2. named before; as, the said witness, the said sum of money.

sail (sāl), 1. piece of cloth spread to the wind to make a ship move through the water. 2. something like a sail. 3. a ship; ships; as, a fleet numbering 30 sail. 4. a trip on a boat with sails. Let's go for a sail. 5. travel on water by the action of wind on sails. 6. travel on a steamboat. 7. travel through the air. 8. move smoothly like a ship with sails. The swans sail along the lake. The eagle sailed by. Mrs. Grand sailed into the room. 9. sail upon, over, or through; as, to sail the seas. 10. manage a ship. The boys are learning to sail. 11. begin a trip by water. Grace sails from New York today. 12. Some special meanings are:

make sail, spread out the sails of a ship.

set sail, begin a trip by water.

under sail, with the sails spread out.

sail boat (sāl′bōt′), boat that is moved by sails. See the pictures of **schooner** and **sloop.**

sail or (sāl′ər), 1. person whose work is sailing. In these days most sailors are on steamships. The men in our navy are called sailors if they are not officers. 2. like a sailor's. Little boys wear sailor suits and sailor caps. Her blouse has a sailor collar.

Sailor collar on a blouse

saint (sānt), 1. very holy person; true Christian. 2. person who has gone to heaven. 3. person declared a saint by the Roman Catholic Church.

saint ly (sānt′li), like a saint; very holy; very good.

saith (seth), old form meaning **says.**

sake (sāk). Sake is used with *for*. **For the sake of** means (1) because of. (2) to help; to please. **For your own sake** means because of your own wants; to help yourself.

sal ad (sal′əd), raw green vegetables, such as lettuce and celery, served with a dressing. Often cold meat, fish, eggs, cooked vegetables, or fruits are used along with, or instead of, the raw green vegetables.

sal a ry (sal′ə ri), fixed pay for regular work. Teachers and clerks receive salaries.

sale (sāl), 1. act of selling; exchange of goods for money. The sale of his old home made him sad. **For sale** or **on sale** means to be sold. That car is for sale. 2. amount sold. Today's sales were larger than yesterday's. 3. chance to sell. There is almost no sale for carriages in these days. 4. selling at lower prices than usual. This store is having a sale on suits.

sales man (sālz′mən), person whose work is selling. Four salesmen were showing people suits and sweaters.

sa li va (sə lī′və), the liquid produced by glands in the mouth.

sal low (sal′ō), having a sickly, yellowish color or complexion.

sal ly (sal′i), 1. sudden rushing forth. The men in the fort made a brave sally and returned with many prisoners. 2. rush forth suddenly; go out. We sallied forth at dawn. 3. witty remark. She continued her story undisturbed by the merry sallies of her hearers.

salm on (sam′ən), 1. a large fish with silvery scales and yellowish-pink flesh. Canned salmon is a good food. 2. yellowish pink.

Salmon

sa loon (sə lün′), 1. place where alcoholic drinks are sold and drunk. 2. large room for general or public use. Concerts were often held in the saloon of the steamship. The ship's passengers ate in the dining saloon.

salt (sôlt), 1. a white substance found in the earth and in sea water. Salt is used to season and preserve food. 2. containing salt. 3. tasting like salt. 4. mix or sprinkle with salt. 5. preserve with salt. 6. seasoning. 7. a chemical compound of a metal and an acid. Baking soda is a salt. 8. sailor.

salt pe ter (sôlt′pē′tər), 1. a salty, white mineral, used in making gunpowder, in preserving meat, and in medicine. 2. a kind of fertilizer.

salt-wa ter (sôlt′wô′tər), 1. consisting of or containing salt water. 2. living in the sea or in water like sea water.

salt y (sôl′ti), containing salt; tasting of salt.

sa lu bri ous (sə lü′bri əs), healthful.

sal u tar y (sal′ū tār′i), 1. good for the health; wholesome. Walking is a salutary exercise. 2. beneficial. The teacher gave the boy salutary advice.

sal u ta tion (sal′ū tā′shən), 1. greeting; saluting. A man raises his hat in salutation. 2. something uttered, written, or done to salute. You begin a letter with a salutation, such as "Dear Sir" or "My dear Mrs. Jones." A formal bow was her parting salutation.

sa lute (sə lüt′), 1. honor in a formal manner by raising the hand to the head, by firing guns, or by dipping flags. We salute the flag every day at school. Soldiers salute their officers. 2. meet with kind words, a bow, a kiss, etc.; greet. The old gentleman walked along the avenue saluting his friends and receiving their salutes. 3. a saluting; sign of welcome or honor. 4. position of the hand, gun, etc., in saluting.

Soldier saluting

sal va tion (sal vā′shən), 1. saving; being saved. 2. saving the soul; deliverance from sin and from punishment for sin. 3. person or thing that saves. Christians believe that Christ is the salvation of the world.

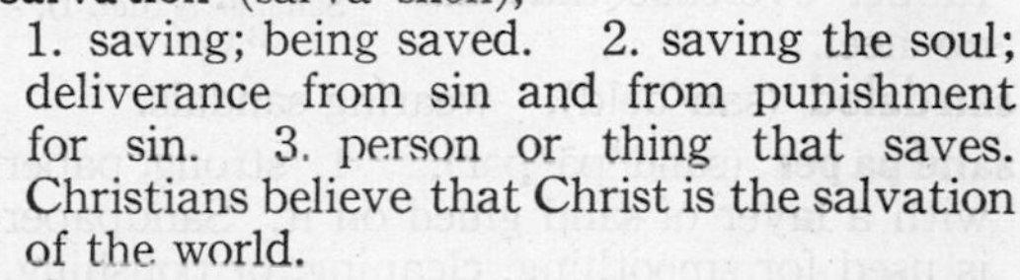

salve (sav), 1. a soft, greasy substance put on wounds and sores; a healing ointment. Is this salve good for burns? 2. put salve on. 3. something soothing. The kind words were salve to his hurt feelings. 4. soothe. He salved his conscience by the thought that his lie harmed no one.

same (sām), 1. not another. We came back the same way we went. 2. just alike; not different. Her name and mine are the same. 3. just spoken of. The boys were talking about a queer man. This same man wore his hair very long and always dressed in white. 4. same person or thing.

samp (samp), coarsely ground corn.

sam ple (sam′pəl), 1. a part to show what the rest is like; one thing to show what the others are like. Get samples of blue silk for a new dress. The salesman showed samples. 2. take a part of; test a part of. We sampled the cake and found it very good.

sanc tion (sangk′shən), 1. permission with authority; support; approval. We have the sanction of the law to play ball in this park. 2. approve; authorize; allow. Her conscience does not sanction stealing.

sanc ti ty (sangk′ti ti), 1. holiness; saintliness; as, the sanctity of a saint. 2. sacredness; holy character; as, the sanctity of a temple, the sanctity of the home.

sanc tu ar y (sangk′chü ãr′i), 1. sacred place. A church is a sanctuary. 2. the part of a church about the altar. 3. place to which people can go for refuge or protection. 4. refuge or protection. The escaped prisoner found sanctuary in the temple.

sand (sand), 1. tiny grains of worn-down rocks. We have all heard of the sands of the seashore, the sands of the desert, sandbanks, and sandstorms. Sand is used for scraping and cleaning, and so are sandpaper and sand soap. 2. sprinkle with sand. People used to sand the kitchen floor; they also sanded letters to dry the ink.

san dal (san′dəl), 1. a kind of shoe made of a sole fastened to the foot by straps. 2. a kind of slipper. 3. a light, low, rubber overshoe that has no heel.

Sandals: A (def. 1); B (def. 2).

san daled (san′dəld), wearing sandals.

sand pa per (sand′pā′pər), 1. strong paper with a layer of sand glued on it. Sandpaper is used for smoothing, cleaning, or polishing. 2. to smooth, clean, or polish with this.

sand pip er (sand′pīp′ər), a small bird with a long bill, living on sandy shores.

Sandpiper (about 7 in. long)

sand stone (sand′stōn′), a kind of rock formed mostly of sand.

sand wich (sand′wich), 1. two slices of bread with meat, jelly, cheese, or some other filling between them. 2. put in (between). John was sandwiched between two fat women.

sand y (san′di), 1. containing sand; consisting of sand. 2. covered with sand. Most of the shore is rocky, but there is a sandy beach. 3. yellowish-red. Alec has sandy hair.

sane (sān). 1. having a healthy mind. 2. having good sense; sensible.

sang (sang). See **sing.** The bird sang for us yesterday.

san guine (sang′gwin), 1. naturally cheerful and hopeful; as, a sanguine disposition. 2. confident; hopeful; as, sanguine of success. 3. having a healthy red color; ruddy; as, a sanguine complexion.

san i tar i um (san′i tãr′i əm), 1. place, especially in a good climate, for treatment of the sick. Sick people who are getting better, or who are suffering from a long, slow disease like tuberculosis, often go to a sanitarium. 2. health resort.

san i tar y (san′i tãr′i), 1. of health; about health. 2. favorable to health; preventing disease. 3. free from dirt and filth. Food should be kept in a sanitary place.

sank (sangk). See **sink.** The ship sank before help reached her.

San ta Claus (san′tə klôz′), Saint Nicholas, the saint of Christmas giving. On Christmas father dresses up as Santa Claus.

sap[1] (sap), the life-giving juice of a plant. Sap does for trees what blood does for us. Maple sugar is made from the sap of some maple trees.

sap[2] (sap), 1. dig under or wear away the foundation of. The walls of the boathouse had been sapped by the waves. 2. weaken; use up. The extreme heat sapped her strength.

sap ling (sap′ling), young tree.

sap phire (saf′īr), 1. a bright-blue precious stone. A sapphire is hard and clear like a diamond. 2. bright blue; as, a sapphire sky.

sar casm (sär′kazm), 1. a sneering or cutting remark. 2. act of making fun of a person to hurt his feelings; harsh or bitter irony. "How unselfish you are!" said Ellen in sarcasm as Mary took the biggest piece of cake.

sar cas tic (sär kas′tik), using sarcasm; sneering; bitterly cutting. "Don't hurry!" was his father's sarcastic comment as Dick began to dress at his usual slow rate.

sar dine (sär dēn′), a kind of small fish preserved in oil for food.

Window sash

sash[1] (sash), a long broad strip of cloth or ribbon, worn as an ornament around the waist or over one shoulder. She wore a white dress with a blue sash around her waist.

sash[2] (sash), frame for the glass of a window or door. The sash in the picture has four panes of glass. See the picture above.

sat (sat). See **sit.** Yesterday I sat in a train all day. The cat has sat at that mouse hole for hours.

Sa tan (sā′tən), the evil spirit; the enemy of goodness; the Devil.

satch el (sach′əl), small bag for carrying clothes, books, etc.

sate (sāt), 1. satisfy fully (any appetite or desire). A long drink sated Joe's thirst. 2. supply with more than enough.

sat el lite (sat′ə līt), 1. a follower or attendant upon a person of importance. 2. small planet that revolves around a larger planet.

sat in (sat′ən), 1. silk or rayon cloth with one very smooth glossy side. 2. of satin; like satin; smooth and glossy.

sat is fac tion (sat′is fak′shən), 1. condition of being satisfied, or pleased and contented. Mary felt satisfaction at winning a prize. 2. anything that makes us feel pleased or contented. It is a great satisfaction to have things turn out just the way you want. 3. fulfillment; satisfying. The satisfaction of hunger requires food. 4. payment of debt; discharge of obligation; a making up for wrong or injury done.

sat is fac to ri ly (sat′is fak′tə ri li), in a satisfactory manner.

sat is fac to ry (sat′is fak′tə ri), satisfying; good enough to satisfy.

sat is fy (sat′is fī), 1. give enough to; fulfill (desires, hopes, demands, etc.); put an end to (needs, wants, etc.). He is satisfying his hunger with bread and milk. 2. make contented; please. Are you satisfied now? 3. pay; make right. After the accident he satisfied all claims for the damage he had caused. 4. convince. The teacher is satisfied that Jack's statement was true.

sat u rate (sach′ů rāt), soak thoroughly; fill full. During a fog, the air is saturated with moisture. Saturate the moss with water before planting the bulbs in it.

Sat ur day (sat′ər di), the seventh day of the week.

sat yr (sat′ər), 1. a merry creature of the woods, part man and part beast. The satyrs were followers of Bacchus, the god of wine. 2. a man who is beastly in thought and action.

Satyr

sauce (sôs), 1. something, usually a liquid, served with a food to make it taste better. We have cranberry sauce with turkey, mint sauce with lamb, egg sauce with fish, and many different sauces with puddings. 2. stewed fruit; as, applesauce. 3. saucy behavior.

sauce pan (sôs′pan′), a metal dish with a handle, used for stewing, boiling, etc.

Saucepan

sau cer (sô′sər), 1. shallow dish to set a cup on. 2. a small round dish with its edge curved up. 3. something round and shallow like a saucer.

sau cy (sô′si), 1. rude; showing lack of respect. 2. pert; smart. She wore a saucy hat with a saucy smile.

saun ter (sôn′tər), stroll; walk along slowly and happily. People saunter through the park on summer evenings.

sau sage (sô′sij), chopped pork, beef, or other meats, seasoned and usually stuffed into a thin tube.

sav age (sav′ij), 1. wild. He likes savage mountain scenery. 2. not civilized; barbarous. Gaudy colors please a savage taste. 3. person living somewhat as wild animals do. 4. fierce; cruel; ready to fight. The savage lion attacked the hunter. 5. a fierce, brutal, or cruel person.

sav age ry (sav′ij ri), savage state; cruelty.

save[1] (sāv), 1. make safe; keep or rescue from harm, danger, hurt, loss, etc. The dog saved the boy's life. The woman saved her jewels from the fire. 2. set free from sin and its results. Christ came to save the world. 3. lay aside; as, to save money. She saves pieces of string. 4. keep from spending or wasting. Save your strength. 5. avoid expense or waste. She saves in every way she can. 6. prevent; make less; as, to save work, to save trouble, to save expense. 7. treat carefully to lessen wear, weariness, etc. Large print saves one's eyes.

save[2] (sāv), except. He works every day save Sundays.

sav ing (sāv′ing), 1. that saves. 2. economical; avoiding waste; tending to save up money. 3. way of saving money, time, etc. It will be a saving to take this path. 4. except; with the exception of. Saving a few crusts, we had eaten nothing all day.

sav ings (sāv′ingz), money saved.

sav ior or **sav iour** (sāv′yər), one who saves or rescues.

Sav iour or **Sav ior** (sāv′yər), Jesus Christ.

sa vor (sā′vər), 1. taste or smell; flavor. The soup has a savor of onion. 2. to taste; to smell. He savored the soup with pleasure. 3. have the quality or nature (of). The plot savored of treason. 4. give flavor to; season.

sa vor y[1] (sā′vər i), pleasing in taste or smell. The savory smell of roasting turkey greeted us as we entered the house.

sa vor y[2] (sā′vər i), a fragrant herb used for seasoning food.

saw[1] (sô), 1. a tool for cutting, made of a thin blade with sharp teeth on the edge. 2. cut with a saw. The man saws wood. 3. make with a saw. Boards are sawed from logs. 4. use a saw. Can you saw straight? 5. be sawed. Pine wood saws more easily than oak.

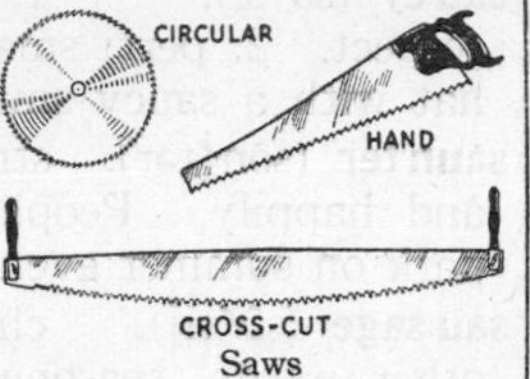

Saws

saw[2] (sô). See **see**[1]. I saw a robin yesterday.

saw[3] (sô), wise saying; proverb. "A stitch in time saves nine" is a familiar saw.

saw dust (sô′dust′), particles of wood made by sawing.

saw mill (sô′mil′), building where machines saw timber into planks, boards, etc.

sax o phone (sak′sə fōn), a brass musical instrument with keys and a reed mouthpiece. See the picture.

Saxophone

say (sā). Say "Please" and "Thank you." Say your prayers. The Bible says to do good unto all men. It is hard to say which dress is prettier. You can learn to dance in, say, ten lessons. James said his say and sat down.

say est (sā′ist), an old form meaning **say.** "Thou sayest" means "you say."

say ing (sā′ing), 1. something said; a statement. 2. a proverb.

says (sez). See **say.** He says "No" to everything.

sayst (sāst), an old form meaning **say.** "Thou sayst" means "you say."

scab (skab), 1. the crust that forms over a sore as it heals. A scab formed on the spot where Joe was vaccinated. 2. a skin disease in animals, especially sheep.

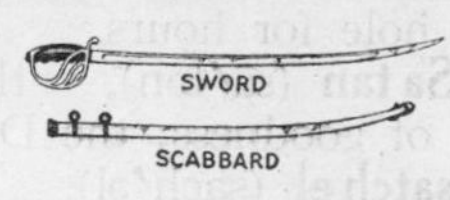

scab bard (skab′ərd), a sheath or case for the blade of a sword, dagger, etc.

scaf fold (skaf′əld), 1. temporary structure for holding workmen and materials. 2. raised platform on which criminals are put to death. 3. any raised framework.

Scaffold for holding workmen

scald (skôld), 1. pour boiling liquid over. Scald the dishes before drying them. 2. burn with hot liquid or steam. She scalded herself with hot grease. 3. heat almost to boiling, but not quite. Scald the milk. 4. a burn caused by hot liquid or steam. The scald on her hand came from lifting a pot cover carelessly.

scale[1] (skāl), 1. one of the thin, flat, hard plates forming the outer covering of some fishes, snakes, and lizards. 2. thin layer like a scale. Scales of skin peel off after scarlet fever. 3. remove scales from. 4. come off in scales. The paint is scaling off the house. 5. an insect that has a covering under which it hides and feeds.

scale[2] (skāl), 1. the dish or pan of a balance. 2. a balance; an instrument for weighing. She weighed some meat on the scales. 3. weigh. He scales 80 pounds.

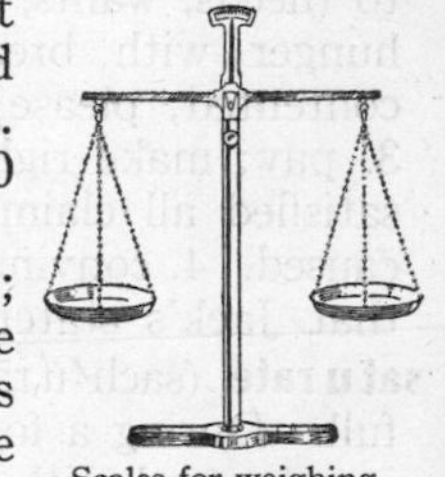
Scales for weighing

scale[3] (skāl), 1. series; graded amounts. The scale of wages in this factory ranges from three dollars to twelve dollars a day. 2. series of marks made along a line at regular distances to use in measuring. A thermometer has a scale. 3. an instrument marked in this way, used for measuring. 4. the size of a plan or map compared with what it represents. This map is drawn to the scale of one inch for each 100 miles. 5. in music, a series of tones ascending or descending in pitch. She practices scales on the piano. 6. climb. They scaled the wall by ladders. 7. relative size or extent. That rich woman entertains on a large scale.

scal lop (skol′əp), 1. a shellfish somewhat like a clam. He ate scallops and bacon. 2. curve on the edge of anything. This cuff has scallops. See the picture below. 3. make with such curves. She scallops the edge of the paper that she covers shelves with. 4. bake with sauce and bread crumbs in a dish; as, scalloped oysters, scalloped tomatoes.

Scallop (def. 1)

scalp (skalp), 1. the skin and hair on the top and back of the head. 2. part of this skin and hair cut off as a token of victory. Indians used to collect the scalps of their enemies. 3. cut or tear the scalp from.

Scallops on a cuff

scal y (skāl′i), covered with scales; having scales like a fish. This iron pipe is scaly with rust.

scamp (skamp), rascal; rogue; worthless person.

scam per (skam′pər), 1. run quickly. The mice scampered when the cat came. 2. a quick run. Let the dog out for a scamper.

scan (skan), 1. look at closely; examine with care. His mother scanned his face to see if he were telling the truth. 2. mark off (lines of poetry) into feet. *Example:* Sing′a | song′of | six′pence.

scan dal (skan′dəl), 1. shameful action that brings disgrace or shocks public opinion. It is a scandal for a city officer to take tax money for his own use. 2. disgrace; damage to reputation. 3. public talk about a person which will hurt his reputation; evil gossip.

scan dal ize (skan′dəl īz), offend by something wrong or improper; shock. Amy scandalized her grandmother by smoking cigarettes.

scan dal ous (skan′dəl əs), 1. disgraceful; shocking. 2. spreading scandal or slander.

scant (skant), 1. not enough in size or quantity. Her coat was short and scant. **Scant of** means having not enough. She was scant of breath. 2. barely enough. Use a scant cup of butter in the cake. You have a scant hour in which to pack. 3. make scant; cut down; limit. Don't scant the butter if you want a rich cake.

scant y (skan′ti), 1. not enough. His scanty clothing did not keep out the cold. 2. barely enough.

scar (skär), 1. the mark left by a healed cut, wound, burn, or sore. 2. any mark like this. See the scars your shoes have made on the chair. 3. mark with a scar. 4. form a scar; heal. Dick's wound is scarring well.

scarce (skãrs), 1. hard to get; rare. Good cooks are scarce. Very old stamps are scarce. 2. scarcely.

scarce ly (skãrs′li), not quite; barely. We could scarcely see through the thick fog.

scar ci ty (skãr′si ti), too small a supply; lack; rarity.

scare (skãr), 1. frighten. We were scared and ran away. 2. a fright. 3. frightened condition.

scarf (skärf), 1. a long broad strip of silk, lace, etc., worn about the neck, shoulders, or head. See the picture. 2. necktie with hanging ends. 3. long strip of linen, etc., used as a cover for a bureau, table, piano, etc.

Woman wearing a scarf

scar let (skär′lit), 1. very bright red. 2. cloth or clothing having this color.

scarlet fever, a very contagious disease that causes a scarlet rash, sore throat, and fever.

scat ter (skat′ər), 1. throw here and there; sprinkle. Mary scatters corn for the chickens. Scatter ashes on the icy sidewalk. 2. separate and drive off in different directions. The police scattered the disorderly crowd. 3. separate and go in different directions. The hens scattered when they saw the hawk.

scav en ger (skav′in jər), 1. person who cleans streets, taking away the dirt and filth. 2. animal that feeds on decaying matter. Vultures are scavengers.

scene (sēn), 1. the time, place, circumstances, etc., of a play or story. The scene is laid in Boston in the year 1775. 2. the painted screens, hangings, etc., used in a theater to represent places. The scene represents a city street. 3. part of an act of a play. The king comes to the castle in Act I, Scene 2. 4. a particular incident of a play. The trial scene is the most exciting one in *The Merchant of Venice*. 5. view; picture. The white sailboats in the blue water made a pretty scene. 6. show of strong feeling. The child kicked and screamed and made such a scene on the train that his mother was ashamed of him.

scen er y (sēn′ər i), 1. general appearance of a place. She enjoys mountain scenery very much. 2. painted hangings, slides, etc., used in a theater to represent places. The scenery pictures a garden in the moonlight.

scent (sent), 1. smell. The scent of roses filled the air. The dog scented a rabbit and ran off. 2. sense of smell. Many dogs have a keen scent. 3. perfume. She used too much scent. She uses scented writing paper. 4. smell left in passing. Dogs follow a fox by the scent. 5. means by which a thing or a person may be traced. The police are on the scent of the thieves. 6. have a suspicion of; be aware of. I scent a trick in his offer.

scep ter or **scep tre** (sep′tər), the rod or staff carried by a ruler as a symbol of royal power or authority.

King holding a scepter

sched ule (skej′ül), 1. written or printed statement of details; a list. A timetable is a schedule of the coming and going of trains. 2. make a schedule of; enter in a schedule.

scheme (skēm), 1. plan; program of action. He has a scheme for extracting gold from sea water. 2. to plan. 3. plot. The men were scheming to cheat the government by bringing the jewels into the country without paying duty. 4. system of connected things, parts, thoughts, etc. The color scheme of the room is blue and gold.

schol ar (skol′ər), 1. pupil at school. 2. learned person; person having much knowledge. 3. student who is given money by a school to help him continue his studies.

schol ar ly (skol′ər li), 1. of a scholar; like that of a scholar. Spectacles gave her a scholarly look. 2. fit for a scholar. 3. learned; having much knowledge. 4. studious; fond of learning. 5. thorough and orderly in methods of study.

schol ar ship (skol′ər ship), 1. possession of knowledge gained by study; quality of learning and knowledge. Good scholarship is more important than good clothes. 2. money given to help a student continue his studies. John passed his college entrance examinations with such high rank that he received a scholarship of two hundred dollars.

school[1] (skül), 1. place for teaching and learning. Children go to school to learn. 2. regular meetings for teaching and learning. 3. pupils who are taught and their teachers. Our school will be in a new building next fall. 4. group of people holding the same beliefs or opinions; as, the French school of painting, a gentleman of the old school. 5. particular department of a university; as, a medical school, a law school. 6. teach. 7. train; discipline. School yourself to control your temper. 8. of a school or schools.

school[2] (skül), 1. large number of fish swimming together; as, a school of mackerel. 2. swim together in large numbers.

school boy (skül′boi′), boy attending school.

school fel low (skül′fel′ō), companion at school.

school girl (skül′gėrl′), girl attending school.

school house (skül′hous′), a building used as a school.

school ing (skül′ing), instruction in school; education received at school.

school mas ter (skül′mas′tər), man who teaches in a school, or is its principal.

school mate (skül′māt′), companion at school.

school room (skül′rüm′), room in which pupils are taught.

school teach er (skül′tēch′ər), person who teaches in a school.

schoon er (skün′ər), a ship with two or more masts and sails set lengthwise.

Schooner with four masts

schwa (shwä), unstressed vowel sound such as *a* in *about* or *o* in *lemon*, represented by the symbol ə.

sci ence (sī′əns), 1. knowledge of facts and principles arranged in an orderly system. 2. a branch of such knowledge.

sci en tif ic (sī′ən tif′ik), 1. using the facts and laws of science; as, a scientific method, a scientific farmer. 2. of science; about science; used in science; as, scientific books, scientific instruments.

Scimitar

sci en tist (sī′ən tist), person who knows much about science.

scim i tar (sim′i tər), a short, curved sword used by certain Oriental peoples. See the picture just above.

scis sors (siz′ərz), a tool or instrument for cutting that has two sharp blades so fastened that they will work toward each other. See the picture.

Scissors

scoff (skôf), mock; make fun to show one does not believe something. We scoffed at the idea of drowning in three inches of water.

scold (skōld), 1. find fault with; blame with angry words. His mother scolded him for tearing his coat in rough play. 2. find fault; talk angrily. Don't scold so much. 3. a noisy, scolding woman. In olden times, scolds were punished by being ducked in ponds.

scoop (sküp), 1. a tool like a shovel. 2. the part of a dredge, machine shovel, etc., that holds coal, sand, etc. 3. a large ladle. 4. a kitchen utensil to take out flour, sugar, etc. 5. amount taken up at one time by a scoop. She used two scoops of flour and one of sugar. 6. take up or out with a scoop. The children scooped up the snow with their hands to build a snow man. Scoop up that spilled grain from the barn floor. 7. act of scooping. 8. hollow out; dig out; make by scooping. The children scooped holes in the sand.

Scoop (def. 4)

scope (skōp), 1. distance the mind can reach; extent of view. Very hard words are not within the scope of a child's understanding. 2. space; opportunity. Football gives scope for courage and quick thinking.

scorch (skôrch), 1. burn slightly; burn on the outside. The cake tastes scorched. The maid scorched the shirt in ironing it. 2. a slight burn. 3. dry up; wither. The grass is scorched by so much hot sunshine.

score (skōr), 1. the record of points made in a game or contest. The score was 9 to 2 in favor of our school. 2. make as points in a game or contest. 3. keep a record of the number of points in a game or contest. The teacher will appoint some pupil to score for both sides. 4. make as an addition to the score; gain; win. James scored five runs for our team. 5. amount owed; debt; account. He paid his score at the inn. 6. to record; mark; set down. The innkeeper scored on a slate every meal each person had. 7. written or printed piece of music. Anne was studying the score of the piece she was learning to play. 8. twenty; set of twenty. A score or more were present at the party. 9. cut or scratch; stroke; mark; line. Moving the furniture across the floor scores the polish. Mistakes are scored in red ink.

scorn (skôrn), 1. look down upon; think of as mean or low; despise. Honest boys scorn sneaks and liars. 2. reject or refuse as low or wrong. The judge scorned to take a bribe. 3. a feeling that a person or act is mean or low; contempt. The big dog walked past the little dog with scorn. Most pupils feel scorn for those who cheat. 4. person, animal, or thing that is scorned or despised. That coward is the scorn of the school.

scorn ful (skôrn′fəl), showing contempt; mocking; full of scorn. He spoke of our old car in a scornful voice.

scor pi on (skôr′pi ən), a small animal belonging to the same group as the spider and having a poisonous sting in its tail.

Scotch (skoch), 1. of Scotland, its people, or their language. *Laird* is a Scotch word. 2. the people of Scotland. 3. English as it is spoken by the people of Scotland.

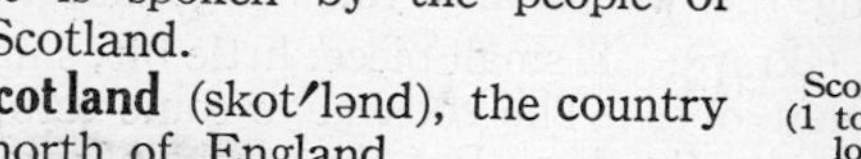

Scot land (skot′lənd), the country north of England.

Scorpion (1 to 8 in. long)

Scot tish (skot′ish), Scotch.

scoun drel (skoun′drəl), very bad person. The scoundrels who set fire to the barn have been caught.

scour[1] (skour), 1. clean or polish by hard rubbing. The maid scours the knives with sand soap, and the floor with a brush and soapsuds. 2. remove dirt and grease from (anything) by rubbing. 3. make clear by flowing through or over. The stream had scoured a channel. 4. clean; cleanse. 5. act of scouring.

scour[2] (skour), 1. move quickly over. Men scoured the country for the lost child. 2. go rapidly in search or pursuit.

scourge (skėrj), 1. whip. 2. any means of punishment. 3. punish. 4. some thing or person that causes great trouble or misfortune.

scout (skout), 1. person sent to find out what the enemy is doing. 2. act as a scout; hunt around to find something. Go and scout for firewood for the picnic. 3. one that acts as a scout. Some ships and airplanes are scouts. 4. A person belonging to the Boy Scouts or Girl Scouts is a **Scout.**

scout mas ter (skout′mas′tər), the leader in charge of a troop or band of Scouts.

scow (skou), a large, flat boat used to carry freight, sand, etc. See the picture.

Scow

scowl (skoul), 1. look angry or sullen by lowering the eyebrows; to frown. 2. an angry, sullen look; a frown. See the picture just below.

scram ble (skram′bəl), 1. make one's way by climbing, crawling, etc. The boys scrambled up the steep, rocky hill. 2. a climb or walk over rough ground. It was a long scramble through bushes and over rocks to the top of the hill. 3. struggle with others for something. The boys scrambled to get the football. 4. a struggle to possess; as, the scramble for wealth and power. 5. scrambling; any disorderly struggle or activity. The pile of boys on the football seemed a wild scramble of arms and legs. 6. cook (eggs), mixing the whites and yolks together.

Man scowling

scrap (skrap), 1. small piece; little bit; small part left over. The cook gave some scraps of meat to the dog. Put the scraps of paper in the waste basket. 2. make into scraps; break up. 3. throw aside as useless or worn out.

scrape (skrāp), 1. rub with something sharp or rough so as to remove; remove in this way. Scrape your muddy shoes with this old knife. The man scraped some paint off the table when he pushed it through the doorway. 2. act of scraping. 3. scraped place. 4. rub with a harsh sound. Don't scrape your feet on the floor. The branch of the tree scraped against the window. 5. give a harsh sound; grate. 6. a harsh, grating sound; as, the scrape of the bow of a violin. 7. dig. The child scraped a hole in the sand. 8. collect by scraping or with difficulty. The hungry boy scraped up the last crumbs from his plate. John has scraped together enough money to buy a bicycle. 9. **Scrape through** means get through with difficulty. Jack barely scraped through the examination. 10. a difficulty; position hard to get out of. Boys often get into scrapes.

scrap er (skrāp′ər), tool for scraping. Wipe your shoes on the scraper. See the pictures in the next column.

scratch (skrach), 1. break, mark, or cut slightly with something sharp or rough. Your feet have scratched the chair. 2. mark made by scratching. There are deep scratches on this desk. 3. tear or dig with the nails or claws. The cat scratched him. 4. very slight cut. That scratch on your hand will soon be well. 5. rub or scrape to relieve itching. Don't scratch your mosquito bites. 6. rub; rub with a harsh noise. He scratched a match on the wall. 7. sound of scratching; as, the scratch of a pen. 8. write in a hurry and carelessly. 9. scrape out; strike out; draw a line through. 10. the starting place of a race. **From scratch** means with no advantages.

A

B

Scrapers: A, for shoes; B, for walls.

scrawl (skrôl), 1. write or draw poorly or carelessly. 2. poor, careless handwriting.

scream (skrēm), 1. make a loud, sharp, piercing cry. People scream in fright, in anger, and in sudden pain. 2. a loud, sharp, piercing cry.

screech (skrēch), 1. cry out sharply in a high voice; shriek. "Help! help!" she screeched. 2. a shrill harsh scream. The woman's screeches brought the police.

screen (skrēn), 1. covered frame that hides, protects, or separates. She keeps her trunk behind a screen. 2. wire woven together with small openings in between. We have screens at the windows to keep out flies. 3. anything like a screen. A screen of trees hides our house from the road. 4. shelter, protect, or hide with a screen. We have screened our porch to keep out flies. She screened her face from the fire with a fan. The mother tried to screen her guilty son. 5. surface on which moving pictures, etc., are shown. 6. sieve for sifting sand, gravel, coal, seed, etc. 7. sift by using a sieve or screen.

Screen door (def. 2)

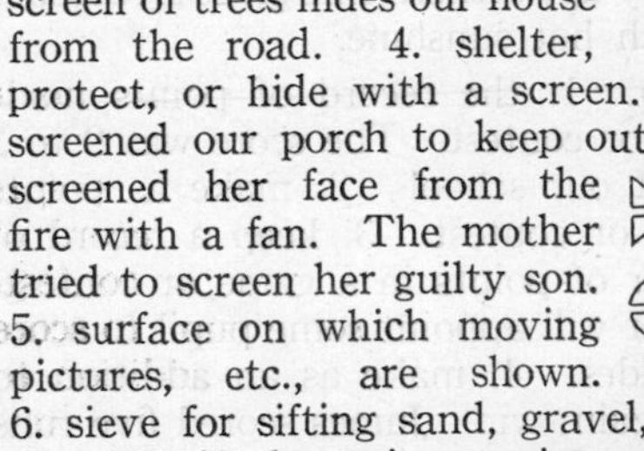

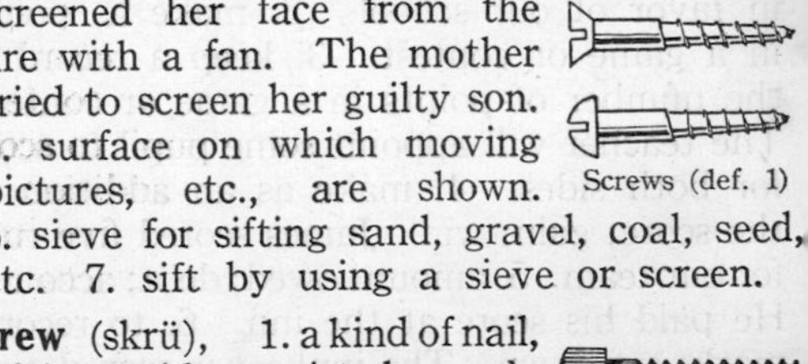
Screws (def. 1)

screw (skrü), 1. a kind of nail, with a ridge twisted evenly round its length. Turn the screw to the right to tighten it. See the pictures above. 2. cylinder with a ridge winding around it. See the picture above. 3. anything that

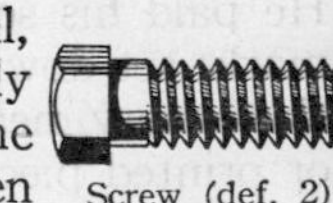
Screw (def. 2)

turns like a screw or looks like one. 4. turn as a screw does; twist. Screw the lid on the jar. 5. fasten with a screw or screws. The carpenter screwed the hinges to the door. 6. propeller that moves a boat.

screw driv er (skrü′drīv′ər), tool for putting in or taking out screws by turning them.

scrib ble (skrib′əl), 1. write or draw carelessly or hastily. 2. make marks that do not mean anything. 3. something scribbled.

scribe (skrīb), 1. person whose occupation is writing. Before printing was invented, there were many scribes. 2. teacher of the Jewish law.

Script (skript), handwriting.

Scrip ture (skrip′chər), 1. the Bible. **The Scriptures** or **Holy Scripture** means the Bible. 2. Any sacred writing may be called a scripture.

scroll (skrōl), 1. roll of parchment or paper, especially one with writing on it. He slowly unrolled the scroll as he read from it. 2. ornament resembling a partly unrolled sheet of paper, or having a spiral or coiled form.

Scroll (def. 1)

Three scrolls in a border

scrub[1] (skrub), 1. rub hard; wash or clean by rubbing. She scrubbed the floor with a brush and soapsuds. 2. a scrubbing. Give your face and hands a good scrub.

scrub[2] (skrub), 1. low, stunted trees or shrubs. Scrub pine was coming up in the pasture. 2. anything small or below the usual size. He is a little scrub of a man. 3. small; poor; inferior.

scru ple (skrü′pəl), 1. a feeling of doubt about what one ought to do. No scruple ever holds him back from having his own way. 2. a feeling of uneasiness that keeps a person from doing something. She has scruples about playing cards for money. 3. hesitate or be unwilling (to do something). A dishonest man does not scruple to deceive others.

scru pu lous (skrü′pū ləs), 1. very careful to do what is right. 2. attending thoroughly to details; very careful. A soldier must pay scrupulous attention to orders.

scru ti nize (skrü′ti nīz), examine closely; inspect carefully. The jeweler scrutinized the diamond for flaws.

scru ti ny (skrü′ti ni), close examination; careful inspection. Careless work will not bear scrutiny.

scud (skud), 1. run or move rapidly. Clouds scud across the sky when there is a high wind. 2. a scudding. 3. clouds or spray driven by the wind.

scuf fle (skuf′əl), 1. struggle or fight in a confused manner. 2. such a fight or struggle. 3. shuffle.

scull (skul), 1. an oar worked with a side twist over the end of a boat to make it go. 2. one of a pair of oars used, one on each side, by a single rower. 3. make (a boat) go by a scull or by sculls.

Man sculling

scul lion (skul′yən), servant who does the dirty, rough work in a kitchen.

sculp tor (skulp′tər), person who carves or models figures. Sculptors make statues of marble and bronze.

sculp ture (skulp′chər), 1. the art of carving or modeling figures. Sculpture includes the cutting of statues from blocks of marble or stone, casting in bronze, and modeling in clay or wax. 2. carve or model. 3. sculptured work; a piece of such work. There are sculptures in the museums. 4. cover or ornament with sculpture. **Sculptured** means carved or ornamented with sculpture.

scum (skum), 1. thin layer that rises to the top of a liquid. When mother makes jelly, she skims off the scum. Green scum rises to the top of the pond. 2. low, worthless people. The saloon was filled with the scum of the town.

scur ry (skėr′i), 1. run quickly; scamper; hurry. We could hear the mice scurry about in the walls. 2. hasty running; hurrying. With much fuss and scurry, Aunt Martha at last got started.

scur vy (skėr′vi), 1. a disease caused by a lack of vegetables and fruits. It causes swollen and bleeding gums, extreme weakness, and livid spots on the skin. 2. mean; contemptible; base; as, a scurvy fellow, a scurvy trick.

Scuttle

scut tle[1] (skut′əl), a kind of bucket for holding or carrying coal. See the picture.

scut tle[2] (skut′əl), 1. an opening in the deck of a ship with a lid or cover; such an opening in the side of a ship or in a wall or roof. 2. the lid or cover. 3. cut holes through the bottom or sides of (a ship) to sink it. After the pirates captured the ship, they scuttled it.

scut tle[3] (skut′əl), scamper; scurry. The dogs scuttled off into the woods.

scythe (sīᴛʜ), a long, curved blade on a long handle, for cutting grass, etc.

Farmer using a scythe

sea (sē), 1. the great body of salt water that covers almost three fourths of the earth's surface; the ocean. 2. any large body of salt water, smaller than an ocean; as, the North Sea, the Mediterranean Sea, the Black Sea. 3. a large, heavy wave; the swell of the ocean. A high sea swept away the ship's masts. 4. Some special meanings are:

at sea, 1. out on the sea. 2. puzzled; confused.

follow the sea, be a sailor.

go to sea, 1. become a sailor. 2. begin a voyage.

put to sea, begin a voyage.

sea board (sē′bōrd′), land near the sea; seacoast.

sea coast (sē′kōst′), land along the sea.

sea far ing (sē′fãr′ing), that goes, travels, works, or lives on the sea. Sailors are seafaring men.

seal[1] (sēl), 1. design used to show ownership or authority. The seal of the United States is attached to important government papers. 2. stamp for marking things with such a design. 3. piece of wax, etc., on which the design is stamped. 4. anything representing such a design. 5. mark with a seal. 6. close tightly; shut; fasten. She sealed the letter. We seal jars of fruit. His eyes were sealed with sleep. Her promise sealed her lips. 7. authorize. 8. settle; determine. The judge's words sealed the prisoner's fate. 9. give a sign that (a thing) is true; as, to seal a promise with a kiss.

Seal of the United States

seal[2] (sēl), 1. a kind of sea animal with flippers. See the picture. Some kinds are hunted for their valuable fur. 2. the fur. 3. leather made from the skin of a seal. 4. hunt seals.

Fur seal (6 ft. long)

sealing wax, a kind of wax, soft when heated, used for sealing letters, packages, etc.

sea lion, a large seal of the Pacific Coast.

seam (sēm), 1. the line formed by sewing two pieces of cloth, canvas, leather, etc., together; as, the seams of a coat, seams of a sail. 2. any line where the edges join. The seams of the boat must be filled in or they will leak. 3. any mark or line like a seam. The old sword cut had left a seam in his face. 4. mark (the face, etc.) with wrinkles, scars, etc. 5. a layer; as, a seam of coal.

Seam in cloth

sea man (sē′mən), 1. sailor. 2. sailor who is not an officer.

sea men (sē′mən), sailors.

seam stress (sēm′stris), woman who earns her living by sewing; a sewing woman.

sea plane (sē′plān′), airplane that can rise from and alight on water; hydroplane.

sea port (sē′pōrt′), a port or harbor on the seacoast; a city or town with a harbor that ships can reach from the sea. San Francisco and New Orleans are seaports.

sear (sēr), 1. burn the surface of. The hot iron seared his flesh. 2. make hard or unfeeling. That cruel man must have a seared conscience. 3. dry up; wither. 4. dried up; withered.

search (sėrch), 1. try to find by looking; seek; look for (something); look through; go over carefully; examine. We searched all day for the lost kitten. The police searched the prisoner to see if he had a gun. The doctor searched the wound for the bullet. 2. searching; examination. John found his book after a long search. **In search of** means trying to find; looking for.

search ing (sėr′ching), 1. examining carefully; thorough; as, a searching gaze, a searching examination. 2. piercing; sharp; as, a searching wind.

search light (sėrch′līt′), 1. powerful light that can throw a beam in any direction. 2. the beam of light so thrown.

sea shore (sē′shōr′), land along the sea.

sea sick (sē′sik′), sick because of a ship's motion.

sea side (sē′sīd′), 1. land along the sea; seacoast. 2. of or at the seaside; as, a seaside hotel.

sea son (sē′zən), 1. The four seasons of the year are spring, summer, autumn, and winter. 2. any period of time marked by something special; as, the Christmas season, the harvest season. 3. suitable or fit time. **In season** means at the right time. 4. improve the flavor of. Season your egg with salt. 5. make or become fit for use by a period of keeping or treatment. Wood is seasoned for building by drying and hardening it. 6. make less severe; soften. Season justice with mercy.

sea son ing (sē′zən ing), something that gives a better flavor. Salt, pepper, and spices are seasonings. We like conversation with a seasoning of humor.

seat (sēt), 1. thing to sit on. Chairs, benches, and stools are seats. Take a seat, please. 2. place in which one has the right to sit. Our seats are in the fifth row of the first balcony. When we say that a man has a seat in Congress, we mean that he is a member of Congress. 3. that part of a chair, bench, stool, etc., on which one sits. This bench has a broken seat. 4. that part of the body on which one sits, or the clothing covering it. The seat of his trousers was patched. 5. manner of sitting on horseback. That rider has a good seat. 6. established place or center. Our county seat has a large high school. 7. residence; home. The seat of our government is in Washington, D.C. 8. to set or place on a seat. He seated himself in the most comfortable chair. 9. have seats for. Our school assembly seats one thousand pupils.

sea ward (sē′wərd), 1. toward the sea. Our house faces seaward. 2. direction toward the sea. The island lies a mile to seaward.

sea wards (sē′wərdz), seaward.

sea weed (sē′wēd′), any plant or plants growing in the sea.

se clude (si klüd′), keep apart from company; shut off from others. He secludes himself and sees only his close friends.

se clud ed (si klüd′id), shut off from others; undisturbed.

se clu sion (si klü′zhən), 1. a secluding or being secluded; retirement. She lives in seclusion apart from her friends. 2. secluded place.

sec ond[1] (sek′ənd), 1. next after the first; as, the second seat from the front, the second prize. 2. below the first; inferior; as, the second officer on a ship, cloth of second quality. 3. another; other. Ella says her friend Amy is her second self. 4. person or thing that is second. 5. goods below first quality. These stockings are seconds and have some slight defects. 6. person who supports or aids another. The prize fighter had a second. 7. support; back up; assist. A man seconded the motion to adjourn.

sec ond[2] (sek′ənd). Sixty seconds make one minute.

sec ond ar y (sek′ən dãr′i), 1. in second place; next after the first in order, place, time, or importance. A high school is a secondary school; it comes after the elementary school. 2. having less importance. Reading fast is secondary to reading well.

sec ond-hand (sek′ənd hand′), 1. not original; obtained from another; as, second-hand information. 2. not new; used already by someone else; as, second-hand clothes. 3. dealing in used goods; as, a second-hand store.

sec ond ly (sek′ənd li), in the second place.

se cre cy (sē′krə si), 1. condition of being secret or being kept secret. 2. ability to keep things secret.

se cret (sē′krit), 1. kept from sight; hidden; as, a secret room, a secret drawer, a secret spring. 2. kept from knowledge of others; as, a secret errand, a secret marriage. 3. known only to a few; as, a secret sign. 4. something secret or hidden. Can you keep a secret? 5. hidden cause or reason; as, the secret of his success, the secret of her charm.

sec re tar y (sek′ri tãr′i), 1. person who writes letters, keeps records, etc., for a person, company, club, etc. Mr. Jones keeps three secretaries busy. 2. person who has charge of a department of a government. 3. a writing desk with a set of drawers, and often with shelves for books.

se crete (si krēt′), 1. hide; keep secret. 2. make; prepare; produce. Glands in the mouth secrete saliva.

se cret ly (sē′krət li), without knowledge by others.

sect (sekt), group of people holding certain principles, beliefs, or opinions. There are many religious sects.

sec tion (sek′shən), 1. part cut off; part; division; slice. His section of the family estate was larger than his brother's. Mother cut the pie into eight equal sections. Anna divided the orange into sections. 2. division of a book. Our arithmetic has several sections on fractions. 3. region; part of a country, city, etc. A town has a business section and sections for homes. 4. act of cutting. 5. cut into sections; divide into sections. 6. a representation of a thing as it would appear if cut straight through. 7. a district one mile square. A township contains 36 sections.

Section of an apple (def. 6)

se cure (si kūr′), 1. free from care or fear. The old couple lived a quiet, secure life. 2. safe against loss, attack, escape, etc. Keep the prisoner secure within the dungeon. This is a secure hiding place. Land in a growing city is a secure investment. 3. firmly fastened; not liable to break or fall. Are the prisoner's bonds secure? Are the boards of this bridge secure? 4. sure; certain; that can be counted on. We know in advance that our victory is secure. He felt secure of salvation. 5. make firm or fast. Secure the locks on doors and windows. 6. make safe. You cannot secure yourself against all risks and dangers. 7. get; obtain. We have secured our tickets for the school play.

se cu ri ty (si kūr′i ti), 1. freedom from danger, care, or fear; feeling or condition of being safe. You may cross the street in security when a policeman holds up his hand. 2. something that secures or makes safe. A watchdog is a security against burglars. Rubber soles are a security against slipping.

se dan (si dan′), 1. a closed automobile seating four or more persons. 2. a covered chair carried on poles by two men. Sedan chairs were much used during the 17th and 18th centuries.

Sedan chair

se date (si dāt′), quiet; calm; serious. She is very sedate for a child and would rather read or sew than play.

sedge (sej), a grasslike plant that grows in wet places.

sed i ment (sed′i mənt), matter that settles to the bottom of a liquid. When a river overflows, it leaves sediment on the land it covers.

se duce (si dūs′ or si dūs′), 1. tempt to wrongdoing; persuade to do wrong. General Arnold was seduced by the offer of great wealth, and betrayed his country to the enemy. 2. lead away; lead astray; beguile.

see[1] (sē), 1. look at; be aware of by using the eyes. See that black cloud. 2. have the power of sight. The blind do not see. 3. understand. I see what you mean. 4. find out. See what you can do for him. 5. take care; make sure. See that the work is done properly. See that you come home early. 6. have knowledge or experience of. That coat has seen hard wear. 7. go with; attend. Dick will see you home. 8. call on. I went to see a friend. 9. receive a call from. Mrs. Brown is too ill to see anyone. **saw** and **seen** are formed from **see**[1].

see[2] (sē), 1. the position or authority of a bishop. 2. the district under a bishop's authority.

seed (sēd), 1. thing from which anything grows. We plant seeds in the garden. Part of every crop is saved for seed. 2. thing grown; children; descendants. The Jews are the seed of Abraham. 3. sow with seed; scatter seed over. The farmer seeded the field with corn. Dandelions seed themselves. 4. remove seeds from. Mary seeded the raisins for the cake. 5. produce seeds; shed seeds. 6. **Go to seed** means (1) come to the time of yielding seed. (2) come to the end of vigor, usefulness, prosperity, etc.

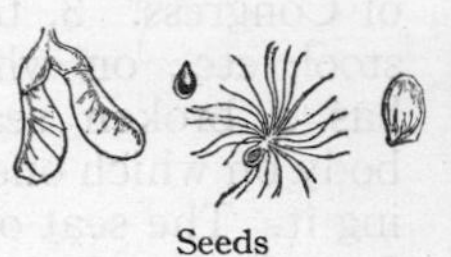
Seeds

seed ling (sēd′ling), 1. young plant grown from a seed. 2. small young tree less than three feet high.

seek (sēk), 1. try to find; look for; hunt. The boys are seeking a good camping place. 2. try to get. Most men seek wealth; all men seek happiness. He seeks your advice. 3. try; attempt. We sought to make peace between Fred and Tom. **sought** is formed from **seek.**

seem (sēm). This apple seemed good but was rotten inside. Does this room seem hot to you? The dog seems to like that bone. Men far off seem small; they look like dots.

seem ing ly (sēm′ing li), apparently; as far as appearances go. This hill is, seemingly, the highest around here.

seen (sēn). See **see**[1]. Have you seen William?

seep (sēp), ooze; trickle. Water seeps through sand.

seer (sēr), prophet; person who foresees or foretells future events.

Children seesawing

see saw (sē′sô′), 1. plank resting on a support near its middle so that the ends can move up and down. 2. move up and down on such a plank. 3. a moving up and down on such a plank. See the picture. 4. a moving up and down or back and forth. 5. move up and down or back and forth.

seethe (sēᴛʜ), 1. boil. The cook seethed the mutton. 2. bubble and foam. The seething waters carried the light boat down over the falls. 3. be excited; be disturbed. The pirate crew was seething with discontent and ready for open rebellion.

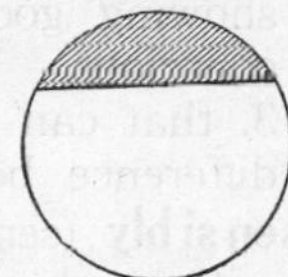
The shaded part is a segment of the circle.

seg ment (seg′mənt), piece or part cut off, marked off, or broken off; division; section. See the picture. An orange is easily pulled apart into its segments.

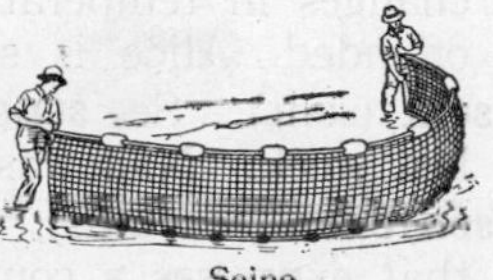
Seine

seine (sān), 1. a fishing net that hangs straight down in the water. A seine has floats at the upper edge and weights at the lower. 2. fish with a seine. 3. catch with a seine.

seize (sēz), 1. take hold of suddenly; grasp. In fright she seized his arm. 2. take possession of. The soldiers seized the city.

sei zure (sē′zhər), 1. act of seizing. 2. condition of being seized. 3. sudden attack of disease.

sel dom (sel′dəm), rarely; not often. He is seldom ill.

se lect (si lekt′), 1. choose; pick out. John's uncle let him select his own Christmas present. 2. picked as best; chosen specially. The captain needs a select crew for this dangerous job. 3. careful in choosing; particular as to friends, company, etc. She belongs to a very select club.

se lec tion (si lek′shən), choice. Her selection of a hat took a long time. The shop offered a very good selection of hats. The plain blue hat was Helen's selection.

self (self), 1. Your self is you. My self is I. Jane does not seem like her former self. It is a good thing to think more of others and less of self. 2. *Self* is used with other words to mean (1) of self; as, self-control. (2) in self; as, self-confidence. (3) by self; as, self-government. 3. *Self* is also used in special meanings; as, selfsame.

self-con fi dence (self′kon′fi dəns), belief in one's own ability, power, judgment, etc.; confidence in oneself.

self -con scious (self′kon′shəs), made conscious of how one is appearing to others; embarrassed, especially by the presence or the thought of other people and their attitude toward one; shy.

self-con trol (self′kən trōl′), control of one's actions, feelings, etc.

self-de fense or **self-de fence** (self′di fens′), defense of one's own person, property, reputation, etc.

self-gov ern ment (self′guv′ərn mənt), 1. government of a group by its own members. 2. self-control.

self ish (sel′fish), caring too much for oneself; caring too little for others. A selfish person puts his own interests first.

self ish ness (sel′fish nis), too great care for oneself; too little care for others.

self-pos ses sion (self′pə zesh′ən), control of one's feelings and actions; calmness.

self-re spect (self′ri spekt′), respect for one's self; proper pride.

self-re straint (self′ri strānt′), self-control.

self same (self′sām′), very same. We study the selfsame books that you do.

self-sat is fac tion (self′sat′is fak′shən), satisfaction with oneself.

sell (sel), 1. give up for money or other payment. Mr. Jones will sell his house. The butcher sells meat. The traitor sold his country for money. 2. be on sale; be sold. Strawberries sell at a high price in January.

sell er (sel′ər), 1. person who sells. A druggist is a seller of drugs. 2. a thing considered with reference to its sale. This book is a best seller.

selves (selvz), more than one self. He had two selves—a good self and a bad self.

sem blance (sem′bləns), likeness; appearance. These clouds have the semblance of a huge head. His story had the semblance of truth, but was really false.

sem i cir cle (sem′i sėr′kəl), a half circle. We sat in a semicircle about the fire.

sem i nar y (sem′i nãr′i), 1. school, especially an academy or boarding school for young women. 2. school to educate men for the ministry or priesthood.

sen ate (sen′it), 1. a governing or law-making assembly. 2. the upper and smaller branch of an assembly that makes laws.

sen a tor (sen′ə tər), member of a senate.

send (send), 1. cause to go. Mother sends Harold on errands. Send a messenger. 2. cause to be carried. We sent the letter by air mail. 3. cause to come. Send help at once!

sen es chal (sen′i shəl), steward of a prince or great noble in the Middle Ages. Seneschals often had the powers of judges or generals.

sen ior (sēn′yər), 1. older. 2. the older; a father whose son has the same given name; as, John Parker, Senior. 3. an older person. Paul is his brother's senior by two years. 4. higher in rank or longer in service. Mr. Jones is the senior member of the firm. 5. person of higher rank or longer service. 6. member of the graduating class of a high school or college. 7. of the graduating class.

se ñor (se nyôr′), a Spanish word meaning Mr. or sir, or a gentleman.

se ño ra (se nyō′rä), a Spanish word meaning Mrs., or madame or a lady.

se ño ri ta (sen′yō rē′tä), a Spanish word meaning Miss, or a young lady.

sen sa tion (sen sā′shən), 1. action of the senses; power to see, hear, feel, taste, smell, etc. Blindness is the loss of the sensation of sight. 2. feeling. Ice gives a sensation of coldness; polished wood gives a sensation of smoothness; sugar gives a sensation of sweetness. 3. strong or excited feeling. The announcement of war caused a sensation throughout the nation. 4. cause of such feeling. The election of a President for a fourth term was a great sensation.

sen sa tion al (sen sā′shən əl), 1. exciting; startling. 2. trying to cause excitement.

sense (sens), 1. Sight, smell, taste, hearing, and touch are the five senses. A dog has a keen sense of smell. 2. feeling. Duty well done brings a sense of pleasure. He seems to have no sense of shame. 3. understanding; appreciation. She has a poor sense of duty. 4. a clear or sound state of mind. He must be out of his senses to act so. 5. judgment; intelligence. He is a man of sense. He hasn't sense enough to come in when it rains. Common sense would have prevented the accident. 6. meaning. Mr. Trent is a gentleman in the true sense of the word. **Make sense** means have a meaning; be reasonable. The sentence James wrote on the board didn't make sense. 7. feel; understand. Mother sensed that Father was tired.

sense less (sens′lis), 1. unconscious. A hard blow knocked him senseless. 2. stupid; foolish.

sen si bil i ty (sen′si bil′i ti), 1. ability to feel or perceive. Some drugs lessen a person's sensibilities. 2. fineness of feeling. She has an unusual sensibility for colors.

sen si ble (sen′si bəl), 1. having good sense; showing good judgment; wise. 2. aware; conscious. I am sensible of your kindness. 3. that can be noticed. There is a sensible difference between yellow and orange.

sen si bly (sen′si bli), 1. in a sensible manner; with good sense. 2. so as to be felt.

sen si tive (sen′si tiv), 1. receiving impressions readily. The eye is sensitive to light. 2. easily affected or influenced. The mercury in the thermometer is sensitive to changes in temperature. 3. easily hurt or offended. Alice is sensitive when scolded.

sent (sent). See **send.** They sent the trunks last week. Nan was sent on an errand.

sen tence (sen′təns), 1. group of words that expresses a complete thought. "Boys and girls" is not a sentence. "The boys are here" is a sentence. 2. decision. 3. decision by a judge on the punishment of a criminal. 4. the punishment itself. 5. pronounce punishment on. The judge sentenced the thief to five years in prison.

sen ti ment (sen′ti mənt), 1. mixture of thought and feeling. Admiration, patriotism, and loyalty are sentiments. 2. feeling, especially refined or tender feeling. 3. a thought or saying that expresses feeling. 4. mental attitude. 5. personal opinion.

sen ti men tal (sen′ti men′təl), 1. having or showing much tender feeling. 2. likely to act from feelings rather than from logical thinking; having too much sentiment. 3. of sentiment; dependent on sentiment. She values her mother's gift for sentimental reasons.

sen ti nel (sen′ti nəl), one stationed to keep watch and guard against surprises.

sen try (sen′tri), soldier stationed at a place to keep watch and guard against surprises.

sep a rate (sep′ə rāt for 1, 2, and 3, sep′ə rit for 4), 1. be between; keep apart; divide. The Atlantic Ocean separates America from Europe. 2. go apart. After school the children separated in all directions. 3. put apart; take away. Separate your things from mine. 4. apart from others; divided; not joined. A person's teeth are separate.

sep a rate ly (sep′ə rit li), one by one; one at a time; not together.

sep a ra tion (sep′ə rā′shən), 1. act of separating; dividing; taking apart. 2. condition of being apart; being separated. The friends were glad to meet after so long a separation.

Sep tem ber (sep tem′bər), the ninth month. It has 30 days.

sep ul cher or **sep ul chre** (sep′əl kər), tomb; grave; place for putting the bodies of persons who have died.

se quel (sē′kwəl), 1. something that follows as a result of some earlier happening; a result of something. Among the sequels of the party were many stomach aches. 2. complete story continuing an earlier one about the same people.

se quence (sē′kwəns), 1. succession; the coming of one thing after another; order of succession. Arrange the names in alphabetical sequence. 2. connected series; as, a sequence of lessons on one subject. 3. something that follows; result. Crime has its sequence of misery.

se quent (sē′kwənt), following.

se quoi a (si kwoi′ə), a very tall evergreen tree of California.

sere (sēr), dried up; withered.

se rene (si rēn′), 1. peaceful; calm; as, serene happiness, a serene smile. 2. clear; bright; not cloudy.

se ren i ty (si ren′i ti), 1. calmness; peacefulness. 2. clearness; quietness.

serf (sėrf), 1. a slave who cannot be sold off the land but passes from one owner to another with the land. 2. person treated almost like a slave.

serge (sėrj), a kind of cloth woven with slanting ridges in it.

ser geant (sär′jənt), 1. army officer ranking next above a corporal. The sergeant drilled his men. 2. a police officer ranking next above a common policeman.

se ries (sēr′iz), 1. things alike in a row. A series of rooms opened off the hall. 2. things placed one after another. Our names were listed in an alphabetical series. 3. things happening one after the other. Two series of rainy days spoiled our vacation.

se ri ous (sēr′i əs), 1. thoughtful; grave; as, a serious face. 2. in earnest; not fooling. Are you joking or serious? 3. important; needing thought. Raising money for our club is a serious matter. 4. important because it may do much harm; dangerous.

se ri ous ness (sēr′i əs nis), state or quality of being serious; earnestness; importance.

ser mon (sėr′mən), 1. a public talk on religion or something connected with religion. Ministers preach sermons in church. 2. a serious talk; a moral lecture; a warning. The teacher gave us a sermon on cheating.

ser pent (sėr′pənt), 1. snake; big snake. 2. a sly, treacherous person.

ser pen tine (sėr′pən tēn), 1. of or like a serpent. 2. winding; twisting; as, the serpentine course of a creek. 3. a mineral, usually green and sometimes spotted like a serpent's skin.

serv ant (sėr′vənt), 1. person employed in a household. Cooks and nursemaids are servants. 2. person employed by another. Policemen and firemen are public servants. 3. person devoted to any service. Ministers are called servants of God.

serve (sėrv), 1. work for; be a servant; work. A slave serves his master. Good citizens serve their country. The soldier served three years in the army. 2. be useful; be what is needed; be used. A flat stone served as a table. 3. be favorable or suitable; satisfy. The ship will sail when wind and tide serve. 4. wait on at table; bring food to. 5. put (food or drink) on the table. The waiter served the soup. Dinner is served. 6. supply; furnish. The dairy serves us with milk. 7. deliver; present. Mr. White was served with a summons to appear in court. 8. treat; act toward. The punishment serves George right. 9. pass; spend. The thief served a term in prison.

serv er (sėr′vər), 1. person who serves. 2. tray for dishes.

serv ice (sėr′vis), 1. helpful act or acts; aid; being useful to others. "Service" is the motto of our school. 2. supply; arrangements for supplying. The train service was good. 3. occupation or employment as a servant. Mary is in service with Mrs. Brown. 4. work for others; work; performance of duties. Mrs. Brown no longer needs the services of a doctor. He was in active service during the war. 5. advantage; benefit; use. Would this coat be of service to you? 6. department of government or public employment; the persons working in it. **The service** often means the army or the navy. The air service was very important in the war. 7. religious meeting; religious ceremony. We attend church services twice a week. The marriage service was performed at the home of the bride. 8. manner of serving food; the food served. The service in this restaurant is excellent. 9. set of dishes, etc. She has a silver tea service. 10. make fit for service. The mechanic serviced our automobile.

serv ice a ble (sėr′vis ə bəl), useful; capable of giving good service.

ser vile (sėr′vil), 1. of slaves; as, a servile revolt, servile work. 2. like that of slaves; fit for a slave; mean; as, servile flattery.

ser vi tude (sėr′vi tūd or sėr′vi tüd), 1. slavery; bondage. 2. forced labor as a punishment. The criminal was sentenced to five years' servitude.

ses sion (sesh′ən), 1. a sitting or meeting of a court, council, legislature, etc. 2. a series of such sittings. 3. the term or period of such sittings. 4. a single, continuous course or period of lessons. Our school has two sessions, one in the morning and one in the afternoon.

set (set), 1. put in some place; put; place. Set the box on its end. 2. put in the right place, position, or condition for use; arrange; put in proper order. The hunter sets his traps. Set the table for dinner. Set the clock. The doctor will set Dan's broken leg. 3. put in some condition or relation. A spark set the woods on fire. The slaves were set free. 4. fix. If he sets his mind on it, he will do it. 5. become fixed; become firm or hard. Jelly sets as it cools. 6. form; shape; the way a thing is put or placed. There was a stubborn set to his jaw. 7. direction; tendency; course; drift. The set of opinion was toward building a new bridge. 8. tend; have a certain direction. The current sets to the south. 9. group; things or people belonging together; as, a set of dishes. 10. go down; sink. The sun sets in the west. 11. begin to move; start. He set out to cross the river. 12. young plant. 13. that has been set; fixed; arranged; formal; as, a set smile, a set speech. 14. Some special meanings are:

set about, begin; start work upon.

set forth, 1. declare. 2. start to go.

set in, 1. begin. 2. blow or flow toward the shore.

set off, 1. explode. 2. start to go. 3. increase by contrast.

setting hen, a hen sitting on eggs to hatch them.

set up, 1. build. 2. begin; start. 3. put up; raise in place, position, power, pride, etc.

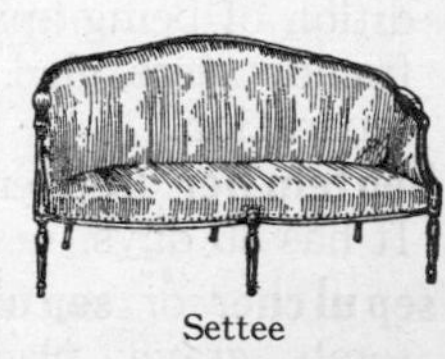
Settee

set tee (se tē′), a sofa or long bench with a back.

set ter (set′ər), 1. person who sets; as, a setter of type or of jewels. 2. a long-haired hunting dog, trained to stand motionless and point his nose toward the game that he scents.

English setter (about 2 ft. high at the shoulder)

set ting (set′ing), 1. frame or other thing in which something is set. The mounting of a jewel is a setting. 2. scenery of a play. 3. place, time, etc., of a play or story. 4. surroundings; background. 5. music composed to go with certain words. 6. the eggs that a hen sits on for hatching. 7. See **set.** Mary was setting the table.

set tle[1] (set′əl), 1. set or be set in a fairly permanent position, place, or way of life. At last we are settled in our new home. Our cousin intends to settle in California. 2. place in a desired or comfortable position. The cat settled herself down in the chair for a nap. 3. put in order; arrange. I must settle all my affairs before going away for the winter. 4. make quiet; become quiet. A vacation will settle your nerves. After the excitement over the Christmas presents had settled down, the children went out to play. 5. clear (a liquid). A beaten egg or cold water will settle coffee. 6. determine; decide; agree upon. Children bring their disputes to mother to settle. Have you settled on a day for the picnic? 7. pay. He settled all his bills before leaving town. Let us settle up our expenses for the trip. 8. establish colonies in; take up residence in (a new country or place) as colonists. The English settled New England. 9. sink. Our house has settled several inches since it was built. 10. come to rest in a particular place; become set or fixed. His cold is settling in his lungs.

Settle

set tle[2] (set′əl), a long bench.

set tle ment (set′əl mənt), 1. act of settling or state of being settled. 2. putting in order; arrangement. No settlement of the dispute is possible unless each side yields some point. 3. payment. 4. the settling of persons in a new country. 5. a group of buildings and the people living in them. Indians often attacked the little settlements of the colonists.

set tler (set′lər), 1. one who settles. 2. person who settles in a new country. The early settlers in America had to fight the Indians.

sev en (sev′ən), one more than six; 7.

sev en teen (sev′ən tēn′), seven more than ten; 17.

sev en teenth (sev′ən tēnth′), 1. next after the 16th. 2. one of 17 equal parts.

sev enth (sev′ənth), 1. next after the sixth. Saturday is the seventh day of the week. 2. one of seven equal parts. A day is one seventh of a week.

sev en ty (sev′ən ti), seven times ten; 70.

sev er (sev′ər), 1. cut apart; separate. The sailor severed the rope with a knife. The rope severed, and the swing fell down. 2. break off. The two nations severed friendly relations.

sev er al (sev′ər əl), 1. some; a few; more than two or three but not many. 2. different; individual. The boys went their several ways, each minding his own business.

se vere (si vēr′), 1. very strict; stern; harsh. The teacher was severe with the children and used severe punishment. 2. serious; dangerous; as, a severe illness. 3. very plain or simple; without ornament. Her haircut is severe like a boy's. 4. sharp; violent. I have a severe headache. That was a severe storm. 5. difficult. The new gun had to pass a series of severe tests.

se vere ly (si vēr′li), in a severe way; violently; hard.

se ver i ty (si ver′i ti), 1. strictness; sternness; harshness. The children feared their father because of his severity. 2. simplicity of style or taste; plainness. The severity of a nun's dress is often becoming. 3. violence; sharpness; as, the severity of storms, pain, or grief. 4. seriousness.

sew (sō), 1. work with a needle and thread; fasten with stitches. You can sew by hand or with a machine. 2. close with stitches. The doctor sewed up the wound.

sew er (sü′ər), a drain to carry off waste water and refuse.

sew ing (sō′ing), work done with a needle and thread; something to be sewed.

sewn (sōn), sewed.

sex (seks), the character of being male or female. A boy is of the male sex; a girl is of the female sex.

sex ton (seks′tən), man who takes care of a church. The sexton keeps the church clean and warm.

shab by (shab′i), 1. much worn. His old suit looks shabby. 2. wearing old or much worn clothes. She is always shabby. 3. mean; not generous; unfair. It is shabby not to speak to an old friend because he is poor.

shack (shak), roughly built hut; house in bad condition.

shack le (shak′əl), 1. See the picture. 2. put shackles on. 3. anything that prevents freedom of action, thought, etc. 4. restrain; hamper. 5. thing for fastening or coupling.

Shackles

shad (shad), food fish of the North Atlantic Coast of America. Shad have many small loose bones.

shade (shād), 1. partly dark place, not in the sunshine. He sat in the shade of a big tree. 2. something that shuts out light. Pull down the shades of the windows. 3. keep light from. A big hat shades the eyes. 4. depth of color; lightness or darkness of color. I want to see silks in all shades of blue. 5. make darker than the rest; darken. A person shades one side of a dish when he draws or paints it. 6. very small difference; little bit. Your coat is a shade longer than your dress. 7. show very small differences; change little by little. This scarf shades from deep rose to pale pink.

shad ing (shād′ing), 1. covering from the light. 2. use of black or color to give the effect of shade in a picture. 3. slight variation or difference of color, character, etc.

shad ow (shad′ō), 1. shade made by some person or thing. Sometimes a person's shadow is much longer than he is, and sometimes much shorter. 2. darkness; partial shade. Don't turn on the light; we like to sit in the shadow. 3. little bit; small degree; slight suggestion. There's not a shadow of a doubt about his guilt. 4. ghost; faint image. You look worn to a shadow. 5. protect from light; shade. The grass is shadowed by huge oaks. 6. follow closely.

shad ow y (shad′ō i), 1. having much shadow or shade; shady. We are glad to leave the hot sunshine and come into the cool shadowy room. 2. like a shadow; dim. He saw a shadowy outline on the window curtain.

shad y (shād′i), 1. in the shade. 2. giving shade. 3. of doubtful morality. That man is a shady character, if not an actual criminal.

shaft[1] (shaft). A shaft is always a long, slender part or piece. It may be: 1. the long, slender stem of an arrow, spear, etc. 2. arrow; spear. 3. one of the two wooden poles between which a horse is harnessed to a carriage, etc. 4. the main part of a column. See the picture under **column.** 5. a bar to support parts of a machine that turn, or to help move parts.

shaft[2] (shaft), 1. deep passage sunk in the earth. The entrance to a mine is called a shaft. 2. a passage that is like a well; a long, narrow space; as, an elevator shaft.

S, shaft in a mine; T, tunnel.

shag gy (shag′i), 1. covered with a thick rough mass of hair, wool, etc.; as, a shaggy dog. 2. long, thick, and rough; as, shaggy eyebrows.

shake (shāk), 1. move quickly backwards and forwards, up and down, or from side to side. The woman shakes the bad boy. John shook his fist in Tom's face. 2. tremble or make tremble. He is shaking with cold. 3. disturb; make less firm. His lie shook my faith in his honesty. 4. act of shaking. A shake of the head was her answer.

shak y (shāk′i), 1. shaking; as, a shaky voice. 2. liable to break down; weak; as, a shaky chair. 3. not reliable; not to be depended on; as, a shaky bank.

shale (shāl), rock formed from hardened clay, etc., that splits easily into thin layers.

shall (shal). We shall come soon. You shall go to the party, I promise you. She shall drink her milk, even if I have to pour it down her throat. Shall is used to express future time, command, obligation, and necessity.

shal lop (shal′əp), a small, light boat.

shal low (shal′ō), 1. not deep; as, shallow water, a shallow dish, a shallow mind. 2. shallow place. The boys splashed in the shallows of the pond.

shalt (shalt), old form meaning **shall.**

sham (sham), 1. fraud; pretense. His goodness is all a sham. 2. false; pretended; imitation. The soldiers had a sham battle. 3. pretend. John is not really sick; he is only shamming.

sham ble (sham′bəl), 1. walk awkwardly or unsteadily. The tired old man shambles. 2. shambling walk.

sham bles (sham′bəlz), 1. place where animals are killed for food. 2. place of butchery or great bloodshed.

shame (shām), 1. painful feeling of having done something wrong, improper, or silly. The child blushed with shame when he was caught stealing candy. 2. cause to feel shame. My silly mistake shamed me. 3. drive or force by shame. Bill was shamed into combing his hair. 4. disgrace; dishonor. That young man's arrest has brought shame to a fine family. 5. bring disgrace upon. He has shamed his parents. 6. a fact to be sorry about; a pity. It is a shame to be so wasteful. What a shame you can't come to the party!

shame ful (shām′fəl), causing shame; bringing disgrace.

shame less (shām′lis), 1. without shame. 2. not modest.

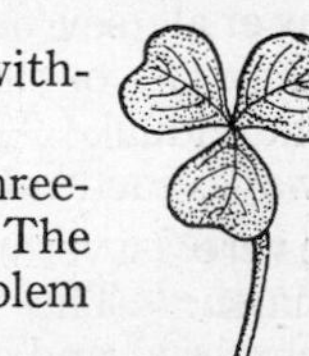
Shamrock

sham rock (sham′rok), a three-leaved plant like clover. The shamrock is the national emblem of Ireland.

shank (shangk), 1. the part of the leg between the knee and the ankle. 2. the corresponding part in animals. 3. the whole leg. 4. any part like a leg, stem, or shaft; as, the shank of an anchor.

shan't (shant), shall not.

shan ty (shan′ti), roughly built hut or cabin.

shape (shāp), 1. form; figure; appearance. An apple is different in shape from a banana. A witch could take the shape of a cat or a bat. A white shape stood at his bedside. 2. condition; order. Take time to get your thoughts into shape. 3. to form. The child shapes clay into balls. The hat is shaped to fit her head. 4. **Take shape** means have or take on a definite form. 5. develop; take shape. His plan is shaping well.

shape less (shāp′lis), 1. without definite shape. 2. having a shape that is not attractive. She wore a shapeless old hat.

shape ly (shāp′li), having a pleasing shape; well-formed.

share (shãr), 1. part; portion; part belonging to one person. The father left each child an equal share of his property. John does more than his share of the work and does not always get his share of the praise. 2. each of the parts into which the ownership of a company or corporation is divided. The ownership of this railroad is divided into several million shares. 3. divide into parts, each taking a part. The knight shared his bread with the beggar. 4. use together; enjoy together; have in common. The sisters share the same room. 5. have a share; take part. Everyone shared in making the picnic a success.

shark (shärk), 1. a large fish that eats other fish and is said to attack people. 2. a dishonest person who preys on others.

Blue shark (about 15 ft. long)

sharp (shärp), 1. having a thin cutting edge or a fine point; as, a sharp knife, a sharp pin. 2. having a point; not rounded; as, a sharp nose, a sharp corner on a box. 3. with a sudden change of direction; as, a sharp turn. 4. very cold; as, sharp weather, a sharp morning. 5. severe; biting; as, sharp words. 6. feeling somewhat like a cut or prick; acting sharply on the senses; as, a sharp taste, a sharp noise, a sharp pain. 7. clear; distinct; as, the sharp contrast between black and white. 8. quick; brisk; as, a sharp walk or run. 9. fierce; violent; as, a sharp struggle. 10. keen; eager; as, a sharp desire, a sharp appetite. 11. being aware of things quickly; as, a sharp eye, sharp ears. 12. watchful; wide-awake. 13. quick in mind; shrewd; clever; as, a sharp boy, a sharp lawyer, sharp at a bargain. 14. promptly; exactly. Come at one o'clock sharp. 15. in music, above the true pitch; as, to sing sharp. 16. a tone one half step above a given tone. 17. the sign (♯) that shows this. 18. in a sharp manner; suddenly.

sharp en (shär′pən), 1. make sharp. Sharpen the pencil. Sharpen your wits. 2. become sharp.

sharp ness (shärp′nis), quality or condition of being sharp.

sharp shoot er (shärp′shüt′ər), 1. person who shoots very well. 2. soldier chosen to do accurate shooting.

shat ter (shat′ər), 1. break into pieces. A stone shattered the window. 2. destroy; disturb greatly; as, shattered hopes, a shattered mind.

shave (shāv), 1. cut hair from (the face, chin, etc.) with a razor. 2. cutting off hair with a razor. 3. cut off (hair) with a razor. 4. cut off in thin slices. She shaved the chocolate. 5. come very close to; graze. The car shaved the corner. 6. narrow miss or escape. The shot missed him, but it was a close shave.

shav en (shāv′ən), shaved.

shav ing (shāv′ing), 1. very thin piece or slice. Shavings of wood are cut off by a plane. 2. act or process of cutting hair from the face, chin, etc., with a razor.

shawl (shôl), square or oblong piece of material worn about the shoulders or head.

she (shē), the girl, woman, or female animal spoken about. My sister says she likes to read and her reading helps her in school.

sheaf (shēf), bundle of things of the same sort; as, a sheaf of arrows. We were bringing sheaves of wheat.

shear (shēr), 1. cut with shears or scissors. 2. cut the wool or fleece from. The farmer sheared his sheep. 3. cut close; cut off.

Shears

shears (shērz), 1. large scissors. 2. any cutting instrument resembling scissors.

sheath (shēth), 1. a case or covering for the blade of a sword or knife. 2. any similar covering.

sheathe (shēᴛʜ), 1. put (a sword, etc.) into a sheath. 2. enclose in a case or covering; as, a mummy sheathed in linen, doors sheathed in metal.

sheaves (shēvz), more than one sheaf.

shed[1] (shed), a building used for shelter, storage, etc., usually having only one story; as, a train shed, a woodshed.

shed[2] (shed), 1. pour out; let fall. He is shedding his blood for his country. The girl had shed tears. 2. throw off. A snake sheds its skin. An umbrella sheds water. 3. cause to flow. He shed his enemy's blood. 4. scatter abroad; give forth. The sun sheds light. Flowers shed perfume. 5. did shed.

sheen (shēn), brightness; luster; shine. Satin and polished silver have a sheen.

sheep (shēp), 1. an animal raised for wool and mutton. Farmer Jones has a hundred sheep. 2. person who is weak, timid, or stupid. "Are you men or are you sheep?" cried the captain. 3. leather made from the skin of a sheep.

Sheep

sheep ish (shēp′ish), 1. awkwardly bashful or embarrassed; as, a sheepish smile. 2. like a sheep; timid; weak; stupid.

sheep skin (shēp′skin′), 1. the skin of a sheep, especially with the wool on it. 2. leather or parchment made from it.

sheer[1] (shēr), 1. very thin; almost transparent. She wore a sheer white dress. 2. unmixed; complete. She fainted from sheer weariness. 3. straight up and down; steep. From the top of the wall was a sheer drop of 100 feet to the water below. 4. completely.

sheer[2] (shēr), 1. swerve; turn aside; turn from a course. 2. a turning of a ship from its course.

sheet[1] (shēt), 1. large piece of linen or cotton cloth used to sleep on or under. 2. a broad thin piece of anything; as, a sheet of paper, a sheet of glass. 3. single piece of paper. 4. newspaper. 5. a broad flat surface; as, a sheet of water.

sheet[2] (shēt), a rope that controls the angle at which a sail is set.

sheet iron, iron in sheets or thin plates.

sheik or **sheikh** (shēk), title given to a chief or head of a family, village, or tribe in parts of Asia and Africa.

shelf (shelf), 1. a thin, flat piece of wood, stone, etc., fastened to a wall or frame to hold things, such as books, dishes, etc. 2. anything like a shelf.

Shelf holding a vase, a clock, and a pitcher.

shell (shel), 1. hard outside covering. Nuts, eggs, oysters, turtles, and beetles all have shells. 2. something like a shell. The framework of a house, a very light racing boat, the pods or husks of some vegetables, and a case filled with gunpowder to be fired from a cannon are all called shells. 3. take out of a shell. The cook is shelling peas. 4. separate (grains of corn) from the cob. 5. fire cannon at. The enemy shelled the town.

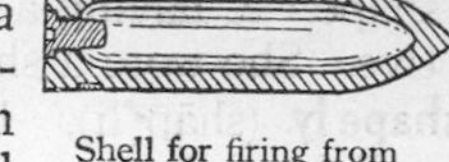
Shell for firing from a cannon

she'll (shēl), 1. she shall. 2. she will.

shel lac (shə lak′), 1. a varnish made with alcohol. 2. put shellac on.

shell fish (shel′fish′), a water animal with a shell. Oysters, clams, crabs, and lobsters are shellfish. Shellfish are very different from regular fish.

shel ter (shel′tər), 1. something that covers or protects from weather, danger, or attack. Trees are a shelter from the sun. 2. protection; refuge. We took shelter from the storm in a barn. 3. protect; shield; as, to shelter runaway slaves. 4. find shelter.

shelve[1] (shelv), 1. put on a shelf. 2. lay aside. Let us shelve that argument. 3. furnish with shelves.

shelve[2] (shelv), slope gradually.

shelves (shelvz), more than one shelf.

shep herd (shep′ərd), 1. man who takes care of sheep. 2. take care of. He will shepherd his flock. 3. guide; direct. The teacher shepherded the children safely out of the burning building. 4. person who cares for and protects. The **Good Shepherd** means Jesus.

shep herd ess (shep′ər dis), woman who takes care of sheep.

sher bet (shėr′bət), 1. frozen mixture of fruit juice, sugar, and water or milk. 2. a drink of fruit juice, sugar, and water, popular in the Orient.

sher iff (sher′if), the most important law-enforcing officer of a county. The sheriff pursued the thieves.

sher ry (sher′i), a strong, light-colored wine.

shew (shō), show.

shied (shīd). See **shy.**

shield (shēld), 1. piece of armor carried on the arm to protect the body in battle. 2. anything used to protect. A windshield on a car keeps off the wind. 3. something shaped like a shield. 4. protect; defend. His mother shielded him from punishment.

Knight holding a shield

shift (shift), 1. change from one place, position, person, etc., to another; to change. He shifted the suitcase from one hand to the other. He always tries to shift the blame to someone else. The wind has shifted to the southeast. 2. a change; substituting in the place of another person or thing. There are two shifts of work in the factory. 3. group of workmen; a group. This man is on the night shift. 4. manage to get along. When his parents died, Tom had to shift for himself. 5. way of getting on; scheme; trick.

shift less (shift′lis), lazy; inefficient.

shil ling (shil′ing), a British silver coin. In ordinary times it was worth about 24 cents in United States money.

shim mer (shim′ər), 1. gleam faintly. The satin shimmers. 2. faint gleam or shine. Pearls have a beautiful shimmer.

shin (shin), 1. the front part of the leg from the knee to the ankle. 2. climb. Tom shinned up the tree.

shine (shīn), 1. send out light; be bright with light. The sun shines. John's face is shining with soap and water. 2. light; brightness; as, the shine of a lamp. 3. sunshine; fair weather. He goes to school rain or shine. 4. luster; polish. Silk has a shine. 5. do very well; be bright. Mary shines in school. Fred is a shining athlete. 6. make bright or light; polish. We shined the silver. **shone** is formed from **shine.**

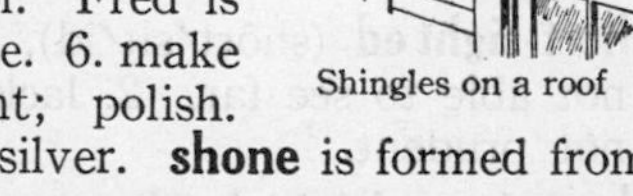
Shingles on a roof

shin gle[1] (shing′gəl), 1. a thin piece of wood, etc., used to cover roofs, etc. See the picture. 2. cover with such pieces. 3. cut (the hair) short. She has had her hair shingled.

shin gle[2] (shing′gəl), loose stones or pebbles such as lie on the seashore; coarse gravel.

shin y (shīn′i), bright; shining. A new penny is shiny. A coat may get shiny from hard wear.

ship (ship), 1. a large vessel with masts and sails. 2. any large vessel for use on water or in air; as, a steamship, a battleship, an airship. 3. a sailing vessel with three or more masts. 4. put or take on board a ship. 5. travel on a ship; sail. 6. send or carry from one place to another by a ship, train, truck, etc. Did he ship it by express or by freight? 7. engage for service on a ship. The captain is shipping a new crew. 8. take a job on a ship. He shipped as cook. 9. take in (water) over the side. A boat ships water when waves break over it. 10. fix in a ship or boat in its proper place for use; as, to ship a rudder.

ship board (ship′bōrd′), ship. **On shipboard** means on a ship.

ship ment (ship′mənt), 1. sending; being sent. A thousand boxes of oranges were ready for shipment. 2. goods sent. The shipment of boxes from the factory has not reached us.

ship per (ship′ər), one who ships goods.

ship ping (ship′ing), 1. the sending of goods by water, rail, etc. 2. ships; the ships of a nation, city, or business. 3. See **ship.**

ship wreck (ship′rek′), 1. destruction or loss of a ship. Only two people were saved from the shipwreck. 2. wrecked ship. 3. destruction; ruin. The shipwreck of his plans discouraged him. 4. wreck, ruin, or destroy. 5. suffer shipwreck.

ship yard (ship′yärd′), place near the water where ships are built or repaired.

shirk (sherk), 1. avoid or get out of doing (work, a duty, etc.). Tom lost his job because he shirked his work. 2. person who shirks or does not do his share.

shirt (shert), 1. a garment for the upper part of a man's body. 2. an undergarment for the upper part of the body.

shiv er[1] (shiv′ər), 1. shake with cold, fear, etc. 2. shaking from cold, fear, etc.

shiv er[2] (shiv′ər), 1. break into small pieces. He shivered the mirror with a hammer. 2. small piece; splinter.

shoal[1] (shōl), 1. shallow. 2. place where the water is shallow. 3. a sandbank or sand bar which makes the water shallow. The ship was wrecked on the shoals. 4. become shallow.

shoal[2] (shōl), 1. large number; crowd. We saw a shoal of fish in the water. 2. form into a shoal; crowd together.

shock[1] (shok), 1. a sudden, violent shake. The two trains collided with a terrible shock. 2. a sudden, violent disturbance. His death was a great shock to his family. 3. disturbance produced by an electric current passing through the body. 4. sudden attack of illness that makes a person senseless or takes away the power to move or speak. 5. give a shock to; cause to feel surprise, horror, or disgust. That child's bad language shocks everyone.

shock[2] (shok), 1. group of stalks of corn or bundles of grain set up on end together. 2. make into shocks.

shock[3] (shok), a thick bushy mass. He has a shock of red hair.

shock ing (shok′ing), 1. causing intense and painful surprise. 2. offensive; disgusting.

shod (shod), furnished with shoes; put shoes on. See **shoe.** The blacksmith shod the horses.

shoe (shü), 1. an outer covering for a person's foot. 2. something used like a shoe; as, a horseshoe. 3. furnish with shoes. A blacksmith shoes horses. May's feet were shod with silver slippers.

A, lady's shoe; B, child's shoe.

shoe mak er (shü′māk′ər), man who makes or mends shoes.

shone (shōn). See **shine.** The sun shone all last week. It has not shone since.

shook (shu̇k). See **shake.** They shook hands.

shoot (shüt), 1. move suddenly and rapidly. A car shot by us. Flames shoot up from a burning house. Pain shot up his arm from his hurt finger. 2. come forth from the ground; grow; grow rapidly. Buds shoot forth in the spring. The corn is shooting up during the warm weather. 3. send swiftly. A bow shoots an arrow. He shot question after question at us. 4. fire (a gun, etc.). The boys shot at the mark. 5. hit with a bullet, arrow, etc. John shot a rabbit. 6. new part growing out; young branch. See the new shoots on that bush.

shop (shop), 1. place where things are sold; a store. 2. visit stores to look at or to buy things. We shopped all morning for new coats. 3. place where things are made or repaired. He works in a carpenter's shop. 4. place where a certain kind of work is done; as, a barber shop.

shop keep er (shop′kēp′ər), person who carries on business in a shop or store.

shop ping (shop′ing), visiting stores to look at or to buy things.

shore (shōr), 1. land at the edge of a sea, lake, etc. **Off shore** means in or on the water, not far from the shore. 2. land near a sea. 3. land.

shorn (shōrn). See **shear.** The sheep was shorn of its wool.

short (shôrt), 1. not long; as, a short time, a short life, a short street. 2. not tall; as, a short man, short grass. 3. not coming up to the right amount, measure, or standard. They say that butcher sometimes gives short weight. Nothing short of your best work will satisfy me. 4. so brief as to be rude. He was so short with me that I felt hurt. 5. breaking or crumbling easily. Pastry is made short with butter and lard. 6. in a short manner; suddenly. He stopped short. 7. Some special meanings are:

cut short, end suddenly.

fall short, 1. fail to reach. 2. be insufficient.

for short, to make shorter.

in short, briefly.

run short, 1. not have enough. 2. not be enough.

short com ing (shôrt′kum′ing), fault; defect.

short en (shôr′tən), 1. make shorter; cut off; take in. She has had all her dresses shortened. 2. become shorter. The days shorten in November in this country.

short en ing (shôr′tən ing), butter, lard, etc., used to make pastry, cake, etc., crumbly.

short ly (shôrt′li), 1. soon; in a short time. 2. in few words; briefly.

shorts (shôrts), 1. breeches that reach only to the knees. 2. short loose trousers worn by boys and girls in sports; trunks. 3. baby's short clothes. 4. mixture of bran and coarse meal.

short-sight ed (shôrt′sīt′id), 1. near-sighted; not able to see far. 2. lacking in foresight; not prudent.

short stop (shôrt′stop′), baseball player between second and third base.

shot[1] (shot), 1. act of shooting. 2. tiny balls of lead; bullets; single ball of lead for a gun or cannon. 3. discharge of a gun or cannon. He heard two shots. 4. an attempt to hit by shooting. That was a good shot, and it hit the mark. 5. the distance a weapon can shoot. We were within rifle shot of the fort. 6. person who shoots. Mr. Smith is a good shot. 7. something like a shot. An aimed stroke or throw in a game is sometimes called a shot. 8. a remark aimed at some person or thing. 9. a heavy metal ball.

shot[2] (shot), 1. See **shoot.** Many years ago he shot a rival and was himself shot in revenge. 2. woven so as to show a play of colors; as, silk shot with gold.

shot gun (shot′gun′), a gun for firing cartridges filled with very small shot.

should (shu̇d), 1. See **shall.** "I said that I should come next week" means that I said, "I shall come next week." 2. ought to. You should try to make fewer mistakes. 3. **Should** is used to express uncertainty. If it should rain, I should not go. 4. **Should** is used in speaking of something which might have happened but did not. I should have gone if you had asked me.

shoul der (shōl′dər), 1. the part of the body to which an arm or foreleg is attached. 2. **Shoulders** often means the two shoulders and the upper part of the back. The man carried a trunk on his shoulders. 3. take on the shoulders; bear (a burden, blame, etc.). Uncle James shouldered the responsibility and expense of sending Jim to college. 4. push with the shoulders. He shouldered his way through the crowd. 5. something that sticks out like a shoulder. Don't drive on the shoulder of the road.

shoulder blade, flat bone of the shoulder.

should n't (shu̇d′ənt), should not.

shouldst (shu̇dst), an old form meaning **should.** "Thou shouldst" means "You should."

shout (shout), 1. call or cry loudly and vigorously. The drowning boy shouted for help. We shouted, "Fire!" The crowd shouted with laughter. 2. a loud, vigorous call or cry. Shouts of joy rang through the halls. 3. talk or laugh very loudly.

shove (shuv), push. The people shoved to get on the crowded car. Fred gave the boat a shove which sent it far out into the water.

shov el (shuv′əl), 1. tool for lifting and throwing loose matter; as, a snow shovel, a coal shovel. See the picture. A steam shovel is worked by steam. 2. lift and throw with a shovel. The men shoveled the sand into a cart. 3. make with a shovel. They shoveled a path through the snow.

Coal shovel

show (shō), 1. let be seen; put in sight. The little girl showed us her dolls. The dog showed his teeth. 2. be in sight. The hole in Jack's stocking shows above his shoe. 3. point out; direct; guide. A boy showed us the way to town. 4. make clear; explain. The teacher showed the children how to do the problem. 5. grant; give; as, to show mercy, to show favor. 6. showing. The club voted by a show of hands. 7. **Show off** means display; as, to show off fine clothes. 8. display. The jewels made a fine show. 9. display for effect. The Smiths' house is furnished for show, not for comfort. 10. appearance. There is some show of truth in Joe's argument. 11. pretense; false appearance. The boy made a show of interest. 12. any kind of public exhibition or display. We are going to the flower show and to the automobile show.

show er (shou′ər), 1. short fall of rain. 2. anything like a fall of rain; as, a shower of hail, a shower of tears, a shower of sparks from an engine. 3. come in a shower. 4. send in a shower; pour down. Grace's rich aunt showered gifts upon her.

shown (shōn), showed. See **show.** The clerk has shown the lady many hats. We were shown many tricks.

show y (shō′i), 1. making a display; likely to attract attention; conspicuous. A peony is a showy flower. 2. too bright and gay to be in good taste.

shrank (shrangk). See **shrink.** That shirt shrank in the wash.

shred (shred), 1. very small piece torn off or cut off; very narrow strip; scrap. The wind tore the sail to shreds. 2. fragment; particle; bit. There's not a shred of evidence that he took the money. 3. tear or cut into small pieces.

Shrew (about 5 in. long with the tail)

shrew (shrü), 1. a bad-tempered, quarrelsome woman. 2. a small animal like a mouse, that has a long snout and eats insects. See the picture above.

shrewd (shrüd), sharp; keen; able to think what should be done. He is shrewd in his business.

shrewd ness (shrüd′nis), sharpness; keenness; practical sense.

shriek (shrēk), 1. a loud, sharp, shrill sound. We heard the shriek of the engine's whistle. 2. make such a sound. People sometimes shriek because of terror, anger, or pain.

shrill (shril), 1. having a high pitch; high and sharp in sound; piercing. Crickets, locusts, and katydids make shrill noises. 2. make a shrill sound; sound sharply.

Shrimp (2 in. long)

shril ly (shril′li), in shrill tones.

shrimp (shrimp), 1. a small shellfish, used for food. See the picture just above. 2. a small or insignificant person.

shrine (shrīn), 1. sacred place; place where sacred things are kept. A shrine may be the tomb of a saint, an altar in a church, or a box holding a holy object. 2. any place or object sacred because of its history; something sacred because of memories connected with it. America sometimes is called freedom's shrine.

Shrine

shrink (shringk), 1. become smaller; make smaller. Wool shrinks in washing. 2. draw back. The dog shrank from the whip. She shrinks from meeting strangers. **shrank, shrunk,** and **shrunken** are formed from **shrink.**

shriv el (shriv′əl), dry up; wither; wrinkle. The hot sunshine shriveled the grass.

shroud[1] (shroud), 1. cloth or garment in which a dead person is wrapped for burial. 2. wrap for burial. 3. something that covers, conceals, or veils. The fog was a shroud over everything. 4. cover; conceal; veil. The earth is shrouded in darkness.

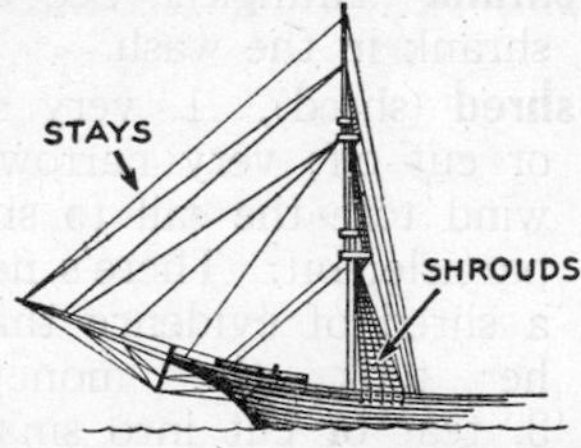

shroud[2] (shroud), a rope from a mast to the side of a ship. Shrouds help support the mast. See the picture just above.

shrub (shrub), a bush; a woody plant smaller than a tree, with many separate stems starting from or near the ground. A lilac bush is a shrub.

shrub ber y (shrub′ər i), 1. shrubs. 2. place planted with shrubs.

shrug (shrug), 1. raise (the shoulders) as an expression of dislike, doubt, indifference, or impatience. He merely shrugged his shoulders in answer to our request for help. 2. raising the shoulders in this way.

shrunk (shrungk). See **shrink.** His wool stockings have shrunk so that he can't get them on.

shrunk en (shrungk′ən), grown smaller; shriveled. See **shrink.**

shud der (shud′ər), 1. tremble with horror, fear, cold, etc. She shudders at the sight of a snake. 2. a trembling; a quivering.

shuf fle (shuf′əl), 1. walk without lifting the feet; scrape or drag the feet. The old man shuffles feebly along. 2. a scraping or dragging movement of the feet. 3. mix; jumble together. He shuffled the pack of cards. 4. push about. 5. move this way and that; as, to shuffle into your clothes. 6. movement this way and that. After a hasty shuffle through his papers, the speaker began to talk.

shun (shun), keep away from; avoid. She was lazy and shunned work.

shut (shut), 1. close. Shut your eyes. You can shut a door, window, book, knife, etc. 2. keep (from coming in). The curtains shut out the light. Shut the dog out of this room. 3. close tight; close securely. When our house was shut up for the summer, we locked all doors and windows. 4. enclose; confine; keep (from going out). Shut the kitten in the basket. 5. check; turn off. Shut off the radio. 6. be closed; become closed.

shut ter (shut′ər), 1. a movable cover for a window. 2. device that opens and closes in front of the lens of a camera. 3. any movable cover, slide, etc., for closing an opening.

shut tle (shut′əl), 1. an instrument that carries the thread from one side of the web to the other in weaving. 2. an instrument on which thread is wound. Shuttles are often used in making lace. 3. something that goes back and forth. 4. move quickly to and fro.

Shuttle for weaving: A, yarn, B, bobbin; C, eye through which the yarn is led; D, yarn.

shy[1] (shī), 1. bashful; uncomfortable in

company. John is shy and dislikes parties. 2. easily frightened away. A deer is a shy animal. 3. start back or aside suddenly. A horse will often shy at a newspaper blowing along the ground.

shy[2] (shī), throw. The boy shied a stone at the tree.

shy ly (shī′li), in a shy manner.

shy ness (shī′nis), shy behavior; quality or state of being shy.

sick (sik), 1. in poor health; having some disease; ill. 2. vomiting; inclined to vomit; feeling nausea. 3. for a sick person. 4. sick people. The sick need special care. 5. weary; tired. He is sick of school. 6. affected with sorrow or longing. She is sick at heart.

sick en (sik′ən), 1. become sick. The bird sickened when kept in the cage. 2. make sick. The sight of blood sickened him.

sick le (sik′əl), tool consisting of a short, curved blade on a short handle, for cutting grass, etc.

Sickle

sick ly (sik′li), 1. often sick; not strong; not healthy. 2. of sickness. Her skin is a sickly yellow. 3. causing sickness; as, a sickly climate. 4. faint; weak; pale.

sick ness (sik′nis), 1. illness; poor health; disease. 2. nausea; vomiting.

side (sīd), 1. a surface or line bounding a thing; as, the sides of a square, a side of a box. 2. one of the two surfaces of an object that is not the front, back, top, or bottom. There is a door at the side of the house. 3. either of the two surfaces of paper, cloth, etc. Write only on one side of the paper. 4. a particular surface; as, the outer and inner sides of a hollow ball, the side of the moon turned toward the earth. 5. either the right or the left part of the body of a person or an animal. The man was wounded in the side. 6. either the right or the left part of a thing; either part or region beyond a central line; as, the east side of a city, our side of the street, to turn to one side. 7. the slope of a hill or bank. 8. group of persons who stand up for their beliefs, opinions, ways of doing things, etc., against another group. 9. the position, course, or part of one person or party against another. It is pleasant to be on the winning side. 10. part of a family; a line of descent. The man is English on his mother's side. 11. at one side; on one side; as, a side door, a side aisle. 12. from one side; as, a side view. 13. toward one side; as, a side glance. 14. less important; as, a side issue. 15. take sides; place oneself with a side or group. The sisters always side with each other when the children quarrel.

side board (sīd′bōrd′), piece of dining-room furniture. A sideboard has drawers and shelves for holding silver and linen, and space on top for dishes.

side long (sīd′lông′), to one side; toward the side.

side walk (sīd′wôk′), place to walk at the side of a street.

side ways (sīd′wāz′), 1. to one side; toward one side. 2. from one side. 3. with one side toward the front.

side wise (sīd′wīz′), sideways.

sid ing (sīd′ing), a short railroad track to which cars can be switched from a main track.

si dle (sī′dəl), move sideways. Tom shyly sidled up to the visitor.

siege (sēj), 1. the surrounding of a fortified place by an army trying to capture it. 2. any long or persistent effort to overcome resistance. **Lay siege to** means (1) besiege. The Greeks laid siege to Troy for ten years. (2) attempt to win or get by long and persistent effort.

si er ra (si er′ə), chain of hills or mountains whose peaks suggest the teeth of a saw.

si es ta (si es′tə), a nap or rest taken at noon or in the afternoon.

sieve (siv), a utensil used to separate large pieces from small, or solids from liquids. See the picture. We shake flour through a sieve and pour soup through a sieve.

Sieve

sift (sift), 1. separate large pieces from small by shaking in a sieve. Sift the ashes. 2. put through a sieve. Sift sugar on the top of the cake. 3. fall through, or as if through, a sieve. The snow sifted softly down. 4. examine very carefully. The teacher will sift the evidence and decide which boy copied from the other.

sigh (sī), 1. let out a very long deep breath because one is sad, tired, relieved, etc. 2. act or sound of sighing; as, a sigh of regret, a sigh of relief. 3. make a sound like a sigh. The wind sighed in the treetops. 4. wish very much; long. She sighed for home and friends.

sight (sīt), 1. power of seeing. Birds have better sight than dogs. 2. act of seeing. **At sight** or **on sight** means as soon as seen. She reads music at sight. 3. range of seeing; view. We live in sight of the school. 4. thing seen. 5. something worth seeing. Niagara Falls is one of the sights of the world. 6. something that looks queer. Jane is a sight in that ugly dress. 7. see. At last the sailors sighted land. 8. device to guide the eye; as, the sights on a rifle. 9. the aim or observation taken by such devices. 10. look at through sights; point to; aim at. The hunter sighted carefully before firing his gun. 11. way of looking or thinking; regard. Dolls are precious in a little girl's sight.

sight less (sīt′lis), blind.

sign (sīn), 1. any mark, thing, or motion used to mean, represent, or point out something. See the sign over the door. The sign reads, "Keep off the grass." The signs for add, subtract, multiply, and divide are +, −, ×, ÷. The robin is a sign of spring. There are no signs of life about the house. The hunters found no signs of deer. The Star in the East was the sign of Christ's coming. She made the sign of the cross. A nod is a sign of agreement. The deaf and dumb talk by signs. He gave the sign of the secret society. A thing or act that stands for something else is a sign of it. 2. put one's name on; write one's name. A man signs a letter, a note promising to pay a debt, a check, etc. We sign for telegrams, parcels, etc. A man **signs up** for a job. 3. **Sign off** means stop broadcasting. 4. give a sign to. The teacher signed me to enter.

sig nal (sig′nəl), 1. sign giving notice of something. A red light is a signal of danger. 2. make a signal or signals (to). He signaled the car to stop by raising his hand. 3. make known by a signal or signals. A bell signals the end of a school period. 4. used as a signal or in signaling. 5. remarkable; striking. The airplane was a signal invention.

sig na ture (sig′nə chər), 1. person's name written by himself. 2. a series of sounds that is always a part of a certain radio program and identifies it. 3. signs printed at the beginning of a staff to show the pitch, key, and time of a piece of music.

sig net (sig′nit), a seal. The order was sealed with the king's signet.

sig nif i cance (sig nif′i kəns), 1. meaning. She did not understand the significance of my nod. 2. importance; consequence.

sig nif i cant (sig nif′i kənt), 1. full of meaning; important; of consequence. July 4, 1776, is a significant date for Americans. 2. having a meaning; expressive. Smiles are significant of pleasure. 3. having or expressing a hidden meaning. A significant nod from his friend warned him to stop talking.

sig ni fy (sig′ni fī), 1. mean; be a sign of. "Oh!" signifies surprise. 2. make known by signs, words, or actions. He signified his consent with a nod. 3. be important; have importance. What a fool says does not signify.

si gnor (sē′nyōr), an Italian word meaning Mr., or gentleman.

si gno ra (sē nyō′rä), an Italian word meaning Mrs., or lady.

si gno ri na (sē′nyō rē′nä), an Italian word meaning Miss, or young lady.

sign post (sīn′pōst′), post having signs, notices, or directions on it.

si lence (sī′ləns), 1. absence of sound or noise. The teacher asked for silence. 2. keeping still; not talking; not mentioning. Silence gives consent. Mother passed over Tom's foolish remarks in silence. 3. stop the noise of; make silent; to quiet. The nurse silenced the baby's crying. 4. "Silence!" means "Keep still!" or "Be still!"

si lent (sī′lənt), 1. not speaking; saying little or nothing. The stranger was silent about his early life. Pupils must be silent during the study hour. 2. quiet; still; noiseless; as, a silent house. 3. not spoken; not said out loud; as, a silent prayer. The *e* in *time* is a silent letter. 4. taking no open or active part. A silent partner in a business has no share in managing the business.

sil hou ette (sil′ü et′), 1. outline portrait cut out of black paper or filled in with some single color. 2. dark image outlined against a lighter background. 3. show in outline. The mountain was silhouetted against the sky.

Silhouette

silk (silk), 1. a fine soft thread spun by silkworms. 2. cloth made from it. She sewed the silk dress with silk thread. 3. thread or cloth like silk, made artificially. 4. anything like silk; as, artificial silk, corn silk. 5. of silk; like silk.

silk en (sil′kən), 1. made of silk. The king

wore silken robes. 2. like silk; smooth, soft, and glossy. She has silken hair.

silk worm (silk′wėrm′), a caterpillar that spins silk to form a cocoon.

COCOON

SILKWORM

silk y (sil′ki), like silk; smooth, soft, and glossy. A kitten has a silky fur.

sill (sil), piece of wood or stone across the bottom of a door, window, or house frame.

sil ly (sil′i), foolish; without sense or reason.

sil van (sil′vən), sylvan.

sil ver (sil′vər), 1. a shining white precious metal. Silver is used for making coins, jewelry, spoons, knives, forks, dishes, etc. 2. coins made from silver; as, a pocketful of silver. 3. utensils or dishes made from silver; as, table silver. 4. made of silver; as, a silver spoon. 5. to cover or coat with silver. 6. the color of silver. 7. having the color of silver; as, a silver slipper. 8. make the color of silver. Moonlight silvered the lake. 9. become the color of silver. The old lady's hair had silvered. 10. having a clear ringing sound.

sil ver y (sil′vər i), like silver; like that of silver. Moonbeams are silvery. The bell has a silvery sound.

sim i lar (sim′i lər), alike; like; much the same. A river and a brook are similar. A gas stove is similar to an oil stove.

sim i lar i ty (sim′i lar′i ti), likeness; resemblance.

sim mer (sim′ər), 1. make a murmuring sound while boiling gently. The kettle simmered on the stove. 2. boil gently; keep at or just below the boiling point. 3. process of cooking at or just below the boiling point. Do not let the soup cook faster than a simmer. 4. be on the point of breaking out; as, simmering anger, simmering rebellion.

sim ple (sim′pəl), 1. easy to do or understand. This book is in simple language. 2. not divided into parts; single; not compound. An oak leaf is a simple leaf. "John called his dog" is a simple sentence. 3. bare; mere; with nothing added. My answer is the simple truth. 4. plain; without ornament; not rich or showy. He eats simple food and wears simple clothing. 5. natural; not affected; not showing off. She has a pleasant, simple manner. 6. common; ordinary. His parents were simple people. 7. dull; weak in mind. "Simple Simon met a pieman."

sim ple ton (sim′pəl tən), silly person; fool.

sim plic i ty (sim plis′i ti), 1. being simple. 2. clearness; freedom from difficulty. The simplicity of the book makes it suitable for children. 3. plainness. A room in a hospital should be furnished with great simplicity. 4. absence of show or pretense; sincerity. 5. lack of shrewdness. His simplicity made him easily fooled.

sim pli fy (sim′pli fī), make simple or more simple; make plainer or easier. *Tho* is a simplified spelling of *though.*

sim ply (sim′pli), 1. in a simple manner. 2. plainly; without much ornament; without pretense or affectation. Mary was simply dressed. 3. merely; only. The baby did not simply cry; he yelled. 4. foolishly. He acted as simply as an idiot. 5. absolutely; as, simply perfect.

si mul ta ne ous (sī′məl tā′ni əs), existing, done, or happening at the same time. All the people in the audience burst into simultaneous applause.

sin (sin), 1. breaking the law of God. 2. break the law of God. 3. wrongdoing of any kind; immoral act. Lying, stealing, dishonesty, and cruelty are sins. 4. do wrong.

since (sins), 1. from then till now. John caught cold Saturday and has been in bed ever since. 2. at some time between then and now. Mr. Cole at first refused the position, but since has accepted it. 3. ago; before now. Old Rover died long since. 4. from (a past time) till now. We have been up since five. 5. after. Charles has worked hard since he left school. 6. after the time that; from the time when. He has been home only once since he went to New York. 7. because. Since you feel tired, you should rest.

sin cere (sin sēr′), free from pretense or deceit; genuine; honest.

sin cer i ty (sin ser′i ti), freedom from pretense or deceit; honesty. No one doubts the sincerity of Abraham Lincoln.

sin ew (sin′ū), 1. a tough, strong band or cord that joins muscle to bone. You can see the sinews in a cooked chicken leg. 2. strength; energy. 3. means of strength; source of power. Men and money are the sinews of war.

sin ew y (sin′ū i), having strong sinews; strong; vigorous. A blacksmith has sinewy arms.

sin ful (sin′fəl), full of sin; wicked; wrong. The sinful man repented.

sing (sing), 1. make music with the voice. People sing in church. 2. make pleasant, musical sounds. Birds sing. 3. bring, send, or put by singing. The baby was sung to sleep. 4. tell in poetry. The poet sang of war and heroes. 5. make a ringing, whistling, humming, or buzzing sound. The teakettle sang. **sang** and **sung** are formed from **sing.**

sing er (sing′ər), 1. person who sings. You can hear famous singers on the radio. 2. bird that sings. Our canary is a fine singer.

sin gle (sing′gəl), 1. only one; one and no more. The spider hung by a single thread. Each child spoke a single line of the poem. 2. for only one; individual. The sisters share one room with two single beds in it. 3. not married. They rent rooms to single men. 4. having only one on each side. The knights engaged in single combat. 5. having only one set of petals. Most cultivated roses have double flowers with many petals; wild roses have single flowers with five petals. 6. sincere; honest; genuine. She showed single devotion to her religion. 7. pick from others. The teacher singled Harry out. 8. something single.

sin gly (sing′gli), 1. by itself; separately. Let us consider each point singly. 2. one by one; one at a time. Misfortunes never come singly. 3. by one's own efforts; without help.

sin gu lar (sing′gū lər), 1. extraordinary; unusual. *Treasure Island* is a story of singular interest to boys. 2. strange; queer; peculiar. 3. being the only one of its kind. 4. one in number. *Boy* is singular; *boys* is plural.

sin gu lar ly (sing′gū lər li), unusually; extraordinarily; peculiarly.

sin is ter (sin′is tər), 1. threatening; showing ill will; as, a sinister rumor, a sinister look. 2. bad; evil.

sink (singk), 1. go down; fall slowly; go lower and lower; go under. She sank to the floor in a faint. The sun is sinking in the west. The swimmer is sinking. 2. make go down; make fall; make go under. The enemy has sunk our ships. 3. become lower or weaker. The wind has sunk down. 4. make lower. Sink your voice to a whisper. 5. go deeply. Let the lessons sink into your mind. 6. make go deep; dig. The men are sinking a well. 7. a shallow basin or tub with a pipe to drain it. The dishes are in the kitchen sink. 8. place where dirty water or any filth collects. **sank** and **sunk** are formed from **sink.**

sin ner (sin′ər), person who sins or does wrong. The sinner who repented was forgiven.

sip (sip), 1. drink little by little. She sipped her tea. 2. a very small drink.

sir (sėr), 1. a title of respect or honor. A boy calls an older man "Sir." We begin business letters with "Dear Sir." 2. the title of a knight or baronet; as, Sir Walter Scott. 3. Mr. or Master. You, sir, do not belong here.

sire (sīr), 1. father; male ancestor. "Fight for the green graves of your sires!" 2. male parent. Lightning was the sire of the race horse Danger. 3. be the father of. Lightning sired Danger. 4. a title of respect used to a great noble, or a king.

si ren (sī′rən), 1. a nymph who lured sailors to destruction upon the rocks by her sweet singing. 2. woman who lures, tempts, or entices. 3. of a siren; tempting; enticing. 4. a kind of whistle that makes a loud piercing sound. We heard the sirens of the fire engines.

sir rah (sir′ə), fellow. "Silence, sirrah!" said the prince to the stable boy.

sir up (sir′əp or sėr′əp), a sweet thick liquid; sugar boiled in water; a liquid made of sugar and fruit juices. We have sugar sirup, maple sirup, and corn sirup. Vanilla sirup, chocolate sirup, etc., are used at soda fountains. Also spelled **syrup.**

sis ter (sis′tər), 1. A girl or woman is sister to the other children of her parents. 2. close friend. 3. members of the same church are often called sisters. 4. nun; as, Sisters of Charity.

sit (sit), 1. I sit in a chair. My cat sits on the rug. 2. seat; cause to sit. The woman sat the little boy down hard. 3. sit on. He sat his horse well. 4. be placed; be. The clock has sat on that shelf for years. 5. have a seat in an assembly; be a member of a council; as, to sit in Congress. 6. hold a session. The court sits next month. 7. place oneself in a position for having one's picture made; pose; as, to sit for a portrait. 8. press or weigh.

Care sat heavy on his brow. 9. perch. The birds were sitting on the fence rail. 10. cover eggs so that they will hatch; brood. 11. fit. The coat sits well.

site (sīt), position or place (of anything). A new school is to be built on the site of the old town hall.

sit ting (sit′ing), 1. a meeting or session of a court, etc. 2. a time of remaining seated.

sitting room, a room to sit in; a parlor; a living room.

sit u at ed (sich′ü āt′id), placed; located. The school is so situated that it can be reached easily from all parts of town.

sit u a tion (sich′ü ā′shən), 1. position; location. Our house has a beautiful situation on a hill. 2. circumstances; case; condition. It is a very disagreeable situation to be alone and without money in a strange city. 3. place to work; job. She is trying to find a situation.

six (siks). Six is one more than five. Six means 6.

six pence (siks′pəns), 1. six pence; six British pennies. Sixpence equals about 12 cents in American money. 2. a silver coin worth six pence.

six teen (siks′tēn′), six more than ten; 16.

six teenth (siks′tēnth′), 1. next after the 15th. 2. one of 16 equal parts. An ounce is one sixteenth of a pound.

sixth (siksth), 1. next after the 5th. 2. one of 6 equal parts.

six ty (siks′ti), six times ten; 60.

size (sīz), 1. amount of space a thing takes up. The two boys are of the same size. The library contains books of all sizes, big and little. We need a house of larger size. 2. one of a series of measures. The size of card I want is 3 by 5 inches. His collar size is fourteen.

siz zle (siz′əl), 1. make a hissing sound, as when fat is frying or burning. 2. such a sound.

Ice skate

skate (skāt), 1. a frame with a blade that can be fastened to a shoe so that a person can glide over ice. 2. a similar frame with small wheels for use on any smooth, hard surface. 3. glide or move along on skates.

Roller skate

skein (skān), small bundle of yarn or thread.

skel e ton (skel′i tən), 1. the bones of a body, fitted together in their natural places. 2. frame; as, the steel skeleton of a building.

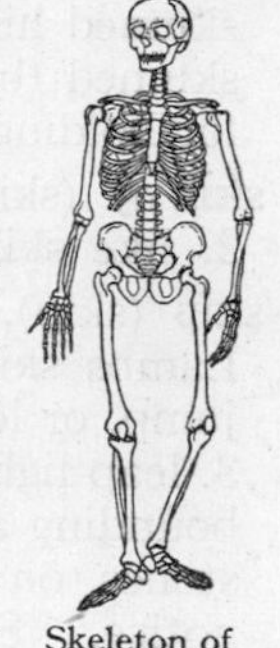
Skeleton of a man

sketch (skech), 1. a rough drawing or design; an outline; a plan. 2. a short description, story, or play. 3. make a sketch of; draw roughly; outline.

ski (skē), 1. one of a pair of long, slender pieces of hard wood fastened to the shoes to enable a person to walk or glide over snow. See the picture just below. 2. glide over the snow on skis.

skid (skid), 1. slip or slide sideways while moving. 2. slide along without turning. 3. timber or frame on which something may slide. 4. piece of wood or metal to prevent a wheel from turning.

skies (skīz). See **sky.**

skiff (skif), 1. small light boat. 2. light rowboat.

skill (skil), 1. ability gained by practice or knowledge. The trained teacher managed the children with skill. 2. ability to do things well with one's body or with tools. It takes skill to tune a piano.

Boys on skis

skilled (skild), 1. having skill; trained; experienced. A carpenter is a skilled workman. 2. showing skill; requiring skill. Plastering is skilled labor.

skil let (skil′it), 1. a shallow pan with a handle, used for frying. 2. long-handled saucepan.

skill ful or **skil ful** (skil′fəl), 1. having skill; expert. He is a very skillful workman. 2. showing skill. That is a skillful piece of work.

skim (skim), 1. remove from the top. The cook skims the cream from the milk and the fat from the soup. 2. take something from the top of. She skims the milk to get cream. 3. move lightly over. The skaters were skimming over the ice. 4. glide along. The swallows went skimming by. 5. read hastily; read with omissions. I skimmed the book.

skin (skin), 1. the covering of the body in persons, animals, and plants. Cows have thick skins. He slipped on the banana skin. 2. hide; pelt. 3. take the skin off. Jack skinned his knees when he fell. The hunter skinned the deer. 4. container made of skin for holding liquids.

skin ny (skin′i), 1. very thin; very lean. 2. like skin.

skip (skip), 1. leap lightly; spring; jump. Lambs skip in the fields. 2. a light spring, jump, or leap. The child gave a skip of joy. 3. leap lightly over. Girls skip rope. 4. send bounding along a surface. Boys like to skip stones on the lake. 5. pass over; fail to notice. She skips the hard words when she reads. Answer the questions in order without skipping. 6. change quickly from one task, pleasure, subject, etc., to another.

skip per (skip′ər), 1. the captain of a ship, especially of a small trading or fishing boat. 2. any captain or leader.

skir mish (skėr′mish), 1. slight fight between small groups of soldiers. 2. any slight conflict. 3. take part in a skirmish.

skirt (skėrt), 1. the part of a dress that hangs from the waist. 2. woman's or girl's garment that hangs from the waist. 3. border; edge. 4. outer part of a place, group of people, etc. 5. pass along the border or edge of. The boys skirted the forest instead of going through it.

skulk (skulk), 1. sneak; lurk; hide because of fear; hide for a bad purpose. 2. move in a stealthy, sneaking way. The wolf was skulking in the woods near the sheep.

skull (skul), 1. the bones of the head. 2. the bones around the brain.

skunk (skungk), 1. a bushy-tailed animal of North America about the size of a cat, black with white stripes along the back. Skunks give off a very strong smell when frightened or attacked. 2. fur of this animal, used on coats, etc. 3. a mean, contemptible person.

Skunk (length about 2 ft. with the tail)

sky (skī), 1. the covering over the world; the region of the clouds or the upper air; the heavens; as, a blue sky, cloudy skies. 2. heaven; place where God and His angels live.

sky lark (skī′lärk′), 1. a small bird that sings very sweetly as it flies toward the sky. 2. play pranks; frolic. The children were skylarking in the orchard.

sky light (skī′līt′), window in a roof or ceiling.

sky scrap er (skī′skrāp′ər), a very tall building. New York is famous for its skyscrapers.

slab (slab), 1. a broad, flat, thick piece (of stone, wood, meat, etc.). Some sidewalks are made of slabs of stone. He ate a slab of cheese as big as my hand. 2. rough outside piece cut from a log.

slack (slak), 1. loose. The rope hung slack. 2. part that hangs loose. He pulled in the slack of the rope. 3. careless. She is a slack housekeeper. 4. slow. The horse was moving at a slack pace. **Slack water** is the time when there is least tide. 5. not active; not brisk; dull. Business is slack at this season.

slack en (slak′ən), 1. make slower. Don't slacken your efforts till the work is done. 2. become slower. Work slackens on a hot day. 3. make looser. Slacken the rope. 4. become loose. The rope slackened as the wave sent the boat toward the pier.

slacks (slaks), loose trousers.

slag (slag), 1. the rough hard waste left after metal is taken from ore by melting it. 2. light, spongy lava.

slain (slān). See **slay.** The sheep were slain by the wolves.

slake (slāk), 1. satisfy (thirst, revenge, wrath, etc.). We slaked our thirst at the spring. 2. put out (a fire). 3. change (lime) by leaving it in the air or putting water on it. Plaster contains slaked lime and sand.

slam (slam), 1. shut with force and noise; bang. He slammed the window down. The door slammed. 2. throw hard with force. Joe slammed himself down on his bed. 3. violent and noisy closing; bang. John threw his books down with a slam.

slan der (slan′dər), 1. false statement meant to do harm. 2. talk falsely about. 3. the spreading of false reports.

slang (slang), 1. words, phrases, etc., not accepted as good English. Slang is mostly made up of new words or meanings that are popular for only a short time. 2. special talk of a particular class of people. **Crib** often means **cheat** in students' slang.

slant (slant), 1. slope. Most handwriting

slants to the right. Has your roof a sharp slant? 2. sloping.

slap (slap), 1. a blow with the open hand or with something flat. 2. strike with the open hand or with something flat. He slapped at the fly with a folded newspaper. 3. put with force. She slapped the book down on the table.

slash (slash), 1. cut with a sweeping stroke of a sword, knife, whip, etc.; gash; lash. He slashed the bark off the tree with his sword. 2. make a slashing stroke. 3. a sweeping, slashing stroke. 4. a cut or wound made by such a stroke. 5. reduce a great deal.

slat (slat), a long, thin, narrow piece of wood or metal.

slate (slāt), 1. a bluish-gray rock that splits easily into thin smooth layers. Slate is used to cover roofs and for blackboards. 2. thin piece of this rock. Children used to write on slates, but now they use paper. The roof was covered with slates. 3. cover with slate. 4. dark, bluish gray.

slaugh ter (slô′tər), 1. killing; butchering. The battle resulted in a frightful slaughter. 2. kill; butcher. Millions of cattle are slaughtered in Chicago every year.

slave (slāv), 1. person who is the property of another. Slaves could be bought and sold like horses. 2. person who works like a slave. 3. work like a slave. Many mothers slave for their children. 4. of slaves; done by slaves; as, slave labor. 5. person who is controlled or ruled by some desire, habit, or influence. A drunkard is a slave of drink.

slav er y (slāv′ər i), 1. condition of being a slave. Many African Negroes were captured and sold into slavery. 2. the custom of keeping slaves. Where slavery is permitted, certain men own others. 3. condition like that of a slave. 4. hard work like that of a slave.

slav ish (slāv′ish), 1. like a slave; mean; base; weakly submitting. 2. like that of slaves; fit for slaves.

slay (slā), kill with violence. A hunter slays wild animals. Jack slew the giant. **slew** and **slain** are formed from **slay.**

Sled for one person

sled (sled), framework of boards mounted on runners for use on snow or ice. See the picture just above.

sledge[1] (slej), sled; sleigh.

sledge[2] (slej), a large, heavy hammer. See the picture below.

Sledge

sleek (slēk), 1. smooth; soft and glossy; as, sleek hair. 2. having smooth, soft skin, hair, fur, etc.; as, a sleek cat. 3. smooth in speech and manners; as, a sleek salesman. 4. to smooth. He sleeked down his hair.

sleep (slēp), 1. rest body and mind; be without ordinary thought or movement. We sleep at night. All animals sleep. 2. rest of body and mind occurring naturally and regularly. Most people need eight hours of sleep a day. 3. be in a condition like sleep. The seeds slept in the ground all winter. 4. state or condition like sleep. The **last sleep** means death. 5. spend in sleeping. **Sleep away** means pass or spend in sleeping. **Sleep off** means get rid of by sleeping. She was sleeping off a headache. **slept** is formed from **sleep.**

sleep er (slēp′ər), 1. one that sleeps. The noise woke the sleepers. 2. a railroad car that has berths for passengers to sleep in. 3. horizontal beam. Sleepers support the rails of a railroad track.

sleep less (slēp′lis), without sleep; not sleeping; restless.

sleep y (slēp′i), 1. ready to go to sleep; inclined to sleep. 2. quiet; not active. We lived in a sleepy little town beside a slow and sleepy stream.

sleet (slēt), 1. half-frozen rain; snow or hail mixed with rain. 2. to rain and snow or hail at the same time.

sleeve (slēv), the part of a garment that covers the arm. **Laugh in one's sleeve** means be amused but not show it.

sleigh (slā), 1. a carriage or cart mounted on runners for use on snow or ice. In northern countries people use sleighs in the winter. 2. travel or ride in a sleigh.

Sleigh

slen der (slen′dər), 1. long and thin; not big around. A boy 6 feet tall and weighing only 130 pounds is very slender. A pencil is a slender piece of wood. 2. slight; small; as, a slender meal, a slender income, a slender hope.

slept (slept). See **sleep.** The baby has slept soundly for several nights.

slew (slü), killed. See **slay.**

slice (slīs), 1. a thin, flat, broad piece cut from something; as, a slice of bread, a slice of meat. 2. cut into slices. Slice the bread. We ate sliced peaches. 3. cut (off).

slick er (slik′ər), a long, loose waterproof coat.

slid (slid). See **slide.** The minutes had slid rapidly by.

slide (slīd), 1. move smoothly as a sled moves on snow or ice. The bureau drawers slide in and out. 2. move easily and quietly. The thief quickly slid behind the curtains. 3. slip. He slid a pistol into his pocket. 4. act of sliding. The children each take a slide in turn. 5. smooth surface for sliding on. The frozen brook makes a good slide. 6. track, rail, etc., on which something slides. 7. mass of earth, snow, etc., sliding down. 8. a small thin sheet of glass.

slight (slīt), 1. slender; not big around. She is a slight girl. 2. small; not much; not important. One slice of bread is a very slight lunch. I have a slight headache. 3. pay too little attention to. This maid slights her work. She felt slighted because she was not asked to the party. 4. slighting treatment; an act of neglect. Cinderella suffered many slights from her sisters.

slight ly (slīt′li), 1. in a slight manner. 2. to a slight degree; somewhat; a little.

slim (slim), 1. slender; thin. He was very slim, being 6 feet tall and weighing only 130 pounds. 2. small; slight; weak. We had a slim attendance because of the rain.

slime (slīm), 1. soft, sticky mud or something like it. His shoes were covered with slime from the swamp. 2. a sticky substance given off by snails, snakes, fish, etc.

slim y (slīm′i), 1. of slime; like slime. 2. covered with slime. The pond is too slimy to swim in.

sling (sling), 1. strip of leather with a string fastened to each end, for throwing stones. 2. throw with a sling; throw; cast; hurl. Cruel boys sling stones at cats. 3. a rope, band, or chain by which heavy objects are lifted, carried, or held. The men lowered the boxes into the cellar by a sling. 4. hanging loop of cloth fastened around the neck to support a hurt arm. 5. hang in a sling; hang so as to swing loosely. The soldier's gun was slung over his shoulder.

A B

A, sling for lifting; B, sling lifting a barrel.

sling shot (sling′shot′), Y-shaped stick with a rubber band fastened to its prongs, used to shoot pebbles, etc.

slink (slingk), move in a secret, guilty manner; sneak. After stealing the meat, the dog slunk away. He was slinking around the house.

slip (slip), 1. go or move smoothly and easily. The ship slips through the waves. The drawer is slipping into place. He slipped back the bolt on the door. She slipped the ring from her finger. 2. slide; move out of place. The knife slipped and cut him. 3. slide suddenly without wanting to. He slipped on the icy sidewalk. 4. go or move quietly, easily, or quickly; escape. She slipped out of the room. Time slips by. Don't let this opportunity slip. Your name has slipped my mind. 5. put quietly or secretly. Slip the note into Mary's hand. 6. **Slip on** or **off** means put on or take off (something) easily or quickly. Slip on your coat and come with us. 7. slipping. His broken leg was caused by a slip on a banana peel. 8. make a mistake or error. **Let slip** means tell without meaning to. 9. mistake; an error in conduct. Bill makes slips in pronouncing words. That remark was a slip of the tongue. 10. thing that can be slipped on or off; covering. During the summer many people put slips on furniture. We put white slips on pillows. Grace wore a pink slip under her party dress. 11. narrow strip of paper, wood, etc. 12. a small branch or twig cut from a plant to grow a new plant. She has promised us slips from that bush.

slip per (slip′ər), a light shoe. She has pretty dancing slippers and comfortable bedroom slippers.

slip per y (slip′ər i), 1. causing slipping. A wet street is slippery. The steps are slippery with ice. 2. slipping away easily. Wet soap is slippery. 3. not to be depended on; tricky.

slit (slit), 1. cut or tear along a line; make a long cut in; as, to slit cloth strips, to slit a skirt to make a pocket. 2. a straight, narrow cut or opening; as, a slit in a bag, the slit in the letter box.

slo gan (slō′gən), 1. a word or phrase used like a war cry by any group, party, class, or business. "Safety First" is our slogan. 2. war cry; battle cry.

sloop (slüp), a sailboat having one mast, a mainsail, a jib, and sometimes other sails. See the picture.

Sloop

slop (slop), 1. spill; splash. He slopped water on me. 2. liquid carelessly spilled or splashed about. 3. dirty water; liquid garbage; as, the kitchen slops. 4. weak liquid food. I am tired of slops; I want a good thick steak.

slope (slōp), 1. go up or down as shown in the picture. The land slopes toward the sea. The house has a sloping roof. 2. any line, surface, or land that goes up or down from a level. If you roll a ball up a slope, it will roll down again. 3. amount of slope. The floor of the theater has a slope of four feet from the back seats to the front.

Slope of a hill

slot (slot), 1. a small, narrow opening. Put a penny in the slot to get a stick of gum from this machine. 2. make a slot or slots in.

sloth (slōth), 1. slowness; laziness; idleness. Percy's sloth keeps him from taking part in sports. 2. a very slow-moving animal of South America that lives in trees. Sloths hang upside down from tree branches.

Sloth (about 2 ft. long)

sloth ful (slōth′fəl), lazy; sluggish.

slouch (slouch), 1. to stand, sit, walk, or move in an awkward, drooping manner. The weary beggar slouched. 2. droop or bend downward. 3. an awkward, drooping way of standing, sitting, or walking. 4. person who slouches.

slov en ly (sluv′ən li), untidy, dirty, or careless in dress, appearance, habits, work, etc.

slow (slō), 1. taking a long time. 2. behind time. 3. dull; stupid; not interesting. 4. make slow; become slow; go slower. 5. slowly.

Common garden slug (about 1 in. long)

slug (slug), 1. a slow-moving creature like a snail, without a shell. 2. a caterpillar or larva that looks like a slug. 3. lump of metal. 4. piece of lead or other metal for firing from a gun.

slug gard (slug′ərd), a lazy, sluggish person.

slug gish (slug′ish), slow; lazy; not active. The stream was so sluggish that I could hardly tell which way it flowed. He has a sluggish mind and shows little interest in anything.

sluice (slüs), 1. structure with a gate for holding back or controlling the water of a canal, river, or lake. 2. gate that holds back or controls the flow of water. When the water behind a dam gets too high, the sluices are opened. 3. let out or draw off (water) by opening a sluice; rush out. 4. flush or cleanse with a rush of water; pour or throw water over. 5. channel for carrying off water. 6. a long, sloping trough through which water flows, used to wash gold from sand or gravel.

Sluice for washing gold

slum (slum), a crowded, dirty part of a city or town. Poverty, disease, and crime are common in slums.

slum ber (slum′bər), 1. sleep. He awoke from his slumber. 2. light sleep. 3. pass in sleep. Baby slumbers away for hours. 4. be like a person asleep. The volcano had slumbered for years.

slung (slung). See **sling.** They slung some stones and ran away. The boy had slung his books over his shoulder.

slunk (slungk), sneaked. See **slink.** The dog had slunk away ashamed.

slur (slėr), 1. pass lightly over; go through hurriedly or in a careless way. 2. pronounce in an incomplete or indistinct way. Many persons slur "ing" and "How do you do." 3. slurred pronunciation, sound, etc. 4. a blot or stain (upon reputation); an insulting or slighting remark.

slush (slush), partly melted snow.

sly (slī), 1. able to do things without letting others know; acting secretly. That girl is as sly as a fox. The sly cat stole the meat while the cook's back was turned. 2. such as a sly person would use. She asked sly questions. 3. playfully mischievous or knowing. The week before Christmas the children exchanged many sly looks and smiles. 4. **On the sly** means secretly.

sly ly (slī′li), in a sly manner; secretly.

smack[1] (smak), 1. slight taste or flavor. This sauce has a smack of lemon. 2. trace; touch. The old sailor still had a smack of the sea about him. 3. have a taste, trace, or touch (of). His speech smacked of the old country.

smack[2] (smak), 1. pull (the lips) apart quickly so as to make a sharp sound. 2. such a movement. 3. sharp sound made in this way. 4. kiss loudly. 5. loud kiss. 6. slap. 7. crack (a whip, etc.).

smack[3] (smak), a small sailboat with one mast.

Smack

small (smôl), 1. not large; little. A cent is a small amount of money. 2. not important. A man who keeps a little shop is a small dealer. 3. having little strength; as, the still small voice of conscience. 4. mean. A boy with a small nature is not generous. 5. Some special meanings are:

small hours, early hours of the morning.

small letters, ordinary letters, not capitals.

small talk, talk about matters having little importance; chat.

the small of the back, the narrowest part of the back.

small pox (smôl′poks′), a very contagious disease with eruptions on the skin that often leave permanent scars shaped like little pits. Tom was inoculated against smallpox.

smart (smärt), 1. feel sharp pain. He smarted from the scolding. 2. cause sharp pain. The cut smarts. 3. sharp pain. The smart of the hurt kept him awake. 4. sharp; severe. He gave the horse a smart blow. 5. keen; active; lively. They walked at a smart pace. 6. clever; bright. Jack is a smart boy. 7. fresh and neat; in good order. 8. stylish; fashionable. 9. in a smart manner.

smash (smash), 1. break into pieces with violence and noise. The boy smashed a window with a stone. 2. destroy; shatter. 3. be broken to pieces. The dishes smashed as the tray upset. 4. become ruined. 5. rush violently; crash. The car smashed into the store window. 6. a smashing or the sound made by it; a crash. We heard a smash as the other automobile hit ours. 7. crushing defeat; disaster; destruction.

smear (smēr), 1. cover with anything sticky, greasy, or dirty. Mary smeared her fingers with jam. 2. rub or spread (oil, grease, paint, etc.). 3. a mark or stain left by smearing. There are smears of paint on the wallpaper.

smell (smel), 1. Can you smell the smoke? We smell with our noses. 2. She picked a rose and smelled it. The dog smelled the tramp's legs. 3. The hall smelled of onions. Roses smell sweet. 4. Smell is keener in dogs than in men. 5. The smell of burning cloth is not pleasant. 6. Have a smell of this rose.

smelt[1] (smelt), 1. melt (ore) in order to get metal out of it. 2. obtain (metal) from ore. 3. refine (impure metal) by melting.

smelt[2] (smelt), smelled.

smelt[3] (smelt), a small food fish with silvery scales.

smile (smīl), 1. look pleased or amused; show pleasure, favor, kindness, amusement, etc., by an upward curve of the mouth. 2. a pleased look. 3. show scorn or disdain by a curve of the mouth. She smiled bitterly. 4. bring, put, drive, etc., by smiling. Smile your tears away. 5. act of smiling.

smite (smīt), strike; strike hard; hit hard. The hero smites the giant with his sword. His conscience smote him. She was smitten with curiosity about the forbidden room. **smote** and **smitten** are formed from **smite.**

smith (smith), 1. man who makes or shapes things out of metal; as, a goldsmith, a tinsmith. 2. blacksmith.

smith y (smith′i), workshop of a smith, especially a blacksmith.

smit ten (smit′ən), 1. struck; hard hit. 2. See **smite.** The giant was smitten by the sword of the knight.

smock (smok), 1. loose outer garment worn to protect clothing. 2. draw (cloth) into a honeycomb pattern by stitches.

Smock

smoke (smōk), 1. cloud from anything burning, or something like it. 2. give off smoke or steam, or something like it. The fireplace smokes. The turkey was brought smoking hot to the table. 3. draw the smoke from (a pipe, cigar, etc.) into the mouth and puff it out again. 4. act of smoking tobacco. 5. expose to smoke. People smoke fish to preserve them. 6. drive (out) by smoke. We tried to smoke the woodchuck out of its hole.

smok er (smōk′ər), 1. person who smokes tobacco. 2. a car or a part of a car where smoking is allowed.

smoke stack (smōk′stak′), tall chimney.

smok y (smōk′i), 1. sending out much smoke; as, a smoky fire. 2. full of smoke. 3. darkened or stained with smoke. 4. like smoke or suggesting smoke; as, a smoky gray, a smoky taste.

smooth (smüᴛʜ), 1. even, like glass, silk, or still water. 2. free from unevenness or roughness; as, smooth sailing, a smooth voyage. 3. without lumps; as, smooth gravy. 4. easy; flowing; polished; pleasant; polite. That salesman is a smooth talker. 5. make smooth; make flat. Smooth this dress with a hot iron. He smoothed out the crushed paper and read what was on it. 6. cure or get rid of (roughness, difficulties, troubles, etc.); make easy. He smoothed away all objections to the plan. She smoothed down her father's temper. 7. in a smooth manner.

smote (smōt). See **smite.** God smote the wicked city with fire from heaven.

smoth er (smuᴛʜ′ər), 1. make unable to get air; kill by depriving of air. The wicked king smothered the two little princes. The fire is smothered by ashes. 2. be unable to breathe freely; suffocate. We are smothering in this stuffy room. 3. cover thickly. In the fall the grass is smothered with leaves. 4. keep back; check. He smothered a sharp reply. His smothered anger suddenly broke out. 5. cloud of dust or smoke.

smug gle (smug′əl), 1. bring in or take out of a country secretly and against the law. It is a crime to smuggle opium into the United States. 2. bring, take, put, etc., secretly. Robert tried to smuggle his puppy into the house.

smug gler (smug′lər), 1. one who smuggles. 2. ship used in smuggling.

snag (snag), 1. a tree or branch held fast in a river or lake. Snags are dangerous to boats. 2. any sharp or rough projecting point.

Snail

snail (snāl), 1. a small soft animal that crawls very slowly. Most snails have shells on their backs. See the picture. 2. a lazy, slow-moving person.

snake (snāk), 1. a long, slender, crawling reptile without limbs. See the picture below. 2. a sly, treacherous person. 3. to move, wind, or curve like a snake.

Snake

snap (snap), 1. make a sudden, quick bite or snatch; seize suddenly. The dog snaps at the child's hand. The dog snapped up the meat. She snapped at the chance to go to college. 2. a quick, sudden bite or snatch. The dog made a snap at a fly. 3. speak quickly and sharply. "Silence!" snapped the captain. 4. make or cause to make a sudden, sharp sound. This wood snaps as it burns. 5. a quick, sharp sound. 6. break suddenly. The violin string snapped. 7. sudden breaking. One snap made the knife useless. 8. a quick, sharp way. She moves with snap and energy. 9. A **cold snap** is a few days of cold weather. 10. fastener; a clasp. One of the snaps of your dress is unfastened. 11. a thin crisp cooky; as, a gingersnap. 12. made or done suddenly.

snap pish (snap′ish), 1. apt to snap. 2. impatient; sharp in speech or manner.

snare (snãr), 1. noose for catching small animals and birds; a trap. The boys made snares to catch rabbits. 2. catch with a snare; to trap. One day they snared a skunk.

Snare

snarl[1] (snärl), 1. growl sharply and show one's teeth. The dog snarled at the stranger. 2. speak in a sharp, angry tone; say with a snarl. 3. sharp growl; angry words. A snarl was his only reply.

snarl[2] (snärl), tangle. My sewing silks are all in a snarl.

snatch (snach), 1. seize suddenly. The hawk snatched the chicken and flew away. 2. grasp (at). He snatched at the rail. 3. act of snatching. The boy made a snatch at the ball. 4. short time. He had a snatch of sleep sitting in his chair. 5. small amount; bit; scrap. We heard snatches of their conversation.

sneak (snēk), 1. move in a stealthy way. The man sneaked about the barn watching for a chance to steal the cow. 2. act like a thief or a person who is ashamed to be seen. Roy sneaked in by the back way. 3. person who sneaks; a sneaking, cowardly person.

sneer (snēr), 1. show scorn or contempt by looks or words. The mean girls sneered at poor Dora's clothes. "Bah!" he sneered with a curl of his lip. 2. a look or words expressing scorn or contempt. Shy Tim feared sneers more than blows.

Man sneering

sneeze (snēz), 1. expel air suddenly and violently through the nose and mouth. A person sneezes when he has a cold. Pepper makes you sneeze. 2. a sneezing.

sniff (snif), 1. draw air through the nose in short breaths that can be heard. A person with a cold sniffs. She sniffed at the present to show her contempt. 2. draw in through the nose with the breath. He sniffed the medicine. 3. smell; try the smell of. The dog sniffed at the stranger. 4. act or sound of sniffing. He cleared his nose with a loud sniff. 5. a single breathing in of something; a breath.

snip (snip), 1. cut with a small, quick stroke with scissors. She snipped the thread. 2. act of snipping. With a few snips she cut out a paper doll. 3. small piece cut off. Pick up the snips of cloth and thread from the floor.

Snipe (about 11 in. long from tip of beak to tip of tail)

snipe (snīp), 1. a marsh bird with a long bill. 2. shoot at soldiers as a sportsman shoots at game; shoot from under cover.

snood (snüd), 1. a band or ribbon formerly worn around the hair by young, unmarried women. 2. bind up (hair) with a snood. 3. a net that is worn over the back of the hair.

snore (snōr), 1. breathe during sleep with a harsh, rough sound. 2. the sound so made.

snort (snôrt), 1. force the breath violently through the nose with a loud harsh sound. The horse snorted. 2. make a sound like this. The engine snorted. 3. act of snorting; the sound made.

snout (snout), 1. the long nose of an animal; the nose and mouth of an animal; as, the snout of a pig. 2. anything like a snout.

snow (snō), 1. frozen water in soft white flakes. Rain falls in summer; snow falls in winter. 2. a fall of snow. 3. fall as snow; as, to snow all day. 4. **Snowed in** means shut in by snow.

snow ball (snō′bôl′), 1. ball made of snow. 2. throw balls of snow at. They snowballed each other. 3. a shrub with white flowers in large clusters like balls.

snow flake (snō′flāk′), a small, feathery piece of snow.

snow shoe (snō′shü′), a light wooden frame with strips of leather stretched across it. Trappers in the far north wear snowshoes on their feet to keep from sinking in deep, soft snow.

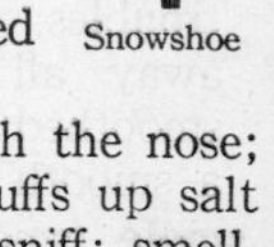
Snowshoe

snow y (snō′i), 1. having snow. 2. covered with snow. 3. like snow; snow-white. The old lady has snowy hair.

snub (snub), 1. treat coldly, scornfully, or with contempt. 2. cold, scornful, or disdainful treatment. 3. short and turned up at the tip; as, a snub nose.

snuff[1] (snuf), 1. draw in through the nose; draw up into the nose. He snuffs up salt and water to cure a cold. 2. sniff; smell. The dog snuffed at the track of the fox. 3. powdered tobacco to be taken into the nose.

snuff[2] (snuf), 1. cut or pinch off the burned part of the wick of a candle. 2. **Snuff out** means put an end to suddenly and completely.

snug (snug), 1. comfortable; warm; sheltered. The cat has found a snug corner behind the stove. 2. neat; trim; compact. The cabins on the boat are snug. 3. fitting closely. That coat is a little too snug. 4. in a snug manner.

snug gle (snug′əl), nestle; cuddle. Baby snuggles close to mother.

so (sō), 1. in that way; in the same way or degree; as stated; as shown. Hold your pen so. The chair is broken and has been so for a long time. Do not walk so fast. Jack is not so tall as his brother. Grace is sick. Is that so? 2. in such a way; to such a degree. 3. very. You are so kind. 4. very much. My head aches so! 5. therefore; accordingly; on this account. The dog seemed hungry; so we fed him. 6. **So** is sometimes used alone to ask a question or to exclaim. So! late again! The train is late. So? 7. Some special meanings are:

and so, 1. likewise; also. Dick is here, and so is John. 2. accordingly. I said I would go, and so I shall.

or so, more or less. It happened a day or so ago.

So as and **so that** express purpose or result. Work so as to succeed. Work so that you will succeed.

soak (sōk), 1. make very wet; become very wet. Soak the clothes all night before you wash them. 2. take up; suck. A sponge soaks up water. 3. soaking. Give the clothes a long soak. 4. go; enter; make its way. Water will soak through the earth.

soap (sōp), 1. a substance used for washing, made of a fat and lye. 2. rub with soap.

soap suds (sōp′sudz′), soap and water mixed and foaming.

soar (sōr), 1. fly upward; fly at a great height. An eagle soars. 2. aspire; rise beyond what is common and ordinary. His ambition soared to the throne.

sob (sob), 1. cry or sigh with short quick breaths. Jane is sobbing herself to sleep. "I have lost my penny," the child sobbed. 2. make a sound like a sob. The wind sobbed. 3. a catching the breath from grief, etc. We saw her tears and heard her sobs.

so ber (sō′bər), 1. not drunk. 2. temperate; moderate. John's parents led sober, hard-working lives. 3. quiet; serious; solemn. John looked sober at the thought of missing the picnic. 4. calm; sensible; free from exaggeration. The judge's sober opinion was not influenced by prejudice or strong feeling. 5. make sober; become sober. The class sobered down as the teacher came in.

so-called (sō′kôld′), 1. called so. 2. called so, but really not so. Her so called friend hasn't even written to her.

so cia ble (sō′shə bəl), 1. liking company. The Smiths are a sociable family and entertain a great deal. 2. friendly; with conversation and companionship. We had a sociable afternoon together. 3. an informal social gathering.

so cial (sō′shəl), 1. for companionship or friendliness; pertaining to companionship or friendliness. Ten of us girls have formed a social club. 2. liking company. She has a social nature. 3. connected with fashionable society. Mrs. Walker is the social leader in our town. 4. a social gathering or party. 5. living or liking to live with others. Man is a social being. 6. concerned with human beings as a group.

so ci e ty (sə sī′ə ti), 1. company; companionship. I enjoy your society. 2. all the people; the people of any particular time or place; their customs. The good of society demands that wrongdoing be punished. 3. a group of persons united by a common purpose or interest. A club, a fraternity, a lodge, and an association may be called societies. 4. the fashionable class; its doings. Grace's mother is a leader of society.

sock (sok), short stocking.

sock et (sok′it), a hollow part or piece for receiving and holding something. A candlestick has a socket in which to set a candle. Your eyes are set in sockets.

sod (sod), 1. ground covered with grass. 2. piece or layer of this containing the grass and its roots. Some pioneers built houses of sods. 3. cover with sods. We must have the bare spots of our lawn sodded.

so da (sō′də), 1. a substance used in cleaning and in making soap. 2. a substance used in cooking and as a medicine. 3. a drink flavored with fruit juice or syrup.

sod den (sod′ən), 1. soaked through. His clothing was sodden with rain. 2. heavy and moist. This bread is sodden because it was not baked well. 3. stupid; dull-looking.

so fa (sō′fə), long, upholstered seat or couch having a back and arms.

soft (sôft), 1. Feathers, cotton, and wool are soft, not hard. 2. Pine wood is softer than oak. Copper and lead are softer than steel. 3. Silk is soft, not rough or coarse. A kitten's fur is soft and pleasant to touch. 4. quietly pleasant; mild; as, a soft spring morning, soft air, soft words, the soft light of candles. 5. gentle; kind; tender; as, soft voice, soft eyes, soft heart. 6. weak. The army had become soft from idleness and luxury. 7. softly; gently. 8. Some special meanings are:

soft coal, coal that burns with a yellow, smoky flame.

soft drinks, drinks that do not contain alcohol.

soft water, water that is easy to wash with.

soft en (sôf′ən), make softer; become softer.

soft ly (sôft′li), in a soft manner; with a soft voice.

soft ness (sôft′nis), 1. being soft. 2. ease; comfort. 3. gentleness. 4. weakness.

soil[1] (soil), ground; earth; dirt; land. Most plants grow best in rich soil.

soil[2] (soil), make dirty; become dirty. Mary soiled her dress. White gloves soil easily.

so journ (sō′jėrn), 1. dwell for a time. The Jews sojourned in the land of Egypt. 2. brief stay; a stay that is not permanent. During his sojourn in Africa the missionary learned about the native customs.

sol ace (sol′is), 1. comfort; relief. She found solace from her troubles in music. 2. to comfort; cheer; relieve. She solaced herself with a book.

sold (sōld). See **sell.** He has sold his car. He sold it a week ago.

sol der (sod′ər), 1. metal that can be melted and used for joining or mending. 2. fasten with solder; mend with solder. He soldered four small holes in the kettle.

sol dier (sōl′jər), 1. man who serves in an army. 2. enlisted man in the army, not a commissioned officer. 3. one who serves in any cause; as, Christian soldiers. 4. act or serve as a soldier. 5. pretend to work but do very little.

sol dier y (sōl′jər i), 1. soldiers. 2. military training or knowledge.

sole[1] (sōl), 1. one and only; single. 2. only. We three were the sole survivors from the wreck.

sole[2] (sōl), 1. the bottom or under surface of the foot. 2. the bottom of a shoe, slipper, boot, etc. 3. piece cut in the same shape. 4. put a sole on. I must have my shoes soled.

sole[3] (sōl), a kind of flatfish. See the picture.

European sole (about 1 ft. long)

sole ly (sōl′li), 1. alone. I am solely responsible for providing the lunch. 2. only. Bananas grow outdoors solely in the tropics.

sol emn (sol′əm), 1. serious; grave; earnest. He gave his solemn promise never to return. That minister speaks in a solemn voice. 2. causing serious thoughts.

so lem ni ty (sə lem′ni ti), 1. solemn feeling; seriousness; impressiveness. The solemnity of the church service was felt even by the children. 2. solemn, formal ceremony. Easter is observed with solemnities.

so lic it (sə lis′it), ask earnestly; make appeals. The tailor has sent around cards soliciting trade.

sol id (sol′id), 1. not a liquid or a gas. Iron, wood, and ice are solids. 2. not hollow. A bar of iron is solid; a pipe is hollow. 3. hard; firm; strongly put together. They were glad to leave the boat and put their feet on solid ground. 4. alike throughout. The cloth is a solid blue. 5. that can be depended on. He is a solid citizen. 6. firmly united. The country was solid for defending itself. 7. whole; undivided; continuous. He spent a solid hour on his arithmetic.

so lid i fy (sə lid′i fī), make solid; become solid; harden.

sol i tar y (sol′i tãr′i), 1. alone; single; only. A solitary rider was seen in the distance. 2. without companions; lonely; away from people. He leads a solitary life in his hut in the mountains. The house is in a solitary spot miles from a town.

sol i tude (sol′i tūd or sol′i tüd), 1. being alone. Alice likes company and hates solitude. 2. lonely place. This forest has many solitudes.

so lo (sō′lō), piece of music for one voice or instrument. Anne sang three solos.

sol u ble (sol′ū bəl), 1. that can be dissolved. Salt is soluble in water. 2. that can be solved; as, soluble puzzles.

so lu tion (sə lü′shən), 1. solving a problem. That problem was hard; its solution required many hours. 2. explanation. The police are seeking a solution of the crime. 3. dissolving; changing a solid or gas to a liquid by treatment with a liquid. 4. being dissolved. Sugar and salt can be held in solution in water. 5. a liquid or mixture formed by dissolving.

solve (solv), clear up; explain; find the answer to. The detective solved the mystery. He has solved all the problems in the lesson.

som ber or **som bre** (som′bər), 1. dark; gloomy. It was a somber room with dark furniture and heavy black hangings. A cloudy winter day is somber. 2. melancholy; dismal. His losses made him very somber.

some (sum), 1. a; any. Ask some girl to come here. 2. a number of. Ask some boys to help you. 3. a quantity of. Drink some milk. 4. particular, but not known or named. Some dogs are large; some are small. 5. about. Some twenty men asked for work. 6. a certain number or quantity. Jack ate some, and threw the rest away.

some bod y (sum′bod i), 1. person not known or named; some person. Somebody has taken my pen. 2. person of importance. She acts as if she were somebody since she won the prize.

some how (sum′hou), in a way not known or not stated; in one way or another. I'll finish this work somehow.

some one (sum′wun), some person; somebody. Someone has to lock up the house.

som er sault (sum′ər sôlt), turn heels over head.

som er set (sum′ər set), somersault.

some thing (sum′thing), 1. some thing; a particular thing not named or known. I'm sure I've forgotten something. 2. a part; a certain amount; a little.

some time (sum′tīm), 1. at one time or another. Come to see us sometime. 2. former. Alice Brown, a sometime pupil of our school, is now a teacher there.

some times (sum′tīmz), now and then; at times.

some what (sum′hwot), 1. in some degree; slightly. My hat is somewhat like yours. 2. some part; some amount. A joke loses somewhat of its fun when you hear it the second time.

some where (sum′hwãr), 1. in some place; in one place or another. John is somewhere about the house. 2. at some time. It happened somewhere in the last century.

son (sun), 1. A boy is the son of his father and mother. 2. male descendant. 3. a boy or man attached to a country, cause, etc., as a child is to its parents; as, sons of America, sons of liberty.

song (sông), 1. something to sing; a short poem set to music. 2. singing. The canary burst into song. 3. poetry that has a musical sound. 4. **For a song** sometimes means very cheap.

song bird (sông′bėrd′), bird that sings.

song ster (sông′stər), 1. singer. 2. writer of songs or poems. 3. songbird.

son-in-law (sun′in lô′), the husband of one's daughter. Mrs. Jones has three sons-in-law.

so no rous (sə nō′rəs), 1. giving out a deep, loud sound. 2. full and rich in sound.

soon (sün), 1. in a short time; before long. 2. early. Why have you come so soon? 3. quickly. As soon as I hear, I will let you know. 4. readily; willingly. The brave soldier would sooner die than yield.

soot (sůt), black substance in the smoke from burning coal, wood, oil, etc. Soot makes smoke dark and collects on the inside of chimneys.

sooth (süth), truth. He speaks sooth. Are you in sooth his grandfather?

soothe (süᴛʜ), 1. quiet; calm; comfort. The mother soothed the crying child. 2. make less painful.

so pran o (sə pran′ō), 1. the highest singing voice in women and boys. 2. part to be sung by such a voice. 3. singer with such a voice. 4. of the soprano or sopranos. 5. for sopranos. 6. having something to do with the soprano or sopranos.

sor cer er (sôr′sər ər), magician; person who practices magic with the aid of evil spirits.

sor cer y (sôr′sər i), magic by the aid of evil spirits; witchcraft. The prince had been changed into a lion by sorcery.

sor did (sôr′did), 1. dirty; filthy. The poor family lived in a sordid hut. 2. mean; base; caring too much for money.

sore (sōr), 1. painful. The suffering of the poor makes her heart sore. 2. causing pain; causing great pain; severe. Mary has a bad cold and a sore throat. 3. causing sorrow. Their defeat is a sore subject with the members of the team. 4. hurt; offended. He is sore at missing the game. 5. painful place on the body where the skin or flesh is broken or bruised. 6. a hurt to the feelings.

sor rel[1] (sor′əl), 1. reddish brown; as, a sorrel horse. 2. horse having this color.

sor rel[2] (sor′əl), a plant with sour leaves.

sor row (sor′ō), 1. grief; sadness; regret. Mary felt sorrow at the loss of her kitten. She expressed sorrow at her mistake. 2. cause of grief; trouble. Her sorrows have aged her. 3. feel or show grief, sadness, or regret. She sorrowed over the lost money.

sor row ful (sor′ō fəl), sad; full of sorrow; feeling sorrow; causing sorrow. A funeral is a sorrowful occasion.

sor ry (sor′i), 1. I am sorry that you are sick. We are sorry that we cannot come to the party. Everyone is sorry for a blind man. 2. wretched; poor; pitiful. The blind beggar in his ragged clothes was a sorry sight.

sort (sôrt), 1. kind; class. What sort of work does he do? I like this sort of candy best. 2. arrange by kinds or classes; arrange in order. Sort these cards according to their colors. 3. put; separate from others. The farmer sorted out the best apples for eating. 4. **Out of sorts** means uncomfortable, ill, or cross.

S O S (es′ō′es′), call for help.

sought (sôt). See **seek.** For days she sought a safe hiding place. He was sought and found.

soul (sōl), 1. the part of the human being that thinks, feels, and makes the body act; the spiritual part of man. Death separates soul and body. Christians believe that the soul lives forever. 2. energy of mind or feelings; spirit. She puts her whole soul into her work. 3. cause of inspiration and energy. Florence Nightingale was the soul of the movement to reform nursing. 4. person. Don't tell a soul.

sound[1] (sound), 1. what can be heard; as, the sound of music, the sound of thunder. 2. make a sound or noise. The trumpet sounds for battle. The wind sounds like an animal howling. 3. cause to sound. Sound the trumpets. 4. utter; call. Sound the alarm. 5. make known. The trumpets sounded the call to battle. 6. seem. That excuse sounds queer. 7. **Within sound of** means near enough to hear.

sound[2] (sound), 1. healthy; free from disease; as, a sound body, a sound mind. 2. free from injury, decay, or defect; as, sound walls, a sound ship, sound fruit. 3. strong; safe; secure; as, a sound bank. 4. correct; right; reasonable; reliable; as, sound advice, sound religious teaching. 5. thorough; hearty; as, a sound whipping, a sound sleep. 6. soundly; thoroughly. Sleep sound, my child.

sound[3] (sound), 1. measure the depth of (water) by letting down a weight fastened on the end of a line. 2. examine or test by a line arranged to bring up a sample. 3. try to find out the views of; test; examine. We sounded mother on the subject of a picnic. 4. go toward the bottom; dive. The whale sounded.

sound[4] (sound), 1. long, narrow strip of water joining two larger bodies of water. 2. an inlet or arm of the sea.

sound ly (sound′li), 1. in a sound manner; without weakness or defect. 2. with unbroken, deep sleep. 3. vigorously; heartily; thoroughly. Mother scolded us soundly. 4. with good judgment. Dick decided soundly and so kept out of trouble.

soup (süp), liquid food made by boiling meat, vegetables, fish, etc.

sour (sour), 1. having a taste like vinegar or lemon juice. Green fruit is sour. 2. fermented; spoiled. Sour milk is healthful, but most foods are not good to eat when they have become sour. 3. disagreeable; bad-tempered; peevish; as, a sour face, a sour remark. 4. become sour; make sour; turn sour. 5. make or become peevish, bad-tempered, or disagreeable.

source (sōrs), 1. fountain; spring; beginning of a brook or river. 2. place from which anything comes or is obtained. A newspaper gets news from many sources. Mines are the chief source of diamonds.

south (south), 1. the direction to your right as you face the rising sun; away from the North Pole. 2. toward the south; farther toward the south. Drive south forty miles. 3. **South of** means farther south than. New York is south of Boston. 4. from the south; as, a south wind. 5. in the south; living in the south. 6. the part of any country toward the south. **The South** means the southern part of the United States.

NORTH
WEST EAST
SOUTH

South Africa. The Union of South Africa is a British dominion in southern Africa.

South America, the continent of the western world southeast of North America.

South American, of South America; as, a South American nation.

south east (south′ēst′), 1. halfway between south and east. 2. a southeast direction. 3. place that is in the southeast part or direction. 4. toward the southeast. 5. from the southeast; as, a southeast wind.

south east ern (south′ēs′tərn), 1. toward the southeast. 2. from the southeast. 3. of the southeast.

south er ly (suᴛʜ′ər li), 1. toward the south. The windows face southerly. 2. from the south. 3. of the south.

south ern (suᴛʜ′ərn), 1. toward the south; as, the southern side of a building. 2. from the south; as, a southern breeze. 3. of the south. He has traveled in southern countries. 4. of the South of the United States; as, a Southern city.

south ward (south′wərd), toward the south; south. He walked southward. The orchard is on the southward slope of the hill.

south wards (south′wərdz), southward.

south west (south′west′), 1. halfway between south and west. 2. a southwest direction. 3. place that is in the southwest part or direction. 4. toward the southwest. 5. from the southwest; as, a southwest wind.

south west ern (south′wes′tərn), 1. toward the southwest. 2. from the southwest. 3. of the southwest.

sou ve nir (sü′və nēr′), something given or kept for remembrance; a remembrance.

sov er eign (sov′rin), 1. above all others; supreme; greatest. Character is of sovereign importance. 2. greatest in rank or power. 3. supreme ruler; king; queen; monarch. 4. independent of the control of other governments. 5. a British gold coin worth 20 shillings, or one pound.

sov er eign ty (sov′rin ti), supreme power or authority.

sow[1] (sō), 1. scatter (seed) on the ground; plant (seed); plant seed in. He sows more wheat than oats. The farmer sowed the field with oats. 2. scatter (anything); spread abroad. The enemy tried to sow discontent in our men.

sow[2] (sou), fully grown female pig.

sown (sōn). See **sow**[1]. The field had been sown with oats.

soy bean (soi′bēn′), 1. a bean widely grown in Asia and the United States. Soybeans are used in making foods and other things. 2. the plant it grows on.

space (spās), 1. unlimited room or place extending in all directions. Our earth moves through space. 2. limited place or room. This brick will fill a space 2½ by 4 by 8 inches. Is there space in the car for another person? 3. distance. The road is bad for a space of two miles. The trees are set at equal spaces apart. 4. length of time. He has not seen his brother for the space of ten years. Many changes occur within the space of one man's life. 5. fix the space of; separate by spaces; divide into spaces. Space your words evenly when you write.

spa cious (spā′shəs), containing much space; with plenty of room; vast. The rooms of the palace were spacious.

spade (spād), 1. a tool for digging; a kind of shovel. 2. dig with a spade. Spade up the garden.

Spade

spa ghet ti (spə get′i), the same mixture of flour and water as macaroni, but made up in slender sticks.

Spain (spān), a country in southwestern Europe.

spake (spāk), did speak. Thus spake the Lord.

span[1] (span), 1. the distance between the tip of a man's thumb and the tip of his little finger when the hand is spread out; 9 inches. 2. measure by the hand spread out. This post can be spanned by one's two hands. 3. short space of time. His span of life is nearly over. 4. part between two supports. The bridge crossed the river in a single span. 5. extend over. A bridge spanned the railroad tracks.

span[2] (span), pair of horses or other animals harnessed and driven together.

span gle (spang′gəl), 1. small piece of glittering metal used for decoration. The dress was covered with spangles. 2. any small bright bit. This rock shows spangles of gold. 3. decorate with spangles. The dress was spangled with gold. 4. sprinkle with small bright bits. The sky is spangled with stars.

Span iard (span′yərd), person born in Spain or having Spanish parents.

span iel (span′yəl), a dog of small or medium size with long, silky hair and drooping ears. Spaniels are very gentle and affectionate.

Cocker spaniel

Span ish (span′ish), 1. of Spain; pertaining to Spain, its people, or their language. 2. the people of Spain. 3. the language of Spain.

spank (spangk), 1. strike with the open hand, a slipper, etc. The nurse spanked the naughty child. 2. a slap.

spar[1] (spär), stout pole used to support or extend the sails of a ship; mast, yard, boom, etc., of a ship.

spar[2] (spär), 1. make motions of attack and defense with the arms and fists; to box. 2. a boxing match. 3. dispute.

spare (spãr), 1. use in small quantities or not at all; be saving of. 2. small in quantity. Fat people should live on a spare diet. 3. do without; omit; get along without. Father couldn't spare the car; so John had to walk. 4. show mercy to. He spared his enemy. Her cruel tongue spares nobody. 5. extra; in reserve; as, a spare tire. 6. thin; lean. Lincoln was a tall, spare man.

spar ing (spãr′ing), economical; frugal; as, a sparing use of sugar.

spar ing ly (spãr′ing li), in an economical way; without using much.

spark (spärk), 1. small bit of fire. Burning wood throws off sparks. 2. flash given off when electricity jumps across an open space. An electric spark explodes the gas in the engine of an automobile. 3. flash; gleam. 4. small amount. I haven't a spark of interest in the plan. The doctor tried to keep a spark of life alive in the sick child. 5. glittering bit. The moving sparks we saw were fireflies. 6. send out small bits of fire; produce sparks.

spar kle (spär′kəl), 1. send out little sparks. The fireworks sparkled. 2. little spark. 3. shine; glitter; flash. Diamonds sparkle. A sparkling drink bubbles. I like the sparkle of her eyes. He has a sparkling wit.

spar row (spar′ō), a small, brownish-gray bird. English sparrows have driven away many of our native American birds.

English sparrow (about 6 in. long)

sparse (spärs), thinly scattered; occurring here and there; as, a sparse population, sparse hair.

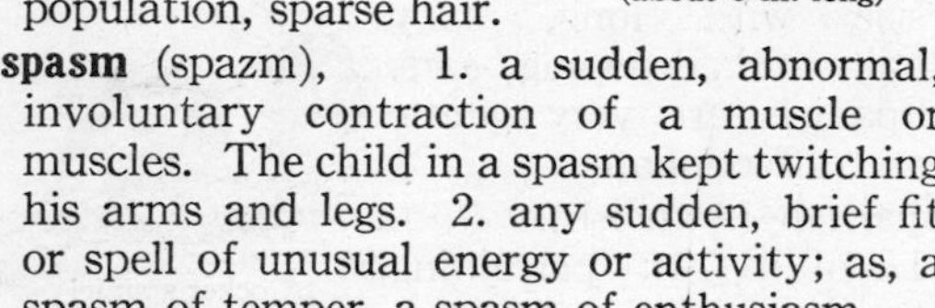

spasm (spazm), 1. a sudden, abnormal, involuntary contraction of a muscle or muscles. The child in a spasm kept twitching his arms and legs. 2. any sudden, brief fit or spell of unusual energy or activity; as, a spasm of temper, a spasm of enthusiasm.

spat[1] (spat), 1. slight quarrel. 2. light blow; slap.

spat[2] (spat). See **spit**[1]. The cat spat at the dog.

spat[3] (spat), a short gaiter, covering the ankle.

Spats

spat ter (spat′ər), 1. scatter or dash in drops; as, to spatter mud. 2. fall in drops. Rain spatters on the sidewalk. 3. strike in a shower. Bullets spattered the wall. 4. spattering; as, a spatter of bullets. 5. sound of spattering. 6. splash or spot with mud, slander, disgrace, etc. 7. splash or spot.

spawn (spôn), 1. the eggs of fish, frogs, shellfish, etc.; the young newly hatched. 2. produce eggs. 3. bring forth; give birth to. 4. offspring; a swarming brood.

speak (spēk), 1. say words; talk. A cat cannot speak. Speak distinctly. 2. make a speech. John spoke for the group that wanted a picnic. 3. say; tell; express; make known. Speak the truth. 4. use (a language). Do you speak French? 5. **Speak out** or **speak up** means speak loudly, clearly, or freely. 6. make sounds. The cannon spoke. **spoke** and **spoken** are formed from **speak.**

speak er (spēk′ər), 1. person who speaks. 2. person who presides over an assembly.

spear[1] (spēr), 1. weapon with a long shaft and a sharp-pointed head. 2. pierce with a spear. The Indians speared the fish.

spear[2] (spēr), a sprout or shoot of a plant; as, a spear of grass.

Spear

spe cial (spesh′əl), 1. of a particular kind; distinct from others; not general. This desk has a special lock. Have you any special color in mind for your new coat? 2. for a particular person, thing, purpose, etc. The railroad ran special trains on holidays. Send the letter by a special messenger. 3. unusual; exceptional; more than ordinary. Today's topic is of special interest. 4. special train, car, bus, etc.

spe cial ly (spesh′əl i), in a special manner or degree; particularly; unusually.

spe cial ty (spesh′əl ti), 1. special line of work, profession, trade, etc. 2. thing to which special attention is given. This store makes a specialty of children's clothes.

spe cies (spē′shiz), group of animals or plants that have certain permanent characteristics in common; distinct sort or kind. Wheat is a species of grass.

spe cif ic (spi sif′ik), definite; precise; particular. There was no specific reason for the quarrel.

spec i fi ca tion (spes′i fi kā′shən), detailed statement of particulars; detailed description of the dimensions, materials, etc., for something to be made.

spec i fy (spes′i fī), mention or name definitely. Did you specify any particular time for us to call? John delivered the paper as specified.

spec i men (spes′i mən), part taken to show the kind or quality of the whole; sample. Arthur collects specimens of all kinds of rocks and minerals.

speck (spek), 1. small spot; stain. Can you clean the specks off this wallpaper? 2. tiny bit. I have a speck in my eye. 3. mark with specks. This fruit is badly specked.

speck le (spek′əl), 1. small spot or mark. This hen is gray with white speckles. 2. mark with speckles. The boy is speckled with freckles.

spec ta cle (spek′tə kəl), 1. thing to look at; sight. The children at play among the flowers made a charming spectacle. A quarrel is an unpleasant spectacle. 2. public show or display. A big army parade is a fine spectacle.

Spectacles

spec ta cles (spek′tə kəlz), pair of glasses to help a person's sight or to protect his eyes. See the picture.

spec tac u lar (spek tak′ū lər), making a great display. Moving pictures present spectacular scenes like battles, processions, storms, or races.

spec ta tor (spek′tā tər), person who looks on. There were many spectators at the game.

spec ter or **spec tre** (spek′tər), ghost.

spec trum (spek′trəm), the band of colors formed when a beam of light is broken up by being passed through a prism or by some other means. A rainbow has all the colors of the spectrum: red, orange, yellow, green, blue, indigo, and violet.

spec u late (spek′ū lāt), 1. reflect; meditate; conjecture. The philosopher speculated about time and space. 2. buy or sell when there is a large risk.

spec u la tion (spek′ū lā′shən), 1. thought; reflection; conjecture. Former speculations about electricity were often mere guesses. 2. buying or selling at a large risk.

sped (sped), speeded. See **speed.** The police car sped down the road.

speech (spēch), 1. act of speaking; talk. 2. power of speaking. Animals lack speech. 3. manner of speaking. His speech showed that he was Southern. 4. what is said; the words spoken. We made the usual farewell speeches. 5. a public talk. The President gave an excellent speech. 6. language.

speech less (spēch′lis), 1. not able to speak. Animals are speechless. George was speechless with anger. 2. silent. Her frown gave a speechless message.

speed (spēd), 1. swift or rapid movement. 2. go fast. He was arrested for speeding. 3. make go fast. Speed up the work. 4. rate of movement. The boys ran at full speed. 5. success; good luck. 6. give success to. God speed you. **sped** is formed from **speed.**

speed i ly (spēd′i li), quickly; with speed; soon.

speed y (spēd′i), fast; rapid; quick; swift.

spell[1] (spel), 1. write or say the letters of (a word) in order. We learn to spell in school. 2. mean. Those clouds spell a storm. Delay spells danger.

spell[2] (spel), 1. word or words having magic power. 2. fascination; charm. We were under the spell of the beautiful music.

spell[3] (spel), 1. period of work or duty. The sailor's spell at the wheel was four hours. 2. a period or time of anything. The child has spells of coughing. 3. work in place of (another person) for a while. I'll spell you at cutting the grass.

spell bound (spel′bound′), too interested to move; fascinated; enchanted.

spell ing (spel′ing), 1. writing or saying the letters of a word in order. John is poor at spelling. 2. the way in which a word is spelled. Ax has two spellings, **ax** and **axe.**

spelling bee, spelling contest.

spend (spend), 1. pay out. She spent ten dollars today. 2. pay out money. She would rather spend than save. 3. use; use up. Don't spend any more time on that lesson. The storm has spent its force.

spent (spent), 1. tired; used up; as, a spent swimmer, a spent horse. 2. See **spend.** Saturday was spent in playing.

Sperm whale (about 60 ft. long)

sperm whale (spėrm′ hwāl′), a large whale that is valuable for its oil.

sphere (sfēr), 1. round body whose surface is at all points equally distant from the center. 2. ball; globe. The sun, moon, earth, and stars are spheres. A baseball is a sphere. 3. place or surroundings in which a person or thing exists, acts, or works. The waitress changed to a higher social sphere after she married the rich man. 4. range; extent; region; as, England's sphere of influence.

Sphinx

sphinx (sfingks), a mythical monster with the head of a woman, the body of a lion, and wings.

spice (spīs), 1. seasoning. Pepper, cinnamon, cloves, ginger, and nutmeg are common spices. 2. put spice in; season; as, spiced peaches, spiced pickles. 3. something that adds flavor or interest. "Variety is the spice of life." 4. add flavor or interest to. The governor spiced his speech with stories and jokes.

spic y (spīs′i), 1. flavored with spice. The cookies were rich and spicy. 2. like that of spice. Some apples have a spicy smell and taste. 3. like spice; lively; keen; as, spicy conversation.

spi der (spī′dər), 1. a small animal with eight legs and no wings. Spiders spin webs to catch insects for food. 2. something like or suggesting a spider. A kind of frying pan is called a spider.

Garden spider. Line shows actual length.

spied (spīd). See **spy.** The hunter spied the stag in the distance.

spike[1] (spīk), 1. a large, strong nail. 2. fasten with spikes. The men spiked the rails to the ties when laying the track. 3. sharp-pointed piece or part. Some baseball players wear shoes with spikes. 4. provide with spikes. Runners wear spiked shoes to keep from slipping. 5. pierce or injure with a spike. 6. make (a cannon) useless by driving a spike into the opening where the powder is set off. 7. make useless. The extra guard spiked the spy's attempt to escape.

Spike (def. 1)

spike[2] (spīk), 1. ear of grain. 2. long, pointed flower cluster.

Spike: A, of grain; B, of flower.

spill (spil), 1. let (liquid or any matter in loose pieces) run or fall; as, to spill milk or salt. 2. fall or flow out. Water spilled from the pail. 3. cause to fall from a horse, carriage, car, boat, etc. The boat upset and spilled the boys into the water. 4. such a fall. John got a bad spill trying to ride.

spilt (spilt), spilled.

spin (spin), 1. draw out and twist (cotton, flax, wool, etc.) into thread. A spider spins a web. 2. produce; draw out; tell. The old sailor used to spin yarns about his adventures at sea. 3. make turn around rapidly. The boy spins his top. 4. turn around rapidly. The wheel spun round. 5. feel as if one were whirling around. My head is spinning. 6. a spinning. 7. rapid run, ride, drive, etc. Get your bicycle and come for a spin with me.

spin ach (spin′ich), a plant whose green leaves are boiled and eaten.

spin dle (spin′dəl), 1. the rod or pin used in spinning to twist, wind, and hold thread. 2. any rod or pin that turns around or on which something turns. Axles and shafts are spindles. 3. grow very long and thin.

spine (spīn), 1. the backbone. See the picture on p. 543. 2. a thorn or something like it. A cactus has spines; so has a porcupine.

spinning wheel, a wheel arranged for spinning wool, cotton, or flax into thread or yarn.

Spinning wheel

spin ster (spin′stər), unmarried woman; old maid.

spi ral (spī′rəl), 1. a coil. See the picture below. A watch spring is a spiral. The thread of a screw is a spiral. 2. coiled. A snail's shell has a spiral shape.

spire (spīr), 1. the top part of a tower or steeple that narrows to a point. See the picture below. 2. anything tapering and pointed. A blade of grass is sometimes called a spire of grass. The sunset shone on the rocky spires of the mountains.

Spirals

spir it (spir′it), 1. supernatural being. God is a spirit. Ghosts and fairies are spirits. 2. soul; moral and religious nature. 3. courage; vigor; liveliness. A race horse must have spirit. 4. state of mind; disposition; temper. He is in good spirits. **Out of spirits** means sad; gloomy. 5. person; personality. He is a brave spirit. He was one of the leading spirits of the revolution. 6. influence that stirs up and rouses. A spirit of progress is good for people. 7. what is really meant as opposed to what is said or written. The spirit of a law is more important than its words. 8. strong alcoholic liquor. Whiskey or brandy is called spirits. 9. carry (away or off) secretly. The child has been spirited away.

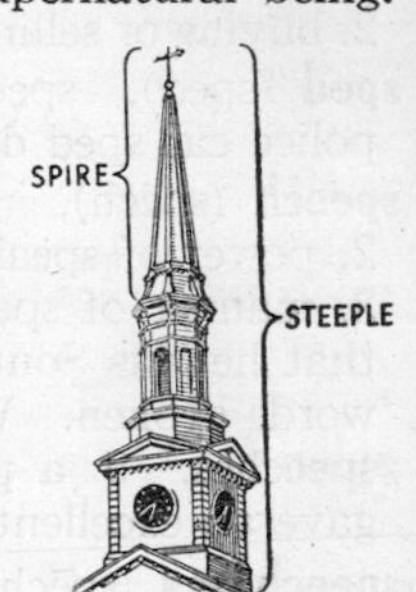

spir it ed (spir′i tid), lively; dashing; brave.

spir i tu al (spir′i chü əl), 1. of the spirit or spirits. 2. caring much for things of the soul or spirit. 3. sacred; religious. 4. a religious song; as, a Negro spiritual.

spit[1] (spit), 1. throw out saliva from the mouth. The cat spits when angry. 2. throw out. The gun spits fire. He spat curses. 3. the liquid produced in the mouth; saliva.

spit[2] (spit), 1. a sharp-pointed, slender rod or bar on which meat is roasted. 2. run a spit through; pierce; stab. The hunters spitted two rabbits. 3. narrow point of land running into the water.

Spits for roasting

spite (spīt), 1. ill will; grudge. Joan stayed away from May's party out of spite. 2. annoy; show ill will toward. He left his yard dirty to spite the people who lived next door. 3. **In spite of** means not prevented by; notwithstanding. The children went to school in spite of the rain.

spite ful (spīt′fəl), full of spite; eager to annoy; behaving with ill will and malice. Spiteful Lulu tore up her sister's papers.

splash (splash), 1. dash liquid about. The baby likes to splash in his tub. The waves splashed on the beach. 2. to wet, spatter, or soil. Our car is all splashed with mud. 3. splashing; sound of splashing. The splash of the wave knocked him over. The boat upset with a loud splash. 4. spot of liquid splashed upon a thing. Jane has splashes of grease on her dress. 5. spot; patch. The dog is white with brown splashes.

splen did (splen′did), brilliant; glorious; magnificent; grand; as, a splendid sunset, a splendid palace, a splendid victory.

splen dor (splen′dər), 1. great brightness; brilliant light. The sun set in a golden splendor. 2. magnificent show; pomp; glory.

splice (splīs), 1. join together (ropes) by weaving together ends which have been pulled out into separate strands. 2. join together (two pieces of timber) by overlapping. 3. joining of ropes or timbers by splicing. How neat a splice can you make?

Splicing

splint (splint), thin strip of wood. The man's broken arm was set in splints to hold it in position. My basket is woven from splints.

splin ter (splin′tər), 1. a thin, sharp piece of wood, bone, glass, etc. John got a splinter in his hand. The mirror broke into splinters. 2. split or break into splinters.

split (split), 1. break or cut from end to end or in layers. The man is splitting wood. She split the cake and filled it with jelly. 2. separate into parts; divide. The old farm has been split up into house lots. The two men split the cost of the dinner between them. 3. splitting; break; crack. Frost caused the split in the rock. 4. division in a group, party, etc. There was a split in the church for a time, but harmony was soon restored.

spoil (spoil), 1. damage; injure; destroy. He spoils a dozen pieces of paper before he writes a letter. The rain spoiled the picnic. That child is spoiled by too much attention. 2. be damaged; become bad or unfit for use. Fruit spoils if kept too long. 3. rob. 4. steal; take by force. 5. things taken by force; things won. The soldiers carried the spoils back to their own land.

spoilt (spoilt), spoiled.

spoke[1] (spōk). See **speak.** She spoke of that yesterday.

spoke[2] (spōk), one of the bars from the center of a wheel to the rim.

SPOKE
HUB
AXLE
FELLOE OR FELLY

spo ken (spō′kən), 1. uttered; told; expressed with the mouth. A child understands a spoken direction better than a written one. 2. See **speak.** They have spoken about having a picnic.

spokes man (spōks′mən), person who speaks for another or others. Mr. Smith was the spokesman for the factory workers.

sponge (spunj), 1. a kind of sea animal. 2. its light framework used for soaking up water in bathing or cleaning. 3. something like a sponge, such as bread dough, a kind of cake, a pudding, etc. 4. wipe or rub with a wet sponge. Sponge the mud spots off the car. Sponge up the spilled water. 5. clean in this way; make damp. 6. live or profit at the expense of another in a mean way. That big boy won't work, but sponges on his mother.

Human spine

spon gy (spun′ji), 1. like a sponge; soft, light, and full of holes; as, spongy moss, spongy dough. 2. hard and full of holes; as, a spongy rock.

spon sor (spon′sər), 1. person who is responsible for a person or thing; as, the sponsor of a law. The sponsor of a radio program pays for it. 2. person who takes vows for an infant at baptism; a godfather or godmother. 3. act as sponsor for.

spon ta ne ous (spon tā′ni əs), of one's own choice; natural; of itself. Both sides burst into spontaneous cheers at the skillful play. A pile of oily rags will sometimes break into a spontaneous flame. Spontaneous combustion occurs when something sets itself on fire.

Spool of thread

spook (spük), ghost; specter.

spool (spül), small cylinder of wood or metal on which thread or wire is wound. See the picture just above.

spoon (spün), 1. See the pictures. 2. take up in a spoon.

spoon ful (spün′fül), as much as a spoon can hold.

spore (spōr), 1. a single cell capable of growing into a new plant or animal. Ferns produce spores. 2. germ; seed.

Spoons

sport (spōrt), 1. a game; outdoor play. Baseball, golf, tennis, swimming, racing, hunting, and fishing are familiar sports. 2. fun; play; amusement. 3. to play. Lambs sport in the fields. The kitten sports with its tail. 4. joking. The man teased the child in sport. 5. ridicule. Don't make sport of the lame boy. 6. the object of jokes and ridicule. A very fat boy is the sport of other boys. 7. sportsman.

sport ing (spōr′ting), 1. of or interested in sports. 2. playing fair. 3. willing to take a chance. 4. involving risk.

sports man (spōrts′mən), 1. person who takes part in sports, especially hunting, fishing, or racing. 2. person who likes sports. 3. person who plays fair.

spot (spot), 1. mark; stain; speck. You have grease spots on your suit. That spot on her cheek is a bruise. His character is without spot. 2. small part unlike the rest. His tie is blue with white spots. 3. make spots on; become spotted; have spots. He has spotted the tablecloth. This silk spots from rain. 4. place. From this spot you can see the ocean. **On the spot** means at that very place or at once. 5. ready; on hand. He paid spot cash for the horse.

spot less (spot′lis), without a spot. She wore a spotless white apron.

spouse (spouz), husband or wife. Mr. Smith is Mrs. Smith's spouse, and she is his spouse.

spout (spout), 1. throw out a liquid in a stream or spray. The fountain spouted up high. A whale spouts water. 2. flow out with force. Water spouted from the break in the pipe. 3. stream; jet. A spout of water shot up from the hole in the pipe. 4. a pipe for carrying off water. Rain runs down a spout from our roof to the ground. 5. a tube or lip by which liquid is poured. A teakettle, a coffee pot, and a syrup jug have spouts. 6. speak in loud and emotional tones.

SPOUT

sprain (sprān), 1. injure (a joint or muscle) by a sudden twist or wrench; as, to sprain your ankle. 2. injury caused in this way.

sprang (sprang). See **spring.** The tiger sprang at the man.

sprawl (sprôl), 1. toss or spread the limbs about. 2. lie or sit with the limbs spread out. The people sprawled on the beach in their bathing suits. 3. spread out in an irregular or awkward manner. The vine sprawled over the grass. 4. act or position of sprawling.

spray[1] (sprā), 1. liquid going through the air in fine drops. We were wet with the sea spray. 2. something like this. A spray of bullets hit the tree behind which he was hiding. 3. an instrument that sends a liquid out as spray. 4. sprinkle; scatter spray on. Spray this liquid on your throat. Spray the apple tree.

spray[2] (sprā), a small branch or piece of some plant with its leaves, flowers, or fruit; as, a spray of ivy, a spray of lilacs, a spray of fern, a spray of berries.

spread (spred), 1. stretch out; open out. The bird spreads its wings. 2. extend; lie. Fields of corn spread out before us. 3. cover with a thin layer. He ate bread spread with butter. 4. put as a thin layer. Spread the paint evenly. 5. scatter; distribute. The Jewish race is spread all over the world. 6. push farther apart. Spread out your fingers. 7. width; extent; amount of spreading. The airplane's spread was sixty feet. 8. covering for a bed or table. 9. food put on the table; a feast. 10. put food on (a table).

spree (sprē), 1. lively frolic. 2. a spell of drinking intoxicating liquor.

sprig (sprig), a shoot, twig, or small branch. He wore a sprig of lilac in his buttonhole.

spright ly (sprīt′li), lively; gay. A kitten is sprightly.

spring (spring), 1. a leap or jump. 2. to leap or jump; rise or move suddenly and lightly. The dog springs at the thief. The boy sprang to his feet. 3. elastic quality. There is no spring left in these old rubber bands. The old man's knees have lost their spring. 4. fly back or away. A bent branch will spring back into place. 5. elastic device that returns to its original shape after being pulled or held out of shape. Beds have wire springs. The spring in a clock makes it go. See the picture. 6. cause to spring; as, to spring a trap. 7. bring out, produce, or make suddenly; as, to spring a surprise on someone. 8. To **spring a mine** is to cause the gunpowder or other explosive in it to explode. 9. the season after winter when plants begin to grow. 10. small stream of water coming from the earth. 11. source; beginning; cause. 12. come from some source; arise; grow. A wind has sprung up. Plants spring from seeds. 13. split; crack; break; bend; strain. To **spring a leak** means to crack and begin to let water through. 14. of or having something to do with a spring or springs. **sprang** and **sprung** are formed from **spring.**

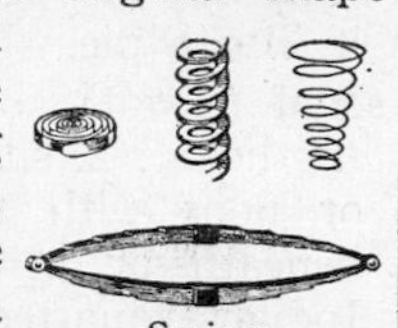
Springs

spring time (spring′tīm′), the season of spring. Flowers bloom in the springtime.

sprin kle (spring′kəl), 1. scatter in drops or tiny bits. He sprinkled ashes on the icy sidewalk. 2. spray or cover with small drops. Helen sprinkled the flowers with water. 3. sprinkling; small quantity. The cook put a sprinkle of nuts on the cake. 4. rain a little. 5. light rain.

sprite (sprīt), elf; fairy; goblin.

sprout (sprout), 1. begin to grow; shoot forth. Seeds sprout. Buds sprout in the spring. Weeds have sprouted in the garden. 2. cause to grow. The rain has sprouted the corn. 3. a shoot of a plant. The gardener was setting out sprouts.

Branch of spruce with cones

spruce[1] (sprüs), 1. a kind of evergreen tree. See the picture on this page. 2. its wood.

spruce[2] (sprüs), 1. neat; trim. John looked very spruce in his new suit. 2. make spruce; make oneself spruce; become spruce. John spruced up for dinner.

sprung (sprung). See **spring.** The trap was sprung.

spun (spun). See **spin.** She spun all day yesterday. The thread was spun from silk.

spur (spėr), 1. a pricking instrument worn on a horseman's heel for urging a horse on. 2. prick with spurs. The rider spurred his horse on. 3. ride quickly. 4. something like a spur; a point sticking out. A cock has spurs on his legs. A spur of rock stuck out from the mountain. 5. anything that urges on. Ambition was the spur that made him work. 6. urge on. Pride spurred the man to fight.

Horseman's spur

spurn (spėrn), 1. strike with the foot; kick away. The king spurned the kneeling slave. 2. scorn; refuse with scorn. The judge spurned the bribe.

spurt (spėrt), 1. flow suddenly in a stream or jet; gush out; squirt. Blood spurted from the wound. 2. sudden rushing forth; jet. Spurts of flame broke out all over the building. 3. a great increase of effort or activity for a short time. 4. put forth great energy for a short time. The swimmers spurted near the end of the race.

sput ter (sput′ər), 1. make spitting or popping noises; as, sputtering firecrackers, fat sputtering in the frying pan. 2. throw out drops of spit, bits of food, etc., in excitement or in talking too fast. 3. say words or sounds in haste and confusion. 4. a sputtering. 5. confused talk.

spy (spī), 1. person who keeps secret watch on the actions of others. 2. person who, in time of war, tries to get information about the enemy, usually by visiting the enemy's territory in disguise. 3. find out or try to find out by careful observation. She spies out everything that goes on in the neighborhood. 4. keep secret watch. Mr. Smith saw two men spying on him from behind a tree. 5. catch sight of; see. He was the first to spy the rescue party in the distance.

spy glass (spī′glas′), small telescope.

squab (skwob), very young bird, especially a young pigeon.

squab ble (skwob′əl), 1. a petty, noisy quarrel. Children's squabbles annoy their parents. 2. take part in a petty, noisy quarrel. I won't squabble over three cents.

squad (skwod), 1. small number of soldiers grouped for drill, inspection, or work. 2. any small group of persons. He hired a squad of boys to work for him.

squad ron (skwod′rən), 1. a part of a naval fleet used for special service; as, the Atlantic squadron of the navy. 2. a body of cavalry usually having from 120 to 200 men. 3. a number of airplanes that fly or fight together. 4. group.

squal id (skwol′id), filthy; degraded; poor; wretched.

squall[1] (skwôl), sudden, violent gust of wind, often with rain, snow, or sleet.

squall[2] (skwôl), 1. cry out loudly; scream violently. The baby squalled. 2. loud, harsh cry. The parrot's squall was heard all over the house.

squal or (skwol′ər), filth; misery and dirt.

squan der (skwon′dər), spend foolishly; waste. He squandered his time and money in gambling.

square (skwãr), 1. a figure with four equal sides and four right angles; having this shape □; anything having this shape, or nearly this shape. The troops were drawn up in a square. 2. space in a city or town, bounded by streets on four sides. This square is full of stores. 3. distance along one side of such a space; a block. We live three squares from the school. 4. open space in a city or town bounded by streets on four sides, often planted with grass, trees, etc. The soldiers' monument is in the square opposite the city hall. 5. any similar open space, as at the meeting of streets. 6. instrument for drawing right angles and testing the squareness of anything. 7. just; fair; honest. You will get a square deal at this shop. 8. settle. Let us square our accounts. 9. satisfying; as, a square meal. 10. make square in shape. 11. mark in squares. The children squared off the sidewalk for their game. 12. forming a right angle; as, a square corner. 13. make straight or level. 14. agree; conform. His acts do not square with his promises. 15. A **square dance** is a dance performed by couples arranged about a square space or in some set form. 16. A **square foot** equals a space a foot long and a foot wide. A rug 9 ft. long and 6 ft. wide covers 54 square feet.

Square (def. 6)

squash[1] (skwosh), 1. crush; press until soft or flat. The boy squashed the bug. This package was squashed in the mail. 2. something squashed; a crushed mass. The grapes are just a squash and not fit to eat. 3. a game somewhat like handball and tennis.

squash[2] (skwosh), a vegetable that grows on a vine. We eat squash as a vegetable or make it into a pie.

Summer squash

Winter squash

squat (skwot), 1. crouch on the heels. 2. sit on the ground or floor with the legs drawn up closely beneath or in front of the body. The Indians squatted around the fire. 3. settle on another's land without title or right. 4. settle on public land to acquire ownership of it. 5. crouching. A squat figure sat in front of the fire. 6. short and thick; low and broad. The Italian was a squat dark man. 7. act of squatting.

squaw (skwô), an American Indian woman or wife.

squawk (skwôk), 1. make a loud, harsh sound. Hens and ducks squawk when frightened. 2. a loud, harsh sound.

squeak (skwēk), 1. make a short, sharp, shrill sound. A mouse squeaks. 2. such a sound. We heard the squeak of the rocking chair.

squeak y (skwēk′i), squeaking.

squeal (skwēl), 1. make a long, sharp, shrill cry. A pig squeals when it is hurt. 2. such a cry.

squeeze (skwēz), 1. press hard. Don't squeeze the kitten; you will hurt it. 2. force by pressing. I can't squeeze another thing into my trunk. 3. a tight pressure. She gave her sister's arm a squeeze. 4. hug. 5. crush; crowd. It's a tight squeeze to get five people in that little car. 6. force a way. He squeezed through the crowd. 7. yield to pressure. Sponges squeeze easily.

squint (skwint), 1. look with the eyes partly closed. 2. sidelong look; hasty look; look. 3. look sideways. 4. tendency to look sideways. She would be very pretty except for her squint. 5. looking sideways. 6. be cross-eyed. 7. cross-eyed.

squire (skwīr), 1. in England, a country gentleman, especially the chief landowner in a district. 2. in the United States, a justice of the peace or a local judge. 3. young man of noble family who attended a knight till he himself was made a knight. 4. woman's escort. 5. to escort (a lady).

squirm (skwėrm), wriggle; writhe; twist. The boy squirmed in his seat.

squir rel (skwėr′əl), 1. a small, bushy-tailed animal that lives in trees. Some kinds live mostly on the ground. 2. its gray, reddish, or dark-brown fur.

Common gray squirrel (about 1½ ft. long with the tail)

squirt (skwėrt), 1. force out (liquid) through a narrow opening; as, to squirt water through a tube. 2. come out in a jet or stream; as, water squirting from a hose. 3. squirting. Dick soaked Ben with squirts of water from the hose. 4. jet.

St., 1. Street. 2. Saint.

stab (stab), 1. pierce or wound with a pointed weapon. 2. a thrust or blow made with a pointed weapon. 3. wound made by stabbing. 4. wound sharply or deeply in the feelings. The mother was stabbed to the heart by her son's lack of gratitude.

sta bil i ty (stə bil′i ti), 1. firmness; being fixed in position. A concrete wall has more stability than a light wooden fence. 2. permanence. 3. steadfastness; as, the stability of Washington's character and devotion.

sta ble[1] (stā′bəl), 1. a building where horses or cattle are kept and fed. 2. group of animals housed in such a building. The black race horse is one of Mr. King's stable. 3. put or keep in a stable.

sta ble[2] (stā′bəl), firm; steady; not likely to move or change. Concrete reinforced with steel is stable.

stack (stak), 1. large pile of hay, straw, etc. Haystacks are often round and arranged so as to shed water. 2. pile of anything; as, a stack of wood. 3. number of rifles arranged to form a cone or pyramid. 4. pile or arrange in a stack; as, to stack hay, to stack firewood, to stack guns. 5. chimney.

Stack of rifles

sta di um (stā′di əm), place for athletic games, consisting of tiers of seats around an open field.

staff (staf), 1. stick; pole; rod. The old man leaned on his staff. The flag hangs on a staff. 2. something that supports or sustains. Bread is called the staff of life because it will support life. 3. group assisting a chief; group of employees. Our school has a staff of ten teachers. 4. group of officers that makes plans for an army but does no fighting. 5. provide with officers or employees. 6. the five lines and the spaces between them on which music is written.

Musical staff

stag (stag), 1. a full-grown male deer. 2. male. A stag dinner is attended by men only.

Stag (about 4 ft. high at the shoulder)

stage (stāj), 1. a platform; flooring. 2. the raised flooring in a theater on which the actors perform. 3. the theater; the drama; actor's profession. 4. scene of action. Bunker Hill was the stage of a famous battle. 5. arrange. The play was very well staged. Mother had staged a surprise for the children's party by hiring a magician to perform. 6. place of rest on a journey; a regular stopping place. 7. the distance between two places on a journey. We climbed the mountain **by easy stages** means we often stopped to rest. 8. one step or degree in a process; a period of development. Frogs pass through a tadpole stage. 9. stagecoach; bus.

stage coach (stāj′kōch′), a coach carrying passengers and parcels over a regular route.

Stagecoach

stag ger (stag′ər), 1. sway or reel (from weakness, a heavy load, or being drunk). 2. make sway or reel. The blow staggered him for the moment. 3. swaying or reeling. 4. become unsteady; waver. The troops staggered under the severe attack. 5. hesitate. 6. cause to hesitate or become confused. The difficulty of the examination staggered him. 7. make helpless. 8. arrange in a zigzag order or way.

stag nant (stag′nənt), 1. not running or flowing; foul from standing still. The water in a stagnant pool is not good to drink. 2. not active; sluggish; dull.

staid (stād), 1. having a settled, quiet character. We think of Quakers as staid people. 2. old form of **stayed.**

stain (stān), 1. soil; spot. He has ink stains on his shirt. The tablecloth is stained where food has been spilled. 2. spot by wrongdoing or disgrace. His character is without stain. His crimes stained the family honor. 3. color. She stained the chair with a green stain.

stair (stãr), 1. one of a series of steps for going from one level or floor to another. A broken stair may make someone fall. 2. a set of such steps. We climbed the winding stair to the tower.

stair case (stãr′kās′), stairs; a flight of stairs.

stair way (stãr′wā′), stairs; a way up and down by stairs. The servants use the back stairway.

stake[1] (stāk), 1. a stick or post pointed at one end for driving into the ground. 2. fasten to a stake or with a stake. 3. mark with stakes; mark the boundaries of. The miner staked off his claims.

stake[2] (stāk), 1. risk (money or something valuable) on the result of a game or on any chance. He staked all his money on the black horse. 2. the money risked; what is staked. The men played for high stakes. He has much **at stake** means he has much to win or lose. 3. the prize in a race or contest. The stakes were divided up among the winners. 4. something to gain or lose; an interest; a share in a property. Each of us has a stake in the future of our country.

sta lac tite (stə lak′tīt), a formation of lime, shaped like an icicle, hanging from the roof of a cave. Stalactites are formed by dripping water that contains lime.

sta lag mite (stə lag′mīt), a formation of lime, shaped like a cone, built upon the floor of a cave.

stale (stāl), 1. not fresh; as, stale bread, a stale joke. 2. out of condition. The horse has gone stale from too much running.

stalk[1] (stôk), 1. the stem of a plant. 2. any stemlike part. A flower or leaf blade may have a stalk.

stalk[2] (stôk), 1. approach wild animals without being seen by them. The hunters stalked the lion. 2. pursue an animal or a person without being seen. 3. spread silently and steadily. Disease stalked through the land. 4. walk with slow, stiff, or haughty strides. 5. stalking.

stall (stôl), 1. place in a stable for one animal. 2. small place for selling things. At the public market different things are sold in different stalls under one big roof. 3. seat in the choir of a church. 4. seat in the front part of a theater. 5. put or keep in a stall. The horses were safely stalled. 6. stop against one's wish. He had stalled the engine of his automobile. We were stalled in the mud.

Stalls for animals

stal wart (stôl′wərt), 1. strongly built. 2. strong and brave. 3. firm; steadfast.

sta men (stā′mən), the part of a flower that contains the pollen.

S, stamen.

stam mer (stam′ər), 1. repeat the same sound in an effort to speak; hesitate in speaking. *Example:* I s-s-see a d-d-dog. 2. stammering; stuttering. John has a nervous stammer.

stamp (stamp), 1. bring down one's foot with force. Jack stamped on the spider. 2. act of stamping. 3. pound; crush. She stamped out the fire. 4. mill or machine that crushes rock, etc. 5. make a mark on; the mark made; the thing making it. She stamped the papers with a stamp that had her name on it. 6. show to be of a certain quality or character. His speech stamps him as a man of education. 7. impression; marks. Her face bore the stamp of suffering. 8. small piece of paper with a sticky back which is put on letters, papers, parcels, etc., to show that a charge has been paid; as, a postage stamp. 9. put a stamp on.

stam pede (stam pēd′), 1. a sudden scattering or headlong flight of a frightened herd of cattle or horses. 2. any headlong flight of a large group; as, a stampede of a frightened crowd from a burning building. 3. scatter or flee in a stampede. 4. general rush; as, a stampede to newly discovered gold fields. 5. make a general rush. 6. cause to stampede.

stanch[1] (stänch), 1. stop or check the flow

of (blood, etc.). 2. stop the flow of blood from (a wound). Also spelled **staunch.**

stanch[2] (stänch), 1. strong; firm; as, stanch walls, a stanch defense, stanch friends, a stanch supporter of the law. 2. watertight; as, a stanch boat. Also spelled **staunch.**

stand (stand), 1. be on one's feet. Don't stand if you are tired, but sit down. 2. rise to one's feet. The children stand to salute the flag. 3. set upright. Stand the box here. 4. be set upright. 5. be in a certain place, rank, scale, etc. Pillars stand on each side of the door. John stood first in his class for service to the school. 6. be in a special condition. He stands innocent of any wrong. The poor man stood in need of food and clothing. 7. take a certain position. "Stand back!" called the policeman to the crowd. 8. stay in place; last. The old house has stood for a hundred years. 9. bear; endure. Many plants cannot stand cold, and die in the winter. 10. be unchanged; hold good; remain the same. The rule against being late will stand. 11. stop moving; halt; stop. 12. a halt; a stop; a stop for defense. We made a last stand against the enemy. 13. place where a person stands; position. The policeman took his stand at the street corner. 14. place or fixtures for a small business; as, a newsstand or a fruit stand. 15. something to put things on or in. Leave your wet umbrella in the stand in the hall. 16. raised place where people may stand or sit. 17. Some special meanings are:

stand by, 1. be near. 2. side with; help.

stand for, 1. represent; mean. 2. be on the side of; take the part of; uphold. Our school stands for fair play.

stand out, 1. project. 2. be noticeable or prominent. 3. refuse to yield.

stood is formed from **stand.**

stand ard (stan′dərd), 1. anything taken as a basis of comparison; model; rule. Your work is not up to the class standard. 2. used as a standard; according to rule. Standard English is better than slang. 3. having recognized excellence or authority. Scott and Dickens are standard authors. 4. flag, emblem, or symbol. 5. upright support. The floor lamp has a long standard.

stand ing (stan′ding), 1. position; reputation; as, men of good standing. 2. duration. **Of long standing** means having lasted a long time. 3. erect; straight up. 4. done from an erect position; as, a standing jump. 5. not flowing; stagnant; as, standing water. 6. established; permanent; as, a standing army.

stand point (stand′point′), the point at which a person stands to look at something; point of view; mental attitude. From Bill's standpoint, combing your hair is a waste of time.

stand still (stand′stil′), stop; halt; pause.

stank (stangk), had a bad smell. See **stink.**

stan za (stan′zə), verse of a poem; group of lines of poetry. They sang the first and last stanzas of "America."

sta ple[1] (stā′pəl), 1. piece of metal with pointed ends bent into a U shape. Staples are driven into doors, etc., to hold hooks, pins, or bolts. 2. bent piece of wire used to hold together papers, parts of a book, etc. 3. fasten with staples.

Staple (def. 1)

sta ple[2] (stā′pəl), 1. the most important or principal article grown or manufactured in a place. Cotton is the staple in many Southern States. 2. most important; principal. Bread is a staple food. The weather is a staple subject of conversation. 3. raw material. 4. fiber of cotton or wool.

star (stär), 1. any of the bright points seen in the sky at night. 2. a heavenly body that is not a planet, comet, or meteor. 3. person having brilliant qualities; a famous actor, singer, etc.; as, a movie star. 4. be a leading performer. She has starred in many pictures. 5. a figure having usually five points, sometimes six, like these: ☆✡. 6. thing having this shape. 7. a sign like this (*). Smith's name was starred twice means that it was printed like this: Smith**. 8. ornament with stars. Nan's card was starred for perfect attendance.

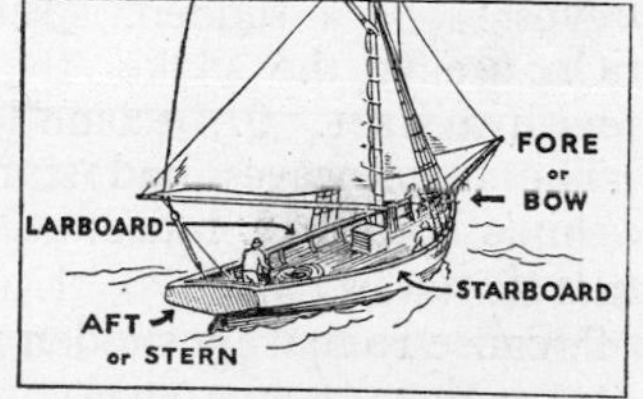

star board (stär′bərd), 1. the right side of a ship. 2. on the right side of a ship.

starch (stärch), 1. a white, tasteless food substance. Potatoes, wheat, rice, and corn contain much starch. 2. preparation of it used to stiffen clothes. 3. stiffen (clothes) with it. Men's collars are often starched.

starch y (stär′chi), 1. like starch; containing starch. 2. stiff with starch. 3. stiff in manner; formal.

stare (stãr), 1. look directly with the eyes wide open. A person stares in wonder, surprise, stupidity, curiosity, or from mere rudeness. The little girl stared at the toys in the window. 2. fixed look with the eyes wide open. The doll's eyes were set in an unchanging stare. 3. be very striking or glaring.

Starfish (about 5 in. across)

star fish (stär′fish′), a star-shaped sea animal. It is not a fish.

stark (stärk), 1. stiff. The dog lay stark in death. 2. downright; complete. That fool is talking stark nonsense. 3. entirely; completely. The boys went swimming stark naked.

star light (stär′līt′), 1. light from the stars. 2. lighted by the stars.

star ling (stär′ling), 1. a common European bird which nests about buildings and is easily tamed. 2. a kind of American blackbird.

star lit (stär′lit′), lighted by the stars.

star ry (stär′i), 1. lighted by stars; containing many stars; as, a starry sky. 2. shining like stars; as, starry eyes.

Stars and Stripes, the flag of the United States.

start (stärt), 1. begin to move, go, or act; set going; put in action. The train started on time. I started a fire. 2. setting in motion. 3. begin. 4. beginning to move, go, or act. 5. move suddenly. Mrs. Jones started in surprise. 6. a sudden, jerking movement. I awoke with a start. 7. come or rise suddenly; spring suddenly. Tears started from her eyes. 8. a sudden, springing movement. On seeing the snake, the man sprang up with a start. 9. become loose; make loose. The huge waves had started some of the ship's bolts. 10. rouse; as, to start a rabbit.

star tle (stär′təl), 1. surprise; frighten. 2. cause to make a sudden movement.

star va tion (stär vā′shən), 1. starving. The starvation of prisoners of war is barbarous. 2. being starved; suffering from extreme hunger. Starvation caused his death.

starve (stärv), 1. die because of hunger; suffer severely because of hunger. 2. weaken or kill with hunger. That cruel man half starves his horses. The enemy starved the men in the fort into surrendering. 3. **Starve for** sometimes means suffer from the lack of. That child is starving for affection.

state (stāt), 1. condition of a person or thing. He is in a poor state of health. The house is in a bad state of repair. 2. nation. 3. one of several organized political groups of people which together form a nation. The State of Texas is one of the United States. 4. rank; person's position in life. 5. dignity; pomp; high style of living. Kings live in great state. 6. tell in speech or writing. State your opinion of the new school rules. 7. with ceremony; of ceremony.

stat ed (stāt′id), fixed; settled.

state ly (stāt′li), having dignity; imposing; majestic. The Capitol at Washington is a stately building.

state ment (stāt′mənt), 1. something stated; account; report. His statement was correct. 2. stating; manner of stating something. The statement of an idea helps me to remember it.

states man (stāts′mən), man skilled in the management of public or national affairs. Abraham Lincoln was a famous American statesman.

states man ship (stāts′mən ship), skill in the management of public affairs.

sta tion (stā′shən), 1. place to stand in. The policeman took his station at the corner. 2. a building or place used for a definite purpose. A place where soldiers live, a harbor for ships, and the police headquarters of a district are all called stations. 3. place or equipment for sending out or receiving programs, messages, etc., by radio. 4. regular stopping place. She met her at the railroad station. 5. social position; rank. A street cleaner is a man of humble station in life. 6. place. He stationed himself just outside the main doorway of the hotel.

sta tion ar y (stā′shən ãr′i), 1. having a fixed station or place; standing still; not movable. A factory engine is stationary. 2. not changing in size, number, activity, etc. The population of this town has been stationary for ten years at about 5000 people.

sta tion er y (stā′shən ãr′i), writing materials; paper, cards, and envelopes.

stat u ar y (stach′ü ãr′i), statues.

stat ue (stach′ü), image of a person or animal carved in stone or wood, cast in bronze, or modeled in clay or wax. Nearly every city has a statue of some famous man.

stat ure (stach′ər), height. A man 6 feet tall is above average stature.

sta tus (stā′təs), condition; position.

stat ute (stach′üt), a law. The statutes for the United States are made by Congress.

staunch[1] (stônch), 1. stop the flow of (blood, etc.). 2. stop the flow of blood from (a wound). Also spelled **stanch.**

staunch[2] (stônch), 1. strong; firm; as, staunch walls, a staunch defense, staunch friends, a staunch supporter of the law. 2. watertight. Also spelled **stanch.**

stave (stāv), 1. one of the curved pieces of wood which form the sides of a barrel, tub, etc. 2. stick or staff. 3. break a hole in (a barrel, boat, etc.). 4. become smashed or broken in. 5. keep (off); put (off). The lost campers ate birds' eggs to stave off starvation. 6. a verse or stanza of a poem or song.

staves (stāvz), 1. more than one staff. 2. more than one stave.

stay[1] (stā), 1. remain. Stay here till I tell you to move. The cat stayed out all night. Shall I go or stay? 2. live for a while; dwell. Alice is staying with her aunt while her mother is ill. 3. put an end to for a while; stop; satisfy. Jim ate some bread and butter to stay his hunger till time for dinner. 4. put off; hold back; delay. The teacher stayed judgment till she could hear both sides. 5. endure. 6. staying; stop; time spent; as, a pleasant stay at the seashore.

stay[2] (stā), 1. a strong rope, often made of wire, which supports the mast of a ship. 2. any rope or chain attached to something to steady it.

stay[3] (stā), support; prop; brace. The oldest son was the family's stay.

stead (sted), 1. place. Our laundress could not come, but sent her sister in her stead. 2. **Stand** (a person) **in good stead** means be an advantage to him. His ability to swim stood him in good stead when the boat upset.

stead fast (sted′fast), firmly fixed; constant; not moving or changing. George Washington was a steadfast servant of his country.

stead i ly (sted′i li), in a steady manner; firmly; uniformly.

stead i ness (sted′i nis), being steady.

stead y (sted′i), 1. firmly fixed; firm; not swaying or shaking. This post is steady as a rock. 2. changing little; uniform; regular. John is making steady progress at school. 3. reliable; having good habits. Fred is a steady young man. 4. make steady; keep steady. Steady the stepladder while I take down the dishes from the shelves. 5. become steady. The wind steadied.

steak (stāk), slice of meat or fish for broiling or frying. Steak often means beefsteak.

steal (stēl), 1. take something that does not belong to one; take dishonestly. Robbers steal. 2. take, get, or do secretly. Jane stole time from her lessons to read a story. 3. move secretly or quietly. She had stolen softly out of the room. **stole** and **stolen** are formed from **steal.**

stealth (stelth), secret action. He obtained the letter by stealth, taking it while his sister was out of the room.

stealth y (stel′thi), done in a secret manner; secret; sly. The cat crept in a stealthy way toward the bird.

steam (stēm), 1. water in the form of vapor or gas. Boiling water gives off steam. Steam is used to heat houses, run engines, etc. 2. give off steam; as, a cup of steaming coffee. 3. move by steam. The ship steamed off. 4. cook, soften, or freshen by steam. She steamed what was left of the pudding.

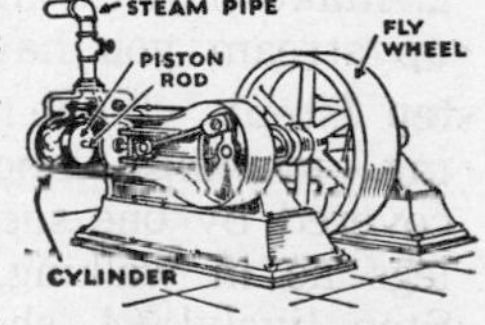

Steam engine

steam boat (stēm′bōt′), boat moved by steam.

steam engine, engine worked by steam.

steam er (stēm′ər), 1. steamboat; steamship. 2. engine or car run by steam. 3. container in which something is steamed.

steam ship (stēm′ship′), ship moved by steam.

steed (stēd), horse; high-spirited horse; war horse; riding horse.

steel (stēl), 1. iron mixed with carbon so that it is very hard, strong, and tough. Most tools are made from steel. 2. something made from steel. A sword or a piece of steel for making sparks can be called a steel. 3. made of steel. 4. make hard or strong like steel. He steeled his heart against the sufferings of the poor.

steep[1] (stēp), having a sharp slope; almost straight up and down. The hill is steep.

steep[2] (stēp), soak. She steeped the tea in boiling water. His sword was steeped in blood.

stee ple (stē′pəl), high tower on a church. Steeples usually have spires.

steer[1] (stēr), 1. guide; as, to steer a ship, to steer a sled, to steer an automobile, to steer an airplane. The pilot steered for the harbor. 2. be guided. This car steers easily. 3. direct one's way or course.

steer[2] (stēr), 1. young ox, usually two to four years old. 2. any male of beef cattle.

stem[1] (stem), 1. the main part of a plant above the ground, which supports the other parts. The trunk of a tree and the stalks of corn are stems. 2. the part of a flower, a fruit, or a leaf that joins it to the plant or tree. 3. remove the stem from (a leaf, fruit, etc.). 4. anything like the stem of a plant; as, the stem of a goblet, the stem of a pipe, etc. 5. line of descent of a family. 6. bow or front end of a boat.

stem[2] (stem), 1. stop; check; dam up. 2. make progress against. When you swim up stream you have to stem the current.

step (step), 1. one motion of the leg in walking, running, dancing, etc. 2. distance covered by one such motion. 3. move the legs as in walking, running, dancing, etc. Step lively! 4. short distance; little way. 5. walk a short distance. Step this way. Dick stepped toward the door. 6. way of stepping; as, a quick step, a dance with fancy steps. 7. **Keep step** means move the same leg at the same time that another person does. **In step** means making one's steps fit those of some other person. **Out of step** means not in step. 8. measure (off) by taking steps. Step off the distance from the door to the window. 9. place for the foot in going up or coming down. A stair or a rung of a ladder is a step. 10. sound made by putting the foot down. 11. footprint. 12. an action. The principal took steps to stop needless absence from school. 13. a degree in a scale; a grade in rank. A colonel is two steps above a captain.

step fa ther (step′fä′ᴛʜər), man who has married one's mother after the death or divorce of one's real father.

step lad der (step′lad′ər), ladder with flat steps instead of rungs.

step moth er (step′muᴛʜ′ər), woman who has married one's father after the death or divorce of one's real mother.

steppe (step), 1. one of the vast treeless plains in southeastern Europe and Siberia. 2. a vast treeless plain.

ster ile (ster′il), 1. barren; not fertile. Sterile land does not produce good crops. 2. free from living germs. A doctor's instruments must be kept sterile.

ster i lize (ster′i līz), make free from living germs. The water had to be sterilized by boiling to make it fit to drink.

ster ling (stėr′ling), 1. British money. 2. of British money; that may be paid in British money. 3. of standard quality; containing 92.5 per cent pure silver. *Sterling* is stamped on solid silver knives, forks, etc. 4. sterling silver. 5. made of sterling silver. 6. genuine; excellent; reliable. Everybody admired Washington's sterling character.

stern[1] (stėrn), 1. severe; strict; harsh. His father was a stern man. His stern frown frightened the children. 2. hard; not yielding; firm.

stern[2] (stėrn), the hind part of a ship or boat.

stew (stū or stü), 1. cook by slow boiling. The cook stewed the chicken for a long time. 2. food cooked by slow boiling; as, beef stew.

stew ard (stū′ərd or stü′ərd), 1. man who manages another's property. He is the steward of that great estate. 2. man who takes charge of the food and table service for a club, a ship, etc. 3. servant on a ship. A dining-room steward is a waiter.

stew ard ess (stū′ər dis or stü′ər dis), a woman steward on a ship or airplane.

stick[1] (stik), 1. a long, thin piece of wood. Put some sticks on the fire. 2. such a piece of wood shaped for a special use; as, a walking stick or a golf stick. 3. something like a stick in shape; as, a stick of candy, a drumstick. 4. A stiff, awkward, or stupid person is called a stick in free and easy talk.

stick[2] (stik), 1. stab; pierce with a pointed instrument. He stuck his fork into the potato. 2. fasten by thrusting the point or end into or through something. He stuck a flower in his buttonhole. 3. put into a position. Don't stick your head out of the train window. 4. fasten; attach; be fastened. Stick a stamp on the letter. Two pages of the book stuck together. 5. keep on; hold fast. John sticks to a task until he finishes it. He sticks to his friends in trouble. 6. puzzle. That problem in arithmetic stuck me. 7. be puzzled; hesitate. He sticks at nothing to get his own way. 8. bring to a stop; become fixed; be at a standstill. The car was stuck in the mud. 9. **Stick up for** means stand up for.

stick y (stik′i), that sticks; as, sticky flypaper.

stiff (stif), 1. not easily bent; hard to move. He wore a stiff collar. The old man's joints were stiff. 2. firm. The jelly is stiff enough to stand alone. 3. not easy in manner; formal. He made a stiff bow. He writes in a stiff style. 4. hard to deal with; hard. A stiff breeze was blowing. It was a stiff examination. 5. more than seems suitable. He asks a stiff price for his house.

stiff en (stif′ən), 1. make stiff. She stiffened the shirt with starch. 2. become stiff. The jelly will stiffen as it cools. He stiffened with anger.

sti fle (stī′fəl), 1. stop the breath of; smother. The smoke stifled the firemen. 2. be unable to breathe freely. I am stifling in this close room. 3. stop; suppress; keep back; as, to stifle a cry, to stifle a yawn.

stile (stīl), 1. step or steps for getting over a fence or wall. 2. turnstile.

Stile

still (stil), 1. without motion; without noise; quiet. Sit still. The lake is still today. The room was so still that you could have heard a pin drop. 2. to quiet. The mother stilled the crying baby. The people prayed that the storm might be stilled. 3. even to this time; even to that time. Was the store still open? 4. and yet; but yet; nevertheless. He was hungry; still he would not eat. Though she has new dolls, still Mary loves her old one best. 5. even; yet. You can read still better if you try.

still ness (stil′nis), 1. quiet; silence. 2. absence of motion; calm.

stilt (stilt), one of a pair of poles, each with a support for the foot at some distance above the ground. Stilts are used in walking through shallow water, or by children for amusement.

stim u late (stim′ū lāt), excite; spur on; rouse to action. Praise stimulated Mary to work hard.

stim u lus (stim′ū ləs), something that stirs to action or effort. Ambition is a great stimulus.

sting (sting), 1. prick; wound. Bees, wasps, and hornets sting. A bee stung John. John put mud on the sting to take away the pain. 2. sharp-pointed part of an animal that pricks or wounds and often poisons. 3. pain sharply. Jim was stung by the mockings of the other children. 4. sharp pain. The ball team felt the sting of defeat. 5. cause a feeling like that of a prick. Mustard stings the tongue.

stin gy (stin′ji), mean about spending or giving money.

stink (stingk), 1. very bad smell. 2. have a bad smell. Decaying fish stink. **stank** and **stunk** are formed from **stink.**

stint (stint), 1. to limit; keep on short allowance; be saving or careful in using or spending. The parents stinted themselves of food to give it to the children. 2. limit. That generous man gives without stint. 3. task assigned. Mary had to wash the supper dishes as her daily stint.

stir (stėr), 1. move. The wind stirs the leaves. No one was stirring in the house. 2. mix by moving around with a spoon, fork, stick, etc. He stirs the sugar in his tea with his spoon. 3. set going; excite; affect strongly. Joe stirred up the other children to mischief. 4. movement; excitement. The coming of the queen caused a great stir. 5. a stirring. Mary gave the mixture a stir.

stir rup (stėr′əp), a support for the rider's foot, hung from a saddle.

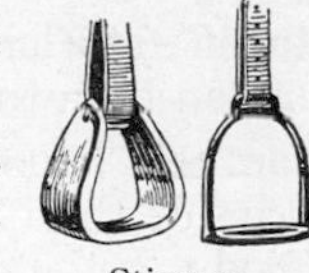
Stirrups

stitch (stich), 1. one complete movement of a threaded needle through cloth in sewing. Take short stitches. 2. one complete movement in knitting, crocheting, embroidering, etc. 3. result of such a movement. Rip out these long stitches. The doctor will take the stitches out of the wound tomorrow. 4. make stitches in; fasten with stitches; sew. 5. a sudden, sharp pain.

stock (stok), 1. things for use or for sale; supply used as it is needed. This store keeps a large stock of toys. 2. cattle or other farm animals. The farm was sold with all its livestock. 3. lay in a supply of; supply. Our camp is well stocked with food. 4. keep regularly for use or for sale. A toy store stocks toys. 5. kept regularly in stock to be sold; as, stock sizes of dresses. 6. in common use; commonplace; everyday. The weather is a stock subject of conversation. 7. shares in a company. Father owns some stock in that railroad. 8. family; race. She is of old New England stock. 9. part used as a support or handle; as, the wooden stock of a rifle. 10. an old-fashioned stiff necktie. 11. lifeless and stupid thing. "You stocks and stones!" 12. trunk of a tree. 13. **The stocks** was a framework with holes for the feet, and sometimes for the hands, used as a punishment.

Man in the stocks

stock ade (stok ād′), 1. a defense or pen made of strong posts fixed upright in the ground. 2. protect, fortify, or surround with a stockade.

Stockade

stock ing (stok′ing), close-fitting knitted covering for the foot and leg.

stock y (stok′i), having a solid or sturdy form or build; thick for its height.

stole (stōl). See **steal.** He stole the money years ago.

sto len (stō′lən). See **steal.** The money was stolen by a thief.

stom ach (stum′ək), 1. the most important part of the body for receiving and digesting food. 2. the part of the body containing the stomach. Dick hit Bill in the stomach. 3. appetite. I have no stomach for killing harmless creatures. 4. bear; endure. He could not stomach such an insult.

stone (stōn), 1. hard mineral matter which is not a metal; rock; piece of rock. Stone is much used in building. 2. made of stone; as, a stone wall, a stone house. 3. having something to do with stone. The **Stone Age** means the period when tools and weapons were made of stone. 4. put stone on; line with stone. 5. gem; jewel. The queen's diamonds were very fine stones. 6. something hard and rounded like a stone, which sometimes forms in the kidneys, bladder, etc., causing sickness and pain. 7. throw stones at; kill by throwing stones. The cruel boys stoned the dog. Stephen was stoned. 8. hard seed; as, peach stones, plum stones. 9. take stones or seeds out of; as, to stone cherries. 10. made of stoneware or coarse clay.

stone ware (stōn′wãr′), coarse, hard, glazed pottery.

ston y (stōn′i), 1. having many stones. The beach is stony. 2. hard like stone. That cruel man has a stony heart.

stood (stu̇d). See **stand.** Tom stood in the corner for five minutes.

stool (stül), seat without back or arms.

Stool

stoop[1] (stüp), 1. bend forward. He stooped to pick up the money. She stoops over her work. 2. a forward bend. My uncle walks with a stoop. 3. carry head and shoulders bent forward. The old man stoops. 4. lower oneself; descend. He stooped to cheating.

stoop[2] (stüp), a porch or platform at the entrance of a house.

stop (stop), 1. close (a hole or opening) by filling (it). Ben will stop up the rats' holes. 2. block (a way). A big box stops up the doorway. 3. keep (from moving, doing, being, working, etc.). The men stopped the boys from teasing the cat. I stopped the clock. 4. put an end to; as, to stop a noise. 5. come to an end; cease. The rain is stopping. 6. stay. Mrs. Blank stopped at the bank for a few minutes. 7. any act of stopping; a closing; a filling up; a blocking; a hindering; a checking. 8. thing that stops, such as a block, a plug, etc. 9. a device that controls the pitch of a musical instrument.

stop per (stop′ər), a plug or cork for closing a bottle, tube, etc.

stor age (stōr′ij), 1. place for storing. She has put her furniture in storage. 2. price for storing. She paid $30 storage on her furniture. 3. act or fact of storing goods. 4. condition of being stored. Cold storage is used to keep eggs and meat from spoiling.

store (stōr), 1. place where goods are kept for sale; as, a clothing store. 2. supply; stock; something put away for use later. She puts up stores of preserves and jellies every year. **In store** means ready for use now or in the future. 3. put away for use later; lay up. The squirrel stores away nuts. 4. place where supplies are kept for future use; a storehouse.

store house (stōr′hous′), place where things are stored. The factory has many storehouses for its products. A library is a storehouse of information.

store keep er (stōr′kēp′ər), person who has charge of a store or stores.

Stork (about 3 ft. tall)

store room (stōr′rüm′), room where things are stored.

stork (stôrk), a large, long-legged bird with a long neck and a long bill.

storm (stôrm), 1. strong wind with rain, snow, hail, or thunder and lightning. In deserts there are storms of sand. 2. heavy fall of rain, snow, or hail; violent outbreak of thunder and lightning. 3. blow hard; rain; snow; hail. 4. violent outburst or disturbance; as, a storm of tears, a storm of angry words. 5. be violent; rage. 6. attack violently. The enemy stormed the castle. 7. violent attack. The castle was taken by storm.

storm y (stôr′mi), 1. having storms; likely to have storms; troubled by storms; as, a stormy sea, a stormy night. 2. violent; rough and disturbed; as, stormy quarrels.

sto ry[1] (stō′ri), 1. an account of some happening or group of happenings. The man told the story of his life. 2. such an account, either true or made-up, intended to interest the reader or hearer; as, fairy stories, ghost stories, stories of adventure, funny stories. 3. falsehood. That boy is a liar; he tells stories.

sto ry[2] (stō′ri), the set of rooms on the same level or floor of a building. The house has two stories.

stout (stout), 1. fat and large. 2. firm; strong; strongly built. The fort has stout walls. 3. brave; bold. Robin Hood was a stout fellow. 4. a dark-brown beer.

stove[1] (stōv), apparatus for cooking and heating. There are coal, gas, oil, and electric stoves. We sat near the stove to get warm. See the pictures on this page.

stove[2] (stōv), staved. See **stave.** That barrel was stove in when it dropped off the truck.

stow (stō), 1. pack. The cargo was stowed in the ship's hold. 2. fill by packing. The boys stowed the little cabin with supplies for the trip. 3. **Stow away** means hide on a ship, airplane, etc., to get a free ride.

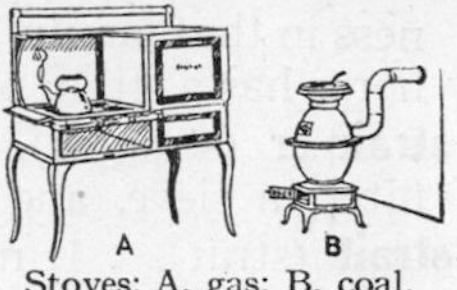

Stoves: A, gas; B, coal.

strad dle (strad′əl), 1. walk, stand, or sit with the legs wide apart. 2. have a leg on each side of (a horse, bicycle, chair, etc.).

strag gle (strag′əl), 1. wander in a scattered fashion. Cows straggled along the road. 2. spread in an irregular, rambling manner. Vines straggled over the yard. It was a straggling little town.

straight (strāt), 1. without a bend or curve; as, a straight line, a straight path, straight hair. 2. directly. Harry went straight home. 3. frank; honest; upright. 4. frankly; honestly. 5. in the proper order or condition. Set the room straight. Our accounts are straight. He kept a straight face, though he wanted to laugh. 6. **Straight away** or **straight off** means at once.

straight en (strāt′ən), 1. make straight. He straightened the bent pin. Straighten your shoulders. 2. put in the proper order or condition. Straighten up your room. We must straighten out our accounts and see how much we owe each other. 3. become straight.

straight for ward (strāt′fôr′wərd), 1. honest; frank. 2. direct; going straight ahead.

straight way (strāt′wā′), at once. The captain read the letter and burned it straightway.

strain[1] (strān), 1. draw tight; stretch. The weight strained the rope. 2. stretch as much as possible. She strained the truth in telling that story. 3. use to the utmost. He strained every muscle to lift the rock. 4. injure by too much effort or by stretching. The runner strained his heart. 5. injury caused by too much effort or by stretching; a sprain. The doctor said the injury to John's ankle was only a slight strain. 6. press or pour through a strainer. Strain the soup before serving it. 7. force or weight that stretches. The strain on the rope made it break. 8. any severe or wearing effort; its effect. The strain of sleepless nights made her ill. 9. a part of a piece of music; melody; song. 10. manner or style; as, a playful strain.

strain[2] (strān), 1. line of descent; race; stock. The Irish strain in him makes him like jokes. 2. inherited quality. There is a strain of madness in that family. 3. trace or streak. That horse has a strain of meanness.

strain er (strān′ər), thing that strains. A filter, a sieve, and a colander are strainers.

strait (strāt), 1. narrow channel connecting two larger bodies of water. 2. difficulty. He was in desperate straits for money.

strand[1] (strand), 1. shore; land bordering a sea, lake, or river. 2. run aground; drive on the shore. The ship was stranded on the rocks. 3. bring into a helpless position. He was stranded a thousand miles from home with no money.

strand[2] (strand), 1. one of the threads, strings, or wires that are twisted together to make a rope. This is a rope of three strands. 2. thread or string; as, a strand of hair, a strand of pearls.

strange (strānj), 1. not known, seen, or heard of before. She is moving to a strange place. A strange cat is on our steps. 2. unusual; queer. What a strange experience! 3. out of place; not at home. The poor child felt strange in the palace. He is strange to the work but will soon learn.

strange ly (strānj′li), in a strange or peculiar way.

stran ger (strān′jər), 1. person not known, seen, or heard of before. She is a stranger to us. 2. person or thing new to a place. He is a stranger in New York. 3. person from another country. The king received the strangers with kindness.

stran gle (strang′gəl), 1. kill by squeezing the throat to stop the breath; choke. Hercules strangled a snake with each hand. His high collar seemed to be strangling him. 2. choke down; suppress; keep back. Tom strangled an impulse to cough.

strap (strap), 1. narrow strip of leather or other material that bends easily. He has a strap around his books. Put a strap around the trunk. 2. a narrow band or strip of cloth. The general wore shoulder straps. 3. fasten with a strap. We strapped the trunk. 4. beat with a strap.

strap ping (strap′ing), tall, strong, and healthy; as, a fine strapping girl.

stra ta (strā′tə), stratums; layers. See **stratum.**

strat a gem (strat′ə jəm), a scheme or trick for deceiving the enemy; trick. The spy got into the castle by the stratagem of dressing as a beggar.

stra te gic (strə tē′jik), 1. of strategy; based on strategy; useful in strategy. 2. important in strategy. The Panama Canal is a strategic link in our national defense.

strat e gy (strat′i ji), 1. the planning and directing of military movements and operations. 2. skillful planning and management of anything. Strategy is needed to keep the boys at work.

stra tum (strā′təm), a layer of material; especially, one of several parallel layers placed one upon another. In digging the well, the men struck first a stratum of sand, then several strata of rock. Tramps are from the lowest stratum of society.

straw (strô), 1. the stalks or stems of grain after drying and threshing. Straw is used for bedding for horses and cows, for making hats, and for many other purposes. 2. hollow stem or stalk; something like it. Straws made of waxed paper are used for sucking up drinks. 3. made of straw; as, a straw hat. 4. a bit; a trifle. He doesn't care a straw.

straw ber ry (strô′ber′i), 1. a small, juicy, red fruit. 2. the plant strawberries grow on.

Strawberry

stray (strā), 1. wander; roam; lose one's way. Our dog has strayed off somewhere. 2. wandering; lost. A stray cat is crying at the door. 3. wanderer. That cat is a stray that we took in. 4. scattered; here and there. There were a few stray huts along the beach.

streak (strēk), 1. a long thin mark or line. He has a streak of dirt on his face. We saw the streaks of lightning. 2. layer. Bacon has streaks of fat and streaks of lean. 3. vein; strain; element. He has a streak of humor, though he looks very serious. 4. put long thin marks or lines on. The Indians used to streak their faces with paint.

stream (strēm), 1. running water; flow of liquid. Small rivers and large brooks are both called streams. **Up stream** means against the current of the water; **down stream** means with the current. 2. any steady flow; as, a stream of lava, a stream of light, a stream of words. 3. flow. Tears streamed from her eyes. 4. wave. The flags streamed in the wind.

stream er (strēm′ər), 1. any long, flowing thing. Streamers of ribbon hung from her hat. 2. a long, narrow flag.

street (strēt), 1. road in a city or town, usually with buildings on both sides. 2. people who live in the buildings on a street. All Oak Street was out to welcome Dick.

street car (strēt′kär′), passenger car that runs on rails in the streets.

strength (strength), being strong; power; force; vigor. Because of his strength he could lift great weights. He did not have enough strength of mind to refuse to do wrong. The strength of the dog's love for his master is well known. Flavorings lose their strength in cooking. **On the strength of** means relying on. Father bought the dog on the strength of Tom's promise to take care of it.

strength en (streng′thən), 1. make stronger. The soldiers strengthened their defenses. 2. grow stronger.

stren u ous (stren′ū əs), very active; full of energy. We had a strenuous day moving into our new house. Mr. Churchill is a strenuous man.

stress (stres), 1. pressure; force; strain. Under the stress of hunger the man stole some food. 2. emphasis; importance. That school lays stress on arithmetic and reading. 3. accent. In *hero*, the stress is on the first syllable. 4. lay stress on; emphasize. Stress the important words of a sentence.

stretch (strech), 1. draw out; extend. The bird stretched its wings. The blow stretched him out on the ground. 2. extend one's body or limbs. John arose and stretched. 3. reach out; hold out. He stretched out a hand for the money. 4. draw tight; strain. He stretched the violin string until it broke. 5. draw out to greater length or size. Rubber stretches. Stretch this shoe a little. 6. continue over a distance; extend from one place to another; fill space; spread. The forest stretches for miles to the westward. 7. act of stretching; condition of being stretched. With a sudden stretch, John took Tom's cap. 8. unbroken length; extent. A stretch of sand hills lay between the road and the ocean.

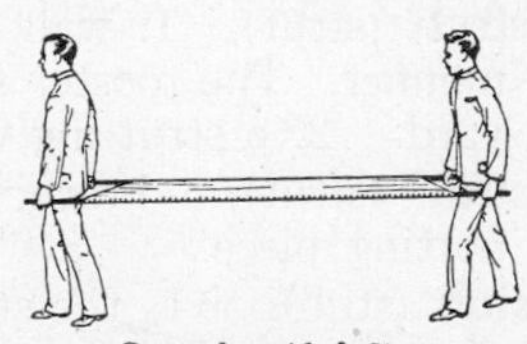
Stretcher (def. 2)

stretch er (strech′ər), 1. person or thing that stretches. A glove stretcher makes gloves larger. 2. canvas stretched on a frame for carrying the sick, wounded, or dead.

strew (strü), 1. scatter; sprinkle. She strewed seeds in her garden. 2. cover with something scattered or sprinkled. The ground was strewn with leaves.

strewn (strün), strewed. See **strew.**

strick en (strik′ən), 1. affected by (wounds, diseases, trouble, sorrows, etc.). Help was rushed to the fire-stricken city. 2. **Stricken in years** means old. 3. struck.

strict (strikt), 1. very careful in following a rule or in making others follow it. Some parents are very strict. 2. harsh; severe. 3. exact; precise. He told the strict truth. 4. perfect; complete. The secret was told him in strict confidence.

strid den (strid′ən). See **stride.** John had stridden away angrily.

stride (strīd), 1. walk with long steps. The tall man strides rapidly down the street. 2. pass with one long step. He strode over the brook. 3. sit or stand with one leg on each side of; as, to stride a fence. 4. long step. The child could not keep up with his father's stride. **strode** and **stridden** are formed from **stride.**

strife (strīf), struggle; quarreling; fighting.

strike (strīk), 1. hit. Jim struck his enemy. The ship struck a rock. 2. set on fire by hitting or rubbing. Strike a match. 3. make by stamping, printing, etc. They will strike a medal in memory of the great victory. 4. influence; overcome (by death, disease, suffering, terror, fear, etc.). All were struck with terror at her wild cry. 5. occur to. She smiled as an amusing thought struck her. 6. sound. The clock strikes twelve times at noon. 7. **Strike up** means begin. Dick and Bob struck up a friendship. 8. **Strike out** means (1) cross out; rub out. (2) fail to hit three times. 9. lower or take down (a sail, flag, tent, etc.). The ship struck her flag as a sign of surrender. 10. go; advance. We will walk along the road a mile, then strike out across the fields. 11. stop work to get better pay, shorter hours, etc. The coal miners struck. 12. stopping work in this way. 13. make; decide; enter upon. The employer and the workmen have struck an agreement. 14. find or come upon (ore, oil, water, etc.).

strik ing (strīk′ing), 1. attracting attention; very noticeable. 2. on a strike. The striking miners will soon return to work.

strik ing ly (strīk′ingli), in a way that attracts attention.

string (string), 1. small cord or very thin rope. The package is tied with red string. 2. such a thread with things on it. She wore a string of beads around her neck. 3. put on a string. The child is stringing beads. 4. special cord for musical instruments, bows, etc. 5. furnish with strings. He had his tennis racket strung. 6. anything used for tying; as, shoestrings, apron strings. 7. tie with string or rope. The horse thief was strung up on a tree. 8. stringy part of plants. String beans have little strings in them. 9. remove strings from. String the beans. 10. number of things in a line or row. A string of cars came down the street. 11. stretch; extend. The program was strung out too long.

stringed (stringd), having strings. A harp is a stringed instrument.

string y (string′i), like a string or strings.

strip[1] (strip), 1. make bare or naked; undress. 2. take off the covering of. The boy stripped the skin from a banana. 3. take away. The boys stripped the fruit from the trees. 4. rob. Thieves stripped the house of everything valuable.

strip[2] (strip), a long, narrow, flat piece (of cloth, paper, bark, etc.).

stripe (strīp), 1. a long, narrow band. A tiger has stripes. The American flag has thirteen stripes. Stripes on an army officer's sleeve show his rank. 2. mark with stripes. The stick of candy was striped with red.

striped (strīpt or strīp′id), having stripes. Zebras are striped.

strip ling (strip′ling), a youth; lad.

strive (strīv), 1. try hard; work hard. Strive to succeed. 2. struggle; fight. The swimmer strove with the tide. **strove** and **striven** are formed from **strive.**

striv en (striv′ən). See **strive.** She has striven hard to make the party a success.

strode (strōd). See **stride.** He strode down the street an hour ago.

stroke[1] (strōk), 1. act of striking; a blow. He drove in the nail with one stroke of the hammer. The house was hit by a stroke of lightning. 2. sound made by striking. We arrived at the stroke of three. 3. single complete movement to be made again and again. He rowed with a strong stroke of the oars. He swims a fast stroke. 4. a movement or mark made by a pen, pencil, brush, etc. He writes with a heavy down stroke. 5. single effort; very successful effort; as, a stroke of work. 6. sudden attack (of disease); as, a stroke of paralysis.

stroke[2] (strōk), 1. move the hand gently along. She likes to stroke her kitten. 2. such a movement. Helen brushed away the crumbs with one stroke.

stroll (strōl), 1. walk; take a quiet walk for pleasure. 2. leisurely walk. We went for a stroll in the park. 3. go from place to place; as, strolling gypsies.

strong (strông). A strong man can lift heavy things. A strong wind blew down the trees. A strong nation is one that has much power because of its wealth and numbers. A strong fort is one that cannot be easily captured. A strong acid is one that contains much acid and little water. Strong tea has more flavor than weak tea. Anything that has much force or power may be called strong.

strong hold (strông′hōld′), strong place; safe place; fort. The robbers have a stronghold in the mountains.

strove (strōv). See **strive.** They strove hard, but did not win the game.

struck (struk). See **strike.** The clock struck four. The barn was struck by lightning.

struc ture (struk′chər), 1. way parts are put together; manner of building; construction. The structure of the schoolhouse was excellent 2. a building; a framework; something built. The city hall is a large stone structure. 3. anything composed of parts arranged together. The human body is a wonderful structure.

strug gle (strug′əl), 1. try hard; work hard. The swimmer struggled against the tide. Amy struggled to keep back the tears. 2. great effort; hard work. 3. fighting.

strung (strung). See **string.** The children strung along after the teacher. The vines were strung on poles.

strut[1] (strut), 1. walk in a vain, important manner. The rooster struts about the barnyard. 2. a strutting walk.

strut[2] (strut), brace; supporting piece.

STRUT

stub (stub), 1. the stump of a tree, a broken tooth, etc. 2. short piece that is left; as, the stub of a pencil. 3. short piece of a leaf in a book kept as a record. 4. pen having a short blunt point. 5. strike (one's toe) against something.

stub ble (stub′əl), 1. the lower ends of stalks of grain left in the ground after the grain is cut. The stubble hurt the boy's bare feet. 2. any short rough growth.

stub born (stub′ərn), 1. fixed in purpose or opinion; not giving in to argument or requests. 2. hard to deal with.

stuc co (stuk′ō), 1. plaster for covering walls. 2. cover with stucco.

stuck (stuk). See **stick**[2]. She stuck out her tongue. We were stuck in the mud.

stud (stud), 1. a nail, knob, etc., sticking out from a surface. The belt was ornamented with silver studs. 2. a kind of small button used in men's shirts. 3. set with studs or something like studs. He plans to stud the sword hilt with jewels. 4. be set or scattered over. Little islands studded the harbor.

stu dent (stū′dənt or stü′dənt), person who studies. That school has 3000 students. Mrs. Smith is a student of birds.

stud ied (stud′id), 1. did study. 2. carefully planned; done on purpose. What Lulu said to me was a studied insult.

stu di o (stū′di ō or stü′di ō), 1. workroom of a painter, sculptor, photographer, etc. 2. place where moving pictures are made. 3. place where a radio program is given.

stu di ous (stū′di əs or stü′di əs), 1. fond of study. He is a studious boy and likes school. 2. careful; showing careful consideration. The clerk made a studious effort to please customers. Mary is always studious of her mother's comfort.

stud y (stud′i), 1. effort to learn by reading or thinking. After an hour's hard study he knew his lesson. 2. make an effort to learn. Helen studied her spelling lesson for half an hour. James is studying to be a doctor. 3. subject that is studied; branch of learning. History, music, and law are studies. 4. room to study in. The preacher was reading in his study. 5. earnest effort. Her constant study is to please her parents. 6. think (out); plan; consider with care. The prisoner studied ways to escape. 7. give care and thought to; try hard. The grocer studies to please his customers. 8. examine carefully. We studied the map to find the shortest road home. 9. investigation; careful examination.

stuff (stuf), 1. material; what a thing is made of. She bought some white stuff for curtains. That boy has good stuff in him. 2. worthless material; useless things. Their attic is full of old stuff. 3. fill; pack full. She stuffed the pillow with feathers. 4. fill (a chicken, turkey, etc.) with bread crumbs, etc. The turkey was stuffed with chestnuts. 5. fill the skin of (a dead animal) to make it look as it did when alive. We saw many stuffed birds at the museum. 6. stop (up); block; choke (up). My head is stuffed up by a cold. 7. eat too much.

stuff y (stuf′i), 1. lacking fresh air; as, a stuffy room. 2. lacking freshness or interest; dull; as, a stuffy speech. 3. stopped up. A cold makes my head feel stuffy.

stum ble (stum′bəl), 1. trip by striking the foot against something. The horse stumbled on a stone and fell. 2. walk in an unsteady way. The tired old man stumbled along. 3. speak, act, etc., in a clumsy or hesitating way. The boy made many blunders as he stumbled through his recitation. 4. make a mistake; do wrong. Even the best men sometimes stumble. 5. come by accident or chance. While in the country, she stumbled upon some fine old pieces of linen.

stump (stump), 1. the lower end of a tree or plant left after the main part is cut off. We sat on top of a stump. 2. anything left after the main or important part is removed. The dog wagged his stump of a tail. 3. walk in a stiff, clumsy way. The lame man stumped along.

stun (stun), make senseless; bewilder; shock; overwhelm. He was stunned by the fall. The sound of the cannon stunned the new soldier. The loss of his money was a stunning blow to Percy.

stung (stung). See **sting.** A wasp stung John. He was stung on the neck.

stunk (stungk), smelled nasty. See **stink.**

stun ning (stun′ing), 1. that stuns. 2. excellent; very attractive.

stunt[1] (stunt), check in growth. Lack of proper food stunts a child.

stunt[2] (stunt), feat; performance. The members of the circus did all sorts of stunts.

stu pe fy (stū′pi fī or stü′pi fī), make stupid, dull, or senseless.

stu pen dous (stū pen′dəs or stü pen′dəs), amazing; marvelous; immense. Niagara Falls is a stupendous sight.

stu pid (stū′pid or stü′pid), dull; not intelligent; not interesting.

stu pid i ty (stū pid′i ti or stü pid′i ti), 1. lack of intelligence. 2. a stupid act, idea, etc.

stu por (stū′pər or stü′pər), dazed condition; loss or lessening of the power to feel. The injured man lay in a stupor, unable to tell what had happened to him.

stur dy (stėr′di), 1. strong; stout. 2. firm; not yielding.

stur geon (stėr′jən), large food fish whose long body has a tough skin with rows of bony plates. Caviar and isinglass are obtained from sturgeons.

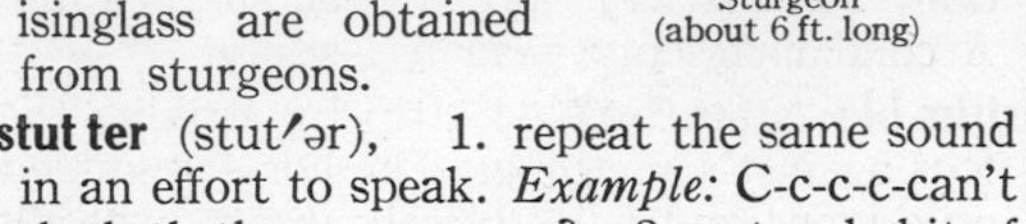

Sturgeon (about 6 ft. long)

stut ter (stut′ər), 1. repeat the same sound in an effort to speak. *Example:* C-c-c-c-can't th-th-th-they c-c-c-come? 2. act or habit of stuttering.

sty[1] (stī), 1. pen for pigs. We clean the sties often, but they soon get dirty again. 2. any filthy place.

sty[2] (stī), a small, painful swelling on the edge of the eyelid. A sty is like a small boil.

style (stīl), 1. fashion. Paris set the style in dress for the world. Her dress is out of style. 2. manner of speaking, writing, doing, building, etc. Books for children should have a clear, easy style. Jane learned several styles of swimming. 3. name; call. Joan of Arc was styled "the Maid of Orléans."

styl ish (stīl′ish), having style; fashionable.

sub di vide (sub′di vīd′), divide into smaller parts.

sub di vi sion (sub′di vizh′ən), 1. division into smaller parts. 2. part of a part.

sub due (səb dū′ or səb dü′), 1. conquer; overcome. Our army subdued the enemy. We subdued a desire to laugh. 2. soften; tone down. The window curtains give the room a subdued light.

sub ject (sub′jikt for 1, 2, 4, 5, and 6, səb jekt′ for 3 and 7), 1. person who is under the power, control, or influence of another. The people are the subjects of the king. 2. under some power or influence. We are subject to our country's laws. 3. bring under some power or influence. Rome subjected all Italy to her rule. 4. something thought about, discussed, studied, etc. The subject for our composition was "An Exciting Moment." 5. the word or words that perform or receive the action of the verb. *I* is the subject of the following sentences: I see the cat. I am seen by the cat. I can see. 6. **Subject to** means (1) likely to have. I am subject to colds. Japan is subject to earthquakes. (2) depending on; on the condition of. I bought the car subject to your approval. 7. To **subject to** sometimes means to cause to undergo or experience something. The savages subjected their captives to torture.

sub lime (səb līm′), lofty; noble; majestic; grand. Mountain scenery is often sublime.

sub ma rine (sub′mə rēn′), 1. a boat that can go under water. 2. under the surface of the sea; under water; as, submarine plants, submarine warfare.

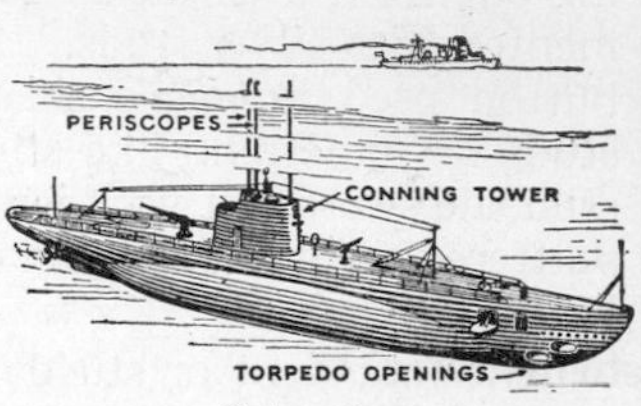

Submarine

sub merge (səb mėrj′), 1. put under water. A big wave submerged us. 2. cover with water. At high tide this path is submerged. 3. go below the surface of the water. The submarine submerged to escape being destroyed.

sub mis sion (səb mish′ən), 1. yielding to power or authority. The defeated general showed his submission by giving up his sword. 2. humble obedience. He bowed in submission to the king's order.

sub mis sive (səb mis′iv), yielding to authority; obedient; humble.

sub mit (səb mit′), 1. yield to some person or group. The thief submitted to arrest by the police. 2. refer to the consideration or judgment of others. The secretary was submitting a report of the last meeting.

sub or di nate (sə bôr′di nit for 1, 2, and 3, sə bôr′di nāt for 4), 1. in a lower order or rank; having less importance; secondary; dependent. An errand boy has a subordinate position. 2. under the authority of a superior. Captains are subordinate to their colonel. 3. subordinate person or thing. 4. place in a lower order or rank; make subject to or dependent on. We must subordinate our wishes to Mother's this time.

sub scribe (səb skrīb′), 1. write underneath; sign (one's name). The men who subscribed to the Declaration of Independence are now famous. 2. agree. He could not subscribe to their unfair plan. 3. promise to give or pay. He subscribed $5 to the hospital fund. 4. promise to take. We subscribe for several magazines.

sub scrib er (səb skrīb′ər), person who subscribes. The magazines make a special offer to new subscribers.

sub scrip tion (səb skrip′shən), 1. subscribing. 2. money subscribed. His subscription to the Fresh Air Fund was $5. 3. the right obtained for the money. His subscription to the newspaper expires next week. 4. sum of money raised by a number of persons. We are raising a subscription for the family of the workman who was killed.

sub se quent (sub′si kwənt), later; following; coming after. Subsequent events proved that Fred was right. The story will be continued in subsequent chapters.

sub se quent ly (sub′si kwənt li), later; afterward.

sub side (səb sīd′), 1. sink to a lower level. After the rain stopped, the flood waters subsided. 2. grow less; become less active. The waves subsided when the wind stopped. Mary's fever subsided after she took the medicine. 3. fall to the bottom; settle.

sub sist (səb sist′), 1. exist; continue to be. A club cannot subsist without members. 2. live; keep alive. People in the far north subsist on fish and meat.

sub sist ence (səb sis′təns), 1. living. Selling papers was the cripple's only means of subsistence. 2. means of keeping alive; food and clothing. The sea provides a subsistence for fishermen.

sub soil (sub′soil′), the layer of earth that lies just under the surface soil.

sub stance (sub′stəns), 1. the real, main, or important part of anything. The substance of an education is its effect on your life, not just learning lessons. 2. real meaning. Give the substance of the speech in your own words. 3. what a thing consists of; matter; material. Ice and water are the same substance in different forms. 4. wealth.

sub stan tial (səb stan′shəl), 1. real; actual. People and things are substantial; dreams and ghosts are not. 2. strong; firm; solid. That house is substantial enough to last a hundred years. 3. large; important; ample. John has made a substantial improvement in arithmetic. 4. well-to-do; wealthy. 5. in the main; in substance. The stories told by the two boys were in substantial agreement.

sub stan tial ly (səb stan′shəl i), 1. essentially; mainly. This report is substantially correct. 2. really; actually. 3. strongly; solidly. This house is substantially built.

sub sti tute (sub′sti tūt or sub′sti tüt), 1. thing used instead of another; person taking the place of another. A substitute was our teacher at school today. 2. put in the place of another. We substituted brown sugar for molasses in these cookies. 3. take the place of another. She substituted for Miss Brown, who is ill.

sub ter ra ne an (sub′tə rā′ni ən), underground. A subterranean passage led from the castle to a cave.

sub tle (sut′əl), 1. thin; delicate; fine. Some subtle odors are hard to recognize. Subtle jokes are hard to understand. 2. faint; mysterious; as, a subtle smile. 3. having a quick, acute, and discerning mind. She is a subtle observer of slight differences in things. 4. sly; crafty; tricky; as, a subtle scheme to get some money.

sub tle ty (sut′əl ti), 1. subtle quality. 2. something subtle.

sub tly (sut′li), in a subtle manner.

sub tract (səb trakt′), take away. Subtract 2 from 10 and you have 8.

sub trac tion (səb trak′shən), taking one number or quantity from another; finding the difference between two quantities. $10-2=8$ is a simple subtraction.

sub urb (sub′ėrb), district lying outside a city or town. Many people who work in the city live in the suburbs.

sub ur ban (səb ėr′bən), of a suburb; in a suburb. We have excellent suburban train service.

sub way (sub′wā′), 1. underground passage. 2. underground electric railroad.

suc ceed (sək sēd′), 1. turn out well; do well; have success. Washington's plans succeeded. 2. come next after; follow; take the place of. John Adams succeeded Washington as President.

suc cess (sək ses′), 1. favorable result; wished-for ending; good fortune. Success in school comes from intelligence and work. What success did you have in finding a new cook? 2. person or thing that succeeds. The circus was a great success.

suc cess ful (sək ses′fəl), having success; prosperous; fortunate.

suc ces sion (sək sesh′ən), 1. the coming of one person or thing after another. **In succession** means one after another. 2. things happening one after another; a series. A succession of accidents spoiled our automobile trip. 3. the right of succeeding to an office, property, or rank. Succession to the command of a company belongs to the first lieutenant.

suc ces sive (sək ses′iv), following in order. It has rained for three successive days.

suc ces sive ly (sək ses′iv li), one after another; in order.

suc ces sor (sək ses′ər), one who follows or succeeds another in office, position, or ownership of property; thing that comes after another in a series. John Adams was Washington's successor as President.

suc cor (suk′ər), help; aid.

suc cu lent (suk′ū lənt), juicy.

suc cumb (sə kum′), 1. give way; yield. He succumbed to the temptation and stole the money. 2. die.

such (such), 1. of that kind; of the same kind or degree. Such men as Washington and Lincoln are rare. The child had such a fever that he nearly died. The food, such as it was, was plentiful. 2. of the kind already spoken of or suggested. The ladies took only tea and coffee and such drinks. 3. so great, so bad, so good, etc. Dan is such a liar! Such weather! 4. some; certain. The bank was robbed at such a time in such and such a town by such and such persons. 5. such a person or thing. Take from the blankets such as you need.

suck (suk), 1. draw into the mouth. Lemonade can be sucked through a straw. 2. draw something from with the mouth; as, to suck oranges. 3. drink; take; absorb. Plants suck up moisture from the earth. A sponge sucks in water. 4. act of sucking. The baby took one suck at the empty bottle and pushed it away.

suck er (suk′ər), 1. an animal or thing that sucks. 2. a fish that sucks in food or has a mouth that suggests sucking. 3. a shoot from an underground stem or root. 4. a lump of hard candy.

Sucker (about 2 ft. long)

suc tion (suk′shən), process of drawing in liquids or gases by sucking out the air. We draw lemonade through a straw by suction. Some pumps work by suction.

sud den (sud′ən), 1. not expected. Our army made a sudden attack on the fort. 2. quick; rapid. The cat made a sudden jump at the mouse.

sue (sü), 1. beg or ask (for). Messengers came suing for peace. 2. start a lawsuit against. He sued the railroad because his cow was killed by the engine.

suf fer (suf′ər), 1. have or feel pain, grief, etc. She suffers from headache. 2. experience harm or loss. Ruth suffered from being out in the storm. His business suffered greatly during the war. 3. allow; permit. Jesus said, "Suffer the little children to come unto me."

suf fer ing (suf′ər ing), pain. Hunger causes suffering.

suf fice (sə fīs′), be enough; satisfy. Fifty dollars a month sufficed for the old lady's needs.

suf fi cient (sə fish′ənt), enough; as much as is needed. The poor child did not have sufficient clothing for the winter.

suf fi cient ly (sə fish′ənt li), enough; as much as is needed.

suf fix (suf′iks), an addition made to the end of a word such as *ly* in badly, *ness* in goodness, *ful* in spoonful, and *ment* in amazement.

suf fo cate (suf′ə kāt), 1. choke. 2. kill by stopping the breath. 3. keep from breathing; hinder in breathing.

suf frage (suf′rij), 1. vote. The voters gave their suffrage to Roosevelt. 2. right to vote. The United States granted the suffrage to women in 1920.

sug ar (shůg′ər), 1. a sweet substance made from sugar cane or sugar beets. Other kinds of sugar are made from cornstarch, grapes, etc. 2. sweeten with sugar. She sugared her tea. 3. cover with sugar; sprinkle with sugar. 4. form sugar. Maple syrup will sugar if cooked.

Sugar cane

sugar cane, a tall plant with a strong, jointed stem and flat leaves, growing in warm regions. Sugar cane is the chief source of sugar.

sug gest (səg jest′), 1. bring (a thought, plan, etc.) to a person's mind. John suggested a game of tag. 2. show in an indirect way; hint. Joe's bad manners suggest a lack of proper home training.

sug ges tion (səg jes′chən), 1. a suggesting. The suggestion of a walk made the dog jump with joy. 2. thing suggested. The picnic was Jane's suggestion.

sug ges tive (səg jes′tiv), 1. tending to suggest ideas, acts, or feelings. The children made an interesting and suggestive list of things to write about. 2. tending to suggest something improper.

su i cide (sü′i sīd), 1. killing oneself on purpose. 2. person who kills himself on purpose.

suit (süt), 1. set of clothes or armor. A man's suit consists of coat, vest, and trousers. 2. case in a law court. 3. make fit; make suitable. The teacher suited the punishment to the fault by making Dick sweep the room after he threw bits of paper on the floor. 4. be good for. A cold climate suits apples and wheat, but not oranges and tea. 5. be becoming to. Her blue hat suits her fair skin. 6. please; be convenient for; satisfy. It is hard to suit everybody. 7. request; wooing. The prince's suit was successful, and Cinderella married him.

suit a ble (süt′ə bəl), fitting; right for the occasion. A simple dress is suitable for school wear. The park gives the children a suitable playground.

suit case (süt′kās′), a flat traveling bag. See the picture.

Man carrying a suitcase

suite (swēt), 1. group of attendants. The queen traveled with a suite of twelve. 2. number of things forming a series or set. She has a suite of rooms at the hotel—a living room, bedroom, and bath.

suit or (süt′ər), man courting a woman. The princess had many suitors.

sul fur (sul′fər), sulphur.

sulk (sulk), 1. be sulky. 2. bad humor shown by sullen silence; sulky mood. Mary has a fit of the sulks.

sulk y (sul′ki), 1. sullen; silent because of bad humor. Peter gets sulky and won't play if he can't be leader. 2. a light carriage with two wheels, for one person. See the picture just above.

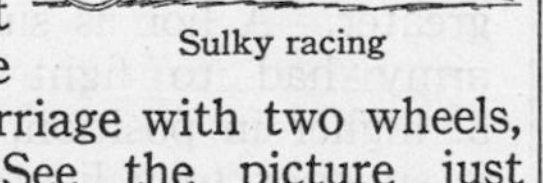

Sulky racing

sul len (sul′ən), 1. silent because of bad humor. Harry becomes sullen if he is punished. 2. gloomy; dismal. The sullen skies threatened rain.

sul phur (sul′fər), a light-yellow substance that burns with a blue flame and a stifling odor. Sulphur is used in making matches and gunpowder.

sul tan (sul′tən), the ruler of a Mohammedan country. Turkey was ruled by a sultan until 1922.

sul tan a (sul tan′ə), 1. wife of a sultan. 2. mother, sister, or daughter of a sultan.

sul try (sul′tri), 1. hot, close, and moist. We expect some sultry weather during July. 2. hot.

sum (sum), 1. the total of two or more numbers or things taken together. The sum of 2 and 3 and 4 is 9. 2. problem in arithmetic. Dick can do easy sums in his head, but he has to use pencil and paper for hard ones. 3. amount of money. He paid the sum of $7 for a new hat. 4. **Sum up** often means express or tell briefly. Sum up the main points of the lesson in three sentences. The judge summed up the evidence.

su mac or **su mach** (shü′mak), a shrub or small tree with leaves that turn scarlet in the autumn and long clusters of red fruit. See the picture.

Sumac

sum ma rize (sum′ə rīz), make a summary of; express briefly.

sum ma ry (sum′ə ri), 1. brief statement giving the main points. This history has a summary at the end of each chapter. 2. brief; short. 3. direct and prompt; without delay. The Indian took summary vengeance by killing both his enemies.

sum mer (sum′ər), 1. the warmest season of the year. 2. spend the summer; as, to summer at the seashore. 3. of summer; for summer; in summer; as, summer heat; summer clothes; summer holidays.

sum mit (sum′it), highest point; top. We could see the summit of the mountain twenty miles away. The summit of her ambition was to be an actress.

sum mon (sum′ən), 1. call; send for. The church bells summon people to worship. A telegram summoned him home. 2. rouse. Jack summoned his courage and entered the deserted house.

sum mons (sum′ənz), 1. an order to appear at a certain place. Mr. Black received a summons to be at the police court at 10 A.M., October 5. 2. a command.

sump ter (sump′tər), a horse or mule for carrying baggage.

sump tu ous (sump′chü əs), costly; magnificent; rich. The king gave a sumptuous banquet.

sun (sun), 1. the brightest object in the sky. The sun lights and warms the earth. 2. the light and warmth of the sun. The cat likes to sit in the sun. 3. put in the light and warmth of the sun. The swimmers sunned themselves on the beach. 4. any heavenly body like the sun. Many stars are suns and have their worlds that travel around them.

sun beam (sun′bēm′), ray of sunlight. A sunbeam brightened the child's hair to gold.

sun burn (sun′bėrn′), 1. a burning of the skin by the sun's rays. His sunburn was red and painful. 2. burn the skin by the sun's rays. He is sunburned from a day on the beach.

sun dae (sun′di), individual portion of ice cream with syrup, crushed fruit, nuts, etc., over it.

Sun day (sun′di), the first day of the week; the day of rest and worship among Christians.

sun der (sun′dər), 1. separate. Time often sunders friends. 2. **In sunder** means apart. Lightning tore the tree in sunder.

sun di al (sun′dī′əl), an instrument for telling the time of day by the position of a shadow cast by the sun.

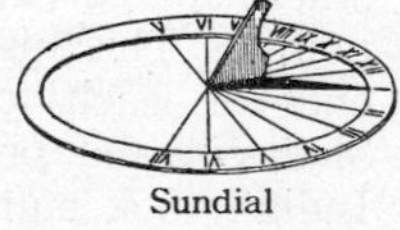
Sundial

sun down (sun′doun′), sunset. We'll be home by sundown.

sun dries (sun′driz), sundry things; items not named; odds and ends. We spent almost two dollars for sundries.

sun dry (sun′dri), various; several. From sundry hints, Jack guessed he was to have a bicycle on his birthday.

sun flow er (sun′flou′ər), a tall plant having large yellow flowers with brown centers.

Sunflower

sung (sung). See **sing.** Many songs were sung at the concert.

sunk (sungk). See **sink.** The ship had sunk to the bottom.

sunk en (sungk′ən), 1. sunk; as, a sunken ship. 2. submerged; under water; as, a sunken rock. 3. situated below the general level; as, a sunken garden. 4. fallen in; hollow; as, sunken eyes.

sun light (sun′līt′), the light of the sun. Outdoor sunlight is very good for the health.

sun lit (sun′lit′), lighted by the sun.

sun ny (sun′i), 1. having much sunshine. 2. like the sun. 3. bright; cheerful. The baby gave her sunniest smile.

sun rise (sun′rīz′), the rising of the sun; the first appearance of the sun in the morning.

sun set (sun′set′), the going down of the sun; the last appearance of the sun in the evening.

sun shine (sun′shīn′), 1. the shining of the sun; the light of the sun. 2. brightness; cheerfulness.

sup[1] (sup), eat the evening meal. He supped alone on bread and milk.

sup[2] (sup), 1. sip; take (liquid) into the mouth a little at a time. He supped his soup from the spoon. 2. mouthful; spoonful.

su perb (sü pėrb′), 1. grand; stately; majestic. Mountain scenery is superb. The queen's jewels are superb. 2. very fine; excellent. The actor gave a superb performance.

su per fi cial (sü′pər fish′əl), 1. of the surface; on the surface. His burns were superficial and soon got well. 2. shallow; not thorough. Girls used to receive only a superficial education.

su per flu ous (sü pėr′flü əs), needless; more than is needed. Do not use superfluous words.

su per in tend (sü′pər in tend′), oversee and direct (work or workers); manage (a place, institution, etc.).

su per in tend ent (sü′pər in ten′dənt), person who oversees or manages; as, a superintendent of schools, a superintendent of a factory.

su pe ri or (sə pēr′i ər), 1. above the average. Bert has a superior mind. This hotel serves a superior grade of coffee. 2. better; higher; greater. A lion is superior to a wolf. Our army had to fight off a superior force. 3. higher in position, rank, etc. A captain is superior to a lieutenant. 4. person who is superior. As a violin player, he has no superior. A captain is a lieutenant's superior

5. showing a feeling of being above others; proud. The other girls disliked Ann's superior manner. 6. not giving in; above yielding (to). A wise man is superior to flattery. 7. the head of a monastery or convent.

su pe ri or i ty (sə pēr′i or′i ti), superior state or quality. No one doubts the superiority of modern ways of traveling over those of olden times.

su per la tive (sü pėr′lə tiv), 1. of the highest kind; above all others. Solomon is said to have been a man of superlative wisdom. 2. *Fairest, fastest,* and *best* are the superlatives of *fair, fast,* and *good.*

su per man (sü′pər man′), man having more than human powers.

su per nat u ral (sü′pər nach′ə rəl), above or beyond what is natural. Angels and devils are supernatural beings.

su per sede (sü′pər sēd′), 1. take the place of; replace. A new governor superseded the old. 2. displace; set aside. Gas light has been superseded by electric light in most cities.

su per sti tion (sü′pər stish′ən), 1. unreasoning fear of what is unknown or mysterious; unreasoning expectation. Superstition made people sacrifice to idols. As knowledge increases, superstition decreases. 2. a belief or practice founded on ignorant fear or mistaken reverence. A common superstition considered it bad luck to sleep in a room numbered 13.

su per sti tious (sü′pər stish′əs), full of superstition; likely to believe superstitions; caused by superstition.

su per vise (sü′pər vīz), direct (work or workers, a process, etc.); oversee; manage. Study halls are supervised by teachers.

su per vi sion (sü′pər vizh′ən), management; direction; oversight. The camp was built under the careful supervision of the scout leader.

su per vi sor (sü′pər vī′zər), person who supervises. The music supervisor has charge of the school band, chorus, and orchestra.

sup per (sup′ər), 1. an evening meal. 2. a meal eaten early in the evening if dinner is near noon, or late in the evening if dinner is at six or later.

sup plant (sə plant′), 1. take the place of. Machinery has supplanted hand labor in making shoes. 2. take the place of by unfair methods. The prince plotted to supplant the king.

sup ple (sup′əl), 1. bending easily; as, a supple birch tree, supple leather, a supple dancer, supple joints. 2. adapting oneself readily to different ideas, circumstances, people, etc.; yielding. Jane gets along well with people because of her supple nature.

sup ple ment (sup′li mənt for 1, sup′li ment for 2), 1. something added to complete a thing, or to make it larger or better. This history has a supplement containing an account of what has happened since 1940. 2. add to; complete. Ben supplements his regular meals by eating between meals.

sup pli ant (sup′li ənt), 1. asking humbly and earnestly. He sent a suppliant message for help. 2. person who asks humbly and earnestly. She knelt as a suppliant at the altar.

sup pli ca tion (sup′li kā′shən), a humble, earnest request. Supplications to God arose from all the churches.

sup ply (sə plī′), 1. furnish; provide. The school supplies books for the children. Joe is supplying us with ice. 2. quantity ready for use; stock; store. Our school gets its supplies of books, paper, pencils, chalk, etc., from the city. The United States has very large supplies of coal and oil. 3. make up for; fill. Rocks and stumps supplied the place of chairs at the picnic.

sup port (sə pōrt′), 1. hold up; keep from falling. Walls support the roof. 2. keep up; help; give strength or courage to. Hope supports us in trouble. 3. provide for. A healthy man should support his family. 4. be in favor of. He supports the President. 5. help prove; bear out. The facts support his claim. 6. bear; endure. She couldn't support life without friends. 7. help; aid. He needs our support. 8. person or thing that supports; prop. The neck is the support of the head.

sup port er (sə pōr′tər), person or thing that supports. He is a firm supporter of justice.

sup pose (sə pōz′), 1. consider as possible. Let's suppose we have three wishes. Suppose we are late, what will the teacher say? 2. believe; think; imagine. I suppose Helen will come as usual.

sup posed (sə pōzd′), accepted as true; assumed; considered as possible or probable. The supposed beggar was really a prince.

sup pos ing (sə pōz′ing), supposing that; if. Supposing it rains, shall we go?

sup press (sə pres′), 1. put an end to; put down; stop by force. The police suppressed a riot. The troops suppressed the rebellion by firing on the mob. 2. keep in; hold back; keep from appearing. Mary suppressed a yawn.

sup pres sion (sə presh′ən), 1. putting down by force or authority; putting an end to. Troops were used in the suppression of the revolt. 2. keeping in; holding back. The suppression of facts may be as dishonest as the telling of lies.

su prem a cy (sə prem′ə si), supreme authority or power.

su preme (sə prēm′), 1. highest in rank or authority; as, a supreme ruler, a supreme court. 2. highest in degree; greatest; utmost; extreme. With supreme courage Clara snatched the baby from in front of the car.

sure (shür), 1. I know it; I am sure of it. Are you sure you locked the door? 2. You can trust John; he is a sure messenger. Air mail is not quite so sure as ordinary mail. 3. firm; as, to stand on sure ground. 4. surely.

sure-foot ed (shür′fůt′id), not liable to stumble, slip, or fall.

sure ly (shür′li), 1. certainly. Half a loaf is surely better than none at all. 2. firmly; without missing, slipping, etc. The goat leaped surely from rock to rock.

sure ty (shür′ti), 1. certainty. 2. security. 3. person who agrees to be responsible for another. Will you be surety for me if I get in trouble?

surf (sėrf), the waves or swell of the sea breaking on the shore. The surf is high just after a storm.

Surf

sur face (sėr′fis), 1. the outside of anything. An egg has a smooth surface. 2. any face or side of a thing. A cube has six surfaces. The upper surface of the plate has pictures on it. 3. outward appearance. He seems rough, but you will find him very kind if you get below the surface. 4. of the surface; on the surface; having something to do with the surface; as, a surface view.

surge (sėrj), 1. rise and fall; move like waves. A great wave surged over us. The crowd surged through the streets. 2. a wave; a sweep or rush of waves; something like a wave. Our boat was upset by the surge. A surge of anger rushed over him.

sur geon (sėr′jən), doctor who performs operations. A surgeon took out Fred's tonsils.

sur ger y (sėr′jər i), treating diseases, injuries, etc., by operations and instruments. Malaria can be cured by medicine, but cancer usually requires surgery.

sur ly (sėr′li), bad-tempered and unfriendly; rude. The surly dog growled at the child. The rude servant grumbled a surly reply.

sur mise (sėr mīz′), guess. His guilt was a matter of surmise; there was no proof. We surmised that the delay was caused by some accident.

sur mount (sər mount′), 1. rise above. Mt. Washington surmounts all the peaks near it. 2. be on top of. A statue surmounts the monument. 3. overcome. Lincoln surmounted many difficulties before he rose to be President.

sur name (sėr′nām′), 1. a last name; a family name. Smith is the surname of John Smith. 2. give an added name to. Simon was surnamed Peter.

sur pass (sər pas′), 1. do better than; be better than. Anna surpasses her sister in arithmetic. 2. be more than; exceed. The glory of heaven surpasses description. Helen was of surpassing beauty.

sur plus (sėr′plus), 1. amount over and above what is needed; extra quantity left over; excess. The bank keeps a large surplus of money in reserve. 2. more than is needed; extra.

sur prise (sər prīz′), 1. catch unprepared; come upon suddenly. Our army surprised the enemy while they were sleeping. 2. astonish. The victory surprised us. 3. catching unprepared; coming upon suddenly. The fort was captured by surprise. 4. feeling caused by something unexpected. His face showed surprise at the news. 5. something unexpected. Mother always has a surprise for the children on holidays. 6. surprising; that is not expected; as, a surprise party, a surprise visit.

sur pris ing (sər prīz′ing), causing surprise or wonder.

sur ren der (sə ren′dər), 1. give up; give oneself up; yield. The captain had to surrender his ship to the enemy. As the storm increased, the men on the raft surrendered all hope. 2. act of surrendering. The surrender of the soldiers saved them from being shot.

sur round (sə round′), be around; shut in on all sides. Our men surrounded the Indians' camp. The surrounding country is flat and sandy.

sur round ings (sə roun′dingz), surrounding things, conditions, etc. The poor child had never had cheerful surroundings.

sur vey (sər vā′ for 1 and 3, sėr′vā for 2, 4, and 5), 1. look over; view; examine. Grandma surveyed Lulu with a stern look. The buyers surveyed the goods offered for sale. 2. general look; view; examination; inspection. We were pleased with our first survey of the house. 3. measure for size, shape, position, boundaries, etc. Men are surveying the land before it is divided into house lots. 4. careful measurement. Surveys showed that the northern boundary was not correct. 5. plan or description of such a measurement. He pointed out the route of the railroad on the government survey.

sur vey ing (sər vā′ing), the business or act of making surveys of land.

sur vey or (sər vā′ər), person who surveys. The surveyor set up his instruments and began to make a survey of the road.

sur viv al (sər vīv′əl), 1. surviving; continuance of life; living or lasting longer than others. 2. a person, thing, custom, belief, etc., that has lasted from an earlier time. Belief in the evil eye is a survival of ancient magic.

sur vive (sər vīv′), 1. live longer than; remain alive after. Only ten of the crew survived the shipwreck. 2. continue to exist. Books have survived from the time of the ancient Greeks.

sur vi vor (sər vī′vər), person, animal, or plant that remains alive. He is the only survivor of a family of nine.

sus cep ti ble (sə sep′ti bəl), 1. easily influenced by feelings or emotions; very sensitive. Poetry appealed to his susceptible nature. 2. **Susceptible of** means capable of receiving or undergoing. Oak is susceptible of a high polish. 3. **Susceptible to** means easily affected by; especially liable to; open to. Vain people are susceptible to flattery.

sus pect (səs pekt′ for 1, 2, and 3, sus′pekt for 4), 1. imagine to be so; think likely. The mouse suspected danger and did not touch the trap. I suspect that some accident has delayed him. 2. believe guilty, false, bad, etc., without proof. The policeman suspected the thief of lying. The elevator boy is the suspected thief. 3. doubt. The judge suspected the truth of the thief's excuse. 4. person suspected. The police have arrested two suspects in connection with the bank robbery.

sus pend (səs pend′), 1. hang down by attaching to something above. The lamp was suspended from the ceiling. 2. hold in place as if by hanging. We saw the smoke suspended in the still air. 3. stop for a while. We suspended building operations during the winter. 4. remove or exclude for a while from some privilege or job. Roy was suspended from school for a week for bad conduct. 5. keep undecided; put off. Let us suspend judgment until we know all the facts.

sus pense (səs pens′), 1. condition of being uncertain. This detective story keeps you in suspense till the last chapter. 2. anxious uncertainty; anxiety. Mothers feel suspense when their children are sick.

sus pen sion (səs pen′shən), a suspending or being suspended; as, the suspension of a boy from school for bad conduct.

Suspension bridge

suspension bridge, bridge hung on cables or chains between towers.

sus pi cion (səs pish′ən), 1. suspecting; the state of mind of one who suspects. The real thief tried to turn suspicion toward others. 2. being suspected. Our old servants are all above suspicion. 3. very small amount; a suggestion. She spoke with a suspicion of spite.

sus pi cious (səs pish′əs), 1. causing one to suspect. A man was hanging about the house in a suspicious manner. 2. suspecting; feeling suspicion. The dog is suspicious of strangers. 3. showing suspicion. He gives suspicious sniffs at their legs.

sus tain (səs tān′), 1. hold up; support. Arches sustain the weight of the roof. 2. keep up; keep going. Hope sustains him in his misery. She eats barely enough to sustain life. 3. bear; endure. The sea wall sustains the shock of the waves. 4. suffer; experience. She sustained a great loss in the death of her husband. 5. allow; admit; favor. The court sustained his claim. 6. agree with; confirm. The facts sustain his theory.

sus te nance (sus′ti nəns), 1. food. He has gone for a week without sustenance. 2. support. He gave money for the sustenance of a poor family.

swag ger (swag′ər), 1. walk with a bold, rude, or superior air. The bully swaggered into the yard. 2. boast or brag noisily. 3. swaggering way of walking or acting.

swain (swān), 1. young man who lives in the country. 2. lover.

swal low[1] (swol′ō), 1. take into the stomach through the throat. We swallow all our food and drink. 2. take in; absorb. The waves swallowed up the swimmer. 3. believe too easily; accept without question or suspicion. He will swallow any story. 4. put up with; accept without opposing or resisting. He swallowed the insults of the bully without saying anything. 5. take back; as, to swallow words said in anger. 6. keep back; keep from expressing. She swallowed her displeasure and smiled. 7. swallowing. He took the medicine at one swallow. 8. amount swallowed at one time. There are only about four swallows of water left in the bottle.

swal low[2] (swol′ō), a small bird with a forked tail. It can fly very fast.

Barn swallow (about 7 in. long)

swam (swam). See **swim.** When the boat sank, we swam to shore.

swamp (swomp), 1. wet, soft land. The farmer will drain the swamp so that he can plant crops there. 2. plunge or sink in a swamp or in water. The horses were swamped in the stream. 3. fill with water and sink. Their boat swamped. 4. overwhelm as a flood would; make helpless. Mr. Ford was swamped with letters asking for money.

swamp y (swomp′i), 1. like a swamp; soft and wet. 2. containing swamps.

Swan (nearly 5 ft. long with the head and neck)

swan (swon), a large, graceful water bird with a long, slender, curving neck.

sward (swôrd), grassy surface; turf.

swarm (swôrm), 1. group of bees that leave a hive and fly off together to start a new colony. 2. group of bees settled together in a hive. 3. large group of insects flying or moving about together. 4. crowd; great number. Swarms of children were playing in the park. 5. fly off together to start a new colony. 6. fly or move about in a swarm; move about in great numbers; be in very great numbers. The mosquitoes swarmed about us. 7. be crowded. The swamp swarms with mosquitoes and other insects.

swarth y (swôr′ᴛʜi), having a dark skin. A swarthy Italian kept the fruit store.

sway (swā), 1. swing back and forth; swing from side to side, or to one side. The frightened girl swayed and fell in a faint. The pail swayed in Jack's hands as he ran. 2. a swinging back and forth or from side to side. The sway of the pail caused some milk to spill out. 3. make move; cause to sway. The wind sways the grass. 4. move to one side; turn aside. Nothing could sway him after he had made up his mind. 5. influence; control; rule. A mob is swayed by its feelings. Few countries are now under the sway of kings.

swear (swãr), 1. make a solemn statement, appealing to God or some other sacred being or object. A witness at a trial has to swear, "I promise to tell the truth, the whole truth, and nothing but the truth, so help me God." 2. promise; vow. The knights had sworn to be true to their king. 3. bind by an oath; require to promise. Members of the club were sworn to secrecy. 4. curse; use profane language. The pirate raged and swore. **swore** and **sworn** are formed from **swear.**

sweat (swet), 1. give out moisture through the pores of the skin. We sweat when it is very hot. 2. cause to sweat. He sweated his horse by riding him too hard. 3. moisture coming through the skin. He wiped the sweat from his face. 4. a fit or condition of sweating. He was in a cold sweat from fear. 5. cause to work hard and under bad conditions. That employer sweats his workers. 6. give out moisture; collect moisture from the air. A pitcher of ice water sweats on a hot day. 7. moisture given out by something or gathered on its surface.

Sweater

sweat er (swet′ər), a knitted jacket, usually of wool. See the picture just above.

sweep (swēp), 1. to clean with a broom; to brush. The maid sweeps the floor. 2. move drive, or take away with a broom; remove with a sweeping motion; carry along. The maid sweeps the dust into a pan. A flood swept away the bridge. 3. act of sweeping; clearing away; removing. He made a clean sweep of all his debts. 4. pass over with a steady movement. Her fingers sweep the harp strings. His eye swept the sky, searching for signs of rain. 5. move swiftly; pass swiftly. Pirates swept down on the town. The wind sweeps over the valley. 6. move with dignity. The lady swept out of the room. 7. a steady, driving motion or swift onward course of something. The sweep of the wind kept trees from growing tall. 8. move or extend in a long course or curve. The shore sweeps to the south for miles. 9. swinging or curving motion. He cut the grass with strong sweeps of his scythe. 10. reach; range. The mountain is beyond the sweep of your eye. 11. stretch; continuous extent. The house looks upon a wide sweep of farming country. 12. person who sweeps chimneys, streets, etc. 13. long oar. 14. long pole used to raise or lower a bucket from a well.

sweep ing (swēp′ing), 1. passing over a wide space. Her sweeping glance took in the whole room. 2. having wide range; as, a sweeping victory, a sweeping statement.

sweet (swēt), 1. having a taste like sugar or honey. Pears are sweeter than lemons. 2. having a pleasant taste or smell. 3. pleasant; as, a sweet child, a sweet smile, sweet music. 4. fresh; not sour, salt, bitter, or spoiled. John drinks sweet milk and likes sweet butter better than salted. Ice helps to keep food sweet. 5. something sweet. 6. dear; darling. 7. sweetly.

sweet en (swēt′ən), 1. make sweet. He sweetened his coffee with two lumps of sugar. 2. become sweet. Those pears will sweeten as they ripen.

sweet en ing (swēt′ning), something that sweetens. Sugar is the most common sweetening.

sweet heart (swēt′härt′), loved one; lover.

sweet ish (swēt′ish), somewhat sweet.

sweet meats (swēt′mēts′), candy; candied fruits; sugar-covered nuts; bonbons.

sweet potato, a yellow root with a sweetish taste, used as a vegetable.

swell (swel), 1. grow bigger; make bigger. Rain swelled the river. Bread dough swells as it rises. His head is swollen where he bumped it. 2. stick out; be larger or thicker in a particular place. A barrel swells in the middle. 3. increase in amount, degree, force, etc. His fortune had swollen during the war. 4. rise above the level. Rounded hills swell gradually from the village plain. 5. part that rises or swells out. 6. long, unbroken wave or waves. The boat rocked in the swell. 7. grow louder; make louder. The sound swelled from a murmur to a roar. All joined in to swell the chorus. 8. swelling tone or sound. 9. Swell is used in free and easy talk to mean a fashionable person; stylish; grand; very satisfactory. **swollen** is formed from **swell.**

swell ing (swel′ing), an increase in size; swollen part. There is a swelling on Dick's head where he bumped it.

swept (swept). See **sweep.** She swept the room. It was swept clean.

swerve (swėrv), 1. turn aside. The car swerved and hit a tree. Nothing could swerve Dan from doing his duty. 2. a swerving.

swift (swift), 1. moving very fast; coming quickly; quick; rapid. 2. swiftly. 3. a small bird with long wings. A swift looks somewhat like a swallow.

Chimney swift (about 5 in. long)

swift ness (swift′nis), speed; rapid motion; quickness. He turned with the swiftness of a cat.

swim[1] (swim), 1. move along on or in the water by using arms, legs, fins, etc. Fish swim. Most boys like to swim. 2. swim across. He swam the river. 3. make swim. He swam his horse across the stream. 4. float. The ham was swimming in gravy. 5. overflow. Her eyes were swimming with tears. 6. act of swimming. May's swim had tired her. She had had an hour's swim. 7. **In the swim** means having a part in what is going on. **swam** and **swum** are formed from **swim.**

swim[2] (swim), be dizzy. The close air and noise made my head swim.

swim mer (swim′ər), person or animal that swims.

swin dle (swin′dəl), 1. cheat; defraud. Honest merchants will not swindle you. 2. an act of swindling; a cheat or fraud.

swine (swīn), 1. hogs. 2. a hog. 3. coarse or beastly person.

swing (swing), 1. move back and forth. The hammock swings. He swings his arms as he walks. 2. move in a curve. He swings the club twice around his head. He swung the automobile around the corner. 3. move with a free, swaying motion. The soldiers came swinging down the street. 4. act or manner of swinging. He brought the hammer down with a long swing. 5. a swinging gait or movement; steady, marked rhythm. The song "Dixie" has a swing. 6. movement; activity. By five o'clock the party was in full swing. 7. seat hung from ropes in which one may sit and swing. **swung** is formed from **swing.**

swirl (swėrl), 1. move or drive along with a twisting motion; whirl; as, dust swirling in the air, a stream swirling over rocks. 2. a whirl; eddy; swirling movement. 3. twist. Her hat had a swirl of lace around it.

swish (swish), 1. move with a hissing sound; make a hissing sound. The whip swished through the air. The cow swished her tail. 2. such a movement or sound; as, the swish of little waves on the shore.

switch (swich), 1. slender stick used in whipping. 2. whip. He switched the boys with a birch switch. 3. stroke; lash. The big dog knocked a vase off the table with a switch of his tail. 4. move like a switch. The horse switched his tail to drive off the flies. 5. device for changing the direction of something, or for making or breaking a connection. A railroad switch shifts a train from one track to another. An electric switch turns the current off or on. 6. change, turn, or shift by using a switch. 7. change; turn.

Switz er land (swit′sər lənd), a small country in Europe, north of Italy.

swol len (swōl′ən), swelled; as, a swollen ankle. See **swell.**

swoon (swün), faint. She swoons at the sight of blood. Cold water will bring her out of the swoon.

swoop (swüp), 1. come down with a rush, as a hawk does; sweep rapidly down upon. The pirates swooped down on the towns. 2. a rapid downward sweep of a bird of prey upon its victim; a sudden, swift descent or attack.

sword (sōrd), a weapon with a long, sharp blade. The sword has come to stand for fighting in general or for military power. "Those that live by the sword shall perish by the sword." "The pen is mightier than the sword."

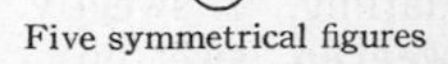
Sword

swore (swōr). See **swear.** He swore to be a loyal American when he became a citizen.

sworn (swōrn), 1. bound by an oath. There were ten sworn witnesses. 2. declared, promised, etc., with an oath. We have his sworn statement. 3. See **swear.** A solemn oath of loyalty was sworn by all the knights.

swum (swum). See **swim.** He had never swum before.

swung (swung). See **swing.** He swung his arms as he walked. The door had swung open.

syc a more (sik′ə mōr), a kind of shade tree with large leaves and light-colored bark.

syl la ble (sil′ə bəl), part of a word pronounced as a unit, consisting of a vowel alone or with one or more consonants. *A mer i can* and *Al a bam a* are words of four syllables. *Do, this,* and *stretch* are words of one syllable.

syl van (sil′vən), of the woods; in the woods; having woods. The fairies had a sylvan home.

sym bol (sim′bəl), something that stands for or represents something else. The lion is the symbol of courage; the lamb, of meekness; the olive branch, of peace; the cross, of Christianity. The marks +, −, ×, and ÷ are symbols for add, subtract, multiply, and divide.

sym met ri cal (si met′ri kəl), having symmetry.

sym me try (sim′i tri), 1. regular form or arrangement. A swollen cheek spoiled the symmetry of his face. 2. well-balanced arrangement of parts; harmony.

Five symmetrical figures

sym pa thet ic (sim′pə thet′ik), 1. having or showing kind feelings toward others. 2. enjoying the same things and getting along well together.

sym pa thet i cal ly (sim′pə thet′i kəl i), in a sympathetic way; with kindness. The doctor spoke sympathetically while he bandaged my leg.

sym pa thize (sim′pə thīz), 1. feel or show sympathy; as, to sympathize with a child who has hurt himself. 2. share in or agree with a feeling or opinion. My mother sympathizes with my plan to be a doctor.

sym pa thy (sim′pə thi), 1. having the same feeling. The sympathy between the twins was so great that they always smiled or cried at the same things. 2. sharing another's sorrow or trouble. Sick people arouse our sympathies. 3. agreement; favor. Mother is in sympathy with my plan.

sym pho ny (sim′fə ni), 1. an elaborate musical composition for an orchestra. 2. harmony of sounds. 3. harmony of colors.

symp tom (simp′təm), sign; indication. Fever is a symptom of illness.

syn a gogue (sin′ə gog), 1. assembly of Jews for religious instruction and worship. 2. place used by Jews for instruction and worship.

syn o nym (sin′ə nim), word that means the same or nearly the same as another word. *Keen* is a synonym of *sharp*.

syr up (sir′əp or sėr′əp), a sweet, thick liquid; sugar boiled in water; a liquid made of sugar and fruit juices or other flavoring. Maple syrup is made from the sap of maple trees.

sys tem (sis′təm), 1. set of things or parts forming a whole; as, a mountain system, a railroad system, the digestive system, etc. 2. ordered group of facts, principles, beliefs, etc.; as, a system of government, system of education, etc. 3. plan; method. 4. orderly way of getting things done. Fred works by a system, not by chance.

sys tem at ic (sis′təm at′ik), 1. according to a system; having a system. 2. orderly in arranging things or in getting things done.

sys tem at i cal ly (sis′təm at′i kəl i), with system; according to some plan or method.

T

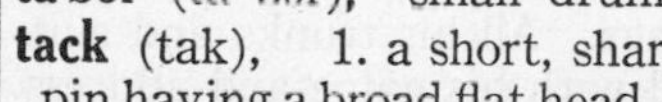

tab er nac le (tab′ər nak əl), 1. place of worship for a large audience. 2. Jewish temple.

ta ble (tā′bəl), 1. piece of furniture having a smooth flat top on legs. 2. food to be eaten. Mrs. Brown sets a good table. 3. the persons seated at a table. 4. put on a table. 5. a list; information in a very brief form; as, a table of contents in the front of a book, the multiplication table, a timetable. 6. a thin flat piece of wood, stone, metal, etc. The Ten Commandments were written on tables of stone.

ta ble cloth (tā′bəl klôth′), cloth for covering a table. Spread the tablecloth and set the table for dinner.

Tablet with inscription

ta ble land (tā′bəl land′), high plain; plateau.

ta ble spoon (tā′bəl spün′), large spoon used to serve vegetables, etc.

tab let (tab′lit), 1. a small flat surface with an inscription. See the picture just above. 2. a small flat sheet of stone, wood, ivory, etc., used to write or draw on. The ancient Romans used tablets as we use pads of paper. 3. number of sheets of paper fastened together at the edge. 4. a small flat piece of medicine or candy.

ta bor (tā′bər), small drum.

tack (tak), 1. a short, sharp-pointed nail or pin having a broad flat head. We bought some carpet tacks. 2. fasten with tacks. She tacked mosquito netting over the windows. 3. attach; add. He tacked a postscript to the end of the letter. 4. sail in a zigzag course against the wind. The ship was tacking, trying to make the harbor. 5. direction in which a ship moves in regard to the position of her sails. 6. course of action or conduct. He took the wrong tack to get what he wanted.

tack le (tak′əl), 1. equipment; apparatus; gear. Ropes and pulleys for lifting furniture through windows are called tackle; so are the ropes that work the sails of a ship. **Fishing tackle** means the rod, line, hooks, etc. 2. try to deal with. Everyone has his own problems to tackle. 3. seize; lay hold of. John tackled the boy with the football and threw him. 4. act of tackling. 5. player between the guard and the end on either side of the line in football.

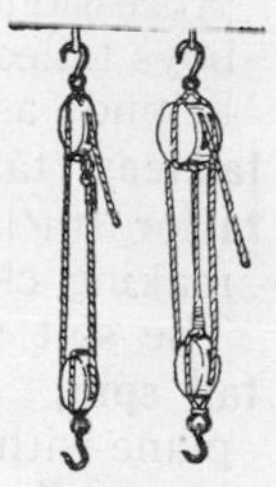
Tackles for lifting

tact (takt), ability to say and do the right thing; skill in dealing with people or handling difficult situations. Mother's tact kept her from talking about things likely to be unpleasant to her guests.

tact ful (takt′fəl), 1. having tact; as, a tactful person. 2. showing tact; as, a tactful reply.

tac tics (tak′tiks), 1. the art or science of disposing military or naval forces in action; the operations themselves. 2. procedures to gain advantage or success; methods. When coaxing failed, Helen changed her tactics and began to cry.

tad pole (tad′pōl′), very young frog or toad. See the pictures.

Tadpole, showing different stages of growth.

taf fe ta (taf′i tə), 1. rather stiff silk cloth with a smooth, glossy surface. 2. similar cloth of linen, rayon, etc.

tag[1] (tag), 1. piece of card, paper, leather, etc., to be tied or fastened to something. Each coat in the store has a tag with the price mark on it. 2. a small, hanging piece; a loosely attached piece; a loose end. We saw only the tag end of the parade. 3. furnish with a tag or tags. All his trunks and suitcases are tagged with his name and address. 4. follow closely. The baby tagged after Helen.

tag[2] (tag), 1. a children's game in which one child chases the rest of the children until he touches one of them. 2. touch or tap with the hand.

tail (tāl), 1. Mice have long tails. 2. something like an animal's tail; as, the tail of a kite. 3. hind part of anything; back; rear. Boys fastened their sleds to the tail of the cart. A crowd of small boys formed the tail of the procession. 4. follow close behind. Some boys tailed after the parade. 5. coming from behind; as, a tail wind.

tail less (tāl′lis), having no tail.

tai lor (tā′lər), 1. man whose business is making clothes. 2. make by tailor's work. The suit was well tailored.

tail spin, downward movement of an airplane with the nose first and the tail spinning in a circle above.

taint (tānt), 1. stain or spot; trace of decay, corruption, or disgrace. No taint of dishonor ever touched George Washington. 2. give a taint to; spoil. Flies sometimes taint what they touch. His mind was tainted from reading bad books. 3. decay; become tainted.

take (tāk), 1. lay hold of. A little child takes its mother's hand in walking. 2. seize; capture. Wild animals are taken in traps. 3. catch hold; lay hold. 4. accept. The man won't take a cent less for the car. 5. receive. George took first prize. 6. win. 7. get; have. Mr. Jones took a holiday. 8. use; make use of. Dick hates to take medicine. Take care not to fall. We took a train to go to Boston. 9. need; require. It takes time and patience to learn how to drive an automobile. 10. choose; select. Take the shortest way home. 11. remove. Please take the waste basket away and empty it. If you take 2 from 7, you have 5. 12. go with. Harry likes to take his dog out for a walk. 13. carry. We take flowers to sick friends. 14. do; make. Take a walk. Please take my photograph. 15. feel. Mary takes pride in her schoolwork. 16. act; have effect. The inoculation did not take. 17. suppose. I take it you won't go to school since you feel sick. 18. regard; consider. Let us take an example. 19. engage; hire. We have taken a cottage for the summer. 20. become affected by. Marble takes a high polish. I take cold easily. 21. please; attract. The song took the fancy of the public. 22. amount taken; as, a great take of fish. 23. Some special meanings are:

take after, be like; resemble. Mary takes after her mother.

take in, 1. make smaller. 2. understand.

take off, leave the ground or the water. Three airplanes took off at the same time.

take to, 1. form a liking for. 2. go to. The cat took to the woods and became wild.

take up, 1. soak up; absorb. 2. make smaller. 3. begin; undertake.

took and **taken** are formed from **take.**

tak en (tāk′ən). See **take.** I have taken this toy from the shelf.

tale (tāl), 1. story. Grandfather told the children tales of his boyhood. 2. falsehood; lie. To **tell tales** often means to tell something about a person to get him into trouble. 3. number; count. His tale of sheep amounted to three hundred.

tal ent (tal′ənt), 1. special natural ability; ability. She has a talent for music. 2. an ancient weight. A talent of silver was worth about $2000.

tal ent ed (tal′ən tid), having natural ability; gifted; as, a talented musician.

tal is man (tal′is mən), a stone, ring, etc., engraved with figures or characters supposed to have magic power; a charm.

talk (tôk), 1. use words; speak. A very

small baby cannot talk. 2. the use of words; spoken words; speech; conversation. The old friends met for a good talk. 3. informal speech. 4. discuss. The men talked politics. 5. spread ideas by other means than speech; as, to talk by signs. 6. gossip; report; rumor.

tall (tôl). The man is 5 feet 8 inches tall. The tree is a hundred feet tall. A giant is a very tall man.

tal low (tal′ō), hard fat from sheep, cows, etc. Tallow is used for making candles and soap.

tal ly (tal′i), 1. stick of wood with notches cut into it. Tallies were formerly used to show the amount of a debt or payment. 2. anything on which a score or account is kept. 3. a notch or mark made on a tally; mark made for a certain number of objects in keeping account. 4. to mark on a tally; count up. 5. account; reckoning; score. 6. agree; correspond. Your account tallied with mine.

tal on (tal′ən), claw of a bird of prey; claw. The eagle seized a chicken with its talons.

tam bou rine (tam′bə rēn′), a small drum with metal disks, played by striking it with the knuckles or by shaking it.

Tambourine

tame (tām), 1. taken from the wild state and made obedient. The man has a tame bear. 2. gentle; without fear. The birds are so tame that they will eat from our hands. 3. make tame; break in. The lion was tamed for the circus. 4. become tame. White rats tame easily. 5. subdue; deprive of courage; tone down. Harsh punishment in childhood had tamed him and broken his will. 6. without spirit; dull. The party was tame because all the people were sleepy.

tam per (tam′pər), meddle; meddle in a bad or improper way. Do not tamper with the lock.

tan (tan), 1. make (a hide) into leather by soaking in a special liquid. 2. bark used in tanning hides, and also for covering riding tracks and circus rings. 3. yellowish brown. He wore tan shoes. 4. make or become brown by exposure to sun and air. Sun and wind had tanned the sailor's face. 5. the change in a person's skin caused by being in the sun and air. John's arms and legs had a dark tan.

tan gle (tang′gəl), 1. twist and twine together in a confused mass. The kitten tangled the ball of yarn. 2. such a confused mass. The climbing vines are all one tangle and need to be pruned and tied up.

tank (tangk), 1. large container for liquid or gas. Our school has a swimming tank. He always kept plenty of gasoline in the tank of his automobile. 2. put or store in a tank. 3. a small, self-moving steel fort used to attack in war. Tanks are mounted on caterpillar wheels so they can travel over rough ground, fallen trees, etc.

Tank used in war

tank ard (tangk′ərd), a large drinking mug with a handle and hinged cover.

Tankard

tan ner (tan′ər), person whose work is tanning hides.

tap[1] (tap), 1. strike lightly. He tapped on the floor with his foot. 2. light blow. There was a tap at the door.

tap[2] (tap), 1. a stopper or plug to close a hole in a cask containing liquid. 2. a means of turning on or off a flow of liquid; faucet. 3. make a hole in to let out liquid. Maple trees are tapped when the sap begins to flow.

Tap (def. 1)

tape (tāp), 1. a long, narrow strip of cloth, paper, etc. That candy store uses fancy tape to tie all packages. 2. something like such a strip. The strip stretched across the finish line in a race is called the tape. A tape of cloth or steel, marked in inches, feet, etc., is used for measuring. 3. fasten with tape.

ta per (tā′pər), 1. become gradually smaller toward one end; make gradually smaller toward one end. A church spire tapers off to a point. 2. very slender candle; long wick coated with wax. The maid used one taper to light all the candles.

tap es try (tap′is tri), fabric with pictures or designs woven in it, used to hang on walls, cover furniture, etc.

tap i o ca (tap′i ō′kə), a starchy food obtained from the root of a tropical plant, used for puddings.

ta pir (tā′pər), a large piglike animal of tropical America that has a flexible snout.

tap root (tap′rüt′), main root growing downward.

tar[1] (tär), 1. a black, sticky substance obtained from wood or coal. The rope was coated with tar. 2. cover with tar; soak in tar. Tarred paper is used on sheds to keep out water. To **tar and feather** is to pour heated tar on and cover with feathers as a punishment.

tar[2] (tär), sailor.

tar dy (tär′di), 1. late; behind time. Tom was tardy for school four times last year. 2. slow. The old coach was tardier than ever.

tar get (tär′git), 1. mark for shooting at; thing aimed at. Anything may be used as a target. The poor boy was made the target of his step-father's anger and scorn. 2. small shield.

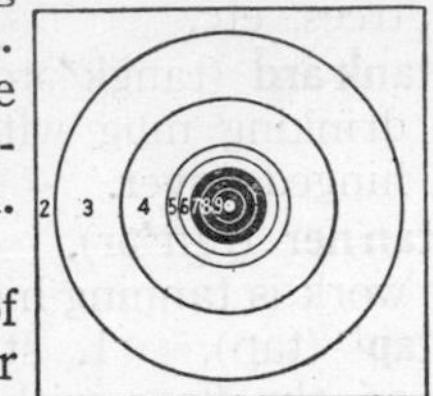

Target for shooting

tar iff (tar′if), 1. list of taxes on imports or exports. There is a very high tariff on imported jewelry. 2. any table or scale of prices. The tariff at the Grand Hotel ranges from $3 to $5 a day for room and bath.

tarn (tärn), a small lake or pool in the mountains.

tar nish (tär′nish), 1. dull the brightness of. Salt will tarnish silver. 2. lose brightness. Brass will tarnish. 3. loss of brightness.

tar ry[1] (tar′i), 1. remain; stay. He tarried at the inn till he felt strong enough to travel. 2. wait; delay. Why do you tarry so long?

tar ry[2] (tär′i), 1. of tar; like tar. 2. covered with tar.

tart[1] (tärt), 1. sour; having a sharp taste. Some apples are tart. 2. sharp. Her reply was too tart to be polite.

tart[2] (tärt), pastry filled with cooked fruit, jam, etc. In the United States, a tart is small and the fruit shows; in England, any fruit pie is a tart.

tar tan (tär′tən), 1. plaid woolen cloth. In parts of Scotland, each clan has its own pattern of tartan. 2. of tartan.

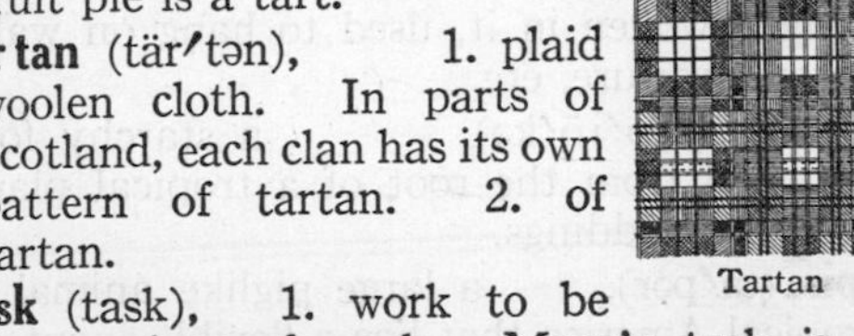

Tartan

task (task), 1. work to be done; piece of work. Mary's task is to set the table. 2. put work on; force to work. 3. burden. The master tasked his slaves beyond their strength. 4. **Take to task** means blame or reprove. The teacher took John to task for not studying.

tas sel (tas′əl), 1. a hanging bunch of threads, small cords, beads, etc. See the picture. 2. something like this. Corn has tassels. 3. grow tassels.

taste (tāst), 1. flavor. Sweet, sour, salt, and bitter are the four most important tastes. 2. try the flavor of (something) by taking a little into the mouth. The cook tastes everything to see if it is right. 3. the sense by which the flavor of things is perceived. Her taste is unusually keen. 4. get the flavor of by the sense of taste. I taste almond in this cake. When I have a cold I can taste nothing. 5. have a particular flavor. The soup tastes of onion. 6. eat or drink a little bit of. The children barely tasted their breakfast Christmas morning. 7. little bit; sample. The snowstorm will give you a taste of northern winter. 8. to experience; have. Having tasted freedom, the bird would not return to its cage. 9. liking. The taste for snails is rare. 10. ability to perceive and enjoy what is beautiful and excellent. Good books and pictures appeal to people of taste. 11. a manner or style that shows such ability. Her house is furnished in excellent taste.

taste less (tāst′lis), 1. without taste. 2. without good taste; in poor taste.

tat ter (tat′ər), 1. torn piece; rag. After the storm the flag hung in tatters upon the mast. 2. wear or tear to tatters.

tat tle (tat′əl), 1. tell tales or secrets. 2. talk foolishly; gossip. 3. idle or foolish talk; gossip; telling tales or secrets.

tat too[1] (ta tü′), 1. a signal on a drum or bugle calling soldiers or sailors to their quarters at night. 2. series of raps, taps, etc. The hail beat a loud tattoo on the windowpane.

tat too[2] (ta tü′), mark (the skin) in patterns by pricking it and putting in colors. The sailor had a ship tattooed on his arm.

Tattooed face

taught (tôt). See **teach.** Miss Jones taught my mother. She was taught well.

taunt (tônt), 1. jeer at; mock; reproach. Some mean girls taunted Jane with being poor. 2. a bitter or insulting remark; mocking; jeering.

taut (tôt), 1. drawn tight; tense; as, a taut rope. 2. neat.

tav ern (tav′ərn), 1. place where alcoholic drinks are sold and drunk. 2. inn. Hotels have taken the place of the old taverns.

taw ny (tô′ni), brownish yellow. A lion has a tawny skin.

tax (taks), 1. money paid by people for the support of the government; money taken from people by their rulers. 2. put a tax on. People who own property are taxed in order to provide clean streets, good roads, protection against crime, and free education. 3. a burden, duty, or demand that oppresses; strain. Climbing stairs is a tax on a weak heart. 4. lay a heavy burden on; be hard for. The work taxed her strength. Reading in a poor light taxes the eyes. 5. reprove; accuse. The teacher taxed Tom with having neglected his work.

tax a tion (taks ā′shən), 1. taxing. Taxation is necessary to provide roads, schools, and police. 2. amount people pay for the support of the government; taxes.

tax i (tak′si), 1. automobile with a meter for recording the fare. 2. ride in a taxi. 3. move over the surface of the ground or water. The airplane taxied to get into a position for rising.

tea (tē), 1. a common drink. 2. the dried and prepared leaves of a shrub from which this drink is made. Tea is raised chiefly in China, Japan, and India. 3. the shrub itself. 4. a meal in the late afternoon or early evening, at which tea is commonly served. The English have afternoon tea. 5. afternoon reception. 6. something to drink prepared from some thing named; as, sage tea, pepper tea. Beef tea is a strong broth made from beef.

teach (tēch), 1. help to learn; show how to do; make understand. John is teaching his dog to shake hands. 2. give lessons in. Miss Stern teaches music. 3. give lessons. She has taught for many years.

teach er (tēch′ər), person who teaches. Our school has fifty teachers.

teach ing (tēch′ing), 1. work or profession of a teacher. 2. what is taught.

tea cup (tē′kup′), cup for drinking tea.

tea ket tle (tē′ket′əl), rather small kettle with a spout, for heating water.

teal (tēl), small fresh-water duck.

team (tēm), 1. number of people working or acting together; as, a football team, a debating team. 2. two or more horses or other animals harnessed together to work. 3. join together in a team. 4. drive a team.

team ster (tēm′stər), man whose work is driving a team of horses.

tea pot (tē′pot′), a container with a handle and a spout for making and serving tea.

tear[1] (tãr), 1. pull apart by force. Don't tear up paper, but put it in the waste basket. 2. make by pulling apart. He tore a hole in his coat. 3. pull hard; pull violently. He tore down the enemy's flag. 4. scratch badly. He tore his hand on a nail. 5. make miserable; distress. His heart was torn by sorrow. 6. become torn. Lace tears easily. 7. torn place. She has a tear in her dress. 8. move with great force or haste. An automobile came tearing down the road. **tore** and **torn** are formed from **tear.**

tear[2] (tēr), drop of salty water coming from the eye.

tear ful (tēr′fəl), weeping.

tease (tēz), 1. annoy; vex or worry by jokes, questions, requests, etc. Don't tease the cat by rubbing her fur the wrong way. The other boys teased Jim about his curly hair. 2. beg. That child teases for everything he sees. 3. person who teases.

tea spoon (tē′spün′), small spoon commonly used to stir tea or coffee.

te di ous (tē′di əs or tē′jəs), long and tiring. A long talk that you cannot understand is tedious.

teem (tēm), be full; abound; swarm. The swamp teemed with mosquitoes.

tee pee (tē′pē), tepee; wigwam.

tee ter (tē′tər), seesaw.

teeth (tēth), 1. more than one tooth. You often show your teeth when you smile. 2. **By the skin of one's teeth** means just barely. 3. **In the teeth of** means straight against. He advanced in the teeth of the wind.

tel e gram (tel′i gram), message sent by telegraph. Mother sent a telegram telling us what train to take.

tel e graph (tel′i graf), 1. a means for sending messages by electricity. 2. send (a message) by telegraph. When you want to telegraph, you give the message to an operator who telegraphs it to the distant city.

tel e phone (tel′i fōn), 1. a means for transmitting sound by electricity. A man in New York can talk to a man in Chicago by using a telephone. 2. talk through a telephone; send (a message) by telephone.

tel e scope (tel′i skōp), 1. an instrument for making distant objects appear nearer and larger. The stars are studied by means of telescopes. 2. force together, one inside another, like the sliding tubes of some telescopes. When two railroad trains crash into each other, the cars are sometimes telescoped. 3. be forced together in this way.

Man using a telescope

tel e vi sion (tel′i vizh′ən), a means for seeing objects at a distance by electricity. We can see things or people in another city by television.

tell (tel), 1. put in words; say. Tell us a story. Tell the truth. 2. inform; tell to. Tell us about it. Tell him the story. 3. make known. Don't tell where the candy is. 4. recognize; know. Can you tell time? 5. order; command. Do as you are told. 6. count; count one by one. The officer told off ten men for special duty. The nun tells her beads. 7. have effect or force. Every blow told. The strain was telling on the man's health. **told** is formed from **tell.**

tell er (tel′ər), 1. person who tells. Our teacher is a good teller of stories. 2. person who counts. A teller in a bank takes in, gives out, and counts money.

tell tale (tel′tāl′), 1. person who tells tales on others; person who reveals private or secret matters from malice. 2. telling what is not supposed to be told; revealing.

te mer i ty (ti mer′i ti), rashness; reckless boldness.

tem per (tem′pər), 1. bring to a proper or desired condition by mixing or preparing. A painter tempers his colors by mixing them with oil. Steel is tempered by heating it and working it till it has the proper degree of hardness and toughness. Temper justice with mercy. 2. the hardness or toughness of the mixture. The temper of the clay was right for shaping. 3. state of mind; disposition; condition. She has a sweet temper. She was in no temper to be kept waiting. 4. angry state of mind. He flies into a temper at trifles.

tem per a ment (tem′pər ə mənt), a person's nature; make-up; disposition. She has a nervous temperament.

tem per ance (tem′pər əns), 1. being moderate in action, speech, habits, etc.; self-control. Temperance should be applied, not only to food and drink, but to work and play. 2. being moderate in the use of alcoholic drinks. 3. the principle and practice of not using alcoholic drinks at all.

tem per ate (tem′pər it), 1. not very hot, and not very cold. The United States is mostly in the north temperate zone. 2. moderate. He spoke in a temperate manner, not favoring either side especially. 3. using self-control. Mr. Gray is a temperate man, and never eats or drinks too much. 4. moderate in using alcoholic drinks.

tem per a ture (tem′pər ə chər), degree of heat or cold. The temperature of freezing water is 32 degrees. The temperature of a person with fever is over 98½ degrees.

tem pest (tem′pist), 1. violent storm with much wind. The tempest drove the ship on the rocks. 2. violent disturbance. She burst into a tempest of anger.

tem pes tu ous (tem pes′chü əs), 1. stormy. It was a tempestuous night. 2. violent. She was in a tempestuous fit of anger.

tem ple[1] (tem′pəl), 1. a building used for the service or worship of a god or gods. Greek temples were beautifully built. 2. any of three temples in ancient Jerusalem built at different times by the Jews. 3. a church.

tem ple[2] (tem′pəl), the flattened part on either side of the forehead.

tem po rar i ly (tem′pə rãr′i li), for a short time; for the present. They are living in a hotel temporarily.

tem po rar y (tem′pə rãr′i), lasting for a short time only. The hunter made a temporary shelter out of branches.

tempt (tempt), 1. make, or try to make, (a person) do something. The sight of the food tempted the hungry man to steal. The serpent tempted Eve to pick the forbidden fruit. 2. attract; appeal strongly to. That candy tempts me. What a tempting couch! 3. provoke. It is tempting Providence to go in that old boat.

temp ta tion (temp tā′shən), 1. tempting. No temptation could make him false to a friend.

2. being tempted. The Lord's Prayer says, "Lead us not into temptation." 3. thing that tempts. Money left carelessly about is a temptation.

ten (ten). Ten is one more than nine. Ten means 10. Five and five make ten.

te na cious (ti nā′shəs), holding fast; as, the tenacious jaws of a bulldog, a person tenacious of his rights, a tenacious memory.

te nac i ty (ti nas′i ti), 1. firmness in holding fast. 2. firmness in holding together. 3. sticky quality; sticky condition.

ten ant (ten′ənt), 1. person paying rent for the use of land or buildings. That building has apartments for one hundred tenants. 2. one that occupies. Birds are tenants of the trees. 3. hold or occupy as a tenant. That old house has not been tenanted for many years.

tend[1] (tend), 1. be apt; be likely; incline (to). Fruit tends to decay. Homes tend to use more machinery now. 2. move (toward); be directed. The road tends to the south here.

tend[2] (tend), take care of; look after; attend to. He tends shop for his father. A shepherd tends his flock. A nurse tends the sick.

tend en cy (ten′dən si), inclination; leaning. Boys have stronger tendencies to fight than girls. Wood has a tendency to swell if it gets wet.

ten der[1] (ten′dər), 1. soft; not hard or tough. The meat is tender. 2. delicate; not strong and hardy. The leaves in spring are green and tender. Stones hurt the little child's tender feet. 3. kind; affectionate; loving. She sent tender messages to her friends. 4. gentle; not rough or crude. These young plants need tender care. 5. young. Two years old is a tender age. 6. sensitive. Automobiles are a tender subject with John since he wrecked his. The elbow joint is a tender spot. 7. feeling pain or grief easily. She has a tender heart and would never hurt anyone.

ten der[2] (ten′dər), 1. offer formally. He tendered his thanks. 2. offer. She refused his tender of marriage. 3. thing offered.

tend er[3] (ten′dər), 1. person or thing that tends another. Dick did not like his job as baby tender. 2. a small boat carried or towed by a big one and used for landing passengers. 3. a small ship used for carrying supplies and passengers to and from larger ships. 4. the car attached behind a locomotive and used for carrying coal, oil, and water.

ten der foot (ten′dər fu̇t′), 1. newcomer to the pioneer life of the western United States. 2. person not used to rough living and hardships. 3. beginner; inexperienced person.

ten der ness (ten′dər nis), 1. being tender. A steak is judged by its flavor and tenderness. 2. tender feeling. She has a tenderness for cats.

ten don (ten′dən), a tough, strong band or cord that joins a muscle to a bone; a sinew.

ten dril (ten′dril), 1. a threadlike part of a climbing plant, that attaches itself to something and supports the plant. 2. something similar; as, tendrils of hair curling about a child's face.

Tendrils on a grapevine

ten e ment (ten′i mənt), 1. a dwelling, or part of a dwelling, occupied by a tenant. A two-family house has two tenements. 2. a building divided into cheap apartments. The tenements are in a poor section of the city.

ten fold (ten′fōld′), ten times as much or as many.

ten nis (ten′is), a game played by two or four players, in which a ball is driven back and forth over a net with rackets.

ten or (ten′ər), 1. course; general tendency. The calm tenor of her life has never been disturbed by excitement or trouble. 2. general meaning. I understand French well enough to get the tenor of his speech. 3. the highest adult male voice. Bass and tenor are two parts for men's voices. 4. part sung by, or written for, such a voice. 5. man who sings this part.

tense (tens), stretched tight; strained; as, a tense rope, tense nerves, a tense moment.

ten sion (ten′shən), 1. a stretching. 2. stretched condition. The tension of the spring is caused by the weight. 3. strain. A mother feels tension when her baby is sick.

Tents

tent (tent), 1. movable shelter made of cloth or skins supported by a pole or poles. 2. live in a tent. "We are tenting tonight on the old campground."

ten ta cle (ten′tə kəl), 1. a feeler; a long, slender, flexible growth on the head or around the mouth of an animal, used to touch, hold, or move. 2. a sensitive, hairlike growth on a plant.

tenth (tenth), 1. next after the ninth. 2. one of 10 equal parts.

te pee (tē′pē), tent of the American Indians.

tep id (tep′id), slightly warm; lukewarm.

term (tėrm), 1. word or group of words used in connection with some special subject; as, medical terms, terms about radio. 2. word; expression. She praised his book in flattering terms. 3. name; call. John might be termed handsome. 4. a set time; length of time. The President's term of office is four years. Most schools have a fall term and a spring term. 5. **Terms** sometimes means (1) conditions. The terms of the peace were very hard for the defeated nation. (2) personal relations. 6. **Not on speaking terms** means not speaking to one another.

ter mi nal (tėr′mi nəl), 1. at the end; forming the end. Terminal buds grow at the end of stems. 2. the end. A railroad terminal is the station, sheds, tracks, etc., at either end of the line.

ter mi nate (tėr′mi nāt), 1. bring to an end; put an end to; end. A policeman terminated the quarrel by sending the boys home. 2. come to an end. The evening's entertainment will terminate in a dance. 3. form the end of; bound; limit.

ter mi na tion (tėr′mi nā′shən), ending; end.

ter mi nus (tėr′mi nəs), 1. an end of a railroad line, bus line, etc. 2. boundary; goal; end.

ter mite (tėr′mīt), white ant. Termites are very destructive to buildings, furniture, provisions, etc.

ter race (ter′əs), 1. a flat, raised piece of land; raised level. 2. form into a terrace or terraces; furnish with terraces. They made a terraced garden. 3. a row of houses or a short street running along the side or top of a slope. She lives at 7 Oak Terrace.

Terraces

ter res tri al (tə res′tri əl), 1. of the earth; not of the heavens; as, this terrestrial globe. 2. of land, not water. 3. living on the ground, not in the air or water or in trees.

ter ri ble (ter′i bəl), causing great fear; dreadful; awful. The terrible storm destroyed many lives.

ter ri bly (ter′i bli), in a terrible manner; dreadfully.

ter ri er (ter′i ər), a kind of small, active, intelligent, and courageous dog that pursues prey into its burrow. The best known kinds are fox terriers, Irish terriers, and Scotch terriers.

Wire-haired terrier (about 15 in. high at the shoulder)

ter rif ic (tə rif′ik), causing great fear; terrifying; very severe. A terrific earthquake shook the island.

ter ri fy (ter′i fī), fill with great fear; frighten very much. Terrified by the sight of the lion, Bill climbed a tree.

ter ri to ry (ter′i tō′ri), 1. land; region. Much territory in Africa is desert. 2. land under the rule of a distant government. Alaska is a territory of the United States.

ter ror (ter′ər), 1. great fear. The child has a terror of thunder. 2. cause of great fear. Pirates were once the terror of the sea.

terse (tėrs), brief and full of meaning.

test (test), 1. examination; trial. The teacher gave the children a test in arithmetic. People who want to drive an automobile must pass a test. 2. means of trial. Trouble is a test of character. 3. examination of a substance to see what it is or what it contains. A test showed that the water from our well was pure. 4. put to a test of any kind; try out. He tested the boy's honesty by leaving money about. That food was tested for poison.

tes ta ment (tes′tə mənt), written instructions telling what to do with a person's property after his death; a will.

Tes ta ment (tes′tə mənt). The Bible consists of two parts, the Old Testament and the New Testament. Testament used alone means the New Testament.

tes ti fy (tes′ti fī), give evidence; say as a witness; declare. The witness testified that the larger car had crowded the smaller one into the ditch. He hated to testify against a friend.

tes ti mo ny (tes′ti mō′ni), 1. statement used for evidence or proof. A witness gave testimony that Mr. Doe was at home from 9 to 11 P.M. 2. evidence. The pupils presented their teacher with a watch in testimony of their respect and affection.

tes ty (tes′ti), easily irritated; impatient.

teth er (teᴛʜ′ər), 1. rope or chain by which an animal is fastened. The cow had broken her tether and was in the garden. 2. fasten with a tether. The horse is tethered to a stake.

text (tekst), 1. the main body of reading matter in a book. This history contains 300 pages of text, and about 50 pages of notes, explanations, and questions for study. 2. a short passage in the Bible used as the subject of a sermon, or as proof of some belief. The minister preached on the text "Blessed are the merciful." 3. topic. Town improvement was the speaker's text.

text book (tekst′bůk′), book for regular study by pupils. Most arithmetics and geographies are textbooks.

tex tile (teks′til), 1. woven. Cloth is a textile fabric. 2. woven fabric. Beautiful textiles were sold in Paris. 3. material that can be woven. 4. suitable for weaving. Linen, cotton, silk, and wool are common textile materials. 5. of or having to do with weaving; as, the textile art.

tex ture (teks′chər), 1. arrangement of threads woven together. Homespun is cloth which has a loose texture. This linen tablecloth has a fine texture. 2. arrangement of the parts of anything; structure. Jane's skin has a fine texture. The texture of marble makes it take a polish.

than (ᴛʜan). John is taller than his sister. Ruth would rather read than play. *Than* shows comparison. You know better than I do. How else can we come than by train?

thank (thangk). Say "thank you" when someone does you a favor. Helen thanked her teacher for helping her. **Have oneself to thank** means be to blame. You have yourself to thank if you eat too much.

thank ful (thangk′fəl), feeling thanks; grateful. He is thankful for good health.

thank less (thangk′lis), 1. ungrateful. The thankless boy did almost nothing for his mother. 2. not likely to get thanks. Giving advice is usually a thankless act.

thanks (thangks), 1. I thank you. 2. act of thanking; expression of pleasure and gratitude. 3. **Thanks to** sometimes means owing to or because of. Thanks to John's efforts, the garden is a great success.

thanks giv ing (thangks giv′ing), 1. giving thanks. 2. expression of thanks. They offered thanksgiving to God for their escape. 3. In the United States, **Thanksgiving** is usually the last Thursday in November, a day set apart every year to thank God for his kindness. Many people forget the original purpose of Thanksgiving.

that (ᴛʜat), 1. *That* is used to point out some one person or thing or idea. We use *this* for the thing nearer us, and *that* for the thing farther away from us. Do you know that boy? Shall we buy this book or that one? I like that better. 2. who; whom. Is he the man that sells dogs? She is the girl that you saw in school. 3. which. Bring the box that will hold most. 4. *That* is also used to connect a group of words. I know that 6 and 4 are 10. 5. *That* is used to show purpose. He ran fast that he might not be late to school. 6. *That* is used to show result. He ran so fast that he was five minutes early. 7. so. The baby cannot stay up that long. 8. when. It was the day that school began.

thatch (thach), 1. straw, rushes, or the like, used to cover roofs or stacks. 2. cover with thatch.

Thatched roof

that's (ᴛʜats), that is.

thaw (thô), 1. melt (ice, snow, or anything frozen); free from frost. The sun at noon thaws the ice on the streets. It thawed early last spring. 2. weather above the freezing point (32 degrees); time of melting. In January we usually have a thaw. 3. become less cold, less formal, or less reserved. His shyness thawed under the teacher's kindness.

the (ᴛʜə or ᴛʜi, or ᴛʜē). The dog I saw had no tail. The boys on the horses are my brothers. The longer you work, the more you get. The later I sit up, the sleepier I become.

the a ter or **the a tre** (thē′ə tər), 1. place where plays are acted; place where moving pictures are shown. 2. place that looks like a theater in its arrangement of seats. 3. place of action. France has been the theater for many wars. 4. plays; the drama. Tony was interested in the theater and tried to write plays himself.

the at ri cal (thi at′ri kəl), 1. of the theater or actors; as, theatrical performances, a theatrical company. 2. suggesting a theater or acting; artificial; for display or effect. 3. **Theatricals** are dramatic performances given by amateurs.

thee (ᴛʜē), you. "The Lord bless thee and keep thee."

theft (theft), stealing. The theft of the jewels caused much excitement. People are put in prison for theft.

their (ᴛʜãr), of them; belonging to them. They like their school and do their lessons well.

theirs (ᴛʜãrz), 1. of them; belonging to them. Those books are theirs, not mine. 2. the one or ones belonging to them. Our house is white; theirs is brown.

them (ᴛʜem). The books are new; take care of them. *They* and *them* mean the persons, animals, or things spoken about.

theme (thēm), 1. subject; topic. Patriotism was the speaker's theme. 2. short written composition. Our school themes must be written in ink and on white paper. 3. principal melody in a piece of music.

them selves (ᴛʜem selvz′), 1. *Themselves* is used to make a statement stronger. The teachers themselves said the test was too hard. 2. *Themselves* is sometimes used instead of *they* or *them.* The boys hurt themselves sliding downhill.

then (ᴛʜen), 1. at that time. 2. that time. By then we shall know the result of the election. 3. soon afterward. The noise stopped and then began again. 4. next in time or place. First comes spring, then summer. 5. at another time. Now one boy does best and then another. 6. also; besides. The dress seems too good to throw away, and then it is so becoming. 7. in that case; therefore. If Harry broke the window, then he should pay for it.

thence (ᴛʜens), 1. from that place. He went to Italy; thence he went to France. 2. for that reason. 3. from that time.

thence forth (ᴛʜens′fōrth′), from then on; from that time forward. Women were given the same rights as men. Thenceforth they could vote.

the ol o gy (thē ol′ə ji), doctrines concerning God and His relations to the universe; the study of divine things or religious truth.

the o ry (thē′ə ri), 1. explanation based on thought. There were several theories about the way in which the fire started. 2. the principles or methods of a science or art rather than its practice; as, the theory of music. 3. idea or opinion about something.

there (ᴛʜãr), 1. in that place; at that place; at that point. Sit there. Finish reading the page and stop there. 2. to that place. Have you seen the new house? We are going there tomorrow. 3. that place. We go to New York first and from there to Boston. 4. in that matter. You are mistaken there. 5. *There* is also used in sentences in which the verb comes before its subject. There are three new houses on our street. Is there a drug store near here? 6. *There* is used to call attention to something. There goes the bell. 7. *There* is also used to express some feeling. There, there! don't cry.

there a bouts (ᴛʜãr′ə bouts′), 1. near that place. 2. near that time. 3. near that number or amount.

there af ter (ᴛʜãr af′tər), after that; afterward. He was very ill as a child and was considered delicate thereafter.

there at (ᴛʜãr at′), 1. when that happened; at that time. 2. because of that; because of it. 3. at that place; there.

there by (ᴛʜãr bī′), 1. by means of that; in that way. He wished to travel and thereby study the customs of other countries. 2. in connection with that. **Thereby hangs a tale** means there is a story connected with that. 3. near there.

there for (ᴛʜãr fôr′), for that; for this; for it. He promised to give a building for a hospital and as much land as should be necessary therefor.

there fore (ᴛʜãr′fōr), for that reason; as a result of that. Louise went to a party and therefore did not study her lessons.

there from (ᴛʜãr from′), from that; from this; from it. He opened his bag and took therefrom an apple.

there in (ᴛʜãr in′), 1. in that place; in it. God created the sea and all that is therein. 2. in that matter; in that way. The captain thought all danger was past. Therein he made a mistake.

there of (ᴛʜãr ov′), 1. of that; of it. 2. from it; from that source.

there on (ᴛʜãr on′), 1. on that; on it. Before the window was a table. A huge book lay thereon. 2. immediately after that. Jesus touched the sick man. Thereon he was healed and arose from his bed.

there's (ᴛʜãrz), there is.

there to (ᴛʜãr tü′), 1. to that; to it. The castle stands on the hill. The road thereto is steep and rough. 2. in addition to that. The king gave his faithful servant rich garments and added thereto a bag of gold.

there un to (ᴛʜãr un′tü), to that; to it.

there up on (ᴛʜãr′ə pon′), 1. immediately after that. The President appeared. Thereupon the people clapped. 2. because of that; therefore. The stolen jewels were found in his room; thereupon he was put in jail. 3. upon that; upon it. The knight carried a shield with a cross painted thereupon.

there with (ᴛʜãr wiᴛʜ′), 1. with that; with it. The lady gave him a rose and a smile therewith. 2. then. "Avenge me!" said the ghost and therewith disappeared.

ther mom e ter (thər mom′i tər), instrument for measuring temperature. On the thermometer shown in the picture 0° is the freezing point of water and 100° is the boiling point of water.

Thermometer

ther mos (thėr′məs), a trade name for a kind of container that will keep hot liquids hot and keep cold liquids cold.

these (ᴛʜēz). *These* is used to point out persons, things, etc. These days are cold. These two problems are hard. These are my books.

they (ᴛʜā), 1. the persons, animals, things, or ideas spoken about. 2. people; persons. They say we should have a new school.

they'd (ᴛʜād), 1. they had. 2. they would.

they'll (ᴛʜāl), 1. they will. 2. they shall.

they're (ᴛʜãr), they are.

they've (ᴛʜāv), they have.

thick (thik), 1. with much space from one side to the opposite side; not thin. The castle has thick stone walls. 2. measuring between two opposite sides. This brick is 8 inches long, 4 inches wide, and $2\frac{1}{2}$ inches thick. 3. set close together; dense. She has thick hair. It is a thick forest. 4. many and close together; abundant. Bullets came thick as hail. 5. like glue or syrup; not like water. Thick liquids pour much more slowly than thin liquids. 6. not clear; foggy. The weather was thick. 7. not clear in sound; hoarse; as, a thick voice. 8. stupid; dull. He has a thick head. 9. thickly. 10. thickest part. King Arthur was in the thick of the fight. 11. very friendly; intimate. *Meaning 11 is not used in formal writing.*

thick en (thik′ən), make thick; become thick. The cook thickens the gravy with flour. The pudding will thicken as it cools.

thick et (thik′it), shrubs, bushes, or small trees growing close together. We crawled into the thicket and hid.

thick ly (thik′li), 1. in a thick manner; closely; densely. Most of New York is a thickly settled region. 2. in great numbers. Weeds grow thickly in the rich soil. 3. frequently. 4. in tones that are hoarse or hard to understand.

thick ness (thik′nis), 1. being thick. The thickness of the walls shuts out all sound. 2. the third measurement of a solid, not length nor breadth. The length of the board is 10 feet, the width 6 inches, the thickness 2 inches. 3. thick part. 4. layer. The pad was made up of three thicknesses of cloth.

thief (thēf), person who steals. Thieves steal secretly and usually without using force.

thieve (thēv), steal. Tom saw a boy thieving at school today.

thieves (thēvz), more than one thief.

thigh (thī), the part of the leg between the hip and the knee.

thim ble (thim′bəl), a small metal cap worn on the finger to protect it when pushing the needle in sewing.

Thimble

thin (thin), 1. with little space from one side to the opposite side; not thick. The ice on the pond is too thin for skating. 2. having little flesh; as, a thin man. 3. not set close together; scanty. He has thin hair. 4. not dense. The air on the tops of high mountains is thin. 5. few and far apart; not abundant. The actors played to a thin audience. 6. like water; not like glue or syrup. This gravy is too thin. 7. having little depth, fullness, or intensity. She speaks in a shrill thin voice. 8. easily seen through. It was a thin excuse that satisfied no one. 9. make thin; become thin.

thine (ᴛʜīn), 1. yours; your; thy. "My daughter shall be thine," said the king to the knight. 2. the one or ones belonging to you; yours. Thine is the swiftest steed. 3. your; thy (used only before a vowel or *h*); as, thine eyes.

thing (thing). All the things in the house were burned. Put these things away. If you can see or hear or touch or taste or smell it, you can call it a thing. A strange thing happened. It was a good thing to do. **Things** sometimes means (1) personal belongings. (2) clothes. I packed my things and took the train.

think (thingk), 1. have ideas; use the mind. I want to think about that question before I answer it. 2. have an opinion; believe. Do you think it will rain? We thought it might snow. 3. consider; have in mind. Think of me when I am away. **thought** is formed from **think.**

third (thėrd), 1. next after the second. C is the third letter of the alphabet. 2. one of three equal parts. Mother divided the cake into thirds.

third ly (thėrd′li), in the third place.

thirst (thėrst), 1. a painful feeling caused by having nothing to drink. The traveler in the desert suffered from thirst. 2. desire for something to drink. He satisfied his thirst at the spring. 3. feel thirst. 4. strong desire. Many boys have a thirst for adventure. 5. have a strong desire.

thirst y (thėrs′ti), 1. feeling thirst; having thirst. The dog is thirsty; please give him some water. 2. without water or moisture; dry. The land seemed thirstier than a desert.

thir teen (thėr′tēn′), three more than ten; 13. Some people think thirteen is an unlucky number.

thir teenth (thėr′tēnth′), 1. next after the 12th. 2. one of 13 equal parts.

thir ti eth (thėr′ti ith), 1. next after the 29th. 2. one of 30 equal parts. A day is about one thirtieth of a month.

thir ty (thėr′ti), three times ten; 30.

this (ᴛʜis). *This* is used to point out some one person, thing, or idea as present, or near, or spoken of before. School begins at eight this year. This is my brother. Shall we buy this or that? **This much** means as much as this.

Thistle

this tle (this′əl), a plant with a prickly stalk and leaves. See the picture just above.

thith er (ᴛʜiᴛʜ′ər), to that place; toward that place; there.

tho or **tho'** (ᴛʜō), though.

thong (thông), 1. narrow strip of leather, used as a fastening. 2. the lash of a whip, a rein, etc.

tho rax (thō′raks), 1. the part of the body between the neck and the abdomen. A man's chest is his thorax. 2. the second division of an insect's body, between the head and the abdomen.

HEAD
THORAX
ABDOMEN
The three parts of an insect

thorn (thôrn), 1. sharp point on a plant. Roses have thorns. 2. a plant that has thorns on it. Thorns sprang up and choked the wheat. 3. A **thorn in the flesh** often means a trouble or annoyance.

thorn y (thôr′ni), 1. full of thorns. He scratched his hands on the thorny bush. He tried to make his way through the thorny thicket. 2. troublesome. The boys argued over the thorny points in the lesson.

thor ough (thėr′ō), complete; doing all that should be done. Please make a thorough search for the lost money. He is a thorough gentleman.

thor ough bred (thėr′ō bred′), 1. of pure breed or stock. 2. a thoroughbred animal, especially a horse. 3. well-bred; thoroughly trained.

thor ough fare (thėr′ō fãr′), 1. a passage, road, or street open at both ends. 2. main road; highway. The Lincoln Highway is a famous thoroughfare of the United States. 3. The sign **No Thoroughfare** means that people are not allowed to go through.

thor ough ly (thėr′ōli), in a thorough manner; completely.

those (ᴛʜōz). *Those* is used to point out several persons or things. She owns that dog; the boys own those dogs. That is his book; those are my books.

thou (ᴛʜou), you. "Thou art fair," said the knight to the lady. God is addressed as Thou. "Thou, God, hear my prayer."

though (ᴛʜō), 1. We take our medicine, though we do not like it. Though it was pouring, the girls went to school. 2. even supposing that. Though I fail, I shall try again. 3. however. I am sorry for our quarrel; you began it, though. 4. **As though** means as if. You look as though you were tired. Also spelled **tho** or **tho'.**

thought (thôt), 1. idea; notion. Her thought was to have a picnic. 2. thinking. Thought helps us solve problems. 3. care; attention; regard. Show some thought for others than yourself. 4. See **think.** We thought it would snow yesterday.

thought ful (thôt′fəl), 1. thinking; full of thought. George was thoughtful for a while and then replied, "No." 2. careful; heedful; careful of others; considerate. She is always thoughtful of her mother.

thought less (thôt′lis), 1. without thought; doing things without thinking; careless. He is a thoughtless boy and is always making blunders. 2. showing little or no care or regard for others. It is thoughtless of her to keep us waiting so long.

thou sand (thou′zənd), ten hundred; 1000.

thou sandth (thou′zəndth), 1. last in a series of a thousand. 2. one of a thousand equal parts; .001.

thrall (thrôl), 1. person in bondage; slave. The thralls did the work of the castle. 2. bondage; slavery. An enchantress had the prince in thrall.

thrash (thrash), 1. beat the grain or seeds from (wheat, etc.); thresh. 2. beat. The man thrashed the boy for stealing apples.

thread (thred), 1. cotton, silk, flax, etc., spun out into a fine cord. You sew with thread. 2. pass a thread through. She threaded her needle. Mary threaded a hundred beads. 3. something long and slender like a thread. The spider hung by a thread. 4. main thought that connects the parts of a story or speech. 5. make one's way through. He threaded the forest. **Thread one's way** means go carefully. The cat threaded its way among the dishes on the shelf. 6. the winding, sloping ridge of a screw. See the picture.

Screws showing threads

thread bare (thred′bãr′), 1. having the nap worn off; worn so much that the threads show; as, a threadbare coat. 2. wearing clothes worn to the threads; shabby; as, a threadbare beggar. 3. old and worn; as, a threadbare excuse.

threat (thret), 1. statement of what will be done to hurt or punish someone. The boys stopped playing ball in the street because of the policeman's threats to arrest them. 2. a sign or cause of possible evil or harm. Those black clouds are a threat of rain.

threat en (thret′ən), 1. make a threat against; say what will be done to punish or harm. The farmer threatened to shoot any dog that killed one of his sheep. He threatens and scolds too much. 2. give warning of (coming trouble). The clouds threaten rain. 3. be a cause of possible evil or harm to. A flood threatened the city.

three (thrē). Three is one more than two. Three means 3. Three feet make one yard.

three fold (thrē′fōld′), 1. three times as much. 2. having three parts.

three score (thrē′skōr′), three times twenty; sixty.

thresh (thresh), 1. separate the grain or seeds from (wheat, etc.). Nowadays most farmers use a machine to thresh their wheat. 2. toss about; move violently.

thresh old (thresh′ōld), 1. piece of wood or stone under a door. 2. doorway. 3. point of entering; beginning point. He was on the threshold of an important discovery.

threw (thrü). See **throw.** He threw a stone and ran away.

thrice (thrīs), three times. He knocked thrice. Bob is thrice as strong as his little brother.

thrift (thrift), absence of waste; saving; economical management; habit of saving. By thrift she managed to get along on her small salary. A bank account encourages thrift.

thrift y (thrif′ti), 1. saving; careful in spending; economical. 2. thriving; prosperous; as, a thrifty plant.

thrill (thril), 1. a shivering, exciting feeling. She gets thrills from the movies. 2. give a shivering, exciting feeling. Stories of adventure thrilled him. 3. have a shivering, exciting feeling. The children thrilled with joy at the sight of the Christmas tree. 4. tremble. Her voice thrilled with terror.

thrive (thrīv), prosper; be successful; grow rich; grow strong. Flowers will not thrive without sunshine.

thro' or **thro** (thrü), through.

throat (thrōt), 1. the front of the neck. 2. the passage from the mouth to the stomach or the lungs. A bone stuck in his throat. 3. any narrow passage. The throat of the valley was blocked by fallen rocks.

throb (throb), 1. beat rapidly or strongly. Climbing stairs makes her heart throb. His wounded arm throbbed with pain. 2. a rapid or strong beat. A throb of pain shot through his head.

throne (thrōn), 1. the chair on which a king, queen, bishop, or other person of high rank sits during ceremonies. 2. the power or authority of a king, queen, etc.

throng (thrông), 1. a crowd; a multitude. 2. to crowd; fill with a crowd. People thronged the theater to see the famous actress. 3. come together in a crowd; go or press in large numbers. The people thronged to see the king.

thros tle (thros′əl), a thrush.

throt tle (throt′əl), 1. choke; strangle. The thief throttled the dog to keep it from barking. 2. a valve or lever for regulating the supply of steam or gasoline to an engine. 3. stop or check by closing a valve; as, to throttle a steam engine.

through (thrü), 1. from end to end of; from side to side of; between the parts of. The soldiers marched through the town. The man went through a doorway. Fish swim through the water. The carpenter bored holes through a board. We look through windows. 2. from beginning to end. Elizabeth read the book through. 3. here and there in; over. We traveled through New England visiting many old towns. 4. because of; by reason of; by means of. The woman refused help through pride. He became rich through hard work and ability. 5. going all the way without change; as, a through train from New York to Chicago. 6. having reached the end of; finished with. We are through school at three o'clock.

through out (thrü out′), 1. all the way through; through all; in every part of. The Fourth of July is celebrated throughout the United States. 2. in every part. The house is well built throughout.

throve (thrōv), thrived; prospered.

throw (thrō), 1. the boy is throwing a ball to his brother. The fire hose threw water on the burning house. He was thrown from his horse. The tree throws a shadow on the grass. He was thrown into prison. He lost two dollars on a throw of dice. 2. Some special meanings are:

throw cold water on, discourage.

throw in, add as a gift.

throw over, give up; discard; abandon.

threw and **thrown** are formed from **throw.**

thrown (thrōn). See **throw.** Mary has thrown her old toys away.

thru (thrü), through.

thrush (thrush), a common songbird. See the picture. A robin is a kind of thrush.

Song thrush (about 9 in. long)

thrust (thrust), 1. push with force; pushed with force. Jack thrusts his hands into his pockets. Frances thrust past me into the room. A soldier thrusts himself into danger. 2. a push with force. She hid the book behind the pillow with a quick thrust. 3. stab; pierce; stabbed; pierced. He thrust the villain through with his sword. 4. a stab. A thrust with the sword killed him.

thud (thud), a dull sound. A heavy blow or fall may cause a thud.

thumb (thum), 1. the short thick finger. 2. part that covers the thumb. There was a hole in the thumb of his mitten. 3. soil or wear by handling with the thumbs. Some of the books were badly thumbed. 4. **Under the thumb of** means under the power or influence of.

thump (thump), 1. strike with something thick and heavy; pound. He thumped the table with his fist. Tom thumped on the piano. 2. a blow with something thick and heavy; heavy knock. He hit the thief a thump on the head. 3. the dull sound made by a blow, knock, or fall. We heard the thump as he fell. 4. make a dull sound. His heart thumped as he walked past the graveyard at night.

thun der (thun′dər), 1. the loud noise which often follows a flash of lightning. 2. give forth thunder. It thundered, but no rain fell. 3. any noise like thunder; as, the thunder of Niagara Falls, a thunder of applause. 4. make a noise like thunder. The cannon thundered.

thun der bolt (thun′dər bōlt′), 1. a flash of lightning and the thunder that follows it. 2. something sudden, startling, and terrible.

thun der ous (thun′dər əs), 1. producing thunder. 2. making a noise like thunder.

thun der storm (thun′dər stôrm′), storm with thunder and lightning.

Thurs day (thėrz′di), the fifth day of the week. Thanksgiving always comes on Thursday.

thus (ᴛʜus), 1. in this way. He spoke thus: "Friends, Romans, Countrymen." 2. therefore. He studied hard; thus he got high marks. **3.** to this extent; to this degree. Thus far may you go and no farther.

thwack (thwak), 1. strike vigorously with a stick or something flat. 2. sharp blow with a stick or something flat.

thwart (thwôrt), 1. oppose and defeat; keep from doing something. The boy's family thwarted his plans for college. 2. a seat across a boat, on which a rower sits. 3. lying across; across.

thy (ᴛʜī), your. "Thy kingdom come, Thy will be done."

thyme (tīm), a low shrub. Its sweet-smelling leaves are used for seasoning.

Thyme

thy self (ᴛʜī self′), yourself. 1. *Thyself* is used to make a statement stronger. "Thou, thyself, must choose between us," said the knight to the lady. 2. *Thyself* is used instead of thee or thou when thee or thou has already been used in the sentence. "Thou forgettest thyself," she replied in haughty tones.

tick[1] (tik), 1. a sound made by a clock or watch. 2. make such a sound. The clock ticked. 3. a sound like it. 4. small mark. We use √ or / as a tick. 5. mark with a tick; check. He ticked off the items one by one.

tick[2] (tik), a tiny insect that lives on animals and sucks their blood.

Tick. Line shows actual length.

tick[3] (tik), the cloth covering of a mattress or pillow.

tick et (tik′it), 1. a card or piece of paper that gives a right or privilege. In his pocket he has a railroad ticket for his trip home, a ticket to the theater, and a ticket to the ball game. 2. a card or piece of paper attached to something to show its price, etc. 3. put a ticket on. All articles in the store are ticketed with the price.

tick le (tik′əl), 1. touch lightly, causing little thrills, shivers, or wriggles. John tickled the baby's feet and made her laugh. 2. have a feeling like this. My nose tickles. 3. tingling or itching feeling. 4. amuse; excite pleasantly. The story tickled him. The child was tickled with his new toys.

tick lish (tik′lish), 1. sensitive to tickling. The bottoms of the feet are ticklish. 2. requiring careful handling; delicate; risky. 3. easily upset; unstable.

tid al (tīd′əl), of tides; having tides; caused by tides. A tidal river is affected by the ocean's tide.

tid bit (tid′bit′), very pleasing bit of food, news, etc.

tide (tīd), 1. the rise and fall of the ocean about every twelve hours, caused by the attraction of the moon and the sun. We go swimming at high tide; at low tide we dig clams. 2. anything that rises and falls like the tide. 3. **Tide over** means help along to the end of. This money will tide him over his illness.

ti di ness (tī′di nis), neatness.

ti dings (tī′dingz), news; information. The messenger brought tidings from the battle front.

ti dy (tī′di), 1. neat. Cats are tidier than pigs. 2. make neat; put in order. She tidied the room. 3. considerable; as, a tidy sum of money.

tie (tī), 1. fasten; bind. Please tie this bundle with string. Tie up your shoes. He is tying his horse to a tree. Tie the ribbon in a pretty bow. He refused to be tied down to a steady position. 2. thing that ties; fastening; bond; connection. Family ties have kept him from success. 3. necktie. 4. equality in points. The game ended in a tie, 3 to 3. 5. make the same score; be equal in points. The two teams tied. **Be tied** means be alike in scores. 6. heavy piece of timber or iron. The rails rest on ties about a foot apart. 7. a curved line joining two notes of the same pitch.

Musical tie

tier (tēr), one of a series of rows arranged one above another; as, tiers of seats at a baseball game.

ti ger (tī′gər), a large fierce animal of Asia which has dull-yellow fur striped with black.

Bengal tiger (about 10 ft. long with the tail)

tight (tīt), 1. firm; held firmly; packed or put together firmly. The sailor made a tight knot. 2. firmly. 3. stretched. He performed on the tight rope. 4. fitting closely; too close; close. This hat is tight. 5. not letting water, air, or gas in or out. A boat should be watertight. 6. scarce; hard to get. Money is tight just now.

tight en (tīt′ən), 1. make tight. He tightened his belt. 2. become tight. The rope tightened when I pulled on it.

ti gress (tī′gris), a female tiger.

tile (tīl), 1. thin piece of baked clay. Tiles are used for covering roofs, paving floors, and for ornament. 2. pipe for draining land. 3. put tiles on or in.

till[1] (til), until; up to the time of; to the time when. The child played till eight. Walk till you come to a white house.

till[2] (til), cultivate (land); plow. Farmers till the land.

till[3] (til), a drawer for money. The till is under or behind the counter.

til ler (til′ər), bar or handle used to turn the rudder in steering a boat.

tilt (tilt), 1. slope; slant. You tilt your head forward when you bow. You tilt your cup when you drink. This table tilts. 2. a slope; a slant. 3. rush, charge, or fight with lances. Knights used to tilt on horseback. 4. a fight on horseback with lances.

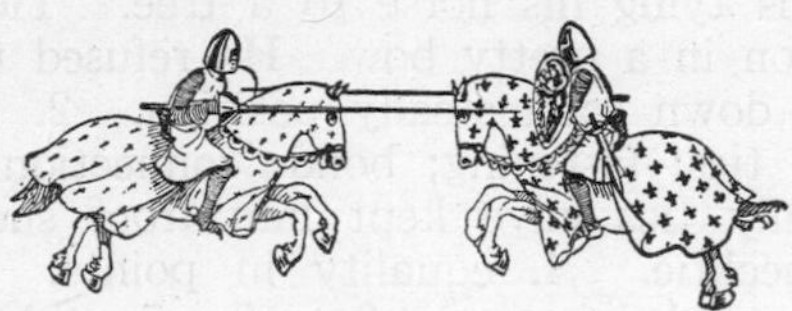

Tilt (def. 4)

tim ber (tim′bər), 1. wood for building and making things. Houses, ships, and furniture are made from timber. 2. large piece of wood used in building. Beams and rafters are timbers. 3. growing trees; forests. Half of his land is covered with timber.

time (tīm), 1. all the days there have been or ever will be; the past, present, and future. 2. a part of time. A minute is a short time. A long time ago people lived in caves. 3. a long time. What a time it took you! 4. some point in time. The time the game begins is two o'clock, November 8. 5. the right part or point of time. It is time to go to bed. 6. occasion. Ann got the right answer every time. Do it five times. 7. way of reckoning time; as, standard time, daylight-saving time. 8. condition of life. War brings hard times. 9. rate of movement in music; rhythm; as, march time, waltz time. 10. measure the time of. He timed the horse for each half mile. 11. do at regular times; set the time of. The dancers time their steps to the music. 12. choose the moment or occasion for. The lady timed her entrance so that she went in just after the prince did. 13. Some special meanings are:

at times, now and then; once in a while.

in time, 1. after a while. 2. soon enough. 3. in the right rate of movement in music, dancing, marching, etc.

on time, at the right time; punctual.

time ly (tīm′li), at the right time. The timely arrival of the police stopped the riot.

time ta ble (tīm′tā′bəl), a schedule showing the times when trains, boats, busses, or airplanes come and go.

tim id (tim′id), easily frightened; shy. The timid child was afraid of the dark. Deer are timid animals.

ti mid i ty (ti mid′i ti), timid behavior; shyness.

tim o thy (tim′ə thi), a kind of coarse grass grown for hay.

tin (tin), 1. a metal that shines like silver but is softer and cheaper. 2. thin sheets of iron or steel coated with tin. 3. made of tin. We cleaned up all the old tin cans. 4. cover with tin. 5. any can, box, pan, or pot made of tin.

tin der (tin′dər), anything that catches fire easily.

tinge (tinj), 1. color slightly. A drop of ink will tinge a glass of water. 2. slight coloring. There is a tinge of red in her cheeks. 3. give a slight taste or smell to; change a very little. Her remarks were tinged with envy. 4. trace; very small amount. She likes just a tinge of lemon in her tea. There was a tinge of blame in his voice.

tin gle (ting′gəl), 1. have a feeling of thrills or a pricking, stinging feeling. Joe tingled with excitement on his first train trip. 2. such a feeling. The cold caused a tingle in my ears.

tink er (tingk′ər), 1. man who mends pots, pans, etc. 2. mend; patch. 3. work or repair in an unskilled or clumsy way.

tin kle (ting′kəl), 1. make sounds like a little bell. 2. cause to tinkle. 3. series of short, light, ringing sounds; as, the tinkle of sleigh bells.

tin sel (tin′səl), 1. glittering copper, brass, etc., in thin sheets, strips, threads, etc. Tinsel is used to trim Christmas trees. 2. anything showy but having little value. 3. showy but not worth much. 4. thin cloth woven with threads of gold, silver, or copper. She wore a beautiful dress of gold tinsel.

tin smith (tin′smith′), person who works with tin; maker of tinware.

tint (tint), 1. variety of a color. The picture was painted in several tints of blue. 2. delicate or pale color. 3. color. The walls were tinted a pale yellow.

tin ware (tin′wãr′), articles made of tin.

ti ny (tī′ni), very small; wee. Grace has the tiniest dog you ever saw.

tip[1] (tip), 1. end, point; as, the tips of the fingers. 2. small piece put on the end of something. 3. put a tip on; furnish with a tip. The spears were tipped with steel.

tip[2] (tip), 1. slope; slant. She tipped the table toward her. 2. upset; overturn. We saw Tom tip Sam into the water. 3. empty out; dump. She tipped all the money in her purse on to the table.

tip[3] (tip), 1. small present of money. He gave the waiter a tip. 2. give a small present of money to. Did you tip the porter? 3. piece of secret information. Fred had a tip that the black horse would win the race.

tip sy (tip′si), 1. unsteady; tipping easily. 2. intoxicated; drunk.

tip toe (tip′tō′), 1. the tips of the toes. **On tiptoe** sometimes means (1) in a secret manner. (2) eager. The children were on tiptoe for vacation to begin. 2. walk on the tips of the toes. Mary tiptoed quietly up the stairs.

tire[1] (tīr), 1. make weary. The long walk tired her. 2. become weary.

tire[2] (tīr), 1. a band of rubber or metal around a wheel. Put more air in all four tires. 2. furnish with a tire.

tired (tīrd), weary; wearied; exhausted.

tire less (tīr′lis), 1. never becoming tired; requiring little rest; as, a tireless worker. 2. never stopping; as, tireless efforts.

tire some (tīr′səm), tiring; not interesting.

'tis (tiz), it is.

tis sue (tish′ü), 1. a fine, light cloth. Alice's dress was of silk tissue. 2. web; network. Her whole story was a tissue of lies. 3. tissue paper. 4. mass of cells forming some part of an animal or plant. The teacher showed pictures of muscle tissues, brain tissues, and skin tissues.

tissue paper, very thin soft paper used for wrapping or covering things.

tit bit (tit′bit′), very pleasing bit of food, news, etc.

ti tle (tī′təl), 1. the name of a book, poem, picture, song, etc. 2. name showing rank, occupation, or condition in life. King, duke, lord, countess, captain, doctor, professor, Madame, and Miss are titles. 3. championship; first-place position; as, the tennis title. 4. claim; right.

to (tü), 1. in the direction of. Go to the right. 2. as far as. This apple is rotten to the core. 3. for the purpose of; for. Mother came to the rescue. 4. *To* is also used (1) to show action toward. Give the book to me. (2) with verbs. John likes to read. (3) to show result. He tore it to pieces. (4) to show addition, or to mean with. He hummed to the music. 5. **To and fro** means first one way and then back again; back and forth.

Toad (about 3 in. long)

toad (tōd), a small animal somewhat like a frog, which lives on land. See the picture above.

toad stool (tōd′stül′), poisonous mushroom. See the picture.

Toadstools

toast (tōst), 1. brown by heat. We toast bread. 2. slices of bread browned by heat. 3. heat thoroughly. He toasted his feet before the open fire. 4. drink a health to; take a drink and wish good fortune to. We toasted grandfather by lifting our glasses, smiling at him, and drinking a little. 5. person or thing whose health is proposed and drunk. "The King" was the first toast drunk by the officers. 6. act of drinking to the health of a person or thing.

to bac co (tə bak′ō), a plant whose leaves are used for smoking or chewing or as snuff.

to bog gan (tə bog′ən), 1. a long, narrow, flat sled without runners. 2. slide downhill on such a sled.

Toboggan

to day or **to-day** (tü dā′), 1. this day. What are you doing today? 2. the present time; now. Many girls wear their hair short today.

toe (tō), 1. one of the five end parts of the foot. 2. the part of a stocking, shoe, etc., that covers the toes. 3. anything like a toe. 4. touch or reach with the toes. Toe this mark. Don't toe in so much.

to geth er (tu̇ geтн′ər), 1. with each other; in company. The girls were walking together. 2. into one gathering, company, mass, or body. The pastor called the people together. The woman will sew these pieces together and make a dress. 3. at the same time. You cannot have day and night together. 4. without a stop or break; continuously. He reads for hours together.

toil[1] (toil), 1. hard work. 2. work hard. 3. move with difficulty, pain, or weariness. Carrying heavy loads, they toiled up the mountain.

toil[2] (toil), net; snare. A lion was caught in the toils. The thief was caught in the toils of the law.

toil er (toil′ər), hard worker.

toi let (toi′lit), 1. process of dressing. She made a hurried toilet. Combs and brushes are toilet articles. 2. person's dress; costume. 3. bathroom or water closet.

toil some (toil′səm), requiring hard work; laborious; as, a long, toilsome climb up the mountain.

to ken (tō′kən), 1. a mark or sign (of something). Black is a token of mourning. 2. sign of friendship. She received many birthday tokens. 3. piece of metal stamped for a higher value than the metal is worth. Tokens are used for some purposes instead of money. 4. piece of metal indicating a right or privilege. This token will admit you to the swimming pool.

told (tōld). See **tell.** You told me that last week. We were told to wait.

tol er a ble (tol′ər ə bəl), 1. that can be endured. The pain has become tolerable. 2. fairly good. She is in tolerable health.

tol er ance (tol′ər əns), 1. willingness to be tolerant and patient toward people whose opinions or ways differ from one's own. 2. action of tolerating.

tol er ant (tol′ər ənt), willing to let other people do as they think best; willing to endure beliefs and actions of which one does not approve. The United States government is tolerant toward all religious beliefs.

tol er ate (tol′ər āt), 1. put up with; allow; permit. The teacher won't tolerate any disorder. 2. bear; endure.

toll[1] (tōl), 1. sound with single strokes slowly and regularly repeated. Bells were tolled at the President's death. 2. such a stroke or sound of a bell.

toll[2] (tōl), a tax or fee paid for some right or privilege. We pay a toll when we use that bridge.

Tomahawk

tom a hawk (tom′ə hôk), 1. light ax used by North American Indians as a weapon and a tool. 2. strike or kill with a tomahawk.

to ma to (tə mā′tō or tə mä′tō), 1. a juicy fruit used as a vegetable. Most tomatoes are red, but some are yellow. 2. the plant it grows on.

tomb (tüm), place for a dead body.

tomb stone (tüm′stōn′), stone that marks a tomb or grave.

to mor row (tu̇ mor′ō), 1. the day after today. 2. the near future.

ton (tun), measure of weight, 2000 pounds in the United States and Canada, 2240 pounds in England. A **long ton** is 2240 pounds; a **short ton** is 2000 pounds. A **metric ton** is 1000 kilograms.

tone (tōn), 1. sound; quality of sound; as, low, angry, or gentle tones, the deep tone of the organ. 2. musical sound. 3. difference in pitch between two notes. F is three tones higher than C. 4. manner of speaking or writing. We disliked the haughty tone of her letter. 5. spirit; character; style. A tone of quiet elegance prevails in her home. 6. vigor; normal healthy condition. 7. effect of color and of light and shade in a picture. I like the soft green tone of that painting. 8. shade of color. The room is furnished in tones of brown. 9. harmonize. This rug tones in well with the wall-paper and furniture. 10. **Tone down** means soften. Tone down your voice. Tone down the colors in that painting. 11. **Tone up** means to give more sound, color, or vigor to. Bright curtains would tone up this dull room.

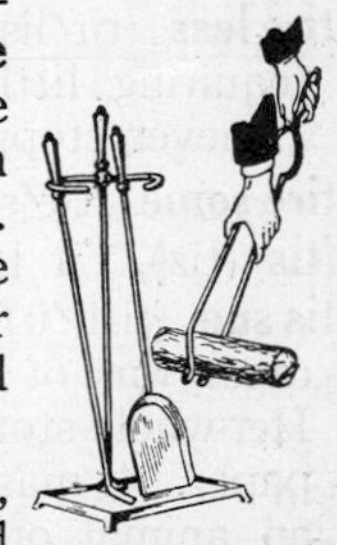

Lifting log with fire tongs

tongs (tôngz), tool for seizing, holding, or lifting. He changed the position of the burning log with the tongs.

tongue (tung), 1. the movable piece of flesh in the mouth. The tongue is used in tasting and, by people, for talking. We eat the tongues of some animals. 2. power of speech. Have you lost your tongue? 3. way of speaking. 4. the language of a people; as, the English tongue. 5. something shaped or used like a tongue. The tongue of a shoe is the strip of leather under the laces. Tongues of flame leaped from the fire. 6. To **hold one's tongue** is to keep still.

ton ic (ton′ik), 1. anything that gives strength; medicine to give strength. Cod-liver oil is a tonic. 2. giving strength; bracing. The mountain air is tonic.

to night or **to-night** (tü nīt′), 1. this night; the night of this day. I am going to bed early tonight. 2. on or during this night.

ton nage (tun′ij), 1. carrying capacity of a ship. A ship of 50,000 cubic feet of space for freight has a tonnage of 500 tons. 2. total amount of shipping in tons.

ton sil (ton′səl), either of the two small oval masses at the back of the mouth.

too (tü), 1. also. The dog is hungry, and thirsty too. We, too, are going away. 2. more than enough. My dress is too long for you. Jack ate too much. The summer passed too quickly. 3. very. I am only too glad to help you.

took (tuk). See **take.** She took the car an hour ago.

tool (tül), 1. a knife, hammer, saw, shovel, or any instrument used in doing work. 2. person or thing used like a tool. He is a tool of the party boss. Books are a scholar's tools. 3. use a tool on.

toot (tüt), 1. sound of a horn, whistle, etc. 2. sound (a horn, whistle, etc.).

tooth (tüth), 1. one of the hard bonelike parts in the mouth, used for biting and chewing. 2. something like a tooth. Each one of the projecting parts of a comb, rake, or saw is a tooth. 3. To **fight tooth and nail** means to fight fiercely, with all one's force.

tooth ache (tüth′āk′), pain in a tooth or the teeth.

tooth pick (tüth′pik′), small pointed piece of wood or sharpened quill for removing bits of food from between the teeth.

top[1] (top), 1. highest part; as, the top of a mountain. Henry is at the top of his class. The boys were yelling at the top of their voices. 2. upper part; as, a shoe top, a carriage top. 3. the part of a plant above ground. 4. head. The girl was dressed in brown from top to toe. 5. highest; greatest. The runners set off at top speed. 6. put a top on. 7. be on top of; be the top of. A church tops the hill. 8. reach the top of; rise above. Call me when you see a gray car topping the hill. 9. be higher or greater than; do better than. Frank's story topped all the rest. 10. remove the top of. 11. a platform around the upper part of a lower mast on a ship.

top[2] (top), toy that spins on a point.

Spinning top

to paz (tō′paz), a precious stone. Topazes are usually yellow.

top ic (top′ik), subject that people think, write, or talk about. The main topics at Mother's party were the weather, clothes, the church, and diseases.

top mast (top′məst or top′mast′), second section of a mast above the deck.

top most (top′mōst), highest. The best cherries always seem to grow on the topmost branches.

top ple (top′əl), 1. fall. The chimney toppled over on the roof. 2. throw down; overturn.

top sail (top′səl or top′sāl′), the second sail above the deck on a mast.

top sy-tur vy (top′si tėr′vi), 1. upside down. 2. in confusion or disorder.

torch (tôrch), light to be carried about or stuck in a holder on a wall. A piece of pine wood or anything that burns easily makes a good torch. "Liberty" is represented as holding up a torch. An electric torch is a flashlight. Torches with very hot flames are used to burn off paint, to solder metal, and to melt metal.

tore (tōr). See **tear**[1]**.** Yesterday Mabel tore her dress on a nail.

tor ment (tôr ment′ for 1 and 4, tôr′ment for 2 and 3), 1. cause very great pain to. Headaches tormented him. 2. cause of very great pain. A bad burn can be a torment. 3. very great pain. He suffered torments from his aching teeth. 4. worry or annoy very much. Tom torments everyone with silly questions.

torn (tōrn). See **tear**[1]**.** He has torn up the plant by the roots. His coat was old and torn.

tor na do (tôr nā′dō), violent whirlwind; a violent, destructive wind.

tor pe do (tôr pē′dō), 1. a large cigar-shaped shell that contains explosives and travels by its own power. Torpedoes are sent under water to blow up enemy ships.

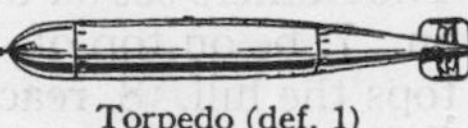
Torpedo (def. 1)

2. a shell containing explosives. 3. attack or destroy with a torpedo. 4. explosive which makes a bang when it is thrown against something hard. Children used to play with torpedoes on the Fourth of July. 5. an explosive put on a railroad track, which makes a very loud noise for a signal when a wheel of the engine runs over it.

tor pid (tôr′pid), 1. inactive; sluggish. 2. not moving or feeling.

tor rent (tor′ənt), 1. a violent, rushing stream of water. The mountain torrent dashed over the rocks. 2. any violent, rushing stream; a flood; as, a torrent of lava from a volcano or a torrent of questions.

tor rid (tor′id), very hot. July was a torrid month.

tor toise (tôr′təs), 1. turtle. 2. turtle living on land.

Tortoise (def. 2)

tor ture (tôr′chər), 1. act of inflicting very severe pain. Torture was formerly used to make people give evidence about crimes, or to make them confess. 2. very severe pain. She suffered tortures from earache. 3. cause very severe pain to. That cruel boy tortures animals. 4. twist the meaning of. 5. twist or force out of its natural form.

toss (tôs), 1. throw; cast; fling. Mary tossed the ball to the baby. 2. throw about; pitch about. The ship is tossed by the waves. He tossed on his bed all night. 3. throw upward. She tossed her head. He was tossed by the bull. 4. a throw; a tossing. A toss of a coin decided who should play first.

tot (tot), little child.

to tal (tō′təl), 1. whole; entire. The total cost of the house and land will be $25,000. 2. the whole amount. His expenses reached a total of $100. Add the different sums to get the total. 3. find the sum of; add. Total that column of figures. 4. reach an amount of; amount to. The money spent yearly on chewing gum totals millions of dollars. 5. complete. He is a total failure. We were in total darkness.

to tal ly (tō′təl i), wholly; entirely; completely. We were totally unprepared.

tot ter (tot′ər), be unsteady; walk with shaky, unsteady steps; shake; tremble. Babies and very old people totter as they walk. The old wall tottered in the gale and fell.

touch (tuch), 1. put the hand or a finger on and feel. She touched the pan to see whether it was still hot. 2. put (one thing) against another. He touched the post with his umbrella. 3. be against; come against. Your sleeve is touching the butter. 4. touching or being touched. A bubble bursts at a touch. The touch of a snake makes her shrink. 5. the sense by which a person perceives things by feeling, handling, or coming against them. The blind develop a keen touch. 6. connection. A newspaper keeps one in touch with the world. 7. slight amount; little bit. We had a touch of frost. 8. a stroke with a brush, pencil, pen, etc.; a detail. The artist finished my picture with a few touches. 9. strike lightly or gently. She touched the strings of her harp. 10. injure slightly. The flowers were touched by the frost. 11. affect with some feeling. The poor woman's story touched our hearts. 12. have to do with; concern. The matter touches your interests. 13. **Touch on** means speak of; treat lightly. Our conversation touched on Mrs. Brown. 14. reach; come up to. 15. act or manner of playing a musical instrument. The girl playing the piano has an excellent touch. 16. **Touch up** means change a little; improve.

touch ing (tuch′ing), 1. arousing tender feeling. *A Christmas Carol* is a touching story. 2. concerning; about. He asked many questions touching my home, parents, and school life.

tough (tuf), 1. bending without breaking. Leather is tough; cardboard is not. 2. strong; hardy. Donkeys are tough little animals and can carry big loads. 3. hard; difficult. Dragging the load uphill was tough work for the horses. 4. hard to influence; stubborn; as, a tough customer. 5. rough; disorderly; as, a tough part of the city. 6. rough person. A gang of toughs attacked the policeman.

tour (tür), 1. travel from place to place. They are making a tour of California. Last year they toured Mexico. 2. short journey; walk around. The children made a tour of the ship.

tour ist (tür′ist), any person traveling for pleasure.

tour na ment (tėr′nə mənt), 1. contest between two groups of knights on horseback who fought for a prize. 2. contest of many persons in some sport; as, a golf tournament.

tou sle (tou′zəl), muss; put into disorder; as, tousled hair.

tow[1] (tō), 1. pull by a rope. The tug is towing three barges. 2. act of towing. 3. condition of being pulled along in this way. The launch had the sailboat in tow. 4. what is towed. Each tug had a tow of three barges. 5. the rope used.

tow[2] (tō), the coarse and broken parts of flax or hemp. This string is made of tow.

to ward (tōrd or tu̇ wôrd′), 1. in the direction of. He walked toward the north. 2. with respect to; about. What is his attitude toward war? 3. near. It must be toward four o'clock. 4. for. Will you give something toward our new hospital?

to wards (tōrdz or tu̇ wôrdz′), toward.

tow el (tou′əl), a piece of cloth or paper for wiping and drying something wet. We have hand towels, bath towels, and dish towels.

tow er (tou′ər), 1. a high structure. See the picture. A tower may stand alone or form part of a church, castle, or other building. 2. defense; a protection. 3. rise high up.

Tower

tow er ing (tou′ər ing), 1. very high. 2. very great. 3. very violent.

town (toun), 1. large group of houses and buildings, smaller than a city. Do you live in a city, a town, a village, or in the country? 2. any large place with many people living in it. Father says New York is a fine town. 3. the people of a town. The whole town was having a holiday.

town ship (toun′ship), part of a county having certain powers of government.

towns man (tounz′mən), 1. person who lives in a town. 2. person who lives in one's own town.

toy (toi), 1. something for a child to play with; plaything. 2. thing that has little value or importance. 3. of, made as, or like a toy. 4. play; amuse oneself; trifle. She toyed with her string of beads.

trace[1] (trās), 1. mark left. We saw traces of rabbits and squirrels on the snow. 2. follow by means of marks, tracks, or signs. The dog traced the fox to its den. 3. follow the course of. He traced the river to its source. The Aldens trace their family back three hundred years to John Alden. 4. mark out. The spy traced a plan of the fort. 5. copy. By putting thin paper over the map, John traced it. 6. very small amount. There was not a trace of color in her cheeks.

trace[2] (trās), either of the two straps, ropes, or chains by which an animal pulls a wagon or carriage.

trac er y (trās′ər i), ornamental work or designs consisting of lines. Stonework, carving, and embroidery often have tracery.

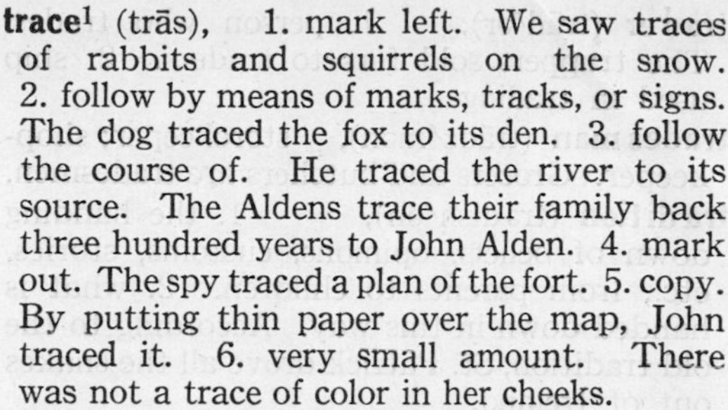

Tracery

trac ing (trās′ing), a copy.

track (trak), 1. a line of metal rails for cars to run on; as, a railroad track. 2. mark left. The dirt road showed many automobile tracks. 3. footprint. We saw wild animals' tracks near the camp. 4. follow by means of marks, footprints, smell, etc. The hunter tracked the bear and killed it. 5. To **keep track of** is to keep within one's sight, knowledge, or attention. 6. make tracks on. 7. path; road. A track runs through the woods to the farmhouse. 8. course for running or racing.

track less (trak′lis), 1. without a track. 2. without paths or trails. Much of Alaska is a trackless wilderness.

tract[1] (trakt), stretch of land, water, etc.; area; as, a wild mountain tract.

tract[2] (trakt), 1. little book or pamphlet on a religious topic. 2. any little book or pamphlet.

trac tor (trak′tər), 1. something used for pulling. 2. engine on wheels for pulling wagons, trucks, plows, etc. A tractor can do the work of many horses on a farm.

trade (trād), 1. buying and selling; commerce. The United States has much trade with foreign countries. 2. buy and sell. The settlers traded with the savages. 3. exchange. 4. bargain; deal. English ships trade all over the world. He made a good trade. 5. kind of work; business. He is learning the carpenter's trade. 6. people in the same kind of work or business. 7. **Trade on** sometimes means take advantage of.

trad er (trād′ər), 1. person who trades. The trappers sold furs to traders. 2. ship used in trading.

trades man (trādz′mən), storekeeper; shopkeeper. Grocers and butchers are tradesmen.

tra di tion (trə dish′ən), 1. the handing down of beliefs, opinions, customs, stories, etc., from parents to children. 2. what is handed down in this way. According to the old tradition, St. Patrick drove all the snakes out of Ireland.

tra di tion al (trə dish′ən əl), 1. of tradition. 2. handed down by tradition. 3. according to tradition. 4. customary.

traf fic (traf′ik), 1. people, automobiles, wagons, ships, etc., coming and going along a way of travel. Police control the traffic in large cities. 2. buying and selling; commerce; trade. 3. buy; sell; exchange; carry on trade. The men trafficked with the natives for ivory. 4. business done by a railroad line or steamship line; number of passengers or amount of freight carried.

traf fick ing (traf′ik ing), trading.

trag e dy (traj′i di), 1. serious play having an unhappy ending. 2. very sad or terrible happening. The father's sudden death was a tragedy to his family.

trag ic (traj′ik), 1. of tragedy; having something to do with tragedy; as, a tragic actor, a tragic poet. 2. very sad; dreadful; as, a tragic death, a tragic accident.

trail (trāl), 1. pull or drag along behind. The child trailed a toy horse after him. 2. grow along. Poison ivy trailed by the road. 3. anything that follows along behind. The car left a trail of dust behind it. 4. track or smell. The dogs found the trail of the rabbit. 5. hunt by track or smell; follow along behind. The dogs trailed the rabbit. 6. path across a wild region. The men had followed desert trails for days.

trail er (trāl′ər), 1. person or animal that follows a trail. 2. vine that grows along the ground. 3. wagon or cart pulled by an automobile, truck, etc. 4. a van fitted up for people to live in and pulled by an automobile.

train (trān), 1. line of cars; as, a railroad train. 2. part that hangs down and drags along; as, the train of a lady's gown. 3. group of followers; as, the king and his train. 4. series; succession. A train of misfortunes overcame the hero. 5. bring up. "Train up a child in the way he should go." 6. teach; make skillful by teaching and practice. Saint Bernard dogs were trained to hunt for travelers lost in the snow. 7. make or become fit by exercise and diet. Runners train for races. 8. point; aim; as, to train guns upon a fort. 9. bring into a particular position. We trained the vines around the post. 10. line of gunpowder that acts as a fuse.

train ing (trān′ing), 1. practical education in some art, profession, etc.; as, training for teachers. 2. developing strength and endurance. 3. good condition maintained by exercise and care.

trait (trāt), feature; quality; characteristic. Courage, love of fair play, and common sense are desirable traits.

trai tor (trā′tər), person who betrays a friend, a duty, his country, etc.

trai tor ous (trā′tər əs), like a traitor; treacherous; faithless.

tramp (tramp), 1. walk heavily. We heard soldiers tramping by. 2. step heavily (on). He tramped on the dog's foot. 3. sound of a heavy step; as, the tramp of marching feet. 4. walk; go on foot. We tramped a hundred miles. 5. a long, steady walk. The boys took a tramp together over the hills. 6. man who wanders about and begs. A tramp came to the door and asked for food. 7. freight ship which takes a cargo when and where it can.

tram ple (tram′pəl), 1. tread heavily; tread on; crush. The man was trampled to death by the herd of wild cattle. 2. **Trample on** sometimes means treat with scorn or cruelty. The selfish king trampled on the rights of his people. 3. act or sound of trampling. We heard the trample of many feet.

trance (trans), 1. state or condition somewhat like sleep, in which the mind seems to have left the body. A person may be in a trance from illness, from the influence of some other person, or from his own will. 2. dreamy or absorbed condition which is like a trance. The old man sat before the fire in a trance, thinking of his past life.

tran quil (trang′kwil), calm; peaceful; quiet.

tran quil li ty (trang kwil′i ti), tranquil condition; calmness; peacefulness; quiet.

trans act (tran zakt′), do; manage; attend to; carry on (business). He transacts business with stores all over the country. A lawyer will transact many affairs connected with the purchase of a home.

trans ac tion (tran zak′shən), 1. carrying on (of business). Mr. Smith attends to the transaction of important matters himself. 2. piece of business. A record is kept of all the firm's transactions.

trans con ti nen tal (trans′kon ti nen′təl), 1. crossing a continent; as, a transcontinental railroad. 2. on the other side of a continent.

trans fer (trans fėr′ for 1, 2, and 5, trans′fər for 3, 4, 6, and 7), 1. convey or remove from one person or place to another; hand over. This farm has been transferred from father to son for generations. Please have my trunks transferred to the Union Station. 2. convey (a drawing, design, pattern) from one surface to another. You transfer the embroidery design from the paper to cloth by pressing it with a warm iron. 3. a transferring or being transferred. 4. thing transferred. 5. change from one streetcar, bus, or train to another. 6. ticket allowing a passenger to continue his journey on another streetcar, bus, or train. 7. a point or place for transferring.

trans form (trans fôrm′), 1. change in form or appearance. A tadpole becomes transformed into a frog. 2. change in condition, nature, or character. The witch transformed men into pigs.

trans for ma tion (trans′fər mā′shən), transforming; as, the transformation of a caterpillar into a butterfly, the transformation of a thief into an honest man.

trans gress (trans gres′), 1. go beyond (a limit or bound). Her manners transgressed the bounds of good taste. 2. break (a law); act against (a command); sin.

tran sient (tran′shənt), 1. passing soon; fleeting; not lasting. Joy and sorrow are often transient. 2. a visitor or boarder who stays for a short time.

tran sit (tran′sit), 1. passing across or through. 2. carrying across or through. The goods were damaged in transit.

tran si tion (tran zish′ən), a change or passing from one condition, place, or thing to another. The life of Lincoln illustrates a transition from poverty to power. Abrupt transitions in a book confuse the reader. In music, a transition is a change of key.

trans late (trans lāt′), 1. change from one language into another. 2. change into other words. 3. change from one place, position, or condition to another. She was translated to the fairy palace in a second.

trans la tion (trans lā′shən), 1. act of translating; change into another language; change from one position or condition to another. 2. result of translating; version.

trans lu cent (trans lü′sənt), letting light through, but not transparent. Frosted glass is translucent.

trans mis sion (trans mish′ən), 1. sending over; passing along. Mosquitoes are the only means of transmission of malaria. 2. the part of an automobile which transmits power from the engine to the rear axle. 3. passing through space of radio waves. When transmission is good, foreign stations can be received.

trans mit (trans mit′), 1. send over; pass on; pass along; let through. I transmitted the money by special messenger. Rats transmit disease. 2. send out (signals, voice, music, etc.) by radio. Some station is transmitting every hour of the day.

trans par ent (trans pãr′ənt), easily seen through. Window glass is transparent. Oscar offered a transparent excuse.

trans plant (trans plant′), 1. plant again in a different place. We start the flowers indoors and then transplant them to the garden. 2. remove from one place to another. All the people in the village were transplanted from Canada to Louisiana.

trans port (trans pōrt′ for 1, 5, and 7, trans′pōrt for 2, 3, 4, and 6), 1. carry from one place to another. Wheat is transported from the farms to the mills. 2. carrying from one place to another. Trucks are much used for transport. 3. ship used to carry men and supplies. 4. airplane that transports passengers, mail, freight, etc. 5. carry away by strong feeling. She was transported with joy by the good news. 6. strong feeling. 7. send away to another country as a punishment.

trans por ta tion (trans′pōr tā′shən), 1. transporting; being transported. The railroad gives free transportation for a certain amount of baggage. 2. means of transport. 3. cost of transport; ticket for transport. 4. sending away to another country as a punishment.

trans verse (trans vėrs′), 1. lying across; placed crosswise; crossing from side to side; as, transverse beams. 2. something transverse.

trap (trap), 1. thing or means for catching animals. 2. trick or other means for catching someone off guard. The police set traps to make the thief tell where the money was. 3. catch in a trap. The bear was trapped. 4. set traps for animals. Some Indians make their living by trapping. 5. door in a floor or roof. 6. a U-shaped bend in a pipe to prevent the escape of air or gas. 7. a light, two-wheeled carriage.

trap door, door in a floor or roof.

tra peze (trə pēz′), a short, horizontal bar hung by ropes like a swing, used in gymnasiums and circuses. See the picture.

Trapeze

trap per (trap′ər), one who traps; especially, a man who traps wild animals for their furs.

trap pings (trap′ingz), 1. ornamental coverings for a horse. 2. ornaments; things worn; as, trappings of a king and his court.

trash (trash), 1. worthless stuff; rubbish. That magazine is simply trash. 2. broken or torn bits. Rake up the trash in the yard and burn it.

trav ail (trav′āl), 1. toil; labor. 2. trouble; hardship.

trav el (trav′əl), 1. go from one place to another; journey. She is traveling in Europe this summer. 2. going from one place to another. She loves travel.

trav el er or **trav el ler** (trav′əl ər), one who travels.

trav erse (trav′ərs or trə vėrs′), 1. pass across; go across. We traversed the desert. 2. something put or lying across.

tray (trā), a flat, shallow holder with a rim around it. The waiter carries the dishes on a tray. She keeps her brush and comb in one tray, and her hairpins in another. Her trunk has two trays.

treach er ous (trech′ər əs), 1. not to be trusted; not faithful. The treacherous soldier carried reports to the enemy. 2. deceiving; not reliable; having a false appearance of strength, security, etc. Thin ice is treacherous.

treach er y (trech′ər i), 1. deceit; breaking faith; treacherous behavior. Arthur's kingdom was destroyed by treachery. 2. treason.

trea cle (trē′kəl), molasses.

tread (tred), 1. walk; step; set the foot down. Don't tread on the flower beds. 2. press under the feet; trample; crush. Tread out the fire before you go away. Joe trod on the snake and killed it. 3. make or form by walking. Cattle had trodden a path to the pond. 4. way of walking; step. He walks with a heavy tread. 5. the part of stairs or a ladder that a person steps on. The stair treads were covered with rubber to prevent slipping. 6. the part of a wheel or tire that touches the ground.

trod and **trodden** are formed from **tread.**

trea son (trē′zən), 1. a being false to one's country or to one's king. Helping the enemies of one's country is treason. 2. betraying a trust; treachery.

treas ure (trezh′ər), 1. wealth or riches stored up; valuable things. The pirates buried treasure along the coast. The palace contains treasures. 2. anything that is much valued; person loved. The silver teapot was the old lady's chief treasure. 3. value highly. She treasures that doll more than all her other toys. 4. put away for future use; store up.

treas ur er (trezh′ər ər), person in charge of money. The treasurer of a club pays its bills.

treas ur y (trezh′ər i), 1. place where money is kept. The national treasury is in Washington, D.C. 2. funds; money owned. We voted to pay for the party out of the club treasury. 3. department which has charge of the income and expenses of a country. 4. place where treasure is kept.

treat (trēt), 1. act toward. The driver treats his horses well. 2. deal with to relieve or cure. The dentist is treating my tooth. 3. discuss; express in literature or art. *The Medical Journal* treats of the progress of medicine. 4. discuss terms; arrange terms. Messengers came to treat for peace. 5. give food, drink, or amusement. He treated his friends to ice cream. 6. gift of food, drink, or amusement. "This is my treat," said Helen. 7. anything that gives pleasure. Being in the country is a treat to Jane.

trea tise (trē′tis), a book or other writing treating of some subject. A treatise is more formal and systematic than most books.

treat ment (trēt′mənt), 1. act or process of treating. My cold won't yield to treatment. 2. way of treating. This cat has suffered from bad treatment. 3. thing done or used to treat something else.

trea ty (trē′ti), an agreement between nations.

tre ble (treb′əl), 1. three times. His salary is treble mine. 2. make or become three times as much. He trebled his money by buying a dog for $5 and selling it for $15. 3. the highest part in music; soprano. The treble and the bass sang a duet.

tree (trē), 1. a large plant with a woody trunk, branches, and leaves. 2. anything like a tree. A **family tree** is a diagram with branches showing how the members of a family are related. 3. drive up a tree. The cat was treed by a dog.

trel lis (trel′is), frame of light strips of wood or metal crossing one another with open spaces in between; lattice.

Trellis

trem ble (trem′bəl), 1. shake because of fear, excitement, weakness, cold, etc. The old woman's hands trembled. Her voice trembled with fear. 2. move gently. The leaves trembled in the breeze. 3. a trembling. There was a tremble in her voice as she began to recite.

tre men dous (tri men′dəs), 1. dreadful; very severe. The army suffered a tremendous defeat. 2. very great.

trem or (trem′ər), 1. a shaking or trembling; as, a nervous tremor in the voice. 2. thrill of emotion or excitement.

trem u lous (trem′ū ləs), 1. trembling; quivering. The child's voice was tremulous with sobs. 2. timid; feeling fear.

trench (trench), 1. a long, narrow ditch with earth thrown up in front to protect soldiers. 2. ditch. 3. dig a trench in.

trench er (tren′chər), wooden platter on which meat was formerly served and carved.

trend (trend), 1. general direction; course; tendency. The hills have a western trend. The trend of modern living is away from many old customs. 2. have a general direction; tend; run. The road trends to the north.

trep i da tion (trep′i dā′shən), 1. fear; fright. 2. trembling.

tres pass (tres′pəs), 1. go on somebody's property without any right. The farmer put up "No Trespassing" signs to keep people off his farm. 2. go beyond the limits of what is right. I won't trespass on your time any longer. 3. a trespassing. 4. do wrong; sin; a wrong; a sin. "Forgive us our trespasses as we forgive those who trespass against us."

tress (tres), a lock, curl, or braid of hair; as, golden tresses.

tres tle (tres′əl), frame used as a support.

Trestle

tri al (trī′əl), 1. process of trying or testing. He gave the machine another trial to see if it would work. 2. for a try or test; as, a trial trip. 3. examining and deciding a case in court. Many thieves are caught and brought to trial. 4. trouble; hardship. Her life has been full of trials—sickness, poverty, and loss of loved ones.

tri an gle (trī′ang′gəl), 1. a figure having three sides and three angles. 2. a musical instrument made of a triangle of steel that is struck with a steel rod.

Triangles

tri an gu lar (trī ang′gū lər), shaped like a triangle; three-cornered.

trib al (trīb′əl), of a tribe.

tribe (trīb), 1. group of people united by race and customs under the same leaders. America was once the home of savage tribes of Indians. 2. class or set of people; as, the tribe of artists, the whole tribe of gossips. 3. class, kind, or sort of animals, plants, or other things. The feathered tribe is a name for birds.

trib u la tion (trib′u lā′shən), affliction; great trouble; severe trial. The early Christians suffered many tribulations.

tri bu nal (tri bū′nəl), court of justice; place of judgment. He was brought before the tribunal for trial.

trib u tar y (trib′ū tãr′i), 1. stream that flows into a larger stream or body of water. The Ohio River is one of the tributaries of the Mississippi River. 2. flowing into a larger stream or body of water. 3. paying tribute; required to pay tribute. 4. one that pays tribute.

trib ute (trib′ūt), 1. money paid by one nation to another for peace or protection or because of some agreement. 2. any forced payment. 3. an acknowledgment of thanks or respect; compliment. Memorial Day is a tribute to our dead soldiers.

trick (trik), 1. something done to deceive or cheat. The false message was a trick to get him to leave the house. 2. deceive; cheat. We were tricked into buying a poor car. 3. clever act; feat of skill. We enjoyed the tricks of the trained animals. 4. piece of mischief. Stealing John's lunch was a mean trick. 5. a peculiar habit or way of acting. He has a trick of pulling at his collar. 6. the cards played in one round. 7. a turn at steering a ship. 8. dress. Alice was tricked out in her mother's clothes.

trick er y (trik′ər i), use of tricks; deception; cheating.

trick le (trik′əl), 1. flow or fall in drops or in a small stream. Tears trickled down her cheeks. The brook trickled through the valley. 2. small flow or stream.

trick y (trik′i), 1. full of tricks; deceiving. A fox is trickier than a sheep. 2. not doing what is expected. The back door has a tricky lock.

tri col or (trī′kul′ər), 1. having three colors. 2. flag having three colors.

tri cy cle (trī′si kəl), three-wheeled vehicle worked by pedals or handles. Sometimes tricycles are used by lame people.

tri dent (trī′dənt), spear with three prongs.

tried (trīd), 1. tested; proved. 2. See **try.**

tri fle (trī′fəl), 1. thing having little value or importance. Do not worry about trifles. 2. small amount; little bit. Dick was a trifle late. 3. small amount of money. The picture cost only a trifle. 4. talk or act lightly, not seriously. Don't trifle with serious matters. 5. play (with); handle. He trifled with his pencil and pen. 6. spend (time, effort, money, etc.) on things having little value. She had trifled away the whole morning.

tri fler (trī′flər), person who trifles.

tri fling (trī′fling), 1. having little value; not important; small. 2. frivolous; shallow.

trig ger (trig′ər), 1. the lever pulled back by the finger in firing a gun. 2. a lever which releases a spring when pulled or pressed.

T, trigger of a gun.

trill (tril), 1. sing, play, sound, or speak with a tremulous, vibrating sound. Some birds trill their songs. 2. act or sound of trilling.

trim (trim), 1. put in good order; make neat by cutting away parts. The gardener trims the hedge. The barber trimmed Father's hair and beard. 2. neat; in good condition or order. A trim maid appeared. 3. good condition or order. 4. decorate. The children were trimming the Christmas tree. 5. balance (a boat) by arranging the load carried. 6. arrange (the sails) to fit wind and direction. 7. change (opinions, etc.) to suit circumstances.

trim ming (trim′ing), ornament; anything used to trim or decorate; as, the trimmings of a Christmas tree, trimming for a dress.

trin ket (tring′kit), 1. any small fancy article, bit of jewelry, or the like. 2. a trifle.

tri o (trē′ō), 1. piece of music for three voices or instruments. 2. three singers or players. 3. any group of three.

trip (trip), 1. journey; as, a trip to Europe. 2. stumble. He tripped on a tree root. 3. cause to stumble. Dick tripped Harry. 4. make a mistake; commit a fault. 5. cause to make a mistake. Father tripped me by that question. 6. loss of footing; stumble; blunder. 7. take light quick steps. The children came tripping down the path to meet us. 8. light quick step.

tripe (trīp), the stomach of an ox, etc., used for food.

tri ple (trip′əl), 1. having three parts. 2. three times as much. 3. a number or amount three times as large. 4. make or become three times as much. Mary's brother has tripled his earnings—from $10 to $30 a week.

tri pod (trī′pod), a stool, frame, or stand with three legs. A camera is sometimes supported on a tripod.

tri umph (trī′umf), 1. victory; success. 2. gain victory; win success. Our team triumphed over theirs. 3. joy because of victory or success. John brought home the prize in triumph. 4. rejoice because of victory or success.

tri um phal (trī um′fəl), celebrating a victory.

tri um phant (trī um′fənt), 1. victorious; successful. 2. rejoicing because of victory or success. The winner spoke in triumphant tones to his defeated rival.

triv i al (triv′i əl), not important. Your composition has only a few trivial mistakes.

trod (trod). See **tread.** He trod on a tack. The path was trod by many feet.

trod den (trod′ən). See **tread.** The cattle had trodden down the corn.

troll[1] (trōl), 1. sing in a full, rolling voice. 2. sing in succession. When three people troll a song or catch, the soprano sings one line, the alto comes in next with the same line, and then the bass sings it, and so on, while the others keep on singing. 3. song whose parts are sung in succession. "Three Blind Mice" is a well-known troll. 4. to fish with a moving line. He trolled for bass. In trolling, a man usually trails the line behind his boat near the surface.

troll[2] (trōl), ugly giant or dwarf living in caves or underground.

Troll

trol ley (trol′i), 1. pulley moving against a wire to carry electricity to a streetcar, electric engine, etc. 2. electric streetcar. 3. pulley running on an overhead track, used to support and move a load.

troop (trüp), 1. a company; a group; as, a troop of boys, a troop of deer. 2. **Troops** often means soldiers. 3. cavalry unit having 60 to 100 men commanded by a captain. 4. unit of 16 or 32 Boy Scouts. 5. gather in troops or bands; move together. The children trooped around the teacher. 6. walk; go; go away. The young boys trooped off after the older ones.

troop er (trüp′ər), 1. soldier in a troop of cavalry. 2. mounted policeman.

tro phy (trō′fi), memorial of victory. The hunter kept the lion's skin and head as trophies.

trop i cal (trop′i kəl), of the tropics. Bananas are tropical fruit.

trop ics (trop′iks), regions near the equator, between 23½ degrees north and 23½ degrees south of it.

trot (trot), 1. go by lifting the right forefoot and the left hind foot at about the same time. Horses trot. 2. the motion of a trotting horse. 3. ride at a trot. 4. make (a horse) trot. 5. run, but not fast. The child trotted along after his mother.

troth (trôth), 1. faithfulness; fidelity; loyalty. "I plight my troth" means "I promise to be faithful." 2. promise. 3. truth.

trou ble (trub′əl), 1. disturb; cause distress or worry to. We sailed on troubled waters. She is troubled by headaches. Don't let what George says trouble you. 2. disturbance; distress; worry; difficulty. That boy makes trouble for his teachers. Jim has stomach trouble. 3. extra work; bother; effort. We have gone to a great deal of trouble for her. If she won't take the trouble to answer our letters, we shall stop writing. 4. cause extra work or effort to. May I trouble you to pass the sugar? 5. cause oneself inconvenience. Don't trouble to come to the door.

trou ble some (trub′əl səm), causing trouble; annoying; full of trouble.

trou blous (trub′ləs), 1. disturbed; restless. 2. troublesome.

trough (trôf), 1. a long, narrow container for holding food or water. He led the horses to the watering trough. 2. something shaped like this. The baker uses a trough for kneading dough. 3. channel for carrying water; gutter. A wooden trough under the eaves of the house carries off rain water. 4. a long hollow between two ridges; as, the trough between two waves.

troupe (trüp), troop; band; company; especially, a group of actors, singers, or acrobats.

trou sers (trou′zərz), a two-legged outer garment reaching from the waist to the ankles or knees. Bob wears long trousers.

trout (trout), a fresh-water food fish. Dick caught nine trout in the brook.

trow (trō), believe; think.

trow el (trou′əl), 1. a tool for spreading or smoothing plaster or mortar. 2. a tool for taking up plants, loosening dirt, etc.

A

B

Trowels: A, for plaster; B, for plants.

troy (troi). One pound troy equals a little over four fifths of an ordinary pound. 12 troy ounces = 1 troy pound. Troy weight is used for gems and precious metals.

tru ant (trü′ənt), 1. child who stays away from school without permission. 2. person who neglects duty. 3. neglecting duty. The truant shepherd left his sheep. 4. wandering. That truant dog won't stay at home.

truce (trüs), 1. a stop in fighting; peace for a short time. A truce was declared between the two armies. 2. a rest from trouble or pain. The hot weather gave the old man a truce from rheumatism.

truck[1] (truk), 1. an automobile, big cart, or wagon for carrying heavy loads. 2. carry on a truck. 3. frame with two or more pairs of wheels for supporting the end of a railroad car, locomotive, etc. 4. small wheel.

truck[2] (truk), 1. vegetables raised for market. 2. rubbish; trash.

trudge (truj), 1. walk. 2. walk wearily or with effort. 3. a hard or weary walk. It was a long trudge up the hill.

true (trü), 1. agreeing with fact; not false. It is true that 6 and 4 are 10. 2. real; genuine; as, true gold, true kindness. 3. faithful; loyal; as, my truest friend, true to your promises. 4. agreeing with a standard; correct; exact. This is a true copy of my letter. 5. rightful; lawful; as, the true heir to the property. 6. in a true manner; truly; exactly. His words ring true.

tru ly (trü′li), 1. in a true manner; exactly; rightly; faithfully. Tell me truly what you think. 2. really; in fact. It was truly a beautiful party.

trum pet (trum′pit), 1. a musical wind instrument that has a powerful tone. 2. thing shaped like a trumpet. The deaf old lady has an ear trumpet to help her hearing. 3. blow a trumpet. 4. a sound like that of a trumpet. 5. make a sound like a trumpet. The elephant trumpeted. 6. proclaim loudly or widely. She'll trumpet that story all over town.

Man playing a trumpet

trum pet er (trum′pit ər), person who blows a trumpet.

trun dle (trun′dəl), roll along; push along. The workman trundled a wheelbarrow hour after hour.

trunk (trungk), 1. the main stem of a tree. 2. the main part of anything; as, the trunk of a column. 3. main; chief; as, the trunk line of a railroad. 4. big box for holding clothes, etc., when traveling. 5. a body without the head, arms, and legs. 6. elephant's snout. 7. **Trunks** sometimes means very short trousers or breeches worn by athletes, swimmers, acrobats, etc.

Trunk for clothes

truss (trus), 1. tie; fasten. The cook trussed up the chicken before roasting it. 2. beams connected to form a support for a roof, bridge, etc. 3. bandage or pad used for support. 4. bundle of hay or straw.

trust (trust), 1. faith; firm belief in someone's honesty, truth, justice, or power. A child puts trust in his mother. 2. believe firmly in the honesty, truth, justice, or power of another; have faith in. "In God we trust." 3. rely on; depend on. A forgetful man should not trust his memory, but should write things down in a notebook. 4. person or thing believed in. God is our trust. 5. obligation assumed by a person who takes charge of another's property. Mr. Adams will be faithful to his trust. 6. commit to the care of; let be with. Can I trust the keys to Jack? 7. hope; believe. I trust you will soon feel better. 8. business credit. When you buy anything and do not pay for it until later, you are getting it on trust. 9. give business credit to. The butcher will trust us for the meat.

trus tee (trus tē′), person responsible for the property or affairs of another person, a company, or an institution. A trustee will manage the children's property until they grow up.

trust ful (trust′fəl), trusting; ready to confide. Trustful Paul would lend money to any of his friends.

trust ing (trus′ting), that trusts; trustful.

trust wor thy (trust′wėr′ᴛʜi), that can be depended on; reliable. The class chose a trustworthy boy for treasurer.

trust y (trus′ti), 1. that can be depended on; reliable. The master left his money with a trusty servant. 2. a prisoner who is given special privileges because of his good behavior. Two trusties were sent to town on an errand.

truth (trüth), 1. that which is true. Tell the truth. 2. true, exact, honest, sincere, or loyal quality or nature.

truth ful (trüth′fəl), telling the truth. George is a truthful boy and will tell what really happened.

try (trī), 1. attempt; make an effort. If at first you don't succeed, try, try again. 2. an attempt. Each boy had three tries at the high jump. 3. experiment on; make trial. Try this candy and see if you like it. 4. test; find out about. We try each car before we sell it. 5. **Try on** means put on to test the fit, etc. Helen tried on her new dress. 6. investigate in a law court. The man was tried and found guilty of murder. 7. strain. Don't try your eyes by reading in a poor light. Her mistakes try my patience. 8. make pure by melting or boiling. The lard was tried in a big kettle.

try ing (trī′ing), hard to endure; annoying; distressing; as, a trying day.

tub (tub), 1. open container for washing or bathing. 2. a round wooden container for holding butter, lard, etc. 3. as much as a tub can hold. 4. bathtub. 5. bath. He takes a cold tub every morning.

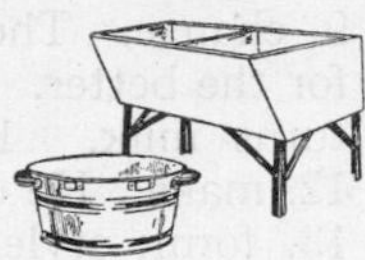
Tubs for washing

tube (tūb or tüb), 1. long pipe of metal, glass, rubber, etc. Tubes are mostly used to hold or carry liquids or gases. 2. small cylinder of thin, easily bent metal with a cap that screws on the open end, used for holding tooth paste, ointment, paint, etc. 3. a pipe or tunnel through which something is sent. The railroad runs under the river in a tube. 4. thing like a tube; as, a radio tube.

tu ber (tū′bər or tü′bər), thick part of an underground stem. A potato is a tuber.

tu ber cu lo sis (tū bėr′kū lō′sis or tü bėr′kū-lō′sis), a disease affecting various tissues of the body, but most often the lungs. Tuberculosis of the lungs is often called consumption. Rest, good food, and sunshine will usually cure tuberculosis.

tuck (tuk), 1. thrust into some narrow space or into some out-of-the-way place. She tucked her purse under her arm. He tucked the letter in his pocket. The little cottage is tucked away under the hill. 2. thrust the edge or end of (a garment or covering) closely into place. Jack tucked a napkin under his chin. Mother comes every night to tuck in the bedclothes. 3. draw close together; fold. A bird tucks his head under his wing when he sleeps. **Tuck up** means draw together and up. He tucked up his sleeves before washing his hands. 4. a fold sewed in a garment. The dress was too long; so mother took a tuck in it. 5. sew a fold in a garment for trimming or to make it shorter. The baby's dress was beautifully tucked with tiny stitches.

Tues day (tūz′di or tüz′di), the third day of the week.

tuft (tuft), 1. bunch of feathers, hair, grass, etc., held together at one end. A goat has a tuft of hair on its chin. 2. clump of bushes, trees, etc. 3. put tufts on; furnish with tufts.

tug (tug), 1. pull with force or effort; pull hard. We tugged the boat in to shore. The child tugged at his mother's hand. 2. hard pull. The baby gave a tug at Mary's hair. 3. a small and powerful steamboat used to tow other boats. 4. tow by a tug. 5. one of a pair of long leather straps by which a horse pulls a wagon, cart, etc. See the diagram under **harness.**

Tug

tu i tion (tū ish′ən or tü ish′ən), 1. teaching; instruction. 2. money paid for instruction.

tu lip (tū′lip or tü′lip), a spring flower having various colors. Tulips are grown from bulbs.

Tulip

tum ble (tum′bəl), 1. fall. The child tumbled down the stairs. The tumble hurt him badly. 2. throw over or down; cause to fall. 3. roll or toss about. The sick child tumbled restlessly in his bed. 4. move in a hurried or awkward way. Jim tumbled out of bed. 5. perform leaps, springs, somersaults, etc. 6. turn over; rumple. 7. confusion; disorder.

tum bler (tum′blər), 1. person who performs leaps or springs; acrobat. 2. a drinking glass.

tu mult (tū′mult or tü′mult), 1. noise; uproar. The sailors' voices could not be heard above the tumult of the storm. 2. violent disturbance or disorder. The cry of "Fire! Fire!" caused a tumult in the theater.

tu mul tu ous (tū mul′chü əs or tü mul′chü əs), 1. very noisy or disorderly. The football team celebrated its victory in a tumultuous fashion. 2. greatly disturbed. 3. rough; stormy. Tumultuous waves beat upon the rocks.

tu na (tü′nə), large sea fish used for food. Some tunas are ten feet long.

tun dra (tun′drə), a vast, level, treeless plain in the Arctic regions. The ground beneath the surface of the tundras is frozen even in summer.

tune (tūn or tün), 1. piece of music; an air or melody; as, hymn tunes. 2. the proper pitch. The piano is out of tune. He can't sing in tune. 3. agreement; harmony. A person out of tune with his surroundings is unhappy. 4. put in tune. A man is tuning the piano. 5. **Tune in** means adjust a radio to hear (what is wanted).

tune ful (tūn′fəl or tün′fəl), musical; melodious. A lark has a tuneful song.

tu nic (tū′nik or tü′nik), 1. garment like a shirt or gown, worn by the ancient Greeks and Romans; any garment like it. 2. woman's dress, coat, or blouse extending below the waist. 3. soldier's coat.

Tunic

tun nel (tun′əl), 1. underground passage. The railroad passes under the mountain through a tunnel. 2. make a tunnel. A mole tunnels in the ground. The workmen are tunneling under the river.

tun ny (tun′i), a large sea fish used for food; the tuna.

tur ban (tėr′bən), 1. a scarf wound around the head or around a cap, worn by men in Oriental countries. 2. a headdress like this. The old woman wore a bright-colored turban. 3. small hat with little or no brim, worn by women and children.

Oriental turban

tur bu lent (tėr′bū lənt), 1. disorderly; unruly; violent. A turbulent mob rushed into the store. 2. greatly disturbed.

turf (tėrf), 1. grass with its roots; sod. We cut some turfs from a field and covered a bare spot with them. 2. piece of this. 3. cover with turf. 4. peat. 5. place where horses race. 6. horse racing.

tur key (tėr′ki), 1. a large American bird. See the picture. 2. the flesh of the turkey, used for food. We ate two turkeys on Christmas day.

Turkey (2 to 4 ft. long)

tur moil (tėr′moil), commotion; disturbance; trouble. Six robberies in one night put our village in a turmoil.

turn (tėrn), 1. move round as a wheel does. 2. cause to move round as a wheel does. I turned the crank three times. 3. motion like that of a wheel. At each turn the screw goes in further. 4. move part way round. Turn over on your back. 5. take a new direction. The road turns to the north here. 6. give a new direction to. Turn your thoughts to work. 7. change of direction. A turn to the left brought him in front of us. 8. change; change and become. She turned pale. 9. change. The sick man has taken a turn for the better. 10. spoil; sour. Hot weather turns milk. 11. become sour or spoiled. 12. make. He can turn pretty compliments. 13. form; style. He has a serious turn of mind. 14. unsettle; put out of order. Too much praise turned his head. 15. depend. The success of the picnic turns on the weather. 16. twist. 17. opportunity; occasion. It is Bob's turn to read. 18. deed; act. One good turn deserves another. 19. a walk, drive, or ride. 20. make sick. The sight of blood turns my stomach. 21. become dizzy. 22. Some special meanings are:

by turns, one after another.

in turn, in proper order.

turn off, 1. discharge. 2. shut off. 3. put out (light).

turn out, 1. put out. 2. drive out. 3. come out; go out. 4. make; produce. 5. result. 6. be found or known.

turn over, 1. think about. 2. give.

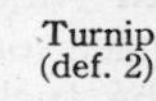

Turnip (def. 2)

tur nip (tėr′nip), 1. a plant with a large roundish root that is used as a vegetable. 2. this root.

turn pike (tėrn′pīk′), 1. gate where toll is paid. 2. road that has, or used to have, a gate where toll is paid.

turn spit (tėrn′spit′), one that turns a roast of meat on a spit.

turn stile (tėrn′stīl′), post with two crossed bars that turn, set in an entrance.

tur pen tine (tėr′pən tīn), an oil obtained from pines and similar trees. Turpentine is used in mixing paints and varnishes, and in medicine.

Turrets of a building

tur quoise (tėr′koiz), 1. a sky-blue or greenish-blue precious stone. 2. sky blue; greenish blue.

tur ret (tėr′it), 1. small tower, often on the corner of a building. See the picture just above.

2. a low armored structure which revolves and within which guns are mounted.

tur tle (tėr′təl), an animal having a hard shell and a soft body. To **turn turtle** is to turn bottom side up.

Turtle

tusk (tusk), a very long, pointed, projecting tooth. Elephants, walruses, and wild boars have tusks. See the picture just below.

tus sle (tus′əl), struggle; wrestle; scuffle.

tut (tut), an exclamation of impatience, contempt, or rebuke.

Tusks of a walrus

tu tor (tū′tər or tü′tər), 1. private teacher. Rich children sometimes have tutors instead of going to school. 2. teach; instruct. In some schools, the bright pupils tutor the dull ones.

twain (twān), an old or poetic word for two. Sir Richard broke his sword in twain.

twang (twang), 1. a sharp ringing sound. The bow made a twang when I shot the arrow. 2. make a sharp ringing sound. The banjos twanged. 3. a sharp nasal tone; as, the twang of a Yankee farmer. 4. speak with a sharp nasal tone.

'twas (twoz), it was.

tweed (twēd), 1. a woolen cloth with a rough surface. Tweed is sometimes made of wool and cotton, and usually has two or more colors. 2. **Tweeds** are clothes made of tweed.

twelfth (twelfth), 1. next after the 11th. Lincoln's birthday comes on February twelfth. 2. one of 12 equal parts. Two is a twelfth of twenty-four.

twelve (twelv), one more than 11; 12. A year has twelve months.

twelve month (twelv′munth′), 12 months; a year.

twen ti eth (twen′ti ith), 1. next after the 19th. 2. one of 20 equal parts.

twen ty (twen′ti), two times ten; 20.

'twere (twėr), it were.

twice (twīs), 1. two times. Twice two is four. 2. doubly.

twig (twig), slender shoot of a tree or other plant; very small branch. Dry twigs are good to start a fire with.

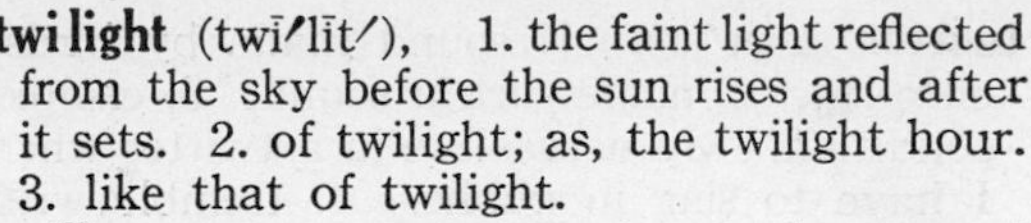

twi light (twī′līt′), 1. the faint light reflected from the sky before the sun rises and after it sets. 2. of twilight; as, the twilight hour. 3. like that of twilight.

twill (twil), cloth woven in raised diagonal lines. Serge is a twill.

'twill (twil), it will.

twin (twin), 1. one of two children or animals born at the same time from the same mother. Twins sometimes look just alike. 2. being one of two things very much alike. Twin candlesticks stood on the shelf. 3. having two like parts.

twine (twīn), 1. a strong thread or string made of two or more strands twisted together. 2. twist together. She twined holly into wreaths. 3. wind. The vine twines around the tree.

twinge (twinj), 1. a sudden sharp pain; as, a twinge of rheumatism, a twinge of remorse. 2. feel such pain.

twin kle (twing′kəl), 1. shine with quick little gleams. Stars twinkle. Jack's eyes twinkled when he laughed. 2. a twinkling; sparkle. Santa Claus has a merry twinkle in his eye. 3. move quickly. The dancer's feet twinkled.

twirl (twėrl), 1. revolve rapidly; spin; whirl. 2. turn round and round idly. 3. twirling; spin; whirl; turn; as, a twirl in a dance.

twist (twist), 1. turn; wind. She twisted her ring on her finger. 2. wind together. This rope is twisted from many threads. Mary twisted flowers into a wreath. 3. have a winding shape; curve or bend in any way. The path twists in and out among the rocks. 4. curve; crook; bend. 5. force out of shape or place. His face was twisted with pain. The lawyer confused the witness by twisting his words into different meanings. 6. twisting; being twisted. 7. anything made by twisting; as, a twist of bread. 8. a thread, cord, or rope made of two or more strands twisted together.

twitch (twich), 1. move with a quick jerk. The child's mouth twitched as if she were about to cry. 2. a quick jerky movement of some part of the body. 3. pull with a sudden tug or jerk; pull (at). She twitched the curtain aside. 4. a short sudden pull or jerk. He felt a twitch at his watch chain.

twit ter (twit′ər), 1. sound made by birds; chirping. 2. make such a sound. 3. excited condition. My nerves are in a twitter when I have to sing in public. 4. tremble with excitement.

two (tü). We count one, two, three, four. Two means 2.

two fold (tü′fōld′), 1. two times as much or as many; double. 2. having two parts.

two pence (tup′əns), two British pennies. Twopence equals about four cents.

'twould (twu̇d), it would.

ty ing (tī′ing). See **tie.** He is tying his shoes.

type (tīp), 1. a kind, class, or group alike in some important way. Some men prefer women of the blonde type. 2. person or thing having the characteristics of a kind, class, or group; representative; symbol. John is a fine type of schoolboy. 3. the general form, style, or character of some kind, class, or group. Mary is above the ordinary type of servant. 4. piece of metal or wood having on its upper surface a letter for use in printing. 5. collection of such pieces. 6. write with a typewriter.

type writ er (tīp′rīt′ər), 1. machine for making letters on paper. 2. person who writes with a typewriter.

ty phoid (tī′foid), 1. **Typhoid fever** is an infectious, often fatal, fever, with intestinal inflammation, caused by a germ taken into the body with food or drink. People can be inoculated against typhoid. 2. of typhoid fever.

typ i cal (tip′i kəl), being a type; representative. The typical Thanksgiving dinner consists of turkey, cranberry sauce, several vegetables, and mince pie or pumpkin pie.

typ i fy (tip′i fī), 1. be a symbol of. The lamb typifies Christ's sacrifice. 2. have the common characteristics of. Daniel Boone typifies the pioneer.

ty ran ni cal (ti ran′i kəl), of a tyrant; like a tyrant; arbitrary; cruel or unjust.

tyr an ny (tir′ə ni), 1. cruel or unjust use of power. The boy ran away to sea to escape his father's tyranny. 2. tyrannical act. The colonists rebelled against the king's tyrannies. 3. government by an absolute ruler.

ty rant (tī′rənt), 1. cruel or unjust ruler; cruel master. 2. absolute ruler.

U

U-boat (ū′bōt′), German submarine.

ud der (ud′ər), the bag of a cow or goat from which the milk comes.

ugh (u̇h or u), an exclamation expressing disgust or horror.

ug li ness (ug′li nis), ugly appearance; being ugly.

ug ly (ug′li), 1. bad to look at; as, an ugly weed, an ugly toad. 2. disagreeable; unpleasant; bad; offensive; as, an ugly task, an ugly scowl, ugly curses. 3. threatening; dangerous; as, an ugly wound. 4. cross; bad-tempered; quarrelsome; as, an ugly dog.

um brel la (um brel′ə), a light, folding frame covered with cloth, used as a protection against rain or sun.

um pire (um′pīr), 1. person who rules on the plays in a game. The umpire called the ball a foul. 2. person chosen to settle a dispute. 3. act as umpire in (a game, dispute, etc.).

un a ble (un ā′bəl), not able. A little baby is unable to walk or talk.

un ac count a ble (un′ə koun′tə bəl), 1. that cannot be accounted for or explained. 2. not responsible.

un ac cus tomed (un′ə kus′təmd), 1. not accustomed. 2. unusual.

un aid ed (un ād′id), not aided; without help.

u na nim i ty (ū′nə nim′i ti), complete accord or agreement.

u nan i mous (ū nan′i məs), in complete accord or agreement; agreed. The children were unanimous in their wish to ride to the beach. George was elected president of his class by a unanimous vote.

u nan i mous ly (ū nan′i məs li), with complete agreement; without a single opposing vote.

un arm (un ärm′), 1. take weapons or armor from; disarm. 2. take off (one's) armor.

un armed (un ärmd′), without weapons; without armor.

un as sum ing (un′ə süm′ing), modest; not putting on airs.

un at tend ed (un′ə ten′did), 1. without

attendants; alone. 2. not accompanied. 3. not taken care of; not attended to.

un a vail ing (un′ə vāl′ing), not successful; useless.

un a void a ble (un′ə void′ə bəl), that cannot be avoided.

un a ware (un′ə wãr′), 1. not aware; unconscious. The child was unaware of any danger from the snake. 2. without thought; unawares.

un a wares (un′ə wãrz′), 1. without knowing; as, "to entertain angels unawares." 2. without being expected; by surprise. The police caught the burglar unawares.

un bar (un bär′), unlock; remove the bars from.

un bear a ble (un bãr′ə bəl), that cannot be borne. The pain from a severe toothache is almost unbearable.

un be com ing (un′bi kum′ing), 1. not suiting; not appropriate. 2. not fitting; not proper.

un be liev ing (un′bi lēv′ing), not believing; doubting.

un bend (un bend′), 1. make or become straight; as, to unbend the fingers. 2. release from strain; as, to unbend a bow. 3. unfasten; as, to unbend a sail. 4. relax. The judge unbent and behaved like a boy.

un bid den (un bid′ən), 1. not bidden; not invited. 2. not commanded.

un bind (un bīnd′), untie; unfasten; let loose; release from bonds or restraint.

un bolt (un bōlt′), draw back the bolts of (a door, etc.).

un born (un bôrn′), not yet born; still to come; of the future.

un bos om (un bu̇z′əm), disclose; reveal. **Unbosom oneself** means tell one's feelings, thoughts, or secrets.

un bound (un bound′), 1. not bound. Unbound sheets of music were scattered about the room. 2. unfastened.

un bro ken (un brō′kən), 1. not broken; whole. 2. continuous; not interrupted. He had eight hours of unbroken sleep. 3. not tamed; as, an unbroken colt.

un buck le (un buk′əl), 1. unfasten the buckle or buckles of. 2. unfasten.

un but ton (un but′ən), unfasten the button or buttons of.

un called-for (un kôld′fôr′), 1. not called for. 2. unnecessary and improper.

un can ny (un kan′i), strange and mysterious; weird. The trees took uncanny shapes in the half darkness.

un ceas ing (un sēs′ing), continual.

un cer tain (un sėr′tən), 1. not certain; doubtful. Alice came so late that she was uncertain of her welcome. 2. likely to change; not to be depended on. This dog has an uncertain temper.

un cer tain ly (un sėr′tən li), in an uncertain way. Joe spoke slowly and uncertainly.

un cer tain ty (un sėr′tən ti), 1. uncertain state or condition; doubt. 2. something uncertain.

un chain (un chān′), free from chains; let loose; set free.

un change a ble (un chān′jə bəl), that cannot be changed.

un changed (un chānjd′), not changed; the same.

un clasp (un klasp′), 1. unfasten. 2. release from a clasp or grasp.

un cle (ung′kəl), 1. brother of one's father or mother. 2. husband of one's aunt.

un clean (un klēn′), 1. dirty; not clean. 2. not pure morally; evil.

Uncle Sam, the government or people of the United States.

un coil (un koil′), unwind.

un com fort a ble (un kum′fər tə bəl), 1. not comfortable. 2. uneasy. 3. disagreeable; causing discomfort.

un com mon (un kom′ən), 1. rare; unusual. 2. remarkable.

un com mon ly (un kom′ən li), 1. rarely; unusually. 2. especially. She is an uncommonly good cook.

un com pro mis ing (un kom′prə mīz′ing), unyielding; firm.

un con cern (un′kən sėrn′), lack of concern; lack of interest.

un con cerned (un′kən sėrnd′), not concerned; not interested; free from care or anxiety; indifferent.

un con quer a ble (un kong′kər ə bəl), that cannot be conquered.

un con scious (un kon′shəs), 1. not conscious. 2. not aware. 3. not meant; not intended; as, unconscious neglect.

un con scious ly (un kon′shəs li), without consciousness; without being aware of what one is doing.

un couth (un küth′), 1. awkward; clumsy; crude; as, uncouth manners. 2. unusual and unpleasant; strange. The poor idiot made uncouth noises.

un cov er (un kuv′ər), 1. remove the cover from. 2. reveal; expose; make known. 3. remove one's hat or cap. The men uncovered as the flag passed by.

un cul ti vat ed (un kul′ti vāt′id), not cultivated; wild; undeveloped.

un curl (un kėrl′), straighten out.

un daunt ed (un dôn′tid), not afraid; not discouraged; fearless. The captain was an undaunted leader.

un de cid ed (un′di sīd′id), 1. not decided; not settled. 2. having one's mind not made up.

un de ni a ble (un′di nī′ə bəl), that cannot be denied.

un der (un′dər), 1. below; beneath. The book fell under the table. 2. less than. The coat will cost under ten dollars. 3. lower; as, the under lip. 4. *Under* is used in many expressions that suggest the idea of being below or beneath. Some are: The witness spoke under oath. The soldiers acted under orders. We learned a great deal under her teaching.

un der brush (un′dər brush′), bushes, small trees, etc., growing under large trees in woods or forests.

un der fed (un′dər fed′), fed too little; not well nourished.

un der foot (un′dər fu̇t′), 1. under one's feet; on the ground. 2. in the way.

un der gar ment (un′dər gär′mənt), garment worn under a dress or suit.

un der go (un′dər gō′), 1. go through; pass through; be subjected to. The town has undergone a great change during the last five years. 2. endure; suffer. Soldiers undergo many hardships.

un der gone (un′dər gôn′). See **undergo.**

un der ground (un′dər ground′ for 1 and 4, un′dər ground′ for 2, 3, and 5), 1. beneath the surface of the ground. Miners work underground. 2. being, working, or used beneath the surface of the ground. 3. place or space beneath the surface of the ground. 4. secretly. 5. secret.

un der growth (un′dər grōth′), bushes, small trees, etc., growing under large trees in woods or forests.

un der hand (un′dər hand′), 1. secret; sly; not open or honest. 2. secretly; slyly. 3. with the hand below the shoulder; as, to pitch underhand.

un der mine (un′dər mīn′), 1. dig under; make a passage or hole under. The soldiers undermined the wall. 2. wear away the foundations of. The cliff was undermined by the waves. 3. weaken by secret or unfair means. Some people tried to undermine the President's influence by spreading lies about him. 4. weaken or destroy gradually. Many severe colds had undermined Jane's health.

un der neath (un′dər nēth′), beneath; below; under.

un der shirt (un′dər shėrt′), shirt worn next the skin under other clothing.

un der stand (un′dər stand′), 1. get the meaning. 2. get the meaning of. He does not understand the question. 3. know well; know how to deal with. A good teacher should understand children. 4. be informed; learn. I understand that Mr. Jones is leaving town. 5. take as a fact; believe. It is understood that you will come.

un der stand ing (un′dər stan′ding), 1. comprehension; knowledge; as, a clear understanding of the problem. 2. intelligence; ability to learn and know. Edison was a man of understanding. 3. knowledge of each other's meaning and wishes; agreement. You and I must come to an understanding. 4. that understands; intelligent.

un der stood (un′dər stu̇d′). See **understand.** Have all of you understood today's lesson?

un der take (un′dər tāk′), 1. try; attempt. 2. agree to do; promise. **undertook** and **undertaken** are formed from **undertake.**

un der tak er (un′dər tāk′ər for 1, un′dər-tāk′ər for 2), 1. person who undertakes something. 2. person who prepares the dead for burial and takes charge of funerals.

un der tak ing (un′dər tāk′ing), 1. a task; an enterprise. 2. a promise; a pledge.

un der tone (un′dər tōn′), 1. low tone; as, to talk in undertones. 2. a subdued color; a color seen through other colors. There was an undertone of brown beneath all the gold and crimson of autumn. 3. something beneath the surface; as, an undertone of sadness in her gaiety.

un der took (un′dər tu̇k′). See **undertake.** John undertook more than he could do.

un der wear (un′dər wãr′), clothing worn under one's outer clothes.

un der went (un′dər went′), passed through; endured. See **undergo.**

un der wood (un′dər wu̇d′), shrubs or small trees growing under larger trees; underbrush.

un de sir a ble (un′di zīr′ə bəl), objectionable; disagreeable.

un did (un did′), untied; destroyed. See **undo.**

un dig ni fied (un dig′ni fīd), not dignified; lacking dignity.

un dis put ed (un′dis pūt′id), not disputed; not doubted.

un dis turbed (un′dis tėrbd′), not disturbed; not troubled; calm.

un do (un dü′), 1. unfasten; untie. Please undo the package. I undid the string. 2. do away with; spoil; destroy. We mended the road, but a heavy storm undid our work. 3. bring to ruin. **undid** and **undone** are formed from **undo.**

un do ing (un dü′ing), 1. doing away with; spoiling; destroying. 2. cause of destruction or ruin. Drink was this man's undoing.

un done (un dun′), 1. not done; not finished. 2. ruined. Alas! We are undone. 3. See **undo.**

un doubt ed (un dout′id), not doubted; accepted as true.

un doubt ed ly (un dout′id li), beyond doubt; surely; certainly.

un dress (un dres′), take the clothes off; strip.

un due (un dū′ or un dü′), 1. not fitting; improper; not right. 2. too great; too much.

un du late (un′jů lāt), 1. move in waves; as, undulating water. 2. have a wavy form or surface; as, an undulating prairie.

un du ly (un dū′li or un dü′li), 1. improperly. 2. excessively; too much.

un dy ing (un dī′ing), deathless; immortal; eternal.

un earth (un ėrth′), 1. dig up; as, to unearth a buried city. 2. discover; find out; as, to unearth a plot.

un earth ly (un ėrth′li), 1. not of this world; supernatural. 2. strange; wild; weird; ghostly.

un eas i ly (un ēz′i li), in an uneasy manner; restlessly.

un eas i ness (un ēz′i nis), lack of ease or comfort; restlessness; anxiety.

un eas y (un ēz′i), 1. not comfortable. 2. restless; disturbed; anxious. 3. not easy in manner; awkward.

un em ployed (un′em ploid′), 1. not employed; not in use; having no work. 2. people out of work. Some of the unemployed sought aid from the government.

un em ploy ment (un′em ploi′mənt), lack of employment; being out of work.

un end ing (un en′ding), continuing; endless.

un e qual (un ē′kwəl), 1. not the same in amount, size, number, or value. 2. not fair; one-sided. 3. not enough. 4. not regular.

un e qualed or **un e qualled** (un ē′kwəld), that has no equal or superior; matchless.

un err ing (un ėr′ing), making no mistakes; exactly right.

un e ven (un ē′vən), 1. not level; as, uneven ground. 2. not equal. 3. that cannot be divided by 2 without a remainder. 27 and 9 are uneven numbers.

un e vent ful (un′i vent′fəl), without important or striking occurrences.

un ex pect ed (un′eks pek′tid), not expected.

un ex pect ed ly (un′eks pek′tid li), without being expected; in a way or to a degree that is not expected.

un fail ing (un fāl′ing), never failing; always ready when needed.

un fair (un fãr′), unjust.

un faith ful (un fāth′fəl), not faithful; not true to duty or one's promises; faithless.

un fa mil iar (un′fə mil′yər), 1. not well known; unusual; strange. That face is unfamiliar to me. 2. not acquainted. He is unfamiliar with the Greek language.

un fas ten (un fas′ən), undo; untie; loosen; open.

un fath om a ble (un faᴛʜ′əm ə bəl), so deep that the bottom cannot be reached; too mysterious to be understood.

un fa vor a ble (un fā′vər ə bəl), not favorable; adverse; harmful.

un feel ing (un fēl′ing), 1. hard-hearted; cruel. 2. not able to feel.

un feigned (un fānd′), sincere; real.

un fin ished (un fin′isht), 1. not finished; not complete. 2. without some special finish; rough; not polished.

un fit (un fit′), 1. not fit; not suitable; not good enough. 2. make unfit; spoil.

un flinch ing (un flin′ching), not drawing back from difficulty, danger, or pain; firm; resolute.

un fold (un fōld′), 1. open the folds of; spread out; as, to unfold a napkin, to unfold your arms. 2. reveal; show; explain.

un fore seen (un′fôr sēn′), unexpected; not known beforehand.

un for get ta ble (un′fər get′ə bəl), that can never be forgotten.

un for tu nate (un fôr′chə nit), 1. not lucky; having bad luck. 2. not suitable; not fitting. 3. an unfortunate person.

un found ed (un foun′did), without foundation; without reason; as, an unfounded complaint.

un fre quent ed (un′fri kwen′tid), seldom visited; rarely used.

un friend ly (un frend′li), 1. not friendly. 2. not favorable.

un furl (un fėrl′), spread out; shake out; unfold. Unfurl the sail. The flag unfurls in the breeze.

un fur nished (un fėr′nisht), not furnished; without furniture.

un gain ly (un gān′li), awkward; clumsy.

un god ly (un god′li), not religious; wicked; sinful.

un gra cious (un grā′shəs), 1. rude; not polite. 2. unpleasant; disagreeable.

un grate ful (un grāt′fəl), not grateful; not thankful.

un guard ed (un gär′did), 1. not protected. 2. careless.

un guent (ung′gwənt), salve; ointment for sores, burns, etc.

un hand (un hand′), let go; take the hands from.

un hap pi ly (un hap′i li), 1. not happily. 2. unfortunately. 3. in an unsuitable way.

un hap pi ness (un hap′i nis), 1. sadness; sorrow. 2. bad luck.

un hap py (un hap′i), 1. sad; sorrowful. 2. unlucky. 3. not suitable.

un har ness (un här′nis), take harness off from (a horse, etc.).

un health y (un hel′thi), 1. not possessing good health; not well; as, an unhealthy child. 2. hurtful to health; unwholesome; as, an unhealthy climate.

un heard (un hėrd′), 1. not listened to. 2. not heard of; unknown.

un heard-of (un hėrd′ov′), never heard of; not known before.

un heed ed (un hēd′id), not heeded; disregarded; unnoticed.

un heed ing (un hēd′ing), not heeding; not attentive.

un hes i tat ing ly (un hez′i tāt′ing li), without hesitation; promptly.

un hinge (un hinj′), 1. take (a door, etc.) off its hinges. 2. unsettle; upset. Trouble has unhinged this poor man's mind.

un hitch (un hich′), free from being hitched; unfasten.

un hook (un hůk′), 1. loosen from a hook. 2. undo by loosening a hook or hooks.

un horse (un hôrs′), throw from a horse's back; cause to fall from a horse.

u ni form (ū′ni fôrm), 1. always the same; not changing. The earth turns around at a uniform rate. 2. all alike; not varying. All the bricks have a uniform size. 3. clothes that are uniform in style, etc. Soldiers, policemen, and nurses wear uniforms. 4. clothe or furnish with a uniform.

u ni form i ty (ū′ni fôr′mi ti), uniform condition or character.

u ni form ly (ū′ni fôrm li), in a uniform manner; alike; in all cases.

u ni fy (ū′ni fī), unite; make or form into one. Several small states were unified into one nation.

un im por tant (un′im pôr′tənt), not important; insignificant; trifling.

un in hab it ed (un′in hab′i tid), not lived in; without inhabitants.

un in tel li gi ble (un′in tel′i ji bəl), that cannot be understood.

un ion (ūn′yən), 1. joining of two or more persons or things into one. The United States was formed by the union of thirteen States. 2. number of persons, groups, states, etc., joined together for some common purpose; a combination. The American colonies formed a union against England. **The Union** often means the United States. 3. group of workers joined together to protect and promote their interests.

Union Jack, the British national flag.

u nique (ū nēk′), 1. having no like or equal; being the only one of its kind. 2. rare; unusual.

u ni son (ū′ni sən), 1. agreement. The feet of marching soldiers move in unison. 2. agreement in pitch of two or more tones, voices, etc.; a sounding together at the same pitch.

u nit (ū′nit), 1. a single thing or person. 2. any group of things or persons considered as one. The family is a social unit.

3. a standard quantity or amount. A foot is a unit of length; a pound is a unit of weight. 4. smallest whole number; 1.

u nite (ū nīt′), join together; make one; become one. Several firms united to form one company. The class united in singing "America."

United States, country in North America, extending from the Atlantic to the Pacific and from the Gulf of Mexico to Canada; United States of America.

United States of America, United States.

u ni ty (ū′ni ti), 1. oneness. A circle has more unity than a row of dots. A nation has more unity than a group of tribes. 2. harmony. Brothers and sisters should live together in unity.

u ni ver sal (ū′ni vėr′səl), of all; belonging to all; concerning all; done by all. Food, fire, and shelter are universal needs.

u ni ver sal ly (ū′ni vėr′səl i), 1. in every instance; without exception. 2. everywhere.

u ni verse (ū′ni vėrs), all things; everything there is. Our world is but a small part of the universe.

u ni ver si ty (ū′ni vėr′si ti), institution of learning of the highest grade. Universities usually have schools of law, medicine, teaching, business, etc., as well as colleges for general instruction.

un just (un just′), not just; not fair.

un kempt (un kempt′), 1. not combed. 2. neglected; untidy; as, the unkempt clothes of a tramp.

un kind (un kīnd′), harsh; cruel.

un kind ly (un kīnd′li), 1. unkind. 2. in an unkind manner.

un kind ness (un kīnd′nis), 1. harsh treatment; cruelty. 2. an unkind act.

un known (un nōn′), not known; not familiar; strange.

un lace (un lās′), undo the laces of.

un law ful (un lô′fəl), contrary to the law; against the law; forbidden.

un learn ed (un lėr′nid for 1, un lėrnd′ for 2), 1. not educated; ignorant. 2. not learned; known without being learned.

un less (un les′), if not. We shall go unless it rains.

un like (un līk′), 1. not like; different. 2. different from.

un like ly (un līk′li), 1. not likely; not probable. 2. not likely to succeed.

un like ness (un līk′nis), being unlike; difference.

un lim it ed (un lim′i tid), without limits; boundless.

un load (un lōd′), 1. remove (a load). 2. take the load from. 3. get rid of. Alice began to unload her troubles onto her mother. 4. remove powder, shot, etc., from (gun). 5. discharge a cargo. The ship is unloading.

un lock (un lok′), open the lock of; open (anything firmly closed).

un looked-for (un lu̇kt′fôr′), unexpected; unforeseen.

un loose (un lüs′), let loose; set free; release.

un love ly (un luv′li), without beauty or charm; unpleasing in appearance; unpleasant; objectionable; disagreeable.

un luck y (un luk′i), not lucky; unfortunate; bringing bad luck.

un mar ried (un mar′id), not married.

un mask (un mask′), 1. remove a mask or disguise. The guests unmasked at midnight. 2. take off a mask or disguise from. 3. show the real nature of; expose. We unmasked the hypocrite.

un mer ci ful (un mėr′si fəl), having no mercy; cruel.

un mind ful (un mīnd′fəl), regardless; heedless; careless.

un mis tak a ble (un′mis tāk′ə bəl), that cannot be mistaken; clear; plain; evident.

un mixed (un mikst′), not mixed; pure.

un mo lest ed (un′mō les′tid), not molested; undisturbed.

un moved (un müvd′), 1. not moved; firm. 2. not disturbed; indifferent.

un nat u ral (un nach′ə rəl), not natural; not normal.

un nec es sar y (un nes′ə sãr′i), not necessary; needless.

un nerve (un nėrv′), deprive of nerve, firmness, self-control, etc. The sight of so much blood unnerved her.

un no ticed (un nō′tist), 1. not observed. 2. not receiving any attention.

un num bered (un num′bərd), 1. not numbered; not counted. 2. too many to count.

un ob served (un′əb zėrvd′), not observed; not noticed; disregarded.

un oc cu pied (un ok′ū pīd), not occupied; vacant; idle.

un pack (un pak′), 1. take out (things packed in a box, trunk, etc.); as, to unpack your clothes. 2. take things out of; as, to unpack a trunk.

un paid (un pād′), not paid. His unpaid bills amounted to $20.

un par al leled (un par′ə leld), having no parallel; unequaled; matchless.

un pin (un pin′), take out a pin or pins from; unfasten. Ruth unpinned baby's bib.

un pleas ant (un plez′ənt), not pleasant; disagreeable.

un pop u lar (un pop′ū lər), not popular; not generally liked.

un prac ticed or **un prac tised** (un prak′tist), 1. not skilled; not expert. 2. not put into practice; not used.

un prec e dent ed (un pres′i den′tid), having no precedent; never done before; never known before. Going to school on Saturdays would be unprecedented.

un pre pared (un′pri pãrd′), not made ready; not ready.

un prin ci pled (un prin′si pəld), lacking good moral principles; bad.

un prof it a ble (un prof′it ə bəl), producing no gain or advantage.

un ques tion a ble (un kwes′chən ə bəl), beyond dispute or doubt; certain. Size is sometimes an unquestionable advantage.

un ques tion a bly (un kwes′chən ə bli), beyond dispute or doubt; certainly.

un rav el (un rav′əl), 1. separate the threads of; pull apart. The kitten unraveled grandma's knitting. 2. come apart. This sweater is unraveling at the elbow. 3. bring out of a tangled state; as, to unravel a mystery.

un re al (un rē′əl), not real; imaginary.

un re al i ty (un′ri al′i ti), unreal quality; lack of reality.

un rea son a ble (un rē′zən ə bəl), 1. not reasonable. 2. not moderate.

un rea son a bly (un rē′zən ə bli), 1. in a way that is not reasonable; contrary to reason; foolishly. 2. extremely.

un re mit ting (un′ri mit′ing), never stopping; not slackening; maintained steadily. Driving in this traffic requires unremitting attention.

un re serv ed ly (un′ri zėr′vid li), 1. frankly; openly. 2. without reservation or restriction.

un rest (un rest′), restlessness; lack of ease and quiet; a disturbed condition.

un re strained (un′ri strānd′), not held back; not checked.

un ri valed or **un ri valled** (un rī′vəld), having no rival; without an equal.

un roll (un rōl′), 1. open or spread out (something rolled). 2. lay open; display.

un ru ly (un rü′li), hard to rule or control; lawless; as, an unruly horse, a disobedient and unruly boy, an unruly section of a country.

un sad dle (un sad′əl), 1. take the saddle off (a horse). 2. cause to fall from a horse.

un safe (un sāf′), dangerous.

un said (un sed′), not said.

un sat is fac to ry (un′sat is fak′tə ri), not good enough to satisfy.

un say (un sā′), take back (something said).

un screw (un skrü′), 1. take out the screw or screws from. 2. loosen or take off by turning.

un scru pu lous (un skrü′pū ləs), careless about right and wrong. The unscrupulous boys cheated.

un seal (un sēl′), 1. break or remove the seal of; as, to unseal a letter. 2. open. The threat of punishment unsealed her lips.

un seat (un sēt′), 1. displace from a seat. 2. throw (a rider) from a saddle. 3. remove from office.

un seem ly (un sēm′li), not proper; not suitable. Laughing in church is unseemly.

un seen (un sēn′), 1. not seen. 2. not visible.

un self ish (un sel′fish), caring for others; generous.

un set tle (un set′əl), disturb; make unstable; shake; weaken.

un set tled (un set′əld), 1. disordered; not in proper condition or order. Our house is still unsettled. 2. not inhabited. Some parts of the world are still unsettled. 3. liable to change; uncertain. The weather is unsettled. 4. not adjusted or disposed of; as, an unsettled estate, an unsettled bill. 5. not determined or decided; as, an unsettled question.

un shak en (un shāk′ən), not shaken; firm; as, an unshaken belief in Santa Claus.

un sheathe (un shēᴛʜ′), draw (a sword, knife, or the like) from a sheath.

un shod (un shod′), without shoes.

un sight ly (un sīt′li), ugly or unpleasant to look at.

un skilled (un skild′), not trained; not expert. Unskilled workers earn little.

un so phis ti cat ed (un′sə fis′ti kāt′id), simple; natural; artless.

un sound (un sound′), not sound; not in good condition; not well supported.

un speak a ble (un spēk′ə bəl), 1. that cannot be expressed in words; as, unspeakable joy, an unspeakable loss. 2. extremely bad; so bad that it is not spoken of.

un speak a bly (un spēk′ə bli), beyond words; extremely.

un sta ble (un stā′bəl), not firmly fixed; easily moved, shaken, or overthrown.

un stead y (un sted′i), not steady; shaky; likely to change; not reliable.

un suc cess ful (un′sək ses′fəl), not successful; having no success.

un suit a ble (un süt′ə bəl), not suitable; unfit.

un sus pect ed (un′səs pek′tid), 1. not suspected. 2. not thought of.

un taught (un tôt′), 1. not taught; not educated. 2. known without being taught; learned naturally.

un think a ble (un thingk′ə bəl), that cannot be imagined.

un ti dy (un tī′di), not neat; not in order.

un tie (un tī′), unfasten; undo. Grace was untying bundles.

un til (un til′), 1. up to the time of. It was cold from Christmas until April. 2. up to the time when. He waited until the sun had set. 3. before. She did not leave until morning. 4. to the degree or place that. He worked until he was too tired to do more.

un time ly (un tīm′li), 1. at a wrong time or season. Snow in May is untimely. 2. too early; too soon.

un tir ing (un tīr′ing), tireless.

un to (un′tü), to. The soldier was faithful unto death.

un told (un tōld′), 1. not told; not revealed. 2. too many to be counted; very great. Wars do untold harm.

un touched (un tucht′), not touched. The cat left the milk untouched. The miser was untouched by the poor man's story. The last topic was left untouched.

un to ward (un tōrd′), 1. unfavorable; unfortunate; as, an untoward wind, an untoward accident. 2. perverse; stubborn; willful. The untoward child was hard to manage.

un trained (un trānd′), not trained; without education.

un tried (un trīd′), not tried; not tested.

un true (un trü′), 1. false; incorrect. 2. not faithful.

un truth (un trüth′), 1. falsity. 2. a lie.

un used (un ūzd′), 1. not used; as, an unused room. 2. not accustomed; as, hands unused to labor.

un u su al (un ū′zhü əl), not common; rare; beyond the ordinary.

un u su al ly (un ū′zhü əl i), uncommonly; rarely; extremely.

un ut ter a ble (un ut′ər ə bəl), unspeakable; that cannot be expressed.

un veil (un vāl′), remove a veil from; uncover; disclose; reveal. The statue was unveiled the day the graduating class presented it to the school. The sun broke through the mist and unveiled the mountains.

un war y (un wãr′i), not cautious; unguarded; not careful.

un wea ried (un wēr′id), 1. not weary; not tired. 2. never growing weary.

un wel come (un wel′kəm), not welcome; not wanted.

un well (un wel′), ill; sick.

un whole some (un hōl′səm), not wholesome; unhealthy; bad for the body or the mind.

un wield y (un wēl′di), hard to handle or manage; not easy to use or control because of size, shape, or weight; clumsy. The armor worn by knights seems unwieldy to us today.

un will ing (un wil′ing), not willing; not consenting.

un will ing ly (un wil′ing li), against one's will; though not wishing to.

un will ing ness (un wil′ing nis), fact or condition of being unwilling.

un wind (un wīnd′), 1. wind off; take from a spool, ball, etc. 2. become unwound.

un wise (un wīz′), not wise; foolish; not showing good judgment.

un wise ly (un wīz′li), in an unwise way; in foolish ways; not as a wise person would do.

un wit ting ly (un wit′ing li), not knowingly; unconsciously; not intentionally.

un wont ed (un wun′tid), 1. not customary; not usual. 2. not accustomed.

un wor thy (un wėr′ᴛʜi), not worthy; not deserving. Such a silly story is unworthy of belief.

un wound (un wound′), 1. not wound; loose. 2. wound off. 3. became loose.

un wrap (un rap′), take a wrapping off from; open.

un yield ing (un yēl′ding), firm; not giving in.

up (up), 1. to a higher place; in a higher place. The bird flew up. 2. in an erect position. Stand up. Get up. 3. to the top of; near the top of; at the top of. He went up the hill to get a good view. 4. not back of. Keep up with the times. 5. completely. The house burned up. 6. at an end. His time is up now. 7. **Up to** sometimes means doing; about to do. Lulu is up to some mischief. 8. in action. 9. into storage or a safe place; aside; by. Squirrels lay up nuts for the winter.

up braid (up brād′), blame; reprove; find fault with. The captain upbraided his men for falling asleep.

up held (up held′), held up; supported. See **uphold.**

up hill (up′hil′ for 1 and 2, up′hil′ for 3), 1. up the slope of a hill; upward. It is an uphill road all the way. 2. difficult. 3. upward. We walked a mile uphill.

up hold (up hōld′), 1. hold up; raise; keep from falling; support. Walls uphold the roof. We try to uphold the good name of our school. 2. confirm. The principal upheld the teacher's decision.

up hol ster (up hōl′stər), 1. provide (furniture) with coverings, cushions, springs, stuffing, etc. 2. furnish (a room) with curtains, rugs, etc.

up hol ster y (up hōl′stər i), 1. coverings for furniture; curtains, cushions, carpets, and hangings. 2. the business of upholstering.

up keep (up′kēp′), 1. maintenance. 2. cost of operating and repair. The upkeep of a big automobile is expensive.

up land (up′lənd), 1. high land. 2. of high land.

up lift (up lift′ for 1, up′lift′ for 2), 1. lift up; raise; elevate. The reformer wanted to uplift the stage and make it better. 2. elevation; movement toward improvement.

up on (ə pon′), on.

up per (up′ər), 1. higher; as, the upper lip, the upper floor, the upper notes of a singer's voice. 2. The **upper hand** means control.

up per most (up′ər mōst), 1. highest. 2. most prominent; having the most force or influence. 3. in the highest place. 4. first.

up raise (up rāz′), raise up; lift.

up rear (up rēr′), rear up; lift up; raise.

up right (up′rīt′), 1. standing up straight; erect. Hold yourself upright. 2. good; honest; just; as, an upright man. 3. something standing erect; a vertical piece of timber.

up right ness (up′rīt′nis), 1. honesty; righteousness. 2. erect position.

up ris ing (up rīz′ing), 1. rising up. 2. revolt; as, an uprising of the savage tribes.

up roar (up′rōr′), 1. noisy disturbance. Main Street was in an uproar when the lion escaped during the circus parade. 2. loud or confused noise.

up root (up rüt′), tear up by the roots. The storm uprooted many trees. Cheating must be uprooted from our games.

up set (up set′ for 1, 4, and 7, up′set′ for 2, 3, 5, and 6), 1. tip over; overturn. Jack upset the milk pitcher. Moving about in a boat may upset it. 2. a tipping over; overturn. 3. tipped over; overturned. 4. disturb greatly; disorder. Rain upset our plans for a picnic. The shock was upsetting to mother's nerves. 5. great disturbance; disorder. 6. greatly disturbed; disordered; as, an upset stomach. 7. overthrow; defeat.

up shot (up′shot′), 1. conclusion; result. 2. the essential facts.

up side (up′sīd′), the upper side.

upside down, 1. having what should be on top at the bottom. The slice of bread and butter fell upside down on the floor. 2. in complete disorder. The children turned the house upside down.

up stairs (up′stãrz′ for 1, up′stãrz′ for 2 and 3), 1. up the stairs. 2. on an upper floor. 3. upper story.

up start (up′stärt′), 1. person who has suddenly risen from a humble position to wealth, power, or importance. 2. an unpleasant and conceited person who puts himself forward too much.

up stream (up′strēm′), against the current of a stream; up a stream. It is hard to swim upstream.

up-to-date (up′tü dāt′), 1. extending to the present time; as, an up-to-date record. 2. keeping up with the times in style, ideas, etc.; as, an up-to-date store.

up turn (up tėrn′ for 1, up′tėrn′ for 2), 1. turn up. 2. upward turn.

up ward (up′wərd), 1. toward a higher place.

Jack climbed upward till he reached the apple. 2. toward a higher or greater rank, amount, age, etc. From ten years of age upward, Jane had studied French. 3. above; more. Children of twelve years and upward must pay full fare. 4. **Upward of** means more than.

up wards (up′wərdz), upward.

ur ban (ėr′bən), 1. of or pertaining to cities or towns. 2. living in cities. 3. characteristic of cities.

ur chin (ėr′chin), 1. small boy. 2. mischievous boy. 3. a poor, ragged child. Urchins played in the street.

urge (ėrj), 1. push; force; drive. The driver urged on the horses. Hunger urged him to steal. 2. ask earnestly; plead with; recommend strongly. Mrs. Jones urged us to stay longer. Mr. Smith's doctor urges a change of climate. The lawyer urged the boy's youth as an excuse for his crime.

ur gent (ėr′jənt), demanding immediate action or attention; pressing; as, an urgent duty, an urgent message.

u rine (ūr′in), the fluid that is secreted by the kidneys, goes to the bladder, and is then discharged from the body.

urn (ėrn), 1. a kind of vase with a foot. Urns were used in Greece and Rome to hold the ashes of the dead. 2. a coffee pot or teapot with a faucet, used for making coffee or tea at the table.

Urn for ornament

Urn for hot drinks

us (us). We learn. The teacher helps us. Mother went with us. *We* and *us* mean the persons speaking.

U.S., United States.

U.S.A., 1. United States of America. 2. United States Army.

us age (ūs′ij or ūz′ij), 1. manner of using; treatment. This car has had rough usage. 2. habit; customary use; long-continued practice. Strangers living in a country should learn many of its usages. Usage determines what is good English.

use (ūz for 1 and 2, ūs for 4, 5, 6, and 7), 1. We use our legs in walking. We use a knife to cut meat. 2. Use others as you would have them use you. 3. **Used to** (ūst′tü′) means (1) accustomed to. Eskimos are used to cold weather. (2) formerly did. You used to come at ten o'clock. 4. He had the use of his friend's books. 5. Use forms habits. 6. A hunter often has use for a gun. 7. There is no use in crying.

use ful (ūs′fəl), of use; helpful. A handkerchief is a useful present. A good guide makes himself useful.

use ful ness (ūs′fəl nis), condition of being useful; practical value.

use less (ūs′lis), of no use; worthless.

us er (ūz′ər), one that uses.

ush er (ush′ər), 1. person who shows people to their seats in a church, theater, etc. 2. to conduct; bring in. The footman ushered the visitors to the door.

u su al (ū′zhü əl), in common use; common; ordinary.

u su al ly (ū′zhü əl i), commonly; ordinarily.

u surp (ū zėrp′), seize and hold (power, position, or authority) by force or without right. The king's brother tried to usurp the throne.

u ten sil (ū ten′səl), 1. container, implement, or tool used for practical purposes. Pots, pans, kettles, and mops are kitchen utensils. 2. implement or tool used for some special purpose. Pens and pencils are writing utensils.

u til i ty (ū til′i ti), 1. usefulness. 2. useful thing. 3. a public service. Railroads, streetcar and bus lines, and gas and electric companies are public utilities.

u ti lize (ū′ti līz), use; put to use. Mother will utilize the bones for soup.

ut most (ut′mōst), 1. farthest; extreme. He walked to the utmost edge of the cliff. 2. greatest; highest. Sunshine is of the utmost importance to health. 3. the extreme limit; the most that is possible. Dick enjoyed himself to the utmost at the circus.

ut ter[1] (ut′ər), complete; total; absolute; as, utter surprise.

ut ter[2] (ut′ər), speak; make known; express. Alice uttered a cry of pain.

ut ter ance (ut′ər əns), 1. expression in words or sounds. The child gave utterance to his grief. 2. way of speaking. Stammering hinders clear utterance. 3. something uttered; a spoken word or words.

ut ter ly (ut′ər li), completely; totally; absolutely.

ut ter most (ut′ər mōst), utmost.

V

va can cy (vā′kən si), 1. being vacant; emptiness. 2. unoccupied position. The death of two policemen made two vacancies in our police force. 3. a room, space, or apartment for rent; empty space.

va cant (vā′kənt), 1. empty; not filled; not occupied; as, a vacant chair, a vacant house. 2. empty of thought or intelligence; as, a vacant smile.

va cate (vā′kāt), go away from and leave empty; make vacant. They will vacate the house at the end of the month.

va ca tion (vā kā′shən), freedom from school, business, or other duties. There is a vacation from school every year at Christmas time.

vac ci nate (vak′si nāt), 1. inoculate against smallpox. 2. take similar measures against other diseases.

vac il late (vas′i lāt), 1. move first one way and then another; waver. 2. waver in mind or opinion. A vacillating person finds it hard to make up his mind.

vac u um (vak′ū əm), empty space without even air in it.

vacuum cleaner, apparatus for cleaning carpets, curtains, floors, etc., by suction.

vag a bond (vag′ə bond), 1. wanderer; idle wanderer; tramp. 2. wandering. The gypsies lead a vagabond life.

va gar y (və gãr′i), extravagant or fanciful notion; as, the vagaries of a dream.

va grant (vā′grənt), 1. wanderer. 2. wandering. Gypsies are vagrant people. 3. idle wanderer; tramp. 4. wandering without proper means of earning a living.

vague (vāg), not definite; not clear; not distinct. In a fog everything looks vague. Nobody can be sure just what a vague statement means.

vain (vān), 1. having too much pride in one's looks, ability, etc. She is vain of her beauty. 2. of no use; unsuccessful. I made vain attempts to reach her by telephone. 3. **In vain** means without effect or without success. The drowning man shouted in vain, for no one could hear him.

vain ly (vān′li), 1. without success. 2. with conceit.

vale (vāl), valley.

val en tine (val′ən tīn), 1. a card or small gift sent on Saint Valentine's Day, February 14. Some valentines make fun of the person to whom they are sent. 2. a sweetheart chosen on this day.

val et (val′it or val′ā), 1. servant who takes care of a man's clothes and gives him personal service. 2. servant in a hotel who cleans or presses clothes. 3. serve as a valet.

val iant (val′yənt), brave; as, a valiant soldier, a valiant deed.

val id (val′id), 1. true; supported by facts or authority. 2. having force; holding good; effective. Illness is a valid excuse for being absent from school.

va lise (və lēs′), traveling bag.

val ley (val′i), 1. low land between hills or mountains. Most large valleys have rivers running through them. 2. wide region drained by a great river system; as, the Mississippi valley.

val or (val′ər), bravery; courage.

val u a ble (val′ū ə bəl), 1. having value; being worth something; as, a valuable ring, valuable information, a valuable friend. 2. an article of value. She keeps her jewelry and other valuables in a safe.

val u a tion (val′ū ā′shən), 1. act of valuing. 2. the value fixed. The jeweler's valuation of the necklace was $10,000.

val ue (val′ū), 1. worth; excellence; usefulness; importance; as, the value of education, the value of milk as a food. 2. real worth; proper price. He bought the house for less than its value. 3. power to buy. The value of the dollar lessened from 1900 to 1920. 4. rate at a certain value or price. The land is valued at $5000. 5. think highly of; regard highly. John values Tom's friendship.

valve (valv), 1. movable part that controls the flow of a liquid or gas through a pipe by opening and closing the passage. A faucet is one kind of valve. 2. something that works like a faucet. 3. one of the parts of shells like those of oysters and clams.

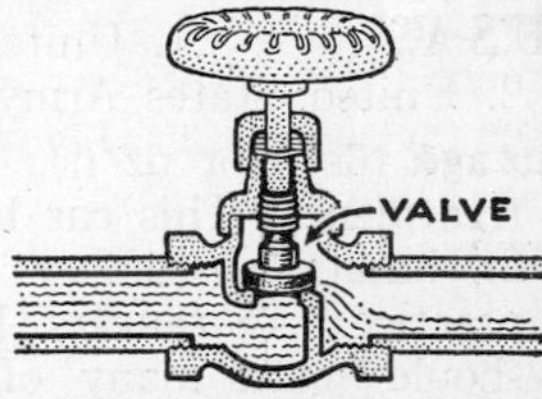

van[1] (van), the front part of an army, fleet, or other advancing group.

van[2] (van), a covered truck or wagon for moving furniture, etc.

van dal (van′dəl), person who destroys or damages beautiful things on purpose. People who break branches from trees in the parks are vandals.

vane (vān), 1. movable device to show which way the wind is blowing. 2. blade of a windmill, a ship's propeller, etc.

Vane (def. 1)

van guard (van′gärd′), 1. the front part of an army; soldiers marching in front to clear the way and guard against surprise. 2. foremost or leading position. 3. leaders of a movement.

va nil la (və nil′ə), 1. a flavoring extract used in candy, ice cream, perfume, etc. 2. the tropical plant which yields the beans used in making this flavoring. 3. the bean itself.

van ish (van′ish), 1. disappear; disappear suddenly. The sun vanished behind a cloud. 2. pass away; cease to be. Many kinds of animals have vanished from the earth.

van i ty (van′i ti), 1. too much pride in one's looks, ability, etc. Louise's vanity made her look in the mirror often. 2. lack of real value.

van quish (vang′kwish), conquer; defeat.

van tage (van′tij), advantage; better position or condition.

va por (vā′pər), 1. steam from boiling water; moisture in the air that can be seen; fog; mist. 2. a gas formed from a substance that is usually liquid or solid.

var i a ble (vãr′i ə bəl), 1. apt to change; changeable; uncertain. The weather is more variable in New York than it is in California. 2. a thing or quantity that varies. Temperature and rainfall are variables.

var i ance (vãr′i əns), 1. difference; disagreement. Roy's actions are at variance with his promises. 2. a varying; a change.

var i a tion (vãr′i ā′shən), 1. a varying; a change. 2. amount of change. There was a variation of 30 degrees in the temperature yesterday.

var ied (vãr′id), 1. of different kinds; having variety; as, a varied assortment of candies. 2. changed; altered. 3. was different.

va ri e ty (və rī′ə ti), 1. difference or change. Variety is the spice of life. 2. number of different kinds. This shop has a variety of toys. 3. kind or sort. Which varieties of cake did you buy?

var i ous (vãr′i əs), 1. different; differing from one another. 2. several; many.

var let (vär′lit), low fellow; rascal.

var nish (vär′nish), 1. a liquid that gives a smooth, glossy appearance to wood, metal, etc. Varnish is often made from substances like resin dissolved in oil or alcohol. 2. the smooth hard surface made when this liquid dries. The varnish on the car has been scratched. 3. put varnish on. 4. favorable appearance; pretense. She covers her selfishness with a varnish of good manners. 5. give a false or deceiving appearance.

var y (vãr′i), 1. change; make different. The driver can vary the speed of an automobile. The singer is varying her style of singing. 2. be different; differ. Stars vary in brightness.

vase (vās), a holder or container used for ornament or for holding flowers.

Ancient Roman vase

vas sal (vas′əl), 1. person who held land from a lord or superior, to whom in return he gave help in war or some other service. A great noble could be a vassal of the king and have many other men as his vassals. 2. like a vassal; like that of a vassal. 3. servant.

vast (vast), very, very large. Texas is a vast State. A billion dollars is a vast amount of money.

vast ly (vast′li), very greatly; to a vast extent; to a vast degree.

vast ness (vast′nis), very great size; being vast.

vat (vat), tank; large container for liquids; as, a vat of dye.

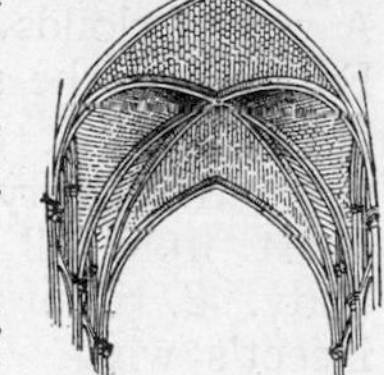
Vault of a roof

vault[1] (vôlt), 1. arched roof or ceiling; series of arches. 2. arched space or passage. 3. something like an arched roof. The vault of heaven means the sky. 4. make in the form of a vault. The roof was vaulted. 5. underground cellar or storehouse. 6. place for storing valuable things and keeping them safe. Vaults are often made of steel. 7. place for burial.

vault[2] (vôlt), 1. to jump or leap over by using the hands or a pole. He vaulted the fence. 2. such a jump or leap. 3. to jump; to leap. He vaulted over the wall.

vaunt (vônt), boast.

veal (vēl), meat from a calf.

veer (vēr), 1. change direction; shift; turn. The wind veered to the south. The talk veered to ghosts. 2. shift; turn.

veg e ta ble (vej′i tə bəl), 1. plant grown for food. Peas, corn, lettuce, tomatoes, and beets are vegetables. 2. any plant. 3. of plants; like plants; pertaining to plants; as, the vegetable kingdom, vegetable life, vegetable oils, a vegetable dinner.

veg e tar i an (vej′i tãr′i ən), 1. person who eats vegetables but no meat. 2. eating vegetables but no meat. 3. containing no meat.

veg e ta tion (vej′i tā′shən), plant life; growing plants; growth of plants. There is not much vegetation in deserts.

ve he mence (vē′i məns), vehement nature; violence; strong feeling.

ve he ment (vē′i mənt), 1. showing strong feeling; caused by strong feeling; eager. 2. forceful; violent.

ve hi cle (vē′i kəl), 1. carriage, cart, wagon, automobile, sled, or any other conveyance used on land. 2. a means of carrying or conveying. Language is the vehicle of thought.

veil (vāl), 1. piece of very thin material worn to protect or hide the face, or as an ornament. 2. piece of material worn so as to fall over the head and shoulders. **Take the veil** means become a nun. 3. cover with a veil. 4. anything that screens or hides. A veil of clouds hid the sun. 5. cover; hide. Fog veiled the shore.

vein (vān), 1. one of the little pipes or tubes that carry blood to the heart from all parts of the body. 2. rib of a leaf or of an insect's wing. 3. a crack or seam in rock filled with a different mineral; as, a vein of copper. 4. any streak or marking of a different shade or color in wood, marble, etc. 5. special character or disposition; mood; as, a vein of cruelty, a joking vein. 6. cover with veins; mark with veins.

A

B

Veins: A, of leaf; B, of insect's wing.

vel lum (vel′əm), 1. the finest kind of parchment, used for writing and binding books. 2. paper or cloth imitating this.

ve loc i ty (vi los′i ti), 1. speed; swiftness; quickness. 2. rate of motion. A bullet goes from this gun with a velocity of 3000 feet a second.

vel vet (vel′vit), 1. cloth with a thick, soft pile. Velvet may be made of silk, rayon, cotton, or some combination of these. 2. made of velvet. Grace wore a velvet hat. 3. like velvet; as, a cat's velvet paws.

vel vet een (vel′vi tēn′), velvet made of cotton or of silk and cotton.

vel vet y (vel′vi ti), smooth and soft like velvet.

vend (vend), sell; peddle. He vends fruit from a cart.

vend er (ven′dər), seller; peddler.

ven dor (ven′dər), seller; peddler.

ven er a ble (ven′ər ə bəl), worthy of reverence; as, a venerable priest, venerable customs.

ven er ate (ven′ər āt), regard with reverence; revere. He venerates his father's memory.

ven er a tion (ven′ər ā′shən), reverence.

venge ance (ven′jəns), 1. revenge; punishment in return for a wrong. The Indian swore vengeance against the men who murdered his father. 2. **With a vengeance** sometimes means with great force or violence. By six o'clock it was raining with a vengeance.

ven i son (ven′i zən), deer meat; the flesh of a deer, used for food.

ven om (ven′əm), 1. the poison of snakes, spiders, etc. 2. spite; malice. She hated the rich and spoke of them with venom.

ven om ous (ven′əm əs), 1. poisonous. Rattlesnakes are venomous. 2. spiteful; malicious.

vent (vent), 1. hole; opening. 2. outlet; way out. Her grief found vent in tears. 3. let out; express freely. He vented his anger on the dog.

ven ti late (ven′ti lāt), 1. change the air in. We ventilate a room by opening windows. 2. purify by fresh air. The lungs ventilate the blood.

ven ti la tion (ven′ti lā′shən), 1. change of air; act or process of supplying with fresh air. 2. means of supplying fresh air.

ven ti la tor (ven′ti lā′tər), any apparatus or means for changing or improving the air.

ven ture (ven′chər), 1. a risky or daring undertaking. A lucky venture in oil stock made his fortune. His courage was equal to any venture. 2. expose to risk or danger. Men venture their lives in war. 3. dare. No one ventured to interrupt the speaker. 4. dare to say or make. He ventured an objection.

ven ture some (ven′chər səm), inclined to take risks; rash; daring.

Ve nus (vē′nəs), 1. the Roman goddess of love and beauty. 2. the most brilliant planet. 3. very beautiful woman.

ve ran da or **ve ran dah** (və ran′də), large porch along one or more sides of a house.

Veranda

verb (vėrb), a word that tells what is or what is done; the part of speech that expresses action or being. *Do, go, come, be, sit, think, know,* and *eat* are verbs.

ver bal (vėr′bəl), 1. in words; of words. A description is a verbal picture. 2. expressed in spoken words; oral; as, a verbal message, a verbal promise.

ver bal ly (vėr′bəl i), 1. in words. 2. in spoken words. The dumb boy could not reply verbally but used signs. 3. word for word. The child reported the conversation verbally. 4. in regard to words only.

ver be na (vər bē′nə), low-growing garden plant with flowers having various colors.

Verbena

ver dant (vėr′dənt), green. The fields are covered with verdant grass.

ver dict (vėr′dikt), 1. the decision of a jury. The jury returned a verdict of "Not Guilty." 2. decision; judgment.

ver dure (vėr′jər), fresh growth of green grass, plants, or leaves.

verge (vėrj), 1. edge; rim; brink. His business is on the verge of ruin. 2. be on the verge; border. Bill's talk was so poorly prepared that it verged on the ridiculous. 3. tend; incline. She was plump, verging toward fat.

ver i fy (ver′i fī), 1. prove to be true; confirm. The driver's report of the accident was verified by two women. 2. find out the truth of; test the correctness of. Amy is verifying her results by using an adding machine.

ver i ly (ver′i li), in truth; truly; really.

ver i ta ble (ver′i tə bəl), true; real; actual.

ver i ty (ver′i ti), 1. truth. 2. true statement or fact. 3. reality.

ver mil ion (vər mil′yən), 1. bright red. 2. bright-red coloring matter.

ver min (vėr′min), small, troublesome, or destructive animals. Fleas, lice, wasps, rats, and mice are vermin. People who are very unpleasant and troublesome are sometimes called vermin.

ver sa tile (vėr′sə til), able to do many things well. Theodore Roosevelt was a versatile man; he was successful as a statesman, soldier, sportsman, explorer, and author.

verse (vėrs), 1. lines of words with a regularly repeated accent; poetry. 2. a single line of poetry. 3. a group of lines of poetry. Sing the first verse of "America." 4. a short division of a chapter in the Bible.

versed (vėrst), experienced; practiced; skilled. A doctor should be well versed in medicine.

ver sion (vėr′zhən), 1. a translation from one language to another; as, a version of the Bible. 2. one particular statement, account, or description. Each of the three boys gave his own version of the quarrel.

ver te bra (vėr′ti brə), one of the bones of the backbone.

ver te brae (vėr′ti brē), vertebras.

Three vertebrae

ver ti cal (vėr′ti kəl), 1. straight up and down; perpendicular to the surface of still water. A person standing up straight is in a vertical position. 2. vertical line, circle, position, part, etc.

ver y (ver′i), 1. much; greatly; extremely. The sun is very hot. 2. real; true; genuine. She cries from very shame. 3. actual. He was caught in the very act of stealing. 4. same. The very people who used to love her hate her now. 5. even. The very thought of blood makes her sick. 6. absolutely; exactly. He stood in the very same place for an hour.

ves pers or **Ves pers** (ves′pərz), a church service held in the evening or late afternoon.

ves sel (ves′əl), 1. hollow holder or container. Cups, bowls, pitchers, bottles, barrels, tubs, etc., are vessels. 2. ship; large boat. 3. tube carrying blood or other fluid.

vest (vest), 1. a short, sleeveless garment worn by men under the coat. 2. garment like this worn by women. 3. undershirt. 4. clothe or robe. The vested priest stood before the altar. 5. furnish with powers, authority, rights, etc. Congress is vested with the power to declare war. 6. put in the possession or control of a person or persons. The management of the hospital is vested in a board of trustees.

ves ti bule (ves′ti būl), 1. passage or hall between the outer door and the inside of a building. 2. the enclosed space at the end of a railroad passenger car.

ves tige (ves′tij), trace; mark. A blackened, charred stump was a vestige of the fire. Ghost stories are vestiges of a widespread belief in ghosts.

vest ment (vest′mənt), garment; especially, a garment worn by a clergyman in performing sacred duties.

ves try (ves′tri), 1. room in a church, where vestments are kept. 2. room in a church or an attached building, used for Sunday school, prayer meetings, etc. 3. a meeting of church members on church business. 4. committee that helps manage church business.

vet er an (vet′ər ən), 1. grown old in service; experienced; as, a veteran farmer. 2. having had much experience in war. Veteran troops fought side by side with the young soldiers. 3. person who has been in the army or navy a long time.

vet er i nar y (vet′ər i nãr′i), 1. pertaining to the medical or surgical treatment of animals. 2. doctor who treats animals.

ve to (vē′tō), 1. the power or right to forbid or prevent. The President has the power of veto over most bills passed in Congress. 2. use the power of veto against; refuse to consent to. Father vetoed our plan to buy a big snake. 3. a prohibition; refusal of consent. Our plan met with three vetoes—from father, mother, and teacher.

vex (veks), 1. annoy; anger by trifles; provoke. It is vexing to have to wait for anyone. 2. disturb. Cape Hatteras is much vexed by storms. 3. A **vexed question** means a question about which people disagree and which is much discussed.

vex a tion (veks ā′shən), 1. vexing; being vexed. His face showed his vexation at the delay. 2. thing that vexes. These three vexations had annoyed mother: the milk had not come, the cat had upset a lamp, and the cake had burned.

vi a (vī′ə), by way of. He is going from New York to California via the Panama Canal.

vi a duct (vī′ə dukt), bridge for carrying a road or railroad over a valley, a part of a city, etc.

vi al (vī′əl), small glass bottle for holding medicines or the like; bottle.

vi and (vī′ənd), article of food, especially of choice food.

vi brant (vī′brənt), 1. vibrating. 2. resounding; resonant.

vi brate (vī′brāt), 1. move rapidly to and fro. A snake's tongue vibrates. A piano string vibrates and makes a sound when a key is struck. 2. quiver; be moved. 3. thrill.

vi bra tion (vī brā′shən), rapid movement to and fro; quivering motion; vibrating. The busses shake the house so much that we feel the vibration.

vic ar (vik′ər), clergyman of a certain sort.

vice[1] (vīs), 1. evil habit or tendency. Lying and cruelty are vices. 2. evil; wickedness. 3. fault; bad habit. Mr. Jones said that his horse had no vices.

vice[2] (vīs), vise.

vice-pres i dent (vīs′prez′i dənt), officer next in rank to the president, who takes the president's place when necessary. If the President of the United States dies, the Vice-President becomes President.

vice roy (vīs′roi), person ruling a country or province as the deputy of the sovereign.

vi ce ver sa (vī′si vėr′sə), the other way round. John blamed Harry, and vice versa (Harry blamed John).

vi cin i ty (vi sin′i ti), 1. region near or about a place; neighborhood. There are no houses for sale in this vicinity. 2. nearness in place; closeness.

vi cious (vish′əs), 1. evil; wicked. The drunkard led a vicious life. 2. having bad habits or a bad disposition; as, a vicious horse. 3. not correct; having faults. This argument contains vicious reasoning. 4. spiteful; malicious.

vi cis si tude (vi sis′i tūd or vi sis′i tüd), change in circumstances; a great variation. The vicissitudes of life may suddenly make a rich man very poor.

vic tim (vik′tim), 1. person or animal sacrificed, injured, or destroyed; as, victims of war, victims of a swindle, victims of an accident. 2. person or animal killed as a sacrifice to a god.

vic tor (vik′tər), 1. winner; conqueror. 2. victorious.

vic to ri ous (vik tō′ri əs), 1. conquering; having won a victory; as, a victorious army. 2. having victories; as, a victorious war.

vic to ry (vik′tə ri), defeat of an enemy; success in a contest. In ten games, our team had seven victories.

vict ual (vit′əl), supply with food. The captain victualed his ship for the voyage.

vict uals (vit′əlz), food.

vie (vī), strive for superiority; contend in rivalry; compete.

view (vū), 1. act of seeing; sight. It was our first view of the ocean. 2. power of seeing; range of the eye. A ship came into view. 3. see; look at. 4. thing seen; a scene. The view from our house is beautiful. 5. picture of some scene. Various views of the coast hung on the walls. 6. a mental picture; an idea. This book will give you a general view of the last war. 7. way of looking at or considering a matter; opinion. Children take a different view of school from that of their teachers. 8. consider; regard. 9. Some special meanings are:

in view, 1. as a purpose or intention. 2. as a hope; as an expectation.

in view of, considering; because of.

on view, to be seen; open for people to see.

with a view to, with the purpose or intention of; with a hope of.

view point (vū′point′), 1. place from which one looks at something. 2. attitude of mind. A heavy rain that is good from the viewpoint of farmers may be bad from the viewpoint of tourists.

vig il (vij′əl), 1. keeping awake during the usual hours of sleep; act of watching. All night the mother kept vigil over the sick child. 2. **Vigils** sometimes means devotions, prayers, services, etc., on the night before a religious festival. 3. the day and night before a solemn religious festival.

vig i lance (vij′i ləns), watchfulness; alertness; caution. The cat watched the mouse hole with vigilance.

vig i lant (vij′i lənt), watchful; alert; wide-awake. The dog kept a vigilant guard over the house.

vig or (vig′ər), active strength or force; healthy energy or power. A man's vigor lessens as he grows old.

vig or ous (vig′ər əs), full of vigor; strong and active; energetic; forcible. He keeps himself vigorous by taking exercise. Doctors wage a vigorous war against disease.

vile (vīl), 1. very bad; disgusting; as, vile weather, a vile smell. 2. evil; immoral. The criminal used vile language. 3. poor; mean; lowly. The king's son stooped to the vile tasks of the kitchen.

vil la (vil′ə), a house in the country or suburbs. A villa is usually a large or elegant residence.

vil lage (vil′ij), 1. group of houses, smaller than a town. 2. the people of a village.

vil lag er (vil′ij ər), person who lives in a village.

vil lain (vil′ən), wicked person. The villain stole the money and cast the blame on his friend.

vil lain ous (vil′ən əs), extremely bad; very wicked; vile.

vil lain y (vil′ən i), 1. great wickedness. 2. very wicked act; a crime.

vil lein (vil′ən), one of a class of half-free peasants in the Middle Ages. A villein was under the control of his lord, but otherwise had the rights of a freeman.

vim (vim), force; energy; vigor.

vin di cate (vin′di kāt), 1. clear from suspicion, dishonor, or any charge of wrongdoing. The verdict of "Not guilty" vindicated him. 2. defend successfully against opposition; uphold; justify. The heir vindicated his claim to the fortune.

vin di ca tion (vin′di kā′shən), defense; justification.

vin dic tive (vin dik′tiv), 1. bearing a grudge; wanting revenge. Roy was so vindictive that he never forgave anybody. 2. showing a strong tendency toward revenge. Vindictive acts rarely do much good.

vine (vīn), 1. a plant that grows along the ground or that climbs by attaching itself to a wall, tree, or other support. Melons and pumpkins grow on vines. Ivy is a vine. 2. a grapevine.

vin e gar (vin′i gər), a sour liquid made from cider, wine, etc. Vinegar is used in salad dressing, in flavoring food, and in preserving food.

vine yard (vin′yərd), place planted with grapevines.

vin tage (vin′tij), 1. the wine from a certain crop of grapes. Some vintages are better than others. 2. a year's crop of grapes. 3. the season of gathering grapes and making wine.

vi ol (vī′əl), a stringed musical instrument played with a bow. The largest kind of viol is called the double bass.

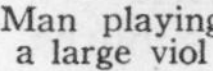
Man playing a large viol

vi o la (vī ō′lə), a musical instrument shaped like a violin, but slightly larger.

vi o late (vī′ə lāt), 1. use force against. 2. break (a law, rule, agreement, promise, etc.); act contrary to; fail to perform. Speeding violates the traffic regulations. 3. break in upon; disturb. The sound of guns violated the usual calm of Sunday morning. 4. treat with disrespect or contempt. The soldiers violated the church by using it as a stable.

vi o la tion (vī′ə lā′shən), 1. use of force; violence. 2. breaking a law, rule, agreement, promise, etc. 3. treatment of a holy thing with contempt.

vi o la tor (vī′ə lā′tər), one who violates.

vi o lence (vī′ə ləns), 1. rough force in action. Tom slammed the door with violence. 2. rough or harmful action or treatment. The policeman had to use violence in arresting the murderer. 3. injury. It would do violence to her principles to work on Sunday.

vi o lent (vī′ə lənt), 1. acting or done with strong rough force; as, a violent blow. 2. caused by strong rough force; as, a violent death. 3. showing or caused by very strong feeling, action, etc.; as, violent language. 4. severe; extreme; very great; as, a violent pain, violent heat.

vi o lent ly (vī′ə lənt li), in a violent way; with violence.

vi o let (vī′ə lit), 1. a plant with purple, blue, yellow, or white flowers. 2. bluish purple. Violet is red and blue mixed.

vi o lin (vī′ə lin′), the commonest musical instrument with four strings played with a bow. See the picture just above.

Man playing a violin

vi o lin ist (vī′ə lin′ist), violin player.

vi o lon cel lo (vī′ə lən chel′ō), a musical instrument like a violin, but very much larger. It is commonly called a cello. See the picture.

Man playing a violoncello

vi per (vī′pər), 1. a poisonous snake. 2. a spiteful, treacherous person.

vir gin (vėr′jin), 1. a maiden; a pure, unmarried woman. 2. of a virgin; as, virgin modesty. 3. pure; spotless. Virgin snow is newly fallen snow. 4. not yet used; as, virgin soil, a virgin forest.

vir tu al (vėr′chü əl), real; being something in effect, though not so in name. Mr. Smith is the virtual president, though his title is secretary. The battle was won with so great a loss of soldiers that it was a virtual defeat.

vir tu al ly (vėr′chü əl i), actually; really; in effect, though not in name. England is virtually a democracy now, for the king has no real power.

vir tue (vėr′chü), 1. goodness; moral excellence; purity. 2. a particular moral excellence. Justice and kindness are virtues. 3. a good quality. Jack praised the virtues of his car. 4. power to produce good results. There is little virtue in that medicine.

vir tu ous (vėr′chü əs), good; moral; righteous; pure.

vis age (viz′ij), face.

vis count (vī′kount), a nobleman ranking next below an earl or count and next above a baron.

vise (vīs), a tool having two jaws moved by a screw, used to hold an object firmly while work is being done on it.

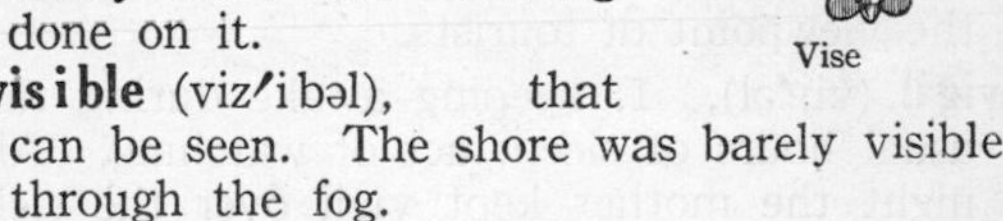
Vise

vis i ble (viz′i bəl), that can be seen. The shore was barely visible through the fog.

vis i bly (viz′i bli), so as to be visible; plainly.

vi sion (vizh′ən), 1. power of seeing; sense of sight. The old man wears glasses because his vision is poor. 2. power of perceiving by the imagination or by clear thinking; as, the vision of a prophet, a man of great vision. 3. something seen in the imagination, in a dream, etc. The beggar had visions of great wealth.

vi sion ar y (vizh′ən ãr′i), 1. not practical;

dreamy. Most plans for bringing about world peace are visionary. 2. person who is not practical; dreamer.

vis it (viz′it), 1. go to see; come to see. 2. make a call; stay with; make a stay; be a guest. I shall visit my aunt next week. 3. act of visiting; short stay. 4. go to; come to; come upon. The poor old man was visited by many troubles.

vis it a tion (viz′i tā′shən), 1. act of visiting. 2. an official visit and inspection. 3. a punishment or reward sent by God. When the escaping murderer was struck by lightning, people said it was a visitation.

vis i tor (viz′i tər), person who visits; person who is visiting; guest.

vi sor (vī′zər), 1. the movable front part of a helmet, covering the face. 2. the brim of a cap, the part that sticks out in front.

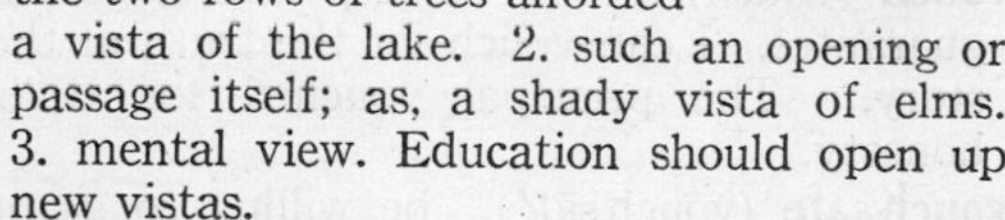

vis ta (vis′tə), 1. view seen through a narrow opening or passage. The opening between the two rows of trees afforded a vista of the lake. 2. such an opening or passage itself; as, a shady vista of elms. 3. mental view. Education should open up new vistas.

vis u al (vizh′ü əl), 1. of sight; having something to do with sight. Telescopes and microscopes are visual aids. 2. visible; that can be seen.

vi tal (vī′təl), 1. of life; as, vital forces. 2. necessary to life. Eating is a vital function. The heart is a vital organ. 3. very necessary; essential; very important. The making of immigrants into good Americans is a vital problem. 4. causing death, failure, or ruin; as, a vital wound, a vital blow to an industry. 5. full of life and spirit; lively. What a vital boy Jack is—never idle, never dull!

vi tal i ty (vī tal′i ti), 1. vital force; power to live; strength. Her vitality was lessened by illness. 2. power to endure and act.

vi tals (vī′təlz), 1. parts or organs necessary to life. The brain, heart, lungs, and stomach are vitals. 2. essential parts or features.

vi ta min or **vi ta mine** (vī′tə min), any of certain special substances necessary for the proper nourishment of the body, found especially in milk, butter, raw fruits and vegetables, cod-liver oil, and the outside part of wheat and other grains.

vit i ate (vish′i āt), injure the quality of; spoil. Gas vitiated the air.

vi va cious (vi vā′shəs), lively; sprightly; animated; gay.

vi vac i ty (vi vas′i ti), liveliness; gaiety.

viv id (viv′id), 1. bright; strong and clear. Dandelions are a vivid yellow. 2. lively; full of life. Her description of the party was so vivid that I almost felt I had been there.

vix en (vik′sən), 1. female fox. 2. bad-tempered or quarrelsome woman.

viz. (viz), namely. He had four sisters, viz., Ella, Alice, Mary, and Jane.

vi zier or **vi zir** (vi zēr′), a high official in Mohammedan countries; a minister of state.

vi zor (vī′zər), visor.

vo cab u lar y (vō kab′ū lãr′i), 1. the stock of words used by a people, class, or person. Reading will increase your vocabulary. 2. a list of words with their meanings.

vo cal (vō′kəl), 1. of the voice. The tongue is a vocal organ. 2. made with the voice. I like vocal music better than instrumental. 3. having a voice; giving forth sound. Men are vocal beings. The zoo was vocal with the roar of the lions. 4. aroused to speech; inclined to talk freely. He became vocal with anger.

vo ca tion (vō kā′shən), a particular occupation, business, profession, or trade. She chose teaching as her vocation.

vo cif er ous (vō sif′ər əs), loud and noisy; shouting; clamoring; as, a vociferous person, vociferous cheers.

vogue (vōg), 1. the fashion. Big hats were in vogue some years ago. 2. popularity. That song had a great vogue at one time.

voice (vois), 1. sound made through the mouth. 2. power to make sounds through the mouth. 3. anything like speech or song; as, the voice of the wind. 4. express; utter. They voiced their approval of the plan. 5. expression. They gave voice to their joy. 6. expressed opinion or choice. His voice was for compromise. 7. the right to express an opinion or choice. Have we any voice in this matter?

void (void), 1. empty; vacant; as, a void space. 2. an empty space. The death of his dog left an aching void in Bob's heart. 3. empty out. 4. without force; not binding in law. A contract made by a boy under legal age is void.

vol a tile (vol′ə til), 1. evaporating rapidly; passing off readily in the form of vapor. Gasoline is volatile. 2. light and changeable in spirits. Pat has a volatile disposition. He changes from gay to sad very quickly.

vol can ic (vol kan′ik), 1. of or caused by a volcano; having to do with volcanoes; as, a volcanic eruption. 2. like a volcano; liable to break out violently; as, a volcanic temper.

Volcano

vol ca no (vol kā′nō), mountain having an opening through which steam, ashes, and lava are forced out.

vol ley (vol′i), 1. shower of stones, bullets, arrows, words, oaths, etc. 2. the discharge of a number of guns at once. 3. discharge or be discharged in a volley. Cannon volleyed on all sides.

vol ley ball (vol′i bôl′), 1. game played with a large ball and a high net. The ball is hit with the hands back and forth over the net without letting it touch the ground. 2. the ball.

vol u ble (vol′ū bəl), ready to talk much; having the habit of talking much; having a great flow of words.

vol ume (vol′ūm), 1. book. We own a library of five hundred volumes. 2. a book forming part of a set or series. 3. space occupied. The storeroom has a volume of 400 cubic feet. 4. amount; quantity. Volumes of smoke poured from the chimneys of the factory. 5. amount of sound; fullness of tone. A pipe organ gives much more volume than a violin or flute.

vo lu mi nous (və lü′mi nəs), 1. forming or filling a large book or many books; as, a voluminous report. 2. writing much; as, a voluminous author. 3. of great size; very bulky. A voluminous cloak covered him from top to toe.

vol un tar i ly (vol′ən tãr′i li), by one's own choice; without force or compulsion.

vol un tar y (vol′ən tãr′i), 1. not forced; not compelled. The thief's confession was voluntary. 2. intended; done on purpose. 3. controlled by the will. Speaking is voluntary; breathing is only partly so.

vol un teer (vol′ən tēr′), 1. person who enters any service by his own choice. 2. offer one's services. As soon as war was declared, many men volunteered. 3. offer freely. Jack volunteered to carry the water. 4. of volunteers. Our village has a volunteer fire department.

vom it (vom′it), 1. throw up what has been eaten. 2. the substance thrown up from the stomach. 3. throw out with force. The chimneys vomited forth smoke.

vo ra cious (vō rā′shəs), eating much; greedy in eating; ravenous.

vote (vōt), 1. a formal expression of a wish or choice. The person receiving the most votes is elected. 2. the right to give such an expression. Not everybody has the vote. 3. votes considered together; as, the labor vote, the women's vote. 4. give a vote. He voted for the Democrats. 5. pass, determine, or grant by a vote. Money for a new school was voted by the board. 6. ballot. More than a million votes were cast. 7. declare. The children all voted the trip a great success.

vot er (vōt′ər), 1. person who votes. 2. person who has the right to vote.

vouch (vouch), be responsible; give a guarantee. I can vouch for the truth of the story. The principal vouched for Bill's honesty.

vouch safe (vouch sāf′), be willing to grant or give; deign (to do or give). Proud Tom vouchsafed no reply.

vow (vou), 1. solemn promise; as, a vow of secrecy, marriage vows. 2. promise made to God; as, a nun's vows. 3. make a vow. 4. declare earnestly or emphatically. She vowed never to leave home again.

vow el (vou′əl), 1. an open sound produced by the voice. A vowel can form a syllable by itself. 2. a letter representing such a sound. *A*, *e*, *i*, *o*, and *u* are vowels. 3. of a vowel. *Voluntary* has four vowel sounds; *strength* has only one.

voy age (voi′ij), 1. journey by water; travel by water. We had a pleasant voyage to England. Columbus voyaged on unknown seas. 2. journey or travel through the air.

voy ag er (voi′ij ər), person who makes a voyage; traveler.

vul gar (vul′gər), 1. not refined; coarse. The tramp used vulgar words. 2. of the common people. The vulgar language differs from the language used by lawyers and preachers.

vul gar i ty (vul gar′i ti), lack of fineness of feeling; lack of good breeding, manners, taste, etc.; vulgar behavior. Talking loudly in a streetcar and chewing gum at a dance are signs of vulgarity.

vul ner a ble (vul′nər ə bəl), 1. that can be wounded or injured; open to attack. The army was vulnerable in two places. 2. sensitive to criticism, temptations, influences, etc. Most people are vulnerable to ridicule.

vul ture (vul′chər), 1. a large bird of prey that eats the flesh of dead animals. See the picture on this page. 2. a greedy, ruthless person.

vy ing (vī′ing), competing. See **vie.**

W

wab ble (wob′əl), 1. move unsteadily from side to side; shake; tremble. 2. waver; be uncertain, unsteady, or inconstant. 3. wabbling motion. Also spelled **wobble.**

wad (wod), 1. a little piece or mass. A wad is used to hold the powder and shot in place in a gun or cartridge. 2. a small, soft mass. 3. make into a wad. 4. stuff with a wad. 5. pad.

wad dle (wod′əl), 1. walk with short steps and a swaying motion, as a duck does. A very fat man with very fat legs waddled across the street. 2. act of waddling. Tony made us laugh by imitating the waddle of a duck.

wade (wād), 1. walk through water, snow, sand, mud, or anything that hinders free motion. 2. make one's way with difficulty. Must I wade through that dull book? 3. go across by wading.

Vulture (about 2½ ft. long)

wa fer (wā′fər), 1. very thin cake or biscuit. 2. the thin round piece of bread used in the Catholic Mass and Communion service. 3. piece of sticky paper, dried paste, etc., used as a seal.

waf fle (wof′əl), a batter cake cooked in a special griddle that makes the cakes very thin in places.

waft (waft), 1. carry over water or through air. The waves wafted the boat to shore. 2. a breath or puff of air, etc. 3. waving movement. A waft of the hand was her only farewell.

wag (wag), 1. move from side to side or up and down. A dog wags his tail. 2. wagging motion. The Indian refused with a wag of his head. 3. person who is fond of making jokes.

wage (wāj), 1. amount paid for work. His wages are $25 a week. 2. something given in return. 3. carry on. Doctors wage war against disease.

wa ger (wā′jər), bet. The wager of $10 was promptly paid. I'll wager the black horse will win the race.

Wagon

wag gish (wag′ish), 1. fond of making jokes. 2. funny; humorous. Jack had a waggish look as he told about the waggish trick.

wag gle (wag′əl), 1. move quickly and repeatedly from side to side; wag. 2. waggling motion.

wag on (wag′ən), four-wheeled vehicle for carrying loads; as, a milk wagon.

wag on er (wag′ən ər), person who drives a wagon.

waif (wāf), 1. person without home or friends; homeless or neglected child. 2. anything without an owner; stray thing, animal, etc.

wail (wāl), 1. cry loud and long because of grief or pain. The baby wailed. 2. long cry of grief or pain. 3. a sound like such a cry. 4. make such a sound. 5. lament; mourn.

wain (wān), old word meaning wagon.

wain scot (wān′skət), 1. lining of wood on the walls of a room. A wainscot usually has panels. 2. line with wood; as, a room wainscoted in oak.

waist (wāst), 1. the part of the body between the ribs and the hips. 2. waistline. 3. a garment or part of a garment covering the body from the neck or shoulders to the waistline. 4. the middle part; as, the waist of a ship.

waist coat (wāst′kōt′), man's vest.

waist line (wāst′līn′), the line around the body between the ribs and hips.

wait (wāt), 1. stay till someone comes or something happens. 2. delay or put off. Mother waited dinner for us. 3. be ready; look forward. Tom is waiting for vacation. 4. act as a servant; change plates, pass food, etc., at table. 5. act or time of waiting. John had a long wait at the doctor's office. 6. **Lie in wait** means stay hidden ready to attack. Robbers lay in wait for the travelers. 7. **Wait on** or **wait upon** means be a servant to. It also means call upon or visit (a superior). The general waited upon the emperor at the palace.

wait er (wāt′ər), 1. one who waits. 2. man who waits on table in a hotel or restaurant.

wait ing (wāt′ing), 1. that waits. The waiting crowd rushed to the train as soon as it was ready. 2. used to wait in; as, a waiting room. 3. time that one waits. **In waiting** means in attendance on a king, queen, prince, princess, etc.

wait ress (wāt′ris), woman who waits on table in a hotel or restaurant.

wake[1] (wāk), 1. stop sleeping. She wakes at seven every morning. 2. cause to stop sleeping. The noise will wake the baby. 3. be awake; stay awake. 4. become alive or active. Flowers wake in the spring. 5. make alive or active. John needs some interest to wake him up. 6. keep watch. 7. watching; all-night watch kept beside the body of a dead person.

wake[2] (wāk), 1. track left behind a moving ship; trace or trail. 2. **In the wake of** means following; behind; after.

wake ful (wāk′fəl), 1. not able to sleep. 2. without sleep. 3. watchful.

wake ful ness (wāk′fəl nis), inability to sleep; wakeful condition.

wak en (wāk′ən), wake.

walk (wôk), 1. go on foot. In walking, a person always has one foot on the ground. 2. go over, on, or through. The man walked the floor in pain from toothache. 3. make go slowly. The rider walked his horse up the hill. 4. act of going on foot. The children went for a walk. 5. distance to walk. It is a mile walk from our house to the school. 6. way of walking. We knew the man was a sailor from his rolling walk. 7. place for walking. There are many pretty walks in the park. 8. way of living. A doctor and a street cleaner are in different walks of life.

wall (wôl), 1. the side of a house, room, or other hollow thing. 2. stone, brick, or other material built up to enclose, divide, support, or protect. Cities used to be surrounded by high walls to keep out enemies. 3. anything like a wall in looks or use. The flood came in a wall of water twelve feet high. The soldiers kept their ranks a solid wall. 4. enclose, divide, protect, or fill with a wall. The garden is walled. Workmen walled up the doorway. 5. **Drive to the wall** means make desperate or helpless.

wal let (wol′it), 1. folding pocketbook for paper money, papers, etc.; flat leather case. 2. bag for carrying things when on a journey.

Wallet (def. 1)

wal low (wol′ō), 1. roll about. The pigs wallowed in the mud. The boat wallowed helplessly in the stormy sea. 2. live in filth and wickedness. 3. act of wallowing. 4. place where an animal wallows.

wall pa per (wôl′pā′pər), 1. paper for covering walls. 2. put wallpaper on.

wal nut (wôl′nut), 1. a kind of nut that is good to eat. 2. the tree it grows on. 3. the wood of this tree. Black walnut is used in making furniture.

wal rus (wôl′rəs), a large sea animal of the Arctic regions, resembling a seal but having long tusks. See the picture. Walrus hide is made into leather for suitcases, bags, etc.

Walrus (about 10 ft. long)

waltz (wôlts), 1. a smooth, even, gliding dance. 2. music for it. 3. dance a waltz.

wam pum (wom′pəm), beads made from shells, formerly used by North American Indians as money and for ornament.

A string of seven pieces of wampum

wan (won), 1. pale. 2. faint; weak; looking worn or tired. The sick boy gave the doctor a wan smile.

wand (wond), slender stick or rod. The fairy had a magic wand.

wan der (won′dər), 1. move about without any special purpose. 2. go from the right way; stray. The dog wandered off and got lost. Mrs. White wanders away from her subject when she talks. A person's mind wanders during very high fever.

wan der er (won′dər ər), person or animal that wanders.

wane (wān), 1. lose size, strength, power, or importance. The moon wanes after it has become full. Many great empires have waned. 2. a decrease; a decline.

want (wont), 1. to wish for; wish. The child wants his dinner. 2. thing desired or needed. Mr. Jones is a man of few wants and is happy with simple pleasures. 3. lack; be without. The fund for a new church wants only a few hundred dollars of the sum needed. 4. lack; need; condition of being without something desired or needed. The plant died from want of water. 5. to need. That plant wants water. 6. great poverty. The old soldier is now in want. 7. be in need of food, clothing, and shelter; be very poor.

want ing (won′ting), 1. lacking; missing. The machine had some of its parts wanting. 2. without; less; minus; as, a year wanting three days. 3. not satisfactory; not coming up to a standard or need. Some boys are wanting in courtesy.

wan ton (won′tən), 1. reckless; heartless. That bad boy hurts animals from wanton cruelty. 2. not moral; not chaste. 3. playful; not restrained; as, a wanton child, a wanton breeze, a wanton mood. 4. act in a wanton manner. The wind wantoned with the leaves.

war (wôr), 1. a fight carried on by force between nations or parts of a nation. 2. fighting; strife; conflict. Doctors carry on war against disease. 3. the occupation or art of fighting with weapons. Soldiers are trained for war. 4. fight; make war. Germany warred against France. 5. used in war; having to do with war; caused by war.

war ble (wôr′bəl), 1. sing like a bird; as, the warbling brook. 2. a bird's song or a sound like it.

war bler (wôr′blər), 1. one that warbles. 2. any of several kinds of songbirds.

ward (wôrd), 1. person under the care of a guardian or of a court. 2. a district of a city or town. 3. a division of a hospital or prison. 4. guard. The soldiers kept watch and ward over the castle. 5. **Ward off** means keep away or turn aside. He warded off the blow with his arm.

ward en (wôr′dən), 1. keeper; guard. The man in charge of a prison is called the warden. 2. a high officer in certain colleges or other institutions.

ward er (wôr′dər), 1. guard; watchman. 2. warden; jailer.

ward robe (wôrd′rōb′), 1. a room, closet, or piece of furniture for holding clothes. 2. stock of clothes. She is shopping for her spring wardrobe.

ware (wãr), 1. manufactured thing; article for sale. The peddler sold his wares cheap. 2. kind of manufactured thing or article for sale; goods; as, silverware and tinware. 3. pottery.

ware house (wãr′hous′), place where goods are kept; storehouse.

war fare (wôr′fãr′), war; fighting.

war i ly (wãr′i li), cautiously. The soldiers climbed warily up the dangerous path.

war i ness (wãr′i nis), caution.

war like (wôr′līk′), 1. fit for war; ready for war; fond of war; as, warlike tribes. 2. threatening war; as, a warlike speech. 3. of war; having to do with war.

warm (wôrm), 1. Sunshine is warm. A fire is warm. 2. We wear warm clothes in winter. 3. easily excited; exciting; lively; as, a warm temper, a warm dispute. 4. having or showing lively feelings; enthusiastic; as, a warm welcome, a warm friend, a warm heart. 5. suggesting heat. Red and yellow are warm colors. 6. make warm. 7. become warm. The speaker warmed to his subject.

warmth (wôrmth), a being warm. We enjoyed both the warmth of the open fire and the warmth of our host's welcome.

warn (wôrn), give notice to; put on guard against danger, evil, or harm. The clouds warned us that a storm was coming up. She warned the king of the plot against his life.

warn ing (wôr′ning), something that warns; notice given in advance.

warp (wôrp), 1. bend or twist out of shape. This floor has warped so that it is not level. Prejudice warps our judgment. 2. a bend or twist. 3. move (a ship, etc.) by ropes fastened to something fixed. 4. rope used in moving a ship. 5. the threads running lengthwise in a fabric. See the picture. The warp is crossed by the woof.

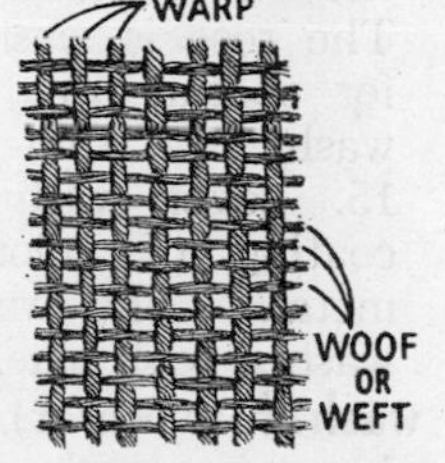

war rant (wor′ənt), 1. that which gives a right; authority. He had no warrant for his action. 2. a written order giving authority for something; as, a warrant to search the house, a warrant for a man's arrest, a warrant for the payment of money. 3. guarantee; promise; good and sufficient reason. He had no warrant for his hopes. 4. justify. Nothing can warrant such rudeness. 5. give one's word for; guarantee; promise. "I'll warrant Dick will behave," said Mr. Black.

war ren (wor′ən), piece of land where rabbits breed or are plentiful.

war ri or (wor′i ər), fighting man; experienced soldier.

war ship (wôr′ship′), ship used in fighting.

wart (wôrt), 1. a small hard lump on the skin. 2. a similar lump on a plant.

war y (wãr′i), 1. on one's guard against danger or deception; as, a wary fox. 2. cautious; careful. He gave wary answers to all of the stranger's questions.

was (woz). Once there was a king. I was late to school yesterday. The candy was eaten.

wash (wosh), 1. clean with water; as, wash one's face, wash dishes, wash clothes. 2. wash oneself. 3. wash clothes; cleanse anything with water. 4. a washing. 5. quantity of clothes washed or to be washed. She hung the wash on the line. 6. undergo washing without damage. Some silks wash perfectly. 7. that can be washed without damage. 8. carry (by a liquid). Wood is washed up by the sea. 9. material carried and then dropped by water. A delta is formed by the wash of a river. 10. wear by water. The cliffs are being slowly washed away by the waves. 11. motion or rush of water. We listened to the wash of the waves against the boat. 12. make wet. The rose is washed with dew. 13. liquid for special use; as, a mouthwash, a hairwash. 14. thin coating of color or metal. 15. cover with a thin coating of color or of metal. The walls were washed with blue.

wash er (wosh′ər), 1. person who washes. 2. machine that washes. 3. a flat ring of metal, rubber, leather, etc. Washers are used with bolts or nuts, or to make joints tight. See the picture.

Washer (def. 3)

wash ing (wosh′ing), 1. cleaning with water. 2. clothes, etc., washed or to be washed.

was n't (woz′ənt), was not.

wasp (wosp), a kind of insect that has a slender body and a powerful sting. See the picture.

Wasp (about life size)

wast (wost), an old form meaning **was.** "Thou wast" means "you were."

waste (wāst), 1. make poor use of; throw away. Don't waste food. 2. failure to use well. 3. not used. 4. useless. 5. something not used; useless stuff. 6. waste material; stuff that is left over; refuse. Bunches of cotton waste are used to clean machinery. 7. bare; wild. **Lay waste** means destroy; damage greatly. 8. desert; wilderness. We traveled through treeless wastes. Before us stretched a waste of snow and ice. 9. spoil; ruin; destroy. The soldiers wasted the fields of the enemy. 10. wearing down little by little; gradual destruction or decay. Both waste and repair are constantly going on in our bodies. 11. wear away. The man was wasted by disease.

waste ful (wāst′fəl), using or spending too much.

watch (woch), 1. look. 2. look at. We watched the kittens play. 3. look or wait with care and attention; be very careful. The boy watched for a chance to cross the street. 4. careful looking; attitude of attention. Be on the watch for automobiles when you cross the street. 5. keep guard. The dog watches over his master's house. 6. protecting; guarding. A man keeps watch over the bank at night. 7. person or persons kept to guard. The man's cry aroused the town watch who came running to his aid. 8. period of time for guarding; as, a watch in the night. 9. stay awake for some purpose. The nurse watches with the sick. 10. staying awake for some purpose. 11. thing for telling time, small enough to be carried in a pocket or worn on the wrist. 12. the time of duty of one part of a ship's crew. A watch usually lasts four hours. 13. the part of a ship's crew on duty at the same time.

watch dog (woch′dôg′), dog kept to guard property.

watch er (woch′ər), one that watches.

watch ful (woch′fəl), on the lookout; wide-awake; watching carefully. "Watchful waiting catches mice." said the cat.

watch man (woch′mən), man set to keep watch. A watchman guards the bank at night.

watch tow er (woch′tou′ər), tower from which a man watches for enemies, fires, ships, etc.

watch word (woch′wėrd′), 1. secret word that allows a person to pass a guard. We gave the watchword, and the sentinel let us pass. 2. motto; slogan. "Forward" is our watchword.

wa ter (wô′tər), 1. the ocean, rivers, lakes, ponds, and rain are water. We use water for drinking and washing. 2. a liquid like water. When you cry, water runs from your eyes. 3. sprinkle or wet with water; as, to water a street, to water grass. 4. supply with water. Our valley is well watered by rivers and brooks. 5. weaken by adding water. It is against the law to sell watered milk. 6. fill with water; discharge water. Strong sunlight will make your eyes water. The cake made the boy's mouth water. 7. take a supply of water. A ship waters before sailing. 8. the clearness and brilliance of a precious stone. A diamond of the first water is a very clear and brilliant one. 9. wavy marking on silk, metal, etc. 10. make a wavy marking on. Grandmother had a dress of watered silk.

water bird, bird that swims or wades in water.

wa ter course (wô′tər kōrs′), 1. stream of water; river; brook. 2. channel for water. In the summer many watercourses dry up.

water cress, a plant that grows in water, used for salad and as a garnish.

wa ter fall (wô′tər fôl′), fall of water from a high place.

wa ter fowl (wô′tər foul′), 1. water bird. 2. water birds; especially, birds that swim.

water lily, a water plant having flat, floating leaves and showy, fragrant flowers. The flowers of the common American water lily are white, or sometimes pink.

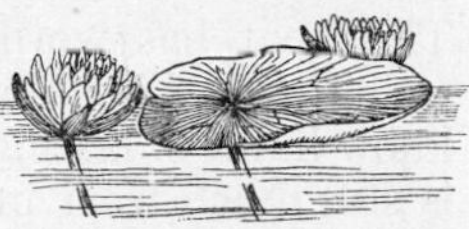
Common American water lily

wa ter man (wô′tər mən), 1. boatman; man who works on a boat. 2. man who rows.

wa ter mel on (wô′tər mel′ən), a large juicy melon with red or pink pulp and hard green rind.

wa ter proof (wô′tər prüf′), 1. that will not let water through. 2. waterproof material. 3. waterproof coat; raincoat. 4. make waterproof.

wa ter tight (wô′tər tīt′), 1. so tight that no water can get in or out. Steamboats are often divided into watertight compartments by watertight partitions. 2. leaving no opening for misunderstanding, criticism, etc.; perfect.

wa ter way (wô′tər wā′), 1. a river, canal, or other body of water that ships can go on. 2. channel for water.

wa ter y (wô′tər i), 1. of water. 2. wet; full of water. 3. containing too much water. 4. like water. 5. indicating rain; as, a watery sky.

watt (wot), a unit of electric power. My lamp uses 60 watts; my heater uses 660 watts.

wave (wāv), 1. a moving ridge or swell of water. 2. any movement like this. Light, heat, and sound move in waves. A cold wave is sweeping over the country. 3. move as waves do; sway. The tall grass waved in the breeze. Mary waved to Alice as she passed. 4. move back and forth. Wave your hand. 5. signal by waving. 6. waving; as, a wave of the hand. 7. curve or series of curves; as, waves in a girl's hair. 8. give a wavelike form to. Girls wave their hair.

wa ver (wā′vər), 1. move to and fro. Helen's choice wavered between the blue dress and the green one. 2. become unsteady; begin to give way. The battle line wavered and broke. 3. a wavering.

wav y (wāv′i), having waves; having many waves; as, a wavy line, wavy hair.

Wavy line

wax[1] (waks), 1. a yellowish substance made by bees. Wax is hard when cold, but can be easily shaped when warm. 2. any substance like this. Most of the wax used for candles, for keeping air from jelly, etc., is really paraffin. Sealing wax and shoemaker's wax are other common waxes. 3. rub, stiffen, polish, etc., with wax. We wax that floor once a month.

wax[2] (waks), 1. grow; increase. The moon waxes till it becomes full, and then wanes. 2. become. The party waxed merry.

wax en (wak′sən), 1. made of wax. 2. like wax. Her skin was waxen.

way (wā), 1. manner; style. Mary is wearing her hair in a new way. 2. means; method. Men of science are trying to find ways to prevent disease. 3. respect; particular. The plan is bad in several ways. 4. direction. Look this way. 5. coming or going; progress. The beggar made his way from door to door. 6. distance. The moon is a long way off. 7. path; road. The hunter found a way through the forest. 8. space for passing or going ahead. Automobiles must make way for a fire engine. 9. habit; custom. Don't mind Joe's teasing; it's only his way. 10. one's wish; will. A spoiled child wants his own way all the time. 11. condition; state. That sick man is in a bad way. 12. movement of a ship through water. The boat slowly gathered way as it slid through the water. 13. Some special meanings are:

by way of, 1. by the route of; through. 2. as; for.

give way, 1. retreat; make way; yield. 2. break down or fail. 3. abandon oneself to emotion.

ways, timbers on which a ship is built and launched.

way far er (wā′fãr′ər), traveler.

way far ing (wā′fãr′ing), traveling.

way laid (wā′lād′). See **waylay.**

way lay (wā′lā′), 1. lie in wait for; attack on the way. Robin Hood waylaid travelers and robbed them. 2. stop (a person) on his way. Newspaper reporters waylaid the famous actor and asked him many questions.

way side (wā′sīd′), 1. edge of a road or path. We ate lunch on the wayside. 2. along the edge of a road or path. We slept in a wayside inn.

way ward (wā′wərd), 1. turning from the right way; disobedient; willful. In a wayward mood, Bill ran away from home. 2. irregular; unsteady.

we (wē), 1. the persons speaking. We are glad to see you. 2. an author, a king, or a judge sometimes uses *we* when he means *I*.

weak (wēk). A weak old man totters as he walks. A person with weak eyes cannot see far. A weak mind is a feeble one. A weak fort can be easily captured. A weak nation has very little power because it is poor and small. Weak tea has less flavor than strong tea. A weak acid contains much water and little acid.

weak en (wēk′ən), 1. make weaker. You can weaken the tea by adding water. 2. become weaker.

weak ling (wēk′ling), 1. weak person or animal. 2. weak.

weak ly (wēk′li), 1. weak; feeble; sickly. 2. in a weak manner.

weak ness (wēk′nis), 1. being weak; lack of power, force, or vigor. Weakness kept Mr. Smith in bed. 2. weak point; slight fault. Putting things off is her weakness. 3. fondness; a liking that one is a little ashamed of. Grace has a weakness for sweets.

weal (wēl), well-being; prosperity; happiness. Good citizens act for the public weal. A loyal man stands by his friends in weal or woe.

wealth (welth), 1. riches; many valuable possessions; property; as, a man of wealth, the wealth of a city. 2. abundance; large quantity; as, a wealth of hair, a wealth of words.

wealth y (wel′thi), having wealth; rich.

wean (wēn), 1. accustom (a child or young animal) to food other than its mother's milk. 2. accustom (a person) to do without something; cause to turn away. Tom was sent away to school to wean him from bad companions.

weap on (wep′ən), thing used in fighting. Swords, spears, arrows, clubs, guns, cannon, shields, claws, horns, teeth, and stings are weapons.

wear (wãr), 1. have on the body. Men wear coats, hats, collars, watches, beards. She wears black since her husband died. 2. have; show. The house wore an air of sadness. 3. wearing; being worn. Clothing for summer wear is being shown in the shops. This suit has been in constant wear for two years. 4. clothing; things worn; as, underwear. Children's wear is sold in this store. 5. last long; give good service. This coat has worn well. A person wears well if you like him better the longer you know him. 6. lasting quality; service. There is still much wear in these shoes. 7. use up; be used up. The pencil is worn to a stub. The paint wears off the house. 8. damage from use. The rug shows wear. 9. make by rubbing, scraping, or washing away. Walking wore a hole in my shoe. 10. tire. She is worn out by too much work. Teaching is wearing work. **wore** and **worn** are formed from **wear.**

wear er (wãr′ər), person or thing that wears.

wea ri ly (wēr′i li), in a weary manner. The tired old man walked along wearily.

wea ri ness (wēr′i nis), weary condition; tired feeling.

wea ri some (wēr′i səm), wearying; tiring; tiresome.

wea ry (wēr′i), 1. tired; as, weary feet, a weary brain. 2. tiring; as, a weary wait. 3. make weary; tire. Walking up hill wearied grandfather.

wea sel (wē′zəl), a small animal with a slender body, that eats rats, mice, birds, and eggs. Weasels are quick and sly.

Weasel (6 to 8 in. long without the tail)

weath er (weᴛʜ′ər), 1. condition of the air; as, hot weather, windy weather. 2. expose to the weather. Wood turns gray if weathered for a long time. 3. go or come through safely. The ship weathered the storm. 4. sail to the windward of. The ship weathered the cape. 5. toward the wind. It was very cold on the weather side of the ship.

weath er-beat en (weᴛʜ′ər bēt′ən), worn by the wind, rain, and other forces of the weather.

weath er cock (weᴛʜ′ər kok′), device to show which way the wind is blowing.

Weathercock

weather vane, weathercock.

weave (wēv), 1. form (threads or strips) into a thing or fabric; make (cloth, etc.) out of thread, etc. People weave thread into cloth, straw into hats, and reeds into baskets. A spider weaves a web. 2. combine into a whole. The author wove three plots together into one story. 3. make by combining parts. 4. method or pattern of weaving. Homespun is a cloth of coarse weave. **wove** and **woven** are formed from **weave.**

weav er (wēv′ər), 1. one that weaves. 2. person who weaves as a regular occupation.

web (web), 1. something woven. A spider spins a web. 2. whole piece of cloth made at one time. 3. anything like a web. His story was a web of lies. 4. the skin joining the toes of ducks, geese, and other swimming birds.

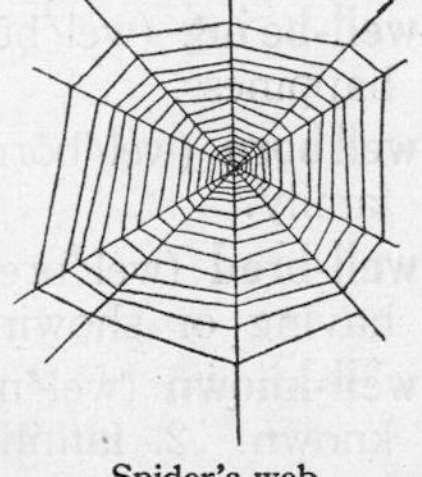
Spider's web

webbed (webd), 1. formed like a web or with a web. 2. having the toes joined by a web. Ducks have webbed feet.

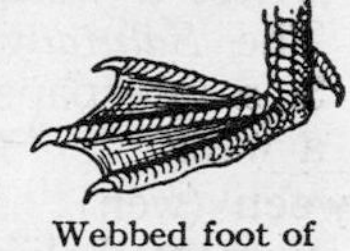
Webbed foot of a duck

wed (wed), marry; married.

we'd (wēd), 1. we had. 2. we should; we would.

wed ded (wed′id), 1. married. 2. united. 3. devoted.

wed ding (wed′ing), 1. marriage ceremony. 2. an anniversary of it. A golden wedding is the fiftieth anniversary of a marriage.

wedge (wej), 1. piece of wood or metal with a thin edge used in splitting, separating, etc. See the picture. 2. something shaped like a wedge or used like a wedge. Wild geese fly in a wedge. Her grand party was an entering wedge into society. 3. split or separate with a wedge. 4. fasten with a wedge. 5. thrust or pack in tight. He wedged himself through the narrow window. The man's foot was wedged between the rocks, so that he could not get away.

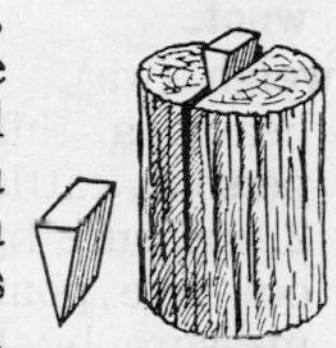
Wedge; wedge splitting a log.

wed lock (wed′lok), married life; marriage.

Wednes day (wenz′di), the fourth day of the week.

wee (wē), very, very small; tiny.

weed (wēd), 1. a useless or troublesome plant. Weeds choke out the vegetables and flowers. 2. take weeds out of. Please weed the garden now. 3. take out weeds.

weeds (wēdz), mourning garments; as, a widow's weeds.

weed y (wēd′i), 1. full of weeds; as, a weedy garden. 2. of weeds; like weeds. 3. thin and lanky; weak.

week (wēk), 1. seven days, one after another. 2. the six working days. He is away all the week but comes home for Sundays.

week day (wēk′dā′), any day of the week except Sunday.

week end (wēk′end′), Saturday and Sunday as a time for recreation, visiting, etc.; as, a weekend in the country.

week ly (wēk′li), 1. of a week; for a week; lasting a week. His weekly wage is $30. 2. once each week; every week. Mary writes a weekly letter to her grandmother. The *Saturday Evening Post* comes weekly. 3. a newspaper or magazine published once a week.

ween (wēn), old word meaning think; suppose; believe; expect.

weep (wēp), 1. cry; shed tears. 2. shed tears for; mourn. **wept** is formed from **weep.**

wee vil (wē′vəl), a small beetle whose larvae eat grain, nuts, fruits, etc. Weevils do much damage to the corn and cotton crops.

Weevil (line shows actual length)

weft (weft), the threads running from side to side across a fabric; the woof. See the picture under **woof.**

weigh (wā), 1. find out how heavy a thing is. We weigh persons, cattle, coal, and many other things. 2. measure by weight. The grocer weighed out five pounds of butter. 3. have as a measure by weight. I weigh 110 pounds. 4. have importance. The amount of his salary does not weigh with Mr. Black at all, because he is very rich. 5. bend by weight. The boughs of the apple tree are weighed down with fruit. She is weighed down with many troubles. 6. balance in the mind; consider carefully. Mr. Jones weighs his words before speaking. 7. lift up (an anchor). The ship weighed anchor and sailed away.

weight (wāt), 1. how heavy a thing is; the amount a thing weighs. The dog's weight is 50 pounds. 2. heaviness. 3. system of units for weight. 4. piece of metal used in weighing things; as, a pound weight. 5. heavy thing or mass. A weight keeps the papers in place. 6. load; burden. The pillars support the weight of the roof. She sank under the weight of troubles. 7. influence; importance; value. A wise man's opinion has great weight. 8. add weight to; put too much weight on; burden. The elevator is weighted too heavily. Job was weighted with troubles.

weight y (wāt′i), 1. heavy. 2. too heavy. 3. important; influential.

weird (wērd), unearthly; mysterious; wild; strange. The shadows made weird figures on the wall. The witches moved in a weird dance.

wel come (wel′kəm), 1. kindly greeting. Welcome home! 2. greet kindly. 3. kind reception. You will always have a welcome here. 4. receive gladly. 5. gladly received; as, a welcome visitor, a welcome letter, a welcome rest. 6. gladly or freely permitted. Everybody is welcome to walk in the public park. 7. You say "You are welcome" when someone thanks you.

weld (weld), 1. join together by hammering or pressing while soft and hot. He welded the broken rod. 2. a welded joint. 3. unite closely. Working together for a month welded them into a strong team. 4. be capable of being welded. Iron welds; wood does not. Copper welds easily.

wel fare (wel′fãr′), health, happiness, and prosperity; being well; doing well. Uncle Charles asked about the welfare of everyone in our family.

well[1] (wel), 1. all right; in a satisfactory, favorable, or good manner. Is everything going well at school? Boston is well supplied with parks. 2. fairly; reasonably. Jim's brother can't well refuse to help him. 3. thoroughly. Shake the medicine well before taking it. 4. much; to a considerable degree. The fair brought in well over a hundred dollars. 5. in good health. Dick is well. 6. satisfactory; good; right. It is well you came along. 7. *Well* is sometimes used to show mild surprise or merely to fill in. Well! well! here's Jack. Well, I'm not sure. 8. **Well off** means (1) in a good condition. (2) fairly rich.

well[2] (wel), 1. hole dug or bored in the ground to get water, oil, gas, etc. The farmer pumped all his water from a well. 2. spring; fountain. 3. something like a well in shape or use. An elevator's shaft is called a well. 4. spring; rise; gush. Water wells from a spring beneath the rock. Tears welled up in her eyes.

we'll (wēl), we shall; we will.

well-be ing (wel′bē′ing), welfare; health and happiness.

well born (wel′bôrn′), belonging to a good family.

well-bred (wel′bred′), well brought up; having or showing good manners.

well-known (wel′nōn′), 1. clearly or fully known. 2. familiar. 3. generally or widely known.

well-nigh (wel′nī′), very nearly; almost.

well-to-do (wel′tə dü′), having enough money to live well; prosperous.

welt (welt), 1. a strip of leather between the upper part and the sole of a shoe. 2. a streak or ridge made on the skin by a stick or whip. 3. beat severely.

wel ter (wel′tər), 1. roll or tumble about; wallow. 2. a rolling or tumbling about. All we saw was a welter of arms, legs, and bodies. 3. commotion; confusion.

wench (wench), 1. girl or young woman. 2. woman servant.

wend (wend), direct (one's way); go. We wended our way home.

went (went), did go. I went home.

wept (wept), cried; shed tears. See **weep.**

were (wėr). The officers were obeyed by the soldiers. If I were rich, I would help the poor.

we're (wēr), we are.

weren't (wėrnt), were not.

wert (wėrt), an old form meaning **were.** "Thou wert" means "you were."

west (west), 1. the direction of the sunset. 2. toward the west; farther toward the west. Walk west three blocks. 3. **West of** means farther west than. Ohio is west of Pennsylvania. 4. from the west; as, a west wind. 5. in the west; living in the west. 6. the part of any country toward the west. 7. **The West** sometimes means the states or countries in the west.

NORTH
WEST ←→ EAST
SOUTH

west er ly (wes′tər li), 1. toward the west. 2. from the west.

west ern (wes′tərn), 1. toward the west. 2. from the west. 3. of the west. 4. of the west of the United States.

west ward (west′wərd), toward the west; west. He walked westward. The orchard is on the westward slope of the hill. Rocks lay westward of the ship's course.

west wards (west′wərdz), westward.

wet (wet), 1. covered or soaked with water or other liquid; watery. Don't touch wet paint. Her eyes were wet with tears. 2. make wet. Have you wet your feet? 3. water. 4. rainy; as, wet weather. 5. wetness; rain. Come in out of the wet.

wet ness (wet′nis), wet condition.

we've (wēv), we have.

whack (hwak), 1. a sharp, resounding blow. 2. strike with a sharp, resounding blow.

whale (hwāl), 1. an animal shaped like a huge fish and living in the sea. Men get oil from whales. 2. hunt and catch whales.

Greenland whale (about 60 ft. long)

whal er (hwāl′ər), 1. hunter of whales. 2. ship used for hunting whales.

wharf (hwôrf), platform built on the shore or out from the shore, beside which ships can load and unload. See the picture.

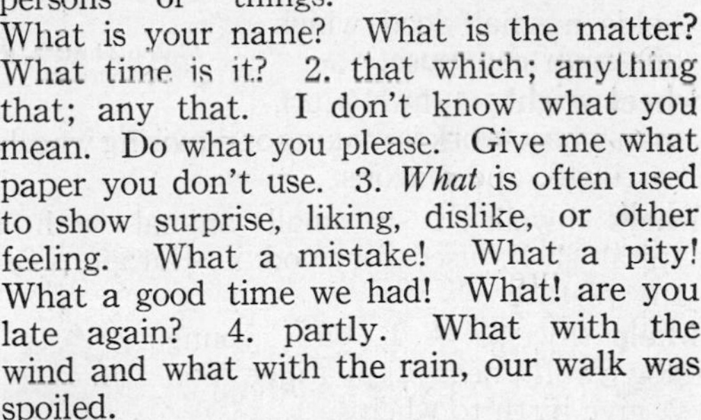

Wharf

wharves (hwôrvz), wharfs.

what (hwot), 1. *What* is used in asking questions about persons or things. What is your name? What is the matter? What time is it? 2. that which; anything that; any that. I don't know what you mean. Do what you please. Give me what paper you don't use. 3. *What* is often used to show surprise, liking, dislike, or other feeling. What a mistake! What a pity! What a good time we had! What! are you late again? 4. partly. What with the wind and what with the rain, our walk was spoiled.

what e'er (hwot ãr′), whatever.

what ev er (hwot ev′ər), 1. anything that; any that. Do whatever you like. Ask whatever girls you like to the party. 2. no matter what; no matter who. Do it, whatever happens. Any person whatever can tell you the way.

what's (hwots), what is.

what so ev er (hwot′sō ev′ər), whatever.

wheat (hwēt), 1. a grain from which flour is made. See the picture. 2. the plant which the grain grows on.

A B
Wheat: A, bearded; B, beardless.

whee dle (hwē′dəl), 1. coax; persuade by flattery, smooth words, caresses, etc. The children wheedled their mother into letting them go to the picnic. 2. get by wheedling. They finally wheedled the secret out of him.

wheel (hwēl), 1. round frame that turns on its center. See the picture. 2. anything round like a wheel or moving like one. A bicycle is often called a wheel. Clay is shaped into dishes on a potter's wheel. The wheels of trade began to turn. A turn of fortune's wheel made Alice's father rich. 3. turn. The rider wheeled his horse about. He wheeled around suddenly. 4. move on wheels. The workman was wheeling a load of bricks on a wheelbarrow. 5. **At the wheel** means (1) at the steering wheel. (2) in control.

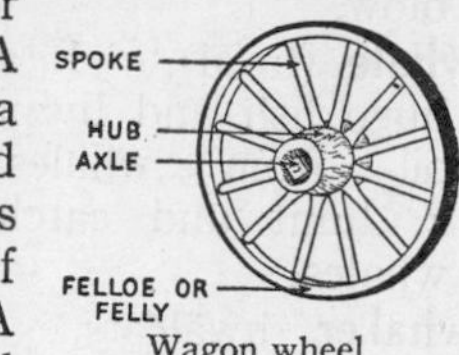

Wagon wheel

wheel bar row (hwēl′bar′ō), a small vehicle which has one wheel and two handles. A wheelbarrow holds a small load which one man can push.

Man pushing a wheelbarrow

wheel wright (hwēl′rīt′), man whose work is making or repairing wheels, carriages, and wagons.

whelk (hwelk), a small animal with a spiral shell, used for food in Europe. See the picture.

Whelk (shell 2 to 3 in. long)

whelp (hwelp), 1. cub; young dog, wolf, bear, lion, tiger, etc. 2. give birth to whelps.

when (hwen), 1. at what time. When does school close? 2. at the time that; at any time that. The dog comes when he is called. 3. at which time; and then. The dog growled till his master spoke, when he gave a joyful bark. 4. although. We have only three books when we need five. 5. what time; which time. Since when have the Browns had a car? 6. the time or occasion; as, the when and where of an act.

whence (hwens), 1. from what place; from where. 2. from what source or cause; from what. 3. from which. Let him return to that land whence he came.

when e'er (hwen ãr′), whenever.

when ev er (hwen ev′ər), when; at whatever time; at any time that.

where (hwãr), 1. in what place; at what place. Where do you live? 2. to what place. Where are you going? 3. from what place. Where did you get that story? 4. in what way; in what respect. Where is the harm in trying? 5. what place. Where did he come from? 6. in which; at which. 7. to which. 8. in the place in which; at the place at which.

where a bouts (hwãr′ə bouts′), 1. where; near what place. Whereabouts are my books? 2. place where a person or thing is. Do you know the whereabouts of the Jones cottage?

where as (hwãr az′), 1. but; while; on the contrary. Some children like school, whereas others do not. 2. considering that; since.

where at (hwãr at′), at what; at which.

where by (hwãr bī′), by what; by which. There is no other way whereby he can be saved.

where fore (hwãr′fōr), 1. for what reason; why. 2. for which reason; therefore; so. 3. reason.

where in (hwãr in′), in what; in which; how.

where of (hwãr ov′), of what; of which; of whom. Solomon knew whereof he spoke.

where on (hwãr on′), on which; on what. Summer cottages occupy the land whereon the old farmhouse stood.

where so ev er (hwãr′sō ev′ər), wherever.

where un to (hwãr un′tü), 1. to which; where. 2. for what purpose; why.

where up on (hwãr′ə pon′), 1. upon what; upon which. 2. at which; after which.

wher ev er (hwãr ev′ər), where; to whatever place; in whatever place. He goes wherever he wishes.

where with (hwãr wiᴛʜ′), with what; with which.

wher ry (hwer′i), 1. a light rowboat. 2. a large fishing boat or barge.

whet (hwet), 1. sharpen by rubbing; as, to whet a knife. 2. make keen or eager. The smell of food whetted my appetite. An exciting story whets your interest.

wheth er (hweᴛʜ′ər). *Whether* is used in expressing choices. Whether we go or whether we stay matters very little. He does not know whether to go or not. I doubt whether we can find a prettier hat elsewhere. Whether sick or well, she is always cheerful. He asked whether he might be excused.

whet stone (hwet′stōn′), a stone for sharpening knives or tools.

whew (hwū), a word expressing surprise, dismay, etc. Whew! it's cold!

whey (hwā), the watery part of milk that separates from the curd when milk sours or when cheese is made.

which (hwich), 1. *Which* is used in asking questions about persons or things. Which boy won the prize? Which books are yours? Which seems the best plan? 2. *Which* is also used in connecting a group of words with some word in the sentence. Read the book which you have. Tom now has the dog which used to belong to his cousin. 3. the one that; any that. Here are three boxes. Choose which you like best.

which ev er (hwich ev′ər), 1. any one; any that. Buy whichever hat you like. Whichever you take will be becoming. 2. no matter which. Whichever side wins, I shall be satisfied.

whiff (hwif), 1. slight puff of air, smoke, odor, etc. 2. blow; puff.

while (hwīl), 1. time. He kept us waiting a long while. The postman came a while ago. 2. during the time that; in the time that. While I was speaking, he said nothing. Summer is pleasant while it lasts. 3. although. While I like the color of the hat, I do not like its shape. 4. pass in some easy or pleasant manner; spend. The children while away many afternoons on the beach. 5. **Worth while** means worth time, attention, or effort.

whilst (hwīlst), while.

whim (hwim), sudden fancy or notion. She has a whim for gardening, but it won't last.

whim per (hwim′pər), 1. cry with low, broken sounds, in the way that a sick child or dog does; make weak complaints. 2. a whimpering cry.

whim si cal (hwim′zi kəl), having many odd notions or fancies; fanciful; odd.

whine (hwīn), 1. make a low, complaining cry or sound. The dog whined to go out with us. 2. low, complaining cry or sound. 3. say with a whine. 4. complain in a peevish, childish way. Some people are always whining about trifles.

whin ny (hwin′i), 1. the sound that a horse makes. 2. make such a sound.

whip (hwip), 1. strike; beat. 2. thing to whip with. 3. beat (cream, eggs, etc.) to a froth. 4. move quickly and suddenly. He whipped off his coat and whipped out his knife.

whip poor will (hwip′pər wil′), American bird whose call sounds somewhat like its name. It is active at night or twilight. See the picture.

Whippoorwill
(9 to 10 in. long)

whir or **whirr** (hwėr), 1. a noise that sounds like *whir-r-r;* as, the whir of machinery. 2. move quickly with such a noise. The motor whirs.

whirl (hwėrl), 1. turn around and around; spin. The leaves whirled in the wind. 2. move around and around. We whirled about the room. He whirled the club. 3. move or carry quickly. We were whirled away in an airplane. 4. whirling movement. We saw whirls of smoke. 5. confused condition. His thoughts are in a whirl.

whirl pool (hwėrl′pül′), water whirling around and around rapidly and violently. Four swimmers got caught in a whirlpool, and had hard work to keep from being drowned.

whirl wind (hwėrl′wind′), air whirling violently around and around; whirling storm of wind.

whisk (hwisk), 1. sweep; brush. She whisked the crumbs from the table. 2. quick sweep. She whisked away the dirt with a few whisks of her broom. 3. move quickly. The mouse whisked into its hole. She whisked the letter out of sight. 4. a light, quick movement. 5. a small brush or broom. We brush our coats with a whisk. 6. beat or whip to a froth.

whisk er (hwis′kər), 1. hair growing on a man's face. 2. long stiff hair growing near the mouth of a cat, rat, etc.

whis key (hwis′ki), a strong intoxicating liquor made from grain. Whiskey is about half alcohol.

whis ky (hwis′ki), whiskey.

whis per (hwis′pər), 1. speak very softly and low. 2. very soft, low spoken sound. 3. speak to in a whisper. 4. tell secretly or privately. It is whispered that Mr. Smith's business is failing. 5. something told secretly or privately. No whisper about having a new teacher has come to our ears. 6. make a soft, rustling sound. The wind whispered in the pines. 7. a soft, rustling sound. The wind was so gentle that we could hear the whisper of the leaves.

whis tle (hwis′əl), 1. make a clear, shrill sound. The policeman whistled for the automobile to stop. The engine whistled before it started off. A blackbird whistles. 2. the sound made by whistling. 3. an instrument for making whistling sounds. See the picture. 4. blow a whistle. 5. move with a shrill sound. The wind whistled around the house.

Steam whistle

whit (hwit), very small bit. The sick man is not a whit better.

white (hwīt), 1. the color of snow. 2. having this color. She turned white with fear. 3. white clothing. 4. something white. Take the whites of four eggs. 5. having a light-colored skin; not black, brown, or yellow. 6. white person. 7. spotless; pure; innocent.

white ant, termite. White ants eat wood and are very destructive to buildings.

white cap (hwīt′kap′), wave with a foaming white crest.

white flag, a flag that means "We want a truce" or "We surrender."

White House, 1. the official residence of the President of the United States, in Washington, D.C. 2. office, authority, opinion, etc., of the President of the United States.

whit en (hwīt′ən), make white; become white.

white wash (hwīt′wosh′), 1. liquid for whitening walls, woodwork, etc. Whitewash is usually made of lime and water. 2. whiten with whitewash. 3. cover up the faults or mistakes of.

whith er (hwiᴛʜ′ər), where; to what place; to which place.

whit ish (hwīt′ish), somewhat white.

whit tle (hwit′əl), 1. cut or shape (wood) with a knife. The old sailor whittled a boat for Jim. 2. cut with a knife for fun.

whiz or **whizz** (hwiz), 1. make a humming or hissing sound; move or rush with such a sound. An arrow whizzed past. 2. humming or hissing sound.

who (hü), 1. *Who* is used in asking questions about persons. Who goes there? Who is your friend? Who told you? 2. *Who* is also used in connecting a group of words with some word in the sentence. The girl who spoke is my best friend. We saw men who were working in the fields. 3. the person that; any person that; one that. Who is not for us is against us.

whoa (hwō), stop!

who ev er (hü ev′ər), 1. who; any person that. Whoever wants the book may have it. 2. no matter who. Whoever else goes hungry, he won't.

whole (hōl), 1. having all its parts; complete. He gave her a whole set of dishes. 2. all of a thing; the total. Four quarters make a whole. 3. thing complete in itself; a system. 4. not broken; in one piece. 5. well; healthy.

whole heart ed (hōl′här′tid), earnest; sincere; hearty; cordial. The returning soldiers were given a wholehearted welcome.

whole sale (hōl′sāl′), 1. sale of goods in large quantities at a time. He buys at wholesale and sells at retail. 2. in large lots or quantities. The wholesale price of this coat is $20; the retail price is $30. 3. selling in large quantities; as, a wholesale fruit business. 4. sell in large quantities.

whole some (hōl′səm), 1. healthful; good for the health. Milk is a wholesome food. 2. healthy-looking; suggesting health.

who'll (hül), who will; who shall.

whol ly (hōl′i), completely; entirely; totally. The sick boy was wholly cured.

whom (hüm), what person; which person. *Whom* is made from *who*, just as *him* is made from *he*. Whom do you like best? He does not know whom to believe. The girl to whom I spoke is my cousin.

whoop (hüp), 1. loud cry or shout. The Indian gave a whoop of rage. 2. shout loudly. 3. the noise a person makes when he has whooping cough. 4. make this noise.

whooping cough, an infectious disease of children and rarely of adults, that causes fits of coughing that end with a loud, gasping sound.

whose (hüz), of whom; of which. The girl whose work got the prize is the youngest in her class. Whose book is this?

who so (hü′sō), old word meaning whoever. Whoso seeks may find.

why (hwī). Why did the baby cry? Harry does not know why he failed. The reason why Harry failed was his laziness. Why! Why! the cage is empty! Why, yes, I will if you wish. Tell me all the whys and wherefores.

wick (wik), the part of an oil lamp or candle that is lighted. See the picture. The oil or melted wax is drawn up the wick and burned.

Candle cut to show the wick

wick ed (wik′id), 1. bad; evil; sinful. 2. mischievous.

wick ed ness (wik′id nis), 1. sin; being wicked. 2. wicked thing or act.

wick er (wik′ər), 1. a slender, easily bent branch or twig. 2. twigs or branches woven together. Wicker is used in making baskets and furniture. 3. made of wicker.

wick et (wik′it), 1. small door or gate. The big door has a wicket in it. 2. small window. Buy your tickets at this wicket. 3. in croquet, a hoop or arch. 4. in cricket, either of the two sets of sticks that one side tries to hit with the ball. See the picture.

A B

Wickets: A, for croquet; B, for cricket.

wide (wīd), 1. Broadway is a wide street. They sail on the wide ocean. The door is three feet wide. They went forth into the wide world. A trip around the world gives wide experience. Wide reading gives wide culture. 2. far open. The child stared with wide eyes. 3. far from a named point or object; as, a guess wide of the truth, a shot wide of the mark. 4. to the full extent. Open your mouth wide. The gates stand wide open.

wide-a wake (wīd′ə wāk′), 1. fully awake; with the eyes wide open. 2. alert; keen; knowing.

wide-eyed (wīd′īd′), with the eyes wide open. The baby gazed at the Christmas tree with wide-eyed surprise.

wide ly (wīd′li), to a wide extent; as, a widely distributed plant, a man who is widely known, to be widely read, widely opened eyes. Tom and Jim gave two widely different accounts of the quarrel.

wid en (wīd′ən), make wide or wider; become wide or wider. He widened the path through the forest. The river widens as it flows.

wide spread (wīd′spred′), 1. spread widely; as, widespread wings. 2. spread over a wide space; as, a widespread flood. 3. occurring in many places far apart; as, a widespread belief.

wid ow (wid′ō), 1. woman whose husband is dead and who has not married again. 2. make a widow of. She was widowed when she was only thirty years old.

wid ow er (wid′ō ər), man whose wife is dead and who has not married again.

width (width), 1. how wide a thing is; distance across; breadth. The room is 12 feet in width. 2. piece of a certain width. It will take two widths of cloth to make the curtains.

wield (wēld), hold and use; manage; control. A soldier wields the sword. A writer wields the pen. The people wield the power in a democracy.

wife (wīf), married woman.

wig (wig), covering of hair for the head. Dolls have wigs. The bald man wore a wig.

Judge's wig

wig gle (wig′əl), 1. wriggle; move with short quick movements from side to side. The restless child wiggled in his chair. 2. such a movement.

wight (wīt), old word meaning person or human being.

wig wam (wig′wom), a hut of poles covered with bark, mats, or skins, made by American Indians.

Wigwam

wild (wīld), 1. living or growing in the forests or fields; not tamed; not cultivated. The tiger is a wild animal. The daisy is a wild flower. 2. with no people living in it. 3. waste; desert. Much of northern Canada is wild land. **The wilds** means wild country. 4. not civilized; savage. 5. not checked; not restrained; as, a wild rush for the ball. 6. violent; as, a wild storm. 7. rash; crazy. 8. wildly.

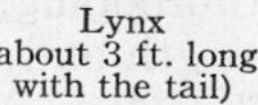

Lynx (about 3 ft. long with the tail)

wild cat (wīld′kat′), 1. a wild animal like a common cat, but larger. A lynx is one kind of wildcat. 2. wild; reckless; not safe.

wil der ness (wil′dər nis), wild place; region with no people living in it.

wild fire (wīld′fīr′), fire hard to put out, formerly used in warfare. **Like wildfire** means very rapidly. The news spread like wildfire.

wild fowl, birds ordinarily hunted, such as wild ducks or geese, partridges, quail, and pheasants.

wild ly (wīld′li), in a wild way; without restraint. People rushed wildly out of the burning building. Insane people talk wildly.

wile (wīl), 1. a trick to deceive; cunning way. The witch by her wiles persuaded the prince to go with her. 2. coax; lure; entice. The sunshine wiled me from my work. 3. **Wile away** means pass time, etc., pleasantly.

will[1] (wil). We cannot always do as we will. Most men feel good will toward their friends and ill will toward their enemies. He will go tomorrow. I will be there. You will do it at once! Mary will read for hours at a time.

will[2] (wil), 1. the power of the mind to decide and do. 2. decide by using this power; use the will. Jane willed to keep awake. 3. determine; decide. Fate has willed it otherwise. 4. a legal statement of a person's wishes about what shall be done with his property after he is dead. 5. give by such a statement. Mr. Black willed all his property to his two daughters.

will ful or **wil ful** (wil′fəl), 1. wanting or taking one's own way; stubborn. The willful child would not eat his supper. 2. intended; done on purpose; as, willful murder, willful waste.

will ing (wil′ing), 1. ready; consenting. He is willing to wait. 2. cheerfully ready; as, willing obedience.

will ing ly (wil′ing li), readily; gladly.

will ing ness (wil′ing nis), being willing; readiness.

wil low (wil′ō), 1. a kind of tree or shrub. See the picture. The branches of most willows bend easily and are used to make furniture, baskets, etc. 2. its wood.

Weeping willow

wilt[1] (wilt), become limp and drooping; wither; lose strength and vigor.

wilt[2] (wilt), an old form meaning **will.** "Thou wilt" means "you will."

wil y (wīl′i), tricky; cunning; crafty; sly. The wily fox got away.

win (win), 1. We win fame, a victory, a prize, sympathy, favor, or a bet. 2. be successful over others. 3. get to; reach; as, to win the summit of a mountain. 4. gain the favor of; persuade. The speaker soon won his audience. Mary has won her mother over to her side. **won** is formed from **win.**

wince (wins), 1. draw back suddenly; shrink. It is hard to keep from wincing when the doctor cleans a cut. 2. act of wincing.

winch (winch), machine for lifting or pulling, turned by a crank.

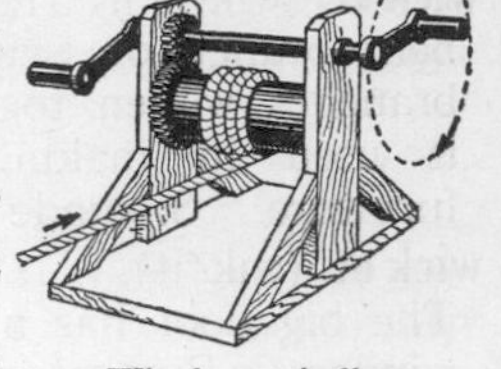

Winch or windlass. The arrows show the way the handles go.

wind[1] (wind), 1. air in motion. The wind bends the branches. 2. air filled with some smell. The deer got wind of the hunter and ran off. 3. **Get wind of** sometimes means find out about. 4. smell; follow by scent. 5. breath; power of breathing. A runner needs good wind. 6. put out of breath; cause difficulty in breathing. The fat man was winded by walking up the steep hill.

wind[2] (wīnd), 1. move this way and that; go in a crooked way; change direction; turn. A brook winds through the woods. We wound our way through the narrow streets. 2. twist or turn around something. The vine winds around a pole. 3. roll into a ball or on a spool. Grandma was winding yarn. Thread comes wound on spools. 4. fold, wrap, or place about something. The mother wound her arms about the child. The man's arm is wound with bandages. 5. make (some machine) go by turning some part of it; as, to wind a clock. 6. a bend; a turn; a twist. 7. **Wind up** sometimes means to end; settle; conclude. **wound** is formed from **wind.**

wind[3] (wīnd), blow. The hunter winds his horn.

wind break (wind′brāk′), protection from the wind.

wind fall (wind′fôl′), 1. fruit blown down by the wind. 2. unexpected piece of good luck.

wind instrument, musical instrument sounded by blowing air into it. Horns, flutes, and cornets are wind instruments.

wind lass (wind′ləs), a winch. See the picture of **winch** on this page.

wind mill (wind′mil′), a mill or machine worked by the wind. Windmills are mostly used to pump water. See the picture.

Windmill for pumping water

win dow (win′dō), 1. an opening in a wall or roof to let in light or air. 2. such an opening with its frame and glass.

win dow pane (win′dō pān′), piece of glass in a window.

window sill, piece of wood or stone across the bottom of a window.

wind pipe (wind′pīp′), the passage from the throat to the lungs.

wind shield (wind′shēld′), a sheet of glass, etc., to keep off the wind. Automobiles have windshields.

wind ward (wind′wərd), 1. toward the wind. 2. the side toward the wind. 3. on the side toward the wind. 4. in the direction from which the wind is blowing. 5. direction from which the wind is blowing.

wind y (win′di), 1. having much wind; as, a windy street, windy weather. 2. made of wind; empty; as, windy talk.

wine (wīn), 1. the juice of grapes which has fermented and contains alcohol. 2. the fermented juice of other fruits or plants; as, currant wine, dandelion wine. 3. entertain with wine.

wing (wing), 1. the part of a bird or insect used in flying. 2. anything like a wing in shape or use; as, the wings of an airplane. 3. part that sticks out from the main thing or body. The house has a wing at each side. Either of the side portions of an army or fleet ready for battle is called a wing. The spaces to the right or left of the stage in a theater are called wings. 4. fly. The bird wings its way to the south. 5. flying; flight. 6. give wings to; make able to fly. Terror winged Tom's steps as the bear drew nearer. 7. wound in the wing. The bullet winged the bird but did not kill it.

winged (wingd or wing′id), 1. having wings. 2. swift; rapid.

wing less (wing′lis), without wings.

wink (wingk), 1. close the eyes and open them again quickly. The bright light made him wink. 2. close and open one eye on purpose as a hint or signal. Father winked at Dick as a sign for him to keep still. 3. **Wink at** sometimes means pretend not to see. One boss winked at a good deal of dishonesty among his men. 4. twinkle. The stars winked. 5. winking. 6. a hint or signal given by winking. 7. very short time. I didn't sleep a wink.

win ner (win′ər), person or thing that wins. The winner got a prize.

win ning (win′ing), 1. that wins; as, a winning team. 2. charming; attractive. 3. **Winnings** means what is won; money won. He pocketed his winnings.

win now (win′ō), 1. blow off the chaff from (grain); drive or blow away (chaff). 2. separate; sift; sort out; as, to winnow truth from lies.

win some (win′səm), charming; attractive; pleasing.

win ter (win′tər), 1. the coldest of the four seasons. 2. of the winter. 3. keep during the winter. We wintered our cattle in the warm valley. 4. pass the winter. Robins winter in the South.

win try (win′tri), of winter; like winter; as, wintry weather, a wintry sky, a wintry manner.

wipe (wīp), 1. rub in order to clean or dry. We wipe our shoes on the mat. We wipe the dishes with a towel. 2. take (away, off, or out) by rubbing. Wipe away your tears. She wiped off the dust. 3. **Wipe out** sometimes means destroy. 4. act of wiping. Dick gave his face a hasty wipe.

wire (wīr), 1. metal drawn out into a thread; as, a telephone wire. 2. made of wire; as, a wire fence. 3. furnish with wire; as, to wire a house for electricity. 4. fasten with wire. He wired the two pieces together. 5. telegraph. He sent a message by wire. Wire your answer at once. 6. telegram.

wire less (wīr′lis), 1. having no wire. 2. radio. 3. message sent by radio. 4. send by radio.

wir y (wīr′i), 1. made of wire. 2. like wire. 3. lean, strong, and tough.

wis dom (wiz′dəm), 1. being wise; knowledge and good judgment based on experience. 2. wise conduct; wise words.

wise[1] (wīz), 1. having or showing knowledge and good judgment; as, a wise judge, wise advice, wise plans. 2. having knowledge or information. We are none the wiser for his explanations.

wise[2] (wīz), way; manner.

wish (wish). I wish I had more money. His wish is for Christmas to come. Kitty's wish is for more milk. Mary sends you best wishes for a Happy New Year. The girl got her wish.

wisp (wisp), small bundle; small bunch; bit; as, a wisp of hair, a wisp of hay, a wisp of smoke.

wist (wist), old word meaning knew. He wist not who had spoken.

wis tar i a (wis tãr′i ə), a climbing shrub with large clusters of purple flowers.

wis te ri a (wis tēr′i ə), wistaria.

wist ful (wist′fəl), 1. longing; yearning. A child stood looking with wistful eyes at the toys in the window. 2. pensive.

wit (wit), 1. understanding; mind; sense. People with quick wits learn easily. The child was out of his wits with fright. That poor man hasn't wit enough to earn a living. 2. the power to perceive quickly and express cleverly ideas that are unusual, striking, and amusing. His wit made even troubles seem amusing. 3. person with such power. Benjamin Franklin was a wit.

witch (wich), 1. woman supposed to have magic power. Witches generally used their power to do evil. 2. an ugly old woman. 3. a charming or fascinating girl or woman.

witch craft (wich′kraft′), what a witch does or can do; magic power.

witch er y (wich′ər i), 1. witchcraft; magic. 2. charm; fascination.

witch ing (wich′ing), bewitching; magical; enchanting.

with (wiᴛʜ or with). *With* shows that persons or things are taken together in some way. 1. in the company of. Come with me. Do you wish sugar with your tea? 2. among. They will mix with the crowd. 3. having. Mr. Wise is a man with brains. 4. in the keeping or service of. Leave the dog with me. 5. in proportion to. The army's power increases with its size. 6. in regard to. We are pleased with the house. 7. using; showing. Work with care. 8. by means of. The man cut the meat with a knife. 9. because of. The man almost died with thirst. The child is shaking with cold. 10. from. I hate to part with my favorite things. 11. against. The English fought with the Germans.

with al (wiᴛʜ ôl′), 1. with it all; also; as well; besides. The lady is rich and fair and wise withal. 2. with.

with draw (wiᴛʜ drô′), 1. draw back; draw away. The child quickly withdraws his hand from the hot stove. 2. take back; remove. Mr. Green agreed to withdraw the charge of theft if they returned the money. Worn-out paper money is withdrawn from use by the government. Will's parents withdrew him from school. 3. go away. She withdrew from the room.

with draw al (wiᴛʜ drô′əl), a withdrawing.

with drawn (wiᴛʜ drôn′). See **withdraw.**

with drew (wiᴛʜ drü′). See **withdraw.** Bill withdrew from the game because he was hurt.

with er (wiᴛʜ′ər), 1. make or become dry and lifeless; fade; shrivel; blight. The hot sun withers the grass. Flowers wither after they are cut. Age had withered the old lady's face. 2. cause to feel ashamed or confused. Mary blushed under her aunt's withering look.

with held (with held′), refused to give; held back. See **withhold.**

with hold (with hōld′), 1. refuse to give. There will be no school play if the principal withholds his consent. 2. hold back; keep back. The captain withholds his men from attack.

with in (wiᴛʜ in′), 1. not beyond; not more than. The task was within the man's powers. He guessed my weight within five pounds. 2. inside of; in the inner part of. By the X ray, doctors can see what is within the body. 3. inside; in the inner part. The house has been painted within and without. The curtains were white without and green within.

with out (wiᴛʜ out′), 1. with no; lacking; free from. A cat walks without noise. I drink tea without sugar. 2. not having. Eat what is on the table or go without. 3. outside; on the outside. The house is painted without and within. 4. outside of; beyond. Soldiers are camped within and without the city walls.

with stand (with stand′), stand against; hold out against; resist; oppose; endure. Soldiers have to withstand hardships. These shoes will withstand hard wear. **withstood** is formed from **withstand.**

with stood (with stůd′). See **withstand.** The soldiers withstood the attack for hours.

wit less (wit′lis), lacking sense; stupid; foolish.

wit ness (wit′nis), 1. person or thing able to give evidence; person who saw something happen. 2. see. He witnessed the accident. 3. person who takes an oath to tell the truth in a court of law. 4. evidence; testimony. 5. give evidence of. Her whole manner witnessed her surprise. 6. person writing his name on a document to show that he saw the maker sign it. 7. sign (a document) as witness. The two servants witnessed Mr. Smith's will.

wit ty (wit′i), full of wit; clever and amusing. A witty person makes witty remarks.

wives (wīvz), more than one wife.

wiz ard (wiz′ərd), man supposed to have magic power. Edison was called a wizard because he made such marvelous inventions.

wob ble (wob′əl), 1. move unsteadily from side to side; shake; tremble. A baby wobbles when it begins to walk alone. 2. waver; be uncertain, unsteady, or inconstant. 3. wobbling motion.

wob bly (wob′li), unsteady; shaky.

woe (wō), 1. great grief, trouble, or distress. Sickness and poverty are common woes. 2. an exclamation of grief, trouble, or distress. "Woe! woe is me!" the miserable beggar cried.

woe ful or **wo ful** (wō′fəl), 1. full of woe; sad; sorrowful; wretched. 2. pitiful.

woke (wōk), waked. See **wake.** John woke before we did.

wolf (wůlf), 1. a wild animal somewhat like a dog. Wolves kill sheep and sometimes even attack men. 2. a cruel, greedy person. 3. **Keep the wolf from the door** means keep safe from hunger or want.

Timber wolf (2 ft. high at the shoulder)

wolf hound (wůlf′hound′), a large dog of any of various breeds once used in hunting wolves.

wolf ish (wůl′fish), like a wolf; savage; as, a wolfish-looking dog, wolfish cruelty.

Wolfhound (about 2½ ft. high at the shoulder)

wolves (wůlvz), more than one wolf.

wom an (wům′ən), 1. female human being. A woman is a girl grown up. 2. women as a group. 3. female servant. The princess told her woman to wait outside.

wom an hood (wům′ən hůd), 1. condition or time of being a woman. 2. character or qualities of a woman. 3. women as a group. Joan of Arc was an honor to womanhood.

wom an kind (wům′ən kīnd′), women; the female sex.

wom an ly (wům′ən li), 1. like a woman. 2. like a woman's. 3. proper or becoming for a woman; as, womanly sympathy.

wom en (wim′in), more than one woman.

wom en folk (wim′in fōk′), women.

won (wun). See **win.** Which side won yesterday? We have won four games.

won der (wun′dər), 1. strange and surprising thing or event. The pyramids are one of the wonders of the world. It is a wonder that he refused such a good offer. No wonder that child is sick; he eats too much candy. 2. the feeling caused by what is strange and surprising. The baby looked with wonder at the Christmas tree. 3. feel wonder. We wonder at the splendor of the stars. I shouldn't wonder if it rained before night. 4. be surprised. I wonder that you came at all. 5. be curious about; wish to know. I wonder what time it is. I wonder where Nell bought her new hat.

won der ful (wun′dər fəl), causing wonder; marvelous; remarkable. The works of God are wonderful. The explorer had wonderful experiences.

won der ment (wun′dər mənt), wonder; surprise.

won drous (wun′drəs), wonderful.

wont (wunt), 1. accustomed. He was wont to read the paper at breakfast. 2. custom; habit. He rose early, as was his wont.

won't (wōnt), will not.

wont ed (wun′tid), accustomed; customary; usual.

woo (wü), 1. make love to; seek to marry. 2. seek to win; try to get. Some people woo fame; some woo wealth. 3. seek to persuade; urge.

wood (wůd), 1. the hard substance beneath the bark of trees. Wood is used for making houses, boats, boxes, and furniture. 2. trees cut up for use. The carpenter brought wood to build a playhouse. Put some wood on the fire. 3. made of wood. 4. a large number of growing trees. The children go to the wood for wild flowers and for nuts.

wood bine (wu̇d′bīn′), 1. honeysuckle. 2. a climbing vine that has leaves with five leaflets and bluish-black berries.

Honeysuckle woodbine

wood chuck (wu̇d′chuk′), a bushy-tailed, thick-set animal, somewhat like rats and rabbits. See the picture just below. Woodchucks grow fat in summer and sleep in their holes in the ground all winter.

wood cock (wu̇d′kok′), a small game bird with a long bill and short legs. See the picture on this page.

wood craft (wu̇d′kraft′), knowledge about how to obtain food and shelter in the woods; skill in hunting, trapping, finding one's way, etc.

Woodchuck (1¼ to 1½ ft. long without the tail)

wood cut ter (wu̇d′kut′ər), man who cuts down trees or chops wood.

wood ed (wu̇d′id), covered with trees. The house stood on a wooded hill.

wood en (wu̇d′ən), 1. made of wood. 2. stiff as wood; awkward. 3. dull; stupid.

wood land (wu̇d′lənd), 1. land covered with trees. 2. of the woods; as, woodland sounds.

American woodcock (nearly 1 ft. long with the long bill). The European woodcock is longer.

wood man (wu̇d′mən), 1. man who cuts down trees. 2. person who lives in the woods. 3. person who takes care of forests.

wood peck er (wu̇d′pek′ər), a bird with a hard, pointed bill for pecking holes in trees to get insects. See the picture.

woods (wu̇dz), a large number of growing trees; a forest.

wood shed (wu̇d′shed′), shed for storing wood.

woods man (wu̇dz′mən), 1. man used to life in the woods and skilled in hunting, fishing, trapping, etc. 2. man whose work is cutting down trees; lumberman.

Woodpecker (about 9 in. long)

wood thrush, thrush common in the thickets and woods of eastern North America.

wood work (wu̇d′wėrk′), things made of wood; wooden parts inside of a house, especially doors, stairs, moldings, etc.

wood y (wu̇d′i), 1. having many trees; covered with trees; as, a woody hillside. 2. consisting of wood; as, the woody parts of a shrub. 3. like wood. Turnips become woody when they are old.

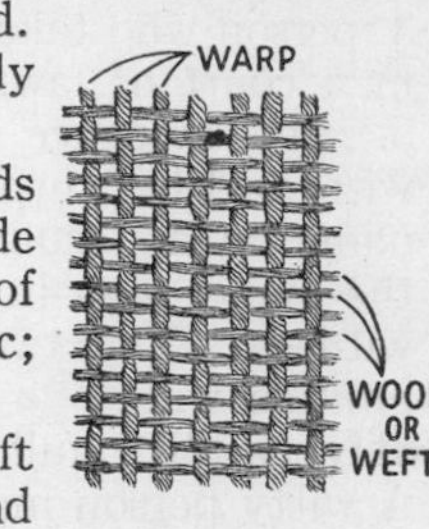

woof (wüf), 1. the threads running from side to side across a fabric. The woof crosses the warp. 2. fabric; cloth; texture.

wool (wu̇l), 1. the soft hair or fur of sheep and some other animals. 2. short, thick, curly hair. 3. something like wool. 4. yarn, cloth, or garments made of wool. He wears wool in winter.

wool en or **wool len** (wu̇l′ən), 1. made of wool. 2. cloth made of wool. 3. of wool; having something to do with wool; as, a woolen mill.

wool ly or **wool y** (wu̇l′i), 1. consisting of wool; as, the woolly coat of a sheep. 2. like wool. 3. covered with wool or something like it.

word (wėrd), 1. a sound or a group of sounds that has meaning. We speak words when we talk. 2. the writing or printing that stands for a word. This page is filled with words. 3. **Words** sometimes means angry talk. 4. short talk. I want a word with you. 5. brief expression. The teacher gave us a word of advice. 6. command; order. Father's word is law. 7. promise. The boy kept his word. A **man of his word** is a man who keeps his promises. 8. news. No word has come from the battle front. 9. put into words. Fred worded his message clearly.

wore (wōr). See **wear.** He wore out his shoes in two months.

work (wėrk), 1. effort in doing or making something. Few people like hard work. 2. something to do; occupation; employment. The man is out of work. 3. that on which effort is put. The dressmaker took her work out on the porch. 4. something made or done. A picture is a work of art. 5. do work; labor; be employed. Most people must work to live. Henry works in a bank. 6. put effort on. He worked on his farm with success. 7. cause to do work. He works his men long hours. 8. act; operate. This pump will not work. The plan worked well. 9. make or get by effort. 10. bring about; cause; do. The plan worked harm. 11. go slowly or with effort. The ship worked to windward. 12. become (up, round, loose, etc.). The window catch has worked loose. 13. ferment. Yeast makes beer work.

work er (wėr′kər), one that works.

work ing (wėr′king), 1. operation; action; method of work. Do you understand the working of this machine? 2. that works. 3. used in working.

work ing man (wėr′king man′), 1. man who works. 2. man who works with his hands or with machines.

work man (wėrk′mən), 1. worker. 2. man who works with his hands or with machines.

work man like (wėrk′mən līk′), skillful; done well.

work man ship (wėrk′mən ship), 1. the art or skill in a worker or his work. Good workmanship deserves good pay. 2. quality or manner of work. 3. the work done.

work men (wėrk′mən), more than one workman.

work room (wėrk′rüm′), a room where work is done.

works (wėrks), 1. factory; place for doing some kind of work. 2. acting or moving parts of a machine; as, the works of a clock.

work shop (wėrk′shop′), shop where work is done.

world (wėrld), 1. the earth. Ships can sail around the world. 2. all of certain things or parts of the earth; as, the insect world, woman's world, the world of fashion. The **Old World** is Europe, Asia, and Africa. The **New World** is North America and South America. 3. all people; the public. The whole world knows it. 4. the things of this life and the people devoted to them. Monks and nuns live apart from the world. 5. star; planet. 6. all created things; everything; the universe. 7. great deal; very much. Sunshine does children a world of good.

world ly (wėrld′li), 1. of this world; not of heaven; as, worldly wealth. 2. caring much for the interests and pleasures of this world.

worm (wėrm), 1. a small, slender crawling or creeping animal. 2. a small crawling animal without legs. 3. something like a worm in shape or movement, such as the thread of a screw. 4. move like a worm; crawl or creep like a worm. The soldiers wormed their way through the tall grass. He wormed himself into our confidence. 5. get by persistent and secret means. John tried to worm the secret out of me. 6. person who deserves contempt or pity.

Worm

worn (wōrn), 1. damaged by use; as, worn rugs. 2. tired; wearied; as, a worn face. 3. See **wear.** He has worn that suit for two years.

worn-out (wōrn′out′), used until no longer fit for use.

wor ry (wėr′i), 1. feel anxious; be uneasy. She worries about little things. 2. bother; annoy; vex; trouble. Don't worry your father with so many questions. 3. care; anxiety; trouble. 4. seize and shake with the teeth; bite at; snap at. The dog worried the rat.

worse (wėrs). Bill is a bad boy, but his brother is worse. We say bad, worse, worst. It is raining worse than ever. Job thought the loss of his property bad enough, but worse followed.

wor ship (wėr′ship), 1. great honor and respect; as, the worship of God, hero worship. 2. pay great honor and respect to. People go to church to worship God. 3. ceremonies or services in honor of God. Services, prayers, and hymns are worship. 4. take part in a religious service. 5. consider extremely precious; hold very dear. A miser worships money. Helen worships her mother.

wor ship er or **wor ship per** (wėr′ship ər), person who worships. The church was filled with worshipers.

wor ship ful (wėr′ship fəl), honorable. We beg you, worshipful gentlemen, to grant our request.

worst (wėrst), 1. Fred is the worst boy in school. This is the worst cold I ever had. This child acts worst when there is company about. The mean boy kept the best of the fruit for himself and gave the worst to his friends. At the worst, you will only have to do the work over again. If worst comes to worst, Mary will quit school and go to work. 2. beat; defeat. The hero worsted his enemies.

wor sted (wu̇s′tid), 1. firmly twisted woolen thread or yarn. 2. cloth made from such thread or yarn. 3. woolen yarn for knitting, crocheting, and needlework.

worth (wėrth), 1. good or important enough for; deserving of. New York is a city worth visiting. 2. merit; usefulness; importance. We should read books of real worth. 3. value; power to buy. Jane got her money's worth out of that coat. He bought a dollar's worth of stamps. 4. equal in value to. This book is worth two dollars. That toy is worth little. 5. having property that amounts to. Mr. Dix was worth a million dollars.

wor thi ness (wėr′ŦHi nis), worth; merit.

worth less (wėrth′lis), without worth; good-for-nothing; useless. Throw those worthless, broken toys away. Don't read that worthless book.

wor thy (wėr′ŦHi), 1. having worth or merit. She helps the worthy poor. 2. deserving; meriting. His courage was worthy of high praise. Bad acts are worthy of punishment. 3. person of great merit; admirable person. Abraham Lincoln stands high among American worthies.

wot (wot), an old form meaning know. "I wot" means "I know."

would (wu̇d), 1. was willing to; were willing to. He would if they would. 2. wished to. 3. was determined to; were determined to. He would go in spite of our warning. 4. should. He said he would come in ten minutes. 5. *Would* is also used (1) to express action done again and again. The children would play for hours on the beach. (2) to express a wish. I would I were rich. (3) to sound more polite than *will* sounds. Would you help us, please?

would n't (wu̇d′ənt), would not.

wouldst (wu̇dst), an old form meaning would. "Thou wouldst" means "you would."

wound[1] (wünd), 1. a hurt or injury caused by cutting, stabbing, shooting, etc. The man has a knife wound in his arm. 2. injure by cutting, stabbing, shooting, etc.; hurt. The hunter wounded the deer. Unkind words wound the feelings. 3. any hurt or injury to feelings, reputation, etc. The loss of his job was a wound to Mr. Black's pride.

wound[2] (wound). See **wind**[2]. She wound the string into a ball some time ago. It is wound too loosely.

wove (wōv). See **weave.** The spider wove a new web after the first was destroyed.

wo ven (wō′vən). See **weave.** This cloth is closely woven.

wraith (rāth), 1. specter; ghost. 2. ghost of a person seen before or soon after his death.

wran gle (rang′gəl), 1. argue or dispute in a noisy or angry way; quarrel. The children wrangled about who should sit on the front seat. 2. a noisy or angry dispute; a quarrel.

wrap (rap), 1. cover by winding or folding something around. She wrapped herself in a shawl. The mountain peak is wrapped in clouds. 2. **Wrapped up in** sometimes means devoted to; thinking chiefly of. Mrs. Jones is wrapped up in her children. 3. an outer covering. Shawls, scarfs, coats, and furs are wraps.

wrap per (rap′ər), 1. person or thing that wraps. 2. a covering or cover. Magazines are mailed in paper wrappers. 3. a woman's loose garment to wear in the house.

wrath (rath), very great anger; rage.

wrath ful (rath′fəl), very angry; showing wrath. The wrathful lion turned on the hunters. His wrathful eyes flashed.

wreak (rēk), 1. give expression to; work off (feelings, desires, etc.). The cruel boy wreaked his bad temper on his dog. 2. inflict (vengeance, punishment, etc.).

wreath (rēth), 1. a ring of flowers or leaves twisted together. We hang wreaths in the windows at Christmas. 2. something suggesting a wreath; as, a wreath of smoke.

Girl wearing a wreath

wreathe (rēŦH), 1. make into a wreath. The children wreathed flowers to put on the soldiers' graves. 2. decorate or adorn with wreaths. The inside of the schoolhouse was wreathed with Christmas greens. 3. make a ring around; encircle. The hills are wreathed in mist. **Wreathed in smiles** means smiling greatly.

wreck (rek), 1. destruction of a ship. The storm caused many wrecks. 2. destruction or ruin of a building, train, automobile, or airship. 3. destruction or serious injury. Heavy rains caused the wreck of many crops. 4. what is left of anything that has been destroyed or much injured. The wrecks of six ships were cast upon the shore by the waves. 5. cause the wreck of; destroy; ruin. Robbers wrecked the mail train.

wreck age (rek′ij), 1. a wrecking; a being wrecked. She wept at the wreckage of her hopes. 2. remains of a wreck. The shore was covered with the wreckage of a ship.

wren (ren), a small songbird. Wrens often build their nests near houses. See the picture.

House wren (about 5 in. long with the tail)

wrench (rench), 1. a violent twist or twisting pull. He gave his ankle a wrench when he jumped off the car. It was a wrench to leave the old home. 2. twist or pull violently. He wrenched the knob off when he was trying to open the door. The policeman wrenched the gun out of the man's hand. 3. tool to hold and turn nuts, bolts, etc. See the picture.

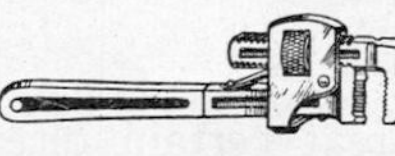
Wrench

wrest (rest), 1. twist, pull, or tear away with force; wrench away. Tom bravely wrested the knife from the crazy girl. 2. take by force. An enemy wrested the power from the duke. 3. twist; turn. You wrest my words from their real meanings.

wres tle (res′əl), 1. try to throw or force an opponent to the ground. The rules for wrestling do not allow using the fists or certain holds on the body. 2. wrestling match. 3. struggle. We wrestle with temptation.

wres tler (res′lər), one who wrestles.

wretch (rech), 1. a very unfortunate or unhappy person. 2. very bad person.

wretch ed (rech′id), 1. very unfortunate or unhappy. 2. very unsatisfactory; miserable; as, a wretched hut. 3. very bad; as, a wretched traitor.

wretch ed ness (rech′id nis), wretched condition or quality; as, the wretchedness of a poor, sick cripple with no friends.

wrig gle (rig′əl), 1. turn and twist. Children wriggle when they are restless. 2. move by twisting and turning, as a worm does. 3. make one's way by shifts and tricks. That boy can wriggle out of any difficulty. 4. a wriggling.

wright (rīt), maker of something. A wheelwright makes wheels. A playwright makes plays for the theater.

wring (ring), 1. twist with force; squeeze hard. Wring out your wet bathing suit. His soul was wrung with grief. 2. get by twisting or squeezing; force out. The laundress wrings water from the clothes. 3. get by force, effort, or persuasion. The old beggar wrung money from us by his sad story. 4. a twist; a squeeze. **wrung** is formed from **wring.**

wring er (ring′ər), machine for squeezing water from clothes.

wrin kle (ring′kəl), 1. ridge; fold. An old man's face has wrinkles. I must press out the wrinkles in this dress. 2. make a wrinkle or wrinkles in. He wrinkled his forehead. 3. have wrinkles; acquire wrinkles. The sleeves wrinkle.

wrist (rist), the joint connecting hand and arm.

wrist band (rist′band′), the band of a sleeve fitting around the wrist.

writ (rit), 1. something written; a writing. The Bible is Holy Writ. 2. a formal order directing a person to do or avoid something. 3. old word meaning written. Their names are writ in gold.

write (rīt), 1. make letters or words with pen, pencil, or chalk. You can read and write. 2. mark with words. Please write on both sides of the paper. 3. put down the words of. Write your name. 4. make up stories, books, etc.; compose. Mr. Blank writes for the magazines. 5. be a writer. Her ambition was to write. 6. write a letter. Mary writes to her mother every week. 7. Some special meanings are:

write down, put into writing.

write out, 1. put into writing. 2. write in full.

write up, 1. write a description or account of. 2. write in detail. 3. bring up to date in writing.

wrote and **written** are formed from **write.**

writ er (rīt′ər), 1. person who writes. 2. person whose occupation is writing; author.

writhe (rīᴛʜ), twist; twist out of shape; twist about. The wounded man writhed with pain.

writ ing (rīt′ing), 1. act of making letters or words with pen, pencil, chalk, etc. 2. written form. Put your ideas in writing. 3. handwriting. 4. something written; a letter, paper, document, etc. 5. literary work; a book or other literary production; as, the writings of Benjamin Franklin.

writ ten (rit′ən). See **write.** He has written a letter.

wrong (rông), 1. not right; wicked. Stealing is wrong. 2. not true; not correct. John gave a wrong answer. 3. not proper; not fit. That is the wrong way to throw a ball. 4. not meant to be seen; least important; as, the wrong side of cloth. 5. out of order. Something is wrong with the car. 6. anything not right. Two wrongs do not make a right. 7. injury; harm. Mrs. Brown is doing her child a wrong by spoiling him so. 8. in a wrong manner; ill; badly. Everything went wrong today. 9. do wrong to; treat unfairly; harm. He forgave those who had wronged him.

wrong do ing (rông′dü′ing), doing wrong; bad acts.

wrong ful (rông′fəl), wrong.

wrote (rōt). See **write.** He wrote his mother a long letter last week.

wroth (rôth), angry.

wrought (rôt), 1. made. The gate was wrought with great skill. 2. worked.

wrung (rung). See **wring.** She wrung out the wet cloth and hung it up. Her heart is wrung with pity for the poor.

wry (rī), twisted; turned to one side. She made a wry face to show her disgust.

X

Xmas (kris′məs), Christmas.

X ray, 1. a ray which goes through substances that ordinary lights cannot penetrate. X rays are used to locate breaks in bones or bullets lodged in the body, and to treat certain diseases. 2. a picture made by means of X rays.

X-ray (eks′rā′), 1. of or by X rays; as, an X-ray examination of one's teeth. 2. examine, photograph, or treat with X rays.

Y

yacht (yot), 1. boat for pleasure trips or for racing. 2. to sail or race on a yacht.

yacht ing (yot′ing), sailing on a yacht.

yam (yam), 1. the starchy root of a vine grown for food in warm countries. 2. the vine itself. 3. a kind of sweet potato.

Yan kee (yang′ki), 1. a native of New England. 2. a native of any of the Northern States. 3. a native of the United States.

yap (yap), 1. snappish bark; a yelp. 2. bark in a snappish way; yelp.

yard[1] (yärd), 1. piece of ground near or around a house. 2. piece of enclosed ground for some special purpose or business; as, barnyard, graveyard, navy yard. 3. space with tracks where railroad cars are stored, shifted around, etc. John's brother works in the railroad yards.

yard[2] (yärd), 1. 36 inches; 3 feet. 2. a beam or pole fastened across a mast, used to support a sail.

yard stick (yärd′stik′), 1. a stick one yard long, used for measuring. 2. standard of judgment or comparison. We need a yardstick for health.

yarn (yärn), 1. any spun thread, especially that prepared for weaving or knitting. The woman knits stockings from yarn. 2. tale; story. The old sailor made up his yarns as he told them.

yawl (yôl), 1. a boat with a large mast near the bow and a small mast near the stern. 2. a ship's boat rowed by four or six oars.

Yawl (def. 1)

yawn (yôn), 1. open the mouth wide because one is sleepy, tired, or bored. 2. act of doing so. 3. open wide. The canyon yawned beneath our feet.

ye (yē), you. If ye are thirsty, drink.

yea (yā), 1. yes. 2. indeed.

year (yēr), 12 months or 365 days. Leap year has 366 days.

year ling (yēr′ling), 1. an animal one year old. 2. one year old; as, a yearling colt.

year ly (yēr′li), 1. once a year; in every year. Mr. Davis takes a yearly trip to New York. 2. lasting a year. The earth makes a yearly revolution around the sun. 3. for a year. He is paid $300 a month, or $3600 yearly.

yearn (yėrn), 1. feel a longing or desire; desire earnestly. He yearns for home. 2. feel pity; have tender feelings. Her heart yearned for the starving children.

yearn ing (yėr′ning), strong desire; longing.

yeast (yēst), 1. the substance used in raising bread and in making beer. Yeast consists of very small plants or cells that grow quickly in a liquid containing sugar. 2. flour or meal mixed with this substance and pressed into small cakes.

yell (yel), 1. cry out with a strong, loud sound. He yelled with pain. 2. a strong, loud cry. 3. say with a yell. We yelled our good-bys as the bus moved away. 4. special shout or cheer used by a school or college.

yel low (yel′ō), 1. the color of gold, butter, or lemons. 2. having this color. 3. having a yellowish skin. The Chinese and Japanese belong to the yellow race. 4. make yellow. Buttercups yellowed the field. 5. become yellow.

yellow fever, a dangerous infectious disease of warm climates, transmitted by the bite of a certain kind of mosquito.

yel low ish (yel′ō ish), somewhat yellow.

yelp (yelp), 1. the quick sharp bark or cry of a dog, fox, etc. 2. make such a bark or cry.

yeo man (yō′mən), 1. a servant or attendant of a lord or king. 2. in England, a person who owns land, but not a large amount. 3. in the United States Navy, a petty officer who has charge of supplies, accounts, etc.

yeo man ry (yō′mən ri), yeomen.

yes (yes). "Yes, I do," said Tom. "Yes, five and two are seven," said sister. "Your work is good, yes, very good," said the teacher.

yes ter day (yes′tər di), 1. the day before today. 2. on the day before today. 3. the near past; as, fashions of yesterday.

yet (yet), 1. Don't go yet. It was not yet dark. The thief will be caught yet. She is talking yet. 2. also; again. Yet once more I forbid you to go. 3. moreover. He won't do it for you nor yet for me. 4. even. The king spoke yet more harshly. 5. but; nevertheless; however. The work is good, yet it could be better.

yew (ū), 1. an evergreen tree of Europe and Asia. 2. the wood of this tree. Bows used to be made of yew.

yield (yēld), 1. produce. This land yields good crops. Mines yield ore. 2. amount yielded; product. This year's yield from the silver mine was very large. 3. give; grant. Mary's mother yielded her consent to the plan. 4. give up; surrender. The enemy yielded to our soldiers. 5. give way. The door yielded to his touch. 6. give place We yield to nobody in love of freedom.

yield ing (yēl′ding), submissive; not resisting.

yoke (yōk), 1. a wooden frame to fasten two work animals together. See the picture. 2. A **yoke of oxen** means two oxen. 3. any frame connecting two other parts. The man carried two buckets on a yoke, one at each end. 4. put a yoke on. 5. harness or fasten a work animal (to). 6. part of a garment fitting the neck and shoulders closely. 7. top piece to a skirt, fitting the hips. 8. something that binds together. 9. join. 10. something that holds people in slavery or submission. Throw off your yoke and be free. 11. rule; dominion. Slaves are under the yoke of their masters.

Yoke on a pair of oxen

Yoke of a dress

yolk (yōk), the yellow part of an egg.

yon (yon), yonder.

yon der (yon′dər), over there; within sight, but not near. Look at that wild duck yonder! The sky is getting black yonder in the west. On yonder hill stands a ruined castle.

yore (yōr), long ago; years ago. Knights wore armor in days of yore.

you (ū), 1. the person or persons spoken to. Are you ready? Then you may go. 2. one; anybody. You never can tell. You push this button to get a light.

you'd (ūd), 1. you had. 2. you would.

you'll (ūl), 1. you will. 2. you shall.

young (yung), 1. in the early part of life; not old. A puppy is a young dog. 2. young ones. An animal will fight to protect its young. 3. having the looks or qualities of youth or of a young person. Mrs. Jones is young for her age. 4. not so old as another. Young Mr. Jones worked for his father.

young ster (yung′stər), 1. child. Jack is a lively youngster. 2. young person.

your (ūr), 1. belonging to you. Wash your hands. 2. having to do with you. We enjoyed your visit.

you're (ūr), you are.

yours (ūrz), 1. of you; belonging to you. The red book is yours. 2. the one or ones belonging to you. My hands are clean; yours are dirty. I like ours better than yours. 3. *Yours* is used at the end of a letter with some other word; as, Yours truly, Sincerely yours.

your self (ūr self′), 1. *Yourself* is used to make a statement stronger. You yourself know the story is not true. 2. *Yourself* is used instead of *you* when *you* has already been used in the sentence. Did you hurt yourself?

your selves (ūr selvz′). You can all see for yourselves that the room is empty.

youth (ūth), 1. being young. He has the vigor of youth. She keeps her youth well. 2. the time between childhood and manhood or womanhood. 3. young man. 4. young people.

Yucca

youth ful (ūth′fəl), 1. young. 2. having the looks or qualities of youth; fresh; lively. The old man had a youthful spirit. 3. of youth; as, youthful faults, youthful energy, youthful pleasures.

you've (ūv), you have.

yuc ca (yuk′ə), a plant having large white flowers. See the picture above.

Yule (ūl), 1. Christmas. 2. Christmas time.

Z

zeal (zēl), eager desire or effort. A good citizen feels zeal for his country's interests. Joseph worked with zeal at his business.

zeal ous (zel′əs), full of zeal; eager; earnest. The new cook seems zealous to please. The children made zealous efforts to clean up the house for the party.

ze bra (zē′brə), a wild animal like a horse but striped with dark bands on white.

Zebra (4 to 4½ ft. high at the shoulder)

ze nith (zē′nith), 1. the point in the heavens directly overhead; the point where a vertical line would pierce the sky. 2. the highest point.

zeph yr (zef′ər), 1. the west wind. 2. any soft, gentle wind. 3. a fine, soft yarn.

ze ro (zēr′ō), 1. naught; 0. There are three zeros in 40,006. 2. point marked as 0 on the scale of a thermometer, etc. 3. of or at zero. 4. nothing. 5. not any; none at all. 6. a very low point. The team's spirit sank to zero after its third defeat.

zest (zest), keen enjoyment; relish. The hungry man ate with zest.

zig zag (zig′zag′), 1. with short, sharp turns from one side to the other. The path ran zigzag up the hill. 2. move in a zigzag way. Lightning zigzagged across the sky. 3. zigzag line or course. 4. one of the short, sharp turns of a zigzag.

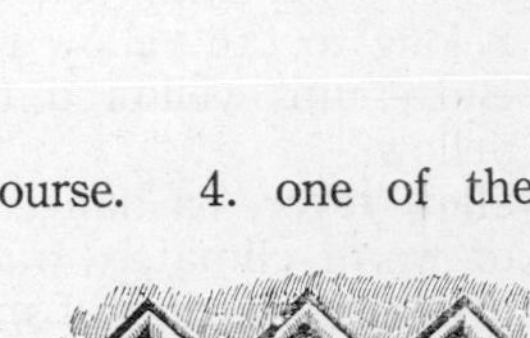

Zigzag design

zinc (zingk), a bluish-white metal very little affected by air and moisture. Zinc is used as a coating for iron, in mixture with other metals, as a roofing material, in electric batteries, in paint, and in medicine.

zin ni a (zin′i ə), a garden plant grown for its showy flowers of many colors.

zip per (zip′ər), sliding fastener for clothing, shoes, etc.

zo di ac (zō′di ak), a belt of the heavens divided into 12 equal parts, named after 12 groups of stars.

Zone (def. 1)

zone (zōn), 1. any of the five great divisions of the earth's surface, bounded by circles parallel to the equator. See the diagram. 2. any region or area especially considered or set off. A war zone is a district where fighting is going on. 3. divide into zones. The city was zoned for factories and residences.

zoo (zü), place where wild animals are kept and shown. We saw lions and tigers in the zoo.

zo ö log i cal (zō′ə loj′i kəl), 1. of animals and animal life. 2. having to do with zoölogy.

zoölogical garden, zoo.

zo öl o gy (zō ol′ə ji), the science of animals; the study of animals and animal life.

zoom (züm), 1. move suddenly upward. The airplane zoomed. 2. sudden upward flight.

45678910111213141516171819202122232425——5453525150494847